African Development Indicators 1997

The World Bank
Washington, D.C.

Manufactured in the United States of America
First printing August 1997

This volume was prepared by the Knowledge, Networks, Information, and Technology Department of the World Bank.

The findings, interpretations, and conclusions expressed in this publication do not necessarily represent the views of the World Bank's Board of Executive Directors or the countries they represent. The World Bank does not guarantee the accuracy of the data in this publication and accepts no responsibility whatsoever for any consequences of their use. Some sources cited in this document may be informal documents that are not readily available.

ISSN 1020-2927
ISBN 0-8213-3932-x

Contents

Table des matières

Prix

Commerce de marchandises

Graphiques

Acknowledgments

This volume was produced by the Knowledge, Networks, Information, and Technology Department of the Africa Region, in collaboration with the Development Data Group of Development Economics Vice Presidency.

The volume was prepared by a team led by Maria Cristina Germany and comprising Ronnie Hammad, Vildan Demiraydin, David Zuaiter, Joan Pandit, and Yanick Brierre. Tariqul Khan developed the systems programs, and Reza Farivari provided aggregation routines. The chapters on national accounts, balance of payments, trade, and government finance draw heavily on the work of World Bank country desks. The chapter on environment was prepared with data from the World Resources Institute. The chapter on household welfare indicators was provided by the Institutional and Social Policy Group of the Africa Region, with the financial support of the Norwegian and Belgian Trust Fund. Virginia Hitchcock provided assistance in editing and production of the volume. Gaudencio Dizon desktopped the text.

In addition, many World Bank staff provided information on their countries or related to their economic or sectoral specialties. Other staff aided and advised on the design and content of this volume.

Preface

African Development Indicators 1997 continues the data publication series started by the World Bank in 1989 with *African Economic and Financial Data* (published jointly with the United Nations Development Programme), followed by *African Development Indicators 1992, 1994–95*, and *1996*. These data books are intended to provide Africans and those interested in Africa with a consistent and convenient set of data to monitor development programs and aid flows in the region. They provide access to more focused information and represent an improvement in the quality and availability of the data.

The data in this volume derive from a variety of sources. In most cases, the original source is national statistical services in Africa. In addition, many international agencies collect or compile data on African countries and organize national data in a standardized framework. This volume draws heavily from such sources. The data have been supplemented by World Bank staff estimates to help address problems of missing or inconsistent data from standard sources. Some of the estimation methods used here differ from methods used in other sources. Throughout the volume, in introductions to chapters or in technical notes, such differences in methodologies are discussed.

In the tradition of the first four volumes, this data book is intended to serve as a prime source of information on Africa. Its wide dissemination to African and non-African analysts and policymakers will contribute to a better understanding of Africa and to development on that continent.

Kevin Cleaver
Technical Director
Africa Region

Acronyms and Abbreviations

ADB	African Development Bank
ADI	*African Development Indicators*
AEFD	*African Economic and Financial Data* (UNDP/World Bank 1989)
AFESD	Arab Fund for Economic and Social Development
BADEA	Arab Bank for Economic Development in Africa
BESD	Bank Economic and Social Database (World Bank)
BIS	Bank for International Settlements
CDIAC	Carbon Dioxide Information Analysis Center
CFA	Communauté Financière Africane (franc zone)
CIDA	Canadian International Development Agency
c.i.f.	Cost, insurance, freight
CITES	Convention on International Trade in Endangered Species of Wild Flora and Fauna
CMEA	Council for Mutual Economic Assistance
COMTRADE	Commodity Trade database (United Nations)
CPI	Consumer price index
DAC	Development Assistance Committee of the OECD
DRS	Debtor Reporting System (World Bank)
ECA	Economic Commission for Africa
FAO	UN Food and Agriculture Organization
f.o.b.	Free on board
GDI	Gross domestic investment
GDP	Gross domestic product
GDS	Gross domestic savings
GFS	*Government Finance Statistics* (IMF)
GNFS	Goods and nonfactor services
GNP	Gross national product
GNS	Gross national savings
IBRD	International Bank for Reconstruction and Development
IDA	International Development Association
IEA	International Energy Agency
DDG	Development Data Group, World Bank

IFAD	International Fund for Agricultural Development
IFS	*International Financial Statistics* (IMF)
ILO	International Labour Organization
IMF	International Monetary Fund
ISIC	UN International Standard Industrial Classification
ITU	International Telecommunications Union
IUCN	International Union for Conservation of Nature and Natural Resources
LIBOR	London interbank offered rate
LIMIC	Low-income and middle-income countries
MBO	Management employee buyout
METMIN	Metals and minerals database (World Bank)
ODA	Official development assistance
OECD	Organization for Economic Cooperation and Development
OPEC	Organization of Petroleum Exporting Countries
ORT	Oral rehydration therapy
PE	Public enterprise
SAF	Structural adjustment facility
SDA	Social dimensions of adjustment
SDR	Special drawing right
SITC	UN Standard International Trade Classification
SNA	System of national accounts
☆STARS☆	Socioeconomic Time-series Access and Retrieval System (World Bank)
UNCTAD	United Nations Conference on Trade and Development
UNDP	United Nations Development Programme
UNECE	United Nations Economic Commission for Europe
UNEP	United Nations Environment Programme
UNESCO	United Nations Education, Scientific, and Cultural Organization
UNFPA	
UNHCR	United Nations High Commissioner for Refugees
UNICEF	United Nations Children's Fund
UNIDO	United Nations Industrial Development Organization
UNSO	United Nations Statistical Office
UNSTAT	United Nations Statistical Department
UNTA	United Nations Technical Assistance
WFP	World Food Programme
WHO	World Health Organization
WRI	World Resources Institute
ZIMCO	Zambia Industrial and Mining Corporation

Introduction

The task of monitoring Africa's development progress and aid flows requires basic empirical data that can be readily used by analysts. This publication—which is the fifth in a series that began with the *African Economic and Financial Data (AEFD)* and was followed by *African Development Indicators (ADI) 1992, 1994–95*, and *1996*—is meant to provide a starting point to fulfill that task.

This volume has been able to extend the work of the previous volumes in this series. In particular:

- Most macroeconomic data (in particular, national accounts, balance of payments, government finance statistics, and trade) reflect data maintained by World Bank country desks, often referred to as operational data. These data are often more up to date and offer better country coverage than the data stored in the Bank's central files, BESD, which were used in past publications. BESD is a large database that contains some, but not all, data produced by Bank staff—operational and other—and some, but not all, data produced by UN agencies.
- The chapter on industry has been replaced by a chapter on power, communications, and transport.
- The chapter on public enterprises has been redesigned.
- The chapter on household welfare indicators has been improved, with new countries added.
- The coverage of many of the data series has been improved, reflecting improvements in the underlying data series, as well as estimates made by Bank staff.
- New sectoral indicators have been added.

However, substantial data gaps remain, notably in areas such as public enterprises, gender, and labor. Strengthening the statistical capacity in African countries is an ongoing process, and greater efforts and institutional support will be required if substantial improvements are to be made.

This volume presents the available relevant data for 1970–96, grouped into 15 chapters: background data; national accounts; prices and exchange rates; money and banking; external sector; external debt and related flows; government finance; agriculture; power, communications, and transportation; public enterprises; labor force and employment; aid flows; social indicators; environmental indicators; and household welfare indicators. Chapter 14 was once again taken from the World Resources Institute's *World Resources 1996–97*. Chapter 15 is presented on a country basis.

Each chapter begins with a brief introduction on the nature of the data, followed by a set of charts, statistical tables, and technical notes. These define the indicators and identify specific sources.

A companion set of ☆STARS☆ diskettes (expected to be available later through the World Bank) will provide year-by-year time series of most chapters back to 1970. These series will provide analysts with data needed to help place the most recent years in an historical context.

The data in this volume incorporate numerous revisions to those published previously in the series. There are several reasons for this.

- Many of the data that were based on estimates in the earlier volumes have been replaced with updated actual data or improved estimates. In most cases, these reflect revisions made by the original reporting authorities or sources, but it also includes corrections of errors in previous volumes.
- Data series expressed in constant US dollars and exchange rates use a base year of 1987; *AEFD* was based on 1980 exchange rates and prices.
- Some series expressed in constant prices have been revised as a result of updated or revised deflators.
- Macroeconomic data now reflect country desk information. The difference will be most noticeable in the chapter on government finance, as figures reflect consolidated government data instead of only central government data.

Considerable effort has been made to standardize and to harmonize related data sets drawn from diverse sources. Because statistical methods, coverage, practices, and definitions differ widely among sources, full comparability cannot be assured, and the indicators must be interpreted with care. In addition, the statistical systems in many developing economies are still weak, and this affects the availability and reliability of the data they report. Moreover, intercountry and intertemporal comparisons always involve complex technical problems, which have no full and unequivocal solution.

The data are drawn from sources thought to be the most authoritative, but many data sources are subject to considerable margins of error. To provide reasonably timely data required for meaningful monitoring, the World Bank, the International Monetary Fund (IMF), and other agencies sometimes make estimates on the basis of available secondary information to fill critical gaps in national reporting, especially for the most recent years, when data cannot be readily produced by national statistical sources. Nonetheless, data gaps exist for many indicators, and some countries are covered only sporadically.

Readers are urged to take these limitations into account in using the data and interpreting the indicators, particularly when making comparisons across economies. Weaknesses in the data point to the need for strengthened statistical systems throughout the region.

As a visual aid to data interpretation and cross-country comparisons, figures for selected indicators are included. As with time series, the figures should also be interpreted with caution, in particular in cross-country analysis, because countries with missing data are excluded from the charts.

As in the two previous publications, this volume contains a special chapter on household welfare indicators. The data in this chapter all come directly from national household surveys. A number of improvements have been made to the layout of the country tables, including the complete standardization of the table formats and the inclusion of selective welfare indicators. In the tables, all indicators are presented by urban and rural expenditure quintiles, which makes it possible to make comparisons within a country between poor and non-poor household groups.

Throughout this volume (except when otherwise stated), the symbol ".." indicates that data are not available or not applicable. A zero (0) indicates either zero value or an insignificant value, that is, less than one-half of the smallest unit shown. The symbol "MR" indicates "most recent year available." In chapter 13, columns headed by a period (for example, 1990–93) show data for the latest available year in the period.

To facilitate cross-country comparisons, values of many national series have been converted from the national currencies to US dollars, using the *World Bank Atlas* methodology.

Indicators in this volume generally follow standard definitions as far as possible and cover years through 1996, depending on the chapter. 1996 data are preliminary and therefore may not be internally consistent within and across accounts, and may not be available for all countries. Because data are continually updated, the statistics here may be different from those in other publications.

Shares and ratios are always calculated using current price series; when gross domestic product (GDP) is used as the denominator for these calculations, it is always expressed at market prices (except in Figure 2-3).

In all but the last chapter, the data are arranged by indicator to facilitate cross-country comparisons. For country-specific work, data can be arranged to show all indicators together for each country.

In this volume, the statistical tables are usually arranged as time series, by country and by country groups. The largest country group is All Africa, consisting of two subgroups: North Africa and Sub-Saharan Africa (including South Africa). In turn, the Sub-Saharan Africa group is shown excluding South Africa and Nigeria. These two subgroups correspond to the Sub-Saharan Africa and Sub-Saharan Africa excluding Nigeria groups shown in the *AEFD* and *ADI 1992*, where South Africa was listed separately.

Annual data shown for country groups are totals, averages, or medians for the countries included in the group, as indicated on the table. These group aggregates can be either simple (arithmetic)—where missing data are treated as zeros—or gap-filled—where weights are used to adjust group totals for missing countries. In the latter case, when values are missing for a country or a year, estimates are made to maintain the same country composition of the groups through time. However, the implicit estimated values for the countries with missing data are not shown separately in the tables. These gap-fill estimates are made, and the aggregate statistics shown, only if the countries for which data are available for a given year account for at least two-thirds of the full group, as defined by benchmarks in 1987. This procedure is standard for many World Bank statistical publications.

Most group averages are weighted according to the relative importance of the countries in the group total for that indicator, based on simple addition across countries when the indicator is expressed in reasonably comparable units. Group averages for analytical ratios (for example, imports to GDP) can be either weighted or simple (arithmetic). Usually they are calculated from the group totals for both the numerator and the denominator, which is analytically equivalent to calculating weighted averages, where the weight for each country is its share in the group total for the denominator. Sometimes, however, when it is appropriate to treat the experiences of different countries equally in determining a representative value for the group, these group averages are arithmetic, that is, each country is assigned equal weight.

Period averages—shown for 1975–84, 1985–89, and 1990 to most recent year—are calculated from time series (levels, ratios, growth rates, or medians) for both countries and country groups. They are either simple averages or average annual percentage growth rates. These growth rates always use the least-squares method and are usually computed from real-term series. In this publication, the least-squares growth rates are computed using the level for the year before the first year shown in the label. The least-squares growth rate, r, is estimated by fitting a least-squares linear regression trend line to the logarithmic annual values of the variable in the relevant period. More specifically, the regression equation takes the form: $\log X_t = a + bt + e_t$, where this is equivalent to the logarithmic transformation of the compound growth rate equation, $X_t = X_o (1 + r)^t$. In these equations X is the variable, t is time, and $a = \log X_o$ and $b = \log (1 + r)$ are the parameters to be estimated; e is the error term. If b^* is the least-squares estimate of b, then the annual average growth rate, r, is obtained as [anti log (b^*)] – 1 and multiplied by 100 to express it in percentage terms. The least-squares

growth rate dampens the influence of exceptional values, particularly at the end points. Least-square growth rates are calculated only if more two-thirds of consecutive data—carrying the same sign—are present in the time series.

Throughout this volume, data for Ethiopia include Eritrea up to 1992, except when otherwise indicated. Zaire, the former name of the newly renamed Democratic Republic of the Congo, is used in this volume.

1

Selected Background Data

The first two tables of the volume provide selected indicators, including a series on population, as background to the data in the rest of the volume. Table 1-1 provides a comparative view, across indicators, of some of the more important indicators for all countries in the most recent year for which relatively complete information is available.

1-1. Basic indicators

	Population mid-1996 (millions)	Land area (thousands of square km.)	GNP per capita: Atlas dollars 1996	GNP per capita: Av. annual percentage growth 1986-96	Life expectancy at birth (years) 1995	School enrollment: Primary 1980	School enrollment: Primary 1992-93	School enrollment: Secondary 1980	School enrollment: Secondary 1992-93	Total net ODA per capita 1995
SUB-SAHARAN AFRICA	599.9	23,628	481	-1.0	52	79	73	13	25	31
excluding South Africa	557.6	22,407	273	-0.8	51	78	69	14	20	32
excl. S.Africa & Nigeria	443.2	21,496	287	-1.3	51	71	62	13	16	40
Angola	11.1	1,247	340	-6.5	47	175	..	20	..	39
Benin	5.6	111	360	0.0	50	64	72	16	..	51
Botswana	1.5	567	..	5.9	68	91	115	19	57	63
Burkina Faso	10.7	274	220	-0.1	49	18	39	3	9	47
Burundi	6.4	26	140	-2.3	49	26	69	3	7	46
Cameroon	13.7	465	610	-6.0	57	98	91	18	27	33
Cape Verde	0.4	4	1,090	11.2	65	114	131	8	27	293
Central African Republic	3.3	623	310	-2.1	48	71	..	14	..	51
Chad	6.6	1,259	160	-3.2	48	..	56	..	8	37
Comoros	0.5	2	460	-1.5	56	88	75	23	19	88
Congo	2.7	342	660	-3.2	51	..	..	..	..	48
Côte d'Ivoire	14.3	318	620	-2.0	55	79	69	19	25	87
Djibouti	0.7	23	..	..	50	37	36	12	12	168
Equatorial Guinea	0.4	28	510	2.3	49	135	..	..	..	85
Eritrea	3.7	101	..	..	48	..	47	..	15	42
Ethiopia	58.1	1,000	110	0.4	49	34	27	8	11	16
Gabon	1.1	258	3,620	-2.5	55	..	..	..	..	132
Gambia, The	1.1	10	..	1.0	46	51	67	11	19	43
Ghana	17.5	228	360	1.4	59	80	..	41	..	38
Guinea	6.8	246	560	1.7	44	36	46	17	12	63
Guinea-Bissau	1.1	28	250	1.6	38	68	..	6	..	111
Kenya	27.3	569	330	0.2	58	115	91	20	25	27
Lesotho	2.0	30	670	0.3	61	102	98	18	26	58
Liberia	2.8	96	..	..	54	48	..	22	..	45
Madagascar	14.1	582	240	-2.0	52	136	73	0	14	22
Malawi	10.0	94	180	-0.1	43	60	82	3	5	44
Mali	10.1	1,220	240	0.1	50	26	30	8	8	56
Mauritania	2.3	1,025	470	0.7	51	37	69	11	15	102
Mauritius	1.1	2	3,690	4.9	71	93	106	50	59	20
Mozambique	16.6	784	90	3.2	47	99	60	5	7	68
Namibia	1.6	823	2,080	3.2	59	..	134	..	59	121
Niger	9.3	1,267	200	-2.2	47	25	28	5	7	30
Nigeria	114.4	911	240	1.7	53	105	90	16	29	2
Rwanda	6.7	25	190	-5.4	39	63	..	3	..	111
São Tomé and Principe	0.1	1	350	-0.3	69	..	..	..	..	609
Senegal	8.7	193	560	-0.5	50	46	60	11	16	79
Seychelles	0.1	0	6,960	3.5	72	..	..	..	..	177
Sierra Leone	4.6	72	200	-3.8	40	52	..	14	..	46
Somalia	9.8	627	..	..	49	19	..	8	..	20
South Africa	42.4	1,221	3,140	-0.9	64	85	115	0	77	9
Sudan	27.3	2,376	..	0.3	54	50	55	16	..	9
Swaziland	0.9	17	..	-0.7	58	103	120	38	51	62
Tanzania	30.5	884	130	1.2	51	93	70	3	5	30
Togo	4.2	54	300	-2.7	56	118	102	33	23	46
Uganda	19.7	200	290	3.0	42	50	67	5	11	43
Zaire	45.3	2,267	..	-8.9	..	92	68	24	24	4
Zambia	9.2	743	430	-0.9	46	90	..	16	..	227
Zimbabwe	11.2	387	620	-0.9	57	85	115	8	44	44
NORTH AFRICA	129.6	5,738	1,366	-0.2	65	84	96	40	62	23
Algeria	28.5	2,382	1,570	-2.3	70	94	104	33	62	11
Egypt, Arab Republic	59.3	995	1,090	2.9	63	73	97	50	76	35
Libya	5.6	1,760	..	..	65	125	110	76	97	2
Morocco	27.1	446	1,280	1.0	65	83	77	26	37	19
Tunisia	9.1	155	2,000	1.8	69	103	118	27	52	8
ALL AFRICA	729.5	29,367	639	-0.8	55	80	78	18	33	29

Note: 1996 data are preliminary (see page 3).

1-2. Population

	Millions of people											Average annual percentage growth		
	1980	1987	1988	1989	1990	1991	1992	1993	1994	1995	1996	75-84	85-89	90-MR
SUB-SAHARAN AFRICA	380.55	466.61	480.11	494.00	511.51	525.54	540.80	553.14	567.50	583.70	599.93	3.0	2.9	2.7
excluding South Africa	351.38	431.97	444.67	457.75	474.44	487.64	502.04	513.50	526.96	542.24	557.55	3.0	2.9	2.7
excl. S.Africa & Nigeria	280.23	343.70	353.81	364.25	378.24	388.65	400.16	408.60	418.95	430.97	443.15	3.0	2.9	2.6
Angola	7.02	8.44	8.68	8.94	9.23	9.52	9.82	10.13	10.45	10.77	11.09	2.7	2.8	3.1
Benin	3.46	4.31	4.45	4.59	4.74	4.88	5.03	5.18	5.33	5.48	5.63	2.9	3.2	2.9
Botswana	0.90	1.15	1.20	1.24	1.28	1.32	1.35	1.39	1.42	1.45	1.48	3.6	3.6	2.6
Burkina Faso	6.96	8.31	8.53	8.77	9.02	9.27	9.53	9.80	10.09	10.38	10.66	2.4	2.7	2.8
Burundi	4.13	5.03	5.18	5.33	5.49	5.64	5.80	5.96	6.11	6.26	6.43	2.5	2.9	2.7
Cameroon	8.70	10.54	10.84	11.15	11.48	11.83	12.18	12.54	12.91	13.29	13.70	3.0	2.8	3.0
Cape Verde	0.29	0.32	0.33	0.33	0.34	0.35	0.36	0.36	0.37	0.38	0.39	1.0	1.9	2.1
Central African Republic	2.31	2.72	2.79	2.86	2.93	3.00	3.07	3.14	3.21	3.28	3.35	2.4	2.4	2.3
Chad	4.48	5.27	5.40	5.54	5.68	5.83	5.98	6.13	6.29	6.45	6.61	2.2	2.5	2.6
Comoros	0.34	0.40	0.41	0.42	0.43	0.44	0.46	0.47	0.48	0.49	0.50	..	2.7	2.6
Congo	1.67	2.07	2.13	2.20	2.28	2.35	2.42	2.49	2.56	2.63	2.71	2.9	3.3	3.0
Côte d'Ivoire	8.19	10.72	11.13	11.54	11.97	12.40	12.81	13.21	13.60	13.98	14.32	3.9	3.9	3.1
Djibouti	0.28	0.43	0.45	0.47	0.50	0.52	0.55	0.57	0.60	0.63	0.66	6.7	5.2	4.9
Equatorial Guinea	0.22	0.34	0.34	0.35	0.35	0.36	0.36	0.37	0.39	0.40	0.41	2.4	3.4	2.5
Eritrea	..	..	..	..	3.14	3.22	3.31	3.39	3.48	3.57	3.67	..	..	2.6
Ethiopia	37.72	46.09	47.64	49.34	51.18	52.95	54.79	53.30	54.89	56.40	58.12	2.8	3.2	2.1
Gabon	0.69	0.85	0.87	0.89	0.94	0.99	1.02	1.05	1.07	1.10	1.13	3.1	2.7	3.3
Gambia, The	0.64	0.81	0.84	0.88	0.92	0.96	1.00	1.04	1.08	1.11	1.14	3.1	4.1	3.8
Ghana	10.74	13.53	13.98	14.43	14.87	15.31	15.76	16.20	16.64	17.08	17.53	2.3	3.5	2.8
Guinea	4.46	5.27	5.43	5.59	5.76	5.92	6.09	6.26	6.42	6.59	6.78	1.7	2.8	2.8
Guinea-Bissau	0.81	0.92	0.93	0.95	0.97	0.98	1.00	1.02	1.05	1.07	1.09	3.9	1.8	2.0
Kenya	16.56	21.36	22.03	22.70	23.35	24.02	24.68	25.35	26.02	26.69	27.35	3.8	3.3	2.7
Lesotho	1.37	1.65	1.69	1.74	1.78	1.82	1.86	1.90	1.94	1.98	2.02	2.8	2.6	2.2
Liberia	1.88	2.30	2.35	2.39	2.44	2.48	2.54	2.60	2.66	2.73	2.82	3.2	2.2	2.4
Madagascar	8.71	10.61	10.95	11.30	11.67	12.05	12.45	12.85	13.25	13.65	14.06	2.7	3.1	3.2
Malawi	6.14	7.68	7.95	8.22	8.51	8.74	8.99	9.24	9.49	9.76	10.01	3.2	3.4	2.8
Mali	6.59	7.78	7.99	8.22	8.46	8.71	8.96	9.23	9.50	9.79	10.09	2.2	2.7	3.0
Mauritania	1.55	1.86	1.91	1.95	2.00	2.05	2.11	2.16	2.22	2.27	2.33	2.5	2.6	2.6
Mauritius	0.97	1.03	1.04	1.05	1.06	1.07	1.08	1.10	1.11	1.13	1.14	1.6	0.7	1.3
Mozambique	12.10	13.84	13.95	14.06	14.18	14.39	14.69	15.08	15.57	16.17	16.58	2.7	1.0	2.5
Namibia	1.03	1.24	1.28	1.32	1.35	1.39	1.43	1.47	1.51	1.55	1.58	2.7	2.8	2.7
Niger	5.52	6.99	7.22	7.44	7.67	7.91	8.17	8.44	8.72	9.03	9.33	3.4	3.2	3.3
Nigeria	71.15	88.27	90.87	93.50	96.20	98.98	101.88	104.89	108.01	111.27	114.40	3.1	3.0	2.9
Rwanda	5.16	6.44	6.62	6.79	6.95	7.15	7.35	7.54	6.23	6.40	6.73	3.3	3.0	-1.0
São Tomé and Principe	0.09	0.11	0.11	0.11	0.11	0.12	0.12	0.12	0.13	0.13	0.13	2.6	1.9	2.5
Senegal	5.54	6.76	6.97	7.18	7.40	7.62	7.84	8.05	8.26	8.47	8.70	2.9	3.0	2.8
Seychelles	0.06	0.07	0.07	0.07	0.07	0.07	0.07	0.07	0.07	0.07	0.08	1.1	0.8	1.6
Sierra Leone	3.24	3.75	3.84	3.92	4.00	4.09	4.19	4.29	4.40	4.51	4.63	2.0	2.3	2.4
Somalia	6.71	8.23	8.38	8.51	8.62	8.05	8.30	8.62	9.01	9.49	9.79	3.9	2.1	2.2
South Africa	29.17	34.63	35.43	36.25	37.07	37.91	38.76	39.64	40.54	41.46	42.38	2.6	2.4	2.3
Sudan	18.68	22.52	23.04	23.55	24.06	24.58	25.10	25.63	26.16	26.71	27.33	3.1	2.4	2.1
Swaziland	0.57	0.71	0.74	0.77	0.79	0.81	0.83	0.86	0.88	0.90	0.92	3.1	3.8	2.6
Tanzania	18.58	23.20	23.95	24.70	25.48	26.28	27.10	27.93	28.78	29.65	30.49	3.2	3.2	3.1
Togo	2.62	3.22	3.32	3.42	3.52	3.63	3.74	3.85	3.99	4.11	4.23	2.8	3.1	3.1
Uganda	12.81	14.84	15.27	15.77	16.33	16.89	17.46	18.03	18.60	19.17	19.72	2.4	2.6	3.2
Zaire	27.01	33.87	35.02	36.20	37.41	38.64	39.90	41.19	42.50	43.85	45.34	3.1	3.4	3.3
Zambia	5.74	7.25	7.42	7.60	7.78	8.01	8.24	8.48	8.73	8.98	9.18	3.7	2.5	2.8
Zimbabwe	7.01	8.89	9.18	9.47	9.75	10.02	10.28	10.54	10.78	11.01	11.21	3.1	3.3	2.5
NORTH AFRICA	88.35	106.41	109.02	111.55	114.20	116.83	119.46	122.05	124.60	127.10	129.58	2.7	2.5	2.1
Algeria	18.67	23.15	23.78	24.39	25.01	25.63	26.25	26.85	27.42	27.96	28.52	3.1	2.8	2.3
Egypt, Arab Republic	40.88	48.88	50.06	51.25	52.44	53.62	54.78	55.93	57.06	58.18	59.27	2.5	2.5	2.1
Libya	3.04	4.10	4.25	4.40	4.55	4.70	4.87	5.04	5.22	5.41	5.59	4.5	3.9	3.5
Morocco	19.38	22.60	23.07	23.56	24.04	24.53	25.03	25.54	26.05	26.56	27.06	2.3	2.2	2.0
Tunisia	6.38	7.69	7.86	7.97	8.16	8.35	8.53	8.69	8.85	8.99	9.14	2.6	2.5	2.0
ALL AFRICA	468.90	573.02	589.13	605.55	625.71	642.37	660.26	675.19	692.10	710.80	729.51	2.9	2.8	2.6

Note: 1996 data are preliminary (see page 3).

Figure 1-1. Development diamonds for all African countries, 1996 (or most recent available year)
(sorted by life expectancy)

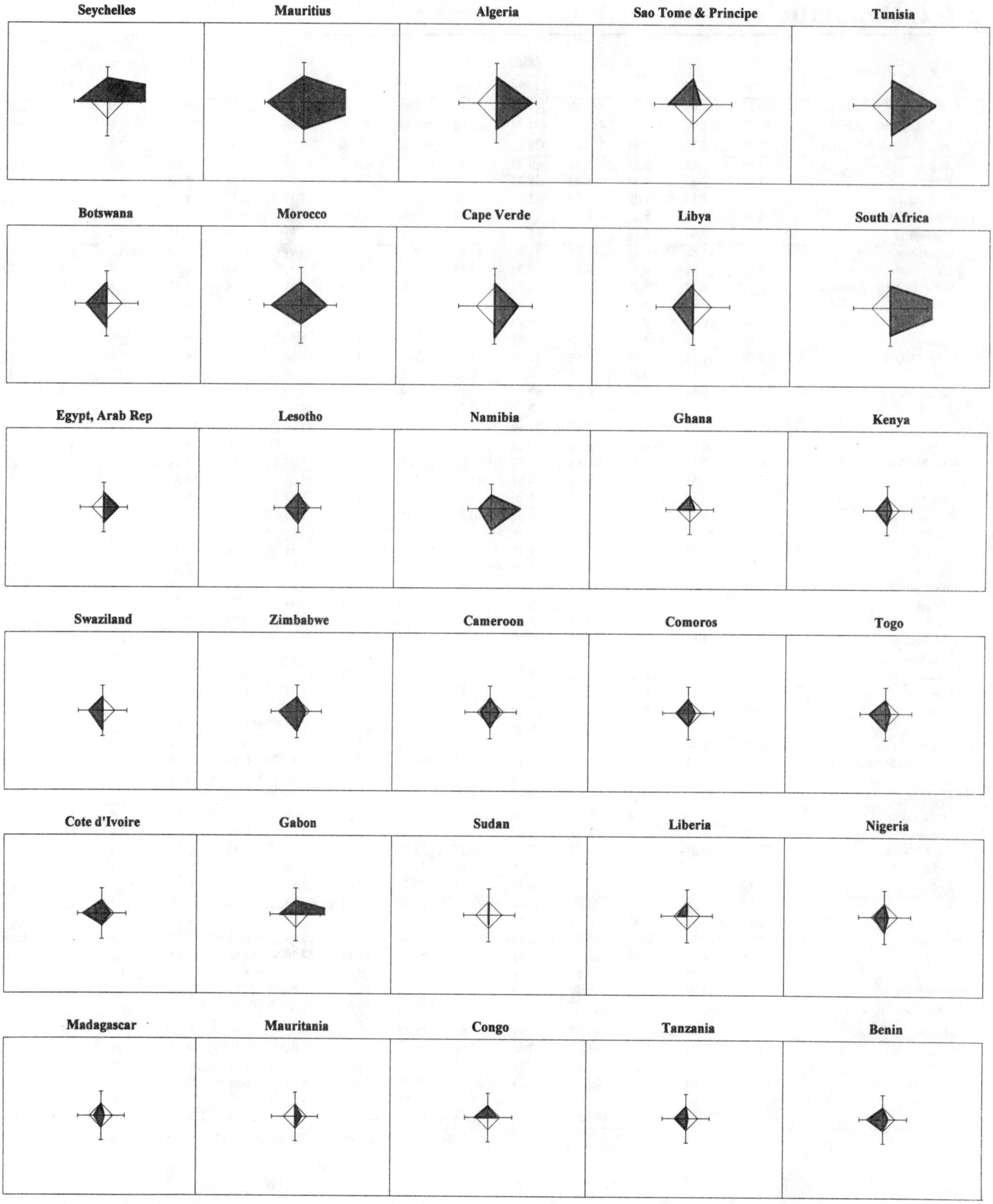

(Graph to be continued on the following page.)

Figure 1-1. (continued)

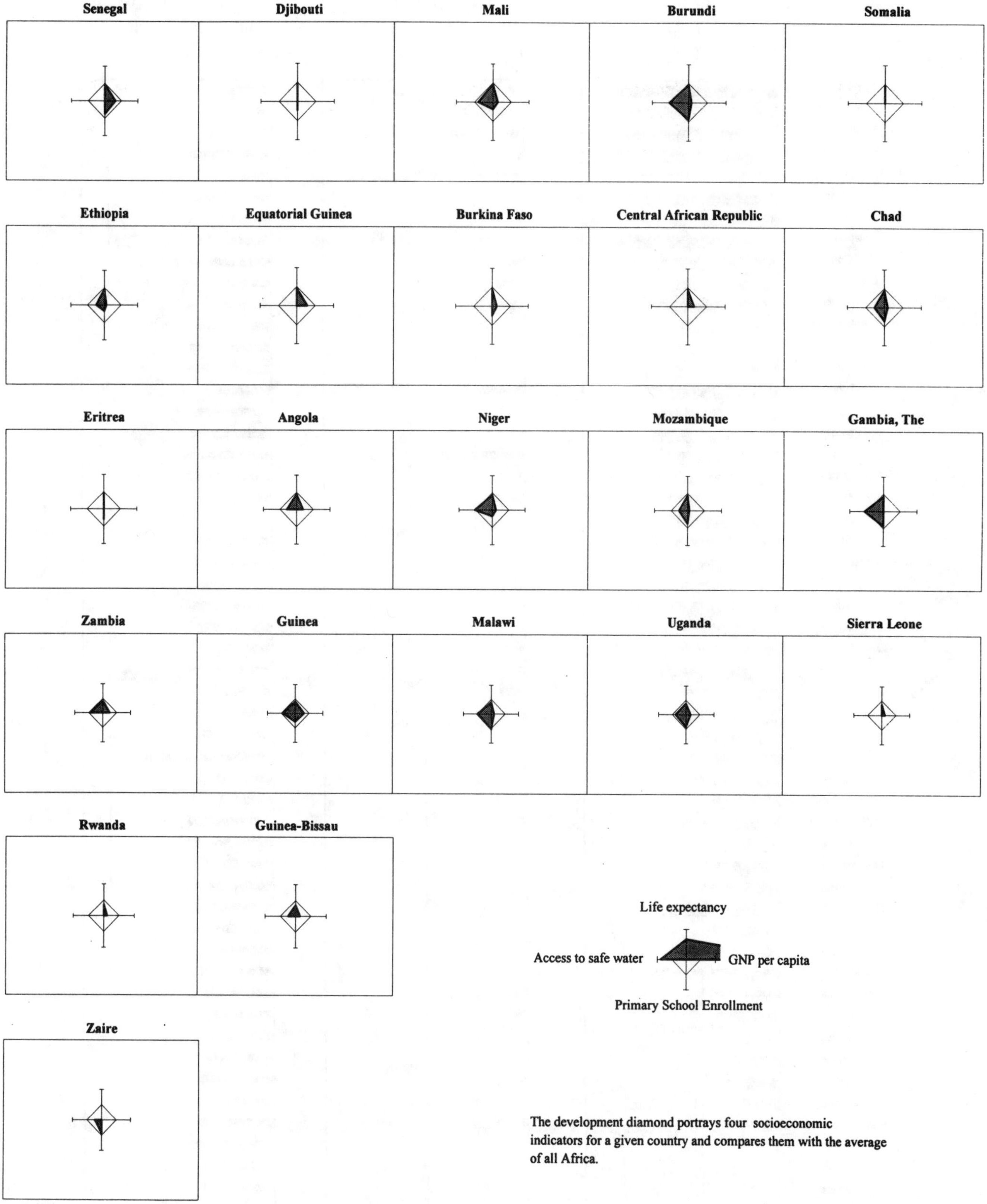

The development diamond portrays four socioeconomic indicators for a given country and compares them with the average of all Africa.

Figure 1-2. Selected basic indicators, 1996*

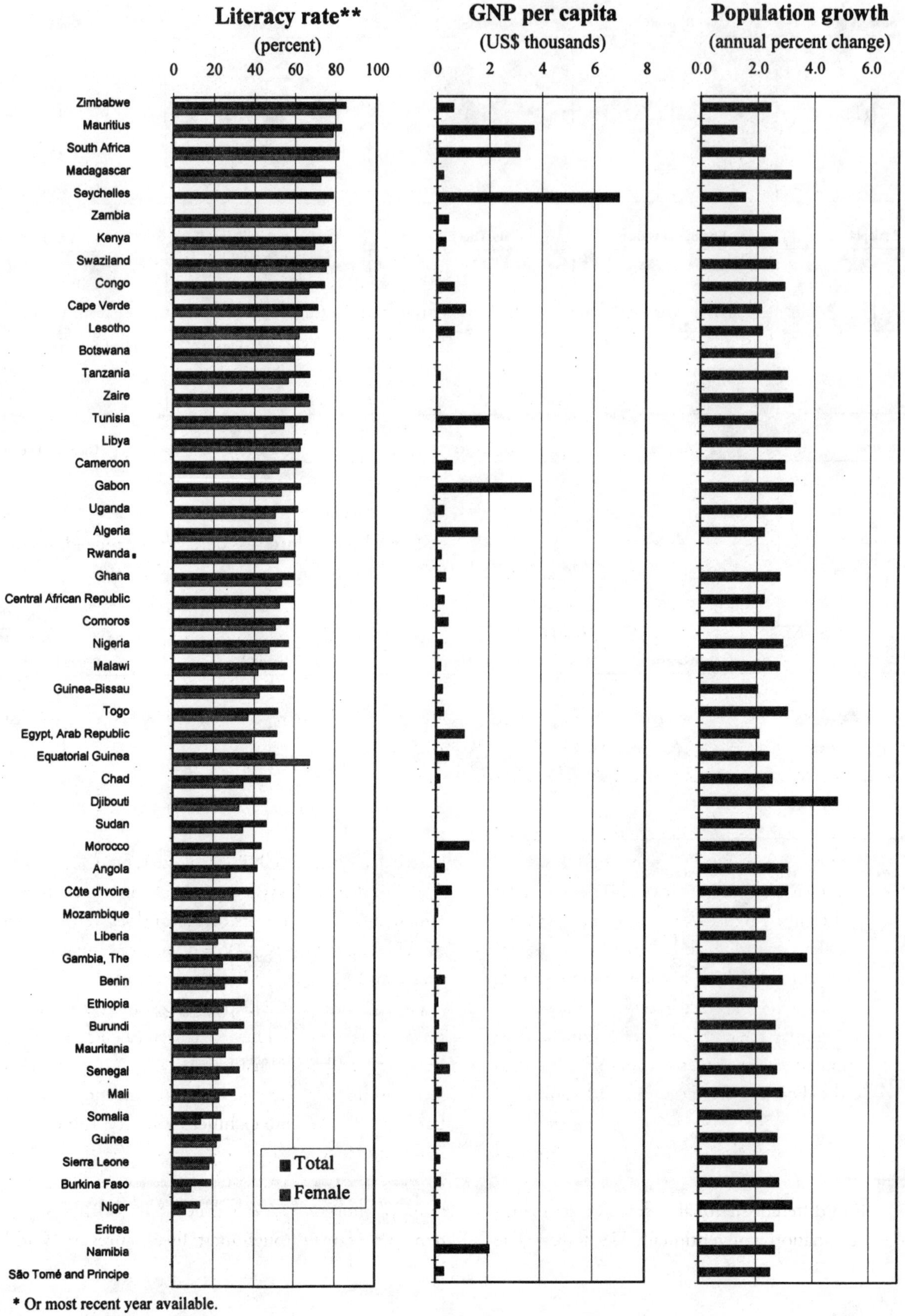

* Or most recent year available.

** Sorted by total literacy rate.

Technical Notes

Tables

Table 1-1. Basic indicators. The data for this table are from the World Bank's Economic and Social Database (BESD), except for official development assistance (ODA), which are from the OECD, Geographical Distribution of Financial Flows to Developing Countries database (see technical notes to Chapter 12). Regional aggregates for GNP per capita, life expectancy, and education are weighted by population.

Population estimates for mid-1995 are World Bank estimates. These are usually projections from the most recent population censuses or surveys (mostly from 1980–95). Refugees not permanently settled in the country of asylum are generally considered to be part of the population of their country of origin (see technical notes to Tables 13-1, 13-4, and 13-5).

Land area refers to the land surface area of a country, excluding inland waters.

GNP per capita figures in US dollars are calculated according to the *World Bank Atlas* method described below. GNP measures the total domestic and foreign value added claimed by residents. It comprises GDP (defined in the note for Table 2-5) plus net factor income from abroad, which is the income residents receive from abroad for factor services (labor and capital) less similar payments made to nonresidents who contributed to the domestic economy. The data are from the Food and Agriculture Organization (FAO).

The *World Bank Atlas* method uses a three-year average of conversion factors to convert GNP data, expressed in different national currencies, to a common denomination, conventionally US dollars. The *Atlas* conversion factor for any year is the average of the official exchange rate (Table 3-4) or alternative conversion factor (Table 3-6) for that year and for the two preceding years, after adjusting them for differences in relative inflation between that country and the United States. This three-year average smoothes fluctuations in prices and exchange rates for each country. The resulting GNP in US dollars is divided by the midyear population for the latest of the three years to derive GNP per capita.

The following formulas describe the procedures for computing the conversion factor for year *t*:

$$\left[e^*_{t-2,t} = \frac{1}{3}\; e_{t-2}\left(\frac{P_t}{P_{t-2}} \Big/ \frac{P^\$_t}{P^\$_{t-2}}\right) + e_{t-1}\left(\frac{P_t}{P_{t-1}} \Big/ \frac{P^\$_t}{P^\$_{t-1}}\right) + e_t\right]$$

and for calculating per capita GNP in US dollars for year *t*:

$$Y^\$_t = (Y_t / N_t) + e^*_{t-2,t}$$

where Y_t = current GNP (local currency) for year t, P_t = GNP deflator for year t, e = average annual exchange rate or alternative conversion factor (local currency to the US dollar) for year t, N_t = midyear population for year t, and $P^\$_t$ = US GNP deflator for year t.

Growth rates of GNP per capita for this table are shown in real terms. They have been calculated by the least-squares method using constant GNP per capita series in 1987 prices in national currency (World Bank, BESD). See also technical notes for Table 2-19.

Life expectancy at birth indicates the number of years a newborn infant would live if prevailing patterns of mortality at the time of its birth were to remain the same throughout its life. Figures are World

Bank estimates based on data from the UN Population Division, the UN Statistical Office, and national statistical offices.

Primary school enrollment is the ratio of children of all ages enrolled in primary school to the population of children of primary school age. While many countries consider the primary school age to be 6 to 11 years, others use different age groups. These different country practices are also reflected in the ratios. Gross enrollment may be reported in excess of 100 percent if some pupils are younger or older than the country's standard range of primary school age. In practice, enrollment does not necessarily equal attendance, nor does it remain constant throughout the year. Data are from the United Nations Education, Scientific, and Cultural Organization (UNESCO).

Secondary school enrollment is the ratio of children of all ages enrolled in secondary schools to the population of children of secondary school age. The definition of secondary school age differs among countries. It is most commonly considered to be 12 to 17 years. Data are from UNESCO.

Total net ODA per capita consists of net disbursements of loans and grants from all official sources on concessional financial terms, divided by the midyear population for the corresponding year (see the technical notes to Chapter 12).

Table 1-2. Population. Average annual percentage growth shown in this table was calculated using the least-squares method.

Statistical background for the population estimates is available in the UN Population and Vital Statistics Report and the World Bank's *World Population Projections* (World Bank 1994–95) (see also the technical notes to Chapter 13).

Figures

The following indicators have been used to derive the figures in this chapter.

Figure 1-1. Life expectancy (Table 1-1); access to safe water (Table 13-10); GNP per capita (Table 2-19); primary school enrollment (Table 1-1).

Figure 1-2. Literacy rate (Table 13-13); GNP per capita (Table 2-19); population growth (Table 1-2).

Methodology used for regional aggregations and period averages in chapter 1

	Aggregations[a]					Period averages[b]	
Table	*(1)*	*(2)*	*(3)*	*(4)*	*(6)*	*(2)*	*(3)*
Table 1-1							
Column 1	x						
Column 2	x						
Column 3				x			
Column 4				x			x
Column 5					x		
Column 6					x		
Column 7					x		
Column 8					x		
Column 9					x		
Column 10		x					
Table 1-2	x					x	

Note: Regional aggregations are shown in the rows for Sub-Saharan Africa, North Africa, and All Africa. Period averages are shown in column 4 for Table 1-1 and in the last three columns for Table 1-2. This table shows only the methodologies used in this chapter.

a. Regional aggregations: (1) simple total; (2) simple total of the first indicator divided by the simple total of the second indicator (same country coverage); (3) simple total of the gap-filled indicator; (4) simple total of the gap-filled main indicator divided by the simple total of the gap-filled secondary indicator; (5) simple total of the first gap-filled main indicator less the simple total of the second gap-filled main indicator, all divided by the simple total of the secondary indicator; (6) weighted total (by population); (7) median; (8) no aggregation; (9) simple arithmetic mean.

b. Period averages: (1) arithmetic mean (using the same series as shown in the table, i.e., ratio if the rest of the table is shown as ratio, level if the rest of the table is shown as level, growth rate if the rest of the table is shown as growth rate); (2) least-squares growth rate (using main indicator); (3) least-squares growth rate (using main indicator in constant terms, with the rest of the table in current terms).

2

National Accounts

National accounts data provide the broadest picture of a nation's economic performance. National accounts provide information on the structure of production in the form of gross domestic product (GDP) and its components by industrial origin, GDP and its components by expenditure, and information on a nation's economic relations with the outside world. These are the key statistics for assessing a nation's economic condition at a given point in time or the trends in a nation's economic performance over time. Moreover, national accounts data provide a quantitative basis for forecasting and policymaking and as such are used widely both by analysts and policymakers.

GDP and its components by industrial origin are compiled following the widely used System of National Accounts (SNA). The SNA methodology accounts for virtually all activities pertinent to the production of goods and the provision of services in an economy by residents and nonresidents, regardless of the allocation to domestic and foreign claims. GDP does not account for the depreciation of fixed capital.

There are three methods of compiling GDP figures: income, expenditure, and production methods. Because of technical and resource constraints, the income method is not used in most developing countries. In this volume, GDP and its components by industrial origin are compiled using the production method. The three components of GDP by industrial origin are value added in agriculture, value added in industry, and value added in services. (See the technical notes at the end of this chapter.) The national accounts are constructed in national currencies and in current prices. Figures reported in this chapter are, however, in US dollars, usually converted from national currency series at the official exchange rate. If the official exchange rate is significantly different from the prevailing market rate or shows extreme volatility, the local currency is converted into US dollars by using an alternative conversion factor. The conversion factors used for this purpose are presented in Table 3-6. Reporting currencies in a common denominator facilitates cross-country comparisons and aggregations in country groups.

In addition, estimates of GDP and its components by industrial origin are converted into constant prices. Reporting figures in constant prices is essential for monitoring real changes in the structure of production and for analyzing relations among prices, production, employment, and so forth.

Constant price series in US dollars use a 1987 base

year and are converted from national currency series using 1987 exchange rates. To establish a common base year for all countries, national accounts in national currencies at constant prices based on years other than 1987 have been partially rebased to 1987 by rescaling constant price series of components of GDP.

Using a single base year raises problems when there are profound structural changes or significant changes in relative prices. For example, values expressed in constant US dollars necessarily reflect the exchange rates prevailing during the base year. Where subsequent exchange rate changes have been substantial, as they have for many African countries since 1980, comparisons among countries and aggregate trends will be affected. For this reason alone, the data should be used with considerable caution.

Monitoring resource allocations across sectors in any given point in time requires the use of current prices. Accordingly, in addition to GDP in constant prices, GDP in current prices is provided. Following GDP in current prices are components of GDP by expenditure. Data on consumption, investment, and savings are constructed using the SNA's convention. Conceptually, all income is either consumed or saved, and as such the sum of total consumption and gross domestic saving equals GDP.

When viewed from a production point of view, by definition savings equals investment. Investment measures additions to fixed assets of an economy, whether it represents additions to the stock of capital or merely replenishes depreciated capital stock, plus net changes in the level of inventories. It is financed either through domestic savings or by drawing on the savings of foreigners. Data on gross domestic investment and gross domestic savings thus shed light not only on the nature of the domestic inter-temporal resource allocation but also on the size of the resource gap. Gross national savings, however, indicates the amount of savings generated by the residents of a nation.

Although this volume includes a chapter on international trade, the fact that balance of payments is an integral part of the national accounts warrants the inclusion of the resource balance and its components in this chapter. Moreover, a closer examination of the fifth edition of the IMF's *Balance of Payments Manual* (1993) reflects differences in concepts, definitions, and classifications from the UN's SNA guidelines. For instance, in the SNA, factor services rendered by residents of another country are excluded from goods and services, but this practice is not universally followed. The tables on resource balance, and on values of exports (f.o.b.) and imports (c.i.f.) of goods and nonfactor services in current US dollars provide a comprehensive and systematic framework for macroeconomic analysis in general. Those interested in a more specialized and rigorous study of international trade transactions should use the data provided in Chapter 5.

The rate of growth of real domestic product is an important indicator of economic progress and as such is widely monitored. Because these growth rates are calculated from national series, they are suitable for both cross-country comparisons and trend analysis for individual countries. Aggregate values and trends, however, reflect the choice of the base year, as explained above.

Gross national income per capita, which is GDP per capita adjusted for changes in international terms of trade and which include net factor income from abroad, and total consumption per capita are also widely monitored indicators of economic progress. When expressed in current US dollars to facilitate comparison and aggregation, however, the values for these indicators necessarily reflect exchange rate fluctuations as well as underlying economic and demographic changes. These indicators may be used with caution for cross-country comparison during any single year. They require special attention when used for trend analysis.

Data for Chapter 2 are from the World Bank's country desks. Estimates are based on data obtained from national sources, usually collected by World Bank staff who review the quality of national accounts data and, in some instances, help adjust national series.

2-1. Gross domestic product, real

	Millions of U.S. dollars, constant 1987 prices											Average annual percentage growth		
	1980	1987	1988	1989	1990	1991	1992	1993	1994	1995	1996	75-84	85-89	90-MR
SUB-SAHARAN AFRICA	218,879	241,327	249,814	258,176	260,957	262,829	263,110	266,059	272,043	282,608	294,937	2.3	2.5	1.7
excluding South Africa	143,033	159,228	164,643	170,849	174,076	176,852	179,378	181,025	184,612	192,595	202,204	2.2	3.0	2.2
excl. S. Africa & Nigeria	115,355	135,832	138,910	143,251	144,194	145,531	147,134	147,902	151,157	158,487	167,609	2.8	2.6	2.0
Angola	..	7,383	7,799	7,833	7,812	7,871	7,986	6,038	6,502	7,320	..	..	4.7	-2.9
Benin	1,242	1,564	1,623	1,652	1,703	1,785	1,857	1,916	2,004	2,096	2,214	3.8	2.2	4.2
Botswana	813	1,543	1,786	2,017	2,137	2,327	2,479	2,474	2,574	2,693	..	11.3	10.5	4.8
Burkina Faso	1,615	2,155	2,282	2,307	2,280	2,492	2,555	2,531	2,564	2,673	2,819	4.1	4.4	2.7
Burundi	806	1,131	1,188	1,205	1,248	1,313	1,349	1,268	1,184	1,139	992	3.8	5.1	-2.6
Cameroon	7,542	12,307	11,350	11,130	10,446	10,065	9,767	9,460	9,234	9,555	10,030	8.5	-0.1	-1.7
Cape Verde	120	236	250	264	266	270	279	290	301	316	328	10.3	12.5	3.3
Central African Republic	1,073	1,181	1,196	1,237	1,224	1,218	1,187	1,160	1,250	1,280	1,253	0.4	1.0	0.4
Chad	574	819	952	1,004	968	1,041	1,123	946	1,039	1,080	1,111	-1.4	5.2	1.3
Comoros	153	196	202	195	205	194	209	217	212	207	209	..	1.3	1.0
Congo	1,505	2,298	2,339	2,401	2,425	2,460	2,525	2,500	2,363	2,415	2,531	9.6	-1.0	0.3
Côte d'Ivoire	9,570	10,088	10,212	10,516	10,390	10,399	10,386	10,362	10,569	11,309	12,081	2.3	2.2	1.7
Djibouti	..	..	..	..	..	..	..	..	..	..	..	..	..	..
Equatorial Guinea	..	120	123	122	126	124	142	152	162	180	..	..	2.7	7.0
Eritrea	..	..	..	..	..	..	..	..	..	..	..	..	..	..
Ethiopia	..	7,488	7,520	7,548	7,834	7,467	7,204	8,104	8,287	8,748	9,791	..	4.2	3.4
Gabon	4,279	3,846	4,009	4,305	4,487	4,824	4,660	4,765	4,907	5,090	5,252	0.2	-3.8	2.5
Gambia, The	169	220	223	234	248	249	266	284	287	269	..	3.3	2.6	3.0
Ghana	4,654	5,075	5,355	5,619	5,791	6,095	6,314	6,617	6,862	7,166	7,528	-0.8	5.1	4.3
Guinea	..	2,042	2,170	2,257	2,355	2,412	2,483	2,600	2,704	2,823	2,949	..	4.7	3.8
Guinea-Bissau	121	168	175	186	197	205	210	215	219	229	242	1.5	2.8	3.4
Kenya	6,159	7,972	8,462	8,859	9,232	9,365	9,296	9,329	9,583	10,005	10,431	4.8	5.8	1.9
Lesotho	326	370	422	477	490	512	510	535	597	651	..	4.7	7.0	5.0
Liberia	1,265	1,139	..	..	..	..	..	..	..	..	..	0.5	-1.2	..
Madagascar	2,708	2,566	2,653	2,761	2,849	2,659	2,691	2,745	2,744	2,792	2,848	-0.3	2.3	0.3
Malawi	1,052	1,161	1,197	1,204	1,310	1,391	1,252	1,442	1,256	1,426	1,655	3.2	1.4	3.0
Mali	1,764	1,965	1,960	2,191	2,200	2,189	2,363	2,307	2,360	2,510	2,610	2.3	3.9	2.5
Mauritania	811	910	926	965	945	972	989	1,047	1,093	1,145	1,196	1.7	3.3	3.5
Mauritius	1,252	1,881	2,010	2,099	2,250	2,346	2,491	2,627	2,738	2,855	3,028	3.7	7.7	5.2
Mozambique	..	1,353	1,464	1,559	1,574	1,651	1,638	1,946	2,033	2,061	2,193	..	6.0	5.5
Namibia	1,849	1,909	1,913	1,959	1,966	2,111	2,276	2,245	2,395	2,491	2,616	..	2.8	4.3
Niger	2,544	2,233	2,345	2,262	2,379	2,438	2,280	2,312	2,403	2,479	2,571	2.8	1.9	1.3
Nigeria	26,385	23,441	25,762	27,617	29,880	31,301	32,215	33,082	33,421	34,196	35,000	-0.4	5.0	3.1
Rwanda	1,756	2,152	2,294	2,282	2,199	2,100	2,274	2,047	1,043	1,337	1,489	6.9	3.1	-8.7
São Tomé and Principe	54	55	57	58	57	58	58	59	60	61	62	3.5	7.5	1.2
Senegal	3,667	4,600	4,833	4,766	4,981	4,946	5,087	4,982	5,081	5,324	5,597	2.3	3.6	1.8
Seychelles	223	249	260	287	308	316	338	358	352	346	352	3.6	5.2	2.9
Sierra Leone	828	834	850	892	915	836	757	757	784	707	741	1.6	1.0	-3.2
Somalia	818	1,010	1,004	1,002	988	..	..	..	..	..	..	4.1	3.0	..
South Africa	75,684	82,070	85,139	87,302	86,869	85,989	83,781	85,077	87,468	90,156	93,136	2.6	1.6	0.8
Sudan	14,653	16,268	15,567	16,714	16,460	16,567	18,439	19,841	20,932	..	..	3.5	0.5	5.3
Swaziland	410	586	608	630	652	646	660	679	695	720	728	3.5	5.8	2.1
Tanzania	..	3,443	3,596	3,728	3,885	4,051	4,154	4,255	4,412	4,589	..	..	4.0	3.4
Togo	1,240	1,249	1,333	1,387	1,385	1,375	1,322	1,082	1,220	1,306	1,387	2.1	3.4	-1.0
Uganda	..	6,283	6,786	7,217	7,677	8,093	8,355	9,053	9,602	10,675	11,683	..	3.3	6.9
Zaire	6,514	7,653	7,689	7,592	7,093	6,496	5,816	5,029	4,835	4,805	4,869	-0.5	1.7	-7.0
Zambia	2,155	2,265	2,386	2,365	2,372	2,362	2,364	2,421	2,382	2,309	2,407	0.2	2.1	0.0
Zimbabwe	4,417	5,380	5,876	6,247	6,161	6,504	5,973	6,121	6,489	6,375	6,846	2.9	3.9	1.0
NORTH AFRICA	140,721	156,598	159,729	165,800	169,513	171,199	175,004	175,177	180,074	184,582	..	5.1	1.5	1.7
Algeria	50,099	64,474	63,418	66,593	65,624	64,696	65,877	64,605	63,957	66,785	..	5.6	1.0	-0.2
Egypt, Arab Republic	27,727	40,508	42,625	44,686	47,180	47,680	49,757	51,192	53,163	55,614	..	8.7	4.1	3.5
Libya	40,227	23,174	23,336	23,486	..	..	..	..	..	..	..	1.6	-3.9	..
Morocco	15,157	18,746	20,665	21,137	22,014	23,464	22,611	22,367	24,850	23,134	..	4.7	4.7	1.7
Tunisia	7,512	9,696	9,684	9,898	10,683	11,108	11,969	12,199	12,596	12,903	..	5.4	2.4	4.4
ALL AFRICA	359,266	397,921	409,528	423,965	430,290	433,807	437,585	440,852	451,644	466,791	..	3.4	2.1	1.4

Note: 1996 data are preliminary (see page 3).

2-2. Value added in agriculture

	Millions of U.S. dollars, constant 1987 prices											Average annual percentage growth		
	1980	1987	1988	1989	1990	1991	1992	1993	1994	1995	1996	75-84	85-89	90-MR
SUB-SAHARAN AFRICA	50,047	54,446	55,637	58,278	58,724	60,169	58,828	61,068	62,364	63,573	68,480	0.6	3.6	2.0
excluding South Africa	45,475	49,714	50,772	52,685	53,541	54,750	55,073	56,265	56,909	59,063	62,524	0.7	3.2	2.2
excl. S. Africa & Nigeria	36,648	41,315	41,523	42,982	43,418	44,264	44,344	45,404	45,763	47,622	51,031	1.9	2.6	2.2
Angola	..	949	923	957	954	1,000	1,110	799	895	1,036	..	..	0.5	-0.4
Benin	435	521	595	652	654	709	733	747	826	832	895	3.0	4.9	4.7
Botswana	113	79	131	130	135	139	142	140	139	142	..	-3.5	12.2	1.1
Burkina Faso	552	659	778	767	716	864	874	886	884	876	922	1.0	4.6	2.9
Burundi	435	572	581	568	600	613	632	587	524	497	460	2.0	4.1	-3.5
Cameroon	2,156	2,952	2,578	2,762	2,734	2,625	2,756	2,811	2,924	2,982	3,131	4.5	0.6	2.0
Cape Verde	16	38	46	45	29	29	29	28	28	28	28	12.7	27.1	-4.1
Central African Republic	476	531	554	559	565	579	584	590	617	638	671	0.6	2.0	2.5
Chad	310	304	398	386	326	438	504	394	500	492	484	-1.0	5.1	4.6
Comoros	57	75	78	80	82	83	83	83	84	86	88	..	3.7	1.1
Congo	218	274	293	304	308	283	301	275	286	300	322	3.4	4.8	0.3
Côte d'Ivoire	3,128	2,958	3,110	3,249	3,404	3,443	3,500	3,500	3,515	3,866	4,035	2.7	3.5	2.7
Djibouti	..	..	..	..	..	..	..	..	..	..	..	..	..	..
Equatorial Guinea	..	76	73	74	75	70	67	67	71	..	..	..	1.0	-1.7
Eritrea	..	..	..	..	..	..	..	..	..	..	..	..	..	..
Ethiopia	..	3,437	3,356	3,352	3,526	3,603	3,505	3,717	3,582	3,703	4,350	..	3.9	2.5
Gabon	344	361	386	387	384	388	385	380	374	333	332	..	1.5	-2.3
Gambia, The	50	69	67	66	73	63	74	66	74	73	..	2.6	-2.1	1.3
Ghana	2,626	2,568	2,660	2,773	2,717	2,873	2,838	2,904	2,983	3,109	3,234	0.2	2.3	2.3
Guinea	..	487	505	532	550	570	591	621	652	675	708	..	4.2	4.2
Guinea-Bissau	57	93	95	98	100	104	108	112	119	126	136	-2.6	3.4	4.7
Kenya	1,704	2,166	2,265	2,358	2,441	2,422	2,342	2,266	2,335	2,450	2,553	4.1	4.4	0.5
Lesotho	65	59	75	81	74	62	43	57	70	57	..	-5.1	6.3	-4.4
Liberia	..	..	..	..	..	..	..	..	..	..	..	..	..	..
Madagascar	720	810	828	871	889	893	909	938	934	959	995	0.2	2.8	1.8
Malawi	463	510	520	533	531	599	449	686	485	623	804	2.2	1.2	4.2
Mali	843	841	854	1,031	1,018	964	1,110	1,016	1,092	1,191	1,205	3.2	8.9	2.6
Mauritania	216	264	272	275	257	267	272	299	308	323	334	2.9	4.5	3.7
Mauritius	147	228	217	201	221	217	231	215	199	214	238	-2.5	1.3	0.8
Mozambique	..	..	..	..	..	..	..	..	..	..	..	..	..	..
Namibia	216	236	233	255	251	268	261	297	339	344	360	..	5.4	5.9
Niger	757	786	912	873	847	955	884	890	980	991	1,034	1.3	2.8	2.5
Nigeria	8,409	8,440	9,268	9,720	10,131	10,489	10,704	10,850	11,111	11,424	11,653	-3.0	6.4	2.5
Rwanda	766	811	857	820	799	846	890	756	446	540	599	5.6	1.1	-7.2
São Tomé and Principe	..	13	16	17	19	16	15	13	..	..	..	..	19.3	-6.2
Senegal	684	896	987	882	956	914	940	898	1,015	1,013	1,080	-1.4	5.3	2.4
Seychelles	15	13	12	13	15	15	14	14	12	12	12	-2.3	-2.5	-1.8
Sierra Leone	313	418	420	418	414	389	329	331	352	359	370	7.9	0.9	-2.2
Somalia	454	620	641	624	632	..	..	..	..	..	..	8.1	3.5	..
South Africa	4,315	4,733	4,866	5,581	5,183	5,415	3,939	4,884	5,470	4,655	5,858	0.2	7.6	0.1
Sudan	4,545	5,636	4,614	4,970	4,793	4,592	..	..	..	..	..	1.5	-1.1	..
Swaziland	67	72	69	75	78	81	66	73	73	74	74	1.7	0.8	-0.7
Tanzania	..	1,596	1,666	1,741	1,839	1,988	2,115	2,225	2,303	2,214	..	..	5.0	4.7
Togo	320	418	457	482	497	491	497	527	460	469	530	2.8	4.3	0.3
Uganda	..	3,440	3,630	3,854	4,056	4,173	4,132	4,516	4,596	4,867	5,070	..	2.7	3.9
Zaire	1,875	2,219	2,285	2,349	2,410	2,477	2,555	2,603	2,581	2,881	..	1.7	2.5	2.9
Zambia	205	247	294	286	261	274	184	330	264	229	264	0.5	5.6	-0.9
Zimbabwe	646	676	848	841	785	809	611	908	935	757	1,069	-0.1	1.5	2.8
NORTH AFRICA	16,173	20,161	20,385	22,135	21,905	24,303	23,037	22,666	23,876	23,110	..	2.7	5.0	0.8
Algeria	4,772	6,495	5,925	7,024	6,372	7,354	7,509	7,179	6,382	7,658	..	3.6	7.2	0.9
Egypt, Arab Republic	6,639	7,943	8,230	8,471	8,705	8,918	9,093	9,319	9,677	9,957	..	2.8	2.7	2.7
Libya	..	..	..	..	..	..	..	..	..	..	..	..	..	..
Morocco	2,598	2,880	3,784	3,958	3,761	4,577	2,953	2,814	4,586	2,481	..	1.3	10.0	-5.2
Tunisia	1,163	1,597	1,185	1,314	1,713	1,951	2,058	1,953	1,756	1,585	..	1.2	-1.2	2.2
ALL AFRICA	66,200	74,588	76,009	80,378	80,604	84,407	81,774	83,593	86,124	86,517	..	1.2	4.0	1.2

Note: 1996 data are preliminary (see page 3).

2-3. Value added in industry

	Millions of U.S. dollars, constant 1987 prices											Average annual percentage growth		
	1980	1987	1988	1989	1990	1991	1992	1993	1994	1995	1996	75-84	85-89	90-MR
SUB-SAHARAN AFRICA	69,079	71,410	74,597	76,953	76,888	76,225	75,700	74,996	76,009	79,015	80,925	2.4	1.8	0.6
excluding South Africa	35,123	38,259	39,789	41,610	42,102	42,632	42,808	41,872	42,438	44,023	45,920	2.4	3.1	1.0
excl. S. Africa & Nigeria	23,491	30,625	31,383	32,437	32,337	32,013	32,154	31,271	32,174	33,654	35,454	3.5	3.4	1.0
Angola	..	3,048	3,422	3,397	3,371	3,369	3,674	3,148	3,440	3,910	..	..	8.1	1.4
Benin	143	204	216	198	216	222	240	251	258	274	284	5.4	-4.1	5.1
Botswana	353	880	941	1,097	1,085	1,159	1,192	1,141	1,188	1,188	..	18.0	7.7	1.4
Burkina Faso	363	502	497	488	479	480	503	494	506	535	564	1.6	4.8	2.1
Burundi	119	178	179	180	194	211	218	191	172	158	150	8.9	3.7	-3.6
Cameroon	1,612	3,576	3,322	3,245	3,018	2,807	2,554	2,376	2,186	2,177	2,297	18.2	0.7	-5.6
Cape Verde	21	18	46	53	36	34	34	34	34	34	34	8.5	13.2	-4.2
Central African Republic	165	174	173	190	185	181	171	168	186	181	150	1.4	1.6	-2.0
Chad	85	151	169	216	232	201	198	174	167	188	202	-2.0	2.5	-2.6
Comoros	21	21	19	16	16	19	23	25	25	26	26	..	-9.0	8.1
Congo	539	822	847	934	978	974	1,000	1,040	1,009	1,068	1,103	11.5	-0.3	2.1
Côte d'Ivoire	1,752	2,242	2,308	2,386	2,216	2,246	2,312	2,331	2,351	2,428	2,677	6.5	5.8	1.7
Djibouti	..	..	..	..	..	..	..	..	..	..	..	..	..	..
Equatorial Guinea	..	10	11	11	12	14	14	16	19	..	..	..	11.1	10.5
Eritrea	..	..	..	..	..	..	..	..	..	..	..	..	..	..
Ethiopia	..	1,056	1,019	994	953	626	582	747	799	864	937	..	2.3	0.1
Gabon	1,743	1,603	1,491	1,811	2,109	1,939	1,902	1,982	2,161	2,273	2,324	..	-2.8	3.0
Gambia, The	22	27	26	28	30	31	31	33	34	30	..	1.6	10.0	2.1
Ghana	877	828	888	912	975	1,011	1,074	1,132	1,163	1,202	1,252	-7.5	9.1	4.6
Guinea	..	702	725	749	771	779	784	808	833	864	901	..	3.3	2.5
Guinea-Bissau	25	21	25	32	36	35	40	41	24	24	25	3.2	-3.5	-5.4
Kenya	1,010	1,270	1,338	1,421	1,487	1,524	1,524	1,527	1,562	1,626	1,667	4.7	5.2	2.0
Lesotho	87	96	113	154	168	183	197	203	245	286	..	13.3	14.3	10.2
Liberia	..	..	..	..	..	..	..	..	..	..	..	..	..	..
Madagascar	364	307	312	316	314	313	310	320	316	320	323	-2.9	2.8	0.4
Malawi	239	259	274	295	323	336	344	318	326	344	359	2.7	3.7	1.8
Mali	206	296	298	288	307	346	363	377	381	411	447	1.6	1.4	6.0
Mauritania	164	218	220	248	231	230	225	244	262	275	283	0.6	3.7	2.8
Mauritius	264	511	558	595	644	681	729	768	817	850	894	3.6	13.0	5.9
Mozambique	..	..	..	..	..	..	..	..	..	..	..	..	..	..
Namibia	674	576	579	562	540	586	678	577	638	667	695	..	1.9	3.2
Niger	483	418	402	420	434	430	407	414	416	426	440	9.3	0.7	0.2
Nigeria	10,877	7,665	8,427	9,187	9,767	10,605	10,641	10,568	10,284	10,421	10,630	0.0	2.1	1.5
Rwanda	313	384	368	378	386	298	340	299	150	153	176	7.4	0.3	-13.5
São Tomé and Principe	..	..	..	..	..	..	..	..	..	..	..	..	..	..
Senegal	585	738	803	795	832	807	848	839	866	940	1,000	2.7	5.8	2.9
Seychelles	35	39	43	46	51	56	55	62	51	52	53	15.3	3.4	1.1
Sierra Leone	152	138	142	155	200	148	152	148	150	120	124	-3.1	2.2	-4.8
Somalia	..	..	..	..	..	..	..	..	..	..	..	..	..	..
South Africa	33,826	33,152	34,805	35,351	34,803	33,626	32,964	33,149	33,597	35,012	35,224	2.5	0.5	0.0
Sudan	1,817	2,504	2,478	2,588	2,435	2,801	..	..	..	..	..	5.3	2.0	..
Swaziland	72	162	196	212	240	250	260	259	262	273	281	3.4	26.3	3.3
Tanzania	..	414	455	457	486	550	616	677	696	726	..	..	4.4	8.6
Togo	295	250	285	304	290	311	287	203	256	307	323	1.5	6.2	-0.3
Uganda	..	611	728	759	803	869	942	1,022	1,150	1,383	1,649	..	6.4	11.4
Zaire	1,751	2,111	2,070	1,979	1,605	1,286	901	770	754	676	..	-2.0	0.3	-17.1
Zambia	897	932	994	986	1,031	1,019	1,117	1,022	966	997	1,013	-0.4	2.7	-0.3
Zimbabwe	1,363	1,625	1,684	1,797	1,875	1,917	1,760	1,636	1,798	1,660	1,683	-1.0	5.0	-1.6
NORTH AFRICA	42,633	54,024	54,292	56,845	58,426	59,949	60,723	59,678	60,731	62,718	..	6.2	1.5	1.3
Algeria	18,113	22,660	21,704	22,687	22,628	23,006	23,007	21,961	21,545	21,975	..	5.3	-0.4	-0.9
Egypt, Arab Republic	7,551	10,495	11,085	11,765	12,401	13,058	13,255	13,550	14,288	15,005	..	11.0	4.2	3.8
Libya	..	..	..	..	..	..	..	..	..	..	..	..	..	..
Morocco	5,239	6,164	6,671	6,594	7,180	7,222	7,385	7,288	7,600	7,836	..	3.6	3.1	2.3
Tunisia	2,380	2,858	2,925	3,332	3,404	3,515	3,759	3,791	3,978	4,148	..	7.1	2.6	3.8
ALL AFRICA	112,517	125,343	129,080	133,884	135,181	135,772	135,890	134,200	136,232	141,253	..	3.7	1.7	0.6

Note: 1996 data are preliminary (see page 3).

2-4. Value added in services

	Millions of U.S. dollars, constant 1987 prices											Average annual percentage growth		
	1980	*1987*	*1988*	*1989*	*1990*	*1991*	*1992*	*1993*	*1994*	*1995*	*1996*	*75-84*	*85-89*	*90-MR*
SUB-SAHARAN AFRICA	88,376	103,350	106,761	109,687	111,791	112,977	113,392	113,341	115,657	120,653	125,536	3.3	2.3	1.7
excluding South Africa	57,435	66,359	68,597	70,764	72,631	73,747	74,220	73,870	75,161	78,688	82,537	3.4	2.6	1.8
excl. S. Africa & Nigeria	51,263	59,461	61,000	62,500	63,109	64,029	63,719	62,442	63,340	66,646	70,100	3.5	2.0	1.2
Angola	..	3,386	3,454	3,478	3,486	3,502	3,202	2,090	2,167	2,373	..	..	2.8	-8.9
Benin	664	839	813	802	833	854	884	918	920	991	1,035	3.8	2.2	3.5
Botswana	347	584	714	790	917	1,029	1,145	1,193	1,247	1,363	..	9.7	14.7	8.9
Burkina Faso	624	931	945	988	1,022	1,072	1,110	1,087	1,105	1,173	1,240	10.0	4.0	2.8
Burundi	191	288	296	308	343	351	357	348	345	314	290	5.3	4.1	-1.1
Cameroon	3,774	5,780	5,450	5,123	4,694	4,633	4,457	4,274	4,124	4,397	4,602	7.1	-0.9	-1.7
Cape Verde	83	180	158	167	201	207	217	229	240	254	267	10.4	9.4	6.1
Central African Republic	375	397	398	413	394	388	361	335	381	389	372	0.4	0.0	-1.1
Chad	179	318	325	348	340	350	361	322	332	347	365	-0.2	6.8	0.2
Comoros	75	101	105	99	107	92	103	108	102	96	95	..	2.0	-0.5
Congo	747	1,201	1,200	1,163	1,138	1,204	1,223	1,185	1,068	1,047	1,106	10.0	-2.7	-1.4
Côte d'Ivoire	4,689	4,888	4,794	4,881	4,771	4,710	4,574	4,531	4,702	5,015	5,370	1.0	0.1	1.1
Djibouti	..	..	..	..	..	..	..	..	..	..	..	..	..	..
Equatorial Guinea	..	33	38	37	39	41	60	69	73	..	..	..	3.9	17.2
Eritrea	..	..	..	..	..	..	..	..	..	..	..	..	..	..
Ethiopia	..	2,450	2,594	2,653	2,807	2,847	2,725	3,199	3,458	3,708	3,973	..	5.8	6.1
Gabon	2,192	1,883	2,132	2,107	1,993	2,497	2,373	2,402	2,372	2,484	2,596	..	-5.4	2.9
Gambia, The	79	98	104	103	109	116	107	128	127	123	..	4.1	3.6	3.4
Ghana	1,151	1,679	1,807	1,935	2,099	2,211	2,402	2,582	2,716	2,855	3,042	2.2	7.8	6.6
Guinea	..	853	940	976	1,034	1,063	1,108	1,171	1,218	1,284	1,339	..	6.1	4.6
Guinea-Bissau	38	53	55	56	61	67	62	61	76	78	81	13.6	5.7	5.2
Kenya	2,469	3,430	3,616	3,806	3,976	4,119	4,240	4,333	4,482	4,651	4,856	5.9	5.6	3.3
Lesotho	98	139	146	152	163	172	178	187	197	217	..	6.5	4.4	5.6
Liberia	..	..	..	..	..	..	..	..	..	..	..	..	..	..
Madagascar	1,279	1,122	1,175	1,222	1,272	1,182	1,195	1,221	1,228	1,245	1,259	0.0	1.8	0.3
Malawi	228	271	280	290	310	328	331	314	309	303	276	3.7	3.7	-0.8
Mali	622	724	709	762	757	753	776	801	781	795	839	1.5	0.0	1.3
Mauritania	352	334	341	351	364	379	394	396	413	431	461	1.9	3.6	3.6
Mauritius	841	1,141	1,234	1,303	1,385	1,448	1,531	1,643	1,723	1,790	1,896	5.7	6.8	5.5
Mozambique	..	..	..	..	..	..	..	..	..	..	..	..	..	..
Namibia	792	902	885	892	898	968	1,018	1,012	1,044	1,081	1,136	..	0.6	3.4
Niger	1,305	1,029	1,031	968	1,098	1,053	989	1,009	1,007	1,062	1,097	2.0	1.6	0.7
Nigeria	6,097	6,905	7,595	8,252	9,488	9,683	10,347	11,115	11,470	11,730	12,160	3.0	7.6	5.3
Rwanda	453	770	820	851	820	836	884	872	382	526	615	10.9	6.7	-7.8
São Tomé and Principe	..	..	..	..	..	..	..	..	..	..	..	..	..	..
Senegal	2,398	2,966	3,043	3,090	3,194	3,226	3,299	3,246	3,199	3,371	3,517	3.4	2.6	1.4
Seychelles	173	197	205	228	242	246	269	282	289	281	286	1.4	6.1	3.5
Sierra Leone	269	238	247	264	242	234	209	205	208	178	193	1.6	-3.3	-4.8
Somalia	..	..	..	..	..	..	..	..	..	..	..	..	..	..
South Africa	30,996	37,019	38,193	38,959	39,205	39,283	39,254	39,507	40,502	42,012	43,199	3.1	1.9	1.4
Sudan	8,291	8,127	8,475	9,155	9,231	9,174	..	..	..	..	..	4.4	1.1	..
Swaziland	271	353	343	342	334	315	334	347	361	374	372	3.9	-0.1	1.9
Tanzania	..	994	1,019	1,067	1,078	1,042	1,016	994	1,036	1,220	..	..	1.7	1.0
Togo	625	581	591	601	598	573	538	352	504	530	534	2.0	1.5	-2.6
Uganda	..	2,010	2,156	2,295	2,445	2,634	2,827	3,028	3,262	3,690	4,043	..	3.2	8.3
Zaire	2,888	3,323	3,335	3,264	3,079	2,733	2,360	1,656	1,499	1,248	..	-0.9	2.1	-15.8
Zambia	1,053	1,087	1,098	1,092	1,080	1,069	1,064	1,069	1,153	1,082	1,131	0.6	0.8	0.6
Zimbabwe	2,079	2,525	2,642	2,759	2,826	2,962	2,966	2,978	3,079	3,249	3,332	5.6	3.1	2.6
NORTH AFRICA	49,815	71,688	74,791	77,458	80,083	80,208	84,569	85,647	88,377	91,537	..	7.5	3.2	2.8
Algeria	16,972	23,134	23,657	24,703	24,478	24,286	25,120	24,817	25,427	26,164	..	5.7	1.8	1.0
Egypt, Arab Republic	13,537	22,070	23,310	24,450	26,074	25,703	27,410	28,323	29,198	30,652	..	11.0	4.5	3.6
Libya	..	..	..	..	..	..	..	..	..	..	..	..	..	..
Morocco	7,319	9,702	10,209	10,585	11,074	11,665	12,274	12,266	12,664	12,816	..	6.8	4.0	3.2
Tunisia	3,969	5,242	5,575	5,252	5,566	5,642	6,153	6,455	6,862	7,171	..	5.8	3.2	5.5
ALL AFRICA	138,487	174,679	181,109	186,631	191,240	192,614	197,193	198,166	203,149	211,298	..	4.7	2.7	1.9

Note: 1996 data are preliminary (see page 3).

2-5. Gross domestic product, nominal

	Millions of U.S. dollars, current prices											Annual average		
	1980	*1987*	*1988*	*1989*	*1990*	*1991*	*1992*	*1993*	*1994*	*1995*	*1996*	*75-84*	*85-89*	*90-MR*
SUB-SAHARAN AFRICA	266,235	241,234	250,207	255,962	282,992	281,625	284,996	270,633	264,421	292,529	314,380	200,704	230,140	284,511
excluding South Africa	187,694	159,163	162,039	164,209	176,272	169,200	165,235	152,793	142,076	157,830	190,979	141,482	154,160	164,912
excl. S.Africa & Nigeria	119,929	135,722	139,191	140,365	147,775	141,863	135,934	129,676	116,959	134,112	159,992	98,377	130,379	138,044
Angola	..	7,383	7,975	9,283	9,113	4,519	5,366	4,250	6,870	6,187	..	..	7,560	6,051
Benin	1,405	1,564	1,626	1,502	1,845	1,899	1,628	2,125	1,527	2,075	2,200	1,035	1,415	1,900
Botswana	971	1,543	2,248	2,749	3,176	3,688	3,700	3,813	4,011	4,318	..	762	1,789	3,784
Burkina Faso	1,709	2,155	2,379	2,363	2,765	2,789	2,990	2,811	1,854	2,330	..	1,311	2,038	2,590
Burundi	920	1,131	1,082	1,114	1,132	1,167	1,087	940	971	1,061	899	778	1,136	1,037
Cameroon	6,741	12,307	12,493	11,140	11,152	12,437	11,396	11,890	7,854	7,964	9,032	5,630	10,942	10,247
Cape Verde	107	236	265	268	305	319	358	331	347	420	426	86	204	358
Central African Republic	797	1,181	1,251	1,240	1,462	1,379	1,384	1,259	898	1,139	1,095	618	1,122	1,231
Chad	727	819	1,044	1,009	1,224	1,321	1,325	1,030	830	1,052	1,172	653	870	1,136
Comoros	124	196	207	199	250	247	264	280	201	233	230	113	176	243
Congo	1,706	2,298	2,213	2,384	2,798	2,725	2,933	1,919	1,769	2,098	2,388	1,451	2,181	2,376
Côte d'Ivoire	10,175	10,088	10,255	9,757	10,797	10,493	11,167	10,405	7,666	9,992	10,688	7,172	9,247	10,173
Djibouti	..	376	399	401	425	456	470	471	487	491	485	..	376	469
Equatorial Guinea	..	120	127	112	132	131	159	157	129	169	..	104	107	146
Eritrea	..	..	..	..	..	..	..	..	..	..	..	..	..	..
Ethiopia	..	7,488	7,728	8,151	8,608	9,573	7,365	7,240	5,850	5,933	6,218	5,602	7,413	7,255
Gabon	4,279	3,846	3,810	4,186	5,952	5,403	5,593	4,381	4,191	5,117	5,704	3,211	3,968	5,192
Gambia, The	233	220	233	241	291	331	323	365	359	363	..	183	203	339
Ghana	4,445	5,075	5,195	5,249	5,886	6,600	6,414	5,662	5,174	6,179	6,343	3,762	5,150	6,037
Guinea	..	2,042	2,384	2,432	2,818	2,982	2,974	3,178	3,395	3,673	3,950	..	2,213	3,281
Guinea-Bissau	105	168	158	201	236	237	222	237	236	254	271	131	163	242
Kenya	7,265	7,972	8,519	8,341	8,572	8,152	8,209	5,753	7,399	9,095	9,272	5,550	7,641	8,065
Lesotho	368	370	448	510	622	589	671	707	766	841	..	279	370	699
Liberia	1,117	1,139	1,194	1,202	..	..	..	..	..	..	..	987	1,143	..
Madagascar	4,042	2,566	2,442	2,498	3,081	2,677	3,001	3,371	2,979	3,198	4,156	3,057	2,724	3,209
Malawi	1,238	1,161	1,334	1,522	1,858	2,178	1,858	2,031	1,283	1,465	..	1,018	1,266	1,779
Mali	1,686	1,965	1,982	2,050	2,477	2,418	2,847	2,666	1,853	2,467	2,660	1,212	1,789	2,484
Mauritania	709	910	957	982	1,020	1,130	1,191	944	1,027	1,068	1,094	645	867	1,067
Mauritius	1,132	1,881	2,134	2,182	2,642	2,831	3,102	3,201	3,514	3,940	4,292	990	1,747	3,360
Mozambique	2,028	1,353	1,203	1,330	1,443	1,433	1,242	1,410	1,433	1,462	1,715	1,988	1,893	1,448
Namibia	2,172	1,909	2,096	2,132	2,270	2,388	2,758	2,556	2,926	3,162	3,026	1,900	1,797	2,727
Niger	2,538	2,233	2,260	2,203	2,480	2,328	2,345	2,220	1,563	1,880	1,987	1,720	2,008	2,115
Nigeria	65,003	23,441	22,848	23,844	28,472	27,313	29,239	23,294	25,068	23,911	30,746	42,173	23,750	26,863
Rwanda	1,163	2,152	2,396	2,410	2,592	1,837	1,918	1,847	730	1,230	1,330	1,091	2,123	1,640
São Tomé and Principe	43	55	49	46	50	57	46	48	50	45	45	32	50	49
Senegal	3,016	4,600	4,981	4,628	5,702	5,494	4,012	4,074	3,882	4,867	5,143	2,361	4,110	4,739
Seychelles	147	249	284	308	373	376	444	491	488	518	515	112	244	458
Sierra Leone	1,199	834	1,286	1,181	897	807	691	771	928	866	940	1,044	1,081	843
Somalia	604	1,010	1,038	1,092	917	..	..	..	..	..	..	677	989	917
South Africa	78,744	82,070	88,168	91,753	106,682	112,309	119,569	117,456	121,619	133,927	126,301	59,582	75,986	119,695
Sudan	6,760	16,268	10,540	10,884	9,014	7,310	5,989	..	..	..	..	7,025	12,361	7,438
Swaziland	582	586	696	725	888	892	967	938	988	1,073	1,069	442	563	974
Tanzania	..	3,443	3,470	3,984	3,869	4,195	4,123	3,727	3,378	4,192	..	6,283	4,682	3,914
Togo	1,136	1,249	1,379	1,353	1,628	1,602	1,689	1,215	929	1,294	1,420	813	1,161	1,397
Uganda	1,267	6,283	6,509	5,252	4,304	3,321	2,856	3,220	3,981	5,655	6,005	2,154	5,097	4,192
Zaire	14,922	7,653	8,853	9,020	9,348	9,086	8,204	8,975	5,829	6,140	19,437	11,730	8,163	9,574
Zambia	3,884	2,265	3,729	3,995	3,288	3,377	3,183	3,564	3,714	4,108	4,168	3,159	2,781	3,629
Zimbabwe	5,355	5,380	6,336	6,552	6,806	6,595	5,464	5,574	5,819	6,606	7,509	4,805	5,553	6,339
NORTH AFRICA	128,366	156,598	147,224	149,398	167,688	145,471	163,551	162,159	164,046	178,473	..	99,997	148,107	163,564
Algeria	42,345	64,474	58,788	54,937	61,902	46,301	49,116	49,762	42,063	41,435	..	34,782	59,855	48,430
Egypt, Arab Republic	22,913	40,508	35,045	39,648	43,130	36,971	46,367	47,197	51,898	60,472	..	20,312	37,154	47,673
Libya	35,545	23,174	21,097	21,864	..	..	..	..	..	..	..	24,534	22,902	..
Morocco	18,821	18,746	22,198	22,847	25,825	27,836	28,558	26,865	30,349	32,412	..	13,468	18,731	28,641
Tunisia	8,742	9,696	10,096	10,102	12,291	13,075	15,575	14,604	15,728	18,035	..	6,901	9,465	14,885
ALL AFRICA	392,855	397,832	397,431	405,360	450,442	428,848	448,802	432,487	427,721	470,417	..	299,362	378,256	443,119

Note: 1996 data are preliminary (see page 3).

2-6. Total consumption

	Percentage of GDP											Annual average		
	1980	1987	1988	1989	1990	1991	1992	1993	1994	1995	1996	75-84	85-89	90-MR
SUB-SAHARAN AFRICA	73.9	81.8	81.6	81.2	81.2	83.0	84.5	85.8	84.2	84.5	83.8	78.7	81.8	83.9
excluding South Africa	78.3	85.7	85.5	85.0	83.7	85.6	86.1	88.9	86.2	86.8	84.8	82.4	85.9	86.0
excl. S. Africa & Nigeria	85.2	86.8	86.4	86.9	86.3	88.6	90.4	91.0	87.6	88.1	86.5	84.7	86.6	88.4
Angola	..	70.0	74.5	73.1	70.3	71.9	71.8	70.0	67.7	66.2	..	..	74.1	69.6
Benin	105.1	96.4	98.3	96.4	94.5	94.2	95.8	94.8	90.6	90.7	90.8	100.0	97.5	93.0
Botswana	72.3	60.9	57.1	45.7	62.6	63.4	55.7	76.9	75.2	77.4	..	79.1	58.0	68.5
Burkina Faso	105.8	99.4	95.7	92.9	92.3	93.9	92.8	95.0	93.9	93.0	92.4	101.7	97.6	93.3
Burundi	100.6	93.4	98.3	96.7	105.4	104.2	102.2	103.1	109.9	107.1	111.6	95.9	96.6	106.2
Cameroon	79.6	79.2	79.0	80.0	79.1	78.0	81.0	82.5	82.1	79.4	60.7	78.0	77.1	77.5
Cape Verde	124.0	101.5	90.0	95.1	90.2	91.0	86.6	84.5	87.4	90.7	89.6	119.8	100.0	88.6
Central African Republic	108.9	99.5	98.9	97.6	98.8	97.3	100.4	96.8	90.9	93.1	98.9	101.6	99.1	96.6
Chad	..	119.6	113.5	116.0	104.1	110.3	111.1	111.8	108.0	98.5	97.4	100.2	118.1	105.9
Comoros	110.1	102.0	102.0	107.0	99.1	97.1	97.7	100.0	108.0	107.9	105.9	106.5	102.5	102.3
Congo	64.3	77.2	81.2	72.4	78.3	81.1	76.6	77.0	74.9	72.2	69.7	73.9	76.8	75.7
Côte d'Ivoire	79.6	81.6	82.4	86.2	87.0	89.0	90.6	90.3	77.6	79.7	80.0	75.7	79.7	84.9
Djibouti	..	..	..	..	..	110.2	113.8	111.0	111.3	108.7	107.7	..	..	110.4
Equatorial Guinea	..	116.9	122.9	111.8	110.9	114.5	97.2	92.5	83.6	..	..	92.4	112.7	99.7
Eritrea	..	..	..	..	..	..	..	121.6	137.6	127.2	125.8	..	..	128.0
Ethiopia	..	93.8	91.6	95.8	95.7	100.0	96.9	93.8	95.0	93.2	92.4	96.6	95.2	95.3
Gabon	39.4	71.3	69.4	69.1	63.1	59.5	65.3	63.3	54.7	57.9	56.9	41.9	68.5	60.1
Gambia, The	99.3	90.2	91.5	97.7	93.9	93.6	99.9	96.2	95.0	95.1	..	96.0	93.5	95.6
Ghana	95.1	94.2	94.3	94.4	94.5	92.7	98.7	102.2	96.0	90.1	91.0	93.8	94.3	95.0
Guinea	..	82.8	87.1	81.5	82.3	84.4	88.8	89.1	91.0	89.9	90.0	..	83.4	87.9
Guinea-Bissau	106.0	95.8	97.7	104.1	100.3	99.0	99.0	95.4	101.8	100.6	94.3	104.6	100.7	98.6
Kenya	81.9	80.8	80.3	82.7	81.0	80.3	83.6	77.5	78.7	87.1	83.1	80.7	79.4	81.6
Lesotho	159.7	170.0	169.0	146.6	130.2	151.0	139.7	129.6	109.1	100.8	..	173.6	167.2	126.7
Liberia	72.7	..	..	..	..	..	..	..	..	..	..	76.7	83.6	..
Madagascar	101.4	94.1	91.6	90.0	96.2	98.4	97.1	97.9	96.9	97.3	96.0	98.1	93.5	97.1
Malawi	89.2	86.7	90.8	95.3	90.6	87.6	99.9	104.2	102.4	97.9	89.1	84.4	90.0	96.0
Mali	101.8	95.9	97.5	94.3	93.8	93.6	95.6	93.5	93.0	90.3	88.2	100.5	100.2	92.6
Mauritania	93.1	88.2	82.9	87.4	94.4	90.0	92.8	90.3	92.8	93.0	86.1	97.7	88.4	91.3
Mauritius	89.5	72.4	73.9	76.2	76.4	75.1	73.9	75.3	76.4	77.3	78.1	81.5	74.5	76.1
Mozambique	123.6	102.4	102.1	106.7	98.5	95.5	94.4	89.6	94.1	82.6	78.1	106.6	101.2	90.4
Namibia	61.1	93.9	82.8	81.7	84.7	90.9	88.0	90.2	80.7	86.0	85.3	86.3	83.6	86.5
Niger	77.4	92.0	82.0	89.6	96.0	92.5	99.0	99.0	98.3	98.5	96.2	90.5	89.9	97.1
Nigeria	67.7	80.1	80.9	74.7	70.6	70.7	66.7	77.3	79.4	79.1	76.2	78.4	82.3	74.3
Rwanda	95.8	96.0	96.5	97.7	96.6	99.3	98.6	100.5	160.1	111.1	102.5	93.2	94.7	109.8
São Tomé and Principe	114.9	117.3	125.8	141.1	137.2	127.3	127.8	123.2	118.0	122.1	123.4	109.0	122.4	125.6
Senegal	100.4	94.9	93.6	92.7	92.3	94.7	93.4	95.1	92.8	89.6	89.1	96.6	95.1	92.4
Seychelles	72.9	69.0	68.1	70.2	62.3	79.0	83.5	82.5	79.6	79.3	80.1	75.7	69.9	78.1
Sierra Leone	100.2	97.6	98.6	101.7	91.7	91.9	93.7	96.7	96.6	109.1	109.7	98.4	98.1	98.5
Somalia	112.9	91.2	93.5	106.9	112.5	..	..	..	..	..	..	111.4	94.4	112.5
South Africa	63.5	74.1	74.3	74.2	76.9	78.9	82.0	81.3	81.3	81.3	81.7	69.7	73.2	80.5
Sudan	96.6	87.2	92.7	93.3	93.4	102.6	..	..	..	..	..	93.7	93.7	98.0
Swaziland	93.5	73.7	71.0	75.0	85.4	90.5	89.3	85.4	86.5	90.9	96.8	83.5	79.6	89.3
Tanzania	..	97.2	94.8	90.6	85.7	91.2	97.8	96.8	96.7	107.1	..	85.7	93.5	95.9
Togo	76.8	91.8	92.9	84.7	85.3	91.0	94.7	102.5	90.6	91.5	93.6	78.6	90.9	92.7
Uganda	100.4	100.1	99.4	99.0	99.4	99.3	99.6	98.9	95.9	92.6	93.7	96.1	97.0	97.1
Zaire	89.9	88.7	87.9	85.0	90.7	98.2	93.9	96.0	89.0	89.9	91.9	89.5	86.7	92.8
Zambia	80.7	83.5	81.8	96.2	82.2	85.5	93.6	91.4	90.0	94.1	93.5	81.1	85.1	90.1
Zimbabwe	73.1	78.6	73.1	78.5	76.6	80.5	86.4	80.5	81.9	85.2	81.6	76.9	75.3	81.8
NORTH AFRICA	60.8	77.2	79.2	78.7	79.7	77.9	79.3	81.9	83.4	83.0	..	65.9	77.0	80.9
Algeria	56.9	68.1	73.0	70.7	72.5	63.3	67.6	72.2	73.0	71.2	..	61.1	69.2	70.0
Egypt, Arab Republic	84.8	84.1	82.9	82.7	83.9	86.8	84.6	86.8	88.6	86.0	..	84.6	84.3	86.1
Libya	43.1	..	..	..	..	..	..	..	..	..	..	53.5	..	..
Morocco	86.3	83.2	79.3	81.7	80.8	82.8	83.9	84.5	84.3	86.6	..	87.1	81.8	83.8
Tunisia	76.0	77.5	78.9	79.4	80.0	79.0	77.7	78.6	77.9	79.7	..	75.8	78.4	78.8
ALL AFRICA	70.6	80.2	81.2	80.8	81.1	81.9	83.3	84.9	84.4	84.5	..	75.5	80.1	83.4

Note: 1996 data are preliminary (see page 3). Since 1994, Nigeria's ratios are distorted because the official exchange rate used by the Government for oil exports and oil value added is significantly overvalued.

2-7. General government consumption

	Percentage of GDP											*Annual average*		
	1980	*1987*	*1988*	*1989*	*1990*	*1991*	*1992*	*1993*	*1994*	*1995*	*1996*	*75-84*	*85-89*	*90-MR*
SUB-SAHARAN AFRICA	14.3	16.2	16.3	16.2	17.2	17.0	17.6	18.1	17.4	16.9	15.8	15.1	16.1	17.2
excluding South Africa	14.8	15.1	15.4	14.9	16.1	15.1	15.4	15.9	14.1	13.7	12.4	15.3	15.2	14.7
excl. S. Africa & Nigeria	16.3	15.9	15.8	15.7	16.3	15.8	16.9	15.6	14.9	14.3	12.8	15.6	15.7	15.2
Angola	..	27.9	31.5	28.6	34.5	29.0	47.1	32.9	33.9	37.0	..	..	30.9	35.7
Benin	8.6	15.5	11.8	11.1	11.0	10.7	10.7	10.3	9.9	10.9	11.2	9.9	13.8	10.7
Botswana	19.3	25.7	27.7	22.1	30.9	31.5	27.5	31.2	31.5	31.9	..	22.1	24.3	30.8
Burkina Faso	10.4	14.9	14.3	14.0	14.9	14.6	15.0	15.2	15.6	14.2	..	12.8	14.2	14.9
Burundi	9.2	9.6	10.7	10.2	10.5	10.3	10.0	10.8	11.3	12.0	13.1	10.3	9.6	11.1
Cameroon	9.7	12.2	10.7	10.8	12.8	13.3	12.8	12.8	10.0	8.6	7.8	9.7	10.8	11.2
Cape Verde	8.2	17.8	16.5	18.0	19.4	19.7	19.8	21.8	24.2	28.8	24.2	10.0	17.4	22.6
Central African Republic	15.1	15.6	14.8	13.7	14.0	17.5	15.1	11.9	14.6	11.8	8.0	15.0	14.5	13.3
Chad	..	22.5	18.1	21.4	14.3	12.7	13.1	14.3	15.6	13.8	12.8	18.4	19.7	13.8
Comoros	30.9	27.3	27.1	27.6	25.1	22.1	21.0	18.6	21.6	21.2	19.1	29.7	27.4	21.2
Congo	17.6	20.6	21.0	19.5	20.1	24.2	21.1	21.2	16.2	12.7	10.9	17.3	20.5	18.1
Côte d'Ivoire	16.9	16.6	17.1	18.2	16.8	16.4	17.4	16.5	13.0	11.9	12.1	16.5	16.3	14.9
Djibouti	..	..	..	..	..	32.0	44.2	44.1	40.1	38.3	33.5	..	..	38.7
Equatorial Guinea	..	29.3	30.1	38.5	39.6	39.3	35.2	41.4	9.9	..	..	28.3	31.5	33.1
Eritrea	..	..	..	..	..	..	..	..	..	..	..	..	..	..
Ethiopia	..	14.8	17.2	18.5	18.5	15.4	10.4	10.6	11.1	10.8	11.3	15.3	16.0	12.6
Gabon	13.2	16.4	16.8	14.2	12.8	14.3	15.5	15.3	12.0	11.4	10.9	14.5	14.8	13.2
Gambia, The	20.1	26.6	24.6	25.7	23.2	20.9	17.8	14.6	17.9	18.5	..	17.9	23.2	18.8
Ghana	11.2	10.0	9.4	9.8	9.3	9.5	12.1	15.2	14.1	12.7	13.7	9.9	9.9	12.4
Guinea	..	11.9	11.2	11.7	11.9	11.5	10.7	9.6	8.7	8.4	8.1	..	11.6	9.9
Guinea-Bissau	29.0	11.1	10.0	11.9	10.6	11.5	9.1	8.6	9.1	8.7	9.2	23.8	12.5	9.6
Kenya	19.8	18.6	18.1	17.9	18.6	16.8	15.7	14.5	14.6	14.8	17.4	18.4	18.1	16.1
Lesotho	35.8	29.8	27.9	22.4	19.9	28.3	30.7	29.9	29.7	32.3	..	25.8	29.3	28.5
Liberia	16.3	..	..	..	..	..	..	..	..	..	..	15.8	19.0	..
Madagascar	12.1	9.1	8.1	8.8	8.0	8.7	8.3	7.9	6.9	6.6	6.4	11.1	8.9	7.5
Malawi	19.3	19.5	16.2	17.1	15.2	14.0	18.5	17.1	22.9	20.5	..	16.4	18.0	18.0
Mali	10.1	13.8	12.9	13.4	13.5	14.6	13.4	12.9	12.1	11.0	10.6	9.6	12.9	12.6
Mauritania	25.3	11.1	11.0	9.9	11.1	10.9	10.4	11.0	10.2	10.0	9.9	25.2	12.0	10.5
Mauritius	14.1	11.7	12.7	12.3	11.8	11.7	11.5	12.1	12.5	12.2	9.8	13.5	11.7	11.6
Mozambique	21.0	17.2	18.2	19.7	20.2	18.4	19.1	16.7	20.0	12.6	12.0	24.5	19.6	17.0
Namibia	17.4	32.6	30.6	28.7	31.7	34.9	36.4	35.9	31.5	32.2	26.3	26.1	30.4	32.7
Niger	10.3	15.4	15.6	17.7	15.0	14.6	17.1	15.8	16.0	14.1	11.3	11.6	15.9	14.8
Nigeria	11.9	11.1	13.1	10.4	15.1	12.2	8.9	17.7	10.6	10.3	10.0	14.4	12.5	12.1
Rwanda	12.5	13.5	13.5	12.7	10.1	12.6	13.7	12.3	8.5	9.6	10.3	14.7	12.6	11.0
São Tomé and Principe	23.6	26.7	42.1	30.5	32.6	28.0	30.3	32.6	33.4	42.9	22.7	20.6	32.6	31.8
Senegal	22.0	15.6	14.7	14.7	14.7	13.5	15.2	14.3	12.4	11.2	10.2	18.2	15.4	13.1
Seychelles	28.7	34.4	31.8	32.9	27.5	29.1	30.8	37.2	35.1	27.9	28.5	28.5	34.5	30.9
Sierra Leone	20.9	8.6	7.5	9.3	9.9	9.4	10.3	11.2	11.1	14.0	11.0	12.3	9.0	11.0
Somalia	15.6	..	..	..	..	..	..	..	..	..	..	19.8	..	..
South Africa	13.3	18.3	17.9	18.6	19.1	19.7	20.6	20.9	21.2	20.6	20.9	14.7	18.0	20.4
Sudan	16.0	13.4	12.3	13.5	11.0	8.9	..	..	..	..	..	12.4	12.6	10.0
Swaziland	19.1	17.4	16.7	15.6	18.0	19.3	23.9	26.4	26.2	26.6	25.5	20.1	18.4	23.7
Tanzania	..	13.9	10.7	8.5	7.3	7.4	7.4	8.2	8.3	10.3	..	13.3	13.2	8.1
Togo	22.4	18.0	13.5	13.8	14.2	14.2	12.4	16.3	13.9	12.4	13.2	20.0	15.2	13.8
Uganda	..	8.0	8.1	7.0	7.5	8.8	9.7	9.8	10.4	9.6	9.8	10.8	9.3	9.4
Zaire	8.3	9.9	12.7	10.1	11.5	13.3	21.7	15.4	4.4	4.9	4.3	9.1	9.7	10.8
Zambia	25.5	20.4	14.9	13.7	19.0	31.8	15.0	9.6	9.7	9.5	8.4	25.7	19.9	14.7
Zimbabwe	26.6	28.6	23.7	23.5	23.6	20.4	21.0	20.1	18.5	19.2	19.1	21.6	25.8	20.3
NORTH AFRICA	12.3	17.0	17.0	15.7	14.9	14.4	14.9	15.3	14.6	13.9	..	14.1	16.6	14.7
Algeria	13.8	18.5	18.7	16.9	16.2	15.0	17.2	17.4	16.8	15.7	..	13.8	17.5	16.4
Egypt, Arab Republic	15.7	14.3	13.9	12.6	11.3	11.2	10.4	10.2	10.3	10.5	..	19.5	14.9	10.6
Libya	21.8	..	..	..	..	..	..	..	..	..	..	27.8	..	..
Morocco	18.3	15.7	15.4	15.7	15.5	15.2	16.3	18.0	16.9	15.5	..	18.9	15.6	16.2
Tunisia	14.5	16.9	16.6	17.3	16.4	16.6	16.0	16.4	15.9	16.4	..	15.7	17.1	16.3
ALL AFRICA	13.4	16.5	16.6	16.1	16.5	16.3	16.8	17.2	16.5	16.0	..	14.7	16.3	16.6

Note: 1996 data are preliminary (see page 3). Since 1994, Nigeria's ratios are distorted because the official exchange rate used by the Government for oil exports and oil value added is significantly over-valued.

2-8. Gross domestic investment

	Percentage of GDP											Annual average		
	1980	*1987*	*1988*	*1989*	*1990*	*1991*	*1992*	*1993*	*1994*	*1995*	*1996*	*75-84*	*85-89*	*90-MR*
SUB-SAHARAN AFRICA	23.0	17.7	18.7	18.4	17.0	17.3	16.8	16.0	17.6	18.5	17.8	22.9	17.7	17.3
excluding South Africa	20.9	17.6	17.9	17.2	17.0	18.0	18.9	16.9	18.3	18.4	18.1	21.0	16.9	17.9
excl. S. Africa & Nigeria	19.9	17.9	17.9	17.1	17.4	17.0	16.7	16.5	18.3	18.4	17.8	19.9	17.3	17.5
Angola	..	18.5	14.6	12.2	11.7	15.0	14.5	14.5	14.2	14.0	..	..	16.3	14.0
Benin	15.2	12.9	12.8	11.8	14.2	14.3	13.7	15.2	15.5	19.0	17.5	17.7	12.0	15.6
Botswana	37.7	24.5	7.3	40.8	40.8	40.8	40.8	26.6	24.6	24.8	..	36.0	23.8	33.1
Burkina Faso	17.0	20.9	19.8	21.6	20.6	20.6	21.3	19.8	19.3	22.2	24.9	20.2	21.7	21.2
Burundi	13.9	22.6	15.0	16.5	14.5	14.4	17.8	17.6	9.3	11.0	7.8	14.3	15.9	13.2
Cameroon	21.0	24.7	20.9	17.1	17.8	16.7	13.5	16.6	15.3	14.5	16.1	25.1	22.6	15.8
Cape Verde	51.6	30.0	40.4	38.7	40.1	39.9	53.5	55.0	60.5	57.4	52.6	49.1	42.3	51.3
Central African Republic	7.0	13.7	11.8	11.8	14.3	12.7	12.5	11.7	13.2	14.4	3.9	10.5	12.9	11.8
Chad	..	10.2	7.9	9.0	17.9	7.3	8.4	11.0	18.7	17.9	19.3	13.3	8.9	14.4
Comoros	33.2	25.2	21.8	17.4	19.7	20.3	22.4	16.7	16.9	17.1	17.2	33.4	24.2	18.6
Congo	35.8	19.7	18.6	14.2	17.2	19.7	20.6	28.9	52.9	36.0	60.7	36.2	22.4	33.7
Côte d'Ivoire	26.5	14.6	15.0	10.8	8.5	8.0	5.5	8.3	12.5	15.0	13.7	23.6	13.7	10.2
Djibouti	..	..	..	..	..	14.4	19.1	17.3	11.7	8.6	9.2	..	..	13.4
Equatorial Guinea	..	20.6	18.7	20.4	26.6	43.3	24.2	25.1	23.1	..	..	13.9	15.9	28.4
Eritrea	..	..	..	..	..	..	..	11.8	13.1	20.5	26.4	..	..	18.0
Ethiopia	..	14.3	16.4	9.7	8.9	7.1	9.4	14.8	15.1	16.3	20.5	10.7	12.3	13.2
Gabon	27.5	30.8	35.7	26.3	21.7	26.5	22.4	22.4	21.9	21.2	20.1	42.9	34.5	22.3
Gambia, The	26.2	19.6	17.4	17.6	18.3	19.7	19.7	21.0	21.0	21.0	..	20.5	18.1	20.1
Ghana	5.6	13.4	11.3	13.2	14.4	15.9	12.8	14.8	15.9	18.6	18.7	6.9	11.4	15.9
Guinea	..	16.3	17.1	17.2	17.5	16.5	16.5	16.2	13.6	14.5	13.0	..	16.4	15.4
Guinea-Bissau	29.6	36.5	46.5	41.3	30.9	33.6	49.2	30.9	16.1	22.9	26.9	23.9	37.8	30.1
Kenya	29.2	24.3	25.0	24.7	24.2	21.0	16.9	17.6	18.6	19.2	19.3	23.4	24.3	19.5
Lesotho	42.4	45.4	47.9	60.7	70.7	77.6	82.2	77.6	85.1	100.6	..	35.1	49.9	82.3
Liberia	27.3	..	..	..	..	..	..	..	..	..	..	23.8	9.2	..
Madagascar	15.0	10.1	13.3	13.4	14.8	10.6	11.3	11.4	10.9	10.8	10.0	10.2	10.9	11.4
Malawi	24.7	15.7	18.7	21.2	19.1	20.1	18.8	12.2	13.2	15.2	17.6	25.3	17.3	16.6
Mali	16.4	20.4	21.0	21.3	22.4	22.8	21.9	21.9	26.0	26.0	26.5	15.7	20.0	23.9
Mauritania	36.2	29.2	28.0	18.5	20.0	17.9	20.5	23.5	14.5	18.1	22.0	34.0	27.0	19.5
Mauritius	20.7	25.6	31.0	31.1	30.9	28.7	29.3	30.9	32.4	25.3	25.8	25.3	26.6	29.0
Mozambique	0.0	36.1	43.3	40.6	44.6	45.7	48.8	54.4	52.2	50.7	50.3	17.5	30.6	49.5
Namibia	29.2	15.3	17.8	17.5	26.7	19.1	22.6	17.4	24.2	20.5	21.2	23.2	14.1	21.7
Niger	36.6	10.5	19.2	13.5	8.1	9.2	5.4	5.7	10.4	7.5	9.7	18.8	14.4	8.0
Nigeria	22.2	16.0	18.0	17.7	14.7	23.4	28.7	19.3	18.3	18.4	19.3	22.4	15.1	20.3
Rwanda	16.1	15.7	14.5	13.4	11.8	11.9	14.8	15.9	0.0	13.2	13.6	14.8	15.4	11.6
São Tomé and Principe	34.2	15.3	19.7	26.3	29.4	31.4	38.7	40.6	41.1	57.5	49.8	33.4	24.0	41.2
Senegal	15.3	12.4	12.7	12.8	13.6	12.3	14.0	13.2	13.7	15.6	16.6	14.6	12.0	14.1
Seychelles	38.3	19.8	25.5	27.1	24.3	22.1	20.6	27.4	23.0	23.4	22.8	33.5	23.6	23.4
Sierra Leone	17.2	8.1	8.0	9.8	9.4	10.5	8.2	7.7	8.5	5.6	9.3	14.5	9.3	8.5
Somalia	42.4	33.3	23.9	30.3	15.5	..	..	..	..	..	..	27.1	28.5	15.5
South Africa	28.3	17.9	20.2	20.5	17.1	16.1	13.9	14.8	16.9	18.6	17.5	27.1	19.4	16.4
Sudan	15.1	15.4	14.9	14.1	13.6	12.7	..	..	..	..	..	16.7	12.4	13.2
Swaziland	30.3	14.8	23.6	23.2	21.1	18.8	21.7	22.6	17.8	17.1	12.7	31.5	21.6	18.8
Tanzania	..	24.4	28.3	29.9	36.4	34.6	31.3	32.4	31.3	31.0	..	22.6	23.9	32.8
Togo	28.4	17.6	16.0	24.5	26.6	17.1	14.6	5.3	13.3	14.3	13.7	29.8	18.7	15.0
Uganda	6.0	9.7	10.8	11.1	12.7	15.2	15.9	15.2	14.7	16.4	16.7	6.9	9.8	15.3
Zaire	10.0	14.2	14.4	14.3	9.0	5.6	6.9	1.8	7.9	7.6	6.3	12.7	13.7	6.4
Zambia	23.3	12.7	11.1	10.8	17.3	11.0	11.9	10.4	13.8	13.0	11.9	22.3	14.7	12.8
Zimbabwe	22.7	17.2	21.8	18.9	23.2	25.0	25.5	21.2	20.0	17.5	17.9	20.2	20.7	21.5
NORTH AFRICA	28.8	27.6	28.4	29.1	28.8	26.2	25.0	23.6	23.5	23.0	..	31.7	28.7	25.0
Algeria	39.1	30.0	27.2	29.0	29.3	31.0	30.0	29.2	31.7	32.0	..	41.5	30.6	30.5
Egypt, Arab Republic	27.5	26.1	34.9	31.8	28.8	21.2	18.2	16.2	16.6	16.3	..	29.9	28.6	19.5
Libya	22.1	..	..	..	..	..	..	..	..	..	..	26.3	..	..
Morocco	24.2	21.1	21.0	23.7	25.2	22.7	22.5	21.0	21.3	21.0	..	26.5	23.1	22.3
Tunisia	29.4	23.5	20.7	23.9	27.1	26.0	29.2	28.5	24.9	24.0	..	31.2	25.0	26.6
ALL AFRICA	24.5	21.2	22.0	22.0	21.0	20.1	19.6	18.7	19.8	20.1	..	25.4	21.6	19.9

Note: 1996 data are preliminary (see page 3). Since 1994, Nigeria's ratios are distorted because the official exchange rate used by the Government for oil exports and oil value added is significantly overvalued.

2-9. Gross public investment

	Percentage of GDP											Annual average		
	1980	*1987*	*1988*	*1989*	*1990*	*1991*	*1992*	*1993*	*1994*	*1995*	*1996*	*75-84*	*85-89*	*90-MR*
SUB-SAHARAN AFRICA	..	7.8	7.4	7.3	6.9	6.3	5.7	5.8	5.5	5.1	5.0	..	7.7	5.8
excluding South Africa	..	..	..	..	..	..	..	..	..	..	..	..	..	..
excl. S. Africa & Nigeria	..	7.1	6.9	5.9	5.9	5.4	5.6	5.4	6.1	5.9	5.0	..	6.7	5.6
Angola	..	..	..	..	..	..	..	..	..	..	..	..	..	..
Benin	..	..	..	5.4	5.4	5.5	4.4	4.4	6.7	7.6	6.4	..	5.4	5.7
Botswana	12.2	..	..	..	..	..	..	..	..	..	..	13.2	..	..
Burkina Faso	..	10.5	7.8	5.4	4.4	6.3	9.0	8.0	7.0	9.4	10.9	..	7.6	7.8
Burundi	12.8	16.4	13.4	14.7	12.5	12.0	14.5	14.2	8.5	9.7	6.3	14.1	13.5	11.1
Cameroon	4.4	11.4	9.2	6.1	5.5	4.0	2.7	1.8	1.3	1.2	0.7	4.7	9.0	2.4
Cape Verde	..	24.3	12.7	10.1	9.1	16.0	28.9	30.2	34.3	31.9	25.0	..	20.7	25.0
Central African Republic	3.7	7.6	6.4	6.3	7.0	7.4	7.4	6.7	7.3	7.6	1.8	4.7	7.1	6.5
Chad	..	9.8	7.5	8.6	17.4	6.9	7.9	10.2	12.9	12.5	12.4	3.8	8.5	11.5
Comoros	23.2	12.9	11.6	8.0	5.2	11.6	12.7	6.7	9.8	6.4	5.8	23.3	14.2	8.3
Congo	..	5.0	6.7	4.5	2.7	0.9	0.8	1.7	2.8	3.0	5.2	..	8.6	2.4
Côte d'Ivoire	11.4	7.4	7.0	6.3	5.3	4.0	4.3	3.8	4.1	4.2	4.3	10.5	6.3	4.3
Djibouti	..	..	..	..	..	..	..	..	..	..	..	..	..	..
Equatorial Guinea	..	..	..	..	..	..	..	..	..	..	..	..	..	..
Eritrea	..	..	..	..	..	..	..	10.8	8.9	12.0	12.5	..	..	11.1
Ethiopia	..	..	..	9.1	6.4	4.3	3.4	5.0	9.0	7.2	7.4	..	9.1	6.1
Gabon	5.3	8.4	6.8	4.2	3.9	5.2	5.3	5.1	5.6	5.3	5.6	15.8	12.8	5.2
Gambia, The	..	..	..	..	..	..	..	..	..	..	..	..	..	..
Ghana	..	7.9	8.0	7.8	7.5	8.3	10.3	11.7	14.0	14.7	13.8	..	7.0	11.4
Guinea	..	7.4	8.2	8.3	9.2	7.8	7.5	7.1	6.1	6.5	5.5	..	7.5	7.1
Guinea-Bissau	..	28.9	31.9	32.1	22.2	25.1	28.9	24.6	20.4	15.2	17.1	..	31.0	21.9
Kenya	10.4	7.1	8.3	8.1	9.7	8.5	7.3	7.3	8.7	6.0	6.0	9.1	7.8	7.7
Lesotho	..	..	..	..	43.3	51.6	51.0	46.4	53.8	..	..	20.0	..	49.2
Liberia	..	..	..	..	..	..	..	..	..	..	..	..	..	..
Madagascar	..	7.0	6.9	9.7	7.9	5.9	7.6	7.8	6.2	5.7	5.8	6.4	7.0	6.7
Malawi	17.5	..	..	..	..	..	..	..	..	..	..	14.0	..	..
Mali	..	10.1	9.4	9.6	10.3	12.1	9.5	9.3	13.0	12.5	12.1	7.1	10.6	11.3
Mauritania	..	9.2	6.8	5.5	6.2	5.1	4.5	5.7	5.8	5.1	5.5	..	8.0	5.4
Mauritius	8.4	7.3	12.0	7.1	11.4	8.2	9.6	7.9	9.0	8.1	5.4	7.9	7.9	8.5
Mozambique	13.3	17.3	22.2	21.6	20.9	19.7	17.7	16.4	20.9	19.0	16.8	18.0	14.9	18.8
Namibia	15.7	7.9	7.2	6.0	8.4	7.6	10.0	8.2	8.2	8.0	5.3	13.9	7.7	8.0
Niger	..	..	8.4	9.5	7.4	3.7	3.9	4.2	6.6	5.4	4.6	..	9.0	5.1
Nigeria	..	..	..	..	..	11.4	8.1	13.4	8.6	6.1	7.2	..	..	9.1
Rwanda	12.2	8.2	6.1	5.4	3.8	4.1	4.6	5.1	0.0	4.0	4.1	13.7	10.2	3.7
São Tomé and Principe	..	..	..	..	..	24.4	24.9	22.1	26.9	40.8	32.0	..	..	28.5
Senegal	6.0	4.1	3.9	4.3	4.1	4.6	5.1	4.1	4.6	4.8	4.8	4.5	4.0	4.6
Seychelles	..	..	..	..	..	..	..	..	..	..	..	16.3	7.6	..
Sierra Leone	..	3.5	2.0	3.1	3.5	4.4	4.7	5.3	4.4	2.6	3.3	3.2	3.0	4.0
Somalia	..	..	..	..	..	..	..	..	..	..	..	..	..	..
South Africa	12.9	7.3	6.7	7.4	6.8	5.9	5.2	4.7	4.3	4.3	4.4	12.9	8.0	5.1
Sudan	7.0	4.1	3.6	2.8	2.3	1.4	..	..	..	..	..	5.8	3.1	1.9
Swaziland	..	..	..	..	..	..	..	..	..	..	..	..	..	..
Tanzania	..	..	..	..	..	..	..	..	..	..	..	..	..	..
Togo	20.2	9.7	7.7	7.4	7.3	4.5	3.5	2.4	2.4	3.5	2.9	12.2	10.2	3.8
Uganda	..	4.3	5.6	5.4	6.2	7.4	7.4	6.7	5.5	5.4	6.3	..	4.4	6.4
Zaire	5.1	4.9	6.7	..	..	..	..	..	..	..	..	3.9	4.7	..
Zambia	..	..	..	..	..	..	..	..	..	..	..	..	..	..
Zimbabwe	4.3	3.3	4.1	3.6	4.4	4.5	4.7	4.3	3.7	3.1	3.0	4.4	3.9	4.0
NORTH AFRICA	..	..	..	..	..	..	..	..	..	..	..	..	..	..
Algeria	..	..	12.2	10.2	8.2	6.1	6.8	8.7	7.9	7.3	..	..	11.2	7.5
Egypt, Arab Republic	..	12.1	15.2	10.5	10.2	9.2	8.5	7.1	6.1	5.5	..	..	12.6	7.8
Libya	19.4	..	..	..	..	..	..	..	..	..	..	21.1	..	..
Morocco	..	..	..	..	..	..	..	..	..	..	..	..	..	..
Tunisia	15.0	10.4	9.0	10.0	11.0	10.2	12.0	15.3	13.6	..	..	17.2	11.4	12.4
ALL AFRICA	..	..	..	..	..	..	..	..	..	..	..	..	..	..

Note: 1996 data are preliminary (see page 3). Since 1994, Nigeria's ratios are distorted because the official exchange rate used by the Government for oil exports and oil value added is significantly over-valued.

2-10. Gross private investment

	Percentage of GDP											Annual average		
	1980	*1987*	*1988*	*1989*	*1990*	*1991*	*1992*	*1993*	*1994*	*1995*	*1996*	*75-84*	*85-89*	*90-MR*
SUB-SAHARAN AFRICA	8.8	10.2	10.8	10.8	..	..	..	..	..	..	..	10.3	10.1	..
excluding South Africa	..	9.5	9.3	9.2	9.1	11.0	12.7	10.4	11.1	11.9	12.0	8.4	8.8	11.2
excl. S. Africa & Nigeria	..	10.1	9.8	9.5	10.4	11.0	10.6	11.6	11.6	12.0	12.2	10.2	9.5	11.3
Angola	..	..	..	..	..	..	..	..	..	..	..	..	..	..
Benin	..	..	..	7.1	8.1	8.1	9.0	10.1	8.8	9.1	10.6	..	7.1	9.1
Botswana	20.0	..	..	..	..	..	..	..	..	..	..	15.0	..	..
Burkina Faso	..	11.3	11.7	15.4	15.3	14.2	13.3	10.7	14.1	14.6	15.0	..	13.0	13.9
Burundi	1.1	4.4	1.7	1.9	2.7	2.9	2.9	3.0	1.4	1.3	1.5	1.5	2.7	2.2
Cameroon	15.6	13.1	11.6	12.0	11.9	12.7	11.6	13.8	14.0	13.3	15.4	24.2	12.1	13.2
Cape Verde	..	5.7	27.6	28.6	31.0	23.9	24.6	24.9	26.2	25.5	27.6	..	18.7	26.2
Central African Republic	3.2	6.0	3.7	6.1	6.8	4.8	4.6	4.5	5.1	5.8	1.3	4.1	5.3	4.7
Chad	..	0.5	0.4	0.4	0.4	0.4	0.5	0.8	5.8	5.4	6.9	0.2	0.4	2.9
Comoros	5.3	5.3	5.9	6.4	6.7	7.2	7.6	7.3	6.6	9.6	10.3	5.4	5.7	7.9
Congo	..	15.9	12.9	10.0	14.5	18.8	19.8	26.7	48.6	33.0	55.5	..	13.8	31.0
Côte d'Ivoire	13.0	6.7	6.8	5.9	4.9	5.1	4.4	4.0	7.0	8.7	9.9	12.3	7.1	6.3
Djibouti	..	..	..	..	..	5.1	9.7	9.1	6.2	4.9	5.3	..	..	6.7
Equatorial Guinea	..	..	..	..	..	..	..	..	..	..	..	..	..	..
Eritrea	..	..	..	..	..	..	..	1.0	4.2	8.5	13.9	..	..	6.9
Ethiopia	..	..	..	0.7	2.5	2.8	6.0	9.8	6.1	9.1	13.1	..	0.7	7.1
Gabon	21.4	23.2	29.4	21.8	17.6	20.9	16.7	17.8	15.4	15.9	14.5	24.0	21.8	17.0
Gambia, The	9.3	12.6	8.8	12.3	15.3	14.5	13.5	13.2	13.7	13.3	..	7.2	8.9	13.9
Ghana	..	5.4	3.2	5.4	6.9	7.5	2.4	3.1	1.9	3.9	4.9	..	4.3	4.4
Guinea	..	8.9	8.9	8.9	8.3	8.6	9.0	9.1	7.5	8.1	7.5	..	8.9	8.3
Guinea-Bissau	..	7.6	14.7	9.2	8.7	8.5	20.4	6.3	1.4	7.1	7.1	..	10.5	8.5
Kenya	12.6	12.5	11.8	11.2	10.9	10.5	9.2	9.6	9.5	12.8	12.6	11.7	11.6	10.7
Lesotho	..	..	..	..	28.0	26.5	31.6	31.2	31.3	..	..	7.1	..	29.7
Liberia	..	..	..	..	..	..	..	..	..	..	..	..	..	..
Madagascar	..	3.1	6.4	3.7	6.9	4.6	3.7	3.7	4.7	5.1	4.2	2.2	3.9	4.7
Malawi	4.7	7.9	9.7	11.2	11.3	12.1	10.2	5.9	4.8	6.2	9.9	7.3	7.9	8.6
Mali	..	10.2	11.6	11.7	12.1	10.7	12.4	12.6	13.0	13.5	14.4	6.0	9.4	12.7
Mauritania	..	19.9	21.2	13.0	13.7	12.8	15.9	17.8	8.7	13.1	16.5	..	19.0	14.1
Mauritius	14.9	14.1	16.2	19.0	19.2	20.4	18.3	20.6	21.6	16.4	19.5	15.3	15.0	19.4
Mozambique	-13.3	18.8	21.1	18.9	23.7	26.0	31.2	38.0	31.3	31.8	33.5	-0.5	15.7	30.8
Namibia	11.4	6.8	8.3	11.0	13.5	8.9	10.9	14.4	13.4	14.3	17.2	8.3	7.5	13.2
Niger	..	..	4.6	3.8	4.0	4.1	1.9	1.9	2.3	1.8	4.7	..	4.2	3.0
Nigeria	..	7.3	7.2	8.3	3.8	12.0	20.5	5.8	9.7	12.4	12.1	5.2	6.1	10.9
Rwanda	0.0	7.5	7.8	8.0	8.9	9.5	10.7	11.8	0.0	9.2	9.5	0.0	4.7	8.5
São Tomé and Principe	..	..	..	..	..	8.9	14.5	18.4	14.2	16.7	17.8	..	..	15.1
Senegal	9.8	8.2	8.8	9.2	8.8	8.7	8.8	9.1	9.0	10.8	11.5	8.8	8.3	9.5
Seychelles	..	..	..	..	14.6	8.4	11.2	14.9	14.7	15.2	15.5	5.4	14.9	13.5
Sierra Leone	..	4.5	6.0	6.7	5.9	6.1	3.6	2.4	4.1	3.0	6.0	..	5.7	4.4
Somalia	..	..	..	..	..	..	..	..	..	..	..	..	..	..
South Africa	13.3	11.2	13.2	13.2	..	..	..	..	..	..	..	14.4	12.4	..
Sudan	4.5	8.3	8.3	8.3	8.3	8.3	..	..	..	..	..	8.3	8.3	8.3
Swaziland	13.3	11.0	16.5	15.4	13.4	11.2	12.5	12.5	11.2	3.9	2.4	13.4	11.7	9.6
Tanzania	..	20.7	21.2	18.0	22.6	21.8	18.8	19.8	19.6	17.1	..	13.3	17.1	20.0
Togo	8.0	8.9	10.1	18.4	18.0	13.5	12.6	8.8	9.1	10.0	10.3	8.0	9.2	11.8
Uganda	..	5.4	5.2	5.7	6.5	7.8	8.5	8.5	9.2	10.1	11.2	..	5.4	8.8
Zaire	3.7	9.0	7.9	..	..	..	..	..	..	..	..	5.8	8.4	..
Zambia	..	5.9	3.3	1.5	7.2	3.5	3.8	7.9	10.2	8.6	7.3	9.0	4.1	7.0
Zimbabwe	14.4	15.5	13.6	13.8	15.2	18.6	19.0	20.5	15.8	14.4	13.9	13.6	14.4	16.8
NORTH AFRICA	..	16.5	14.7	16.5	16.2	14.6	14.1	13.0	13.7	13.4	..	12.4	15.1	14.2
Algeria	22.8	17.8	13.3	15.8	17.6	19.0	19.4	18.4	21.0	21.3	..	25.3	16.8	19.4
Egypt, Arab Republic	..	15.2	19.2	20.1	16.7	13.1	10.5	9.2	10.5	10.5	..	7.1	13.3	11.7
Libya	1.8	..	..	..	..	..	..	..	..	..	..	3.6	..	..
Morocco	..	..	..	..	..	..	..	..	..	..	..	..	..	..
Tunisia	13.3	11.3	11.5	12.5	13.4	13.9	15.2	12.9	13.0	..	..	13.2	12.2	13.7
ALL AFRICA	..	12.3	12.1	12.7	..	..	..	..	..	..	..	11.5	11.8	..

Note: 1996 data are preliminary (see page 3). Since 1994, Nigeria's ratios are distorted because the official exchange rate used by the Government for oil exports and oil value added is significantly over-valued.

2-11. Gross domestic savings

	Percentage of GDP											Annual average		
	1980	*1987*	*1988*	*1989*	*1990*	*1991*	*1992*	*1993*	*1994*	*1995*	*1996*	*75-84*	*85-89*	*90-MR*
SUB-SAHARAN AFRICA	26.1	18.2	18.4	18.8	18.8	17.0	15.5	14.2	15.8	15.5	16.2	21.3	18.2	16.1
excluding South Africa	21.7	14.3	14.5	15.0	16.3	14.4	13.9	11.1	13.8	13.2	15.2	17.6	14.1	14.0
excl. S. Africa & Nigeria	14.8	13.2	13.6	13.1	13.7	11.4	9.6	9.0	12.4	11.9	13.5	15.3	13.4	11.6
Angola	..	30.0	25.5	26.9	29.7	28.1	28.2	30.0	32.3	33.8	..	..	25.9	30.4
Benin	-5.1	3.6	1.7	3.6	5.5	5.8	4.2	5.2	9.4	9.3	9.2	0.0	2.5	7.0
Botswana	27.7	39.1	42.9	54.3	37.4	36.6	44.3	23.1	24.8	22.6	..	20.9	42.0	31.5
Burkina Faso	-5.8	0.6	4.3	7.1	7.7	6.1	7.2	5.0	6.1	7.0	7.6	-1.7	2.4	6.7
Burundi	-0.6	6.6	1.7	3.3	-5.4	-4.2	-2.2	-3.1	-9.9	-7.1	-11.6	4.1	3.4	-6.2
Cameroon	20.4	20.8	21.0	20.0	20.9	22.0	19.0	17.5	17.9	20.6	39.3	22.0	22.9	22.5
Cape Verde	-24.0	-1.5	10.0	4.9	9.8	9.0	13.4	15.5	12.6	9.3	10.4	-19.8	0.0	11.4
Central African Republic	-8.9	0.5	1.1	2.4	1.2	2.7	-0.4	3.2	9.1	6.9	1.1	-1.6	0.9	3.4
Chad	..	-19.6	-13.5	-16.0	-4.1	-10.3	-11.1	-11.8	-8.0	1.5	2.6	-0.2	-18.1	-5.9
Comoros	-10.1	-2.0	-2.0	-7.0	0.9	2.9	2.3	0.0	-8.0	-7.9	-5.9	-6.5	-2.5	-2.3
Congo	35.7	22.8	18.8	27.6	21.7	18.9	23.4	23.0	25.1	27.8	30.3	26.1	23.2	24.3
Côte d'Ivoire	20.4	18.4	17.6	13.8	13.0	11.0	9.4	9.7	22.4	20.3	20.0	24.3	20.3	15.1
Djibouti	..	..	..	..	..	-10.2	-13.8	-11.0	-11.3	-8.7	-7.7	..	..	-10.4
Equatorial Guinea	..	-16.9	-22.9	-11.8	-10.9	-14.5	2.8	7.5	16.4	..	..	7.6	-12.7	0.3
Eritrea	..	..	..	..	..	..	..	-21.6	-37.6	-27.2	-25.8	..	..	-28.0
Ethiopia	..	6.2	8.4	4.2	4.3	0.0	3.1	6.2	5.0	6.8	7.6	3.4	4.8	4.7
Gabon	60.6	28.7	30.6	30.9	36.9	40.5	34.7	36.7	45.3	42.1	43.1	58.1	31.5	39.9
Gambia, The	0.7	9.8	8.5	2.3	6.1	6.4	0.1	3.8	5.0	4.9	..	4.0	6.5	4.4
Ghana	4.9	5.8	5.7	5.6	5.5	7.3	1.3	-2.2	4.0	9.9	9.0	6.2	5.7	5.0
Guinea	..	17.2	12.9	18.5	17.7	15.6	11.2	10.9	9.0	10.1	10.0	..	16.6	12.1
Guinea-Bissau	-6.0	4.2	2.3	-4.1	-0.3	1.0	1.0	4.6	-1.8	-0.6	5.7	-4.6	-0.7	1.4
Kenya	18.1	19.2	19.7	17.3	19.0	19.7	16.4	22.5	21.3	12.9	16.9	19.3	20.6	18.4
Lesotho	-59.7	-70.0	-69.0	-46.6	-30.2	-51.0	-39.7	-29.6	-9.1	-0.8	..	-73.6	-67.2	-26.7
Liberia	27.3	..	..	..	..	..	..	..	..	..	..	23.3	16.4	..
Madagascar	-1.4	5.9	8.4	10.0	3.8	1.6	2.9	2.1	3.1	2.7	4.0	1.9	6.5	2.9
Malawi	10.8	13.3	9.2	4.7	9.4	12.4	0.1	-4.2	-2.4	2.1	10.9	15.6	10.0	4.0
Mali	-1.8	4.1	2.5	5.7	6.2	6.4	4.4	6.5	7.0	9.7	11.8	-0.5	-0.2	7.4
Mauritania	6.9	11.8	17.1	12.6	5.6	10.0	7.2	9.7	7.2	7.0	13.9	2.3	11.6	8.7
Mauritius	10.5	27.6	26.1	23.8	23.6	24.9	26.1	24.7	23.6	22.7	21.9	18.5	25.5	23.9
Mozambique	-23.6	-2.4	-2.1	-6.7	1.5	4.5	5.6	10.4	5.9	17.4	21.9	-6.6	-1.2	9.6
Namibia	38.9	6.1	17.2	18.3	15.3	9.1	12.0	9.8	19.3	14.0	14.7	13.7	16.4	13.5
Niger	22.6	8.0	18.0	10.4	4.0	7.5	1.0	1.0	1.7	1.5	3.8	9.5	10.1	2.9
Nigeria	32.3	19.9	19.1	25.3	29.4	29.3	33.3	22.7	20.6	20.9	23.8	21.6	17.7	25.7
Rwanda	4.2	4.0	3.5	2.3	3.4	0.7	1.4	-0.5	-60.1	-11.1	-2.5	6.8	5.3	-9.8
São Tomé and Principe	-14.9	-17.3	-25.8	-41.1	-37.2	-27.3	-27.8	-23.2	-18.0	-22.1	-23.4	-9.0	-22.4	-25.6
Senegal	-0.4	5.1	6.4	7.3	7.7	5.3	6.6	4.9	7.2	10.4	10.9	3.4	4.9	7.6
Seychelles	27.1	31.0	31.9	29.8	37.7	21.0	16.5	17.5	20.4	20.7	19.9	24.3	30.1	21.9
Sierra Leone	-0.2	2.4	1.4	-1.7	8.3	8.1	6.3	3.3	3.4	-9.1	-9.7	1.6	1.9	1.5
Somalia	-12.9	8.8	6.5	-6.9	-12.5	..	..	..	..	..	..	-11.4	5.6	-12.5
South Africa	36.5	25.9	25.7	25.8	23.1	21.1	18.0	18.7	18.7	18.7	18.3	30.3	26.8	19.5
Sudan	3.4	12.8	7.3	6.7	6.6	-2.6	..	..	..	..	..	6.3	6.3	2.0
Swaziland	6.5	26.3	29.0	25.0	14.6	9.5	10.7	14.6	13.5	9.1	3.2	16.5	20.4	10.7
Tanzania	..	2.8	5.2	9.4	14.3	8.8	2.2	3.2	3.3	-7.1	..	14.3	6.5	4.1
Togo	23.2	8.2	7.1	15.3	14.7	9.0	5.3	-2.5	9.4	8.5	6.4	21.4	9.1	7.3
Uganda	-0.4	-0.1	0.6	1.0	0.6	0.7	0.4	1.1	4.1	7.4	6.3	3.9	3.0	2.9
Zaire	10.1	11.3	12.1	15.0	9.3	1.8	6.1	4.0	11.0	10.1	8.1	10.5	13.3	7.2
Zambia	19.3	16.5	18.2	3.8	17.8	14.5	6.4	8.6	10.0	5.9	6.5	18.9	14.9	9.9
Zimbabwe	26.9	21.4	26.9	21.5	23.4	19.5	13.6	19.5	18.1	14.8	18.4	23.1	24.7	18.2
NORTH AFRICA	39.2	22.8	20.8	21.3	20.3	22.1	20.7	18.1	16.6	17.0	..	34.1	23.0	19.1
Algeria	43.1	31.9	27.0	29.3	27.5	36.7	32.4	27.8	27.0	28.8	..	38.9	30.8	30.0
Egypt, Arab Republic	15.2	15.9	17.1	17.3	16.1	13.2	15.4	13.2	11.4	14.0	..	15.4	15.7	13.9
Libya	56.9	..	..	..	..	..	..	..	..	..	..	46.5	..	..
Morocco	13.7	16.8	20.7	18.3	19.2	17.2	16.1	15.5	15.7	13.4	..	12.9	18.2	16.2
Tunisia	24.0	22.5	21.1	20.6	20.0	21.0	22.3	21.4	22.1	20.3	..	24.2	21.6	21.2
ALL AFRICA	29.4	19.8	18.8	19.2	18.9	18.1	16.7	15.1	15.6	15.5	..	24.5	19.9	16.6

Note: 1996 data are preliminary (see page 3). Since 1994, Nigeria's ratios are distorted because the official exchange rate used by the Government for oil exports and oil value added is significantly over-valued.

2-12. Gross national savings

	Percentage of GDP											Annual average		
	1980	*1987*	*1988*	*1989*	*1990*	*1991*	*1992*	*1993*	*1994*	*1995*	*1996*	*75-84*	*85-89*	*90-MR*
SUB-SAHARAN AFRICA	21.9	13.4	13.7	13.5	13.1	12.3	10.8	9.9	11.3	11.4	11.6	17.9	13.3	11.5
excluding South Africa	17.6	9.0	9.3	8.8	9.5	8.5	7.8	5.2	7.1	7.3	8.6	14.7	8.9	7.7
excl. S. Africa & Nigeria	11.3	8.7	8.0	7.4	7.6	6.1	4.2	3.5	5.6	5.7	6.2	12.1	8.4	5.5
Angola	..	24.5	9.1	10.7	9.4	10.0	4.6	1.9	-6.6	..	..	..	15.7	3.9
Benin	2.3	7.0	5.2	10.2	12.1	11.6	9.2	10.8	13.0	12.2	12.8	4.9	6.8	11.6
Botswana	20.5	30.6	29.5	42.6	30.2	31.9	46.0	20.2	21.5	24.1	..	14.5	30.3	29.0
Burkina Faso	0.0	7.8	11.5	12.5	11.2	9.3	12.4	10.0	10.6	11.3	11.8	4.0	10.2	10.9
Burundi	..	..	..	..	..	..	..	..	..	..	..	..	..	..
Cameroon	11.9	16.4	16.4	16.4	13.7	15.0	13.6	11.3	11.1	12.3	33.5	15.9	18.1	15.8
Cape Verde	16.4	-10.7	24.7	21.6	28.4	27.3	33.2	35.7	34.8	31.8	32.8	10.8	10.5	32.0
Central African Republic	-8.5	-3.1	-3.2	-1.7	-2.4	-0.6	-3.3	-1.1	4.7	2.6	-3.2	-3.8	-1.9	-0.5
Chad	..	-25.0	-21.6	-22.0	-18.7	-9.7	-3.5	-23.3	-10.6	-7.2	-5.8	-6.5	-20.0	-11.3
Comoros	..	..	..	..	..	..	..	..	..	..	..	..	..	..
Congo	26.0	9.1	2.3	10.0	..	..	..	..	..	..	..	16.2	11.0	..
Côte d'Ivoire	7.9	6.2	4.1	-2.5	..	..	..	..	..	..	..	14.0	7.1	..
Djibouti	..	..	..	..	..	..	..	..	..	..	..	..	..	..
Equatorial Guinea	..	-20.7	-15.4	-13.4	-9.6	-18.1	-6.0	0.4	3.4	..	..	..	-13.2	-6.0
Eritrea	..	..	..	..	..	..	..	18.8	14.8	10.5	10.1	..	..	13.6
Ethiopia	..	8.3	9.7	6.1	6.1	1.9	9.5	11.3	9.8	14.0	14.2	4.9	7.0	9.6
Gabon	..	..	..	..	..	..	..	..	..	..	..	..	..	..
Gambia, The	..	2.0	5.1	-5.8	4.9	9.5	1.4	5.1	6.4	8.7	..	0.1	-2.9	6.0
Ghana	5.0	7.1	6.5	7.2	7.0	8.8	3.6	0.4	7.1	12.1	..	6.2	5.9	6.5
Guinea	..	8.3	4.4	8.3	8.4	8.2	4.1	5.4	4.5	5.5	..	..	7.4	6.0
Guinea-Bissau	..	15.1	14.7	4.5	14.5	5.1	10.3	8.7	5.8	6.7	12.3	..	11.4	9.1
Kenya	17.0	16.3	16.5	14.4	15.7	15.9	12.5	17.8	18.0	13.9	18.1	17.4	17.8	16.0
Lesotho	59.6	44.2	30.3	42.3	35.8	13.8	24.2	28.4	42.6	53.8	..	33.9	41.3	33.1
Liberia	25.8	..	..	..	..	..	..	..	..	..	..	22.2	16.3	..
Madagascar	..	5.1	8.8	7.9	3.8	-0.3	3.5	3.2	1.2	0.4	3.1	2.4	5.8	2.1
Malawi	..	..	..	..	..	..	..	..	..	..	..	..	..	..
Mali	6.1	9.4	8.9	11.7	13.6	15.4	13.1	13.9	16.9	14.9	17.0	7.6	7.0	15.0
Mauritania	14.3	4.8	18.7	30.6	5.1	8.7	10.0	11.4	8.9	9.3	17.3	11.5	13.4	10.1
Mauritius	8.4	29.0	28.2	26.5	26.7	28.1	29.2	27.6	26.0	24.7	23.3	17.4	26.6	26.5
Mozambique	-21.1	..	..	..	..	..	..	..	..	..	..	-5.5	0.4	..
Namibia	27.4	17.3	17.9	24.1	27.7	24.5	25.7	22.1	29.8	24.0	26.1	24.5	21.1	25.7
Niger	25.1	..	..	..	..	..	..	..	..	..	..	12.8	13.1	..
Nigeria	..	..	..	..	..	..	..	..	..	..	..	23.9	..	..
Rwanda	..	..	..	..	..	..	..	..	..	..	..	..	..	..
São Tomé and Principe	-7.5	-27.8	-33.4	-51.1	-47.2	-37.3	-36.2	-31.6	-22.2	-35.0	-28.2	-4.2	-28.3	-34.0
Senegal	-4.4	0.4	2.3	3.3	4.5	2.9	5.0	3.0	6.9	9.5	9.4	-0.2	0.5	5.9
Seychelles	23.5	25.4	25.8	..	..	..	..	..	..	..	..	19.6	27.3	..
Sierra Leone	-0.5	-1.5	-3.7	-8.5	-1.8	-1.3	-6.2	-7.0	-7.4	-11.9	-5.7	-0.1	-2.4	-5.9
Somalia	-5.8	24.3	15.7	17.0	..	..	..	..	..	..	..	-4.0	18.7	..
South Africa	..	22.2	21.9	22.0	17.5	16.9	14.8	16.0	16.6	16.8	..	24.8	22.6	16.4
Sudan	6.1	15.1	9.5	5.9	5.6	-3.4	..	..	..	..	..	8.3	9.2	1.1
Swaziland	12.5	32.5	41.9	29.1	26.5	22.9	26.3	24.9	20.3	15.4	5.2	24.7	32.4	20.2
Tanzania	..	32.2	35.9	35.1	38.5	14.5	8.4	13.7	17.6	-5.7	..	17.6	26.7	14.5
Togo	27.2	..	..	..	..	..	..	..	..	..	..	25.7	..	..
Uganda	-0.8	0.8	1.6	1.9	0.6	1.4	2.1	3.6	10.4	12.2	12.6	-3.5	3.8	6.1
Zaire	8.0	2.8	3.6	7.3	0.8	-7.1	-4.3	-4.0	-2.1	-3.6	..	8.3	6.1	-3.4
Zambia	..	..	..	..	..	..	..	..	..	..	..	..	..	..
Zimbabwe	..	..	..	..	..	..	..	..	..	..	..	..	..	..
NORTH AFRICA	36.4	19.1	17.3	17.9	18.0	18.5	18.1	15.8	14.5	14.8	..	31.1	19.1	16.6
Algeria	..	..	..	..	..	..	..	..	..	..	..	..	..	..
Egypt, Arab Republic	..	11.6	16.3	17.1	19.4	23.7	30.1	28.1	19.1	21.0	..	..	15.0	23.6
Libya	53.5	..	..	..	..	..	..	..	..	..	..	39.8	..	..
Morocco	17.0	22.1	23.2	20.2	24.4	21.3	20.3	19.0	18.9	16.1	..	16.5	21.6	20.0
Tunisia	25.1	22.8	22.3	22.9	21.7	21.5	21.4	19.6	20.8	19.5	..	25.0	22.2	20.8
ALL AFRICA	25.6	15.4	14.6	14.6	14.2	13.8	12.8	11.5	12.0	12.1	..	21.2	15.3	12.7

Note: 1996 data are preliminary (see page 3). Since 1994, Nigeria's ratios are distorted because the official exchange rate used by the Government for oil exports and oil value added is significantly over-valued.

2-13. Resource balance

	Percentage of GDP											Annual average		
	1980	1987	1988	1989	1990	1991	1992	1993	1994	1995	1996	75-84	85-89	90-MR
SUB-SAHARAN AFRICA	2.8	0.4	-0.4	0.3	1.7	-0.3	-0.9	-1.3	-1.4	-2.6	-1.2	-1.8	0.4	-0.9
excluding South Africa	0.6	-3.5	-3.6	-2.3	-0.8	-3.8	-4.4	-5.3	-4.1	-4.7	-2.3	-3.8	-3.0	-3.6
excl. S. Africa & Nigeria	-5.5	-4.8	-4.4	-4.0	-3.8	-5.7	-6.3	-6.8	-5.5	-6.1	-3.8	-5.1	-4.0	-5.5
Angola	..	11.5	10.9	14.7	18.0	13.1	13.7	15.5	18.2	19.8	..	..	9.6	16.4
Benin	-20.3	-9.3	-11.2	-8.2	-8.7	-8.5	-9.5	-10.0	-6.0	-9.7	-8.3	-17.8	-9.5	-8.7
Botswana	-10.0	14.6	35.6	13.5	-3.4	-4.1	3.5	-3.4	0.2	-2.2	..	-15.1	18.1	-1.6
Burkina Faso	-22.9	-20.3	-15.5	-14.5	-12.9	-14.5	-14.1	-14.8	-13.1	-15.2	-17.3	-21.8	-19.3	-14.6
Burundi	-14.5	-16.0	-13.4	-13.2	-19.9	-18.6	-20.0	-20.8	-19.2	-18.1	-19.4	-10.2	-12.6	-19.4
Cameroon	-0.6	-3.9	0.1	2.9	3.1	5.4	5.5	1.0	2.6	6.1	23.2	-3.0	0.3	6.7
Cape Verde	-75.6	-31.5	-30.3	-33.8	-30.3	-30.9	-40.1	-39.5	-47.9	-48.1	-42.2	-68.9	-42.3	-39.9
Central African Republic	-15.9	-13.2	-10.6	-9.4	-13.1	-10.0	-12.9	-8.5	-4.1	-7.4	-2.8	-12.0	-12.0	-8.4
Chad	-16.9	-29.8	-21.4	-25.0	-22.0	-17.7	-19.5	-22.7	-26.7	-16.4	-16.7	-14.6	-27.0	-20.2
Comoros	-43.2	-27.3	-23.8	-24.4	-18.8	-17.4	-20.1	-16.7	-24.9	-25.0	-23.1	-39.8	-26.7	-20.9
Congo	-0.1	3.1	0.2	13.5	4.5	-0.8	2.8	-5.9	-27.9	-8.3	-30.4	-10.2	0.7	-9.4
Côte d'Ivoire	-6.2	3.8	2.6	3.0	4.6	3.0	3.9	1.3	9.8	5.4	6.3	0.7	6.6	4.9
Djibouti	..	..	..	..	..	-24.6	-32.8	-28.2	-23.0	-17.2	-16.9	..	..	-23.8
Equatorial Guinea	..	-37.6	-41.6	-32.2	-37.5	-57.8	-21.4	-17.6	-6.6	..	..	-6.3	-28.5	-28.2
Eritrea	..	..	..	..	..	..	-55.6	-33.4	-50.7	-47.7	-52.2	..	..	-47.9
Ethiopia	..	-8.1	-8.1	-5.6	-4.6	-7.1	-6.3	-8.6	-10.1	-9.5	-12.9	-7.4	-7.5	-8.5
Gabon	33.1	-2.2	-5.1	4.6	15.2	14.0	12.3	14.2	23.4	20.9	23.0	15.2	-3.0	17.6
Gambia, The	-25.5	-9.7	-8.8	-15.2	-12.2	-13.3	-19.7	-17.2	-16.0	-16.1	..	-16.5	-11.6	-15.7
Ghana	-0.7	-7.6	-5.6	-7.6	-9.0	-8.6	-11.5	-17.0	-11.9	-8.7	-9.7	-0.6	-5.8	-10.9
Guinea	..	0.9	-4.2	1.3	0.2	-0.9	-5.3	-5.3	-4.6	-4.4	-3.0	..	0.3	-3.3
Guinea-Bissau	-35.6	-32.3	-44.3	-45.4	-31.2	-32.5	-48.3	-26.3	-17.8	-23.5	-21.2	-28.4	-38.5	-28.7
Kenya	-11.1	-5.1	-5.3	-7.4	-5.2	-1.3	-0.5	4.9	2.7	-6.3	-2.4	-4.1	-3.7	-1.1
Lesotho	-102.1	-115.4	-116.9	-107.3	-101.0	-128.6	-121.9	-107.2	-94.1	-101.3	..	-108.7	-117.1	-109.0
Liberia	0.0	..	..	..	..	..	..	..	..	..	..	-0.5	7.2	..
Madagascar	-16.4	-4.2	-4.9	-3.4	-11.0	-8.9	-8.3	-9.3	-7.8	-8.1	-6.0	-8.2	-4.4	-8.5
Malawi	-14.0	-2.4	-9.5	-16.4	-9.8	-7.8	-18.6	-16.4	-15.6	-13.1	-6.7	-9.7	-7.2	-12.6
Mali	-18.2	-16.3	-18.5	-15.6	-16.2	-16.4	-17.5	-15.4	-19.0	-16.3	-14.7	-16.2	-20.2	-16.5
Mauritania	-29.3	-17.3	-11.0	-5.9	-14.3	-7.9	-13.2	-13.8	-7.3	-11.1	-8.1	-31.8	-15.4	-10.8
Mauritius	-10.3	2.1	-5.0	-7.3	-7.2	-3.8	-3.3	-6.2	-8.8	-2.6	-3.8	-6.8	-1.1	-5.1
Mozambique	-23.6	-38.5	-45.4	-47.3	-43.2	-41.2	-43.3	-44.0	-46.3	-33.4	-28.4	-24.1	-31.8	-40.0
Namibia	9.7	-9.1	-0.5	0.8	-11.4	-10.0	-10.6	-7.6	-4.9	-6.5	-6.5	-9.6	2.3	-8.2
Niger	-14.1	-2.6	-1.2	-3.1	-4.1	-1.7	-4.4	-4.7	-8.7	-6.1	-5.9	-9.3	-4.3	-5.1
Nigeria	10.1	3.9	1.1	7.5	14.6	5.9	4.6	3.4	2.3	2.4	4.5	-0.8	2.6	5.4
Rwanda	-11.9	-11.7	-11.0	-11.1	-8.4	-11.1	-13.4	-16.4	-60.1	-24.3	-16.2	-8.0	-10.1	-21.4
São Tomé and Principe	-49.1	-32.6	-45.5	-67.4	-66.6	-58.7	-66.5	-63.8	-59.0	-79.6	-73.2	-42.4	-46.3	-66.8
Senegal	-15.7	-7.3	-6.4	-5.4	-5.9	-6.9	-7.3	-8.3	-6.4	-5.3	-5.7	-11.1	-7.2	-6.6
Seychelles	-11.2	11.3	6.3	2.6	13.4	-1.1	-4.1	-9.9	-2.6	-2.7	-2.9	-9.2	6.5	-1.4
Sierra Leone	-17.5	-5.7	-6.6	-11.5	-1.2	-2.4	-1.9	-4.5	-5.1	-14.7	-19.0	-12.9	-7.4	-7.0
Somalia	-55.3	-24.5	-17.4	-37.2	-28.0	..	..	..	..	..	..	-38.5	-22.9	-28.0
South Africa	8.2	8.0	5.4	5.2	6.0	5.0	4.1	3.9	1.8	0.0	0.7	3.1	7.4	3.1
Sudan	-11.6	-2.6	-7.5	-7.4	-7.1	-15.3	..	..	..	..	..	-10.4	-6.1	-11.2
Swaziland	-23.8	11.5	5.5	1.8	-6.5	-9.4	-11.0	-8.0	-4.4	-8.0	-9.5	-15.0	-1.2	-8.1
Tanzania	..	-21.6	-23.1	-20.5	-22.1	-25.8	-29.1	-29.2	-28.0	-38.1	..	-8.4	-17.5	-28.7
Togo	-5.3	-9.4	-8.9	-9.2	-11.9	-8.1	-9.2	-7.8	-3.9	-5.7	-7.3	-8.4	-9.6	-7.7
Uganda	-6.5	-9.8	-10.2	-10.1	-12.1	-14.5	-15.5	-14.1	-10.7	-9.0	-10.4	-3.0	-6.8	-12.3
Zaire	0.1	-2.9	-2.3	0.7	0.3	-3.7	-0.8	2.2	3.1	2.5	1.8	-2.2	-0.4	0.8
Zambia	-4.0	3.8	7.1	-7.0	0.5	3.5	-5.5	-1.8	-3.8	-7.1	-5.4	-3.4	0.3	-2.8
Zimbabwe	4.2	4.2	5.1	2.6	0.3	-5.5	-11.9	-1.7	-1.9	-2.7	0.5	2.9	4.0	-3.3
NORTH AFRICA	..	..	..	..	..	..	..	..	..	..	..	..	..	..
Algeria	4.0	1.9	-0.2	0.3	-1.8	5.6	2.3	-1.4	-4.7	-3.2	..	-2.7	0.2	-0.5
Egypt, Arab Republic	-12.4	-10.2	-17.8	-14.5	-12.7	-8.0	-2.8	-3.0	-5.2	-2.3	..	-14.5	-12.9	-5.7
Libya	34.8	..	..	..	..	..	..	..	..	..	..	20.1	..	..
Morocco	-10.5	-4.3	-0.3	-5.4	-5.9	-5.6	-6.4	-5.5	-5.5	-7.6	..	-13.6	-5.0	-6.1
Tunisia	-5.4	-1.0	0.4	-3.3	-7.0	-5.0	-6.9	-7.1	-2.8	-3.6	..	-7.0	-3.4	-5.4
ALL AFRICA	3.7	0.2	-1.0	-0.6	0.2	0.3	-0.2	-0.9	-1.5	-1.9	..	-1.8	-0.4	-0.6

Note: 1996 data are preliminary (see page 3). Since 1994, Nigeria's ratios are distorted because the official exchange rate used by the Government for oil exports and oil value added is significantly overvalued.

2-14. Exports of goods and nonfactor services, nominal

	Millions of U.S. dollars, current prices											*Annual average*		
	1980	*1987*	*1988*	*1989*	*1990*	*1991*	*1992*	*1993*	*1994*	*1995*	*1996*	*75-84*	*85-89*	*90-MR*
SUB-SAHARAN AFRICA	81,615	60,983	63,688	67,892	78,974	73,777	74,232	69,489	73,428	81,211	91,030	51,907	59,035	77,449
excluding South Africa	53,463	37,146	38,266	42,791	51,760	46,977	46,561	41,588	44,422	48,030	58,540	34,310	36,626	48,268
excl. S.Africa & Nigeria	33,023	30,494	33,071	35,057	39,411	36,851	35,230	33,311	38,836	44,326	53,916	25,020	31,103	40,269
Angola	..	2,415	2,634	3,144	3,546	1,383	2,454	2,027	4,542	3,771	..	..	2,417	2,954
Benin	323	457	476	306	402	459	388	478	411	531	546	244	396	459
Botswana	516	1,010	1,848	1,862	2,228	2,605	2,464	2,331	2,079	2,133	..	401	1,259	2,306
Burkina Faso	173	229	267	244	352	337	302	326	244	312	..	126	214	312
Burundi	81	110	136	109	89	116	95	87	138	132	72	86	125	104
Cameroon	1,810	2,055	2,003	2,307	2,275	2,487	2,304	2,016	1,734	2,059	2,159	1,524	2,313	2,148
Cape Verde	19	47	40	47	56	47	49	48	61	83	86	18	40	61
Central African Republic	201	197	196	214	220	176	165	182	202	234	201	145	194	197
Chad	175	180	223	198	234	224	209	195	190	313	325	143	173	242
Comoros	11	30	37	30	24	37	36	53	38	45	42	15	29	39
Congo	1,024	959	899	1,160	1,433	1,226	1,257	848	1,115	1,252	1,599	782	996	1,247
Côte d'Ivoire	3,561	3,372	3,127	3,126	3,421	3,147	3,566	3,006	3,291	4,108	4,763	2,701	3,301	3,615
Djibouti	..	..	..	..	..	249	213	233	215	200	200	..	..	218
Equatorial Guinea	..	45	51	41	42	42	58	62	68	..	..	34	39	55
Eritrea	..	..	..	..	..	..	..	..	..	..	..	..	..	..
Ethiopia	..	623	629	745	672	543	340	603	665	854	796	560	642	639
Gabon	2,770	1,401	1,408	1,918	2,740	2,554	2,577	2,136	2,585	2,916	3,398	1,877	1,603	2,701
Gambia, The	109	117	144	169	201	241	216	217	159	210	..	79	124	207
Ghana	376	943	958	879	993	1,120	1,105	1,208	1,383	1,581	1,669	334	826	1,294
Guinea	..	646	641	756	870	848	720	713	672	798	746	..	666	767
Guinea-Bissau	9	21	22	21	26	33	18	26	39	30	28	11	17	29
Kenya	2,030	1,701	1,864	1,923	2,234	2,200	2,154	2,234	2,645	2,967	3,090	1,533	1,782	2,503
Lesotho	74	60	81	84	89	89	133	157	167	183	..	44	59	136
Liberia	614	..	..	..	..	..	..	..	..	..	..	508	466	..
Madagascar	539	424	398	450	489	461	496	516	656	746	755	415	399	588
Malawi	307	301	322	299	447	513	417	334	387	421	..	258	293	420
Mali	263	320	319	334	415	442	440	424	404	538	553	174	290	459
Mauritania	265	448	490	499	473	502	462	433	432	538	587	258	461	490
Mauritius	579	1,214	1,382	1,401	1,724	1,780	1,860	1,899	2,010	2,349	2,622	471	1,092	2,035
Mozambique	429	175	189	213	230	313	294	300	334	406	472	308	174	336
Namibia	1,661	1,086	1,177	1,269	1,222	1,362	1,499	1,515	1,591	1,728	1,765	1,185	1,084	1,526
Niger	619	463	472	405	420	396	315	298	257	317	314	397	404	331
Nigeria	18,859	6,707	5,283	7,796	12,366	10,165	11,337	8,329	5,725	3,918	4,861	8,898	5,563	8,100
Rwanda	168	160	159	148	145	140	113	102	44	70	81	144	179	99
São Tomé and Principe	20	9	12	11	8	11	10	12	12	9	10	13	11	10
Senegal	853	1,108	1,133	1,234	1,512	1,358	924	875	1,277	1,539	1,593	805	1,048	1,297
Seychelles	100	153	182	201	256	214	268	287	256	262	261	77	157	258
Sierra Leone	334	264	239	299	215	213	215	187	166	105	111	267	326	173
Somalia	200	68	50	84	90	..	..	..	..	..	..	142	64	90
South Africa	28,267	23,883	25,463	25,173	27,327	26,883	27,741	27,928	29,044	33,200	33,419	17,752	22,450	29,363
Sudan	810	711	661	750	653	397	..	..	..	..	..	712	703	525
Swaziland	404	474	523	578	665	694	770	823	899	893	970	290	417	816
Tanzania	..	386	458	529	525	525	554	675	805	1,250	..	633	477	722
Togo	580	517	602	537	545	536	456	301	300	445	439	401	498	432
Uganda	242	518	493	418	312	248	250	227	351	677	726	258	483	399
Zaire	2,456	1,989	2,258	2,299	2,758	1,852	1,368	1,017	1,414	1,890	6,828	1,638	2,105	2,447
Zambia	1,608	894	1,242	1,071	1,227	1,160	822	930	1,174	1,297	1,249	1,138	946	1,123
Zimbabwe	1,600	1,607	1,989	2,076	2,174	3,028	1,974	2,121	2,433	2,924	3,319	1,411	1,702	2,568
NORTH AFRICA	..	..	..	..	..	..	..	..	..	..	..	..	..	..
Algeria	14,541	9,443	8,436	10,224	14,425	13,346	12,195	10,880	9,966	11,063	..	10,568	9,996	11,979
Egypt, Arab Republic	6,992	5,087	6,069	7,094	8,647	10,284	13,459	13,071	11,904	13,304	..	5,294	6,161	11,778
Libya	23,523	..	..	..	..	..	..	..	..	..	..	13,757	..	..
Morocco	3,273	4,420	5,771	5,409	6,849	6,716	7,161	7,124	7,688	8,841	..	2,584	4,527	7,396
Tunisia	3,518	3,377	4,242	4,480	5,353	5,278	6,158	5,995	7,034	8,088	..	2,441	3,504	6,318
ALL AFRICA	127,298	93,183	98,668	106,385	127,829	122,424	126,708	119,276	123,128	137,110	..	82,566	93,093	126,079

Note: 1996 data are preliminary (see page 3).

2-15. Imports of goods and nonfactor services, nominal

	Millions of U.S. dollars, current prices											Annual average		
	1980	1987	1988	1989	1990	1991	1992	1993	1994	1995	1996	75-84	85-89	90-MR
SUB-SAHARAN AFRICA	74,153	59,967	64,789	67,020	74,069	74,687	76,785	73,039	77,226	88,943	94,957	55,224	58,307	79,958
excluding South Africa	52,248	42,709	44,091	46,647	53,222	53,451	53,875	49,635	50,181	55,456	62,982	39,422	41,264	54,115
excl. S.Africa & Nigeria	39,562	36,997	39,155	40,734	45,083	44,946	43,858	42,181	45,256	52,519	60,047	30,080	36,430	47,699
Angola	..	1,563	1,765	1,782	1,907	791	1,717	1,366	3,294	2,548	..	..	1,652	1,937
Benin	608	603	657	428	562	621	543	691	503	732	728	433	531	626
Botswana	613	784	1,048	1,490	2,337	2,757	2,336	2,461	2,071	2,227	..	500	912	2,365
Burkina Faso	564	667	635	587	709	743	724	741	488	667	..	413	596	679
Burundi	214	291	281	256	314	333	312	283	325	324	246	175	267	305
Cameroon	1,847	2,538	1,994	1,980	1,931	1,820	1,673	1,903	1,531	1,572	64	1,680	2,300	1,499
Cape Verde	100	121	120	137	148	146	192	179	227	285	265	77	118	206
Central African Republic	327	352	329	330	411	314	344	289	239	318	232	220	327	307
Chad	298	424	446	450	503	458	467	429	411	486	521	240	404	468
Comoros	64	83	87	78	71	80	89	99	88	103	95	60	75	89
Congo	1,026	888	895	838	1,307	1,248	1,176	962	1,609	1,425	2,325	872	965	1,436
Côte d'Ivoire	4,190	2,988	2,860	2,836	2,927	2,833	3,136	2,866	2,538	3,570	4,090	2,714	2,742	3,137
Djibouti	..	..	..	..	..	361	367	366	327	284	282	..	..	331
Equatorial Guinea	..	90	104	77	92	118	92	90	77	..	..	49	72	94
Eritrea	..	..	..	..	..	..	..	..	..	..	..	..	..	..
Ethiopia	..	1,227	1,252	1,200	1,069	1,226	806	1,226	1,257	1,420	1,600	973	1,195	1,229
Gabon	1,354	1,484	1,603	1,726	1,837	1,798	1,890	1,513	1,603	1,847	2,089	1,338	1,718	1,797
Gambia, The	168	138	165	205	236	285	279	280	216	268	..	111	148	261
Ghana	407	1,329	1,250	1,278	1,522	1,685	1,845	2,172	1,999	2,116	2,283	360	1,124	1,946
Guinea	..	627	741	724	864	875	878	880	829	960	867	..	663	879
Guinea-Bissau	46	75	92	112	100	111	125	88	81	89	86	48	81	97
Kenya	2,837	2,108	2,315	2,540	2,679	2,302	2,193	1,953	2,447	3,539	3,308	1,791	2,087	2,632
Lesotho	450	487	605	632	717	847	951	915	888	1,036	..	353	487	892
Liberia	614	..	..	..	..	..	..	..	..	..	..	514	387	..
Madagascar	1,202	531	518	535	827	700	746	830	888	1,005	1,006	692	517	857
Malawi	480	329	449	549	629	683	763	667	587	613	..	352	392	657
Mali	570	639	686	654	817	838	937	836	756	939	945	374	636	867
Mauritania	473	606	595	557	619	591	620	563	507	657	676	463	589	605
Mauritius	695	1,176	1,487	1,561	1,915	1,887	1,962	2,098	2,320	2,454	2,787	541	1,122	2,203
Mozambique	909	696	735	842	853	903	831	920	997	895	959	787	670	908
Namibia	1,451	1,260	1,188	1,253	1,482	1,600	1,792	1,710	1,734	1,934	1,962	1,356	1,060	1,745
Niger	976	520	499	474	523	434	418	402	393	431	430	560	482	433
Nigeria	12,324	5,783	5,033	5,998	8,203	8,559	9,989	7,530	5,150	3,334	3,487	8,996	4,898	6,607
Rwanda	307	412	422	417	364	344	371	404	483	369	296	237	397	376
São Tomé and Principe	41	27	35	42	42	44	41	42	41	46	42	27	33	43
Senegal	1,327	1,445	1,450	1,486	1,847	1,740	1,219	1,213	1,527	1,797	1,886	1,078	1,328	1,604
Seychelles	117	125	164	193	206	218	286	335	269	276	276	89	141	267
Sierra Leone	543	311	324	435	226	232	228	222	213	232	290	407	409	235
Somalia	534	315	230	490	346	..	..	..	..	..	..	400	296	346
South Africa	21,838	17,282	20,685	20,380	20,886	21,271	22,894	23,313	26,840	33,137	32,481	15,866	17,053	25,832
Sudan	1,597	1,142	1,456	1,560	1,291	1,513	..	..	..	..	..	1,440	1,408	1,402
Swaziland	543	406	485	565	722	778	876	897	942	979	1,071	371	412	895
Tanzania	..	1,131	1,260	1,345	1,380	1,607	1,754	1,763	1,752	2,846	..	1,155	1,232	1,850
Togo	640	634	725	661	738	666	612	396	337	520	543	471	609	544
Uganda	324	1,134	1,157	950	834	729	694	682	775	1,186	1,348	364	873	892
Zaire	2,444	2,208	2,463	2,241	2,730	2,192	1,438	818	1,233	1,736	6,476	1,844	2,140	2,375
Zambia	1,764	808	976	1,351	1,211	1,041	997	995	1,316	1,590	1,477	1,249	941	1,232
Zimbabwe	1,377	1,383	1,663	1,908	2,157	3,390	2,622	2,216	2,544	3,100	3,284	1,257	1,479	2,759
NORTH AFRICA	39,953	31,968	37,804	41,973	54,106	46,678	51,402	50,958	53,064	57,656	..	32,530	36,698	52,311
Algeria	12,847	8,227	8,553	10,038	15,529	10,738	11,048	11,557	11,940	12,393	..	10,816	9,883	12,201
Egypt, Arab Republic	9,822	9,222	12,322	12,827	14,109	13,234	14,761	14,488	14,604	14,690	..	8,159	10,934	14,314
Libya	11,167	..	..	..	..	..	..	..	..	..	..	8,634	..	..
Morocco	5,247	5,218	5,831	6,641	8,384	8,271	8,986	8,590	9,368	11,315	..	4,372	5,378	9,152
Tunisia	3,986	3,473	4,206	4,815	6,220	5,926	7,237	7,032	7,479	8,746	..	2,950	3,813	7,107
ALL AFRICA	112,581	92,303	102,613	108,684	126,943	121,012	127,471	123,102	129,428	145,962	..	86,797	94,709	128,986

Note: 1996 data are preliminary (see page 3).

2-16. Exports of goods and non factor services, real

	Millions of U.S. dollars, constant 1987 prices											Average annual percentage growth		
	1980	1987	1988	1989	1990	1991	1992	1993	1994	1995	1996	75-84	85-89	90-MR
SUB-SAHARAN AFRICA	63,474	60,931	64,925	69,014	71,395	71,776	72,295	75,379	76,175	81,889	88,437	1.0	2.6	3.2
excluding South Africa	39,568	37,131	38,767	41,456	43,388	43,794	43,577	45,267	45,756	48,613	52,568	1.2	2.4	2.9
excl. S. Africa & Nigeria	26,917	30,523	31,730	33,690	34,913	34,911	34,374	35,804	37,062	39,460	43,241	2.8	2.4	3.1
Angola	..	2,415	3,066	3,080	3,171	3,442	3,658	3,216	3,480	3,944	..	..	16.2	3.1
Benin	463	457	418	255	265	382	398	391	410	434	521	4.0	-6.2	9.6
Botswana	..	1,010	1,022	858	..	..	..	..	..	..	..	..	-17.7	..
Burkina Faso	249	229	237	201	278	287	248	296	214	230	228	4.7	-0.2	-0.9
Burundi	60	110	122	118	112	130	131	112	106	108	66	5.5	2.1	-5.7
Cameroon	1,295	2,055	2,149	2,647	2,387	2,308	2,428	2,376	2,634	2,587	2,750	14.0	-1.5	1.3
Cape Verde	22	47	37	46	49	40	38	42	53	62	66	11.5	-2.2	5.8
Central African Republic	244	197	170	194	181	166	147	171	210	205	201	-0.4	-2.9	2.1
Chad	139	180	202	213	187	180	173	185	186	241	259	-0.3	5.2	3.4
Comoros	10	30	34	29	19	29	26	38	43	47	48	..	10.2	12.1
Congo	690	959	1,084	1,167	1,187	1,132	1,199	1,256	1,230	1,264	1,359	10.1	2.2	2.0
Côte d'Ivoire	3,170	3,372	3,309	3,839	4,248	3,916	3,907	3,493	4,223	4,239	5,260	8.5	0.7	2.8
Djibouti	..	..	..	..	..	..	..	..	..	..	..	..	..	..
Equatorial Guinea	..	..	..	..	..	..	..	..	..	..	..	..	..	..
Eritrea	..	..	..	..	..	..	..	..	..	..	..	..	..	..
Ethiopia	..	623	651	663	649	495	263	484	567	625	680	..	1.6	1.2
Gabon	1,362	1,401	1,449	1,742	1,946	2,003	2,054	2,312	2,416	2,541	2,553	0.7	0.5	5.7
Gambia, The	131	117	145	177	181	188	189	180	183	176	..	4.8	9.1	-0.1
Ghana	1,007	943	994	1,117	1,186	1,296	1,331	1,558	1,565	1,618	1,859	-9.4	11.3	7.2
Guinea	..	646	692	733	766	790	737	824	771	859	831	..	6.6	1.8
Guinea-Bissau	38	21	26	23	30	39	19	29	58	46	50	-1.8	5.8	11.5
Kenya	1,489	1,701	1,782	1,958	2,334	2,320	2,333	3,099	2,399	2,652	2,840	-0.2	5.7	4.4
Lesotho	64	60	75	86	75	80	77	89	93	96	..	6.3	17.3	3.2
Liberia	..	..	..	..	..	..	..	..	..	..	..	..	..	..
Madagascar	673	424	389	455	509	533	535	564	621	641	703	-4.1	0.5	5.8
Malawi	290	301	307	261	326	344	334	317	349	383	389	2.7	-1.7	4.4
Mali	235	320	312	341	371	413	440	449	430	496	527	8.9	3.2	5.7
Mauritania	283	448	427	437	408	407	383	429	371	417	447	5.8	1.8	0.1
Mauritius	658	1,214	1,361	1,404	1,519	1,584	1,638	1,769	1,822	1,960	2,080	3.8	15.5	5.5
Mozambique	..	175	192	223	235	302	295	305	327	381	426	..	2.7	9.0
Namibia	1,060	1,086	1,043	1,069	1,021	1,201	1,343	1,441	1,337	1,506	1,536	..	3.4	6.0
Niger	743	463	478	475	467	497	402	389	373	384	..	0.8	-2.0	-4.6
Nigeria	11,587	6,707	7,136	7,864	8,556	8,944	9,241	9,510	8,804	9,275	9,567	-2.9	2.3	2.1
Rwanda	105	160	127	134	129	119	109	94	43	41	58	6.5	1.8	-16.0
São Tomé and Principe	10	9	14	19	10	11	12	11	8	6	6	2.6	17.6	-13.0
Senegal	844	1,108	1,150	1,213	1,441	1,508	1,388	1,285	1,336	1,444	1,540	4.0	1.8	1.5
Seychelles	..	153	174	240	272	255	236	260	219	218	224	..	21.7	-2.3
Sierra Leone	282	264	175	251	302	313	304	234	206	102	109	-8.8	-2.5	-14.1
Somalia	166	68	50	56	..	..	..	..	..	..	..	9.3	-5.5	..
South Africa	24,248	23,883	26,226	27,637	28,113	28,097	28,809	30,196	30,505	33,337	35,945	0.7	2.8	3.6
Sudan	959	711	560	594	422	355	356	..	..	..	..	1.3	-7.2	..
Swaziland	242	474	482	526	522	526	503	516	529	544	571	2.6	20.3	1.0
Tanzania	..	..	..	..	..	..	..	..	..	..	..	..	..	..
Togo	564	517	563	508	468	481	409	316	316	447	443	4.6	4.2	-3.2
Uganda	..	518	538	569	598	565	652	623	820	1,044	1,245	..	1.2	11.8
Zaire	1,028	1,989	2,026	1,905	1,886	1,563	910	830	768	926	1,202	4.2	1.0	-10.2
Zambia	1,118	894	842	830	770	805	833	1,187	1,207	1,157	1,239	-2.9	-2.9	7.9
Zimbabwe	1,312	1,607	1,765	1,878	1,844	1,762	1,824	2,062	2,481	2,555	2,779	5.4	3.9	6.8
NORTH AFRICA	..	..	..	..	..	..	..	..	..	..	..	..	..	..
Algeria	7,016	9,443	9,478	10,236	10,584	10,488	10,898	10,691	10,327	10,885	..	1.9	3.0	0.6
Egypt, Arab Republic	4,410	5,087	5,656	6,599	7,070	7,306	8,248	8,845	8,416	8,539	..	5.5	7.1	4.8
Libya	..	..	..	..	..	..	..	..	..	..	..	..	..	..
Morocco	3,035	4,420	5,327	4,838	5,827	5,843	5,992	6,492	6,437	6,698	..	3.3	7.8	4.7
Tunisia	2,745	3,377	4,101	4,304	4,494	4,454	4,812	5,032	5,606	5,700	..	5.6	10.5	5.2
ALL AFRICA	89,868	93,152	100,130	106,288	111,212	111,769	114,466	119,158	119,726	127,248	..	1.6	3.5	2.7

Note: 1996 data are preliminary (see page 3).

2-17. Imports of goods and non factor services, real

	Millions of U.S. dollars, constant 1987 prices											Average annual percentage growth		
	1980	1987	1988	1989	1990	1991	1992	1993	1994	1995	1996	75-84	85-89	90-MR
SUB-SAHARAN AFRICA	80,088	60,062	65,094	66,789	65,770	67,634	69,339	70,533	72,398	80,029	86,159	1.6	-1.1	3.6
excluding South Africa	59,064	42,849	43,975	45,628	45,924	47,375	47,944	47,499	45,302	48,286	52,031	3.4	-2.6	1.2
excl. S. Africa & Nigeria	38,635	37,264	38,489	39,610	39,144	39,782	40,172	39,908	39,253	42,327	45,562	2.1	0.7	1.6
Angola	..	1,563	1,567	1,640	2,033	1,941	2,682	1,983	1,942	2,039	..	..	-2.1	2.1
Benin	964	603	631	398	527	621	673	676	469	642	612	2.8	-6.7	3.8
Botswana	..	784	916	1,124	..	..	..	..	..	..	..	..	-4.7	..
Burkina Faso	499	667	595	540	626	675	644	696	497	623	657	3.2	4.3	0.6
Burundi	209	291	287	245	281	294	310	385	392	357	274	7.1	0.3	3.7
Cameroon	1,527	2,538	2,325	2,860	2,673	2,544	2,615	2,254	2,156	2,141	2,423	10.5	-0.6	-3.4
Cape Verde	112	121	113	135	129	123	150	157	197	214	204	11.9	-3.3	8.5
Central African Republic	499	352	295	303	348	267	284	256	209	246	174	3.0	-7.3	-7.4
Chad	247	424	448	439	415	385	380	363	305	312	338	-4.0	7.9	-4.7
Comoros	76	83	84	79	58	76	67	101	84	91	88	..	-3.2	4.5
Congo	907	888	895	874	894	986	1,120	1,035	1,147	914	1,519	8.0	-11.9	5.3
Côte d'Ivoire	3,535	2,988	2,787	2,701	2,443	2,561	2,625	2,575	2,615	3,034	3,678	3.2	-0.1	4.0
Djibouti	..	..	..	..	..	..	..	..	..	..	..	..	..	..
Equatorial Guinea	..	..	..	..	..	..	..	..	..	..	..	..	..	..
Eritrea	..	..	..	..	..	..	..	..	..	..	..	..	..	..
Ethiopia	..	1,227	1,334	1,377	1,107	1,226	1,015	1,228	1,072	1,146	1,478	..	3.0	0.5
Gabon	1,430	1,484	1,555	1,480	1,410	1,383	1,398	1,460	1,229	1,262	1,447	4.0	-9.4	-1.2
Gambia, The	271	138	163	194	206	214	234	223	202	229	..	0.5	7.5	1.8
Ghana	1,784	1,329	1,322	1,384	1,456	1,602	1,708	1,996	1,833	1,856	1,999	-9.8	9.9	5.3
Guinea	..	627	713	689	756	760	741	782	723	761	700	..	5.0	0.1
Guinea-Bissau	79	75	83	98	83	94	104	78	77	72	73	0.1	-5.9	-4.3
Kenya	2,691	2,108	2,298	2,523	2,608	2,491	2,433	3,255	3,803	4,805	4,569	-3.9	9.4	11.0
Lesotho	451	487	600	605	571	632	619	585	559	607	..	7.2	4.2	-0.4
Liberia	..	..	..	..	..	..	..	..	..	..	..	..	..	..
Madagascar	1,230	531	480	484	644	548	556	634	637	644	631	-3.6	-4.3	2.9
Malawi	535	329	397	481	495	521	566	523	474	505	477	-2.1	2.2	-0.4
Mali	465	639	677	669	748	771	819	750	696	799	814	7.0	0.6	1.6
Mauritania	474	606	556	519	546	521	529	490	430	494	509	2.9	-4.6	-1.5
Mauritius	682	1,176	1,410	1,431	1,593	1,567	1,613	1,730	1,823	1,757	1,859	-1.1	20.6	3.4
Mozambique	..	696	680	752	703	719	664	719	745	652	681	..	1.2	-1.0
Namibia	1,183	1,260	1,212	1,216	1,284	1,336	1,401	1,384	1,412	1,465	1,447	..	4.5	2.4
Niger	663	520	475	427	417	384	358	345	333	349	..	3.5	-6.5	-4.1
Nigeria	18,837	5,783	5,705	6,225	6,916	7,674	7,845	7,678	6,286	6,274	6,799	5.8	-15.1	-0.6
Rwanda	275	412	410	385	325	599	616	708	914	420	426	10.4	-0.1	4.1
São Tomé and Principe	26	27	40	53	48	45	40	46	43	44	36	6.2	16.3	-3.4
Senegal	1,198	1,445	1,453	1,499	1,564	1,530	1,555	1,449	1,316	1,361	1,434	4.7	2.1	-1.8
Seychelles	..	125	160	205	199	216	294	316	179	176	178	..	14.2	-2.5
Sierra Leone	595	311	282	376	402	359	305	334	281	328	423	-5.1	4.3	-1.0
Somalia	416	315	202	293	..	..	..	..	..	..	..	16.9	-1.3	..
South Africa	21,079	17,282	21,068	21,135	19,902	20,328	21,415	22,918	26,608	31,012	33,349	-1.4	2.8	7.8
Sudan	1,834	1,142	1,342	1,394	1,126	1,357	1,208	..	..	..	..	10.6	-12.5	..
Swaziland	336	406	448	540	544	556	582	623	512	524	546	8.8	7.9	-0.3
Tanzania	..	..	..	..	..	..	..	..	..	..	..	..	..	..
Togo	570	634	697	630	647	592	538	367	304	423	449	6.0	5.7	-7.9
Uganda	..	1,134	1,260	1,231	1,214	1,157	1,139	1,100	1,322	1,899	2,082	..	7.3	7.8
Zaire	1,013	2,208	2,517	2,520	1,903	1,772	1,094	710	530	682	911	4.2	9.5	-17.6
Zambia	1,061	808	807	676	633	514	541	663	682	737	696	-10.7	3.8	2.4
Zimbabwe	1,129	1,383	1,519	1,616	1,587	1,880	1,954	1,753	2,019	2,230	2,352	3.7	3.9	5.4
NORTH AFRICA	37,571	31,968	33,898	37,114	37,995	36,046	37,375	38,121	39,629	40,503	..	4.7	-4.4	1.4
Algeria	11,235	8,227	8,505	9,934	8,960	7,356	7,695	7,179	7,617	7,686	..	5.1	-10.1	-3.9
Egypt, Arab Republic	11,447	9,222	9,505	9,662	10,016	10,134	9,662	10,430	10,626	10,735	..	4.5	-5.9	1.7
Libya	..	..	..	..	..	..	..	..	..	..	..	..	..	..
Morocco	4,456	5,218	5,675	6,131	6,978	7,158	7,811	7,981	8,395	8,734	..	1.5	7.6	5.7
Tunisia	3,585	3,473	4,034	4,620	5,114	4,827	5,394	5,581	5,766	5,964	..	8.5	2.0	4.2
ALL AFRICA	117,861	92,361	99,427	104,111	103,843	104,026	107,033	108,970	112,314	121,102	..	2.6	-2.2	2.4

Note: 1996 data are preliminary (see page 3).

2-18. GDP growth

	Percent annual change											Average annual percentage growth		
	1980	1987	1988	1989	1990	1991	1992	1993	1994	1995	1996	75-84	85-89	90-MR
SUB-SAHARAN AFRICA	3.6	2.1	3.5	3.3	1.1	0.7	0.1	1.1	2.2	3.9	4.4	2.3	2.5	1.7
excluding South Africa	1.2	1.7	3.4	3.8	1.9	1.6	1.4	0.9	2.0	4.3	5.0	2.2	3.0	2.2
excl. S.Africa & Nigeria	0.5	2.2	2.3	3.1	0.7	0.9	1.1	0.5	2.2	4.8	5.8	2.8	2.6	2.0
Angola	..	7.9	5.6	0.4	-0.3	0.8	1.5	-24.4	7.7	12.6	..	..	4.7	-2.9
Benin	6.4	-1.7	3.8	1.8	3.0	4.8	4.1	3.2	4.6	4.6	5.6	3.8	2.2	4.2
Botswana	14.3	8.8	15.7	12.9	5.9	8.9	6.6	-0.2	4.0	4.6	..	11.3	10.5	4.8
Burkina Faso	-0.3	-0.7	5.9	1.1	-1.2	9.3	2.6	-0.9	1.3	4.2	5.5	4.1	4.4	2.7
Burundi	1.0	5.6	5.0	1.4	3.6	5.2	2.7	-6.0	-6.6	-3.8	-12.9	3.8	5.1	-2.6
Cameroon	-2.0	-2.3	-7.8	-1.9	-6.1	-3.6	-3.0	-3.1	-2.4	3.5	5.0	8.5	-0.1	-1.7
Cape Verde	37.7	36.8	5.9	5.7	0.7	1.4	3.3	4.2	3.8	4.7	4.0	10.3	12.5	3.3
Central African Republic	-4.6	-4.9	1.3	3.4	-1.1	-0.5	-2.6	-2.3	7.8	2.4	-2.1	0.4	1.0	0.4
Chad	-6.1	-2.8	16.2	5.4	-3.5	7.5	7.9	-15.8	9.8	4.0	2.8	-1.4	5.2	1.3
Comoros	..	1.7	2.7	-3.2	5.1	-5.5	7.7	3.8	-2.3	-2.3	1.0	..	1.3	1.0
Congo	18.8	0.2	1.8	2.6	1.0	1.5	2.6	-1.0	-5.5	2.2	4.8	9.6	-1.0	0.3
Côte d'Ivoire	-11.4	-0.5	1.2	3.0	-1.2	0.1	-0.1	-0.2	2.0	7.0	6.8	2.3	2.2	1.7
Djibouti	..	..	..	..	..	..	..	..	..	..	..	..	..	..
Equatorial Guinea	..	6.4	3.0	-1.3	3.3	-1.0	13.7	7.3	6.8	11.2	..	..	2.7	7.0
Eritrea	..	..	..	..	..	..	..	..	..	..	..	..	..	..
Ethiopia	..	13.7	0.4	0.4	3.8	-4.7	-3.5	12.5	2.3	5.6	11.9	..	4.2	3.4
Gabon	2.1	-16.2	4.2	7.4	4.2	7.5	-3.4	2.2	3.0	3.7	3.2	0.2	-3.8	2.5
Gambia, The	-9.8	2.8	1.1	5.2	5.8	0.5	7.0	6.7	1.0	-6.5	..	3.3	2.6	3.0
Ghana	0.6	4.6	5.5	4.9	3.1	5.3	3.6	4.8	3.7	4.4	5.0	-0.8	5.1	4.3
Guinea	..	3.3	6.3	4.0	4.3	2.4	3.0	4.7	4.0	4.4	4.5	..	4.7	3.8
Guinea-Bissau	-18.9	1.1	4.5	6.2	5.6	4.4	2.2	2.6	1.5	4.8	5.5	1.5	2.8	3.4
Kenya	5.4	5.9	6.2	4.7	4.2	1.4	-0.7	0.4	2.7	4.4	4.3	4.8	5.8	1.9
Lesotho	-2.7	5.7	14.1	12.9	2.8	4.5	-0.4	4.9	11.4	9.2	..	4.7	7.0	5.0
Liberia	-4.5	-1.0	..	..	..	..	..	..	..	..	..	0.5	-1.2	..
Madagascar	0.8	1.2	3.4	4.1	3.2	-6.7	1.2	2.0	0.0	1.8	2.0	-0.3	2.3	0.3
Malawi	-0.2	1.1	3.1	0.6	8.8	6.2	-10.0	15.2	-12.9	13.5	16.1	3.2	1.4	3.0
Mali	-4.7	1.3	-0.2	11.8	0.4	-0.5	8.0	-2.4	2.3	6.4	4.0	2.3	3.9	2.5
Mauritania	4.0	2.2	1.8	4.2	-2.1	2.8	1.8	5.9	4.4	4.7	4.5	1.7	3.3	3.5
Mauritius	-9.5	8.6	6.8	4.4	7.2	4.2	6.2	5.5	4.2	4.3	6.1	3.7	7.7	5.2
Mozambique	..	14.6	8.2	6.5	0.9	4.9	-0.8	18.8	4.5	1.4	6.4	..	6.0	5.5
Namibia	..	4.3	0.2	2.4	0.4	7.4	7.9	-1.4	6.7	4.0	5.0	..	2.8	4.3
Niger	4.8	-2.7	5.0	-3.5	5.2	2.5	-6.5	1.4	3.9	3.2	3.7	2.8	1.9	1.3
Nigeria	3.9	-0.7	9.9	7.2	8.2	4.8	2.9	2.7	1.0	2.3	2.3	-0.4	5.0	3.1
Rwanda	9.0	-1.2	6.6	-0.5	-3.7	-4.5	8.3	-10.0	-49.1	28.2	11.4	6.9	3.1	-8.7
São Tomé and Principe	13.8	21.2	2.0	3.1	-2.2	1.5	0.7	1.1	2.2	2.0	1.5	3.5	7.5	1.2
Senegal	-2.2	4.0	5.1	-1.4	4.5	-0.7	2.8	-2.1	2.0	4.8	5.1	2.3	3.6	1.8
Seychelles	-4.2	4.5	4.2	10.3	7.5	2.7	6.9	5.8	-1.6	-1.8	1.7	3.6	5.2	2.9
Sierra Leone	5.3	2.5	2.0	4.9	2.6	-8.7	-9.4	0.1	3.6	-9.9	4.8	1.6	1.0	-3.2
Somalia	-4.2	5.1	-0.6	-0.2	-1.5	..	..	..	..	..	..	4.1	3.0	..
South Africa	7.5	2.7	3.7	2.5	-0.5	-1.0	-2.6	1.5	2.8	3.1	3.3	2.6	1.6	0.8
Sudan	1.0	2.2	-4.3	7.4	-1.5	0.7	11.3	7.6	5.5	..	..	3.5	0.5	5.3
Swaziland	2.3	7.4	3.7	3.6	3.5	-1.0	2.2	2.8	2.5	3.6	1.0	3.5	5.8	2.1
Tanzania	..	4.5	4.4	3.7	4.2	4.3	2.5	2.4	3.7	4.0	..	..	4.0	3.4
Togo	14.7	0.5	6.7	4.1	-0.2	-0.7	-3.9	-18.2	12.8	7.1	6.2	2.1	3.4	-1.0
Uganda	..	3.8	8.0	6.3	6.4	5.4	3.2	8.3	6.1	11.2	9.4	..	3.3	6.9
Zaire	2.4	2.7	0.5	-1.3	-6.6	-8.4	-10.5	-13.5	-3.9	-0.6	1.3	-0.5	1.7	-7.0
Zambia	3.0	3.1	5.3	-0.9	0.3	-0.4	0.1	2.4	-1.6	-3.1	4.3	0.2	2.1	0.0
Zimbabwe	15.0	-1.4	9.2	6.3	-1.4	5.6	-8.2	2.5	6.0	-1.8	7.4	2.9	3.9	1.0
NORTH AFRICA	3.8	0.2	2.0	3.8	2.2	1.0	2.2	0.1	2.8	2.5	..	5.1	1.5	1.7
Algeria	0.9	-0.1	-1.6	5.0	-1.5	-1.4	1.8	-1.9	-1.0	4.4	..	5.6	1.0	-0.2
Egypt, Arab Republic	10.4	2.5	5.2	4.8	5.6	1.1	4.4	2.9	3.9	4.6	..	8.7	4.1	3.5
Libya	0.6	-3.2	0.7	0.6	..	..	..	..	..	..	..	1.6	-3.9	..
Morocco	9.1	-2.3	10.2	2.3	4.2	6.6	-3.6	-1.1	11.1	-6.9	..	4.7	4.7	1.7
Tunisia	7.4	6.6	-0.1	2.2	7.9	4.0	7.7	1.9	3.3	2.4	..	5.4	2.4	4.4
ALL AFRICA	3.7	1.3	2.9	3.5	1.5	0.8	0.9	0.7	2.4	3.4	. . .	3.4	2.1	1.4

Note: 1996 data are preliminary (see page 3).

2-19. GNP per capita

	U.S. dollars, Atlas method											Annual average		
	1980	1987	1988	1989	1990	1991	1992	1993	1994	1995	1996	75-84	85-89	90-MR
SUB-SAHARAN AFRICA	660	480	529	534	518	497	513	495	478	481	493	536	489	496
excluding South Africa	532	356	377	371	355	325	327	300	274	273	290	422	354	306
excl. S.Africa & Nigeria	450	381	405	397	376	338	339	313	285	287	302	363	369	320
Angola	..	880	820	830	780	590	500	..	..	..	340	..	843	553
Benin	410	320	380	360	370	380	370	380	340	360	360	313	326	366
Botswana	940	1,230	1,530	1,900	2,270	2,620	2,990	2,830	2,850	3,020	..	808	1,346	2,763
Burkina Faso	250	240	290	290	290	310	280	230	200	210	220	201	242	249
Burundi	200	260	250	230	220	220	210	180	160	160	140	183	246	184
Cameroon	700	1,030	1,110	1,060	920	900	910	760	630	570	610	619	978	757
Cape Verde	430	500	650	680	660	740	970	990	990	1,030	1,090	320	514	924
Central African Republic	340	400	460	470	470	460	470	430	370	350	310	272	388	409
Chad	170	140	190	180	180	200	210	190	170	160	160	153	154	181
Comoros	370	420	520	510	540	530	610	620	520	480	460	348	418	537
Congo	890	1,030	1,030	990	990	1,010	1,090	900	690	630	660	825	1,004	853
Côte d'Ivoire	1,290	750	840	850	800	760	770	720	620	620	620	889	778	701
Djibouti	..	..	..	..	..	..	..	..	..	..	..	..	..	..
Equatorial Guinea	..	..	370	360	360	350	400	440	370	380	510	..	365	401
Eritrea	..	..	..	..	..	..	..	..	..	..	..	..	..	..
Ethiopia	..	190	180	170	170	130	110	120	110	110	110	..	164	123
Gabon	4,750	3,680	4,430	4,630	4,620	5,060	4,940	4,840	3,460	3,490	3,620	4,273	4,188	4,290
Gambia, The	370	270	310	320	330	350	340	360	340	320	..	292	274	340
Ghana	430	420	430	400	390	410	430	410	360	350	360	356	402	387
Guinea	..	..	420	420	450	470	490	510	520	540	560	..	420	506
Guinea-Bissau	140	190	190	200	230	240	250	240	240	240	250	176	184	241
Kenya	450	370	410	400	380	350	340	270	270	280	330	341	362	317
Lesotho	440	370	460	550	560	560	580	580	620	650	670	391	418	603
Liberia	620	490	..	..	..	..	..	..	..	..	..	526	470	..
Madagascar	460	280	260	230	230	210	230	240	230	230	240	354	274	230
Malawi	190	160	170	170	200	230	210	240	170	170	180	164	164	200
Mali	250	220	260	280	280	270	310	300	250	250	240	185	214	271
Mauritania	470	440	500	510	490	510	530	500	480	460	470	406	446	491
Mauritius	1,240	1,620	2,070	2,220	2,440	2,610	2,960	3,080	3,200	3,390	3,690	1,149	1,646	3,053
Mozambique	..	140	110	90	90	90	80	90	90	80	90	133	130	87
Namibia	..	1,400	1,440	1,860	1,770	1,860	1,980	1,900	2,030	2,090	2,080	..	1,455	1,959
Niger	480	280	330	320	320	310	290	240	210	200	200	321	280	253
Nigeria	790	260	270	270	270	270	280	250	230	220	240	606	292	251
Rwanda	250	330	380	380	360	310	310	260	150	180	190	207	334	251
São Tomé and Principe	520	540	560	440	490	490	520	490	520	420	350	399	454	469
Senegal	540	570	720	690	720	700	650	550	490	530	560	438	558	600
Seychelles	2,140	3,330	4,070	4,650	5,100	5,300	6,170	6,530	6,730	6,770	6,960	1,680	3,454	6,223
Sierra Leone	370	270	270	280	260	200	160	160	160	170	200	316	290	187
Somalia	100	120	130	120	110	..	..	..	..	..	..	110	116	110
South Africa	2,300	2,020	2,440	2,590	2,600	2,710	2,910	2,990	3,090	3,150	3,140	1,967	2,170	2,941
Sudan	430	640	590	540	430	360	310	..	..	..	..	381	522	367
Swaziland	880	750	940	900	1,060	1,100	1,190	1,140	1,140	1,170	..	810	820	1,133
Tanzania	..	230	190	160	150	160	150	140	130	130	130	..	228	141
Togo	440	330	420	430	430	430	430	350	300	300	300	324	338	363
Uganda	..	330	420	430	350	260	200	190	190	240	290	..	324	246
Zaire	640	240	250	240	230	190	170	130	120	110	..	479	242	158
Zambia	630	260	330	420	450	400	380	390	380	400	430	560	322	404
Zimbabwe	760	590	690	720	710	680	570	540	540	540	620	694	642	600
NORTH AFRICA	1,361	1,477	1,514	1,452	1,420	1,328	1,352	1,298	1,338	1,366	1,469	1,110	1,414	1,367
Algeria	2,080	2,870	2,800	2,590	2,400	2,040	1,980	1,800	1,670	1,590	1,570	1,773	2,676	1,864
Egypt, Arab Republic	530	800	830	800	790	750	790	800	880	990	1,090	485	752	870
Libya	10,460	6,110	5,810	5,540	..	..	..	..	..	..	..	7,927	5,968	..
Morocco	990	750	950	970	1,030	1,100	1,100	1,060	1,170	1,110	1,280	727	790	1,121
Tunisia	1,360	1,270	1,340	1,310	1,430	1,490	1,700	1,680	1,740	1,820	2,000	1,092	1,244	1,694
ALL AFRICA	784	665	711	703	682	649	666	641	633	639	666	637	660	654

Note: 1996 data are preliminary (see page 3).

2-20. Total consumption per capita

	Current U.S. dollars											Annual average		
	1980	1987	1988	1989	1990	1991	1992	1993	1994	1995	1996	75-84	85-89	90-MR
SUB-SAHARAN AFRICA	517	423	425	421	449	445	446	420	392	424	439	415	402	431
excluding South Africa	418	316	312	305	311	297	283	265	232	253	291	333	306	276
excl. S.Africa & Nigeria	365	343	340	335	337	323	307	289	244	274	312	299	328	298
Angola	..	612	685	759	694	341	392	293	445	380	..	..	658	424
Benin	426	350	359	315	368	366	310	389	260	344	355	300	318	342
Botswana	778	814	1,075	1,016	1,558	1,776	1,524	2,112	2,125	2,304	..	645	858	1,900
Burkina Faso	260	258	267	250	283	283	291	272	173	209	..	193	238	252
Burundi	224	210	206	202	217	216	192	163	175	181	156	179	219	186
Cameroon	616	926	911	799	768	820	758	782	500	476	400	498	800	643
Cape Verde	458	745	728	762	805	834	872	770	817	1,002	985	349	619	869
Central African Republic	375	431	444	424	493	447	453	388	255	324	324	274	407	383
Chad	..	186	219	211	224	250	246	188	143	161	173	145	194	198
Comoros	406	502	516	505	574	541	567	599	451	511	483	343	450	532
Congo	658	858	842	782	963	941	929	593	518	575	615	586	806	733
Côte d'Ivoire	989	768	760	729	784	753	790	711	438	569	597	671	688	663
Djibouti	..	..	..	..	..	964	978	911	899	841	795	..	..	898
Equatorial Guinea	..	417	455	359	416	419	423	387	279	..	..	446	365	385
Eritrea	..	..	..	..	..	..	..	..	..	..	..	..	..	..
Ethiopia	..	152	149	158	161	181	130	127	101	98	99	134	153	128
Gabon	2,438	3,245	3,049	3,250	4,020	3,249	3,584	2,655	2,141	2,699	2,886	1,949	3,210	3,033
Gambia, The	362	246	253	268	296	321	321	337	316	310	..	277	233	317
Ghana	393	353	351	343	374	399	402	357	299	326	329	327	360	355
Guinea	..	321	383	355	403	425	434	452	481	501	525	..	344	460
Guinea-Bissau	138	175	166	221	246	239	220	221	229	239	234	177	179	233
Kenya	359	302	311	304	297	273	278	176	224	297	282	271	284	261
Lesotho	429	382	448	431	455	489	504	483	431	428	..	353	368	465
Liberia	432	..	..	..	..	..	..	..	..	..	..	407	410	..
Madagascar	471	228	204	199	254	218	234	257	218	228	284	347	242	242
Malawi	180	131	152	176	198	218	206	229	138	147	..	141	148	190
Mali	260	242	242	235	275	260	303	270	181	227	233	186	227	250
Mauritania	426	432	417	439	480	495	524	394	430	436	405	408	410	452
Mauritius	1,049	1,318	1,517	1,586	1,909	1,992	2,122	2,198	2,412	2,701	2,940	849	1,254	2,325
Mozambique	207	100	88	101	100	95	80	84	87	75	81	167	138	86
Namibia	1,289	1,440	1,356	1,324	1,423	1,562	1,700	1,573	1,569	1,760	1,631	1,491	1,206	1,602
Niger	356	294	257	265	311	272	284	260	176	205	205	279	256	245
Nigeria	619	213	203	191	209	195	191	172	184	170	205	464	223	189
Rwanda	216	321	349	347	360	255	257	246	187	213	203	196	312	246
São Tomé and Principe	528	609	565	585	605	620	487	481	466	430	419	383	566	501
Senegal	547	646	669	597	711	682	478	481	436	515	527	417	571	547
Seychelles	1,703	2,600	2,900	3,219	3,422	4,314	5,312	5,710	5,380	5,593	5,496	1,462	2,562	5,032
Sierra Leone	371	217	331	307	206	181	154	174	204	209	223	318	283	193
Somalia	102	112	116	137	120	..	..	..	..	..	..	114	114	120
South Africa	1,715	1,756	1,850	1,880	2,213	2,338	2,529	2,408	2,440	2,628	2,435	1,410	1,603	2,427
Sudan	350	630	424	431	350	305	..	..	..	..	..	354	512	328
Swaziland	964	609	670	710	955	993	1,034	935	974	1,084	1,121	671	611	1,014
Tanzania	..	144	137	146	130	146	149	129	113	151	..	268	190	136
Togo	334	356	386	335	394	401	427	323	211	288	314	246	325	337
Uganda	99	424	424	330	262	195	163	177	205	273	285	156	333	223
Zaire	497	200	222	212	227	231	193	209	122	126	394	394	208	215
Zambia	546	261	411	506	347	360	361	384	383	431	424	453	328	385
Zimbabwe	558	476	505	544	535	530	459	426	442	511	547	520	469	493
NORTH AFRICA	883	1,135	1,069	1,053	1,170	970	1,086	1,088	1,099	1,166	..	738	1,072	1,096
Algeria	1,291	1,896	1,804	1,592	1,795	1,144	1,265	1,337	1,119	1,055	..	1,115	1,792	1,286
Egypt, Arab Republic	476	697	580	640	690	599	716	732	806	893	..	417	641	739
Libya	5,040	..	..	..	..	..	..	..	..	..	..	4,323	..	..
Morocco	838	690	763	792	867	940	958	888	982	1,057	..	608	674	949
Tunisia	1,041	977	1,013	1,007	1,204	1,237	1,420	1,321	1,386	1,599	..	820	969	1,361
ALL AFRICA	592	557	548	541	584	547	566	544	522	559	..	481	528	554

Note: 1996 data are preliminary (see page 3).

Figure 2-1. Gross domestic product, 1996*

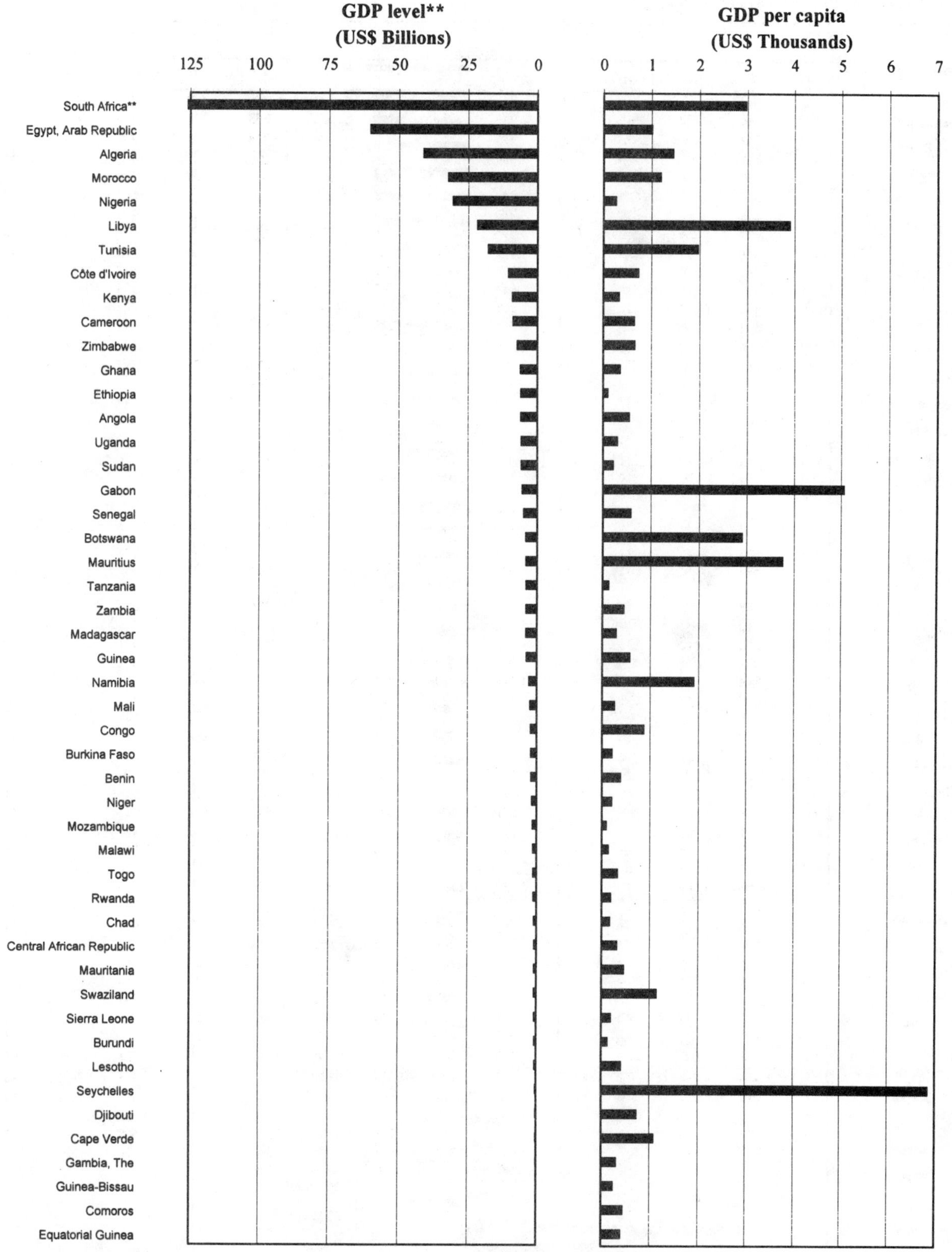

* Or most recent year available.

** Sorted by GDP level.

*** GDP level greater than $125 billion.

Figure 2-2. GDP and export growth rates, average 1990-96*

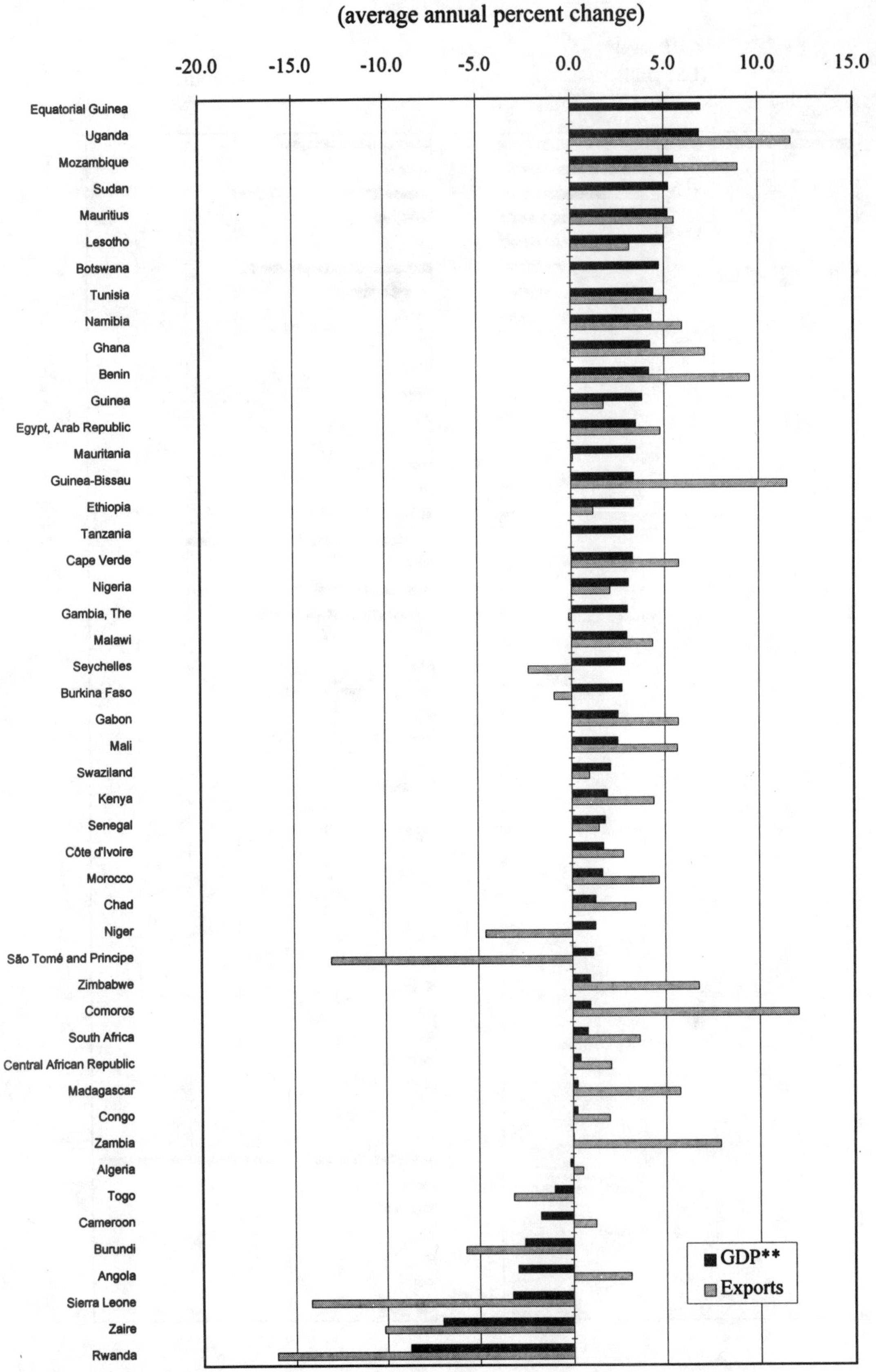

* Or most recent year available

** Sorted by GDP.

Figure 2-3. Composition of GDP, 1996*

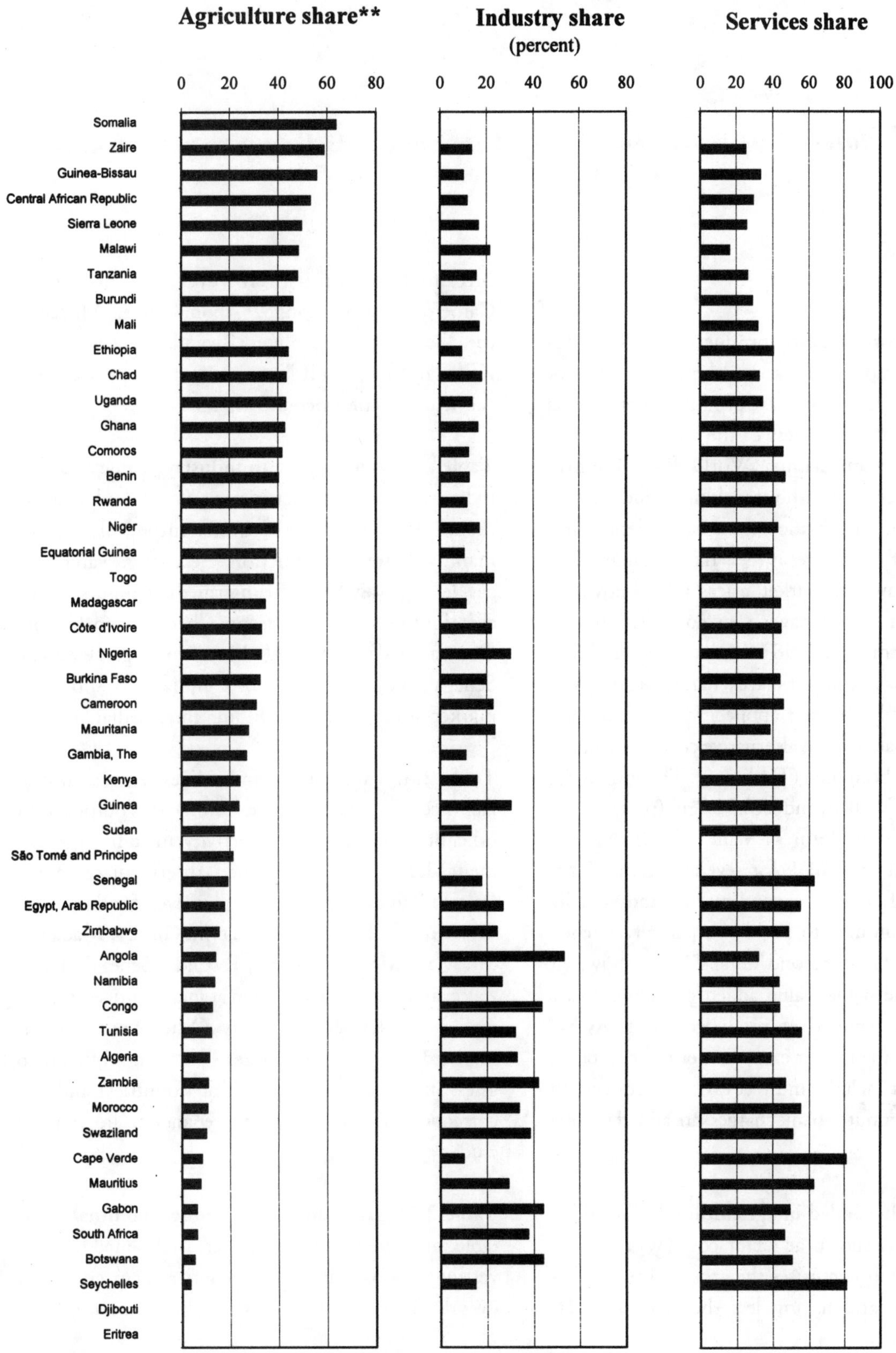

* Or most recent year available ** Sorted by Agriculture Share.

Note: Nigeria's shares are distorted because of official exchange rate over-valuation affecting oil exports and oil value added.

Technical Notes

Tables

Table 2-1. Gross domestic product, real. Gross domestic product (GDP) measures the total output of goods and services for final use produced by residents and nonresidents, regardless of the allocation to domestic and foreign claims (World Bank country desks). It is calculated without making deductions for depreciation of "manmade" assets or depletion and degradation of natural resources. In this table, GDP figures are shown at market prices (also known as purchaser values) and have been converted to US dollars using constant (1987) exchange rates. For a few countries where the official exchange rate does not reflect effectively the rate applied to actual foreign exchange transactions, an alternative currency conversion factor has been used (Table 3-6). The sum of the components of GDP by industrial origin (presented in this volume in the form of value added) will not normally equal total GDP for several reasons. First, components of GDP by expenditure are individually rescaled and summed to provide a partially rebased series for total GDP. Second, total GDP is shown at purchaser value, while value added components are conventionally reported at producer prices. As explained above, the former excludes net indirect taxes, while the latter includes indirect taxes. Third, certain items, such as imputed bank charges, are added in total GDP.

Table 2-2. Value added in agriculture. Value added in agriculture is shown at factor cost (World Bank country desks). It comprises the gross output of forestry, hunting, and fishing less the value of their intermediate inputs. However, for Botswana, Cameroon, Chad, Congo, Gabon, Guinea, Madagascar, Mali, Morocco, Niger, Rwanda, Senegal, Togo, Zaire, and Zambia it is shown at market prices, that is, including intermediate inputs.

Table 2-3. Value added in industry. Value added in industry is shown at factor cost (World Bank country desks). It comprises the gross output of mining, manufacturing, construction, electricity, water, and gas, less the value of their intermediate inputs. However, for Botswana, Cameroon, Chad, Congo, Gabon, Guinea, Madagascar, Mali, Morocco, Niger, Rwanda, Senegal, Togo, Zaire, and Zambia it is shown at market prices, that is, including intermediate inputs.

Table 2-4. Value added in services. Also shown at factor cost, this table consists of the gross output of all other branches of economic activity, including government, less the value of their intermediate inputs (World Bank country desks). However, for Botswana, Cameroon, Chad, Congo, Gabon, Guinea, Madagascar, Mali, Morocco, Niger, Rwanda, Senegal, Togo, Zaire, and Zambia it is shown at market prices, that is, including intermediate inputs. Other items, such as imputed bank service charges (which are difficult to assess in the same fashion for all countries) and any corrections for statistical discrepancies, are not included.

Table 2-5. Gross domestic product, nominal. This table, presented at market prices, is obtained by converting national currency GDP series in current prices (World Bank country desks) to US dollars at official annual exchange rates (Table 3-4; see also the note for Table 2-1). GDP growth rates are presented in real terms.

Table 2-6. Total consumption. Total consumption is the sum of private consumption (World Bank country desks) and general government consumption (Table 2-7). Private consumption, not separately shown here, is the value of all goods and services purchased or received as income in kind by households and nonprofit institutions. It excludes purchases of dwellings, but includes imputed rent for owner-occupied dwellings. In practice, it includes any statistical discrepancy in the use of resources.

Table 2-7. General government consumption. This indicator includes all current expenditure for purchases of goods and services by all levels of government, including capital expenditure on national defense and security (World Bank country desks). Other capital expenditure by government is included in investment.

Tables 2-8, 2-9, and 2-10. Gross domestic, public, and private investment. Gross domestic investment (GDI) consists of gross domestic fixed capital formation plus net changes in the level of inventories (World Bank country desks). GDI comprises outlays by the public sector (Table 2-9) and the private sector (Table 2-10). Examples include improvements in land, dwellings, machinery, and other equipment. For some countries the sum of gross private investment and gross public investment does not add up to gross domestic investment due to statistical discrepancies.

Table 2-11. Gross domestic savings. Gross domestic savings (GDS) is calculated by deducting total consumption (Table 2-6) from gross domestic product in current prices (Table 2-5).

Table 2-12. Gross national savings. Gross national savings (GNS) is the sum of gross domestic savings (Table 2-11), net factor income from abroad (World Bank country desks) and net private transfers from abroad (Table 5-5). The estimate here also includes net public transfers from abroad (Table 5-6).

Table 2-13. Resource balance. The table indicates the difference between exports f.o.b. (Table 2-14) and imports c.i.f. (Table 2-15) of goods and nonfactor services (or the difference between GDS and GDI). The resource balance is shown as a share of GDP in US dollars at current prices (Table 2-5).

Tables 2-14 and 2-15. Exports and imports of goods and nonfactor services, nominal. Data for exports and imports of goods and nonfactor services are from the World Bank country desks and refer to all goods and nonfactor services (GNFS) provided to, or by, the rest of the world, including merchandise, freight, insurance, travel, and other nonfactor services. The value of factor services, such as investment income, interest, and labor income, is not included. These series are generally estimated on the basis of foreign trade statistics from customs declarations. They are not fully comparable with the series from the balance of payments, which are based on changes in ownership between residents of a country and the rest of the world. Exports, as well as imports of GNFS, are shown in current US dollars.

Tables 2-16 and 2-17. Exports and imports of goods and nonfactor services, real. These are defined as in Tables 2-14 and 2-15, but expressed in constant 1987 US dollars.

Table 2-18. GDP growth. This table (World Bank country desks) provides average annual growth rates calculated from GDP at constant 1987 prices (Table 2-1).

Table 2-19. GNP per capita. Figures presented here (World Bank country desks) are calculated using the *World Bank Atlas* method, as described in the technical notes for Table 1-1; they are similar in concept to GNP per capita in current prices, except that the use of three-year averages of exchange rates smoothes out sharp fluctuations from year to year.

Table 2-20. Total consumption per capita. This table is obtained by dividing total consumption at current US dollars (Table 2-6) by the corresponding midyear population (Table 1-2).

Figures

The following indicators have been used to derive the figures in this chapter.

Figure 2-1. Gross domestic product (Table 2-5); GDP per capita (Tables 1-2 and 2-5).

Figure 2-2. GDP growth (Table 2-1); export growth (Table 2-16).

Figure 2-3. Value added in agriculture (Table 2-2); value added in industry (Table 2-3); value added in services (Table 2-4); gross domestic product (Table 2-1).

Methodology used for regional aggregations and period averages in chapter 2

	Aggregations[a]			*Period averages*[b]	
Table	*(3)*	*(4)*	*(5)*	*(1)*	*(2)*
2-1	x				x
2-2	x				x
2-3	x				x
2-4	x				x
2-5	x			x	
2-6		x		x	
2-7		x		x	
2-8		x		x	
2-9		x		x	
2-10		x		x	
2-11		x		x	
2-12		x		x	
2-13			x	x	
2-14	x			x	
2-15	x			x	
2-16	x				x
2-17	x				x
2-18	x				x
2-19		x		x	
2-20		x		x	

Note: Regional aggregations are shown in the rows for Sub-Saharan Africa, North Africa, and All Africa. Period averages are shown in the last three columns. This table shows only the methodologies used in this chapter.

a. Regional aggregations: (1) simple total; (2) simple total of the first indicator divided by the simple total of the second indicator (same country coverage); (3) simple total of the gap-filled indicator; (4) simple total of the gap-filled main indicator divided by the simple total of the gap-filled secondary indicator; (5) simple total of the first gap-filled main indicator less the simple total of the second gap-filled main indicator, all divided by the simple total of the secondary indicator; (6) weighted total (by population); (7) median; (8) no aggregation; (9) simple arithmetic mean.

b. Period averages: (1) arithmetic mean (using the same series as shown in the table, i.e., ratio if the rest of the table is shown as ratio, level if the rest of the table is shown as level, growth rate if the rest of the table is shown as growth rate); (2) least-squares growth rate (using main indicator); (3) least-squares growth rate (using main indicator in constant terms, with the rest of the table in current terms).

3

Prices and Exchange Rates

Information on prices and exchange rates are important in monitoring national economic performance. This chapter provides three sets of price deflators and six exchange rate indicators. The GDP deflator for national currency series shows changes in domestic prices only. The US dollar series GDP deflator includes the effects of both domestic price changes, as reflected in the national currency series GDP implicit deflator, and changes in the exchange rate between national currencies and US dollars. The consumer price index measures the change in prices of a selected bundle of consumer goods, which differs among countries.

The US dollar exchange rate (units of national currency per US dollar) is reported because of extensive use of US dollars to denominate international transactions; US dollars are also widely used for statistical comparisons across countries. The SDR exchange rate index (based on SDRs per unit of national currency) is a broader measure of the changes in the international value of domestic currencies because it is based on five major currencies. For Sub-Saharan Africa, it may be more representative of movements in non-dual exchange rates than that expressed in US dollars alone because a large share of the region's foreign trade and debt is not denominated in US dollars. A decrease in the index shows that the currency has depreciated, which indicates that foreign goods have become relatively more expensive than domestic goods. We have included information on the parallel market exchange rate and the ratio of the parallel to the official exchange rates to provide a measure of the premium on the official rate. It is tempting to view the divergence between the official and parallel rates as a measure of the disequilibrium in the official exchange rate. However, this is not necessarily true. Conversion factors are sometimes used in place of official exchange rates when the latter are considered to be especially unrepresentative of rates effectively applied to international transactions.

3-1. GDP deflator (local currency series)

	Index 1987=100											Annual average		
	1980	1987	1988	1989	1990	1991	1992	1993	1994	1995	1996	75-84	85-89	90-MR
SUB-SAHARAN AFRICA	53.2	100.0	108.9	122.9	135.5	150.1	166.8	175.5	203.2	226.1	221.9	51.7	101.5	182.7
excluding South Africa	53.6	100.0	108.8	120.8	133.4	146.7	164.0	168.3	193.2	207.9	209.7	52.3	101.1	174.8
excl. S. Africa & Nigeria	53.9	100.0	108.7	118.7	131.3	146.1	159.4	167.7	186.1	189.7	197.6	53.0	100.9	168.3
Angola	..	100.0	102.3	118.5	131.3	331.6	1,664.3	17,776.8	369,793.9	7,450,228.3	..	..	103.2	1,306,654.4
Benin	79.5	100.0	99.2	96.5	98.2	99.9	102.3	104.5	140.7	164.4	169.2	76.8	98.6	125.6
Botswana	52.1	100.0	116.7	149.0	157.6	165.1	173.0	188.5	220.4	240.7	..	45.1	107.1	190.9
Burkina Faso	74.4	100.0	103.3	108.7	109.8	105.1	103.0	104.6	133.6	144.8	153.2	73.0	103.5	122.0
Burundi	83.1	100.0	103.5	118.7	125.7	130.6	135.8	145.7	167.7	188.3	221.9	69.8	106.8	159.4
Cameroon	58.7	100.0	100.8	99.0	100.7	104.2	102.7	104.7	116.1	135.6	141.8	58.4	100.8	115.1
Cape Verde	49.4	100.0	105.5	109.2	110.6	116.6	120.5	126.5	130.2	141.1	147.9	51.3	97.6	127.6
Central African Republic	52.2	100.0	103.6	106.4	108.2	106.3	102.7	102.3	132.7	147.9	148.7	52.4	103.5	121.3
Chad	89.1	100.0	108.7	106.7	114.5	119.2	103.9	102.6	147.6	161.9	179.6	87.0	108.2	132.8
Comoros	56.6	100.0	101.9	108.0	110.3	119.4	111.2	121.5	131.1	140.3	140.2	70.8	99.4	124.9
Congo	79.7	100.0	93.8	105.4	104.6	104.0	102.3	101.2	138.4	144.3	160.6	81.7	104.7	122.2
Côte d'Ivoire	74.8	100.0	99.5	98.5	94.1	94.7	94.7	94.6	134.0	146.7	150.6	68.1	102.0	115.6
Djibouti	..	..	..	..	..	..	..	..	..	..	..	..	..	..
Equatorial Guinea	..	100.0	102.3	97.7	95.2	98.5	98.8	97.1	146.6	155.1	..	..	100.3	115.2
Eritrea	..	..	..	..	..	..	..	..	..	..	..	..	..	..
Ethiopia	..	100.0	102.8	108.0	109.9	128.2	136.2	159.1	165.3	188.1	191.3	84.5	105.6	154.0
Gabon	70.3	100.0	94.2	103.2	120.2	105.1	105.7	107.0	157.8	167.0	184.9	65.7	104.6	135.4
Gambia, The	35.9	100.0	108.9	122.9	141.6	156.5	164.0	168.3	176.0	189.7	..	34.8	93.7	166.0
Ghana	6.3	100.0	133.5	171.6	225.6	270.9	302.0	377.8	490.7	704.2	938.4	11.5	105.5	472.8
Guinea	..	100.0	121.7	148.8	184.4	217.6	252.2	272.6	286.2	301.1	312.6	..	112.3	261.0
Guinea-Bissau	7.8	100.0	179.0	349.7	470.0	756.2	1,313.8	1,983.9	2,485.3	3,582.9	5,290.2	8.9	141.7	2,268.9
Kenya	53.2	100.0	108.6	117.7	129.3	145.5	172.9	217.4	263.0	284.1	308.5	54.0	101.7	217.3
Lesotho	43.2	100.0	118.4	137.9	161.4	158.3	184.3	211.7	223.7	230.1	..	43.0	104.5	194.9
Liberia	88.3	100.0	..	..	..	..	..	..	..	..	..	80.2	95.9	..
Madagascar	29.5	100.0	121.2	135.7	151.1	172.9	194.4	219.8	311.3	456.9	553.4	34.6	101.9	294.3
Malawi	43.3	100.0	129.3	157.9	175.2	198.7	242.0	280.7	404.1	710.9	920.7	44.9	109.9	418.9
Mali	67.2	100.0	100.2	99.3	102.0	103.7	106.1	108.9	145.1	163.2	173.5	66.1	100.8	128.9
Mauritania	54.3	100.0	105.3	114.3	117.7	129.0	141.8	147.3	157.1	163.8	169.9	54.4	99.0	146.7
Mauritius	53.9	100.0	110.8	123.1	135.5	146.7	154.7	167.0	179.0	186.3	197.6	50.0	100.8	166.7
Mozambique	..	100.0	148.3	218.6	293.0	428.5	656.5	965.7	1,464.0	2,201.8	3,038.1	21.9	106.8	1,292.5
Namibia	44.9	100.0	122.4	140.2	146.7	153.4	169.7	182.7	213.1	226.1	244.2	54.4	107.5	190.9
Niger	70.1	100.0	95.5	103.4	94.5	89.6	90.6	90.5	120.2	126.0	131.6	68.2	98.9	106.1
Nigeria	41.5	100.0	121.4	175.2	187.8	225.7	370.4	457.9	594.6	935.8	1,191.1	40.4	106.2	566.2
Rwanda	77.2	100.0	100.2	106.0	122.2	137.4	141.1	163.3	193.2	302.8	343.9	77.3	102.0	200.6
São Tomé and Principe	50.8	100.0	137.8	181.7	232.1	366.1	461.1	641.2	1,112.2	1,941.3	2,927.8	50.2	116.6	1,097.4
Senegal	57.8	100.0	102.1	103.1	103.7	104.3	105.5	106.0	141.2	151.9	156.4	56.9	98.9	124.1
Seychelles	75.5	100.0	105.0	108.5	115.5	112.0	120.1	126.9	125.0	127.5	130.1	66.3	100.1	122.5
Sierra Leone	4.7	100.0	153.5	247.4	463.3	890.5	1,423.0	1,802.8	2,165.4	2,886.9	3,647.1	5.5	116.0	1,897.0
Somalia	12.8	100.0	169.8	335.3	1,057.8	..	..	..	..	..	..	14.1	147.4	1,057.8
South Africa	39.8	100.0	115.6	135.4	156.1	177.1	199.9	221.5	242.4	264.6	286.4	38.2	103.0	221.1
Sudan	15.4	100.0	160.6	233.2	380.0	677.4	1,282.7	2,378.9	4,534.3	..	..	17.6	125.8	1,850.7
Swaziland	54.4	100.0	127.1	147.9	173.1	187.2	205.1	221.6	247.7	265.3	310.3	49.9	109.0	230.0
Tanzania	..	100.0	155.2	249.5	337.7	408.5	486.0	582.2	714.7	957.7	..	46.0	128.5	581.1
Togo	64.4	100.0	102.5	103.5	106.5	109.4	112.5	105.8	140.8	164.5	174.2	66.5	99.5	130.5
Uganda	..	100.0	290.6	626.3	905.0	1,141.7	1,658.9	2,159.3	2,296.9	2,494.8	2,627.1	6.1	213.5	1,897.7
Zaire	5.5	100.0	191.6	402.8	841.7	19379	809450	14275436	3838791037	23932983356	163042766014	8.6	159.4	27261377931
Zambia	14.9	100.0	135.7	245.1	501.9	970.9	2,530.5	7,002.9	10,962.6	16,022.5	21,891.2	14.3	115.3	8,554.6
Zimbabwe	46.9	100.0	117.2	133.4	162.7	209.2	280.4	354.7	439.9	540.0	663.7	49.1	104.8	378.7
NORTH AFRICA	58.5	100.0	107.9	116.9	141.1	157.0	178.9	192.9	205.4	224.5	..	58.8	102.2	183.3
Algeria	66.9	100.0	113.0	129.4	174.2	272.6	335.7	370.8	475.4	609.7	..	60.8	106.0	373.1
Egypt, Arab Republic	46.7	100.0	113.7	135.0	160.1	183.3	219.6	241.3	258.6	289.6	..	41.6	98.5	225.4
Libya	88.8	100.0	87.8	94.6	..	..	..	..	..	..	..	74.3	96.2	..
Morocco	58.5	100.0	105.5	109.8	115.7	123.6	129.0	133.6	134.5	143.1	..	57.4	99.8	129.9
Tunisia	56.9	100.0	107.9	116.9	122.2	130.7	138.2	144.5	152.2	159.5	..	58.2	102.3	141.2
ALL AFRICA	54.1	100.0	108.8	120.8	135.5	150.1	166.8	175.5	203.2	226.1	221.9	53.3	101.5	182.7

Note: 1996 data are preliminary (see page 3). Group data are medians of individual country values for each year.

3-2. GDP deflator (U.S. dollar series)

	Index 1987=100											Annual average		
	1980	1987	1988	1989	1990	1991	1992	1993	1994	1995	1996	75-84	85-89	90-MR
SUB-SAHARAN AFRICA	121.6	100.0	100.2	99.1	108.4	107.2	108.3	101.7	97.2	103.5	106.6	93.4	94.4	104.7
excluding South Africa	131.2	100.0	98.4	96.1	101.3	95.7	92.1	84.4	77.0	81.9	94.4	100.6	96.0	89.5
excl. S. Africa & Nigeria	104.0	100.0	100.2	98.0	102.5	97.5	92.4	87.7	77.4	84.6	95.5	84.5	95.9	91.1
Angola	..	100.0	102.3	118.5	116.7	57.4	67.2	70.4	105.7	84.5	..	..	103.2	83.6
Benin	113.1	100.0	100.1	90.9	108.4	106.4	87.6	110.9	76.2	99.0	99.4	84.4	88.4	98.3
Botswana	119.4	100.0	125.9	136.3	148.6	158.5	149.2	154.1	155.9	160.4	..	93.4	107.5	154.5
Burkina Faso	105.8	100.0	104.2	102.4	121.2	111.9	117.0	111.1	72.3	87.2	..	80.3	92.8	103.5
Burundi	114.2	100.0	91.1	92.4	90.7	88.9	80.6	74.1	82.0	93.1	90.6	93.0	101.3	85.7
Cameroon	89.4	100.0	110.1	100.1	106.8	123.6	116.7	125.7	85.1	83.3	90.1	69.9	92.7	104.5
Cape Verde	89.1	100.0	106.1	101.5	114.5	118.4	128.5	114.1	115.2	133.0	129.8	83.2	91.1	121.9
Central African Republic	74.3	100.0	104.6	100.3	119.4	113.2	116.6	108.6	71.8	89.0	87.3	56.3	92.8	100.9
Chad	126.7	100.0	109.6	100.6	126.4	127.0	117.9	108.9	79.9	97.4	105.5	96.0	96.3	109.0
Comoros	80.5	100.0	102.8	101.8	121.8	127.2	126.3	128.9	94.6	112.6	109.8	67.2	89.8	117.3
Congo	113.3	100.0	94.6	99.3	115.4	110.7	116.2	76.8	74.9	86.9	94.3	88.1	92.5	96.5
Côte d'Ivoire	106.3	100.0	100.4	92.8	103.9	100.9	107.5	100.4	72.5	88.4	88.5	74.2	91.1	94.6
Djibouti	..	..	..	..	..	..	..	..	..	..	..	..	..	..
Equatorial Guinea	..	100.0	103.2	92.1	105.1	104.9	112.0	103.0	79.4	93.4	..	..	95.8	99.6
Eritrea	..	..	..	..	..	..	..	..	..	..	..	..	..	..
Ethiopia	..	100.0	102.8	108.0	109.9	128.2	102.2	89.3	70.6	67.8	63.5	84.5	105.6	90.2
Gabon	100.0	100.0	95.0	97.2	132.7	112.0	120.0	91.9	85.4	100.5	108.6	70.3	92.6	107.3
Gambia, The	138.1	100.0	104.5	103.0	117.6	133.0	121.1	128.4	125.1	135.1	..	101.6	92.1	126.7
Ghana	95.5	100.0	97.0	93.4	101.6	108.3	101.6	85.6	75.4	86.2	84.3	85.5	101.2	91.9
Guinea	..	100.0	109.9	107.7	119.7	123.7	119.8	122.2	125.5	130.1	133.9	..	104.6	125.0
Guinea-Bissau	87.4	100.0	90.2	108.0	120.2	115.5	105.9	110.0	107.8	110.8	112.1	91.7	94.4	111.8
Kenya	118.0	100.0	100.7	94.1	92.9	87.0	88.3	61.7	77.2	90.9	88.9	94.4	95.6	83.8
Lesotho	112.9	100.0	106.0	107.1	127.0	115.1	131.5	132.1	128.3	129.2	..	91.0	92.6	127.2
Liberia	88.3	100.0	..	..	..	..	..	..	..	..	..	80.2	95.9	..
Madagascar	149.3	100.0	92.1	90.5	108.2	100.7	111.5	122.8	108.6	114.5	145.9	122.0	105.2	116.0
Malawi	117.7	100.0	111.5	126.4	141.8	156.5	148.3	140.8	102.2	102.7	..	101.4	107.6	132.1
Mali	95.6	100.0	101.1	93.5	112.6	110.5	120.5	115.6	78.5	98.2	101.9	71.8	90.4	105.4
Mauritania	87.4	100.0	103.3	101.7	107.9	116.3	120.3	90.1	93.9	93.3	91.5	81.2	95.3	101.9
Mauritius	90.4	100.0	106.2	104.0	117.4	120.7	124.5	121.9	128.3	138.0	141.8	75.6	92.6	127.5
Mozambique	..	100.0	82.2	85.3	91.7	86.8	75.8	72.5	70.5	70.9	78.2	153.9	147.1	78.1
Namibia	117.5	100.0	109.6	108.8	115.5	113.1	121.2	113.9	122.2	126.9	115.7	106.0	95.6	118.3
Niger	99.8	100.0	96.4	97.4	104.3	95.5	102.9	96.0	65.1	75.8	77.3	74.6	88.7	88.1
Nigeria	246.4	100.0	88.7	86.3	95.3	87.3	90.8	70.4	75.0	69.9	87.8	177.6	96.8	82.4
Rwanda	66.3	100.0	104.4	105.6	117.9	87.5	84.3	90.2	70.0	92.0	89.3	65.5	96.5	90.2
São Tomé and Principe	79.2	100.0	86.5	79.0	87.8	98.3	78.1	80.8	82.3	74.1	72.0	75.1	96.7	81.9
Senegal	82.3	100.0	103.1	97.1	114.5	111.1	78.9	81.8	76.4	91.4	91.9	62.6	89.2	92.3
Seychelles	66.1	100.0	109.3	107.6	121.2	118.8	131.3	137.1	138.5	150.0	146.6	55.4	95.1	134.8
Sierra Leone	144.8	100.0	151.3	132.5	98.0	96.6	91.3	101.8	118.3	122.5	126.9	128.2	128.6	107.9
Somalia	73.8	100.0	103.4	109.0	92.9	..	..	..	..	..	..	83.5	100.7	92.9
South Africa	104.0	100.0	103.6	105.1	122.8	130.6	142.7	138.1	139.0	148.6	135.6	80.1	91.3	136.8
Sudan	46.1	100.0	67.7	65.1	54.8	44.1	32.5	..	..	..	..	45.5	77.4	43.8
Swaziland	142.1	100.0	114.4	115.1	136.2	138.3	146.5	138.2	142.1	148.9	147.0	106.2	96.6	142.5
Tanzania	..	100.0	96.5	106.9	99.6	103.6	99.3	87.6	76.6	91.3	..	211.7	137.7	93.0
Togo	91.7	100.0	103.5	97.5	117.6	116.5	127.8	112.3	76.2	99.0	102.3	73.3	89.7	107.4
Uganda	..	100.0	95.9	72.8	56.1	41.0	34.2	35.6	41.5	53.0	51.4	46.7	78.4	44.7
Zaire	229.1	100.0	115.1	118.8	131.8	139.9	141.1	178.4	120.6	127.8	399.2	176.7	108.7	177.0
Zambia	180.3	100.0	156.3	168.9	138.6	143.0	134.6	147.2	155.9	177.9	173.1	144.9	120.7	152.9
Zimbabwe	121.2	100.0	107.8	104.9	110.5	101.4	91.5	91.1	89.7	103.6	109.7	107.2	97.6	99.6
NORTH AFRICA	91.2	100.0	92.2	90.1	98.9	85.0	93.5	92.6	91.1	96.7	..	75.2	93.2	93.0
Algeria	84.5	100.0	92.7	82.5	94.3	71.6	74.6	77.0	65.8	62.0	..	68.4	92.5	74.2
Egypt, Arab Republic	82.6	100.0	82.2	88.7	91.4	77.5	93.2	92.2	97.6	108.7	..	74.9	90.4	93.4
Libya	88.4	100.0	90.4	93.1	..	..	..	..	..	..	..	73.9	95.1	..
Morocco	124.2	100.0	107.4	108.1	117.3	118.6	126.3	120.1	122.1	140.1	..	94.2	95.3	124.1
Tunisia	116.4	100.0	104.3	102.1	115.0	117.7	130.1	119.7	124.9	139.8	..	95.3	99.3	124.5
ALL AFRICA	109.3	100.0	97.0	95.6	104.7	98.9	102.6	98.1	94.7	100.8	..	86.3	93.9	99.9

Note: 1996 data are preliminary (see page 3). Group data are obtained by dividing GDP in current US$ by GDP in constant US$ series for each group.

3-3. Consumer price index

	Index 1987=100											Average annual percentage growth		
	1980	*1987*	*1988*	*1989*	*1990*	*1991*	*1992*	*1993*	*1994*	*1995*	*1996*	*75-84*	*85-89*	*90-MR*
SUB-SAHARAN AFRICA	46.9	100.0	110.4	120.9	135.4	150.1	168.4	189.1	218.8	250.5	341.0	12.1	9.5	15.6
excluding South Africa	47.4	100.0	109.6	120.9	135.1	149.7	162.0	188.6	216.7	248.5	403.0	12.3	9.1	17.8
excl. S. Africa & Nigeria	48.4	100.0	109.4	120.9	134.9	149.5	161.7	180.6	209.8	246.4	403.0	12.4	9.3	17.6
Angola	..	..	..	..	..	..	..	..	..	..	..	..	..	..
Benin	..	..	..	..	..	..	..	..	..	..	..	..	..	..
Botswana	49.3	100.0	108.4	120.9	134.7	150.5	174.8	199.9	221.0	244.2	268.8	12.1	9.5	12.5
Burkina Faso	72.1	100.0	104.1	103.8	102.9	105.5	103.4	103.9	130.1	139.7	148.3	11.0	0.5	5.7
Burundi	60.2	100.0	104.5	116.7	124.8	136.1	138.6	152.0	174.5	208.2	263.2	13.4	5.4	11.4
Cameroon	46.4	100.0	101.7	100.0	101.1	101.1	101.1	97.9	132.2	150.6	..	11.5	6.4	6.4
Cape Verde	..	100.0	104.1	108.8	120.4	131.9	136.0	150.3	153.8	166.6	..	..	5.8	7.0
Central African Republic	71.5	100.0	96.0	96.8	96.4	94.4	93.0	90.3	112.5	134.1	..	..	-0.7	4.5
Chad	..	100.0	115.5	110.9	110.7	115.4	111.8	103.9	145.9	159.1	..	..	-1.3	5.6
Comoros	..	..	..	..	..	..	..	..	..	..	..	..	..	..
Congo	56.3	100.0	103.8	108.1	102.9	112.3	114.6	116.9	175.1	212.5	..	11.1	3.4	11.8
Côte d'Ivoire	64.9	100.0	106.9	108.1	107.2	109.0	113.6	84.9	107.1	122.4	125.4	12.9	6.0	1.6
Djibouti	75.1	100.0	..	..	..	..	..	..	..	..	..	2.8	8.9	..
Equatorial Guinea	..	100.0	102.3	108.4	109.6	106.1	98.5	102.4	..	..	..	..	-6.0	-2.2
Eritrea	..	..	..	..	..	..	..	..	..	..	..	..	..	..
Ethiopia	78.9	100.0	107.1	115.5	121.4	164.8	182.1	188.6	202.9	223.2	..	10.6	2.2	11.9
Gabon	59.5	100.0	91.2	97.4	104.9	110.5	105.1	95.7	130.4	143.3	..	12.5	1.0	5.3
Gambia, The	27.5	100.0	111.7	120.9	135.7	147.4	161.4	171.8	174.7	186.9	..	10.5	24.3	7.3
Ghana	6.3	100.0	131.4	164.5	225.8	266.6	293.3	366.5	457.6	797.9	1069.6	67.9	27.7	28.8
Guinea	..	..	..	..	..	..	..	..	..	..	..	..	..	..
Guinea-Bissau	..	100.0	160.3	289.8	385.4	607.4	1030.0	1525.5	1757.0	2554.1	..	..	..	45.4
Kenya	47.4	100.0	111.2	125.6	145.2	173.9	225.3	328.5	423.9	427.2	464.9	13.6	9.3	23.3
Lesotho	40.7	100.0	111.5	127.9	142.7	168.0	196.9	222.8	241.1	263.4	..	14.1	13.7	13.3
Liberia	78.0	100.0	109.6	119.6	..	..	..	..	..	..	..	8.1	5.5	..
Madagascar	30.5	100.0	126.9	138.3	154.6	167.8	192.2	211.5	293.8	438.0	524.6	15.3	15.9	21.4
Malawi	37.9	100.0	133.9	150.6	168.3	189.6	232.6	278.3	374.8	687.1	..	..	20.4	26.3
Mali	..	..	..	..	..	..	..	..	..	..	..	..	..	..
Mauritania	..	100.0	101.3	114.4	122.0	128.8	141.9	155.1	161.5	..	..	..	6.8	7.5
Mauritius	63.4	100.0	109.2	123.0	139.6	149.4	156.3	172.7	185.4	196.5	209.4	14.9	5.3	7.6
Mozambique	..	100.0	150.1	210.4	309.3	411.2	598.2	850.7	1388.1	2143.7	..	..	67.6	46.5
Namibia	43.2	100.0	112.9	129.9	145.5	162.9	191.7	208.1	230.5	253.6	..	..	13.1	12.0
Niger	77.1	100.0	98.6	95.8	95.1	87.6	83.7	82.7	112.5	124.4	131.0	12.6	-3.3	5.2
Nigeria	35.4	100.0	154.5	232.5	249.6	282.1	407.9	641.0	1006.6	1739.5	..	17.7	23.2	41.1
Rwanda	70.9	100.0	103.0	104.0	108.4	129.7	142.0	159.6	..	317.5	341.0	11.1	1.9	20.3
São Tomé and Principe	..	..	..	..	..	..	..	..	..	..	..	..	..	..
Senegal	56.1	100.0	98.2	98.6	98.9	97.2	97.1	96.5	127.7	137.7	141.5	9.7	1.7	6.1
Seychelles	79.7	100.0	101.8	103.4	107.5	109.7	113.2	114.7	116.8	116.4	..	10.6	1.5	2.0
Sierra Leone	2.6	100.0	134.3	215.9	455.5	923.3	1528.0	1867.4	2319.2	2922.0	3600.1	22.7	85.1	46.3
Somalia	9.0	100.0	181.9	..	..	..	..	..	..	..	..	29.6	41.9	..
South Africa	37.7	100.0	112.8	129.4	148.1	170.7	194.5	213.4	232.6	252.5	271.3	12.8	15.7	11.1
Sudan	16.7	100.0	164.7	274.6	453.5	1013.9	2206.6	4443.8	..	..	..	22.9	40.3	104.4
Swaziland	38.4	100.0	112.4	121.7	135.1	149.7	162.0	189.6	216.7	248.5	279.7	14.4	13.5	12.8
Tanzania	15.6	100.0	131.2	165.1	224.2	288.6	351.6	440.5	590.7	752.7	910.6	19.6	30.7	27.5
Togo	69.7	100.0	99.8	99.0	100.0	100.4	101.8	100.8	..	..	..	11.1	0.5	0.5
Uganda	0.9	100.0	296.1	478.1	636.4	815.0	1242.4	1317.9	1446.2	1569.9	1684.6	..	159.5	19.7
Zaire	6.3	100.0	171.1	349.1	633.0	14270.0	603501	12594490	3006698771	19305654721	146216598052	57.3	63.0	2243.3
Zambia	..	100.0	151.0	337.3	698.4	1380.3	3667.6	10390.8	16065.6	21673.4	31013.4	..	63.0	97.6
Zimbabwe	38.7	100.0	107.4	121.3	142.3	175.5	249.4	318.2	389.0	476.9	579.1	11.9	11.2	26.3
NORTH AFRICA	53.6	100.0	106.6	115.6	129.0	151.5	182.3	200.3	214.1	240.5	169.1	11.3	7.9	7.0
Algeria	53.6	100.0	105.9	115.8	135.0	170.0	223.8	269.7	348.1	460.1	..	10.9	8.9	26.1
Egypt, Arab Republic	35.0	100.0	117.7	142.7	166.6	199.5	226.7	254.1	274.8	318.1	340.9	13.2	19.3	13.2
Libya	..	..	..	..	..	..	..	..	..	..	..	..	..	..
Morocco	56.0	100.0	102.4	105.6	112.9	121.9	128.9	135.6	142.5	151.3	155.8	9.9	4.7	5.8
Tunisia	..	100.0	107.2	115.5	123.1	133.1	140.9	146.5	153.4	163.0	169.1	..	7.3	5.6
ALL AFRICA	47.4	100.0	109.4	120.9	135.0	150.1	168.4	189.1	218.8	250.5	310.3	12.2	9.4	14.5

Note: 1996 data are preliminary (see page 3). Group data are medians of individual country values for each year.

3-4. Official exchange rate

	National currency per U.S. dollar											Annual average		
	1980	*1987*	*1988*	*1989*	*1990*	*1991*	*1992*	*1993*	*1994*	*1995*	*1996*	*75-84*	*85-89*	*90-MR*
SUB-SAHARAN AFRICA	..	..	..	..	..	..	..	..	..	..	..	..	..	..
excluding South Africa	..	..	..	..	..	..	..	..	..	..	..	..	..	..
excl. S. Africa & Nigeria	..	..	..	..	..	..	..	..	..	..	..	..	..	..
Angola	29.9	29.9	29.9	29.9	29.9	55.1	251.4	2,660.2	59,515.0	..	..	29.4	29.9	12,502.3
Benin	211.3	300.5	297.8	319.0	272.3	282.1	264.7	283.2	555.2	499.1	511.6	276.7	342.6	381.2
Botswana	0.8	1.7	1.8	2.0	1.9	2.0	2.1	2.4	2.7	2.8	3.3	0.9	1.9	2.5
Burkina Faso	211.3	300.5	297.8	319.0	272.3	282.1	264.7	283.2	555.2	499.1	511.6	276.7	342.6	381.2
Burundi	90.0	123.6	140.4	158.7	171.3	181.5	208.3	242.8	252.7	249.8	302.7	91.8	131.5	229.9
Cameroon	211.3	300.5	297.8	319.0	272.3	282.1	264.7	283.2	555.2	499.1	511.6	276.7	342.6	381.2
Cape Verde	40.2	72.5	72.1	78.0	70.0	71.4	68.0	80.4	81.9	76.9	82.6	46.6	78.9	75.9
Central African Republic	211.3	300.5	297.8	319.0	272.3	282.1	264.7	283.2	555.2	499.1	511.6	276.7	342.6	381.2
Chad	211.3	300.5	297.8	319.0	272.3	282.1	264.7	283.2	555.2	499.1	511.6	276.7	342.6	381.2
Comoros	211.3	300.5	297.8	319.0	272.3	282.1	264.7	283.2	416.4	374.4	383.7	276.7	342.6	325.2
Congo	211.3	300.5	297.8	319.0	272.3	282.1	264.7	283.2	555.2	499.1	511.6	276.7	342.6	381.2
Côte d'Ivoire	211.3	300.5	297.8	319.0	272.3	282.1	264.7	283.2	555.2	499.1	511.6	276.7	342.6	381.2
Djibouti	177.7	177.7	177.7	177.7	177.7	177.7	177.7	177.7	177.7	177.7	177.7	177.7	177.7	177.7
Equatorial Guinea	211.3	300.5	297.8	319.0	272.3	282.1	264.7	283.2	555.2	499.1	511.6	276.7	342.6	381.2
Eritrea	..	..	..	..	..	..	..	..	..	..	..	..	..	..
Ethiopia	2.1	2.1	2.1	2.1	2.1	2.1	2.8	5.0	5.5	6.2	6.4	2.1	2.1	4.3
Gabon	211.3	300.5	297.8	319.0	272.3	282.1	264.7	283.2	555.2	499.1	511.6	276.7	342.6	381.2
Gambia, The	1.7	7.1	6.7	7.6	7.9	8.8	8.9	9.1	9.6	9.5	..	2.3	6.4	9.0
Ghana	2.8	153.7	202.3	270.0	326.3	367.8	437.1	649.1	956.7	1,200.4	1,637.2	6.1	153.9	796.4
Guinea	19.0	428.4	474.4	591.6	660.2	753.9	902.0	955.5	976.6	991.4	1,004.0	21.1	370.4	891.9
Guinea-Bissau	33.8	559.0	1,109.7	1,810.1	2,185.5	3,658.6	6,933.9	10,081.9	12,892.1	18,072.5	26,373.4	41.6	768.4	11,456.9
Kenya	7.4	16.5	17.7	20.6	22.9	27.5	32.2	58.0	56.1	51.4	57.1	9.4	17.5	43.6
Lesotho	0.8	2.0	2.3	2.6	2.6	2.8	2.9	3.3	3.6	3.6	4.3	1.0	2.3	3.3
Liberia	1.0	1.0	1.0	1.0	1.0	1.0	1.0	1.0	1.0	1.0	1.0	1.0	1.0	1.0
Madagascar	211.3	1,069.2	1,407.1	1,603.4	1,494.1	1,835.4	1,864.0	1,913.8	3,067.3	4,265.6	4,061.3	297.7	1,083.7	2,643.1
Malawi	0.8	2.2	2.6	2.8	2.7	2.8	3.6	4.4	8.7	15.3	..	1.0	2.2	6.3
Mali	211.3	300.5	297.8	319.0	272.3	282.1	264.7	283.2	555.2	499.1	511.6	276.7	342.6	381.2
Mauritania	45.9	73.9	75.3	83.1	80.6	81.9	87.0	120.8	123.6	129.8	137.2	49.0	76.7	108.7
Mauritius	7.7	12.9	13.4	15.2	14.9	15.7	15.6	17.6	18.0	17.4	17.9	8.5	14.1	16.7
Mozambique	32.4	290.7	524.6	744.9	929.1	1,434.5	2,516.5	3,874.2	6,038.6	9,024.3	11,293.8	34.3	328.8	5,015.9
Namibia	0.8	2.0	2.3	2.6	2.6	2.8	2.9	3.3	3.6	3.6	4.3	1.0	2.3	3.3
Niger	211.3	300.5	297.8	319.0	272.3	282.1	264.7	283.2	555.2	499.1	511.6	276.7	342.6	381.2
Nigeria	0.5	4.0	4.5	7.4	8.0	9.9	17.3	22.1	22.0	21.9	..	0.6	3.7	16.9
Rwanda	92.8	79.7	76.4	80.0	82.6	125.1	133.4	144.3	..	262.2	306.8	93.7	85.0	175.7
São Tomé and Principe	34.8	54.2	86.3	124.7	143.3	201.8	321.3	429.9	732.6	1,420.3	2,203.2	36.5	69.7	778.9
Senegal	211.3	300.5	297.8	319.0	272.3	282.1	264.7	283.2	555.2	499.1	511.6	276.7	342.6	381.2
Seychelles	6.4	5.6	5.4	5.6	5.3	5.3	5.1	5.2	5.1	4.8	5.0	6.7	6.0	5.1
Sierra Leone	1.0	34.0	32.5	59.8	151.4	295.3	499.4	567.5	586.7	755.2	920.7	1.3	29.5	539.5
Somalia	6.3	105.2	170.5	490.7	..	..	..	..	..	..	..	9.1	175.6	..
South Africa	0.8	2.0	2.3	2.6	2.6	2.8	2.9	3.3	3.6	3.6	4.3	1.0	2.3	3.3
Sudan	0.5	3.0	4.5	4.5	4.5	7.0	97.4	159.3	289.6	..	1,250.8	0.6	3.4	301.4
Swaziland	0.8	2.0	2.3	2.6	2.6	2.8	2.9	3.3	3.6	3.6	4.3	1.0	2.3	3.3
Tanzania	8.2	64.3	99.3	143.4	195.1	219.2	297.7	405.3	509.6	574.8	580.0	9.2	71.4	397.4
Togo	211.3	300.5	297.8	319.0	272.3	282.1	264.7	283.2	555.2	499.1	511.6	276.7	342.6	381.2
Uganda	0.1	42.8	106.1	223.1	428.9	734.0	1,133.8	1,195.0	979.4	968.9	1,046.1	0.7	78.6	926.6
Zaire	0.0	0.0	0.0	0.0	0.0	0.0	0.2	2.5	1,194.1	7,024.4	..	0.0	0.0	1,370.2
Zambia	0.8	9.5	8.3	13.8	30.3	64.6	172.2	452.8	669.4	857.2	1,203.7	0.9	8.5	492.9
Zimbabwe	0.6	1.7	1.8	2.1	2.5	3.6	5.1	6.5	8.2	8.7	10.0	0.8	1.8	6.4
NORTH AFRICA	..	..	..	..	..	..	..	..	..	..	..	..	..	..
Algeria	3.8	4.8	5.9	7.6	9.0	18.5	21.8	23.3	35.1	47.7	54.7	4.3	5.6	30.0
Egypt, Arab Republic	0.7	0.7	0.7	0.9	1.6	3.1	3.3	3.4	3.4	3.4	3.4	0.6	0.7	3.1
Libya	0.3	0.3	0.3	0.3	0.3	0.3	0.3	0.3	0.3	0.3	0.4	0.3	0.3	0.3
Morocco	3.9	8.4	8.2	8.5	8.2	8.7	8.5	9.3	9.2	8.5	8.7	5.2	8.8	8.7
Tunisia	0.4	0.8	0.9	0.9	0.9	0.9	0.9	1.0	1.0	0.9	1.0	0.5	0.9	0.9
ALL AFRICA	..	..	..	..	..	..	..	..	..	..	..	..	..	..

Note: 1996 data are preliminary (see page 3). New Ugandan shilling = 100 old Ugandan shilling was introduced in May 1987.

3-5. SDR exchange rate index

	SDRs per unit of national currency, index 1987=100											Annual average		
	1980	1987	1988	1989	1990	1991	1992	1993	1994	1995	1996	75-84	85-89	90-MR
SUB-SAHARAN AFRICA	..	..	..	..	..	..	..	..	..	..	..	..	..	..
excluding South Africa	..	..	..	..	..	..	..	..	..	..	..	..	..	..
excl. S.Africa & Nigeria	..	..	..	..	..	..	..	..	..	..	..	..	..	..
Angola	..	..	..	..	..	..	..	..	..	..	..	..	..	..
Benin	141	100	97	95	105	101	104	98	49	51	52	126	95	80
Botswana	215	100	89	84	86	79	72	64	56	52	45	207	97	65
Burkina Faso	141	100	97	95	105	101	104	98	49	51	52	126	95	80
Burundi	136	100	85	78	69	65	54	47	44	42	..	150	103	54
Cameroon	141	100	97	95	105	101	104	98	49	51	52	126	95	80
Cape Verde	179	100	97	94	99	96	98	84	80	80	78	193	98	88
Central African Republic	141	100	97	95	105	101	104	98	49	51	52	126	95	80
Chad	141	100	97	95	105	101	104	98	49	51	52	126	95	80
Comoros	141	100	97	95	105	101	104	98	65	68	70	126	95	87
Congo	141	100	97	95	105	101	104	98	49	51	52	126	95	80
Côte d'Ivoire	141	100	97	95	105	101	104	98	49	51	52	126	95	80
Djibouti	99	100	96	101	95	95	92	93	90	85	89	111	107	91
Equatorial Guinea	141	100	97	95	105	101	104	98	49	51	52	126	95	80
Eritrea	..	..	..	..	..	..	..	..	..	..	..	..	..	..
Ethiopia	99	100	96	101	95	95	78	38	34	29	..	111	107	62
Gabon	141	100	97	95	105	101	104	98	49	51	52	126	95	80
Gambia, The	408	100	102	94	86	76	73	72	67	63	..	358	129	73
Ghana	5,346	100	71	56	43	38	31	21	14	11	..	8,110	152	26
Guinea	2,242	100	87	73	62	54	44	41	40	37	..	2,238	528	46
Guinea-Bissau	..	..	..	..	..	..	..	..	..	..	..	..	..	..
Kenya	220	100	89	81	68	57	47	28	27	28	26	201	102	40
Lesotho	260	100	87	78	75	70	66	58	52	48	42	244	96	59
Liberia	99	100	96	101	95	95	92	93	90	85	89	111	107	91
Madagascar	470	100	69	63	64	52	49	48	32	20	..	406	118	44
Malawi	270	100	83	81	77	74	58	46	26	12	..	256	112	49
Mali	141	100	97	95	105	101	104	98	49	51	52	126	95	80
Mauritania	160	100	95	88	87	85	79	58	54	48	48	168	103	66
Mauritius	166	100	92	85	83	78	76	68	65	63	64	179	98	71
Mozambique	..	..	..	..	..	..	..	..	..	..	..	..	..	..
Namibia	260	100	87	78	75	70	66	58	52	48	42	244	96	59
Niger	141	100	97	95	105	101	104	98	49	51	52	126	95	80
Nigeria	728	100	86	55	48	38	23	17	16	16	..	689	228	26
Rwanda	85	100	100	100	91	60	55	51	32	28	23	94	100	49
São Tomé and Principe	135	100	54	39	31	24	14	10	6	3	2	146	93	13
Senegal	141	100	97	95	105	101	104	98	49	51	52	126	95	80
Seychelles	87	100	100	100	100	100	100	100	100	100	100	92	100	100
Sierra Leone	2,914	100	95	53	20	11	6	5	5	4	3	2,821	296	8
Somalia	1,621	100	69	24	..	..	..	..	..	..	..	1,490	138	..
South Africa	260	100	87	78	75	70	66	58	52	48	42	244	96	59
Sudan	559	100	60	63	60	49	4	2	1	..	..	612	101	23
Swaziland	260	100	87	78	75	70	66	58	52	48	42	244	97	59
Tanzania	767	100	62	45	31	27	20	15	11	9	..	787	186	19
Togo	141	100	97	95	105	101	104	98	49	51	52	126	95	80
Uganda	37,511	100	31	13	6	4	2	2	3	2	..	25,313	185	3
Zaire	3,926	100	58	29	17	2	0	0	0	0	..	8,453	134	3
Zambia	1,122	100	104	70	29	14	5	2	1	1	1	1,125	165	8
Zimbabwe	257	100	89	79	65	46	30	24	18	16	15	254	102	31
NORTH AFRICA	..	..	..	..	..	..	..	..	..	..	..	..	..	..
Algeria	125	100	80	65	52	25	20	19	13	9	8	126	96	21
Egypt, Arab Republic	99	100	96	87	47	22	19	19	19	18	18	145	104	23
Libya	100	100	100	100	100	100	96	90	84	73	73	111	108	88
Morocco	211	100	98	99	97	91	90	83	82	83	85	187	101	87
Tunisia	203	100	93	88	90	85	86	76	74	75	76	190	105	80
ALL AFRICA	..	..	..	..	..	..	..	..	..	..	..	..	..	..

Note: 1996 data are preliminary (see page 3).

3-6. Currency conversion factor

	Units of national currency per US dollar											Annual average		
	1980	1987	1988	1989	1990	1991	1992	1993	1994	1995	1996	75-84	85-89	90-MR
SUB-SAHARAN AFRICA	..	..	..	..	..	..	..	..	..	..	..	..	..	..
excluding South Africa	..	..	..	..	..	..	..	..	..	..	..	..	..	..
excl. S. Africa & Nigeria	..	..	..	..	..	..	..	..	..	..	..	..	..	..
Angola	29.9	29.9	29.9	29.9	33.7	172.8	..	..	152,775.0	2,728,571.9	127,362,417.5	29.5	29.9	26,048,794.2
Benin	211.3	300.5	297.9	319.0	272.3	282.1	351.0	283.2	555.2	499.2	511.6	276.7	342.6	393.5
Botswana	0.8	1.8	1.7	2.0	1.9	1.9	2.0	2.2	2.6	2.7	3.0	0.9	1.8	2.3
Burkina Faso	211.3	300.5	297.8	319.0	272.3	282.1	397.0	388.8	555.2	499.2	511.6	276.7	342.6	415.2
Burundi	90.0	123.6	140.4	158.7	171.3	181.5	208.3	242.8	252.7	249.8	302.8	91.8	131.5	229.9
Cameroon	209.2	318.7	291.7	315.4	300.7	268.6	280.0	411.5	434.3	518.6	501.9	265.6	356.7	387.9
Cape Verde	40.2	72.5	72.1	78.0	70.0	71.4	68.0	80.4	81.9	76.9	83.6	46.6	78.9	76.0
Central African Republic	211.3	300.5	297.8	319.0	272.3	282.1	264.7	283.2	555.2	499.2	511.6	276.7	342.6	381.2
Chad	211.3	300.5	297.8	319.0	272.3	282.1	264.7	283.2	555.2	499.2	511.6	276.7	342.6	381.2
Comoros	211.3	300.5	297.8	319.0	272.3	282.1	265.0	283.2	416.4	374.4	383.7	274.7	342.6	325.3
Congo	211.3	300.5	297.8	319.0	272.3	282.1	265.0	362.3	555.2	499.2	511.6	276.7	342.6	392.5
Côte d'Ivoire	211.3	300.5	297.8	319.0	272.3	282.1	264.7	283.2	555.2	499.2	511.6	276.7	342.6	381.2
Djibouti	177.7	177.7	177.7	177.7	177.7	177.7	178.0	177.7	177.7	177.7	177.7	177.7	177.7	177.8
Equatorial Guinea	110.6	300.5	297.9	319.0	272.3	282.1	265.0	283.2	555.2	499.1	511.6	146.9	342.6	381.2
Eritrea	..	..	..	..	..	..	..	..	..	..	..	..	..	..
Ethiopia	..	2.1	2.1	2.1	2.1	2.1	3.0	4.3	5.8	6.3	6.3	2.1	2.1	4.3
Gabon	211.3	300.5	297.8	319.0	272.3	282.1	264.7	349.6	555.2	499.2	511.6	276.7	342.6	390.7
Gambia, The	1.8	6.7	7.0	8.1	8.1	7.9	9.0	8.8	9.5	9.5	9.7	2.4	6.8	8.9
Ghana	9.6	147.0	202.3	270.0	326.3	367.8	437.0	649.1	956.7	1,200.4	1,637.2	17.5	157.0	796.4
Guinea	19.0	428.4	474.4	591.6	660.2	753.9	902.0	955.5	976.7	991.4	1,000.0	21.1	370.4	891.4
Guinea-Bissau	49.9	559.0	1,109.7	1,810.1	2,185.5	3,658.6	6,934.0	10,081.9	12,892.1	18,072.5	26,373.4	54.0	802.4	11,456.9
Kenya	7.4	16.5	17.7	20.6	22.9	27.5	32.0	58.0	56.1	51.4	57.1	9.4	17.5	43.6
Lesotho	0.8	2.0	2.3	2.6	2.6	2.8	3.0	3.3	3.5	3.6	4.3	1.0	2.3	3.3
Liberia	1.0	1.0	1.0	1.0	1.0	1.0	..	..	..	..	..	1.0	1.0	1.0
Madagascar	211.3	1,069.2	1,407.1	1,603.4	1,494.2	1,835.4	1,864.0	1,913.8	3,067.3	4,265.6	4,061.3	297.7	1,083.7	2,643.1
Malawi	0.8	2.2	2.6	2.8	2.7	2.8	4.0	4.5	8.7	15.3	15.3	1.0	2.2	7.6
Mali	211.3	300.5	297.8	319.0	272.3	282.1	265.0	283.2	555.2	499.2	511.6	276.7	342.6	381.2
Mauritania	45.9	73.9	75.3	83.1	80.6	81.9	87.0	120.8	123.6	129.8	137.2	49.0	76.7	108.7
Mauritius	7.7	12.9	13.4	15.3	14.9	15.7	16.0	17.6	18.0	17.4	17.9	8.5	14.1	16.8
Mozambique	32.4	290.7	524.6	744.9	929.1	1,434.5	2,517.0	3,874.2	6,038.6	9,024.3	11,293.8	34.3	328.8	5,015.9
Namibia	0.8	2.0	2.3	2.6	2.6	2.8	3.0	3.3	3.6	3.6	4.3	0.9	2.3	3.3
Niger	211.3	300.5	297.8	319.0	272.3	282.1	264.7	283.2	555.2	499.2	511.6	276.7	342.6	381.2
Nigeria	0.8	4.6	6.4	9.4	9.2	12.0	19.0	30.2	36.8	62.2	63.0	1.1	5.3	33.2
Rwanda	92.8	79.7	76.4	80.0	82.6	125.1	133.4	144.3	220.0	262.2	306.8	93.7	85.0	182.1
São Tomé and Principe	34.8	54.2	86.3	124.7	143.3	201.8	320.0	430.0	732.6	1,420.3	2,203.2	36.5	69.7	778.8
Senegal	211.3	300.5	297.8	319.0	272.3	282.1	402.0	389.4	555.2	499.2	511.6	276.7	342.6	416.0
Seychelles	6.4	5.6	5.4	5.6	5.3	5.3	5.0	5.2	5.1	4.8	5.0	6.7	6.0	5.1
Sierra Leone	1.0	32.0	32.5	59.8	151.4	295.3	499.4	567.5	586.7	755.2	920.7	1.3	29.1	539.5
Somalia	28.8	166.5	273.4	512.2	1,896.1	..	..	..	..	..	..	28.1	236.3	1,896.1
South Africa	0.8	2.0	2.3	2.6	2.6	2.8	3.0	3.3	3.5	3.6	4.3	1.0	2.3	3.3
Sudan	0.6	1.8	4.2	6.3	12.2	27.0	69.0	..	..	..	1,250.8	0.7	3.1	339.7
Swaziland	0.8	2.0	2.3	2.6	2.6	2.8	3.0	3.3	3.5	3.6	4.3	1.0	2.3	3.3
Tanzania	..	51.2	82.3	119.4	173.5	201.8	250.0	340.1	477.6	536.4	581.4	9.8	57.9	365.8
Togo	211.3	300.5	297.8	319.0	272.3	282.1	264.7	283.2	555.2	499.2	511.6	276.7	342.6	381.2
Uganda	1.0	19.8	60.0	170.4	319.6	550.9	961.0	1,201.8	1,097.0	932.5	1,012.0	2.1	53.2	867.8
Zaire	0.0	0.0	0.0	0.0	0.0	0.0	0.2	3.0	1,194.0	7,024.0	15,314.4	0.0	0.0	3,362.2
Zambia	0.8	9.5	8.3	13.8	34.5	64.6	179.0	452.8	669.4	857.2	1,203.7	0.9	8.5	494.5
Zimbabwe	0.6	1.7	1.8	2.1	2.4	3.4	5.1	6.5	8.2	8.7	10.1	0.8	1.8	6.3
NORTH AFRICA	..	..	..	..	..	..	..	..	..	..	..	..	..	..
Algeria	3.8	4.9	5.9	7.6	9.0	18.5	22.0	23.3	35.1	47.7	51.3	4.3	5.6	29.5
Egypt, Arab Republic	0.7	1.3	1.8	1.9	2.2	3.0	3.0	3.3	3.4	3.4	3.4	0.7	1.4	3.1
Libya	0.3	0.3	0.3	0.3	0.3	0.3	..	..	..	..	0.4	0.3	0.3	0.3
Morocco	3.9	8.4	8.2	8.5	8.2	8.7	9.0	9.3	9.2	8.5	8.7	5.2	8.8	8.8
Tunisia	0.4	0.8	0.9	0.9	0.9	0.9	1.0	1.0	1.0	0.9	1.0	0.5	0.9	1.0
ALL AFRICA	..	..	..	..	..	..	..	..	..	..	..	..	..	..

Note: 1996 data are preliminary (see page 3). Based on the official exchange rate, adjusted for certain countries to more accurately reflect the rate at which international transactions are carried out.

3-7. Parallel market exchange rate

	National currency per U.S. dollar											Annual average		
	1980	1987	1988	1989	1990	1991	1992	1993	1994	1995	1996	75-84	85-89	90-MR
SUB-SAHARAN AFRICA	..	..	..	..	..	..	..	..	..	..	..	..	..	..
excluding South Africa	..	..	..	..	..	..	..	..	..	..	..	..	..	..
excl. S. Africa & Nigeria	..	..	..	..	..	..	..	..	..	..	..	..	..	..
Angola	..	2,000.0	1,850.0	..	..	1,266.7	1,087.5	31,740.0	203,137.5	569,573.8	163,370.0	900.0	1,837.5	161,695.9
Benin	209.5	305.0	302.1	324.8	281.8	289.0	270.1	288.0	586.4	499.3	516.4	304.2	343.9	390.1
Botswana	0.8	2.2	2.1	2.3	1.9	2.4	2.5	2.8	2.9	2.8	3.4	1.2	2.4	2.7
Burkina Faso	209.5	305.0	302.1	324.8	281.8	17.1	16.8	288.0	586.4	499.3	516.4	304.2	343.9	315.1
Burundi	106.0	137.3	169.6	214.0	186.1	269.3	310.9	370.7	409.4	340.8	369.6	122.3	161.7	322.4
Cameroon	209.5	305.0	302.1	324.8	281.8	289.0	270.1	288.0	586.4	499.3	516.4	304.2	343.9	390.1
Cape Verde	..	..	..	..	..	88.0	79.5	87.0	92.0	89.3	89.5	..	..	87.6
Central African Republic	209.5	305.0	302.1	324.8	281.8	289.0	270.1	288.0	586.4	499.3	516.4	304.2	343.9	390.1
Chad	209.5	305.0	302.1	324.8	281.8	289.0	270.1	288.0	586.4	499.3	516.4	304.2	343.9	390.1
Comoros	209.5	305.0	302.1	324.8	281.8	289.0	270.1	288.0	446.0	390.6	415.6	304.2	343.9	340.2
Congo	209.5	305.0	302.1	324.8	281.8	289.0	270.1	288.0	586.4	499.3	516.4	304.2	343.9	390.1
Côte d'Ivoire	209.5	305.0	302.1	324.8	281.8	289.0	270.1	288.0	586.4	499.3	516.4	304.2	343.9	390.1
Djibouti	..	225.7	213.5	217.9	191.8	213.8	205.8	212.0	208.6	198.5	192.1	..	207.8	203.2
Equatorial Guinea	209.5	305.0	302.1	324.8	281.8	289.0	270.1	288.0	586.4	586.4	516.4	304.2	343.9	402.6
Eritrea	..	..	..	..	..	..	..	..	..	..	..	..	..	..
Ethiopia	2.8	4.6	6.6	5.9	6.0	6.7	9.5	13.3	12.0	10.7	10.2	3.5	5.1	9.8
Gabon	209.5	305.0	302.1	324.8	281.8	289.0	270.1	288.0	586.4	499.3	516.4	334.6	343.9	390.1
Gambia, The	1.7	7.7	8.6	7.4	8.3	8.8	11.5	9.1	9.0	10.4	10.8	2.5	7.1	9.7
Ghana	15.9	213.3	252.2	328.8	360.8	382.2	451.6	665.7	976.4	1,224.3	1,663.4	41.7	222.1	817.8
Guinea	41.7	443.3	538.9	580.1	693.3	793.0	1,608.1	1,156.9	1,074.1	1,017.9	1,025.9	102.9	453.8	1,052.7
Guinea-Bissau	..	..	1,800.0	..	..	4,172.5	6,075.0	9,883.3	14,012.5	19,166.7	26,855.0	..	1,800.0	13,360.8
Kenya	8.2	17.5	21.8	22.4	23.3	30.0	44.4	91.7	66.8	53.4	59.5	11.9	19.0	52.7
Lesotho	..	2.4	2.4	2.7	2.7	2.9	3.0	3.5	3.8	3.7	4.5	1.4	2.5	3.4
Liberia	..	..	1.5	..	..	..	..	40.0	45.0	42.3	45.8	..	1.5	43.3
Madagascar	265.0	850.0	1,671.7	1,639.1	1,589.2	2,071.3	2,239.2	2,217.9	3,122.9	4,397.5	4,551.7	521.1	1,133.5	2,884.2
Malawi	1.6	2.5	3.1	3.6	3.3	3.9	4.6	5.9	9.2	16.7	16.5	1.7	2.8	8.6
Mali	209.5	305.0	302.1	324.8	281.8	289.0	270.1	288.0	586.4	499.3	516.4	304.2	343.9	390.1
Mauritania	65.0	170.0	200.0	..	..	213.3	221.7	247.5	145.0	139.3	144.0	93.2	178.0	185.1
Mauritius	..	13.7	14.1	16.0	15.7	17.1	16.8	18.3	18.4	18.2	19.4	..	14.5	17.7
Mozambique	80.0	2,225.0	..	1,250.0	..	2,100.0	2,800.0	3,950.0	6,875.0	9,865.7	12,172.5	322.2	1,793.8	6,293.9
Namibia	..	..	..	..	..	..	..	..	..	..	..	..	..	..
Niger	209.5	305.0	302.1	324.8	281.8	289.0	270.1	288.0	586.4	499.3	516.4	304.2	343.9	390.1
Nigeria	0.9	6.7	6.7	10.7	9.3	6.7	21.9	56.8	71.7	78.3	81.8	1.4	6.4	46.6
Rwanda	115.0	101.0	98.7	109.8	104.2	209.1	238.9	297.4	286.5	268.1	331.8	135.4	111.4	248.0
São Tomé and Principe	..	..	..	..	..	222.5	360.0	432.5	810.0	1,503.3	2,407.5	..	..	956.0
Senegal	209.5	305.0	302.1	324.8	281.8	289.0	270.1	288.0	586.4	499.3	516.4	304.2	343.9	390.1
Seychelles	..	..	..	..	5.9	5.7	5.5	5.4	5.5	5.5	5.4	..	..	5.6
Sierra Leone	1.4	100.0	131.6	180.9	470.6	535.7	845.1	647.5	618.7	741.3	942.1	2.1	86.5	685.9
Somalia	9.9	150.0	319.2	398.8	1,982.1	4,675.0	6,095.0	7,456.3	6,961.3	6,549.2	7,789.8	14.7	224.0	5,929.8
South Africa	0.9	2.4	2.4	2.7	2.7	2.9	3.0	3.5	3.8	3.7	4.5	1.2	2.5	3.4
Sudan	1.0	5.2	11.2	15.9	43.6	105.3	62.4	31.6	45.3	77.5	147.2	1.3	8.4	73.3
Swaziland	..	2.4	2.4	3.0	2.7	3.1	3.3	3.8	3.9	3.9	4.7	..	2.5	3.6
Tanzania	21.0	175.0	211.0	263.5	292.4	348.5	405.9	443.5	523.2	587.3	604.7	30.5	175.4	457.9
Togo	209.5	305.0	302.1	324.8	281.8	289.0	270.1	288.0	586.4	499.3	516.4	304.2	343.9	390.1
Uganda	75.7	11,750.0	470.8	597.5	685.8	859.2	1,365.4	1,515.8	1,289.2	1,076.2	1,135.2	203.8	3,681.6	1,132.4
Zaire	6.4	91.0	235.8	469.4	738.1	19,318.8	756,558.3	3,112,920.4	1,209.8	7,452.1	52,429.4	14.3	182.6	564,375.3
Zambia	1.3	15.0	30.3	107.8	121.2	133.3	104.2	531.0	805.4	935.6	1,281.8	1.7	33.5	558.9
Zimbabwe	1.1	2.6	3.1	3.5	3.3	5.3	6.7	7.7	9.4	8.9	10.8	1.7	2.8	7.4
NORTH AFRICA	..	..	..	..	..	..	..	..	..	..	..	..	..	..
Algeria	10.9	23.6	29.7	37.1	29.8	33.8	87.4	106.8	128.7	131.9	127.6	13.6	27.2	92.3
Egypt, Arab Republic	0.8	2.0	2.2	2.6	2.6	3.4	3.4	3.4	3.4	3.4	3.6	0.9	2.0	3.3
Libya	0.5	1.3	1.0	0.9	1.0	1.2	1.6	1.7	1.6	1.3	2.0	0.5	1.0	1.5
Morocco	4.1	8.6	8.5	9.2	9.3	9.2	8.9	9.4	9.4	8.6	8.8	6.0	9.1	9.1
Tunisia	0.4	0.8	0.9	1.0	0.9	1.0	1.0	1.0	1.1	0.9	1.0	0.6	0.9	1.0
ALL AFRICA	..	..	..	..	..	..	..	..	..	..	..	..	..	..

Notes: 1996 data are preliminary (see page 3). Rates are annual averages of month-end estimates, based on a sample of transactions. New Ugandan shilling = 100 old Ugandan shilling was introduced in 1987.

-8. Ratio of parallel market to official exchange rate

	Ratio of parallel market to official exchange rates											*Annual average*		
	1980	*1987*	*1988*	*1989*	*1990*	*1991*	*1992*	*1993*	*1994*	*1995*	*1996*	*75-84*	*85-89*	*90-MR*
B-SAHARAN AFRICA	..	..	..	..	..	..	..	..	..	..	..	..	..	..
cluding South Africa	..	..	..	..	..	..	..	..	..	..	..	..	..	..
cl. S. Africa & Nigeria	..	..	..	..	..	..	..	..	..	..	..	..	..	..
ngola	..	66.85	61.84	..	..	22.99	4.33	11.93	3.41	..	..	30.08	61.42	10.67
enin	0.99	1.01	1.01	1.02	1.04	1.02	1.02	1.02	1.06	1.00	1.01	1.03	1.01	1.02
otswana	1.03	1.31	1.15	1.14	1.02	1.19	1.19	1.16	1.08	1.01	1.02	1.23	1.27	1.09
urkina Faso	0.99	1.01	1.01	1.02	1.04	0.06	0.06	1.02	1.06	1.00	1.01	1.03	1.01	0.75
urundi	1.18	1.11	1.21	1.35	1.09	1.48	1.49	1.53	1.62	1.36	1.22	1.28	1.22	1.40
ameroon	0.99	1.01	1.01	1.02	1.04	1.02	1.02	1.02	1.06	1.00	1.01	1.03	1.01	1.02
ape Verde	..	..	..	..	..	1.23	1.17	1.08	1.12	1.16	1.08	..	..	1.14
entral African Republic	0.99	1.01	1.01	1.02	1.04	1.02	1.02	1.02	1.06	1.00	1.01	1.03	1.01	1.02
had	0.99	1.01	1.01	1.02	1.04	1.02	1.02	1.02	1.06	1.00	1.01	1.03	1.01	1.02
omoros	0.99	1.01	1.01	1.02	1.04	1.02	1.02	1.02	1.07	1.04	1.08	1.03	1.01	1.04
ongo	0.99	1.01	1.01	1.02	1.04	1.02	1.02	1.02	1.06	1.00	1.01	1.03	1.01	1.02
ôte d'Ivoire	0.99	1.01	1.01	1.02	1.04	1.02	1.02	1.02	1.06	1.00	1.01	1.03	1.01	1.02
jibouti	..	1.27	1.20	1.23	1.08	1.20	1.16	1.19	1.17	1.12	1.08	..	1.17	1.14
quatorial Guinea	0.99	1.01	1.01	1.02	1.04	1.02	1.02	1.02	1.06	1.17	1.01	1.03	1.01	1.05
ritrea	..	..	..	..	..	..	..	..	..	..	..	..	..	..
hiopia	1.35	2.22	3.19	2.85	2.90	3.24	3.39	2.66	2.20	1.74	1.61	1.70	2.48	2.53
abon	0.99	1.01	1.01	1.02	1.04	1.02	1.02	1.02	1.06	1.00	1.01	1.02	1.01	1.02
ambia, The	0.99	1.09	1.28	0.98	1.05	1.00	1.29	1.00	0.94	1.09	..	1.06	1.10	1.06
hana	5.78	1.39	1.25	1.22	1.11	1.04	1.03	1.03	1.02	1.02	1.02	7.98	1.67	1.04
uinea	2.20	1.03	1.14	0.98	1.05	1.05	1.78	1.21	1.10	1.03	1.02	4.62	3.42	1.18
uinea-Bissau	..	..	1.62	..	..	1.14	0.88	0.98	1.09	1.06	1.02	..	1.62	1.03
enya	1.11	1.06	1.23	1.09	1.02	1.09	1.38	1.58	1.19	1.04	1.04	1.18	1.08	1.19
esotho	..	1.18	1.06	1.03	1.04	1.05	1.05	1.07	1.07	1.02	1.05	1.09	1.09	1.05
iberia	..	..	1.50	..	..	..	..	40.00	45.00	42.30	45.80	..	1.50	43.28
Madagascar	1.25	0.80	1.19	1.02	1.06	1.13	1.20	1.16	1.02	1.03	1.12	1.53	1.05	1.10
Malawi	1.97	1.13	1.21	1.30	1.21	1.39	1.28	1.34	1.05	1.09	..	1.77	1.25	1.23
Mali	0.99	1.01	1.01	1.02	1.04	1.02	1.02	1.02	1.06	1.00	1.01	1.03	1.01	1.02
Mauritania	1.42	2.30	2.66	..	..	2.60	2.55	2.05	1.17	1.07	1.05	1.79	2.37	1.75
Mauritius	..	1.06	1.05	1.05	1.06	1.09	1.08	1.04	1.02	1.05	1.08	..	1.03	1.06
Mozambique	2.47	7.65	..	1.68	..	1.46	1.11	1.02	1.14	1.09	1.08	8.19	24.52	1.15
amibia	..	..	..	..	..	..	..	..	..	..	..	..	..	..
iger	0.99	1.01	1.01	1.02	1.04	1.02	1.02	1.02	1.06	1.00	1.01	1.03	1.01	1.02
igeria	1.65	1.67	1.48	1.45	1.16	0.68	1.27	2.57	3.26	3.58	..	2.09	2.24	2.08
wanda	1.24	1.27	1.29	1.37	1.26	1.67	1.79	2.06	..	1.02	1.08	1.44	1.31	1.48
ão Tomé and Principe	..	..	..	..	..	1.10	1.12	1.01	1.11	1.06	1.09	..	..	1.08
enegal	0.99	1.01	1.01	1.02	1.04	1.02	1.02	1.02	1.06	1.00	1.01	1.03	1.01	1.02
eychelles	..	..	..	..	1.11	1.08	1.07	1.04	1.09	1.16	1.09	..	..	1.09
ierra Leone	1.33	2.94	4.05	3.02	3.11	1.81	1.69	1.14	1.05	0.98	1.02	1.42	2.46	1.54
omalia	1.57	1.43	1.87	0.81	..	..	..	..	..	..	..	1.45	1.76	..
outh Africa	1.16	1.18	1.06	1.03	1.04	1.05	1.05	1.07	1.07	1.02	1.05	1.12	1.09	1.05
udan	2.00	1.73	2.49	3.53	9.69	15.14	0.64	0.20	0.16	..	0.12	1.63	2.35	4.32
waziland	..	1.18	1.06	1.14	1.04	1.12	1.16	1.16	1.10	1.08	1.09	..	1.11	1.11
anzania	2.56	2.72	2.13	1.84	1.50	1.59	1.36	1.09	1.03	1.02	1.04	3.02	3.08	1.23
ogo	0.99	1.01	1.01	1.02	1.04	1.02	1.02	1.02	1.06	1.00	1.01	1.03	1.01	1.02
ganda	1,020.63	274.27	4.44	2.68	1.60	1.17	1.20	1.27	1.32	1.11	1.09	535.92	151.70	1.25
aire	..	..	..	..	..	..	..	..	1.01	1.06	..	..	..	..
ambia	1.65	1.58	3.67	7.80	4.00	2.06	0.61	1.17	1.20	1.09	1.06	1.69	3.17	1.60
imbabwe	1.71	1.56	1.72	1.65	1.35	1.46	1.31	1.19	1.15	1.03	1.08	2.09	1.55	1.22
ORTH AFRICA	..	..	..	..	..	..	..	..	..	..	..	..	..	..
lgeria	2.84	4.87	5.02	4.88	3.33	1.83	4.00	4.57	3.67	2.77	2.33	3.08	4.82	3.21
gypt, Arab Republic	1.14	2.86	3.14	3.00	1.68	1.08	1.02	1.01	1.00	1.00	1.06	1.42	2.74	1.12
ibya	1.69	4.76	3.50	3.00	3.53	4.27	5.62	5.57	4.99	3.76	5.53	1.64	3.54	4.75
Morocco	1.04	1.03	1.04	1.08	1.13	1.06	1.04	1.01	1.02	1.01	1.01	1.07	1.03	1.04
unisia	0.99	0.97	1.05	1.05	1.02	1.08	1.13	1.00	1.09	0.95	1.03	1.02	1.03	1.04
L AFRICA	..	..	..	..	..	..	..	..	..	..	..	..	..	..

Notes: 1996 data are preliminary (see page 3). New Ugandan shilling = 100 old Ugandan shilling was introduced in 1987. Numbers for Zaire are expressed in integrals.

3-9. Real effective exchange rate index

	Index 1990=100											Annual average		
	1980	*1987*	*1988*	*1989*	*1990*	*1991*	*1992*	*1993*	*1994*	*1995*	*1996*	*75-84*	*85-89*	*90-MR*
SUB-SAHARAN AFRICA	126.6	107.1	104.2	100.9	100.0	96.9	94.6	93.2	76.9	79.3	82.4	126.1	108.2	89.0
excluding South Africa	123.7	107.2	104.4	101.1	100.0	96.8	94.6	93.1	74.2	78.3	82.3	123.5	108.8	88.5
excl. S. Africa & Nigeria	120.7	107.1	104.2	100.9	100.0	96.9	94.6	93.2	73.1	77.7	80.9	119.4	108.2	88.0
Angola	..	..	..	..	..	..	..	..	..	..	..	..	..	..
Benin	..	100.1	100.4	98.0	100.0	96.4	102.5	99.7	67.3	77.2	79.6	..	99.7	89.0
Botswana	..	97.8	95.4	96.0	100.0	104.8	111.1	118.1	117.0	112.8	101.5	..	97.6	109.3
Burkina Faso	..	104.3	104.7	100.1	100.0	97.6	96.0	94.4	57.8	62.1	64.3	..	105.7	81.7
Burundi	128.3	128.0	112.5	113.9	100.0	102.7	87.2	86.8	93.1	98.2	110.9	157.6	135.5	97.0
Cameroon	88.2	108.1	105.1	97.1	100.0	95.7	96.5	89.8	57.6	66.4	67.3	83.9	98.8	81.9
Cape Verde	..	100.4	99.4	96.0	100.0	104.1	109.1	102.2	99.4	101.9	90.9	..	99.0	101.1
Central African Republic	106.0	105.1	102.9	97.7	100.0	94.4	94.6	89.9	56.7	63.2	64.5	100.7	101.8	80.5
Chad	..	101.8	108.1	98.5	100.0	100.4	99.2	89.2	60.0	64.4	68.8	..	110.2	83.1
Comoros	..	..	..	..	..	..	..	..	..	..	..	..	..	..
Congo	..	105.1	105.3	105.3	100.0	103.3	105.1	104.3	81.8	94.2	84.5	..	105.0	96.2
Côte d'Ivoire	106.1	102.1	104.0	98.5	100.0	96.5	100.8	99.2	60.9	70.3	70.5	90.0	94.5	85.4
Djibouti	..	..	..	..	..	..	..	..	..	..	..	..	..	..
Equatorial Guinea	..	107.2	102.2	100.0	100.0	92.1	88.3	93.1	71.0	75.7	79.4	..	116.1	85.7
Eritrea	..	..	..	..	..	..	..	..	..	..	..	..	..	..
Ethiopia	..	101.1	101.3	108.6	100.0	132.5	116.6	59.8	52.7	52.1	48.5	..	117.9	80.3
Gabon	113.4	105.4	90.8	92.0	100.0	87.1	87.3	84.1	56.5	62.5	63.9	103.8	98.7	77.3
Gambia, The	133.6	99.6	108.5	104.5	100.0	95.6	97.8	105.7	97.9	94.8	94.0	128.9	107.6	98.0
Ghana	..	111.2	106.5	100.2	100.0	102.2	90.3	79.3	63.5	72.9	79.4	..	142.6	83.9
Guinea	..	93.8	104.4	106.6	100.0	103.4	95.5	99.5	96.7	91.2	93.0	..	100.0	97.0
Guinea-Bissau	..	143.3	98.0	106.6	100.0	91.2	74.4	80.8	71.9	66.5	69.5	..	115.9	79.2
Kenya	..	115.5	110.5	108.8	100.0	98.0	102.6	89.4	112.2	111.1	108.6	..	120.5	103.2
Lesotho	112.4	103.1	101.9	102.0	100.0	106.8	115.6	114.3	109.6	109.0	99.5	110.9	104.4	107.8
Liberia	..	..	..	..	..	..	..	..	..	..	..	..	..	..
Madagascar	..	114.1	100.2	95.7	100.0	87.0	91.5	101.1	88.8	80.3	102.2	..	130.9	93.0
Malawi	110.7	89.3	94.9	100.7	100.0	103.5	95.3	97.1	68.8	59.7	82.3	108.1	97.6	86.7
Mali	..	98.0	102.2	97.8	100.0	96.3	90.9	88.9	55.1	62.0	64.1	..	107.6	79.6
Mauritania	..	114.1	105.0	102.9	100.0	101.2	100.9	81.5	79.6	72.7	72.5	..	115.0	86.9
Mauritius	..	97.6	96.9	97.6	100.0	98.5	96.9	97.6	98.6	96.6	92.8	..	102.1	97.3
Mozambique	..	150.0	96.6	99.7	100.0	84.8	65.3	63.6	61.5	58.8	67.5	..	208.7	71.6
Namibia	..	..	..	..	..	..	..	..	..	..	..	..	..	..
Niger	..	115.7	109.1	101.2	100.0	87.5	84.8	82.8	55.1	61.1	63.1	..	117.7	76.3
Nigeria	350.6	120.2	120.5	107.6	100.0	85.0	70.5	77.2	142.8	122.1	150.0	431.4	282.8	106.8
Rwanda	..	110.7	111.7	109.5	100.0	76.0	73.4	80.5	64.6	85.0	79.6	..	112.9	79.8
São Tomé and Principe	..	..	..	..	..	..	..	..	..	..	..	..	..	..
Senegal	..	109.5	103.0	98.4	100.0	93.7	93.9	90.6	58.8	63.7	64.1	..	106.6	80.7
Seychelles	..	107.0	105.8	103.2	100.0	98.8	98.9	103.2	103.6	101.2	96.4	..	108.3	100.3
Sierra Leone	120.7	131.0	154.8	134.9	100.0	101.1	92.3	102.7	116.9	105.6	106.1	451.7	164.1	103.5
Somalia	..	..	..	..	..	..	..	..	..	..	..	..	..	..
South Africa	133.9	102.6	97.0	97.4	100.0	104.3	107.9	106.0	101.3	98.2	90.4	134.6	97.3	101.2
Sudan	..	37.9	43.4	66.9	100.0	176.8	28.2	28.0	33.1	25.5	16.6	..	47.1	58.3
Swaziland	..	111.3	107.7	101.1	100.0	96.8	92.6	94.3	98.3	101.6	103.2	..	108.6	98.1
Tanzania	..	167.6	132.0	115.5	100.0	98.8	86.9	94.1	93.8	97.1	117.9	..	249.5	98.4
Togo	126.6	109.4	103.7	96.5	100.0	95.0	96.6	93.3	62.1	71.9	71.5	120.7	104.4	84.3
Uganda	925.1	212.8	192.1	162.9	100.0	76.6	70.4	75.7	94.2	91.7	93.1	437.9	178.3	86.0
Zaire	381.3	116.4	121.3	120.3	100.0	96.9	94.6	125.4	91.1	83.5	82.6	378.0	125.8	96.3
Zambia	132.7	62.5	94.7	120.9	100.0	93.2	89.5	101.6	98.6	94.6	98.3	136.0	90.4	96.5
Zimbabwe	..	126.2	117.4	112.7	100.0	84.0	76.5	79.7	74.2	78.3	84.3	..	126.2	82.4
NORTH AFRICA	156.7	118.6	104.9	104.7	100.0	99.4	102.5	103.2	105.1	107.9	108.6	139.6	120.7	103.8
Algeria	..	166.8	137.6	118.1	100.0	59.7	61.4	74.0	63.7	53.3	54.5	..	163.0	66.7
Egypt, Arab Republic	..	129.9	97.0	103.4	100.0	96.6	102.1	117.0	121.2	120.0	128.3	..	122.5	112.2
Libya	..	..	..	..	..	..	..	..	..	..	..	..	..	..
Morocco	156.7	107.3	105.7	106.0	100.0	102.2	103.0	105.9	109.1	112.4	113.2	139.6	109.2	106.5
Tunisia	..	106.2	104.2	102.8	100.0	102.1	104.5	100.6	101.2	103.4	103.9	..	116.3	102.2
ALL AFRICA	127.5	107.3	104.3	101.6	100.0	96.9	95.0	93.7	80.7	81.9	83.4	127.6	109.1	90.2

Note: 1996 data are preliminary (see page 3).

Figure 3-1. Real effective exchange rate, 1996

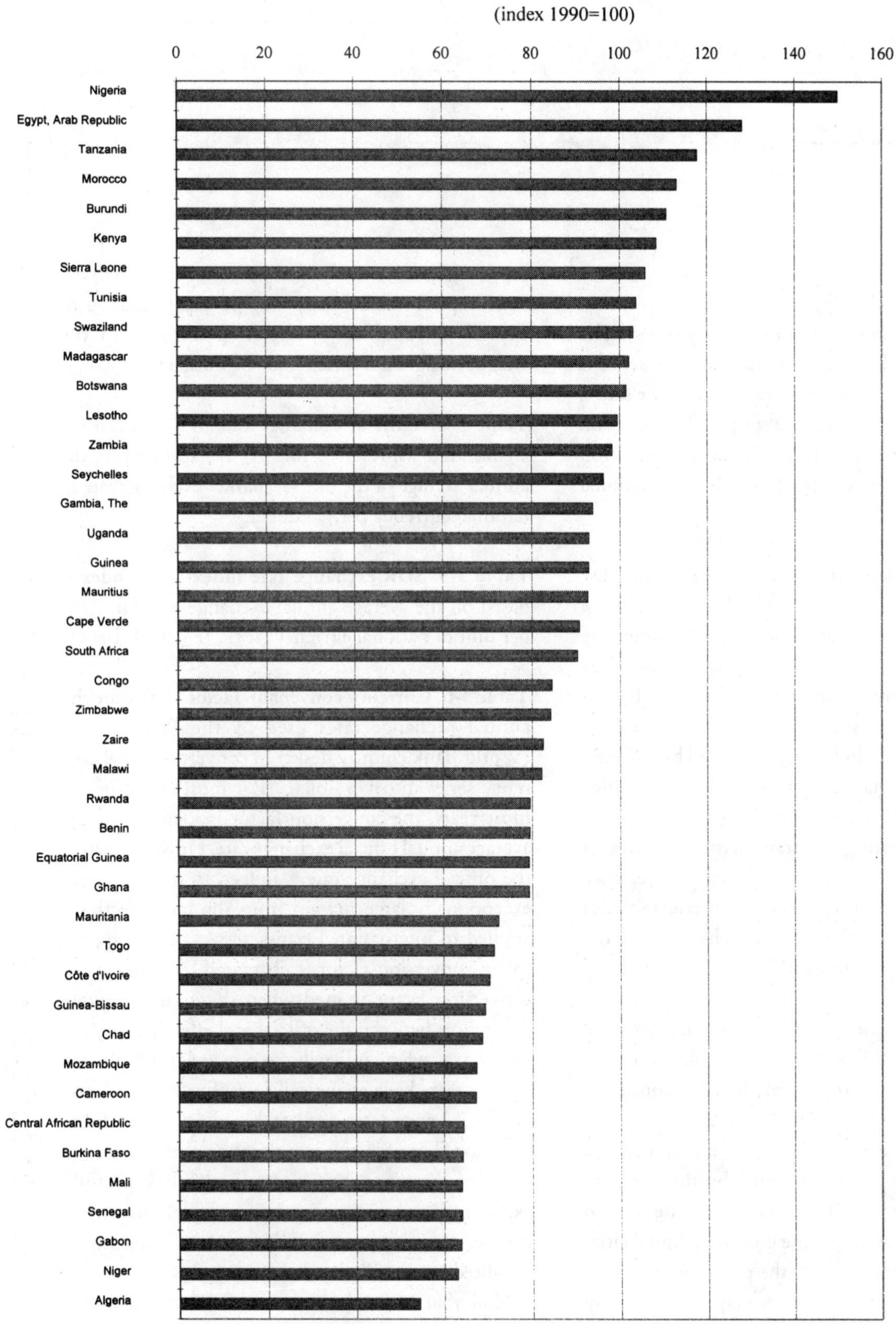

Technical Notes

Tables

Table 3-1. GDP deflator (local currency series). The implicit GDP deflator for national currency series is obtained by dividing, for each year of the time series, the value of GDP at current prices (World Bank country desks) by the value of GDP at constant 1987 prices (World Bank country desks), both in national currency.

Table 3-2. GDP deflator (US dollar series). The GDP deflator for US dollar series (with base year 1987 = 100) (World Bank country desks) is obtained by dividing, for each year of the time series, the value of GDP at current US dollars (Table 2-5) by the value of GDP at constant 1987 dollars (Table 2-1). GDP at current US dollars was obtained by converting current national series at single-year exchange rates, while GDP at constant 1987 dollars was obtained by converting constant national series at 1987 prices at a fixed (1987) exchange rate. As a result, the GDP deflator for US dollar series includes both the effects of domestic price changes and the effects of exchange rate variations.

Table 3-3. Consumer price index. Consumer price indexes (IMF, *IFS*, line 64) are generally compiled using the Laspeyres formula: goods in the consumption basket selected according to consumption patterns in the base year, derived from household expenditure surveys, are weighted by their relative prices in the base year. The data often relate only to selected representative income groups in capital cities or major urban areas. Thus, the consumer price indexes shown for some countries may not accurately represent price movements because the underlying consumption basket may not be representative of overall national consumption patterns, and the weights assigned to prices may be outdated.

Table 3-4. Official exchange rate. The official exchange rate (IMF, *IFS*, line rf) is expressed as the annual average of the official market exchange rate in national currency per US dollar.

Table 3-5. SDR exchange rate index. This index is based on the average annual exchange rate for SDRs per unit of national currency (IMF, *IFS*, line rd-zf).

Table 3-6. Currency conversion factor. These are the annual exchange rates used by the World Bank (World Bank country desks) to convert national currency series into US dollars. For most countries, in most years, the conversion factor is identical to the average annual official exchange rate. However, where the official exchange rate is judged to diverge by an exceptionally large margin from the rate effectively applied to international transactions, a more appropriate conversion factor is estimated. An alternative conversion factor is used when there are egregious differences between the official and effective transaction rates, when officially recognized multiple exchange rates have analytically significant spreads, or when exchange rates need to be adjusted to a fiscal year base. The objective in estimating alternative conversion factors is to approximate as closely as possible exchange rates actually used. For example, where multiple exchange rates are maintained, a transaction-weighted rate is calculated.

Note that national statistical compilers sometimes

use an official exchange rate to assign a national currency value to international transactions originally denominated in foreign currencies. In these cases, the official rate must be used to convert the same items back to dollars, regardless of whether it was the rate actually applied to the international transactions, even if an alternative conversion factor is used for other components of GDP.

Table 3-7. Parallel market exchange rate. Data reported here are from *Pick's Currency Yearbooks* and *Currency Alerts* (now discontinued) and *Global Currency Report*. They are averages of month-end rates for the period covered, based on a sample of transactions, usually in a capital city or a financial center of the country. They include the rates at the Bureaux de Change that have been established in some countries with auction markets as semi-official foreign exchange windows for small transactions. The current table corrects some errors contained in *ADI 1994-95*.

Table 3-8. Ratio of parallel market to official exchange rates. This ratio is obtained by dividing parallel market exchange rates (Table 3-7) by official exchange rates (Table 3-4), to measure the premium on the official exchange rate. The premium is usually high in the presence of an overvalued exchange rate. The current table reflects the corrected series for Table 3-7.

Table 3-9. Real effective exchange rate index. This index (IMF, *IFS* Database) gives a measure of price competitiveness of the country's exports relative to its trading partners. A decline (increase) in the index indicates real depreciation (appreciation) of the exchange rate. The data have been rebased to 1990. The year 1987 coincided with the early period of massive devaluations in the process of adjustment by several Sub-Saharan African countries. As a result, the substantial devaluations that continued to take place after 1987 may not be very pronounced in the data. Relative movements in the inflation rates between a country and the trading partner(s) may diminish the real impact of a devaluation, particularly if inflationary tendencies are stronger domestically than abroad.

Figure

The following indicator has been used to derive the figure in this chapter.

Figure 3-1. Real effective exchange rate (Table 3-9).

Methodology used for regional aggregations and period averages in chapter 3

	Aggregations[a]			*Period averages*[b]	
Table	*(4)*	*(7)*	*(8)*	*(1)*	*(2)*
3-1		x		x	
3-2	x			x	
3-3		x		x	x
3-4			x	x	
3-5			x	x	
3-6			x	x	
3-7			x	x	
3-8			x	x	
3-9		x		x	

Note: Regional aggregations are shown in the rows for Sub-Saharan Africa, North Africa, and All Africa. Period averages are shown in the last three columns. This table shows only the methodologies used in this chapter.

a. Regional aggregations: (1) simple total; (2) simple total of the first indicator divided by the simple total of the second indicator (same country coverage); (3) simple total of the gap-filled indicator; (4) simple total of the gap-filled main indicator divided by the simple total of the gap-filled secondary indicator; (5) simple total of the first gap-filled main indicator less the simple total of the second gap-filled main indicator, all divided by the simple total of the secondary indicator; (6) weighted total (by population); (7) median; (8) no aggregation; (9) simple arithmetic mean.

b. Period averages: (1) arithmetic mean (using the same series as shown in the table, i.e., ratio if the rest of the table is shown as ratio, level if the rest of the table is shown as level, growth rate if the rest of the table is shown as growth rate); (2) least-squares growth rate (using main indicator); (3) least-squares growth rate (using main indicator in constant terms, with the rest of the table in current terms).

4

Money and Banking

Monetary variables directly affect prices and exchange rates and indirectly affect real economic performance. Money plays a vital role in any modern economy. Data in this chapter are concerned with the creation of the types of assets that transactors in the economy wish to hold from the types of liabilities that debtors are willing to incur. However, emphasis here is on the creation of the means of payment, that is, on the more liquid end of the liquidity spectrum for assets.

Money and the institutions that deal in money provide cover against credit risks, limit transactions costs, help mobilize savings, allocate credit, and facilitate investment and hence growth of the economy. Data on money and banking help to assess the prevailing financial conditions of a country and to arrive at a proper evaluation of the financial policy options open to a country for achieving its macroeconomic objectives. The government usually intervenes in finance to control the supply of money and credit. The primary objective of such intervention is to maintain price stability. However, the government may also intervene to finance a budget deficit that in turn may threaten price stability. The government also ensures that financial institutions are properly supervised to ensure continued confidence in the financial system and to avoid destabilizing runs on the banking system. Time series are provided for nine indicators in this section.

4-1. Domestic Credit

	Level	*Percentage annual change*										*Average annual percentage growth*		
	1980	*1980*	*1988*	*1989*	*1990*	*1991*	*1992*	*1993*	*1994*	*1995*	*1996*	*75-84*	*85-89*	*90-MR*
SUB-SAHARAN AFRICA	..	19	11	13	11	10	11	6	20	11	15	18	17	8
excluding South Africa	..	19	11	13	11	10	11	6	20	11	15	18	20	7
excl. S. Africa & Nigeria	..	19	10	13	11	10	11	5	20	12	15	13	23	6
Angola	..	..	..	..	..	..	..	..	..	..	..	..	..	..
Benin	69,800	49	5	-30	11	-30	-4	-26	74	22	..	21	-4	-1
Botswana	6	-27	29	28	28	0	14	11	20	-3	16	7	..	..
Burkina Faso	57,700	3	12	25	1	-10	-16	-5	4	-14	..	21	5	-8
Burundi	13,100	19	19	-1	10	7	-5	4	16	..	..	28	6	5
Cameroon	379,000	28	21	9	-2	21	-34	-3	-1	-1	..	21	5	-7
Cape Verde	1,120	39	9	21	15	27	16	19	23	25	..	40	15	19
Central African Republic	40,000	39	-3	6	1	18	-18	0	32	-4	..	11	-2	3
Chad	50,400	-1	-12	-11	-22	35	11	-15	30	-9	..	9	1	5
Comoros	..	..	25	24	18	12	8	-20	9	-1	..	..	6	2
Congo	80,400	18	3	13	-4	4	3	-32	3	10	..	19	1	-6
Côte d'Ivoire	845,000	22	6	-6	-4	-1	2	-3	6	12	..	19	1	2
Djibouti	..	..	3	3	-3	3	8	-2	10	17	..	..	4	5
Equatorial Guinea	..	..	-6	3	-7	108	-10	-33	46	1	..	..	-4	8
Eritrea	..	..	..	..	..	..	..	..	..	..	..	..	..	..
Ethiopia	3,400	19	11	13	19	10	14	6	8	12	..	21	10	10
Gabon	178,000	11	-10	4	-14	2	-7	1	25	16	..	14	8	3
Gambia, The	196	23	17	-10	-61	..	..	-17	-13	41	..	25	-18	10
Ghana	9,490	28	-4	24	4	82	45	53	19	53	14	36	32	34
Guinea	..	..	..	..	..	..	34	9	22	29	..	..	..	19
Guinea-Bissau	..	..	71	132	65	7	21	32	20	-19	..	..	60	18
Kenya	16,200	13	7	6	26	19	18	-2	50	37	19	18	14	20
Lesotho	58	..	40	20	-12	-6	-51	-74	-294	217	81	..	25	-53
Liberia	284	19	25	15	..	..	14	10	6	..	..	19	15	..
Madagascar	341,000	50	4	-3	6	12	28	16	29	-3	-2	25	10	13
Malawi	333	12	-16	19	3	21	65	14	36	-3	..	21	5	22
Mali	138,000	5	-26	8	-17	-3	2	12	19	15	..	8	-2	5
Mauritania	11,700	14	6	62	11	10	0	7	-1	-37	..	18	12	-1
Mauritius	4,440	14	17	13	16	25	20	25	23	13	6	23	10	18
Mozambique	..	..	..	..	..	..	..	..	..	..	..	..	..	..
Namibia	..	..	..	..	..	11	90	29	28	31	23	..	..	30
Niger	84,200	45	0	-5	-4	-10	-4	-17	25	-17	..	27	-3	-5
Nigeria	10,700	23	26	-9	34	14	129	67	41	11	..	33	10	41
Rwanda	3,480	12	24	18	16	-15	33	23	-7	-7	-2	9	17	6
São Tomé and Principe	..	..	0	..	..	..	..	..	..	..	..	..	47	..
Senegal	302,000	17	7	-3	-9	-2	-1	-2	7	2	..	18	2	-1
Seychelles	190	12	25	23	11	10	11	25	20	15	..	18	15	15
Sierra Leone	413	35	46	53	203	24	-8	1	1,076	-12	6	28	43	54
Somalia	3,880	31	48	94	..	..	..	..	..	..	..	25	49	..
South Africa	32,300	21	26	18	15	..	..	12	21	12	18	15	16	15
Sudan	1,770	22	33	58	38	56	152	66	47	..	..	24	34	56
Swaziland	37	0	-3	-30	40	-68	68	109	163	-36	-45	26	-3	16
Tanzania	18,200	24	37	39	72	14	23	40	11	11	..	22	29	23
Togo	71,500	13	5	-22	14	10	-8	2	21	44	..	15	6	9
Uganda	211	64	..	..	..	..	..	-8	-14	-47	51	34	..	-17
Zaire	0	22	186	134	341	1,404	2,862	1,650	5,285	183	..	36	64	281
Zambia	1,860	17	192	100	89	136	..	..	76	97	..	20	49	..
Zimbabwe	645	..	12	28	20	27	44	61	20	19	26	..	15	28
NORTH AFRICA	..	18	11	24	7	8	11	7	11	15	10	26	18	11
Algeria	102,000	18	12	8	13	17	32	17	3	25	..	21	10	16
Egypt, Arab Republic	14,100	42	20	25	26	7	4	7	13	16	14	26	18	10
Libya	1,220	-41	11	83	7	5	6	4	11	6	..	19	11	6
Morocco	31,200	18	9	10	-1	19	11	8	11	15	6	17	9	10
Tunisia	1,570	19	4	24	6	8	11	5	6	7	..	18	10	7
ALL AFRICA	..	19	11	15	11	10	11	7	20	12	14	20	15	19

Note: 1996 data are preliminary (see page 3). Levels for 1980 are expressed in millions of units of national currency. Group data are medians of individual country values in each year or period.

4-2. Credit to the private sector

	Level	*Percentage annual change*										*Average annual percentage growth*		
	1980	*1980*	*1988*	*1989*	*1990*	*1991*	*1992*	*1993*	*1994*	*1995*	*1996*	*75-84*	*85-89*	*90-MR*
SUB-SAHARAN AFRICA	..	15	13	17	14	12	6	10	14	17	12	16	34	10
excluding South Africa	..	14	13	17	14	12	6	10	14	17	13	16	32	9
excl. S. Africa & Nigeria	..	14	13	18	13	12	6	9	13	17	13	14	35	4
Angola	..	..	..	..	..	..	..	..	..	..	..	..	..	..
Benin	85,000	34	10	-25	-1	-15	-19	-2	11	7	..	20	-2	-6
Botswana	93	10	23	36	52	43	35	12	12	-3	4	15	16	18
Burkina Faso	60,200	4	13	18	4	-23	-12	-9	-16	9	..	15	10	-11
Burundi	6,410	14	34	32	36	21	6	35	8	..	..	20	18	18
Cameroon	417,000	29	-11	-1	1	0	-55	-8	0	0	..	24	2	-19
Cape Verde	506	-14	-30	30	19	15	20	59	1	35	..	19	11	21
Central African Republic	23,500	51	-5	8	-4	-9	-37	-5	18	24	..	10	-2	-8
Chad	37,500	-2	-58	-7	-3	12	-4	-31	13	17	..	8	-13	-3
Comoros	..	..	44	-8	43	7	4	-12	-2	10	..	..	6	4
Congo	56,000	23	-43	5	7	3	-1	-46	15	13	..	21	-12	-8
Côte d'Ivoire	876,000	11	0	-3	-4	0	-12	-5	-5	19	..	15	1	-3
Djibouti	..	..	2	4	-5	-3	-1	-6	2	13	..	..	4	-1
Equatorial Guinea	..	..	-2	6	1	58	-36	-75	13	51	..	..	2	-24
Eritrea	..	..	..	..	..	..	..	..	..	..	..	..	..	..
Ethiopia	875	-1	4	-2	-5	-1	23	97	27	48	..	8	9	27
Gabon	143,000	16	-34	9	1	6	-28	-2	-1	25	..	14	-7	-4
Gambia, The	99	19	13	12	16	14	-24	59	7	-10	..	19	5	8
Ghana	940	18	40	151	14	-6	57	35	46	44	73	28	48	30
Guinea	..	..	..	..	..	..	34	21	12	26	..	..	..	20
Guinea-Bissau	..	..	90	120	45	18	-2	63	73	5	..	..	66	27
Kenya	11,800	21	16	17	12	22	31	5	28	48	25	16	13	21
Lesotho	21	-10	29	18	22	31	16	59	39	6	-10	22	18	23
Liberia	89	-39	-17	65	..	..	53	-12	64	..	..	-1	7	..
Madagascar	164,000	26	4	11	28	12	6	15	26	16	2	17	12	14
Malawi	184	8	28	46	35	28	34	-12	54	4	..	17	9	19
Mali	82,000	8	-26	20	0	2	7	3	-9	52	..	8	1	5
Mauritania	10,100	14	9	51	13	11	2	3	3	-27	..	13	13	1
Mauritius	1,880	9	27	22	19	17	23	28	20	15	5	16	23	18
Mozambique	..	..	..	..	..	..	..	..	..	..	..	..	..	..
Namibia	..	..	..	..	..	17	30	30	31	34	19	..	..	25
Niger	90,700	20	-1	-16	-8	-9	-4	-10	10	-41	..	19	-2	-10
Nigeria	6,150	38	18	10	16	26	83	17	76	50	..	24	15	37
Rwanda	6,210	46	21	8	-17	-18	26	17	-7	71	1	19	10	9
São Tomé and Principe	..	..	18	..	..	..	..	..	..	..	..	..	29	..
Senegal	270,000	16	7	2	-7	-3	6	2	-18	2	..	16	3	-3
Seychelles	160	3	9	32	8	9	5	10	21	17	..	9	0	11
Sierra Leone	91	28	95	124	19	153	28	44	11	5	23	13	65	31
Somalia	426	-5	59	203	..	..	..	..	..	..	..	17	67	..
South Africa	27,300	26	27	21	14	..	..	12	18	16	17	16	16	15
Sudan	593	29	19	10	55	83	91	69	96	49	..	26	25	57
Swaziland	98	15	28	29	39	40	3	9	22	2	6	17	16	14
Tanzania	1,140	11	438	183	29	32	-13	40	20	-10	..	12	84	14
Togo	65,900	13	4	-3	3	12	0	-8	-1	28	..	14	7	3
Uganda	49	85	..	..	..	..	..	34	18	24	35	31	..	23
Zaire	0	32	62	74	77	744	4,696	1,889	22,446	473	..	29	58	307
Zambia	509	5	77	114	54	61	..	..	38	81	..	13	41	..
Zimbabwe	107	-9	43	37	28	70	42	44	29	29	20	..	24	32
NORTH AFRICA	..	13	6	13	12	9	14	11	25	9	18	26	7	25
Algeria	68,500	14	6	9	18	32	-77	2	25	6	..	19	5	-19
Egypt, Arab Republic	2,170	-10	16	18	20	1	25	19	32	37	25	26	18	20
Libya	1,140	7	-4	6	2	4	8	11	27	7	..	16	3	10
Morocco	12,400	13	..	..	..	34	15	11	11	15	10	14	..	13
Tunisia	1,350	22	6	27	5	9	14	7	8	9	..	18	10	9
ALL AFRICA	..	14	13	18	14	12	7	11	18	16	18	20	28	14

Note: 1996 data are preliminary (see page 3). Data exclude credit to other financial institutions. 1980 levels are in millions of local currency. Group data are medians of individual country values for each year or period.

4-3. Credit to the government

	Level	Percentage annual change										Average annual percentage growth		
	1980	*1980*	*1988*	*1989*	*1990*	*1991*	*1992*	*1993*	*1994*	*1995*	*1996*	*75-84*	*85-89*	*90-MR*
SUB-SAHARAN AFRICA	..	23	11	-1	7	7	19	8	34	-3	8	25	13	18
excluding South Africa	..	24	11	2	7	7	19	8	34	-2	8	24	18	17
excl. S. Africa & Nigeria	..	24	11	2	6	7	19	8	34	-1	8	23	13	19
Angola	..	..	..	..	..	..	..	..	..	..	..	..	..	..
Benin	-15,200	-8	-48	-141	-513	-177	-172	-309	-274	73	..	..	8	28
Botswana	-92	17	29	30	31	7	19	11	19	-3	12	..	..	..
Burkina Faso	-3,380	46	13	3	6	-51	5	-25	-115	-703	..	..	..	..
Burundi	4,630	24	1	-31	-25	2	-41	-55	176	..	..	38	-8	-21
Cameroon	-38,100	40	-72	-66	73	-676	79	8	1	-4	..	..	..	13
Cape Verde	30	-59	3	34	29	90	34	27	122	18	..	71	28	42
Central African Republic	16,500	26	-22	-7	-21	111	15	2	39	-22	..	13	-11	17
Chad	13,000	2	-132	-374	-119	-963	398	16	45	-24	..	9	-2	46
Comoros	..	..	-26	187	-24	24	23	-41	49	-24	..	..	5	-2
Congo	24,400	7	263	67	-18	7	35	-6	-4	4	..	5	38	4
Côte d'Ivoire	-54,700	-52	43	-13	-11	6	70	2	35	1	..	50	1	17
Djibouti	..	..	-1	1	-15	-48	-132	210	126	40	..	..	..	77
Equatorial Guinea	..	..	8	-6	-29	296	19	-10	53	-5	..	..	-6	29
Eritrea	..	..	..	..	..	..	..	..	..	..	..	..	..	..
Ethiopia	1,736	19	14	17	26	13	15	-1	5	-4	..	27	11	8
Gabon	35,000	-4	30	-4	-39	-9	75	7	54	9	..	-31	61	15
Gambia, The	97	28	59	-170	797	65	-113	-453	38	-60	..	30	-92	..
Ghana	6,520	33	-6	-26	8	166	44	63	3	61	-1	38	23	38
Guinea	..	..	..	..	..	..	37	-16	52	36	..	..	..	20
Guinea-Bissau	..	..	11	219	116	-2	45	18	-49	-144	..	..	44	14
Kenya	3,988	8	-7	-5	56	13	0	-12	97	18	7	22	12	18
Lesotho	37	329	46	21	-29	-40	-182	294	78	32	18	50	30	-43
Liberia	151	63	31	12	..	..	10	13	1	..	..	43	18	..
Madagascar	177,000	81	2	-14	-20	11	68	16	34	-24	-7	41	8	12
Malawi	92	31	-33	2	-34	-22	300	31	43	-21	..	27	-4	30
Mali	55,900	2	-25	-19	-77	-80	-373	-239	639	-84	..	7	-15	0
Mauritania	1,630	13	-5	112	4	5	-6	25	-17	-85	..	22	19	-19
Mauritius	2,550	18	2	-5	4	49	11	20	32	12	9	30	-6	19
Mozambique	..	..	..	..	..	..	..	..	..	..	..	..	..	..
Namibia	..	..	..	..	..	60	-245	30	4	17	56	..	..	20
Niger	-7,490	-59	11	91	8	-13	-6	-40	102	50	..	15	-6	3
Nigeria	3,540	7	30	-27	55	4	208	96	29	-7	..	38	6	48
Rwanda	-2,811	131	25	37	63	-13	41	28	-7	-50	-6	9	43	1
São Tomé and Principe	..	..	-25	..	..	..	..	..	..	..	..	..	0	..
Senegal	28,700	53	5	-16	-15	2	-26	-23	174	2	..	40	-3	5
Seychelles	29	118	30	21	12	11	13	28	19	15	..	52	18	16
Sierra Leone	318	37	38	40	260	11	-16	-14	1,688	-12	5	33	33	56
Somalia	3,450	37	34	-57	..	..	..	..	..	..	..	29	12	..
South Africa	5,060	0	-2	-22	51	..	..	51	112	-60	80	0	-2	15
Sudan	777	13	51	95	41	62	175	68	34	..	..	23	41	58
Swaziland	-61	27	281	148	38	104	-3	-6	-28	50	34	..	..	..
Tanzania	17,040	26	37	-30	120	1	54	40	7	23	..	23	17	29
Togo	4,530	14	42	-475	-59	58	67	-57	-277	178	..	13	-27	..
Uganda	162	58	..	..	..	..	..	-20	-30	-105	-243	37	..	-80
Zaire	0	19	277	154	396	1,399	2,945	1,628	3,733	-30	..	39	79	261
Zambia	1,350	23	259	96	98	154	..	..	85	101	..	21	62	..
Zimbabwe	367	..	-16	15	35	-32	118	102	17	-2	43	..	13	30
NORTH AFRICA	..	14	20	10	10	5	5	1	1	2	1	20	20	5
Algeria	33,000	24	20	7	6	-5	44	133	-11	-14	..	23	18	22
Egypt, Arab Republic	8,250	14	24	30	26	4	5	-7	7	2	-1	20	20	3
Libya	70	-93	55	218	10	6	4	1	1	5	..	15	25	4
Morocco	18,800	21	9	10	-9	5	8	7	10	14	3	18	8	6
Tunisia	219	2	-6	6	13	6	-13	-14	-12	-16	..	18	6	-8
ALL AFRICA	..	19	12	6	8	6	15	7	29	-1	8	25	19	15

Note: 1996 data are preliminary (see page 3). Data exclude credit to other financial institutions. 1980 levels are in millions of local currency. Group data are medians of individual country values for each year or period.

4-4. Net foreign assets

	Billions of units of national currency											*Annual average*		
	1980	*1987*	*1988*	*1989*	*1990*	*1991*	*1992*	*1993*	*1994*	*1995*	*1996*	*75-84*	*85-89*	*90-MR*
SUB-SAHARAN AFRICA	..	..	..	..	..	..	..	..	..	..	..	..	..	..
excluding South Africa	..	..	..	..	..	..	..	..	..	..	..	..	..	..
excl. S.Africa & Nigeria	..	..	..	..	..	..	..	..	..	..	..	..	..	..
Angola	..	..	..	..	..	..	..	..	..	..	..	..	..	..
Benin	-23	-57	-56	-24	4	41	65	70	160	146	..	-17	-43	81
Botswana	0	3	4	5	6	8	9	11	11	12	19	0	3	11
Burkina Faso	0	67	80	67	66	76	90	106	164	236	..	6	58	123
Burundi	5	5	6	12	11	18	30	35	45	..	..	3	6	28
Cameroon	-14	-12	-206	-194	-185	-174	-170	-224	-294	-320	..	13	-60	-228
Cape Verde	2	5	6	5	5	4	5	6	6	5	..	2	5	5
Central African Republic	3	16	14	20	19	16	16	24	92	99	..	1	14	44
Chad	-4	9	11	23	32	22	14	-1	14	48	..	0	12	21
Comoros	..	7	7	8	7	7	7	11	16	16	..	4	6	11
Congo	8	-7	-34	-40	-4	-18	-15	0	13	23	..	-3	-19	0
Côte d'Ivoire	-223	-384	-488	-487	-495	-474	-511	-515	-72	58	..	-211	-409	-335
Djibouti	..	33	36	36	42	45	35	37	36	34	..	21	32	38
Equatorial Guinea	..	-5	-6	-3	-6	-5	-6	-7	-14	-10	..	..	-5	-8
Eritrea	..	..	..	..	..	..	..	..	..	..	..	..	..	..
Ethiopia	0	0	0	0	0	0	1	2	5	5	..	0	0	2
Gabon	16	-11	-67	-47	21	36	-21	-24	70	25	..	35	-12	18
Gambia, The	0	0	0	0	0	0	1	1	1	1	..	0	0	0
Ghana	0	-131	-153	-181	-152	-91	-228	-295	-164	-14	349	-2	-111	-85
Guinea	..	..	..	..	..	81	113	162	121	109	..	..	..	117
Guinea-Bissau	..	-77	-108	-55	-41	-133	-261	-329	-367	-274	..	..	-65	-234
Kenya	2	-2	-4	-2	-5	-8	-6	30	16	10	32	1	-2	10
Lesotho	0	0	0	0	0	0	1	1	1	2	2	0	0	1
Liberia	0	0	0	0	..	-1	-1	-1	-1	..	..	0	0	-1
Madagascar	-110	-1,720	-1,960	-1,990	-2,200	-2,810	-133	-11	1	309	860	-150	-1,459	-569
Malawi	0	0	0	0	0	0	0	0	-1	1	..	0	0	0
Mali	-8	-46	-28	14	27	65	69	74	107	120	..	-29	-33	77
Mauritania	-2	-11	-12	-12	-16	-24	-32	-30	-33	-25	..	-3	-11	-26
Mauritius	0	3	6	8	12	15	16	17	16	19	20	0	3	16
Mozambique	..	..	..	..	..	..	..	..	..	..	..	..	..	..
Namibia	..	..	..	..	0	1	0	0	0	0	0	..	..	0
Niger	5	17	29	24	26	26	28	24	23	22	..	5	16	25
Nigeria	6	7	8	18	41	54	18	52	56	100	..	3	8	54
Rwanda	15	12	9	6	3	12	10	5	1	24	34	9	10	13
São Tomé and Principe	..	-1	-1	..	..	..	..	..	..	..	..	0	-1	..
Senegal	-97	-211	-258	-213	-188	-179	-172	-207	-130	-70	..	-102	-233	-158
Seychelles	0	0	0	0	0	0	0	0	0	0	..	0	0	0
Sierra Leone	0	-8	-13	-21	-64	-145	-188	-204	-339	-396	-159	0	-11	-214
Somalia	0	-20	-56	-214	..	..	..	..	..	..	..	0	-63	..
South Africa	6	4	1	0	1	..	-11	-17	-21	-18	-31	2	1	-16
Sudan	0	-7	-10	-10	-12	-25	-367	-587	-1,220	-2,020	..	-1	-7	-705
Swaziland	0	0	0	1	1	1	1	1	1	1	2	0	0	1
Tanzania	0	-80	-153	-105	-131	-159	-295	-384	-278	-207	..	0	-80	-242
Togo	0	63	43	68	70	74	54	23	43	33	..	21	62	49
Uganda	0	..	..	..	..	..	-243	-193	-52	53	112	0	-3	-65
Zaire	0	0	0	0	0	0	0	-18	-1,790	-8,810	..	0	0	-1,770
Zambia	-1	-8	-12	-26	-51	-102	..	-496	-788	-1,090	..	-1	-12	-505
Zimbabwe	0	0	0	0	0	-2	-3	-3	-2	-3	-3	0	0	-2
NORTH AFRICA	..	..	..	..	..	..	..	..	..	..	..	..	..	..
Algeria	17	9	9	7	7	24	23	20	60	26	..	12	10	27
Egypt, Arab Republic	-1	2	2	-1	-1	17	34	46	51	49	54	-1	1	35
Libya	5	2	1	1	2	1	2	1	2	2	..	2	2	2
Morocco	0	-3	-1	0	15	23	30	35	40	34	36	-1	-3	30
Tunisia	0	0	1	1	1	1	1	1	1	1	..	0	0	1
ALL AFRICA	..	..	..	..	..	..	..	..	..	..	..	..	..	..

Note: 1996 data are preliminary (see page 3).

4-5. Growth of money supply

	Level	Percentage annual change										Average annual percentage growth		
	1980	1980	1988	1989	1990	1991	1992	1993	1994	1995	1996	75-84	85-89	90-MR
SUB-SAHARAN AFRICA	..	16	13	16	9	12	11	11	34	15	..	13	15	-7
excluding South Africa	..	16	13	16	9	12	11	12	34	15	..	14	15	-7
excl. S. Africa & Nigeria	..	14	12	16	9	11	10	11	33	14	..	13	13	-6
Angola	..	..	..	..	..	..	..	..	..	..	..	..	..	..
Benin	44,681	32	16	17	24	12	10	-13	67	-13	..	17	-3	11
Botswana	91	10	30	25	16	5	-1	15	11	7	..	16	25	8
Burkina Faso	41,669	20	11	4	-2	6	1	12	39	25	..	13	10	12
Burundi	10,045	11	5	4	9	11	10	12	28	..	..	16	7	12
Cameroon	210,993	13	8	7	-7	3	-28	-14	35	-12	..	18	0	-6
Cape Verde	2,302	26	6	6	8	9	31	7	8	17	..	18	8	13
Central African Republic	34,628	32	-9	14	-4	-3	-4	16	74	8	..	15	2	12
Chad	26,478	-16	-13	8	0	4	-9	-28	32	43	..	12	-1	0
Comoros	..	..	14	16	6	-9	9	0	14	-4	..	..	9	3
Congo	54,560	37	-6	-1	25	-7	6	-20	40	0	..	16	-2	4
Côte d'Ivoire	438,730	1	-4	-12	3	-3	-4	1	62	18	..	11	-2	9
Djibouti	..	..	7	-7	9	16	11	4	3	-2	..	..	6	7
Equatorial Guinea	..	..	-42	39	-57	-16	35	-29	135	58	..	..	-8	7
Eritrea	..	..	..	..	..	..	..	..	..	..	..	..	..	..
Ethiopia	1,568	0	11	16	22	18	15	4	21	3	..	11	12	13
Gabon	94,879	10	21	5	6	8	-27	-3	42	12	..	11	-1	2
Gambia, The	61	6	8	22	14	33	11	6	-12	16	..	11	17	9
Ghana	6,087	30	45	53	11	14	53	28	50	33	..	35	39	28
Guinea	..	..	..	..	..	..	20	19	-3	9	..	..	..	10
Guinea-Bissau	..	..	84	31	61	34	83	27	58	47	..	..	52	41
Kenya	8,434	-8	1	13	27	15	47	27	13	4	..	12	11	21
Lesotho	48	..	40	12	8	18	12	23	12	7	..	..	17	14
Liberia	..	..	..	..	..	..	..	..	..	..	..	..	..	..
Madagascar	151,296	22	22	32	-4	31	22	12	57	15	..	14	19	21
Malawi	97	7	46	4	6	31	19	35	51	44	..	7	24	27
Mali	59,519	5	5	-4	-11	9	1	9	48	14	..	12	0	11
Mauritania	5,677	12	5	21	3	10	4	4	-5	-8	..	13	10	2
Mauritius	1,720	21	16	18	24	20	8	3	19	8	..	8	18	12
Mozambique	..	..	..	..	..	..	..	..	..	..	..	..	..	..
Namibia	..	..	..	..	..	34	22	46	15	8	54	..	..	24
Niger	64,594	13	12	7	-12	3	-10	11	15	9	..	16	1	3
Nigeria	9,227	50	44	24	30	41	56	53	47	17	..	19	16	36
Rwanda	12,026	7	3	-13	5	8	25	11	16	41	..	11	5	15
São Tomé and Principe	..	..	-6	..	..	..	..	..	..	..	..	..	6	..
Senegal	137,939	14	0	7	-12	4	2	-9	54	4	..	11	3	6
Seychelles	159	38	21	17	-1	23	10	14	-3	3	..	13	9	8
Sierra Leone	..	..	..	..	..	..	..	..	..	..	..	..	..	..
Somalia	2,783	19	51	208	..	..	..	..	..	..	..	22	62	..
South Africa	8,398	36	25	9	16	37	3	7	25	18	..	18	15	15
Sudan	1,097	31	44	68	46	60	101	76	55	67	..	26	37	53
Swaziland	50	22	14	18	17	7	20	14	7	17	..	13	19	13
Tanzania	13,346	28	37	30	35	23	34	33	33	..	..	19	29	27
Togo	55,336	5	-29	-2	19	4	-27	-18	105	38	..	15	-7	8
Uganda	140	31	125	60	50	50	68	26	35	15	..	34	84	34
Zaire	0	73	119	75	176	2,387	4,114	2,461	5,635	407	..	47	57	308
Zambia	519	0	63	52	61	78	..	..	45	62	..	11	45	..
Zimbabwe	633	37	28	20	28	23	6	95	18	52	..	12	16	29
NORTH AFRICA	..	21	13	9	17	8	9	5	11	7	..	22	12	10
Algeria	84,434	17	13	-1	8	20	16	19	8	7	..	19	7	13
Egypt, Arab Republic	6,775	56	13	9	17	8	9	12	11	9	..	22	12	10
Libya	2,899	29	-12	17	26	-4	16	4	13	6	..	15	3	9
Morocco	25,312	8	14	11	37	14	6	5	11	6	..	12	12	11
Tunisia	951	21	17	1	6	1	7	4	11	10	..	16	6	6
ALL AFRICA	..	20	13	13	11	11	10	11	25	10	..	14	14	-7

Note: 1996 data are preliminary (see page 3). 1980 levels are in millions of local currency. Group data are medians of individual country values in each year or period.

4-6. Discount rate

	Percentage											Annual average		
	1980	*1987*	*1988*	*1989*	*1990*	*1991*	*1992*	*1993*	*1994*	*1995*	*1996*	*75-84*	*85-89*	*90-MR*
SUB-SAHARAN AFRICA	8.5	9.0	9.5	11.0	11.0	11.7	12.5	12.0	12.5	13.2	..	8.4	9.8	12.9
excluding South Africa	8.5	9.0	9.5	11.0	11.0	11.3	12.5	11.8	12.0	13.0	..	8.3	9.8	12.8
excl. S. Africa & Nigeria	8.5	8.8	9.5	11.0	11.0	11.2	12.5	11.5	12.0	12.5	..	8.4	9.8	12.6
Angola	..	..	..	..	..	..	..	..	..	..	..	..	..	..
Benin	10.5	8.5	9.5	11.0	11.0	11.0	12.5	10.5	10.0	7.5	..	9.5	9.6	10.4
Botswana	5.8	8.5	6.5	6.5	8.5	12.0	14.3	14.3	13.5	13.0	..	8.3	7.9	12.6
Burkina Faso	10.5	8.5	9.5	11.0	11.0	11.0	12.5	10.5	10.0	7.5	..	9.5	9.6	10.4
Burundi	7.0	7.0	7.0	7.0	8.0	10.7	9.8	9.8	9.4	9.9	..	6.4	6.6	9.6
Cameroon	8.5	8.0	9.5	10.0	11.0	10.8	12.0	11.5	7.8	8.6	..	7.6	8.9	10.3
Cape Verde	..	..	..	..	..	..	..	..	..	..	..	..	..	..
Central African Republic	8.5	8.0	9.5	10.0	11.0	10.8	12.0	11.5	7.8	8.6	..	7.6	8.9	10.3
Chad	8.5	8.0	9.5	10.0	11.0	10.8	12.0	11.5	7.8	8.6	..	7.7	8.9	10.3
Comoros	..	8.5	8.5	..	..	..	..	..	..	..	..	10.0	9.3	..
Congo	8.5	8.0	9.5	10.0	11.0	10.8	12.0	11.5	7.8	8.6	..	7.6	8.9	10.3
Côte d'Ivoire	10.5	8.5	9.5	11.0	11.0	11.0	12.5	10.5	10.0	7.5	..	9.5	9.6	10.4
Djibouti	..	..	..	..	..	..	..	..	..	..	..	..	..	..
Equatorial Guinea	..	8.0	9.5	10.0	11.0	10.8	12.0	11.5	7.8	8.6	..	..	8.9	10.3
Eritrea	..	..	..	..	..	..	..	..	..	..	..	..	..	..
Ethiopia	..	3.0	3.0	3.0	3.0	3.0	5.3	12.0	12.0	12.0	..	..	4.2	7.9
Gabon	8.5	8.0	9.5	10.0	11.0	10.8	12.0	11.5	7.8	8.6	..	7.6	8.9	10.3
Gambia, The	8.0	21.0	19.0	15.0	16.5	15.5	17.5	13.5	13.5	14.0	..	7.6	18.0	15.1
Ghana	13.5	23.5	26.0	26.0	33.0	20.0	30.0	35.0	33.0	45.0	..	12.7	22.9	32.7
Guinea	..	10.0	10.0	13.0	15.0	19.0	19.0	17.0	17.0	18.0	..	..	10.5	17.5
Guinea-Bissau	..	..	..	..	42.0	42.0	45.5	41.0	26.0	39.0	54.0	..	..	41.4
Kenya	8.0	12.5	16.0	16.5	19.4	20.3	20.5	45.5	21.5	24.5	..	9.9	14.0	25.3
Lesotho	8.0	9.0	15.5	17.0	15.8	18.0	15.0	13.5	13.5	15.5	..	11.8	12.6	15.2
Liberia	..	..	..	..	..	..	..	..	..	..	..	..	..	..
Madagascar	5.5	11.5	11.5	..	..	..	..	..	..	..	..	8.0	11.5	..
Malawi	10.0	14.0	11.0	11.0	14.0	13.0	20.0	25.0	40.0	50.0	..	8.5	11.6	27.0
Mali	10.5	8.5	9.5	11.0	11.0	11.0	12.5	10.5	10.0	7.5	..	9.5	9.6	10.4
Mauritania	6.0	6.5	6.5	7.0	7.0	7.0	7.0	..	..	..	..	5.5	6.6	7.0
Mauritius	10.5	10.0	10.0	12.0	12.0	11.3	8.3	8.3	13.8	11.4	..	9.5	10.8	10.9
Mozambique	..	..	..	..	..	..	..	..	..	..	..	..	..	..
Namibia	..	..	..	..	..	20.5	16.5	14.5	15.5	17.5	17.8	..	..	17.0
Niger	10.5	8.5	8.5	11.0	11.0	11.0	12.5	10.5	10.0	7.5	..	9.5	9.4	10.4
Nigeria	6.0	12.8	12.8	18.5	18.5	15.5	17.5	26.0	13.5	13.5	..	5.9	12.8	17.4
Rwanda	9.0	9.0	9.0	9.0	14.0	14.0	11.0	11.0	11.0	16.0	16.0	7.4	9.0	13.3
São Tomé and Principe	..	..	..	..	..	..	..	..	..	..	..	..	..	..
Senegal	10.5	8.5	9.5	11.0	11.0	11.0	12.5	10.5	10.0	7.5	..	9.5	9.6	10.4
Seychelles	..	..	..	..	..	..	..	..	..	..	..	..	..	..
Sierra Leone	12.0	16.0	16.0	16.0	55.0	..	..	..	..	..	..	10.2	15.6	55.0
Somalia	4.0	12.0	45.0	45.0	..	..	..	..	..	..	..	5.2	25.2	..
South Africa	6.5	9.5	14.5	18.0	18.0	17.0	14.0	12.0	13.0	15.0	17.0	11.1	12.9	15.1
Sudan	..	..	..	..	..	..	..	..	..	..	..	..	..	..
Swaziland	7.0	9.0	11.0	12.0	12.0	13.0	12.0	11.0	12.0	15.0	..	11.1	10.8	12.5
Tanzania	4.8	11.3	12.7	15.2	..	..	..	14.5	34.6	48.4	..	4.5	10.0	32.5
Togo	10.5	8.5	9.5	11.0	11.0	11.0	12.5	10.5	10.0	7.5	..	9.5	9.6	10.4
Uganda	8.0	31.0	45.0	55.0	50.0	46.0	41.0	24.0	15.0	13.3	15.9	13.7	38.2	29.3
Zaire	12.0	29.0	37.0	50.0	45.0	55.0	55.0	95.0	145.0	125.0	..	14.7	33.6	86.7
Zambia	6.5	15.0	15.0	..	..	..	47.0	72.5	..	..	..	7.5	21.3	59.8
Zimbabwe	4.5	9.0	9.0	9.0	10.3	20.0	..	28.5	29.5	29.5	27.0	6.3	9.0	24.1
NORTH AFRICA	5.9	8.9	8.9	11.4	11.9	11.9	11.4	8.9	8.9	11.2	..	6.0	9.4	10.7
Algeria	..	..	..	..	..	..	..	..	..	..	..	..	..	..
Egypt, Arab Republic	11.0	13.0	13.0	14.0	14.0	20.0	18.4	16.5	14.0	13.5	..	9.7	13.2	16.1
Libya	5.0	5.0	5.0	5.0	5.0	5.0	5.0	5.0	..	..	..	5.0	5.0	5.0
Morocco	6.0	8.5	8.5	..	..	..	..	..	7.0	..	..	5.6	8.5	7.0
Tunisia	5.8	9.3	9.3	11.4	11.9	11.9	11.4	8.9	8.9	8.9	..	6.1	9.7	10.3
ALL AFRICA	8.5	9.0	9.5	11.0	11.0	11.9	12.5	11.8	12.0	13.2	..	8.2	9.8	12.8

Note: 1996 data are preliminary (see page 3). Group data are medians of individual country values in each year or period.

4-7. Real discount rate

	Percentage											Annual average		
	1980	1987	1988	1989	1990	1991	1992	1993	1994	1995	1996	75-84	85-89	90-MR
SUB-SAHARAN AFRICA	-3.6	-0.6	1.5	3.0	3.7	2.1	3.5	5.5	-2.0	-0.3	..	-4.0	0.9	2.9
excluding South Africa	-3.5	-0.1	1.9	3.1	3.8	2.2	3.5	6.1	-3.4	-0.4	..	-4.3	1.2	2.8
excl. S. Africa & Nigeria	-3.4	-0.6	2.4	3.1	3.7	3.0	5.4	6.6	-2.0	-0.3	..	-4.1	1.1	3.5
Angola	..	..	..	..	..	..	..	..	..	..	..	..	..	..
Benin	..	..	..	..	..	..	..	..	..	..	..	..	..	..
Botswana	-6.9	-1.2	-1.7	-4.5	-2.6	0.2	-1.7	-0.1	2.7	2.3	..	-3.1	-1.5	0.1
Burkina Faso	-1.5	11.5	5.2	11.3	11.9	8.3	14.8	9.9	-12.1	0.1	..	-0.5	8.6	5.5
Burundi	4.4	-0.1	2.4	-4.2	0.9	1.6	7.8	0.1	-4.7	-7.9	..	-5.4	0.9	-0.4
Cameroon	-1.0	-4.5	7.7	11.9	9.8	10.7	12.0	15.2	-20.2	-4.7	..	-3.8	3.1	3.8
Cape Verde	..	..	..	..	..	..	..	..	..	..	..	..	..	..
Central African Republic	..	16.0	14.0	9.1	11.4	13.2	13.6	14.8	-13.5	-8.9	..	1.2	8.7	5.1
Chad	..	14.9	-5.2	14.5	11.2	6.3	15.6	20.0	-23.3	-0.4	..	-9.4	10.4	4.9
Comoros	..	..	..	..	..	..	..	..	..	..	..	..	..	..
Congo	1.1	5.7	5.5	5.6	16.6	1.5	9.8	9.3	-28.1	-10.5	..	-3.4	5.1	-0.2
Côte d'Ivoire	-3.7	1.5	2.4	9.8	11.9	9.2	7.9	47.8	-12.8	-5.9	..	-2.1	4.2	9.7
Djibouti	..	..	..	..	..	..	..	..	..	..	..	..	..	..
Equatorial Guinea	..	24.0	7.0	3.9	9.8	14.4	20.6	7.2	..	..	..	..	16.6	13.0
Eritrea	..	..	..	..	..	..	..	..	..	..	..	..	..	..
Ethiopia	..	5.6	-3.8	-4.5	-2.0	-24.1	-4.8	8.2	4.1	1.8	..	..	0.8	-2.8
Gabon	-3.4	9.0	20.0	3.1	3.0	5.1	17.8	22.4	-20.9	-1.2	..	-4.9	7.1	4.4
Gambia, The	1.1	-2.0	6.5	6.2	3.8	6.4	7.3	6.6	11.6	6.6	..	-4.2	-3.1	7.0
Ghana	-24.4	-11.7	-4.1	0.6	-3.1	1.6	18.2	8.0	6.5	-16.8	..	-30.2	-2.2	2.4
Guinea	..	..	..	..	..	..	..	..	..	..	..	..	..	..
Guinea-Bissau	..	..	..	..	6.8	-9.9	-14.2	-4.8	9.4	-4.4	..	..	..	-2.9
Kenya	-5.1	4.5	4.3	3.1	3.3	0.4	-7.0	-0.2	-5.8	23.5	..	-3.4	3.8	2.4
Lesotho	-6.6	-2.5	3.6	2.0	3.7	0.3	-1.9	0.3	4.9	5.7	..	-1.6	-1.0	2.2
Liberia	..	..	..	..	..	..	..	..	..	..	..	..	..	..
Madagascar	-10.8	-3.0	-12.1	..	..	..	..	..	..	..	..	-5.3	-4.2	..
Malawi	..	-8.9	-17.1	-1.3	2.0	0.3	-2.2	4.5	4.0	-18.2	..	-3.2	-5.9	-1.6
Mali	..	..	..	..	..	..	..	..	..	..	..	..	..	..
Mauritania	..	-1.5	5.1	-5.3	0.4	1.3	-2.8	..	..	..	..	..	-0.6	-0.4
Mauritius	-22.2	9.4	0.8	-0.6	-1.3	4.0	3.5	-2.0	6.0	5.1	..	-3.4	4.6	2.5
Mozambique	..	..	..	..	..	..	..	..	..	..	..	..	..	..
Namibia	..	..	..	..	..	7.7	-1.0	5.5	4.3	6.8	..	..	..	4.6
Niger	0.2	16.3	10.0	14.2	11.9	20.4	17.8	11.9	-19.1	-2.8	..	-2.1	12.8	6.7
Nigeria	-3.6	1.3	-27.0	-21.2	10.4	2.2	-18.7	-19.8	-27.7	-34.3	..	-11.7	-8.1	-14.7
Rwanda	1.6	4.7	5.8	7.9	9.4	-4.7	1.3	-1.2	..	..	8.0	-3.6	7.2	2.6
São Tomé and Principe	..	..	..	..	..	..	..	..	..	..	..	..	..	..
Senegal	1.6	13.2	11.5	10.5	10.6	13.0	12.6	11.2	-16.9	-0.3	..	-1.2	7.0	5.0
Seychelles	..	..	..	..	..	..	..	..	..	..	..	..	..	..
Sierra Leone	-0.8	-58.4	-13.6	-27.9	-26.5	..	..	..	..	..	..	-11.9	-34.2	-26.5
Somalia	-34.5	-12.6	-20.3	..	..	..	..	..	..	..	..	-18.9	-17.3	..
South Africa	-6.4	-5.7	1.5	2.9	3.1	1.5	0.1	2.1	3.7	5.9	8.9	-1.4	-2.4	3.6
Sudan	..	..	..	..	..	..	..	..	..	..	..	..	..	..
Swaziland	-9.8	-3.9	-1.2	3.4	0.9	2.0	3.5	-5.2	-2.0	0.3	..	-2.4	-2.4	-0.1
Tanzania	-19.5	-14.3	-14.1	-8.5	..	..	..	-8.6	0.4	16.5	..	-13.2	-15.7	2.8
Togo	-1.6	8.4	9.7	11.9	9.9	10.6	11.0	11.6	..	..	..	-0.8	9.4	10.8
Uganda	..	-56.3	-51.0	-4.0	12.7	14.0	-7.5	16.9	4.8	4.4	8.0	-23.2	-42.2	7.6
Zaire	-23.6	-27.8	-19.9	-26.5	-20.0	-93.1	-96.3	-90.7	-99.0	-65.0	..	-25.6	-17.0	-77.3
Zambia	..	-21.8	-23.8	..	..	..	-44.7	-39.1	..	..	..	..	-20.7	-41.9
Zimbabwe	-0.9	-3.1	1.5	-3.4	-6.1	-2.7	..	0.7	5.9	5.6	4.6	-5.5	-1.8	1.3
NORTH AFRICA	-5.6	0.9	1.9	-1.3	1.3	1.8	4.7	4.3	4.0	0.3	..	-3.4	0.4	2.7
Algeria	..	..	..	..	..	..	..	..	..	..	..	..	..	..
Egypt, Arab Republic	-8.0	-5.6	-4.0	-6.0	-2.4	0.2	4.2	3.9	5.4	-1.9	..	-3.1	-4.7	1.6
Libya	..	..	..	..	..	..	..	..	..	..	..	..	..	..
Morocco	-3.1	5.6	6.0	..	..	..	..	..	1.8	..	..	-3.9	3.0	1.8
Tunisia	..	0.9	1.9	3.4	5.0	3.4	5.2	4.7	4.0	2.5	..	-1.7	2.2	4.1
ALL AFRICA	-3.6	-0.1	1.7	3.0	3.7	2.1	3.8	4.7	1.1	-0.3	..	-4.1	1.0	3.3

Note: 1996 data are preliminary (see page 3). Real discount rate in each year is the nominal discount rate deflated by the annual change in the CPI.

4-8. Commercial bank lending rate

	Percentage											Annual average		
	1980	*1987*	*1988*	*1989*	*1990*	*1991*	*1992*	*1993*	*1994*	*1995*	*1996*	*75-84*	*85-89*	*90-MR*
SUB-SAHARAN AFRICA	12.0	13.5	13.6	15.1	18.3	18.1	17.6	17.5	17.5	18.0	..	12.1	14.0	19.0
excluding South Africa	12.0	13.5	13.6	15.1	18.0	18.1	17.5	17.5	17.5	18.3	..	12.0	14.0	19.9
excl. S. Africa & Nigeria	12.3	13.5	13.6	15.1	17.0	17.9	17.3	17.5	17.5	18.0	..	12.2	14.0	19.6
Angola	..	..	..	..	..	..	..	..	..	..	..	..	..	..
Benin	14.5	13.5	13.6	15.1	16.0	16.0	16.8	..	..	..	..	13.8	14.0	16.3
Botswana	8.5	10.0	7.8	7.7	7.9	11.8	14.0	14.9	13.9	14.3	..	13.5	9.6	12.8
Burkina Faso	14.5	13.5	13.6	15.1	16.0	16.0	16.8	..	..	..	..	13.8	14.0	16.3
Burundi	12.0	12.0	12.0	12.0	12.3	12.8	13.7	13.8	14.2	15.3	..	12.0	12.0	13.7
Cameroon	13.0	13.0	13.5	15.0	18.5	18.1	17.8	17.5	17.5	16.0	..	13.0	13.9	17.6
Cape Verde	6.5	10.0	10.0	10.0	10.0	10.0	10.0	10.0	10.7	12.0	..	6.5	10.0	10.4
Central African Republic	10.5	11.4	12.3	13.0	18.5	18.1	17.8	17.5	17.5	16.0	..	11.1	12.2	17.6
Chad	11.0	10.5	10.8	11.5	18.5	18.1	17.8	17.5	17.5	16.0	..	10.7	11.1	17.6
Comoros	..	13.0	13.0	..	..	..	..	..	..	..	..	15.0	14.0	..
Congo	11.0	11.1	11.8	12.5	18.5	18.1	17.8	17.5	17.5	16.0	..	11.3	11.8	17.6
Côte d'Ivoire	14.5	13.5	13.6	15.1	16.0	16.0	16.8	..	..	..	..	13.8	14.0	16.3
Djibouti	..	..	..	..	..	..	3.0	2.6	..	..	..	..	..	2.8
Equatorial Guinea	..	14.1	14.8	15.5	18.5	18.1	17.8	17.5	17.5	16.0	..	..	14.8	17.6
Eritrea	..	..	..	..	..	..	..	..	..	..	..	..	..	..
Ethiopia	..	6.0	6.0	6.0	6.0	6.0	8.0	14.0	14.3	15.1	..	..	6.8	10.6
Gabon	12.5	11.1	11.8	12.5	18.5	18.1	17.8	17.5	17.5	16.0	..	11.8	11.9	17.6
Gambia, The	15.0	27.9	29.5	26.8	26.5	26.5	26.8	26.1	25.0	25.0	..	16.7	25.4	26.0
Ghana	19.0	25.5	25.6	..	..	..	..	..	..	..	..	19.3	23.1	..
Guinea	..	15.0	15.0	17.3	21.2	24.5	27.0	24.5	22.0	21.5	..	..	15.8	23.4
Guinea-Bissau	..	18.0	30.0	38.3	45.8	47.0	50.3	63.6	36.3	32.9	51.8	..	26.1	46.8
Kenya	10.6	14.0	15.0	17.3	18.8	19.0	21.1	30.0	36.2	28.8	..	11.8	14.9	25.6
Lesotho	11.0	11.1	13.7	18.8	20.4	20.0	18.3	15.8	14.3	16.4	..	15.2	15.3	17.5
Liberia	18.4	13.6	13.4	13.8	..	..	..	..	14.5	..	..	19.9	14.9	14.5
Madagascar	..	..	..	..	..	..	..	..	..	..	..	..	..	..
Malawi	16.7	19.5	22.3	23.0	21.0	20.0	22.0	29.5	31.0	47.3	..	17.7	20.4	28.5
Mali	14.5	13.5	13.6	15.1	16.0	16.0	16.8	..	..	..	..	13.8	14.0	16.3
Mauritania	12.0	12.0	12.0	10.0	10.0	10.0	10.0	..	..	..	..	12.0	11.6	10.0
Mauritius	..	14.1	15.0	16.1	18.0	17.8	17.1	16.6	18.9	20.8	..	13.5	14.7	18.2
Mozambique	..	..	..	..	..	..	..	..	..	..	..	..	..	..
Namibia	..	..	..	..	..	23.4	20.2	18.0	17.1	18.5	19.2	..	..	19.4
Niger	14.5	13.5	13.6	15.1	16.0	16.0	16.8	..	..	..	..	13.8	14.0	16.3
Nigeria	8.4	14.0	16.6	20.4	25.3	20.0	24.8	31.7	20.5	20.2	..	8.0	14.1	23.7
Rwanda	13.5	13.0	12.0	12.0	13.2	19.0	16.7	15.0	..	..	..	13.3	13.0	16.0
São Tomé and Principe	..	..	..	..	..	..	..	..	..	..	..	..	..	..
Senegal	14.5	13.5	13.6	15.1	16.0	16.0	16.8	..	..	..	..	13.8	14.0	16.3
Seychelles	..	..	..	15.5	15.6	15.6	15.6	15.7	15.6	..	..	..	15.5	15.6
Sierra Leone	11.0	28.5	28.0	29.7	52.5	56.3	62.8	50.5	27.3	28.8	32.1	12.7	24.1	44.3
Somalia	7.5	22.0	33.7	..	..	..	..	..	..	..	..	8.9	23.8	..
South Africa	9.5	12.5	15.3	19.8	21.0	20.3	18.9	16.2	15.6	17.9	19.5	14.1	16.7	18.5
Sudan	..	..	..	..	..	..	..	..	..	..	..	..	..	..
Swaziland	9.5	11.9	15.0	14.5	14.5	16.3	15.0	14.0	15.0	18.0	..	13.2	14.2	15.5
Tanzania	11.5	27.5	29.6	31.0	..	..	..	31.0	39.0	42.8	..	11.4	23.8	37.6
Togo	14.5	13.5	14.5	16.0	16.0	16.0	17.5	..	..	..	..	13.8	14.4	16.5
Uganda	10.8	34.7	35.0	40.0	38.7	34.4	..	..	..	20.2	..	15.2	33.4	31.1
Zaire	..	..	..	..	..	..	..	..	..	..	..	..	..	..
Zambia	9.5	21.2	18.4	18.4	35.1	..	54.6	113.3	..	..	..	9.7	20.8	67.7
Zimbabwe	17.5	13.0	13.0	13.0	11.7	15.5	..	36.3	34.9	34.7	..	20.3	13.8	26.6
NORTH AFRICA	7.1	10.0	9.4	9.0	9.0	8.0	13.7	12.6	13.3	16.5	..	7.5	9.2	12.2
Algeria	..	..	..	..	..	..	..	..	..	..	..	..	..	..
Egypt, Arab Republic	13.3	16.3	17.0	18.3	19.0	..	20.3	18.3	16.5	16.5	..	12.5	16.3	18.1
Libya	7.0	7.0	7.0	7.0	7.0	7.0	7.0	7.0	..	..	..	7.0	7.0	7.0
Morocco	7.0	9.0	9.0	9.0	9.0	9.0	..	..	10.0	..	..	7.0	8.7	9.3
Tunisia	7.3	11.1	9.9	..	..	..	..	..	..	..	..	7.9	9.9	..
ALL AFRICA	11.8	13.5	13.6	15.1	18.0	17.9	17.6	17.5	17.5	17.9	..	11.6	14.0	18.9

Note: 1996 data are preliminary (see page 3). Group data are medians of individual country values in each year or period.

4-9. Commercial bank deposit rate

	Percentage											Annual average		
	1980	*1987*	*1988*	*1989*	*1990*	*1991*	*1992*	*1993*	*1994*	*1995*	*1996*	*75-84*	*85-89*	*90-MR*
SUB-SAHARAN AFRICA	6.2	7.3	7.8	8.4	7.5	8.8	7.8	9.6	10.2	11.5	..	6.5	7.8	9.9
excluding South Africa	6.2	7.2	7.6	8.0	7.5	8.1	7.8	9.5	10.0	11.2	..	6.5	7.6	9.7
excl. S. Africa & Nigeria	6.2	7.2	7.4	7.8	7.5	7.5	7.8	9.0	9.6	10.8	..	6.6	7.5	9.4
Angola	..	..	..	..	..	..	..	..	..	..	..	..	..	..
Benin	6.2	5.3	5.3	6.4	7.0	7.0	7.8	..	..	..	..	6.5	6.1	7.3
Botswana	5.0	7.5	5.0	5.6	6.1	11.4	12.5	13.5	10.4	10.0	..	9.3	7.2	10.6
Burkina Faso	6.2	5.3	5.3	6.4	7.0	7.0	7.8	..	..	..	..	6.5	6.1	7.3
Burundi	2.5	5.3	4.0	..	..	..	..	..	..	..	..	3.4	4.9	..
Cameroon	7.5	7.1	7.2	7.5	7.5	7.5	7.5	7.8	8.1	5.5	..	7.3	7.3	7.3
Cape Verde	..	4.0	4.0	4.0	4.0	4.0	4.0	4.0	4.0	5.0	..	..	4.0	4.2
Central African Republic	5.5	7.2	7.4	7.5	7.5	7.5	7.5	7.8	8.1	5.5	..	6.4	7.4	7.3
Chad	5.5	5.3	4.3	4.3	7.5	7.5	7.5	7.8	8.1	5.5	..	5.3	5.0	7.3
Comoros	..	6.5	6.5	..	..	..	..	..	..	..	..	7.5	7.0	..
Congo	6.5	7.8	7.8	8.0	7.5	7.5	7.5	7.8	8.1	5.5	..	6.5	8.0	7.3
Côte d'Ivoire	6.2	5.3	5.3	6.4	7.0	7.0	7.8	..	..	..	..	6.5	6.1	7.3
Djibouti	..	..	..	..	..	..	3.0	2.6	..	..	..	..	..	2.8
Equatorial Guinea	..	7.9	6.3	6.5	7.5	7.5	7.5	7.8	8.1	5.5	..	..	7.3	7.3
Eritrea	..	..	..	..	..	..	..	..	..	..	..	..	..	..
Ethiopia	..	6.7	6.7	6.7	2.4	5.0	3.6	11.5	11.5	11.5	..	..	6.5	7.6
Gabon	7.5	7.9	8.2	8.8	7.5	7.5	7.5	7.8	8.1	5.5	..	7.4	8.1	7.3
Gambia, The	5.0	15.8	15.0	12.9	11.3	12.7	13.8	13.0	12.6	12.5	..	7.1	13.9	12.7
Ghana	11.5	17.6	16.5	..	..	21.3	16.3	23.6	23.1	28.7	..	12.0	16.7	22.6
Guinea	..	15.0	16.8	19.5	21.0	22.0	23.0	19.8	18.0	17.5	..	..	17.1	20.2
Guinea-Bissau	..	..	23.0	28.0	32.7	36.0	39.3	53.9	28.7	26.5	47.3	..	25.5	37.8
Kenya	5.8	10.3	10.3	12.0	13.7	..	..	..	..	13.6	..	7.7	11.0	13.6
Lesotho	..	7.0	9.6	12.8	13.0	13.0	10.6	8.1	8.4	13.3	..	10.3	10.0	11.1
Liberia	10.3	5.9	5.4	6.8	..	..	..	..	6.3	..	..	10.4	6.9	6.3
Madagascar	..	..	..	..	..	..	..	..	..	..	..	..	..	..
Malawi	7.9	14.3	13.5	12.8	12.1	12.5	16.5	21.8	25.0	37.3	..	9.8	13.2	20.9
Mali	6.2	5.3	5.3	6.4	7.0	7.0	7.8	..	..	..	..	6.5	6.1	7.3
Mauritania	..	6.0	6.0	5.0	5.0	5.0	5.0	..	..	..	..	5.5	6.2	5.0
Mauritius	..	9.4	10.0	11.1	12.6	12.3	10.1	8.4	11.0	12.2	..	10.7	9.9	11.1
Mozambique	..	..	..	..	..	..	..	..	..	..	..	..	..	..
Namibia	..	..	..	..	..	12.8	11.4	9.6	9.2	10.8	12.6	..	..	11.1
Niger	6.2	5.3	5.3	6.4	7.0	7.0	7.8	..	..	..	..	6.5	6.1	7.3
Nigeria	5.3	13.1	13.0	14.7	19.8	14.9	18.0	23.2	13.1	13.5	..	5.1	11.8	17.1
Rwanda	6.3	6.3	6.3	6.3	6.9	8.8	7.7	5.0	..	..	10.9	5.1	6.3	7.9
São Tomé and Principe	3.0	..	..	..	..	..	..	..	..	..	..	3.0	..	..
Senegal	6.2	5.3	5.3	6.4	7.0	7.0	7.8	..	..	..	..	6.5	6.1	7.3
Seychelles	..	10.0	10.0	9.6	9.5	9.6	9.6	9.5	..	..	..	9.1	9.8	9.5
Sierra Leone	9.2	12.7	16.3	20.0	40.5	47.8	54.7	27.0	11.6	7.0	14.0	9.2	14.9	28.9
Somalia	4.5	16.3	20.6	25.0	..	..	..	..	..	..	..	5.5	18.2	..
South Africa	5.5	8.7	13.5	18.1	18.9	17.3	13.8	11.5	11.1	13.5	..	10.0	13.7	14.4
Sudan	6.0	..	..	..	..	..	..	..	..	..	..	9.2	..	..
Swaziland	4.5	4.8	9.2	8.9	8.9	10.9	9.0	7.4	8.0	10.3	..	9.0	7.8	9.1
Tanzania	4.0	15.8	17.5	17.0	..	..	..	..	..	24.6	..	4.0	12.6	24.6
Togo	6.2	5.3	5.3	6.4	7.0	7.0	7.8	..	..	..	..	6.5	6.1	7.3
Uganda	6.8	20.0	21.5	32.2	31.3	31.2	35.8	16.3	10.0	7.6	..	9.9	23.4	22.0
Zaire	..	..	..	..	..	..	..	..	..	..	..	..	..	..
Zambia	7.0	13.2	11.4	11.4	25.7	..	48.5	..	..	..	..	6.2	13.8	37.1
Zimbabwe	3.5	9.6	9.7	8.9	8.8	14.1	..	29.4	26.8	25.9	21.6	6.6	9.7	21.1
NORTH AFRICA	5.0	7.9	7.9	8.5	8.5	8.5	8.8	8.8	11.8	10.9	..	4.9	7.7	9.5
Algeria	..	..	..	..	..	..	..	..	..	..	..	..	..	..
Egypt, Arab Republic	8.3	11.0	11.0	11.7	12.0	12.0	12.0	12.0	11.8	10.9	..	8.0	11.1	11.8
Libya	5.1	5.5	5.5	5.5	5.5	5.5	5.5	5.5	..	..	..	4.7	5.5	5.5
Morocco	4.9	8.5	8.5	8.5	8.5	8.5	..	..	..	..	..	5.6	8.4	8.5
Tunisia	2.5	7.2	7.4	..	..	..	..	..	..	..	..	3.4	6.7	..
ALL AFRICA	6.2	7.4	7.8	8.5	7.5	8.6	7.8	9.6	10.4	11.2	..	6.3	7.9	9.9

Note: 1996 data are preliminary (see page 3). Group data are medians of individual country values in each year or period.

Figure 4-1. Credit to private and public sectors as a share of GDP, 1996*

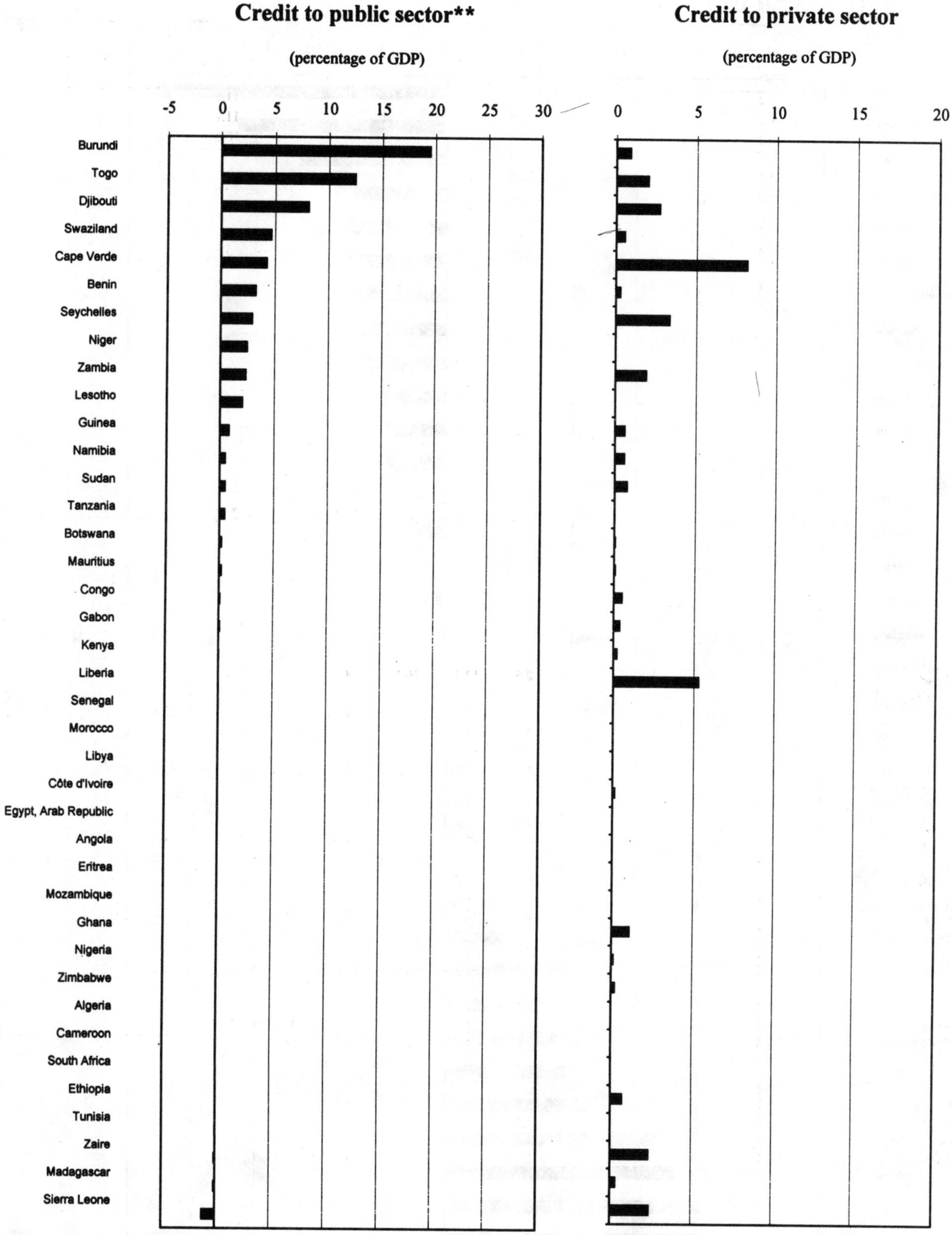

* Or most recent year available

** Sorted by credit to public sector.

Note: Nigeria's ratios are distorted because of official exchange rate over-valuation affecting oil exports and oil value added .

Figure 4-2. Real discount rate, average 1990-96*

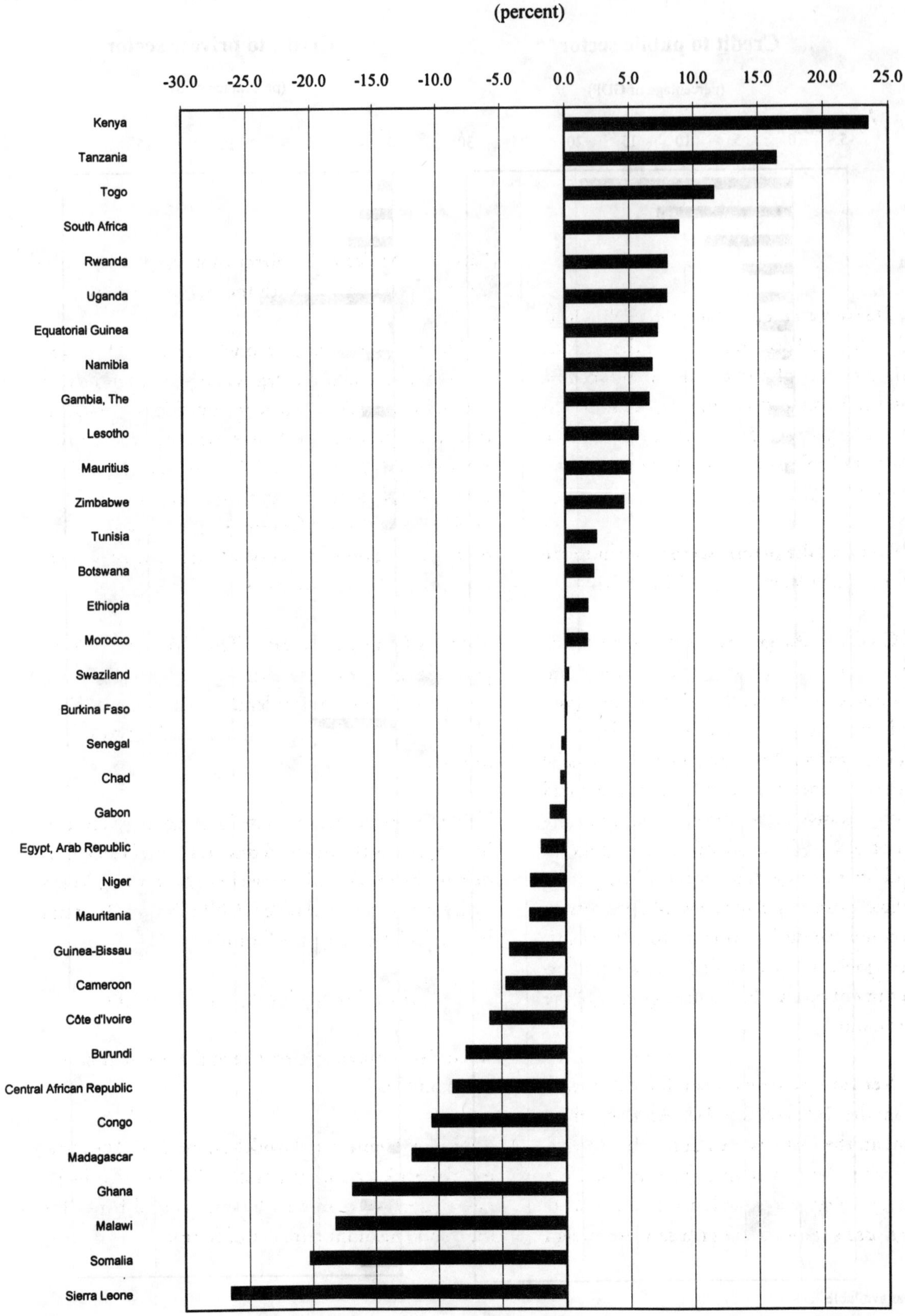

* Or most recent year available

Technical Notes

Tables

Table 4-1. Domestic credit. Domestic credit (IMF, *IFS*, line 32) includes all domestic assets of the banking system. It is the sum of the claims on the central government (net), on official entities, and on the private sector. Domestic credit is made up of credit to the private sector (Table 4-2) and credit to the government (Table 4-3).

Table 4-2. Credit to the private sector. Credit to the private sector is taken from IMF, *IFS*, line 32d.

Table 4-3. Credit to the government. Credit to the government sector is taken from IMF, *IFS*, line 32an. Negative numbers for net claims on the central government indicate that government is a net depositor to the banking system. The government's financial position with the monetary system is always presented on a net basis because its recourse to the monetary system cannot always be analyzed meaningfully in terms of liquidity preferences or by considering debtor and creditor positions separately. Movements in net claims on the central government (that is, claims or credits less government deposits) indicate the impact of government operations on the liquidity of the rest of the economy.

Table 4-4. Net foreign assets. Data for net foreign assets are from the IMF, *IFS*, line 31n. As for credit to the government, the financial position of the foreign sector with the monetary system is presented on a net basis for the same reason as noted above. Movements in net foreign assets (that is, foreign assets less foreign liabilities) indicate the direct monetary impact of a country's transactions with the rest of the world.

Table 4-5. Growth of money supply. This table shows the annual percentage change in money (M1), defined as the sum of currency outside of banks and demand deposits other than those of the central government (IMF, *IFS*, line 34). The presentation of the money supply in the form of growth rates rather than levels reflects the importance from the point of view of macroeconomic stability of the rate of growth rather than the stock of money.

Table 4-6. Discount rate. The discount rate reported here is the nominal interest rate at which the monetary authorities lend to (or discount eligible paper from) deposit money banks (IMF, *IFS*, line 60).

Table 4-7. Real discount rate. The real discount rate in each year is the nominal discount rate (Table 4-6) deflated by the annual change in inflation as reflected by the consumer price index (CPI) (Table 3-3). It has been calculated using the formula:

$$\left\{ [l + (i/100)] \,/\, [(\pi_t/\pi_{t-1})] - 1 \right\} x\ 100$$

where i is nominal interest rate and π is inflation rate based on the CPI.

Table 4-8. Commercial bank lending rate. The commercial bank lending rate (IMF, *IFS*, line 60p) is the rate charged to borrowers by commercial banks for short- and medium-term use of funds.

Table 4-9. Commercial bank deposit rate. The deposit rate (IMF, *IFS*, line 60l) is the rate paid to depositors on time savings and demand deposits by deposit money banks and similar financial institutions.

Figures

The following indicators have been used to derive the figures in this chapter.

Figure 4-1. Credit to the private sector (Table 4-2); credit to the public sector (Table 4-3); gross domestic product (Table 2-5).

Figure 4-2. Real discount rate (Table 4-7).

Methodology used for regional aggregations and period averages in chapter 4

	Aggregations[a]		*Period averages*[b]	
Table	*(7)*	*(8)*	*(1)*	*(2)*
4-1	x			x
4-2	x			x
4-3	x			x
4-4		x	x	
4-5	x			x
4-6	x		x	
4-7	x		x	
4-8	x		x	
4-9	x		x	

Note: Regional aggregations are shown in the rows for Sub-Saharan Africa, North Africa, and All Africa. Period averages are shown in the last three columns. This table shows only the methodologies used in this chapter. The definitions of the methodologies used throughout the book are given below.

a. Regional aggregations: (1) simple total; (2) simple total of the first indicator divided by the simple total of the second indicator (same country coverage); (3) simple total of the gap-filled indicator; (4) simple total of the gap-filled main indicator divided by the simple total of the gap-filled secondary indicator; (5) simple total of the first gap-filled main indicator less the simple total of the second gap-filled main indicator, all divided by the simple total of the secondary indicator; (6) weighted total (by population); (7) median; (8) no aggregation; (9) simple arithmetic mean.

b. Period averages: (1) arithmetic mean (using the same series as shown in the table, i.e., ratio if the rest of the table is shown as ratio, level if the rest of the table is shown as level, growth rate if the rest of the table is shown as growth rate); (2) least-squares growth rate (using main indicator); (3) least-squares growth rate (using main indicator in constant terms, with the rest of the table in current terms).

5

External Sector

The external sector provides data on economic and financial relations between African countries and the rest of the world, with detailed accounting of commodity trade, one of the principal components of the current account within the balance of payments framework. Commodity trade and price data can also provide a partial basis for analyzing Africa's constraints and performance in the international marketplace, including its terms of trade. Commodity exports are a major source of foreign exchange. Other sources of foreign exchange include receipts from factor and nonfactor services, borrowing from abroad, incoming foreign investment, and foreign transfers and grants.

The balance of payments is a system of accounts, covering a given period, that is intended to record systematically: flows of real resources, including the services of the original factors of production, between the domestic economy of a country and the rest of the world; changes in the country's foreign assets and liabilities that arise from economic transactions; and transfer payments, which are the counterpart of real resources or financial claims provided to, or received from, the rest of the world that carry no provision for repayment.

The tables provide gross entries for goods and services and net entries for unrequited transfers (official and private) and other financial flows; a table for current account balance as traditionally defined (with transfers above the line) is also shown. The information is presented for broad aggregates; fuller detail can be found in the IMF's *Balance of Payments Manual* (1993) and *Balance of Payments Yearbooks*.

Unit values for exports (f.o.b.) and imports (c.i.f.) measure changes in the aggregate price level of a country's exports and imports of goods and nonfactor services over time. Unit values reflect average price changes for broad groups of commodities, rather than for any single commodity. The terms of trade indicate relative movements in export and import unit values (here, they are based on goods and nonfactor services from the national accounts). If the prices of exports rise while the prices of imports rise more slowly, stay constant, or decline, the same quantity of exports "buys" a bigger quantity of imports. The effect of such price changes is equivalent to an increase in the real value of output (or increased productivity in value terms) of the export sector. Were import prices to rise more quickly than export prices, the reverse would be true. Export figures for specific commodities show physical quantities rather than value in either current or constant prices. Most of the key nonagricultural primary commodities are exported from a few countries with substantial mineral resources. Variations in export prices and earnings for the five major oil-exporting countries in Sub-Saharan Africa (which in the 1980s have accounted for about half of Sub- Saharan export earnings) have dominated trends in this region as a whole.

5-1. Merchandise exports, f.o.b.

	Millions of U.S. dollars (current prices)											*Average annual percentage growth*		
	1980	*1987*	*1988*	*1989*	*1990*	*1991*	*1992*	*1993*	*1994*	*1995*	*1996*	*75-84*	*85-89*	*90-MR*
SUB-SAHARAN AFRICA	78,989	54,607	56,537	61,407	62,950	60,097	60,716	57,404	57,941	65,623	..	6.9	2.9	0.0
excluding South Africa	53,414	33,523	34,102	39,029	45,948	42,658	42,246	39,177	39,700	46,754	53,359	5.3	0.6	2.4
excl. S. Africa & Nigeria	26,575	25,993	27,061	29,202	31,977	30,493	29,897	27,842	30,157	35,838	39,136	5.9	3.8	3.0
Angola	..	2,322	2,520	3,014	3,884	3,449	3,833	2,900	3,002	3,519	..	..	7.0	-0.8
Benin	222	366	376	215	287	337	371	341	308	405	424	7.1	6.0	7.6
Botswana	545	1,592	1,478	1,820	1,753	1,903	1,725	1,725	1,880	1,848	..	20.1	24.4	0.3
Burkina Faso	161	193	238	205	283	269	238	263	188	243	305	8.1	11.1	1.3
Burundi	66	98	124	93	73	90	77	73	124	116	60	..	-1.0	0.2
Cameroon	1,418	1,729	1,670	1,837	1,906	2,159	1,937	1,651	1,432	1,662	1,721	16.9	-5.0	-3.0
Cape Verde	9	8	3	8	6	4	4	4	5	8	10	15.5	2.9	3.8
Central African Republic	147	129	134	148	151	126	116	132	151	173	135	8.6	3.9	0.9
Chad	71	109	144	156	194	194	182	152	135	250	259	0.8	13.4	4.4
Comoros	11	12	22	18	18	24	21	22	11	11	6	..	15.7	-13.4
Congo	911	877	844	1,155	1,328	1,108	1,179	1,119	959	1,173	1,517	22.9	-3.2	1.0
Côte d'Ivoire	3,013	3,091	2,664	2,697	3,003	2,705	2,945	2,519	2,869	3,870	4,316	6.4	0.0	5.6
Djibouti	..	..	..	..	..	72	53	71	56	38	40	..	..	-11.4
Equatorial Guinea	..	39	45	33	38	36	52	52	65	86	172	..	9.5	23.3
Eritrea	..	..	..	..	..	..	15	36	65	81	82	..	..	51.9
Ethiopia	459	391	381	444	366	276	154	222	281	454	410	6.3	-0.1	1.1
Gabon	2,531	1,286	1,196	1,629	2,490	2,230	2,257	2,326	2,365	2,643	3,111	8.9	-6.5	6.2
Gambia, The	..	79	74	96	119	146	156	125	123	127	..	..	8.3	2.7
Ghana	1,104	825	881	808	897	998	986	1,064	1,236	1,431	1,571	-3.8	8.5	9.0
Guinea	500	635	609	731	817	790	657	665	626	753	..	4.7	6.5	-2.2
Guinea-Bissau	..	15	16	14	19	20	7	16	33	24	22	..	..	7.8
Kenya	1,363	907	1,014	922	993	1,052	1,008	1,099	1,482	1,875	2,050	5.8	-2.0	12.5
Lesotho	58	30	64	66	59	58	105	95	136	168	..	10.7	24.8	19.4
Liberia	600	375	..	..	..	..	..	..	..	..	..	1.4	-5.6	..
Madagascar	437	329	280	318	318	334	324	332	447	502	513	2.0	-1.1	8.1
Malawi	281	279	294	269	412	476	397	321	373	410	436	8.8	-0.4	2.9
Mali	205	256	252	269	330	371	362	349	335	459	473	10.9	8.9	6.4
Mauritania	196	402	441	448	422	438	414	400	394	493	485	6.8	7.5	1.2
Mauritius	434	893	1,001	995	1,201	1,213	1,303	1,303	1,344	1,539	1,652	2.9	24.5	6.3
Mozambique	281	97	103	105	126	162	139	132	164	174	226	..	4.5	8.6
Namibia	1,534	994	1,074	1,155	1,086	1,214	1,327	1,280	1,337	1,431	1,464	..	8.5	4.0
Niger	576	412	369	308	313	290	269	248	231	281	280	14.6	3.9	-2.3
Nigeria	25,956	7,532	7,053	9,812	13,914	12,127	12,307	11,297	9,534	10,916	13,752	3.8	-7.1	0.4
Rwanda	..	114	110	97	103	96	69	68	32	47	62	..	-8.9	-11.5
São Tomé and Principe	17	6	11	6	4	6	5	7	6	5	5	-3.0	-7.6	-0.5
Senegal	422	671	679	758	894	803	828	707	794	969	1,022	2.0	6.0	2.8
Seychelles	6	8	17	15	28	19	20	22	27	22	23	-1.8	32.2	3.9
Sierra Leone	214	121	106	142	145	145	150	118	118	42	50	-1.0	0.0	-15.6
Somalia	133	94	58	61	58	..	..	..	..	..	..	3.6	-2.7	..
South Africa	25,698	21,088	22,432	22,399	17,099	17,514	18,536	18,280	18,296	18,976	..	10.3	7.4	-1.1
Sudan	594	482	486	550	443	342	349	351	503	..	..	3.4	-5.6	-3.2
Swaziland	368	424	466	494	554	580	608	626	827	781	842	6.3	22.6	8.1
Tanzania	508	337	338	423	389	394	414	411	486	593	..	0.1	1.6	5.5
Togo	476	403	460	409	395	393	327	215	226	355	345	7.9	9.8	-4.4
Uganda	319	384	298	282	210	176	172	157	254	595	590	1.3	-6.1	14.5
Zaire	2,269	1,813	2,460	2,417	2,326	1,649	1,246	1,144	1,256	1,632	1,936	5.9	5.8	-4.9
Zambia	1,457	867	1,155	1,410	1,264	1,085	1,111	949	1,067	1,190	1,128	-0.9	10.2	-2.4
Zimbabwe	281	1,455	1,668	1,692	1,753	1,785	1,530	1,610	1,947	2,216	2,500	0.0	9.3	5.1
NORTH AFRICA	44,234	22,434	21,947	25,266	35,369	37,428	36,950	35,264	33,707	40,900	..	9.7	-6.0	4.7
Algeria	13,652	8,737	7,811	9,569	12,889	12,387	11,439	10,410	8,899	10,260	..	14.3	-7.7	-2.5
Egypt, Arab Republic	3,854	2,200	2,069	1,660	2,657	4,227	4,629	4,854	3,808	5,368	..	9.4	-17.6	16.9
Libya	21,919	6,292	5,653	7,274	11,352	..	..	..	..	..	..	6.7	-10.5	..
Morocco	2,415	3,068	4,017	3,851	4,955	5,094	5,010	4,936	5,538	6,676	..	5.3	14.2	6.8
Tunisia	2,395	2,137	2,396	2,913	3,517	3,708	4,014	3,746	4,643	5,470	..	12.0	10.7	9.2
ALL AFRICA	123,144	77,040	78,477	86,672	98,370	96,741	97,071	92,030	91,434	105,674	..	7.9	-0.1	1.4

Note: 1996 data are preliminary (see page 3).

5-2. Merchandise imports, f.o.b.

	Millions of U.S. dollars (current prices)											Average annual percentage growth		
	1980	1987	1988	1989	1990	1991	1992	1993	1994	1995	1996	75-84	85-89	90-MR
SUB-SAHARAN AFRICA	..	46,046	51,108	51,685	62,344	63,691	64,761	62,754	59,659	68,497	..	..	3.9	2.7
excluding South Africa	42,950	32,123	33,870	34,857	39,012	39,807	41,282	38,652	38,122	43,972	47,717	8.2	2.6	3.1
excl. S. Africa & Nigeria	28,129	26,355	28,108	28,960	31,949	31,903	32,522	30,501	31,438	36,860	40,117	6.5	6.1	3.5
Angola	..	1,303	1,372	1,338	1,578	1,347	1,988	1,463	1,633	1,748	..	..	-1.8	3.5
Benin	499	463	508	317	428	483	561	539	373	557	548	8.3	6.9	5.3
Botswana	603	804	1,032	1,187	1,606	1,793	1,540	1,458	1,351	1,752	..	17.5	18.6	2.2
Burkina Faso	368	475	477	442	542	490	516	541	349	485	519	8.1	10.3	-0.5
Burundi	165	159	166	151	189	196	182	172	203	209	165	..	-1.8	1.4
Cameroon	1,452	1,853	1,631	1,352	1,454	1,251	1,024	1,021	1,016	1,074	1,200	12.5	5.5	-3.5
Cape Verde	80	93	102	110	120	128	167	152	195	232	209	10.1	5.9	11.3
Central African Republic	185	198	178	186	242	179	189	158	139	188	117	8.7	4.6	-6.3
Chad	55	226	231	240	259	250	243	205	212	278	301	-1.8	12.7	1.5
Comoros	22	40	43	36	45	49	58	50	45	54	49	..	6.1	3.2
Congo	545	420	523	503	515	507	439	500	613	650	1,364	15.2	-5.0	11.1
Côte d'Ivoire	2,614	1,852	1,693	1,777	1,705	1,825	1,984	1,784	1,608	2,420	2,847	6.1	4.4	5.6
Djibouti	..	..	..	..	..	258	259	255	237	205	201	..	..	-5.7
Equatorial Guinea	..	55	65	45	52	90	62	52	34	76	96	..	12.3	5.1
Eritrea	..	..	..	..	..	..	331	275	396	404	456	..	..	10.8
Ethiopia	692	1,081	1,099	1,020	881	1,029	875	1,051	915	1,064	1,413	16.4	1.0	3.7
Gabon	829	732	791	812	805	861	887	845	777	898	969	4.6	0.0	1.7
Gambia, The	..	108	106	113	154	193	214	194	163	201	..	..	9.1	6.7
Ghana	908	938	998	1,011	1,200	1,313	1,457	1,728	1,578	1,687	1,938	-1.6	11.2	8.8
Guinea	339	500	604	587	723	735	740	731	711	795	..	5.0	9.1	3.2
Guinea-Bissau	..	45	59	69	68	68	84	54	54	59	57	..	..	-3.7
Kenya	2,585	1,898	2,101	2,156	2,309	1,682	1,608	1,385	1,761	2,644	2,448	8.1	7.9	1.9
Lesotho	425	387	565	593	743	851	877	867	989	1,115	..	13.6	12.0	9.3
Liberia	478	312	..	..	..	..	..	..	..	..	..	1.8	-1.5	..
Madagascar	764	313	327	320	566	440	465	510	546	628	629	5.4	-3.1	7.4
Malawi	308	291	370	405	491	616	712	628	555	549	538	2.7	8.7	2.6
Mali	308	335	359	351	442	491	512	475	440	557	558	9.7	5.3	4.9
Mauritania	321	354	360	353	405	385	424	375	340	417	435	7.0	2.6	1.3
Mauritius	516	909	1,163	1,206	1,470	1,419	1,473	1,559	1,760	1,797	1,932	4.6	27.6	6.1
Mozambique	720	592	694	761	878	791	745	830	883	727	802	..	12.8	-0.2
Namibia	1,094	946	852	933	1,118	1,120	1,263	1,212	1,279	1,467	1,508	..	8.1	6.2
Niger	677	138	169	162	338	281	266	256	263	274	272	11.0	-14.5	2.8
Nigeria	14,735	5,774	5,776	5,912	7,070	7,892	8,737	8,129	6,675	7,131	7,655	12.5	-8.9	1.5
Rwanda	..	261	273	245	256	228	241	268	367	194	202	..	4.0	-1.4
São Tomé and Principe	16	17	21	27	21	24	23	26	24	24	19	12.4	2.1	-1.9
Senegal	875	956	956	998	1,165	1,114	1,192	1,087	1,027	1,218	1,325	4.6	4.7	2.2
Seychelles	84	96	135	140	158	146	163	202	174	159	172	12.4	14.2	2.7
Sierra Leone	334	140	156	183	155	158	155	148	149	137	209	1.4	2.6	0.1
Somalia	402	350	234	352	211	..	..	..	..	..	..	15.0	-6.3	..
South Africa	..	13,925	17,210	16,810	23,260	23,809	23,416	24,031	21,479	24,467	..	6.1	7.0	3.5
Sudan	1,339	707	1,040	1,040	1,035	1,535	1,290	1,068	1,226	..	..	8.1	-2.3	2.1
Swaziland	537	369	441	515	587	631	698	777	798	897	982	16.5	9.9	9.3
Tanzania	1,089	935	1,003	1,151	1,144	1,381	1,444	1,472	1,591	1,510	..	3.6	9.0	5.6
Togo	524	444	521	465	511	453	409	251	212	350	370	9.4	13.8	-7.2
Uganda	318	514	545	562	584	545	451	531	718	1,086	1,218	4.5	9.9	12.0
Zaire	1,519	1,774	1,610	1,925	1,739	1,304	935	614	667	951	1,110	0.0	10.7	-10.5
Zambia	1,114	669	788	901	889	952	1,302	950	1,003	1,228	1,154	0.3	6.9	3.9
Zimbabwe	308	1,073	1,166	1,323	1,512	1,700	1,781	1,512	1,778	2,128	2,213	1.4	6.5	6.5
NORTH AFRICA	34,001	28,308	28,665	32,641	38,059	36,038	38,740	37,928	40,664	48,722	..	8.1	-2.2	5.1
Algeria	9,596	7,399	7,592	9,362	9,659	7,747	8,541	7,990	9,158	10,100	..	5.6	-3.1	0.5
Egypt, Arab Republic	6,814	8,055	7,004	7,052	8,817	9,390	8,959	9,656	9,583	11,531	..	10.2	-8.8	6.1
Libya	10,368	5,820	5,762	6,509	7,575	..	..	..	..	..	..	12.0	-3.1	..
Morocco	3,770	4,006	4,615	5,345	6,815	6,834	7,451	6,977	7,619	9,936	..	8.3	8.7	7.8
Tunisia	3,453	3,028	3,692	4,372	5,193	4,895	6,079	5,757	6,210	7,458	..	13.2	7.2	7.9
ALL AFRICA	93,851	74,357	79,757	84,337	100,407	100,087	103,599	100,726	99,764	116,337	..	7.3	1.4	3.5

Note: 1996 data are preliminary (see page 3).

5-3. Exports of total services

	Millions of U.S. dollars (current prices)											Average annual percentage growth		
	1980	*1987*	*1988*	*1989*	*1990*	*1991*	*1992*	*1993*	*1994*	*1995*	*1996*	*75-84*	*85-89*	*90-MR*
SUB-SAHARAN AFRICA	11,405	9,969	10,584	11,410	21,148	20,372	19,951	20,284	21,110	22,920	..	7.4	4.9	7.7
excluding South Africa	8,784	7,247	7,338	7,863	9,057	9,087	9,354	9,205	8,919	10,149	11,017	6.7	2.6	3.5
excl. S. Africa & Nigeria	6,991	7,242	6,904	7,543	8,679	8,610	9,132	9,064	8,744	9,909	10,564	8.4	4.3	3.7
Angola	..	..	128	150	119	186	159	117	119	132	..	..	..	-3.0
Benin	84	94	99	88	115	123	143	137	103	126	122	11.3	8.9	2.7
Botswana	203	272	301	335	468	455	693	712	476	699	..	14.4	16.5	10.1
Burkina Faso	65	36	29	39	69	68	65	63	70	80	64	9.2	5.8	5.2
Burundi	26	15	15	24	25	35	31	25	27	31	22	..	7.3	-0.4
Cameroon	395	370	396	490	383	343	399	379	325	409	450	21.7	-1.7	-0.6
Cape Verde	14	47	42	45	58	49	52	49	60	78	79	43.1	11.6	7.3
Central African Republic	58	71	65	66	70	56	56	54	56	67	63	7.0	10.9	-0.7
Chad	0	73	81	44	44	40	44	47	60	69	76	-13.0	10.2	9.3
Comoros	3	17	19	22	9	15	21	35	30	37	38	..	48.5	17.5
Congo	119	128	100	7	114	118	79	68	160	84	87	7.6	-29.0	22.4
Côte d'Ivoire	588	319	493	542	596	675	810	773	536	619	659	9.4	-0.9	1.0
Djibouti	..	..	..	..	..	194	178	192	182	188	184	..	..	-0.4
Equatorial Guinea	..	8	9	11	8	10	7	8	7	5	10	..	118.6	-4.3
Eritrea	..	..	..	..	..	..	73	103	80	99	69	..	..	-1.6
Ethiopia	131	249	267	314	311	271	305	291	285	354	413	5.0	11.5	3.2
Gabon	350	131	228	308	270	352	369	344	231	286	300	12.2	10.1	-1.4
Gambia, The	..	36	55	39	47	68	72	82	40	73	..	..	20.7	6.3
Ghana	110	80	65	72	87	103	137	156	159	164	179	-5.8	14.7	15.9
Guinea	54	13	34	27	56	60	64	51	52	53	..	..	53.1	6.4
Guinea-Bissau	..	12	12	12	30	27	25	21	17	17	21	..	..	-0.6
Kenya	835	804	871	1,008	1,221	1,147	1,154	1,146	1,184	1,118	1,070	7.1	9.9	0.1
Lesotho	305	305	419	413	496	519	509	497	526	552	..	13.8	5.9	3.4
Liberia	13	58	..	..	..	..	..	..	..	..	..	18.0	17.0	..
Madagascar	82	105	132	161	209	151	177	187	208	251	293	2.6	24.1	7.5
Malawi	34	26	38	40	45	45	27	19	18	25	37	-7.4	5.5	-7.6
Mali	58	65	73	72	108	96	106	99	78	88	91	10.7	13.9	-0.1
Mauritania	74	48	54	57	55	66	53	34	40	48	103	9.6	9.8	1.9
Mauritius	150	337	410	453	589	643	691	664	711	849	884	8.1	31.6	8.4
Mozambique	118	79	85	95	103	147	165	180	191	233	253	..	9.3	15.1
Namibia	206	178	236	304	320	392	375	461	488	532	582	..	8.8	9.9
Niger	68	94	75	71	71	59	56	49	38	41	37	7.4	10.5	-10.0
Nigeria	1,069	315	430	319	379	478	228	147	166	225	382	-0.1	-10.7	-5.7
Rwanda	..	56	57	60	52	47	50	37	19	38	24	..	7.0	-12.3
São Tomé and Principe	6	2	2	5	4	4	5	5	6	4	6	20.1	4.8	3.9
Senegal	409	467	488	517	651	583	616	527	508	601	644	8.8	10.8	0.7
Seychelles	97	148	168	190	232	199	252	268	272	250	265	15.4	14.2	4.5
Sierra Leone	21	52	53	39	70	69	66	70	49	64	62	5.4	-3.9	2.2
Somalia	71	13	23	27	33	..	..	..	..	..	..	13.9	-15.9	..
South Africa	3,560	3,109	3,245	3,544	12,026	11,227	10,547	11,032	12,138	12,714	..	8.3	4.5	14.7
Sudan	231	240	175	203	210	68	40	52	106	..	..	14.6	-3.7	-20.4
Swaziland	82	151	185	217	273	260	252	128	189	190	199	15.4	16.4	-4.7
Tanzania	179	106	108	122	134	141	141	206	369	511	..	-1.1	1.8	27.0
Togo	95	133	162	152	180	172	161	115	81	95	105	17.9	10.8	-9.4
Uganda	12	22	26	22	36	26	27	85	90	88	157	9.0	1.4	31.6
Zaire	135	279	255	231	258	226	135	151	66	73	73	3.1	13.3	-19.3
Zambia	168	56	72	103	79	87	94	107	123	112	140	3.7	1.7	6.2
Zimbabwe	33	236	239	276	291	295	342	396	456	536	625	7.0	11.5	12.9
NORTH AFRICA	7,196	7,186	8,077	8,660	10,287	11,504	15,668	17,086	16,279	18,228	..	13.6	5.7	13.5
Algeria	978	866	606	689	587	504	729	746	808	800	..	7.4	3.1	5.4
Egypt, Arab Republic	2,662	2,775	2,909	4,101	5,156	6,678	8,262	9,189	8,266	9,728	..	19.9	0.3	14.8
Libya	1,446	912	891	565	783	..	..	..	..	..	..	12.8	1.9	..
Morocco	896	1,368	1,772	1,590	1,977	1,821	2,444	2,412	2,374	2,455	..	8.6	15.1	7.2
Tunisia	1,214	1,265	1,899	1,715	1,783	1,507	2,107	2,143	2,364	2,657	..	11.2	14.5	8.3
ALL AFRICA	19,015	17,198	18,665	20,075	31,421	31,725	34,612	36,151	36,328	39,995	..	9.8	4.8	9.3

Note: 1996 data are preliminary (see page 3).

5-4. Imports of total services

	Millions of U.S. dollars (current prices)											Average annual percentage growth		
	1980	1987	1988	1989	1990	1991	1992	1993	1994	1995	1996	75-84	85-89	90-MR
SUB-SAHARAN AFRICA	..	29,048	29,333	33,303	31,557	30,516	32,751	30,776	36,224	40,000	..	..	5.0	3.0
excluding South Africa	23,470	21,509	21,922	25,575	29,449	29,265	29,237	27,694	26,575	30,086	31,478	7.8	5.4	1.5
excl. S. Africa & Nigeria	16,189	17,740	19,895	20,990	23,673	23,514	24,086	22,789	21,959	24,896	26,349	9.5	7.4	1.9
Angola	..	717	1,750	1,963	2,587	2,912	2,917	2,435	2,529	2,665	..	..	20.3	2.5
Benin	112	171	174	150	174	169	219	192	165	219	221	11.2	4.1	4.5
Botswana	351	571	587	691	753	778	768	576	746	915	..	18.0	15.7	1.9
Burkina Faso	228	201	171	158	-159	-244	-196	-187	170	204	244	9.1	5.1	..
Burundi	58	163	141	131	149	158	158	133	146	141	102	..	14.1	-2.8
Cameroon	1,026	1,101	783	1,083	1,347	1,516	1,468	1,611	1,098	1,178	1,265	19.0	-12.1	-0.5
Cape Verde	8	29	24	33	35	24	31	36	40	62	61	29.3	20.3	11.3
Central African Republic	144	182	181	171	192	157	175	158	127	160	136	7.0	12.3	-3.8
Chad	28	212	230	222	260	219	239	240	232	254	273	-7.6	16.7	1.8
Comoros	12	45	46	43	29	34	34	52	45	52	48	..	2.8	6.3
Congo	650	818	873	699	1,244	1,188	1,115	1,219	1,254	1,178	1,476	16.3	5.1	6.4
Côte d'Ivoire	2,110	2,065	2,149	2,226	2,939	2,519	2,726	2,484	1,638	2,150	2,228	11.2	10.4	-3.4
Djibouti	..	..	..	..	..	110	117	118	97	88	90	..	..	-5.7
Equatorial Guinea	..	41	47	41	49	36	41	51	45	117	155	..	69.3	19.0
Eritrea	..	..	..	..	..	..	0	1	7	44	35	..	..	..
Ethiopia	105	201	229	270	260	275	290	314	274	293	317	-1.9	16.5	2.2
Gabon	1,414	1,011	1,104	1,167	1,668	1,519	1,781	1,688	1,336	1,733	2,013	10.8	-3.3	4.3
Gambia, The	..	5	61	60	69	79	83	77	64	74	..	..	84.1	1.6
Ghana	355	392	384	386	417	461	513	568	545	574	620	0.4	8.9	7.1
Guinea	238	273	317	345	355	320	285	270	265	286	..	..	9.0	-4.6
Guinea-Bissau	..	39	43	55	42	60	55	50	41	48	48	..	..	-1.9
Kenya	872	501	555	713	759	1,011	947	940	1,069	1,241	1,156	4.9	-0.1	7.4
Lesotho	58	55	85	92	104	240	77	89	119	123	..	12.6	13.9	0.6
Liberia	97	263	..	..	..	..	..	..	..	..	..	12.6	7.5	..
Madagascar	368	423	416	437	436	440	421	457	480	532	536	10.1	8.7	3.4
Malawi	330	93	104	103	100	121	96	84	84	111	116	11.5	-0.9	0.1
Mali	229	336	361	348	440	404	495	411	372	456	460	8.1	11.9	2.1
Mauritania	172	332	320	270	277	270	267	258	215	294	298	13.2	4.1	0.3
Mauritius	207	326	391	429	519	542	619	609	623	721	809	8.7	22.1	8.0
Mozambique	130	310	275	331	261	287	330	342	373	395	390	..	11.6	4.9
Namibia	787	506	731	639	515	631	694	646	586	617	641	..	5.2	0.7
Niger	339	326	278	206	258	197	189	177	193	201	191	10.7	7.9	-2.2
Nigeria	7,025	3,775	2,072	4,589	5,770	5,743	5,154	4,909	4,631	5,217	5,246	2.8	-4.4	-0.3
Rwanda	..	172	171	190	129	131	147	155	129	153	115	..	7.7	-3.1
São Tomé and Principe	7	11	12	19	26	26	23	22	22	28	26	14.9	8.1	2.6
Senegal	462	723	747	741	897	802	832	743	660	762	783	11.9	9.5	-1.3
Seychelles	43	57	50	72	69	91	131	141	142	130	135	14.6	19.7	11.3
Sierra Leone	95	104	111	133	183	173	180	163	180	152	100	4.0	4.1	-3.4
Somalia	139	201	198	242	222	..	..	..	..	..	..	10.3	10.2	..
South Africa	..	7,549	7,423	7,755	2,221	1,375	3,611	3,167	9,674	9,976	..	8.3	4.0	17.6
Sudan	343	967	1,066	1,229	1,023	881	890	927	983	..	..	19.1	5.6	-3.9
Swaziland	122	189	217	279	293	303	268	164	285	242	245	9.8	22.7	-3.0
Tanzania	160	491	554	600	604	379	635	723	805	821	..	5.1	19.5	8.0
Togo	227	258	277	259	288	273	262	200	183	219	216	14.1	9.9	-4.8
Uganda	132	133	194	217	169	187	221	221	247	371	450	6.1	11.9	12.5
Zaire	1,160	1,393	1,685	1,547	1,556	1,552	1,282	1,196	1,141	1,308	1,466	8.5	11.3	-2.6
Zambia	872	572	668	806	799	693	623	559	566	620	574	3.0	7.5	-5.1
Zimbabwe	330	606	668	706	784	931	961	836	1,016	1,120	1,199	8.8	7.5	6.9
NORTH AFRICA	14,611	16,725	15,895	16,272	18,034	20,342	18,012	18,126	17,167	18,555	..	13.8	4.9	0.6
Algeria	5,035	3,653	4,254	3,978	3,984	4,211	4,065	3,507	3,769	4,329	..	16.1	-3.1	-0.1
Egypt, Arab Republic	2,931	8,177	6,231	6,869	8,136	9,590	7,346	7,647	6,464	7,457	..	20.4	17.1	-1.6
Libya	3,650	1,944	2,074	1,869	1,878	..	..	..	..	..	..	11.3	-8.8	..
Morocco	2,077	1,995	2,271	2,487	2,637	2,752	3,047	3,063	3,143	2,878	..	7.0	11.8	3.3
Tunisia	918	956	1,065	1,070	1,399	1,461	1,701	2,012	2,138	2,250	..	11.5	6.6	12.9
ALL AFRICA	46,049	45,772	45,218	49,552	49,590	50,491	50,825	48,838	53,889	59,200	..	9.7	4.9	2.4

Note: 1996 data are preliminary (see page 3).

5-5. Net private transfers

	Millions of U.S. dollars (current prices)											Annual average		
	1980	*1987*	*1988*	*1989*	*1990*	*1991*	*1992*	*1993*	*1994*	*1995*	*1996*	*75-84*	*85-89*	*90-MR*
SUB-SAHARAN AFRICA	..	..	..	..	..	..	..	..	..	..	..	..	..	..
excluding South Africa	..	..	..	..	..	..	..	..	..	..	..	..	..	..
excl. S.Africa & Nigeria	..	..	..	..	..	..	..	..	..	..	..	411	..	..
Angola	..	-8	-4	-68	-140	-30	12	-14	-22	-24	..	26	-19	-36
Benin	107	81	82	78	86	84	95	94	51	68	67	60	77	78
Botswana	-1	7	-16	-31	-41	-39	-19	-65	-85	103	..	0	-9	-24
Burkina Faso	112	164	184	140	105	98	169	155	97	112	115	75	164	122
Burundi	3	7	10	9	10	13	13	17	24	25	19	6	9	17
Cameroon	19	-111	-134	-17	-67	-59	-72	-88	-38	-17	26	11	-69	-45
Cape Verde	40	34	39	43	55	58	70	71	81	100	100	30	32	76
Central African Republic	0	-19	-27	-25	-31	-30	-27	-31	-17	-25	-22	0	-14	-26
Chad	-4	-10	-17	-20	-13	-20	-34	-35	2	-2	11	-6	-9	-13
Comoros	..	..	..	..	..	..	..	..	..	..	..	..	..	..
Congo	..	..	..	..	11	-60	-19	-9	0	26	..	..	..	-8
Côte d'Ivoire	-706	-490	-507	-386	..	..	..	..	..	..	..	-403	-414	..
Djibouti	..	..	..	..	..	..	..	..	..	..	..	..	..	..
Equatorial Guinea	..	0	15	4	8	1	-4	-3	0	-3	-3	..	5	0
Eritrea	..	..	..	..	..	..	181	165	276	215	254	..	..	218
Ethiopia	20	148	119	188	171	200	316	247	248	311	313	37	162	258
Gabon	..	..	..	..	..	..	..	..	..	..	..	..	..	..
Gambia, The	..	..	17	8	..	..	..	..	..	..	..	3	12	..
Ghana	-3	202	172	202	202	220	255	261	271	263	276	7	136	250
Guinea	-3	-37	-25	-43	-51	-42	-64	-54	-41	-35	..	-3	-34	-48
Guinea-Bissau	..	3	5	5	5	1	5	4	6	6	7	..	4	5
Kenya	27	72	89	101	167	144	68	147	148	405	373	41	80	207
Lesotho	2	72	4	4	5	3	3	4	15	200	..	29	29	38
Liberia	-29	-21	..	..	..	..	..	..	..	..	..	-32	-25	..
Madagascar	-21	52	64	72	77	67	109	114	46	75	87	-14	54	82
Malawi	..	..	..	..	..	..	..	..	..	..	..	..	..	..
Mali	41	50	59	64	102	70	74	94	85	96	96	25	53	88
Mauritania	-28	-25	-28	-24	-14	-15	27	-1	6	30	40	-25	-26	10
Mauritius	0	41	72	68	82	79	87	85	93	99	110	4	47	91
Mozambique	28	..	..	..	..	..	..	..	..	..	..	38	16	..
Namibia	0	0	0	0	0	0	0	0	0	0	0	0	0	0
Niger	-57	..	..	..	..	..	..	..	..	..	..	-40	-51	..
Nigeria	..	..	..	..	..	..	..	..	..	..	..	-211	..	..
Rwanda	..	..	..	..	..	..	..	..	..	..	..	..	..	..
São Tomé and Principe	1	0	0	0	0	1	1	2	3	0	1	1	0	1
Senegal	-20	6	6	6	8	14	26	36	38	40	38	-3	7	29
Seychelles	..	..	..	..	..	..	..	..	..	..	..	..	..	..
Sierra Leone	0	2	0	0	0	0	0	0	0	0	0	3	1	0
Somalia	57	..	..	..	..	..	..	..	..	..	..	43	..	..
South Africa	..	97	7	41	-1,658	-1,389	-779	-461	-1	277	..	21	61	-669
Sudan	209	250	445	297	188	79	169	169	55	..	..	246	354	132
Swaziland	-2	0	4	2	0	-1	1	0	0	72	74	-1	1	21
Tanzania	22	446	519	467	461	408	456	463	485	365	..	22	364	440
Togo	1	..	..	..	..	..	..	..	..	..	..	-1	..	..
Uganda	-2	100	120	114	78	81	136	129	312	330	407	7	95	210
Zaire	-79	-69	-67	-109	-81	-82	-97	-123	-98	-102	-74	-47	-72	-94
Zambia	..	..	..	..	..	..	..	..	..	..	..	..	..	..
Zimbabwe	..	..	..	..	..	..	..	..	..	..	..	..	..	..
NORTH AFRICA	..	..	..	..	..	..	..	..	..	..	..	..	..	..
Algeria	..	..	..	..	..	..	..	..	..	..	..	..	..	..
Egypt, Arab Republic	..	3,005	3,496	3,510	3,954	3,996	5,713	6,204	3,426	3,439	..	..	3,337	4,455
Libya	-1,089	-508	-497	-472	-446	..	..	..	..	..	..	-1,075	-571	-446
Morocco	1,070	1,691	1,423	1,461	2,146	2,152	2,388	2,120	2,070	2,115	..	812	1,419	2,165
Tunisia	348	484	558	503	613	563	570	597	688	753	..	255	435	631
ALL AFRICA	..	..	..	..	..	..	..	..	..	..	..	..	..	..

Note: 1996 data are preliminary (see page 3).

5-6. Net official current transfers

	Millions of U.S. dollars (current prices)											Annual average		
	1980	*1987*	*1988*	*1989*	*1990*	*1991*	*1992*	*1993*	*1994*	*1995*	*1996*	*75-84*	*85-89*	*90-MR*
SUB-SAHARAN AFRICA	..	..	..	..	..	..	..	..	..	..	..	..	..	..
excluding South Africa	..	..	..	..	..	..	..	..	..	..	..	..	..	..
excl. S.Africa & Nigeria	..	..	..	..	..	..	..	..	..	..	..	..	..	..
Angola	..	60	36	64	63	58	90	180	191	259	..	..	67	140
Benin	0	0	0	58	74	56	73	64	39	37	48	0	12	56
Botswana	..	..	..	..	..	..	..	..	..	..	..	..	..	..
Burkina Faso	0	0	0	0	0	0	0	0	0	0	1	0	0	0
Burundi	42	74	62	88	105	120	104	111	148	132	119	45	65	120
Cameroon	83	31	48	85	131	119	250	70	56	-26	47	46	56	100
Cape Verde	0	0	0	0	0	0	0	0	0	0	0	0	0	0
Central African Republic	0	..	..	..	..	..	..	..	..	..	..	0	0	..
Chad	0	84	83	53	75	59	98	62	65	74	54	0	44	69
Comoros	..	..	..	..	..	..	..	..	..	..	..	..	..	..
Congo	..	..	..	..	..	..	..	..	..	..	..	..	..	..
Côte d'Ivoire	-1	132	54	197	226	74	9	88	-31	-27	-27	23	92	45
Djibouti	..	..	..	..	..	..	..	..	..	..	..	..	..	..
Equatorial Guinea	..	..	..	..	..	..	..	..	..	..	..	..	..	..
Eritrea	..	..	..	..	..	..	0	0	0	0	0	..	..	0
Ethiopia	60	56	50	50	50	61	211	108	86	148	133	40	57	114
Gabon	..	25	11	9	21	14	6	14	15	0	0	..	16	10
Gambia, The	..	..	..	..	..	..	..	..	..	..	..	..	..	..
Ghana	83	..	..	..	..	..	..	..	..	..	..	65	..	..
Guinea	17	..	..	..	..	..	..	..	..	..	..	13	..	..
Guinea-Bissau	..	18	19	19	17	12	16	10	14	19	16	..	19	15
Kenya	118	0	0	0	0	0	0	0	0	0	0	64	0	0
Lesotho	173	4	77	107	0	0	0	0	0	0	..	36	53	0
Liberia	36	45	..	..	..	..	..	..	..	..	..	57	78	..
Madagascar	..	102	125	64	70	77	54	70	44	17	33	53	92	52
Malawi	..	..	..	..	..	..	..	..	..	..	..	..	..	..
Mali	110	86	98	97	124	180	215	132	146	97	106	85	98	143
Mauritania	118	38	115	261	67	61	72	86	56	46	55	119	111	63
Mauritius	0	27	12	17	6	9	5	13	9	6	0	3	19	7
Mozambique	..	..	..	..	..	..	..	..	..	..	..	..	..	..
Namibia	101	319	275	253	249	275	338	237	205	232	252	360	294	255
Niger	154	142	..	..	..	..	..	..	..	..	..	127	168	..
Nigeria	..	-20	64	128	48	22	-57	54	-48	-66	-67	-14	8	-16
Rwanda	..	119	90	84	89	109	92	165	354	231	64	..	104	158
São Tomé and Principe	0	0	0	0	0	0	0	0	0	0	0	0	0	0
Senegal	0	-22	3	10	-5	1	8	-9	83	70	23	0	-2	25
Seychelles	..	..	..	..	..	..	..	..	..	..	..	..	..	..
Sierra Leone	26	15	10	8	21	21	20	10	15	31	56	11	13	25
Somalia	143	343	244	357	265	..	..	..	..	..	..	111	291	265
South Africa	..	116	33	37	71	92	130	168	126	100	..	66	37	115
Sudan	84	280	369	299	342	205	269	124	88	..	..	139	330	206
Swaziland	79	46	69	86	98	99	131	115	93	20	30	46	59	84
Tanzania	108	436	489	512	525	..	..	..	..	..	..	138	377	525
Togo	86	71	58	59	77	68	56	28	16	26	24	62	62	42
Uganda	0	0	0	0	0	0	0	0	0	0	0	6	0	0
Zaire	267	55	56	69	54	25	8	7	99	102	83	137	113	54
Zambia	..	..	..	..	..	..	..	..	..	..	..	..	..	..
Zimbabwe	..	..	..	..	..	..	..	..	..	..	..	..	..	..
NORTH AFRICA	..	..	..	..	1,109	..	..	..	..	..	..	..	..	1,109
Algeria	0	0	0	0	0	0	0	0	0	0	..	0	0	0
Egypt, Arab Republic	..	496	678	668	970	1,349	1,123	1,353	814	919	..	..	614	1,088
Libya	-46	-60	-37	-16	-35	..	..	..	..	..	..	-85	-39	-35
Morocco	144	68	173	142	174	118	77	30	55	-19	..	90	95	73
Tunisia	42	35	60	206	0	0	0	0	0	0	..	36	75	0
ALL AFRICA	..	..	..	..	..	..	..	..	..	..	..	..	..	..

Note: 1996 data are preliminary (see page 3).

5-7. Current account balance, excluding net capital grants

	Millions of U.S. dollars (current prices)											Annual average		
	1980	*1987*	*1988*	*1989*	*1990*	*1991*	*1992*	*1993*	*1994*	*1995*	*1996*	*75-84*	*85-89*	*90-MR*
SUB-SAHARAN AFRICA	-4,124	-7,169	-8,962	-7,268	-6,723	-10,529	-12,506	-11,619	-11,848	-12,711	-5,693	-8,269	-6,969	-10,233
excluding South Africa	-4,124	-10,105	-10,046	-8,724	-8,780	-12,789	-13,913	-13,440	-11,253	-10,335	-5,693	-8,212	-9,218	-10,886
excl. S.Africa & Nigeria	-8,980	-8,862	-10,357	-9,264	-11,429	-12,912	-13,318	-12,597	-10,235	-9,787	-7,565	-6,691	-8,341	-11,120
Angola	..	447	-442	-142	-239	-596	-811	-715	-872	-527	..	..	-49	-627
Benin	-197	-93	-125	-27	-39	-52	-98	-95	-38	-141	-108	-174	-75	-82
Botswana	-207	496	144	246	-179	-251	92	338	174	-17	..	-129	196	26
Burkina Faso	-259	-283	-197	-215	74	190	151	127	-165	-254	-277	-203	-227	-22
Burundi	-86	-128	-96	-68	-126	-95	-114	-78	-27	-45	-47	-98	-90	-76
Cameroon	-564	-934	-434	-39	-448	-205	21	-620	-338	-171	-220	-453	-416	-283
Cape Verde	-25	-33	-42	-46	-36	-40	-73	-64	-89	-108	-82	-38	-41	-70
Central African Republic	-43	-134	-90	-123	-189	-111	-157	-110	-26	-95	-46	-31	-96	-105
Chad	-16	-181	-170	-229	-220	-196	-192	-219	-182	-141	-174	-80	-210	-189
Comoros	-9	-16	-5	6	-22	-12	-36	-7	-24	-30	-23	-14	-9	-22
Congo	-167	-295	-513	-99	-370	-524	-315	-541	-670	-569	-1,253	-248	-351	-606
Côte d'Ivoire	-1,830	-865	-1,139	-966	-1,321	-1,257	-1,323	-1,193	-131	-542	-594	-844	-616	-909
Djibouti	..	..	..	..	..	-111	-155	-120	-106	-78	-77	..	..	-108
Equatorial Guinea	..	-50	-43	-38	-48	-80	-48	-46	-7	-104	-71	..	-33	-58
Eritrea	..	..	..	..	..	..	-62	28	18	-53	-85	..	..	-31
Ethiopia	-126	-437	-512	-294	-243	-495	-180	-497	-290	-90	-460	-176	-376	-322
Gabon	514	-449	-616	-168	150	91	-226	-58	336	100	211	157	-490	86
Gambia, The	..	-40	-21	-74	-47	-47	-57	-50	-48	-55	..	-61	-44	-51
Ghana	29	-225	-264	-315	-432	-454	-592	-815	-456	-402	-532	-95	-254	-526
Guinea	-9	-162	-303	-217	-257	-248	-367	-339	-339	-309	..	-49	-202	-310
Guinea-Bissau	..	-36	-50	-74	-39	-68	-87	-52	-24	-41	-40	..	-53	-50
Kenya	-1,115	-616	-683	-838	-687	-351	-325	67	-17	-487	-111	-430	-609	-273
Lesotho	56	-31	-86	-95	-287	-512	-337	-360	-431	-468	..	-4	-42	-399
Liberia	46	-118	..	..	..	..	..	..	..	..	..	15	-15	..
Madagascar	..	-147	-143	-143	-329	-251	-222	-263	-280	-316	-240	-146	-156	-272
Malawi	-310	-60	-110	-213	-145	-250	-371	-342	-230	-227	-188	-163	-110	-250
Mali	-124	-216	-239	-196	-218	-179	-249	-213	-169	-273	-252	-124	-224	-222
Mauritania	-133	-222	-98	118	-152	-105	-125	-114	-58	-94	-51	-133	-111	-100
Mauritius	-139	64	-59	-102	-111	-17	-6	-103	-227	-25	-95	-81	-6	-83
Mozambique	-423	-693	-735	-848	-864	-738	-738	-825	-865	-677	-667	-489	-668	-768
Namibia	-40	39	2	139	23	130	85	120	165	111	149	20	112	112
Niger	-429	..	-3	11	-261	-167	-170	-170	-227	-177	-175	-247	-98	-192
Nigeria	4,856	-1,243	311	540	2,649	123	-595	-844	-1,018	-548	1,872	-1,521	-878	234
Rwanda	..	-136	-176	-187	-135	-87	-158	-130	-46	-14	-151	..	-124	-103
São Tomé and Principe	1	-20	-21	-36	-38	-39	-34	-34	-31	-42	-34	-6	-25	-36
Senegal	-526	-556	-527	-448	-513	-514	-546	-569	-263	-300	-381	-374	-484	-441
Seychelles	-23	3	..	2	41	-12	-25	-55	-22	-25	-18	-17	7	-17
Sierra Leone	-168	-55	-98	-127	-101	-96	-100	-113	-148	-152	-141	-136	-77	-122
Somalia	-136	-114	-101	-153	-81	..	..	..	..	..	..	-117	-121	-81
South Africa	..	2,936	1,084	1,456	2,057	2,260	1,407	1,821	-594	-2,376	..	-96	2,250	762
Sudan	-564	-422	-630	-920	-875	-1,722	-1,353	-1,299	-1,457	..	..	-546	-551	-1,341
Swaziland	-132	62	65	4	45	3	25	-72	26	-76	-82	-70	21	-19
Tanzania	-540	-538	-592	-735	-764	-818	-1,068	-1,115	-1,076	-862	..	-442	-585	-950
Togo	-95	-87	-110	-95	-137	-79	-119	-84	-64	-82	-97	-88	-85	-94
Uganda	-121	-141	-295	-361	-429	-449	-338	-381	-309	-444	-514	-57	-221	-409
Zaire	-88	-1,089	-591	-863	-738	-1,037	-925	-632	-485	-554	-559	-366	-514	-704
Zambia	-538	-347	-264	-222	-388	-513	-753	-472	-398	-564	-477	-377	-306	-509
Zimbabwe	-444	-2	51	-78	-258	-547	-837	-311	-318	-369	-133	-353	-46	-396
NORTH AFRICA	6,223	-8,656	-7,119	-6,917	-1,506	-1,485	2,773	3,274	-2,934	-4,191	..	-3,626	-6,475	-678
Algeria	242	39	-1,903	-1,030	1,352	2,223	1,020	802	-1,820	-2,240	..	-1,008	-1,123	223
Egypt, Arab Republic	-438	-7,757	-4,083	-3,982	-4,216	-2,730	3,422	4,296	266	466	..	-1,765	-4,478	251
Libya	8,259	-1,067	-1,789	-1,010	2,236	..	..	..	..	..	..	1,034	-408	2,236
Morocco	-1,467	194	499	-789	-200	-400	-580	-542	-726	-1,587	..	-1,379	-220	-673
Tunisia	-373	-64	156	-106	-679	-577	-1,089	-1,283	-654	-830	..	-508	-246	-852
ALL AFRICA	2,099	-15,825	-16,081	-14,185	-8,230	-12,014	-9,733	-8,346	-14,782	-16,902	-5,693	-11,895	-13,444	-10,814

Note: 1996 data are preliminary (see page 3).

5-8. Current account balance, excluding net capital grants/GDP

	Percentage											Annual average		
	1980	1987	1988	1989	1990	1991	1992	1993	1994	1995	1996	75-84	85-89	90-MR
SUB-SAHARAN AFRICA	..	-3.0	-3.6	-2.9	-2.4	-3.8	-4.4	-3.9	-4.1	-4.5	..	-4.8	-3.0	-3.8
excluding South Africa	-2.2	-6.5	-6.3	-5.4	-5.0	-7.7	-8.5	-8.4	-7.3	-6.8	-3.4	-6.3	-6.1	-6.7
excl. S. Africa & Nigeria	-8.9	-6.7	-7.5	-6.7	-7.8	-9.2	-9.9	-9.3	-8.0	-7.7	-6.0	-8.0	-6.5	-8.3
Angola	..	6.1	-5.5	-1.5	-2.6	-13.2	-15.1	-16.8	-12.7	-8.5	..	..	-0.6	-11.5
Benin	-14.0	-5.9	-7.7	-1.8	-2.1	-2.7	-6.0	-4.5	-2.5	-6.8	-4.9	-16.6	-5.2	-4.2
Botswana	-21.4	32.1	6.4	8.9	-5.6	-6.8	2.5	8.9	4.3	-0.4	..	-16.6	11.1	0.5
Burkina Faso	-15.2	-13.1	-8.3	-9.1	2.7	6.8	5.0	4.5	-8.9	-10.9	..	-15.6	-11.4	-0.1
Burundi	-9.3	-11.3	-8.9	-6.1	-11.1	-8.2	-10.5	-8.3	-2.8	-4.3	-5.2	-9.8	-8.0	-7.2
Cameroon	-8.4	-7.6	-3.5	-0.3	-4.0	-1.7	0.2	-5.2	-4.3	-2.1	-2.4	-8.3	-3.7	-2.8
Cape Verde	-23.5	-14.1	-15.6	-17.1	-11.7	-12.6	-20.2	-19.3	-25.7	-25.7	-19.3	-42.3	-22.5	-19.2
Central African Republic	-5.4	-11.3	-7.2	-9.9	-12.9	-8.1	-11.3	-8.7	-2.9	-8.3	-4.2	-4.3	-8.4	-8.1
Chad	-2.2	-22.1	-16.3	-22.7	-18.0	-14.9	-14.5	-21.3	-21.9	-13.4	-14.8	-12.2	-24.9	-17.0
Comoros	-7.2	-8.2	-2.3	2.8	-8.7	-5.0	-13.5	-2.4	-11.9	-12.9	-9.8	-13.0	-6.0	-9.2
Congo	-9.8	-12.9	-23.2	-4.1	-13.2	-19.2	-10.7	-28.2	-37.8	-27.1	-52.5	-20.7	-16.9	-27.0
Côte d'Ivoire	-18.0	-8.6	-11.1	-9.9	-12.2	-12.0	-11.9	-11.5	-1.7	-5.4	-5.6	-10.8	-6.1	-8.6
Djibouti	..	..	..	..	..	-24.3	-33.0	-25.5	-21.8	-15.9	-16.0	..	..	-22.8
Equatorial Guinea	..	-41.4	-34.0	-33.9	-36.0	-61.5	-30.3	-29.6	-5.7	-61.6	..	..	-29.1	-37.4
Eritrea	..	..	..	..	..	..	..	..	..	..	..	..	..	..
Ethiopia	..	-5.8	-6.6	-3.6	-2.8	-5.2	-2.4	-6.9	-5.0	-1.5	-7.4	-5.8	-5.1	-4.5
Gabon	12.0	-11.7	-16.2	-4.0	2.5	1.7	-4.0	-1.3	8.0	2.0	3.7	4.2	-12.5	1.8
Gambia, The	..	-18.3	-9.2	-30.7	-16.2	-14.2	-17.6	-13.7	-13.3	-15.0	..	-30.4	-22.2	-15.0
Ghana	0.7	-4.4	-5.1	-6.0	-7.3	-6.9	-9.2	-14.4	-8.8	-6.5	-8.4	-2.4	-5.0	-8.8
Guinea	..	-7.9	-12.7	-8.9	-9.1	-8.3	-12.3	-10.7	-10.0	-8.4	..	..	-9.0	-9.8
Guinea-Bissau	..	-21.4	-31.8	-36.8	-16.3	-28.4	-38.9	-22.1	-10.3	-16.1	-14.6	..	-30.0	-21.0
Kenya	-15.3	-7.7	-8.0	-10.0	-8.0	-4.3	-4.0	1.2	-0.2	-5.4	-1.2	-7.2	-7.9	-3.1
Lesotho	15.3	-8.4	-19.1	-18.7	-46.1	-87.0	-50.1	-51.0	-56.3	-55.7	..	-2.8	-8.9	-57.7
Liberia	4.1	-10.3	..	..	..	..	..	..	..	..	..	1.9	-1.2	..
Madagascar	..	-5.7	-5.8	-5.7	-10.7	-9.4	-7.4	-7.8	-9.4	-9.9	-5.8	-4.6	-5.8	-8.6
Malawi	-25.0	-5.2	-8.2	-14.0	-7.8	-11.5	-20.0	-16.8	-17.9	-15.5	..	-15.6	-8.4	-14.9
Mali	-7.4	-11.0	-12.0	-9.6	-8.8	-7.4	-8.8	-8.0	-9.1	-11.1	-9.5	-10.7	-12.9	-8.9
Mauritania	-18.8	-24.4	-10.2	12.1	-14.9	-9.3	-10.5	-12.1	-5.6	-8.8	-4.7	-19.9	-13.8	-9.4
Mauritius	-12.3	3.4	-2.8	-4.7	-4.2	-0.6	-0.2	-3.2	-6.5	-0.6	-2.2	-7.6	0.0	-2.5
Mozambique	-20.9	-51.2	-61.1	-63.7	-59.9	-51.5	-59.5	-58.5	-60.4	-46.3	-38.9	-24.6	-42.8	-53.6
Namibia	-1.8	2.0	0.1	6.5	1.0	5.4	3.1	4.7	5.6	3.5	4.9	1.3	7.0	4.0
Niger	-16.9	..	-0.2	0.5	-10.5	-7.2	-7.3	-7.6	-14.5	-9.4	-8.8	-13.7	-6.3	-9.3
Nigeria	7.5	-5.3	1.4	2.3	9.3	0.5	-2.0	-3.6	-4.1	-2.3	6.1	-3.9	-4.2	0.5
Rwanda	..	-6.3	-7.4	-7.8	-5.2	-4.7	-8.2	-7.0	-6.3	-1.2	-11.3	..	-5.6	-6.3
São Tomé and Principe	2.3	-36.6	-42.3	-77.3	-76.6	-68.7	-74.7	-72.3	-63.4	-92.5	-76.6	-18.5	-51.1	-75.0
Senegal	-17.4	-12.1	-10.6	-9.7	-9.0	-9.4	-13.6	-14.0	-6.8	-6.2	-7.4	-15.4	-12.2	-9.5
Seychelles	-15.9	1.1	..	0.6	10.9	-3.3	-5.7	-11.3	-4.4	-4.8	-3.5	-15.8	3.4	-3.2
Sierra Leone	-14.0	-6.5	-7.6	-10.8	-11.3	-11.9	-14.4	-14.7	-15.9	-17.5	-15.0	-13.7	-7.0	-14.4
Somalia	-22.6	-11.3	-9.7	-14.0	-8.8	..	..	..	..	..	..	-17.3	-12.2	-8.8
South Africa	..	3.6	1.2	1.6	1.9	2.0	1.2	1.6	-0.5	-1.8	..	-0.6	3.2	0.7
Sudan	-8.3	-2.6	-6.0	-8.4	-9.7	-23.6	-22.6	..	..	..	..	-7.8	-4.7	-18.6
Swaziland	-22.6	10.6	9.4	0.6	5.1	0.4	2.6	-7.6	2.6	-7.1	-7.7	-12.4	2.4	-1.7
Tanzania	..	-15.6	-17.0	-18.4	-19.7	-19.5	-25.9	-29.9	-31.8	-20.6	..	-8.7	-13.6	-24.6
Togo	-8.4	-7.0	-8.0	-7.1	-8.4	-4.9	-7.1	-6.9	-6.8	-6.3	-6.8	-10.5	-7.2	-6.8
Uganda	-9.6	-2.2	-4.5	-6.9	-10.0	-13.5	-11.8	-11.8	-7.8	-7.9	-8.6	-5.8	-4.0	-10.2
Zaire	-0.6	-14.2	-6.7	-9.6	-7.9	-11.4	-11.3	-7.0	-8.3	-9.0	-2.9	-3.6	-6.2	-8.3
Zambia	-13.8	-15.3	-7.1	-5.6	-11.8	-15.2	-23.7	-13.2	-10.7	-13.7	-11.4	-11.9	-13.0	-14.3
Zimbabwe	-8.3	0.0	0.8	-1.2	-3.8	-8.3	-15.3	-5.6	-5.5	-5.6	-1.8	-6.2	-1.0	-6.5
NORTH AFRICA	4.8	-5.5	-4.8	-4.6	-2.6	-1.2	2.0	2.4	-2.1	-2.8	..	-4.0	-4.3	-0.7
Algeria	0.6	0.1	-3.2	-1.9	2.2	4.8	2.1	1.6	-4.3	-5.4	..	-4.5	-1.9	0.2
Egypt, Arab Republic	-1.9	-19.1	-11.7	-10.0	-9.8	-7.4	7.4	9.1	0.5	0.8	..	-9.6	-11.9	0.1
Libya	23.2	-4.6	-8.5	-4.6	..	..	..	..	..	..	..	4.8	-2.2	..
Morocco	-7.8	1.0	2.2	-3.5	-0.8	-1.4	-2.0	-2.0	-2.4	-4.9	..	-10.4	-1.5	-2.3
Tunisia	-4.3	-0.7	1.5	-1.0	-5.5	-4.4	-7.0	-8.8	-4.2	-4.6	..	-7.4	-2.8	-5.7
ALL AFRICA	1.0	-4.0	-4.1	-3.5	-2.5	-3.0	-2.3	-1.8	-3.4	-3.9	..	-4.7	-3.5	-2.8

Note: 1996 data are preliminary (see page 3). Since 1994, Nigeria's ratios are distorted because the official exchange rate used by the Government for oil exports and oil value added is significantly overvalued.

5-9. Net capital grants

	Millions of U.S. dollars (current prices)											Annual average		
	1980	1987	1988	1989	1990	1991	1992	1993	1994	1995	1996	75-84	85-89	90-MR
SUB-SAHARAN AFRICA	1,058	2,798	3,195	3,401	3,919	4,848	5,998	5,127	4,710	4,432	2,774	952	2,762	4,544
excluding South Africa	1,058	2,798	3,195	3,401	3,919	4,848	5,998	5,127	4,710	4,432	2,774	952	2,762	4,544
excl. S.Africa & Nigeria	1,058	2,798	3,195	3,401	3,919	4,848	5,998	5,127	4,710	4,432	2,774	952	2,762	4,544
Angola	0	0	0	0	0	0	0	0	0	0	0	0	0	0
Benin	63	62	76	108	59	45	59	63	55	71	68	63	63	60
Botswana	207	163	241	251	316	298	335	338	359	71	..	125	173	286
Burkina Faso	211	195	213	224	227	274	347	303	211	260	253	151	193	268
Burundi	34	34	26	44	59	66	63	53	18	24	6	38	37	41
Cameroon	0	0	0	0	0	0	0	0	0	0	0	0	0	0
Cape Verde	29	47	39	28	32	37	67	54	60	69	63	20	39	54
Central African Republic	0	0	0	0	0	0	0	0	0	0	0	0	0	0
Chad	28	125	121	129	88	77	76	95	78	75	67	76	140	79
Comoros	0	0	0	0	14	11	21	14	15	11	6	0	0	13
Congo	0	0	0	0	0	0	0	0	0	0	0	0	0	0
Côte d'Ivoire	..	..	..	..	0	53	57	53	54	70	78	..	..	52
Djibouti	0	0	0	0	0	90	84	91	66	60	57	0	0	64
Equatorial Guinea	..	25	29	22	35	35	27	30	7	8	2	..	20	21
Eritrea	..	..	..	..	..	..	168	70	80	73	106	..	..	99
Ethiopia	0	156	138	159	112	230	221	293	198	280	259	26	183	227
Gabon	0	0	0	0	0	0	0	0	0	0	0	0	0	0
Gambia, The	..	0	0	44	45	31	34	31	31	31	0	0	9	29
Ghana	83	122	175	219	214	202	216	256	201	260	206	69	144	222
Guinea	..	83	84	98	101	110	136	118	120	148	..	..	77	122
Guinea-Bissau	..	32	27	43	30	33	29	37	44	56	41	..	34	38
Kenya	0	159	256	250	205	204	214	94	80	90	123	12	185	144
Lesotho	..	..	..	..	156	152	266	225	251	357	..	..	..	234
Liberia	..	..	..	..	..	..	..	..	..	..	..	..	..	..
Madagascar	0	0	0	68	91	36	72	87	72	85	99	16	14	77
Malawi	50	30	92	75	81	59	147	120	111	152	100	33	50	110
Mali	0	117	145	109	106	138	144	106	99	126	136	14	109	122
Mauritania	0	59	35	25	21	22	21	20	26	27	10	0	42	21
Mauritius	11	18	16	18	25	15	19	2	0	13	13	5	18	12
Mozambique	56	349	377	388	448	502	499	503	565	339	283	90	293	449
Namibia	0	0	0	0	43	29	33	27	43	44	45	0	0	38
Niger	0	0	-154	-137	-184	-158	-129	-154	-134	-115	-118	0	-58	-142
Nigeria	0	0	0	0	0	0	0	0	0	0	0	0	0	0
Rwanda	..	0	75	33	24	67	60	0	41	64	120	..	22	54
São Tomé and Principe	0	2	1	2	11	12	13	10	14	24	26	0	1	16
Senegal	140	250	270	250	321	315	328	290	267	273	280	130	224	296
Seychelles	15	24	29	32	35	24	24	34	36	15	15	10	23	26
Sierra Leone	11	6	5	4	9	9	8	19	11	1	16	5	5	10
Somalia	0	0	0	0	0	0	0	0	0	0	0	0	0	0
South Africa	..	..	..	..	..	..	..	..	..	..	..	..	..	..
Sudan	0	280	369	299	342	205	269	124	88	0	0	36	330	147
Swaziland	0	46	69	86	98	99	131	115	93	0	0	7	59	77
Tanzania	0	0	0	0	..	549	809	759	634	525	..	0	0	655
Togo	..	26	17	47	37	24	26	4	7	8	7	20	27	16
Uganda	38	40	92	131	153	262	206	269	251	303	277	47	72	246
Zaire	0	165	169	207	163	76	24	19	41	51	23	0	108	57
Zambia	23	105	100	72	296	521	636	384	338	318	230	13	91	389
Zimbabwe	58	80	66	79	108	95	242	173	181	167	85	50	68	150
NORTH AFRICA	141	35	150	206	970	695	81	133	171	175	..	529	618	371
Algeria	0	0	0	0	0	0	0	0	0	0	..	0	0	0
Egypt, Arab Republic	2	0	0	0	0	0	0	0	0	0	0	182	461	0
Libya	0	0	0	0	0	0	0	0	0	0	0	0	0	0
Morocco	98	0	90	0	760	573	0	30	68	105	..	139	81	256
Tunisia	42	35	60	206	210	122	81	104	103	70	..	27	75	115
ALL AFRICA	1,199	2,833	3,345	3,607	4,888	5,542	6,079	5,260	4,881	4,607	2,774	1,678	3,380	4,862

Note: 1996 data are preliminary (see page 3).

5-10. Net foreign direct investment

	Millions of U.S. dollars (current prices)											Annual average		
	1980	1987	1988	1989	1990	1991	1992	1993	1994	1995	1996	75-84	85-89	90-MR
SUB-SAHARAN AFRICA	-54	1,404	1,695	3,689	627	561	38	1,499	1,417	2,003	1,630	884	1,800	1,111
excluding South Africa	-54	1,567	1,597	3,679	878	1,523	1,428	680	1,402	1,953	1,630	834	1,934	1,356
excl. S.Africa & Nigeria	685	954	1,238	1,236	276	935	592	66	820	1,197	718	752	1,076	658
Angola	..	119	131	200	-336	665	288	302	326	329	..	346	192	262
Benin	4	1	1	1	2	4	26	-7	8	4	-6	2	1	4
Botswana	109	-147	154	135	158	153	47	-269	7	..	..	46	53	19
Burkina Faso	0	0	0	1	6	0	1	0	1	3	7	1	0	3
Burundi	1	1	1	1	1	1	1	0	0	0	0	1	1	0
Cameroon	105	345	350	436	13	-115	-64	-98	-48	-2	57	58	322	-37
Cape Verde	..	3	0	-1	0	1	-1	3	2	10	10	..	1	4
Central African Republic	5	9	-9	-3	1	-8	4	-15	-2	0	6	6	2	-2
Chad	0	0	0	14	25	6	3	21	17	12	18	11	19	15
Comoros	0	8	4	3	-1	3	-1	0	0	1	1	0	3	0
Congo	40	43	9	0	-29	-57	..	..	..	..	..	24	18	-43
Côte d'Ivoire	83	88	56	22	26	45	35	24	52	94	223	51	53	71
Djibouti	..	..	..	..	..	..	..	..	..	..	..	..	..	..
Equatorial Guinea	..	0	0	0	10	40	-4	-12	-19	190	..	..	0	34
Eritrea	..	..	..	..	..	..	..	..	..	..	..	..	..	..
Ethiopia	0	0	0	0	0	0	0	0	0	0	0	3	0	0
Gabon	24	267	368	85	80	-150	-87	-114	-100	-113	-136	59	219	-88
Gambia, The	..	3	11	3	9	11	11	7	5	..	..	1	5	8
Ghana	16	5	5	15	15	20	22	25	30	35	20	13	7	24
Guinea	34	64	60	43	64	61	106	100	82	96	..	12	52	85
Guinea-Bissau	..	0	0	0	1	0	0	0	0	0	0	..	0	0
Kenya	78	32	9	101	58	19	6	2	4	13	16	25	36	17
Lesotho	5	2	21	13	17	7	15	8	19	19	..	4	8	14
Liberia	..	39	..	..	..	..	..	..	..	..	..	47	2	..
Madagascar	0	0	0	13	22	14	21	15	6	10	10	-1	3	14
Malawi	10	0	0	0	0	0	0	0	0	0	0	4	0	0
Mali	2	-6	1	15	-14	-8	-9	-7	38	30	29	0	1	9
Mauritania	27	2	1	4	8	5	7	16	3	7	0	1	3	7
Mauritius	1	16	24	36	35	14	-16	-19	10	26	17	2	19	10
Mozambique	0	6	5	3	9	23	25	32	35	45	73	0	3	35
Namibia	..	..	..	..	28	114	117	49	60	51	52	..	..	67
Niger	44	3	-15	1	-12	0	0	0	0	4	0	17	-5	-1
Nigeria	-739	613	359	2,443	602	588	836	614	582	756	912	212	857	699
Rwanda	..	18	21	22	7	5	6	6	0	2	3	..	19	4
São Tomé and Principe	..	0	0	0	0	0	1	4	2	2	2	..	0	2
Senegal	13	0	0	0	37	5	-42	-85	88	34	-17	8	0	3
Seychelles	6	14	18	15	19	..	..	..	..	..	..	5	11	19
Sierra Leone	10	0	0	2	3	3	5	18	17	18	24	4	1	13
Somalia	..	..	..	..	..	..	..	..	..	..	..	-1	..	..
South Africa	..	-163	98	10	-251	-962	-1,390	819	15	50	..	-123	-134	-287
Sudan	..	..	..	..	..	..	..	..	..	..	..	..	..	..
Swaziland	18	54	42	60	19	34	42	26	46	30	28	15	38	32
Tanzania	..	..	..	..	..	..	..	..	..	..	..	..	..	..
Togo	42	13	6	17	8	12	19	2	6	5	11	23	13	9
Uganda	0	28	10	13	6	1	2	4	5	2	113	1	22	19
Zaire	0	10	11	12	13	0	0	0	0	0	0	91	9	2
Zambia	..	0	0	0	0	0	0	0	40	75	146	6	0	37
Zimbabwe	10	-86	-57	-47	-34	10	6	27	80	168	32	1	-43	41
NORTH AFRICA	65	41	357	560	563	648	1,352	1,518	2,542	1,506	..	145	321	1,355
Algeria	281	-109	-48	-25	-39	-34	3	-2	0	0	..	-2	-67	-12
Egypt, Arab Republic	541	176	124	124	136	141	359	453	1,285	677	..	456	171	508
Libya	-1,136	-230	42	90	54	..	..	..	..	..	..	-564	-33	54
Morocco	143	112	129	226	227	376	503	522	815	535	..	73	122	496
Tunisia	236	92	110	144	185	166	487	545	442	295	..	182	128	353
ALL AFRICA	11	1,445	2,051	4,249	1,190	1,209	1,390	3,016	3,959	3,509	..	1,036	2,121	2,379

Note: 1996 data are preliminary (see page 3).

5-11. Net long-term borrowing

	Millions of U.S. dollars (current prices)											Annual average		
	1980	1987	1988	1989	1990	1991	1992	1993	1994	1995	1996	75-84	85-89	90-MR
SUB-SAHARAN AFRICA	11,421	6,302	4,546	6,347	4,012	3,460	3,483	2,002	4,793	4,723	..	5,560	4,807	4,364
excluding South Africa	7,746	6,516	5,908	6,639	5,105	4,394	3,738	4,950	2,698	2,467	..	5,658	5,552	3,619
excl. S.Africa & Nigeria	6,236	5,712	5,686	5,658	5,358	4,470	5,081	4,985	2,845	2,844	..	4,643	5,349	3,990
Angola	..	679	620	375	629	128	493	632	280	164	..	..	741	388
Benin	56	56	46	126	102	84	89	60	79	68	..	74	57	80
Botswana	21	68	18	34	-37	49	22	45	-5	2	..	28	37	13
Burkina Faso	55	95	73	82	61	121	128	119	80	83	..	48	73	99
Burundi	35	117	80	85	69	60	86	58	31	27	..	37	85	55
Cameroon	500	174	243	664	449	220	520	264	249	-101	..	313	237	267
Cape Verde	3	3	6	7	8	-1	10	7	24	14	..	10	8	10
Central African Republic	24	82	85	56	105	94	41	47	36	30	..	17	68	59
Chad	3	40	58	77	101	88	139	51	54	53	..	21	41	81
Comoros	13	13	8	4	5	-3	14	4	6	9	..	11	14	6
Congo	488	92	319	-15	-42	-167	33	383	30	-67	..	222	141	29
Côte d'Ivoire	1,017	213	126	340	521	389	351	278	524	205	..	636	141	378
Djibouti	8	21	12	3	19	13	17	18	9	8	..	8	17	14
Equatorial Guinea	18	18	20	19	9	7	13	9	4	2	..	8	17	7
Eritrea	..	..	..	..	..	..	..	..	..	..	..	..	..	..
Ethiopia	93	336	375	297	208	345	259	312	186	145	..	126	322	243
Gabon	-109	196	241	131	152	68	8	58	29	133	..	52	207	75
Gambia, The	51	29	13	17	3	12	37	7	2	6	..	18	21	11
Ghana	143	262	281	242	291	387	351	328	291	343	..	69	242	332
Guinea	47	70	187	186	100	145	149	245	120	55	..	44	132	136
Guinea-Bissau	77	42	45	37	34	42	37	21	18	13	..	26	41	28
Kenya	424	371	400	547	317	545	178	103	-307	226	..	250	335	177
Lesotho	10	40	37	40	43	46	58	40	37	42	..	15	32	44
Liberia	61	27	4	-1	-1	-13	0	20	-14	0	..	61	22	-1
Madagascar	320	253	150	148	148	150	79	83	48	55	..	168	157	94
Malawi	120	73	82	93	87	109	90	148	72	59	..	75	70	94
Mali	89	119	110	157	133	109	103	38	42	126	..	79	126	92
Mauritania	109	95	69	33	49	23	81	81	82	43	..	101	77	60
Mauritius	79	77	138	53	103	81	3	23	87	268	..	37	60	94
Mozambique	..	332	150	184	190	76	169	142	194	195	..	..	279	161
Namibia	..	..	..	..	..	..	..	..	..	..	..	..	..	..
Niger	223	144	121	90	92	-24	56	47	32	-6	..	107	104	33
Nigeria	1,510	803	222	981	-253	-76	-1,343	-35	-148	-376	..	1,015	203	-372
Rwanda	25	92	76	50	53	76	65	38	19	43	..	28	71	49
São Tomé and Principe	9	9	11	16	16	43	20	15	14	12	..	6	11	20
Senegal	171	270	118	243	81	26	218	97	9	23	..	166	215	76
Seychelles	12	12	3	1	3	3	6	-4	-1	-3	..	7	11	1
Sierra Leone	54	10	25	16	44	52	37	87	59	47	..	30	20	54
Somalia	106	72	63	64	43	13	0	0	0	0	..	136	83	9
South Africa	..	..	..	..	..	..	..	..	..	..	..	..	..	..
Sudan	658	160	324	191	171	116	94	91	9	36	..	495	164	86
Swaziland	21	-9	-8	-4	-13	2	-10	-8	-3	0	..	22	-1	-5
Tanzania	318	181	299	123	217	164	229	141	174	147	..	289	188	178
Togo	82	17	88	36	56	47	34	10	33	18	..	88	30	33
Uganda	51	355	90	240	234	118	204	298	182	161	..	62	197	200
Zaire	271	301	330	353	267	263	54	53	1	0	..	281	239	106
Zambia	391	85	132	100	64	127	146	147	55	55	..	210	175	99
Zimbabwe	93	30	-2	131	177	238	373	300	22	84	..	164	44	199
NORTH AFRICA	5,063	3,131	4,488	2,615	1,504	314	1,524	597	1,287	1,044	..	5,187	3,616	1,358
Algeria	869	641	1,587	448	158	-698	450	-422	1,591	929	..	1,435	811	335
Egypt, Arab Republic	2,337	1,327	1,471	656	312	312	-51	286	165	-396	..	2,162	1,459	105
Libya	..	..	..	..	..	..	..	..	..	..	..	..	..	..
Morocco	1,394	776	736	878	883	490	516	96	-112	-151	..	1,116	818	287
Tunisia	352	10	245	187	145	351	353	262	150	586	..	373	212	308
ALL AFRICA	16,484	9,433	9,034	8,961	5,516	3,774	5,007	2,599	6,079	5,768	..	10,747	8,422	5,721

5-12. Other capital flows

	Millions of U.S. dollars (current prices)											Annual average		
	1980	1987	1988	1989	1990	1991	1992	1993	1994	1995	1996	75-84	85-89	90-MR
SUB-SAHARAN AFRICA	..	283	-290	-3,121	1,061	2,486	-2,122	2,016	3,335	3,285	..	..	-336	1,677
excluding South Africa	..	283	-290	-3,121	1,061	2,486	-2,122	2,016	3,335	3,285	..	..	-336	1,677
excl. S.Africa & Nigeria	..	534	932	-429	1,960	2,835	613	1,694	2,624	2,519	..	..	-296	2,041
Angola	..	-1,067	-261	-439	-92	-149	181	-412	252	-99	..	..	-845	-53
Benin	54	-61	-29	-104	-24	7	-7	-35	-80	-17	..	25	-41	-26
Botswana	-40	-18	-176	-87	49	44	-422	-144	-229	..	..	-16	-42	-141
Burkina Faso	5	26	-54	-133	-366	-542	-565	-475	-11	94	..	15	-26	-311
Burundi	8	55	-10	-12	-5	-11	-41	-28	32	21	..	-10	4	-5
Cameroon	103	-102	-234	-1,188	-68	71	-535	237	-187	288	..	114	-244	-32
Cape Verde	..	-8	-3	-6	-7	-8	5	-10	-14	30	..	..	-4	-1
Central African Republic	24	24	25	76	79	16	116	107	126	77	..	4	24	87
Chad	-19	33	10	38	5	18	-53	20	83	60	..	-25	16	22
Comoros	-8	5	-7	-15	0	-3	2	3	-1	5	..	-2	-5	1
Congo	-302	155	187	119	441	703	..	..	..	..	..	2	190	572
Côte d'Ivoire	..	..	..	..	625	820	646	926	295	394	..	..	..	618
Djibouti	..	..	..	..	..	..	..	..	..	..	..	..	..	..
Equatorial Guinea	..	-7	-7	-6	-6	2	5	18	17	-88	..	..	-8	-9
Eritrea	..	..	..	..	..	..	..	..	..	..	..	..	..	..
Ethiopia	-7	-76	-191	-173	-151	68	-235	86	136	-279	..	-6	-131	-62
Gabon	-337	165	347	417	-331	57	84	35	-128	-161	..	-259	245	-74
Gambia, The	..	12	-3	14	-19	-12	-25	-16	29	..	..	36	13	-8
Ghana	-366	-26	-72	-35	30	16	-121	248	98	46	..	-81	-96	53
Guinea	..	-22	-55	-88	43	-50	-20	-74	-17	41	..	..	-62	-13
Guinea-Bissau	..	-27	-9	-12	-11	0	26	-14	-45	-28	..	..	-16	-12
Kenya	483	489	388	160	514	-508	2	65	344	25	..	136	280	74
Lesotho	..	..	..	..	97	352	89	87	543	270	..	..	..	240
Liberia	..	..	..	..	..	..	..	..	..	..	..	..	..	..
Madagascar	..	-37	62	-52	-70	69	67	94	155	226	..	0	27	90
Malawi	113	-17	20	5	6	93	41	81	36	100	..	27	-9	59
Mali	25	8	44	41	35	82	17	99	77	59	..	-3	15	61
Mauritania	-27	62	-20	-152	36	82	13	-25	-80	51	..	15	-16	13
Mauritius	74	-1	19	126	110	85	68	42	75	-138	..	14	22	40
Mozambique	..	64	230	270	222	151	85	101	124	157	..	..	109	140
Namibia	..	..	..	..	..	..	..	..	..	..	..	..	..	..
Niger	109	..	90	20	388	352	257	267	337	293	..	117	102	316
Nigeria	-1,083	-251	-1,223	-2,692	-900	-349	-2,735	322	711	766	..	-156	-41	-364
Rwanda	..	8	-42	42	-5	-6	0	43	-11	-48	..	..	1	-4
São Tomé and Principe	..	6	6	17	12	-13	2	10	-1	4	..	..	11	2
Senegal	147	16	153	30	121	210	62	156	139	56	..	43	57	124
Seychelles	-1	-48	-53	-46	-94	..	..	..	..	..	..	-4	-50	-94
Sierra Leone	61	40	80	105	46	42	70	3	54	68	..	79	55	47
Somalia	..	..	..	..	..	..	..	..	..	..	..	-8	..	..
South Africa	..	..	..	..	..	..	..	..	..	..	..	..	..	..
Sudan	..	..	..	..	..	..	..	..	..	..	..	..	..	..
Swaziland	130	-133	-155	-96	-139	-125	-94	-106	-130	46	..	32	-99	-91
Tanzania	..	..	..	..	..	..	..	..	..	..	..	..	..	..
Togo	..	39	10	64	40	12	-45	-56	6	63	..	-7	35	3
Uganda	-23	-304	117	-41	26	32	-73	-162	-38	124	..	-78	-103	-15
Zaire	-149	730	118	492	294	654	849	545	427	464	..	-81	218	539
Zambia	..	421	352	315	140	-106	73	15	157	113	..	-10	29	65
Zimbabwe	267	130	54	-94	-11	331	90	-38	51	205	..	63	71	105
NORTH AFRICA	-3,367	4,163	1,145	2,159	672	4,824	545	-692	1,891	689	..	-2,376	1,658	1,322
Algeria	-50	-523	-432	-35	-1,556	-965	-1,406	-426	718	387	..	-385	142	-541
Egypt, Arab Republic	-2,611	5,435	2,944	2,769	2,045	6,037	1,340	-1,014	390	8	..	-1,455	2,225	1,468
Libya	..	..	..	..	..	..	..	..	..	..	..	..	..	..
Morocco	-513	-793	-1,174	-242	127	-85	360	335	468	397	..	-251	-596	267
Tunisia	-192	44	-194	-334	56	-164	250	412	314	-102	..	-26	-112	128
ALL AFRICA	..	4,445	855	-963	1,733	7,310	-1,577	1,324	5,227	3,974	..	..	1,322	2,998

Note: Includes all capital account flows, except changes in reserves, that are not included in the tables on foreign investment or long-term borrowing.

5-13. Use of reserves

	Millions of U.S. dollars (current prices)											Annual average		
	1980	1987	1988	1989	1990	1991	1992	1993	1994	1995	1996	75-84	85-89	90-MR
SUB-SAHARAN AFRICA	-4,215	-1,766	-763	-3,801	-3,406	-3,128	3,926	542	-2,204	-6,779	-4,201	984	-1,298	-2,178
excluding South Africa	-4,215	-1,766	-1,537	-3,301	-3,061	-1,667	4,020	-502	-3,114	-2,918	-4,201	928	-1,353	-1,635
excl. S.Africa & Nigeria	330	-1,844	-1,868	-2,029	-963	-1,380	182	-445	-2,987	-2,321	-1,701	479	-1,211	-1,374
Angola	0	-178	-49	6	37	-48	-150	193	14	133	0	33	-40	26
Benin	19	35	30	-103	-99	-87	-70	14	-24	16	-48	10	-5	-42
Botswana	-90	-562	-382	-578	-307	-293	-74	-309	-306	-576	..	-63	-417	-311
Burkina Faso	-11	-33	-34	41	-2	-43	-61	-73	-117	-186	-97	-13	-14	-83
Burundi	8	-79	-1	-50	2	-20	5	-4	-54	-27	-30	10	-37	-18
Cameroon	-145	516	75	126	53	30	57	218	324	-14	-82	-33	100	84
Cape Verde	0	-12	0	18	3	11	-9	10	17	-15	-13	-1	-2	1
Central African Republic	-10	19	-11	-6	4	10	-4	-29	-134	-12	-20	-4	4	-26
Chad	5	-17	-18	-30	2	8	27	32	-50	-59	4	-3	-5	-5
Comoros	4	-9	0	2	3	4	0	-14	4	4	-9	0	-3	-1
Congo	-59	5	-2	-6	0	45	27	5	-47	-7	-14	1	2	1
Côte d'Ivoire	112	-145	-107	18	150	-50	235	-88	-794	-222	-51	92	-75	-117
Djibouti	..	..	..	..	..	-6	17	8	-4	7	-1	..	..	3
Equatorial Guinea	13	15	1	3	-1	-4	8	2	-1	-8	..	2	3	-1
Eritrea	..	..	..	..	..	..	-120	-115	-78	58	75	..	..	-36
Ethiopia	40	21	190	10	73	-147	-66	-194	-229	-56	-55	27	2	-96
Gabon	-93	-179	-340	-466	-51	-67	222	79	-137	42	-83	-9	-180	1
Gambia, The	..	-3	0	-4	8	5	1	21	-19	0	..	5	-4	3
Ghana	96	-138	-125	-127	-118	-171	124	-41	-164	-284	19	25	-44	-91
Guinea	-30	-33	27	-22	-51	-18	-3	-49	34	-31	..	-2	-10	-20
Guinea-Bissau	..	-11	-12	6	-15	-7	-5	9	6	0	-11	..	-6	-3
Kenya	131	-435	-371	-221	-408	91	-76	-331	-104	133	-408	7	-227	-158
Lesotho	-43	0	-1	4	-25	-44	-92	0	-419	-219	..	-7	-6	-133
Liberia	41	1	-1	-10	-1	..	0	-1	-3	..	..	27	-3	-1
Madagascar	-83	-69	-69	-33	137	-17	-17	-16	0	-60	-134	6	-44	-15
Malawi	17	-26	-84	40	-29	-11	94	-7	11	-84	-101	16	-1	-18
Mali	8	-21	-61	-127	-42	-142	-6	-23	-87	-68	-83	4	-28	-64
Mauritania	24	4	14	-28	37	-27	3	22	27	-33	-50	16	4	-3
Mauritius	-25	-174	-139	-131	-161	-179	-68	54	55	-144	-36	24	-112	-68
Mozambique	32	-58	-25	3	-6	-13	-40	46	-52	-60	-158	46	-17	-40
Namibia	..	..	..	..	-37	12	7	-91	-75	-29	-131	..	..	-49
Niger	53	-14	-39	16	-22	-4	-13	9	-8	0	0	6	5	-5
Nigeria	-4,545	78	331	-1,272	-2,098	-287	3,838	-57	-127	-597	-2,500	449	-142	-261
Rwanda	..	18	47	41	56	-55	27	43	-3	-46	-18	..	13	1
São Tomé and Principe	12	3	3	1	0	-2	-2	-5	2	1	2	0	2	-1
Senegal	55	20	-15	-75	-46	-42	-20	111	-241	-85	-25	26	-12	-49
Seychelles	-8	-4	4	-4	-4	-11	-3	-2	8	4	1	-1	-1	-1
Sierra Leone	32	-1	-12	1	-1	-10	-21	-13	7	18	21	17	-4	0
Somalia	18	15	-72	-24	-51	..	..	..	..	..	..	5	-12	-51
South Africa	..	..	774	-501	-344	-1,461	-94	1,044	911	-3,860	..	111	137	-634
Sudan	140	220	281	172	102	112	101	39	62	..	..	86	152	83
Swaziland	-37	-20	-13	-50	-11	-13	-95	45	-32	1	-18	-8	-17	-18
Tanzania	66	5	-61	65	-57	-86	133	118	-107	-46	..	9	-2	-7
Togo	2	-8	-11	-68	-3	-15	86	125	11	-12	-41	-18	-21	22
Uganda	55	22	-14	18	10	37	-2	-29	-90	-146	-73	25	-10	-42
Zaire	-35	-118	-37	-202	1	43	-1	14	17	39	-12	76	-60	14
Zambia	0	-264	-320	-265	-111	-29	-101	-75	-192	3	-44	49	12	-78
Zimbabwe	17	-152	-112	9	17	-126	127	-151	-16	-254	43	13	-93	-51
NORTH AFRICA	-7,299	1,448	1,073	613	-1,064	-4,987	-6,539	-4,489	-3,464	852	..	560	55	-3,282
Algeria	-1,341	-48	796	642	85	-527	-67	48	-489	924	..	-39	237	-4
Egypt, Arab Republic	168	819	-456	433	1,723	-3,760	-5,070	-4,022	-2,106	-754	0	421	161	-1,998
Libya	-6,407	1,082	1,392	-292	-1,158	150	-520	-35	..	..	..	73	-81	-391
Morocco	346	-288	-281	-74	-1,797	-953	-800	-441	-513	702	..	126	-206	-634
Tunisia	-65	-116	-378	-97	83	103	-82	-39	-355	-19	..	-20	-57	-52
ALL AFRICA	-11,513	-318	310	-3,189	-4,470	-8,115	-2,614	-3,947	-5,667	-5,926	-4,201	1,544	-1,243	-4,991

Note: Excludes IMF credit transactions, which appear in the Table on long-term borrowing.

5-14. Import coverage ratio of reserves

	Reserves in months of imports of goods and services											Annual average		
	1980	*1987*	*1988*	*1989*	*1990*	*1991*	*1992*	*1993*	*1994*	*1995*	*1996*	*75-84*	*85-89*	*90-MR*
SUB-SAHARAN AFRICA	..	5	5	6	6	6	7	9	9	7	..	3	5	7
excluding South Africa	5	7	7	7	7	8	9	11	10	9	3	3	6	8
excl. S.Africa & Nigeria	3	8	7	9	9	9	10	12	11	10	3	3	7	9
Angola	..	..	..	..	..	..	..	..	..	..	..	..	..	..
Benin	0	0	0	0	1	4	4	4	6	3	3	1	0	4
Botswana	4	18	17	18	17	18	20	24	26	21	..	4	16	21
Burkina Faso	2	6	6	5	10	17	13	13	6	6	5	2	5	10
Burundi	6	3	3	5	4	5	6	7	7	7	7	3	3	6
Cameroon	1	0	1	0	0	0	0	0	0	0	..	1	1	0
Cape Verde	6	8	8	6	6	5	5	4	2	2	2	6	7	4
Central African Republic	2	3	4	4	3	4	3	4	10	8	..	2	3	5
Chad	2	2	2	3	3	3	2	1	2	3	..	1	2	2
Comoros	2	4	3	5	5	4	4	5	6	5	..	2	3	5
Congo	1	0	0	0	0	0	0	0	0	0	..	0	0	0
Côte d'Ivoire	0	0	0	0	0	0	0	0	1	1	1	0	0	1
Djibouti	..	..	..	..	..	3	3	2	3	3	3	..	..	3
Equatorial Guinea	..	0	1	0	0	1	2	0	0	0	..	..	0	0
Eritrea	..	..	..	..	..	..	..	..	..	..	..	..	..	..
Ethiopia	4	2	1	1	1	1	3	4	6	7	5	5	2	4
Gabon	1	0	0	0	1	2	0	0	1	1	..	1	1	1
Gambia, The	..	3	1	1	3	3	4	..	5	5	..	0	1	4
Ghana	3	3	3	4	2	4	3	3	4	4	..	3	5	3
Guinea	..	..	..	..	..	1	1	2	1	1	..	..	..	1
Guinea-Bissau	..	1	2	2	2	1	2	2	2	2	..	..	2	2
Kenya	2	1	1	1	1	1	0	2	2	1	3	2	2	1
Lesotho	1	2	1	1	1	1	2	3	4	4	..	1	1	3
Liberia	0	0	..	..	..	..	..	..	..	..	..	0	0	..
Madagascar	0	3	4	4	1	1	..	..	1	1	2	1	3	1
Malawi	1	2	4	2	3	3	1	1	1	2	..	1	2	2
Mali	1	0	1	2	3	4	4	5	3	4	5	1	1	4
Mauritania	4	1	1	2	1	1	1	1	1	2	2	3	1	1
Mauritius	2	4	4	4	5	6	5	4	4	4	4	2	3	4
Mozambique	..	2	2	2	2	3	..	..	2	2	4	1	2	3
Namibia	..	..	..	..	..	..	0	1	1	1	1	..	..	1
Niger	2	7	6	7	5	5	6	5	3	3	3	2	6	4
Nigeria	6	2	1	2	4	4	1	2	2	2	..	3	2	2
Rwanda	..	5	3	2	1	4	2	1	1	4	6	..	4	3
São Tomé and Principe	..	..	..	..	..	..	..	..	..	..	..	..	..	..
Senegal	0	0	0	0	0	0	0	0	1	2	2	0	0	1
Seychelles	2	1	1	1	1	1	1	1	1	1	1	1	1	1
Sierra Leone	1	0	0	0	0	0	1	1	1	1	1	1	0	1
Somalia	1	0	1	0	..	..	..	..	..	..	..	2	0	..
South Africa	..	2	1	1	1	2	1	1	1	2	..	2	1	1
Sudan	0	0	0	0	0	0	0	0	0	..	..	0	0	0
Swaziland	3	3	3	3	3	2	4	3	3	3	2	3	3	3
Tanzania	0	0	1	0	1	1	2	1	2	1	..	1	0	1
Togo	1	6	4	5	5	6	5	4	3	3	3	3	6	4
Uganda	0	1	1	0	1	1	2	2	4	4	4	1	1	2
Zaire	2	2	1	1	1	1	1	0	1	1	0	1	2	1
Zambia	1	1	1	1	1	1	..	2	..	..	..	1	1	1
Zimbabwe	8	3	2	2	2	1	2	3	3	3	3	3	2	2
NORTH AFRICA	9	7	5	5	5	..	6	7	8	8	..	5	7	7
Algeria	6	5	3	3	2	3	3	4	4	3	..	4	4	3
Egypt, Arab Republic	3	2	2	2	3	4	9	10	11	11	..	2	2	8
Libya	13	12	9	8	9	..	..	..	..	..	..	7	11	9
Morocco	2	2	1	1	3	4	4	5	5	4	..	1	1	4
Tunisia	2	2	2	2	2	2	1	1	2	2	..	2	2	2
ALL AFRICA	8	6	5	6	6	5	7	8	8	8	..	5	6	7

Note: 1996 data are preliminary (see page 3). Based on total reserves, excluding gold, at year-end and on imports of all goods and services at current prices and exchange rates.

5-15. Export unit values

	Index 1987=100											Average annual percentage growth		
	1980	1987	1988	1989	1990	1991	1992	1993	1994	1995	1996	75-84	85-89	90-MR
SUB-SAHARAN AFRICA	128.6	100.0	98.1	98.4	110.6	102.8	102.7	92.2	96.4	99.2	102.9	6.1	5.6	-1.2
excluding South Africa	135.1	100.0	98.7	103.2	119.3	107.3	106.8	91.9	97.1	98.8	111.4	4.3	4.8	-1.7
excl. S. Africa & Nigeria	122.7	100.0	104.2	104.1	112.9	105.6	102.5	93.0	104.8	112.3	124.7	4.0	3.1	1.6
Angola	..	100.0	85.9	102.1	111.8	40.2	67.1	63.0	130.5	95.6	..	..	-3.9	2.0
Benin	69.7	100.0	113.8	119.6	151.9	120.2	97.4	122.4	100.3	122.2	104.7	5.9	10.1	-2.7
Botswana	..	100.0	180.7	217.0	..	..	..	..	..	..	..	..	60.0	..
Burkina Faso	69.4	100.0	112.8	121.5	126.5	117.4	122.0	110.1	114.2	135.5	..	5.1	12.3	0.2
Burundi	135.8	100.0	111.9	91.7	79.8	89.1	72.1	77.5	130.2	121.8	107.8	5.4	-2.7	5.4
Cameroon	139.8	100.0	93.2	87.2	95.3	107.8	94.9	84.8	65.8	79.6	78.5	3.5	-3.0	-3.8
Cape Verde	89.1	100.0	106.1	101.5	114.5	118.4	128.5	114.1	115.2	133.0	129.8	7.1	11.8	2.7
Central African Republic	82.4	100.0	115.1	110.2	121.2	106.4	112.0	106.0	96.0	114.1	100.0	8.4	9.5	-1.6
Chad	126.2	100.0	110.2	92.8	125.7	124.7	120.7	105.4	102.1	129.6	125.5	-0.7	3.2	1.8
Comoros	110.6	100.0	108.8	102.4	122.1	128.5	139.7	138.3	88.5	95.1	88.1	..	12.8	-4.0
Congo	148.4	100.0	82.9	99.3	120.7	108.4	104.9	67.5	90.7	99.1	117.7	9.7	-6.1	-0.9
Côte d'Ivoire	112.3	100.0	94.5	81.4	80.5	80.4	91.3	86.1	77.9	96.9	90.5	-1.1	-1.1	1.8
Djibouti	..	..	..	..	..	..	..	..	..	..	..	..	..	..
Equatorial Guinea	..	..	..	..	..	..	..	..	..	..	..	..	..	..
Eritrea	..	..	..	..	..	..	..	..	..	..	..	..	..	..
Ethiopia	..	100.0	96.6	112.3	103.5	109.8	129.1	124.6	117.3	136.7	117.0	..	2.2	2.2
Gabon	203.3	100.0	97.2	110.1	140.8	127.5	125.4	92.4	107.0	114.8	133.1	8.8	-4.6	-0.6
Gambia, The	82.9	100.0	99.3	95.5	111.2	127.6	114.6	120.6	86.9	119.1	..	4.0	6.7	0.4
Ghana	37.4	100.0	96.4	78.7	83.8	86.4	83.0	77.5	88.4	97.7	89.8	0.5	10.7	2.0
Guinea	..	100.0	92.7	103.2	113.5	107.3	97.7	86.6	87.2	92.9	89.8	..	-0.5	-3.2
Guinea-Bissau	23.4	100.0	85.4	90.1	86.7	86.9	93.5	87.6	66.5	64.9	57.3	13.5	3.0	-6.3
Kenya	136.4	100.0	104.6	98.2	95.7	94.8	92.3	72.1	110.3	111.9	108.8	5.5	-1.8	2.1
Lesotho	116.9	100.0	108.1	98.3	118.5	111.3	172.8	176.3	178.9	191.6	..	4.8	4.1	12.4
Liberia	..	..	..	..	..	..	..	..	..	..	..	..	..	..
Madagascar	80.1	100.0	102.3	98.9	96.0	86.5	92.5	91.4	105.7	116.5	107.3	6.5	3.3	2.6
Malawi	106.1	100.0	104.8	114.2	137.0	149.1	125.1	105.4	110.7	109.9	..	3.8	1.4	-3.1
Mali	112.2	100.0	102.3	98.1	111.8	106.9	100.0	94.5	94.0	108.5	104.8	3.4	6.1	-0.1
Mauritania	93.4	100.0	114.9	114.0	115.9	123.3	120.8	100.9	116.6	129.0	131.3	1.7	5.4	1.4
Mauritius	88.0	100.0	101.5	99.8	113.5	112.4	113.6	107.4	110.3	119.9	126.0	0.5	8.9	2.2
Mozambique	..	100.0	98.6	95.5	98.0	103.7	99.6	98.3	102.1	106.8	110.8	..	4.8	1.7
Namibia	156.7	100.0	112.8	118.7	119.7	113.4	111.7	105.1	119.0	114.7	115.0	..	4.5	-0.4
Niger	83.3	100.0	98.7	85.3	90.1	79.7	78.3	76.5	68.9	82.3	..	9.4	11.2	-2.4
Nigeria	162.8	100.0	74.0	99.1	144.5	113.7	122.7	87.6	65.0	42.2	50.8	3.1	10.3	-14.2
Rwanda	159.7	100.0	124.6	110.6	112.7	117.2	103.9	108.4	101.7	168.6	139.7	8.0	-8.3	4.0
São Tomé and Principe	202.8	100.0	86.5	56.0	87.8	98.3	89.1	107.1	151.0	156.6	164.9	0.4	-17.1	15.3
Senegal	101.1	100.0	98.5	101.7	104.9	90.1	66.6	68.1	95.6	106.6	103.4	-0.8	6.8	0.5
Seychelles	..	100.0	104.2	83.8	94.0	84.0	113.3	110.4	117.3	120.5	116.1	..	-5.3	5.5
Sierra Leone	118.2	100.0	136.5	118.9	71.3	67.8	70.6	79.9	80.7	102.4	101.9	18.9	-11.8	1.6
Somalia	120.8	100.0	101.1	151.1	..	..	..	..	..	..	..	-1.2	0.4	..
South Africa	116.6	100.0	97.1	91.1	97.2	95.7	96.3	92.5	95.2	99.6	93.0	9.1	5.0	0.3
Sudan	84.4	100.0	118.1	126.3	154.8	111.8	..	..	..	..	..	4.1	3.8	..
Swaziland	167.0	100.0	108.5	109.9	127.3	131.9	153.0	159.6	169.9	164.1	169.9	3.8	1.5	6.3
Tanzania	..	..	..	..	..	..	..	..	..	..	..	..	..	..
Togo	102.8	100.0	106.9	105.6	116.5	111.4	111.4	95.1	95.0	99.5	99.1	-1.9	5.9	-2.2
Uganda	..	100.0	91.6	73.4	52.1	43.9	38.4	36.5	42.8	64.8	58.3	..	-2.1	-0.8
Zaire	238.8	100.0	111.5	120.7	146.2	118.5	150.3	122.5	184.3	204.1	567.9	3.0	1.7	17.6
Zambia	143.7	100.0	147.5	129.0	159.4	144.0	98.7	78.3	97.3	112.2	100.8	2.4	9.3	-5.7
Zimbabwe	122.0	100.0	112.7	110.5	117.9	171.9	108.2	102.8	98.0	114.4	119.4	4.2	4.2	-1.6
NORTH AFRICA	..	..	..	..	..	..	..	..	..	..	..	..	..	..
Algeria	207.2	100.0	89.0	99.9	136.3	127.2	111.9	101.8	96.5	101.6	..	11.3	-10.2	-3.0
Egypt, Arab Republic	158.5	100.0	107.3	107.5	122.3	140.8	163.2	147.8	141.4	155.8	..	9.8	-7.5	5.3
Libya	..	..	..	..	..	..	..	..	..	..	..	..	..	..
Morocco	107.8	100.0	108.3	111.8	117.5	114.9	119.5	109.7	119.4	132.0	..	2.6	6.2	1.7
Tunisia	128.2	100.0	103.4	104.1	119.1	118.5	128.0	119.1	125.5	141.9	..	5.3	1.6	3.8
ALL AFRICA	141.6	100.0	98.5	100.1	114.9	109.5	110.7	100.1	102.8	107.8	..	6.9	2.7	-1.7

Note: 1996 data are preliminary (see page 3).

5-16. Import unit values

	Index 1987=100											Average annual percentage growth		
	1980	*1987*	*1988*	*1989*	*1990*	*1991*	*1992*	*1993*	*1994*	*1995*	*1996*	*75-84*	*85-89*	*90-MR*
SUB-SAHARAN AFRICA	92.6	100.0	99.5	100.3	112.6	110.4	110.7	103.6	106.7	111.1	110.2	4.9	9.0	-0.3
excluding South Africa	88.5	100.0	100.3	102.2	115.9	112.8	112.4	104.5	110.8	114.8	121.0	2.4	10.0	0.5
excl. S. Africa & Nigeria	102.4	100.0	101.7	102.8	115.2	113.0	109.2	105.7	115.3	124.1	131.8	4.4	6.0	2.3
Angola	..	100.0	112.6	108.6	93.8	40.8	64.0	68.9	169.6	125.0	..	..	5.0	7.9
Benin	63.0	100.0	104.1	107.6	106.8	100.1	80.6	102.2	107.3	114.1	118.9	6.3	13.4	1.8
Botswana	..	100.0	114.5	132.6	..	..	..	..	..	..	..	..	42.0	..
Burkina Faso	113.0	100.0	106.8	108.8	113.2	110.1	112.4	106.5	98.1	107.0	..	5.8	4.3	-1.3
Burundi	102.7	100.0	97.9	104.5	112.1	113.1	100.6	73.3	82.9	90.8	89.8	10.2	2.7	-3.9
Cameroon	120.9	100.0	85.8	69.2	72.2	71.5	64.0	84.4	71.0	73.4	2.6	6.5	-4.2	-23.6
Cape Verde	89.1	100.0	106.1	101.5	114.5	118.4	128.5	114.1	115.2	133.0	129.8	-0.5	11.8	2.7
Central African Republic	65.6	100.0	111.4	109.1	118.1	117.5	121.2	112.7	114.3	129.5	133.1	4.4	15.5	2.0
Chad	120.8	100.0	99.7	102.6	121.4	118.9	123.0	118.0	134.8	155.8	154.3	2.2	5.8	5.4
Comoros	84.9	100.0	103.7	99.2	121.1	105.5	133.5	98.7	104.4	113.4	108.9	..	11.9	0.0
Congo	113.1	100.0	100.0	95.9	146.2	126.6	105.0	93.0	140.2	155.9	153.0	5.8	7.5	4.6
Côte d'Ivoire	118.5	100.0	102.6	105.0	119.8	110.6	119.5	111.3	97.1	117.7	111.2	4.4	6.3	-0.2
Djibouti	..	..	..	..	..	..	..	..	..	..	..	..	..	..
Equatorial Guinea	..	..	..	..	..	..	..	..	..	..	..	..	..	..
Eritrea	..	..	..	..	..	..	..	..	..	..	..	..	..	..
Ethiopia	..	100.0	93.9	87.1	96.5	100.0	79.4	99.9	117.2	123.9	108.2	..	-0.7	4.2
Gabon	94.6	100.0	103.0	116.6	130.3	130.0	135.2	103.6	130.5	146.4	144.3	1.3	10.9	2.2
Gambia, The	62.0	100.0	101.1	105.7	114.7	132.7	119.2	125.4	107.0	117.2	..	10.2	6.9	0.4
Ghana	22.8	100.0	94.6	92.3	104.5	105.1	108.0	108.8	109.1	114.0	114.3	2.0	11.9	2.5
Guinea	..	100.0	103.9	105.1	114.2	115.2	118.5	112.5	114.7	126.2	123.8	..	4.6	1.9
Guinea-Bissau	58.6	100.0	110.2	114.1	119.5	117.8	120.0	112.5	105.1	124.8	117.3	8.1	16.3	0.0
Kenya	105.4	100.0	100.7	100.7	102.7	92.4	90.1	60.0	64.4	73.7	72.4	9.6	0.1	-6.3
Lesotho	99.7	100.0	100.9	104.4	125.6	134.0	153.6	156.5	158.8	170.7	..	7.5	6.3	7.8
Liberia	..	..	..	..	..	..	..	..	..	..	..	..	..	..
Madagascar	97.7	100.0	107.9	110.5	128.4	127.7	134.1	130.9	139.4	156.1	159.2	9.7	4.8	4.6
Malawi	89.8	100.0	113.2	114.1	126.9	131.0	134.8	127.6	123.9	121.3	..	6.4	8.7	0.4
Mali	122.7	100.0	101.3	97.8	109.2	108.8	114.4	111.4	108.5	117.6	116.0	1.9	7.2	1.8
Mauritania	99.8	100.0	107.0	107.3	113.4	113.5	117.1	115.1	117.9	133.0	132.8	5.6	6.0	2.9
Mauritius	102.0	100.0	105.5	109.1	120.2	120.4	121.6	121.3	127.3	139.6	149.9	6.1	5.5	3.8
Mozambique	..	100.0	108.2	112.0	121.3	125.7	125.1	128.0	133.8	137.1	140.8	..	8.4	2.9
Namibia	122.7	100.0	98.0	103.0	115.4	119.8	127.9	123.5	122.9	132.0	135.6	..	3.1	3.2
Niger	147.3	100.0	105.1	110.9	125.4	113.0	116.7	116.6	118.0	123.3	..	2.5	12.3	0.8
Nigeria	65.4	100.0	88.2	96.4	118.6	111.5	127.3	98.1	81.9	53.1	51.3	-3.4	31.6	-10.8
Rwanda	111.6	100.0	102.8	108.3	111.8	57.5	60.3	57.1	52.8	87.7	69.6	5.9	6.4	-5.3
São Tomé and Principe	157.9	100.0	86.5	79.0	87.8	98.3	100.5	91.9	94.8	102.8	116.8	5.2	-10.4	4.0
Senegal	110.7	100.0	99.8	99.1	118.1	113.7	78.4	83.7	116.0	132.1	131.5	0.5	5.5	3.2
Seychelles	..	100.0	102.1	94.1	103.3	100.8	97.5	106.1	150.5	157.3	154.7	..	1.8	8.5
Sierra Leone	91.2	100.0	115.0	115.7	56.1	64.6	74.7	66.3	75.8	70.6	68.4	16.5	-14.4	-2.6
Somalia	128.3	100.0	114.2	167.6	..	..	..	..	..	..	..	-3.5	4.7	..
South Africa	103.6	100.0	98.2	96.4	104.9	104.6	106.9	101.7	100.9	106.9	97.4	10.3	4.2	0.0
Sudan	87.1	100.0	108.5	111.9	114.7	111.5	..	..	..	..	..	-1.0	12.7	..
Swaziland	161.6	100.0	108.2	104.7	132.7	139.9	150.6	144.0	183.9	186.7	196.2	4.6	3.2	8.5
Tanzania	..	..	..	..	..	..	..	..	..	..	..	..	..	..
Togo	112.3	100.0	104.1	105.0	114.1	112.4	113.7	107.8	110.7	122.8	120.9	0.2	7.0	1.5
Uganda	..	100.0	91.8	77.2	68.7	63.0	60.9	62.0	58.6	62.4	64.7	..	10.9	-2.2
Zaire	241.3	100.0	97.9	88.9	143.5	123.7	131.5	115.2	232.5	254.4	710.9	-0.7	-4.9	25.6
Zambia	166.3	100.0	120.9	199.9	191.4	202.5	184.3	150.0	193.1	215.6	212.2	11.9	3.7	0.8
Zimbabwe	122.0	100.0	109.5	118.1	135.9	180.3	134.2	126.4	126.0	139.0	139.6	5.2	5.0	0.2
NORTH AFRICA	106.3	100.0	111.5	113.1	142.4	129.5	137.5	133.7	133.9	142.4	..	4.9	7.7	0.2
Algeria	114.3	100.0	100.6	101.0	173.3	146.0	143.6	161.0	156.7	161.2	..	4.7	4.2	4.7
Egypt, Arab Republic	85.8	100.0	129.6	132.8	140.9	130.6	152.8	138.9	137.4	136.8	..	8.6	9.7	0.4
Libya	..	..	..	..	..	..	..	..	..	..	..	..	..	..
Morocco	117.8	100.0	102.7	108.3	120.1	115.6	115.0	107.6	111.6	129.6	..	4.9	1.3	1.1
Tunisia	111.2	100.0	104.3	104.2	121.6	122.8	134.2	126.0	129.7	146.7	..	5.1	4.4	4.3
ALL AFRICA	95.5	100.0	103.2	104.4	122.2	116.3	119.1	113.0	115.2	120.5	..	5.1	8.4	-0.4

Note: 1996 data are preliminary (see page 3).

5-17. Terms of trade

	Index 1987=100											Average annual percentage growth		
	1980	*1987*	*1988*	*1989*	*1990*	*1991*	*1992*	*1993*	*1994*	*1995*	*1996*	*75-84*	*85-89*	*90-MR*
SUB-SAHARAN AFRICA	138.9	100.0	98.6	98.0	98.2	93.1	92.7	89.0	90.4	89.2	93.4	1.2	-3.1	-0.9
excluding South Africa	152.7	100.0	98.4	101.0	102.9	95.1	95.1	87.9	87.6	86.0	92.0	1.8	-4.7	-2.2
excl. S. Africa & Nigeria	119.8	100.0	102.5	101.2	98.0	93.4	93.9	88.0	90.9	90.5	94.6	-0.4	-2.7	-0.7
Angola	..	100.0	76.2	94.0	119.2	98.6	104.8	91.4	76.9	76.5	..	..	-8.5	-5.5
Benin	110.6	100.0	109.4	111.2	142.2	120.1	120.8	119.7	93.5	107.1	88.1	-0.3	-2.9	-4.4
Botswana	..	100.0	157.9	163.6	..	..	..	..	..	..	..	..	12.7	..
Burkina Faso	61.4	100.0	105.7	111.7	111.8	106.7	108.5	103.4	116.3	126.7	..	-0.7	7.7	1.5
Burundi	132.2	100.0	114.2	87.8	71.2	78.7	71.7	105.7	157.0	134.2	120.1	-4.3	-5.3	9.8
Cameroon	115.6	100.0	108.7	125.9	132.0	150.6	148.3	100.5	92.7	108.5	2992.8	-2.9	1.2	25.9
Cape Verde	100.0	100.0	100.0	100.0	100.0	100.0	100.0	100.0	100.0	100.0	100.0	7.6	0.0	0.0
Central African Republic	125.5	100.0	103.3	101.0	102.6	90.6	92.4	94.1	84.0	88.1	75.1	3.9	-5.1	-3.6
Chad	104.5	100.0	110.5	90.5	103.6	104.9	98.1	89.3	75.8	83.2	81.3	-2.8	-2.4	-3.4
Comoros	130.3	100.0	104.9	103.3	100.8	121.7	104.6	140.1	84.8	83.9	81.0	..	0.8	-4.0
Congo	131.2	100.0	82.9	103.6	82.6	85.6	99.9	72.6	64.7	63.5	76.9	3.7	-12.7	-5.3
Côte d'Ivoire	94.8	100.0	92.1	77.5	67.2	72.7	76.4	77.3	80.3	82.4	81.4	-5.2	-7.0	2.0
Djibouti	..	..	..	..	..	..	..	..	..	..	..	..	..	..
Equatorial Guinea	..	..	..	..	..	..	..	..	..	..	..	..	..	..
Eritrea	..	..	..	..	..	..	..	..	..	..	..	..	..	..
Ethiopia	..	100.0	102.9	128.9	107.2	109.7	162.6	124.7	100.1	110.3	108.1	..	2.9	-1.9
Gabon	214.8	100.0	94.4	94.4	108.1	98.1	92.8	89.2	82.0	78.4	92.2	7.5	-14.1	-2.7
Gambia, The	133.7	100.0	98.2	90.3	96.9	96.1	96.1	96.1	81.3	101.7	..	-5.6	-0.2	0.0
Ghana	163.9	100.0	101.9	85.2	80.2	82.2	76.8	71.3	81.1	85.7	78.6	-1.4	-1.0	-0.4
Guinea	..	100.0	89.2	98.1	99.4	93.1	82.4	77.0	76.0	73.7	72.6	..	-4.9	-5.0
Guinea-Bissau	40.0	100.0	77.5	79.0	72.6	73.8	77.9	77.9	63.2	52.1	48.9	5.0	-11.5	-6.3
Kenya	129.4	100.0	103.8	97.5	93.2	102.6	102.4	120.1	171.3	151.9	150.3	-3.8	-1.8	8.9
Lesotho	117.2	100.0	107.1	94.1	94.3	83.1	112.5	112.7	112.7	112.2	..	-2.5	-2.1	4.3
Liberia	..	..	..	..	..	..	..	..	..	..	..	..	..	..
Madagascar	81.9	100.0	94.8	89.5	74.8	67.7	69.0	69.8	75.8	74.6	67.4	-2.9	-1.4	-1.9
Malawi	118.1	100.0	92.6	100.1	108.0	113.9	92.8	82.6	89.3	90.6	..	-2.4	-6.7	-3.5
Mali	91.4	100.0	101.0	100.3	102.4	98.2	87.4	84.9	86.6	92.3	90.4	1.5	-1.0	-2.0
Mauritania	93.6	100.0	107.4	106.2	102.2	108.6	103.2	87.7	98.9	97.0	98.9	-3.6	-0.6	-1.4
Mauritius	86.3	100.0	96.2	91.5	94.4	93.3	93.4	88.5	86.7	85.8	84.1	-5.3	3.2	-1.6
Mozambique	..	100.0	91.2	85.3	80.8	82.5	79.6	76.8	76.3	77.9	78.7	..	-3.4	-1.2
Namibia	127.7	100.0	115.1	115.3	103.8	94.7	87.3	85.1	96.9	86.9	84.8	..	1.3	-3.5
Niger	56.6	100.0	93.9	76.9	71.8	70.5	67.1	65.6	58.4	66.8	..	6.7	-0.9	-3.2
Nigeria	248.8	100.0	83.9	102.9	121.9	101.9	96.3	89.3	79.4	79.5	99.0	6.7	-16.2	-3.8
Rwanda	143.0	100.0	121.3	102.1	100.8	203.9	172.4	189.9	192.5	192.3	200.7	2.0	-13.8	9.8
São Tomé and Principe	128.4	100.0	100.0	70.8	100.0	100.0	88.7	116.5	159.3	152.4	141.1	-4.6	-7.5	10.8
Senegal	91.3	100.0	98.7	102.7	88.9	79.2	85.0	81.4	82.4	80.7	78.7	-1.3	1.2	-2.7
Seychelles	..	100.0	102.1	89.0	90.9	83.3	116.2	104.0	77.9	76.6	75.1	..	-7.0	-2.8
Sierra Leone	129.7	100.0	118.7	102.7	127.1	105.0	94.5	120.5	106.4	145.0	148.9	2.1	3.0	4.3
Somalia	94.1	100.0	88.5	90.1	..	..	..	..	..	..	..	2.4	-4.1	..
South Africa	112.5	100.0	98.9	94.5	92.6	91.4	90.1	90.9	94.4	93.2	95.5	-1.2	0.8	0.2
Sudan	96.9	100.0	108.8	112.8	135.0	100.3	..	..	..	..	..	5.2	-7.9	..
Swaziland	103.3	100.0	100.3	105.0	95.9	94.3	101.6	110.8	92.4	87.9	86.6	-0.7	-1.7	-2.1
Tanzania	..	..	..	..	..	..	..	..	..	..	..	..	..	..
Togo	91.6	100.0	102.7	100.6	102.1	99.1	98.0	88.2	85.8	81.0	81.9	-2.1	-1.0	-3.7
Uganda	..	100.0	99.8	95.1	76.0	69.7	63.0	58.9	73.0	103.8	90.0	..	-11.7	1.5
Zaire	99.0	100.0	113.9	135.7	101.9	95.8	114.3	106.4	79.3	80.3	79.9	3.7	7.0	-6.4
Zambia	86.4	100.0	122.0	64.5	83.3	71.1	53.5	52.2	50.4	52.0	47.5	-8.5	5.4	-6.4
Zimbabwe	100.0	100.0	102.9	93.6	86.7	95.3	80.6	81.3	77.8	82.3	85.5	-1.0	-0.7	-1.8
NORTH AFRICA	..	..	..	..	..	..	..	..	..	..	..	..	..	..
Algeria	181.2	100.0	88.5	98.8	78.6	87.2	77.9	63.2	61.6	63.0	..	6.2	-13.8	-7.4
Egypt, Arab Republic	184.8	100.0	82.8	81.0	86.8	107.8	106.8	106.4	102.9	113.9	..	1.0	-15.6	4.9
Libya	..	..	..	..	..	..	..	..	..	..	..	..	..	..
Morocco	91.6	100.0	105.4	103.2	97.8	99.5	103.9	102.0	107.0	101.9	..	-2.2	4.8	0.6
Tunisia	115.2	100.0	99.2	99.9	98.0	96.5	95.4	94.6	96.8	96.8	..	0.2	-2.7	-0.5
ALL AFRICA	148.3	100.0	95.5	95.9	94.0	94.2	92.9	88.6	89.2	89.4	..	1.8	-5.3	-1.3

Note: 1996 data are preliminary (see page 3).

5-18. Forest products exports

	Thousands of cubic meters											Average annual percentage growth		
	1980	1986	1987	1988	1989	1990	1991	1992	1993	1994	1995	75-84	85-89	90-MR
SUB-SAHARAN AFRICA	8,169	6,554	6,803	8,821	7,032	6,931	6,824	7,170	..	..	..	-2.6	2.4	0.4
excluding South Africa	7,413	5,108	5,283	6,044	5,855	5,794	5,632	5,478	..	..	..	-2.6	-1.3	-2.3
excl. S. Africa & Nigeria	7;402	5,048	5,266	6,028	5,844	5,757	5,583	5,444	..	..	..	-2.5	-1.1	-2.4
Angola	..	1	0	0	3	0	..	2	..	..	..	..	56.3	..
Benin	..	..	..	..	..	..	0	0	..	..	..	..	..	..
Botswana	..	..	..	..	..	..	..	..	..	..	..	..	..	..
Burkina Faso	..	..	..	..	..	..	..	..	..	..	..	..	..	..
Burundi	..	..	..	..	..	..	..	..	..	..	..	..	..	..
Cameroon	934	499	521	652	539	837	1,049	816	..	..	..	-1.9	-4.7	15.8
Cape Verde	..	..	..	..	..	..	..	..	..	..	..	..	..	..
Central African Republic	177	95	74	80	113	67	37	36	..	..	..	-2.3	-5.5	-33.1
Chad	..	..	..	..	..	..	..	..	..	..	..	..	..	..
Comoros	..	..	..	..	..	1	..	0	..	..	..	..	..	..
Congo	385	355	643	941	937	816	609	530	..	..	..	2.8	28.3	-18.1
Côte d'Ivoire	3,394	1,579	1,175	1,138	1,084	1,127	967	878	..	..	..	-2.4	-16.9	-7.6
Djibouti	..	..	..	..	..	..	..	..	..	..	..	..	..	..
Equatorial Guinea	16	133	133	133	142	129	126	143	..	..	..	24.0	12.4	-0.1
Eritrea	..	..	..	..	..	..	..	..	..	..	..	..	..	..
Ethiopia	..	..	..	..	..	..	..	..	..	..	..	..	..	..
Gabon	1,150	1,078	1,353	1,343	1,460	1,244	1,392	1,447	..	..	..	-0.6	0.8	0.9
Gambia, The	..	..	..	..	..	..	0	0	..	..	..	..	..	..
Ghana	183	296	514	531	371	361	390	426	..	..	..	-19.0	26.0	5.0
Guinea	..	8	8	8	8	13	15	17	..	..	..	-14.9	-7.6	26.5
Guinea-Bissau	6	3	5	4	4	6	12	9	..	..	..	-15.1	22.1	38.4
Kenya	33	6	4	4	3	4	3	0	..	..	..	-7.0	-26.5	-48.9
Lesotho	..	..	..	..	..	..	..	..	..	..	..	..	..	..
Liberia	524	378	255	701	729	663	429	642	..	..	..	-3.6	30.0	-7.9
Madagascar	0	1	2	1	2	3	26	6	..	..	..	-17.5	21.2	81.4
Malawi	..	..	..	1	0	0	0	1	..	..	..	1.8	..	45.3
Mali	..	..	..	..	..	..	0	..	..	..	..	..	..	..
Mauritania	..	..	..	..	..	1	..	..	..	..	..	..	..	..
Mauritius	..	..	..	..	..	..	..	2	..	..	..	..	..	..
Mozambique	31	4	5	10	2	5	4	1	..	..	..	-34.2	-3.8	-10.4
Namibia	..	..	..	..	..	..	..	..	..	..	..	..	..	..
Niger	..	..	..	..	..	..	..	..	..	..	..	..	..	..
Nigeria	11	60	17	16	11	37	49	34	..	..	..	-5.0	-32.2	42.8
Rwanda	..	..	..	..	..	..	0	..	..	..	..	..	..	..
São Tomé and Principe	..	..	..	..	..	0	..	..	..	..	..	..	..	..
Senegal	..	..	..	..	..	..	..	..	..	..	..	..	..	..
Seychelles	..	..	..	..	..	0	..	..	..	..	..	..	..	..
Sierra Leone	..	3	1	1	0	0	0	0	..	..	..	..	-8.8	-20.8
Somalia	..	..	..	..	..	..	..	..	..	..	..	..	..	..
South Africa	756	1,446	1,520	2,777	1,177	1,137	1,191	1,692	..	..	..	-2.2	24.9	12.0
Sudan	..	..	..	..	..	..	0	..	..	..	..	..	..	..
Swaziland	421	355	355	293	285	254	254	254	..	..	..	2.8	-13.1	-3.4
Tanzania	5	9	5	6	3	25	14	8	..	..	..	-15.9	3.0	22.4
Togo	..	..	..	..	..	0	..	..	..	..	..	..	..	..
Uganda	0	..	..	..	..	..	..	..	..	..	..	-30.6	..	..
Zaire	116	211	147	163	143	142	172	136	..	..	..	5.7	0.4	0.4
Zambia	..	..	..	..	..	0	0	..	..	..	..	..	..	..
Zimbabwe	26	34	65	17	17	56	83	89	..	..	..	-0.6	-14.1	70.6
NORTH AFRICA	88	74	94	117	95	95	77	105	..	..	..	1.3	6.1	1.1
Algeria	..	..	..	..	..	1	..	..	..	..	..	..	..	..
Egypt, Arab Republic	..	..	..	..	..	0	0	..	..	..	..	..	..	..
Libya	..	..	..	..	..	..	0	0	..	..	..	..	..	..
Morocco	74	65	85	102	88	84	70	98	..	..	..	4.9	6.3	1.3
Tunisia	14	10	10	16	7	10	8	7	..	..	..	-8.4	3.4	0.4
ALL AFRICA	8,258	6,628	6,897	8,938	7,127	7,026	6,901	7,275	..	..	..	-2.5	2.5	0.4

5-19. Petroleum exports

	Thousands of metric tons											Average annual percentage growth		
	1980	1986	1987	1988	1989	1990	1991	1992	1993	1994	1995	75-84	85-89	90-MR
SUB-SAHARAN AFRICA	117,134	102,081	95,764	107,140	122,815	128,631	133,490	134,184	143,805	131,978	..	-4.5	4.7	2.0
excluding South Africa	117,134	102,081	95,764	107,140	122,815	128,631	133,490	134,184	143,805	131,978	..	-4.5	4.7	2.0
excl. S. Africa & Nigeria	20,404	35,872	38,160	44,881	46,866	51,488	53,322	51,178	51,611	51,718	..	3.7	9.0	1.3
Angola	6,334	12,701	15,928	21,177	21,520	22,462	23,738	22,605	23,057	23,057	..	0.3	21.7	1.1
Benin	0	371	317	148	148	296	300	273	307	315	..	..	-13.7	11.4
Botswana	..	..	..	..	..	..	..	..	..	..	..	..	..	..
Burkina Faso	..	..	..	..	..	..	..	..	..	..	..	..	..	..
Burundi	..	..	..	..	..	..	..	..	..	..	..	..	..	..
Cameroon	1,886	7,816	7,273	7,621	7,601	7,267	6,582	5,361	5,185	4,443	..	80.4	1.2	-10.6
Cape Verde	..	..	..	..	..	..	..	..	..	..	..	..	..	..
Central African Republic	..	..	..	..	..	..	..	..	..	..	..	..	..	..
Chad	..	..	..	..	..	..	..	..	..	..	..	..	..	..
Comoros	..	..	..	..	..	..	..	..	..	..	..	..	..	..
Congo	3,383	5,449	5,952	6,711	7,583	7,611	7,427	7,255	8,118	8,195	..	12.3	6.5	1.6
Côte d'Ivoire	122	100	100	49	0	0	0	0	0	0	..	..	-34.8	..
Djibouti	..	..	..	..	..	..	..	..	..	..	..	..	..	..
Equatorial Guinea	..	..	..	..	..	..	..	..	..	..	..	..	..	..
Eritrea	..	..	..	..	..	..	..	..	..	..	..	..	..	..
Ethiopia	..	..	..	..	..	..	..	..	..	..	..	..	..	..
Gabon	7,740	7,884	7,194	7,936	8,750	12,694	14,150	14,690	13,925	14,623	..	-4.3	0.8	8.6
Gambia, The	..	..	..	..	..	..	..	..	..	..	..	..	..	..
Ghana	80	0	0	0	0	0	0	0	0	0	..	..	..	..
Guinea	..	..	..	..	..	..	..	..	..	..	..	..	..	..
Guinea-Bissau	..	..	..	..	..	..	..	..	..	..	..	..	..	..
Kenya	..	..	..	..	..	..	..	..	..	..	..	..	..	..
Lesotho	..	..	..	..	..	..	..	..	..	..	..	..	..	..
Liberia	..	..	..	..	..	..	..	..	..	..	..	..	..	..
Madagascar	..	..	..	..	..	..	..	..	..	..	..	..	..	..
Malawi	..	..	..	..	..	..	..	..	..	..	..	..	..	..
Mali	..	..	..	..	..	..	..	..	..	..	..	..	..	..
Mauritania	..	..	..	..	..	..	..	..	..	..	..	..	..	..
Mauritius	..	..	..	..	..	..	..	..	..	..	..	..	..	..
Mozambique	..	..	..	..	..	..	..	..	..	..	..	..	..	..
Namibia	..	..	..	..	..	..	..	..	..	..	..	..	..	..
Niger	..	..	..	..	..	..	..	..	..	..	..	..	..	..
Nigeria	96,730	66,209	57,604	62,259	75,949	77,143	80,168	83,006	92,194	80,260	..	-6.8	2.2	2.4
Rwanda	..	..	..	..	..	..	..	..	..	..	..	..	..	..
São Tomé and Principe	..	..	..	..	..	..	..	..	..	..	..	..	..	..
Senegal	..	..	..	..	..	..	..	..	..	..	..	..	..	..
Seychelles	..	..	..	..	..	..	..	..	..	..	..	..	..	..
Sierra Leone	..	..	..	..	..	..	..	..	..	..	..	..	..	..
Somalia	..	..	..	..	..	..	..	..	..	..	..	..	..	..
South Africa	..	..	..	..	..	..	..	..	..	..	..	..	..	..
Sudan	..	..	..	..	..	..	..	..	..	..	..	..	..	..
Swaziland	..	..	..	..	..	..	..	..	..	..	..	..	..	..
Tanzania	..	..	..	..	..	..	..	..	..	..	..	..	..	..
Togo	..	..	..	..	..	..	..	..	..	..	..	..	..	..
Uganda	..	..	..	..	..	..	..	..	..	..	..	..	..	..
Zaire	859	1,551	1,395	1,239	1,264	1,158	1,125	995	1,019	1,085	..	0.3	-0.8	-3.6
Zambia	..	..	..	..	..	..	..	..	..	..	..	..	..	..
Zimbabwe	..	..	..	..	..	..	..	..	..	..	..	..	..	..
NORTH AFRICA	145,865	93,093	93,166	91,415	101,229	111,593	114,246	114,092	110,405	112,649	..	-3.7	-0.6	1.4
Algeria	38,918	27,941	28,757	28,114	30,430	32,525	31,870	31,108	32,138	32,217	..	-5.7	1.1	0.6
Egypt, Arab Republic	17,146	21,161	24,431	20,962	20,261	19,929	18,461	20,412	19,924	21,500	..	20.7	-2.8	1.1
Libya	85,054	39,883	36,228	38,971	47,242	55,766	60,403	58,463	54,893	55,661	..	-6.4	-0.4	2.1
Morocco	..	..	..	..	..	..	..	..	..	..	..	..	..	..
Tunisia	4,747	4,108	3,750	3,368	3,296	3,373	3,512	4,109	3,450	3,271	..	-0.5	-3.9	0.5
ALL AFRICA	262,999	195,174	188,930	198,555	224,044	240,224	247,736	248,276	254,209	244,627	..	-4.1	2.0	1.8

5-20. Copper exports

	Thousands of metric tons											Average annual percentage growth		
	1980	1986	1987	1988	1989	1990	1991	1992	1993	1994	1995	75-84	85-89	90-MR
SUB-SAHARAN AFRICA	1,286	1,206	1,178	1,062	1,074	973	792	714	630	495	414	5.2	-3.1	-14.7
excluding South Africa	1,164	1,087	1,061	960	958	883	688	581	517	421	335	4.6	-3.4	-16.1
excl. S. Africa & Nigeria	1,164	1,087	1,061	960	958	883	688	581	517	421	335	4.6	-3.4	-16.1
Angola	0	0	0	0	0	0	0	0	0	0	0	..	..	..
Benin	0	0	0	0	0	0	0	0	0	0	0	..	..	..
Botswana	20	17	19	25	19	19	20	19	22	20	18	..	1.0	-0.2
Burkina Faso	0	0	0	0	0	0	0	0	0	0	0	..	..	..
Burundi	0	0	0	0	0	0	0	0	0	0	0	..	..	..
Cameroon	0	0	0	0	0	0	0	0	0	0	0	..	..	..
Cape Verde	0	0	0	0	0	0	0	0	0	0	0	..	..	..
Central African Republic	0	0	0	0	0	0	0	0	0	0	0	..	..	..
Chad	0	0	0	0	0	0	0	0	0	0	0	..	..	..
Comoros	0	0	0	0	0	0	0	0	0	0	0	..	..	..
Congo	1	0	0	0	0	0	0	0	0	0	0	..	..	..
Côte d'Ivoire	0	0	0	0	0	0	0	0	0	0	0	..	..	..
Djibouti	0	0	0	0	0	0	0	0	0	0	0	..	..	..
Equatorial Guinea	0	0	0	0	0	0	0	0	0	0	0	..	..	..
Eritrea	0	0	0	0	0	0	0	0	0	0	0	..	..	..
Ethiopia	0	0	0	0	0	0	0	0	0	0	0	..	..	..
Gabon	0	0	0	0	0	0	0	0	0	0	0	..	..	..
Gambia, The	0	0	0	0	0	0	0	0	0	0	0	..	..	..
Ghana	0	0	0	0	0	0	0	0	0	0	0	..	..	..
Guinea	0	0	0	0	0	0	0	0	0	0	0	..	..	..
Guinea-Bissau	0	0	0	0	0	0	0	0	0	0	0	..	..	..
Kenya	0	0	0	0	0	0	0	0	0	0	0	..	..	..
Lesotho	0	0	0	0	0	0	0	0	0	0	0	..	..	..
Liberia	0	0	0	0	0	0	0	0	0	0	0	..	..	..
Madagascar	0	0	0	0	0	0	0	0	0	0	0	..	..	..
Malawi	0	0	0	0	0	0	0	0	0	0	0	..	..	..
Mali	0	0	0	0	0	0	0	0	0	0	0	..	..	..
Mauritania	1	0	0	0	0	0	0	0	0	0	0	..	..	..
Mauritius	0	0	0	0	0	0	0	0	0	0	0	..	..	..
Mozambique	0	0	0	0	0	0	0	0	0	0	0	..	..	..
Namibia	41	43	37	38	33	30	34	35	30	26	25	1.9	-7.0	-4.3
Niger	0	0	0	0	0	0	0	0	0	0	0	..	..	..
Nigeria	0	0	0	0	0	0	0	0	0	0	0	..	..	..
Rwanda	0	0	0	0	0	0	0	0	0	0	0	..	..	..
São Tomé and Principe	0	0	0	0	0	0	0	0	0	0	0	..	..	..
Senegal	0	0	0	0	0	0	0	0	0	0	0	..	..	..
Seychelles	0	0	0	0	0	0	0	0	0	0	0	..	..	..
Sierra Leone	0	0	0	0	0	0	0	0	0	0	0	..	..	..
Somalia	0	0	0	0	0	0	0	0	0	0	0	..	..	..
South Africa	121	119	117	103	115	90	104	132	113	74	79	13.2	-0.8	-5.0
Sudan	0	0	0	0	0	0	0	0	0	0	0	..	..	..
Swaziland	0	0	0	0	0	0	0	0	0	0	0	..	..	..
Tanzania	0	0	0	0	0	0	0	0	0	0	0	..	..	..
Togo	0	0	0	0	0	0	0	0	0	0	0	..	..	..
Uganda	0	0	0	0	0	..	..	..	..	..	..	..	..	..
Zaire	461	528	483	461	439	374	252	116	28	14	..	16.8	-2.7	-52.2
Zambia	617	466	499	424	456	460	382	412	437	361	292	-1.8	-3.4	-5.9
Zimbabwe	23	32	22	12	10	0	0	0	0	0	0	3.8	-16.6	..
NORTH AFRICA	6	18	17	13	12	16	16	17	13	19	16	..	-13.1	3.2
Algeria	0	0	0	0	0	0	0	0	0	0	0	..	..	..
Egypt, Arab Republic	0	0	0	0	0	0	0	0	0	0	0	..	..	..
Libya	0	0	0	0	0	0	0	0	0	0	0	..	..	..
Morocco	6	18	17	13	12	16	16	17	13	19	16	..	-12.9	3.2
Tunisia	0	0	0	0	0	0	0	0	0	0	0	..	..	..
ALL AFRICA	1,292	1,224	1,195	1,075	1,086	989	807	730	643	514	430	5.4	-3.3	-14.3

5-21. Iron exports

	Thousands of metric tons											Average annual percentage growth		
	1980	1986	1987	1988	1989	1990	1991	1992	1993	1994	1995	75-84	85-89	90-MR
SUB-SAHARAN AFRICA	28,215	21,111	20,447	22,981	24,956	21,057	17,509	15,778	18,986	19,465	21,397	..	-0.4	-1.9
excluding South Africa	17,482	15,504	14,903	15,734	15,780	9,988	7,474	6,114	6,276	6,722	7,196	..	-2.3	-11.2
excl. S. Africa & Nigeria	17,482	15,504	14,903	15,734	15,780	9,988	7,474	6,114	6,276	6,722	7,196	..	-2.3	-11.2
Angola	0	0	0	0	0	0	0	0	0	0	0	..	..	..
Benin	0	0	0	0	0	0	0	0	0	0	0	..	..	..
Botswana	0	0	0	0	0	0	0	0	0	0	0	..	..	..
Burkina Faso	0	0	0	0	0	0	0	0	0	0	0	..	..	..
Burundi	0	0	0	0	0	0	0	0	0	0	0	..	..	..
Cameroon	0	0	0	0	0	0	0	0	0	0	0	..	..	..
Cape Verde	0	0	0	0	0	0	0	0	0	0	0	..	..	..
Central African Republic	0	0	0	0	0	0	0	0	0	0	0	..	..	..
Chad	0	0	0	0	0	0	0	0	0	0	0	..	..	..
Comoros	0	0	0	0	0	0	0	0	0	0	0	..	..	..
Congo	0	0	0	0	0	0	0	0	0	0	0	..	..	..
Côte d'Ivoire	0	0	0	0	0	0	0	0	0	0	0	..	..	..
Djibouti	0	0	0	0	0	0	0	0	0	0	0	..	..	..
Equatorial Guinea	0	0	0	0	0	0	0	0	0	0	0	..	..	..
Eritrea	0	0	0	0	0	0	0	0	0	0	0	..	..	..
Ethiopia	0	0	0	0	0	0	0	0	0	0	0	..	..	..
Gabon	0	0	0	0	0	0	0	0	0	0	0	..	..	..
Gambia, The	0	0	0	0	0	0	0	0	0	0	0	..	..	..
Ghana	0	0	0	0	0	0	0	0	0	0	0	..	..	..
Guinea	0	0	0	0	0	0	0	0	0	0	0	..	..	..
Guinea-Bissau	0	0	0	0	0	0	0	0	0	0	0	..	..	..
Kenya	0	0	0	0	0	0	0	0	0	0	0	..	..	..
Lesotho	0	0	0	0	0	0	0	0	0	0	0	..	..	..
Liberia	11,695	9,700	9,052	9,231	8,540	2,607	670	853	0	0	0	..	-5.4	-56.3
Madagascar	0	0	0	0	0	0	0	0	0	0	0	..	..	..
Malawi	0	0	0	0	0	0	0	0	0	0	0	..	..	..
Mali	0	0	0	0	0	0	0	0	0	0	0	..	..	..
Mauritania	5,673	5,804	5,851	6,503	7,240	7,381	6,804	5,261	6,276	6,722	7,196	..	3.0	-1.0
Mauritius	0	0	0	0	0	0	0	0	0	0	0	..	..	..
Mozambique	0	0	0	0	0	0	0	0	0	0	0	..	..	..
Namibia	0	0	0	0	0	0	0	0	0	0	0	..	..	..
Niger	0	0	0	0	0	0	0	0	0	0	0	..	..	..
Nigeria	0	0	0	0	0	0	0	0	0	0	0	..	..	..
Rwanda	0	0	0	0	0	0	0	0	0	0	0	..	..	..
São Tomé and Principe	0	0	0	0	0	0	0	0	0	0	0	..	..	..
Senegal	0	0	0	0	0	0	0	0	0	0	0	..	..	..
Seychelles	0	0	0	0	0	0	0	0	0	0	0	..	..	..
Sierra Leone	0	0	0	0	0	0	0	0	0	0	0	..	..	..
Somalia	0	0	0	0	0	0	0	0	0	0	0	..	..	..
South Africa	10,733	5,607	5,544	7,247	9,176	11,069	10,035	9,664	12,710	12,743	14,201	..	4.0	6.7
Sudan	0	0	0	0	0	0	0	0	0	0	0	..	..	..
Swaziland	114	0	0	0	0	0	0	0	0	0	0	..	..	..
Tanzania	0	0	0	0	0	0	0	0	0	0	0	..	..	..
Togo	0	0	0	0	0	0	0	0	0	0	0	..	..	..
Uganda	0	0	0	0	0	0	0	0	0	0	0	..	..	..
Zaire	0	0	0	0	0	0	0	0	0	0	0	..	..	..
Zambia	0	0	0	0	0	0	0	0	0	0	0	..	..	..
Zimbabwe	0	0	0	0	0	0	0	0	0	0	0	..	..	..
NORTH AFRICA	784	23	6	48	62	47	50	55	58	42	21	..	-11.3	-11.2
Algeria	699	23	6	0	10	9	10	20	25	25	5	..	-41.9	3.2
Egypt, Arab Republic	0	0	0	0	0	0	0	0	0	0	0	..	..	..
Libya	0	0	0	0	0	0	0	0	0	0	0	..	..	..
Morocco	85	0	0	48	52	38	40	35	33	17	16	..	..	-17.4
Tunisia	0	0	0	0	0	0	0	0	0	0	0	..	..	..
ALL AFRICA	28,999	21,134	20,453	23,029	25,018	21,104	17,559	15,833	19,044	19,507	21,418	..	-0.6	-1.9

5-22. Phosphates exports

	Thousands of metric tons											Average annual percentage growth		
	1980	1986	1987	1988	1989	1990	1991	1992	1993	1994	1995	75-84	85-89	90-MR
SUB-SAHARAN AFRICA	4,277	4,568	5,023	5,983	5,877	4,995	5,544	4,617	3,747	4,154	4,919	0.4	6.9	-4.5
excluding South Africa	4,274	3,619	3,962	4,715	4,783	3,778	4,378	3,272	2,550	2,881	3,511	-0.6	4.6	-6.9
excl. S. Africa & Nigeria	4,274	3,619	3,962	4,715	4,783	3,778	4,378	3,272	2,550	2,881	3,511	-0.6	4.6	-6.9
Angola	0	0	0	0	0	0	0	0	0	0	0	..	..	..
Benin	0	0	0	0	0	0	0	0	0	0	0	..	..	..
Botswana	0	0	0	0	0	0	0	0	0	0	0	..	..	..
Burkina Faso	0	0	0	0	0	0	0	0	0	0	0	..	..	..
Burundi	0	0	0	0	0	0	0	0	0	0	0	..	..	..
Cameroon	0	0	0	0	0	0	0	0	0	0	0	..	..	..
Cape Verde	0	0	0	0	0	0	0	0	0	0	0	..	..	..
Central African Republic	0	0	0	0	0	0	0	0	0	0	0	..	..	..
Chad	0	0	0	0	0	0	0	0	0	0	0	..	..	..
Comoros	0	0	0	0	0	0	0	0	0	0	0	..	..	..
Congo	0	0	0	0	0	0	0	0	0	0	0	..	..	..
Côte d'Ivoire	0	0	0	0	0	0	0	0	0	0	0	..	..	..
Djibouti	0	0	0	0	0	0	0	0	0	0	0	..	..	..
Equatorial Guinea	0	0	0	0	0	0	0	0	0	0	0	..	..	..
Eritrea	0	0	0	0	0	0	0	0	0	0	0	..	..	..
Ethiopia	0	0	0	0	0	0	0	0	0	0	0	..	..	..
Gabon	0	0	0	0	0	0	0	0	0	0	0	..	..	..
Gambia, The	0	0	0	0	0	0	0	0	0	0	0	..	..	..
Ghana	0	0	0	0	0	0	0	0	0	0	0	..	..	..
Guinea	0	0	0	0	0	0	0	0	0	0	0	..	..	..
Guinea-Bissau	0	0	0	0	0	0	0	0	0	0	0	..	..	..
Kenya	0	0	0	0	0	0	0	0	0	0	0	..	..	..
Lesotho	0	0	0	0	0	0	0	0	0	0	0	..	..	..
Liberia	0	0	0	0	0	0	0	0	0	0	0	..	..	..
Madagascar	0	0	0	0	0	0	0	0	0	0	0	..	..	..
Malawi	0	0	0	0	0	0	0	0	0	0	0	..	..	..
Mali	0	0	0	0	0	0	0	0	0	0	0	..	..	..
Mauritania	0	0	0	0	0	0	0	0	0	0	0	..	..	..
Mauritius	0	0	0	0	0	0	0	0	0	0	0	..	..	..
Mozambique	0	0	0	0	0	0	0	0	0	0	0	..	..	..
Namibia	0	0	0	0	0	0	0	0	0	0	0	..	..	..
Niger	0	0	0	0	0	0	0	0	0	0	0	..	..	..
Nigeria	0	0	0	0	0	0	0	0	0	0	0	..	..	..
Rwanda	0	0	0	0	0	0	0	0	0	0	0	..	..	..
São Tomé and Principe	0	0	0	0	0	0	0	0	0	0	0	..	..	..
Senegal	1,378	1,353	1,453	1,847	1,435	1,356	1,304	1,187	983	648	859	-3.9	4.4	-11.1
Seychelles	0	0	0	0	0	0	0	0	0	0	0	..	..	..
Sierra Leone	0	0	0	0	0	0	0	0	0	0	0	..	..	..
Somalia	0	0	0	0	0	0	0	0	0	0	0	..	..	..
South Africa	4	949	1,061	1,268	1,094	1,217	1,166	1,344	1,197	1,273	1,408	39.6	20.6	3.2
Sudan	0	0	0	0	0	0	0	0	0	0	0	..	..	..
Swaziland	0	0	0	0	0	0	0	0	0	0	0	..	..	..
Tanzania	0	0	0	0	0	0	0	0	0	0	0	..	..	..
Togo	2,896	2,266	2,509	2,868	3,347	2,422	3,074	2,086	1,567	2,234	2,652	1.9	4.5	-5.3
Uganda	0	0	0	0	0	0	0	0	0	0	0	..	..	..
Zaire	0	0	0	0	0	0	0	0	0	0	0	..	..	..
Zambia	0	0	0	0	0	0	0	0	0	0	0	..	..	..
Zimbabwe	0	0	0	0	0	0	0	0	0	0	0	..	..	..
NORTH AFRICA	18,932	15,890	15,284	16,560	14,700	13,297	10,537	11,068	10,096	11,523	11,466	-1.1	-2.3	-3.8
Algeria	768	818	800	877	970	735	804	800	449	575	671	5.6	8.5	-7.5
Egypt, Arab Republic	258	183	180	268	246	297	164	180	134	114	48	12.4	3.8	-22.2
Libya	0	0	0	0	0	0	0	0	0	0	0	..	..	..
Morocco	16,457	13,696	13,061	14,260	12,407	11,672	9,143	9,132	8,398	9,527	9,420	-0.8	-3.1	-4.6
Tunisia	1,449	1,193	1,245	1,156	1,077	593	426	956	1,114	1,308	1,327	-6.9	-0.8	12.0
ALL AFRICA	23,210	20,458	20,307	22,543	20,576	18,292	16,080	15,684	13,843	15,678	16,385	-0.8	-0.2	-4.0

5-23. Cocoa exports

	Thousands of metric tons											*Average annual percentage growth*		
	1980	*1986*	*1987*	*1988*	*1989*	*1990*	*1991*	*1992*	*1993*	*1994*	*1995*	*75-84*	*85-89*	*90-MR*
SUB-SAHARAN AFRICA	870	1,161	1,123	1,081	1,321	1,343	1,353	1,182	1,108	986	1,064	0.4	4.8	-5.1
excluding South Africa	869	1,159	1,122	1,078	1,319	1,341	1,349	1,172	1,095	975	1,057	0.4	4.7	-5.2
excl. S. Africa & Nigeria	718	985	1,005	866	1,211	1,197	1,198	1,070	1,094	973	1,055	1.1	5.2	-3.2
Angola	0	0	0	0	0	0	0	0	0	0	0	-20.5	..	..
Benin	5	13	6	0	0	0	0	0	0	0	0	6.3	-63.7	..
Botswana	0	0	0	0	0	0	0	0	0	0	0	..	..	..
Burkina Faso	0	0	0	0	0	0	0	0	0	0	0	..	..	..
Burundi	0	0	0	0	0	0	0	0	0	0	0	..	..	..
Cameroon	106	107	129	135	107	119	98	68	3	1	4	0.1	3.8	-55.2
Cape Verde	0	0	0	0	0	0	0	0	0	0	0	..	..	..
Central African Republic	0	0	0	0	0	0	0	0	0	0	0	..	..	..
Chad	0	0	0	0	0	0	0	0	0	0	0	..	..	..
Comoros	0	0	0	0	0	0	0	0	0	0	0	..	..	..
Congo	2	1	1	1	1	1	0	0	0	0	0	-5.2	-20.0	-34.1
Côte d'Ivoire	333	601	601	457	795	768	787	723	822	723	803	9.1	5.4	-0.2
Djibouti	0	0	0	0	0	0	0	0	0	0	0	..	..	..
Equatorial Guinea	7	9	7	8	7	6	6	5	3	3	3	-0.2	0.3	-14.0
Eritrea	0	0	0	0	0	0	0	0	0	0	0	..	..	..
Ethiopia	0	0	0	0	0	0	0	0	0	0	0	..	..	..
Gabon	4	2	2	2	2	2	1	2	0	0	0	-4.2	3.1	8.0
Gambia, The	0	0	0	0	0	0	0	0	0	0	0	..	..	..
Ghana	218	211	219	223	266	270	265	244	263	243	241	-7.7	9.0	-1.8
Guinea	4	3	3	3	3	2	2	2	0	0	0	4.3	-6.2	-13.4
Guinea-Bissau	0	0	0	0	0	0	0	0	0	0	0	..	..	..
Kenya	0	0	0	0	0	0	0	0	0	0	0	-7.3	..	7.8
Lesotho	0	0	0	0	0	0	0	0	0	0	0	..	..	..
Liberia	4	4	2	3	3	3	2	1	0	0	0	9.1	-14.8	-46.4
Madagascar	2	2	3	4	2	3	4	3	0	0	0	6.2	7.9	-78.8
Malawi	0	0	0	0	0	0	0	0	0	0	0	..	..	..
Mali	0	0	0	0	0	0	0	0	0	0	0	..	..	..
Mauritania	0	0	0	0	0	0	0	0	0	0	0	..	..	..
Mauritius	0	0	0	0	0	0	0	0	0	0	0	..	..	..
Mozambique	0	0	0	0	0	0	0	0	0	0	0	..	..	..
Namibia	0	0	0	0	0	0	0	0	0	0	0	..	..	..
Niger	0	0	0	0	0	0	0	0	0	0	0	..	..	..
Nigeria	151	175	117	212	108	144	150	102	1	1	2	-2.6	-0.8	-59.9
Rwanda	0	0	0	0	0	0	0	0	0	0	0	..	..	..
São Tomé and Principe	7	3	3	4	3	3	5	4	0	0	0	-4.3	0.4	15.1
Senegal	0	0	0	0	0	0	0	0	0	0	0	..	..	..
Seychelles	0	0	0	0	0	0	0	0	0	0	0	..	..	..
Sierra Leone	9	9	9	9	8	5	13	5	0	0	0	6.0	-4.6	-7.6
Somalia	0	0	0	0	0	0	0	0	0	0	0	..	..	..
South Africa	0	1	1	3	2	3	5	10	12	11	7	-8.3	32.9	29.4
Sudan	0	0	0	0	0	0	0	0	0	0	0	..	..	..
Swaziland	0	0	0	0	0	0	0	0	0	0	0	..	..	..
Tanzania	1	1	1	2	2	3	2	2	0	0	0	8.6	5.4	-0.6
Togo	15	13	13	11	7	8	6	8	0	0	0	-1.7	-12.0	4.2
Uganda	0	0	0	0	0	0	1	1	0	0	0	1.9	6.3	17.9
Zaire	4	6	5	5	5	5	5	3	3	3	4	-0.2	2.6	-9.3
Zambia	0	0	0	0	0	0	0	0	0	0	0	..	..	..
Zimbabwe	0	0	0	0	0	0	0	0	0	0	0	..	..	-31.2
NORTH AFRICA	0	0	1	0	1	1	2	1	0	0	1	..	23.9	-15.5
Algeria	0	0	0	0	0	0	0	0	0	0	0	..	..	..
Egypt, Arab Republic	0	0	0	0	0	1	2	0	0	0	0	..	39.0	-12.0
Libya	0	0	0	0	0	0	0	0	0	0	0	..	..	..
Morocco	0	0	0	0	0	0	0	0	0	0	0	..	..	..
Tunisia	0	0	1	0	1	0	0	0	0	0	0	..	5.7	-20.5
ALL AFRICA	870	1,161	1,123	1,081	1,322	1,344	1,355	1,183	1,108	986	1,065	0.4	4.8	-5.1

5-24. Coffee exports

	Thousands of metric tons											Average annual percentage growth		
	1980	1986	1987	1988	1989	1990	1991	1992	1993	1994	1995	75-84	85-89	90-MR
SUB-SAHARAN AFRICA	895	1,077	917	902	1,008	1,095	876	911	522	0	0	-1.8	0.3	-13.9
excluding South Africa	894	1,077	917	902	1,008	1,095	876	910	522	0	0	-1.8	0.3	-13.9
excl. S. Africa & Nigeria	892	1,076	916	901	1,008	1,095	875	910	522	0	0	-1.8	0.3	-13.9
Angola	47	19	16	11	8	5	5	5	2	0	0	-17.7	-19.0	-27.1
Benin	0	0	0	0	1	0	0	0	0	0	0	16.8	-22.8	..
Botswana	0	0	0	0	0	0	0	0	0	0	0	..	..	..
Burkina Faso	0	0	0	0	0	0	0	0	0	0	0	..	..	..
Burundi	19	37	27	37	29	34	41	40	28	0	0	3.0	-0.2	0.8
Cameroon	92	124	98	95	152	158	113	104	67	0	0	0.0	4.4	-18.6
Cape Verde	0	0	0	0	0	0	0	0	0	0	0	..	..	..
Central African Republic	11	10	11	15	25	13	9	7	8	0	0	2.2	10.5	-25.4
Chad	0	0	0	0	0	0	0	0	0	0	0	..	..	..
Comoros	0	0	0	0	0	0	0	0	0	0	0	..	..	..
Congo	2	1	0	0	0	0	0	0	0	0	0	8.1	-30.0	-44.4
Côte d'Ivoire	207	230	165	204	130	232	199	220	226	0	0	-2.6	-7.4	11.2
Djibouti	0	0	0	0	0	0	0	0	0	0	0	..	..	..
Equatorial Guinea	0	1	1	0	0	0	0	0	0	0	0	-10.3	-18.8	-24.1
Eritrea	0	0	0	0	0	0	0	0	0	0	0	..	..	..
Ethiopia	76	75	74	85	103	64	51	45	0	0	0	5.7	4.2	-23.8
Gabon	1	2	1	2	2	0	0	0	0	0	0	28.3	13.5	-39.4
Gambia, The	0	0	0	0	0	0	0	0	0	0	0	..	..	..
Ghana	0	1	1	1	1	1	1	2	3	0	0	-20.7	13.0	45.8
Guinea	3	4	5	6	10	7	4	5	6	0	0	0.4	105.0	-12.9
Guinea-Bissau	0	0	0	0	0	0	0	0	0	0	0	..	..	..
Kenya	80	127	100	88	94	112	83	78	88	0	0	2.9	-2.6	-4.7
Lesotho	0	0	0	0	0	0	0	0	0	0	0	..	..	..
Liberia	13	8	5	4	5	2	0	0	0	0	0	6.3	-10.9	..
Madagascar	70	47	47	43	60	48	41	49	51	0	0	-2.5	2.6	-2.9
Malawi	0	4	5	4	4	7	5	8	6	0	0	25.1	13.3	11.1
Mali	0	0	0	0	0	0	0	0	0	0	0	..	..	..
Mauritania	0	0	0	0	0	0	0	0	0	0	0	..	..	..
Mauritius	0	0	0	0	0	0	0	0	0	0	0	..	..	..
Mozambique	0	0	0	0	0	0	0	0	0	0	0	..	..	..
Namibia	0	0	0	0	0	0	0	0	0	0	0	..	..	..
Niger	0	0	0	0	0	0	0	0	0	0	0	..	..	..
Nigeria	2	1	1	1	0	0	0	1	1	0	0	-4.2	43.0	25.9
Rwanda	22	41	46	31	36	46	38	34	30	0	0	1.4	1.3	-6.5
São Tomé and Principe	0	0	0	0	0	0	0	0	0	0	0	..	..	..
Senegal	1	0	0	0	0	0	0	0	0	0	0	..	..	..
Seychelles	0	0	0	0	0	0	0	0	0	0	0	..	..	..
Sierra Leone	10	7	6	8	5	8	6	4	3	0	0	-0.8	12.2	-14.6
Somalia	0	0	0	0	0	0	0	0	0	0	0	..	..	..
South Africa	0	0	0	1	0	1	0	1	0	0	0	16.5	-1.6	7.3
Sudan	0	0	0	0	0	0	0	0	0	0	0	..	..	..
Swaziland	0	0	0	0	0	0	0	0	0	0	0	..	..	..
Tanzania	43	49	44	39	50	61	53	53	0	0	0	0.8	-2.1	0.6
Togo	9	8	14	11	13	14	9	19	0	0	0	-6.2	28.5	7.5
Uganda	110	141	148	144	177	142	125	119	0	0	0	-2.8	3.8	-12.3
Zaire	74	130	89	68	99	104	84	104	0	0	0	0.3	2.7	-0.4
Zambia	0	0	0	0	1	1	0	2	0	0	0	..	6.1	3.5
Zimbabwe	3	11	12	6	7	35	9	10	4	0	0	13.1	-9.3	-21.3
NORTH AFRICA	0	0	0	0	2	2	0	0	0	0	0	..	..	..
Algeria	0	0	0	0	0	1	0	0	0	0	0	..	..	..
Egypt, Arab Republic	0	0	0	0	2	1	0	0	0	0	0	..	..	..
Libya	0	0	0	0	0	0	0	0	0	0	0	..	..	..
Morocco	0	0	0	0	0	0	0	0	0	0	0	..	..	..
Tunisia	0	0	0	0	0	0	0	0	0	0	0	..	..	..
ALL AFRICA	895	1,077	917	902	1,010	1,097	876	911	522	0	0	-1.8	0.3	-14.0

5-25. Cotton exports

	Thousands of metric tons											Average annual percentage growth		
	1980	1986	1987	1988	1989	1990	1991	1992	1993	1994	1995	75-84	85-89	90-MR
SUB-SAHARAN AFRICA	466	682	696	662	812	713	661	686	470	492	492	1.3	7.6	-8.8
excluding South Africa	465	680	692	657	804	707	658	681	470	492	492	1.3	7.3	-8.7
excl. S. Africa & Nigeria	465	680	692	657	802	705	656	680	463	489	485	1.4	7.3	-8.8
Angola	0	1	1	1	2	0	0	0	0	0	0	-27.7	10.4	..
Benin	8	38	42	19	56	41	43	58	60	74	99	-0.6	13.3	12.1
Botswana	1	0	0	0	0	0	0	0	1	1	1	22.5	..	56.6
Burkina Faso	28	45	65	55	43	72	64	45	0	0	0	10.8	14.3	0.3
Burundi	1	0	3	1	0	0	0	0	2	2	1	-1.0	8.2	62.6
Cameroon	26	18	21	23	85	38	23	42	51	59	54	15.1	19.6	1.0
Cape Verde	0	0	0	0	0	0	0	0	0	0	0	..	..	..
Central African Republic	14	13	9	6	8	9	13	6	8	5	12	-4.1	-12.7	-1.2
Chad	35	36	33	43	48	57	65	85	40	32	62	-2.4	-0.4	-3.1
Comoros	0	0	0	0	0	0	0	0	0	0	0	..	..	..
Congo	0	0	0	0	0	0	0	0	0	0	0	..	..	..
Côte d'Ivoire	39	80	66	96	89	89	86	67	96	100	88	14.7	15.2	1.1
Djibouti	0	0	0	0	0	0	0	0	0	0	0	..	..	..
Equatorial Guinea	0	0	0	0	0	0	0	0	0	0	0	..	..	..
Eritrea	0	0	0	0	0	0	0	0	0	0	0	..	..	..
Ethiopia	6	2	0	1	0	0	0	0	0	0	0	9.2	..	..
Gabon	0	0	0	0	0	0	0	0	0	0	0	..	..	..
Gambia, The	0	1	0	0	1	1	2	1	1	1	1	..	12.4	-11.2
Ghana	0	0	0	0	0	0	0	0	0	0	0	..	..	..
Guinea	0	0	0	1	1	2	1	5	10	6	7	..	..	44.2
Guinea-Bissau	0	1	1	1	1	0	1	0	1	1	1	..	28.5	-0.4
Kenya	4	1	0	0	0	0	1	6	8	4	1	-20.0	-11.5	2.6
Lesotho	0	0	0	0	0	0	0	0	0	0	0	..	..	..
Liberia	0	0	0	0	0	0	0	0	0	0	0	..	..	..
Madagascar	1	8	6	0	1	0	3	2	0	1	1	21.9	-17.2	3.9
Malawi	3	2	1	0	4	4	9	5	0	0	0	-1.6	-1.4	-74.7
Mali	53	69	76	70	99	93	114	115	133	126	105	9.9	14.2	3.4
Mauritania	0	0	0	0	0	0	0	0	0	0	0	..	..	..
Mauritius	0	0	0	0	0	0	0	0	0	0	0	..	..	..
Mozambique	6	1	4	4	5	6	5	13	13	16	13	-8.0	1.2	23.4
Namibia	0	0	0	0	0	0	0	0	0	0	0	..	..	..
Niger	0	0	2	1	3	2	1	1	1	1	0	-3.4	81.6	-20.6
Nigeria	0	0	0	0	1	3	2	1	7	3	8	..	..	27.2
Rwanda	0	0	0	0	0	0	0	0	0	0	0	..	..	..
São Tomé and Principe	0	0	0	0	0	0	0	0	0	0	0	..	..	..
Senegal	6	7	5	8	8	5	12	17	20	14	13	2.2	-6.5	14.6
Seychelles	0	0	0	0	0	0	0	0	0	0	0	..	..	..
Sierra Leone	0	0	0	0	0	0	0	0	0	0	0	..	..	..
Somalia	0	0	0	0	0	0	0	0	0	0	0	..	..	..
South Africa	1	2	5	5	9	5	3	5	0	0	0	-1.0	163.5	-21.2
Sudan	132	203	204	177	176	126	87	76	0	0	0	0.0	1.2	-25.1
Swaziland	4	2	5	6	9	19	8	8	0	0	0	4.8	40.9	-11.6
Tanzania	32	32	44	52	54	46	39	64	0	0	0	-3.9	17.9	3.3
Togo	5	35	32	29	34	33	36	40	0	0	0	27.1	22.1	5.9
Uganda	2	5	3	2	2	4	8	8	0	0	0	-21.5	-25.4	53.2
Zaire	2	0	0	0	0	0	0	0	0	0	0	..	..	..
Zambia	5	2	3	2	8	3	2	2	0	0	0	17.9	12.6	-36.2
Zimbabwe	54	81	65	59	65	54	34	16	18	47	27	4.2	-0.2	-11.8
NORTH AFRICA	167	146	131	86	66	41	16	16	20	114	67	0.1	-17.1	9.0
Algeria	0	0	0	0	0	0	0	0	0	0	0	..	..	..
Egypt, Arab Republic	164	146	130	80	58	39	13	16	18	113	67	0.2	-18.9	10.9
Libya	0	0	0	0	0	0	0	0	0	0	0	..	..	..
Morocco	3	0	2	6	7	1	3	1	2	1	0	3.7	..	-48.0
Tunisia	0	0	0	0	0	0	0	0	0	0	0	..	..	..
ALL AFRICA	633	827	828	747	878	753	677	702	490	606	560	0.9	3.5	-7.3

5-26. Groundnut exports

	Thousands of metric tons											Average annual percentage growth		
	1980	1986	1987	1988	1989	1990	1991	1992	1993	1994	1995	75-84	85-89	90-MR
SUB-SAHARAN AFRICA	606	361	483	687	581	574	342	330	258	393	417	-8.8	14.8	-7.0
excluding South Africa	561	322	463	662	504	535	310	306	231	333	371	-8.6	14.2	-7.4
excl. S. Africa & Nigeria	560	322	463	661	504	535	309	306	229	326	366	-8.1	14.2	-7.7
Angola	1	0	0	0	0	0	0	0	0	0	0	-4.7	..	..
Benin	2	0	5	2	0	0	0	0	0	0	0	-27.0	..	..
Botswana	1	0	0	0	0	0	0	0	0	0	0	-10.3	27.2	-17.1
Burkina Faso	1	5	6	4	1	1	1	1	0	0	0	-43.8	152.1	-18.1
Burundi	0	0	0	0	0	0	0	0	0	0	0	..	..	..
Cameroon	1	0	0	0	0	0	0	0	0	0	0	-42.1	21.9	13.8
Cape Verde	0	0	0	0	0	0	0	0	0	0	0	..	..	..
Central African Republic	0	0	0	0	0	0	0	0	0	1	1	..	..	..
Chad	0	0	0	3	0	0	0	0	1	2	0	..	..	..
Comoros	0	0	0	0	0	0	0	0	0	0	0	..	..	..
Congo	0	0	0	0	0	0	0	0	0	0	0	..	..	..
Côte d'Ivoire	0	0	0	1	0	0	0	0	0	0	0	-16.0	..	..
Djibouti	0	0	0	0	0	0	0	0	0	0	0	..	..	..
Equatorial Guinea	0	0	0	0	0	0	0	0	0	0	0	..	..	..
Eritrea	0	0	0	0	0	0	0	0	0	0	0	..	..	..
Ethiopia	1	0	0	1	1	0	0	0	0	0	0	-6.7	-49.1	..
Gabon	0	0	0	0	0	0	0	0	0	0	0	..	..	..
Gambia, The	67	25	17	30	24	24	17	18	28	26	33	-7.7	-11.7	5.8
Ghana	2	0	0	0	0	0	0	0	0	0	0	..	..	..
Guinea	0	0	0	0	0	0	0	0	0	0	0	..	..	..
Guinea-Bissau	8	2	3	4	2	2	0	0	0	0	0	-4.4	-18.0	-40.3
Kenya	0	0	0	0	0	0	0	0	1	0	0	-24.6	23.1	46.7
Lesotho	0	0	0	0	0	0	0	0	0	0	0	..	..	..
Liberia	0	0	0	0	0	0	0	0	0	0	0	..	..	..
Madagascar	4	0	0	0	0	0	1	0	0	0	0	-35.4	..	-3.4
Malawi	28	20	19	36	3	0	1	0	0	1	1	-17.9	23.3	1.1
Mali	15	10	10	11	11	12	10	11	12	17	16	-11.7	9.5	7.0
Mauritania	0	0	0	0	0	0	0	0	0	0	0	..	..	..
Mauritius	0	0	0	0	0	0	0	0	0	0	0	..	..	-17.4
Mozambique	10	4	4	2	3	2	0	0	0	0	0	-8.4	22.4	-32.2
Namibia	0	0	0	0	0	0	0	0	0	0	0	..	..	..
Niger	1	0	0	2	6	1	1	1	0	0	0	-39.7	75.7	-33.9
Nigeria	1	0	0	1	0	0	1	0	2	7	5	-38.0	..	93.8
Rwanda	0	0	0	0	0	0	0	0	0	0	0	..	..	..
São Tomé and Principe	0	0	0	0	0	0	0	0	0	0	0	..	..	..
Senegal	175	223	297	396	348	360	215	214	119	182	205	-9.1	21.2	-11.9
Seychelles	0	0	0	0	0	0	0	0	0	0	0	..	..	..
Sierra Leone	0	0	0	0	0	0	0	0	0	0	0	..	..	..
Somalia	0	0	0	0	0	0	0	0	0	0	0	..	..	..
South Africa	45	39	19	25	77	39	32	24	27	59	46	-12.5	23.1	-3.1
Sudan	238	31	73	164	98	109	39	51	65	88	104	-6.0	15.7	1.0
Swaziland	0	0	0	0	0	0	0	0	0	0	0	..	..	..
Tanzania	1	0	0	0	1	7	16	7	0	0	0	..	181.1	-33.1
Togo	0	0	25	1	0	0	0	0	0	0	0	..	..	..
Uganda	0	0	0	0	0	0	0	0	1	0	0	..	..	25.3
Zaire	0	0	0	0	0	0	0	0	0	0	0	..	..	..
Zambia	0	0	0	0	0	0	5	1	0	0	0	-26.0	..	-38.4
Zimbabwe	3	2	4	6	4	16	3	1	3	7	3	-19.5	108.2	-8.2
NORTH AFRICA	13	4	1	1	3	7	5	5	21	15	15	-7.3	-19.9	32.7
Algeria	0	0	0	0	0	0	0	0	0	0	0	..	..	..
Egypt, Arab Republic	13	4	1	1	3	4	2	4	12	7	10	-7.3	-19.9	27.6
Libya	0	0	0	0	0	3	4	1	8	4	5	..	..	18.3
Morocco	0	0	0	0	0	0	0	0	0	0	0	..	..	71.0
Tunisia	0	0	0	0	0	0	0	0	0	3	0	..	..	68.7
ALL AFRICA	620	365	484	687	584	581	347	335	279	407	432	-8.8	14.6	-6.3

5-27. Oil palm products exports

	Thousands of metric tons											Average annual percentage growth		
	1980	*1986*	*1987*	*1988*	*1989*	*1990*	*1991*	*1992*	*1993*	*1994*	*1995*	*75-84*	*85-89*	*90-MR*
SUB-SAHARAN AFRICA	280	222	285	215	220	243	211	209	293	250	174	-12.2	8.0	-1.1
excluding South Africa	280	222	285	215	220	243	211	207	291	246	174	-12.2	8.0	-1.2
excl. S. Africa & Nigeria	184	149	192	112	156	223	187	193	281	236	172	-9.3	3.4	3.0
Angola	0	0	0	0	0	0	0	0	0	0	0	..	..	..
Benin	13	2	12	8	3	6	1	2	3	7	9	-12.5	8.9	15.7
Botswana	0	0	0	0	0	0	0	0	0	0	0	..	..	..
Burkina Faso	0	0	0	0	0	0	0	0	0	0	0	..	..	..
Burundi	0	0	0	0	0	0	0	0	0	0	0	..	..	..
Cameroon	21	20	32	21	31	28	10	18	27	30	8	-7.7	12.3	-9.6
Cape Verde	0	0	0	0	0	0	0	0	0	0	0	..	..	..
Central African Republic	0	0	0	0	0	0	0	0	0	0	0	..	..	..
Chad	0	0	0	0	0	0	0	0	0	0	0	..	..	..
Comoros	0	0	0	0	0	0	0	0	0	0	0	..	..	..
Congo	0	0	0	0	0	0	0	0	0	0	0	-17.6	..	..
Côte d'Ivoire	99	105	122	61	87	166	159	146	173	152	121	-7.9	5.0	3.3
Djibouti	0	0	0	0	0	0	0	0	0	0	0	..	..	..
Equatorial Guinea	0	0	0	0	0	0	0	0	0	0	0	..	..	..
Eritrea	0	0	0	0	0	0	0	0	0	0	0	..	..	..
Ethiopia	0	0	0	0	0	0	0	0	0	0	0	..	..	..
Gabon	0	4	2	1	8	4	2	5	1	0	2	..	9.6	-17.8
Gambia, The	1	0	0	0	0	0	0	0	0	0	0	-19.8	..	..
Ghana	0	1	6	2	8	7	3	8	9	11	12	..	39.0	11.3
Guinea	15	3	4	2	1	1	1	1	7	1	0	-3.6	1.5	-0.6
Guinea-Bissau	6	8	6	8	5	2	5	3	2	3	1	2.0	5.1	-14.6
Kenya	0	0	0	0	0	0	1	5	53	14	12	-52.7	..	131.3
Lesotho	0	0	0	0	0	0	0	0	0	0	0	..	..	..
Liberia	6	2	5	6	8	5	4	5	5	5	5	24.9	12.7	-4.2
Madagascar	0	0	0	0	0	0	0	0	0	0	0	..	..	..
Malawi	0	0	0	0	0	0	0	0	0	0	0	..	..	..
Mali	0	0	0	0	0	0	0	0	0	0	0	..	..	..
Mauritania	0	0	0	0	0	0	0	0	0	0	0	..	..	..
Mauritius	0	0	0	0	0	0	0	0	0	0	0	..	..	75.9
Mozambique	0	0	0	0	0	0	0	0	0	0	0	..	..	..
Namibia	0	0	0	0	0	0	0	0	0	0	0	..	..	..
Niger	0	0	0	0	0	0	0	0	0	0	0	..	..	..
Nigeria	96	74	92	103	64	20	23	14	10	10	2	-16.9	18.0	-36.4
Rwanda	0	0	0	0	0	0	0	0	0	0	0	..	..	..
São Tomé and Principe	0	0	0	0	0	0	0	0	0	0	0	-19.1	..	..
Senegal	0	0	0	0	0	0	0	0	0	0	0	-55.4	18.6	..
Seychelles	0	0	0	0	0	0	0	0	0	0	0	..	..	..
Sierra Leone	1	2	0	1	0	0	0	0	0	11	0	-11.4	-48.9	-2.7
Somalia	0	0	0	0	0	0	0	0	0	0	0	..	..	..
South Africa	0	0	0	0	0	0	0	2	2	3	1	..	..	-24.6
Sudan	0	0	0	0	0	0	0	0	0	0	0	..	..	..
Swaziland	0	0	0	0	0	0	0	0	0	0	0	..	..	..
Tanzania	1	0	0	0	0	0	0	0	0	0	0	..	..	..
Togo	10	1	1	0	0	0	0	0	0	0	0	-13.6	-15.9	21.6
Uganda	0	0	0	0	0	0	0	0	0	0	0	..	..	..
Zaire	10	2	1	2	4	4	1	1	1	3	1	-23.7	-21.9	-21.0
Zambia	0	0	0	0	0	0	0	0	0	0	0	..	..	..
Zimbabwe	0	0	0	0	0	0	0	0	0	0	0	..	..	..
NORTH AFRICA	0	0	0	0	0	0	0	0	0	0	0	..	..	-2.1
Algeria	0	0	0	0	0	0	0	0	0	0	0	..	..	..
Egypt, Arab Republic	0	0	0	0	0	0	0	0	0	0	0	..	..	4.8
Libya	0	0	0	0	0	0	0	0	0	0	0	..	..	..
Morocco	0	0	0	0	0	0	0	0	0	0	0	..	..	..
Tunisia	0	0	0	0	0	0	0	0	0	0	0	..	..	..
ALL AFRICA	280	222	285	215	220	243	211	209	293	250	175	-12.2	8.0	-1.1

5-28. Sisal exports

	Thousands of metric tons											Average annual percentage growth		
	1980	1986	1987	1988	1989	1990	1991	1992	1993	1994	1995	75-84	85-89	90-MR
SUB-SAHARAN AFRICA	109	53	54	51	50	50	42	43	42	41	43	-9.6	-8.7	-3.0
excluding South Africa	109	53	53	50	50	50	42	43	42	41	43	-9.7	-8.7	-3.0
excl. S. Africa & Nigeria	109	53	53	50	50	50	42	43	42	41	43	-9.7	-8.7	-3.0
Angola	3	0	0	0	0	0	0	0	0	0	0	-30.8	..	..
Benin	0	0	0	0	0	0	0	0	0	0	0	..	..	..
Botswana	0	0	0	0	0	0	0	0	0	0	0	..	..	..
Burkina Faso	0	0	0	0	0	0	0	0	0	0	0	..	..	..
Burundi	0	0	0	0	0	0	0	0	0	0	0	..	..	..
Cameroon	0	0	0	0	0	0	0	0	0	0	0	..	..	..
Cape Verde	0	0	0	0	0	0	0	0	0	0	0	..	..	..
Central African Republic	0	0	0	0	0	0	0	0	0	0	0	..	..	..
Chad	0	0	0	0	0	0	0	0	0	0	0	..	..	..
Comoros	0	0	0	0	0	0	0	0	0	0	0	..	..	..
Congo	0	0	0	0	0	0	0	0	0	0	0	..	..	..
Côte d'Ivoire	0	0	0	0	0	0	0	0	0	0	0	..	..	..
Djibouti	0	0	0	0	0	0	0	0	0	0	0	..	..	..
Equatorial Guinea	0	0	0	0	0	0	0	0	0	0	0	..	..	..
Eritrea	0	0	0	0	0	0	0	0	0	0	0	..	..	..
Ethiopia	0	0	0	0	0	0	0	0	0	0	0	..	..	..
Gabon	0	0	0	0	0	0	0	0	0	0	0	..	..	..
Gambia, The	0	0	0	0	0	0	0	0	0	0	0	..	..	..
Ghana	0	0	0	0	0	0	0	0	0	0	0	..	..	..
Guinea	0	0	0	0	0	0	0	0	0	0	0	..	..	..
Guinea-Bissau	0	0	0	0	0	0	0	0	0	0	0	..	..	..
Kenya	40	32	28	31	33	30	28	32	27	25	21	-1.3	-4.8	-5.9
Lesotho	0	0	0	0	0	0	0	0	0	0	0	..	..	..
Liberia	0	0	0	0	0	0	0	0	0	0	0	..	..	..
Madagascar	10	9	7	9	8	12	10	7	9	8	10	-5.9	-8.0	0.3
Malawi	0	0	0	0	0	0	0	0	0	0	0	..	..	..
Mali	0	0	0	0	0	0	0	0	0	0	0	..	..	..
Mauritania	0	0	0	0	0	0	0	0	0	0	0	..	..	..
Mauritius	0	0	0	0	0	0	0	0	0	0	0	..	..	..
Mozambique	7	0	1	1	1	0	0	0	0	0	0	-14.5	-9.4	-11.3
Namibia	0	0	0	0	0	0	0	0	0	0	0	..	..	..
Niger	0	0	0	0	0	0	0	0	0	0	0	..	..	..
Nigeria	0	0	0	0	0	0	0	0	0	0	0	..	..	..
Rwanda	0	0	0	0	0	0	0	0	0	0	0	..	..	..
São Tomé and Principe	0	0	0	0	0	0	0	0	0	0	0	..	..	..
Senegal	0	0	0	0	0	0	0	0	0	0	0	..	..	..
Seychelles	0	0	0	0	0	0	0	0	0	0	0	..	..	..
Sierra Leone	0	0	0	0	0	0	0	0	0	0	0	..	..	..
Somalia	0	0	0	0	0	0	0	0	0	0	0	..	..	..
South Africa	0	1	1	1	0	0	0	0	0	0	0	-4.2	-7.7	-41.3
Sudan	0	0	0	0	0	0	0	0	0	0	0	..	..	..
Swaziland	0	0	0	0	0	0	0	0	0	0	0	..	..	..
Tanzania	48	12	18	10	9	8	5	4	5	7	11	-12.1	-16.9	2.9
Togo	0	0	0	0	0	0	0	0	0	0	0	..	..	..
Uganda	0	0	0	0	0	0	0	0	0	0	0	..	..	..
Zaire	0	0	0	0	0	0	0	0	0	0	0	..	..	..
Zambia	0	0	0	0	0	0	0	0	0	0	0	..	..	..
Zimbabwe	0	0	0	0	0	0	0	0	0	0	0	..	..	..
NORTH AFRICA	0	0	0	0	0	0	0	0	0	0	0	..	..	..
Algeria	0	0	0	0	0	0	0	0	0	0	0	..	..	..
Egypt, Arab Republic	0	0	0	0	0	0	0	0	0	0	0	..	..	..
Libya	0	0	0	0	0	0	0	0	0	0	0	..	..	..
Morocco	0	0	0	0	0	0	0	0	0	0	0	..	..	..
Tunisia	0	0	0	0	0	0	0	0	0	0	0	..	..	..
ALL AFRICA	109	53	54	51	50	50	42	43	42	41	43	-9.6	-8.7	-3.0

5-29. Tea exports

	Thousands of metric tons											Average annual percentage growth		
	1980	1986	1987	1988	1989	1990	1991	1992	1993	1994	1995	75-84	85-89	90-MR
SUB-SAHARAN AFRICA	182	225	232	245	258	269	281	270	298	278	309	3.8	4.8	2.4
excluding South Africa	180	225	231	245	257	268	279	269	297	277	308	3.7	4.8	2.4
excl. S. Africa & Nigeria	180	225	231	245	257	268	279	269	297	277	308	3.7	4.8	2.4
Angola	0	0	0	0	0	0	0	0	0	0	0	..	..	..
Benin	0	0	0	0	0	0	0	0	0	0	0	..	..	..
Botswana	0	0	0	0	0	0	0	0	0	0	0	..	..	..
Burkina Faso	0	0	0	0	0	0	0	0	0	0	0	..	..	..
Burundi	1	4	4	4	4	4	5	6	5	7	5	12.1	2.7	7.0
Cameroon	1	0	0	0	0	3	0	0	0	0	0	22.6	-33.6	-18.6
Cape Verde	0	0	0	0	0	0	0	0	0	0	0	..	..	..
Central African Republic	0	0	0	0	0	0	0	0	0	0	0	..	..	..
Chad	0	0	0	0	0	0	0	0	0	0	0	..	..	..
Comoros	0	0	0	0	0	0	0	0	0	0	0	..	..	..
Congo	0	0	0	0	0	0	0	0	0	0	0	..	..	..
Côte d'Ivoire	0	0	0	0	0	0	0	0	0	0	0	..	..	..
Djibouti	0	0	0	0	0	0	0	0	0	0	0	..	..	..
Equatorial Guinea	0	0	0	0	0	0	0	0	0	0	0	..	..	..
Eritrea	0	0	0	0	0	0	0	0	0	0	0	..	..	..
Ethiopia	0	0	0	0	0	0	0	0	0	0	0	..	..	..
Gabon	0	0	0	0	0	0	0	0	0	0	0	..	..	..
Gambia, The	0	0	0	0	0	0	0	0	0	0	0	..	..	..
Ghana	0	0	0	0	0	0	0	0	0	0	0	..	..	..
Guinea	0	0	0	0	0	0	0	0	0	0	0	..	..	..
Guinea-Bissau	0	0	0	0	0	0	0	0	0	0	0	..	..	..
Kenya	85	133	151	155	165	166	176	172	199	175	218	6.7	8.4	3.9
Lesotho	0	0	0	0	0	0	0	0	0	0	0	..	..	..
Liberia	0	0	0	0	0	0	0	0	0	0	0	..	..	..
Madagascar	0	0	0	0	0	0	0	0	0	0	0	..	0.0	-5.7
Malawi	31	40	33	37	38	43	41	37	35	39	33	3.8	-0.2	-3.0
Mali	0	0	0	0	0	0	0	0	0	0	0	..	..	..
Mauritania	0	0	0	0	0	0	0	0	0	0	0	..	..	..
Mauritius	4	6	7	5	5	4	5	6	4	4	3	8.1	-7.3	-5.8
Mozambique	30	2	1	1	0	1	1	0	0	0	0	-0.2	-48.5	-2.1
Namibia	0	0	0	0	0	0	0	0	0	0	0	..	..	..
Niger	0	0	0	0	0	0	0	0	0	0	0	..	..	..
Nigeria	0	0	0	0	0	0	0	0	0	0	0	..	..	..
Rwanda	7	10	9	12	13	12	13	14	12	8	5	8.6	8.0	-12.6
São Tomé and Principe	0	0	0	0	0	0	0	0	0	0	0	..	..	..
Senegal	0	0	0	0	1	1	0	0	0	0	0	..	..	..
Seychelles	0	0	0	0	0	0	0	0	0	0	0	..	..	..
Sierra Leone	0	0	0	0	0	0	0	0	0	0	0	..	..	..
Somalia	0	0	0	0	0	0	0	0	0	0	0	..	..	..
South Africa	2	1	1	1	1	1	1	1	1	1	1	25.5	11.1	-3.4
Sudan	0	0	0	0	0	0	0	0	0	0	0	..	..	..
Swaziland	0	0	0	0	0	0	0	0	0	0	0	..	..	..
Tanzania	13	11	12	11	12	15	18	19	20	22	22	2.5	1.2	9.9
Togo	0	0	0	0	0	0	0	0	0	0	0	..	..	..
Uganda	1	3	2	3	3	5	7	8	10	11	11	-28.1	11.4	22.3
Zaire	2	3	2	2	3	3	2	2	2	2	2	-8.6	-4.8	-8.3
Zambia	0	0	0	0	0	0	0	0	0	0	0	..	..	..
Zimbabwe	6	12	10	13	13	12	11	6	8	10	9	10.6	5.3	-5.8
NORTH AFRICA	0	0	0	0	0	0	0	0	0	0	0	..	..	4.9
Algeria	0	0	0	0	0	0	0	0	0	0	0	..	..	..
Egypt, Arab Republic	0	0	0	0	0	0	0	0	0	0	0	..	..	-9.5
Libya	0	0	0	0	0	0	0	0	0	0	0	..	..	..
Morocco	0	0	0	0	0	0	0	0	0	0	0	..	..	..
Tunisia	0	0	0	0	0	0	0	0	0	0	0	..	..	..
ALL AFRICA	182	225	232	245	259	269	281	270	298	278	309	3.8	4.8	2.4

5-30. Sugar exports

	Thousands of metric tons											Average annual percentage growth		
	1980	1986	1987	1988	1989	1990	1991	1992	1993	1994	1995	75-84	85-89	90-MR
SUB-SAHARAN AFRICA	1,047	2,458	2,735	2,262	2,490	1,991	1,549	1,190	901	1,260	1,356	4.2	2.6	-11.1
excluding South Africa	1,047	1,497	1,572	1,352	1,400	1,020	838	906	760	941	966	3.4	0.4	-4.8
excl. S. Africa & Nigeria	1,047	1,497	1,572	1,352	1,400	1,020	838	906	760	941	966	3.4	0.4	-4.8
Angola	0	0	0	0	0	0	0	0	0	0	0	..	..	..
Benin	0	0	0	0	0	0	0	0	0	0	0	..	..	..
Botswana	0	0	0	0	0	0	0	0	0	0	0	-14.0	65.9	-5.5
Burkina Faso	0	0	0	0	0	0	0	0	0	0	0	..	..	..
Burundi	0	0	0	0	0	0	0	0	0	0	0	..	..	..
Cameroon	9	21	0	1	1	0	2	0	1	0	1	42.1	-24.4	-32.1
Cape Verde	0	0	0	0	0	0	0	0	0	0	0	..	..	..
Central African Republic	0	0	0	0	0	0	0	0	0	0	0	..	..	..
Chad	0	0	0	0	0	0	0	0	0	0	0	..	..	..
Comoros	0	0	0	0	0	0	0	0	0	0	0	..	..	..
Congo	0	16	18	18	14	26	23	29	18	11	14	-1.3	-14.0	-6.8
Côte d'Ivoire	11	21	28	7	18	23	18	11	39	34	12	142.4	-18.9	0.9
Djibouti	0	0	0	0	0	0	0	0	0	0	0	..	..	..
Equatorial Guinea	0	0	0	0	0	0	0	0	0	0	0	..	..	..
Eritrea	0	0	0	0	0	0	0	0	0	0	0	..	..	..
Ethiopia	0	0	0	0	0	0	0	0	0	0	0	..	..	..
Gabon	2	0	0	0	0	0	8	7	0	0	0	9.3	..	..
Gambia, The	0	0	0	0	0	0	0	0	0	0	0	..	..	..
Ghana	0	0	0	0	0	0	0	0	0	0	0	..	..	..
Guinea	0	0	0	0	0	0	0	0	0	0	0	..	..	..
Guinea-Bissau	0	0	0	0	0	0	0	0	0	0	0	..	..	..
Kenya	56	0	0	0	0	0	0	104	50	0	27	19.0	-15.5	306.3
Lesotho	0	0	0	0	0	0	0	0	0	0	0	..	..	..
Liberia	0	0	0	0	0	0	0	0	0	0	0	8.1	..	..
Madagascar	26	0	52	19	72	47	21	17	11	24	15	-1.1	19.9	-21.3
Malawi	92	100	94	99	54	62	51	22	26	43	65	13.9	-5.4	-3.0
Mali	0	0	0	0	0	0	0	0	0	0	0	..	..	..
Mauritania	0	0	0	0	0	0	0	0	0	0	0	..	..	..
Mauritius	618	626	657	653	637	578	551	598	535	519	524	-0.7	4.4	-2.9
Mozambique	64	20	10	12	13	18	25	52	0	52	54	-12.8	-8.1	27.9
Namibia	0	0	0	0	0	0	0	0	0	0	0	..	..	..
Niger	0	0	0	0	1	1	0	0	0	0	0	..	..	..
Nigeria	0	0	0	0	0	0	0	0	0	0	0	..	..	..
Rwanda	0	0	0	0	0	0	0	0	0	0	0	..	..	..
São Tomé and Principe	0	0	0	0	0	0	0	0	0	0	0	..	..	..
Senegal	0	2	11	8	7	3	0	0	0	0	0	-34.3	244.7	-82.5
Seychelles	0	0	0	0	0	0	0	0	0	0	0	..	..	..
Sierra Leone	0	0	0	0	0	0	0	0	0	0	0	..	..	..
Somalia	0	0	0	0	0	0	0	0	0	0	0	..	..	..
South Africa	0	961	1,163	910	1,089	971	712	284	141	318	390	..	6.2	-21.9
Sudan	0	0	0	0	0	65	49	54	80	58	96	..	..	8.5
Swaziland	0	463	462	375	414	0	0	0	0	0	0	..	1.5	..
Tanzania	0	0	0	0	0	0	0	0	0	0	0	..	..	..
Togo	0	0	0	0	0	0	0	0	0	0	0	..	..	..
Uganda	0	0	0	0	0	0	0	0	0	0	0	..	..	..
Zaire	0	0	0	0	0	0	0	0	0	0	0	..	..	..
Zambia	0	0	0	0	0	0	0	0	0	0	0	..	..	..
Zimbabwe	169	229	241	159	171	197	89	12	0	201	160	3.9	-7.3	-18.4
NORTH AFRICA	10	1	0	1	14	2	8	1	1	7	6	-31.8	155.0	-9.3
Algeria	0	0	0	0	0	0	0	0	0	0	0	..	..	..
Egypt, Arab Republic	10	1	0	0	14	2	8	1	1	7	6	-12.4	134.0	-9.3
Libya	0	0	0	0	0	0	0	0	0	0	0	..	..	..
Morocco	0	0	0	1	0	0	0	0	0	0	0	..	-17.5	18.3
Tunisia	0	0	0	0	0	0	0	0	0	0	0	..	..	..
ALL AFRICA	1,056	2,458	2,735	2,263	2,504	1,994	1,558	1,190	902	1,267	1,362	3.8	2.7	-11.1

5-31. Tobacco exports

	Hundreds of metric tons											Average annual percentage growth		
	1980	1986	1987	1988	1989	1990	1991	1992	1993	1994	1995	75-84	85-89	90-MR
SUB-SAHARAN AFRICA	1,777	1,810	1,818	1,832	1,823	2,264	2,483	2,783	3,164	4,390	3,138	3.0	0.5	12.1
excluding South Africa	1,705	1,705	1,730	1,753	1,727	2,184	2,393	2,702	3,070	4,220	3,028	3.2	0.2	12.3
excl. S. Africa & Nigeria	1,705	1,705	1,730	1,752	1,727	2,182	2,393	2,690	3,068	4,217	3,025	3.2	0.2	12.3
Angola	16	0	0	0	0	0	0	0	0	0	0	-4.7	..	..
Benin	0	0	0	0	0	0	0	0	0	0	0	-36.9	..	..
Botswana	1	0	0	0	1	0	0	0	0	0	0	29.6	-1.9	-0.5
Burkina Faso	0	0	0	0	0	0	0	0	0	0	0	..	..	..
Burundi	0	0	5	9	8	7	11	15	10	4	2	..	89.6	-18.0
Cameroon	21	11	9	5	9	8	7	7	6	1	3	-7.9	-11.6	-23.9
Cape Verde	0	0	0	0	0	0	0	0	0	0	0	..	..	..
Central African Republic	8	7	7	4	2	0	1	1	1	1	2	-8.6	-4.4	9.6
Chad	0	0	0	0	0	0	0	0	0	0	0	..	..	..
Comoros	0	0	0	0	0	0	0	0	0	0	0	..	..	..
Congo	1	0	0	0	0	0	0	0	0	0	0	-23.6	-46.4	..
Côte d'Ivoire	0	0	0	0	0	1	0	0	0	0	0	-2.6	..	..
Djibouti	0	0	0	0	0	0	0	0	0	0	0	..	..	..
Equatorial Guinea	0	0	0	0	0	0	0	0	0	0	0	..	..	..
Eritrea	0	0	0	0	0	0	0	0	0	0	0	..	..	..
Ethiopia	0	0	0	0	0	0	0	0	0	0	0	..	..	..
Gabon	0	0	0	0	0	0	0	0	0	0	0	..	..	..
Gambia, The	0	0	0	0	0	0	0	0	0	0	0	..	..	..
Ghana	0	2	1	1	1	3	3	2	3	5	2	-33.6	-12.6	13.0
Guinea	0	0	0	0	0	0	0	0	0	0	0	..	..	..
Guinea-Bissau	0	0	0	0	0	0	0	0	0	0	0	..	..	..
Kenya	0	5	5	7	9	0	19	23	56	3	25	9.8	31.8	41.1
Lesotho	0	0	0	0	0	0	0	0	0	0	0	..	..	..
Liberia	0	0	0	0	0	0	0	0	0	0	0	3.3	..	..
Madagascar	1	6	5	5	5	0	0	0	0	0	4	-11.2	-6.9	-5.8
Malawi	611	594	618	596	546	891	972	973	957	984	995	8.4	-3.3	7.3
Mali	0	0	0	0	0	0	0	0	0	0	0	-53.9	..	..
Mauritania	0	0	0	0	0	0	0	0	0	0	0	..	..	..
Mauritius	0	0	0	0	0	0	0	0	0	0	0	..	..	..
Mozambique	0	0	0	0	0	0	0	0	0	0	0	..	..	..
Namibia	0	0	0	0	0	0	0	0	0	0	0	..	..	..
Niger	3	0	0	8	8	9	0	0	0	0	0	39.9	..	..
Nigeria	0	0	0	1	0	2	0	12	3	4	3	..	..	42.9
Rwanda	0	0	0	0	0	0	0	0	0	0	0	..	..	..
São Tomé and Principe	0	0	0	0	0	0	0	0	0	0	0	..	..	..
Senegal	0	0	0	0	2	3	0	0	1	1	1	..	..	-15.1
Seychelles	0	0	0	0	0	0	0	0	0	0	0	..	..	..
Sierra Leone	0	3	2	1	2	1	2	7	2	2	2	..	23.3	7.5
Somalia	0	0	0	0	0	0	0	0	0	0	0	..	..	..
South Africa	72	105	87	79	95	80	90	81	94	169	110	-1.8	7.0	7.3
Sudan	0	1	0	0	0	0	0	0	0	0	0	..	..	..
Swaziland	2	2	1	0	0	0	0	0	1	1	1	-17.4	-22.6	11.6
Tanzania	83	77	74	82	77	59	80	114	106	154	178	-7.4	7.6	18.4
Togo	0	0	0	0	0	0	0	0	0	0	0	4.7	..	..
Uganda	3	0	0	0	5	23	25	23	41	41	42	-8.6	-20.7	33.7
Zaire	0	0	0	0	0	0	0	0	0	0	0	..	..	..
Zambia	26	8	19	26	10	20	13	19	41	30	9	-13.6	0.0	5.7
Zimbabwe	930	991	985	1,007	1,041	1,158	1,261	1,505	1,843	2,989	1,760	3.9	2.3	14.7
NORTH AFRICA	15	21	9	10	7	10	11	7	7	9	12	6.5	-7.2	3.3
Algeria	0	0	0	0	0	0	0	0	0	0	0	..	..	..
Egypt, Arab Republic	0	0	0	0	2	1	0	0	0	0	0	..	..	-38.8
Libya	0	0	0	0	0	0	0	0	0	0	0	..	..	..
Morocco	0	0	0	0	0	0	0	3	3	1	0	..	..	-83.3
Tunisia	15	21	9	10	5	9	11	4	4	8	12	26.9	-5.4	4.0
ALL AFRICA	1,792	1,831	1,826	1,842	1,830	2,274	2,495	2,791	3,171	4,399	3,149	3.0	0.4	12.1

5-32. Meat exports

	Hundreds of metric tons											Average annual percentage growth		
	1980	1986	1987	1988	1989	1990	1991	1992	1993	1994	1995	75-84	85-89	90-MR
SUB-SAHARAN AFRICA	1,033	602	554	494	539	541	573	639	854	715	753	-9.0	-7.2	7.2
excluding South Africa	662	520	486	455	487	472	526	579	754	650	689	-9.1	-7.4	7.6
excl. S. Africa & Nigeria	662	520	486	455	487	472	526	579	754	650	689	-9.1	-7.4	7.6
Angola	0	0	0	0	0	0	0	0	0	0	0	..	..	..
Benin	0	0	0	0	0	0	0	0	0	0	0	..	..	..
Botswana	165	273	159	174	189	158	199	193	222	191	177	-1.8	-7.3	1.0
Burkina Faso	3	5	1	0	0	0	0	0	0	0	0	-3.5	-32.5	..
Burundi	0	0	0	0	0	0	0	0	0	0	0	..	..	..
Cameroon	0	0	0	0	0	0	0	0	0	0	0	-15.2	..	..
Cape Verde	0	0	0	0	0	0	0	0	0	0	0	..	..	..
Central African Republic	20	0	0	0	0	0	0	0	0	0	0	-19.8	..	..
Chad	0	0	1	1	2	4	2	2	2	2	2	..	..	-4.8
Comoros	0	0	0	0	0	0	0	0	0	0	0	..	..	..
Congo	0	0	0	0	0	0	0	0	0	0	0	..	..	..
Côte d'Ivoire	0	0	0	0	0	0	0	0	0	0	0	0.0	..	..
Djibouti	0	0	0	0	0	0	0	0	0	0	0	..	..	..
Equatorial Guinea	0	0	0	0	0	0	0	0	0	0	0	..	..	..
Eritrea	0	0	0	0	0	0	0	0	0	0	0	..	..	..
Ethiopia	15	6	16	9	2	2	1	0	0	2	5	-0.1	-26.5	6.5
Gabon	0	0	0	0	0	0	0	0	0	0	0	..	..	..
Gambia, The	0	0	0	0	0	0	0	0	0	0	0	..	..	..
Ghana	0	0	0	0	0	0	0	0	0	0	0	..	..	..
Guinea	0	0	0	0	0	0	0	0	0	0	0	..	..	..
Guinea-Bissau	0	0	0	0	0	0	0	0	0	0	0	..	..	..
Kenya	2	1	1	1	1	3	3	2	6	5	4	-24.5	-19.5	23.8
Lesotho	0	0	0	0	0	0	0	0	0	0	0	..	..	..
Liberia	0	0	0	0	0	0	0	0	0	0	0	..	..	..
Madagascar	65	0	2	0	0	1	4	11	17	23	38	-11.5	..	98.0
Malawi	0	0	0	0	0	0	0	0	0	0	0	..	..	..
Mali	0	0	0	0	0	0	0	0	0	0	0	..	..	..
Mauritania	0	0	0	0	0	0	0	0	0	0	0	..	..	..
Mauritius	0	1	1	0	0	3	2	2	0	0	0	..	-24.2	-66.7
Mozambique	0	0	0	0	0	0	0	0	0	0	0	..	..	..
Namibia	230	153	171	181	247	208	258	262	313	281	251	4.6	8.7	3.1
Niger	0	0	0	0	0	0	0	0	0	0	0	..	..	..
Nigeria	0	0	0	0	0	0	0	0	0	0	0	..	..	..
Rwanda	0	0	0	0	0	0	0	0	0	0	0	..	..	..
São Tomé and Principe	0	0	0	0	0	0	0	0	0	0	0	..	..	..
Senegal	1	1	1	0	3	1	0	0	1	1	1	-4.5	11.0	-16.9
Seychelles	0	0	0	0	0	0	0	0	0	0	0	..	..	..
Sierra Leone	0	0	0	0	0	0	0	0	0	0	0	..	..	..
Somalia	0	0	0	0	0	0	0	0	0	0	0	..	..	..
South Africa	371	82	68	39	52	69	47	60	100	65	64	-10.3	-4.6	4.5
Sudan	0	0	0	0	0	0	0	0	22	24	55	-17.3	..	..
Swaziland	27	32	21	1	1	9	10	2	7	7	6	-3.4	-46.2	18.0
Tanzania	0	0	0	0	0	43	0	0	0	0	0	..	..	..
Togo	0	0	1	0	0	0	0	0	0	0	0	..	..	..
Uganda	0	0	0	0	0	0	0	0	0	0	0	..	..	..
Zaire	0	0	0	0	0	0	0	0	0	0	0	..	..	..
Zambia	0	1	0	0	0	0	2	0	1	1	1	..	..	-22.9
Zimbabwe	134	47	111	88	42	40	45	105	164	112	150	-22.1	-21.2	29.2
NORTH AFRICA	35	1	2	2	17	58	11	42	37	23	16	-1.6	18.4	-3.1
Algeria	0	0	0	0	0	0	0	0	0	0	0	..	..	..
Egypt, Arab Republic	1	1	1	1	16	55	10	40	36	20	14	-0.7	48.6	-4.3
Libya	0	0	0	0	0	2	0	0	0	0	0	..	..	..
Morocco	33	0	0	0	0	0	0	0	0	1	1	-2.3	..	..
Tunisia	1	0	1	1	1	1	1	2	1	2	1	-1.2	0.0	5.6
ALL AFRICA	1,068	603	556	496	556	599	584	681	891	738	769	-8.7	-6.9	6.7

5-33. Manufactured goods exports

	Millions of U.S. dollars (current prices)											*Annual average*		
	1980	*1986*	*1987*	*1988*	*1989*	*1990*	*1991*	*1992*	*1993*	*1994*	*1995*	*75-84*	*85-89*	*90-MR*
SUB-SAHARAN AFRICA	..	..	2,760	2,885	2,858	3,504	2,817	2,999	3,149	2,889	3,127	..	2,834	3,081
excluding South Africa	..	..	2,760	2,885	2,858	3,504	2,817	2,999	3,149	2,889	3,127	..	2,834	3,081
excl. S.Africa & Nigeria	..	..	2,744	2,871	2,839	3,476	2,793	2,986	3,127	2,880	3,105	..	2,818	3,061
Angola	..	0	0	0	0	0	0	0	0	0	0	0	0	0
Benin	..	0	0	0	0	0	0	0	0	0	0	0	0	0
Botswana	..	0	0	0	0	0	0	0	0	43	45	0	0	15
Burkina Faso	..	..	..	..	..	..	..	..	..	..	..	..	..	..
Burundi	1	10	13	7	4	4	4	11	9	6	8	3	8	7
Cameroon	96	162	166	110	175	191	171	155	142	109	137	81	148	151
Cape Verde	..	..	..	..	..	..	..	..	..	..	..	..	..	..
Central African Republic	..	..	0	0	0	0	0	0	0	0	0	..	0	0
Chad	..	5	4	3	3	2	0	1	0	0	1	5	4	1
Comoros	..	0	0	0	0	0	0	0	0	0	0	0	0	0
Congo	..	40	31	36	45	0	0	0	0	0	0	56	40	0
Côte d'Ivoire	0	821	962	904	828	1,204	564	683	752	429	578	365	849	702
Djibouti	..	..	..	..	..	..	..	..	..	..	..	..	..	..
Equatorial Guinea	..	..	..	..	..	..	..	..	..	..	..	..	..	..
Eritrea	..	..	..	..	..	..	..	..	..	..	..	..	..	..
Ethiopia	..	..	..	..	..	..	..	..	..	..	..	..	..	..
Gabon	..	..	..	..	..	0	0	0	0	0	0	..	..	0
Gambia, The	21	30	34	32	41	51	62	67	54	53	55	23	33	57
Ghana	..	..	..	..	..	..	..	..	..	..	..	..	..	..
Guinea	..	0	0	0	0	0	0	0	0	0	0	..	0	0
Guinea-Bissau	..	0	0	0	0	0	0	0	0	0	0	0	0	0
Kenya	..	120	123	139	137	140	146	137	140	159	182	128	127	151
Lesotho	..	3	4	3	0	13	22	23	31	39	43	2	2	29
Liberia	..	..	..	..	..	..	..	..	..	..	..	..	..	..
Madagascar	..	45	62	69	71	103	125	112	103	127	132	45	57	117
Malawi	..	18	0	0	0	0	0	0	0	0	0	14	7	0
Mali	..	0	0	0	0	0	0	0	0	0	0	0	0	0
Mauritania	..	0	0	0	0	0	0	0	0	0	0	0	0	0
Mauritius	..	296	408	487	485	645	645	703	753	756	852	156	369	726
Mozambique	..	..	..	..	..	..	..	..	..	..	5	..	..	5
Namibia	..	112	172	174	148	169	226	292	290	289	0	137	140	211
Niger	..	0	0	0	0	0	0	0	0	0	0	0	0	0
Nigeria	52	41	15	14	20	28	24	12	23	10	22	54	30	20
Rwanda	..	13	2	0	4	4	3	3	2	1	1	5	5	2
São Tomé and Principe	..	..	0	0	0	0	0	0	0	0	0	..	0	0
Senegal	..	4	4	4	6	7	7	26	19	23	40	9	5	20
Seychelles	..	0	4	11	9	10	12	13	11	17	16	0	5	13
Sierra Leone	..	..	..	..	..	..	..	..	..	..	..	..	..	..
Somalia	..	..	..	..	..	..	..	..	..	..	..	..	..	..
South Africa	..	..	..	..	..	..	..	..	..	..	..	..	..	..
Sudan	..	1	31	53	33	11	0	0	42	0	0	31	24	9
Swaziland	..	..	..	..	..	..	..	..	..	..	..	..	..	..
Tanzania	90	39	63	72	86	97	70	61	52	89	95	54	59	77
Togo	..	97	102	115	100	150	145	128	75	60	86	66	92	107
Uganda	..	..	..	..	..	..	..	..	..	..	..	..	..	..
Zaire	..	0	0	11	12	0	0	0	0	0	0	0	5	0
Zambia	..	..	..	0	0	0	0	0	0	0	0	..	0	0
Zimbabwe	..	308	560	642	652	675	590	573	652	682	829	319	495	667
NORTH AFRICA	..	..	3,009	3,941	4,441	5,705	5,837	6,328	5,730	6,622	8,532	..	3,797	6,459
Algeria	..	12	37	216	234	258	226	213	68	28	30	7	105	137
Egypt, Arab Republic	..	..	665	961	978	1,302	1,163	1,461	1,167	1,233	2,202	..	868	1,421
Libya	..	..	..	..	..	..	..	..	..	..	..	..	..	..
Morocco	..	655	876	979	1,130	1,525	1,568	1,551	1,482	1,474	1,600	434	823	1,533
Tunisia	905	1,175	1,431	1,785	2,099	2,621	2,880	3,102	3,012	3,887	4,701	718	1,473	3,367
ALL AFRICA	..	..	5,769	6,826	7,299	9,209	8,654	9,326	8,880	9,511	11,659		6,631	9,540

5-34. Manufactured goods exports, growth

	Percent											Average annual percentage growth		
	1980	1986	1987	1988	1989	1990	1991	1992	1993	1994	1995	75-84	85-89	90-MR
SUB-SAHARAN AFRICA	..	..	..	..	..	..	..	..	..	..	..	..	..	..
excluding South Africa	..	..	..	..	..	..	..	..	..	..	..	..	..	..
excl. S.Africa & Nigeria	..	..	..	..	..	..	..	..	..	..	..	..	..	..
Angola	..	..	..	..	..	..	..	..	..	..	..	..	..	..
Benin	..	..	..	..	..	..	..	..	..	..	..	..	..	..
Botswana	..	..	..	..	..	..	..	..	..	..	..	..	..	..
Burkina Faso	..	..	..	..	..	..	..	..	..	..	..	..	..	..
Burundi	..	128.6	61.3	-19.4	-60.6	-2.4	-15.0	188.2	-17.3	-45.7	0.0	..	12.9	4.6
Cameroon	21.3	-15.6	-21.3	-12.5	69.1	3.5	-6.2	-5.0	1.2	9.9	14.3	13.0	0.2	1.5
Cape Verde	..	..	..	..	..	..	..	..	..	..	..	..	..	..
Central African Republic	..	..	..	..	..	..	..	..	..	..	..	..	..	..
Chad	..	..	..	29.5	8.8	9.7	1.5	-2.9	-4.5	-1.6	23.8	..	..	1.7
Comoros	..	..	..	..	..	..	..	..	..	..	..	..	..	..
Congo	..	..	..	..	..	..	..	..	..	..	..	..	..	..
Côte d'Ivoire	..	..	..	..	..	..	..	..	..	..	..	..	..	..
Djibouti	..	..	..	..	..	..	..	..	..	..	..	..	..	..
Equatorial Guinea	..	..	..	..	..	..	..	..	..	..	..	..	..	..
Eritrea	..	..	..	..	..	..	..	..	..	..	..	..	..	..
Ethiopia	..	..	..	..	..	..	..	..	..	..	..	..	..	..
Gabon	..	..	..	..	..	..	..	..	..	..	..	..	..	..
Gambia, The	..	..	..	29.6	9.8	0.0	-6.0	-6.4	-7.1	-7.4	-7.7	..	..	-6.1
Ghana	..	..	..	..	..	..	..	..	..	..	..	..	..	..
Guinea	..	..	..	..	..	..	..	..	..	..	..	..	..	..
Guinea-Bissau	..	..	..	..	..	..	..	..	..	..	..	..	..	..
Kenya	..	-20.1	3.0	-14.4	-3.6	27.9	10.3	-8.3	7.0	10.2	9.4	..	-9.1	6.9
Lesotho	..	..	..	..	..	..	..	..	..	..	..	..	..	..
Liberia	..	..	..	..	..	..	..	..	..	..	..	..	..	..
Madagascar	..	9.5	34.8	11.3	-1.4	26.5	22.1	-15.2	1.1	8.9	6.1	..	12.4	5.1
Malawi	..	..	..	..	..	..	..	..	..	..	..	..	..	..
Mali	..	..	..	..	..	..	..	..	..	..	..	..	..	..
Mauritania	..	..	..	..	..	..	..	..	..	..	..	..	..	..
Mauritius	..	34.8	-3.9	37.5	-12.5	23.2	6.1	7.4	9.5	1.0	5.0	..	14.7	7.8
Mozambique	..	..	..	..	..	..	..	..	..	..	..	..	..	..
Namibia	..	..	..	..	..	..	..	..	..	..	..	..	..	..
Niger	..	..	..	..	..	..	..	..	..	..	..	..	..	..
Nigeria	-6.3	-45.0	-66.2	-13.2	40.5	34.2	-14.6	-51.2	83.5	-59.3	111.7	-6.5	-32.5	-9.5
Rwanda	..	-20.6	-40.7	0.0	-12.5	-28.6	-20.0	12.5	-22.2	-42.9	175.0	..	-21.8	-9.2
São Tomé and Principe	..	..	..	..	..	..	..	..	..	..	..	..	..	..
Senegal	..	-48.9	-6.5	-14.0	43.2	-1.9	3.8	31.5	-15.5	-1.7	44.1	..	-13.5	6.5
Seychelles	..	..	..	78.4	12.1	-35.1	18.8	47.4	27.4	-60.7	-9.5	..	..	-5.7
Sierra Leone	..	..	..	..	..	..	..	..	..	..	..	..	..	..
Somalia	..	..	..	..	..	..	..	..	..	..	..	..	..	..
South Africa	..	..	..	..	..	..	..	..	..	..	..	..	..	..
Sudan	..	..	..	..	..	..	..	..	..	..	..	..	..	..
Swaziland	..	..	..	..	..	..	..	..	..	..	..	..	..	..
Tanzania	..	..	..	..	..	..	-30.0	-18.1	-23.2	49.9	-29.1	..	..	-11.4
Togo	..	..	..	-15.9	-49.4	10.6	-1.9	-164.5	192.4	-22.7	88.5	..	..	..
Uganda	..	..	..	..	..	..	..	..	..	..	..	..	..	..
Zaire	..	..	..	..	..	..	..	..	..	..	..	..	..	..
Zambia	..	..	..	..	..	..	..	..	..	..	..	..	..	..
Zimbabwe	..	..	..	7.0	2.2	-3.9	-14.6	-7.0	14.3	0.7	12.3	..	..	-0.6
NORTH AFRICA	..	..	..	..	..	..	..	..	..	..	..	..	..	..
Algeria	..	-86.6	230.6	2359.7	-76.4	-9.6	-34.1	8.7	-23.5	-57.7	-1.6	..	99.8	-24.4
Egypt, Arab Republic	..	..	..	33.2	-1.4	30.0	-14.0	21.6	-21.6	3.9	68.4	..	..	5.5
Libya	..	..	..	..	..	..	..	..	..	..	..	..	..	..
Morocco	..	14.7	27.4	4.2	17.8	24.4	2.0	-8.4	-0.1	-4.1	15.5	..	15.1	1.6
Tunisia	..	27.2	13.9	13.9	19.1	10.5	6.8	0.0	1.7	23.2	6.1	..	16.5	7.2
ALL AFRICA	..	..	..	..	..	..	..	..	..	..	..	..	..	..

5-35. Food imports

	Millions of U.S. dollars (current prices)											Annual average		
	1980	*1986*	*1987*	*1988*	*1989*	*1990*	*1991*	*1992*	*1993*	*1994*	*1995*	*75-84*	*85-89*	*90-MR*
SUB-SAHARAN AFRICA	..	2,909	2,921	3,500	3,511	4,047	4,134	4,875	4,435	5,241	5,516	2,507	3,135	4,708
excluding South Africa	..	2,909	2,921	3,500	3,511	4,047	4,134	4,875	4,435	5,241	5,516	2,507	3,135	4,708
excl. S.Africa & Nigeria	..	2,909	2,921	2,951	3,033	3,350	3,409	3,994	3,580	4,370	4,474	2,507	2,930	3,863
Angola	..	246	193	248	242	286	57	244	203	295	354	0	263	240
Benin	..	..	..	..	..	..	..	..	..	..	..	..	..	..
Botswana	..	119	156	0	0	0	0	0	0	306	334	128	75	107
Burkina Faso	..	..	..	..	..	..	..	..	..	..	..	..	..	..
Burundi	18	16	12	15	10	12	15	11	19	55	51	19	14	27
Cameroon	82	110	133	177	155	190	248	224	208	195	222	70	134	215
Cape Verde	0	..	33	29	36	38	42	75	53	65	85	0	25	59
Central African Republic	..	26	28	25	27	34	28	30	25	23	29	20	26	28
Chad	..	..	18	15	15	18	7	0	4	5	4	..	16	6
Comoros	..	7	6	11	11	10	12	13	10	9	18	8	8	12
Congo	..	26	15	18	25	30	31	34	36	15	16	104	23	27
Côte d'Ivoire	..	416	508	502	483	467	490	377	431	317	442	303	436	421
Djibouti	..	..	..	..	..	..	..	..	..	..	..	..	..	..
Equatorial Guinea	..	6	8	10	..	..	..	..	..	..	..	..	7	..
Eritrea	..	..	..	..	..	..	..	..	..	..	..	..	..	..
Ethiopia	..	294	194	137	186	74	152	132	166	127	181	126	219	138
Gabon	..	170	163	137	126	143	157	174	166	166	181	142	151	164
Gambia, The	..	45	49	48	51	69	87	97	87	73	90	..	48	84
Ghana	..	44	73	43	42	39	39	38	43	45	56	39	48	43
Guinea	..	7	15	12	12	12	8	49	53	76	77	..	12	46
Guinea-Bissau	..	13	11	15	16	15	21	32	25	17	26	16	14	23
Kenya	..	118	130	138	125	125	149	156	141	180	209	111	125	160
Lesotho	..	67	0	0	0	0	0	0	0	297	328	102	27	104
Liberia	..	..	..	..	..	..	..	..	..	..	..	..	..	..
Madagascar	89	52	52	17	38	49	35	58	51	106	67	87	42	61
Malawi	..	..	2	3	4	5	7	8	7	60	76	..	3	27
Mali	..	81	64	83	69	114	117	97	97	86	104	131	88	102
Mauritania	..	91	97	110	107	118	112	127	97	100	94	76	100	108
Mauritius	..	88	114	130	173	197	195	214	237	270	307	93	118	237
Mozambique	..	149	168	172	160	155	152	199	172	248	203	135	154	188
Namibia	..	0	0	0	0	229	279	350	326	314	0	0	0	250
Niger	..	..	21	44	27	40	31	22	22	16	18	..	30	25
Nigeria	..	..	..	550	478	697	725	880	855	872	1,042	..	514	845
Rwanda	..	38	24	23	29	32	35	29	59	218	56	27	31	72
São Tomé and Principe	..	5	5	9	7	6	5	5	7	7	7	8	7	6
Senegal	..	195	208	283	334	334	351	363	348	310	394	235	243	350
Seychelles	..	20	24	33	30	34	33	40	46	42	34	17	25	38
Sierra Leone	..	44	45	50	54	45	32	33	43	52	20	39	49	37
Somalia	..	..	..	..	..	..	..	..	..	..	..	..	..	..
South Africa	..	..	..	..	..	..	..	..	..	..	..	..	..	..
Sudan	..	195	140	172	245	231	345	328	168	0	0	219	189	179
Swaziland	..	..	..	..	..	..	..	..	..	..	..	..	..	..
Tanzania	..	95	76	107	55	63	1	49	94	130	139	94	82	79
Togo	..	93	95	92	89	86	91	81	46	41	36	81	91	63
Uganda	..	..	..	..	..	..	..	..	..	..	..	..	..	..
Zaire	..	0	0	0	0	0	0	0	0	0	0	0	0	0
Zambia	..	17	11	14	14	9	..	258	50	55	98	24	16	94
Zimbabwe	..	17	30	32	37	42	47	50	42	50	118	77	31	58
NORTH AFRICA	..	..	4,872	4,125	6,495	5,550	4,623	5,428	5,358	5,522	7,427	..	5,164	5,651
Algeria	..	1,851	1,745	1,808	2,925	2,134	1,894	2,127	2,092	2,206	2,520	1,757	2,102	2,162
Egypt, Arab Republic	..	..	2,338	1,254	2,404	2,328	1,802	1,979	1,878	1,982	2,760	..	1,999	2,121
Libya	..	..	..	..	..	..	..	..	..	..	..	..	..	..
Morocco	..	476	476	509	588	583	591	892	972	799	1,332	660	511	861
Tunisia	..	362	312	554	578	506	336	430	417	536	815	467	428	507
ALL AFRICA	..	5,597	7,792	7,626	10,006	9,596	8,758	10,302	9,793	10,764	12,942	..	7,376	10,359

5-36. Food imports, growth

	Percent											Average annual percentage growth		
	1980	*1986*	*1987*	*1988*	*1989*	*1990*	*1991*	*1992*	*1993*	*1994*	*1995*	*75-84*	*85-89*	*90-MR*
SUB-SAHARAN AFRICA	..	..	..	..	..	..	..	..	..	..	..	..	..	..
excluding South Africa	..	..	..	..	..	..	..	..	..	..	..	..	..	..
excl. S.Africa & Nigeria	..	..	..	..	..	..	..	..	..	..	..	..	..	..
Angola	..	-40.2	-3.8	9.3	7.5	31.3	-79.6	356.6	-17.4	5.6	12.1	..	-7.0	5.3
Benin	..	..	..	..	..	..	..	..	..	..	..	..	..	..
Botswana	..	..	..	..	..	..	..	..	..	..	..	..	..	..
Burkina Faso	..	..	..	..	..	..	..	..	..	..	..	..	..	..
Burundi	..	40.9	-5.3	-29.8	-21.8	-27.9	77.6	-57.5	75.7	92.3	-43.2	..	-5.8	6.3
Cameroon	0.9	12.6	48.2	13.0	-3.8	36.1	33.3	-2.9	-7.9	-32.2	-2.3	-0.9	22.9	-1.1
Cape Verde	..	..	..	-30.9	24.1	13.8	9.6	78.8	-27.7	12.1	19.8	..	..	13.3
Central African Republic	..	..	..	-17.9	5.2	36.0	-21.9	10.5	-16.5	-54.4	26.9	..	..	-13.4
Chad	..	..	..	2.8	3.2	3.1	2.0	-89.6	500.0	25.4	-12.7	..	..	-6.5
Comoros	..	33.3	-25.0	83.3	9.1	-25.0	22.2	0.0	-9.1	30.0	76.9	..	5.8	9.7
Congo	..	39.7	37.6	-5.3	-9.2	-7.8	-2.5	-16.4	32.0	10.9	-0.7	..	-6.4	2.6
Côte d'Ivoire	..	..	..	..	..	-3.4	5.0	-24.9	17.1	-26.4	19.1	..	..	-5.7
Djibouti	..	..	..	..	..	..	..	..	..	..	..	..	..	..
Equatorial Guinea	..	8.1	19.4	8.7	..	..	..	..	..	..	..	..	12.7	..
Eritrea	..	..	..	..	..	..	..	..	..	..	..	..	..	..
Ethiopia	..	-26.2	-6.8	..	..	..	..	..		..	..	..	-11.2	..
Gabon	..	..	..	..	..	..	..	..	..	..	..	..	..	..
Gambia, The	..	..	..	-8.8	15.1	28.6	23.0	7.4	-11.2	-17.7	18.6	..	..	3.8
Ghana	..	5.1	95.9	-42.8	2.7	1.6	2.5	4.3	5.6	4.1	5.3	..	8.4	4.0
Guinea	..	..	86.3	-22.8	-1.7	-9.7	-34.3	511.9	12.9	38.7	-7.3	..	8.1	46.0
Guinea-Bissau	..	..	..	64.0	1.6	-14.1	37.7	43.8	-21.6	-15.4	60.8	..	..	9.2
Kenya	..	44.1	12.6	73.4	-41.7	2.1	13.1	-11.4	8.3	15.3	6.0	..	22.4	4.8
Lesotho	..	..	..	..	..	..	..	..	..	..	..	..	..	..
Liberia	..	..	..	..	..	..	..	..	..	..	..	..	..	..
Madagascar	..	32.1	-25.7	-67.3	158.8	-31.8	23.3	56.8	-22.4	135.6	-31.1	..	-12.4	16.3
Malawi	..	..	..	20.0	41.7	32.4	26.7	14.0	-10.8	722.4	25.4	..	..	61.0
Mali	..	-48.1	-35.0	30.4	-31.3	34.6	18.6	-30.6	1.7	-8.3	13.0	..	-20.7	-1.5
Mauritania	..	9.3	-2.1	-11.3	-3.1	19.5	-4.5	12.3	-22.4	-5.2	-14.3	..	-3.0	-4.3
Mauritius	..	-22.4	-8.7	-11.8	15.2	9.3	5.8	6.9	8.0	6.0	2.5	..	-11.1	6.6
Mozambique	..	-23.8	30.7	8.1	-1.9	-0.7	-0.1	33.6	-11.7	34.6	-16.4	..	1.0	7.1
Namibia	..	..	..	..	..	..	..	..	..	..	..	..	..	..
Niger	..	..	..	..	..	..	..	..	..	..	..	..	..	..
Nigeria	..	..	..	..	-13.7	57.4	5.0	20.3	-1.4	-5.8	9.2	..	..	9.7
Rwanda	..	-22.0	-41.6	-12.8	28.7	5.2	5.4	1.7	0.8	5.0	8.3	..	-12.2	3.8
São Tomé and Principe	..	..	-19.4	26.2	-12.4	-12.7	-11.0	..	..	..	..	..	-1.1	..
Senegal	..	-13.1	-6.5	15.6	10.8	-0.2	5.4	-2.7	-1.4	-13.2	7.7	..	-3.3	-1.7
Seychelles	..	12.4	5.8	27.2	-19.1	9.3	-1.5	14.3	27.4	-16.3	-20.1	..	6.2	3.2
Sierra Leone	..	-14.0	2.5	6.3	16.8	11.2	1.1	2.0	31.1	13.0	-65.3	..	2.7	-1.6
Somalia	..	..	..	..	..	..	..	..	..	..	..	..	..	..
South Africa	..	..	..	..	..	..	..	..	..	..	..	..	..	..
Sudan	..	34.1	51.1	-22.2	5.9	..	..	..	..	..	..	..	10.1	..
Swaziland	..	..	..	..	..	..	..	..	..	..	..	..	..	..
Tanzania	..	..	..	..	..	..	..	..	..	..	..	..	..	..
Togo	..	8.2	13.5	-5.2	-5.9	-2.3	..	..	..	..	..	..	2.6	..
Uganda	..	..	..	..	..	..	..	..	..	..	..	..	..	..
Zaire	..	..	..	..	..	..	..	..	..	..	..	..	..	..
Zambia	..	-27.3	-31.3	18.2	7.7	-35.7	..	..	-80.0	1.8	33.9	..	-11.9	39.3
Zimbabwe	..	-56.3	114.3	-13.3	11.5	24.1	11.1	5.0	-14.3	8.3	138.5	..	-9.3	13.5
NORTH AFRICA	..	..	..	..	..	..	..	..	..	..	..	..	..	..
Algeria	..	-9.7	-10.2	48.0	19.9	-29.4	3.5	8.6	-10.5	7.5	-12.0	..	10.0	-3.7
Egypt, Arab Republic	..	..	..	-55.0	70.7	0.2	-19.2	9.8	-4.8	2.0	27.8	..	..	0.2
Libya	..	..	..	..	..	..	..	..	..	..	..	..	..	..
Morocco	..	-4.4	16.2	-15.5	-6.2	7.9	16.6	46.8	26.5	-24.1	19.2	..	-4.5	14.8
Tunisia	..	23.6	-7.8	50.1	-12.7	-19.1	-35.5	21.9	2.3	21.1	35.1	..	6.6	1.3
ALL AFRICA	..	..	..	..	..	..	..	..	..	..	..	..	..	..

5-37. Non food consumer goods imports

	Millions of U.S. dollars (current prices)											Annual average		
	1980	*1986*	*1987*	*1988*	*1989*	*1990*	*1991*	*1992*	*1993*	*1994*	*1995*	*75-84*	*85-89*	*90-MR*
SUB-SAHARAN AFRICA	..	4,341	4,905	6,163	5,973	6,252	6,554	8,108	7,662	7,383	7,900	..	4,969	7,310
excluding South Africa	..	4,341	4,905	6,163	5,973	6,252	6,554	8,108	7,662	7,383	7,900	..	4,969	7,310
excl. S.Africa & Nigeria	..	4,341	4,905	4,878	4,664	4,859	5,112	5,719	5,377	5,610	6,329	3,000	4,450	5,501
Angola	..	74	502	478	467	551	676	1,009	778	712	856	0	328	764
Benin	..	..	..	..	..	..	..	..	..	..	..	..	..	..
Botswana	..	138	191	0	0	0	0	0	0	156	170	152	89	54
Burkina Faso	..	..	..	..	..	..	..	..	..	..	..	..	..	..
Burundi	53	44	44	45	44	53	52	52	56	57	53	43	42	54
Cameroon	136	254	351	238	193	209	163	83	105	85	157	222	262	133
Cape Verde	..	91	39	42	43	46	57	60	57	65	90	0	43	62
Central African Republic	..	59	42	36	35	62	20	26	26	16	21	30	45	28
Chad	..	..	122	98	104	120	117	102	88	57	69	..	108	92
Comoros	..	24	33	33	27	36	40	49	41	36	35	25	29	40
Congo	..	260	212	234	3	3	2	3	3	5	5	261	212	4
Côte d'Ivoire	..	491	547	472	492	385	454	552	501	470	712	343	482	512
Djibouti	..	..	..	..	..	..	..	..	..	..	..	..	..	..
Equatorial Guinea	..	8	13	13	15	14	15	24	46	..	..	..	11	25
Eritrea	..	..	..	..	..	..	..	..	..	..	..	..	..	..
Ethiopia	..	133	162	156	136	176	168	173	195	183	176	116	140	178
Gabon	..	359	117	176	174	202	224	252	241	71	77	330	236	178
Gambia, The	..	2	2	2	2	3	4	4	4	3	4	..	2	4
Ghana	..	112	131	163	137	160	228	306	519	373	408	80	125	332
Guinea	..	198	218	314	309	339	334	313	318	320	389	..	259	336
Guinea-Bissau	..	0	5	6	14	12	10	7	5	6	7	11	7	8
Kenya	..	561	648	728	795	727	550	537	376	682	941	394	612	636
Lesotho	..	120	0	0	0	0	0	0	0	208	230	132	43	73
Liberia	..	..	..	..	..	..	..	..	..	..	..	..	..	..
Madagascar	104	51	53	56	58	100	70	89	80	97	105	61	54	90
Malawi	..	..	34	42	54	65	81	94	83	66	63	..	43	75
Mali	..	90	95	87	126	118	151	182	188	176	212	40	95	171
Mauritania	..	30	27	29	24	33	23	25	13	12	15	23	27	20
Mauritius	..	69	97	118	110	126	138	152	163	173	187	49	91	156
Mozambique	..	82	68	95	89	96	99	108	120	132	115	47	76	111
Namibia	..	0	0	0	0	0	0	0	0	0	0	0	0	0
Niger	..	..	146	103	89	93	87	94	92	117	128	..	113	102
Nigeria	..	..	..	1,285	1,309	1,393	1,442	2,389	2,286	1,773	1,571	..	1,297	1,809
Rwanda	..	51	40	33	64	72	46	92	88	158	69	31	46	88
São Tomé and Principe	..	9	6	6	15	14	15	14	18	9	7	15	9	13
Senegal	..	141	188	198	203	207	185	212	193	170	199	136	166	194
Seychelles	..	10	17	21	23	26	23	29	39	33	25	8	16	29
Sierra Leone	..	19	20	23	24	23	23	22	13	4	4	14	21	15
Somalia	..	..	..	..	..	..	..	..	..	..	..	..	..	..
South Africa	..	..	..	..	..	..	..	..	..	..	..	..	..	..
Sudan	..	68	81	115	108	53	34	14	8	0	0	120	88	18
Swaziland	..	..	..	..	..	..	..	..	..	..	..	..	..	..
Tanzania	..	118	116	169	139	154	412	427	443	392	397	57	126	371
Togo	..	310	280	271	233	217	200	186	115	100	89	104	263	151
Uganda	..	..	..	..	..	..	..	..	..	..	..	..	..	..
Zaire	..	0	0	0	0	0	0	0	0	0	0	0	0	0
Zambia	..	..	..	..	..	..	..	..	..	39	57	..	..	48
Zimbabwe	..	365	258	281	318	364	409	429	364	428	259	303	300	376
NORTH AFRICA	..	..	5,220	4,136	3,606	4,866	4,678	5,052	5,498	7,242	7,288	..	4,321	5,771
Algeria	..	2,258	1,786	1,841	2,051	2,224	1,501	1,631	1,386	2,041	2,180	2,087	2,034	1,827
Egypt, Arab Republic	..	..	2,166	836	-159	267	799	813	1,448	2,159	1,531	..	948	1,169
Libya	..	..	..	..	..	..	..	..	..	..	..	..	..	..
Morocco	..	381	492	526	591	804	855	714	725	787	958	237	453	807
Tunisia	..	622	777	933	1,123	1,570	1,523	1,895	1,939	2,255	2,619	563	799	1,967
ALL AFRICA	..	7,602	10,125	10,299	9,579	11,118	11,232	13,159	13,161	14,625	15,188	..	9,401	13,080

5-38. Non food consumer goods imports, growth

	Percent											Average annual percentage growth		
	1980	1986	1987	1988	1989	1990	1991	1992	1993	1994	1995	75-84	85-89	90-MR
SUB-SAHARAN AFRICA	..	..	..	..	..	..	..	..	..	..	..	..	..	..
excluding South Africa	..	..	..	..	..	..	..	..	..	..	..	..	..	..
excl. S.Africa & Nigeria	..	..	..	..	..	..	..	..	..	..	..	..	..	..
Angola	..	-37.2	617.2	-18.2	2.1	28.7	26.5	55.6	-24.0	..	..	..	55.6	22.0
Benin	..	..	..	..	..	..	..	..	..	..	..	..	..	..
Botswana	..	..	..	..	..	..	..	..	..	..	..	..	..	..
Burkina Faso	..	..	..	..	..	..	..	..	..	..	..	..	..	..
Burundi	..	13.9	-6.6	8.3	2.8	18.8	5.4	21.9	6.9	4.4	-20.2	..	0.9	7.0
Cameroon	-40.2	-22.3	21.4	-21.5	16.4	-10.6	-17.4	26.9	-0.1	78.0	65.6	-3.7	-3.0	17.6
Cape Verde	..	..	..	-11.9	6.1	16.0	30.2	8.1	-4.5	-6.4	27.9	..	..	8.8
Central African Republic	..	..	..	-21.3	-6.3	93.3	-70.1	40.6	-0.4	-69.8	26.3	..	..	-23.1
Chad	..	..	..	-4.6	-3.1	-7.0	-19.3	-15.9	-9.0	-33.0	4.6	..	..	-15.6
Comoros	..	-33.3	17.9	-3.0	-12.5	17.9	12.1	16.2	-9.3	25.6	-10.2	..	-7.0	8.2
Congo	..	-10.8	-11.1	-4.5	33.5	-7.9	-1.9	-16.5	32.2	10.9	-1.1	..	-0.4	2.7
Côte d'Ivoire	..	..	..	..	..	-467.6	-5.5	3.0	-15.2	-5.8	25.8	..	..	..
Djibouti	..	..	..	..	..	..	..	..	..	..	..	..	..	..
Equatorial Guinea	..	15.4	42.2	-11.7	73.5	..	..	..	..	..	..	..	23.0	..
Eritrea	..	..	..	..	..	..	..	..	..	..	..	..	..	..
Ethiopia	..	..	..	..	..	..	..	..	..	..	..	..	..	..
Gabon	..	..	..	..	..	..	..	..	..	..	..	..	..	..
Gambia, The	..	..	..	-9.1	15.0	26.1	24.1	8.3	-12.8	-17.6	17.9	..	..	3.5
Ghana	..	33.8	16.4	14.7	-15.6	10.0	40.0	28.6	69.6	-30.7	4.8	..	11.8	19.3
Guinea	..	..	-0.4	33.9	-0.6	4.0	-3.7	-9.4	6.3	-3.0	10.6	..	12.1	-0.5
Guinea-Bissau	..	..	..	-9.6	180.9	12.1	-25.7	-32.7	-36.5	17.0	12.7	..	..	-16.6
Kenya	..	43.9	6.7	-5.6	7.4	67.3	-23.5	20.9	-25.3	70.4	-2.9	..	9.0	8.0
Lesotho	..	..	..	..	..	..	..	..	..	..	..	..	..	..
Liberia	..	..	..	..	..	..	..	..	..	..	..	..	..	..
Madagascar	..	-16.2	-7.0	-34.0	60.0	55.4	-28.7	21.0	-5.3	16.9	-16.9	..	-6.7	2.4
Malawi	..	..	..	13.2	30.0	12.3	22.7	11.0	-11.7	-22.8	-12.8	..	..	-1.6
Mali	..	-3.2	-6.3	-13.1	47.0	-14.9	26.7	13.6	4.9	-8.9	12.9	..	9.2	6.1
Mauritania	..	-7.2	-18.8	0.0	-17.3	30.8	-31.1	2.6	-46.5	-12.9	13.5	..	-10.9	-16.3
Mauritius	..	32.0	102.9	86.7	37.9	-7.8	17.3	-3.3	-1.7	6.0	-1.8	..	33.0	1.7
Mozambique	..	17.3	9.7	30.1	-4.8	1.2	1.4	4.3	11.5	7.1	-16.6	..	12.2	2.9
Namibia	..	..	..	..	..	..	..	..	..	..	..	..	..	..
Niger	..	..	..	..	..	..	..	..	..	..	..	..	..	..
Nigeria	..	..	..	..	2.5	0.8	1.2	58.9	-4.1	-25.1	-18.2	..	..	2.0
Rwanda	..	0.0	-29.0	-24.3	99.1	21.7	11.6	3.8	-6.2	3.2	11.5	..	-0.6	5.4
São Tomé and Principe	..	..	8.8	-36.3	141.3	-2.3	-6.7	..	..	..	..	..	11.5	..
Senegal	..	10.4	2.2	3.2	1.8	-2.7	-2.1	3.0	-5.6	-15.1	4.9	..	4.5	-3.6
Seychelles	..	14.3	54.5	19.1	21.4	14.8	-10.1	18.2	46.9	-25.4	-24.9	..	21.2	3.1
Sierra Leone	..	-31.7	-5.7	9.8	2.1	-5.4	1.4	-2.1	-42.4	-75.0	-10.0	..	-6.0	-32.0
Somalia	..	..	..	..	..	..	..	..	..	..	..	..	..	..
South Africa	..	..	..	..	..	..	..	..	..	..	..	..	..	..
Sudan	..	..	..	..	..	..	..	..	..	..	..	..	..	..
Swaziland	..	..	..	..	..	..	..	..	..	..	..	..	..	..
Tanzania	..	..	..	..	..	..	-0.4	1.5	1.5	..	..	..	..	0.9
Togo	..	-7.0	33.1	-39.5	-9.7	-4.5	..	..	..	..	..	..	-9.5	..
Uganda	..	..	..	..	..	..	..	..	..	..	..	..	..	..
Zaire	..	..	..	..	..	..	-15.4	-41.8	-25.2	..	..	..	..	-29.8
Zambia	..	..	..	..	..	..	..	..	..	..	..	..	..	..
Zimbabwe	..	31.3	-25.0	1.6	14.1	6.0	9.8	0.6	-14.9	13.4	-44.1	..	1.6	-4.9
NORTH AFRICA	..	..	..	..	..	..	..	..	..	..	..	..	..	..
Algeria	..	-23.3	-18.0	-44.1	18.1	-8.5	-1.4	-21.9	-9.3	-4.5	16.7	..	-20.3	-7.5
Egypt, Arab Republic	..	..	..	-64.4	-118.4	-264.0	187.8	-1.5	74.7	46.6	-33.1	..	..	37.9
Libya	..	..	..	..	..	..	..	..	..	..	..	..	..	..
Morocco	..	18.0	17.2	0.0	12.5	28.6	4.5	-20.0	-4.8	4.7	-9.5	..	12.2	-2.6
Tunisia	..	2.3	9.5	14.6	22.8	21.0	-5.0	0.9	19.9	11.6	3.1	..	9.7	7.8
ALL AFRICA	..	..	..	..	..	..	..	..	..	..	..	..	..	..

5-39. Fuel imports

	Millions of U.S. dollars (current prices)											Annual average		
	1980	*1986*	*1987*	*1988*	*1989*	*1990*	*1991*	*1992*	*1993*	*1994*	*1995*	*75-84*	*85-89*	*90-MR*
SUB-SAHARAN AFRICA	..	2,472	2,478	2,344	2,599	3,700	3,532	3,206	3,172	4,126	4,319	3,171	2,593	3,676
excluding South Africa	..	2,472	2,478	2,344	2,599	3,700	3,532	3,206	3,172	4,126	4,319	3,171	2,593	3,676
excl. S.Africa & Nigeria	..	2,472	2,478	2,280	2,553	3,645	3,471	3,158	3,127	4,037	4,217	3,171	2,571	3,609
Angola	..	0	0	0	0	0	0	0	0	0	0	0	0	0
Benin	..	..	..	..	..	..	..	..	..	..	..	..	..	..
Botswana	..	60	69	0	0	0	0	0	0	788	860	72	39	275
Burkina Faso	..	..	..	..	..	..	..	..	..	..	..	..	..	..
Burundi	25	27	29	27	20	30	29	26	24	29	32	30	27	28
Cameroon	187	17	16	13	11	16	11	8	8	7	8	96	13	10
Cape Verde	0	0	5	6	6	10	8	8	6	5	11	0	3	8
Central African Republic	..	22	10	14	20	23	16	16	15	13	17	17	18	17
Chad	..	19	38	31	33	37	11	4	3	8	8	20	28	12
Comoros	..	5	8	4	2	6	6	7	6	6	8	5	4	7
Congo	..	10	6	7	3	129	196	104	162	367	187	23	9	191
Côte d'Ivoire	..	322	336	288	449	569	530	511	430	396	486	266	355	487
Djibouti	..	..	..	..	..	..	..	..	..	..	..	..	..	..
Equatorial Guinea	..	6	6	6	6	7	6	7	5	..	..	..	6	6
Eritrea	..	..	..	..	..	..	..	..	..	..	..	..	..	..
Ethiopia	..	122	109	104	103	109	102	120	197	222	169	183	125	153
Gabon	..	84	16	7	7	12	11	12	11	161	173	44	33	63
Gambia, The	..	24	26	25	27	37	46	52	47	39	48	..	26	45
Ghana	..	125	145	148	161	205	175	162	158	176	197	161	156	179
Guinea	..	51	61	55	54	65	68	69	73	69	82	..	55	71
Guinea-Bissau	..	7	5	4	9	8	10	5	3	6	8	9	7	7
Kenya	..	300	348	288	344	466	385	412	407	333	401	476	348	400
Lesotho	..	32	0	0	0	0	0	0	0	195	216	40	13	68
Liberia	..	..	..	..	..	..	..	..	..	..	..	..	..	..
Madagascar	159	58	55	66	35	113	71	72	85	72	81	123	60	82
Malawi	..	..	40	43	42	51	63	73	65	28	33	..	41	52
Mali	..	78	68	66	45	69	79	84	74	53	75	62	67	72
Mauritania	..	27	33	25	35	43	37	33	35	32	30	43	32	35
Mauritius	..	52	76	75	99	131	131	125	120	119	138	78	75	127
Mozambique	..	54	63	61	72	95	80	78	104	83	171	109	65	102
Namibia	..	0	0	0	0	128	110	99	87	81	0	0	0	84
Niger	..	..	19	19	18	27	19	22	23	20	18	..	19	22
Nigeria	..	..	..	64	46	55	61	48	45	89	103	..	55	67
Rwanda	..	55	52	52	48	45	39	37	35	23	22	49	52	34
São Tomé and Principe	..	1	2	1	1	2	4	3	3	2	3	..	1	3
Senegal	..	178	177	165	155	159	148	150	124	142	138	209	170	144
Seychelles	..	18	17	22	30	36	38	33	34	32	48	26	23	37
Sierra Leone	..	23	24	26	28	30	26	22	27	29	24	45	25	26
Somalia	..	..	..	..	..	..	..	..	..	..	..	..	..	..
South Africa	..	..	..	..	..	..	..	..	..	..	..	..	..	..
Sudan	..	266	184	212	204	244	356	225	250	0	0	351	230	179
Swaziland	..	..	..	..	..	..	..	..	..	..	..	..	..	..
Tanzania	..	145	170	147	152	195	160	185	167	149	155	238	167	168
Togo	..	19	30	26	28	48	35	36	26	22	22	30	25	32
Uganda	..	61	63	69	76	78	83	72	58	55	64	91	69	68
Zaire	..	0	0	0	0	157	133	60	61	45	52	0	0	85
Zambia	..	72	67	62	103	119	83	53	47	56	41	144	85	67
Zimbabwe	..	131	106	115	130	149	168	175	149	175	191	213	142	168
NORTH AFRICA	..	..	..	..	..	..	..	..	..	..	..	..	..	..
Algeria	..	274	161	169	127	141	130	147	141	150	200	211	183	151
Egypt, Arab Republic	..	..	..	..	..	..	..	..	..	..	..	..	..	..
Libya	..	..	..	..	..	..	..	..	..	..	..	..	..	..
Morocco	..	596	738	628	843	1,171	991	1,124	957	1,113	1,184	1,021	776	1,090
Tunisia	..	252	318	243	380	487	396	449	455	466	496	373	313	458
ALL AFRICA	..	3,594	3,694	3,384	3,949	5,499	5,049	4,927	4,724	5,853	6,199	4,776	3,864	5,375

5-40. Fuel imports, growth

	Percent											Average annual percentage growth		
	1980	1986	1987	1988	1989	1990	1991	1992	1993	1994	1995	75-84	85-89	90-MR
SUB-SAHARAN AFRICA	..	..	..	..	..	..	..	..	..	..	..	..	..	..
excluding South Africa	..	..	..	..	..	..	..	..	..	..	..	..	..	..
excl. S.Africa & Nigeria	..	..	..	..	..	..	..	..	..	..	..	..	..	..
Angola	..	..	..	..	..	..	..	..	..	..	..	..	..	..
Benin	..	..	..	..	..	..	..	..	..	..	..	..	..	..
Botswana	..	..	..	..	..	..	..	..	..	..	..	..	..	..
Burkina Faso	..	..	..	..	..	..	..	..	..	..	..	..	..	..
Burundi	..	1.5	10.2	1.7	-12.5	37.3	-10.9	-3.5	2.0	-9.3	8.1	..	-0.1	0.1
Cameroon	9.7	329.4	-27.4	3.8	-32.7	16.2	-14.0	-29.7	19.2	-9.7	3.6	-42.6	10.2	-6.1
Cape Verde	..	..	..	30.2	-18.8	44.6	-8.6	-1.4	-9.6	-15.2	103.6	..	..	4.7
Central African Republic	..	..	..	34.7	35.6	24.0	-36.0	5.6	-5.3	-56.3	30.6	..	..	-16.1
Chad	..	..	..	-4.5	-3.3	-6.8	-19.3	-61.0	-21.4	191.4	35.2	..	..	-7.3
Comoros	..	0.0	60.0	-50.0	-25.0	100.0	0.0	0.0	0.0	33.3	25.0	..	-11.9	16.1
Congo	..	26.7	8.8	-53.2	79.3	-7.7	-2.1	-17.0	33.3	11.5	-1.7	..	-2.6	2.7
Côte d'Ivoire	..	..	..	..	..	26.7	-6.8	-3.6	-15.7	-8.0	14.8	..	..	-3.1
Djibouti	..	..	..	..	..	..	..	..	..	..	..	..	..	..
Equatorial Guinea	..	-22.0	87.5	16.7	24.3	-48.3	11.1	0.0	0.0	..	..	..	25.7	-9.5
Eritrea	..	..	..	..	..	..	..	..	..	..	..	..	..	..
Ethiopia	..	-34.9	-20.3	35.3	-26.2	5.0	46.5	20.0	119.8	..	..	..	-10.4	40.0
Gabon	..	..	..	..	..	..	..	..	..	..	..	..	..	..
Gambia, The	..	..	..	-8.9	15.3	28.7	22.9	7.4	-11.3	-17.6	18.6	..	..	3.8
Ghana	..	23.4	-8.6	2.8	17.8	-13.3	4.2	-7.1	3.3	18.9	3.9	..	9.3	1.8
Guinea	..	..	-7.8	13.3	-18.2	-3.7	26.0	1.5	14.1	0.0	10.2	..	-3.4	8.2
Guinea-Bissau	..	..	..	-5.6	94.1	-11.1	17.0	-49.5	-38.5	134.4	45.3	..	..	-4.2
Kenya	..	-37.0	9.0	-15.5	15.7	6.5	29.8	-9.5	2.8	-18.7	8.7	..	-10.2	1.0
Lesotho	..	..	..	..	..	..	..	..	..	..	..	..	..	..
Liberia	..	..	..	..	..	..	..	..	..	..	..	..	..	..
Madagascar	..	33.9	-26.7	50.9	-55.4	124.3	-24.1	0.0	33.3	-11.9	31.1	..	-4.5	11.1
Malawi	..	..	..	32.5	-19.4	-5.7	48.3	18.0	-0.6	-54.7	11.4	..	..	-3.1
Mali	..	-17.3	-0.9	13.8	9.6	28.2	-9.5	2.5	-14.0	12.9	28.2	..	2.7	3.1
Mauritania	..	29.8	-4.4	-1.6	14.3	-12.3	1.4	-7.3	17.1	-2.7	-11.5	..	6.3	-1.2
Mauritius	..	-46.1	3.0	-23.7	28.4	25.6	9.1	-7.9	1.7	4.8	2.3	..	-16.9	3.7
Mozambique	..	-40.5	-4.0	22.5	-1.6	1.4	3.2	-2.8	51.2	-18.0	-26.7	..	-8.5	2.1
Namibia	..	..	..	..	..	..	..	..	..	..	..	..	..	..
Niger	..	..	..	..	..	..	..	..	..	..	..	..	..	..
Nigeria	..	..	..	..	-27.9	13.0	9.3	-24.1	-6.7	90.2	6.9	..	..	8.0
Rwanda	..	-7.7	-14.3	-6.5	-7.2	-12.0	-14.3	0.0	-8.0	-5.4	7.9	..	-7.5	-5.9
São Tomé and Principe	..	..	73.9	-57.5	22.4	96.2	69.1	..	..	..	..	..	-10.9	..
Senegal	..	25.2	-9.5	-4.2	5.0	-16.5	-8.5	18.4	-8.7	30.4	-19.5	..	-0.4	0.5
Seychelles	..	-32.1	0.0	43.8	35.8	-6.1	6.5	0.9	8.1	-3.3	-12.9	..	3.1	0.2
Sierra Leone	..	32.2	25.3	-1.8	-4.0	-14.2	-7.8	0.4	37.2	13.8	-24.5	..	11.6	3.1
Somalia	..	..	..	..	..	..	..	..	..	..	..	..	..	..
South Africa	..	..	..	..	..	..	..	..	..	..	..	..	..	..
Sudan	..	-23.4	-36.1	14.2	-3.4	..	..	..	..	..	..	..	-15.0	..
Swaziland	..	..	..	..	..	..	..	..	..	..	..	..	..	..
Tanzania	..	..	..	..	..	..	..	..	..	..	..	..	..	..
Togo	..	7.6	13.3	2.5	-4.0	57.7	-22.8	..	..	..	..	..	5.3	..
Uganda	..	..	..	..	..	..	..	..	..	..	..	..	..	..
Zaire	..	..	..	..	..	..	..	..	..	..	..	..	..	..
Zambia	..	-38.5	13.6	-13.4	65.5	9.4	-31.4	-38.9	-9.1	12.5	-31.1	..	-5.9	-18.3
Zimbabwe	..	14.4	-36.5	34.0	-6.3	-11.3	33.1	6.4	-3.6	24.2	0.5	..	-1.5	8.6
NORTH AFRICA	..	..	..	..	..	..	..	..	..	..	..	..	..	..
Algeria	..	-8.7	19.8	-2.1	-43.4	87.7	-9.9	8.0	-13.6	6.0	1.3	..	-8.7	4.7
Egypt, Arab Republic	..	..	..	..	..	..	..	..	..	..	..	..	..	..
Libya	..	..	..	..	..	..	..	..	..	..	..	..	..	..
Morocco	..	-1.6	8.8	2.5	14.7	5.4	-0.5	10.4	-3.1	23.3	1.1	..	6.4	6.0
Tunisia	..	7.2	22.6	-11.3	35.5	-0.8	-13.2	15.0	16.5	9.8	7.1	..	9.4	6.3
ALL AFRICA	..	..	..	..	..	..	..	..	..	..	..	..	..	..

5-41. Primary intermediate goods imports

	Millions of U.S. dollars (current prices)											Annual average		
	1980	*1986*	*1987*	*1988*	*1989*	*1990*	*1991*	*1992*	*1993*	*1994*	*1995*	*75-84*	*85-89*	*90-MR*
SUB-SAHARAN AFRICA	..	..	..	..	..	..	..	..	..	..	..	..	..	..
excluding South Africa	..	..	..	..	..	..	..	..	..	..	..	..	..	..
excl. S.Africa & Nigeria	..	..	..	..	..	..	..	..	..	..	..	..	..	..
Angola	..	219	283	310	303	357	254	223	89	214	257	0	292	232
Benin	..	..	..	..	..	..	..	..	..	..	..	..	..	..
Botswana	..	0	0	0	0	0	0	0	0	409	446	0	0	143
Burkina Faso	..	..	..	..	..	..	..	..	..	..	..	..	..	..
Burundi	0	0	0	0	0	0	0	0	0	0	0	0	0	0
Cameroon	55	91	94	74	67	85	65	72	61	60	69	61	76	69
Cape Verde	..	..	0	..	..	..	..	..	..	..	..	..	0	..
Central African Republic	..	..	57	50	53	63	55	53	40	45	58	..	53	52
Chad	..	..	0	0	0	0	0	0	0	0	0	..	0	0
Comoros	..	2	2	2	1	4	3	3	4	4	4	2	2	4
Congo	..	..	..	..	32	32	23	28	28	72	78	..	32	44
Côte d'Ivoire	..	0	0	0	0	0	0	0	0	0	0	0	0	0
Djibouti	..	..	..	..	..	..	..	..	..	..	..	..	..	..
Equatorial Guinea	..	6	7	9	..	..	..	..	..	..	..	..	6	..
Eritrea	..	..	..	..	..	..	..	..	..	..	..	..	..	..
Ethiopia	..	40	24	26	26	28	28	17	20	15	21	35	28	21
Gabon	..	..	..	10	11	9	10	10	10	10	10	..	10	10
Gambia, The	..	13	14	14	15	20	25	28	25	21	26	..	14	24
Ghana	..	..	..	..	..	..	..	..	..	..	..	..	..	..
Guinea	..	0	0	0	0	0	0	0	0	0	0	..	0	0
Guinea-Bissau	..	..	..	..	..	..	..	..	..	..	..	0	0	..
Kenya	..	40	48	56	57	56	57	59	47	51	71	42	48	57
Lesotho	..	3	0	0	0	0	0	0	0	56	62	6	2	20
Liberia	..	..	..	..	..	..	..	..	..	..	..	..	..	..
Madagascar	206	88	102	91	91	142	91	101	114	100	152	129	96	117
Malawi	..	..	110	146	152	184	231	267	235	188	178	..	136	214
Mali	..	..	..	..	..	..	..	..	..	..	..	..	..	..
Mauritania	..	..	..	..	..	..	..	..	..	..	..	..	..	..
Mauritius	..	29	28	30	136	169	162	170	180	192	224	16	49	183
Mozambique	..	102	117	149	155	176	183	136	195	159	50	84	122	150
Namibia	..	0	0	0	0	0	0	0	0	0	0	0	0	0
Niger	..	..	..	..	..	..	..	..	..	..	..	..	..	..
Nigeria	..	..	..	1,439	1,603	1,839	1,782	1,992	1,773	2,121	2,408	..	1,521	1,986
Rwanda	..	0	0	1	0	0	0	0	0	0	0	0	0	0
São Tomé and Principe	..	..	..	..	..	..	..	..	..	..	..	..	..	..
Senegal	..	..	..	..	..	..	..	..	..	..	..	..	..	..
Seychelles	..	..	0	0	0	0	0	0	0	0	23	..	0	4
Sierra Leone	..	..	..	..	..	..	..	..	..	14	28	..	..	21
Somalia	..	..	..	..	..	..	..	..	..	..	..	..	..	..
South Africa	..	..	..	..	..	..	..	..	..	..	..	..	..	..
Sudan	..	207	158	247	167	81	154	179	87	0	0	172	195	83
Swaziland	..	..	..	..	..	..	..	..	..	..	..	..	..	..
Tanzania	..	185	171	360	399	344	121	136	118	178	187	130	257	180
Togo	..	..	..	..	..	..	..	..	..	..	..	..	..	..
Uganda	..	..	..	..	..	..	..	..	..	..	..	..	..	..
Zaire	..	0	0	0	0	0	0	0	0	0	0	0	0	0
Zambia	..	14	45	47	72	49	34	48	20	72	80	..	45	51
Zimbabwe	..	64	69	75	85	97	110	115	97	115	198	39	69	122
NORTH AFRICA	..	..	..	..	..	..	..	..	..	..	..	..	..	..
Algeria	..	554	502	626	851	939	870	981	942	999	1,000	638	652	955
Egypt, Arab Republic	..	..	..	..	..	..	..	..	..	..	..	..	..	..
Libya	..	..	..	..	..	..	..	..	..	..	..	..	..	..
Morocco	..	616	652	781	628	835	807	930	657	815	1,063	515	656	851
Tunisia	..	0	0	0	0	0	0	0	0	0	0	0	0	0
ALL AFRICA	..	..	..	..	..	..	..	..	..	..	..	..	..	..

5-42. Primary intermediate goods imports, growth

	Percent											Average annual percentage growth		
	1980	1986	1987	1988	1989	1990	1991	1992	1993	1994	1995	75-84	85-89	90-MR
SUB-SAHARAN AFRICA	..	..	..	..	..	..	..	..	..	..	..	..	..	..
excluding South Africa	..	..	..	..	..	..	..	..	..	..	..	..	..	..
excl. S.Africa & Nigeria	..	..	..	..	..	..	..	..	..	..	..	..	..	..
Angola	..	-36.2	36.6	-5.9	2.1	28.5	-26.7	-8.6	-60.6	96.4	12.3	..	-1.0	-10.8
Benin	..	..	..	..	..	..	..	..	..	..	..	..	..	..
Botswana	..	..	..	..	..	..	..	..	..	..	..	..	..	..
Burkina Faso	..	..	..	..	..	..	..	..	..	..	..	..	..	..
Burundi	..	..	..	..	..	..	..	..	..	..	..	..	..	..
Cameroon	17.1	68.8	8.6	-32.7	-5.6	39.4	-21.1	16.1	-16.5	-19.4	2.7	15.3	0.6	-4.8
Cape Verde	..	..	..	..	..	..	..	..	..	..	..	..	..	..
Central African Republic	..	..	..	-19.3	3.9	28.0	-17.5	0.2	-24.7	-44.1	26.3	..	..	-13.7
Chad	..	..	..	..	..	..	..	..	..	..	..	..	..	..
Comoros	..	0.0	-50.0	100.0	-50.0	200.0	-33.3	0.0	50.0	33.3	0.0	..	-11.2	20.1
Congo	..	..	..	..	..	..	..	..	..	..	..	..	..	..
Côte d'Ivoire	..	..	..	..	..	..	..	..	..	..	..	..	..	..
Djibouti	..	..	..	..	..	..	..	..	..	..	..	..	..	..
Equatorial Guinea	..	31.4	4.5	11.4	..	..	..	..	..	..	..	..	14.1	..
Eritrea	..	..	..	..	..	..	..	..	..	..	..	..	..	..
Ethiopia	..	..	..	..	..	..	..	..	..	..	..	..	..	..
Gabon	..	..	..	..	..	..	..	..	..	..	..	..	..	..
Gambia, The	..	..	..	-8.6	14.8	29.3	22.6	7.3	-11.2	-17.6	18.6	..	..	3.8
Ghana	..	..	..	..	..	..	..	..	..	..	..	..	..	..
Guinea	..	..	..	..	..	..	..	..	..	..	..	..	..	..
Guinea-Bissau	..	..	..	..	..	..	..	..	..	..	..	..	..	..
Kenya	..	-13.6	-1.7	3.6	16.2	-11.0	9.4	1.6	-17.6	5.1	34.4	..	0.8	0.6
Lesotho	..	..	..	..	..	..	..	..	..	..	..	..	..	..
Liberia	..	..	..	..	..	..	..	..	..	..	..	..	..	..
Madagascar	..	-30.3	3.0	-15.7	0.0	47.7	-34.6	6.0	18.2	-15.4	13.6	..	-10.8	-0.2
Malawi	..	..	..	23.4	4.8	12.4	22.8	10.9	-11.7	-22.8	-12.9	..	..	-1.6
Mali	..	..	..	..	..	..	..	..	..	..	..	..	..	..
Mauritania	..	..	..	..	..	..	..	..	..	..	..	..	..	..
Mauritius	..	17.5	-31.7	-17.3	9.8	40.3	5.2	2.4	10.8	5.1	2.4	..	-8.4	8.7
Mozambique	..	-7.5	24.9	18.7	4.8	7.5	1.8	-28.7	43.9	-20.9	-25.0	..	7.9	-5.5
Namibia	..	..	..	..	..	..	..	..	..	..	..	..	..	..
Niger	..	..	..	..	..	..	..	..	..	..	..	..	..	..
Nigeria	..	..	..	..	4.1	11.2	-2.3	12.7	-20.7	4.9	5.6	..	..	-0.2
Rwanda	..	..	..	..	..	..	..	..	..	..	..	..	..	..
São Tomé and Principe	..	..	..	..	..	..	..	..	..	..	..	..	..	..
Senegal	..	..	..	..	..	..	..	..	..	..	..	..	..	..
Seychelles	..	..	..	..	..	..	..	..	..	..	..	..	..	..
Sierra Leone	..	..	..	..	..	..	..	..	..	..	88.9	..	..	..
Somalia	..	..	..	..	..	..	..	..	..	..	..	..	..	..
South Africa	..	..	..	..	..	..	..	..	..	..	..	..	..	..
Sudan	..	..	..	..	..	..	..	..	..	..	..	..	..	..
Swaziland	..	..	..	..	..	..	..	..	..	..	..	..	..	..
Tanzania	..	..	..	..	..	..	..	..	..	..	..	..	..	..
Togo	..	..	..	..	..	..	..	..	..	..	..	..	..	..
Uganda	..	..	..	..	..	..	..	..	..	..	..	..	..	..
Zaire	..	..	..	..	..	..	..	..	..	..	..	..	..	..
Zambia	..	..	181.3	-2.2	54.5	-35.3	-34.1	37.9	-57.5	247.1	3.4	..	54.0	-1.0
Zimbabwe	..	1.4	-2.8	1.4	14.3	6.3	9.4	1.1	-14.9	13.8	58.2	..	6.6	6.4
NORTH AFRICA	..	..	..	..	..	..	..	..	..	..	..	..	..	..
Algeria	..	-8.3	-21.0	7.0	21.3	-23.3	-10.0	8.0	-13.5	10.1	1.3	..	-2.7	-4.2
Egypt, Arab Republic	..	..	..	..	..	..	..	..	..	..	..	..	..	..
Libya	..	..	..	..	..	..	..	..	..	..	..	..	..	..
Morocco	..	6.3	12.2	20.3	-23.3	24.7	-2.8	19.0	-3.5	-0.6	7.2	..	6.0	5.6
Tunisia	..	..	..	..	..	..	..	..	..	..	..	..	..	..
ALL AFRICA	..	..	..	..	..	..	..	..	..	..	..	..	..	..

5-43. Manufactured goods imports

	Millions of U.S. dollars (current prices)											Annual average		
	1980	1986	1987	1988	1989	1990	1991	1992	1993	1994	1995	75-84	85-89	90-MR
SUB-SAHARAN AFRICA	..	..	..	..	..	..	..	..	..	..	..	..	..	..
excluding South Africa	..	..	..	..	..	..	..	..	..	..	..	..	..	..
excl. S.Africa & Nigeria	..	..	..	..	..	..	..	..	..	..	..	..	..	..
Angola	..	196	116	133	128	151	91	135	72	85	86	0	154	103
Benin	..	..	..	..	..	..	..	..	..	..	..	..	..	..
Botswana	..	0	0	0	0	0	0	0	0	98	107	0	0	34
Burkina Faso	..	..	..	..	..	..	..	..	..	..	..	..	..	..
Burundi	40	53	48	49	48	60	68	55	48	43	47	46	49	54
Cameroon	605	624	680	617	504	603	582	465	459	417	476	511	569	500
Cape Verde	..	..	..	..	..	..	..	..	..	..	..	..	..	..
Central African Republic	..	..	..	..	..	..	..	..	..	..	..	..	..	..
Chad	..	..	98	79	84	96	109	127	105	91	62	..	87	98
Comoros	..	2	3	3	1	1	2	2	2	2	2	0	2	2
Congo	..	129	116	135	115	149	116	142	141	86	94	141	128	121
Côte d'Ivoire	..	..	..	..	..	256	236	301	254	297	404	..	..	291
Djibouti	..	..	..	..	..	..	..	..	..	..	..	..	..	..
Equatorial Guinea	..	5	6	7	..	..	..	..	..	..	..	..	5	..
Eritrea	..	..	..	..	..	..	..	..	..	..	..	..	..	..
Ethiopia	..	125	129	158	172	155	115	113	94	129	183	117	140	132
Gabon	..	..	..	91	79	85	100	103	..	30	32	..	85	70
Gambia, The	..	7	8	7	8	11	14	15	14	11	14	..	7	13
Ghana	..	..	..	..	..	..	..	..	..	..	..	..	..	..
Guinea	..	..	..	..	..	..	..	..	..	..	..	..	..	..
Guinea-Bissau	..	..	..	..	..	..	..	..	..	..	..	0	0	..
Kenya	..	253	291	320	294	265	289	291	307	293	505	186	273	325
Lesotho	..	70	0	0	0	0	0	0	0	23	25	94	30	8
Liberia	..	..	..	..	..	..	..	..	..	..	..	..	..	..
Madagascar	..	12	46	19	29	59	86	99	129	130	194	20	36	116
Malawi	..	..	23	35	36	43	54	63	55	44	42	..	31	50
Mali	..	..	..	..	..	..	..	..	..	..	..	..	..	..
Mauritania	..	..	..	..	..	..	..	..	..	..	..	..	..	..
Mauritius	..	327	474	548	497	554	551	587	626	659	724	181	412	617
Mozambique	..	68	98	106	103	104	109	75	87	64	70	71	84	85
Namibia	..	0	0	0	0	0	0	0	0	0	0	0	0	0
Niger	..	..	..	..	..	..	..	..	..	..	..	..	..	..
Nigeria	..	..	..	1,010	183	673	1,407	1,296	1,665	702	1,074	..	597	1,136
Rwanda	..	93	100	118	104	97	128	92	91	23	41	82	100	79
São Tomé and Principe	..	..	..	..	..	..	..	..	..	..	..	..	..	..
Senegal	..	258	284	290	302	377	345	378	350	325	392	249	272	361
Seychelles	..	..	0	0	0	0	0	0	0	0	29	..	0	5
Sierra Leone	..	..	..	..	..	..	..	..	..	15	27	..	..	21
Somalia	..	..	..	..	..	..	..	..	..	..	..	..	..	..
South Africa	..	..	..	..	..	..	..	..	..	..	..	..	..	..
Sudan	..	102	80	163	145	140	306	182	200	0	0	160	122	138
Swaziland	..	..	..	..	..	..	..	..	..	..	..	..	..	..
Tanzania	..	11	6	4	5	9	37	16	11	12	13	6	7	16
Togo	..	..	..	..	..	..	..	..	..	..	..	..	..	..
Uganda	..	..	..	..	..	..	..	..	..	..	..	..	..	..
Zaire	..	0	0	0	0	1,678	1,390	825	607	584	872	0	0	993
Zambia	..	..	..	..	..	..	..	..	..	127	253	..	..	190
Zimbabwe	..	173	161	175	199	227	256	268	227	267	462	166	175	285
NORTH AFRICA	..	..	..	..	..	..	..	..	..	..	..	..	..	..
Algeria	..	2,300	1,818	1,905	2,011	2,225	2,045	2,306	2,213	2,348	2,100	3,053	2,073	2,206
Egypt, Arab Republic	..	..	..	..	..	..	..	..	..	..	..	..	..	..
Libya	..	..	..	..	..	..	..	..	..	..	..	..	..	..
Morocco	..	951	1,149	1,539	1,783	2,193	2,342	2,488	2,433	2,908	3,546	738	1,247	2,651
Tunisia	..	0	0	0	0	0	0	0	0	0	0	0	0	0
ALL AFRICA	..	..	..	..	..	..	..	..	..	..	..	..	..	..

5-44. Manufactured goods imports, growth

	Percent											Average annual percentage growth		
	1980	*1986*	*1987*	*1988*	*1989*	*1990*	*1991*	*1992*	*1993*	*1994*	*1995*	*75-84*	*85-89*	*90-MR*
SUB-SAHARAN AFRICA	..	..	..	..	..	..	..	..	..	..	..	..	..	..
excluding South Africa	..	..	..	..	..	..	..	..	..	..	..	..	..	..
excl. S.Africa & Nigeria	..	..	..	..	..	..	..	..	..	..	..	..	..	..
Angola	..	-15.6	-46.1	6.9	-3.1	11.7	-41.0	42.4	-45.4	14.3	0.0	..	-18.6	-10.6
Benin	..	..	..	..	..	..	..	..	..	..	..	..	..	..
Botswana	..	..	..	..	..	..	..	..	..	..	..	..	..	..
Burkina Faso	..	..	..	..	..	..	..	..	..	..	..	..	..	..
Burundi	..	4.6	-5.0	1.5	-0.2	13.7	22.0	-10.7	-13.9	-4.1	15.2	..	-0.6	0.1
Cameroon	16.5	30.6	18.4	-15.7	-3.2	-3.4	-5.5	-23.3	0.8	-11.7	10.3	-3.9	2.1	-7.8
Cape Verde	..	..	..	..	..	..	..	..	..	..	..	..	..	..
Central African Republic	..	..	..	..	..	..	..	..	..	..	..	..	..	..
Chad	..	..	..	-4.6	-3.1	-7.0	-19.2	19.1	-12.9	27.1	21.4	..	..	2.6
Comoros	..	..	0.0	0.0	-50.0	0.0	0.0	100.0	0.0	0.0	0.0	..	-18.8	16.0
Congo	..	-35.4	57.7	0.2	-5.3	..	..	..	..	..	..	..	4.7	..
Côte d'Ivoire	..	..	..	..	..	..	..	..	..	..	..	..	..	..
Djibouti	..	..	..	..	..	..	..	..	..	..	..	..	..	..
Equatorial Guinea	..	33.3	7.1	1.7	..	..	..	..	..	..	..	..	12.6	..
Eritrea	..	..	..	..	..	..	..	..	..	..	..	..	..	..
Ethiopia	..	..	..	..	..	..	..	..	..	..	..	..	..	..
Gabon	..	..	..	..	..	..	..	..	..	..	..	..	..	..
Gambia, The	..	..	..	-9.2	14.5	29.1	23.5	7.1	-11.1	-17.5	18.2	..	..	3.9
Ghana	..	..	..	..	..	..	..	..	..	..	..	..	..	..
Guinea	..	..	..	..	..	..	..	..	..	..	..	..	..	..
Guinea-Bissau	..	..	..	..	..	..	..	..	..	..	..	..	..	..
Kenya	..	-8.5	-5.7	6.7	-1.9	-20.6	17.1	-1.5	9.6	-7.7	64.7	..	1.3	6.1
Lesotho	..	..	..	..	..	..	..	..	..	..	..	..	..	..
Liberia	..	..	..	..	..	..	..	..	..	..	..	..	..	..
Madagascar	..	-86.6	253.8	-63.0	64.7	89.3	39.6	12.2	30.1	-2.8	40.0	..	-18.9	27.1
Malawi	..	..	..	38.8	3.7	12.3	22.7	10.9	-11.6	-22.8	-12.9	..	..	-1.6
Mali	..	..	..	..	..	..	..	..	..	..	..	..	..	..
Mauritania	..	..	..	..	..	..	..	..	..	..	..	..	..	..
Mauritius	..	16.7	2.2	-10.5	7.3	8.3	6.1	3.7	13.1	5.0	2.5	..	3.3	6.7
Mozambique	..	17.3	16.4	0.8	-2.1	-4.4	2.6	-34.5	17.4	-28.7	-18.5	..	8.0	-13.0
Namibia	..	..	..	..	..	..	..	..	..	..	..	..	..	..
Niger	..	..	..	..	..	..	..	..	..	..	..	..	..	..
Nigeria	..	..	..	..	-81.8	247.9	104.5	-11.7	28.8	-59.3	41.2	..	..	18.0
Rwanda	..	-4.2	-2.1	9.7	-11.2	-12.1	-19.7	3.9	-6.3	3.3	11.4	..	-1.0	-4.1
São Tomé and Principe	..	..	..	..	..	..	..	..	..	..	..	..	..	..
Senegal	..	-1.2	-8.5	2.5	4.3	4.0	7.2	0.7	-4.0	-10.3	7.9	..	-0.5	-0.2
Seychelles	..	..	..	..	..	..	..	..	..	..	..	..	..	..
Sierra Leone	..	..	..	..	..	..	..	..	..	..	76.0	..	..	..
Somalia	..	..	..	..	..	..	..	..	..	..	..	..	..	..
South Africa	..	..	..	..	..	..	..	..	..	..	..	..	..	..
Sudan	..	..	..	..	..	..	..	..	..	..	..	..	..	..
Swaziland	..	..	..	..	..	..	..	..	..	..	..	..	..	..
Tanzania	..	..	..	..	..	..	..	..	..	..	..	..	..	..
Togo	..	..	..	..	..	..	..	..	..	..	..	..	..	..
Uganda	..	..	..	..	..	..	..	..	..	..	..	..	..	..
Zaire	..	..	..	..	..	..	..	..	..	..	..	..	..	..
Zambia	..	..	-1750.0	15.9	-39.2	51.1	..	..	..	..	83.7	..	..	-7.1
Zimbabwe	..	-12.0	-15.3	1.9	14.0	5.9	10.1	0.5	-15.1	13.4	59.7	..	-4.8	6.4
NORTH AFRICA	..	..	..	..	..	..	..	..	..	..	..	..	..	..
Algeria	..	-0.5	-28.5	-25.0	51.3	-19.9	-10.0	8.1	-13.6	6.7	1.3	..	-12.3	-4.3
Egypt, Arab Republic	..	..	..	..	..	..	..	..	..	..	..	..	..	..
Libya	..	..	..	..	..	..	..	..	..	..	..	..	..	..
Morocco	..	0.2	31.7	33.8	13.8	10.6	9.7	5.1	-2.8	15.3	6.5	..	18.4	6.6
Tunisia	..	..	..	..	..	..	..	..	..	..	..	..	..	..
ALL AFRICA	..	..	..	..	..	..	..	..	..	..	..	..	..	..

5-45. Capital goods imports

	Millions of U.S. dollars (current prices)											*Annual average*		
	1980	*1986*	*1987*	*1988*	*1989*	*1990*	*1991*	*1992*	*1993*	*1994*	*1995*	*75-84*	*85-89*	*90-MR*
SUB-SAHARAN AFRICA	..	5,328	6,008	8,583	9,558	10,253	10,398	10,223	8,951	9,093	10,997	4,381	6,808	9,986
excluding South Africa	..	5,328	6,008	8,583	9,558	10,253	10,398	10,223	8,951	9,093	10,997	4,381	6,808	9,986
excl. S.Africa & Nigeria	..	5,328	6,008	6,537	6,633	7,083	7,078	7,157	6,576	7,261	9,300	4,381	5,814	7,409
Angola	..	351	209	203	198	233	269	378	322	327	657	0	263	364
Benin	..	..	..	..	..	..	..	..	..	..	..	..	..	..
Botswana	..	117	152	0	0	0	0	0	0	311	344	114	74	109
Burkina Faso	..	..	..	..	..	..	..	..	..	..	..	..	..	..
Burundi	33	63	73	70	65	80	91	78	57	56	62	45	67	71
Cameroon	388	505	580	512	424	504	488	390	384	349	460	359	480	429
Cape Verde	0	0	47	46	52	52	65	98	71	98	129	0	29	85
Central African Republic	..	91	61	53	51	59	60	64	53	43	63	73	67	57
Chad	..	42	90	73	77	88	100	97	84	83	85	52	67	90
Comoros	..	..	..	..	..	..	..	..	..	..	..	..	..	..
Congo	..	203	163	244	434	237	180	188	203	113	336	199	249	210
Côte d'Ivoire	..	549	559	542	449	419	394	531	332	423	683	411	509	464
Djibouti	..	..	..	..	..	..	..	..	..	..	..	..	..	..
Equatorial Guinea	..	11	18	21	14	14	19	16	..	..	..	..	15	17
Eritrea	..	..	..	..	..	..	..	..	..	..	..	..	..	..
Ethiopia	..	354	463	518	397	340	466	320	379	239	334	449	396	346
Gabon	..	169	116	371	356	354	360	335	320	320	339	188	245	338
Gambia, The	..	9	10	10	10	14	17	19	18	15	18	..	10	17
Ghana	..	129	167	182	190	226	248	277	318	349	398	200	171	302
Guinea	..	..	..	..	..	..	..	..	..	..	..	..	..	..
Guinea-Bissau	..	16	7	11	20	22	15	24	14	15	16	12	13	18
Kenya	..	433	433	571	542	671	523	411	328	503	940	384	464	563
Lesotho	..	65	0	0	0	0	0	0	0	323	368	68	24	115
Liberia	..	..	..	..	..	..	..	..	..	..	..	..	..	..
Madagascar	333	94	102	131	120	186	165	129	140	128	141	160	109	148
Malawi	..	..	82	103	118	143	179	208	183	168	159	..	101	173
Mali	..	141	159	169	155	194	188	201	183	193	256	80	146	202
Mauritania	..	161	121	101	71	82	72	112	106	81	65	85	107	86
Mauritius	..	118	224	398	310	440	380	377	394	511	397	54	224	416
Mozambique	..	87	129	154	228	252	276	260	277	333	185	94	129	264
Namibia	..	0	0	0	0	0	0	0	0	0	0	0	0	0
Niger	..	..	99	106	118	148	102	85	80	67	64	..	107	91
Nigeria	..	..	..	2,046	2,925	3,170	3,320	3,066	2,376	1,833	1,697	..	2,486	2,577
Rwanda	..	85	96	100	86	58	54	69	72	36	50	50	84	56
São Tomé and Principe	..	..	1	1	1	1	1	2	2	12	12	1	1	5
Senegal	..	139	166	144	173	180	165	176	159	154	180	134	141	169
Seychelles	..	29	29	49	45	49	40	40	60	48	39	16	35	46
Sierra Leone	..	33	34	44	52	44	33	30	29	36	34	54	40	34
Somalia	..	..	..	..	..	..	..	..	..	..	..	..	..	..
South Africa	..	..	..	..	..	..	..	..	..	..	..	..	..	..
Sudan	..	217	189	314	355	286	341	364	355	0	0	348	266	224
Swaziland	..	..	..	..	..	..	..	..	..	..	..	..	..	..
Tanzania	..	494	611	406	481	599	680	701	633	729	772	430	485	685
Togo	..	75	122	111	117	131	113	85	61	91	115	48	95	99
Uganda	..	..	..	..	..	..	..	..	..	..	..	..	..	..
Zaire	..	0	0	0	0	0	0	0	0	0	0	0	0	0
Zambia	..	136	250	292	372	346	285	349	328	365	699	118	243	395
Zimbabwe	..	414	449	488	553	632	711	745	632	743	901	345	440	727
NORTH AFRICA	..	..	5,057	5,839	6,891	9,335	8,398	8,047	7,782	7,746	8,577	..	5,929	8,314
Algeria	..	2,915	1,893	1,967	2,335	3,092	1,888	1,894	1,835	2,118	2,100	3,129	2,444	2,154
Egypt, Arab Republic	..	..	1,764	2,188	2,311	3,151	3,340	2,610	2,545	2,349	3,108	..	2,088	2,851
Libya	..	..	..	..	..	..	..	..	..	..	..	..	..	..
Morocco	..	906	881	1,066	1,409	1,856	1,867	1,965	1,833	1,845	1,854	733	982	1,870
Tunisia	..	636	520	618	836	1,235	1,304	1,578	1,569	1,433	1,516	839	642	1,439
ALL AFRICA	..	9,785	11,065	14,422	16,449	19,588	18,796	18,270	16,734	16,839	19,574	..	12,129	18,300

5-46. Capital goods imports, growth

	Percent											Average annual percentage growth		
	1980	*1986*	*1987*	*1988*	*1989*	*1990*	*1991*	*1992*	*1993*	*1994*	*1995*	*75-84*	*85-89*	*90-MR*
SUB-SAHARAN AFRICA	..	..	..	..	..	..	..	..	..	..	..	..	..	..
excluding South Africa	..	..	..	..	..	..	..	..	..	..	..	..	..	..
excl. S.Africa & Nigeria	..	..	..	..	..	..	..	..	..	..	..	..	..	..
Angola	..	-16.1	-45.8	-9.5	-1.8	11.4	12.9	34.6	-12.9	-1.3	97.8	..	-22.3	14.8
Benin	..	..	..	..	..	..	..	..	..	..	..	..	..	..
Botswana	..	..	..	..	..	..	..	..	..	..	..	..	..	..
Burkina Faso	..	..	..	..	..	..	..	..	..	..	..	..	..	..
Burundi	..	-32.8	10.1	-15.1	-14.6	30.9	22.6	-25.2	-22.8	-36.0	11.4	..	-6.6	-11.4
Cameroon	-7.5	24.3	40.9	-24.9	-8.9	12.7	-5.2	-23.5	0.9	-11.7	19.4	-5.6	9.0	-5.4
Cape Verde	..	..	..	-7.1	12.0	0.0	24.4	49.3	-27.7	36.0	29.4	..	..	14.8
Central African Republic	..	..	..	-20.3	-4.6	24.1	-4.5	12.3	-16.8	-59.4	42.0	..	..	-11.6
Chad	..	..	..	-4.6	-3.1	-7.0	-19.3	-7.0	-7.9	-2.1	29.6	..	..	-5.4
Comoros	..	..	..	..	..	..	..	..	..	..	..	..	..	..
Congo	..	51.4	9.6	22.0	-39.8	-7.8	-1.9	-16.5	32.2	10.9	-1.1	..	7.6	2.7
Côte d'Ivoire	..	..	..	..	..	-6.7	-6.1	35.1	-37.5	27.3	51.2	..	..	3.3
Djibouti	..	..	..	..	..	..	..	..	..	..	..	..	..	..
Equatorial Guinea	..	21.5	9.8	5.6	-32.1	0.8	-23.1	0.0	0.0	..	..	..	0.6	-7.4
Eritrea	..	..	..	..	..	..	..	..	..	..	..	..	..	..
Ethiopia	..	..	..	..	..	..	..	..	..	..	..	..	..	..
Gabon	..	..	..	..	..	..	..	..	..	..	..	..	..	..
Gambia, The	..	..	..	-8.2	14.6	28.4	22.9	7.5	-11.0	-17.5	18.1	..	..	3.8
Ghana	..	-36.1	28.0	5.9	4.3	12.2	7.4	7.3	14.7	6.0	9.1	..	-3.1	9.3
Guinea	..	..	..	..	..	..	..	..	..	..	..	..	..	..
Guinea-Bissau	..	..	..	84.7	71.4	3.5	-36.0	58.9	-40.8	26.1	13.4	..	..	-3.4
Kenya	..	-5.9	2.2	0.3	-16.4	72.9	-19.2	-23.4	-15.9	50.3	78.7	..	-3.7	6.3
Lesotho	..	..	..	..	..	..	..	..	..	..	..	..	..	..
Liberia	..	..	..	..	..	..	..	..	..	..	..	..	..	..
Madagascar	..	-18.6	-2.9	21.6	-8.1	41.2	-9.3	-25.3	13.8	-12.1	12.8	..	3.5	-2.5
Malawi	..	..	..	16.8	15.7	12.4	22.7	10.9	-11.6	-11.2	-13.1	..	..	0.9
Mali	..	1.4	-2.3	2.6	-7.2	11.1	0.7	3.0	-5.0	2.2	20.0	..	3.2	3.2
Mauritania	..	66.7	-31.4	-22.5	-28.6	8.5	-13.7	48.7	-4.9	-26.8	-25.7	..	-14.3	-3.0
Mauritius	..	25.8	33.6	37.7	-25.7	33.1	-4.5	-4.0	6.7	4.0	-20.0	..	19.8	1.1
Mozambique	..	16.5	19.7	11.2	49.7	4.5	7.2	-9.5	6.9	16.6	-46.8	..	17.9	-3.0
Namibia	..	..	..	..	..	..	..	..	..	..	..	..	..	..
Niger	..	..	..	..	..	..	..	..	..	..	..	..	..	..
Nigeria	..	..	..	..	43.9	2.6	2.5	-11.5	-22.3	-25.5	-14.5	..	..	-13.3
Rwanda	..	28.5	3.1	-2.8	-12.8	7.0	-10.3	4.0	-6.4	3.4	11.4	..	5.6	0.0
São Tomé and Principe	..	..	..	-37.0	31.7	-1.2	-3.7	..	..	..	..	..	..	..
Senegal	..	0.8	8.9	-9.3	21.3	-7.5	2.2	-2.4	-6.0	-6.8	4.9	..	3.9	-3.0
Seychelles	..	22.3	13.5	64.7	11.0	-4.0	-9.4	8.8	52.1	-12.7	-19.9	..	23.4	3.9
Sierra Leone	..	-15.5	-4.1	25.4	14.6	-19.0	-17.1	-1.6	9.5	30.5	-11.2	..	5.0	-0.6
Somalia	..	..	..	..	..	..	..	..	..	..	..	..	..	..
South Africa	..	..	..	..	..	..	..	..	..	..	..	..	..	..
Sudan	..	-11.6	7.1	119.2	51.1	..	..	..	..	..	..	..	20.1	..
Swaziland	..	..	..	..	..	..	..	..	..	..	..	..	..	..
Tanzania	..	..	..	..	..	..	..	..	..	..	..	..	..	..
Togo	..	10.0	12.4	4.3	-0.9	15.6	..	..	..	..	..	..	6.7	..
Uganda	..	..	..	..	..	..	..	..	..	..	..	..	..	..
Zaire	..	..	..	..	..	..	..	..	..	..	..	..	..	..
Zambia	..	-29.4	67.8	9.6	27.0	-12.1	-19.3	17.4	-3.8	7.2	76.9	..	16.6	4.9
Zimbabwe	..	17.9	-1.3	1.1	14.3	6.0	10.0	0.5	-14.8	13.3	11.8	..	3.4	2.4
NORTH AFRICA	..	..	..	..	..	..	..	..	..	..	..	..	..	..
Algeria	..	-39.2	-35.7	-9.2	25.6	60.1	-35.2	-13.1	-10.5	7.6	7.0	..	-20.6	-5.9
Egypt, Arab Republic	..	..	..	14.3	2.4	33.1	2.0	-24.3	-4.4	-9.2	24.7	..	..	-2.8
Libya	..	..	..	..	..	..	..	..	..	..	..	..	..	..
Morocco	..	18.4	-11.7	13.1	32.3	24.5	-1.2	0.5	-2.5	-2.9	-12.3	..	5.8	-0.2
Tunisia	..	-15.5	-28.3	13.5	38.0	27.8	3.4	21.2	8.7	-23.7	-4.1	..	-9.2	3.9
ALL AFRICA	..	..	..	..	..	..	..	..	..	..	..	..	..	..

5-47. Direction of trade matrix, imports, 1984

Importers — *Percentage of total imports*

Exporters		DZA	AGO	BEN	BFA	BDI	CMR	CPV	CAF	TCD	COM	COG	CIV	DJI	EGY	GNQ	ETH
Algeria	DZA	**	..	4.62	2.55	..	..	..	..	..	..	..	0.17	0.50	0.02	..	..
Angola	AGO	..	**	..	..	..	..	..	..	..	..	..	..	..	..	..	..
Benin	BEN	..	..	**	0.05	..	0.00	..	..	..	..	..	0.01	..	..	..	..
Burkina Faso	BFA	..	..	0.09	**	..	..	..	..	..	..	..	0.07	..	..	..	..
Burundi	BDI	..	..	..	..	**	0.00	..	..	..	..	..	0.00	..	..	..	0.00
Cameroon	CMR	..	..	0.22	0.05	..	**	..	16.27	10.90	..	2.12	0.35	..	0.00	2.67	..
Cape Verde	CPV	0.01	0.00	0.03	..	..	..	**	0.14	..	..	..	0.04	..	..	..	..
Central African Republic	CAF	..	..	..	..	..	0.02	..	**	..	..	..	0.01	..	0.00	..	..
Chad	TCD	..	..	..	..	..	0.84	..	..	**	..	..	..	..	..	..	..
Comoros	COM	..	..	0.03	..	..	..	..	..	..	**	..	..	..	..	..	..
Congo	COG	0.00	1.53	0.00	..	..	0.00	..	0.00	1.33	..	**	0.01	..	0.00	..	..
Côte d'Ivoire	CIV	..	..	1.45	32.55	..	0.53	..	..	..	..	..	**	..	0.01	..	0.00
Djibouti	DJI	..	..	..	..	..	..	..	..	..	..	..	..	**	..	..	..
Egypt, Arab Rep.	EGY	0.01	..	..	..	..	0.00	..	0.00	..	..	..	..	0.04	**	..	0.08
Equatorial Guinea	GNQ	..	..	..	..	..	0.00	..	..	..	..	..	..	..	..	**	..
Ethiopia	ETH	0.02	..	..	..	..	0.02	..	..	..	..	..	0.00	12.16	0.00	..	**
Gabon	GAB	..	..	0.13	..	..	0.68	..	..	..	..	..	3.23	..	..	..	..
Gambia, The	GMB	..	..	..	..	..	..	..	..	..	..	..	..	..	..	..	..
Ghana	GHA	..	..	1.48	0.64	..	..	..	..	..	..	..	0.02	..	0.02	..	..
Guinea	GIN	..	..	..	0.00	..	1.46	..	..	..	..	..	0.00	..	..	..	..
Guinea-Bissau	GNB	..	..	..	..	..	..	..	..	..	..	..	0.01	..	0.00	..	..
Kenya	KEN	0.01	0.03	0.00	0.00	16.18	0.01	..	0.00	..	4.48	0.00	0.23	1.09	0.22	..	0.46
Liberia	LBR	..	..	0.00	..	..	0.01	..	..	..	..	..	0.01	..	0.00	..	..
Libya	LBY	..	..	..	..	..	..	..	..	..	..	..	..	..	..	..	..
Madagascar	MDG	0.00	..	..	..	0.00	0.00	..	..	..	0.50	0.00	..	0.00	..	..	..
Malawi	MWI	..	..	0.09	..	0.78	0.04	..	0.42	0.11	..	0.02	0.00	..	0.01	..	0.01
Mali	MLI	..	..	..	0.86	..	0.00	..	..	..	..	..	0.27	..	..	..	..
Mauritania	MRT	..	..	..	..	..	0.00	..	..	..	..	..	3.80	..	..	..	..
Mauritius	MUS	..	..	..	..	..	..	..	..	..	..	..	..	..	..	..	..
Morocco	MAR	0.00	0.02	0.19	0.00	..	0.42	..	0.00	..	0.17	0.94	0.38	0.00	0.03	0.76	..
Mozambique	MOZ	..	..	..	..	..	..	..	..	..	..	..	0.02	..	..	..	..
Niger	NER	..	..	0.19	0.18	..	0.00	..	..	..	..	..	0.01	..	..	..	..
Nigeria	NGA	..	..	3.93	0.95	..	0.25	..	..	..	..	..	7.71	..	0.00	..	0.00
Reunion	REU	..	..	..	..	0.00	..	..	..	..	5.80	0.00	..	0.00	..	..	..
Rwanda	RWA	..	..	..	..	..	..	..	..	..	..	..	0.00	..	..	..	..
South Africa	ZAF	..	..	..	..	..	..	..	..	..	..	..	..	..	..	..	..
São Tomé and Principe	STP	..	..	..	..	..	..	..	..	..	..	..	..	..	..	..	..
Senegal	SEN	..	..	2.33	2.36	..	0.34	..	..	..	..	..	3.05	..	0.00	..	0.00
Seychelles	SYC	..	..	..	..	..	..	..	..	..	..	..	..	0.67	..	..	..
Sierra Leone	SLE	..	..	..	..	..	..	..	..	..	..	..	0.05	..	..	..	..
Somalia	SOM	..	..	..	..	..	..	..	..	..	..	..	..	..	0.00	..	..
Sudan	SDN	..	..	..	..	..	..	..	..	..	..	..	..	..	0.98	..	0.04
Tanzania	TZA	..	..	..	..	..	0.00	..	..	..	..	..	0.08	..	0.03	..	0.05
Togo	TGO	..	..	0.82	1.68	..	0.01	..	0.00	0.00	..	0.02	0.32	..	..	..	..
Tunisia	TUN	0.49	..	0.00	0.00	..	0.00	..	..	0.33	..	0.00	0.03	..	0.09	..	..
Uganda	UGA	..	..	..	..	..	..	..	..	..	..	..	..	..	0.00	..	..
Zaire	ZAR	..	..	0.09	..	..	0.00	..	..	..	..	..	0.02	..	0.05	..	..
Zambia	ZMB	..	..	..	..	..	..	..	..	..	..	..	0.06	..	0.00	..	..
Zimbabwe	ZWE	0.03	0.98	..	..	0.70	0.01	0.14	0.42	..	0.50	0.07	0.07	..	0.08	..	0.54
Sub-Saharan Africa	SSA	0.06	2.54	10.91	39.27	17.67	4.22	0.14	17.25	12.46	11.28	2.24	19.45	13.93	1.40	2.67	1.10
European Community	EEC	68.15	63.95	46.64	42.91	62.00	71.74	87.07	70.97	69.19	43.45	79.46	57.44	53.68	43.62	83.59	46.38
North America	NNA	8.90	11.45	4.12	9.41	7.19	6.28	..	1.26	16.02	40.63	2.78	5.69	3.45	20.45	0.00	26.39
Rest Of World	ROW	22.89	22.06	38.34	8.41	13.14	17.76	12.78	10.52	2.22	4.64	15.52	17.41	28.90	34.53	13.74	26.11
World	WLD	100.00	100.00	100.00	100.00	100.00	100.00	100.00	100.00	100.00	100.00	100.00	100.00	100.00	100.00	100.00	100.00

Note: ** means "not applicable."

(Table continues on the following page)

5-47. (continued)

Percentage of total imports

GAB	GMB	GHA	GIN	GNB	KEN	LBR	LBY	MDG	MWI	MLI	MRT	MUS	MAR	MOZ	NER	NGA	REU	RWA	ZAF
..	1.17	..	..	..	0.55	0.05	0.01	..	..	0.05	..	..	..	5.79	0.30	..	..	..	..
..	..	..	..	..	..	..	..	..	..	..	..	..	0.00	..	..	..	..	..	..
..	..	..	..	..	..	0.00	..	..	..	..	..	..	..	..	..	..	..	..	..
..	..	..	..	..	..	..	..	..	..	..	..	..	0.01	..	..	..	..	..	..
..	..	..	..	..	0.32	..	..	..	..	..	..	..	..	..	..	..	..	2.40	..
1.79	..	..	0.07	..	0.00	0.00	..	..	..	..	0.04	..	0.03	..	0.06	0.35	0.01	0.00	..
..	..	..	..	0.00	..	0.00	..	..	..	..	..	..	..	..	..	..	..	..	..
..	..	..	..	..	..	..	..	..	..	..	..	..	0.01	..	..	..	..	..	..
..	..	..	..	..	..	0.00	..	..	..	..	..	..	..	..	..	..	..	..	..
..	..	..	..	..	..	0.00	..	0.03	..	..	..	0.07	0.00	..	..	..	0.01	..	..
0.01	..	..	..	..	..	..	..	..	..	..	..	..	0.03	..	..	0.00	0.35	..	0.00
0.48	..	..	..	..	0.00	1.16	..	..	..	..	..	0.04	0.59	..	..	..	0.06	..	..
..	..	..	..	..	..	..	..	..	..	..	..	..	..	..	..	..	..	..	..
..	0.00	0.02	0.00	..	0.00	0.00	0.00	..	..	..	0.00	..	0.06	..	0.06	0.00	..	..	0.00
..	..	..	..	..	..	..	..	..	..	..	..	..	..	..	..	..	..	..	..
..	..	..	..	..	0.06	..	0.00	..	0.00	..	0.00	0.24	..	..	..	0.00	..	..	..
**	..	..	..	..	..	..	..	..	..	..	..	..	0.31	..	..	..	0.01	..	..
..	**	..	..	..	..	0.00	..	..	..	..	..	0.00	..	..	..	..	..	..	..
..	..	**	..	..	0.00	0.00	..	..	..	..	..	0.02	..	..	..	..	..	..	..
..	..	..	**	..	..	0.02	..	..	..	..	..	..	0.00	..	..	..	..	..	..
..	..	..	..	**	..	..	..	..	..	..	..	..	..	..	..	..	..	..	..
0.00	0.00	0.00	0.04	..	**	0.00	0.01	0.80	0.58	..	0.00	1.12	0.00	1.36	0.00	0.00	0.79	23.14	0.01
..	0.00	0.05	0.18	..	..	**	0.00	..	..	0.00	0.04	..	0.00	..	..	0.16	..	..	..
..	..	..	..	..	..	..	**	..	..	..	0.00	..	0.03	..	..	..	..	..	..
0.03	..	..	..	..	0.07	..	..	**	..	..	..	0.31	0.00	0.00	0.00	..	1.32	..	..
0.07	2.22	0.00	0.18	0.00	0.03	0.04	..	..	**	..	..	0.04	..	1.08	..	..	..	..	0.20
0.00	..	..	..	..	..	0.08	0.01	..	..	**	..	..	0.13	..	..	..	..	..	..
..	..	..	..	..	..	0.04	..	..	..	..	**	..	..	..	..	..	..	..	..
..	..	..	..	..	..	..	..	..	..	..	..	**	..	..	..	..	0.28	..	0.00
0.66	0.00	0.00	1.52	..	0.00	0.02	0.61	..	..	0.38	0.14	0.20	**	..	0.06	0.00	0.19	..	0.00
..	..	..	..	..	..	..	..	0.27	..	..	..	..	..	**	..	..	..	..	..
0.00	..	..	..	..	..	..	..	..	..	..	..	..	..	..	**	..	..	..	..
..	..	..	..	..	0.00	0.39	..	..	..	..	..	..	0.01	..	..	**	..	..	..
0.00	..	0.00	..	..	0.00	..	..	0.83	..	..	..	0.18	0.09	..	..	..	**	..	0.00
..	..	..	..	..	0.25	..	..	..	..	..	..	..	..	..	..	..	..	**	..
..	..	..	..	..	..	..	..	..	..	..	..	..	..	..	..	..	..	..	**
..	..	..	..	..	..	0.00	..	..	..	..	..	..	..	..	..	..	..	..	..
0.42	..	..	..	..	0.00	0.02	0.00	..	..	..	..	0.00	0.01	..	..	..	0.15	..	..
..	..	..	..	..	0.06	..	..	0.00	..	..	..	0.02	..	..	..	..	0.07	..	0.00
..	0.23	..	0.00	..	..	0.07	..	..	..	..	..	..	..	..	..	0.00	..	..	..
..	..	..	..	..	0.01	0.00	..	..	..	..	..	..	0.00	..	..	..	..	..	..
..	..	..	..	..	0.00	..	0.00	..	..	..	..	0.00	..	..	..	..	..	..	..
..	..	..	..	..	0.11	..	..	0.65	..	..	..	0.00	..	..	..	..	0.00	..	..
0.01	..	1.10	0.07	..	..	0.00	..	..	..	0.86	..	..	0.04	..	0.96	0.08	..	..	..
0.10	..	0.00	0.07	..	..	..	0.90	..	..	0.00	0.00	..	0.15	..	0.00	0.00	..	..	..
..	..	..	..	..	0.11	..	0.00	..	..	..	..	0.00	0.00	..	..	..	0.00	..	..
0.01	..	..	..	..	0.09	..	..	..	..	..	..	0.00	0.01	..	..	..	..	..	..
..	..	..	..	..	0.11	..	..	..	..	..	..	..	..	..	..	..	..	..	..
0.01	..	0.19	0.00	..	0.07	0.00	0.05	0.00	12.16	..	..	0.37	0.05	1.22	..	0.01	..	0.63	1.94
2.85	2.45	1.36	0.54	0.00	1.31	1.82	0.08	2.55	12.74	0.86	0.07	2.40	1.33	3.67	1.02	0.60	3.06	26.17	2.17
79.53	51.46	55.95	64.86	47.07	45.68	25.58	58.90	48.31	58.07	77.44	74.37	26.73	53.81	37.26	83.44	57.35	76.36	44.94	48.25
5.61	16.92	16.09	12.74	46.17	7.54	4.10	4.06	12.29	3.70	7.19	10.05	2.01	16.07	11.27	0.90	11.10	0.12	5.63	20.17
12.03	29.17	26.63	21.86	6.92	45.47	68.50	36.96	36.85	25.49	14.47	15.47	68.86	28.79	47.81	14.64	30.95	20.47	23.20	29.41
100.00	100.00	100.00	100.00	100.00	100.00	100.00	100.00	100.00	100.00	100.00	100.00	100.00	100.00	100.00	100.00	100.00	100.00	100.00	100.00

Note: ** means "not applicable."

(Table continues on the following page)

5-47. (continued)

Percentage of total imports

STP	SEN	SYC	SLE	SOM	SDN	TZA	TGO	TUN	UGA	ZAR	ZMB	ZWE	SSA	EEC	NNA	ROW	WLD
..	0.02	0.70	..	..	0.17	1.78	..	2.47	0.84	..	..	..	0.20	1.41	0.70	0.13	**0.69**
..	..	..	..	..	..	..	..	..	..	..	..	..	..	0.11	0.28	0.04	**0.11**
..	..	..	..	..	..	..	..	..	..	..	..	..	0.00	0.02	0.00	0.00	**0.01**
..	..	..	..	..	..	..	..	0.02	..	..	..	..	0.00	0.01	0.00	0.00	**0.00**
..	..	..	..	..	..	0.10	..	..	0.40	0.43	0.02	..	0.04	0.01	0.00	0.00	**0.01**
..	0.21	..	..	..	..	..	0.06	0.01	..	0.01	..	..	0.19	0.10	0.04	0.01	**0.05**
0.00	0.00	..	..	..	..	..	..	..	..	0.00	..	..	0.00	0.00	0.00	0.00	**0.00**
..	..	..	..	..	..	..	..	..	..	..	..	..	0.00	0.01	0.00	0.01	**0.01**
..	..	..	..	..	..	..	..	..	..	..	..	..	0.03	0.01	0.00	0.00	**0.01**
..	..	..	..	..	..	..	..	..	..	..	..	..	0.00	0.00	0.00	0.00	**0.00**
3.67	0.00	..	..	..	..	..	0.00	0.09	0.00	0.22	..	..	0.06	0.04	0.24	0.00	**0.07**
..	..	..	0.06	..	..	..	..	0.37	..	..	..	..	0.31	0.29	0.15	0.05	**0.16**
..	..	..	..	..	..	..	..	..	..	..	..	..	..	..	..	..	**..**
..	0.00	..	0.00	0.00	3.09	0.00	0.00	0.18	0.04	0.06	..	..	0.08	0.22	0.05	0.23	**0.18**
..	..	..	..	..	..	..	..	..	..	..	..	..	0.00	0.01	0.00	0.00	**0.00**
..	0.00	..	..	..	0.52	0.03	0.00	..	0.00	0.00	0.00	0.00	0.10	0.03	0.02	0.02	**0.02**
..	..	..	0.00	..	..	..	..	..	..	..	..	..	0.14	0.18	0.20	0.02	**0.12**
..	..	..	0.00	..	..	..	..	..	..	..	..	..	0.00	0.00	0.00	0.00	**0.00**
..	..	..	0.00	..	..	..	..	..	..	..	..	..	0.02	0.03	0.01	0.02	**0.02**
..	..	..	0.11	..	..	..	..	..	..	..	..	..	0.05	0.05	0.04	0.01	**0.03**
..	..	..	..	..	..	..	..	..	..	..	..	..	0.00	0.00	0.00	0.00	**0.00**
..	0.00	2.24	0.00	1.30	2.62	1.61	0.03	0.23	35.87	1.05	0.27	0.06	0.63	0.08	0.02	0.04	**0.06**
..	0.00	..	0.55	..	..	..	0.16	..	..	..	..	..	0.03	0.05	0.02	0.00	**0.03**
..	..	..	..	..	..	1.97	..	0.88	..	..	..	..	0.04	1.45	0.01	0.37	**0.65**
..	..	0.00	..	0.00	..	0.01	..	0.00	..	..	..	..	0.03	0.04	0.01	0.01	**0.02**
..	0.00	0.00	0.11	..	0.00	0.10	..	..	0.00	0.48	2.09	2.14	0.16	0.03	0.01	0.01	**0.02**
..	..	..	..	..	..	..	..	0.16	..	..	..	..	0.02	0.02	0.00	0.01	**0.01**
..	0.24	..	..	..	..	..	..	..	..	..	..	..	0.15	0.03	0.00	0.01	**0.02**
..	..	..	..	..	..	..	..	..	..	..	..	..	0.01	0.05	0.01	0.01	**0.02**
..	1.00	..	0.06	..	0.11	0.03	0.28	0.72	0.00	0.21	..	..	0.11	0.22	0.01	0.11	**0.13**
..	..	..	..	..	..	..	..	..	..	..	..	..	0.00	0.01	0.00	0.01	**0.01**
..	..	..	..	..	..	..	..	..	..	..	..	..	0.00	0.03	0.00	0.00	**0.01**
..	..	..	32.89	..	..	..	..	..	..	..	..	..	0.51	1.47	0.79	0.33	**0.83**
..	0.00	0.00	..	..	..	..	..	..	..	..	..	..	0.02	0.01	0.00	0.00	**0.00**
..	..	..	..	..	..	..	..	..	..	..	..	..	0.01	0.01	0.00	0.00	**0.00**
..	..	..	..	..	..	..	..	..	..	..	..	..	..	0.59	0.42	1.65	**0.98**
**	..	..	..	..	..	..	..	..	..	..	..	..	0.00	0.00	..	0.00	**0.00**
..	**	..	0.50	..	..	..	..	..	..	..	..	..	0.17	0.07	0.00	0.01	**0.03**
..	..	**	..	..	..	0.00	..	..	..	..	..	..	0.01	0.00	0.00	0.00	**0.00**
..	0.02	..	**	..	..	..	..	..	..	..	..	0.00	0.01	0.01	0.00	0.01	**0.01**
..	..	..	..	**	..	..	..	..	..	..	..	..	0.00	0.00	0.00	0.02	**0.01**
..	..	..	..	..	**	..	..	0.14	..	..	..	..	0.00	0.04	0.01	0.08	**0.05**
..	..	0.00	0.06	..	..	**	..	..	..	..	..	..	0.01	0.04	0.00	0.02	**0.02**
..	0.00	..	..	..	..	..	**	0.20	..	0.00	..	..	0.06	0.02	0.00	0.01	**0.01**
..	0.01	..	..	0.00	0.01	..	0.06	**	..	0.01	..	..	0.01	0.19	0.09	0.05	**0.11**
..	..	..	..	..	..	..	..	..	**	..	..	..	0.00	0.04	0.03	0.01	**0.02**
..	..	..	..	..	..	..	..	0.00	..	**	..	..	0.00	0.05	0.08	0.06	**0.06**
..	..	..	..	..	..	..	..	..	..	..	**	..	0.01	0.04	0.03	0.04	**0.04**
..	0.01	0.70	0.00	0.00	0.23	0.34	0.00	0.02	0.04	1.57	8.27	**	0.88	0.06	0.02	0.03	**0.06**
3.67	**0.51**	**2.94**	**34.27**	**1.30**	**3.37**	**2.22**	**0.22**	**1.24**	**36.35**	**3.77**	**10.66**	**2.17**	**3.68**	**3.69**	**2.44**	**2.55**	**2.94**
76.15	**57.68**	**31.61**	**43.41**	**55.33**	**50.11**	**46.78**	**70.28**	**69.46**	**41.04**	**58.78**	**43.55**	**46.42**	**52.16**	**56.68**	**16.75**	**27.52**	**35.59**
..	**13.45**	**6.15**	**10.69**	**25.16**	**13.74**	**8.39**	**5.29**	**8.92**	**1.68**	**9.20**	**24.62**	**13.32**	**13.02**	**9.20**	**28.84**	**18.38**	**17.47**
20.18	**28.37**	**59.30**	**11.68**	**18.22**	**32.78**	**42.63**	**24.18**	**20.38**	**20.92**	**28.25**	**21.19**	**38.09**	**31.15**	**30.44**	**51.96**	**51.54**	**44.00**
100.00	**100.00**	**100.00**	**100.00**	**100.00**	**100.00**	**100.00**	**100.00**	**100.00**	**100.00**	**100.00**	**100.00**	**100.00**	**100.00**	**100.00**	**100.00**	**100.00**	**100.00**

Note: ** means "not applicable."

5-48. Direction of trade matrix, imports, 1988

Exporters		DZA	AGO	BEN	BFA	BDI	CMR	CPV	CAF	TCD	COM	COG	CIV	DJI	EGY	GNQ	ETH
		Importers							*Percentage of total imports*								
Algeria	DZA	**	..	0.02	0.00	..	0.00	..	..	..	..	0.11	0.00	..	0.01	..	0.00
Angola	AGO	..	**	..	..	..	0.07	..	..	..	..	..	..	..	..	..	..
Benin	BEN	..	..	**	..	..	0.06	..	..	..	..	..	..	..	0.00	..	..
Burkina Faso	BFA	0.00	..	..	**	..	..	..	..	..	..	..	..	..	..	..	..
Burundi	BDI	..	..	..	..	**	..	..	..	..	..	..	..	..	..	..	..
Cameroon	CMR	0.06	..	..	..	..	**	..	..	..	..	..	..	..	0.02	..	..
Cape Verde	CPV	0.09	..	..	..	..	..	**	..	..	..	..	..	..	..	..	..
Central African Republic	CAF	..	..	..	..	..	0.01	..	**	..	..	..	..	..	..	..	..
Chad	TCD	0.00	..	..	..	..	0.47	..	..	**	..	..	..	..	0.00	..	..
Comoros	COM	..	..	..	..	..	..	..	..	..	**	..	..	..	0.00	..	..
Congo	COG	0.05	..	..	..	..	0.07	..	..	..	..	**	..	..	..	..	..
Côte d'Ivoire	CIV	0.07	..	..	..	..	0.62	..	..	..	..	..	**	..	0.02	..	..
Djibouti	DJI	..	..	0.00	..	0.00	..	..	..	..	0.00	..	0.00	**	0.00	..	0.05
Egypt, Arab Rep.	EGY	0.07	0.00	..	..	0.00	0.07	..	0.00	0.00	..	0.00	0.01	0.05	**	..	0.07
Equatorial Guinea	GNQ	0.00	..	..	..	..	0.00	..	..	..	..	..	..	..	0.00	**	..
Ethiopia	ETH	0.01	..	..	..	0.00	..	..	..	0.00	..	..	..	9.33	0.00	..	**
Gabon	GAB	0.09	..	..	..	..	0.27	..	..	..	..	..	..	..	0.00	..	..
Gambia, The	GMB	..	..	..	..	..	0.00	..	..	..	..	..	..	..	..	..	..
Ghana	GHA	..	..	..	..	..	0.00	..	..	..	..	..	..	..	0.00	..	..
Guinea	GIN	..	..	..	..	..	2.44	..	..	..	..	..	..	..	..	..	..
Guinea-Bissau	GNB	..	..	..	..	..	..	..	..	..	..	..	..	..	..	..	..
Kenya	KEN	0.00	0.08	..	0.00	9.13	0.00	0.50	0.00	..	0.75	0.00	0.05	0.55	0.11	0.00	0.57
Liberia	LBR	..	..	..	..	..	..	..	..	..	..	..	..	..	..	..	..
Libya	LBY	0.19	..	..	..	..	..	..	..	..	..	..	0.02	..	..	..	..
Madagascar	MDG	0.04	..	..	..	..	0.00	..	..	..	..	..	..	..	..	..	..
Malawi	MWI	..	0.00	0.00	..	1.90	0.00	..	..	0.00	..	0.00	0.00	..	0.01	..	0.00
Mali	MLI	0.35	..	..	..	..	0.00	..	..	..	..	..	..	..	..	..	..
Mauritania	MRT	0.10	..	..	..	..	0.57	..	..	..	..	..	..	..	0.06	..	..
Mauritius	MUS	..	..	..	..	..	..	..	..	..	1.49	..	..	..	..	..	..
Morocco	MAR	0.15	0.76	0.29	0.12	..	0.71	..	0.60	0.00	0.60	0.89	0.58	0.00	0.06	0.39	..
Mozambique	MOZ	0.00	..	..	..	..	0.06	..	..	..	..	..	..	..	..	..	..
Niger	NER	0.00	..	..	..	..	..	..	..	..	..	..	..	..	..	..	..
Nigeria	NGA	..	..	..	..	..	0.38	..	..	..	..	..	..	..	0.00	..	..
Reunion	REU	..	..	..	..	..	..	..	..	..	12.39	..	0.00	0.09	..	..	..
Rwanda	RWA	..	..	..	0.00	0.07	..	..	..	..	..	..	..	0.00	..	..	0.00
South Africa	ZAF	0.02	..	..	..	..	0.00	..	..	..	..	..	..	..	0.03	..	..
São Tomé and Principe	STP	..	..	..	..	..	..	..	..	..	..	..	..	..	..	..	..
Senegal	SEN	..	..	..	..	..	1.64	..	..	..	..	..	..	..	0.01	..	..
Seychelles	SYC	..	..	..	..	..	..	..	..	..	0.00	..	..	..	..	..	..
Sierra Leone	SLE	0.01	..	..	..	..	0.02	..	..	..	..	..	..	..	..	..	..
Somalia	SOM	..	..	..	..	..	..	..	..	..	..	..	..	..	0.01	..	..
Sudan	SDN	0.00	..	..	..	..	..	..	..	..	..	..	..	..	1.36	..	..
Tanzania	TZA	0.12	..	..	..	..	..	..	..	..	..	..	..	..	0.03	..	..
Togo	TGO	0.00	0.00	2.07	1.98	..	0.09	..	0.00	0.33	..	0.16	0.03	..	..	0.20	..
Tunisia	TUN	0.83	..	0.27	0.31	..	0.55	0.00	0.00	..	..	0.02	0.19	0.00	0.05	..	..
Uganda	UGA	0.06	..	..	..	..	..	..	..	..	..	..	..	..	0.01	..	..
Zaire	ZAR	0.00	..	..	..	..	0.00	..	..	..	..	..	..	..	0.14	..	..
Zambia	ZMB	..	..	..	..	..	..	..	..	..	..	..	..	..	..	..	..
Zimbabwe	ZWE	..	..	..	..	..	0.29	..	..	..	..	..	..	..	0.18	..	..
Sub-Saharan Africa	**SSA**	**1.07**	**0.09**	**2.10**	**2.02**	**11.10**	**7.07**	**0.50**	**0.00**	**0.33**	**14.78**	**0.16**	**0.07**	**9.98**	**1.99**	**0.20**	**0.61**
European Community	**EEC**	**59.41**	**56.21**	**49.89**	**78.45**	**68.19**	**70.65**	**67.93**	**73.30**	**80.31**	**75.67**	**82.43**	**73.51**	**52.29**	**43.03**	**89.57**	**54.89**
North America	**NNA**	**13.49**	**7.81**	**5.39**	**6.37**	**0.98**	**4.06**	**3.39**	**2.81**	**5.72**	**1.19**	**4.73**	**5.55**	**2.45**	**21.86**	**0.98**	**17.44**
Rest Of World	**ROW**	**26.03**	**35.89**	**42.62**	**13.20**	**19.73**	**18.23**	**28.18**	**23.89**	**13.64**	**8.51**	**12.68**	**20.86**	**35.24**	**33.12**	**9.25**	**27.06**
World	**WLD**	**100.00**	**100.00**	**100.00**	**100.00**	**100.00**	**100.00**	**100.00**	**100.00**	**100.00**	**100.00**	**100.00**	**100.00**	**100.00**	**100.00**	**100.00**	**100.00**

Note: ** means "not applicable."

(Table continues on the following page.)

5-48. (continued)

Percentage of total imports

GAB	GMB	GHA	GIN	GNB	KEN	LBR	LBY	MDG	MWI	MLI	MRT	MUS	MAR	MOZ	NER	NGA	REU	RWA	ZAF
..	..	..	0.10	..	..	0.00	0.61	..	..	0.51	12.21	..	0.14	..	0.04	..	..	0.00	..
..	..	..	..	..	..	..	..	..	..	..	..	..	..	..	..	0.00	..	..	..
..	..	..	..	..	..	..	..	..	..	..	..	..	0.00	..	..	0.08	..	..	..
..	..	..	..	..	..	..	..	..	..	..	..	..	0.02	..	..	0.08	..	..	..
..	..	..	..	..	..	..	..	..	..	..	..	..	..	..	..	..	..	..	..
..	..	..	..	..	..	..	..	0.00	..	..	..	..	0.02	..	..	0.06	0.01	..	..
..	..	..	..	..	..	..	..	..	..	..	..	..	..	..	..	..	..	..	..
..	..	..	..	..	..	..	..	..	..	..	..	..	0.00	..	..	..	0.01	..	..
..	..	..	..	..	..	..	..	..	..	..	..	..	0.10	..	..	0.14	..	..	..
..	..	..	..	..	..	..	..	0.00	..	..	..	..	..	..	..	..	0.01	..	..
..	..	..	..	..	..	..	..	..	..	..	..	..	0.20	..	..	..	0.41	..	..
..	..	..	..	..	..	..	..	0.00	..	..	..	..	0.31	..	..	0.08	0.06	..	..
..	..	..	..	..	0.00	..	0.00	0.03	..	..	..	0.00	0.00	..	0.00	0.00	0.01	..	..
0.00	..	0.00	0.00	..	0.04	0.01	0.00	..	0.00	0.00	0.00	0.00	0.07	..	0.00	0.01	..	..	0.00
..	..	..	..	..	..	..	..	..	..	..	..	..	..	..	..	..	..	..	..
..	0.00	0.00	0.00	..	0.03	..	0.00	..	0.00	..	..	0.00	..	..	..	0.00	0.00	0.00	..
**	..	..	..	..	..	..	..	0.03	..	..	..	..	0.33	..	..	0.00	0.02	..	..
..	**	..	..	..	..	..	..	..	..	..	..	..	..	..	..	0.00	..	..	..
..	..	**	..	..	..	..	..	..	..	..	..	..	0.04	..	..	0.01	..	..	..
..	..	..	**	..	..	..	..	..	..	..	..	..	0.00	..	..	..	..	..	..
..	..	..	..	**	..	..	..	..	..	..	..	..	..	..	..	..	..	..	..
0.00	0.00	0.00	0.00	..	**	0.00	0.00	0.22	1.65	0.00	0.00	0.28	0.00	1.66	..	0.04	0.43	12.67	0.02
..	..	..	..	..	..	**	..	..	..	..	..	..	0.01	..	..	0.09	..	..	..
..	..	..	..	..	..	..	**	..	..	..	..	..	0.02	..	..	..	..	..	..
..	..	..	..	..	..	..	..	**	..	..	..	..	0.00	..	..	..	0.65	..	..
..	0.48	0.00	..	..	0.01	0.02	0.00	0.00	**	..	..	0.01	..	0.64	0.00	0.00	..	0.05	0.23
..	..	..	..	..	..	..	..	..	..	**	..	..	0.17	..	..	0.01	..	..	..
..	..	..	..	..	..	..	..	..	..	..	**	..	0.01	..	..	0.00	..	..	..
..	..	..	..	..	0.02	..	..	0.59	..	..	..	**	0.08	..	..	..	1.38	..	0.04
0.81	0.06	0.04	1.86	0.14	0.50	0.05	1.78	0.08	..	0.78	0.71	0.15	**	0.02	0.23	0.30	0.13	..	..
..	..	..	..	..	..	..	..	1.09	..	..	..	..	0.00	**	..	0.00	..	..	..
..	..	..	..	..	..	..	..	..	..	..	..	..	..	..	**	0.35	..	..	..
..	..	..	..	..	..	..	..	..	..	..	..	..	0.04	..	..	**	..	..	..
..	..	..	..	..	..	..	..	1.26	..	..	..	0.14	..	..	..	..	**	..	0.00
0.00	..	0.00	..	..	0.05	0.00	0.00	0.00	..	0.00	..	..	..	..	..	..	0.00	**	0.00
..	..	..	..	..	..	..	..	0.17	..	..	..	..	0.04	..	..	0.00	3.15	..	**
..	..	..	..	..	..	..	..	..	..	..	..	..	..	..	..	..	..	..	..
..	..	..	..	..	..	..	..	..	..	..	..	..	0.01	..	..	0.03	0.03	..	..
..	..	..	..	..	0.00	..	..	..	..	..	..	0.00	..	..	..	..	0.09	..	0.00
..	..	..	..	..	..	..	..	..	..	..	..	..	..	..	..	0.00	..	..	..
..	..	..	..	..	..	..	..	..	..	..	..	..	..	..	..	..	..	..	..
..	..	..	..	..	..	..	..	..	..	..	..	..	0.00	..	..	..	..	..	..
..	..	..	..	..	..	..	..	..	..	..	..	..	..	..	..	0.00	0.06	..	..
0.03	0.00	0.21	0.03	0.00	0.00	0.00	..	..	..	0.10	0.00	..	0.08	0.03	0.77	0.05	..	..	..
0.08	..	0.20	0.05	..	..	0.00	0.69	..	0.00	0.03	0.04	0.01	0.26	0.02	0.04	0.00	..	0.00	..
..	..	..	..	..	..	..	..	..	..	..	..	..	..	..	..	..	0.00	..	..
..	..	..	..	..	..	..	..	0.00	..	..	..	..	0.00	..	..	0.00	..	..	..
..	..	..	..	..	..	..	..	..	..	..	..	..	..	..	..	0.01	..	..	..
..	..	..	..	..	..	..	..	..	..	..	..	..	0.01	..	..	0.02	0.39	..	..
0.03	0.48	0.21	0.03	0.00	0.12	0.02	0.00	3.38	1.65	0.10	0.02	0.43	1.50	2.32	0.77	1.05	6.69	12.72	0.28
77.35	57.45	58.72	70.56	81.55	57.24	23.80	58.54	58.74	60.79	80.40	67.18	38.92	64.19	46.05	73.48	58.27	81.33	55.53	56.57
6.93	9.95	17.94	10.33	3.43	5.89	3.13	0.86	3.61	8.17	7.15	4.18	15.90	12.42	11.90	4.77	8.72	0.07	1.32	13.83
15.70	32.18	23.14	19.06	15.16	36.75	73.06	40.60	34.25	29.39	12.34	28.64	44.77	21.89	39.74	20.98	31.97	11.90	30.43	29.31
100.00	100.00	100.00	100.00	100.00	100.00	100.00	100.00	100.00	100.00	100.00	100.00	100.00	100.00	100.00	100.00	100.00	100.00	100.00	100.00

Note: ** means "not applicable."

(Table continues on the following page.)

5-48. (continued)

Percentage of total imports

STP	SEN	SYC	SLE	SOM	SDN	TZA	TGO	TUN	UGA	ZAR	ZMB	ZWE	SSA	EEC	NNA	ROW	WLD
..	0.03	..	..	..	..	..	..	2.79	0.14	..	0.69	0.42	0.15	0.55	0.30	0.09	0.31
..	4.03	..	..	..	..	..	..	..	..	..	..	0.00	0.10	0.06	0.26	0.02	0.08
..	0.01	..	..	..	..	..	..	..	..	..	..	..	0.01	0.01	0.00	0.00	0.00
..	0.00	..	..	..	..	..	..	0.11	..	..	..	..	0.01	0.01	0.00	0.00	0.00
..	..	..	..	..	..	..	..	0.00	..	..	..	0.03	0.00	0.01	0.00	0.00	0.01
..	0.03	..	..	..	..	..	..	0.05	..	..	..	0.00	0.01	0.07	0.03	0.01	0.04
..	0.00	..	..	..	..	..	..	0.00	..	..	..	..	0.00	0.00	0.00	0.00	0.00
..	..	..	..	..	..	..	..	..	..	..	..	..	0.00	0.01	0.00	0.00	0.00
..	..	..	..	..	..	..	..	0.07	..	..	..	..	0.03	0.01	0.00	0.00	0.01
..	..	..	..	..	..	..	..	..	..	..	..	..	0.00	0.00	0.00	0.00	0.00
..	0.01	..	..	..	..	..	..	0.10	..	..	..	0.01	0.02	0.05	0.08	0.01	0.04
..	4.34	..	..	..	..	..	..	0.44	..	..	..	0.01	0.13	0.20	0.06	0.02	0.10
..	0.00	..	..	0.31	0.00	0.00	..	0.00	0.00	..	0.00	..	0.00	0.00	0.00	0.00	0.00
..	0.00	..	..	0.00	3.69	0.00	0.00	0.36	0.06	0.00	..	0.41	0.13	0.08	0.03	0.11	0.08
..	..	..	..	..	..	..	..	0.01	..	..	..	..	0.00	0.00	0.00	0.00	0.00
..	0.00	..	..	0.00	0.10	0.00	..	0.00	0.06	..	0.00	0.00	0.05	0.02	0.01	0.02	0.02
..	0.07	..	..	..	..	..	..	0.06	..	..	..	0.00	0.01	0.08	0.04	0.01	0.05
..	0.00	..	..	..	..	..	..	..	..	..	..	..	0.00	0.00	0.00	0.00	0.00
..	0.00	..	..	..	..	..	..	..	..	..	..	..	0.00	0.05	0.05	0.02	0.04
..	0.00	..	..	..	..	..	..	..	..	..	..	..	0.06	0.03	0.03	0.00	0.02
..	0.01	..	..	..	..	..	..	..	..	..	..	..	0.00	0.00	0.00	0.00	0.00
..	..	0.95	0.00	3.46	1.67	2.96	0.20	0.00	24.35	0.95	1.08	1.11	0.58	0.05	0.01	0.02	0.04
..	0.02	..	..	..	..	..	..	0.00	..	..	..	..	0.01	0.07	0.02	0.02	0.04
..	..	..	..	..	5.40	..	..	0.41	..	..	..	..	0.16	0.58	0.00	0.08	0.26
..	0.01	0.08	..	..	..	..	..	0.02	..	..	..	..	0.02	0.02	0.01	0.01	0.01
..	0.01	..	0.14	..	0.00	0.10	..	0.00	0.00	0.28	0.26	0.50	0.12	0.01	0.01	0.01	0.01
..	0.10	..	..	..	..	..	..	0.07	..	..	..	0.00	0.00	0.01	0.00	0.00	0.00
..	0.12	..	..	..	..	..	..	..	..	..	..	0.00	0.02	0.02	0.00	0.02	0.02
..	..	0.79	..	..	..	..	..	..	..	..	..	..	0.07	0.08	0.03	0.01	0.04
..	0.85	..	0.07	..	0.00	0.13	0.60	1.51	..	0.41	..	0.00	0.23	0.20	0.02	0.13	0.14
..	0.00	..	..	..	..	..	..	..	..	..	..	0.04	0.01	0.01	0.00	0.02	0.01
..	0.00	..	..	..	..	..	..	..	..	..	..	0.00	0.03	0.04	0.00	0.00	0.02
..	2.74	..	..	..	..	..	..	..	..	..	..	0.00	0.08	0.35	0.72	0.06	0.30
0.00	..	0.71	..	..	..	..	..	..	..	..	..	..	0.04	0.01	0.00	0.00	0.01
..	..	..	..	0.00	..	0.00	..	0.00	0.06	0.14	0.00	..	0.01	0.00	0.00	0.01	0.00
..	..	11.44	..	..	..	..	..	0.00	..	..	..	30.93	0.80	0.63	0.36	0.43	0.50
**	..	..	..	..	..	..	..	..	..	..	..	..	..	0.00	0.00	0.00	0.00
..	**	..	..	..	..	..	..	0.13	..	..	..	..	0.05	0.03	0.00	0.01	0.02
..	..	**	..	..	..	..	..	..	..	..	..	..	0.00	0.00	0.00	0.00	0.00
..	0.00	..	**	..	..	..	..	0.00	..	..	..	..	0.00	0.01	0.01	0.00	0.00
..	..	..	..	**	..	..	..	..	..	..	..	..	..	0.00	0.00	0.01	0.00
..	..	..	..	..	**	..	..	0.07	..	..	..	0.00	0.00	0.02	0.00	0.03	0.02
..	..	0.00	..	..	..	**	..	0.07	..	..	..	0.02	0.00	0.02	0.00	0.01	0.01
..	0.02	..	..	..	..	..	**	0.05	..	0.00	..	..	0.05	0.01	0.01	0.01	0.01
..	0.18	..	0.07	..	0.00	0.01	0.16	**	0.03	0.00	1.10	0.00	0.05	0.18	0.01	0.05	0.09
..	..	..	..	..	..	..	..	0.00	**	..	..	0.00	0.00	0.02	0.01	0.00	0.01
..	0.00	..	..	..	..	..	..	0.01	..	**	..	0.03	0.00	0.08	0.05	0.01	0.04
..	..	0.00	..	..	..	..	..	..	..	..	**	3.99	0.08	0.04	0.01	0.07	0.04
..	0.12	0.08	..	..	..	..	..	0.01	..	..	..	**	0.03	0.05	0.03	0.04	0.04
0.00	11.63	14.06	0.14	3.73	1.78	3.07	0.20	1.28	24.43	1.38	1.34	36.71	2.43	2.20	1.86	0.87	1.60
54.52	63.34	36.62	60.92	60.89	43.15	53.01	60.60	73.13	43.80	67.58	60.99	37.05	57.42	62.23	18.68	29.16	40.29
34.64	7.81	1.91	12.20	12.17	8.94	5.85	4.60	7.36	4.90	11.90	7.80	5.84	9.46	7.98	29.33	17.80	16.15
10.84	17.21	47.42	26.81	23.17	46.14	38.07	34.58	18.23	26.88	19.15	29.86	20.40	30.69	27.59	50.12	52.17	41.96
100.00	100.00	100.00	100.00	100.00	100.00	100.00	100.00	100.00	100.00	100.00	100.00	100.00	100.00	100.00	100.00	100.00	100.00

Note: ** means "not applicable."

5-49. Direction of trade matrix, imports, 1993

Importers — *Percentage of total imports*

Exporters		DZA	AGO	BEN	BFA	BDI	CMR	CPV	CAF	TCD	COM	COG	CIV	DJI	EGY	GNQ	ETH
Algeria	DZA	**	..	..	..	..	0.00	..	..	..	..	0.00	..	..	0.11	..	..
Angola	AGO	..	**	..	..	..	..	..	..	..	..	..	..	..	..	..	..
Benin	BEN	..	..	**	..	..	..	..	..	..	..	..	..	..	..	..	..
Burkina Faso	BFA	..	..	..	**	..	..	..	..	..	..	..	..	..	..	..	..
Burundi	BDI	..	..	..	..	**	..	..	..	..	..	..	..	..	..	..	..
Cameroon	CMR	..	..	..	..	..	**	..	..	..	..	..	..	..	..	..	..
Cape Verde	CPV	..	..	..	..	..	..	**	..	..	..	..	..	..	..	..	..
Central African Republic	CAF	..	..	..	..	..	..	..	**	..	..	..	..	..	..	..	..
Chad	TCD	..	..	..	..	..	..	..	..	**	..	..	..	..	..	..	..
Comoros	COM	..	..	..	..	..	..	..	..	..	**	..	..	..	..	..	..
Congo	COG	..	0.83	0.00	..	..	0.00	..	0.00	..	..	**	0.00	..	..	..	..
Côte d'Ivoire	CIV	..	..	..	..	..	..	..	..	..	..	..	**	..	..	..	..
Djibouti	DJI	..	..	..	..	..	..	..	..	..	..	..	..	**	..	..	..
Egypt, Arab Rep.	EGY	0.35	0.05	0.00	0.00	0.00	0.01	..	0.00	0.11	..	0.00	0.05	0.67	**	0.00	0.22
Equatorial Guinea	GNQ	..	..	..	..	..	..	..	..	..	..	..	..	..	..	**	..
Ethiopia	ETH	..	..	..	..	0.00	..	..	..	0.11	..	..	..	7.12	0.00	..	**
Gabon	GAB	0.00	0.06	0.15	..	..	0.14	..	0.00	..	..	0.00	0.11	..	0.00	0.00	..
Gambia, The	GMB	..	..	..	..	..	..	..	..	..	..	..	..	..	..	..	..
Ghana	GHA	..	..	..	..	..	..	..	..	..	..	..	..	..	..	..	..
Guinea	GIN	..	..	..	..	..	..	..	..	..	..	..	..	..	..	..	..
Guinea-Bissau	GNB	..	..	..	..	..	..	..	..	..	..	..	..	..	..	..	..
Kenya	KEN	0.00	0.00	0.00	0.04	5.43	0.01	..	0.00	..	4.24	0.00	0.01	1.00	0.46	0.00	3.15
Liberia	LBR	..	..	..	..	..	..	..	..	..	..	..	..	..	..	..	..
Libya	LBY	..	..	..	..	..	..	..	..	..	..	..	..	..	..	..	..
Madagascar	MDG	..	0.00	0.00	0.00	0.00	0.00	..	0.00	..	1.20	0.00	0.01	0.00	0.00	..	0.00
Malawi	MWI	..	..	..	..	..	..	..	..	..	..	..	..	..	..	..	..
Mali	MLI	..	..	..	..	..	..	..	..	..	..	..	..	..	..	..	..
Mauritania	MRT	..	..	..	..	..	..	..	..	..	..	..	..	..	..	..	..
Mauritius	MUS	0.00	..	..	..	0.43	0.00	..	..	..	1.68	0.00	0.00	0.00	0.00	..	..
Morocco	MAR	1.11	0.08	0.18	0.25	0.07	0.38	..	0.38	..	0.48	1.26	0.52	0.00	0.02	0.21	..
Mozambique	MOZ	..	..	..	..	..	..	..	..	..	..	..	..	..	..	..	..
Niger	NER	..	..	..	..	..	..	..	..	..	..	..	..	..	..	..	..
Nigeria	NGA	..	..	..	..	..	..	..	..	..	..	..	..	..	..	..	..
Reunion	REU	..	..	..	..	..	0.00	..	..	..	8.01	..	..	0.03	..	..	0.00
Rwanda	RWA	..	..	..	..	..	..	..	..	..	..	..	..	..	..	..	..
South Africa	ZAF	0.00	6.53	0.41	0.50	2.90	1.55	0.91	0.25	0.00	9.05	2.73	2.14	0.03	0.12	2.91	0.13
São Tomé and Principe	STP	..	..	..	..	..	..	..	..	..	..	..	..	..	..	..	..
Senegal	SEN	0.01	0.01	1.68	1.59	0.00	0.90	0.07	1.51	1.68	..	1.07	0.96	0.00	..	0.00	0.65
Seychelles	SYC	..	..	..	..	..	..	..	..	..	..	..	..	..	..	..	..
Sierra Leone	SLE	..	..	..	..	..	..	..	..	..	..	..	..	..	..	..	..
Somalia	SOM	..	..	..	..	..	..	..	..	..	..	..	..	..	..	..	..
Sudan	SDN	..	..	..	..	..	..	..	..	..	..	..	..	..	..	..	..
Tanzania	TZA	..	..	..	..	..	..	..	..	..	..	..	..	..	..	..	..
Togo	TGO	..	..	..	..	..	..	..	..	..	..	..	..	..	..	..	..
Tunisia	TUN	0.95	0.00	0.33	0.17	..	0.96	..	0.13	0.34	..	0.00	0.31	0.03	0.06	0.00	0.00
Uganda	UGA	..	..	..	..	..	..	..	..	..	..	..	..	..	..	..	..
Zaire	ZAR	..	..	..	..	..	..	..	..	..	..	..	..	..	..	..	..
Zambia	ZMB	..	..	..	..	..	..	..	..	..	..	..	..	..	..	..	..
Zimbabwe	ZWE	0.07	0.26	0.00	..	1.16	0.00	0.00	..	..	..	0.00	0.00	0.00	0.17	..	0.03
Sub-Saharan Africa	SSA	0.08	7.68	2.26	2.09	9.99	2.61	0.98	1.77	1.68	24.18	3.80	3.22	8.21	0.76	3.12	3.96
European Community	EEC	67.28	66.01	55.21	71.36	63.00	71.96	76.49	75.79	80.52	65.89	72.24	70.67	45.66	42.81	83.58	52.77
North America	NNA	15.35	13.62	3.88	8.10	1.88	7.47	2.87	6.68	8.62	0.32	5.10	6.52	3.90	23.79	7.28	16.18
Rest Of World	ROW	17.29	12.68	38.65	18.46	25.20	17.96	19.66	15.76	9.07	9.69	18.84	19.59	42.23	32.64	6.03	27.09
World	WLD	100.00	100.00	100.00	100.00	100.00	100.00	100.00	100.00	100.00	100.00	100.00	100.00	100.00	100.00	100.00	100.00

Note: ** means "not applicable."

(Table continues on the following page.)

5-49. (continued)

Percentage of total imports

GAB	GMB	GHA	GIN	GNB	KEN	LBR	LBY	MDG	MWI	MLI	MRT	MUS	MAR	MOZ	NER	NGA	REU	RWA	ZAF
..	..	..	..	..	..	0.22	0.05	..	..	0.00	6.79	..	1.11	..	0.00	..	..	..	..
..	..	..	..	..	..	..	..	..	..	..	..	..	..	..	..	..	..	..	..
..	..	..	..	..	..	..	..	..	..	..	..	..	..	..	..	..	..	..	..
..	..	..	..	..	..	..	..	..	..	..	..	..	..	..	..	..	..	..	..
..	..	..	..	..	..	..	..	..	..	..	..	..	..	..	..	..	..	..	..
..	..	..	..	..	..	..	..	..	..	..	..	..	..	..	..	..	..	..	..
..	..	..	..	..	..	..	..	..	..	..	..	..	..	..	..	..	..	..	..
..	..	..	..	..	..	..	..	..	..	..	..	..	..	..	..	..	..	..	..
..	..	..	..	..	..	..	..	..	..	..	..	..	..	..	..	..	..	..	..
..	..	..	..	..	..	..	..	..	..	..	..	..	..	..	..	..	..	..	..
0.01	..	..	0.06	..	..	..	..	..	..	0.00	..	0.02	0.01	..	0.00	0.00	0.28	..	0.00
..	..	..	..	..	..	..	..	..	..	..	..	..	..	..	..	..	..	..	..
..	..	..	..	..	..	..	..	..	..	..	..	..	..	..	..	..	..	..	..
0.00	0.00	0.04	0.06	0.00	0.01	0.00	1.27	0.05	0.00	0.09	0.02	0.00	0.16	0.08	0.00	0.05	..	0.21	0.02
..	..	..	..	..	..	..	..	..	..	..	..	..	..	..	..	..	..	..	..
0.00	..	0.00	..	..	0.00	..	..	..	..	..	..	..	..	..	..	0.00	..	..	0.00
**	0.11	..	1.13	..	..	0.01	..	0.02	..	0.00	0.07	..	0.23	0.51	0.04	0.01	..	..	0.00
..	**	..	..	..	..	..	..	..	..	..	..	..	..	..	..	..	..	..	..
..	..	**	..	..	..	..	..	..	..	..	..	..	..	..	..	..	..	..	..
..	..	..	**	..	..	..	..	..	..	..	..	..	..	..	..	..	..	..	..
..	..	..	..	**	..	..	..	..	..	..	..	..	..	..	..	..	..	..	..
0.00	0.00	0.03	0.00	0.00	**	0.00	0.00	0.12	0.54	0.03	0.13	0.74	0.00	0.06	0.00	0.04	0.12	12.20	0.05
..	..	..	..	..	..	**	..	..	..	..	..	..	..	..	..	..	..	..	..
..	..	..	..	..	..	..	**	..	..	..	..	..	..	..	..	..	..	..	..
0.00	..	0.00	0.00	..	0.04	..	0.00	**	0.00	..	0.00	0.74	0.00	0.00	0.00	0.00	0.98	0.00	0.01
..	..	..	..	..	..	..	..	..	**	..	..	..	..	..	..	..	..	..	..
..	..	..	..	..	..	..	..	..	..	**	..	..	..	..	..	..	..	..	..
..	..	..	..	..	..	..	..	..	..	..	**	..	..	..	..	..	..	..	..
0.00	..	0.00	..	..	0.27	..	..	6.86	0.15	..	..	**	0.00	0.57	0.00	0.00	1.85	0.68	0.05
1.26	0.29	0.13	1.29	..	..	0.87	2.79	0.07	0.03	1.63	1.50	0.11	**	0.00	0.22	0.14	0.11	..	0.00
..	..	..	..	..	..	..	..	..	..	..	..	..	..	**	..	..	..	..	..
..	..	..	..	..	..	..	..	..	..	..	..	..	..	..	**	..	..	..	..
..	..	..	..	..	..	..	..	..	..	..	..	..	..	..	..	**	..	..	..
..	..	..	..	..	..	..	..	1.16	..	..	..	0.31	0.00	..	..	..	**	..	0.00
..	..	..	..	..	..	..	..	..	..	..	..	..	..	..	..	..	..	**	..
0.92	0.15	1.09	0.12	..	4.44	0.02	..	4.34	46.66	0.51	0.02	11.00	0.11	35.30	0.09	0.20	3.52	0.73	**
..	..	..	..	..	..	..	..	..	..	..	..	..	..	..	..	..	..	..	..
0.56	4.57	0.03	2.42	2.00	0.04	0.02	..	0.02	..	9.30	2.69	0.00	0.07	..	0.13	0.06	..	..	0.00
..	..	..	..	..	0.00	..	..	0.00	..	..	..	0.01	..	..	..	..	0.08	..	0.00
..	..	..	..	..	..	..	..	..	..	..	..	..	..	..	..	..	..	..	..
..	..	..	..	..	..	..	..	..	..	..	..	..	..	..	..	..	..	..	..
..	..	..	..	..	..	..	..	..	..	..	..	..	..	..	..	..	..	..	..
..	..	..	..	..	..	..	..	..	..	..	..	..	..	..	..	..	..	..	..
..	..	..	..	..	..	..	..	..	..	..	..	..	..	..	..	..	..	..	..
0.10	0.11	0.19	0.39	0.06	..	..	3.84	0.00	..	0.03	0.09	..	0.55	..	0.04	0.00	0.01	0.00	..
..	..	..	..	..	..	..	..	..	..	..	..	..	..	..	..	..	..	..	..
..	..	..	..	..	..	..	..	..	..	..	..	..	..	..	..	..	..	..	..
..	..	..	..	..	..	..	..	..	..	..	..	..	..	..	..	..	..	..	..
..	0.00	0.14	0.00	..	0.87	..	0.01	0.30	11.00	0.03	0.00	0.36	0.00	6.45	0.00	0.01	0.01	0.37	1.86
1.48	4.82	1.29	3.73	2.00	5.66	0.05	0.01	12.82	58.36	9.87	2.91	13.17	0.42	42.92	0.31	0.32	6.85	14.03	1.99
74.53	48.69	52.85	64.84	31.38	45.59	15.83	65.17	53.65	22.16	64.90	67.00	38.20	73.32	27.32	74.88	51.83	85.34	59.11	47.16
7.99	3.70	16.51	12.19	1.16	8.89	0.44	1.42	2.67	4.20	11.03	7.77	1.31	10.53	7.80	7.14	14.56	0.10	5.34	16.16
15.99	42.82	29.34	19.21	65.40	39.85	83.68	33.39	30.86	15.28	14.21	22.33	47.32	15.73	21.96	17.72	33.28	7.70	21.52	34.69
100.00	100.00	100.00	100.00	100.00	100.00	100.00	100.00	100.00	100.00	100.00	100.00	100.00	100.00	100.00	100.00	100.00	100.00	100.00	100.00

Note: ** means "not applicable."

(Table continues on the following page.)

5-49. (continued)

Percentage of total imports

STP	SEN	SYC	SLE	SOM	SDN	TZA	TGO	TUN	UGA	ZAR	ZMB	ZWE	SSA	EEC	NNA	ROW	WLD
0.00	0.01	..	..	..	..	..	0.00	1.20	0.26	..	..	..	0.09	0.58	0.26	0.08	0.29
..	..	..	..	..	..	..	..	..	..	..	..	..	..	..	..	..	..
..	..	..	..	..	..	..	..	..	..	..	..	..	..	..	..	..	..
..	..	..	..	..	..	..	..	..	..	..	..	..	..	..	..	..	..
..	..	..	..	..	..	..	..	..	..	..	..	..	..	..	..	..	..
..	..	..	..	..	..	..	..	..	..	..	..	..	..	..	..	..	..
..	..	..	..	..	..	..	..	..	..	..	..	..	..	..	..	..	..
..	..	..	..	..	..	..	..	..	..	..	..	..	..	..	..	..	..
..	..	..	..	..	..	..	..	..	..	..	..	..	..	..	..	..	..
..	..	..	..	..	..	..	..	..	..	..	..	..	..	..	..	..	..
..	0.00	..	..	..	..	0.01	0.00	0.00	..	0.19	..	0.01	0.03	0.03	0.07	0.01	0.03
..	..	..	..	..	..	..	..	..	..	..	..	..	..	..	..	..	..
..	..	..	..	..	..	..	..	..	..	..	..	..	..	..	..	..	..
0.00	0.03	..	0.05	0.00	4.03	0.05	0.00	0.39	0.05	0.05	0.01	0.00	0.09	0.10	0.06	0.09	0.09
..	..	..	..	..	..	..	..	..	..	..	..	..	..	..	..	..	..
..	..	..	..	..	0.35	0.00	..	..	0.00	0.00	0.00	0.00	0.05	0.01	0.00	0.00	0.01
..	1.68	..	0.22	..	..	..	0.54	0.00	..	1.66	..	..	0.09	0.05	0.21	0.03	0.08
..	..	..	..	..	..	..	..	..	..	..	..	..	..	..	..	..	..
..	..	..	..	..	..	..	..	..	..	..	..	..	..	..	..	..	..
..	..	..	..	..	..	..	..	..	..	..	..	..	..	..	..	..	..
..	..	..	..	..	..	..	..	..	..	..	..	..	..	..	..	..	..
..	0.00	0.96	0.05	22.30	3.86	8.42	0.03	0.00	29.70	1.74	0.29	0.28	0.78	0.04	0.01	0.03	0.04
..	..	..	..	..	..	..	..	..	..	..	..	..	..	..	..	..	..
..	..	..	..	..	..	..	..	..	..	..	..	..	..	..	..	..	..
..	0.00	0.26	..	..	0.00	0.01	0.00	0.03	..	0.02	0.00	0.00	0.06	0.01	0.00	0.00	0.01
..	..	..	..	..	..	..	..	..	..	..	..	..	..	..	..	..	..
..	..	..	..	..	..	..	..	..	..	..	..	..	..	..	..	..	..
..	..	..	..	..	..	..	..	..	..	..	..	..	..	..	..	..	..
0.00	0.01	1.40	..	..	0.00	0.20	0.03	0.00	0.21	0.02	0.13	0.38	0.19	0.09	0.04	0.00	0.04
..	0.46	0.04	0.38	0.00	0.00	..	0.37	0.76	0.00	0.71	0.00	0.01	0.24	0.19	0.02	0.07	0.11
..	..	..	..	..	..	..	..	..	..	..	..	..	..	..	..	..	..
..	..	..	..	..	..	..	..	..	..	..	..	..	..	..	..	..	..
..	..	..	..	..	..	..	..	..	..	..	..	..	..	..	..	..	..
..	..	0.09	..	..	..	..	..	..	..	..	..	..	0.04	0.01	0.00	0.00	0.01
..	..	..	..	..	..	..	..	..	..	..	..	..	..	..	..	..	..
6.87	0.09	10.47	0.82	0.28	1.27	1.68	1.24	0.01	0.72	16.52	41.71	53.57	4.58	0.36	0.23	1.05	0.70
**	..	..	..	..	..	..	..	..	..	..	..	..	..	..	..	..	..
0.00	**	..	1.15	..	..	0.00	0.45	0.02	0.00	0.05	0.00	..	0.27	0.02	0.00	0.01	0.02
..	..	**	..	..	..	..	..	0.00	..	..	..	..	0.00	0.00	0.00	0.00	0.00
..	..	..	**	..	..	..	..	..	..	..	..	..	..	..	..	..	..
..	..	..	..	**	..	..	..	..	..	..	..	..	..	..	..	..	..
..	..	..	..	..	**	..	..	..	..	..	..	..	..	..	..	..	..
..	..	..	..	..	..	**	..	..	..	..	..	..	..	..	..	..	..
..	..	..	..	..	..	..	**	..	..	..	..	..	..	..	..	..	..
..	0.25	0.00	..	..	0.20	..	0.03	**	..	0.02	..	..	0.05	0.25	0.00	0.05	0.11
..	..	..	..	..	..	..	..	..	**	..	..	..	..	..	..	..	..
..	..	..	..	..	..	..	..	..	..	**	..	..	..	..	..	..	..
..	..	..	..	..	..	..	..	..	..	..	**	..	..	..	..	..	..
0.76	0.00	0.13	0.00	0.00	0.19	0.46	0.00	0.00	0.72	0.67	6.98	**	0.95	0.03	0.01	0.02	0.04
7.63	1.78	13.30	2.24	22.58	5.68	10.77	2.29	0.07	31.35	20.86	49.11	54.24	7.06	0.66	0.59	1.17	0.96
70.48	67.73	28.22	55.79	32.04	42.64	39.12	37.13	81.37	34.43	52.21	23.05	24.80	47.67	62.83	16.09	29.24	38.75
6.62	8.68	28.65	11.90	18.71	7.58	3.69	3.61	4.74	6.59	6.81	7.74	6.44	10.25	8.24	31.00	18.06	17.03
15.52	21.82	29.87	30.08	26.67	44.10	46.41	56.97	13.82	27.63	20.12	20.10	14.52	35.01	28.28	52.31	51.53	43.25
100.00	100.00	100.00	100.00	100.00	100.00	100.00	100.00	100.00	100.00	100.00	100.00	100.00	100.00	100.00	100.00	100.00	100.00

Note: ** means "not applicable."

5-50. Direction of trade matrix, exports, 1984

Importers — *Percentage of total exports*

Exporters		DZA	AGO	BEN	BFA	BDI	CMR	CPV	CAF	TCD	COM	COG	CIV	DJI	EGY	GNQ	ETH
Algeria	DZA	**	..	0.12	0.05	..	..	..	..	..	..	..	0.02	0.01	0.02	..	..
Angola	AGO	..	**	..	..	..	..	..	..	..	..	..	..	..	..	..	..
Benin	BEN	..	..	**	0.09	..	0.00	..	..	..	..	..	0.09	..	..	..	..
Burkina Faso	BFA	..	..	0.55	**	..	..	..	..	..	..	..	1.84	..	..	..	..
Burundi	BDI	..	..	..	..	**	0.00	..	..	..	..	..	0.00	..	..	..	0.00
Cameroon	CMR	..	..	0.08	0.01	..	**	..	1.31	1.11	..	1.05	0.54	..	0.02	0.08	..
Cape Verde	CPV	23.08	0.00	3.85	..	..	..	**	3.85	..	..	..	19.23	..	..	..	..
Central African Republic	CAF	..	..	..	..	..	0.35	..	**	..	..	..	0.12	..	0.00	..	..
Chad	TCD	..	..	..	..	..	10.91	..	..	**	..	..	..	..	..	..	..
Comoros	COM	..	..	0.78	..	..	..	..	..		**	..	..	..	..	..	..
Congo	COG	0.02	1.18	0.00	..	..	0.00	..	0.00	0.10	..	**	0.02	..	0.00	..	..
Côte d'Ivoire	CIV	..	..	0.17	2.65	..	0.25	..	..	..	..	..	**	..	0.05	..	0.00
Djibouti	DJI	..	..	..	..	..	..	..	..	..	..	..	..	**	..	..	..
Egypt, Arab Rep.	EGY	0.03	..	..	..	..	0.00	..	0.00	..	..	..	..	0.00	**	..	0.02
Equatorial Guinea	GNQ	..	..	..	..	..	0.00	..	..	..	..	..	..	..	..	**	..
Ethiopia	ETH	0.31	..	..	..	..	0.07	..	..	..	..	..	0.00	6.94	0.00	..	**
Gabon	GAB	..	..	0.02	..	..	0.42	..	..	..	..	..	2.17	..	..	..	..
Gambia, The	GMB	..	..	..	..	..	..	..	..	..	..	..	..	..	..	..	..
Ghana	GHA	..	..	1.12	0.33	..	..	..	..	..	..	..	0.07	..	0.55	..	..
Guinea	GIN	..	..	..	0.00	..	3.72	..	..	..	..	..	0.00	..	..	..	..
Guinea-Bissau	GNB	..	..	..	..	..	..	..	..	..	..	..	0.85	..	0.00	..	..
Kenya	KEN	0.08	0.03	0.00	0.00	1.97	0.01	..	0.00	..	0.26	0.00	0.29	0.25	2.50	..	0.33
Liberia	LBR	..	..	0.00	..	..	0.02	..	..	..	..	..	0.02	..	0.00	..	..
Libya	LBY	..	..	..	..	..	..	..	..	..	..	..	..	..	..	..	..
Madagascar	MDG	0.00	..	..	..	0.00	0.00	..	..	..	0.09	0.00	..	0.00	..	..	..
Malawi	MWI	..	..	0.10	..	0.33	0.17	..	0.10	0.03	..	0.03	0.00	..	0.36	..	0.03
Mali	MLI	..	..	..	1.05	..	0.00	..	..	..	..	..	2.04	..	..	..	..
Mauritania	MRT	..	..	..	..	..	0.00	..	..	..	..	..	17.32	..	..	..	..
Mauritius	MUS	..	..	..	..	..	..	..	..	..	..	..	..	..	..	..	..
Morocco	MAR	0.02	0.01	0.03	0.00	..	0.24	..	0.00	..	0.00	0.19	0.23	0.00	0.14	0.01	..
Mozambique	MOZ	..	..	..	..	..	..	..	..	..	..	..	0.35	..	..	..	..
Niger	NER	..	..	0.29	0.20	..	0.00	..	..	..	..	..	0.10	..	..	..	..
Nigeria	NGA	..	..	0.09	0.01	..	0.02	..	..	..	..	..	0.74	..	0.00	..	0.00
Reunion	REU	..	..	..	..	0.00	..	..	..	..	4.40	0.00	..	0.00	..	..	..
Rwanda	RWA	..	..	..	..	..	..	..	..	..	..	..	0.00	..	..	..	..
South Africa	ZAF	..	..	..	..	..	..	..	..	..	..	..	..	..	..	..	..
São Tomé and Principe	STP	..	..	..	..	..	..	..	..	..	..	..	..	..	..	..	..
Senegal	SEN	..	..	1.38	0.97	..	0.78	..	..	..	..	..	7.72	..	0.00	..	0.00
Seychelles	SYC	..	..	..	..	..	..	..	..	..	..	..	..	6.25	..	..	..
Sierra Leone	SLE	..	..	..	..	..	..	..	..	..	..	..	0.47	..	..	..	..
Somalia	SOM	..	..	..	..	..	..	..	..	..	..	..	..	..	0.00	..	..
Sudan	SDN	..	..	..	..	..	..	..	..	..	..	..	..	..	14.82	..	0.04
Tanzania	TZA	..	..	..	..	..	0.00	..	..	..	..	..	0.29	..	1.01	..	0.11
Togo	TGO	..	..	1.31	1.86	..	0.05	..	0.00	0.00	..	0.05	2.17	..	..	..	..
Tunisia	TUN	2.37	..	0.00	0.00	..	0.00	..	..	0.02	..	0.00	0.02	..	0.62	..	..
Uganda	UGA	..	..	..	..	..	..	..	..	..	..	..	..	..	0.10	..	..
Zaire	ZAR	..	..	0.03	..	..	0.00	..	..	..	..	..	0.03	..	0.59	..	..
Zambia	ZMB	..	..	..	..	..	..	..	..	..	..	..	0.12	..	0.05	..	..
Zimbabwe	ZWE	0.22	0.89	..	..	0.09	0.01	0.01	0.03	..	0.03	0.03	0.09	..	0.90	..	0.41
Sub-Saharan Africa	SSA	0.01	0.05	0.07	0.17	0.04	0.11	0.00	0.02	0.02	0.01	0.02	0.53	0.07	0.33	0.00	0.02
European Community	EEC	0.97	0.10	0.02	0.02	0.01	0.15	0.01	0.01	0.01	0.00	0.06	0.13	0.02	0.86	0.00	0.06
North America	NNA	0.26	0.03	0.00	0.01	0.00	0.03	..	0.00	0.00	0.01	0.00	0.03	0.00	0.82	0.00	0.07
Rest Of World	ROW	0.26	0.03	0.02	0.00	0.00	0.03	0.00	0.00	0.00	0.00	0.01	0.03	0.01	0.55	0.00	0.03
World	WLD	0.50	0.05	0.02	0.01	0.01	0.07	0.00	0.00	0.01	0.00	0.03	0.08	0.01	0.70	0.00	0.04

Note: ** means "not applicable."

(Table continues on the following page.)

5-50. (continued)

Percentage of total exports

GAB	GMB	GHA	GIN	GNB	KEN	LBR	LBY	MDG	MWI	MLI	MRT	MUS	MAR	MOZ	NER	NGA	REU	RWA	ZAF
..	0.01	..	..	..	0.06	0.01	0.00	..	..	0.00	..	..	..	0.21	0.00	..	..	..	..
..	..	..	..	..	..	..	..	..	..	..	..	..	0.00	..	..	..	..	..	..
..	..	..	..	..	..	0.00	..	..	..	..	..	..	..	..	..	..	..	..	..
..	..	..	..	..	..	..	..	..	..	..	..	..	0.37	..	..	..	..	..	..
..	..	..	..	..	3.86	..	..	..	..	..	..	..	..	..	..	..	..	3.76	..
1.36	..	..	0.02	..	0.00	0.01	..	..	..	..	0.01	..	0.11	..	0.01	2.22	0.01	0.00	..
..	..	..	..	0.00	..	0.00	..	..	..	..	..	..	..	..	..	..	..	..	..
..	..	..	..	..	..	..	..	..	..	..	..	..	0.47	..	..	..	..	..	..
..	..	..	..	..	..	0.00	..	..	..	..	..	..	..	..	..	..	..	..	..
..	..	..	..	..	..	0.00	..	0.78	..	..	..	2.34	0.78	..	..	..	0.78	..	..
0.01	..	..	..	..	..	..	..	..	..	..	..	..	0.09	..	..	0.02	0.20	..	0.05
0.12	..	..	..	..	0.00	1.04	..	..	..	..	..	0.01	0.73	..	..	..	0.01	..	..
..	..	..	..	..	..	..	..	..	..	..	..	..	..	..	..	..	..	..	..
..	0.00	0.00	0.00	..	0.00	0.00	0.00	..	..	..	0.00	..	0.06	..	0.00	0.00	..	..	0.00
..	..	..	..	..	..	..	..	..	..	..	..	..	..	..	..	..	..	..	..
..	..	..	..	..	0.17	..	0.00	..	0.00	..	0.00	0.26	..	..	..	0.00	..	..	..
**	..	..	..	..	..	..	..	..	..	..	..	..	0.51	..	..	..	0.00	..	..
..	**	..	..	..	..	0.00	..	..	..	..	..	0.00	..	..	..	..	..	..	..
..	..	**	..	..	0.00	0.02	..	..	..	..	..	0.02	..	..	..	..	..	..	..
..	..	..	**	..	..	0.10	..	..	..	..	..	..	0.02	..	..	..	..	..	..
..	..	..	..	**	..	..	..	..	..	..	..	..	..	..	..	..	..	..	..
0.00	0.00	0.00	0.01	..	**	0.01	0.07	0.26	0.06	..	0.00	0.48	0.01	0.56	0.00	0.01	0.51	3.48	0.15
..	0.00	0.04	0.11	..	..	**	0.00	..	..	0.00	0.02	..	0.00	..	..	2.03	..	..	..
..	..	..	..	..	..	..	**	..	..	..	0.00	..	0.01	..	..	..	..	..	..
0.06	..	..	..	..	0.24	..	..	**	..	..	..	0.41	0.00	0.00	0.00	..	2.65	..	..
0.17	0.63	0.00	0.17	0.00	0.13	0.30	..	..	**	..	..	0.07	..	1.56	..	..	..	..	7.91
0.00	..	..	..	..	..	1.05	0.22	..	..	**	..	..	2.49	..	..	..	..	..	..
..	..	..	..	..	..	0.30	..	..	..	..	**	..	..	..	..	..	..	..	..
..	..	..	..	..	..	..	..	..	..	..	..	**	..	..	..	..	0.49	..	0.15
0.20	0.00	0.00	0.19	..	0.00	0.02	1.78	..	..	0.04	0.02	0.04	**	..	0.00	0.00	0.06	..	0.00
..	..	..	..	..	..	..	..	1.04	..	..	..	..	..	**	..	..	..	..	..
0.00	..	..	..	..	..	..	..	..	..	..	..	..	..	..	**	..	..	..	..
..	..	..	..	..	0.00	0.07	..	..	..	..	..	..	0.00	..	..	**	..	..	..
0.00	..	0.00	..	..	0.00	..	..	3.52	..	..	..	1.01	3.89	..	..	..	**	..	0.13
..	..	..	..	..	3.73	..	..	..	..	..	..	..	..	..	..	..	..	**	..
..	..	..	..	..	..	..	..	..	..	..	..	..	..	..	..	..	..	..	**
..	..	..	..	..	..	0.00	..	..	..	..	..	..	..	..	..	..	..	..	..
0.52	..	..	..	..	0.00	0.07	0.00	..	..	..	..	0.00	0.06	..	..	..	0.19	..	..
..	..	..	..	..	2.73	..	..	0.00	..	..	..	0.39	..	..	..	..	1.95	..	0.39
..	0.14	..	0.00	..	..	1.08	..	..	..	..	..	..	..	..	..	0.00	..	..	..
..	..	..	..	..	0.08	0.00	..	..	..	..	..	..	0.00	..	..	..	..	..	..
..	..	..	..	..	0.00	..	0.04	..	..	..	..	0.00	..	..	..	..	..	..	..
..	..	..	..	..	0.37	..	..	0.58	..	..	..	0.00	..	..	..	..	0.00	..	..
0.05	..	2.32	0.10	..	..	0.05	..	..	..	0.91	..	..	0.65	..	0.81	2.22	..	..	..
0.04	..	0.00	0.01	..	..	..	3.18	..	..	0.00	0.00	..	0.27	..	0.00	0.01	..	..	..
..	..	..	..	..	0.32	..	0.02	..	..	..	..	0.00	0.00	..	..	..	0.00	..	..
0.01	..	..	..	..	0.11	..	..	..	..	..	..	0.00	0.02	..	..	..	..	..	..
..	..	..	..	..	0.21	..	..	..	..	..	..	..	..	..	..	..	..	..	..
0.01	..	0.08	0.00	..	0.09	0.00	0.34	0.00	1.24	..	..	0.17	0.18	0.53	..	0.05	..	0.10	23.35
0.04	0.00	0.01	0.00	0.00	0.03	0.09	0.01	0.02	0.03	0.00	0.00	0.02	0.09	0.03	0.00	0.07	0.04	0.08	0.52
0.09	0.01	0.04	0.03	0.01	0.09	0.10	0.61	0.03	0.01	0.03	0.03	0.02	0.30	0.03	0.02	0.53	0.09	0.01	0.96
0.01	0.00	0.02	0.01	0.01	0.03	0.03	0.09	0.01	0.00	0.01	0.01	0.00	0.18	0.02	0.00	0.21	0.00	0.00	0.82
0.01	0.00	0.01	0.01	0.00	0.07	0.22	0.31	0.02	0.00	0.00	0.01	0.04	0.13	0.03	0.00	0.23	0.02	0.00	0.47
0.04	0.01	0.02	0.02	0.00	0.07	0.14	0.37	0.02	0.01	0.01	0.02	0.03	0.20	0.03	0.01	0.33	0.04	0.01	0.71

Note: ** means "not applicable."

(Table continues on the following page.)

5-50. (continued)

Percentage of total exports

STP	SEN	SYC	SLE	SOM	SDN	TZA	TGO	TUN	UGA	ZAR	ZMB	ZWE	SSA	EEC	NNA	ROW	WLD
..	0.00	0.00	..	..	0.01	0.10	..	0.59	0.02	..	..	..	0.63	69.32	22.42	7.63	100.00
..	..	..	..	..	..	..	..	..	..	..	..	..	..	33.59	53.73	12.68	100.00
..	..	..	..	..	..	..	..	..	..	..	..	..	0.09	94.22	0.26	5.34	100.00
..	..	..	..	..	..	..	..	1.29	..	..	..	..	2.39	65.07	0.18	32.35	100.00
..	..	..	..	..	..	0.69	..	..	0.99	4.36	0.10	..	13.86	54.55	2.18	29.41	100.00
..	0.19	..	..	..	..	..	0.02	0.02	..	0.01	..	..	8.05	64.96	18.49	8.49	100.00
0.00	0.00	..	..	..	..	..	..	..	..	0.00	..	..	26.92	46.15	0.00	23.08	100.00
..	..	..	..	..	..	..	..	..	..	..	..	..	0.47	43.49	2.33	53.72	100.00
..	..	..	..	..	..	..	..	..	..	..	..	..	10.91	78.69	0.10	10.29	100.00
..	..	..	..	..	..	..	..	..	..	..	..	..	4.69	66.41	24.22	4.69	100.00
0.03	0.00	..	..	..	..	..	0.00	0.22	0.00	0.19	..	..	1.80	18.35	77.57	2.27	100.00
..	..	..	0.00	..	..	..	..	0.39	..	..	..	..	4.26	62.54	20.71	12.49	100.00
..	..	..	..	..	..	..	..	..	..	..	..	..	..	..	..	..	..
..	0.00	..	0.00	0.00	0.94	0.00	0.00	0.16	0.00	0.02	..	..	1.00	41.74	5.62	51.64	100.00
..	..	..	..	..	..	..	..	..	..	..	..	..	0.00	93.63	2.55	3.82	100.00
..	0.00	..	..	..	1.20	0.05	0.00	..	0.00	0.00	0.00	0.00	8.71	41.42	19.53	30.36	100.00
..	..	..	0.00	..	..	..	..	..	..	..	..	..	2.62	51.20	37.51	8.67	100.00
..	..	..	0.00	..	..	..	..	..	..	..	..	..	0.00	50.84	1.67	47.26	100.00
..	..	..	0.00	..	..	..	..	..	..	..	..	..	1.57	47.39	12.32	38.75	100.00
..	..	..	0.04	..	..	..	..	..	..	..	..	..	3.87	59.04	29.69	7.41	100.00
..	..	..	..	..	..	..	..	..	..	..	..	..	0.85	83.90	7.63	7.63	100.00
..	0.00	0.15	0.00	0.35	2.39	1.03	0.01	0.61	8.51	1.01	0.10	0.03	22.28	45.94	5.85	25.92	100.00
..	0.00	..	0.22	..	..	..	0.11	..	..	..	..	..	2.61	70.47	20.24	6.68	100.00
..	..	..	..	..	..	0.12	..	0.22	..	..	..	..	0.12	75.98	0.39	23.51	100.00
..	..	0.00	..	0.00	..	0.03	..	0.00	..	..	..	..	3.44	61.78	14.80	19.98	100.00
..	0.00	0.00	0.07	..	0.00	0.23	..	..	0.00	1.62	2.78	3.77	20.22	58.93	8.84	12.01	100.00
..	..	..	..	..	..	..	..	2.49	..	..	..	..	4.14	48.67	0.88	46.30	100.00
..	0.67	..	..	..	..	..	..	..	..	..	..	..	18.33	55.43	0.34	25.90	100.00
..	..	..	..	..	..	..	..	..	..	..	..	..	0.64	73.04	13.11	13.21	100.00
..	0.38	..	0.00	..	0.05	0.01	0.04	0.94	0.00	0.10	..	..	1.88	59.47	1.98	36.67	100.00
..	..	..	..	..	..	..	..	..	..	..	..	..	1.39	37.85	15.86	45.02	100.00
..	..	..	..	..	..	..	..	..	..	..	..	..	0.59	96.71	0.25	2.41	100.00
..	..	..	0.42	..	..	..	..	..	..	..	..	..	1.35	60.49	21.38	16.77	100.00
..	0.00	0.00	..	..	..	..	..	..	..	..	..	..	9.05	82.29	0.50	8.17	100.00
..	..	..	..	..	..	..	..	..	..	..	..	..	3.73	69.76	12.77	13.73	100.00
..	..	..	..	..	..	..	..	..	..	..	..	..	..	20.64	9.43	69.93	100.00
**	..	..	..	..	..	..	..	..	..	..	..	..	0.00	93.02	..	5.81	100.00
..	**	..	0.17	..	..	..	..	..	..	..	..	..	11.79	75.32	0.73	12.16	100.00
..	..	**	..	..	..	0.00	..	..	..	..	..	..	11.72	4.69	7.03	76.56	100.00
..	0.14	..	**	..	..	..	..	..	..	..	..	0.00	1.83	56.09	8.80	33.29	100.00
..	..	..	..	**	..	..	..	..	..	..	..	..	0.08	10.19	0.73	89.08	100.00
..	..	..	..	..	**	..	..	0.49	..	..	..	..	0.04	25.91	2.87	71.18	100.00
..	..	0.00	0.03	..	..	**	..	..	..	..	..	..	1.41	60.69	4.01	33.90	100.00
..	0.00	..	..	..	..	..	**	2.92	..	0.00	..	..	11.93	56.09	0.45	31.47	100.00
..	0.01	..	..	0.00	0.01	..	0.01	**	..	0.01	..	..	0.12	60.31	19.11	20.46	100.00
..	..	..	..	..	..	..	..	..	**	..	..	..	0.32	59.95	24.33	15.40	100.00
..	..	..	..	..	..	..	..	0.00	..	**	..	..	0.18	28.87	32.01	38.92	100.00
..	..	..	..	..	..	..	..	..	..	..	**	..	0.34	34.85	16.89	47.92	100.00
..	0.01	0.05	0.00	0.00	0.22	0.23	0.00	0.05	0.01	1.58	3.32	**	32.62	36.15	6.72	24.50	100.00
0.00	0.01	0.00	0.12	0.01	0.06	0.03	0.00	0.07	0.18	0.08	0.09	0.02	2.72	42.72	18.52	36.04	100.00
0.00	0.08	0.00	0.01	0.03	0.08	0.05	0.04	0.32	0.02	0.10	0.03	0.04	3.19	54.25	10.49	32.07	100.00
..	0.04	0.00	0.01	0.02	0.04	0.02	0.01	0.08	0.00	0.03	0.03	0.02	1.62	17.94	36.80	43.64	100.00
0.00	0.03	0.01	0.00	0.01	0.04	0.04	0.01	0.08	0.01	0.04	0.01	0.03	1.54	23.56	26.32	48.58	100.00
0.00	0.05	0.00	0.01	0.02	0.06	0.04	0.02	0.17	0.01	0.06	0.02	0.03	2.17	34.06	22.29	41.48	100.00

Note: ** means "not applicable."

5-51. Direction of trade matrix, exports, 1988

Exporters		*Importers* DZA	AGO	BEN	BFA	BDI	CMR	CPV	CAF	TCD	COM	COG	CIV	DJI	EGY	GNQ	ETH
		Percentage of total exports															
Algeria	DZA	**	..	0.00	0.00	..	0.00	..	..	..	..	0.01	0.00	..	0.01	..	0.00
Angola	AGO	..	**	..	..	..	0.04	..	..	..	..	..	..	..	..	..	..
Benin	BEN	..	..	**	..	..	0.63	..	..	..	..	..	..	..	0.00	..	..
Burkina Faso	BFA	0.32	..	..	**	..	..	..	..	..	..	..	..	..	..	..	..
Burundi	BDI	..	..	..	..	**	..	..	..	..	..	..	..	..	..	..	..
Cameroon	CMR	0.47	..	..	..	..	**	..	..	..	..	..	..	..	0.17	..	..
Cape Verde	CPV	53.85	..	..	..	..	..	**	..	..	..	..	..	..	..	..	..
Central African Republic	CAF	..	..	..	..	..	0.11	..	**	..	..	..	..	..	..	..	..
Chad	TCD	0.07	..	..	..	..	3.76	..	..	**	..	..	..	..	0.00	..	..
Comoros	COM	..	..	..	..	..	..	..	..	..	**	..	..	..	0.00	..	..
Congo	COG	0.35	..	..	..	..	0.08	..	..	..	..	**	..	..	..	..	..
Côte d'Ivoire	CIV	0.19	..	..	..	..	0.27	..	..	..	..	..	**	..	0.08	..	..
Djibouti	DJI	..	..	0.00	..	0.00	..	..	..	..	0.00	..	0.00	**	0.00	..	2.59
Egypt, Arab Rep.	EGY	0.25	0.00	..	..	0.00	0.04	..	0.00	0.00	..	0.00	0.01	0.00	**	..	0.04
Equatorial Guinea	GNQ	0.00	..	..	..	..	0.00	..	..	..	..	..	..	..	0.00	**	..
Ethiopia	ETH	0.12	..	..	..	0.00	..	..	..	0.00	..	..	..	4.80	0.00	..	**
Gabon	GAB	0.53	..	..	..	..	0.25	..	..	..	..	..	..	..	0.03	..	..
Gambia, The	GMB	..	..	..	..	..	0.00	..	..	..	..	..	..	..	..	..	..
Ghana	GHA	..	..	..	..	..	0.00	..	..	..	..	..	..	..	0.00	..	..
Guinea	GIN	..	..	..	..	..	5.14	..	..	..	..	..	..	..	..	..	..
Guinea-Bissau	GNB	..	..	..	..	..	..	..	..	..	..	..	..	..	..	..	..
Kenya	KEN	0.02	0.11	..	0.00	1.26	0.00	0.06	0.00	..	0.05	0.00	0.07	0.12	1.04	0.00	0.66
Liberia	LBR	..	..	..	..	..	..	..	..	..	..	..	..	..	..	..	..
Libya	LBY	0.20	..	..	..	..	..	..	..	..	..	..	0.00	..	..	..	..
Madagascar	MDG	0.95	..	..	..	..	0.00	..	..	..	..	..	..	..	..	..	..
Malawi	MWI	..	0.00	0.00	..	0.97	0.00	..	..	0.00	..	0.00	0.00	..	0.39	..	0.00
Mali	MLI	23.72	..	..	..	..	0.00	..	..	..	..	..	..	..	..	..	..
Mauritania	MRT	1.76	..	..	..	..	1.54	..	..	..	..	..	..	..	1.45	..	..
Mauritius	MUS	..	..	..	..	..	..	..	..	..	0.10	..	..	..	..	..	..
Morocco	MAR	0.30	0.28	0.03	0.01	..	0.22	..	0.02	0.00	0.01	0.11	0.25	0.00	0.17	0.01	..
Mozambique	MOZ	0.11	..	..	..	..	0.25	..	..	..	..	..	..	..	..	..	..
Niger	NER	0.02	..	..	..	..	..	..	..	..	..	..	..	..	..	..	..
Nigeria	NGA	..	..	..	..	..	0.05	..	..	..	..	..	..	..	0.00	..	..
Reunion	REU	..	..	..	..	..	..	..	..	..	5.25	..	0.00	0.13	..	..	..
Rwanda	RWA	..	..	..	0.00	0.10	..	..	..	..	..	..	..	0.00	..	..	0.00
South Africa	ZAF	0.01	..	..	..	..	0.00	..	..	..	..	..	..	..	0.02	..	..
São Tomé and Principe	STP	..	..	..	..	..	..	..	..	..	..	..	..	..	..	..	..
Senegal	SEN	..	..	..	..	..	4.22	..	..	..	..	..	..	..	0.18	..	..
Seychelles	SYC	..	..	..	..	..	..	..	..	..	0.00	..	..	..	..	..	..
Sierra Leone	SLE	0.78	..	..	..	..	0.17	..	..	..	..	..	..	..	..	..	..
Somalia	SOM	..	..	..	..	..	..	..	..	..	..	..	..	..	1.05	..	..
Sudan	SDN	0.00	..	..	..	..	..	..	..	..	..	..	..	..	26.25	..	..
Tanzania	TZA	3.15	..	..	..	..	..	..	..	..	..	..	..	..	1.05	..	..
Togo	TGO	0.00	0.00	3.51	2.10	..	0.41	..	0.00	0.12	..	0.29	0.17	..	..	0.04	..
Tunisia	TUN	2.48	..	0.05	0.03	..	0.25	0.00	0.00	..	..	0.00	0.13	0.00	0.21	..	..
Uganda	UGA	1.32	..	..	..	..	..	..	..	..	..	..	..	..	0.29	..	..
Zaire	ZAR	0.01	..	..	..	..	0.00	..	..	..	..	..	..	..	1.27	..	..
Zambia	ZMB	..	..	..	..	..	..	..	..	..	..	..	..	..	..	..	..
Zimbabwe	ZWE	..	..	..	..	..	0.28	..	..	..	..	..	..	..	1.53	..	..
Sub-Saharan Africa	SSA	0.18	0.00	0.02	0.01	0.04	0.19	0.00	0.00	0.00	0.02	0.00	0.00	0.05	0.47	0.00	0.02
European Community	EEC	0.40	0.07	0.02	0.02	0.01	0.07	0.01	0.01	0.01	0.00	0.04	0.11	0.01	0.40	0.00	0.06
North America	NNA	0.23	0.02	0.01	0.00	0.00	0.01	0.00	0.00	0.00	0.00	0.01	0.02	0.00	0.51	0.00	0.05
Rest Of World	ROW	0.17	0.04	0.02	0.00	0.00	0.02	0.00	0.00	0.00	0.00	0.01	0.03	0.01	0.30	0.00	0.03
World	WLD	0.27	0.05	0.02	0.01	0.01	0.04	0.00	0.00	0.00	0.00	0.02	0.06	0.01	0.38	0.00	0.05

Note: ** means "not applicable."

(Table continues on the following page.)

5-51. (continued)

Percentage of total exports

GAB	GMB	GHA	GIN	GNB	KEN	LBR	LBY	MDG	MWI	MLI	MRT	MUS	MAR	MOZ	NER	NGA	REU	RWA	ZAF
..	..	..	0.00	..	..	0.00	0.41	..	..	0.02	0.68	..	0.08	..	0.00	..	..	0.00	..
..	..	..	..	..	..	..	..	..	..	..	..	..	..	..	..	0.00	..	..	..
..	..	..	..	..	..	..	..		..	..	..	..	0.18	..	..	3.14	..	..	..
..	..	..	..	..	..	..	..	..	..	..	..	..	1.18	..	..	3.86	..	..	..
..	..	..	..	..	..	..	..	..	..	..	..	..	..	..	..	..	..	..	..
..	..	..	..	..	..	..	..	0.00	..	..	..	..	0.11	..	..	0.26	0.01	..	..
..	..	..	..	..	..	..	..	..	..	..	..	..	..	..	..	..	..	..	..
..	..	..	..	..	..	..	..	..	..	..	..	..	0.22	..	..	..	0.11	..	..
..	..	..	..	..	..	..	..	..	..	..	..	..	3.12	..	..	4.11	..	..	..
..	..	..	..	..	..	..	..	0.00	..	..	..	..	..	..	..	..	0.25	..	..
..	..	..	..	..	..	..	..	..	..	..	..	..	0.98	..	..	..	0.64	..	..
..	..	..	..	..	..	..	..	0.00	..	..	..	..	0.57	..	..	0.13	0.04	..	..
..	..	..	..	..	0.00	..	0.00	0.43	..	..	..	0.00	0.00	..	0.00	0.00	0.43	..	..
0.00	..	0.00	0.00	..	0.03	0.01	0.00	..	0.00	0.00	0.00	0.00	0.16	..	0.00	0.01	..	..	0.00
..	..	..	..	..	..	..	..	..	..	..	..	..	..	..	..	..	..	..	..
..	0.00	0.00	0.00	..	0.12	..	0.00	..	0.00	..	..	0.00	..	..	..	0.00	0.00	0.00	..
**	..	..	..	..	..	..	..	0.01	..	..	..	..	1.30	..	..	0.01	0.03	..	..
..	**	..	..	..	..	..	..	..	..	..	..	..	..	..	..	0.00	..	..	..
..	..	**	..	..	..	..	..	..	..	..	..	..	0.19	..	..	0.04	..	..	..
..	..	..	**	..	..	..	..	..	..	..	..	..	0.00	..	..	..	..	..	..
..	..	..	..	**	..	..	..	..	..	..	..	..	..	..	..	..	..	..	..
0.00	0.00	0.00	0.00	..	**	0.00	0.00	0.08	0.26	0.00	0.00	0.25	0.01	0.99	..	0.15	0.63	2.50	0.19
..	..	..	..	..	..	**	..	..	..	..	..	..	0.06	..	..	0.40	..	..	..
..	..	..	..	..	..	..	**	..	..	..	..	..	0.01	..	..	..	..	..	..
..	..	..	..	..	..	..	..	**	..	..	..	..	0.04	..	..	..	3.54	..	..
..	0.29	0.00	..	..	0.04	0.14	0.00	0.00	**	..	..	0.04	..	1.40	0.00	0.04	..	0.04	10.91
..	..	..	..	..	..	..	..	..	..	**	..	..	7.69	..	..	0.28	..	..	..
..	..	..	..	..	..	..	..	..	..	..	**	..	0.07	..	..	0.00	..	..	..
..	..	..	..	..	0.04	..	..	0.21	..	..	..	**	0.37	..	..	..	2.07	..	0.47
0.17	0.00	0.01	0.20	0.00	0.23	0.03	2.65	0.01	..	0.06	0.09	0.04	**	0.00	0.02	0.35	0.06	..	..
..	..	..	..	..	..	..	..	1.37	..	..	..	..	0.00	**	..	0.00	..	..	..
..	..	..	..	..	..	..	..	..	..	..	..	..	..	..	**	3.52	..	..	..
..	..	..	..	..	..	..	..	..	..	..	..	..	0.02	..	..	**	..	..	..
..	..	..	..	..	..	..	..	2.84	..	..	..	0.82	..	..	..	..	**	..	0.13
0.00	..	0.00	..	..	0.79	0.00	0.00	0.00	..	0.00	..	..	..	..	..	..	0.00	**	0.00
..	..	..	..	..	..	..	..	0.00	..	..	..	..	0.02	..	..	0.00	0.36	..	**
..	..	..	..	..	..	..	..	..	..	..	..	..	..	..	..	..	..	..	..
..	..	..	..	..	..	..	..	..	..	..	..	..	0.12	..	..	0.25	0.12	..	..
..	..	..	..	..	0.00	..	..	..	..	..	..	0.00	..	..	..	..	9.93	..	0.00
..	..	..	..	..	..	..	..	..	..	..	..	..	..	..	..	0.00	..	..	..
..	..	..	..	..	..	..	..	..	..	..	..	..	..	..	..	..	..	..	..
..	..	..	..	..	..	..	..	..	..	..	..	..	0.00	..	..	..	..	..	..
..	..	..	..	..	..	..	..	..	..	..	..	..	..	..	..	0.04	0.33	..	..
0.08	0.00	0.70	0.04	0.00	0.00	0.00	..	..	..	0.12	0.00	..	1.44	0.08	0.83	0.83	..	..	..
0.03	..	0.07	0.01	..	..	0.00	1.56	..	0.00	0.00	0.01	0.00	0.50	0.00	0.00	0.00	..	0.00	..
..	..	..	..	..	..	..	..	..	..	..	..	..	..	..	..	..	0.00	..	..
..	..	..	..	..	..	..	..	0.00	..	..	..	..	0.00	..	..	0.00	..	..	..
..	..	..	..	..	..	..	..	..	..	..	..	..	..	..	..	0.05	..	..	..
..	..	..	..	..	..	..	..	..	..	..	..	..	0.05	..	..	0.07	0.52	..	..
0.00	0.00	0.00	0.00	0.00	0.00	0.00	0.00	0.03	0.01	0.00	0.00	0.01	0.17	0.03	0.00	0.11	0.24	0.06	0.09
0.06	0.01	0.05	0.03	0.01	0.09	0.05	0.30	0.02	0.01	0.02	0.03	0.03	0.28	0.03	0.02	0.24	0.12	0.01	0.71
0.01	0.00	0.03	0.01	0.00	0.02	0.02	0.01	0.00	0.00	0.00	0.00	0.04	0.14	0.02	0.00	0.09	0.00	0.00	0.43
0.01	0.00	0.02	0.01	0.00	0.06	0.15	0.20	0.01	0.00	0.00	0.01	0.04	0.09	0.02	0.00	0.12	0.02	0.01	0.35
0.03	0.01	0.03	0.02	0.00	0.06	0.09	0.21	0.01	0.01	0.01	0.02	0.04	0.18	0.02	0.01	0.16	0.06	0.01	0.50

Note: ** means "not applicable."

(Table continues on the following page.)

5-51. (continued)

Percentage of total exports

STP	SEN	SYC	SLE	SOM	SDN	TZA	TGO	TUN	UGA	ZAR	ZMB	ZWE	SSA	EEC	NNA	ROW	WLD
..	0.00	..	..	..	..	..	..	1.10	0.01	..	0.05	0.05	0.81	68.49	18.80	11.90	100.00
..	1.90	..	..	..	..	..	..	..	..	..	..	0.00	1.93	28.46	61.43	8.17	100.00
..	0.09	..	..	..	..	..	..	..	..	..	..	..	3.95	72.24	15.45	8.36	100.00
..	0.00	..	..	..	..	..	..	3.76	..	..	..	..	3.97	80.79	1.72	13.52	100.00
..	..	..	..	..	..	..	..	0.00	..	..	..	0.19	0.19	66.56	0.88	32.38	100.00
..	0.03	..	..	..	..	..	..	0.16	..	..	..	0.00	0.30	76.67	14.62	8.41	100.00
..	0.00	..	..	..	..	..	..	0.00	..	..	..	..	0.00	44.44	0.00	54.70	100.00
..	..	..	..	..	..	..	..	..	..	..	..	..	0.22	90.67	3.71	5.39	100.00
..	..	..	..	..	..	..	..	1.63	..	..	..	..	7.94	85.60	0.14	6.31	100.00
..	..	..	..	..	..	..	..	..	..	..	..	..	0.25	34.49	61.29	3.97	100.00
..	0.01	..	..	..	..	..	..	0.33	..	..	..	0.01	0.74	51.23	42.17	5.87	100.00
..	1.76	..	..	..	..	..	..	0.56	..	..	..	0.00	2.21	77.63	12.74	7.42	100.00
..	0.00	..	..	3.02	0.00	0.00	..	0.00	0.00	..	0.00	..	6.90	58.19	0.00	34.48	100.00
..	0.00	..	..	0.00	2.24	0.00	0.00	0.55	0.01	0.00	..	0.17	2.58	37.13	6.46	53.83	100.00
..	..	..	..	..	..	..	..	1.01	..	..	..	..	0.00	96.97	0.00	3.03	100.00
..	0.00	..	..	0.00	0.31	0.00	..	0.02	0.05	..	0.00	0.00	5.30	44.19	10.14	40.37	100.00
..	0.06	..	..	..	..	..	..	0.15	..	..	..	0.00	0.36	72.46	17.07	10.11	100.00
..	0.00	..	..	..	..	..	..	..	..	..	..	..	0.15	63.44	0.46	35.94	100.00
..	0.00	..	..	..	..	..	..	..	..	..	..	..	0.04	54.00	25.51	20.44	100.00
..	0.00	..	..	..	..	..	..	..	..	..	..	..	5.14	63.61	29.10	2.14	100.00
..	2.17	..	..	..	..	..	..	..	..	..	..	..	2.17	86.96	4.35	8.70	100.00
..	..	0.12	0.00	0.74	2.08	2.37	0.11	0.00	8.46	1.16	0.56	0.97	23.96	48.51	5.86	21.68	100.00
..	0.02	..	..	..	..	..	..	0.00	..	..	..	..	0.41	69.19	11.81	18.59	100.00
..	..	..	..	..	1.04	..	..	0.20	..	..	..	..	1.04	86.78	0.06	12.12	100.00
..	0.04	0.04	..	..	..	..	..	0.18	..	..	..	..	3.58	59.93	15.33	21.17	100.00
..	0.04	..	0.07	..	0.00	0.29	..	0.04	0.00	1.26	0.50	1.61	17.69	49.84	11.73	20.78	100.00
..	0.95	..	..	..	..	..	..	2.18	..	..	..	0.00	1.23	55.50	4.08	39.09	100.00
..	0.29	..	..	..	..	..	..	..	..	..	..	0.00	1.83	54.09	4.17	39.91	100.00
..	..	0.10	..	..	..	..	..	..	..	..	..	..	3.00	76.62	15.08	5.30	100.00
..	0.24	..	0.00	..	0.00	0.03	0.09	1.33	..	0.14	..	0.00	2.71	56.59	2.62	38.08	100.00
..	0.00	..	..	..	..	..	..	..	..	..	..	0.14	1.76	21.03	8.32	68.89	100.00
..	0.00	..	..	..	..	..	..	..	..	..	..	0.00	3.52	94.90	1.37	0.21	100.00
..	0.36	..	..	..	..	..	..	..	..	..	..	0.00	0.41	44.32	47.36	7.91	100.00
0.00	..	0.57	..	..	..	..	..	..	..	..	..	..	9.67	86.60	0.19	3.54	100.00
..	..	..	..	0.00	..	0.00	..	0.00	0.20	1.79	0.00	..	2.98	9.42	0.89	86.81	100.00
..	..	0.11	..	..	..	..	..	0.00	..	..	..	2.12	2.60	48.52	14.32	34.56	100.00
**	..	..	..	..	..	..	..	..	..	..	..	..	..	62.12	30.30	7.58	100.00
..	**	..	..	..	..	..	..	0.95	..	..	..	..	4.57	79.66	1.91	13.83	100.00
..	..	**	..	..	..	..	..	..	..	..	..	..	10.64	80.14	0.71	7.80	100.00
..	0.00	..	**	..	..	..	..	0.00	..	..	..	..	0.17	69.91	26.00	3.91	100.00
..	..	..	..	**	..	..	..	..	..	..	..	..	..	36.96	1.23	61.81	100.00
..	..	..	..	..	**	..	..	0.41	..	..	..	0.00	0.00	37.43	3.91	58.68	100.00
..	..	0.00	..	..	..	**	..	0.83	..	..	..	0.07	0.43	61.27	5.80	32.50	100.00
..	0.08	..	..	..	..	..	**	0.62	..	0.00	..	..	9.45	51.67	12.88	26.00	100.00
..	0.08	..	0.00	..	0.00	0.00	0.04	**	0.00	0.00	0.25	0.00	0.98	74.68	1.12	23.21	100.00
..	..	..	..	..	..	..	..	0.03	**	..	..	0.00	0.00	67.21	20.55	12.25	100.00
..	0.00	..	..	..	..	..	..	0.04	..	**	..	0.03	0.03	68.79	22.59	8.59	100.00
..	..	0.00	..	..	..	..	..	..	..	..	**	3.04	3.08	36.08	2.43	58.41	100.00
..	0.10	0.01	..	..	..	..	..	0.03	..	..	..	**	0.99	46.45	11.96	40.61	100.00
0.00	0.29	0.04	0.00	0.02	0.05	0.06	0.00	0.10	0.21	0.04	0.02	0.78	2.47	52.81	22.75	21.97	100.00
0.00	0.06	0.00	0.01	0.01	0.05	0.04	0.03	0.22	0.01	0.08	0.03	0.03	2.33	59.40	9.08	29.19	100.00
0.00	0.02	0.00	0.00	0.01	0.03	0.01	0.01	0.06	0.00	0.04	0.01	0.01	0.96	19.00	35.57	44.47	100.00
0.00	0.02	0.01	0.00	0.00	0.05	0.03	0.02	0.05	0.01	0.02	0.01	0.02	1.19	25.28	23.39	50.14	100.00
0.00	0.04	0.00	0.01	0.01	0.05	0.03	0.02	0.12	0.01	0.05	0.02	0.03	1.63	38.45	19.58	40.33	100.00

Note: ** means "not applicable."

5-52. Direction of trade matrix, exports, 1993

Exporters		DZA	AGO	BEN	BFA	BDI	CMR	CPV	CAF	TCD	COM	COG	CIV	DJI	EGY	GNQ	ETH
		Importers						*Percentage of total exports*									
Algeria	DZA	**	..	..	..	..	0.00	..	..	..	..	0.00	..	..	0.13	..	..
Angola	AGO	..	**	..	..	..	..	..	..	..	..	..	..	..	..	..	..
Benin	BEN	..	..	**	..	..	..	..	..	..	..	..	..	..	..	..	..
Burkina Faso	BFA	..	..	..	**	..	..	..	..	..	..	..	..	..	..	..	..
Burundi	BDI	..	..	..	..	**	..	..	..	..	..	..	..	..	..	..	..
Cameroon	CMR	..	..	..	..	..	**	..	..	..	..	..	..	..	..	..	..
Cape Verde	CPV	..	..	..	..	..	..	**	..	..	..	..	..	..	..	..	..
Central Afri	CAF	..	..	..	..	..	..	..	**	..	..	..	..	..	..	..	..
Chad	TCD	..	..	..	..	..	..	..	..	**	..	..	..	..	..	..	..
Comoros	COM	..	..	..	..	..	..	..	..	..	**	..	..	..	..	..	..
Congo	COG	..	1.06	0.00	..	..	0.00	..	0.00	..	..	**	0.00	..	..	..	..
Côte d'Ivoire	CIV	..	..	..	..	..	..	..	..	..	..	..	**	..	..	..	..
Djibouti	DJI	..	..	..	..	..	..	..	..	..	..	..	..	**	..	..	..
Egypt	EGY	0.79	0.02	0.00	0.00	0.00	0.00	..	0.00	0.00	..	0.00	0.02	0.07	**	0.00	0.07
Equatorial G	GNQ	..	..	..	..	..	..	..	..	..	..	..	..	..	..	**	..
Ethiopia	ETH	..	..	..	..	0.00	..	..	..	0.05	..	..	..	12.05	0.00	..	**
Gabon	GAB	0.01	0.03	0.03	..	..	0.04	..	0.00	..	..	0.00	0.06	..	0.01	0.00	..
Gambia	GMB	..	..	..	..	..	..	..	..	..	..	..	..	..	..	..	..
Ghana	GHA	..	..	..	..	..	..	..	..	..	..	..	..	..	..	..	..
Guinea	GIN	..	..	..	..	..	..	..	..	..	..	..	..	..	..	..	..
Guinea-Bissa	GNB	..	..	..	..	..	..	..	..	..	..	..	..	..	..	..	..
Kenya	KEN	0.00	0.00	0.00	0.01	0.55	0.01	..	0.00	..	0.39	0.00	0.01	0.25	4.01	0.00	2.16
Liberia	LBR	..	..	..	..	..	..	..	..	..	..	..	..	..	..	..	..
Libya, Aj	LBY	..	..	..	..	..	..	..	..	..	..	..	..	..	..	..	..
Madagascar	MDG	..	0.00	0.00	0.00	0.00	0.00	..	0.00	..	0.57	0.00	0.04	0.00	0.04	..	0.00
Malawi	MWI	..	..	..	..	..	..	..	..	..	..	..	..	..	..	..	..
Mali	MLI	..	..	..	..	..	..	..	..	..	..	..	..	..	..	..	..
Mauritania	MRT	..	..	..	..	..	..	..	..	..	..	..	..	..	..	..	..
Mauritius	MUS	0.00	..	..	..	0.04	0.00	..	..	..	0.14	0.00	0.00	0.00	0.00	..	..
Morocco	MAR	2.11	0.03	0.03	0.02	0.00	0.08	..	0.01	..	0.02	0.19	0.19	0.00	0.05	0.00	..
Mozambique	MOZ	..	..	..	..	..	..	..	..	..	..	..	..	..	..	..	..
Niger	NER	..	..	..	..	..	..	..	..	..	..	..	..	..	..	..	..
Nigeria	NGA	..	..	..	..	..	..	..	..	..	..	..	..	..	..	..	..
Reunion	REU	..	..	..	..	..	0.00	..	..	..	5.69	..	..	0.06	..	..	0.00
Rwanda	RWA	..	..	..	..	..	..	..	..	..	..	..	..	..	..	..	..
South Africa	ZAF	0.00	0.34	0.01	0.01	0.02	0.05	0.01	0.00	0.00	0.05	0.06	0.12	0.00	0.06	0.01	0.01
São Tomé and Principe	STP	..	..	..	..	..	..	..	..	..	..	..	..	..	..	..	..
Senegal	SEN	0.12	0.02	1.69	0.63	0.00	1.21	0.02	0.20	0.25	..	0.98	2.21	0.00	..	0.00	1.01
Seychelles	SYC	..	..	..	..	..	..	..	..	..	..	..	..	..	..	..	..
Sierra Leone	SLE	..	..	..	..	..	..	..	..	..	..	..	..	..	..	..	..
Somalia	SOM	..	..	..	..	..	..	..	..	..	..	..	..	..	..	..	..
Sudan	SDN	..	..	..	..	..	..	..	..	..	..	..	..	..	..	..	..
Tanzania	TZA	..	..	..	..	..	..	..	..	..	..	..	..	..	..	..	..
Togo	TGO	..	..	..	..	..	..	..	..	..	..	..	..	..	..	..	..
Tunisia	TUN	1.75	0.00	0.05	0.01	..	0.21	..	0.00	0.01	..	0.00	0.11	0.00	0.17	0.00	0.00
Uganda	UGA	..	..	..	..	..	..	..	..	..	..	..	..	..	..	..	..
Zaire	ZAR	..	..	..	..	..	..	..	..	..	..	..	..	..	..	..	..
Zambia	ZMB	..	..	..	..	..	..	..	..	..	..	..	..	..	..	..	..
Zimbabwe	ZWE	0.37	0.24	0.00	..	0.12	0.00	0.00	..	..	..	0.00	0.00	0.00	1.58	..	0.02
Total Sub-Saharan Afric	SSA	0.02	0.29	0.04	0.02	0.04	0.06	0.00	0.00	0.00	0.09	0.06	0.14	0.08	0.28	0.00	0.11
European Community	EEC	0.36	0.06	0.03	0.01	0.01	0.04	0.01	0.00	0.01	0.01	0.03	0.07	0.01	0.39	0.00	0.04
North America	NNA	0.18	0.03	0.00	0.00	0.00	0.01	0.00	0.00	0.00	0.00	0.00	0.02	0.00	0.49	0.00	0.03
Rest Of World	ROW	0.08	0.01	0.02	0.00	0.00	0.01	0.00	0.00	0.00	0.00	0.01	0.02	0.01	0.26	0.00	0.02
World	WLD	0.20	0.04	0.02	0.01	0.00	0.02	0.00	0.00	0.00	0.00	0.02	0.04	0.01	0.35	0.00	0.03

Note: ** means "not applicable."

(Table continues on the following page.)

5-52. (continued)

Percentage of total exports

GAB	GMB	GHA	GIN	GNB	KEN	LBR	LBY	MDG	MWI	MLI	MRT	MUS	MAR	MOZ	NER	NGA	REU	RWA	ZAF
..	..	..	..	..	..	0.10	0.02	..	..	0.00	0.31	..	0.70	..	0.00	..	..	..	..
..	..	..	..	..	..	..	..	..	..	..	..	..	..	..	..	..	..	..	..
..	..	..	..	..	..	..	..	..	..	..	..	..	..	..	..	..	..	..	..
..	..	..	..	..	..	..	..	..	..	..	..	..	..	..	..	..	..	..	..
..	..	..	..	..	..	..	..	..	..	..	..	..	..	..	..	..	..	..	..
..	..	..	..	..	..	..	..	..	..	..	..	..	..	..	..	..	..	..	..
..	..	..	..	..	..	..	..	..	..	..	..	..	..	..	..	..	..	..	..
..	..	..	..	..	..	..	..	..	..	..	..	..	..	..	..	..	..	..	..
..	..	..	..	..	..	..	..	..	..	..	..	..	..	..	..	..	..	..	..
..	..	..	..	..	..	..	..	..	..	..	..	..	..	..	..	..	..	..	..
0.01	..	..	0.03	..	..	..	..	..	..	0.00	..	0.02	0.08	..	0.00	0.01	0.49	..	0.04
..	..	..	..	..	..	..	..	..	..	..	..	..	..	..	..	..	..	..	..
..	..	..	..	..	..	..	..	..	..	..	..	..	..	..	..	..	..	..	..
0.00	0.00	0.02	0.01	0.00	0.01	0.00	2.01	0.01	0.00	0.01	0.00	0.00	0.33	0.02	0.00	0.09	..	0.01	0.10
..	..	..	..	..	..	..	..	..	..	..	..	..	..	..	..	..	..	..	..
0.00	..	0.00	..	..	0.00	..	..	..	..	..	..	..	..	..	..	0.00	..	..	0.00
**	0.01	..	0.21	..	..	0.02	..	0.00	..	0.00	0.01	..	0.55	0.16	0.00	0.03	..	..	0.00
..	**	..	..	..	..	..	..	..	..	..	..	..	..	..	..	..	..	..	..
..	..	**	..	..	..	..	..	..	..	..	..	..	..	..	..	..	..	..	..
..	..	..	**	..	..	..	..	..	..	..	..	..	..	..	..	..	..	..	..
..	..	..	..	**	..	..	..	..	..	..	..	..	..	..	..	..	..	..	..
0.00	0.00	0.03	0.00	0.00	**	0.01	0.00	0.04	0.15	0.01	0.04	0.71	0.00	0.04	0.00	0.17	0.15	1.70	0.55
..	..	..	..	..	..	**	..	..	..	..	..	..	..	..	..	..	..	..	..
..	..	..	..	..	..	..	**	..	..	..	..	..	..	..	..	..	..	..	..
0.00	..	0.00	0.00	..	0.19	..	0.00	**	0.00	..	0.00	3.71	0.11	0.00	0.00	0.00	6.19	0.00	0.61
..	..	..	..	..	..	..	..	..	**	..	..	..	..	..	..	..	..	..	..
..	..	..	..	..	..	..	..	..	..	**	..	..	..	..	..	..	..	..	..
..	..	..	..	..	..	..	..	..	..	..	**	..	..	..	..	..	..	..	..
0.00	..	0.00	..	..	0.26	..	..	2.02	0.04	..	..	**	0.01	0.33	0.00	0.01	2.09	0.09	0.52
0.25	0.02	0.05	0.17	..	..	1.13	3.70	0.01	0.00	0.15	0.19	0.04	**	0.00	0.01	0.24	0.05	..	0.01
..	..	..	..	..	..	..	..	..	..	..	..	..	..	**	..	..	..	..	..
..	..	..	..	..	..	..	..	..	..	..	..	..	..	..	**	..	..	..	..
..	..	..	..	..	..	..	..	..	..	..	..	..	..	..	..	**	..	..	..
..	..	..	..	..	..	..	..	2.85	..	..	..	2.33	0.00	..	..	..	**	..	0.40
..	..	..	..	..	..	..	..	..	..	..	..	..	..	..	..	..	..	**	..
0.03	0.00	0.06	0.00	..	0.26	0.00	..	0.08	0.76	0.01	0.00	0.60	0.03	1.23	0.00	0.05	0.24	0.01	**
..	..	..	..	..	..	..	..	..	..	..	..	..	..	..	..	..	..	..	..
0.68	2.08	0.07	1.95	0.51	0.10	0.13	..	0.02	..	5.17	2.05	0.00	0.74	..	0.05	0.63	..	..	0.00
..	..	..	..	..	0.00	..	..	0.00	..	..	..	0.65	..	..	..	..	9.15	..	1.31
..	..	..	..	..	..	..	..	..	..	..	..	..	..	..	..	..	..	..	..
..	..	..	..	..	..	..	..	..	..	..	..	..	..	..	..	..	..	..	..
..	..	..	..	..	..	..	..	..	..	..	..	..	..	..	..	..	..	..	..
..	..	..	..	..	..	..	..	..	..	..	..	..	..	..	..	..	..	..	..
..	..	..	..	..	..	..	..	..	..	..	..	..	..	..	..	..	..	..	..
0.02	0.01	0.07	0.05	0.00	..	..	4.95	0.00	..	0.00	0.01	..	0.92	..	0.00	0.00	0.00	0.00	..
..	..	..	..	..	..	..	..	..	..	..	..	..	..	..	..	..	..	..	..
..	..	..	..	..	..	..	..	..	..	..	..	..	..	..	..	..	..	..	..
..	..	..	..	..	..	..	..	..	..	..	..	..	..	..	..	..	..	..	..
..	0.00	0.15	0.00	..	0.93	..	0.04	0.10	3.24	0.01	0.00	0.36	0.00	4.09	0.00	0.04	0.02	0.05	20.33
0.03	0.04	0.05	0.06	0.01	0.24	0.01	0.00	0.17	0.69	0.10	0.04	0.52	0.08	1.09	0.00	0.06	0.34	0.08	0.87
0.04	0.01	0.06	0.02	0.00	0.05	0.06	0.24	0.02	0.01	0.02	0.02	0.04	0.35	0.02	0.01	0.25	0.11	0.01	0.51
0.01	0.00	0.04	0.01	0.00	0.02	0.00	0.01	0.00	0.00	0.01	0.01	0.00	0.11	0.01	0.00	0.16	0.00	0.00	0.40
0.01	0.01	0.03	0.01	0.01	0.04	0.27	0.11	0.01	0.00	0.00	0.01	0.04	0.07	0.01	0.00	0.14	0.01	0.00	0.34
0.02	0.01	0.04	0.01	0.00	0.04	0.14	0.14	0.01	0.01	0.01	0.01	0.04	0.19	0.02	0.01	0.18	0.05	0.01	0.42

Note: ** means "not applicable."

(Table continues on the following page.)

5-52. (continued)

Percentage of total exports

STP	SEN	SYC	SLE	SOM	SDN	TZA	TGO	TUN	UGA	ZAR	ZMB	ZWE	SSA	EEC	NNA	ROW	WLD
0.00	0.00	..	..	..	..	..	0.00	0.62	0.01	..	..	..	0.43	69.63	17.50	12.45	100.00
..	..	..	..	..	..	..	..	..	..	..	..	..	..	..	..	..	..
..	..	..	..	..	..	..	..	..	..	..	..	..	..	..	..	..	..
..	..	..	..	..	..	..	..	..	..	..	..	..	..	..	..	..	..
..	..	..	..	..	..	..	..	..	..	..	..	..	..	..	..	..	..
..	..	..	..	..	..	..	..	..	..	..	..	..	..	..	..	..	..
..	..	..	..	..	..	..	..	..	..	..	..	..	..	..	..	..	..
..	..	..	..	..	..	..	..	..	..	..	..	..	..	..	..	..	..
..	..	..	..	..	..	..	..	..	..	..	..	..	..	..	..	..	..
..	..	..	..	..	..	..	..	..	..	..	..	..	..	..	..	..	..
..	0.00	..	..	..	..	0.01	0.00	0.01	..	0.11	..	0.01	1.79	35.85	52.15	10.20	100.00
..	..	..	..	..	..	..	..	..	..	..	..	..	..	..	..	..	..
..	..	..	..	..	..	..	..	..	..	..	..	..	..	..	..	..	..
0.00	0.01	..	0.00	0.00	0.97	0.02	0.00	0.66	0.01	0.01	0.00	0.00	1.50	39.67	14.07	44.76	100.00
..	..	..	..	..	..	..	..	..	..	..	..	..	..	..	..	..	..
..	..	..	..	..	1.29	0.00	..	..	0.00	0.00	0.00	0.00	13.44	40.90	10.01	35.65	100.00
..	0.57	..	0.02	..	..	..	0.07	0.00	..	0.36	..	..	1.65	24.70	54.63	19.03	100.00
..	..	..	..	..	..	..	..	..	..	..	..	..	..	..	..	..	..
..	..	..	..	..	..	..	..	..	..	..	..	..	..	..	..	..	..
..	..	..	..	..	..	..	..	..	..	..	..	..	..	..	..	..	..
..	..	..	..	..	..	..	..	..	..	..	..	..	..	..	..	..	..
..	0.00	0.16	0.01	2.90	2.10	6.54	0.01	0.01	8.37	0.74	0.20	0.28	28.26	34.14	4.29	33.31	100.00
..	..	..	..	..	..	..	..	..	..	..	..	..	..	..	..	..	..
..	..	..	..	..	..	..	..	..	..	..	..	..	..	..	..	..	..
..	0.00	0.23	..	..	0.00	0.04	0.00	0.65	..	0.04	0.00	0.00	11.69	61.44	7.72	19.18	100.00
..	..	..	..	..	..	..	..	..	..	..	..	..	..	..	..	..	..
..	..	..	..	..	..	..	..	..	..	..	..	..	..	..	..	..	..
..	..	..	..	..	..	..	..	..	..	..	..	..	..	..	..	..	..
0.00	0.01	0.22	..	..	0.00	0.14	0.01	0.00	0.05	0.01	0.08	0.37	6.42	71.30	18.42	3.85	100.00
..	0.11	0.00	0.02	0.00	0.00	..	0.04	1.06	0.00	0.11	0.00	0.00	3.16	62.44	4.03	30.37	100.00
..	..	..	..	..	..	..	..	..	..	..	..	..	..	..	..	..	..
..	..	..	..	..	..	..	..	..	..	..	..	..	..	..	..	..	..
..	..	..	..	..	..	..	..	..	..	..	..	..	..	..	..	..	..
..	..	0.11	..	..	..	..	..	..	..	..	..	..	11.44	81.62	0.11	6.83	100.00
..	..	..	..	..	..	..	..	..	..	..	..	..	..	..	..	..	..
0.01	0.00	0.10	0.01	0.00	0.04	0.07	0.02	0.00	0.01	0.40	1.67	3.14	9.50	18.11	6.54	65.85	100.00
**	..	..	..	..	..	..	..	..	..	..	..	..	..	..	..	..	..
0.00	**	..	0.35	..	..	0.00	0.26	0.17	0.00	0.05	0.00	..	22.29	40.32	2.97	34.39	100.00
..	..	**	..	..	..	..	..	0.00	..	..	..	..	11.11	80.39	0.65	8.50	100.00
..	..	..	**	..	..	..	..	..	..	..	..	..	..	..	..	..	..
..	..	..	..	**	..	..	..	..	..	..	..	..	..	..	..	..	..
..	..	..	..	..	**	..	..	..	..	..	..	..	..	..	..	..	..
..	..	..	..	..	..	**	..	..	..	..	..	..	..	..	..	..	..
..	..	..	..	..	..	..	**	..	..	..	..	..	..	..	..	..	..
..	0.06	0.00	..	..	0.04	..	0.00	**	..	0.00	..	..	0.67	79.10	0.85	19.37	100.00
..	..	..	..	..	..	..	..	..	**	..	..	..	..	..	..	..	..
..	..	..	..	..	..	..	..	..	..	**	..	..	..	..	..	..	..
..	..	..	..	..	..	..	..	..	..	..	**	..	..	..	..	..	..
0.02	0.00	0.02	0.00	0.00	0.11	0.37	0.00	0.00	0.21	0.30	5.07	**	35.81	31.66	7.39	25.14	100.00
0.01	0.05	0.09	0.01	0.12	0.13	0.35	0.02	0.01	0.37	0.37	1.43	2.31	10.63	24.00	12.12	53.25	100.00
0.00	0.05	0.00	0.01	0.00	0.02	0.03	0.01	0.32	0.01	0.02	0.02	0.03	1.78	57.09	8.15	32.98	100.00
0.00	0.01	0.01	0.00	0.01	0.01	0.01	0.00	0.04	0.00	0.01	0.01	0.02	0.87	17.04	35.72	46.37	100.00
0.00	0.01	0.00	0.00	0.00	0.02	0.03	0.01	0.05	0.01	0.01	0.01	0.01	1.17	23.02	23.73	52.08	100.00
0.00	0.03	0.01	0.01	0.01	0.02	0.03	0.01	0.15	0.01	0.02	0.03	0.04	1.45	35.21	19.62	43.72	100.00

Note: ** means "not applicable."

5-53. Direction of trade matrix, current US dollars, 1984

Importers — *Millions of current US dollars*

Exporters		DZA	AGO	BEN	BFA	BDI	CMR	CPV	CAF	TCD	COM	COG	CIV	DJI	EGY	GNQ	ETH
Algeria	DZA	**	..	15	6	..	..	..	..	..	..	..	2	1	2	..	..
Angola	AGO	..	**	..	..	..	..	..	..	..	..	..	..	..	..	..	..
Benin	BEN	..	..	**	0	..	0	..	..	..	..	..	0	..	..	..	..
Burkina Faso	BFA	..	..	0	**	..	..	..	..	..	..	..	1	..	..	..	..
Burundi	BDI	..	..	..	..	**	0	..	..	..	..	..	0	..	..	..	0
Cameroon	CMR	..	..	1	0	..	**	..	12	10	..	9	5	..	0	1	..
Cape Verde	CPV	1	0	0	..	..	..	**	0	..	..	..	1	..	..	..	..
Central African Republic	CAF	..	..	..	..	..	0	..	**	..	..	..	0	..	0	..	..
Chad	TCD	..	..	..	..	..	11	..	..	**	..	..	..	..	..	..	..
Comoros	COM	..	..	0	..	..	..	..	..	..	**	..	..	..	..	..	..
Congo	COG	0	14	0	..	..	0	..	0	1	..	**	0	..	0	..	..
Côte d'Ivoire	CIV	..	..	5	72	..	7	..	..	..	..	..	**	..	1	..	0
Djibouti	DJI	..	..	..	..	..	..	..	..	..	..	..	..	**	..	..	..
Egypt, Arab Rep.	EGY	1	..	..	..	..	0	..	0	..	..	..	..	0	**	..	1
Equatorial Guinea	GNQ	..	..	..	..	..	0	..	..	..	..	..	..	..	..	**	..
Ethiopia	ETH	1	..	..	..	..	0	..	..	..	..	..	0	29	0	..	**
Gabon	GAB	..	..	0	..	..	9	..	..	..	..	..	44	..	..	..	..
Gambia, The	GMB	..	..	..	..	..	..	..	..	..	..	..	..	..	..	..	..
Ghana	GHA	..	..	5	1	..	..	..	..	..	..	..	0	..	2	..	..
Guinea	GIN	..	..	..	0	..	18	..	..	..	..	..	0	..	..	..	..
Guinea-Bissau	GNB	..	..	..	..	..	..	..	..	..	..	..	0	..	0	..	..
Kenya	KEN	1	0	0	0	21	0	..	0	..	3	0	3	3	26	..	4
Liberia	LBR	..	..	0	..	..	0	..	..	..	..	..	0	..	0	..	..
Libya	LBY	..	..	..	..	..	..	..	..	..	..	..	..	..	..	..	..
Madagascar	MDG	0	..	..	..	0	0	..	..	..	0	0	..	0	..	..	..
Malawi	MWI	..	..	0	..	1	1	..	0	0	..	0	0	..	1	..	0
Mali	MLI	..	..	..	2	..	0	..	..	..	..	..	4	..	..	..	..
Mauritania	MRT	..	..	..	..	..	0	..	..	..	..	..	52	..	..	..	..
Mauritius	MUS	..	..	..	..	..	..	..	..	..	..	..	..	..	..	..	..
Morocco	MAR	0	0	1	0	..	5	..	0	..	0	4	5	0	3	0	..
Mozambique	MOZ	..	..	..	..	..	..	..	..	..	..	..	0	..	..	..	..
Niger	NER	..	..	1	0	..	0	..	..	..	..	..	0	..	..	..	..
Nigeria	NGA	..	..	13	2	..	3	..	..	..	..	..	105	..	0	..	0
Reunion	REU	..	..	..	..	0	..	..	..	..	4	0	..	0	..	..	..
Rwanda	RWA	..	..	..	..	..	..	..	..	..	..	..	0	..	..	..	..
South Africa	ZAF	..	..	..	..	..	..	..	..	..	..	..	..	..	..	..	..
São Tomé and Principe	STP	..	..	..	..	..	..	..	..	..	..	..	..	..	..	..	..
Senegal	SEN	..	..	7	5	..	4	..	..	..	..	..	41	..	0	..	0
Seychelles	SYC	..	..	..	..	..	..	..	..	..	..	..	..	2	..	..	..
Sierra Leone	SLE	..	..	..	..	..	..	..	..	..	..	..	1	..	..	..	..
Somalia	SOM	..	..	..	..	..	..	..	..	..	..	..	..	..	0	..	..
Sudan	SDN	..	..	..	..	..	..	..	..	..	..	..	..	..	117	..	0
Tanzania	TZA	..	..	..	..	..	0	..	..	..	..	..	1	..	4	..	0
Togo	TGO	..	..	3	4	..	0	..	0	0	..	0	4	..	..	..	..
Tunisia	TUN	43	..	0	0	..	0	..	..	0	..	0	0	..	11	..	..
Uganda	UGA	..	..	..	..	..	..	..	..	..	..	..	..	..	0	..	..
Zaire	ZAR	..	..	0	..	..	0	..	..	..	..	..	0	..	6	..	..
Zambia	ZMB	..	..	..	..	..	..	..	..	..	..	..	1	..	0	..	..
Zimbabwe	ZWE	2	9	..	..	1	0	0	0	..	0	0	1	..	9	..	4
Sub-Saharan Africa	SSA	5	23	35	86	23	53	0	12	11	7	10	264	33	168	1	8
European Community	EEC	5882	582	148	94	79	899	61	51	62	26	348	779	128	5219	22	353
North America	NNA	768	104	13	21	9	79	..	1	14	25	12	77	8	2448	0	201
Rest Of World	ROW	1975	201	122	19	17	223	9	8	2	3	68	236	69	4132	4	199
World	WLD	8630	909	318	220	128	1254	70	71	90	60	438	1357	238	11967	26	762

Note: ** means "not applicable."

(Table continues on the following page.)

5-53. (continued)

Millions of current US dollars

GAB	GMB	GHA	GIN	GNB	KEN	LBR	LBY	MDG	MWI	MLI	MRT	MUS	MAR	MOZ	NER	NGA	REU	RWA	ZAF
..	1	..	..	..	7	1	0	..	..	0	..	..	..	25	1	..	..	..	..
..	..	..	..	..	..	..	..	..	..	..	..	..	0	..	..	..	..	..	..
..	..	..	..	..	..	0	..	..	..	..	..	..	..	..	..	..	..	..	..
..	..	..	..	..	..	..	..	..	..	..	..	..	0	..	..	..	..	..	..
..	..	..	..	..	4	..	..	..	..	..	..	..	..	..	..	..	..	4	..
12	..	..	0	..	0	0	..	..	..	..	0	..	1	..	0	20	0	0	..
..	..	..	..	0	..	0	..	..	..	..	..	..	..	..	..	..	..	..	..
..	..	..	..	..	..	..	..	..	..	..	..	..	0	..	..	..	..	..	..
..	..	..	..	..	..	0	..	..	..	..	..	..	..	..	..	..	..	..	..
..	..	..	..	..	..	0	..	0	..	..	..	0	0	..	..	..	0	..	..
0	..	..	..	..	..	..	..	..	..	..	..	..	1	..	..	0	2	..	1
3	..	..	..	..	0	28	..	..	..	..	..	0	20	..	..	..	0	..	..
..	..	..	..	..	..	..	..	..	..	..	..	..	..	..	..	..	..	..	..
..	0	0	0	..	0	0	0	..	..	..	0	..	2	..	0	0	..	..	0
..	..	..	..	..	..	..	..	..	..	..	..	..	..	..	..	..	..	..	..
..	..	..	..	..	1	..	0	..	0	..	0	1	..	..	..	0	..	..	..
**	..	..	..	..	..	..	..	..	..	..	..	..	10	..	..	..	0	..	..
..	**	..	..	..	..	0	..	..	..	..	..	0	..	..	..	..	..	..	..
..	..	**	..	..	0	0	..	..	..	..	..	0	..	..	..	..	..	..	..
..	..	..	**	..	..	1	..	..	..	..	..	..	0	..	..	..	..	..	..
..	..	..	..	**	..	..	..	..	..	..	..	..	..	..	..	..	..	..	..
0	0	0	0	..	**	0	1	3	1	..	0	5	0	6	0	0	5	37	2
..	0	0	1	..	..	**	0	..	..	0	0	..	0	..	..	9	..	..	..
..	..	..	..	..	..	..	**	..	..	..	0	..	1	..	..	..	..	..	..
0	..	..	..	..	1	..	..	**	..	..	..	1	0	0	0	..	9	..	..
1	2	0	1	0	0	1	..	..	**	..	..	0	..	5	..	..	..	..	24
0	..	..	..	..	..	2	0	..	..	**	..	..	5	..	..	..	..	..	..
..	..	..	..	..	..	1	..	..	..	..	**	..	..	..	..	..	..	..	..
..	..	..	..	..	..	..	..	..	..	..	..	**	..	..	..	..	2	..	1
4	0	0	4	..	0	1	39	..	..	1	0	1	**	..	0	0	1	..	0
..	..	..	..	..	..	..	..	1	..	..	..	..	..	**	..	..	..	..	..
0	..	..	..	..	..	..	..	..	..	..	..	..	..	..	**	..	..	..	..
..	..	..	..	..	0	10	..	..	..	..	..	..	0	..	..	**	..	..	..
0	..	0	..	..	0	..	..	3	..	..	..	1	3	..	..	..	**	..	0
..	..	..	..	..	3	..	..	..	..	..	..	..	..	..	..	..	..	**	..
..	..	..	..	..	..	..	..	..	..	..	..	..	..	..	..	..	..	..	**
..	..	..	..	..	..	0	..	..	..	..	..	..	..	..	..	..	..	..	..
3	..	..	..	..	0	0	0	..	..	..	..	0	0	..	..	..	1	..	..
..	..	..	..	..	1	..	..	0	..	..	..	0	..	..	..	..	1	..	0
..	0	..	0	..	..	2	..	..	..	..	..	..	..	..	..	0	..	..	..
..	..	..	..	..	0	0	..	..	..	..	..	..	0	..	..	..	..	..	..
..	..	..	..	..	0	..	0	..	..	..	..	0	..	..	..	..	..	..	..
..	..	..	..	..	1	..	..	2	..	..	..	0	..	..	..	..	0	..	..
0	..	5	0	..	..	0	..	..	..	2	..	..	1	..	2	4	..	..	..
1	..	0	0	..	..	..	57	..	..	0	0	..	5	..	0	0	..	..	..
..	..	..	..	..	1	..	0	..	..	..	..	0	0	..	..	..	0	..	..
0	..	..	..	..	1	..	..	..	..	..	..	0	0	..	..	..	..	..	..
..	..	..	..	..	1	..	..	..	..	..	..	..	..	..	..	..	..	..	..
0	..	1	0	..	1	0	3	0	13	..	..	2	2	5	..	1	..	1	235
19	2	6	2	0	16	44	5	9	13	2	0	11	45	16	2	34	21	41	261
533	44	235	179	31	557	622	3718	163	60	163	210	121	1807	161	140	3250	520	71	5826
38	15	68	35	31	92	100	256	41	4	15	28	9	540	49	2	629	1	9	2435
81	25	112	60	5	554	1666	2333	124	26	30	44	312	967	207	25	1754	139	37	3551
671	86	420	276	67	1218	2432	6312	337	103	210	283	453	3358	433	167	5666	681	158	12074

Note: ** means "not applicable."

(Table continues on the following page.)

5-53. (continued)

Millions of current US dollars

STP	SEN	SYC	SLE	SOM	SDN	TZA	TGO	TUN	UGA	ZAR	ZMB	ZWE	SSA	EEC	NNA	ROW	WLD
..	0	1	..	..	2	12	..	70	2	..	..	..	75	8239	2665	907	11886
..	..	..	..	..	..	..	..	..	..	..	..	..	..	659	1053	249	1960
..	..	..	..	..	..	..	..	..	..	..	..	..	0	108	0	6	114
..	..	..	..	..	..	..	..	1	..	..	..	..	1	35	0	18	54
..	..	..	..	..	..	1	..	..	1	4	0	..	14	55	2	30	101
..	2	..	..	..	..	..	0	0	..	0	..	..	71	574	163	75	883
0	0	..	..	..	..	..	..	..	..	0	..	..	1	1	0	1	3
..	..	..	..	..	..	..	..	..	..	..	..	..	0	37	2	46	86
..	..	..	..	..	..	..	..	..	..	..	..	..	11	76	0	10	96
..	..	..	..	..	..	..	..	..	..	..	..	..	1	9	3	1	13
0	0	..	..	..	..	..	0	3	0	2	..	..	21	217	917	27	1183
..	..	..	0	..	..	..	..	11	..	..	..	..	115	1687	559	337	2698
..	..	..	..	..	..	..	..	..	..	..	..	..	..	..	..	..	..
..	0	..	0	0	30	0	0	5	0	1	..	..	31	1311	177	1621	3140
..	..	..	..	..	..	..	..	..	..	..	..	..	0	29	1	1	31
..	0	..	..	..	5	0	0	..	0	0	0	0	36	173	81	127	417
..	..	..	0	..	..	..	..	..	..	..	..	..	53	1033	757	175	2018
..	..	..	0	..	..	..	..	..	..	..	..	..	0	21	1	20	42
..	..	..	0	..	..	..	..	..	..	..	..	..	7	200	52	163	421
..	..	..	0	..	..	..	..	..	..	..	..	..	19	290	146	36	491
..	..	..	..	..	..	..	..	..	..	..	..	..	0	10	1	1	12
..	0	2	0	4	25	11	0	6	90	11	1	0	234	483	62	273	1052
..	0	..	1	..	..	..	1	..	..	..	..	..	12	317	91	30	449
..	..	..	..	..	..	13	..	25	..	..	..	..	13	8470	44	2621	11148
..	..	0	..	0	..	0	..	0	..	..	..	..	12	210	50	68	340
..	0	0	0	..	0	1	..	..	0	5	8	11	61	178	27	36	302
..	..	..	..	..	..	..	..	5	..	..	..	..	8	88	2	84	181
..	2	..	..	..	..	..	..	..	..	..	..	..	55	165	1	77	297
..	..	..	..	..	..	..	..	..	..	..	..	..	3	284	51	51	388
..	8	..	0	..	1	0	1	20	0	2	..	..	41	1292	43	797	2172
..	..	..	..	..	..	..	..	..	..	..	..	..	1	33	14	39	86
..	..	..	..	..	..	..	..	..	..	..	..	..	1	197	1	5	203
..	..	..	59	..	..	..	..	..	..	..	..	..	191	8544	3020	2368	14124
..	0	0	..	..	..	..	..	..	..	..	..	..	7	66	0	7	80
..	..	..	..	..	..	..	..	..	..	..	..	..	3	58	11	11	83
..	..	..	..	..	..	..	..	..	..	..	..	..	..	3464	1583	11737	16784
**	..	..	..	..	..	..	..	..	..	..	..	..	0	8	..	1	9
..	**	..	1	..	..	..	..	..	..	..	..	..	63	404	4	65	536
..	..	**	..	..	..	0	..	..	..	..	..	..	3	1	2	20	26
..	0	..	**	..	..	..	..	..	..	..	..	0	3	83	13	49	148
..	..	..	..	**	..	..	..	..	..	..	..	..	0	13	1	109	123
..	..	..	..	..	**	..	..	4	..	..	..	..	0	204	23	561	788
..	..	0	0	..	..	**	..	..	..	..	..	..	5	229	15	128	377
..	0	..	..	..	..	..	**	6	..	0	..	..	24	111	1	63	199
..	0	..	..	0	0	..	0	**	..	0	..	..	2	1083	343	368	1796
..	..	..	..	..	..	..	..	..	**	..	..	..	1	242	98	62	404
..	..	..	..	..	..	..	..	0	..	**	..	..	2	290	321	391	1004
..	..	..	..	..	..	..	..	..	..	..	**	..	2	228	111	314	655
..	0	1	0	0	2	2	0	1	0	16	33	**	328	363	68	246	1004
0	4	2	62	4	32	15	1	35	91	38	43	12	1368	21476	9307	18115	50266
8	471	23	78	158	481	314	223	1968	102	595	175	248	19395	330243	63854	195244	608736
..	110	4	19	72	132	56	17	253	4	93	99	71	4841	53602	109941	130403	298787
2	232	42	21	52	314	286	77	578	52	286	85	203	11582	177332	198075	365681	752670
11	817	72	181	285	959	670	318	2834	250	1012	403	534	37185	582653	381177	709443	1710459

Note: ** means "not applicable."

5-54. Direction of trade matrix, current US dollars, 1988

Importers — *Millions of current US dollars*

Exporters		DZA	AGO	BEN	BFA	BDI	CMR	CPV	CAF	TCD	COM	COG	CIV	DJI	EGY	GNQ	ETH
Algeria	DZA	**	..	0	0	..	0	..	..	..	..	1	0	..	1	..	0
Angola	AGO	..	**	..	..	..	1	..	..	..	..	..	..	..	..	..	..
Benin	BEN	..	..	**	..	..	1	..	..	..	..	..	..	..	0	..	..
Burkina Faso	BFA	0	..	..	**	..	..	..	..	..	..	..	..	..	..	..	..
Burundi	BDI	..	..	..	..	**	..	..	..	..	..	..	..	..	..	..	..
Cameroon	CMR	4	..	..	..	..	**	..	..	..	..	..	..	..	2	..	..
Cape Verde	CPV	6	..	..	..	..	..	**	..	..	..	..	..	..	..	..	..
Central African Republic	CAF	..	..	..	..	..	0	..	**	..	..	..	..	..	..	..	..
Chad	TCD	0	..	..	..	..	5	..	..	**	..	..	..	..	0	..	..
Comoros	COM	..	..	..	..	..	..	..	..	..	**	..	..	..	0	..	..
Congo	COG	3	..	..	..	..	1	..	..	..	..	**	..	..	..	..	..
Côte d'Ivoire	CIV	5	..	..	..	..	7	..	..	..	..	..	**	..	2	..	..
Djibouti	DJI	..	..	0	..	0	..	..	..	..	0	..	0	**	0	..	1
Egypt, Arab Rep.	EGY	5	0	..	..	0	1	..	0	0	..	0	0	0	**	..	1
Equatorial Guinea	GNQ	0	..	..	..	..	0	..	..	..	..	..	..	..	0	**	..
Ethiopia	ETH	1	..	..	..	0	..	..	..	0	..	..	..	20	0	..	**
Gabon	GAB	6	..	..	..	..	3	..	..	..	..	..	..	..	0	..	..
Gambia, The	GMB	..	..	..	..	..	0	..	..	..	..	..	..	..	..	..	..
Ghana	GHA	..	..	..	..	..	0	..	..	..	..	..	..	..	0	..	..
Guinea	GIN	..	..	..	..	..	27	..	..	..	..	..	..	..	..	..	..
Guinea-Bissau	GNB	..	..	..	..	..	..	..	..	..	..	..	..	..	..	..	..
Kenya	KEN	0	1	..	0	13	0	1	0	..	1	0	1	1	11	0	7
Liberia	LBR	..	..	..	..	..	..	..	..	..	..	..	..	..	..	..	..
Libya	LBY	13	..	..	..	..	..	..	..	..	..	..	0	..	..	..	..
Madagascar	MDG	3	..	..	..	..	0	..	..	..	..	..	..	..	..	..	..
Malawi	MWI	..	0	0	..	3	0	..	..	0	..	0	0	..	1	..	0
Mali	MLI	25	..	..	..	..	0	..	..	..	..	..	..	..	..	..	..
Mauritania	MRT	7	..	..	..	..	6	..	..	..	..	..	..	..	6	..	..
Mauritius	MUS	..	..	..	..	..	..	..	..	..	1	..	..	..	..	..	..
Morocco	MAR	11	10	1	0	..	8	..	1	0	0	4	9	0	6	0	..
Mozambique	MOZ	0	..	..	..	..	1	..	..	..	..	..	..	..	..	..	..
Niger	NER	0	..	..	..	..	..	..	..	..	..	..	..	..	..	..	..
Nigeria	NGA	..	..	..	..	..	4	..	..	..	..	..	..	..	0	..	..
Reunion	REU	..	..	..	..	..	..	..	..	..	8	..	0	0	..	..	..
Rwanda	RWA	..	..	..	0	0	..	..	..	..	..	..	..	0	..	..	0
South Africa	ZAF	2	..	..	..	..	0	..	..	..	..	..	..	..	3	..	..
São Tomé and Principe	STP	..	..	..	..	..	..	..	..	..	..	..	..	..	..	..	..
Senegal	SEN	..	..	..	..	..	18	..	..	..	..	..	..	..	1	..	..
Seychelles	SYC	..	..	..	..	..	..	..	..	..	0	..	..	..	..	..	..
Sierra Leone	SLE	1	..	..	..	..	0	..	..	..	..	..	..	..	..	..	..
Somalia	SOM	..	..	..	..	..	..	..	..	..	..	..	..	..	1	..	..
Sudan	SDN	0	..	..	..	..	..	..	..	..	..	..	..	..	134	..	..
Tanzania	TZA	9	..	..	..	..	..	..	..	..	..	..	..	..	3	..	..
Togo	TGO	0	0	9	5	..	1	..	0	0	..	1	0	..	..	0	..
Tunisia	TUN	59	..	1	1	..	6	0	0	..	..	0	3	0	5	..	..
Uganda	UGA	4	..	..	..	..	..	..	..	..	..	..	..	..	1	..	..
Zaire	ZAR	0	..	..	..	..	0	..	..	..	..	..	..	..	14	..	..
Zambia	ZMB	..	..	..	..	..	..	..	..	..	..	..	..	..	..	..	..
Zimbabwe	ZWE	..	..	..	..	..	3	..	..	..	..	..	..	..	18	..	..
Sub-Saharan Africa	SSA	77	1	9	5	16	79	1	0	0	10	1	1	22	196	0	7
European Community	EEC	4261	743	204	202	97	789	82	86	73	51	369	1134	113	4228	46	661
North America	NNA	967	103	22	16	1	45	4	3	5	1	21	86	5	2148	1	210
Rest Of World	ROW	1867	475	175	34	28	204	34	28	12	6	57	322	76	3255	5	326
World	WLD	7172	1322	410	258	142	1117	121	118	91	67	448	1543	217	9826	51	1203

Note: ** means "not applicable."

(Table continues on the following page.)

5-54. (continued)

Millions of current US dollars

GAB	GMB	GHA	GIN	GNB	KEN	LBR	LBY	MDG	MWI	MLI	MRT	MUS	MAR	MOZ	NER	NGA	REU	RWA	ZAF
..	..	..	0	..	..	0	33	..	..	2	55	..	6	..	0	..	..	0	..
..	..	..	..	..	..	..	..	..	..	..	..	..	..	..	..	0	..	..	..
..	..	..	..	..	..	..	..	..	..	..	..	..	0	..	..	4	..	..	..
..	..	..	..	..	..	..	..	..	..	..	..	..	1	..	..	4	..	..	..
..	..	..	..	..	..	..	..	..	..	..	..	..	..	..	..	..	..	..	..
..	..	..	..	..	..	..	..	0	..	..	..	..	1	..	..	2	0	..	..
..	..	..	..	..	..	..	..	..	..	..	..	..	..	..	..	..	..	..	..
..	..	..	..	..	..	..	..	..	..	..	..	..	0	..	..	..	0	..	..
..	..	..	..	..	..	..	..	..	..	..	..	..	4	..	..	6	..	..	..
..	..	..	..	..	..	..	..	0	..	..	..	..	..	..	..	..	0	..	..
..	..	..	..	..	..	..	..	..	..	..	..	..	9	..	..	..	6	..	..
..	..	..	..	..	..	..	..	0	..	..	..	..	15	..	..	3	1	..	..
..	..	..	..	..	0	..	0	0	..	..	..	0	0	..	0	0	0	..	..
0	..	0	0	..	1	0	0	..	0	0	0	0	3	..	0	0	..	..	0
..	..	..	..	..	..	..	..	..	..	..	..	..	..	..	..	..	..	..	..
..	0	0	0	..	1	..	0	..	0	..	..	0	..	..	..	0	0	0	..
**	..	..	..	..	..	..	..	0	..	..	..	..	15	..	..	0	0	..	..
..	**	..	..	..	..	..	..	..	..	..	..	..	..	..	..	0	..	..	..
..	..	**	..	..	..	..	..	..	..	..	..	..	2	..	..	0	..	..	..
..	..	..	**	..	..	..	..	..	..	..	..	..	0	..	..	..	..	..	..
..	..	..	..	**	..	..	..	..	..	..	..	..	..	..	..	..	..	..	..
0	0	0	0	..	**	0	0	1	3	0	0	3	0	10	..	2	7	26	2
..	..	..	..	..	..	**	..	..	..	..	..	..	1	..	..	4	..	..	..
..	..	..	..	..	..	..	**	..	..	..	..	..	1	..	..	..	..	..	..
..	..	..	..	..	..	..	..	**	..	..	..	..	0	..	..	..	10	..	..
..	1	0	..	..	0	0	0	0	**	..	..	0	..	4	0	0	..	0	30
..	..	..	..	..	..	..	..	..	..	**	..	..	8	..	..	0	..	..	..
..	..	..	..	..	..	..	..	..	..	..	**	..	0	..	..	0	..	..	..
..	..	..	..	..	0	..	..	2	..	..	..	**	4	..	..	..	21	..	5
6	0	0	7	0	8	1	96	0	..	2	3	1	**	0	1	13	2	..	..
..	..	..	..	..	..	..	..	4	..	..	..	..	0	**	..	0	..	..	..
..	..	..	..	..	..	..	..	..	..	..	..	..	..	..	**	15	..	..	..
..	..	..	..	..	..	..	..	..	..	..	..	..	2	..	..	**	..	..	..
..	..	..	..	..	..	..	..	5	..	..	..	1	..	..	..	..	**	..	0
0	..	0	..	..	1	0	0	0	..	0	..	..	..	..	..	..	0	**	0
..	..	..	..	..	..	..	..	1	..	..	..	..	2	..	..	0	47	..	**
..	..	..	..	..	..	..	..	..	..	..	..	..	..	..	..	..	..	..	..
..	..	..	..	..	..	..	..	..	..	..	..	..	1	..	..	1	1	..	..
..	..	..	..	..	0	..	..	..	..	..	..	0	..	..	..	..	1	..	0
..	..	..	..	..	..	..	..	..	..	..	..	..	..	..	..	0	..	..	..
..	..	..	..	..	..	..	..	..	..	..	..	..	..	..	..	..	..	..	..
..	..	..	..	..	..	..	..	..	..	..	..	..	0	..	..	..	..	..	..
..	..	..	..	..	..	..	..	..	..	..	..	..	..	..	..	0	1	..	..
0	0	2	0	0	0	0	..	..	..	0	0	..	4	0	2	2	..	..	..
1	..	2	0	..	..	0	37	..	0	0	0	0	12	0	0	0	..	0	..
..	..	..	..	..	..	..	..	..	..	..	..	..	..	..	..	..	0	..	..
..	..	..	..	..	..	..	..	0	..	..	..	..	0	..	..	0	..	..	..
..	..	..	..	..	..	..	..	..	..	..	..	..	..	..	..	1	..	..	..
..	..	..	..	..	..	..	..	..	..	..	..	..	1	..	..	1	6	..	..
0	1	2	0	0	2	1	0	12	3	0	0	4	69	14	2	45	100	26	38
591	96	482	277	57	942	535	3168	210	100	237	304	365	2972	282	191	2492	1217	114	7470
53	17	147	41	2	97	70	46	13	13	21	19	149	575	73	12	373	1	3	1826
120	54	190	75	11	605	1643	2197	123	48	36	130	419	1014	244	55	1367	178	62	3870
764	168	820	393	70	1646	2248	5412	358	164	295	452	937	4630	613	260	4277	1496	204	13203

Note: ** means "not applicable."

(Table continues on the following page.)

5-54. (continued)

Millions of current US dollars

STP	SEN	SYC	SLE	SOM	SDN	TZA	TGO	TUN	UGA	ZAR	ZMB	ZWE	SSA	EEC	NNA	ROW	WLD
..	0	..	..	..	..	..	..	89	1	..	4	4	66	5585	1533	970	8155
..	42	..	..	..	..	..	..	..	..	..	..	0	42	622	1343	179	2187
..	0	..	..	..	..	..	..	..	..	..	..	..	4	80	17	9	111
..	0	..	..	..	..	..	..	4	..	..	..	..	4	75	2	13	93
..	..	..	..	..	..	..	..	0	..	..	..	0	0	107	1	52	160
..	0	..	..	..	..	..	..	2	..	..	..	0	3	708	135	78	924
..	0	..	..	..	..	..	..	0	..	..	..	..	0	5	0	6	12
..	..	..	..	..	..	..	..	..	..	..	..	..	0	81	3	5	89
..	..	..	..	..	..	..	..	2	..	..	..	..	11	121	0	9	141
..	..	..	..	..	..	..	..	..	..	..	..	..	0	14	25	2	40
..	0	..	..	..	..	..	..	3	..	..	..	0	7	492	405	56	960
..	45	..	..	..	..	..	..	14	..	..	..	0	56	1971	323	188	2539
..	0	..	..	1	0	0	..	0	0	..	0	..	2	14	0	8	23
..	0	..	..	0	48	0	0	12	0	0	..	4	55	787	137	1142	2120
..	..	..	..	..	..	..	..	0	..	..	..	..	0	38	0	1	40
..	0	..	..	0	1	0	..	0	0	..	0	0	22	186	43	170	421
..	1	..	..	..	..	..	..	2	..	..	..	0	4	855	201	119	1180
..	0	..	..	..	..	..	..	..	..	..	..	..	0	41	0	23	65
..	0	..	..	..	..	..	..	..	..	..	..	..	0	548	259	207	1014
..	0	..	..	..	..	..	..	..	..	..	..	..	27	337	154	11	529
..	0	..	..	..	..	..	..	..	..	..	..	..	0	4	0	0	5
..	..	1	0	8	22	25	1	0	88	12	6	10	248	502	61	224	1034
..	0	..	..	..	..	..	..	0	..	..	..	..	4	685	117	184	990
..	..	..	..	..	70	..	..	13	..	..	..	..	70	5800	4	810	6683
..	0	0	..	..	..	..	..	1	..	..	..	..	10	164	42	58	274
..	0	..	0	..	0	1	..	0	0	4	1	5	49	139	33	58	279
..	1	..	..	..	..	..	..	2	..	..	..	0	1	59	4	41	105
..	1	..	..	..	..	..	..	..	..	..	..	0	8	224	17	166	415
..	..	1	..	..	..	..	..	..	..	..	..	..	30	764	150	53	998
..	9	..	0	..	0	1	3	48	..	5	..	0	98	2052	95	1380	3625
..	0	..	..	..	..	..	..	..	..	..	..	0	5	60	24	196	285
..	0	..	..	..	..	..	..	..	..	..	..	0	15	402	6	1	423
..	28	..	..	..	..	..	..	..	..	..	..	0	32	3478	3717	621	7848
0	..	1	..	..	..	..	..	..	..	..	..	..	15	137	0	6	158
..	..	..	..	0	..	0	..	0	0	2	0	..	3	10	1	88	101
..	..	14	..	..	..	..	..	0	..	..	..	278	340	6337	1870	4514	13061
**	..	..	..	..	..	..	..	..	..	..	..	..	..	4	2	1	7
..	**	..	..	..	..	..	..	4	..	..	..	..	20	346	8	60	434
..	..	**	..	..	..	..	..	..	..	..	..	..	2	11	0	1	14
..	0	..	**	..	..	..	..	0	..	..	..	..	0	80	30	5	115
..	..	..	..	**	..	..	..	..	..	..	..	..	..	42	1	70	114
..	..	..	..	..	**	..	..	2	..	..	..	0	0	191	20	299	509
..	..	0	..	..	..	**	..	2	..	..	..	0	1	169	16	90	276
..	0	..	..	..	..	..	**	2	..	0	..	..	23	125	31	63	242
..	2	..	0	..	0	0	1	**	0	0	6	0	24	1787	27	555	2393
..	..	..	..	..	..	..	..	0	**	..	..	0	0	208	64	38	310
..	0	..	..	..	..	..	..	0	..	**	..	0	0	770	253	96	1120
..	..	0	..	..	..	..	..	..	..	..	**	36	36	425	29	688	1178
..	1	0	..	..	..	..	..	0	..	..	..	**	11	532	137	465	1145
0	120	18	0	8	23	25	1	41	88	17	7	329	1038	22162	9545	9221	41966
18	652	46	86	136	556	438	333	2339	157	850	328	332	24543	626535	95793	307893	1054764
12	80	2	17	27	115	48	25	235	18	150	42	52	4044	80308	150391	188002	422745
4	177	60	38	52	594	315	190	583	97	241	160	183	13118	277742	256950	550844	1098654
33	1030	126	141	223	1288	827	550	3198	359	1258	537	897	42743	1006747	512679	1055960	2618129

Note: ** means "not applicable."

5-55. Direction of trade matrix, current US dollars, 1993

Importers — *Millions of current US dollars*

Exporters		DZA	AGO	BEN	BFA	BDI	CMR	CPV	CAF	TCD	COM	COG	CIV	DJI	EGY	GNQ	ETH
Algeria	DZA	**	..	..	..	..	0	..	..	..	..	0	..	..	14	..	..
Angola	AGO	..	**	..	..	..	..	..	..	..	..	..	..	..	..	..	..
Benin	BEN	..	..	**	..	..	..	..	..	..	..	..	..	..	..	..	..
Burkina Faso	BFA	..	..	..	**	..	..	..	..	..	..	..	..	..	..	..	..
Burundi	BDI	..	..	..	..	**	..	..	..	..	..	..	..	..	..	..	..
Cameroon	CMR	..	..	..	..	..	**	..	..	..	..	..	..	..	..	..	..
Cape Verde	CPV	..	..	..	..	..	..	**	..	..	..	..	..	..	..	..	..
Central Afri	CAF	..	..	..	..	..	..	..	**	..	..	..	..	..	..	..	..
Chad	TCD	..	..	..	..	..	..	..	..	**	..	..	..	..	..	..	..
Comoros	COM	..	..	..	..	..	..	..	..	..	**	..	..	..	..	..	..
Congo	COG	..	10	0	..	..	0	..	0	..	..	**	0	..	..	..	..
Côte d'Ivoire	CIV	..	..	..	..	..	..	..	..	..	..	..	**	..	..	..	..
Djibouti	DJI	..	..	..	..	..	..	..	..	..	..	..	..	**	..	..	..
Egypt	EGY	24	1	0	0	0	0	..	0	0	..	0	1	2	**	0	2
Equatorial G	GNQ	..	..	..	..	..	..	..	..	..	..	..	..	..	..	**	..
Ethiopia	ETH	..	..	..	..	0	..	..	..	0	..	..	..	24	0	..	**
Gabon	GAB	0	1	1	..	..	1	..	0	..	..	0	2	..	0	0	..
Gambia	GMB	..	..	..	..	..	..	..	..	..	..	..	..	..	..	..	..
Ghana	GHA	..	..	..	..	..	..	..	..	..	..	..	..	..	..	..	..
Guinea	GIN	..	..	..	..	..	..	..	..	..	..	..	..	..	..	..	..
Guinea-Bissa	GNB	..	..	..	..	..	..	..	..	..	..	..	..	..	..	..	..
Kenya	KEN	0	0	0	0	8	0	..	0	..	5	0	0	3	55	0	30
Liberia	LBR	..	..	..	..	..	..	..	..	..	..	..	..	..	..	..	..
Libya	LBY	..	..	..	..	..	..	..	..	..	..	..	..	..	..	..	..
Madagascar	MDG	..	0	0	0	0	0	..	0	..	2	0	0	0	0	..	0
Malawi	MWI	..	..	..	..	..	..	..	..	..	..	..	..	..	..	..	..
Mali	MLI	..	..	..	..	..	..	..	..	..	..	..	..	..	..	..	..
Mauritania	MRT	..	..	..	..	..	..	..	..	..	..	..	..	..	..	..	..
Mauritius	MUS	0	..	..	..	1	0	..	..	..	2	0	0	0	0	..	..
Morocco	MAR	78	1	1	1	0	3	..	0	..	1	7	7	0	2	0	..
Mozambique	MOZ	..	..	..	..	..	..	..	..	..	..	..	..	..	..	..	..
Niger	NER	..	..	..	..	..	..	..	..	..	..	..	..	..	..	..	..
Nigeria	NGA	..	..	..	..	..	..	..	..	..	..	..	..	..	..	..	..
Reunion	REU	..	..	..	..	..	0	..	..	..	10	..	..	0	..	..	0
Rwanda	RWA	..	..	..	..	..	..	..	..	..	..	..	..	..	..	..	..
South Africa	ZAF	0	81	3	1	4	13	1	0	0	11	15	30	0	15	1	1
São Tomé and Principe	STP	..	..	..	..	..	..	..	..	..	..	..	..	..	..	..	..
Senegal	SEN	1	0	10	4	0	7	0	1	2	..	6	13	0	..	0	6
Seychelles	SYC	..	..	..	..	..	..	..	..	..	..	..	..	..	..	..	..
Sierra Leone	SLE	..	..	..	..	..	..	..	..	..	..	..	..	..	..	..	..
Somalia	SOM	..	..	..	..	..	..	..	..	..	..	..	..	..	..	..	..
Sudan	SDN	..	..	..	..	..	..	..	..	..	..	..	..	..	..	..	..
Tanzania	TZA	..	..	..	..	..	..	..	..	..	..	..	..	..	..	..	..
Togo	TGO	..	..	..	..	..	..	..	..	..	..	..	..	..	..	..	..
Tunisia	TUN	67	0	2	0	..	8	..	0	0	..	0	4	0	7	0	0
Uganda	UGA	..	..	..	..	..	..	..	..	..	..	..	..	..	..	..	..
Zaire	ZAR	..	..	..	..	..	..	..	..	..	..	..	..	..	..	..	..
Zambia	ZMB	..	..	..	..	..	..	..	..	..	..	..	..	..	..	..	..
Zimbabwe	ZWE	5	3	0	..	2	0	0	..	..	..	0	0	0	21	..	0
Total Sub-Saharan Afric	SSA	6	95	14	5	14	21	1	1	2	30	21	45	28	91	2	37
European Community	EEC	4719	815	335	171	87	585	109	60	72	82	397	987	156	5117	40	497
North America	NNA	1077	168	24	19	3	61	4	5	8	0	28	91	13	2844	4	152
Rest Of World	ROW	1213	157	235	44	35	146	28	13	8	12	104	274	144	3902	3	255
World	WLD	7015	1235	608	240	138	812	143	79	89	125	549	1397	341	11955	48	942

Note: ** means "not applicable."

(Table continues on the following page.)

5-55. (continued)

Millions of current US dollars

GAB	GMB	GHA	GIN	GNB	KEN	LBR	LBY	MDG	MWI	MLI	MRT	MUS	MAR	MOZ	NER	NGA	REU	RWA	ZAF
..	..	..	..	..	..	11	3	..	..	0	31	..	71	..	0	..	..	..	..
..	..	..	..	..	..	..	..	..	..	..	..	..	..	..	..	..	..	..	..
..	..	..	..	..	..	..	..	..	..	..	..	..	..	..	..	..	..	..	..
..	..	..	..	..	..	..	..	..	..	..	..	..	..	..	..	..	..	..	..
..	..	..	..	..	..	..	..	..	..	..	..	..	..	..	..	..	..	..	..
..	..	..	..	..	..	..	..	..	..	..	..	..	..	..	..	..	..	..	..
..	..	..	..	..	..	..	..	..	..	..	..	..	..	..	..	..	..	..	..
..	..	..	..	..	..	..	..	..	..	..	..	..	..	..	..	..	..	..	..
..	..	..	..	..	..	..	..	..	..	..	..	..	..	..	..	..	..	..	..
..	..	..	..	..	..	..	..	..	..	..	..	..	..	..	..	..	..	..	..
0	..	..	0	..	..	..	..	..	..	0	..	0	1	..	0	0	5	..	0
..	..	..	..	..	..	..	..	..	..	..	..	..	..	..	..	..	..	..	..
..	..	..	..	..	..	..	..	..	..	..	..	..	..	..	..	..	..	..	..
0	0	1	0	0	0	0	62	0	0	0	0	0	10	1	0	3	..	0	3
..	..	..	..	..	..	..	..	..	..	..	..	..	..	..	..	..	..	..	..
0	..	0	..	..	0	..	..				..	..	..	..		0	..	..	0
**	0	..	6	..	..	1	..	0	..	0	0	..	15	4	0	1	..	..	0
..	**	..	..	..	..	..	..	..	..	..	..	..	..	..	..	..	..	..	..
..	..	**	..	..	..	..	..	..	..	..	..	..	..	..	..	..	..	..	..
..	..	..	**	..	..	..	..	..	..	..	..	..	..	..	..	..	..	..	..
..	..	..	..	**	..	..	..	..	..	..	..	..	..	..	..	..	..	..	..
0	0	0	0	0	**	0	0	1	2	0	1	10	0	1	0	2	2	23	8
..	..	..	..	..	..	**	..	..	..	..	..	..	..	..	..	..	..	..	..
..	..	..	..	..	..	..	**	..	..	..	..	..	..	..	..	..	..	..	..
0	..	0	0	..	1	..	0	**	0	..	0	10	0	0	0	0	16	0	2
..	..	..	..	..	..	..	..	..	**	..	..	..	..	..	..	..	..	..	..
..	..	..	..	..	..	..	..	..	..	**	..	..	..	..	..	..	..	..	..
..	..	..	..	..	..	..	..	..	..	..	**	..	..	..	..	..	..	..	..
0	..	0	..	..	4	..	..	30	1	..	..	**	0	5	0	0	31	1	8
9	1	2	6	..	..	42	137	0	0	6	7	1	**	0	1	9	2	..	0
..	..	..	..	..	..	..	..	..	..	..	..	..	..	**	..	..	..	..	..
..	..	..	..	..	..	..	..	..	..	..	..	..	..	..	**	..	..	..	..
..	..	..	..	..	..	..	..	..	..	..	..	..	..	..	..	**	..	..	..
..	..	..	..	..	..	..	..	5	..	..	..	4	0	..	..	..	**	..	1
..	..	..	..	..	..	..	..	..	..	..	..	..	..	..	..	..	..	**	..
7	0	15	1	..	62	1	..	19	181	2	0	144	7	296	0	13	58	1	**
..	..	..	..	..	..	..	..	..	..	..	..	..	..	..	..	..	..	..	..
4	13	0	12	3	1	1	..	0	..	31	12	0	5	..	0	4	..	..	0
..	..	..	..	..	0	..	..	0	..	..	..	0	..	..	..	..	1	..	0
..	..	..	..	..	..	..	..	..	..	..	..	..	..	..	..	..	..	..	..
..	..	..	..	..	..	..	..	..	..	..	..	..	..	..	..	..	..	..	..
..	..	..	..	..	..	..	..	..	..	..	..	..	..	..	..	..	..	..	..
..	..	..	..	..	..	..	..	..	..	..	..	..	..	..	..	..	..	..	..
..	..	..	..	..	..	..	..	..	..	..	..	..	..	..	..	..	..	..	..
1	0	3	2	0	..	..	189	0	..	0	0	..	35	..	0	0	0	0	..
..	..	..	..	..	..	..	..	..	..	..	..	..	..	..	..	..	..	..	..
..	..	..	..	..	..	..	..	..	..	..	..	..	..	..	..	..	..	..	..
..	..	..	..	..	..	..	..	..	..	..	..	..	..	..	..	..	..	..	..
..	0	2	0	..	12	..	1	1	43	0	0	5	0	54	0	1	0	1	268
11	13	18	18	3	79	3	1	55	227	33	13	173	27	359	1	20	114	27	286
543	134	740	317	49	637	764	3199	231	86	218	309	501	4661	229	170	3278	1415	113	6780
58	10	231	60	2	124	21	70	12	16	37	36	17	669	65	16	921	2	10	2323
117	118	411	94	102	557	4039	1639	133	59	48	103	621	1000	184	40	2105	128	41	4988
728	276	1400	488	155	1396	4827	4909	431	388	337	461	1312	6356	837	227	6323	1658	191	14377

Note: ** means "not applicable."

(Table continues on the following page.)

5-55. (continued)

Millions of current US dollars

STP	SEN	SYC	SLE	SOM	SDN	TZA	TGO	TUN	UGA	ZAR	ZMB	ZWE	SSA	EEC	NNA	ROW	WLD
0	0	..	..	..	..	..	0	62	1	..	..	..	43	7031	1767	1257	10098
..	..	..	..	..	..	..	..	..	..	..	..	..	..	..	..	..	..
..	..	..	..	..	..	..	..	..	..	..	..	..	..	..	..	..	..
..	..	..	..	..	..	..	..	..	..	..	..	..	..	..	..	..	..
..	..	..	..	..	..	..	..	..	..	..	..	..	..	..	..	..	..
..	..	..	..	..	..	..	..	..	..	..	..	..	..	..	..	..	..
..	..	..	..	..	..	..	..	..	..	..	..	..	..	..	..	..	..
..	..	..	..	..	..	..	..	..	..	..	..	..	..	..	..	..	..
..	..	..	..	..	..	..	..	..	..	..	..	..	..	..	..	..	..
..	..	..	..	..	..	..	..	..	..	..	..	..	..	..	..	..	..
..	0	..	..	..	..	0	0	0	..	1	..	0	17	346	503	99	965
..	..	..	..	..	..	..	..	..	..	..	..	..	..	..	..	..	..
..	..	..	..	..	..	..	..	..	..	..	..	..	..	..	..	..	..
0	0	..	0	0	30	1	0	21	0	0	0	0	47	1232	437	1390	3105
..	..	..	..	..	..	..	..	..	..	..	..	..	..	..	..	..	..
..	..	..	..	..	3	0	..	..	0	0	0	0	27	83	20	72	202
..	15	..	0	..	..	..	2	0	..	10	..	..	43	651	1441	502	2637
..	..	..	..	..	..	..	..	..	..	..	..	..	..	..	..	..	..
..	..	..	..	..	..	..	..	..	..	..	..	..	..	..	..	..	..
..	..	..	..	..	..	..	..	..	..	..	..	..	..	..	..	..	..
..	..	..	..	..	..	..	..	..	..	..	..	..	..	..	..	..	..
..	0	2	0	40	29	90	0	0	115	10	3	4	388	469	59	458	1374
..	..	..	..	..	..	..	..	..	..	..	..	..	..	..	..	..	..
..	..	..	..	..	..	..	..	..	..	..	..	..	..	..	..	..	..
..	0	1	..	..	0	0	0	2	..	0	0	0	31	161	20	50	262
..	..	..	..	..	..	..	..	..	..	..	..	..	..	..	..	..	..
..	..	..	..	..	..	..	..	..	..	..	..	..	..	..	..	..	..
..	..	..	..	..	..	..	..	..	..	..	..	..	..	..	..	..	..
0	0	3	..	..	0	2	0	0	1	0	1	5	94	1046	270	57	1467
..	4	0	1	0	0	..	1	39	0	4	0	0	117	2308	149	1122	3696
..	..	..	..	..	..	..	..	..	..	..	..	..	..	..	..	..	..
..	..	..	..	..	..	..	..	..	..	..	..	..	..	..	..	..	..
..	..	..	..	..	..	..	..	..	..	..	..	..	..	..	..	..	..
..	..	0	..	..	..	..	..	..	..	..	..	..	20	143	0	12	176
..	..	..	..	..	..	..	..	..	..	..	..	..	..	..	..	..	..
3	1	24	2	1	10	18	4	0	3	96	400	753	2273	4334	1565	15757	23930
**	..	..	..	..	..	..	..	..	..	..	..	..	..	..	..	..	..
0	**	..	2	..	..	0	2	1	0	0	0	..	135	244	18	208	605
..	..	**	..	..	..	..	..	0	..	..	..	..	2	12	0	1	15
..	..	..	**	..	..	..	..	..	..	..	..	..	..	..	..	..	..
..	..	..	..	**	..	..	..	..	..	..	..	..	..	..	..	..	..
..	..	..	..	..	**	..	..	..	..	..	..	..	..	..	..	..	..
..	..	..	..	..	..	**	..	..	..	..	..	..	..	..	..	..	..
..	..	..	..	..	..	..	**	..	..	..	..	..	..	..	..	..	..
..	2	0	..	..	2	..	0	**	..	0	..	..	26	3009	33	737	3805
..	..	..	..	..	..	..	..	..	**	..	..	..	..	..	..	..	..
..	..	..	..	..	..	..	..	..	..	**	..	..	..	..	..	..	..
..	..	..	..	..	..	..	..	..	..	..	**	..	..	..	..	..	..
0	0	0	0	0	1	5	0	0	3	4	67	**	472	418	98	332	1319
3	16	31	4	40	42	115	8	4	121	121	471	762	3503	7907	3995	17547	32951
28	606	65	102	57	318	417	132	4230	133	303	221	348	23637	758417	108280	438173	1328507
3	78	66	22	33	57	39	13	246	26	40	74	91	5081	99497	208561	270706	583845
6	195	69	55	48	329	495	202	719	107	117	193	204	17361	341353	351926	772197	1482837
39	895	229	183	179	745	1067	354	5199	387	580	958	1405	49581	1207174	672762	1498623	3428140

Note: ** means "not applicable."

Figure 5-1. Terms of trade gains and losses, average 1990-96*

(annual average percent change)

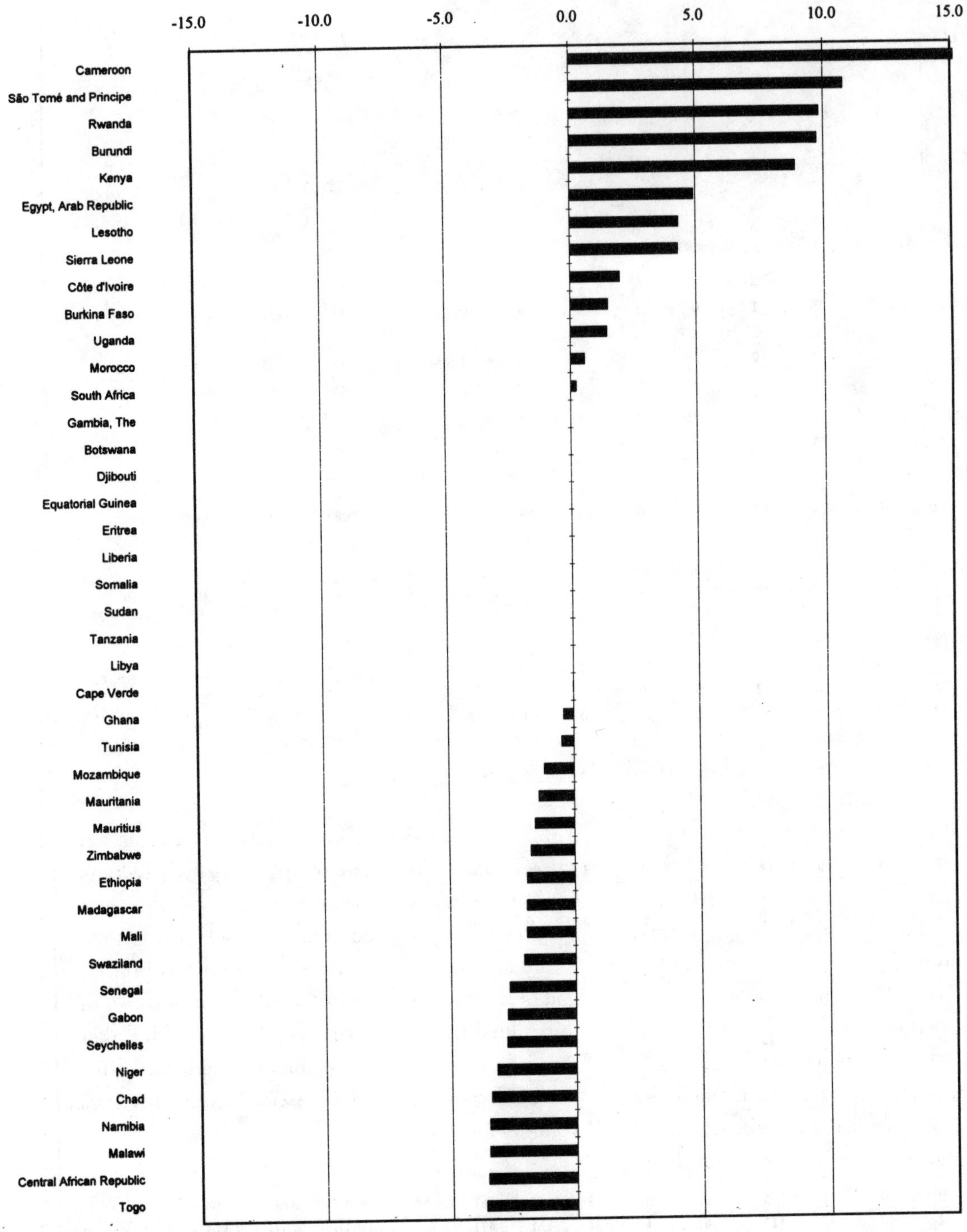

* Or most recent year available

Technical Notes

Tables

Tables 5-1 and 5-2. Merchandise exports and merchandise imports, f.o.b. Merchandise exports and imports (World Bank country desks) are both valued f.o.b. and comprise all transactions involving a change of ownership of goods, including nonmonetary gold, between residents of a country and the rest of the world. These transactions include those in which ownership changes even though goods do not cross customs borders. The few types of goods not covered by the merchandise account include travelers' purchases abroad, which are included in travel, and purchases of goods by diplomatic and military personnel, which are classified under other official goods, services, and income.

Tables 5-3 and 5-4. Exports and imports of total services. Service exports and imports (World Bank country desks) include total nonfactor and factor services, based on transactions involving ownership changes as explained above for goods. Nonfactor services comprise shipment, passenger and other transport services, and travel, as well as current account transactions not separately reported (that is, not classified as merchandise, nonfactor services, or transfers). These include transactions with nonresidents by government agencies and their personnel abroad, as well as transactions by private residents with foreign governments and government personnel stationed in the reporting country. Factor services comprise services of labor and capital, thus covering income from direct investment abroad, interest, dividends, and property and labor income. Net interest is recorded on an accrual basis; that is, interest obligations are included whether payments are made or not.

Table 5-5. Net private transfers. Net private transfers (World Bank country desks) are inflows (from private sources to either private or public recipients) less outflows from private sources to either private or public recipients that carry no provisions for repayments. They include workers' remittances; transfers by migrants; gifts, dowries, and inheritances; and alimony and other support remittances.

Table 5-6. Net current official transfers. Net official transfers (World Bank country desks) are the official sources counterpart of Table 5-5. They include transfers on both current and capital accounts, including government grants of real resources and financial items such as subsidies to current budgets, grants of technical assistance, and government contributions to international organizations for administrative expenses.

Table 5-7. Current account balance, excluding net capital grants. Current account balance (World Bank country desks), as presented here, is the difference between exports of goods and all services plus inflows of unrequited current transfers (official and private) and imports of goods and all services plus outflows of unrequited transfers to the rest of the world. Other common presentations exclude or include both current and capital official transfers. Data in previous volumes included both.

Table 5-8. Current account balance, excluding net capital grants, as a percentage of GDP. It is defined as the ratio of figures presented in Table 5-7 to GDP in current prices (Table 2-5).

Table 5-9. Capital grants. These grants (World Bank country desks) are unrequited transfers, often used to finance balance of payments deficits.

Table 5-10. Net foreign direct investment. Net foreign direct investment (World Bank country desks) is the net amount invested or reinvested by nonresidents to acquire a lasting interest in enterprises in which they exercise significant managerial control. Investment includes equity capital, reinvested earnings, and other capital. The net figures subtract the value of direct investment abroad by residents of the reporting country.

Table 5-11. Net long-term borrowing. Net long-term borrowing is calculated as disbursements less the repayment of principal (amortization) of public, publicly guaranteed, and private nonguaranteed borrowings that have an original or extended maturity of more than one year and that are repayable in foreign currencies, goods, or services. These data are as reported in the World Bank's Debtor Reporting System (DRS) and are in accord with the data on external debt discussed in Chapter 6.

Table 5-12. Other capital flows. Other capital flows comprise the net balance of inflows and outflows of capital not elsewhere included. It covers, for example, changes in the stock of short-term debt, arrears, and other liabilities (all adjusted for valuation changes resulting from exchange rate changes and other factors), and errors and omissions. This table incorporates corrections to data in *ADI 1992.*

Table 5-13. Use of reserves. This table (World Bank country desks) shows the variation from year to year of the net balance of international reserve assets and is valued throughout at year-end London prices (for example, US$37.37 an ounce in 1970 and US$484.10 an ounce in 1987). Positive numbers represent a decrease or use of reserves; negative numbers represent an increase in reserves. This table incorporates corrections to data in *ADI 1996.*

Table 5-14. Import coverage ratio of reserves. This ratio gives the number of months, at current import levels, that can adequately be covered by available foreign exchange reserves (World Bank country desks). It is obtained by dividing the stock of reserves by imports divided by 12.

Tables 5-15 and 5-16. Export and import unit values. The indexes for total export and import unit values (World Bank country desks) are based on exports of goods and nonfactor services from the national accounts. These indexes are calculated by dividing the values of exports and imports expressed in current US dollars (Tables 2-14 and 2-15) by the volume of exports (f.o.b.) and imports (c.i.f.) expressed in constant 1987 US dollars (Tables 2-16 and 2-17). Because of the way these trade unit value indexes are calculated (Paasche indexes, with changing weights), they reflect the composition of exports and imports in each year and may not give a reliable trend in unit values when trade composition changes dramatically. By contrast, this index reflects more accurately shifts in a country's actual composition of trade than would an index using weights based on trade shares in a single year. Data may differ from those in *ADI 1992* and *ADI 1994–95* because a different source was used for this volume.

Table 5-17. Terms of trade. Terms of trade measure the relative movement of export and import prices. This series is calculated as the ratio of a country's export unit values or prices (Table 5-15) to its import unit values or prices (Table 5-16). It shows changes over a base year (1987) in the level of export unit values as a percentage of import unit values. Data may differ from those in *ADI 1992* and *ADI 1994–95* because a different source was used for this volume.

Table 5-18. Forest products exports. Exports of forest production (FAO data) is given as an aggregate including all wood from trees and forests (coniferous and nonconiferous), whether in natural form or partially processed (SITC 245, 246, and 247); sawwood and sleepers (SITC 248); and wood-based panels and fiberwood, compressed or noncompressed (SITC 634 and 641).

Table 5-19. Petroleum exports. This table contains the volumes of crude petroleum exported (World Bank, IEABAL). Data may differ from *ADI 1992* and *ADI 1994–95* because a different source was used for this volume.

Table 5-20. Copper exports. The table presents the unweighted sum of the metal content weights of copper ore and concentrate and of unrefined plus refined copper, metal, and alloys, unwrought (World Bank, METMIN). Data may differ from *ADI 1992* and *ADI 1994–95* because a different source was used for this volume.

Table 5-21. Iron exports. These are exports measured in metal content weight of iron ore (World Bank, METMIN).

Table 5-22. Phosphates exports. These are the volume of phosphates exports, expressed as the weight of mineral content in phosphate rock (World Bank, METMIN).

Table 5-23. Cocoa exports. Cocoa exports include cocoa beans, cocoa powder and cake, cocoa paste, cocoa butter, and chocolate products not elsewhere specified (FAO data).

Table 5-24. Coffee exports. Coffee exports are shown for green and roasted beans (FAO data).

Table 5-25. Cotton exports. Cotton exports refer to cotton lint only (FAO data).

Table 5-26. Groundnut exports. Groundnut exports include the weight of groundnuts in shelled equivalent (using a conversion factor of 70 percent), groundnut oil, and groundnut cake (FAO data).

Table 5-27. Oil palm products exports. Exports of oil palm products consist of palm oil and palm kernels (FAO data).

Table 5-28. Sisal exports. Only sisal fiber exports are included (FAO data).

Table 5-29. Tea exports. Tea exports figures are for processed tea (FAO data).

Table 5-30. Sugar exports. Sugar exports are shown in terms of raw sugar equivalent. The conversion factor to express refined sugar in raw sugar equivalent is 1.087 for all countries (FAO data).

Table 5-31. Tobacco exports. Only tobacco leaves are included (FAO data).

Table 5-32. Meat exports. Meat exports are defined as fresh, chilled, or frozen meat (SITC category 011) (FAO data).

Tables 5-33 and 5-34. Manufactured goods exports. Data reported in these tables follow the classification of manufacturing industries as reported in the UN *International Standard Industrial Classification of All Economic Activities* (ISIC), Revision 2 (World Bank country desks). First table is expressed in current prices; second table shows growth.

Tables 5-35 and 5-36. Food imports. Data refer to the sum of food, beverages, tobacco, oilseeds and oleaginous fruits, animal and vegetable oils, and fats (SITC sections 0, 1, and 4 and division 22) (World Bank country desks). First table is expressed in current prices; second table shows growth.

Tables 5-37 and 5-38. Nonfood consumer goods imports. Data reported in these tables show consumer goods imports other than food. Data are calculated as total merchandise imports less food, fuel, intermediate goods, and capital goods imports (World Bank country desks). First table is expressed in current prices; second table shows growth.

Tables 5-39 and 5-40. Fuel imports. Figures are defined as SITC section 3 (sum of Canada, Mexico, and United States) (World Bank country desks). First table presents data in current prices; second table shows growth.

Tables 5-41 and 5-42. Primary intermediate goods imports. Data on these tables comprise minerals, ores, and metals imports (the sum of SITC divisions 27, 28, and 68 and item 522.56) and agricultural raw materials imports (the sum of SITC section 2, less divisions 22, 27, and 28 and groups 233, 244, 266, and 267). Synthetics are excluded (World Bank country desks). First table presents data in current prices; second table shows growth.

Tables 5-43 and 5-44. Manufactured goods imports. Data reported on these tables follow the classification of manufacturing industries as reported in the UN *International Standard Industrial Classification of All Economic Activities* (ISIC), Revision 2 (World Bank country desks). First table presents data in current prices; second table shows growth.

Tables 5-45 and 5-46. Capital goods imports. Data shown here are for machinery and transport equipment (SITC section 7) (World Bank country desks). First table presents data in current prices; second table shows growth.

Tables 5-47, 5-48, and 5-49. Direction of trade matrix, imports. These tables show, for each importing country, the percentage of the value of its total imports that originates from each of the exporting countries for 1984, 1988, and 1993, respectively. They are calculated from Tables 5-53 to 5-55, below.

In these tables data posted under South Africa are for South Africa Customs Union, which comprises Botswana, Lesotho, Namibia, South Africa, and Swaziland.

Tables 5-50, 5-51, and 5-52. Direction of trade matrix, exports. As with the foregoing, for each exporter, these tables show the percentage of the value of total exports, f.o.b., that goes to each of its trade partners for 1984, 1988, and 1993, respectively. These are calculated from Tables 5-53 to 5-55, below.

In these tables data posted under South Africa are for South Africa Customs Union, which comprises Botswana, Lesotho, Namibia, South Africa, and Swaziland.

Tables 5-53, 5-54, and 5-55. Direction of trade matrix, current US dollars. These are the value of trade in goods and services to or from the countries indicated. Matrixes are shown for 1984, 1988, and 1993. They form the basis for the calculations in the previous six tables (UNSTAT, COMTRADE). Data for South Africa are for the South Africa Customs Union, which comprises Botswana, Lesotho, Namibia, South Africa, and Swaziland.

Figure

The following indicator has been used to derive the figures in this chapter.

Figure 5-1. Terms of trade gains or losses (Table 5-17).

Methodology used for regional aggregations and period averages in chapter 5

	Aggregations[a]				*Period averages*[b]	
Table	*(1)*	*(3)*	*(4)*	*(6)*	*(1)*	*(2)*
5-1		x				x
5-2		x				x
5-3		x				x
5-4		x				x
5-5	x				x	
5-6	x				x	
5-7	x				x	
5-8				x	x	
5-9	x				x	
5-10	x				x	
5-11	x				x	
5-12	x				x	
5-13	x				x	
5-14				x	x	
5-15			x		x	
5-16			x		x	
5-17			x/x		x	
5-18	x					x
5-19	x					x
5-20	x					x
5-21	x					x
5-22	x					x
5-23	x					x
5-24	x					x
5-25	x					x
5-26	x					x
5-27	x					x
5-28	x					x
5-29	x					x
5-30	x					x
5-31	x					x
5-32	x				x	
5-33	x				x	
5-34	x					x
5-35	x				x	
5-36	x					x
5-37	x				x	
5-38	x					x
5-39	x				x	
5-40	x					x
5-41	x				x	
5-42	x					x
5-43	x				x	
5-44	x					x
5-45	x				x	
5-46	x					x
5-47	x					
5-48	x					
5-49	x					
5-50	x					
5-51	x					
5-52	x					
5-53	x					
5-54	x					
5-55	x					

Note: Regional aggregations are shown in the rows for Sub-Saharan Africa, North Africa, and All Africa. Period averages are shown in the last three columns. This table shows only the methodologies used in this chapter.

a. Regional aggregations: (1) simple total; (2) simple total of the first indicator divided by the simple total of the second indicator (same country coverage); (3) simple total of the gap-filled indicator; (4) simple total of the gap-filled main indicator divided by the simple total of the gap-filled secondary indicator; (5) simple total of the first gap-filled main indicator less the simple total of the second gap-filled main indicator, all divided by the simple total of the secondary indicator; (6) weighted total; (7) median; (8) no aggregation; (9) simple arithmetic mean.

b. Period averages: (1) arithmetic mean (using the same series as shown in the table, i.e., ratio if the rest of the table is shown as ratio, level if the rest of the table is shown as level, growth rate if the rest of the table is shown as growth rate); (2) least-squares growth rate (using main indicator); (3) least-squares growth rate (using main indicator in constant terms, with the rest of the table in current terms).

6

External Debt and Related Flows

The tables in this chapter provide a consistent presentation of the structure and terms of external debt and debt servicing. No data are presented on debt owed to domestic lenders. The aggregates and ratios provide various measures of a country's external debt situation. These measures include the size of debt and its servicing requirements, the amount of debt relative to GDP, the ratio of debt-servicing payments to exports, and the interest rate and terms of the stock of debt (including grace period, maturity, and grant element).

Unlike the presentation in the *ADI 1992*, these tables follow the presentation in the *World Debt Tables* and therefore show IMF purchases, repurchases, charges, and net purchases separately from long- and short-term lending, repayments, interests, or net lending. While IMF purchases and repurchases are not strictly lending (they are swaps of currency), they do add to, or subtract from, the resources available for consumption or investment and do impose a liability against future income streams. For this reason, IMF transactions are included here.

Data on debt and related flows are drawn largely from the World Bank's Debtor Reporting System (DRS), to which member countries submit detailed accounts on the annual status, transactions, and terms of debt and related flows. World Bank and IMF staff estimates based on other sources of data supplement DRS data, especially for recent years, on debt not guaranteed by debtor governments and on short-term debt. The figures in this chapter are based mostly on data supplied by debtor countries. Other data series on debt, on which the World Bank may base some of its estimates, are maintained by the Organization for Economic Cooperation and Development (OECD) and the Bank for International Settlements (BIS) from data provided by creditor governments and agencies. No figures are given for Libya, Namibia, and South Africa, which do not report debt information to the DRS. However, totals do include estimates for these countries.

The following definitions apply throughout the chapter. Long-term loans have an original or extended maturity of more than one year, while the maturity on short-term loans is one year or less. Official and private refer to the source of the foreign loans. Official loans are from multilateral organizations (excluding the IMF) and from foreign governments; these loans are either made directly to the government of the borrowing country or guaranteed by it, or its agencies, when made to a third party. Private loans are from the private sector, including foreign parent companies and their affiliates, suppliers, financial markets (such as commercial banks), and other sources. These private loans may or may not be guaranteed by creditor or debtor governments and agencies. "Public and publicly guaranteed" loans, as defined by the DRS, refer to loans from both official and private foreign sources that are made to, or guaranteed by, the debtor government or its agencies. Almost all loans from foreign official sources are public or publicly guaranteed. Some loans from foreign private sources are made to, or guaranteed by, the debtor government or its agencies (these are labeled *private guaranteed* by the DRS). Some loans from foreign private sources are not public or publicly guaranteed (these are labeled *private nonguaranteed* by DRS).

Concessional loans carry a grant element of 25 percent or more (based on a standard 10 percent discount rate), which is consistent with the Development Assistance Committee of the OECD (DAC) definition of ODA (see Chapter 12). Nonconcessional loans carry a grant element of less than 25 percent. In this chapter, private loans are shown separately from official nonconcessional loans.

Additional information, definitions, and methodology are available in the World Bank, *Global Development Finance 1997* (formerly *World Debt Tables*).

6-1. Gross disbursements: official concessional long-term loans

	Millions of U.S. dollars (current prices)											*Annual average*		
	1980	*1986*	*1987*	*1988*	*1989*	*1990*	*1991*	*1992*	*1993*	*1994*	*1995*	*75-84*	*85-89*	*90-MR*
SUB-SAHARAN AFRICA	2,655	4,342	4,784	4,777	4,964	5,005	4,679	4,884	4,909	4,983	4,787	2,412	4,386	4,875
excluding South Africa	2,655	4,342	4,784	4,777	4,964	5,005	4,679	4,884	4,909	4,983	4,787	2,412	4,386	4,875
excl. S.Africa & Nigeria	2,606	4,342	4,782	4,766	4,873	4,895	4,627	4,848	4,841	4,906	4,689	2,387	4,363	4,801
Angola	4	59	49	28	24	48	67	45	38	72	62	4	38	55
Benin	35	65	61	51	121	111	94	74	76	95	87	29	66	89
Botswana	9	3	18	22	38	18	47	21	44	36	60	12	19	38
Burkina Faso	41	79	96	80	85	70	138	134	134	106	111	36	78	115
Burundi	38	93	131	92	106	92	85	107	77	52	45	32	96	76
Cameroon	148	102	92	102	193	108	91	380	311	372	88	122	116	225
Cape Verde	3	10	7	10	11	7	5	18	10	29	17	6	11	14
Central African Republic	19	58	82	79	63	110	95	45	49	43	32	15	65	62
Chad	5	30	38	59	80	96	92	69	57	61	56	16	43	72
Comoros	13	20	13	8	4	5	3	18	5	8	10	11	13	8
Congo	49	73	104	58	40	119	31	17	8	291	14	61	72	80
Côte d'Ivoire	58	52	146	42	188	307	263	400	469	770	587	65	94	466
Djibouti	2	23	30	22	12	27	21	24	23	13	13	7	23	20
Equatorial Guinea	4	19	23	20	19	9	9	15	10	4	2	3	18	8
Eritrea	..	..	..	..	..	..	..	..	..	..	..	..	..	..
Ethiopia	70	275	332	387	314	242	147	180	346	236	206	111	318	226
Gabon	16	34	63	41	16	67	71	10	20	54	146	11	36	61
Gambia, The	28	33	35	22	28	22	29	54	25	22	20	13	26	29
Ghana	118	247	270	326	301	319	380	328	353	326	403	68	253	351
Guinea	56	168	160	233	242	190	217	169	241	137	149	57	176	184
Guinea-Bissau	59	22	37	47	43	37	45	41	22	23	22	19	34	32
Kenya	163	172	178	303	391	418	397	242	301	184	539	121	229	347
Lesotho	8	18	25	28	42	44	44	54	28	37	31	11	28	40
Liberia	39	33	29	3	0	0	2	0	33	0	0	34	20	6
Madagascar	155	155	230	204	210	206	192	116	110	72	82	98	183	130
Malawi	57	118	93	94	100	126	166	135	186	101	118	48	90	139
Mali	78	173	133	130	173	154	115	124	58	121	174	74	142	124
Mauritania	97	145	144	112	85	101	67	92	140	118	103	81	113	103
Mauritius	18	22	51	48	41	79	67	51	36	26	24	15	36	47
Mozambique	1	359	278	156	162	179	98	187	159	254	230	78	255	185
Namibia	..	..	..	..	..	..	..	..	..	..	..	..	..	..
Niger	59	103	132	144	94	90	40	82	92	66	27	40	107	66
Nigeria	49	0	2	11	91	110	53	36	67	77	99	25	22	74
Rwanda	27	76	100	85	64	61	89	76	48	20	54	27	80	58
São Tomé and Principe	8	8	11	12	18	17	44	22	16	15	12	4	11	21
Senegal	118	321	367	256	346	198	132	253	81	97	155	90	280	153
Seychelles	6	14	10	5	7	8	10	8	3	2	2	4	9	5
Sierra Leone	35	22	14	32	6	42	53	48	92	72	105	21	22	69
Somalia	74	104	76	64	71	46	13	0	0	0	0	101	83	10
South Africa	..	..	..	..	..	..	..	..	..	..	..	..	..	..
Sudan	271	208	198	294	219	180	128	93	95	10	27	314	203	89
Swaziland	17	13	12	9	12	16	18	6	3	16	12	10	10	12
Tanzania	171	200	190	326	157	248	263	341	179	226	247	190	200	251
Togo	38	88	44	105	59	82	67	44	17	40	26	36	70	46
Uganda	13	87	193	118	239	246	176	230	335	269	221	34	149	246
Zaire	131	189	290	287	295	214	116	75	58	1	0	127	234	77
Zambia	247	160	97	123	77	50	298	224	256	212	240	101	124	213
Zimbabwe	1	90	101	102	78	87	104	198	199	196	133	29	90	153
NORTH AFRICA	2,084	991	1,136	1,285	1,004	1,597	1,661	1,539	1,553	1,715	1,630	1,746	1,087	1,616
Algeria	74	68	113	44	80	292	161	225	264	522	459	76	62	320
Egypt, Arab Republic	1,074	482	508	762	474	756	963	540	604	500	375	1,089	556	623
Libya	..	..	..	..	..	..	..	..	..	..	..	..	..	..
Morocco	731	264	317	238	219	305	286	466	443	398	484	407	272	397
Tunisia	205	176	199	241	231	243	251	309	242	295	313	173	197	275
ALL AFRICA	4,738	5,332	5,921	6,062	5,968	6,602	6,340	6,423	6,461	6,698	6,418	4,158	5,472	6,490

6-2. Gross disbursements: official nonconcessional long-term loans

	Millions of U.S. dollars (current prices)											Annual average		
	1980	1986	1987	1988	1989	1990	1991	1992	1993	1994	1995	75-84	85-89	90-MR
SUB-SAHARAN AFRICA	1,603	1,947	2,280	1,812	2,114	2,221	1,972	1,913	1,584	1,230	937	1,323	1,957	1,643
excluding South Africa	1,603	1,947	2,280	1,812	2,114	2,221	1,972	1,913	1,584	1,230	937	1,323	1,957	1,643
excl. S.Africa & Nigeria	1,530	1,219	1,758	1,411	1,447	1,689	1,431	1,418	1,108	709	604	1,143	1,418	1,160
Angola	-4	63	106	41	87	115	58	56	21	0	6	-4	87	43
Benin	24	7	7	5	12	10	5	29	2	4	5	8	7	9
Botswana	15	30	80	33	33	11	56	63	28	20	6	16	46	31
Burkina Faso	18	14	13	14	9	9	9	9	5	0	1	11	11	5
Burundi	1	6	11	5	2	2	1	0	0	1	0	3	7	1
Cameroon	102	148	172	107	201	450	228	148	100	68	17	68	142	168
Cape Verde	0	0	0	0	0	5	0	0	0	0	0	4	0	1
Central African Republic	6	20	8	11	1	3	2	1	0	0	1	3	9	1
Chad	0	1	2	1	1	8	0	74	0	0	0	2	1	14
Comoros	0	4	0	0	0	0	0	0	0	0	0	1	1	0
Congo	60	29	50	106	18	9	1	0	0	40	1	38	52	8
Côte d'Ivoire	173	168	415	247	207	452	403	251	154	148	81	175	230	248
Djibouti	3	0	0	0	0	0	0	0	0	0	0	1	0	0
Equatorial Guinea	11	0	0	2	0	1	0	0	0	0	0	3	1	0
Eritrea	..	..	..	..	..	..	..	..	..	..	..	..	..	..
Ethiopia	7	39	28	38	149	68	23	29	21	14	31	11	58	31
Gabon	19	42	62	99	106	73	70	98	70	69	152	35	71	89
Gambia, The	2	2	2	0	1	1	0	2	0	0	0	2	2	0
Ghana	102	28	48	30	52	58	37	57	22	15	15	35	36	34
Guinea	8	19	9	4	13	6	12	30	34	32	31	12	11	24
Guinea-Bissau	0	3	3	1	0	0	0	1	0	0	0	3	5	0
Kenya	69	116	174	84	147	12	65	86	17	35	26	96	127	40
Lesotho	1	5	9	10	5	7	11	23	33	17	20	3	8	18
Liberia	25	11	3	12	0	0	0	0	0	0	0	23	11	0
Madagascar	57	29	92	19	12	4	7	5	7	5	1	48	42	5
Malawi	49	26	16	10	12	5	4	3	2	4	0	23	17	3
Mali	7	3	3	10	7	2	2	0	0	0	0	4	5	1
Mauritania	16	22	17	35	1	36	4	42	16	21	9	26	19	21
Mauritius	18	17	37	75	17	18	30	12	23	11	17	17	36	19
Mozambique	-1	16	18	12	24	7	12	10	13	3	5	-78	16	8
Namibia	..	..	..	..	..	..	..	..	..	..	..	..	..	..
Niger	33	6	19	6	3	1	0	0	11	4	0	26	10	3
Nigeria	73	729	522	402	667	532	541	495	477	522	334	180	539	483
Rwanda	0	0	0	0	0	1	0	0	0	0	0	0	0	0
São Tomé and Principe	2	3	1	0	0	0	0	0	0	0	0	2	1	0
Senegal	68	29	28	13	21	8	27	55	67	34	7	61	28	33
Seychelles	6	4	3	3	3	2	2	6	5	8	7	2	3	5
Sierra Leone	9	0	0	0	12	0	0	0	0	0	0	4	2	0
Somalia	13	2	0	0	0	0	0	0	0	0	0	18	2	0
South Africa	..	..	..	..	..	..	..	..	..	..	..	..	..	..
Sudan	295	2	3	89	17	5	0	15	6	2	24	137	23	9
Swaziland	12	8	9	4	4	7	5	1	5	1	4	14	7	4
Tanzania	74	27	15	11	35	40	14	8	17	22	8	77	25	18
Togo	12	1	5	8	2	1	0	0	0	0	0	14	4	0
Uganda	5	48	66	16	31	16	4	20	54	1	10	15	42	18
Zaire	70	81	83	117	97	99	188	8	0	0	0	61	82	49
Zambia	68	87	69	79	43	67	40	37	24	29	38	92	75	39
Zimbabwe	77	51	72	58	64	71	110	240	353	104	81	31	59	160
NORTH AFRICA	1,577	2,604	1,829	2,124	2,902	3,371	3,527	3,071	2,981	2,771	2,321	1,576	2,446	3,007
Algeria	492	571	406	725	1,058	1,563	1,668	1,250	1,046	1,259	1,021	491	663	1,301
Egypt, Arab Republic	830	965	550	518	572	481	320	467	488	312	94	698	812	360
Libya	..	..	..	..	..	..	..	..	..	..	..	..	..	..
Morocco	136	789	600	581	851	872	889	907	859	619	773	253	663	820
Tunisia	119	278	274	301	421	456	650	448	588	582	433	134	308	526
ALL AFRICA	3,180	4,552	4,109	3,937	5,016	5,592	5,499	4,984	4,566	4,001	3,258	2,899	4,404	4,650

6-3. Gross disbursements: private long-term loans

	Millions of U.S. dollars (current prices)											Annual average		
	1980	1986	1987	1988	1989	1990	1991	1992	1993	1994	1995	75-84	85-89	90-MR
SUB-SAHARAN AFRICA	6,282	3,557	3,345	3,436	3,118	2,480	1,984	1,885	1,864	1,098	1,447	4,336	3,507	1,793
excluding South Africa	6,282	3,557	3,345	3,436	3,118	2,480	1,984	1,885	1,864	1,098	1,447	4,336	3,507	1,793
excl. S.Africa & Nigeria	4,652	2,970	2,607	2,935	2,288	2,195	1,790	1,881	1,864	1,098	1,447	2,938	2,725	1,713
Angola	0	776	621	649	393	643	202	542	633	354	424	0	710	466
Benin	4	1	2	1	0	0	0	0	0	0	0	44	1	0
Botswana	3	7	8	3	1	0	0	0	30	0	0	6	4	5
Burkina Faso	6	1	0	0	4	0	0	0	0	0	0	8	1	0
Burundi	0	0	0	6	1	2	0	0	0	0	0	5	2	0
Cameroon	364	419	302	414	474	160	103	141	88	8	0	230	354	83
Cape Verde	0	1	0	0	0	0	0	0	0	0	0	0	0	0
Central African Republic	0	1	1	1	0	0	0	0	0	0	0	2	1	0
Chad	0	0	3	1	0	0	0	0	0	0	0	5	1	0
Comoros	0	0	0	0	0	0	0	0	0	0	0	0	0	0
Congo	412	223	251	446	127	185	6	114	451	1	0	207	273	126
Côte d'Ivoire	1,508	112	281	238	279	261	236	202	190	317	75	791	219	213
Djibouti	5	0	0	0	0	0	0	0	0	0	0	1	0	0
Equatorial Guinea	5	1	1	0	0	0	0	0	0	0	0	3	0	0
Eritrea	..	..	..	..	..	..	..	..	..	..	..	..	..	..
Ethiopia	33	79	137	147	29	51	261	113	10	4	0	30	97	73
Gabon	135	383	95	133	31	37	16	0	3	2	0	174	174	10
Gambia, The	22	0	0	0	0	0	0	0	0	0	0	5	0	0
Ghana	0	107	54	67	44	59	82	103	77	117	92	12	64	88
Guinea	57	3	3	38	0	0	0	0	11	0	0	29	13	2
Guinea-Bissau	21	0	6	0	0	0	0	0	2	0	0	5	5	0
Kenya	387	231	297	334	302	236	440	175	87	6	130	224	279	179
Lesotho	5	2	14	15	8	7	6	2	0	0	13	4	8	5
Liberia	11	0	0	0	0	0	0	0	0	0	0	23	0	0
Madagascar	155	8	16	14	0	0	1	1	1	0	1	62	10	1
Malawi	48	1	1	13	11	2	0	2	1	7	0	28	6	2
Mali	10	3	1	0	0	0	0	0	0	0	0	6	1	0
Mauritania	14	10	1	2	2	0	0	0	0	0	0	24	4	0
Mauritius	61	12	38	120	48	65	76	63	39	147	370	28	45	127
Mozambique	0	60	65	14	32	44	6	4	8	4	36	0	46	17
Namibia	..	..	..	..	..	..	..	..	..	..	..	..	..	..
Niger	190	67	50	28	49	48	0	0	0	0	0	91	45	8
Nigeria	1,631	587	738	501	830	285	193	4	0	0	0	1,399	782	80
Rwanda	0	0	4	0	0	0	0	0	0	0	0	3	1	0
São Tomé and Principe	0	1	0	0	0	0	0	0	0	0	0	1	0	0
Senegal	141	68	34	14	8	15	11	8	1	1	1	74	29	6
Seychelles	0	15	5	4	5	6	5	5	0	2	2	1	7	3
Sierra Leone	42	0	0	0	0	4	0	0	0	0	0	24	0	1
Somalia	27	0	0	0	0	0	0	0	0	0	0	25	1	0
South Africa	..	..	..	..	..	..	..	..	..	..	..	..	..	..
Sudan	145	0	0	0	0	0	0	0	0	0	0	100	0	0
Swaziland	0	1	0	0	0	0	0	0	0	0	0	3	3	0
Tanzania	122	74	45	36	35	17	4	41	45	21	4	62	48	22
Togo	50	0	0	0	0	0	0	0	0	0	0	63	0	0
Uganda	65	55	140	33	41	38	5	6	18	0	0	36	60	11
Zaire	263	6	10	6	59	3	0	0	0	0	0	176	16	1
Zambia	289	164	12	42	92	48	46	33	11	9	19	157	66	28
Zimbabwe	55	81	113	116	214	266	284	326	158	101	280	167	128	236
NORTH AFRICA	5,013	6,405	5,771	7,599	6,146	6,592	5,989	7,423	6,274	4,408	3,290	4,706	6,310	5,663
Algeria	2,832	3,880	3,936	5,406	4,423	5,084	4,696	6,046	5,191	3,202	1,827	2,743	4,197	4,341
Egypt, Arab Republic	776	1,442	1,091	1,382	1,082	773	674	389	169	262	34	778	1,316	384
Libya	..	..	..	..	..	..	..	..	..	..	..	..	..	..
Morocco	1,117	691	479	458	433	416	375	531	640	745	656	879	475	561
Tunisia	288	392	266	353	208	319	244	456	274	199	773	306	322	378
ALL AFRICA	11,295	9,962	9,116	11,035	9,265	9,072	7,973	9,307	8,138	5,506	4,738	9,043	9,817	7,456

6-4. Disbursements: long-term loans and IMF purchases

	Millions of U.S. dollars (current prices)											Annual average		
	1980	*1986*	*1987*	*1988*	*1989*	*1990*	*1991*	*1992*	*1993*	*1994*	*1995*	*75-84*	*85-89*	*90-MR*
SUB-SAHARAN AFRICA	15,432	11,584	12,004	11,728	12,000	11,175	9,660	10,039	9,639	11,529	13,777	9,683	11,465	10,970
excluding South Africa	11,757	10,581	11,087	11,081	11,058	10,368	9,214	9,209	8,696	8,229	10,191	9,039	10,664	9,318
excl. S.Africa & Nigeria	10,004	9,265	9,825	10,167	9,470	9,441	8,427	8,674	8,152	7,631	9,759	7,435	9,320	8,680
Angola	0	898	776	718	503	806	327	643	692	427	493	0	834	564
Benin	71	73	70	57	141	120	112	104	100	125	105	83	76	111
Botswana	28	40	106	58	71	30	103	84	102	56	66	34	69	74
Burkina Faso	70	93	109	94	98	79	155	143	151	132	139	56	90	133
Burundi	45	109	141	121	120	96	91	126	77	53	45	44	112	81
Cameroon	626	669	565	716	887	718	433	669	499	478	118	427	634	486
Cape Verde	3	11	7	10	11	12	5	18	10	29	17	10	12	15
Central African Republic	40	86	100	103	64	121	98	46	49	59	33	27	82	67
Chad	5	32	51	61	93	112	92	143	57	76	69	26	51	92
Comoros	13	24	13	8	4	5	4	18	5	10	10	12	14	9
Congo	526	336	404	610	185	319	38	132	459	350	15	310	399	219
Côte d'Ivoire	1,777	390	842	648	712	1,172	948	853	813	1,405	924	1,114	599	1,019
Djibouti	10	23	30	22	12	27	21	24	23	13	13	9	24	20
Equatorial Guinea	38	20	24	26	19	10	16	15	14	7	2	12	21	11
Eritrea	..	..	..	..	..	..	..	..	..	..	..	..	..	..
Ethiopia	119	435	496	572	493	360	431	342	407	274	237	170	481	342
Gabon	171	491	240	349	158	186	162	108	93	189	355	222	308	182
Gambia, The	56	46	49	27	38	33	31	55	25	22	20	26	35	31
Ghana	249	421	520	639	574	502	659	487	517	457	551	184	494	529
Guinea	129	207	179	290	278	196	241	210	286	182	211	103	212	221
Guinea-Bissau	80	26	47	48	46	37	45	42	24	24	25	28	45	33
Kenya	713	519	650	898	944	802	950	502	436	257	695	515	716	607
Lesotho	15	24	49	57	60	62	65	86	70	60	64	19	46	68
Liberia	109	43	32	15	0	0	2	0	33	0	0	113	31	6
Madagascar	437	243	382	247	255	228	217	122	118	78	84	235	269	141
Malawi	190	146	110	142	146	158	190	141	189	138	129	121	127	157
Mali	109	190	137	157	186	183	117	139	72	163	219	95	158	149
Mauritania	156	198	187	154	99	148	71	145	168	163	133	141	150	138
Mauritius	143	75	126	243	106	162	173	127	98	183	411	87	129	192
Mozambique	0	434	377	207	234	242	158	265	201	282	271	0	329	237
Namibia	..	..	..	..	..	..	..	..	..	..	..	..	..	..
Niger	290	200	225	189	156	148	40	83	103	86	27	164	179	81
Nigeria	1,753	1,315	1,262	914	1,588	927	787	535	544	599	433	1,603	1,344	637
Rwanda	34	76	104	85	64	62	101	77	48	20	68	31	81	63
São Tomé and Principe	10	12	12	12	19	17	44	22	16	15	12	7	13	21
Senegal	395	477	503	340	440	251	228	316	150	199	247	261	399	232
Seychelles	12	32	17	12	14	16	17	18	8	11	11	7	19	13
Sierra Leone	106	45	14	32	17	46	53	48	92	209	124	66	29	95
Somalia	135	128	94	64	71	46	13	0	0	0	0	158	101	10
South Africa	..	..	..	..	..	..	..	..	..	..	..	..	..	..
Sudan	921	210	201	382	237	185	128	108	101	12	51	655	226	97
Swaziland	31	25	20	13	16	23	23	7	8	17	16	29	21	16
Tanzania	433	340	295	416	227	334	309	481	241	270	259	352	298	316
Togo	122	104	50	137	84	104	67	55	17	55	59	122	89	59
Uganda	161	190	457	241	362	382	264	311	408	322	287	135	287	329
Zaire	603	371	550	410	659	316	304	83	58	1	0	482	461	127
Zambia	693	532	178	244	213	165	384	293	290	249	2,550	487	290	655
Zimbabwe	132	222	286	276	357	424	498	985	776	477	574	257	277	622
NORTH AFRICA	9,124	10,663	9,771	11,853	11,408	12,028	11,997	12,855	11,208	9,809	7,828	8,608	10,851	10,954
Algeria	3,398	4,519	4,455	6,174	6,165	6,939	6,834	7,521	6,501	5,825	3,781	3,310	5,044	6,233
Egypt, Arab Republic	2,743	2,889	2,300	2,662	2,128	2,010	2,039	1,518	1,261	1,074	504	2,624	2,714	1,401
Libya	..	..	..	..	..	..	..	..	..	..	..	..	..	..
Morocco	2,262	1,780	1,604	1,425	1,682	1,659	1,549	1,930	1,943	1,761	1,913	1,703	1,568	1,792
Tunisia	611	1,023	792	915	860	1,018	1,358	1,286	1,104	1,076	1,518	616	877	1,227
ALL AFRICA	24,556	22,246	21,775	23,580	23,408	23,203	21,657	22,893	20,847	21,338	21,605	18,291	22,316	21,924

Note: In 1995, Zambia was able to clear its arrears to the IMF after completing a 3 year Rights Arrangement Program.

6-5. Amortization: official concessional long-term loans

	Millions of U.S. dollars (current prices)											Annual average		
	1980	1986	1987	1988	1989	1990	1991	1992	1993	1994	1995	75-84	85-89	90-MR
SUB-SAHARAN AFRICA	276	591	590	658	627	649	663	655	826	1,032	1,102	263	569	821
excluding South Africa	276	591	590	658	627	649	663	655	826	1,032	1,102	263	569	821
excl. S.Africa & Nigeria	256	575	585	647	619	631	654	646	658	799	955	244	555	724
Angola	0	0	0	1	1	2	4	2	2	7	5	0	1	4
Benin	1	5	6	5	3	7	9	8	12	12	15	2	4	11
Botswana	0	4	4	7	5	6	7	9	13	15	13	1	5	10
Burkina Faso	4	6	7	14	11	13	15	10	12	19	22	2	8	15
Burundi	1	8	10	13	13	14	18	14	15	16	14	1	10	15
Cameroon	14	33	35	26	8	27	26	24	40	16	16	13	25	25
Cape Verde	0	1	2	2	2	2	3	6	2	2	2	0	2	3
Central African Republic	0	2	3	2	2	3	2	2	1	5	2	1	2	3
Chad	3	3	2	2	3	2	3	3	1	6	3	1	3	3
Comoros	0	1	0	0	0	0	1	2	2	2	0	0	0	1
Congo	11	2	1	2	2	3	0	0	1	8	7	10	4	3
Côte d'Ivoire	18	24	38	56	57	80	81	95	80	61	72	15	37	78
Djibouti	2	2	7	8	8	8	8	7	5	5	5	1	5	6
Equatorial Guinea	0	1	1	0	0	1	1	0	0	0	0	0	0	0
Eritrea	..	..	..	..	..	..	..	..	..	..	..	..	..	..
Ethiopia	9	53	64	80	62	22	24	17	16	20	29	12	57	21
Gabon	5	5	4	5	3	2	8	24	8	9	12	6	5	10
Gambia, The	0	2	6	7	10	11	9	9	8	10	7	1	5	9
Ghana	17	38	44	38	28	44	32	38	40	61	62	23	37	46
Guinea	44	27	71	42	39	53	51	19	16	29	91	36	42	43
Guinea-Bissau	0	2	2	1	4	1	1	3	2	4	5	0	2	3
Kenya	7	27	25	33	38	41	48	43	52	79	78	9	29	57
Lesotho	0	3	3	4	4	4	4	5	9	6	11	1	3	6
Liberia	2	2	2	4	1	0	11	0	0	1	0	4	2	2
Madagascar	23	10	15	21	19	21	15	25	17	17	13	22	14	18
Malawi	2	7	4	5	7	9	18	13	13	13	18	2	5	14
Mali	4	13	10	26	20	20	6	17	18	57	41	4	17	26
Mauritania	3	23	35	37	26	30	21	25	42	36	40	3	28	32
Mauritius	2	8	11	13	16	15	19	33	19	22	25	2	11	22
Mozambique	0	44	7	6	7	9	10	13	13	17	32	2	17	15
Namibia	..	..	..	..	..	..	..	..	..	..	..	..	..	..
Niger	16	8	9	10	7	5	5	4	12	9	7	5	8	7
Nigeria	21	16	5	11	8	18	9	9	169	233	146	20	14	97
Rwanda	0	5	7	6	11	8	11	10	10	1	11	1	7	9
São Tomé and Principe	0	0	2	1	1	0	1	1	1	1	1	0	1	1
Senegal	8	21	37	35	41	54	46	35	31	69	66	5	29	50
Seychelles	0	1	0	1	2	2	4	4	5	6	7	0	1	5
Sierra Leone	1	1	0	0	0	1	1	5	2	5	7	1	0	3
Somalia	2	3	3	1	3	2	0	0	0	0	0	2	2	0
South Africa	..	..	..	..	..	..	..	..	..	..	..	..	..	..
Sudan	18	124	39	50	44	14	11	13	9	3	9	21	54	10
Swaziland	2	4	5	6	5	5	10	6	6	6	8	2	4	7
Tanzania	19	25	31	31	66	40	43	38	46	45	46	14	34	43
Togo	2	6	8	8	8	6	9	6	4	4	7	2	7	6
Uganda	3	5	6	7	7	10	13	11	18	24	24	3	6	17
Zaire	3	12	11	10	9	8	5	5	4	0	0	5	10	4
Zambia	7	2	5	7	2	5	14	10	15	25	53	4	4	20
Zimbabwe	5	4	6	14	17	21	25	34	37	49	73	3	9	40
NORTH AFRICA	299	377	348	426	450	585	451	544	601	729	704	268	392	602
Algeria	73	84	88	98	91	103	84	88	87	54	40	72	95	76
Egypt, Arab Republic	119	109	80	127	163	279	158	110	66	79	163	112	124	143
Libya	..	..	..	..	..	..	..	..	..	..	..	..	..	..
Morocco	64	88	59	73	60	61	70	191	293	328	280	44	65	204
Tunisia	43	96	120	129	136	142	139	155	155	269	220	40	109	180
ALL AFRICA	575	968	937	1,084	1,077	1,234	1,114	1,199	1,428	1,761	1,805	531	961	1,423

6-6. Amortization: official nonconcessional long-term loans

	Millions of U.S. dollars (current prices)											Annual average		
	1980	1986	1987	1988	1989	1990	1991	1992	1993	1994	1995	75-84	85-89	90-MR
SUB-SAHARAN AFRICA	395	852	974	1,319	1,185	1,885	1,764	1,382	1,370	1,864	2,022	308	1,089	1,715
excluding South Africa	395	852	974	1,319	1,185	1,885	1,764	1,382	1,370	1,864	2,022	308	1,089	1,715
excl. S.Africa & Nigeria	370	757	832	989	896	1,127	1,222	1,058	1,049	1,442	1,562	280	824	1,243
Angola	0	23	23	38	62	61	56	42	23	35	24	0	30	40
Benin	1	6	5	5	4	11	6	7	6	8	9	2	5	8
Botswana	6	13	30	29	28	42	45	50	43	45	46	3	22	45
Burkina Faso	4	5	4	5	4	4	10	5	8	8	7	2	4	7
Burundi	1	3	6	4	4	5	5	5	3	5	3	0	4	4
Cameroon	15	62	70	62	48	71	83	57	98	116	138	17	58	94
Cape Verde	0	2	2	2	2	2	2	2	2	2	2	0	2	2
Central African Republic	0	4	5	2	5	4	1	2	1	2	0	1	4	2
Chad	0	1	1	1	0	0	1	1	4	2	1	0	1	1
Comoros	0	0	0	0	0	0	5	1	0	0	0	0	0	1
Congo	10	9	11	19	23	68	4	1	0	137	25	11	16	39
Côte d'Ivoire	37	80	93	150	127	167	192	196	213	294	406	29	102	245
Djibouti	1	0	0	0	0	0	0	0	0	0	0	0	0	0
Equatorial Guinea	1	1	6	0	0	0	1	2	1	0	0	1	2	1
Eritrea	..	..	..	..	..	..	..	..	..	..	..	..	..	..
Ethiopia	1	21	31	37	29	24	14	12	12	12	14	3	26	15
Gabon	14	15	9	13	14	16	34	60	23	55	78	13	16	44
Gambia, The	0	2	1	2	1	2	4	6	6	6	7	0	1	5
Ghana	19	18	17	20	21	23	33	41	31	39	41	12	18	35
Guinea	20	12	24	27	17	24	22	22	17	12	20	9	18	20
Guinea-Bissau	0	1	1	1	2	2	2	2	0	1	4	0	1	2
Kenya	23	66	100	116	116	138	141	131	126	171	187	21	91	149
Lesotho	0	3	3	8	4	4	7	8	6	6	7	1	4	6
Liberia	2	12	3	6	1	1	5	0	13	13	0	5	6	5
Madagascar	1	25	39	37	39	25	22	8	10	9	9	8	36	14
Malawi	3	25	22	21	20	31	34	24	19	16	26	4	19	25
Mali	0	1	1	2	2	2	1	2	3	20	8	0	2	6
Mauritania	1	14	25	42	23	56	25	25	34	22	29	6	25	32
Mauritius	3	14	21	24	24	24	29	51	32	32	33	3	19	34
Mozambique	0	5	8	9	9	13	9	13	15	46	35	0	7	22
Namibia	..	..	..	..	..	..	..	..	..	..	..	..	..	..
Niger	2	17	10	11	11	4	3	3	20	6	1	5	12	6
Nigeria	25	96	141	330	289	758	543	324	322	422	460	28	264	471
Rwanda	0	0	0	0	0	0	1	0	0	0	0	0	0	0
São Tomé and Principe	1	1	1	0	1	1	0	0	0	1	0	1	1	0
Senegal	11	39	64	66	32	57	53	25	17	43	49	7	44	40
Seychelles	0	2	2	1	3	3	3	4	3	3	3	0	2	3
Sierra Leone	2	3	2	5	0	2	1	7	2	8	22	2	2	7
Somalia	5	0	1	0	4	0	0	0	0	0	0	2	1	0
South Africa	..	..	..	..	..	..	..	..	..	..	..	..	..	..
Sudan	29	22	2	8	2	1	1	1	1	0	6	20	8	2
Swaziland	3	10	13	13	14	28	10	9	9	12	8	3	11	13
Tanzania	7	33	34	34	30	36	59	45	43	38	50	7	44	45
Togo	8	56	17	15	14	20	11	4	3	3	1	8	27	7
Uganda	8	10	18	36	29	34	25	26	60	48	36	6	20	38
Zaire	100	56	42	48	54	25	23	19	0	0	0	36	52	11
Zambia	30	48	38	31	28	40	190	92	78	94	133	25	36	104
Zimbabwe	0	20	29	38	47	57	49	49	67	77	97	2	29	66
NORTH AFRICA	285	1,724	1,594	1,747	1,957	2,344	2,579	2,540	2,671	2,293	2,716	309	1,661	2,524
Algeria	171	677	799	869	919	1,101	1,207	1,156	1,176	647	635	157	765	987
Egypt, Arab Republic	32	461	224	371	486	611	605	411	334	307	396	53	355	444
Libya	..	..	..	..	..	..	..	..	..	..	..	..	..	..
Morocco	51	409	348	303	365	419	525	663	850	1,002	1,260	57	357	786
Tunisia	30	178	223	204	187	214	242	309	312	336	426	43	184	307
ALL AFRICA	679	2,577	2,567	3,065	3,142	4,229	4,343	3,922	4,042	4,157	4,738	617	2,750	4,238

6-7. Amortization: private long-term loans

	Millions of U.S. dollars (current prices)											*Annual average*		
	1980	*1986*	*1987*	*1988*	*1989*	*1990*	*1991*	*1992*	*1993*	*1994*	*1995*	*75-84*	*85-89*	*90-MR*
SUB-SAHARAN AFRICA	2,123	2,982	2,322	2,163	1,730	2,066	1,814	2,907	1,261	1,672	1,604	1,845	2,639	1,887
excluding South Africa	2,123	2,982	2,322	2,163	1,730	2,066	1,814	2,907	1,261	1,672	1,604	1,845	2,639	1,887
excl. S.Africa & Nigeria	1,926	1,850	2,010	1,812	1,420	1,663	1,503	1,362	1,172	1,581	1,401	1,305	1,776	1,447
Angola	0	41	73	58	66	113	138	106	35	105	300	0	61	133
Benin	3	19	3	0	0	0	0	0	0	0	0	4	8	0
Botswana	0	1	3	5	4	19	3	3	1	2	6	2	6	6
Burkina Faso	2	8	4	2	1	0	1	0	0	0	0	2	5	0
Burundi	3	6	8	7	7	8	3	2	1	1	1	2	6	3
Cameroon	85	334	285	292	147	171	93	67	98	67	53	76	292	91
Cape Verde	0	0	0	0	0	0	0	0	0	0	0	0	0	0
Central African Republic	1	1	1	1	2	1	0	1	0	0	0	1	1	0
Chad	0	0	0	0	1	1	1	0	1	0	0	1	1	1
Comoros	0	0	0	0	0	0	0	0	0	0	0	0	0	0
Congo	12	212	300	270	174	285	200	97	75	157	50	62	236	144
Côte d'Ivoire	667	293	498	194	150	251	240	212	242	356	60	350	264	227
Djibouti	0	2	2	2	1	0	0	0	0	0	0	1	2	0
Equatorial Guinea	0	0	0	1	0	0	0	0	0	0	0	1	0	0
Eritrea	..	..	..	..	..	..	..	..	..	..	..	..	..	..
Ethiopia	7	53	65	80	106	107	48	33	37	36	49	10	68	52
Gabon	260	107	11	15	5	8	48	17	4	33	75	149	55	31
Gambia, The	0	0	2	1	1	8	5	5	4	4	0	1	1	4
Ghana	42	29	50	84	105	79	48	58	52	66	63	11	56	61
Guinea	11	2	6	18	13	19	10	8	8	9	15	8	9	12
Guinea-Bissau	3	0	0	0	0	0	0	0	0	0	0	1	0	0
Kenya	165	212	154	173	139	169	167	151	123	281	204	161	180	183
Lesotho	3	3	2	5	6	7	5	7	6	5	4	2	5	6
Liberia	12	0	0	0	0	0	0	0	0	0	0	9	0	0
Madagascar	23	54	32	28	17	16	12	11	8	5	7	10	28	10
Malawi	28	34	12	9	3	5	10	14	10	11	15	17	19	11
Mali	2	3	7	2	1	1	1	3	0	1	0	1	3	1
Mauritania	13	7	7	1	6	1	2	2	0	0	0	21	5	1
Mauritius	14	17	17	68	13	21	43	40	25	41	85	17	28	42
Mozambique	0	13	15	19	18	18	21	7	10	5	9	0	14	12
Namibia	..	..	..	..	..	..	..	..	..	..	..	..	..	..
Niger	40	39	38	35	38	39	55	20	24	24	24	40	38	31
Nigeria	197	1,132	313	351	310	404	311	1,546	89	91	203	540	863	441
Rwanda	2	5	4	3	3	2	1	1	0	0	0	1	4	1
São Tomé and Principe	0	0	0	0	0	0	0	0	0	0	0	0	0	0
Senegal	137	38	59	64	59	30	45	39	4	10	27	46	49	26
Seychelles	0	3	3	7	8	8	7	5	3	4	4	0	5	5
Sierra Leone	29	1	2	1	1	0	0	0	0	0	29	16	2	5
Somalia	0	0	0	0	0	0	0	0	0	0	0	3	0	0
South Africa	..	..	..	..	..	..	..	..	..	..	..	..	..	..
Sudan	7	5	0	0	0	0	0	0	0	0	0	16	1	0
Swaziland	3	4	12	2	2	2	2	2	2	2	0	2	5	1
Tanzania	23	4	6	9	9	12	13	79	10	13	17	18	6	24
Togo	9	23	8	2	2	0	0	0	0	0	0	16	10	0
Uganda	21	20	20	34	36	22	30	14	32	16	10	15	27	21
Zaire	90	37	29	23	35	15	13	5	0	0	0	42	32	5
Zambia	175	38	51	75	82	57	54	46	51	75	55	111	51	56
Zimbabwe	34	184	221	226	162	169	185	309	305	253	240	58	195	243
NORTH AFRICA	3,137	3,909	4,040	4,795	5,476	7,134	7,691	7,681	7,314	4,079	2,854	2,365	4,489	6,125
Algeria	2,284	2,808	2,927	3,621	4,103	5,577	5,931	5,827	5,661	2,692	1,703	1,646	3,252	4,565
Egypt, Arab Republic	192	673	517	693	824	809	882	925	575	523	340	238	746	676
Libya	..	..	..	..	..	..	..	..	..	..	..	..	..	..
Morocco	475	153	211	165	200	231	464	533	704	544	524	323	169	500
Tunisia	186	275	385	317	350	517	413	395	375	321	286	157	321	385
ALL AFRICA	5,260	6,891	6,363	6,958	7,206	9,201	9,505	10,588	8,574	5,751	4,458	4,210	7,128	8,013

6-8. Amortization: long-term loans and IMF repurchases

	Millions of U.S. dollars (current prices)											Annual average		
	1980	1986	1987	1988	1989	1990	1991	1992	1993	1994	1995	75-84	85-89	90-MR
SUB-SAHARAN AFRICA	3,271	7,940	6,761	7,364	6,095	7,453	6,234	6,559	6,945	6,286	8,473	3,363	7,180	6,991
excluding South Africa	3,177	5,652	5,109	5,355	4,861	5,553	4,854	5,474	3,912	5,081	7,143	2,698	5,447	5,336
excl. S.Africa & Nigeria	2,935	4,409	4,650	4,663	4,254	4,373	3,992	3,595	3,333	4,334	6,334	2,110	4,306	4,327
Angola	0	64	96	97	128	176	199	150	60	146	329	0	93	177
Benin	6	33	17	13	9	21	16	15	18	21	26	7	20	19
Botswana	6	18	38	40	38	67	54	62	57	61	65	6	32	61
Burkina Faso	11	22	18	24	18	19	25	15	20	27	29	7	20	22
Burundi	4	21	29	28	26	28	25	24	23	28	27	5	24	26
Cameroon	131	437	400	388	208	270	214	203	282	204	212	112	381	231
Cape Verde	0	3	4	4	4	4	6	8	4	5	3	0	3	5
Central African Republic	7	16	15	16	22	17	7	7	3	13	10	6	17	10
Chad	5	5	4	5	8	7	4	4	8	10	10	4	8	7
Comoros	0	1	0	0	0	0	6	3	2	2	0	0	0	2
Congo	41	226	315	294	203	362	209	98	77	305	84	86	259	189
Côte d'Ivoire	722	535	777	586	496	621	618	594	585	787	625	405	550	638
Djibouti	2	4	9	10	9	8	8	7	5	5	5	2	7	6
Equatorial Guinea	2	5	8	3	5	4	2	2	1	1	1	2	6	2
Eritrea	..	..	..	..	..	..	..	..	..	..	..	..	..	..
Ethiopia	17	164	180	214	219	177	92	62	66	68	92	30	177	93
Gabon	279	127	24	33	22	40	114	137	71	119	216	169	75	116
Gambia, The	0	21	17	15	17	26	23	22	21	24	20	4	15	23
Ghana	106	118	299	418	338	262	190	200	190	248	273	57	249	227
Guinea	76	53	115	92	78	110	93	51	44	56	134	56	77	81
Guinea-Bissau	3	4	4	4	6	3	4	5	3	6	10	2	4	5
Kenya	205	422	400	423	425	454	396	407	363	546	508	217	411	446
Lesotho	3	10	10	17	15	15	16	20	21	18	25	4	13	19
Liberia	18	14	5	12	5	2	15	0	13	15	0	23	10	8
Madagascar	49	143	126	133	128	113	84	59	49	42	43	47	124	65
Malawi	35	93	72	65	56	65	82	69	47	46	68	30	70	63
Mali	9	39	45	54	45	41	17	28	29	88	55	8	43	43
Mauritania	26	60	79	89	66	103	62	61	82	64	78	35	72	75
Mauritius	19	84	82	146	90	103	113	124	75	96	143	30	99	109
Mozambique	0	62	29	33	34	40	41	34	43	78	90	0	38	54
Namibia	..	..	..	..	..	..	..	..	..	..	..	..	..	..
Niger	58	69	81	89	74	63	75	36	66	48	42	50	74	55
Nigeria	242	1,243	459	692	607	1,180	862	1,878	579	746	809	588	1,141	1,009
Rwanda	3	13	14	12	17	10	13	12	10	1	11	3	13	10
São Tomé and Principe	1	1	2	1	2	1	1	1	1	1	1	1	2	1
Senegal	165	165	226	229	192	197	191	143	80	151	223	67	183	164
Seychelles	0	6	6	9	13	13	14	13	12	12	14	1	8	13
Sierra Leone	49	38	6	8	3	7	9	17	13	93	62	26	13	33
Somalia	11	40	27	2	18	5	0	0	0	0	0	9	20	1
South Africa	..	..	..	..	..	..	..	..	..	..	..	..	..	..
Sudan	131	151	42	58	45	16	12	14	9	3	54	90	63	18
Swaziland	8	23	35	25	21	36	21	17	16	19	17	6	24	21
Tanzania	81	94	86	83	114	116	143	167	106	111	132	59	99	129
Togo	19	91	50	52	49	43	28	20	15	14	19	27	61	23
Uganda	45	122	117	158	141	111	102	80	119	112	99	35	129	104
Zaire	277	240	273	211	441	200	91	29	4	5	1	123	279	55
Zambia	269	241	97	112	130	126	292	184	213	215	2,067	193	130	516
Zimbabwe	40	303	362	356	264	270	266	391	409	380	410	67	306	354
NORTH AFRICA	3,942	6,917	6,636	7,509	8,296	10,846	11,468	11,487	11,102	8,050	6,691	3,276	7,200	9,941
Algeria	2,529	3,568	3,813	4,587	5,114	6,781	7,223	7,237	7,252	3,588	2,548	1,875	4,112	5,772
Egypt, Arab Republic	446	1,300	885	1,249	1,496	1,746	1,724	1,487	975	930	995	449	1,274	1,309
Libya	..	..	..	..	..	..	..	..	..	..	..	..	..	..
Morocco	678	998	966	794	886	938	1,231	1,530	2,003	2,025	2,164	454	866	1,649
Tunisia	290	549	728	650	673	984	930	889	847	926	948	243	615	921
ALL AFRICA	7,213	14,857	13,397	14,872	14,391	18,298	17,702	18,046	18,047	14,335	15,164	6,639	14,380	16,932

Note: In 1995, Zambia was able to clear its arrears to the IMF after completing a 3 year Rights Arrangement Program.

6-9. Interest payments: official concessional long-term loans

	Millions of U.S. dollars (current prices)											Annual average		
	1980	*1986*	*1987*	*1988*	*1989*	*1990*	*1991*	*1992*	*1993*	*1994*	*1995*	*75-84*	*85-89*	*90-MR*
SUB-SAHARAN AFRICA	267	374	391	438	423	757	559	839	773	1,088	797	198	380	802
excluding South Africa	267	374	391	438	423	757	559	839	773	1,088	797	198	380	802
excl. S.Africa & Nigeria	251	363	386	433	414	441	519	473	513	647	656	183	371	542
Angola	0	1	1	3	2	1	3	2	3	6	7	0	1	4
Benin	1	5	5	5	4	7	9	7	9	9	11	1	5	9
Botswana	1	2	3	3	3	4	5	5	6	4	3	1	3	5
Burkina Faso	2	5	7	7	8	7	6	6	6	7	9	2	6	7
Burundi	1	6	9	10	10	7	8	10	9	10	9	1	8	9
Cameroon	18	34	36	20	12	34	30	18	25	20	55	15	26	30
Cape Verde	0	1	1	1	1	1	1	1	1	1	1	0	1	1
Central African Republic	0	3	5	5	3	5	3	6	2	6	3	0	4	4
Chad	0	1	3	3	1	3	4	4	4	5	3	0	2	4
Comoros	0	1	1	0	1	1	2	1	1	1	1	0	1	1
Congo	12	2	3	12	6	30	8	5	4	93	9	6	7	25
Côte d'Ivoire	14	27	12	6	9	6	54	32	33	38	51	14	14	36
Djibouti	1	2	3	4	2	2	2	2	2	1	1	1	3	2
Equatorial Guinea	0	0	0	1	0	1	1	1	0	1	0	0	0	1
Eritrea	..	..	..	..	..	..	..	..	..	..	..	..	..	..
Ethiopia	9	20	27	41	32	19	14	11	12	17	21	9	27	16
Gabon	3	2	2	2	3	2	10	20	5	15	41	3	2	15
Gambia, The	0	1	2	3	3	4	3	4	4	4	3	0	2	4
Ghana	14	18	22	27	22	25	27	34	40	41	30	15	21	33
Guinea	12	6	15	13	16	29	27	20	24	28	29	10	12	26
Guinea-Bissau	0	1	2	1	3	2	2	2	2	3	4	0	2	2
Kenya	10	22	27	33	24	28	60	36	43	54	63	11	25	47
Lesotho	0	2	2	2	2	3	4	6	5	4	5	0	2	4
Liberia	2	2	2	3	0	0	1	0	0	0	0	2	2	0
Madagascar	6	9	14	16	15	20	20	21	16	14	12	9	12	17
Malawi	4	9	8	7	8	10	15	13	14	14	20	4	8	14
Mali	2	10	12	14	12	15	7	11	9	33	22	3	11	16
Mauritania	7	13	12	11	12	13	13	11	21	24	20	7	12	17
Mauritius	2	5	7	9	9	11	13	18	16	17	19	2	7	15
Mozambique	0	28	8	11	12	9	13	18	30	17	25	0	14	19
Namibia	..	..	..	..	..	..	..	..	..	..	..	..	..	..
Niger	2	6	11	11	6	5	5	4	8	7	8	2	7	6
Nigeria	16	11	5	5	9	317	40	365	259	440	141	15	9	260
Rwanda	1	4	6	8	7	6	6	7	4	2	8	1	6	5
São Tomé and Principe	0	0	0	1	0	0	1	1	1	1	1	0	0	1
Senegal	8	19	23	31	75	30	31	20	7	25	22	5	30	23
Seychelles	0	1	1	2	2	3	3	3	3	2	3	0	1	3
Sierra Leone	1	1	0	1	0	2	1	7	3	4	5	1	1	3
Somalia	2	3	3	3	4	4	0	0	0	0	0	2	3	1
South Africa	..	..	..	..	..	..	..	..	..	..	..	..	..	..
Sudan	32	44	16	18	11	8	10	11	7	0	1	17	20	6
Swaziland	1	1	3	2	2	2	3	2	2	2	2	1	2	2
Tanzania	17	16	18	22	19	22	27	25	59	31	32	15	18	33
Togo	1	5	6	10	7	8	8	7	6	5	5	1	6	7
Uganda	1	5	7	7	7	7	10	11	13	19	24	2	6	14
Zaire	47	7	20	15	15	19	15	12	7	0	0	11	13	9
Zambia	16	4	13	13	9	12	20	20	26	40	39	7	9	26
Zimbabwe	1	11	12	16	16	18	18	20	21	25	29	2	12	22
NORTH AFRICA	290	258	170	265	374	373	252	582	671	769	914	239	264	593
Algeria	33	20	17	19	17	20	24	26	27	39	93	30	18	38
Egypt, Arab Republic	154	130	52	130	206	213	85	396	424	475	578	122	134	362
Libya	..	..	..	..	..	..	..	..	..	..	..	..	..	..
Morocco	72	54	41	46	77	65	69	82	141	146	151	56	51	109
Tunisia	32	55	62	70	75	76	74	78	79	109	93	31	61	85
ALL AFRICA	558	633	562	703	797	1,131	810	1,421	1,444	1,856	1,711	437	644	1,395

6-10. Interest payments: official nonconcessional long-term loans

	Millions of U.S. dollars (current prices)											Annual average		
	1980	1986	1987	1988	1989	1990	1991	1992	1993	1994	1995	75-84	85-89	90-MR
SUB-SAHARAN AFRICA	425	1,041	1,331	1,732	1,502	1,961	2,326	1,391	1,159	1,379	1,335	359	1,294	1,592
excluding South Africa	425	1,041	1,331	1,732	1,502	1,961	2,326	1,391	1,159	1,379	1,335	359	1,294	1,592
excl. S.Africa & Nigeria	378	886	945	1,020	929	977	1,116	929	848	1,047	1,016	307	898	989
Angola	0	13	12	30	22	25	19	13	5	4	6	0	17	12
Benin	1	4	3	2	2	7	4	3	4	10	10	1	3	6
Botswana	6	23	30	31	29	32	28	28	26	26	22	5	25	27
Burkina Faso	2	6	7	6	8	3	9	8	10	7	8	2	6	8
Burundi	0	4	4	5	4	4	4	4	3	2	2	0	4	3
Cameroon	24	55	65	65	59	91	99	69	105	115	101	21	57	97
Cape Verde	0	1	3	2	1	1	1	2	1	1	1	1	2	1
Central African Republic	0	5	3	2	5	3	2	1	1	2	0	1	4	2
Chad	0	1	1	0	0	0	1	2	4	2	1	0	0	2
Comoros	0	0	0	0	0	0	1	1	0	0	0	0	0	0
Congo	13	32	23	22	32	39	6	1	0	89	11	8	25	24
Côte d'Ivoire	63	186	150	177	159	181	218	207	185	230	201	48	159	204
Djibouti	0	0	0	0	0	0	0	0	0	0	0	0	0	0
Equatorial Guinea	0	1	2	1	0	0	1	1	0	0	0	0	1	0
Eritrea	..	..	..	..	..	..	..	..	..	..	..	..	..	..
Ethiopia	5	10	10	9	11	6	8	9	9	14	11	4	9	9
Gabon	16	13	20	42	52	65	76	182	25	59	119	11	28	88
Gambia, The	0	2	1	2	1	1	2	2	2	2	1	0	1	2
Ghana	10	14	16	22	22	20	25	28	27	20	21	8	17	24
Guinea	9	6	26	13	13	18	12	13	12	11	12	7	13	13
Guinea-Bissau	0	1	2	2	1	1	1	1	0	1	2	0	1	1
Kenya	43	89	109	115	100	106	94	75	82	107	102	35	96	94
Lesotho	0	2	3	3	4	3	5	6	6	6	8	1	3	6
Liberia	5	13	5	6	1	1	1	0	8	0	0	6	7	2
Madagascar	3	36	72	39	70	51	39	10	8	4	8	5	50	20
Malawi	6	19	16	17	16	18	19	14	11	9	14	7	16	14
Mali	0	2	1	1	2	2	1	1	1	5	1	0	1	2
Mauritania	2	14	18	20	13	22	12	8	21	14	12	4	15	15
Mauritius	6	16	19	22	21	22	22	22	18	17	16	5	18	20
Mozambique	0	4	5	13	18	7	15	20	39	35	51	0	9	28
Namibia	..	..	..	..	..	..	..	..	..	..	..	..	..	..
Niger	5	18	33	32	8	2	6	1	7	3	0	5	21	3
Nigeria	47	155	386	712	573	984	1,210	462	311	332	319	52	396	603
Rwanda	0	0	0	0	0	0	0	0	0	0	0	0	0	0
São Tomé and Principe	0	0	0	0	2	1	0	0	0	0	0	0	1	0
Senegal	14	63	75	63	52	42	43	19	13	27	31	13	56	29
Seychelles	0	2	2	2	2	2	2	2	2	2	3	0	2	2
Sierra Leone	2	1	1	2	0	2	1	4	10	18	14	2	1	8
Somalia	0	0	1	0	7	0	0	0	0	0	0	0	2	0
South Africa	..	..	..	..	..	..	..	..	..	..	..	..	..	..
Sudan	12	2	5	2	1	1	1	0	1	0	2	10	6	1
Swaziland	6	8	10	10	9	7	6	5	4	4	3	4	9	5
Tanzania	17	19	25	24	25	22	24	26	47	32	47	14	21	33
Togo	11	31	19	52	21	21	11	3	2	1	3	8	30	7
Uganda	1	14	15	14	15	11	16	11	16	14	8	2	13	13
Zaire	59	73	61	69	45	58	35	14	1	0	0	33	75	18
Zambia	38	46	36	29	36	31	199	59	54	66	74	30	36	80
Zimbabwe	0	37	38	53	45	49	48	56	76	87	91	6	40	68
NORTH AFRICA	299	1,352	948	1,410	1,587	1,526	1,494	1,732	1,817	1,985	2,325	369	1,256	1,813
Algeria	126	293	289	310	290	298	333	365	356	354	719	105	287	404
Egypt, Arab Republic	67	622	234	524	597	518	319	460	458	556	551	162	477	477
Libya	..	..	..	..	..	..	..	..	..	..	..	..	..	..
Morocco	63	324	287	425	553	539	656	697	774	821	779	67	366	711
Tunisia	42	113	138	151	147	171	187	210	229	254	276	36	127	221
ALL AFRICA	724	2,393	2,279	3,143	3,089	3,487	3,820	3,123	2,976	3,364	3,660	728	2,551	3,405

6-11. Interest payments: private long-term loans

	Millions of U.S. dollars (current prices)											Annual average		
	1980	*1986*	*1987*	*1988*	*1989*	*1990*	*1991*	*1992*	*1993*	*1994*	*1995*	*75-84*	*85-89*	*90-MR*
SUB-SAHARAN AFRICA	1,685	1,429	1,133	1,616	1,722	1,640	1,528	1,621	748	877	777	1,254	1,638	1,198
excluding South Africa	1,685	1,429	1,133	1,616	1,722	1,640	1,528	1,621	748	877	777	1,254	1,638	1,198
excl. S.Africa & Nigeria	1,219	1,089	917	855	825	817	724	617	456	575	530	845	972	620
Angola	0	32	48	72	76	74	62	31	16	39	64	0	50	48
Benin	1	14	7	0	6	0	0	0	0	0	0	3	7	0
Botswana	1	3	3	4	4	3	3	2	1	1	3	1	3	2
Burkina Faso	3	1	1	0	0	0	0	0	0	0	0	1	1	0
Burundi	1	2	3	2	2	1	1	0	0	0	0	1	2	0
Cameroon	78	109	87	128	62	73	41	65	26	21	14	56	93	40
Cape Verde	0	0	0	0	0	0	0	0	0	0	0	0	0	0
Central African Republic	0	1	0	0	0	1	1	0	0	0	0	1	0	0
Chad	0	0	0	0	0	0	0	0	0	0	0	0	0	0
Comoros	0	0	0	0	0	0	0	0	0	0	0	0	0	0
Congo	13	56	58	48	54	52	36	22	17	50	40	36	64	36
Côte d'Ivoire	513	473	310	184	233	256	220	171	163	159	138	343	341	184
Djibouti	0	1	0	0	0	0	0	0	0	0	0	0	0	0
Equatorial Guinea	0	0	0	0	0	0	0	0	0	0	0	0	0	0
Eritrea	..	..	..	..	..	..	..	..	..	..	..	..	..	..
Ethiopia	2	20	21	33	31	24	16	22	3	9	29	4	24	17
Gabon	100	35	20	20	15	11	51	36	6	29	44	52	26	29
Gambia, The	0	1	2	0	0	5	2	1	0	0	0	0	1	1
Ghana	7	14	19	23	19	14	14	19	17	21	8	4	16	16
Guinea	2	0	0	5	3	6	1	0	1	2	1	2	2	2
Guinea-Bissau	1	0	0	0	0	0	0	0	0	0	0	0	0	0
Kenya	110	75	90	90	75	95	92	88	81	128	54	69	81	90
Lesotho	1	0	1	2	2	2	1	1	1	1	3	1	1	2
Liberia	16	0	0	0	0	0	0	0	0	0	0	5	0	0
Madagascar	19	4	19	18	16	13	9	3	1	1	4	12	12	5
Malawi	25	9	4	4	5	5	6	3	1	1	2	13	7	3
Mali	1	1	1	0	0	1	0	0	0	1	0	1	1	0
Mauritania	4	5	1	1	1	1	1	0	0	0	0	3	2	0
Mauritius	15	9	8	12	13	10	16	17	11	10	22	11	11	14
Mozambique	0	5	5	7	6	7	6	5	4	2	4	0	6	5
Namibia	..	..	..	..	..	..	..	..	..	..	..	..	..	..
Niger	58	24	28	32	21	16	10	8	7	6	6	30	26	9
Nigeria	466	341	216	761	897	823	805	1,004	292	303	247	409	667	579
Rwanda	0	1	1	1	0	0	0	0	0	0	0	0	1	0
São Tomé and Principe	0	0	0	0	0	0	0	0	0	0	0	0	0	0
Senegal	46	17	25	25	22	13	18	8	2	2	4	22	22	8
Seychelles	0	1	2	3	2	2	1	1	1	1	1	0	2	1
Sierra Leone	5	0	0	0	0	0	0	0	0	0	0	4	0	0
Somalia	0	0	0	0	0	0	0	0	0	0	0	1	0	0
South Africa	..	..	..	..	..	..	..	..	..	..	..	..	..	..
Sudan	5	2	0	0	0	0	0	0	0	0	0	15	9	0
Swaziland	2	2	2	1	1	1	1	1	0	0	0	1	1	0
Tanzania	13	2	2	4	4	3	4	5	6	0	2	9	3	3
Togo	8	7	4	6	5	5	0	0	0	0	0	7	6	1
Uganda	1	4	2	4	4	1	7	5	3	1	2	2	4	3
Zaire	99	55	32	14	34	12	7	1	0	0	0	61	40	3
Zambia	63	20	24	35	31	29	20	20	15	11	16	43	23	18
Zimbabwe	9	83	87	78	77	83	81	80	71	79	71	30	83	78
NORTH AFRICA	2,078	1,912	1,960	2,152	2,401	2,128	2,148	3,226	1,922	1,689	1,587	1,369	2,058	2,117
Algeria	1,280	1,236	1,262	1,353	1,433	1,466	1,432	1,424	1,316	1,137	922	837	1,282	1,283
Egypt, Arab Republic	129	259	187	263	331	317	257	191	167	137	130	128	278	200
Libya	..	..	..	..	..	..	..	..	..	..	..	..	..	..
Morocco	516	277	366	384	481	197	337	1,501	328	316	416	316	356	516
Tunisia	154	139	145	153	156	147	123	110	110	100	118	88	142	118
ALL AFRICA	3,763	3,341	3,093	3,768	4,123	3,768	3,677	4,846	2,670	2,566	2,364	2,623	3,697	3,315

6-12. Interest payments: long-term loans and IMF charges

	Millions of U.S. dollars (current prices)											Annual average		
	1980	*1986*	*1987*	*1988*	*1989*	*1990*	*1991*	*1992*	*1993*	*1994*	*1995*	*75-84*	*85-89*	*90-MR*
SUB-SAHARAN AFRICA	2,480	3,317	3,182	4,066	3,939	4,597	4,640	4,037	2,817	3,476	3,417	1,939	3,666	3,831
excluding South Africa	2,480	3,317	3,182	4,066	3,939	4,597	4,640	4,037	2,817	3,476	3,417	1,939	3,666	3,831
excl. S.Africa & Nigeria	1,951	2,810	2,574	2,588	2,460	2,473	2,586	2,206	1,955	2,400	2,711	1,463	2,595	2,388
Angola	0	45	61	105	99	101	84	46	24	49	77	0	68	63
Benin	3	22	15	8	12	14	13	11	12	19	21	5	14	15
Botswana	8	28	36	37	36	39	35	36	33	31	28	8	31	34
Burkina Faso	6	12	14	14	16	10	15	14	16	15	18	5	13	15
Burundi	3	12	16	17	15	12	13	15	12	13	11	2	14	13
Cameroon	121	198	188	213	141	209	180	160	159	157	173	92	177	173
Cape Verde	0	2	4	4	2	2	3	3	2	2	2	1	3	2
Central African Republic	1	11	11	9	10	10	7	7	4	9	4	3	10	7
Chad	1	2	4	4	2	4	5	6	8	8	5	1	3	6
Comoros	0	1	1	0	1	1	2	3	1	1	1	0	1	1
Congo	38	91	85	82	92	121	51	29	21	232	62	50	97	86
Côte d'Ivoire	590	737	517	410	439	474	524	436	399	437	398	417	560	445
Djibouti	1	3	3	4	2	2	2	2	2	1	1	1	3	2
Equatorial Guinea	0	2	4	2	1	1	2	1	1	1	1	0	2	1
Eritrea	..	..	..	..	..	..	..	..	..	..	..	..	..	..
Ethiopia	19	55	63	88	77	51	38	42	24	40	62	20	65	43
Gabon	120	51	43	68	79	91	148	246	41	106	209	66	60	140
Gambia, The	1	8	7	7	6	12	7	7	6	6	4	2	6	7
Ghana	35	98	107	119	106	96	96	102	98	93	69	30	100	92
Guinea	24	14	43	32	35	55	40	33	37	41	42	20	29	41
Guinea-Bissau	1	2	5	4	4	4	3	3	2	4	6	1	3	4
Kenya	171	226	257	266	229	254	264	210	211	290	222	125	236	242
Lesotho	2	4	6	7	7	8	10	14	12	11	15	2	6	12
Liberia	24	15	7	9	1	1	2	1	9	0	2	17	10	2
Madagascar	28	62	117	86	113	94	74	37	27	19	24	30	86	46
Malawi	36	47	37	36	35	39	45	32	27	25	37	27	39	34
Mali	4	19	19	20	18	21	11	14	11	38	23	5	19	20
Mauritania	15	34	35	36	29	38	27	20	43	38	33	16	33	33
Mauritius	26	44	46	53	51	47	53	57	45	44	57	24	47	50
Mozambique	0	37	18	30	36	23	34	43	75	55	81	0	29	52
Namibia	..	..	..	..	..	..	..	..	..	..	..	..	..	..
Niger	65	53	77	79	40	27	24	15	24	17	14	37	59	20
Nigeria	529	507	607	1,478	1,480	2,124	2,054	1,831	862	1,075	706	476	1,072	1,442
Rwanda	2	5	7	8	8	6	7	7	4	2	8	1	7	6
São Tomé and Principe	0	1	1	1	3	1	1	1	1	1	1	0	1	1
Senegal	71	118	140	137	165	99	103	53	26	58	60	45	126	66
Seychelles	0	4	5	7	6	7	6	6	6	6	6	0	5	6
Sierra Leone	10	15	2	3	1	4	2	14	15	60	19	8	5	19
Somalia	2	22	9	3	14	5	0	0	0	0	1	5	11	1
South Africa	..	..	..	..	..	..	..	..	..	..	..	..	..	..
Sudan	63	69	35	21	25	9	10	13	11	1	15	57	52	10
Swaziland	9	12	15	13	11	10	9	8	7	7	6	5	12	8
Tanzania	54	41	48	54	54	53	57	57	113	64	82	41	45	71
Togo	19	48	35	74	37	37	23	13	9	7	8	17	47	16
Uganda	7	48	41	41	42	32	41	29	34	36	36	14	44	35
Zaire	220	193	169	147	141	127	67	35	10	2	16	118	179	43
Zambia	142	146	74	79	76	74	304	167	155	158	548	102	88	234
Zimbabwe	10	152	151	156	142	152	147	163	178	201	205	41	150	174
NORTH AFRICA	2,698	3,620	3,169	3,923	4,487	4,199	4,045	5,685	4,512	4,512	4,928	2,015	3,680	4,647
Algeria	1,440	1,549	1,567	1,682	1,762	1,845	1,848	1,884	1,742	1,561	1,803	972	1,592	1,780
Egypt, Arab Republic	367	1,015	479	928	1,147	1,063	672	1,061	1,062	1,178	1,268	422	896	1,051
Libya	..	..	..	..	..	..	..	..	..	..	..	..	..	..
Morocco	663	750	764	923	1,178	873	1,124	2,323	1,274	1,295	1,353	466	851	1,374
Tunisia	229	306	359	391	401	418	402	417	436	478	504	155	341	442
ALL AFRICA	5,179	6,937	6,350	7,989	8,427	8,796	8,685	9,722	7,330	7,987	8,345	3,953	7,346	8,477

6-13. Total external debt service payments: long-term loans & IMF credit

	Millions of U.S. dollars (current prices)											*Annual average*		
	1980	*1986*	*1987*	*1988*	*1989*	*1990*	*1991*	*1992*	*1993*	*1994*	*1995*	*75-84*	*85-89*	*90-MR*
SUB-SAHARAN AFRICA	5,657	8,959	8,282	9,421	8,787	10,150	9,494	9,510	6,729	8,511	10,558	4,637	9,107	9,159
excluding South Africa	5,657	8,959	8,282	9,421	8,787	10,150	9,494	9,510	6,729	8,511	10,558	4,637	9,107	9,159
excl. S.Africa & Nigeria	4,886	7,209	7,215	7,250	6,700	6,847	6,577	5,801	5,288	6,689	9,043	3,573	6,894	6,707
Angola	0	110	158	202	227	277	283	196	84	195	406	0	161	240
Benin	9	55	32	21	21	35	28	26	30	39	47	13	34	34
Botswana	14	46	74	77	73	106	89	98	90	92	92	13	64	95
Burkina Faso	17	34	32	38	33	29	40	29	36	42	46	11	33	37
Burundi	7	33	45	45	42	41	38	38	35	41	38	8	38	39
Cameroon	252	636	588	602	349	479	394	362	441	361	385	203	559	404
Cape Verde	0	5	8	8	7	6	9	11	5	6	5	1	6	7
Central African Republic	8	27	26	25	32	28	14	14	7	21	15	9	27	16
Chad	6	8	8	10	11	11	9	10	16	18	15	5	11	13
Comoros	0	2	1	1	1	1	8	6	2	3	1	1	1	3
Congo	78	317	400	376	295	483	260	127	98	537	146	136	355	275
Côte d'Ivoire	1,312	1,273	1,293	996	934	1,095	1,142	1,030	984	1,224	1,023	822	1,110	1,083
Djibouti	3	7	13	14	12	11	10	9	7	6	6	3	10	8
Equatorial Guinea	2	6	11	5	6	5	4	3	1	2	2	3	7	3
Eritrea	..	..	..	..	..	..	..	..	..	..	..	..	..	..
Ethiopia	36	219	243	301	296	228	131	104	90	107	153	51	242	136
Gabon	399	178	67	101	101	131	261	383	112	225	425	235	134	256
Gambia, The	1	29	24	21	23	37	30	29	28	30	24	5	21	30
Ghana	141	215	405	537	444	358	286	302	288	341	342	87	349	319
Guinea	100	67	158	124	113	165	133	84	81	96	176	76	105	123
Guinea-Bissau	4	6	8	8	10	6	7	9	5	10	16	2	8	9
Kenya	376	648	657	689	654	707	660	617	574	836	730	343	647	687
Lesotho	5	15	15	24	22	23	26	34	33	29	40	6	19	31
Liberia	43	29	13	21	6	3	17	1	22	15	2	41	21	10
Madagascar	77	206	243	219	241	207	157	96	76	61	67	77	210	111
Malawi	71	140	109	101	92	104	127	102	74	70	106	57	109	97
Mali	13	58	64	75	64	62	28	42	41	126	79	13	62	63
Mauritania	40	93	113	125	95	141	88	81	125	102	110	51	104	108
Mauritius	44	128	127	199	141	151	166	181	120	140	200	54	146	159
Mozambique	0	99	47	63	70	63	75	77	118	133	172	0	67	106
Namibia	..	..	..	..	..	..	..	..	..	..	..	..	..	..
Niger	122	122	158	168	114	90	98	51	89	66	57	87	132	75
Nigeria	772	1,750	1,066	2,170	2,087	3,304	2,917	3,709	1,441	1,822	1,515	1,064	2,213	2,451
Rwanda	4	18	21	20	24	17	20	19	14	3	19	4	20	15
São Tomé and Principe	1	1	3	2	4	2	2	2	2	2	2	1	3	2
Senegal	235	284	366	366	358	296	294	195	105	209	282	112	309	230
Seychelles	0	9	11	16	19	20	20	18	17	18	20	1	13	19
Sierra Leone	58	53	8	11	4	11	11	31	28	154	81	34	18	52
Somalia	13	62	37	5	32	10	0	0	0	0	1	14	31	2
South Africa	..	..	..	..	..	..	..	..	..	..	..	..	..	..
Sudan	194	220	77	79	71	25	22	27	20	3	69	147	115	28
Swaziland	17	34	50	38	33	46	30	25	24	26	22	12	36	29
Tanzania	135	135	134	137	168	169	200	224	218	175	214	100	144	200
Togo	38	139	85	126	86	80	50	32	24	20	27	44	108	39
Uganda	52	170	158	199	182	143	143	109	154	148	135	49	172	138
Zaire	497	433	442	358	583	327	158	64	15	6	18	241	458	98
Zambia	411	387	171	191	206	200	596	352	368	373	2,615	296	219	750
Zimbabwe	50	455	513	511	406	422	413	554	587	580	615	107	456	529
NORTH AFRICA	6,640	10,035	9,562	11,202	12,656	14,648	15,153	16,828	15,589	11,981	11,584	5,037	10,547	14,297
Algeria	3,968	5,117	5,381	6,269	6,876	8,626	9,071	9,121	8,994	5,149	4,352	2,848	5,703	7,552
Egypt, Arab Republic	813	2,315	1,364	2,177	2,643	2,809	2,396	2,548	2,036	2,108	2,263	871	2,170	2,360
Libya	..	..	..	..	..	..	..	..	..	..	..	..	..	..
Morocco	1,341	1,748	1,730	1,717	2,064	1,812	2,355	3,853	3,277	3,320	3,517	921	1,717	3,022
Tunisia	518	856	1,087	1,040	1,074	1,402	1,332	1,306	1,283	1,404	1,452	398	956	1,363
ALL AFRICA	12,298	18,994	17,844	20,623	21,443	24,798	24,647	26,339	22,319	20,492	22,142	9,674	19,653	23,456

Note: In 1995, Zambia was able to clear its arrears to the IMF after completing a 3 year Rights Arrangement Program.

6-14. Interest payments: short-term loans

	Millions of U.S. dollars (current prices)											*Annual average*		
	1980	*1986*	*1987*	*1988*	*1989*	*1990*	*1991*	*1992*	*1993*	*1994*	*1995*	*75-84*	*85-89*	*90-MR*
SUB-SAHARAN AFRICA	**2,046**	**1,907**	**1,554**	**1,623**	**1,523**	**1,544**	**1,359**	**1,266**	**1,227**	**1,135**	**1,008**	**1,212**	**1,755**	**1,257**
excluding South Africa	1,031	748	531	656	624	715	603	558	527	386	408	541	692	533
excl. S.Africa & Nigeria	652	448	491	616	593	683	575	518	477	336	352	304	523	490
Angola	..	52	16	31	25	43	53	54	66	55	53	..	35	54
Benin	11	7	8	7	5	4	3	2	1	1	2	5	7	2
Botswana	2	0	0	0	0	0	0	0	0	0	0	0	0	0
Burkina Faso	5	3	4	5	5	6	6	5	2	2	2	2	4	4
Burundi	2	2	2	2	1	2	1	1	1	1	1	1	2	1
Cameroon	28	40	65	74	57	43	33	31	30	24	39	17	54	33
Cape Verde	0	0	1	0	0	0	0	0	0	0	1	0	0	0
Central African Republic	2	2	2	2	2	2	2	2	2	2	1	1	2	2
Chad	0	0	0	0	2	2	2	1	1	0	1	0	0	1
Comoros	0	0	1	1	1	0	0	0	0	0	0	0	0	0
Congo	31	46	52	46	46	48	40	35	30	20	35	12	45	35
Côte d'Ivoire	95	48	75	79	142	167	138	130	110	20	23	47	80	98
Djibouti	1	2	1	2	3	4	4	2	2	4	4	1	2	3
Equatorial Guinea	1	0	0	0	0	0	0	0	0	1	0	1	0	0
Eritrea	..	..	..	..	..	..	..	..	..	..	..	..	..	..
Ethiopia	9	6	6	8	8	8	7	5	5	4	1	4	7	5
Gabon	33	24	30	32	45	45	48	50	45	43	17	13	31	41
Gambia, The	3	2	2	2	1	1	1	1	1	2	1	1	2	1
Ghana	18	13	10	9	10	12	17	19	22	26	28	12	12	21
Guinea	9	5	6	4	4	4	4	4	3	3	5	4	5	3
Guinea-Bissau	1	2	2	2	2	3	1	0	0	0	0	1	2	1
Kenya	58	29	35	46	51	78	55	49	53	38	36	24	39	51
Lesotho	1	0	0	0	0	0	0	0	0	0	0	0	0	0
Liberia	11	4	4	4	0	0	0	0	0	0	0	4	3	0
Madagascar	29	6	4	1	4	7	5	3	3	2	3	9	4	4
Malawi	16	6	6	5	5	4	4	4	1	1	3	5	5	3
Mali	3	4	5	4	4	3	3	2	2	1	2	2	4	2
Mauritania	7	6	6	9	8	9	10	6	4	4	5	5	7	6
Mauritius	8	3	3	3	4	5	5	3	4	10	16	3	3	7
Mozambique	..	6	8	9	12	15	7	5	3	1	1	..	8	5
Namibia	..	..	..	..	..	..	..	..	..	..	..	..	..	..
Niger	19	8	7	7	9	9	10	2	2	2	1	7	7	4
Nigeria	379	300	40	40	31	32	28	40	50	50	56	236	169	43
Rwanda	3	2	2	3	5	5	6	6	6	1	1	1	3	4
São Tomé and Principe	0	0	0	0	1	1	0	0	1	0	0	0	0	0
Senegal	24	17	21	23	24	29	21	15	15	14	14	13	21	18
Seychelles	37	2	3	1	4	4	3	2	1	1	1	5	2	2
Sierra Leone	6	4	6	5	1	5	4	5	4	5	2	3	4	4
Somalia	0	0	0	1	0	0	0	0	0	0	0	0	0	0
South Africa	..	..	..	..	..	..	..	..	..	..	..	..	..	..
Sudan	70	27	20	100	25	25	0	0	0	0	0	39	38	4
Swaziland	2	1	1	1	2	0	0	0	0	0	0	1	1	0
Tanzania	26	20	20	22	7	9	5	5	4	5	4	12	19	5
Togo	14	6	6	6	6	6	5	5	4	4	3	6	6	4
Uganda	5	2	2	3	4	5	5	5	3	3	2	2	3	4
Zaire	45	22	28	34	26	21	20	13	13	9	8	18	27	14
Zambia	0	0	0	0	0	3	3	1	1	2	1	0	0	2
Zimbabwe	15	21	20	22	33	49	48	45	33	28	35	22	25	40
NORTH AFRICA	**869**	**665**	**566**	**851**	**726**	**750**	**527**	**570**	**385**	**333**	**322**	**589**	**736**	**481**
Algeria	116	36	65	272	126	179	100	200	36	33	28	150	125	96
Egypt, Arab Republic	422	390	293	305	300	301	220	168	164	130	132	246	351	186
Libya	..	..	..	..	..	..	..	..	..	..	..	..	..	..
Morocco	105	97	72	73	13	20	18	15	18	18	24	57	71	19
Tunisia	26	21	18	18	27	30	39	37	67	52	38	9	21	44
ALL AFRICA	**2,916**	**2,573**	**2,120**	**2,473**	**2,249**	**2,295**	**1,886**	**1,836**	**1,612**	**1,468**	**1,330**	**1,801**	**2,491**	**1,738**

6-15. Net flows: long-and short-term loans, including IMF

	Millions of U.S. dollars (current prices)											*Annual average*		
	1980	*1986*	*1987*	*1988*	*1989*	*1990*	*1991*	*1992*	*1993*	*1994*	*1995*	*75-84*	*85-89*	*90-MR*
SUB-SAHARAN AFRICA	8,580	6,610	9,772	7,104	6,975	7,122	3,902	4,916	4,987	917	3,848	6,340	7,109	4,282
excluding South Africa	8,580	6,610	9,772	7,104	6,975	7,122	3,902	4,916	4,987	917	3,848	6,340	7,109	4,282
excl. S.Africa & Nigeria	7,069	5,198	6,839	5,467	6,409	7,156	4,064	5,624	4,515	1,577	4,298	5,325	5,884	4,539
Angola	..	513	1,430	800	797	927	259	897	303	322	-144	..	1,013	427
Benin	66	50	67	-21	116	92	106	62	84	107	96	75	52	91
Botswana	21	23	69	18	34	-37	49	22	45	-5	2	28	37	13
Burkina Faso	59	77	110	62	74	70	131	105	109	117	124	50	76	109
Burundi	41	80	126	68	97	65	66	101	45	25	26	39	89	55
Cameroon	495	478	93	329	520	685	70	380	134	304	66	315	283	273
Cape Verde	3	12	6	0	4	11	-1	12	7	26	33	10	8	14
Central African Republic	33	81	81	90	36	107	94	39	53	31	25	21	67	58
Chad	0	30	49	57	95	108	97	120	50	64	59	22	47	83
Comoros	13	24	18	1	4	2	-2	14	5	7	11	11	14	6
Congo	485	112	209	-96	29	95	-266	-35	310	79	166	224	189	58
Côte d'Ivoire	1,055	-83	544	227	924	1,189	561	627	726	-1,002	935	709	351	506
Djibouti	8	-23	44	10	24	22	-16	11	35	15	9	8	22	13
Equatorial Guinea	36	13	17	22	14	10	8	13	13	17	-8	10	12	9
Eritrea	..	..	..	..	..	..	..	..	..	..	..	..	..	..
Ethiopia	102	277	327	396	238	190	346	229	312	206	138	140	310	237
Gabon	-109	542	182	313	296	146	87	-193	19	-27	90	53	295	20
Gambia, The	55	25	29	12	17	15	13	35	25	-21	-9	22	16	10
Ghana	143	300	191	177	346	338	561	303	374	312	348	127	240	373
Guinea	53	151	93	197	220	86	122	143	228	118	104	47	149	133
Guinea-Bissau	77	-2	53	44	33	45	37	23	18	20	14	26	35	26
Kenya	508	-8	458	405	571	642	281	117	146	-354	193	298	341	171
Lesotho	12	14	39	42	41	47	50	66	50	41	39	15	33	49
Liberia	91	29	27	8	-4	-1	-15	-1	10	-14	0	89	23	-4
Madagascar	388	95	245	59	129	198	119	53	59	19	48	188	131	82
Malawi	156	53	47	32	85	106	84	90	104	93	93	91	56	95
Mali	100	155	82	97	136	150	97	91	62	66	187	87	112	109
Mauritania	130	143	111	102	27	98	60	-49	75	96	69	107	86	58
Mauritius	124	-22	39	112	-1	77	60	59	23	264	326	56	29	135
Mozambique	..	382	381	182	234	174	61	235	89	206	192	..	308	159
Namibia	..	..	..	..	..	..	..	..	..	..	..	..	..	..
Niger	233	154	97	128	64	123	-121	48	28	25	-12	114	109	15
Nigeria	1,510	1,412	2,933	1,637	566	-34	-162	-708	472	-660	-450	1,015	1,225	-257
Rwanda	31	64	102	75	51	54	90	67	38	-12	53	28	70	48
São Tomé and Principe	9	12	12	11	28	10	42	23	16	9	13	6	14	19
Senegal	230	372	324	70	220	222	-76	170	67	-28	52	195	214	68
Seychelles	12	41	8	3	1	14	4	-8	-12	-4	-13	6	14	-3
Sierra Leone	58	73	60	19	27	38	57	108	154	102	-147	40	46	52
Somalia	125	73	73	48	53	58	13	0	0	0	0	149	74	12
South Africa	..	..	..	..	..	..	..	..	..	..	..	..	..	..
Sudan	790	-133	113	346	214	169	116	272	91	9	0	565	73	110
Swaziland	24	4	-15	-21	8	-30	1	-9	-8	-2	4	23	-1	-7
Tanzania	352	185	256	382	-136	233	134	316	111	178	106	293	165	180
Togo	104	26	-11	95	113	10	44	27	-60	55	38	95	48	19
Uganda	116	81	338	91	232	277	167	239	244	224	185	100	163	222
Zaire	326	140	421	232	228	89	125	-28	0	-140	61	359	234	18
Zambia	424	684	4	285	-33	-100	147	92	77	34	379	294	254	105
Zimbabwe	93	-99	-106	-40	202	335	201	740	261	-7	350	190	-16	313
NORTH AFRICA	5,072	4,501	640	4,382	2,979	-1,029	1,215	342	-912	2,231	1,395	5,231	3,272	540
Algeria	869	2,241	-1,195	1,892	1,270	-891	58	-163	-844	2,172	1,287	1,435	948	270
Egypt, Arab Republic	2,297	1,413	1,094	1,343	746	-1,237	400	-552	-227	72	-53	2,175	1,387	-266
Libya	..	..	..	..	..	..	..	..	..	..	..	..	..	..
Morocco	1,584	329	650	801	735	806	303	480	-47	-213	-205	1,248	634	187
Tunisia	321	518	91	345	228	293	454	577	205	200	366	373	303	349
ALL AFRICA	13,651	11,111	10,412	11,486	9,953	6,092	5,117	5,258	4,074	3,148	5,243	11,571	10,381	4,822

6-16. Net flows: long-term loans, including IMF

	Millions of U.S. dollars (current prices)											Annual average		
	1980	1986	1987	1988	1989	1990	1991	1992	1993	1994	1995	75-84	85-89	90-MR
SUB-SAHARAN AFRICA	8,579	4,939	5,986	5,705	6,212	4,816	4,360	3,735	4,734	3,194	3,026	6,341	5,219	3,977
excluding South Africa	8,579	4,939	5,986	5,705	6,212	4,816	4,360	3,735	4,734	3,194	3,026	6,341	5,219	3,977
excl. S.Africa & Nigeria	7,069	4,866	5,183	5,483	5,231	5,069	4,436	5,078	4,769	3,342	3,402	5,325	5,016	4,349
Angola	0	834	679	620	375	629	128	493	632	280	164	0	741	388
Benin	66	40	52	43	132	100	96	89	82	104	80	75	56	92
Botswana	21	22	68	18	34	-37	49	22	45	-5	2	28	37	13
Burkina Faso	59	71	92	70	80	60	130	128	131	105	110	50	70	111
Burundi	41	88	112	93	93	68	66	102	53	25	18	39	89	55
Cameroon	495	232	166	328	679	448	219	466	217	275	-94	315	253	255
Cape Verde	3	8	3	6	7	8	-1	10	7	24	14	10	8	10
Central African Republic	33	71	85	87	42	104	91	39	45	46	22	21	65	58
Chad	0	26	47	55	85	106	88	139	49	67	59	22	43	85
Comoros	13	23	13	8	4	5	-2	14	4	8	9	11	14	6
Congo	485	110	89	316	-18	-43	-172	33	383	45	-69	224	141	30
Côte d'Ivoire	1,055	-145	66	62	216	550	330	259	229	618	299	709	49	381
Djibouti	8	19	21	12	3	19	13	17	18	9	8	8	17	14
Equatorial Guinea	36	15	16	24	14	6	14	13	13	6	1	10	15	9
Eritrea	..	..	..	..	..	..	..	..	..	..	..	..	..	..
Ethiopia	102	271	316	358	274	183	339	279	342	206	145	140	304	249
Gabon	-109	364	216	316	136	146	49	-29	22	70	138	53	233	66
Gambia, The	55	25	32	12	21	7	8	34	4	-2	0	22	20	8
Ghana	143	303	221	221	236	240	469	287	327	209	277	127	245	301
Guinea	54	154	64	197	200	86	148	160	242	126	77	47	136	140
Guinea-Bissau	77	21	43	44	39	34	42	37	21	18	15	26	41	28
Kenya	509	97	250	474	519	348	554	96	73	-289	187	298	306	161
Lesotho	12	14	39	40	45	47	49	65	50	41	39	15	33	48
Liberia	91	29	27	3	-4	-2	-13	0	20	-15	0	89	20	-2
Madagascar	388	100	256	114	128	114	133	63	69	36	41	188	145	76
Malawi	156	53	38	77	90	93	108	71	142	92	61	91	57	95
Mali	100	151	91	103	141	142	100	111	43	75	164	87	115	106
Mauritania	130	139	108	65	33	45	10	84	87	100	55	107	79	63
Mauritius	124	-9	44	97	15	59	60	3	23	87	268	56	30	83
Mozambique	0	372	348	174	200	202	118	232	158	204	181	0	291	182
Namibia	..	..	..	..	..	..	..	..	..	..	..	..	..	..
Niger	233	131	144	100	82	85	-35	46	38	38	-16	114	105	26
Nigeria	1,510	73	803	222	981	-253	-76	-1,343	-35	-148	-376	1,015	203	-372
Rwanda	31	64	90	73	48	52	88	65	38	19	56	28	68	53
São Tomé and Principe	9	11	9	11	17	16	43	20	15	14	12	6	11	20
Senegal	230	311	277	111	248	54	37	173	70	49	24	195	216	68
Seychelles	12	26	12	3	1	3	3	6	-4	-1	-3	6	11	1
Sierra Leone	58	7	8	24	15	39	44	32	79	116	63	40	15	62
Somalia	125	88	67	62	53	40	13	0	0	0	0	149	81	9
South Africa	..	..	..	..	..	..	..	..	..	..	..	..	..	..
Sudan	790	59	160	324	191	169	116	94	91	9	-3	565	163	79
Swaziland	24	2	-15	-12	-5	-13	2	-10	-8	-3	0	23	-4	-5
Tanzania	352	245	209	332	113	217	166	314	135	158	127	293	199	186
Togo	104	13	-1	85	36	61	39	35	2	42	40	96	28	36
Uganda	116	68	341	83	221	271	162	231	288	210	189	100	158	225
Zaire	326	131	277	199	218	115	214	54	53	-3	-1	359	182	72
Zambia	424	291	81	132	83	39	92	109	78	34	483	294	159	139
Zimbabwe	93	-81	-76	-80	93	154	231	594	367	97	164	190	-29	268
NORTH AFRICA	5,072	3,795	2,758	3,896	2,666	1,177	671	1,112	-269	2,266	1,060	5,231	3,335	1,003
Algeria	869	951	641	1,587	1,051	158	-390	284	-751	2,237	1,233	1,435	932	462
Egypt, Arab Republic	2,297	1,589	1,415	1,412	632	265	314	31	286	144	-491	2,175	1,440	91
Libya	..	..	..	..	..	..	..	..	..	..	..	..	..	..
Morocco	1,584	782	638	632	796	720	319	400	-60	-264	-252	1,248	702	144
Tunisia	321	473	63	266	187	34	428	397	256	150	570	373	262	306
ALL AFRICA	13,651	8,733	8,744	9,601	8,878	5,993	5,031	4,846	4,465	5,460	4,086	11,572	8,554	4,980

6-17. Net transfers: long- and short-term loans, including IMF

	Millions of U.S. dollars (current prices)											*Annual average*		
	1980	*1986*	*1987*	*1988*	*1989*	*1990*	*1991*	*1992*	*1993*	*1994*	*1995*	*75-84*	*85-89*	*90-MR*
SUB-SAHARAN AFRICA	**5,070**	**2,544**	**6,060**	**2,384**	**2,413**	**1,811**	**-1,341**	**321**	**1,643**	**-2,945**	**23**	**3,862**	**2,752**	**-81**
excluding South Africa	**5,070**	**2,544**	**6,060**	**2,384**	**2,413**	**1,811**	**-1,341**	**321**	**1,643**	**-2,945**	**23**	**3,862**	**2,752**	**-81**
excl. S.Africa & Nigeria	**4,468**	**1,940**	**3,775**	**2,265**	**3,358**	**4,001**	**903**	**2,900**	**2,083**	**-1,160**	**1,235**	**3,559**	**2,768**	**1,660**
Angola	0	415	1,352	664	674	784	123	796	212	218	-274	0	910	310
Benin	51	21	44	-36	99	74	91	49	71	87	72	65	31	74
Botswana	12	-5	33	-19	-2	-77	13	-14	12	-36	-26	20	5	-21
Burkina Faso	48	62	91	44	53	54	110	86	91	100	104	43	59	91
Burundi	37	66	109	49	81	51	52	85	32	12	15	35	74	41
Cameroon	346	239	-160	42	323	433	-143	189	-55	123	-145	207	51	67
Cape Verde	3	10	2	-4	2	9	-3	9	5	24	30	9	5	12
Central African Republic	30	68	68	79	24	95	85	31	48	20	19	17	55	50
Chad	-1	28	45	53	91	103	91	113	41	56	54	21	44	76
Comoros	13	23	17	0	3	2	-4	12	4	6	11	11	13	5
Congo	417	-24	72	-224	-109	-74	-357	-99	258	-173	69	162	47	-62
Côte d'Ivoire	370	-869	-48	-262	344	548	-100	61	217	-1,459	514	245	-290	-37
Djibouti	6	-28	39	3	18	16	-22	7	30	10	3	6	16	7
Equatorial Guinea	35	11	13	20	13	9	6	11	12	15	-9	9	10	8
Eritrea	..	..	..	..	..	..	..	..	..	..	..	..	..	..
Ethiopia	75	217	258	300	153	131	301	182	283	162	75	116	238	189
Gabon	-262	467	108	213	172	11	-109	-489	-67	-176	-136	-26	205	-161
Gambia, The	52	15	21	4	10	3	5	27	18	-29	-14	19	8	2
Ghana	90	189	74	49	229	230	449	182	254	193	251	85	128	260
Guinea	20	132	44	162	182	27	79	106	188	74	57	23	116	89
Guinea-Bissau	75	-5	47	38	28	39	33	19	15	16	8	25	29	22
Kenya	280	-262	167	93	290	311	-38	-142	-118	-682	-64	148	66	-122
Lesotho	10	10	33	34	34	38	40	52	37	30	24	13	27	37
Liberia	56	11	16	-4	-5	-2	-17	-1	1	-14	-2	67	9	-6
Madagascar	331	27	124	-28	12	96	40	13	29	-3	21	149	41	33
Malawi	103	1	4	-9	45	63	35	54	76	68	53	58	12	58
Mali	93	132	58	73	114	126	83	74	49	27	162	80	89	87
Mauritania	108	103	70	57	-11	50	24	-74	28	54	31	86	46	19
Mauritius	90	-69	-9	56	-55	25	2	-1	-26	210	253	30	-22	77
Mozambique	0	339	356	143	186	136	19	187	11	150	109	0	271	102
Namibia	..	..	..	..	..	..	..	..	..	..	..	..	..	..
Niger	149	93	13	42	16	88	-154	31	3	5	-27	69	43	-9
Nigeria	602	605	2,285	118	-945	-2,190	-2,244	-2,579	-440	-1,785	-1,212	303	-16	-1,742
Rwanda	26	56	92	64	38	42	78	54	28	-15	44	25	60	39
São Tomé and Principe	9	12	11	10	24	9	41	22	14	7	11	6	12	17
Senegal	135	237	163	-90	31	94	-200	103	27	-100	-22	136	67	-16
Seychelles	-25	35	0	-6	-10	3	-5	-15	-19	-10	-20	1	7	-11
Sierra Leone	42	54	52	11	26	30	52	89	135	38	-168	28	36	29
Somalia	122	50	63	45	39	53	13	0	0	0	-1	144	62	11
South Africa	..	..	..	..	..	..	..	..	..	..	..	..	..	..
Sudan	657	-229	58	225	164	136	106	259	81	9	-16	470	-17	96
Swaziland	13	-9	-31	-35	-5	-40	-8	-18	-15	-9	-2	16	-14	-15
Tanzania	271	124	188	306	-197	172	71	254	-5	110	20	240	101	103
Togo	70	-28	-52	15	70	-34	17	10	-73	45	26	72	-5	-2
Uganda	104	31	295	48	186	241	121	204	206	185	146	85	117	184
Zaire	61	-75	224	50	61	-59	38	-76	-23	-151	38	223	28	-39
Zambia	282	538	-70	207	-109	-177	-160	-77	-79	-125	-170	191	166	-131
Zimbabwe	67	-272	-277	-217	27	135	7	532	50	-235	110	128	-191	100
NORTH AFRICA	1,704	337	-2,977	-208	-1,974	-5,758	-3,207	-5,763	-5,709	-2,514	-3,755	2,754	-977	-4,451
Algeria	-686	656	-2,828	-62	-618	-2,915	-1,889	-2,247	-2,621	578	-544	313	-769	-1,606
Egypt, Arab Republic	1,508	8	322	111	-701	-2,602	-492	-1,781	-1,452	-1,236	-1,453	1,507	140	-1,503
Libya	..	..	..	..	..	..	..	..	..	..	..	..	..	..
Morocco	817	-518	-186	-194	-456	-87	-840	-1,858	-1,339	-1,525	-1,582	725	-288	-1,205
Tunisia	66	191	-285	-63	-199	-155	14	123	-298	-331	-177	209	-59	-137
ALL AFRICA	6,774	2,882	3,083	2,175	439	-3,947	-4,548	-5,442	-4,067	-5,459	-3,732	6,616	1,775	-4,532

6-18. Net transfers: long-term loans, including IMF

	Millions of U.S. dollars (current prices)											Annual average		
	1980	1986	1987	1988	1989	1990	1991	1992	1993	1994	1995	75-84	85-89	90-MR
SUB-SAHARAN AFRICA	6,099	1,622	2,805	1,638	2,273	219	-280	-302	1,917	-282	-391	4,402	1,553	147
excluding South Africa	6,099	1,622	2,805	1,638	2,273	219	-280	-302	1,917	-282	-391	4,402	1,553	147
excl. S.Africa & Nigeria	5,118	2,056	2,609	2,895	2,771	2,595	1,850	2,872	2,814	942	691	3,863	2,421	1,961
Angola	0	788	618	516	276	529	45	447	607	231	87	0	673	324
Benin	63	18	37	36	120	86	84	78	70	85	58	70	41	77
Botswana	14	-6	33	-19	-2	-77	14	-13	12	-36	-26	20	6	-21
Burkina Faso	53	59	77	56	64	50	115	114	115	90	92	45	57	96
Burundi	38	76	97	76	78	55	53	87	41	12	7	36	75	43
Cameroon	374	34	-23	115	538	239	38	306	58	118	-267	224	75	82
Cape Verde	3	6	-1	2	5	6	-3	7	5	22	12	9	6	8
Central African Republic	32	60	74	77	32	94	84	32	42	37	18	18	55	51
Chad	-1	24	43	51	82	102	83	133	41	58	54	21	40	79
Comoros	13	22	12	8	3	5	-4	12	3	7	9	11	13	5
Congo	448	19	4	234	-110	-164	-223	4	362	-187	-131	174	44	-56
Côte d'Ivoire	465	-882	-451	-348	-223	76	-194	-177	-171	181	-99	292	-511	-64
Djibouti	7	16	18	8	0	17	11	15	16	7	6	7	14	12
Equatorial Guinea	36	14	13	22	13	5	12	11	12	5	0	9	13	8
Eritrea	..	..	..	..	..	..	..	..	..	..	..	..	..	..
Ethiopia	83	216	254	270	197	133	301	237	317	166	84	120	239	206
Gabon	-228	313	173	248	57	56	-99	-275	-19	-36	-70	-13	174	-74
Gambia, The	54	17	25	5	15	-4	1	27	-2	-8	-5	21	14	1
Ghana	108	206	114	102	130	144	373	185	229	115	209	96	145	209
Guinea	30	140	21	166	165	31	108	127	204	86	35	27	107	98
Guinea-Bissau	75	20	39	40	35	30	39	34	19	14	9	25	38	24
Kenya	338	-129	-7	209	290	95	290	-114	-138	-579	-34	172	70	-80
Lesotho	10	10	33	33	38	39	39	52	38	30	24	13	28	37
Liberia	67	15	19	-6	-5	-3	-15	-1	11	-15	-2	72	10	-4
Madagascar	360	38	138	29	14	20	60	26	42	17	17	158	59	30
Malawi	119	6	1	41	55	54	63	39	115	68	23	64	18	60
Mali	96	132	72	82	123	121	89	97	32	36	140	82	96	86
Mauritania	115	105	73	29	4	7	-17	64	44	62	23	90	46	30
Mauritius	98	-53	-2	44	-35	12	7	-54	-22	43	211	33	-17	33
Mozambique	0	335	330	144	164	179	83	189	83	149	100	0	262	130
Namibia	..	..	..	..	..	..	..	..	..	..	..	..	..	..
Niger	168	78	67	21	43	58	-59	32	14	21	-30	77	46	6
Nigeria	981	-435	196	-1,257	-499	-2,377	-2,130	-3,174	-897	-1,223	-1,083	540	-869	-1,814
Rwanda	29	58	82	65	40	46	81	58	34	17	48	27	62	47
São Tomé and Principe	9	11	9	10	15	14	42	20	14	13	11	6	10	19
Senegal	159	193	137	-26	83	-45	-66	121	45	-9	-35	150	90	2
Seychelles	12	22	6	-4	-5	-4	-3	0	-9	-7	-9	6	6	-5
Sierra Leone	48	-9	6	21	14	36	42	18	64	55	44	32	10	43
Somalia	122	66	58	59	40	35	13	0	0	0	-1	144	70	8
South Africa	..	..	..	..	..	..	..	..	..	..	..	..	..	..
Sudan	727	-10	125	303	166	161	106	81	81	9	-18	509	111	70
Swaziland	15	-10	-30	-25	-16	-23	-7	-18	-16	-9	-6	17	-16	-13
Tanzania	297	205	161	278	60	165	109	257	22	95	45	252	153	115
Togo	84	-35	-35	11	-2	24	16	22	-7	35	32	78	-19	20
Uganda	109	20	300	42	180	239	121	202	254	174	153	87	115	191
Zaire	106	-63	108	52	76	-12	146	18	43	-5	-18	241	3	29
Zambia	282	145	7	54	6	-35	-212	-58	-77	-123	-65	191	71	-95
Zimbabwe	82	-233	-227	-235	-49	2	84	432	189	-103	-42	150	-179	94
NORTH AFRICA	2,374	175	-411	-27	-1,822	-3,022	-3,374	-4,574	-4,781	-2,245	-3,868	3,216	-345	-3,644
Algeria	-570	-598	-926	-95	-711	-1,687	-2,237	-1,601	-2,493	676	-570	463	-660	-1,319
Egypt, Arab Republic	1,930	574	936	485	-515	-799	-358	-1,030	-775	-1,034	-1,759	1,754	544	-959
Libya	..	..	..	..	..	..	..	..	..	..	..	..	..	..
Morocco	922	32	-125	-291	-382	-153	-806	-1,923	-1,334	-1,559	-1,605	782	-149	-1,230
Tunisia	92	167	-295	-125	-214	-384	26	-21	-179	-328	66	218	-80	-137
ALL AFRICA	8,473	1,797	2,394	1,612	451	-2,804	-3,654	-4,876	-2,864	-2,527	-4,259	7,618	1,208	-3,497

6-19. Long-term debt: official concessional

	Millions of U.S. dollars (current prices)											Annual average		
	1980	1986	1987	1988	1989	1990	1991	1992	1993	1994	1995	75-84	85-89	90-MR
SUB-SAHARAN AFRICA	15,355	34,420	42,570	44,689	47,255	55,210	59,960	62,472	66,165	72,945	78,704	14,763	39,344	65,909
excluding South Africa	15,355	34,420	42,570	44,689	47,255	55,210	59,960	62,472	66,165	72,945	78,704	14,763	39,344	65,909
excl. S.Africa & Nigeria	14,823	33,939	42,024	44,163	46,731	54,609	58,917	61,430	65,012	71,598	77,274	14,299	38,841	64,807
Angola	..	133	403	631	902	1,205	1,268	1,296	1,317	1,410	1,492	..	426	1,331
Benin	166	371	468	488	868	963	1,062	1,123	1,175	1,298	1,269	156	498	1,148
Botswana	62	109	125	138	168	189	233	237	271	303	351	88	130	264
Burkina Faso	221	447	584	617	532	622	748	841	935	929	1,025	178	505	850
Burundi	104	455	634	683	768	793	850	905	960	1,026	1,062	108	577	933
Cameroon	906	1,297	1,424	1,378	1,637	1,861	1,893	2,317	2,503	3,429	4,207	717	1,371	2,702
Cape Verde	20	77	89	94	100	101	104	113	120	149	167	22	85	125
Central African Republic	59	262	386	442	494	511	609	629	673	720	762	64	354	651
Chad	171	164	217	272	301	410	503	546	599	675	743	141	218	579
Comoros	43	146	173	173	148	159	158	168	162	168	179	44	152	166
Congo	405	772	984	1,001	1,041	1,750	1,827	1,765	1,698	1,992	2,095	374	887	1,855
Côte d'Ivoire	465	1,838	2,274	1,989	2,194	3,132	3,468	3,597	3,779	3,973	4,687	425	1,798	3,773
Djibouti	16	111	148	154	131	156	171	176	192	207	218	20	126	187
Equatorial Guinea	32	60	88	104	127	124	132	138	145	149	155	31	85	140
Eritrea	..	..	..	..	..	..	..	..	..	..	..	..	..	..
Ethiopia	587	1,752	2,157	2,426	2,652	2,949	3,078	3,255	3,583	3,898	4,127	648	2,089	3,482
Gabon	125	184	275	286	306	427	493	452	412	565	983	100	237	556
Gambia, The	68	161	208	214	227	252	274	308	322	348	371	59	187	312
Ghana	815	1,265	1,663	1,662	1,864	2,168	2,448	2,640	2,959	3,418	3,811	720	1,483	2,907
Guinea	678	1,132	1,344	1,492	1,401	1,679	1,842	2,023	2,212	2,399	2,553	734	1,258	2,118
Guinea-Bissau	97	253	326	358	410	500	539	557	583	643	764	77	308	598
Kenya	707	1,593	1,924	2,088	2,048	2,493	2,827	2,899	3,182	3,472	3,971	669	1,792	3,141
Lesotho	44	154	190	207	244	297	339	374	384	436	468	48	186	383
Liberia	216	516	585	563	564	590	581	568	595	617	630	224	536	597
Madagascar	482	1,082	1,416	1,538	1,575	1,820	2,041	2,058	2,048	2,205	2,320	534	1,293	2,082
Malawi	278	671	852	908	981	1,118	1,282	1,358	1,543	1,717	1,849	283	785	1,478
Mali	620	1,493	1,815	1,831	1,970	2,280	2,392	2,424	2,433	2,575	2,784	597	1,667	2,482
Mauritania	513	1,110	1,269	1,292	1,268	1,326	1,380	1,392	1,577	1,735	1,839	499	1,178	1,542
Mauritius	73	170	239	256	280	377	424	412	407	443	469	71	218	422
Mozambique	..	1,687	2,099	2,221	2,288	2,148	2,433	2,665	2,887	3,317	3,043	..	1,928	2,749
Namibia	..	..	..	..	..	..	..	..	..	..	..	..	..	..
Niger	156	507	677	780	694	822	838	885	961	1,006	1,046	174	610	926
Nigeria	531	481	546	526	524	600	1,043	1,042	1,154	1,347	1,430	464	503	1,103
Rwanda	141	406	547	601	572	658	741	780	817	882	940	126	488	803
São Tomé and Principe	20	52	66	76	91	113	158	173	188	209	253	16	66	182
Senegal	411	1,384	1,912	2,041	1,743	1,981	1,951	2,096	2,128	2,269	2,419	420	1,611	2,141
Seychelles	19	55	76	75	78	93	99	94	87	89	89	13	65	92
Sierra Leone	143	260	304	326	320	358	415	460	557	633	759	128	285	530
Somalia	549	1,195	1,398	1,424	1,461	1,562	1,582	1,545	1,551	1,581	1,601	566	1,309	1,570
South Africa	..	..	..	..	..	..	..	..	..	..	..	..	..	..
Sudan	1,776	3,494	3,786	3,959	4,221	4,471	4,614	4,606	4,677	4,781	4,844	1,749	3,767	4,665
Swaziland	100	116	142	135	142	169	175	165	155	176	186	69	126	171
Tanzania	1,322	2,373	2,799	3,133	3,132	3,420	3,525	3,778	3,967	4,293	4,438	1,376	2,707	3,903
Togo	255	406	498	586	556	714	782	810	820	906	944	192	468	829
Uganda	255	600	867	908	1,166	1,464	1,638	1,818	2,148	2,474	2,782	225	805	2,054
Zaire	862	1,634	2,105	2,032	2,635	3,144	3,269	3,214	3,222	3,409	3,519	825	1,954	3,296
Zambia	827	1,474	1,773	1,825	1,618	2,301	2,728	2,676	2,856	3,217	3,473	702	1,586	2,875
Zimbabwe	18	521	717	755	815	942	1,006	1,098	1,220	1,459	1,587	87	638	1,219
NORTH AFRICA	13,512	20,290	22,859	23,843	24,370	23,158	24,988	25,748	26,841	29,848	32,234	12,026	21,949	27,136
Algeria	1,252	548	639	597	583	828	920	1,019	1,186	2,062	3,061	1,022	576	1,513
Egypt, Arab Republic	8,131	12,122	13,630	14,439	14,696	12,533	16,808	17,290	18,163	19,751	20,549	7,134	13,223	17,516
Libya	..	..	..	..	..	..	..	..	..	..	..	..	..	..
Morocco	2,723	5,522	6,143	6,387	6,570	7,003	4,359	4,510	4,537	4,888	5,276	2,606	5,888	5,096
Tunisia	1,405	2,098	2,447	2,420	2,522	2,793	2,900	2,929	2,954	3,147	3,350	1,264	2,262	3,012
ALL AFRICA	28,867	54,710	65,429	68,532	71,625	78,367	84,948	88,220	93,006	102,792	110,938	26,789	61,293	93,045

6-20. Long-term debt: official nonconcessional

	Millions of U.S. dollars (current prices)											Annual average		
	1980	1986	1987	1988	1989	1990	1991	1992	1993	1994	1995	75-84	85-89	90-MR
SUB-SAHARAN AFRICA	8,859	29,701	39,019	38,063	43,312	49,529	51,690	50,706	49,439	53,172	54,506	7,946	33,780	51,507
excluding South Africa	8,859	29,701	39,019	38,063	43,312	49,529	51,690	50,706	49,439	53,172	54,506	7,946	33,780	51,507
excl. S.Africa & Nigeria	8,398	21,729	28,146	27,818	29,155	33,119	33,580	33,420	32,346	34,707	35,443	7,309	24,788	33,769
Angola	14	260	434	548	597	673	672	663	654	811	814	18	407	715
Benin	50	58	69	64	182	191	210	231	222	230	241	30	85	221
Botswana	73	261	370	349	341	341	356	348	333	312	284	74	306	329
Burkina Faso	39	96	124	120	82	90	129	133	127	107	106	33	100	115
Burundi	6	44	55	53	51	49	44	38	36	33	31	8	48	39
Cameroon	331	731	994	953	1,402	2,024	2,172	2,614	2,541	2,814	2,935	272	924	2,516
Cape Verde	1	28	29	25	23	27	24	21	20	18	16	10	27	21
Central African Republic	40	107	127	115	106	92	87	81	78	62	73	37	106	79
Chad	35	24	29	26	37	51	54	123	112	74	94	24	28	85
Comoros	0	13	15	14	13	14	9	7	7	8	8	2	13	9
Congo	199	635	1,007	1,047	1,041	1,301	1,314	1,219	1,176	1,833	1,940	157	810	1,464
Côte d'Ivoire	782	2,431	3,608	3,620	3,872	4,554	4,965	4,999	4,823	4,669	4,527	679	3,089	4,756
Djibouti	5	3	4	3	0	0	0	0	0	0	0	3	2	0
Equatorial Guinea	14	62	64	63	62	68	66	60	55	55	58	13	61	60
Eritrea	..	..	..	..	..	..	..	..	..	..	..	..	..	..
Ethiopia	51	160	170	165	285	338	348	353	374	399	431	56	183	374
Gabon	191	270	852	1,137	1,537	2,008	2,055	1,971	1,925	2,677	2,917	161	801	2,259
Gambia, The	5	31	40	37	37	38	35	30	23	18	12	5	32	26
Ghana	216	234	305	296	322	383	377	373	364	350	332	143	271	363
Guinea	182	403	450	407	446	466	460	336	343	388	339	148	377	389
Guinea-Bissau	5	84	107	109	114	117	123	119	116	101	82	13	98	110
Kenya	496	1,186	1,519	1,360	1,272	1,244	1,174	1,083	984	1,329	1,236	468	1,256	1,175
Lesotho	2	29	41	40	40	47	50	61	84	101	115	5	35	76
Liberia	144	290	334	320	313	334	330	318	307	311	324	128	303	321
Madagascar	91	1,224	1,616	1,575	1,423	1,400	1,375	1,324	1,213	1,262	1,295	244	1,370	1,312
Malawi	156	214	252	241	225	220	189	156	141	138	115	116	223	160
Mali	14	37	43	57	66	71	70	66	79	60	53	11	47	67
Mauritania	73	336	440	418	403	404	383	383	336	343	336	84	370	364
Mauritius	81	199	262	290	267	280	283	235	228	221	213	67	236	243
Mozambique	0	639	858	849	855	1,426	1,436	1,832	1,805	1,825	2,154	62	758	1,746
Namibia	..	..	..	..	..	..	..	..	..	..	..	..	..	..
Niger	99	335	430	407	316	357	370	341	313	304	329	89	352	336
Nigeria	461	7,972	10,874	10,245	14,157	16,411	18,110	17,286	17,093	18,465	19,063	637	8,992	17,738
Rwanda	2	2	2	1	1	2	1	1	1	1	7	1	2	2
São Tomé and Principe	4	23	23	23	22	22	22	21	21	20	8	5	21	19
Senegal	242	923	1,088	976	715	777	768	753	775	674	688	263	902	739
Seychelles	6	23	27	27	26	27	26	27	29	36	40	6	24	31
Sierra Leone	69	152	182	160	172	199	196	253	241	234	205	51	151	221
Somalia	18	272	299	320	318	327	327	318	312	318	323	58	294	321
South Africa	..	..	..	..	..	..	..	..	..	..	..	..	..	..
Sudan	1,517	2,300	2,580	2,614	2,856	3,029	3,023	2,902	2,864	2,984	3,077	1,149	2,496	2,980
Swaziland	65	111	130	109	97	81	76	63	59	51	50	51	109	63
Tanzania	307	1,308	1,515	1,505	1,533	1,721	1,657	1,510	1,314	1,288	1,278	312	1,308	1,461
Togo	230	418	490	424	339	320	309	274	256	274	300	175	416	289
Uganda	38	250	355	338	346	362	345	355	337	300	188	62	297	314
Zaire	1,747	3,398	4,215	4,062	4,453	4,973	5,130	4,882	4,711	5,011	5,225	1,330	3,767	4,989
Zambia	674	1,728	2,064	2,036	2,036	2,105	1,904	1,746	1,532	1,486	1,445	605	1,830	1,703
Zimbabwe	83	401	530	514	514	566	637	796	1,078	1,179	1,199	80	455	909
NORTH AFRICA	8,089	23,572	29,958	30,636	29,856	25,355	26,662	26,821	26,827	32,046	35,959	8,084	26,984	28,945
Algeria	2,243	3,757	4,045	4,101	4,147	4,888	5,549	5,432	5,292	8,939	12,393	1,749	3,874	7,082
Egypt, Arab Republic	4,491	13,589	17,382	17,787	15,797	8,632	8,147	7,891	7,879	8,677	9,056	4,807	15,464	8,380
Libya	..	..	..	..	..	..	..	..	..	..	..	..	..	..
Morocco	799	4,704	6,649	6,898	7,873	9,400	10,031	10,520	10,373	10,685	10,659	1,023	5,946	10,278
Tunisia	556	1,522	1,882	1,849	2,038	2,435	2,935	2,978	3,283	3,744	3,850	505	1,700	3,204
ALL AFRICA	16,948	53,273	68,977	68,699	73,168	74,884	78,352	77,527	76,266	85,218	90,465	16,029	60,764	80,452

6-21. Long-term debt: private

	Millions of U.S. dollars (current prices)											Annual average		
	1980	1986	1987	1988	1989	1990	1991	1992	1993	1994	1995	75-84	85-89	90-MR
SUB-SAHARAN AFRICA	20,772	32,473	41,040	41,597	39,534	40,283	38,613	32,269	32,222	31,546	31,956	17,249	37,240	34,481
excluding South Africa	20,772	32,473	41,040	41,597	39,534	40,283	38,613	32,269	32,222	31,546	31,956	17,249	37,240	34,481
excl. S.Africa & Nigeria	16,396	22,395	25,006	24,294	24,558	25,357	25,098	23,787	23,728	22,879	23,447	12,752	23,261	24,049
Angola	0	3,008	4,186	4,722	5,093	5,605	5,664	6,056	6,620	6,913	7,227	0	3,815	6,347
Benin	118	340	396	362	77	23	12	5	4	4	4	142	298	9
Botswana	8	39	51	48	42	27	25	21	48	50	47	15	43	36
Burkina Faso	20	33	36	30	34	38	6	5	4	4	5	18	34	10
Burundi	8	26	23	19	14	9	6	4	3	2	2	10	22	4
Cameroon	1,014	1,308	1,478	1,525	1,680	1,714	1,716	1,525	1,444	1,220	1,116	727	1,386	1,456
Cape Verde	0	3	3	3	3	3	2	2	2	2	2	0	3	2
Central African Republic	48	23	24	23	21	22	21	20	20	16	17	40	23	19
Chad	54	34	43	39	8	9	8	7	6	6	2	42	31	6
Comoros	0	0	0	0	0	0	0	0	0	0	0	0	0	0
Congo	653	1,392	1,400	1,437	1,421	1,155	900	891	1,240	949	920	546	1,410	1,009
Côte d'Ivoire	5,091	5,696	5,686	5,338	5,489	5,537	5,436	5,263	5,126	5,210	5,345	3,507	5,570	5,320
Djibouti	5	5	3	1	1	0	0	0	0	0	0	3	3	0
Equatorial Guinea	7	18	21	18	16	18	17	16	15	16	17	9	18	16
Eritrea	..	..	..	..	..	..	..	..	..	..	..	..	..	..
Ethiopia	49	328	435	493	409	370	579	559	502	457	400	65	391	478
Gabon	955	977	1,026	878	768	716	676	626	596	268	199	767	851	513
Gambia, The	24	19	17	26	25	18	14	9	5	1	0	16	25	8
Ghana	131	293	357	329	269	257	319	332	345	412	452	132	291	353
Guinea	159	96	100	142	121	108	98	103	104	98	82	133	133	99
Guinea-Bissau	36	46	55	46	36	33	32	30	29	32	3	17	45	26
Kenya	1,286	979	1,320	1,344	1,517	1,903	2,253	1,755	1,687	1,276	1,164	898	1,218	1,673
Lesotho	11	7	21	29	32	34	35	28	21	17	28	9	19	27
Liberia	156	182	196	193	188	192	196	195	200	208	208	115	186	200
Madagascar	338	320	259	207	159	133	119	107	82	81	77	248	259	100
Malawi	192	64	57	56	64	64	53	40	31	28	14	128	67	38
Mali	36	49	48	25	21	18	14	5	3	2	2	30	37	7
Mauritania	131	139	143	122	93	97	94	88	19	9	8	118	125	52
Mauritius	165	104	133	183	214	262	295	311	281	455	767	94	148	395
Mozambique	0	855	818	706	723	675	495	231	167	111	102	0	771	297
Namibia	..	..	..	..	..	..	..	..	..	..	..	..	..	..
Niger	432	377	392	355	362	376	226	206	182	157	133	267	371	213
Nigeria	4,376	10,078	16,034	17,303	14,976	14,926	13,515	8,481	8,495	8,667	8,509	4,496	13,978	10,432
Rwanda	8	9	11	7	5	4	3	2	1	2	2	7	9	2
São Tomé and Principe	0	2	2	2	1	1	1	1	1	1	0	1	3	1
Senegal	461	356	363	270	235	241	202	162	156	154	128	301	303	174
Seychelles	0	30	36	30	27	28	26	25	22	22	22	2	28	24
Sierra Leone	111	81	92	82	81	95	93	32	22	21	4	91	83	44
Somalia	28	88	47	35	35	37	36	35	34	36	37	86	58	36
South Africa	..	..	..	..	..	..	..	..	..	..	..	..	..	..
Sudan	854	1,571	2,049	1,804	1,888	2,151	2,079	1,972	1,949	2,131	2,355	872	1,730	2,106
Swaziland	24	23	12	10	9	7	5	4	2	1	0	14	15	3
Tanzania	341	456	511	482	497	485	465	384	390	396	413	260	475	422
Togo	415	67	64	52	50	52	52	51	50	51	53	247	64	51
Uganda	244	253	366	347	335	335	301	260	115	93	84	149	301	198
Zaire	1,462	886	887	847	878	889	872	852	836	860	878	1,393	877	865
Zambia	726	634	654	599	599	476	418	377	333	207	174	675	612	331
Zimbabwe	595	1,181	1,188	1,029	1,022	1,141	1,233	1,190	1,030	901	955	561	1,113	1,075
NORTH AFRICA	21,535	29,477	32,810	34,957	35,338	36,061	31,647	29,675	27,777	26,662	24,571	16,551	31,480	29,399
Algeria	13,545	15,193	18,412	19,723	19,899	20,719	19,512	19,022	18,383	17,371	14,988	9,882	17,157	18,332
Egypt, Arab Republic	2,070	6,876	6,570	7,155	7,425	7,663	4,851	3,676	2,863	2,485	2,033	2,131	6,752	3,928
Libya	..	..	..	..	..	..	..	..	..	..	..	..	..	..
Morocco	4,491	5,496	5,867	6,160	6,246	6,028	5,797	5,475	5,161	5,492	5,743	3,469	5,724	5,616
Tunisia	1,429	1,911	1,962	1,919	1,768	1,652	1,486	1,502	1,370	1,315	1,807	1,069	1,846	1,522
ALL AFRICA	42,307	61,950	73,851	76,554	74,872	76,344	70,260	61,944	59,999	58,208	56,527	33,800	68,719	63,880

6-22. Total external debt

	Millions of U.S. dollars (current prices)											Annual average		
	1980	1986	1987	1988	1989	1990	1991	1992	1993	1994	1995	75-84	85-89	90-MR
SUB-SAHARAN AFRICA	57,745	117,048	143,744	146,065	152,982	172,562	178,737	177,109	183,314	193,174	204,253	51,151	131,778	184,858
excluding South Africa	57,745	117,048	143,744	146,065	152,982	172,562	178,737	177,109	183,314	193,174	204,253	51,151	131,778	184,858
excl. S.Africa & Nigeria	48,824	94,836	114,722	116,444	122,860	139,123	145,210	148,090	152,615	159,655	169,248	42,636	105,854	152,323
Angola	..	3,662	5,451	6,290	7,205	8,443	8,874	9,940	10,486	11,293	11,482	..	5,120	10,086
Benin	424	947	1,146	1,065	1,203	1,245	1,364	1,407	1,479	1,636	1,646	398	1,036	1,463
Botswana	147	412	550	539	555	563	620	612	660	676	699	182	481	638
Burkina Faso	330	640	828	845	717	834	967	1,040	1,117	1,128	1,267	269	708	1,059
Burundi	166	570	770	801	889	907	964	1,022	1,061	1,123	1,157	153	697	1,039
Cameroon	2,588	4,157	4,678	4,778	5,440	6,679	6,898	7,349	7,452	8,254	9,350	1,976	4,445	7,664
Cape Verde	21	116	132	127	128	135	135	142	149	180	216	33	120	160
Central African Republic	195	462	618	669	694	699	794	814	873	884	944	181	557	835
Chad	285	264	346	392	399	530	634	728	771	825	908	228	324	733
Comoros	44	167	203	199	174	185	180	188	184	189	203	48	175	188
Congo	1,526	3,519	4,307	4,090	4,279	4,953	4,832	4,770	5,081	5,422	6,032	1,227	3,849	5,182
Côte d'Ivoire	7,462	11,450	13,577	13,342	14,821	17,259	18,174	18,547	19,071	17,395	18,952	5,644	12,570	18,233
Djibouti	32	125	183	185	179	206	192	192	225	247	260	33	163	221
Equatorial Guinea	76	159	196	211	229	241	254	255	264	288	293	71	185	266
Eritrea	..	..	..	..	..	..	..	..	..	..	..	..	..	..
Ethiopia	824	2,407	2,936	3,274	3,489	3,809	4,198	4,343	4,661	5,001	5,221	887	2,826	4,539
Gabon	1,514	1,944	2,619	2,845	3,351	3,984	4,223	3,851	3,861	3,986	4,492	1,231	2,393	4,066
Gambia, The	137	270	327	325	338	369	383	403	425	421	426	116	301	405
Ghana	1,398	2,767	3,313	3,128	3,397	3,873	4,371	4,499	4,882	5,463	5,874	1,311	2,972	4,827
Guinea	1,134	1,764	2,072	2,266	2,175	2,476	2,622	2,648	2,848	3,108	3,242	1,119	1,948	2,824
Guinea-Bissau	145	409	527	558	605	712	764	774	802	859	894	120	490	801
Kenya	3,383	4,589	5,755	5,781	5,862	7,056	7,455	6,907	7,118	7,160	7,381	2,643	5,233	7,179
Lesotho	72	198	259	287	328	395	446	493	530	602	659	69	249	521
Liberia	686	1,436	1,705	1,656	1,685	1,849	1,954	1,923	1,957	2,056	2,127	620	1,545	1,977
Madagascar	1,241	2,995	3,672	3,669	3,444	3,720	3,916	3,931	3,818	4,117	4,302	1,206	3,260	3,967
Malawi	821	1,161	1,373	1,361	1,419	1,579	1,670	1,697	1,812	2,009	2,140	651	1,266	1,818
Mali	732	1,756	2,067	2,040	2,159	2,502	2,618	2,623	2,656	2,796	3,066	702	1,898	2,710
Mauritania	843	1,755	2,058	2,082	2,004	2,141	2,233	2,134	2,174	2,329	2,467	807	1,877	2,246
Mauritius	467	672	818	880	855	995	1,058	1,070	1,030	1,411	1,801	359	771	1,227
Mozambique	..	3,466	4,105	4,148	4,354	4,665	4,725	5,138	5,209	5,651	5,781	..	3,784	5,195
Namibia	..	..	..	..	..	..	..	..	..	..	..	..	..	..
Niger	863	1,448	1,697	1,742	1,564	1,793	1,565	1,580	1,614	1,566	1,633	640	1,532	1,625
Nigeria	8,921	22,212	29,021	29,621	30,122	33,440	33,527	29,019	30,699	33,519	35,005	8,515	25,924	32,535
Rwanda	190	452	606	655	623	711	808	849	890	931	1,008	158	540	866
São Tomé and Principe	24	79	98	109	136	153	198	217	239	254	277	22	97	223
Senegal	1,473	3,225	4,028	3,886	3,269	3,731	3,554	3,634	3,766	3,659	3,845	1,269	3,394	3,698
Seychelles	84	148	175	168	166	195	198	180	163	170	164	127	151	178
Sierra Leone	435	886	1,051	1,054	1,088	1,206	1,303	1,313	1,452	1,532	1,226	414	960	1,339
Somalia	660	1,800	2,009	2,086	2,159	2,370	2,449	2,447	2,501	2,616	2,678	785	1,939	2,510
South Africa	..	..	..	..	..	..	..	..	..	..	..	..	..	..
Sudan	5,177	9,631	11,249	11,531	13,359	14,762	15,227	15,450	15,837	16,918	17,623	4,807	10,945	15,969
Swaziland	210	278	307	264	269	262	261	238	224	237	251	149	272	246
Tanzania	2,460	4,609	5,493	5,878	5,733	6,286	6,400	6,495	6,655	7,095	7,333	2,379	5,148	6,711
Togo	1,052	1,070	1,239	1,227	1,184	1,286	1,354	1,352	1,291	1,458	1,486	716	1,132	1,371
Uganda	689	1,414	1,921	1,923	2,177	2,583	2,777	2,928	3,029	3,369	3,564	617	1,733	3,041
Zaire	4,770	7,191	8,758	8,562	9,239	10,270	10,826	10,964	11,270	12,322	13,137	4,319	7,984	11,465
Zambia	3,261	5,744	6,650	6,863	6,729	7,265	7,335	7,001	6,819	6,611	6,853	2,971	6,112	6,981
Zimbabwe	786	2,626	2,853	2,668	2,791	3,247	3,436	4,006	4,210	4,411	4,885	982	2,671	4,033
NORTH AFRICA	51,270	85,993	96,025	99,998	101,777	92,515	90,637	88,452	86,512	94,141	98,811	43,809	91,758	91,845
Algeria	19,365	22,651	24,410	26,041	27,087	27,896	28,216	27,062	26,033	30,167	32,610	14,323	23,690	28,664
Egypt, Arab Republic	19,131	39,855	44,205	46,441	45,963	33,402	33,033	31,575	31,110	33,039	34,116	18,165	42,513	32,713
Libya	..	..	..	..	..	..	..	..	..	..	..	..	..	..
Morocco	9,247	17,544	20,593	20,716	21,753	23,527	21,139	21,273	20,687	21,587	22,147	8,319	19,272	21,727
Tunisia	3,527	5,943	6,817	6,799	6,974	7,691	8,250	8,542	8,682	9,348	9,938	3,002	6,284	8,742
ALL AFRICA	109,015	203,041	239,769	246,062	254,759	265,077	269,374	265,560	269,826	287,315	303,064	94,961	223,537	276,703

6-23. Structure of external debt

	Millions of U.S. dollars (current prices)															
	Bilateral				Multilateral				Private		Short-term		IMF			
	Concessional		Nonconcessional		Concessional		Nonconcessional									
	1980	1995	1980	1995	1980	1995	1980	1995	1980	1995	1980	1995	1980	1995		
SUB-SAHARAN AFRICA	10,916	38,008	5,733	40,118	4,440	40,716	3,126	14,388	20,772	31,956	22,577	42,093	3,033	8,673		
excluding South Africa	10,916	38,008	5,733	40,118	4,440	40,716	3,126	14,388	20,772	31,956	9,761	31,361	3,033	7,760		
excluding South Africa & Nigeria	10,515	36,971	5,711	25,606	4,309	40,323	2,687	9,837	16,396	23,447	6,208	25,358	3,033	7,760		
Angola	..	1,371	1	741	..	121	13	74	0	7,227	..	1,949	0	0		
Benin	82	433	31	216	84	837	20	24	118	4	73	48	16	84		
Botswana	28	134	23	27	34	217	50	258	8	47	4	17	0	0		
Burkina Faso	89	86	30	62	133	939	9	45	20	5	35	57	15	75		
Burundi	49	167	1	0	55	895	5	31	8	2	12	14	36	48		
Cameroon	663	3,556	142	1,912	243	651	189	1,023	1,014	1,116	278	1,041	59	51		
Cape Verde	3	25	1	10	17	142	0	6	0	2	0	31	0	0		
Central African Republic	17	143	28	58	42	619	12	15	48	17	25	57	24	35		
Chad	97	121	35	53	75	622	0	41	54	2	12	20	14	49		
Comoros	21	35	0	0	21	145	0	8	0	0	1	13	0	3		
Congo	355	1,715	132	1,618	50	380	68	323	653	920	247	1,058	22	19		
Côte d'Ivoire	369	3,284	355	2,033	96	1,403	427	2,494	5,091	5,345	1,059	3,966	65	427		
Djibouti	14	80	5	0	2	138	0	0	5	0	6	42	0	0		
Equatorial Guinea	30	59	13	52	2	96	1	5	7	17	7	45	16	19		
Eritrea	..	..	..	..	..	..	..	..	..	..	..	..	..	..		
Ethiopia	281	1,908	18	285	306	2,220	33	146	49	400	57	190	79	74		
Gabon	103	871	173	2,367	23	113	18	550	955	199	228	297	15	97		
Gambia, The	33	57	0	3	36	314	5	9	24	0	23	16	16	26		
Ghana	633	1,073	119	86	182	2,738	97	246	131	452	131	631	105	649		
Guinea	615	1,241	116	186	63	1,313	67	153	159	82	80	173	35	94		
Guinea-Bissau	68	279	5	66	29	486	0	16	36	3	5	40	1	6		
Kenya	414	1,630	159	665	293	2,342	337	572	1,286	1,164	640	636	254	374		
Lesotho	4	92	2	32	40	376	0	83	11	28	8	10	6	38		
Liberia	179	421	50	79	37	209	94	244	156	208	81	630	89	336		
Madagascar	320	710	71	1,218	162	1,609	20	77	338	77	244	538	87	73		
Malawi	102	243	112	35	176	1,606	44	80	192	14	116	47	80	116		
Mali	454	1,408	6	43	166	1,376	7	10	36	2	24	79	39	147		
Mauritania	407	1,060	54	207	106	779	18	129	131	8	65	184	62	100		
Mauritius	39	379	37	34	34	91	44	179	165	767	47	351	102	0		
Mozambique	..	1,804	0	2,078	..	1,239	0	76	0	102	..	281	0	202		
Namibia	..	..	..	..	..	..	..	..	..	..	..	..	..	..		
Niger	42	198	70	309	114	849	29	20	432	133	159	72	16	52		
Nigeria	401	1,038	21	14,511	131	392	440	4,552	4,376	8,509	3,553	6,003	0	0		
Rwanda	51	130	1	7	91	809	0	0	8	2	26	33	14	26		
São Tomé and Principe	9	71	4	8	11	182	0	0	0	0	0	16	0	1		
Senegal	221	803	169	443	190	1,616	73	245	461	128	219	263	140	347		
Seychelles	16	63	4	4	3	27	2	36	0	22	59	13	0	0		
Sierra Leone	103	341	47	202	40	417	22	3	111	4	53	94	59	165		
Somalia	400	828	9	310	150	773	10	14	28	37	47	551	18	167		
South Africa	..	..	..	..	..	..	..	..	..	..	..	..	..	..		
Sudan	1,361	2,910	1,298	2,877	415	1,934	219	200	854	2,355	599	6,388	431	960		
Swaziland	69	110	34	3	31	76	31	47	24	0	15	15	6	0		
Tanzania	972	1,725	93	1,123	350	2,713	214	155	341	413	319	1,007	171	197		
Togo	155	241	210	283	99	702	19	17	415	53	120	85	33	105		
Uganda	191	635	23	134	64	2,147	15	55	244	84	63	93	89	417		
Zaire	667	1,804	1,620	4,558	195	1,715	127	667	1,462	878	326	3,031	373	485		
Zambia	778	1,681	327	1,050	49	1,792	348	394	726	174	586	523	447	1,239		
Zimbabwe	15	1,037	83	133	3	550	0	1,066	595	955	90	684	0	461		
NORTH AFRICA	11,413	28,859	6,123	20,794	2,099	3,376	1,966	15,165	21,535	24,571	8,063	4,705	868	1,926		
Algeria	1,239	2,841	1,973	8,826	14	220	270	3,567	13,545	14,988	2,325	690	0	1,478		
Egypt, Arab Republic	6,231	18,643	3,767	6,734	1,901	1,906	725	2,322	2,070	2,033	4,027	2,375	411	103		
Libya	..	..	..	..	..	..	..	..	..	..	..	..	..	..		
Morocco	2,633	4,449	166	4,656	90	827	633	6,004	4,491	5,743	778	418	457	52		
Tunisia	1,311	2,926	218	579	95	424	338	3,272	1,429	1,807	136	638	0	293		
ALL AFRICA	22,329	66,867	11,856	60,912	6,539	44,092	5,092	29,553	42,307	56,527	30,640	46,798	3,901	10,599		

6-24. Structure of external debt service payments

	Millions of U.S. dollars (current prices)															
	Bilateral				Multilateral				Private		Short-term		IMF			
	Concessional		Nonconcessional		Concessional		Nonconcessional									
	1980	1995	1980	1995	1980	1995	1980	1995	1980	1995	1980	1995	1980	1995		
SUB-SAHARAN AFRICA	424	1,082	455	916	119	817	365	2,440	3,809	2,381	1,029	408	487	2,922		
excluding South Africa	424	1,082	455	916	119	817	365	2,440	3,809	2,381	1,029	408	487	2,922		
excluding South Africa & Nigeria	402	810	439	916	104	802	309	1,662	3,145	1,931	650	352	487	2,922		
Angola	..	12	0	28	..	0	0	2	0	364	0	53	0	0		
Benin	1	7	1	12	1	19	1	6	4	0	11	2	0	2		
Botswana	1	6	2	8	0	10	10	60	1	9	2	0	0	0		
Burkina Faso	3	5	4	6	3	26	2	9	5	0	5	2	0	0		
Burundi	1	8	0	0	0	15	1	5	4	1	2	1	1	9		
Cameroon	25	50	18	48	7	20	21	191	163	67	28	39	19	9		
Cape Verde	0	0	0	1	0	3	0	2	0	0	0	1	0	0		
Central African Republic	0	0	0	0	0	6	0	1	1	0	2	1	7	8		
Chad	1	0	0	1	2	6	0	1	0	0	0	1	3	8		
Comoros	0	0	0	0	0	1	0	0	0	0	0	0	0	0		
Congo	22	13	13	9	1	3	11	27	25	90	31	35	8	3		
Côte d'Ivoire	29	59	55	215	4	64	45	393	1,180	198	95	23	0	94		
Djibouti	2	3	1	0	0	4	0	0	0	0	1	4	0	0		
Equatorial Guinea	0	0	1	0	0	1	0	0	0	0	1	0	0	1		
Eritrea	..	..	..	..	..	..	..	..	..	..	..	..	..	..		
Ethiopia	11	9	1	4	7	42	5	21	9	78	9	1	2	0		
Gabon	6	49	28	132	2	3	2	66	359	119	33	17	1	57		
Gambia, The	0	4	0	5	0	6	0	4	0	0	3	1	1	6		
Ghana	24	44	22	3	7	47	7	60	48	71	18	28	33	117		
Guinea	55	76	7	19	0	44	21	13	14	16	9	5	2	9		
Guinea-Bissau	0	2	0	1	0	7	0	5	4	0	1	0	0	1		
Kenya	13	88	22	115	5	53	44	174	274	258	58	36	17	41		
Lesotho	0	3	0	4	0	13	0	10	4	7	1	0	0	3		
Liberia	3	0	0	0	1	0	7	0	27	0	11	0	5	2		
Madagascar	26	3	2	9	3	22	2	7	42	10	29	3	3	15		
Malawi	4	13	7	13	3	25	2	27	53	17	16	3	3	11		
Mali	4	34	0	6	1	29	0	3	3	0	3	2	4	7		
Mauritania	7	29	2	22	3	31	2	19	17	0	7	5	11	10		
Mauritius	2	36	4	8	1	8	5	41	29	107	8	16	3	0		
Mozambique	..	43	0	75	..	14	0	12	0	13	0	1	0	16		
Namibia	..	..	..	..	..	..	..	..	..	..	..	..	..	..		
Niger	3	2	5	0	16	13	2	1	98	29	19	1	0	11		
Nigeria	22	272	15	0	15	15	56	779	663	450	379	56	0	0		
Rwanda	0	0	0	0	1	19	0	0	3	0	3	1	0	0		
São Tomé and Principe	0	0	1	0	0	1	0	0	0	0	0	0	0	0		
Senegal	13	19	19	25	3	70	7	54	183	31	24	14	12	84		
Seychelles	0	7	0	0	0	2	0	6	0	4	37	1	0	0		
Sierra Leone	1	6	2	35	1	5	2	1	35	29	6	2	19	4		
Somalia	3	0	0	0	1	0	5	0	0	0	0	0	4	1		
South Africa	..	..	..	..	..	..	..	..	..	..	..	..	..	..		
Sudan	37	0	30	0	12	10	11	8	12	0	70	0	92	52		
Swaziland	2	9	6	2	1	2	3	10	5	0	2	0	0	0		
Tanzania	32	29	2	16	5	49	21	81	36	19	26	4	39	21		
Togo	2	2	17	2	1	11	2	1	16	0	14	3	0	12		
Uganda	3	10	8	11	2	38	1	34	22	11	5	2	16	31		
Zaire	48	0	136	0	2	0	22	0	189	0	45	8	101	18		
Zambia	16	55	22	55	6	37	45	152	238	71	0	1	84	2,244		
Zimbabwe	3	78	0	30	3	25	0	159	43	311	15	35	0	13		
NORTH AFRICA	570	1,420	331	2,244	19	198	253	2,797	5,215	4,441	669	222	253	484		
Algeria	104	111	229	664	2	22	69	689	3,564	2,626	116	28	0	240		
Egypt, Arab Republic	265	666	50	460	8	76	50	487	320	470	422	132	121	105		
Libya	..	..	..	..	..	..	..	..	..	..	..	..	..	..		
Morocco	131	376	24	986	5	55	91	1,053	990	940	105	24	100	107		
Tunisia	70	267	28	135	5	46	44	568	340	405	26	38	33	32		
ALL AFRICA	994	2,501	786	3,160	138	1,015	618	5,237	9,023	6,822	1,699	630	739	3,406		

Note: In 1995, Zambia was able to clear its arrears to the IMF after completing a 3 year Rights Arrangement Program.

6-25. Terms of long-term external financing, 1995

	Concessional terms				Nonconcessional terms				Structure of financing (percentage of total)		
	Interest (percent)	Grace period (years)	Maturity (years)	Grant element (percent)	Interest (percent)	Grace period (years)	Maturity (years)	Grant element (percent)	Grants	Conces-sional loans	Noncon-cessional loans
SUB-SAHARAN AFRICA	1.5	9.2	34.4	70.3	7.1	2.5	8.5	10.2	61.1	28.4	10.5
excluding South Africa	1.5	9.2	34.4	70.3	7.1	2.5	8.5	10.2	61.1	28.4	10.5
excluding South Africa & Nigeria	1.5	9.2	34.4	70.3	7.1	2.5	8.5	10.2	61.0	28.5	10.6
Angola	0.0	0.0	0.0	0.0	0.0	0.0	0.0	0.0	100.0	0.0	0.0
Benin	1.3	8.6	33.2	70.6	0.0	0.0	0.0	0.0	57.9	42.1	0.0
Botswana	0.0	0.0	0.0	0.0	0.0	0.0	0.0	0.0	100.0	0.0	0.0
Burkina Faso	0.8	10.4	39.9	80.8	0.0	0.0	0.0	0.0	86.6	13.4	0.0
Burundi	0.8	9.8	38.0	78.4	0.0	0.0	0.0	0.0	85.5	14.5	0.0
Cameroon	2.1	8.7	28.4	61.7	0.0	0.0	0.0	0.0	63.8	36.2	0.0
Cape Verde	0.8	10.3	39.8	80.6	0.0	0.0	0.0	0.0	82.8	17.2	0.0
Central African Republic	0.8	10.2	39.7	0.0	0.0	0.0	0.0	0.0	86.5	13.5	0.0
Chad	0.8	15.4	42.3	82.5	0.0	0.0	0.0	0.0	55.7	44.3	0.0
Comoros	0.0	0.0	0.0	0.0	0.0	0.0	0.0	0.0	100.0	0.0	0.0
Congo	2.2	8.9	31.8	63.7	0.0	0.0	0.0	0.0	73.8	26.2	0.0
Côte d'Ivoire	1.8	8.5	30.0	64.3	7.6	4.5	16.0	16.8	38.8	60.4	0.8
Djibouti	0.0	0.0	0.0	0.0	0.0	0.0	0.0	0.0	100.0	0.0	0.0
Equatorial Guinea	0.0	0.0	0.0	0.0	0.0	0.0	0.0	0.0	100.0	0.0	0.0
Eritrea	0.0	0.0	0.0	0.0	0.0	0.0	0.0	0.0	100.0	0.0	0.0
Ethiopia	0.8	9.9	39.4	80.2	0.0	0.0	0.0	0.0	77.0	23.0	0.0
Gabon	5.3	5.7	24.5	30.7	7.7	5.2	17.9	13.0	34.3	61.6	4.1
Gambia, The	0.2	10.7	34.9	83.5	0.0	0.0	0.0	0.0	71.6	28.4	0.0
Ghana	1.3	9.9	36.8	73.9	6.6	1.7	8.3	11.7	25.1	52.9	22.0
Guinea	1.9	7.1	26.2	60.6	2.7	0.1	3.5	10.8	56.8	32.7	10.5
Guinea-Bissau	1.0	9.7	37.7	77.5	0.0	0.0	0.0	0.0	66.9	33.1	0.0
Kenya	2.1	9.9	35.4	66.7	8.2	0.5	6.3	2.4	38.8	34.5	26.8
Lesotho	0.8	9.4	38.9	79.6	10.0	3.6	20.3	-1.6	71.8	13.5	14.7
Liberia	0.0	0.0	0.0	0.0	0.0	0.0	0.0	0.0	100.0	0.0	0.0
Madagascar	0.8	9.7	37.3	76.8	11.0	2.7	8.2	-5.1	67.3	32.3	0.5
Malawi	0.8	9.8	39.3	80.0	0.0	0.0	0.0	0.0	72.2	27.8	0.0
Mali	1.5	8.8	30.7	68.6	0.0	0.0	0.0	0.0	56.1	43.9	0.0
Mauritania	0.9	9.9	35.5	77.1	0.0	0.0	0.0	0.0	54.7	45.3	0.0
Mauritius	3.6	5.9	19.8	43.7	6.3	4.7	8.0	15.6	3.8	13.0	83.2
Mozambique	1.0	9.0	35.8	74.8	0.0	0.0	0.0	0.0	83.1	16.9	0.0
Namibia	0.0	0.0	0.0	0.0	0.0	0.0	0.0	0.0	100.0	0.0	0.0
Niger	0.7	9.2	36.0	76.1	0.0	0.0	0.0	0.0	95.5	4.5	0.0
Nigeria	0.0	0.0	0.0	0.0	0.0	0.0	0.0	0.0	100.0	0.0	0.0
Rwanda	0.8	10.3	39.7	80.6	0.0	0.0	0.0	0.0	91.9	8.1	0.0
São Tomé and Principe	0.0	0.0	0.0	0.0	0.0	0.0	0.0	0.0	100.0	0.0	0.0
Senegal	1.0	9.5	38.6	76.6	2.0	10.0	29.5	65.6	56.1	42.8	1.1
Seychelles	0.0	0.0	0.0	0.0	8.1	5.0	35.0	13.9	83.0	0.0	17.0
Sierra Leone	0.6	7.8	32.6	70.4	8.6	6.8	23.2	8.7	63.6	34.9	1.5
Somalia	0.0	0.0	0.0	0.0	0.0	0.0	0.0	0.0	100.0	0.0	0.0
South Africa	..	..	..	..	..	..	..	..	..	..	..
Sudan	0.0	0.0	0.0	0.0	0.0	0.0	0.0	0.0	100.0	0.0	0.0
Swaziland	0.0	0.0	0.0	0.0	7.1	5.0	19.5	18.1	36.0	0.0	64.0
Tanzania	0.8	8.8	35.4	74.8	11.8	2.6	10.6	-9.7	74.6	25.4	0.0
Togo	0.8	9.8	39.3	80.0	0.0	0.0	0.0	0.0	65.6	34.4	0.0
Uganda	0.8	10.1	39.6	80.4	0.0	0.0	0.0	0.0	81.0	19.0	0.0
Zaire	2.6	4.4	19.9	48.7	0.0	0.0	0.0	0.0	92.1	7.9	0.0
Zambia	0.8	10.1	39.9	80.4	10.0	2.8	8.3	-1.0	54.4	44.1	1.5
Zimbabwe	0.0	0.0	0.0	0.0	5.9	3.4	7.8	15.2	88.8	0.0	11.2
NORTH AFRICA	3.1	7.4	23.6	45.1	6.6	3.2	12.1	13.5	18.0	20.1	61.9
Algeria	4.0	10.8	29.0	49.8	6.3	2.1	7.0	9.3	3.8	3.0	93.2
Egypt, Arab Republic	0.6	8.0	28.0	69.6	7.1	4.5	18.4	17.2	90.9	6.5	2.5
Libya	..	..	..	..	..	..	..	..	..	..	..
Morocco	3.4	7.2	22.8	41.2	6.4	2.9	13.3	16.8	5.2	53.9	40.9
Tunisia	2.4	7.2	24.8	54.2	6.8	4.5	16.4	16.1	2.9	10.8	86.3
ALL AFRICA	1.9	8.7	31.6	63.9	6.7	3.0	11.2	12.7	47.1	25.7	27.2

Note: Data are averages for new commitments of public and publicly guaranteed long-term loans only, excluding IMF purchases, weighted by the US dollar value of the loans.

6-26. External debt and debt service ratios, 1995

	Debt-GDP ratio		Total external debt per capita (US dollars)	Percentage of debt disbursed	Debt-export ratio		Debt service-export ratio	
	Concessional	Non-concessional			Concessional	Non-concessional	Ex ante	Ex post
SUB-SAHARAN AFRICA	49	75	380	85	131	202	..	20
excluding South Africa	49	75	380	85	131	202	..	20
excl. S. Africa & Nigeria	57	62	397	85	161	176	..	21
Angola	24	13	1,066	90	40	268	..	12
Benin	61	12	301	81	209	62	..	8
Botswana	8	7	482	86	14	14	..	4
Burkina Faso	44	5	122	71	260	61	..	12
Burundi	100	3	185	78	722	65	..	26
Cameroon	53	37	704	88	199	244	..	20
Cape Verde	40	4	569	52	91	27	..	3
Central African Republic	67	6	288	89	310	74	..	6
Chad	71	9	141	71	233	52	..	5
Comoros	77	3	413	88	295	40	..	2
Congo	100	92	2,291	94	167	313	..	14
Côte d'Ivoire	47	45	1,356	93	104	318	..	23
Djibouti	44	0	410	72	96	19	..	5
Equatorial Guinea	92	34	733	84	170	151	..	2
Eritrea	..	..	..	..	..	..	..	..
Ethiopia	70	7	93	81	511	135	..	19
Gabon	19	57	4,091	89	34	120	..	15
Gambia, The	102	3	382	81	186	27	..	13
Ghana	62	5	344	69	238	129	..	23
Guinea	70	9	492	82	314	85	..	22
Guinea-Bissau	301	32	836	87	1,737	295	..	37
Kenya	44	14	277	83	133	114	..	26
Lesotho	56	14	333	57	62	25	..	5
Liberia	..	..	778	99	..	..	..	..
Madagascar	73	40	315	85	306	262	..	9
Malawi	126	8	219	79	426	67	..	25
Mali	113	2	313	81	433	44	..	13
Mauritania	172	31	1,085	86	315	108	..	20
Mauritius	12	5	1,596	70	19	53	..	9
Mozambique	208	147	358	81	653	588	..	37
Namibia	..	..	..	..	..	..	..	..
Niger	56	18	181	83	319	179	..	18
Nigeria	6	80	315	87	13	301	..	14
Rwanda	76	1	157	69	1,103	80	..	23
São Tomé and Principe	556	17	2,150	83	2,974	288	..	25
Senegal	50	14	454	79	144	85	..	18
Seychelles	17	8	2,237	85	33	28	..	8
Sierra Leone	88	24	272	77	717	442	..	78
Somalia	..	..	282	86	..	..	..	..
South Africa	..	..	..	..	..	..	..	..
Sudan	..	..	660	94	..	..	..	..
Swaziland	17	5	279	61	18	6	..	2
Tanzania	106	30	247	82	402	262	..	20
Togo	73	23	362	89	200	115	..	6
Uganda	49	3	186	74	407	115	..	20
Zaire	57	85	300	91	206	564	..	1
Zambia	85	35	763	90	267	260	..	201
Zimbabwe	24	18	444	74	58	120	..	24
NORTH AFRICA	21	44	812	82	64	132	..	23
Algeria	7	30	1,166	79	25	243	..	36
Egypt, Arab Republic	34	15	586	91	112	74	..	13
Libya	..	..	..	..	..	..	..	..
Morocco	16	33	834	81	47	151	..	32
Tunisia	19	21	1,106	69	38	74	..	17
ALL AFRICA	35	59	460	84	99	168	..	22

Figure 6-1. Debt service ratio (ex post), 1995

(percent of exports of goods and services)

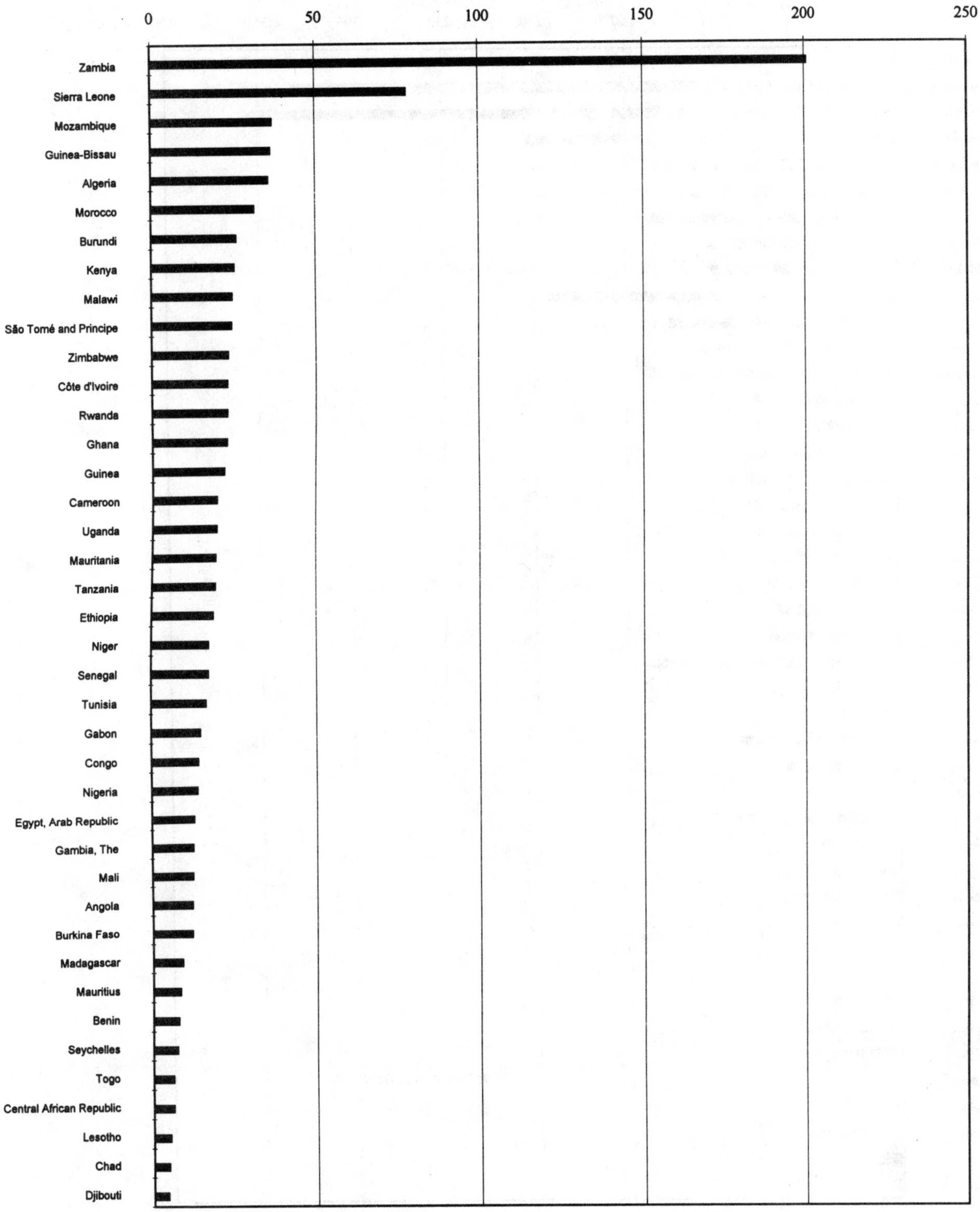

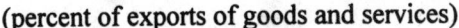

Note: In 1995, Zambia was able to clear its arrears to the IMF after completing a 3 year Rights Arrangement Program.

Figure 6-2. Debt to GDP ratio, 1995

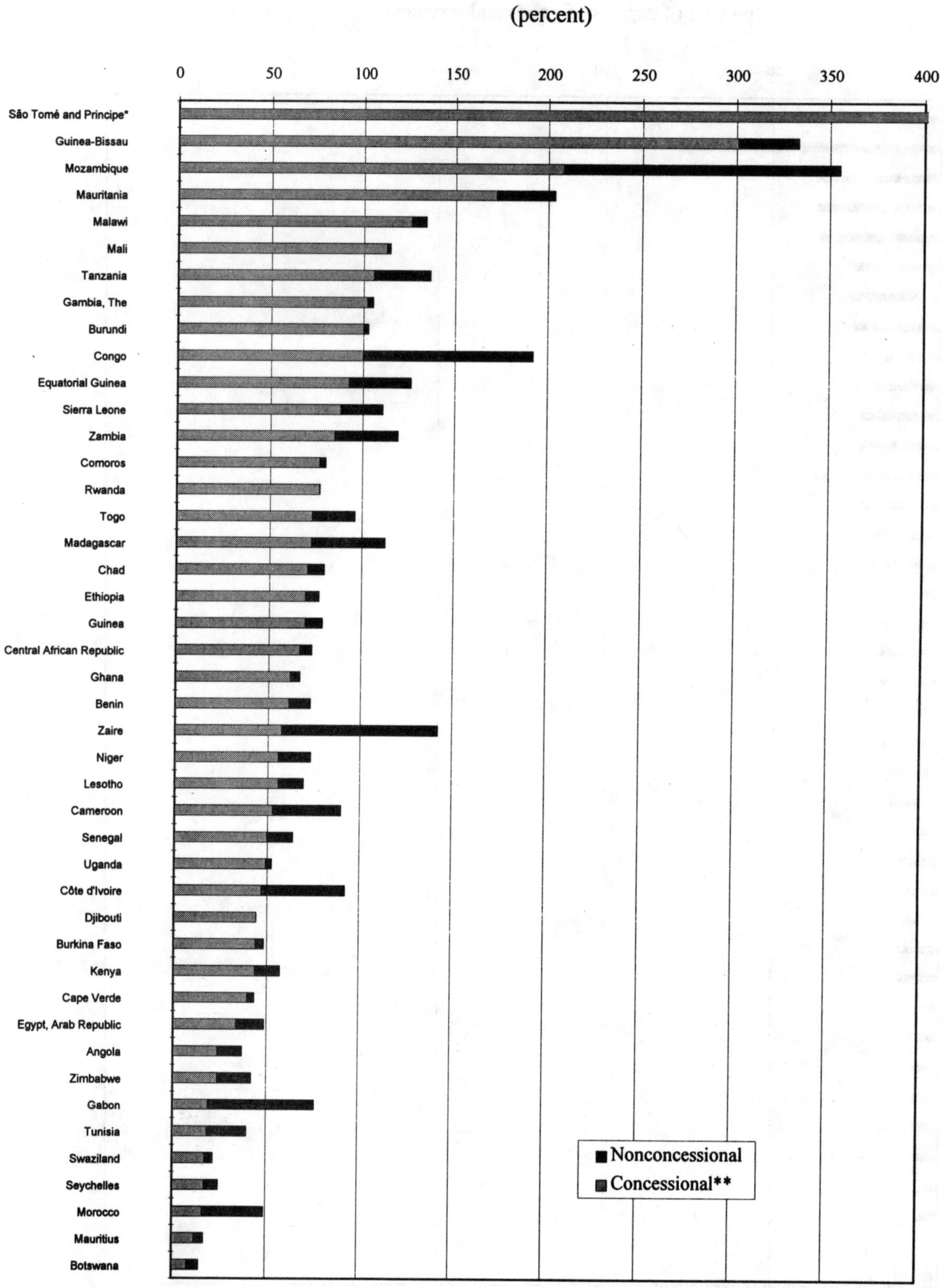

* Debt to GDP ratio is greater than 400.

** Sorted by concessional debt.

Technical Notes

Tables

Tables 6-1, 6-2, and 6-3. Gross disbursements: official concessional, official nonconcessional, and private long-term loans. Gross disbursements are from commitments of long-term external loans by official concessional, official nonconcessional, and private sources, respectively (World Bank, DRS).

Table 6-4. Disbursements: long-term loans and IMF purchases. This is the sum of tables 6-1 through 6-3, plus IMF purchases.

Tables 6-5, 6-6, and 6-7. Amortization: official concessional, official nonconcessional, and private long-term loans. Amortization is the actual repayment of principal made in foreign currencies, goods, or services on outstanding long-term official concessional, official nonconcessional, and private long-term loans as described above (World Bank, DRS).

Table 6-8. Amortization: long-term loans and IMF repurchases. This is the sum of Tables 6-5 to 6-7, plus repurchases of drawings from the IMF.

Tables 6-9, 6-10, and 6-11. Interest payments: official concessional, official non-concessional, and private long-term loans. These are actual payments made in foreign currencies, goods, and services to various lenders described above on interest obligations, including IMF charges on drawings due on disbursed debt and on commitment charges due on undisbursed debt (where information is available), that is, on long-term official concessional, official nonconcessional, and private loans (World Bank, DRS).

Table 6-12. Interest payments: long-term loans and IMF charges. This is the sum of Tables 6-9 through 6-11, plus IMF charges on drawings.

Table 6-13. Total external debt service payments: long-term loans and IMF credit. Total external debt service payments include the sum of amortization on long-term loans and IMF credit and interest payments on long-term loans and IMF credit (World Bank, DRS).

Table 6-14. Interest payments: short-term loans. These are estimated for the respective year based on the estimated year-end stock of short-term debt (which may include interest arrears on long-term debt) and the annual average six-month London interbank offered rate (LIBOR) on notes denominated in US dollars as reported in the *IFS* (with no adjustment for spreads). Actual payments may be different because the LIBOR only approximates actual interest rates on short-term loans, and because not all interest due on short-term loans is actually paid (World Bank, DRS).

Table 6-15. Net flows: long- and short-term loans, including IMF. These flows represent all disbursements of long- and short-term loans net of all repayments of principal on long- and short-term loans and IMF credit (World Bank, DRS).

Table 6-16. Net flows: long-term loans, including IMF. Net flows of long-term loans are as defined above for Table 6-15, but excluding short-term loans (World Bank, DRS).

Table 6-17. Net transfers: long- and short-term loans, including IMF. Net transfers are net flows (Table 6-15) less interest payments (Tables 6-12 and 6-14).

Table 6-18. Net transfers: long-term loans, including IMF. Net transfers include long-term loans and IMF credit only (Table 6-16 less Table 6-12).

Tables 6-19, 6-20, and 6-21. Long-term debt: official concessional, official nonconcessional, and private. This series reflects the total debt outstanding and disbursed of official concessional, official nonconcessional, and private loans (World Bank, DRS). The time series reflects changes in the valuation of year-end debt stocks (because of US dollar exchange rate fluctuation) and debt cancellation, as well as net disbursements. Therefore changes in debt stocks from year to year cannot be used as a measure of net borrowing or vice versa.

Table 6-22. Total external debt. When Tables 6-19 to 6-21 are supplemented with IMF credit and estimates of total short-term debt (which includes interest in arrears on public and publicly guaranteed long-term loans), they sum up to total external debt (World Bank, DRS).

Table 6-23. Structure of external debt. This table summarizes debt structure for 1980 and 1995 (World Bank, DRS). The columns cover the type of creditor and concessionality. The private debt shown includes both the private guaranteed (by an entity of the debtor government) and the private nonguaranteed debt. For each year, all components shown add to the total in Table 6-22.

Table 6-24. Structure of external debt service payments. This summary table compares debt service payments for all types of creditors in 1980 and 1995 (World Bank, DRS). Debt service payments on short-term loans are excluded, to be consistent with Table 6-13. Debt service payments are actual repayments of principal (amortization) and actual payments of interest. The column headings have the same definitions as given above for Table 6-23.

Table 6-25. Terms of long-term external financing, 1995. This table presents the average interest rates, grace periods, maturities, and grant elements shown separately for concessional and nonconcessional long-term loans (official and private); short-term loans are excluded (World Bank, DRS). Grant elements are calculated using a standard 10 percent discount rate. The indicators are weighted averages (based on amount of commitments) across all loans in each category. For the column on structure of financing (that is, total flows), grants are based on sources for Chapter 12 (Aid Flows) and are not comparable with net official transfers shown in Chapter 5.

Table 6-26. External debt and debt service ratios, 1995. This table includes the ratio of debt outstanding and disbursed to GDP; per capita debt; the ratio of debt outstanding and disbursed to debt outstanding, including undisbursed; the ratio of debt outstanding and disbursed to exports of goods and all services, including receipts of workers' remittances; and the ratio of total debt service paid to exports of goods and all services, more commonly called the debt service ratio (World Bank, DRS). Ratios are shown separately for concessional debt and for all nonconcessional (including private) debt. Both the stock of external debt and debt service payments include short- and long-term loans and IMF credit, except for the ratio of debt outstanding to debt outstanding including undisbursed, which is calculated for public and publicly guaranteed debt only. The data for exports of goods and all services, plus receipts of workers' remittances, are taken from balance of payments data in Chapter 5. The debt service ratio is shown for the ex post category, depicting the amount actually paid after debt relief and/or arrears.

Figures

The following indicators have been used to derive the figures in this chapter.

Figure 6-1. Debt service ratio (Table 6-26).

Figure 6-2. Debt to GDP ratio (Table 6-26).

Methodology used for regional aggregations and period averages in chapter 6

	Aggregations[a]			*Period averages*[b]
Table	*(1)*	*(2)*	*(6)*	*(1)*
6-1	x			x
6-2	x			x
6-3	x			x
6-4	x			x
6-5	x			x
6-6	x			x
6-7	x			x
6-8	x			x
6-9	x			x
6-10	x			x
6-11	x			x
6-12	x			x
6-13	x			x
6-14	x			x
6-15	x			x
6-16	x			x
6-17	x			x
6-18	x			x
6-19	x			x
6-20	x			x
6-21	x			x
6-22	x			
6-23	x			
6-24	x			
6-25			x	
6-26		x		

Note: Regional aggregations are shown in the rows for Sub-Saharan Africa, North Africa, and All Africa. Period averages are shown in the last three columns. This table shows only the methodologies used in this chapter.

a. Regional aggregations: (1) simple total; (2) simple total of the first indicator divided by the simple total of the second indicator (same country coverage); (3) simple total of the gap-filled indicator; (4) simple total of the gap-filled main indicator divided by the simple total of the gap-filled secondary indicator; (5) simple total of the first gap-filled main indicator less the simple total of the second gap-filled main indicator, all divided by the simple total of the secondary indicator; (6) weighted total; (7) median; (8) no aggregation; (9) simple arithmetic mean.

b. Period averages: (1) arithmetic mean (using the same series as shown in the table, i.e., ratio if the rest of the table is shown as ratio, level if the rest of the table is shown as level, growth rate if the rest of the table is shown as growth rate); (2) least-squares growth rate (using main indicator); (3) least-squares growth rate (using main indicator in constant terms, with the rest of the table in current terms).

7

Government Finance

The data in this chapter pertain to consolidated government (except when not available) instead of to central government operations, which were reported in previous volumes.

Definitions have been taken from the IMF's *Government Finance Statistics* (*GFS*). For this volume, data are taken from country desks. When not available from country desks, data are taken from the *GFS* and supplemented with data from IMF, World Bank, or staff reports, or from other national government sources. Data from various sources have been harmonized to produce a consistent and comparable time series.

The focus of this chapter is on the principal financial transactions of government—taxing, borrowing, spending, and lending—rather than on the production and consumption of goods and services, the use of labor, or other government activities. Spending covers both current and capital transactions.

The data cover major government finance indicators—fiscal deficit or surplus, expenditure and lending minus repayments, revenue, grants, and domestic and foreign financing—expressed as a percentage of GDP. The chapter also includes information on the major components of revenue and expenditure by economic category, shown as percentages of total revenue and as a percentage of expenditure and lending minus repayments, respectively.

Measures of fiscal deficit or surplus are among the single most important indicators of government fiscal performance. The measure is usually calculated as the difference between total revenue (including grants) and total expenditure (including lending minus repayments). As such, it measures government net financing requirements. *GFS* methodology recommends grouping grants receipts with revenue because they can be spent without incurring an obligation for future payments but lists them separately because grants can sometimes be treated as financing items. Financing includes all government borrowing from others (at home and abroad) minus amortization (government repayment of its borrowing from others and changes in cash balances). Other measures of fiscal balance include the fiscal deficit or surplus without capital grants, which measures the government's ability to operate without foreign capital transfers, and the fiscal deficit or surplus, excluding interest payments from expenditure, referred to as the primary deficit or surplus.

Revenue is divided between taxes—unrequited compulsory payments to government—and nontax revenue. It includes only non- repayable receipts other than grants. Tax revenue is also classified according to the base upon which the tax is levied (for example, income and profits).

Expenditure is classified by economic category (such as wages, purchases, and interest payments). Lending minus repayments—government lending less repayment of past government lending—is grouped with expenditure, except in certain cases (see Technical Notes).

The economic classification of expenditures (for example, on wages) is presented as a percentage of total expenditure and lending minus repayments, because lending minus repayments is itself a separate economic classification.

No attempt was made to reconcile *GFS* data in this chapter with the System of National Accounts (SNA). The fundamental difference between the two systems is that *GFS* focuses on government financial transactions, whereas the SNA considers government transactions as part of total demand and value added. (For further discussion, see World Bank 1988b, box 2.1, p. 45.) Indicators calculated as ratios to GDP use GDP at purchaser values or market prices (see Technical Notes to Chapter 1). Because GDP at purchaser values includes import duties (and GDP at market prices includes indirect taxes), ratios for revenues tend to understate tax burdens, especially where such taxes are an important source of government revenue.

Fiscal year data are compared with the calendar year GDP data that correspond either to the second half of the fiscal year or to the calendar year in which most of the fiscal year falls. Fiscal years do not correspond to calendar years in Botswana, Cameroon, Egypt, Ethiopia, the Gambia, Ghana (before 1982), Kenya, Lesotho, Liberia, Malawi, Mauritius, Niger, Nigeria, Senegal, Sierra Leone, Sudan, Swaziland, Tanzania, Uganda, and Zimbabwe (after 1985).

Tables in this volume contain corrections to mislabeled subtitles in *ADI 1992.* Thus subtitles in tables 7-1 through 7-8 are now correctly labeled percentage of total GDP (instead of revenues).

7-1. Government deficit/surplus (including grants)

	Percentage of GDP											Annual average		
	1980	*1987*	*1988*	*1989*	*1990*	*1991*	*1992*	*1993*	*1994*	*1995*	*1996*	*75-84*	*85-89*	*90-MR*
SUB-SAHARAN AFRICA	-2.2	-4.3	-4.4	-3.4	-3.6	-4.5	-6.1	-8.3	-5.9	-3.8	-2.9	-2.9	-3.4	-5.0
excluding South Africa	-2.1	-3.6	-4.5	-4.4	-3.8	-4.4	-5.2	-7.6	-5.4	-2.8	-4.4	-2.2	-3.2	-4.8
excl. S. Africa & Nigeria	-2.8	-2.5	-2.0	-3.6	-3.9	-3.6	-4.1	-4.4	-4.3	-3.0	-2.6	-1.1	-2.1	-3.7
Angola	..	..	..	..	..	..	..	..	..	..	..	..	..	..
Benin	..	-0.8	1.1	-1.0	-4.1	-3.5	-2.6	-1.1	-2.8	-3.4	-0.3	0.6	-0.7	-2.5
Botswana	..	..	..	..	..	..	..	..	..	..	..	..	..	..
Burkina Faso	..	-5.0	-5.9	2.9	-4.4	-3.6	-2.9	-4.6	-3.2	-1.8	-0.5	-5.5	-3.2	-3.0
Burundi	9.8	-9.8	-6.9	1.3	2.5	5.5	2.9	1.7	-2.9	-1.3	-10.2	9.5	0.7	-0.3
Cameroon	0.4	-13.0	-5.9	-4.5	-7.6	-8.2	-6.6	-6.3	-9.2	-4.9	-2.8	0.9	-5.2	-6.5
Cape Verde	..	-5.5	-1.5	-4.5	-2.0	-7.2	-8.7	-6.8	-14.6	-13.1	-11.3	-7.2	46.7	-9.1
Central African Republic	..	-7.0	-6.2	-5.0	-7.5	-9.4	-9.3	-8.5	-9.5	-5.3	-3.5	0.9	-5.4	-7.6
Chad	..	-6.2	-6.1	-10.1	-10.9	-5.8	-11.6	-12.2	-4.3	-6.1	-4.4	-1.4	-5.6	-7.9
Comoros	..	16.8	14.3	-3.4	-1.1	-2.6	-3.5	2.5	-7.1	-7.4	-5.1	19.1	11.2	-3.5
Congo	..	-12.8	-18.0	-10.1	-7.1	-14.1	-14.2	-13.7	-13.2	-8.3	-2.0	-2.7	-10.7	-10.4
Côte d'Ivoire	-8.5	19.0	17.4	-16.6	-12.0	-12.7	-11.6	-11.8	-6.3	-3.0	-2.4	2.7	13.8	-8.5
Djibouti	..	..	..	..	..	-3.0	-11.7	-13.0	-8.4	-8.1	-4.0	..	..	-8.0
Equatorial Guinea	..	..	..	..	..	..	..	..	..	..	..	..	..	..
Eritrea	..	..	..	..	..	..	-1.8	2.3	4.8	..	-1.4	..	..	0.9
Ethiopia	..	-4.9	-4.9	-6.5	-11.2	-8.9	-7.4	-7.1	-10.2	-4.3	-5.1	-6.6	-5.7	-7.7
Gabon	..	-8.4	-9.4	-6.1	-3.5	-2.2	-5.2	-5.7	-1.6	3.1	2.7	-21.5	-6.5	-1.8
Gambia, The	-4.0	5.3	8.7	-4.2	-7.7	-2.0	..	..	..	..	..	-0.6	3.3	-4.8
Ghana	..	-2.4	-2.8	-2.1	-3.1	-2.3	-9.4	-10.4	-9.3	-6.7	-10.6	-2.3	-2.7	-7.4
Guinea	..	-4.0	-6.8	-5.0	-5.2	-4.6	-3.4	-3.8	-3.6	-2.7	-2.6	..	-5.5	-3.7
Guinea-Bissau	..	12.7	1.2	7.4	6.1	-5.1	-9.2	2.4	13.7	19.8	2.8	..	1.9	4.4
Kenya	-0.4	-0.2	-0.3	-0.2	-0.3	-0.2	-0.5	-0.4	-0.1	0.0	0.1	-0.3	-0.3	-0.2
Lesotho	..	..	..	..	..	..	..	..	..	..	..	..	..	..
Liberia	..	..	..	..	..	..	..	..	..	..	..	..	..	..
Madagascar	-12.8	-3.4	-3.3	-1.4	2.3	-4.2	-4.2	-4.6	-5.8	-3.4	-2.1	-7.4	-3.1	-3.2
Malawi	-8.4	-5.0	2.5	3.0	-1.4	-0.3	-7.8	-3.9	-6.3	0.9	-1.0	-6.4	-2.2	-2.8
Mali	..	-5.3	-4.7	-4.8	-2.7	-3.9	-3.9	-4.1	-4.2	-3.0	-0.8	-3.8	-5.9	-3.2
Mauritania	..	-3.3	-3.5	-8.1	-5.1	-5.1	-2.7	-7.8	-2.5	1.2	7.5	0.0	-4.0	-2.1
Mauritius	..	-0.4	-1.7	-2.3	-1.6	-2.1	-2.2	-2.0	-2.8	-5.4	-5.3	-6.6	-1.8	-3.1
Mozambique	-8.2	-12.8	-12.4	-8.7	-12.3	-5.6	-5.4	-5.1	-8.3	-5.0	-5.2	-15.1	-14.1	-6.7
Namibia	0.0	-7.8	-9.5	-5.7	-2.4	-5.4	-6.3	-9.6	-7.0	-5.1	-4.3	-10.1	-9.5	-5.7
Niger	..	-3.7	-5.1	-5.8	-7.0	-3.6	-4.7	-3.8	-6.7	-3.5	-0.2	-4.9	-4.8	-4.2
Nigeria	-0.2	-7.5	-13.0	-7.2	-3.4	-7.1	-8.9	-18.1	-9.1	-2.4	-9.1	-5.8	-7.0	-8.3
Rwanda	-2.0	-6.5	-3.5	-1.7	-5.4	-4.2	-4.3	-4.0	-9.1	5.8	-0.3	-2.6	-3.7	-3.1
São Tomé and Principe	..	-16.5	-22.1	-40.8	-48.5	-38.5	-41.8	-33.6	-43.0	-37.1	-50.7	..	-26.5	-41.9
Senegal	-0.3	-1.4	-1.1	-1.3	-2.2	2.9	-1.7	-2.9	-1.8	-0.2	0.0	-2.4	-1.9	-0.8
Seychelles	..	-4.6	-4.0	-8.0	0.2	-4.9	-5.6	-7.7	-4.3	-4.9	-3.7	-2.5	-7.7	-4.4
Sierra Leone	..	-8.8	-5.3	-9.6	-8.8	-7.0	-5.6	-5.1	-3.7	-6.1	-3.9	..	-9.3	-5.7
Somalia	..	..	..	..	..	..	..	..	..	..	..	..	..	..
South Africa	-2.3	-6.1	-4.2	-1.3	-3.3	-4.7	-8.0	-9.9	-7.1	-6.0	..	-4.4	-4.0	-6.5
Sudan	..	..	..	..	..	..	..	..	..	..	..	..	..	..
Swaziland	..	..	..	..	..	..	..	..	..	..	..	..	..	..
Tanzania	..	-2.8	-3.9	-0.3	-0.6	0.5	1.1	-6.2	-3.2	-9.0	..	-11.6	-4.7	-2.9
Togo	..	-6.8	-3.3	-2.0	-2.9	-6.5	-4.2	-15.6	-12.2	-6.5	-6.0	-2.1	-3.4	-7.7
Uganda	..	-3.8	-3.9	-3.2	-4.4	-3.4	-7.3	-3.2	-3.8	-3.0	3.2	-2.1	-3.6	-3.1
Zaire	..	..	..	..	..	..	..	..	..	..	..	..	..	..
Zambia	..	-5.4	-9.3	-4.3	-8.3	-7.0	-2.5	-5.1	-5.8	-5.3	-4.0	..	-10.8	-5.4
Zimbabwe	10.3	-9.7	-8.5	-8.8	-7.3	-5.4	-6.2	-4.8	-5.7	-8.3	-7.6	11.2	-8.7	-6.5
NORTH AFRICA	..	-6.1	-9.2	-4.1	-1.6	-2.5	-1.4	-4.8	-2.4	-0.6	..	-3.5	-5.4	-2.2
Algeria	..	-7.2	-12.4	-1.8	3.6	1.7	-1.1	-8.7	-4.4	-1.4	..	-8.1	-8.0	-1.7
Egypt, Arab Republic	..	-12.9	-16.7	-14.1	-13.6	-12.7	-3.1	-1.4	-0.5	0.3	..	..	-14.6	-5.2
Libya	..	..	..	..	..	..	..	..	..	..	..	..	..	..
Morocco	..	..	..	..	..	..	..	..	..	..	..	..	..	..
Tunisia	..	..	..	..	..	..	..	..	..	..	..	..	..	..
ALL AFRICA	-1.3	-5.1	-6.3	-3.7	-2.9	-3.8	-4.4	-7.0	-4.7	-2.6	..	-1.8	-4.2	-4.2

Note: 1996 data are preliminary. Nigeria's data are for federal level; since 1994, ratios are distorted because the official exchange rate used by the Gov. for oil exports oil value added is significantly over-valued.

7-2. Government deficit/surplus (excluding grants)

	Percentage of GDP											Annual average		
	1980	1987	1988	1989	1990	1991	1992	1993	1994	1995	1996	75-84	85-89	90-MR
SUB-SAHARAN AFRICA	-2.4	-5.5	-5.5	-4.7	-4.7	-5.7	-7.4	-9.7	-7.5	-5.4	-4.1	-3.1	-4.5	-6.4
excluding South Africa	-2.4	-5.2	-6.0	-6.2	-5.3	-6.1	-7.2	-9.6	-7.6	-5.1	-6.3	-2.5	-4.7	-6.7
excl. S. Africa & Nigeria	-3.2	-4.6	-3.9	-5.9	-5.9	-5.9	-6.6	-7.0	-7.2	-6.1	-5.2	-1.5	-4.0	-6.3
Angola	..	..	..	..	..	..	..	..	..	..	..	..	..	..
Benin	..	-4.4	-3.4	-10.2	-9.5	-7.1	-6.7	-4.9	-7.3	-7.3	-4.8	-2.1	-5.7	-6.8
Botswana	..	..	..	..	..	..	..	..	..	..	..	..	..	..
Burkina Faso	..	-11.2	-9.6	-15.2	-7.3	-8.2	-9.1	-10.1	-10.6	-9.3	-7.9	-12.9	-10.1	-8.9
Burundi	6.1	-13.7	-9.3	-5.5	-5.6	-3.2	-5.7	-7.4	-5.2	-5.0	-12.2	5.4	-3.4	-6.3
Cameroon	0.4	-13.0	-5.9	-4.5	-7.6	-8.2	-6.6	-6.3	-9.4	-5.1	-3.3	0.9	-5.2	-6.6
Cape Verde	..	-25.3	-16.4	-15.2	-12.7	-19.8	-28.0	-23.6	-32.6	-30.5	-27.0	-45.0	-28.4	-24.9
Central African Republic	0.0	-13.1	-12.2	-9.9	-11.8	-14.1	-15.2	-13.9	-14.2	-11.6	-5.0	-0.4	-10.6	-12.3
Chad	..	-25.5	-19.1	-23.7	-22.3	-12.9	-18.5	-18.7	-20.2	-16.3	-15.4	-1.4	-19.6	-17.7
Comoros	..	-25.2	-18.1	-19.8	-16.2	-18.8	-18.7	-11.1	-22.4	-18.2	-13.3	-19.1	-24.0	-17.0
Congo	..	-12.9	-18.1	-10.2	-7.4	-14.3	-14.2	-13.7	-14.3	-9.3	-2.4	-3.6	-10.8	-10.8
Côte d'Ivoire	-8.5	19.0	17.4	-16.6	-12.0	-13.2	-12.1	-12.3	-6.9	-3.7	-3.1	2.7	13.8	-9.0
Djibouti	..	..	..	..	..	-15.2	-24.1	-21.8	-13.4	-10.1	-5.8	..	..	-15.1
Equatorial Guinea	..	..	..	..	..	..	..	..	..	..	..	..	..	..
Eritrea	..	..	..	..	..	..	-43.9	-32.1	-21.6	..	-5.5	..	..	-25.8
Ethiopia	..	-6.9	-8.8	-11.2	-13.8	-11.3	-9.7	-11.1	-15.0	-8.1	-8.3	-8.7	-9.4	-11.0
Gabon	..	-8.8	-9.9	-6.5	-3.9	-2.4	-5.3	-6.0	-2.0	3.1	2.7	-21.8	-7.0	-2.0
Gambia, The	-32.8	-11.3	-6.7	-11.2	-10.0	-3.7	..	..	..	..	..	-32.5	-17.1	-6.9
Ghana	-18.7	-5.1	-5.3	-5.3	-5.7	-4.9	-12.7	-14.8	-13.0	-10.4	-13.6	-11.8	-5.1	-10.8
Guinea	..	-8.0	-10.0	-8.7	-8.8	-8.2	-7.8	-7.5	-7.1	-6.7	-5.7	..	-8.7	-7.4
Guinea-Bissau	..	-33.7	-43.7	-42.6	-25.2	-35.8	-38.1	-29.9	-23.1	-17.7	-23.5	-77.2	-41.5	-27.6
Kenya	-0.5	-0.4	-0.5	-0.5	-0.5	-0.4	-0.7	-0.5	-0.2	-0.1	0.0	-0.4	-0.5	-0.3
Lesotho	..	..	..	..	..	..	..	..	..	..	..	..	..	..
Liberia	..	..	..	..	..	..	..	..	..	..	..	..	..	..
Madagascar	-12.8	-4.0	-4.1	-5.5	-2.1	-6.3	-7.7	-8.1	-8.8	-6.3	-5.4	-7.7	-4.4	-6.4
Malawi	-11.8	-11.0	-7.9	-7.0	-6.8	-6.3	-13.2	-9.6	-27.8	-15.8	-5.5	-10.6	-9.7	-12.2
Mali	..	-10.6	-10.5	-9.9	-8.5	-12.1	-11.0	-9.6	-13.7	-10.5	-7.9	-8.4	-11.0	-10.5
Mauritania	..	-18.9	-9.9	-12.8	-9.2	-7.9	-6.0	-12.0	-5.4	-1.9	3.1	0.0	-16.5	-5.6
Mauritius	..	-1.2	-2.2	-2.6	-1.9	-2.2	-2.3	-2.2	-3.1	-5.7	-5.7	-7.0	-2.5	-3.3
Mozambique	-11.4	-22.9	-27.0	-24.8	-29.2	-24.9	-26.3	-22.2	-29.7	-20.8	-17.0	-18.3	-23.5	-24.3
Namibia	0.0	-7.8	-9.5	-5.7	-2.4	-7.1	-7.3	-10.5	-7.7	-6.2	-5.4	-10.1	-9.5	-6.6
Niger	..	-8.8	-9.7	-10.5	-12.4	-8.4	-8.6	-9.4	-12.5	-8.2	-5.1	-8.3	-9.4	-9.2
Nigeria	-0.2	-7.5	-13.0	-7.2	-3.4	-7.1	-8.9	-18.1	-9.1	-2.4	-9.1	-5.8	-7.0	-8.3
Rwanda	-2.0	-9.6	-8.0	-5.9	-10.0	-12.0	-14.9	-15.5	-12.8	-14.4	-14.3	-5.8	-7.2	-13.4
São Tomé and Principe	..	-27.3	-29.1	-56.7	-64.3	-51.8	-50.9	-50.3	-60.5	-60.5	-74.2	..	-37.7	-58.9
Senegal	-2.2	-2.5	-2.5	-3.2	-3.4	1.2	-3.0	-4.0	-5.7	-3.2	-1.9	3.7	-3.2	-2.9
Seychelles	0.0	-7.7	-5.6	-9.5	-1.7	-6.4	-6.9	-9.2	-5.1	-6.4	-5.0	-20.4	-9.9	-5.8
Sierra Leone	..	-11.1	-7.7	-10.2	-10.1	-9.6	-8.4	-7.4	-6.2	-9.9	-7.4	..	-11.5	-8.4
Somalia	..	..	..	..	..	..	..	..	..	..	..	..	..	..
South Africa	-2.3	-6.1	-4.2	-1.3	-3.3	-4.7	-8.0	-9.9	-7.1	-6.0	..	-4.4	-4.0	-6.5
Sudan	..	..	..	..	..	..	..	..	..	..	..	..	..	..
Swaziland	..	..	..	..	..	..	..	..	..	..	..	..	..	..
Tanzania	..	-15.8	-9.4	-4.7	-4.7	-2.2	-2.1	-10.8	-8.0	-11.4	..	-11.6	-9.3	-6.5
Togo	-40.5	-9.0	-5.3	-6.1	-6.2	-8.0	-5.9	-15.9	-13.6	-7.9	-6.5	-18.0	-6.9	-9.1
Uganda	..	-4.2	-5.6	-4.8	-5.9	-7.2	-14.4	-11.3	-10.4	-7.6	-1.4	-2.7	-4.7	-8.3
Zaire	..	..	..	..	..	..	..	..	..	..	..	..	..	..
Zambia	-38.1	-5.8	-10.8	-6.6	-12.7	-16.0	-12.6	-12.5	-10.6	-9.7	-6.6	-35.1	-12.0	-11.5
Zimbabwe	8.5	-12.3	-10.3	-10.4	-9.5	-8.3	-10.4	-9.5	-10.2	-12.2	-10.3	8.7	-11.2	-10.0
NORTH AFRICA	..	-6.6	-9.4	-4.4	-2.4	-3.4	-2.1	-5.4	-2.9	-1.1	..	-3.5	-5.7	-2.9
Algeria	..	-7.2	-12.4	-1.8	3.6	1.7	-1.1	-8.7	-4.4	-1.4	..	-8.1	-8.0	-1.7
Egypt, Arab Republic	..	-15.0	-17.6	-15.4	-15.1	-15.2	-5.5	-3.5	-2.1	-1.2	..	..	-16.0	-7.1
Libya	..	..	..	..	..	..	..	..	..	..	..	..	..	..
Morocco	..	..	..	..	..	..	..	..	..	..	..	..	..	..
Tunisia	..	..	..	..	..	..	..	..	..	..	..	..	..	..
ALL AFRICA	-1.4	-5.9	-7.1	-4.6	-3.9	-4.9	-5.5	-8.2	-5.8	-3.8	..	-2.0	-4.9	-5.3

Note: 1996 data are preliminary. Nigeria's data are for federal level; since 1994, ratios are distorted because the official exchange rate used by the Gov. for oil exports oil value added is significantly over-valued.

7-3. Government primary deficit/surplus (-/+)

	Percentage of GDP											Annual average		
	1980	1987	1988	1989	1990	1991	1992	1993	1994	1995	1996	75-84	85-89	90-MR
SUB-SAHARAN AFRICA	-2.0	-8.1	-8.5	-7.7	-8.2	-8.8	-11.4	-13.1	-10.5	-7.7	-4.2	-3.4	-6.9	-9.1
excluding South Africa	-1.8	-8.9	-10.3	-10.5	-10.3	-10.6	-12.8	-14.4	-11.9	-8.6	-6.4	-2.9	-8.1	-10.7
excl. S. Africa & Nigeria	-1.9	-6.0	-6.5	-8.5	-9.0	-8.6	-10.6	-9.9	-10.4	-9.0	-6.3	-1.5	-6.0	-9.1
Angola	..	-9.2	-18.6	-30.6	-32.0	-28.8	-43.3	-26.1	-32.2	-42.8	..	..	-13.6	-34.2
Benin	0.0	-2.4	-1.0	-4.2	-7.2	-6.1	-6.2	-3.7	-5.9	-6.1	-2.8	0.3	-2.7	-5.4
Botswana	0.0	-55.1	-48.1	-46.7	-44.9	-53.5	-48.7	0.0	0.0	18.3	..	0.0	-48.1	-21.5
Burkina Faso	0.0	-6.4	-7.2	1.9	-5.5	-5.0	-4.3	-6.2	-4.7	-3.2	-1.5	-0.6	-4.3	-4.3
Burundi	9.6	-11.8	-8.9	-0.8	0.6	3.9	1.1	0.0	-4.4	-3.0	-13.0	4.4	-1.2	-2.1
Cameroon	0.1	-14.1	-7.9	-6.2	-9.7	-12.3	-12.0	-11.1	-16.3	-13.0	-9.5	0.2	-6.5	-12.0
Cape Verde	0.0	-7.0	-3.1	-6.0	-3.5	-8.5	-10.0	-8.1	-15.7	-16.9	-13.9	-0.7	45.4	-10.9
Central African Republic	4.4	-8.6	-7.9	-6.4	-8.7	-10.9	-11.3	-10.7	-11.8	-7.7	-5.5	1.2	-6.5	-9.5
Chad	0.0	-6.6	-6.4	-10.4	-11.4	-6.7	-12.6	-13.8	-5.9	-7.4	-5.8	0.3	-5.9	-9.1
Comoros	0.0	15.6	12.9	-4.8	-2.3	-3.7	-4.4	1.7	-8.1	-8.4	-6.0	-0.8	7.1	-4.4
Congo	0.0	-19.5	-26.2	-17.5	-17.0	-22.8	-22.1	-21.1	-25.3	-22.5	-14.8	-0.2	-16.7	-20.8
Côte d'Ivoire	-11.6	11.8	8.8	-26.1	-21.8	-23.6	-22.0	-20.5	-14.1	-9.8	-10.1	-1.1	6.0	-17.4
Djibouti	..	0.0	0.0	0.0	0.0	12.2	12.4	8.8	5.0	-8.1	-4.0	..	0.0	3.8
Equatorial Guinea	..	-2.4	-6.6	-10.4	-11.8	-12.8	-16.4	-22.1	-12.4	-6.6	..	0.0	-7.0	-13.7
Eritrea	..	..	..	..	..	..	-1.8	2.3	4.8	0.0	-1.4	..	..	0.8
Ethiopia	..	-6.2	-6.4	-8.0	-12.5	-10.3	-8.9	-9.1	-13.7	-6.9	-7.4	-7.5	-7.2	-9.8
Gabon	0.0	-13.0	-15.5	-11.8	-9.1	-8.2	-11.6	-12.7	-8.4	-4.8	-3.2	-2.4	-11.0	-8.3
Gambia, The	-13.2	-3.6	0.6	-10.9	-14.5	-8.9	0.0	0.0	0.0	0.0	..	-8.7	-5.6	-3.9
Ghana	0.0	-1.2	-1.4	-0.3	-1.8	-1.5	-8.4	-9.6	-10.3	-7.4	-13.3	-0.3	-1.9	-7.5
Guinea	..	-6.6	-10.0	-7.5	-7.7	-6.9	-5.3	-5.1	-5.2	-4.1	-3.9	..	-8.2	-5.5
Guinea-Bissau	0.0	7.8	-3.9	1.5	1.9	-10.8	-14.0	-3.3	8.3	13.1	-3.8	-0.1	-2.1	-1.2
Kenya	-0.5	-0.3	-0.5	-0.4	-0.6	-0.4	-1.1	-1.0	-0.4	-0.3	-0.2	-0.3	-0.4	-0.6
Lesotho	0.0	4.3	5.2	4.1	6.2	4.4	4.4	2.8	8.9	13.1	..	0.0	2.7	6.6
Liberia	0.0	0.0	0.0	0.0	..	..	..	..	..	..	..	0.0	0.0	..
Madagascar	-13.3	-5.4	-5.4	-3.0	0.8	-6.2	-7.6	-8.6	-11.2	-8.5	-6.6	-4.1	-4.9	-6.9
Malawi	-8.4	-11.6	-2.3	-2.2	-5.2	-3.1	-10.9	-7.0	-11.7	-5.5	-6.7	-6.8	-8.0	-7.2
Mali	0.0	-7.1	-6.6	-6.8	-5.0	-5.7	-5.6	-5.7	-6.6	-4.4	-1.9	0.9	-7.6	-5.0
Mauritania	0.0	-6.2	-6.7	-11.4	-7.8	-7.7	-5.8	-11.9	-5.4	-2.1	4.3	0.0	-7.3	-5.2
Mauritius	0.0	-4.8	-5.5	-6.4	-6.1	-6.2	-5.5	-4.8	-5.7	-8.6	-8.5	-1.3	-6.6	-6.5
Mozambique	-8.2	-14.9	-14.9	-11.8	-15.7	-7.8	-9.1	-8.8	-10.0	-7.6	-7.6	-15.1	-15.8	-9.5
Namibia	0.0	-10.7	-11.8	-7.7	-4.7	-5.8	-6.5	-9.9	-7.7	-6.2	-5.1	-11.2	-12.4	-6.6
Niger	0.0	-6.5	-7.8	-8.6	-9.3	-5.5	-6.3	-5.5	-9.0	-5.8	-1.9	-0.7	-7.5	-6.2
Nigeria	-1.6	-18.9	-23.1	-17.1	-14.7	-17.2	-20.1	-29.5	-16.9	-7.4	-6.5	-7.4	-15.1	-16.0
Rwanda	-2.3	-7.6	-4.6	-2.7	-6.4	-6.1	-6.3	-6.3	-13.7	3.3	-1.9	-1.5	-4.7	-5.3
São Tomé and Principe	0.0	-5.4	-29.8	-47.7	-58.7	-49.5	-52.8	-45.1	-54.0	-49.2	-50.1	0.0	-17.6	-51.3
Senegal	-0.3	-4.3	-4.2	-4.5	-4.8	0.4	-3.7	-5.1	-5.1	-2.9	-2.4	-1.8	-5.1	-3.4
Seychelles	-1.8	-13.3	-13.0	-16.0	-7.7	-12.8	-13.3	-15.9	-13.2	-13.6	-13.0	-1.5	-14.3	-12.8
Sierra Leone	-1.8	-14.4	-10.6	-15.6	-14.5	-13.2	-11.3	-9.1	-6.2	-8.2	-6.0	-0.7	-14.0	-9.8
Somalia	0.0	0.0	0.0	0.0	0.0	..	..	..	..	..	..	0.0	0.0	0.0
South Africa	-2.3	-6.1	-4.2	-1.3	-3.3	-4.7	-8.0	-9.9	-7.1	-6.0	0.0	-4.4	-4.0	-5.6
Sudan	0.0	-3.7	-5.0	-4.1	-3.1	-1.8	-6.8	-11.0	-8.9	..	..	-0.3	-4.9	-6.3
Swaziland	0.0	-1.1	-1.1	-0.8	-0.6	-0.1	0.7	0.3	-10.6	0.0	0.0	0.0	-0.9	-1.5
Tanzania	..	-6.5	-13.1	-7.7	-7.2	-4.6	-4.4	-13.9	-11.2	-12.0	..	-14.0	-9.7	-8.9
Togo	-4.2	-10.9	-7.5	-6.2	-6.2	-9.7	-7.1	-19.9	-18.0	-10.0	-8.8	-3.4	-8.2	-11.4
Uganda	0.0	-4.2	-4.5	-3.8	-5.0	-4.4	-10.6	-5.0	-5.2	-4.0	2.2	-0.4	-4.5	-4.6
Zaire	0.0	0.0	0.0	0.0	0.0	0.0	0.0	0.0	0.0	0.0	0.0	0.0	0.0	0.0
Zambia	-4.1	-13.3	-15.7	-9.8	-16.1	-15.4	-11.0	-16.5	-16.3	-14.2	-11.4	-2.1	-20.3	-14.4
Zimbabwe	-4.7	-16.2	-14.6	-15.0	-13.5	-11.4	-13.2	-12.2	-13.6	-18.4	-16.9	-4.6	-14.6	-14.2
NORTH AFRICA	-0.1	-8.9	-12.1	-7.1	-4.8	-6.3	-5.7	-9.7	-7.9	-6.1	..	-3.8	-10.4	-6.7
Algeria	0.0	-8.7	-14.5	-3.5	2.0	-0.2	-3.3	-11.0	-7.2	-4.6	..	-0.9	-9.6	-4.0
Egypt, Arab Republic	0.0	-16.5	-20.4	-18.0	-17.4	-19.0	-9.9	-9.9	-10.0	-6.9	..	-2.3	-20.7	-12.2
Libya	0.0	0.0	0.0	0.0	..	..	..	..	..	..	..	0.0	0.0	..
Morocco	0.0	-11.9	-10.2	-12.2	-6.8	-6.5	-7.7	-8.0	-8.6	-11.3	..	-1.7	-12.5	-8.2
Tunisia	-1.6	0.0	0.0	0.0	0.0	0.0	-3.2	-3.5	-3.6	-3.8	..	-0.3	0.0	-2.3
ALL AFRICA	-1.2	-8.4	-9.9	-7.5	-7.0	-7.9	-9.3	-11.9	-9.6	-7.1	..	-2.5	-8.3	-8.8

Note: 1996 data are preliminary. Nigeria's data are for federal level; since 1994, ratios are distorted because the official exchange rate used by the Gov. for oil exports oil value added is significantly over-valued.

7-4. Government expenditure and lending minus repayments

	Percentage of GDP											Annual average		
	1980	*1987*	*1988*	*1989*	*1990*	*1991*	*1992*	*1993*	*1994*	*1995*	*1996*	*75-84*	*85-89*	*90-MR*
SUB-SAHARAN AFRICA	24.4	27.3	26.7	26.6	27.9	28.0	29.6	31.7	28.3	26.8	..	25.1	26.3	28.7
excluding South Africa	..	23.2	22.9	23.6	24.6	24.3	25.2	27.0	23.0	21.2	22.8	19.0	22.3	24.0
excl. S. Africa & Nigeria	..	23.4	22.3	24.6	24.4	24.1	24.7	24.5	24.3	23.4	22.4	20.2	23.0	24.0
Angola	..	..	..	..	..	..	..	..	..	..	..	..	..	..
Benin	..	17.3	16.0	19.6	19.4	18.5	18.9	17.9	19.9	21.7	20.0	13.2	17.8	19.5
Botswana	..	..	..	..	..	..	..	..	..	..	..	..	..	..
Burkina Faso	..	23.5	20.7	17.2	19.6	21.5	20.9	22.6	21.6	21.1	20.3	22.6	19.2	21.1
Burundi	11.9	30.3	26.7	27.4	25.9	25.8	28.4	30.4	24.3	26.1	24.1	12.6	21.6	26.4
Cameroon	16.0	31.3	22.3	20.6	21.8	23.4	22.3	20.0	19.3	17.8	17.3	21.2	23.9	20.3
Cape Verde	..	42.4	33.4	32.7	31.4	37.5	48.6	49.3	60.8	59.3	53.5	67.4	47.4	48.6
Central African Republic	..	23.8	23.1	20.2	22.6	23.4	24.4	21.9	21.3	20.6	10.9	12.1	20.4	20.7
Chad	..	33.4	27.1	32.6	31.8	21.5	27.5	28.7	27.1	24.8	25.3	13.2	27.2	26.7
Comoros	..	37.4	33.1	33.9	33.3	32.7	34.7	24.8	35.7	31.4	26.5	36.8	36.9	31.3
Congo	..	32.5	37.1	32.2	34.4	39.7	36.6	36.7	36.7	33.1	31.6	38.3	36.7	35.6
Côte d'Ivoire	37.4	7.2	8.6	38.5	33.4	32.9	31.9	30.0	27.1	26.5	27.2	25.9	13.6	29.9
Djibouti	..	..	..	..	..	41.0	51.0	50.1	43.0	39.2	35.3	..	..	43.3
Equatorial Guinea	..	..	..	..	..	..	..	..	..	..	..	..	..	..
Eritrea	..	..	..	..	..	..	173.5	145.0	113.7	..	16.4	..	..	112.2
Ethiopia	..	25.8	30.5	34.3	31.2	25.0	20.4	22.7	28.5	25.3	25.9	26.1	29.3	25.6
Gabon	..	31.2	31.1	25.4	23.5	26.7	28.3	28.6	25.5	25.5	23.2	21.5	33.6	25.9
Gambia, The	69.6	62.5	52.7	45.7	40.5	36.8	..	..	..	..	..	84.3	61.8	38.7
Ghana	18.7	19.1	18.9	18.9	18.2	19.5	24.6	30.6	32.8	31.8	33.0	13.1	18.3	27.2
Guinea	..	23.5	24.4	24.2	24.6	22.9	21.3	19.1	17.5	17.8	16.3	..	23.4	19.9
Guinea-Bissau	..	46.8	57.0	54.4	44.5	49.2	50.2	40.5	35.5	30.4	36.0	58.7	51.5	40.9
Kenya	1.8	1.5	1.6	1.6	1.7	1.6	1.9	2.0	1.6	1.6	1.6	1.6	1.6	1.7
Lesotho	..	..	..	..	..	..	..	..	..	..	..	..	..	..
Liberia	..	..	..	..	..	..	..	..	..	..	..	..	..	..
Madagascar	27.9	18.7	17.1	19.7	17.0	16.4	20.0	20.6	19.8	17.4	16.3	20.6	17.8	18.2
Malawi	30.4	32.8	29.3	29.4	27.1	25.1	32.5	27.0	46.4	33.2	27.5	28.2	31.5	31.3
Mali	..	25.7	25.0	26.7	25.8	28.2	24.3	23.5	27.2	24.9	23.9	19.9	26.0	25.4
Mauritania	..	36.7	31.6	33.7	31.9	28.9	24.8	36.8	27.7	24.8	24.5	0.0	35.0	28.5
Mauritius	..	24.9	25.9	26.3	24.9	25.0	24.5	24.0	23.9	24.7	24.9	29.4	26.1	24.6
Mozambique	34.9	40.3	47.7	47.7	51.5	46.6	47.5	42.2	47.3	39.1	35.0	46.4	42.8	44.2
Namibia	0.0	36.2	35.0	32.0	36.6	36.0	39.5	44.4	36.7	37.7	41.1	23.1	35.0	38.8
Niger	..	20.1	19.9	20.7	22.7	16.9	16.8	16.7	18.6	15.4	12.9	19.2	20.1	17.1
Nigeria	24.0	22.8	24.1	21.0	24.9	24.7	26.5	33.2	19.6	15.8	23.6	23.6	20.6	24.1
Rwanda	14.3	23.1	20.5	18.6	20.1	22.8	25.7	25.2	16.6	21.5	24.0	17.4	20.1	22.3
São Tomé and Principe	..	53.4	54.9	78.5	82.3	68.0	71.1	68.3	73.8	77.0	87.6	..	62.3	75.5
Senegal	24.5	20.7	19.4	20.7	21.0	19.1	22.0	20.2	19.7	18.3	17.2	23.4	20.6	19.6
Seychelles	..	57.4	54.8	57.7	48.7	50.6	50.4	52.2	49.5	46.2	47.5	28.0	57.0	49.3
Sierra Leone	..	18.1	15.3	18.6	19.8	20.9	21.4	21.3	18.9	19.5	17.2	..	18.5	19.8
Somalia	..	..	..	..	..	..	..	..	..	..	..	..	..	..
South Africa	28.6	34.9	34.0	32.2	34.0	34.9	37.9	40.4	38.2	37.3	..	31.5	33.7	37.1
Sudan	..	..	..	..	..	..	..	..	..	..	..	..	..	..
Swaziland	..	..	..	..	..	..	..	..	..	..	..	..	..	..
Tanzania	..	26.9	25.7	19.8	18.8	17.9	18.9	23.8	23.0	26.1	..	29.8	24.7	21.4
Togo	40.5	32.8	29.0	28.8	28.8	25.4	22.1	27.0	26.6	22.8	21.7	34.9	32.4	24.9
Uganda	..	8.9	11.3	10.2	12.7	14.7	21.2	18.6	18.7	17.6	16.3	13.7	11.0	17.1
Zaire	..	..	..	..	..	..	..	..	..	..	..	..	..	..
Zambia	38.1	25.7	27.5	25.2	32.9	34.7	31.0	27.0	28.7	26.6	22.9	35.1	32.1	29.1
Zimbabwe	5.3	48.6	44.1	42.9	44.3	43.2	44.6	41.0	39.2	41.6	38.9	14.3	44.4	41.8
NORTH AFRICA	..	..	..	..	..	..	..	..	..	..	..	..	..	..
Algeria	..	37.6	39.9	30.7	25.2	30.2	30.7	36.2	33.9	31.9	..	46.3	39.3	31.3
Egypt, Arab Republic	..	41.2	43.5	39.3	37.9	40.9	36.6	33.2	32.2	28.4	..	..	41.3	34.9
Libya	..	..	..	..	..	..	..	..	..	..	..	..	..	..
Morocco	..	..	..	..	..	..	..	..	..	..	..	..	..	..
Tunisia	..	..	..	..	..	..	..	..	..	..	..	..	..	..
ALL AFRICA	..	31.3	31.7	29.0	28.5	30.0	30.7	32.9	30.0	28.1	..	29.6	30.5	30.0

Note: 1996 data are preliminary. Nigeria's data are for federal level; since 1994, ratios are distorted because the official exchange rate used by the Gov. for oil exports oil value added is significantly over-valued.

7-5. Government interest payments

	Percentage of GDP											Annual average		
	1980	1987	1988	1989	1990	1991	1992	1993	1994	1995	1996	75-84	85-89	90-MR
SUB-SAHARAN AFRICA	..	..	..	..	..	..	..	..	..	..	..	..	..	..
excluding South Africa	..	6.1	5.9	5.7	6.1	6.1	6.6	6.7	6.1	5.5	4.7	..	5.9	6.0
excl. S. Africa & Nigeria	..	..	..	3.8	3.8	..	4.6	4.7	5.4	5.7	..	..	3.8	4.8
Angola	..	1.1	4.5	5.3	5.2	6.2	5.5	7.9	9.1	14.6	..	..	2.5	8.1
Benin	..	1.6	2.1	3.1	3.0	2.6	3.6	2.6	3.1	2.7	2.5	0.0	2.0	2.9
Botswana	..	55.1	48.1	46.7	44.9	53.5	48.7	0.0	0.0	-6.1	..	0.0	48.1	23.5
Burkina Faso	..	1.3	1.3	1.0	1.1	1.4	1.4	1.6	1.5	1.4	1.0	0.7	1.2	1.3
Burundi	0.2	2.0	2.1	2.2	1.8	1.6	1.8	1.6	1.5	1.7	2.8	0.7	1.9	1.8
Cameroon	0.3	1.1	2.1	1.7	2.1	4.1	5.4	4.8	7.0	8.1	6.7	0.6	1.3	5.5
Cape Verde	..	1.5	1.6	1.5	1.5	1.3	1.2	1.3	1.1	3.7	2.6	0.0	1.3	1.8
Central African Republic	..	1.6	1.7	1.4	1.3	1.5	2.0	2.2	2.3	2.3	2.0	..	1.5	1.9
Chad	..	0.4	0.3	0.3	0.6	0.9	1.0	1.6	1.6	1.4	1.4	..	0.3	1.2
Comoros	..	1.3	1.5	1.4	1.2	1.1	0.9	0.8	1.0	1.0	0.9	1.3	1.3	1.0
Congo	..	6.6	8.2	7.4	10.3	8.8	7.9	7.4	12.1	14.2	12.8	..	7.6	10.5
Côte d'Ivoire	3.0	7.2	8.6	9.4	9.8	10.9	10.4	8.7	7.9	6.9	7.7	4.9	7.8	8.9
Djibouti	..	..	..	..	..	..	..	..	..	..	..	..	..	..
Equatorial Guinea	..	5.2	6.0	6.5	6.6	6.9	7.7	7.4	6.9	4.2	..	..	5.8	6.6
Eritrea	..	..	..	..	..	..	..	..	..	..	..	..	..	..
Ethiopia	..	1.3	1.5	1.6	1.3	1.3	1.5	2.0	3.5	2.6	2.4	0.9	1.5	2.1
Gabon	..	4.6	6.0	5.7	5.6	6.0	6.4	7.0	6.7	7.9	5.9	2.4	4.4	6.5
Gambia, The	9.2	8.9	8.2	6.6	6.8	6.9	..	..	..	..	..	12.3	8.9	6.9
Ghana	..	1.4	1.1	1.3	1.4	1.8	2.2	3.7	4.7	4.4	5.6	1.3	1.5	3.4
Guinea	..	2.6	3.2	2.4	2.6	2.4	1.8	1.4	1.6	1.4	1.3	..	2.7	1.8
Guinea-Bissau	..	..	..	..	..	..	..	..	..	..	..	..	..	..
Kenya	0.1	0.3	0.3	0.3	0.4	0.3	0.7	0.7	0.4	0.4	0.3	0.2	0.3	0.4
Lesotho	..	4.0	4.3	7.3	5.5	4.6	3.0	3.0	1.9	-1.6	..	0.0	3.1	2.7
Liberia	..	..	..	..	..	..	..	..	..	..	..	..	..	..
Madagascar	..	2.1	2.1	1.6	1.5	2.0	3.4	4.0	5.4	5.0	4.5	1.0	1.8	3.7
Malawi	..	6.6	4.8	5.3	3.8	2.8	3.1	3.1	5.5	6.3	5.7	4.2	5.8	4.3
Mali	..	1.8	1.9	2.0	2.3	1.8	1.8	1.6	2.3	1.4	1.1	0.5	1.7	1.8
Mauritania	..	..	..	..	..	..	..	..	..	..	..	..	..	..
Mauritius	..	4.4	3.8	4.1	4.4	4.1	3.4	2.8	2.9	3.2	3.2	6.0	4.8	3.4
Mozambique	0.0	2.1	2.4	3.1	3.3	2.2	3.6	3.6	1.7	2.6	2.4	0.0	1.7	2.8
Namibia	..	..	..	..	..	..	..	..	..	..	0.8	..	..	0.8
Niger	..	2.8	2.6	2.7	2.3	1.9	1.6	1.7	2.3	2.4	1.7	2.1	2.7	2.0
Nigeria	1.4	11.3	10.1	10.0	11.3	10.1	11.2	11.4	7.8	5.0	5.1	1.6	8.0	8.8
Rwanda	0.2	1.1	1.1	1.1	1.0	1.9	2.0	2.3	4.6	2.4	1.6	0.4	1.0	2.2
São Tomé and Principe	..	5.4	7.7	6.9	10.2	11.0	11.0	11.5	11.0	12.0	4.3	..	6.3	10.1
Senegal	..	2.9	3.1	3.2	2.7	2.5	2.0	2.2	3.3	2.7	2.4	3.6	3.2	2.5
Seychelles	1.8	8.7	9.0	7.9	7.9	7.9	7.7	8.2	8.9	8.7	9.4	1.9	6.6	8.4
Sierra Leone	1.8	5.5	5.4	6.0	5.7	6.3	5.8	4.0	2.6	2.1	2.1	2.0	4.7	4.1
Somalia	..	..	..	..	..	..	..	..	..	..	..	..	..	..
South Africa	..	..	..	..	..	..	..	..	..	..	..	..	..	..
Sudan	..	3.7	5.0	4.1	3.1	1.8	6.8	11.0	8.9	..	..	2.9	4.9	6.3
Swaziland	..	1.7	1.4	1.6	1.0	0.9	1.0	0.9	0.8	..	0.0	1.4	1.8	0.8
Tanzania	..	3.7	3.7	3.1	2.5	2.4	2.3	3.1	3.2	4.0	..	2.4	3.0	2.9
Togo	5.8	4.1	4.2	4.2	3.2	3.2	2.8	4.3	5.8	3.5	2.8	6.3	4.8	3.7
Uganda	..	..	..	0.6	0.6	1.0	3.3	1.8	1.5	1.0	1.0	..	0.6	1.5
Zaire	..	..	..	..	..	..	..	..	..	..	..	..	..	..
Zambia	4.1	7.9	6.4	5.6	7.8	8.5	8.5	11.3	10.5	8.9	7.4	4.2	9.5	9.0
Zimbabwe	1.5	6.5	6.1	6.2	6.2	6.0	7.0	7.3	8.0	10.1	9.3	3.2	6.0	7.7
NORTH AFRICA	..	2.8	3.2	3.0	2.9	3.7	4.0	4.6	5.1	4.7	..	..	3.0	4.2
Algeria	..	1.5	2.1	1.7	1.6	1.8	2.2	2.3	2.8	3.1	..	1.2	1.6	2.3
Egypt, Arab Republic	..	3.6	3.7	3.9	3.8	6.3	6.8	8.5	9.4	7.2	..	0.0	3.0	7.0
Libya	..	..	..	..	..	..	..	..	..	..	..	..	..	..
Morocco	..	6.0	6.2	6.2	6.2	5.5	5.5	5.9	5.7	6.1	..	6.1	6.1	5.8
Tunisia	1.6	..	..	..	..	..	3.2	3.5	3.6	3.8	..	1.6	..	3.5
ALL AFRICA	..	..	..	..	..	..	..	..	..	..	..	..	..	..

Note: 1996 data are preliminary. Nigeria's data are for federal level; since 1994, ratios are distorted because the official exchange rate used by the Gov. for oil exports oil value added is significantly over-valued.

7-6. Government revenue (excluding grants)

	Percentage of GDP											Annual average		
	1980	1987	1988	1989	1990	1991	1992	1993	1994	1995	1996	75-84	85-89	90-MR
SUB-SAHARAN AFRICA	..	20.9	20.3	21.0	22.4	21.4	21.0	20.4	19.6	20.9	..	21.1	21.1	21.0
excluding South Africa	..	16.6	15.2	15.7	17.9	16.6	16.2	15.0	13.5	15.3	16.1	14.8	16.4	15.8
excl. S. Africa & Nigeria	..	17.1	16.9	16.5	16.4	16.2	15.7	15.0	14.6	16.1	16.7	16.3	17.5	15.8
Angola	..	..	..	..	..	..	..	..	..	..	..	..	..	..
Benin	..	12.9	12.7	9.4	9.9	11.5	12.2	13.0	12.5	14.4	15.1	11.1	12.2	12.7
Botswana	..	..	..	..	..	..	..	..	..	..	..	..	..	..
Burkina Faso	..	12.2	11.1	2.0	12.3	13.3	11.8	12.6	11.0	11.8	12.4	9.7	9.1	12.2
Burundi	18.1	16.6	17.4	21.9	20.3	22.6	22.7	23.0	19.1	21.1	11.9	18.0	18.3	20.1
Cameroon	16.3	18.4	16.4	16.0	14.3	15.2	15.7	13.7	9.9	12.7	13.9	22.2	18.6	13.6
Cape Verde	..	17.0	17.0	17.6	18.7	17.7	20.6	25.7	28.2	28.8	26.5	22.4	19.0	23.7
Central African Republic	..	10.7	10.9	10.3	10.9	9.3	9.2	8.0	7.1	9.1	5.9	7.8	9.8	8.5
Chad	..	7.9	8.0	8.9	9.5	8.6	9.0	10.0	6.9	8.5	9.9	5.1	7.6	8.9
Comoros	..	12.2	14.9	14.1	17.1	13.9	16.0	13.7	13.3	13.1	13.2	17.6	12.9	14.3
Congo	..	19.6	19.0	22.0	27.0	25.4	22.5	23.0	22.4	23.8	29.3	34.6	25.9	24.8
Côte d'Ivoire	28.9	26.2	25.9	21.8	21.5	19.7	19.8	17.7	20.1	22.9	24.0	28.5	27.4	20.8
Djibouti	..	..	..	..	..	25.8	26.9	28.4	29.5	29.1	29.5	..	..	28.2
Equatorial Guinea	..	..	..	..	..	..	..	..	..	..	..	..	..	..
Eritrea	..	..	..	..	..	..	129.7	112.8	92.1	..	10.9	..	..	86.4
Ethiopia	..	18.9	21.7	23.1	17.4	13.6	10.7	11.6	13.5	17.1	17.6	17.4	20.0	14.5
Gabon	..	22.4	21.2	18.9	19.6	24.3	22.9	22.6	23.5	28.6	25.9	-0.3	26.7	23.9
Gambia, The	36.8	51.2	46.0	34.5	30.5	33.2	..	..	..	..	..	51.8	44.7	31.8
Ghana	..	14.1	13.5	13.6	12.5	14.6	11.9	15.7	19.7	21.4	19.4	8.0	13.2	16.5
Guinea	..	15.5	14.4	15.5	15.8	14.7	13.5	11.6	10.4	11.1	10.6	..	14.7	12.5
Guinea-Bissau	..	13.1	13.3	11.7	19.3	13.4	12.1	10.6	12.4	12.7	12.4	..	10.0	13.3
Kenya	1.3	1.1	1.1	1.1	1.2	1.2	1.2	1.5	1.4	1.5	1.6	1.2	1.1	1.4
Lesotho	..	..	..	..	..	..	..	..	..	..	..	..	..	..
Liberia	..	..	..	..	..	..	..	..	..	..	..	..	..	..
Madagascar	15.1	14.7	13.1	14.2	14.9	10.1	12.4	12.5	10.9	11.1	11.0	12.9	13.4	11.8
Malawi	18.6	21.9	21.4	22.4	20.3	18.8	19.3	17.4	18.6	17.4	22.0	17.6	21.8	19.1
Mali	..	15.1	14.5	16.8	17.2	16.1	13.4	13.9	13.5	14.4	15.9	11.4	15.0	14.9
Mauritania	..	17.9	21.8	21.0	22.6	21.1	18.8	24.7	22.3	23.0	27.6	0.0	18.5	22.9
Mauritius	..	23.7	23.8	23.7	23.1	22.8	22.2	21.8	20.8	18.9	19.2	22.4	23.6	21.3
Mozambique	23.4	17.4	20.7	22.9	22.2	21.7	21.1	20.0	17.6	18.3	18.0	28.0	19.3	19.9
Namibia	0.0	28.4	25.5	26.3	34.1	28.9	32.2	33.9	29.0	31.5	35.7	13.0	25.5	32.2
Niger	..	11.3	10.1	10.2	10.2	8.5	8.2	7.3	6.0	7.2	7.8	11.0	10.7	7.9
Nigeria	23.8	15.2	11.1	13.8	21.6	17.6	17.6	15.1	10.6	13.4	14.6	17.8	13.6	15.8
Rwanda	12.3	13.5	12.5	12.7	10.1	10.9	10.8	9.7	3.8	7.2	9.7	11.6	12.9	8.9
São Tomé and Principe	..	26.1	25.8	21.8	18.0	16.2	20.2	18.0	13.3	16.5	13.4	..	24.6	16.5
Senegal	22.3	18.2	16.9	17.5	17.6	20.3	19.0	16.2	14.0	15.1	15.3	19.3	17.4	16.8
Seychelles	..	49.7	49.2	48.1	47.1	44.2	43.4	43.0	44.4	39.8	42.5	8.0	47.0	43.5
Sierra Leone	..	7.0	7.6	8.4	9.7	11.3	13.0	13.9	12.7	9.5	9.8	..	7.0	11.4
Somalia	..	..	..	..	..	..	..	..	..	..	..	..	..	..
South Africa	26.3	28.9	29.8	30.9	30.7	30.2	29.8	30.5	31.1	31.3	..	27.0	29.8	30.6
Sudan	..	..	..	..	..	..	..	..	..	..	..	..	..	..
Swaziland	..	..	..	..	..	..	..	..	..	..	..	..	..	..
Tanzania	..	11.2	16.3	15.1	14.1	15.7	16.8	12.9	15.0	14.7	..	18.2	15.4	14.9
Togo	..	23.8	23.7	22.6	22.6	17.5	16.2	11.1	12.9	14.9	15.2	28.1	25.5	15.8
Uganda	..	4.7	5.8	5.5	6.8	7.5	6.8	7.3	8.3	10.0	10.3	11.1	6.3	8.1
Zaire	..	..	..	..	..	..	..	..	..	..	..	..	..	..
Zambia	..	19.8	16.7	18.6	20.3	18.7	18.4	14.6	18.1	16.9	16.3	..	20.1	17.6
Zimbabwe	13.8	36.4	33.7	32.5	34.8	34.9	34.2	31.5	29.0	29.4	28.6	23.0	33.2	31.8
NORTH AFRICA	..	..	..	..	..	..	..	..	..	..	..	..	..	..
Algeria	..	30.4	27.6	28.9	28.9	31.8	29.5	27.6	29.4	30.4	..	38.2	31.3	29.6
Egypt, Arab Republic	..	26.2	25.9	23.8	22.8	25.7	31.2	29.7	30.0	27.2	..	..	25.3	27.8
Libya	..	..	..	..	..	..	..	..	..	..	..	..	..	..
Morocco	..	..	..	..	..	..	..	..	..	..	..	..	..	..
Tunisia	..	..	..	..	..	..	..	..	..	..	..	..	..	..
ALL AFRICA	..	23.6	22.6	23.1	23.8	24.2	24.1	23.1	23.0	23.8	..	24.4	23.8	23.7

Note: 1996 data are preliminary. Nigeria's data are for federal level; since 1994, ratios are distorted because the official exchange rate used by the Gov. for oil exports oil value added is significantly overvalued.

7-7. Grants to government

	Percentage of GDP											Annual average		
	1980	*1987*	*1988*	*1989*	*1990*	*1991*	*1992*	*1993*	*1994*	*1995*	*1996*	*75-84*	*85-89*	*90-MR*
SUB-SAHARAN AFRICA	0.2	1.1	1.1	1.3	1.1	1.2	1.4	1.4	1.5	1.6	1.2	0.2	1.0	1.3
excluding South Africa	0.3	1.6	1.5	1.8	1.5	1.7	2.0	2.0	2.2	2.3	1.9	0.4	1.5	1.9
excl. S. Africa & Nigeria	0.4	2.1	1.9	2.4	2.0	2.2	2.5	2.6	2.8	3.1	2.6	0.5	1.9	2.6
Angola	..	0.0	0.0	0.0	0.0	0.0	0.0	0.0	0.0	0.6	..	..	0.0	0.1
Benin	0.0	3.7	4.5	9.2	5.4	3.6	4.1	3.9	4.6	3.9	4.5	1.1	4.9	4.3
Botswana	0.0	0.0	0.0	0.0	0.0	0.0	0.0	0.0	0.0	1.9	..	0.0	0.0	0.3
Burkina Faso	0.0	6.2	3.7	18.1	2.9	4.6	6.2	5.4	7.3	7.6	7.5	0.7	6.9	5.9
Burundi	3.7	4.0	2.4	6.9	8.1	8.7	8.6	9.1	2.3	3.7	2.0	2.0	4.0	6.1
Cameroon	0.0	0.0	0.0	0.0	0.0	0.0	0.0	0.0	0.1	0.2	0.5	0.0	0.0	0.1
Cape Verde	0.0	19.9	14.9	10.7	10.7	12.6	19.3	16.8	18.0	17.4	15.7	3.8	75.1	15.8
Central African Republic	4.4	6.1	6.0	4.9	4.2	4.7	6.0	5.4	4.7	6.2	1.5	1.6	5.3	4.7
Chad	0.0	19.3	13.0	13.6	11.4	7.1	6.9	6.5	15.9	10.2	10.9	1.1	14.0	9.9
Comoros	0.0	42.0	32.5	16.4	15.1	16.3	15.2	13.6	15.4	10.8	8.3	7.7	35.2	13.5
Congo	0.0	0.1	0.1	0.1	0.3	0.2	0.0	0.0	1.1	1.0	0.4	0.2	0.1	0.4
Côte d'Ivoire	0.0	0.0	0.0	0.0	0.0	0.5	0.5	0.5	0.7	0.7	0.7	0.0	0.0	0.5
Djibouti	..	0.0	0.0	0.0	0.0	12.2	12.4	8.8	5.0	2.0	1.9	..	0.0	6.0
Equatorial Guinea	..	2.2	6.2	3.2	0.0	0.0	0.0	0.0	0.0	0.0	..	0.0	3.3	0.0
Eritrea	..	..	..	..	..	..	42.0	34.4	26.4	0.0	4.1	..	..	21.4
Ethiopia	..	2.1	4.0	4.7	2.6	2.4	2.3	4.0	4.8	3.8	3.2	2.1	3.7	3.3
Gabon	0.0	0.4	0.4	0.4	0.4	0.3	0.1	0.3	0.4	0.0	0.0	0.0	0.4	0.2
Gambia, The	28.9	16.6	15.5	7.0	2.4	1.7	0.0	0.0	0.0	0.0	..	25.5	20.3	0.7
Ghana	0.0	2.7	2.5	3.2	2.7	2.6	3.2	4.5	3.7	3.8	3.0	0.1	2.3	3.3
Guinea	..	4.0	3.3	3.6	3.7	3.7	4.4	3.7	3.5	4.0	3.1	..	3.2	3.7
Guinea-Bissau	0.0	46.4	44.9	50.0	31.4	30.7	28.8	32.4	36.8	37.5	26.3	1.9	43.4	32.0
Kenya	0.1	0.2	0.2	0.3	0.2	0.2	0.1	0.1	0.1	0.1	0.1	0.1	0.2	0.1
Lesotho	0.0	8.3	9.5	11.3	11.7	9.0	7.4	5.9	5.1	6.7	..	0.0	5.8	7.6
Liberia	0.0	0.0	0.0	0.0	..	..	..	..	..	..	..	0.0	0.0	..
Madagascar	0.0	0.7	0.7	4.1	4.4	2.1	3.5	3.5	3.0	2.9	3.3	0.2	1.3	3.2
Malawi	3.4	6.0	10.5	10.0	5.4	6.0	5.5	5.7	21.5	16.7	4.6	3.4	7.5	9.3
Mali	0.0	5.3	5.7	5.1	5.9	8.2	7.1	5.6	9.5	7.5	7.1	1.8	5.1	7.3
Mauritania	0.0	15.6	6.4	4.7	4.1	2.8	3.3	4.2	2.9	3.0	4.4	0.0	12.5	3.5
Mauritius	0.0	0.8	0.5	0.3	0.2	0.1	0.1	0.2	0.3	0.4	0.3	0.0	0.8	0.2
Mozambique	3.2	10.1	14.5	16.1	16.9	19.3	20.9	17.1	21.5	15.8	11.8	3.2	9.3	17.6
Namibia	0.0	0.0	0.0	0.0	0.0	1.7	1.0	0.8	0.6	1.0	1.1	0.0	0.0	0.9
Niger	0.0	5.2	4.6	4.7	5.4	4.8	3.9	5.6	5.8	4.7	4.9	0.3	4.6	5.0
Nigeria	0.0	0.0	0.0	0.0	0.0	0.0	0.0	0.0	0.0	0.0	0.0	0.0	0.0	0.0
Rwanda	0.0	3.1	4.5	4.3	4.6	7.7	10.6	11.5	3.7	20.1	14.0	1.6	3.5	10.3
São Tomé and Principe	0.0	10.8	7.0	15.9	15.8	13.3	9.1	16.6	17.6	23.4	23.5	0.0	6.8	17.0
Senegal	1.9	1.1	1.3	1.9	1.3	1.7	1.3	1.1	3.9	3.0	1.9	0.8	1.4	2.0
Seychelles	0.0	3.1	1.6	1.5	1.9	1.5	1.3	1.5	0.8	1.4	1.3	1.0	2.2	1.4
Sierra Leone	0.0	2.2	2.4	0.6	1.3	2.6	2.8	2.3	2.6	3.8	3.5	0.3	2.2	2.7
Somalia	0.0	0.0	0.0	0.0	0.0	..	..	..	..	..	..	0.0	0.0	0.0
South Africa	0.0	0.0	0.0	0.0	0.0	0.0	0.0	0.0	0.0	0.0	0.0	0.0	0.0	0.0
Sudan	0.0	0.0	0.0	0.0	0.0	0.0	0.0	0.0	0.0	..	..	0.0	0.0	0.0
Swaziland	0.0	0.6	0.4	0.7	0.5	0.8	1.7	1.1	0.3	0.0	0.0	0.1	0.8	0.6
Tanzania	..	12.9	5.6	4.4	4.1	2.7	3.2	4.6	4.8	2.4	..	0.0	4.6	3.6
Togo	1.5	2.2	2.0	4.1	3.2	1.5	1.6	0.3	1.5	1.4	0.5	1.4	3.4	1.4
Uganda	0.0	0.5	1.7	1.6	1.5	3.8	7.1	8.1	6.6	4.7	4.6	0.1	1.1	5.2
Zaire	0.0	0.0	0.0	0.0	0.0	0.0	0.0	0.0	0.0	0.0	0.0	0.0	0.0	0.0
Zambia	0.0	0.4	1.5	2.3	4.3	9.0	10.2	7.3	4.8	4.4	2.6	0.0	1.2	6.1
Zimbabwe	1.8	2.6	1.9	1.6	2.2	2.9	4.1	4.6	4.6	3.9	2.7	1.2	2.5	3.6
NORTH AFRICA	..	0.5	0.3	0.3	0.8	1.0	0.7	0.6	0.5	0.4	..	0.0	0.3	0.7
Algeria	0.0	0.0	0.0	0.0	0.0	0.0	0.0	0.0	0.0	0.0	..	0.0	0.0	0.0
Egypt, Arab Republic	0.0	2.1	0.9	1.3	1.5	2.5	2.4	2.1	1.6	1.5	..	0.0	0.9	1.9
Libya	0.0	0.0	0.0	0.0	..	..	..	..	..	..	..	0.0	0.0	..
Morocco	0.0	0.0	0.6	0.0	2.9	2.1	0.0	0.3	0.2	0.1	..	0.0	0.6	0.9
Tunisia	0.0	0.0	0.0	0.0	0.0	0.0	0.0	0.0	0.0	0.0	..	0.0	0.0	0.0
ALL AFRICA	0.1	0.9	0.7	0.9	1.0	1.1	1.1	1.1	1.2	1.1	..	0.1	0.7	1.1

Note: 1996 data are preliminary. Nigeria's data are for federal level; since 1994, ratios are distorted because the official exchange rate used by the Gov. for oil exports oil value added is significantly over-valued.

7-8. Foreign financing

	Percentage of GDP											Annual average		
	1980	*1987*	*1988*	*1989*	*1990*	*1991*	*1992*	*1993*	*1994*	*1995*	*1996*	*75-84*	*85-89*	*90-MR*
SUB-SAHARAN AFRICA	..	..	..	..	..	..	..	..	..	..	..	..	..	..
excluding South Africa	..	2.2	2.8	3.6	3.0	2.0	2.7	2.9	5.4	-0.4	1.1	1.0	2.2	2.4
excl. S. Africa & Nigeria	..	1.8	2.5	3.6	4.2	2.9	4.1	3.0	6.7	0.9	3.0	..	2.2	3.5
Angola	..	-0.3	4.0	3.0	3.9	1.7	5.1	-7.3	0.9	-13.5	..	..	0.6	-1.5
Benin	..	..	..	..	..	..	..	..	..	..	..	..	..	..
Botswana	..	-19.2	-13.5	-14.0	-8.8	-11.4	-2.2	9.4	4.3	0.3	..	0.0	-14.8	-1.4
Burkina Faso	..	4.0	3.0	-7.1	1.4	2.8	2.7	3.4	2.6	4.0	3.4	3.0	1.1	2.9
Burundi	3.3	12.0	8.4	6.5	2.9	2.4	5.8	4.5	3.2	2.8	6.6	5.6	7.5	4.0
Cameroon	2.2	3.0	4.4	4.8	5.3	1.9	8.4	0.1	20.5	-1.7	9.7	1.6	3.0	6.3
Cape Verde	..	3.0	0.5	1.8	0.6	0.7	2.4	3.6	4.4	2.4	5.4	11.5	5.5	2.8
Central African Republic	0.4	3.1	1.5	2.5	3.0	3.1	2.3	2.1	4.0	2.7	0.5	1.0	3.5	2.5
Chad	..	5.8	7.0	11.2	8.8	3.8	2.8	3.9	3.1	6.1	7.3	0.7	5.8	5.1
Comoros	..	3.1	1.2	3.3	2.3	1.5	1.8	2.4	4.4	3.2	3.2	18.9	6.9	2.7
Congo	11.2	14.1	17.3	8.1	8.8	7.5	9.6	13.6	10.5	-20.6	-12.4	5.7	10.2	2.4
Côte d'Ivoire	7.9	-8.2	-8.1	10.5	11.5	10.9	9.8	7.5	11.0	4.2	0.7	2.9	-2.9	7.9
Djibouti	..	..	..	..	..	0.4	0.1	3.0	2.4	4.8	2.7	..	..	2.2
Equatorial Guinea	..	-2.7	3.3	3.0	5.2	2.6	-8.8	9.8	0.8	-3.4	..	..	0.2	1.0
Eritrea	..	..	..	..	..	..	..	..	..	..	0.0	..	..	0.0
Ethiopia	..	2.5	2.5	3.9	3.8	2.2	1.2	3.9	7.4	3.9	3.6	2.6	2.9	3.7
Gabon	..	6.6	7.8	7.6	2.2	-1.5	-2.5	0.6	16.2	2.1	2.8	..	6.3	2.8
Gambia, The	1.7	6.1	2.8	2.6	1.5	1.0	..	..	..	..	..	13.9	7.4	1.3
Ghana	0.9	2.8	3.4	3.2	4.5	4.5	3.5	6.5	4.8	4.5	4.1	0.7	2.7	4.6
Guinea	..	4.3	5.2	5.8	4.1	3.3	7.4	4.9	2.6	3.5	2.1	..	5.3	4.0
Guinea-Bissau	..	10.6	8.9	11.7	4.9	8.7	5.0	-5.3	-8.2	-5.8	-1.7	..	15.4	-0.3
Kenya	0.3	0.1	0.1	0.2	0.1	0.0	0.1	0.0	-0.1	0.0	0.1	0.1	0.1	0.0
Lesotho	..	9.3	7.0	8.3	7.9	7.7	7.4	7.4	3.5	7.9	..	0.0	4.9	7.0
Liberia	..	..	..	..	..	..	..	..	..	..	..	..	..	..
Madagascar	5.6	3.6	3.9	4.6	2.1	3.9	2.7	2.9	1.7	1.8	4.8	4.1	3.4	2.8
Malawi	7.1	3.5	3.2	3.1	4.6	3.6	4.7	6.5	8.5	2.9	4.7	5.1	3.4	5.1
Mali	..	4.8	9.9	11.7	5.9	6.2	4.4	3.4	7.5	7.4	6.0	5.0	8.1	5.8
Mauritania	..	4.5	2.5	2.9	3.5	4.1	4.1	4.9	3.7	4.3	3.1	0.0	3.7	3.9
Mauritius	..	1.5	0.2	-0.9	-0.6	-0.7	-0.6	-0.4	-0.4	1.5	-0.2	-1.0	0.6	-0.2
Mozambique	3.7	8.5	9.8	8.2	10.6	6.2	3.2	3.7	9.1	6.2	7.1	6.5	7.2	6.6
Namibia	..	..	..	..	..	..	..	..	..	0.0	0.0	..	..	0.0
Niger	..	5.8	4.7	3.3	6.8	0.6	1.5	-0.1	12.5	-0.6	4.1	5.4	4.2	3.5
Nigeria	0.6	3.2	3.7	3.6	-0.1	-0.2	-1.6	2.7	2.0	-3.8	-3.1	0.6	1.9	-0.6
Rwanda	-0.3	4.6	2.8	2.1	2.4	3.3	4.1	3.2	1.6	4.3	0.5	0.9	3.4	2.8
São Tomé and Principe	..	20.3	8.9	11.5	37.2	18.5	18.6	17.9	-1.9	-31.6	23.6	..	13.5	11.8
Senegal	-2.7	3.8	3.5	3.2	3.7	0.5	1.5	0.5	8.7	3.3	1.3	1.6	3.2	2.8
Seychelles	..	1.3	-2.9	1.9	-1.8	3.1	-1.5	0.8	-1.4	0.2	0.5	6.6	3.2	0.0
Sierra Leone	..	2.2	2.4	4.7	5.1	3.6	5.8	5.5	3.0	3.0	2.7	..	3.0	4.1
Somalia	..	..	..	..	..	..	..	..	..	..	..	..	..	..
South Africa	..	..	..	..	..	..	..	..	..	..	..	..	..	..
Sudan	..	0.0	0.0	0.0	0.0	0.0	4.6	4.9	0.0	..	..	0.0	0.0	1.9
Swaziland	..	0.5	-0.5	-0.2	-0.2	-0.6	-0.3	-0.6	1.1	..	0.0	-0.8	0.6	-0.1
Tanzania	..	1.4	2.6	-0.7	0.2	1.0	2.2	2.3	3.0	5.3	..	4.1	1.5	2.3
Togo	..	..	0.0	0.0	0.0	0.0	0.0	0.0	0.0	0.0	0.0	..	0.0	0.0
Uganda	..	0.3	2.2	2.2	6.7	3.6	5.2	5.2	5.9	4.8	2.6	0.4	1.3	4.8
Zaire	..	..	..	..	..	..	..	..	..	..	..	..	..	..
Zambia	..	-0.3	4.0	1.1	6.6	0.8	3.1	5.8	4.4	5.0	3.1	..	4.5	4.1
Zimbabwe	0.5	2.0	1.2	1.2	1.4	2.7	4.2	2.4	0.6	0.2	0.1	2.2	2.4	1.7
NORTH AFRICA	..	0.0	0.3	-0.1	-0.3	-0.3	-0.6	-0.3	4.2	-0.6	..	0.9	0.3	0.4
Algeria	..	0.8	1.5	0.6	0.6	0.6	-0.3	0.1	7.9	-0.8	..	0.0	0.6	1.4
Egypt, Arab Republic	..	0.6	-0.5	-0.6	-0.7	-1.1	-1.3	-0.9	0.3	0.0	..	3.7	1.8	-0.6
Libya	..	..	..	..	..	..	..	..	..	..	..	..	..	..
Morocco	..	-4.7	-2.2	-2.0	-3.1	-1.8	-1.3	-0.7	-1.8	-0.9	..	-1.7	-4.0	-1.6
Tunisia	..	..	..	..	..	..	1.0	..	..	..	..	..	..	1.0
ALL AFRICA	..	..	..	..	..	..	1.2	1.5	..	..	..	..	..	1.3

Note: 1996 data are preliminary. Nigeria's data are for federal level; since 1994, ratios are distorted because the official exchange rate used by the Gov. for oil exports oil value added is significantly over-valued.

7-9. Taxes on income and profits

	Percentage of total revenue											Annual average		
	1980	*1987*	*1988*	*1989*	*1990*	*1991*	*1992*	*1993*	*1994*	*1995*	*1996*	*75-84*	*85-89*	*90-MR*
SUB-SAHARAN AFRICA	..	12.3	12.8	13.1	12.2	11.4	11.3	11.5	11.8	11.3	..	8.8	12.4	11.6
excluding South Africa	..	18.8	19.7	20.2	18.8	17.5	17.3	17.7	18.1	17.3	18.0	16.1	19.1	17.8
excl. S. Africa & Nigeria	..	26.5	27.7	28.4	26.4	24.5	24.4	24.9	25.4	24.3	25.2	23.3	26.9	25.0
Angola	..	..	..	..	..	..	..	..	..	..	..	..	..	..
Benin	..	..	..	16.5	26.3	22.8	24.6	24.8	30.7	28.4	27.2	..	16.5	26.4
Botswana	..	..	..	..	..	..	..	..	..	..	..	..	..	..
Burkina Faso	..	19.8	19.7	108.7	21.5	20.4	22.0	18.9	18.7	21.6	24.2	19.6	36.1	21.1
Burundi	18.9	17.9	19.1	12.4	17.7	18.4	17.8	20.5	18.4	17.6	19.5	21.0	17.0	18.6
Cameroon	21.7	45.7	50.9	44.4	44.3	17.3	18.0	17.3	18.8	15.7	15.7	26.9	49.7	21.0
Cape Verde	..	24.1	21.4	20.4	20.8	21.2	20.4	22.2	23.8	23.0	24.3	..	22.0	22.2
Central African Republic	..	26.5	27.6	22.1	24.1	24.0	22.8	22.9	24.3	20.6	24.4	..	25.2	23.3
Chad	..	17.9	17.3	21.9	18.7	26.7	27.7	23.6	28.8	38.8	40.3	..	19.1	29.2
Comoros	..	11.9	21.6	13.8	19.6	13.5	11.1	9.0	12.6	12.2	12.4	6.6	15.4	12.9
Congo	..	..	..	..	..	63.2	51.9	49.2	67.8	57.8	63.4	..	..	58.9
Côte d'Ivoire	..	20.2	19.9	20.5	22.5	20.7	20.6	19.3	14.8	17.7	19.2	17.5	17.8	19.3
Djibouti	..	..	..	..	..	..	..	..	..	..	..	..	..	..
Equatorial Guinea	..	..	..	..	..	..	..	..	..	..	..	..	..	..
Eritrea	..	28.6	28.6	30.7	..	..	..	..	..	..	13.1	22.3	29.4	13.1
Ethiopia	..	31.0	29.2	26.9	29.5	30.5	28.4	22.9	24.3	22.1	25.5	28.6	28.8	26.2
Gabon	..	..	25.5	21.9	27.2	31.3	34.3	29.5	38.4	45.0	51.9	..	23.7	36.8
Gambia, The	21.3	15.7	16.3	20.3	20.5	18.5	..	..	..	..	..	15.8	17.6	19.5
Ghana	..	23.0	28.5	23.8	23.0	17.6	18.6	19.1	17.5	17.4	22.4	18.9	23.0	19.4
Guinea	..	1.2	1.8	2.2	2.1	4.2	6.8	6.9	8.8	9.1	10.6	..	1.6	6.9
Guinea-Bissau	..	7.3	6.4	8.7	7.4	5.9	6.1	7.1	6.7	6.9	7.8	..	14.1	6.9
Kenya	28.5	32.2	32.0	32.6	31.5	31.6	27.5	37.0	36.1	33.4	35.4	28.8	31.6	33.2
Lesotho	..	..	..	..	..	..	..	..	..	..	..	..	..	..
Liberia	..	..	..	..	..	..	..	..	..	..	..	..	..	..
Madagascar	79.6	11.1	11.4	8.2	10.2	13.0	10.4	12.9	15.1	11.1	14.0	31.6	11.8	12.4
Malawi	..	77.6	61.2	53.9	52.6	51.5	51.1	55.1	53.3	48.4	27.6	83.3	71.5	48.5
Mali	..	11.2	11.9	12.1	13.2	14.1	15.9	16.0	15.4	18.3	19.7	16.7	12.7	16.1
Mauritania	..	35.8	31.8	33.3	31.2	28.2	31.8	27.3	27.2	26.4	22.7	..	36.7	27.8
Mauritius	..	10.7	12.4	14.0	14.5	14.6	13.8	12.0	12.5	14.6	16.0	..	11.3	14.0
Mozambique	..	22.0	22.5	20.0	17.8	17.7	15.6	14.4	17.9	16.6	16.2	..	21.4	16.6
Namibia	..	..	..	..	..	..	..	..	..	..	26.3	..	..	26.3
Niger	..	24.5	29.0	27.3	23.6	28.8	33.8	33.7	30.0	30.5	25.3	22.0	25.9	29.4
Nigeria	..	..	..	..	..	..	..	..	..	..	0.0	..	..	0.0
Rwanda	..	20.1	22.7	21.4	22.7	19.4	21.3	22.9	24.0	11.9	25.8	23.6	20.3	21.1
São Tomé and Principe	..	10.8	9.1	9.6	11.8	10.2	6.7	8.9	10.7	14.1	20.9	..	9.8	11.9
Senegal	27.1	22.2	25.0	24.7	24.8	23.7	25.5	26.9	24.8	24.8	23.5	28.6	24.4	24.9
Seychelles	..	19.7	13.4	17.3	22.5	20.7	16.6	15.1	17.9	21.1	18.9	22.6	18.4	19.0
Sierra Leone	..	25.5	26.0	23.4	23.3	22.6	22.7	22.0	17.6	15.7	17.1	..	24.2	20.1
Somalia	..	..	..	..	..	..	..	..	..	..	..	..	..	..
South Africa	..	..	..	..	..	..	..	..	..	..	..	..	..	..
Sudan	..	..	..	..	..	..	..	..	..	..	..	..	..	..
Swaziland	..	..	..	..	..	..	..	..	..	..	..	..	..	..
Tanzania	..	35.6	23.4	23.1	21.3	24.3	23.1	27.7	24.1	23.0	22.0	..	27.4	23.7
Togo	..	33.5	32.1	37.7	31.8	30.4	30.6	30.9	40.1	41.7	30.9	36.6	34.3	33.8
Uganda	..	0.0	0.0	9.8	10.0	10.1	12.7	14.3	15.8	14.7	9.1	0.0	2.0	12.4
Zaire	..	..	..	..	..	..	..	..	..	..	..	..	..	..
Zambia	..	26.5	28.4	24.2	23.1	27.0	33.0	28.6	28.7	28.9	27.2	..	27.5	28.0
Zimbabwe	0.0	46.5	45.8	46.5	47.0	44.2	46.0	48.7	47.7	44.9	44.9	8.6	45.4	46.2
NORTH AFRICA	..	..	..	..	..	..	..	..	..	..	..	..	..	..
Algeria	..	..	..	..	..	..	..	..	..	..	..	..	..	..
Egypt, Arab Republic	..	17.7	17.6	18.7	19.4	22.4	23.0	23.8	22.9	21.8	..	..	18.0	22.2
Libya	..	..	..	..	..	..	..	..	..	..	..	..	..	..
Morocco	..	..	..	..	..	..	..	..	..	..	..	..	..	..
Tunisia	..	..	..	..	..	..	..	..	..	..	..	..	..	..
ALL AFRICA	..	14.8	15.4	14.9	13.4	12.0	12.2	12.9	12.7	16.3	..	..	14.4	13.2

Note: 1996 data are preliminary (see page 3). Total revenue does not include grants. Nigeria's fiscal data are for federal level only.

7-10. Taxes on international trade and transactions

	Percentage of total revenue											Annual average		
	1980	1987	1988	1989	1990	1991	1992	1993	1994	1995	1996	75-84	85-89	90-MR
SUB-SAHARAN AFRICA	..	7.8	7.6	11.1	10.4	10.6	10.6	10.4	11.4	11.9	..	3.1	7.7	10.9
excluding South Africa	..	12.1	11.6	17.1	16.0	16.4	16.3	16.0	17.5	18.4	18.5	6.7	11.9	17.0
excl. S. Africa & Nigeria	..	17.0	16.4	24.0	22.5	23.0	22.9	22.4	24.6	25.8	26.0	9.6	16.7	23.9
Angola	..	..	..	..	..	..	..	..	..	..	..	..	..	..
Benin	..	..	..	39.0	41.7	41.5	40.4	42.5	39.6	40.4	41.3	..	39.0	41.1
Botswana	..	..	..	..	..	..	..	..	..	..	..	..	..	..
Burkina Faso	..	40.7	47.3	213.3	38.3	36.8	33.3	36.4	54.0	52.4	47.0	35.3	79.1	42.6
Burundi	30.5	22.4	27.5	25.7	15.6	18.4	16.3	15.7	26.7	33.0	28.8	22.5	27.2	22.1
Cameroon	..	18.6	22.0	14.9	15.4	13.1	18.0	16.6	18.3	19.8	19.9	..	17.7	17.3
Cape Verde	..	..	39.3	41.6	43.8	48.4	49.1	41.2	39.6	40.0	40.0	..	40.4	43.1
Central African Republic	..	30.2	29.6	31.4	39.8	37.5	34.7	33.1	32.5	42.5	38.9	..	31.9	37.0
Chad	..	26.2	27.8	24.0	24.4	15.2	15.6	13.7	19.4	27.2	31.2	..	26.0	21.0
Comoros	..	..	..	48.4	41.4	38.6	32.2	36.6	36.6	44.0	47.4	..	48.4	39.5
Congo	..	..	..	..	12.1	17.3	21.2	20.9	13.9	19.2	16.3	..	..	17.3
Côte d'Ivoire	..	..	..	34.0	26.2	30.7	25.7	26.1	38.6	37.6	36.6	..	34.0	31.6
Djibouti	..	..	..	..	..	..	..	..	..	..	..	..	..	..
Equatorial Guinea	..	..	..	..	..	..	..	..	..	..	..	..	..	..
Eritrea	..	21.3	21.3	22.8	..	..	..	..	..	..	25.5	20.8	21.5	25.5
Ethiopia	..	..	..	..	..	..	..	..	..	..	..	..	..	..
Gabon	..	..	..	..	19.2	21.1	19.4	21.1	16.0	17.6	19.6	..	..	19.1
Gambia, The	..	70.2	66.5	62.1	59.2	60.3	..	..	..	..	..	54.6	62.7	59.8
Ghana	..	42.5	35.2	39.6	38.7	33.6	33.2	30.4	37.1	31.5	34.8	..	39.1	34.2
Guinea	..	6.2	6.8	6.4	8.7	11.6	12.8	14.5	15.6	14.4	13.4	..	6.4	13.0
Guinea-Bissau	..	43.9	42.9	18.3	25.2	28.7	16.7	29.0	35.8	27.4	32.9	..	35.0	27.9
Kenya	0.0	0.0	0.0	0.0	0.0	0.0	0.0	0.0	0.0	0.0	15.5	0.0	0.0	2.2
Lesotho	..	..	..	..	..	..	..	..	..	..	..	..	..	..
Liberia	..	..	..	..	..	..	..	..	..	..	..	..	..	..
Madagascar	..	38.7	44.7	35.5	37.1	37.6	36.0	33.4	33.7	41.9	40.7	31.3	38.8	37.2
Malawi	..	..	21.4	30.9	32.5	34.7	34.0	30.9	36.8	41.0	12.4	..	26.2	31.8
Mali	..	26.8	25.4	26.4	26.4	41.1	42.9	45.3	39.7	41.2	34.7	31.9	27.2	38.8
Mauritania	..	41.7	35.0	34.5	31.2	34.9	40.5	36.9	35.7	23.6	20.0	..	45.9	31.8
Mauritius	..	51.4	51.2	49.6	48.9	46.3	44.4	44.6	41.0	38.1	37.1	..	51.1	42.9
Mozambique	..	..	..	..	21.9	24.4	25.6	25.5	22.5	24.0	28.7	..	..	24.7
Namibia	..	..	..	..	..	..	..	..	..	..	27.7	..	..	27.7
Niger	..	33.6	32.4	34.3	39.5	39.0	35.4	41.3	41.5	43.2	46.7	36.9	34.7	40.9
Nigeria	..	..	..	..	..	..	..	..	..	..	0.0	..	..	0.0
Rwanda	..	34.1	29.9	28.3	27.5	30.9	31.0	27.8	36.4	38.5	30.0	39.3	36.5	31.7
São Tomé and Principe	..	19.8	39.4	37.2	3.9	4.2	3.4	1.8	4.3	5.8	21.8	..	32.1	6.5
Senegal	37.1	31.9	33.2	28.8	33.4	33.1	36.4	37.2	41.1	42.5	43.4	36.6	33.3	38.2
Seychelles	..	0.0	0.0	0.0	51.7	50.7	54.3	58.9	52.4	48.5	53.4	0.0	0.0	52.8
Sierra Leone	..	44.4	21.1	27.3	25.1	24.7	27.4	31.0	38.6	41.2	42.2	..	29.0	32.9
Somalia	..	..	..	..	..	..	..	..	..	..	..	..	..	..
South Africa	..	..	..	..	..	..	..	..	..	..	..	..	..	..
Sudan	..	..	..	..	..	..	..	..	..	..	..	..	..	..
Swaziland	..	..	..	..	..	..	..	..	..	..	..	..	..	..
Tanzania	..	38.6	23.7	22.9	24.4	23.8	22.2	19.3	20.7	36.6	12.3	..	28.4	22.8
Togo	..	36.7	35.7	34.6	37.8	40.9	34.8	35.3	40.8	37.7	41.2	33.3	34.4	38.4
Uganda	..	..	..	34.5	48.9	55.2	50.8	51.3	48.0	48.9	36.8	..	34.5	48.6
Zaire	..	..	..	..	..	..	..	..	..	..	..	..	..	..
Zambia	..	35.2	30.3	32.5	36.1	32.4	32.9	33.3	30.8	27.4	29.7	..	29.8	31.8
Zimbabwe	..	..	..	..	..	..	..	..	..	..	16.9	..	..	16.9
NORTH AFRICA	..	..	..	..	..	..	..	..	..	..	..	..	..	..
Algeria	..	..	..	..	..	..	..	..	..	..	..	..	..	..
Egypt, Arab Republic	..	14.3	14.9	15.6	13.3	11.4	10.6	10.7	11.6	12.6	..	..	14.9	11.7
Libya	..	..	..	..	..	..	..	..	..	..	..	..	..	..
Morocco	..	..	..	..	..	..	..	..	..	..	..	..	..	..
Tunisia	..	..	..	..	..	..	..	..	..	..	..	..	..	..
ALL AFRICA	..	8.5	8.2	12.7	12.1	12.8	11.7	11.6	12.7	13.5	..	..	8.2	12.4

Note: 1996 data are preliminary (see page 3). Total revenue does not include grants. Nigeria's fiscal data are for federal level only.

7-11. Indirect taxes

	Percentage of total revenue											Annual average		
	1980	1987	1988	1989	1990	1991	1992	1993	1994	1995	1996	75-84	85-89	90-MR
SUB-SAHARAN AFRICA	..	26.3	26.4	29.4	26.5	26.7	26.8	26.8	27.6	27.2	..	18.5	26.2	26.9
excluding South Africa	..	40.4	40.7	45.2	40.8	41.1	41.3	41.2	42.4	41.8	40.8	36.0	40.3	41.3
excl. S. Africa & Nigeria	..	56.8	57.2	63.6	57.3	57.7	58.0	57.9	59.6	58.8	57.3	51.9	56.7	58.1
Angola	..	..	..	..	..	..	..	..	..	..	..	..	..	..
Benin	..	..	..	60.1	53.1	54.0	57.6	60.1	55.7	54.1	55.9	..	60.1	55.8
Botswana	..	..	..	..	..	..	..	..	..	..	..	..	..	..
Burkina Faso	..	62.4	69.3	337.3	60.8	55.4	52.0	53.7	73.0	70.6	67.3	61.8	121.5	61.8
Burundi	53.8	56.1	59.8	54.3	47.0	47.7	46.0	44.1	64.7	66.8	66.5	50.3	57.4	54.7
Cameroon	61.6	42.4	41.2	50.3	52.0	46.0	46.5	52.6	59.5	61.7	61.1	40.4	39.9	54.2
Cape Verde	..	45.5	46.4	49.1	51.2	56.0	55.4	47.4	46.6	47.0	46.8	..	47.0	50.1
Central African Republic	..	61.4	60.1	67.1	73.8	68.0	69.4	70.4	66.4	75.1	74.7	86.2	69.2	71.1
Chad	..	73.8	78.6	71.5	77.2	53.1	53.5	53.8	67.7	49.8	48.8	..	74.7	57.7
Comoros	..	67.8	56.1	58.7	50.5	65.0	71.5	78.5	75.9	74.0	73.5	62.7	71.2	69.9
Congo	..	..	..	..	45.5	35.5	46.2	47.8	30.7	41.7	35.7	..	..	40.4
Côte d'Ivoire	..	64.2	58.9	62.4	59.3	65.1	64.7	64.1	64.5	61.0	60.1	51.4	57.7	62.7
Djibouti	..	..	..	..	..	..	..	..	..	..	..	..	..	..
Equatorial Guinea	..	..	..	..	..	..	..	..	..	..	..	..	..	..
Eritrea	..	34.4	34.3	36.9	..	..	..	..	..	..	47.8	36.7	35.0	47.8
Ethiopia	..	40.5	37.6	33.9	40.3	47.7	44.3	46.2	54.2	44.5	43.9	46.7	38.8	45.9
Gabon	..	..	73.1	73.6	35.5	35.9	35.1	37.0	26.7	26.1	25.3	..	73.4	31.6
Gambia, The	107.0	76.1	72.0	69.3	66.8	68.4	..	..	..	..	..	86.0	86.7	67.6
Ghana	..	67.4	62.4	66.6	68.7	72.5	71.9	69.0	68.7	54.5	63.4	64.1	66.0	66.9
Guinea	..	92.8	89.6	91.2	90.2	89.9	85.7	86.0	84.0	84.3	82.3	..	92.1	86.0
Guinea-Bissau	..	56.1	55.8	27.2	34.0	42.4	26.0	40.6	48.5	46.8	44.4	..	59.2	40.4
Kenya	59.1	66.3	65.2	59.4	61.0	56.1	63.1	55.6	52.1	51.7	49.5	60.8	62.9	55.6
Lesotho	..	..	..	..	..	..	..	..	..	..	..	..	..	..
Liberia	..	..	..	..	..	..	..	..	..	..	..	..	..	..
Madagascar	..	63.6	68.8	54.1	53.1	54.9	59.6	52.5	55.3	63.1	60.4	59.7	62.7	57.0
Malawi	..	0.0	21.4	30.9	32.5	34.7	34.0	30.9	36.8	41.0	47.2	0.0	10.5	36.7
Mali	..	52.4	46.6	46.5	43.6	61.1	61.7	63.9	58.9	55.8	60.0	51.8	50.0	57.9
Mauritania	..	65.8	53.5	50.3	50.0	50.8	55.9	49.3	53.4	47.8	40.8	..	69.4	49.7
Mauritius	..	70.1	71.6	71.2	71.6	70.2	69.3	70.1	66.9	65.7	66.2	..	70.9	68.6
Mozambique	46.8	62.7	61.7	68.3	71.6	67.3	71.3	76.7	73.7	74.7	86.1	46.9	58.1	74.5
Namibia	..	..	..	..	..	..	..	..	..	..	58.5	..	..	58.5
Niger	..	54.5	54.3	55.1	59.5	58.6	52.5	60.4	63.7	63.9	66.2	65.3	58.0	60.7
Nigeria	..	..	..	..	..	..	..	..	..	..	0.0	..	..	0.0
Rwanda	..	67.2	63.6	64.0	64.3	67.8	66.4	69.5	75.4	82.0	66.4	63.2	67.4	70.2
São Tomé and Principe	..	26.8	45.6	41.8	48.1	52.9	59.4	63.4	64.5	45.1	43.9	..	38.1	53.9
Senegal	66.2	55.9	56.8	51.4	55.5	53.1	55.1	58.9	64.0	65.4	67.3	63.6	58.3	59.9
Seychelles	..	50.4	55.6	53.6	57.8	56.8	61.0	65.8	58.9	56.1	60.4	49.2	52.0	59.5
Sierra Leone	..	70.0	64.6	71.7	72.1	73.1	72.5	73.3	78.8	79.4	79.0	..	70.0	75.5
Somalia	..	..	..	..	..	..	..	..	..	..	..	..	..	..
South Africa	..	..	..	..	..	..	..	..	..	..	..	..	..	..
Sudan	..	..	..	..	..	..	..	..	..	..	..	..	..	..
Swaziland	..	..	..	..	..	..	..	..	..	..	..	..	..	..
Tanzania	..	112.5	68.2	64.8	64.8	64.4	65.2	61.5	66.8	73.2	56.4	..	81.8	64.6
Togo	..	49.0	49.7	48.1	50.4	56.8	45.0	49.7	50.5	50.5	58.0	41.2	46.0	51.5
Uganda	..	83.2	87.4	75.0	81.5	83.6	80.7	77.7	77.3	77.7	55.8	93.4	88.4	76.3
Zaire	..	..	..	..	..	..	..	..	..	..	..	..	..	..
Zambia	..	64.6	62.0	71.6	75.1	70.9	62.5	68.0	64.5	62.8	64.9	..	63.9	66.9
Zimbabwe	0.0	40.1	41.0	42.3	41.4	46.1	44.0	39.1	40.3	41.8	44.2	9.2	42.6	42.4
NORTH AFRICA	..	..	..	..	..	..	..	..	..	..	..	..	..	..
Algeria	..	..	..	..	..	..	..	..	..	..	..	..	..	..
Egypt, Arab Republic	..	33.3	33.4	35.3	34.3	31.8	32.9	34.7	36.8	39.7	..	..	34.0	35.0
Libya	..	..	..	..	..	..	..	..	..	..	..	..	..	..
Morocco	..	..	..	..	..	..	..	..	..	..	..	..	..	..
Tunisia	..	..	..	..	..	..	..	..	..	..	..	..	..	..
ALL AFRICA	..	35.4	36.1	40.5	39.9	41.2	41.2	40.8	40.6	37.3	..	..	36.4	40.2

Note: 1996 data are preliminary (see page 3). Total revenue does not include grants. Nigeria's fiscal data are for federal level only.

7-12. Nontax revenue excluding grants

	Percentage of total revenue											Annual average		
	1980	1987	1988	1989	1990	1991	1992	1993	1994	1995	1996	75-84	85-89	90-MR
SUB-SAHARAN AFRICA	..	9.5	9.6	5.8	9.2	10.7	10.4	9.8	8.4	8.5	..	14.2	9.6	9.5
excluding South Africa	..	6.8	6.8	1.8	7.1	9.2	8.7	7.6	5.7	5.8	13.6	14.8	6.9	8.2
excl. S. Africa & Nigeria	..	9.6	9.6	2.6	10.0	12.9	12.2	10.6	8.0	8.1	10.6	21.2	9.7	10.4
Angola	..	..	..	..	..	..	..	..	..	..	..	..	..	..
Benin	..	..	..	-8.5	-9.4	6.3	-2.4	-1.4	-2.4	8.2	4.8	..	-8.5	0.5
Botswana	..	..	..	..	..	..	..	..	..	..	..	..	..	..
Burkina Faso	..	17.8	11.0	-345.3	16.1	15.3	13.3	11.6	-27.0	-19.0	-11.7	18.4	-57.5	-0.2
Burundi	6.7	7.9	7.5	15.2	9.6	9.0	10.5	11.0	7.0	4.9	8.4	7.2	8.2	8.6
Cameroon	16.7	11.9	7.8	5.3	3.8	36.7	35.5	30.1	21.8	22.6	23.2	32.7	10.4	24.8
Cape Verde	..	30.4	17.3	17.7	17.1	16.6	15.5	17.1	16.4	16.6	15.1	..	21.8	16.3
Central African Republic	..	12.1	12.3	10.8	2.1	8.0	8.0	6.7	9.0	4.3	0.9	..	10.7	5.6
Chad	..	8.2	4.0	6.6	4.1	20.2	18.8	22.6	3.8	11.4	10.9	..	6.3	13.1
Comoros	..	-152.6	-86.5	-88.6	-58.0	-95.5	-28.2	-54.5	-59.6	-44.6	-44.0	-93.9	-133.2	-54.9
Congo	..	..	..	..	2.3	0.9	1.9	3.0	1.5	0.6	0.8	..	..	1.6
Côte d'Ivoire	..	15.5	21.2	17.1	18.2	12.8	14.1	15.8	19.7	18.1	16.5	31.1	24.5	16.5
Djibouti	..	..	..	..	..	..	..	..	..	..	..	..	..	..
Equatorial Guinea	..	..	..	..	..	..	..	..	..	..	..	..	..	..
Eritrea	..	32.7	31.9	32.4	..	..	..	..	..	..	39.1	40.1	33.1	39.1
Ethiopia	..	28.5	33.2	39.2	30.2	21.8	27.3	30.9	21.5	33.4	30.7	24.7	32.4	28.0
Gabon	..	..	1.4	4.5	37.3	32.8	30.7	33.5	35.0	28.9	22.8	..	2.9	31.6
Gambia, The	-28.4	-8.1	-5.6	-0.3	5.5	7.1	..	..	..	..	..	-27.5	-13.4	6.3
Ghana	..	9.6	9.1	9.6	8.3	9.8	9.5	11.9	13.8	28.2	14.2	17.5	11.1	13.7
Guinea	..	6.0	8.6	6.5	7.7	5.9	7.2	6.8	2.5	-0.4	5.1	..	6.3	5.0
Guinea-Bissau	..	-169.9	-172.1	-182.4	-38.2	-73.9	-74.6	-108.8	-100.4	-78.5	-45.6	..	-238.4	-74.3
Kenya	12.2	1.3	2.5	6.4	7.5	12.3	9.4	7.3	11.8	14.9	10.9	10.3	5.0	10.6
Lesotho	..	..	..	..	..	..	..	..	..	..	..	..	..	..
Liberia	..	..	..	..	..	..	..	..	..	..	..	..	..	..
Madagascar	20.4	25.2	19.7	17.2	16.0	16.5	9.0	12.7	5.5	1.9	1.6	21.8	21.4	9.0
Malawi	..	8.7	-7.1	-7.1	1.6	-2.2	0.9	-2.5	-48.2	-37.5	4.4	1.2	0.9	-11.9
Mali	..	36.3	41.4	35.5	40.4	23.6	21.5	20.1	23.7	21.7	20.3	31.6	36.1	24.5
Mauritania	..	-15.0	5.1	5.3	10.2	12.8	5.6	6.0	8.8	16.4	32.9	..	-18.1	13.2
Mauritius	..	14.4	10.7	9.1	7.6	9.1	10.9	11.6	14.4	13.1	16.1	..	13.1	11.8
Mozambique	22.1	15.3	15.8	11.8	10.6	15.0	13.2	8.9	8.4	8.7	8.2	30.8	20.5	10.4
Namibia	..	..	..	..	..	..	..	..	..	..	12.1	..	..	12.1
Niger	..	21.0	16.7	17.6	16.9	12.6	13.8	5.9	6.3	5.6	8.5	12.7	16.2	9.9
Nigeria	..	..	..	..	..	..	..	..	..	..	20.8	..	..	20.8
Rwanda	..	-1.9	-11.4	-7.1	-14.1	-31.5	-48.3	-62.5	-24.3	-160.0	-71.7	-11.5	-7.0	-58.9
São Tomé and Principe	..	20.9	18.1	-24.2	-47.7	-45.3	-10.8	-64.5	-107.5	-100.5	-142.3	..	5.0	-74.1
Senegal	-1.7	19.5	14.6	12.8	12.6	14.9	12.7	13.2	-6.8	-2.1	4.2	1.1	12.1	6.9
Seychelles	..	29.8	31.0	29.1	7.8	9.0	13.6	10.0	17.3	19.3	17.6	28.2	29.6	13.5
Sierra Leone	..	4.5	9.4	4.8	4.7	4.3	4.7	4.7	3.6	4.9	3.9	..	5.7	4.4
Somalia	..	..	..	..	..	..	..	..	..	..	..	..	..	..
South Africa	20.6	14.6	14.7	13.0	13.0	13.5	13.4	13.9	13.6	13.6	..	19.4	14.4	13.5
Sudan	..	..	..	..	..	..	..	..	..	..	..	..	..	..
Swaziland	..	..	..	..	..	..	..	..	..	..	..	..	..	..
Tanzania	..	-48.2	-25.9	-17.1	-15.3	-5.9	-7.3	-24.8	-22.6	-6.8	12.2	..	-30.4	-10.1
Togo	..	17.0	15.2	11.2	13.5	12.7	23.8	17.5	3.0	2.9	11.1	18.0	15.8	12.1
Uganda	..	16.8	12.6	15.2	8.5	6.3	6.6	8.0	6.9	7.7	4.2	6.6	9.7	6.9
Zaire	..	..	..	..	..	..	..	..	..	..	..	..	..	..
Zambia	..	8.9	9.6	4.2	1.8	2.1	4.5	3.4	6.8	8.4	8.0	..	8.6	5.0
Zimbabwe	-6.5	9.8	10.5	8.6	8.4	5.7	3.9	4.9	4.1	6.7	6.2	-3.9	8.1	5.7
NORTH AFRICA	..	..	..	..	..	..	..	..	..	..	..	..	..	..
Algeria	..	..	..	..	..	..	..	..	..	..	..	..	..	..
Egypt, Arab Republic	..	26.6	26.7	26.8	24.2	35.4	31.2	35.0	34.3	33.5	..	..	26.7	32.3
Libya	..	..	..	..	..	..	..	..	..	..	..	..	..	..
Morocco	..	..	..	..	..	..	..	..	..	..	..	..	..	..
Tunisia	..	..	..	..	..	..	..	..	..	..	..	..	..	..
ALL AFRICA	..	12.9	12.1	8.2	9.7	11.7	11.1	11.3	11.6	10.8	..	..	11.5	11.0

Note: 1996 data are preliminary (see page 3). Total revenue does not include grants. Nigeria's fiscal data are for federal level only.

7-13. Government expenditure: wages and salaries

	Percentage of total expenditure and lending minus repayments											*Annual average*		
	1980	*1987*	*1988*	*1989*	*1990*	*1991*	*1992*	*1993*	*1994*	*1995*	*1996*	*75-84*	*85-89*	*90-MR*
SUB-SAHARAN AFRICA	..	14.4	14.6	11.0	11.5	13.2	12.7	14.0	13.4	13.2	..	4.4	12.1	13.0
excluding South Africa	..	22.2	22.5	16.9	17.7	20.2	19.5	21.5	20.7	20.3	20.3	10.1	18.7	20.0
excl. S. Africa & Nigeria	..	29.6	29.2	20.9	21.7	25.6	25.5	27.1	24.1	23.3	25.2	14.4	24.4	24.6
Angola	..	..	..	..	..	..	..	..	..	..	..	..	..	..
Benin	..	0.0	0.0	39.3	37.2	37.6	36.3	35.0	27.1	24.0	26.1	33.5	7.9	31.9
Botswana	..	..	..	..	..	..	..	..	..	..	..	..	..	..
Burkina Faso	..	27.8	34.9	42.4	38.8	31.9	30.8	29.0	26.2	25.1	24.5	26.1	34.0	29.5
Burundi	49.1	20.0	23.9	23.2	24.6	26.1	23.0	23.4	29.2	27.5	36.5	49.0	31.8	27.2
Cameroon	31.4	22.8	32.6	40.1	39.2	38.4	41.5	43.6	31.4	26.3	24.1	24.7	29.0	34.9
Cape Verde	..	0.0	19.7	23.8	26.1	25.2	20.0	24.3	19.6	20.6	26.7	0.0	8.7	23.2
Central African Republic	..	30.1	29.5	31.3	26.4	27.7	27.3	29.4	24.2	22.2	41.3	..	30.2	28.4
Chad	..	13.7	14.7	16.7	19.5	25.1	21.1	27.1	20.8	23.1	20.3	..	15.0	22.4
Comoros	..	0.0	0.0	28.9	30.1	31.6	27.0	31.0	23.1	28.2	35.5	0.0	5.8	29.5
Congo	..	37.3	33.2	32.1	30.3	42.6	47.5	48.8	36.3	32.1	27.4	..	30.4	37.8
Côte d'Ivoire	..	154.9	135.9	29.6	34.6	34.4	35.5	35.6	28.5	26.2	26.2	..	110.7	31.6
Djibouti	..	..	..	..	..	46.0	46.6	48.0	56.4	61.6	60.3	..	..	53.1
Equatorial Guinea	..	..	..	..	..	..	..	..	..	..	..	..	..	..
Eritrea	..	29.1	28.4	..	..	..	..	..	..	..	18.6	20.3	28.9	18.6
Ethiopia	..	..	..	..	..	..	..	25.0	21.5	23.9	21.5	..	..	23.0
Gabon	..	29.2	30.2	30.7	32.2	32.4	34.3	34.0	27.9	27.4	27.3	27.9	25.1	30.8
Gambia, The	..	17.3	23.0	23.2	24.6	27.5	..	..	..	..	..	16.3	21.2	26.1
Ghana	..	25.1	24.9	23.5	23.5	22.3	24.8	20.3	18.3	18.3	17.5	17.7	25.6	20.7
Guinea	..	10.4	16.5	17.5	17.1	20.0	23.1	24.2	25.1	23.9	26.9	..	14.3	22.9
Guinea-Bissau	..	12.3	8.4	9.0	9.4	10.3	7.8	8.0	7.5	9.2	6.6	21.4	13.5	8.4
Kenya	..	..	..	..	..	30.5	26.3	24.1	31.6	30.1	29.1	..	..	28.6
Lesotho	..	..	..	..	..	..	..	..	..	..	..	..	..	..
Liberia	..	..	..	..	..	..	..	..	..	..	..	..	..	..
Madagascar	..	27.5	28.2	22.8	24.7	28.2	21.3	19.7	18.3	18.7	18.6	33.0	28.9	21.4
Malawi	..	17.3	15.9	16.9	17.0	18.0	18.8	22.5	17.5	20.2	22.2	16.7	16.2	19.5
Mali	..	26.0	25.7	22.1	22.0	22.0	22.6	23.1	15.9	15.7	15.6	30.9	24.5	19.6
Mauritania	..	17.4	20.2	17.8	19.8	20.1	23.3	15.3	19.0	20.3	20.4	..	18.5	19.8
Mauritius	..	29.0	31.0	31.1	29.6	28.1	28.3	31.4	32.8	30.4	30.4	29.2	29.7	30.1
Mozambique	..	..	..	..	9.4	10.5	9.6	10.4	8.1	10.5	11.9	..	..	10.1
Namibia	..	23.8	22.3	24.1	22.1	38.9	40.2	41.1	41.5	40.6	41.0	17.6	22.2	37.9
Niger	..	21.0	22.6	23.7	24.0	34.9	37.4	38.3	29.4	34.3	25.5	18.8	21.2	32.0
Nigeria	..	4.0	6.0	7.2	7.8	7.0	4.8	7.8	12.3	13.0	8.3	..	5.7	8.7
Rwanda	..	25.5	28.5	30.6	27.2	25.3	22.4	24.1	24.9	19.5	20.1	30.6	28.0	23.4
São Tomé and Principe	..	19.0	14.3	8.5	11.6	10.7	10.1	7.8	7.0	4.3	2.5	..	13.9	7.7
Senegal	42.3	41.9	42.4	41.0	39.7	46.8	39.1	41.4	35.0	35.4	36.0	41.2	41.9	39.1
Seychelles	..	0.0	0.0	0.0	25.1	25.6	27.2	24.8	27.5	28.4	28.2	0.0	0.0	26.7
Sierra Leone	..	8.1	9.9	6.9	7.3	8.2	10.1	12.9	16.2	15.4	19.6	..	9.6	12.8
Somalia	..	..	..	..	..	..	..	..	..	..	..	..	..	..
South Africa	..	..	..	..	..	..	..	..	..	..	..	..	..	..
Sudan	..	..	..	..	..	..	..	..	..	..	..	..	..	..
Swaziland	..	..	..	..	..	..	..	..	..	..	..	..	..	..
Tanzania	..	19.0	16.2	21.4	21.3	20.0	19.3	19.2	21.0	19.0	24.5	21.1	21.4	20.6
Togo	..	27.8	29.8	27.6	28.6	36.5	39.1	41.4	36.1	35.6	34.0	27.1	26.0	35.9
Uganda	..	10.9	8.4	10.7	7.4	9.0	8.2	8.7	10.3	14.6	16.9	10.9	11.9	10.7
Zaire	..	..	..	..	..	..	..	..	..	..	..	..	..	..
Zambia	..	..	..	..	23.3	21.3	25.4	17.7	16.1	19.0	19.3	..	..	20.3
Zimbabwe	..	..	..	..	..	..	..	..	..	..	32.5	..	..	32.5
NORTH AFRICA	..	..	..	..	..	..	..	..	..	..	..	..	..	..
Algeria	..	31.3	28.4	35.2	36.7	27.5	31.8	28.9	29.1	28.5	..	19.1	27.8	30.4
Egypt, Arab Republic	..	17.4	17.0	17.3	16.7	15.6	15.8	18.8	19.7	21.5	..	..	17.2	18.0
Libya	..	..	..	..	..	..	..	..	..	..	..	..	..	..
Morocco	..	..	..	..	..	..	..	..	..	..	..	..	..	..
Tunisia	..	..	..	..	..	..	..	..	..	..	..	..	..	..
ALL AFRICA	..	18.5	17.9	17.1	17.7	16.6	17.3	17.9	17.6	17.6	..	9.7	16.0	17.4

Note: 1996 data are preliminary (see page 3). Nigeria's fiscal data are for federal level only.

7-14. Government expenditure: trends in real wages and salaries

	Index 1980=100											Annual average		
	1980	1987	1988	1989	1990	1991	1992	1993	1994	1995	1996	75-84	85-89	90-MR
SUB-SAHARAN AFRICA	..	100	104	106	107	118	121	135	120	118	105	93	100	118
excluding South Africa	..	100	104	106	107	118	121	135	120	118	105	93	100	118
excl. S.Africa & Nigeria	..	100	104	106	107	117	120	130	119	113	105	93	100	116
Angola	..	..	..	..	..	..	..	..	..	..	..	..	..	..
Benin	..	..	..	..	..	..	..	..	..	..	..	..	..	..
Botswana	..	..	..	..	..	..	..	..	..	..	..	..	..	..
Burkina Faso	..	100	117	126	132	122	117	119	106	104	103	80	100	115
Burundi	95	100	109	114	116	124	125	126	117	107	107	96	102	118
Cameroon	54	100	93	103	101	106	105	100	56	46	..	68	97	86
Cape Verde	..	..	..	..	..	..	..	..	..	..	..	..	..	..
Central African Republic	..	100	104	102	97	105	103	100	90	76	..	..	99	95
Chad	..	100	95	140	165	154	161	193	158	167	..	..	112	166
Comoros	..	..	..	..	..	..	..	..	..	..	..	..	..	..
Congo	..	100	93	87	92	138	141	139	89	62	..	..	95	110
Côte d'Ivoire	..	100	98	97	94	91	87	109	91	84	92	..	95	92
Djibouti	..	..	..	..	..	..	..	..	..	..	..	..	..	..
Equatorial Guinea	..	..	..	..	..	..	..	..	..	..	..	..	..	..
Eritrea	..	..	..	..	..	..	..	..	..	..	..	..	..	..
Ethiopia	..	..	..	..	..	..	..	..	..	..	..	..	..	..
Gabon	..	100	111	102	111	113	130	148	120	118	..	97	106	123
Gambia, The	..	100	110	106	108	112	..	..	..	..	..	168	122	110
Ghana	..	100	105	107	102	110	163	173	181	150	156	28	97	148
Guinea	..	..	..	..	..	..	..	..	..	..	..	..	..	..
Guinea-Bissau	..	100	97	114	104	134	108	95	85	93	..	..	104	103
Kenya	..	..	..	..	..	..	..	..	..	..	..	..	..	..
Lesotho	..	..	..	..	..	..	..	..	..	..	..	..	..	..
Liberia	..	..	..	..	..	..	..	..	..	..	..	..	..	..
Madagascar	..	100	93	92	89	96	88	88	79	72	69	106	96	83
Malawi	..	100	82	95	96	100	121	135	167	151	..	95	94	128
Mali	..	..	..	..	..	..	..	..	..	..	..	..	..	..
Mauritania	..	100	106	100	99	97	98	96	96	..	..	..	100	97
Mauritius	..	100	120	126	119	119	126	140	153	149	159	77	101	138
Mozambique	..	..	..	..	..	..	..	..	..	..	..	..	..	..
Namibia	..	100	99	100	98	170	195	219	205	207	..	68	93	182
Niger	..	100	109	127	136	156	164	172	149	141	90	73	100	144
Nigeria	..	100	136	146	204	202	174	284	221	176	..	..	118	210
Rwanda	..	100	103	105	107	101	102	100	..	42	57	85	99	85
São Tomé and Principe	..	..	..	..	..	..	..	..	..	..	..	..	..	..
Senegal	98	100	104	106	109	119	119	114	97	95	96	93	98	107
Seychelles	..	..	..	..	..	..	..	..	..	..	..	..	..	..
Sierra Leone	..	100	120	107	109	113	124	164	183	171	206	551	143	153
Somalia	..	..	..	..	..	..	..	..	..	..	..	..	..	..
South Africa	..	..	..	..	..	..	..	..	..	..	..	..	..	..
Sudan	..	..	..	..	..	..	..	..	..	..	..	..	..	..
Swaziland	..	..	..	..	..	..	..	..	..	..	..	..	..	..
Tanzania	..	100	101	135	133	117	119	146	146	165	190	148	116	145
Togo	..	100	104	101	107	122	111	112	..	..	..	83	95	113
Uganda	..	100	104	170	170	247	321	396	486	719	828	212	159	453
Zaire	..	..	..	..	..	..	..	..	..	..	..	..	..	..
Zambia	..	..	..	..	..	..	..	..	..	..	..	..	..	..
Zimbabwe	..	..	..	..	..	..	..	..	..	..	..	..	..	..
NORTH AFRICA	..	100	105	106	103	114	127	122	113	107	142	85	98	118
Algeria	..	100	101	106	103	114	127	122	113	106	..	85	97	114
Egypt, Arab Republic	..	100	105	99	99	97	96	105	109	107	..	0	61	102
Libya	..	..	..	..	..	..	..	..	..	..	..	..	..	..
Morocco	..	100	109	121	125	133	132	128	132	135	142	94	103	133
Tunisia	..	..	..	..	..	..	..	..	..	..	..	..	..	..
ALL AFRICA	..	100	104	106	107	117	123	127	119	113	107	92	99	116

Note: 1996 data are preliminary (see page 3). Nigeria's fiscal data are for federal level only.

7-15. Government expenditure: other goods and services

	Percentage of total expenditure and lending minus repayments											Annual average		
	1980	1987	1988	1989	1990	1991	1992	1993	1994	1995	1996	75-84	85-89	90-MR
SUB-SAHARAN AFRICA	..	16.1	15.9	14.3	14.3	13.7	13.2	11.9	11.0	11.1	..	23.4	18.4	12.5
excluding South Africa	..	24.8	24.4	22.0	22.1	21.0	20.2	18.2	17.0	17.1	16.3	42.5	28.4	18.8
excl. S. Africa & Nigeria	..	30.1	28.2	25.6	24.6	21.8	19.9	15.2	17.5	17.4	19.0	44.8	32.3	19.4
Angola	..	..	..	..	..	..	..	..	..	..	..	..	..	..
Benin	..	0.0	0.0	7.7	7.3	8.3	8.3	8.2	6.2	5.1	7.3	9.7	1.5	7.2
Botswana	..	..	..	..	..	..	..	..	..	..	..	..	..	..
Burkina Faso	..	4.7	5.7	7.3	7.2	7.8	8.6	10.8	12.0	10.1	9.5	4.2	6.1	9.4
Burundi	28.0	11.6	16.1	13.9	15.9	13.8	12.4	12.1	17.5	18.4	18.0	22.6	19.8	15.4
Cameroon	22.9	10.5	15.4	16.6	17.4	12.5	10.4	13.8	11.1	18.0	21.0	20.3	13.7	14.9
Cape Verde	..	30.6	3.4	3.9	4.2	3.3	2.5	2.3	1.6	1.5	2.3	23.4	16.5	2.5
Central African Republic	..	..	..	11.5	12.7	11.6	16.8	14.1	13.8	..	12.4	..	11.5	13.6
Chad	..	16.4	19.6	19.6	21.0	34.5	26.4	26.4	21.6	17.2	22.2	..	18.5	24.2
Comoros	..	37.2	49.6	20.3	19.5	22.0	19.1	26.5	20.2	22.3	17.8	36.7	36.7	21.1
Congo	..	9.9	6.0	8.9	9.9	23.9	6.8	6.4	7.6	6.5	7.1	..	10.0	9.8
Côte d'Ivoire	..	79.5	65.1	17.9	15.7	15.4	19.2	19.2	18.7	19.1	17.1	..	65.8	17.7
Djibouti	..	..	..	..	..	31.5	35.1	35.7	30.7	29.0	28.4	..	..	31.7
Equatorial Guinea	..	..	..	..	..	..	..	..	..	..	..	..	..	..
Eritrea	..	..	..	..	..	..	..	..	..	..	..	..	..	..
Ethiopia	..	..	..	..	..	..	..	21.5	17.6	23.7	22.0	..	..	21.2
Gabon	..	23.4	23.8	25.0	22.4	21.0	20.5	19.4	19.2	17.3	19.6	23.8	20.4	19.9
Gambia, The	..	30.9	32.2	33.0	33.0	31.6	..	..	..	..	..	21.8	28.0	32.3
Ghana	..	13.0	13.3	13.3	12.9	12.8	10.0	12.6	10.5	8.1	11.6	34.3	15.4	11.2
Guinea	..	29.9	18.1	19.5	18.9	18.7	15.6	13.9	13.2	11.3	11.6	..	24.7	14.8
Guinea-Bissau	..	11.4	9.2	12.9	14.4	13.1	10.4	9.4	12.6	11.9	11.7	-21.4	12.5	11.9
Kenya	..	..	..	..	..	19.0	0.0	0.0	0.0	0.0	28.5	..	..	7.9
Lesotho	..	..	..	..	..	..	..	..	..	..	..	..	..	..
Liberia	..	..	..	..	..	..	..	..	..	..	..	..	..	..
Madagascar	..	..	..	..	..	..	..	..	..	..	..	20.1	..	..
Malawi	..	42.0	39.6	41.2	39.2	37.6	38.2	40.7	31.9	41.4	40.5	37.6	41.1	38.5
Mali	..	25.6	26.8	33.7	31.4	33.1	31.6	29.3	28.1	27.7	28.8	28.1	26.5	30.0
Mauritania	..	-8.5	-9.6	-5.8	-4.6	-3.0	-4.3	-1.0	-1.4	-0.3	-0.5	..	-8.4	-2.2
Mauritius	..	8.0	8.5	8.5	8.3	9.5	10.1	8.7	8.7	9.5	9.1	7.2	8.1	9.1
Mozambique	..	..	..	..	28.4	27.1	29.1	27.8	35.0	21.2	23.3	..	..	27.4
Namibia	..	21.8	22.2	24.1	19.9	23.9	25.2	22.2	22.7	22.6	23.0	15.7	20.9	22.8
Niger	..	14.5	15.9	14.8	17.4	12.5	21.3	15.3	18.8	16.8	21.4	13.8	14.9	17.6
Nigeria	..	11.7	15.1	13.2	15.8	18.9	21.2	25.9	15.6	16.2	9.4	..	16.4	17.6
Rwanda	..	22.7	20.4	21.3	32.5	31.3	35.7	27.4	27.1	25.0	27.3	16.8	19.6	29.5
São Tomé and Principe	..	31.0	15.5	10.6	3.2	3.0	4.7	3.7	5.0	4.7	15.6	..	19.1	5.7
Senegal	25.8	15.6	16.4	16.5	16.4	11.3	20.4	15.2	11.8	11.4	12.5	18.6	15.5	14.1
Seychelles	..	49.1	44.1	42.2	30.3	30.9	31.6	29.8	31.1	32.1	31.8	53.1	45.9	31.1
Sierra Leone	..	39.5	39.0	43.1	42.7	36.8	37.8	39.5	42.7	56.5	44.6	..	39.2	42.9
Somalia	..	..	..	..	..	..	..	..	..	..	..	..	..	..
South Africa	..	..	..	..	..	..	..	..	..	..	..	..	..	..
Sudan	..	..	..	..	..	..	..	..	..	..	..	..	..	..
Swaziland	..	..	..	..	..	..	..	..	..	..	..	..	..	..
Tanzania	..	31.8	28.3	32.3	26.2	40.2	36.2	..	45.0	31.1	27.7	32.1	32.7	34.4
Togo	..	14.1	14.6	14.7	14.5	16.0	15.0	19.0	16.4	18.9	26.9	8.5	13.2	18.1
Uganda	..	47.1	42.2	49.4	43.9	32.6	31.8	26.6	29.7	32.8	33.0	35.0	45.2	32.9
Zaire	..	..	..	..	..	..	..	..	..	..	..	..	..	..
Zambia	..	..	..	..	12.5	10.7	10.7	11.9	10.4	16.4	17.4	..	..	12.8
Zimbabwe	..	..	..	..	..	..	..	..	..	..	16.0	..	..	16.0
NORTH AFRICA	..	..	..	..	..	..	..	..	..	..	..	..	..	..
Algeria	..	2.2	2.1	2.6	2.7	3.1	2.3	4.0	4.8	5.8	..	2.3	2.3	3.8
Egypt, Arab Republic	..	16.2	14.4	14.8	14.1	12.4	13.0	15.3	15.5	16.1	..	..	15.1	14.4
Libya	..	..	..	..	..	..	..	..	..	..	..	..	..	..
Morocco	..	..	..	..	..	..	..	..	..	..	..	..	..	..
Tunisia	..	..	..	..	..	..	..	..	..	..	..	..	..	..
ALL AFRICA	..	13.1	12.7	11.8	11.8	11.2	10.8	10.5	10.2	10.6	..	20.8	14.6	10.8

Note: 1996 data are preliminary (see page 3). Nigeria's fiscal data are for federal level only.

7-16. Government expenditure: interest payments

	Percentage of total expenditure and lending minus repayments											Annual average		
	1980	1987	1988	1989	1990	1991	1992	1993	1994	1995	1996	75-84	85-89	90-MR
SUB-SAHARAN AFRICA	..	18.2	17.2	14.9	14.9	14.6	16.0	14.6	16.6	15.5	..	7.3	15.4	15.4
excluding South Africa	..	28.0	26.4	23.0	22.9	22.4	24.5	22.5	25.6	23.8	20.2	20.5	23.8	23.1
excl. S. Africa & Nigeria	..	19.2	20.2	13.0	13.7	14.9	17.3	17.8	19.9	20.7	19.7	18.4	18.0	17.7
Angola	..	..	..	..	..	..	..	..	..	..	..	..	..	..
Benin	..	9.4	13.4	16.0	15.7	14.0	19.2	14.7	15.5	12.4	12.3	..	11.2	14.8
Botswana	..	..	..	..	..	..	..	..	..	..	..	..	..	..
Burkina Faso	..	5.7	6.2	6.1	5.7	6.5	6.8	6.9	6.9	6.7	4.9	3.1	6.2	6.3
Burundi	2.0	6.6	7.7	7.9	7.1	6.1	6.4	5.3	6.1	6.3	11.7	5.3	9.6	7.0
Cameroon	2.0	3.6	9.2	8.2	9.7	17.6	24.2	24.0	36.5	45.2	38.6	2.9	5.7	28.0
Cape Verde	..	3.7	4.7	4.5	4.9	3.4	2.6	2.7	1.8	6.3	4.8	0.0	3.2	3.8
Central African Republic	..	6.5	7.2	7.1	5.6	6.3	8.3	9.9	10.8	11.3	18.1	..	6.5	10.0
Chad	..	1.1	1.1	0.9	1.8	4.1	3.7	5.7	6.1	5.6	5.5	..	1.0	4.7
Comoros	..	3.4	4.4	4.0	3.7	3.4	2.6	3.3	2.9	3.2	3.3	3.4	3.6	3.2
Congo	..	20.4	22.1	22.9	29.9	22.1	21.6	20.1	33.0	43.0	40.3	..	21.1	30.0
Côte d'Ivoire	8.1	100.0	100.0	24.6	29.3	33.2	32.7	29.0	29.0	25.9	28.4	46.1	84.9	29.6
Djibouti	..	..	..	..	..	..	..	..	..	..	..	..	..	..
Equatorial Guinea	..	..	..	..	..	..	..	..	..	..	..	..	..	..
Eritrea	..	..	..	..	..	..	..	..	..	..	..	..	..	..
Ethiopia	..	5.1	5.0	4.6	4.2	5.4	7.3	8.9	12.5	10.3	9.2	3.4	5.0	8.3
Gabon	..	14.6	19.4	22.6	23.7	22.6	22.5	24.4	26.4	30.9	25.6	11.4	14.1	25.2
Gambia, The	13.2	14.2	15.5	14.5	16.8	18.7	..	..	..	..	..	13.1	14.5	17.8
Ghana	..	7.4	6.0	7.0	7.8	9.0	8.9	12.0	14.2	13.9	16.9	11.3	8.3	11.8
Guinea	..	11.2	13.0	10.1	10.4	10.3	8.6	7.2	9.0	8.1	7.9	..	11.6	8.8
Guinea-Bissau	..	..	..	..	..	..	..	..	..	..	..	..	..	..
Kenya	7.0	18.5	19.0	18.2	21.7	21.4	33.6	35.6	23.5	24.4	19.2	11.1	17.6	25.6
Lesotho	..	..	..	..	..	..	..	..	..	..	..	..	..	..
Liberia	..	..	..	..	..	..	..	..	..	..	..	..	..	..
Madagascar	..	11.0	12.2	8.3	8.9	12.3	17.1	19.4	27.3	29.0	27.6	5.6	9.9	20.2
Malawi	..	20.1	16.5	17.9	14.1	11.0	9.6	11.7	11.8	19.1	20.7	13.5	18.4	14.0
Mali	..	7.0	7.7	7.4	9.1	6.3	7.3	6.9	8.5	5.7	4.5	2.4	6.5	6.9
Mauritania	..	..	..	..	..	..	..	..	..	..	..	..	..	..
Mauritius	..	17.7	14.6	15.7	17.7	16.4	13.7	11.8	12.2	12.9	12.7	20.4	18.3	13.9
Mozambique	0.0	5.2	5.1	6.5	6.5	4.8	7.6	8.6	3.7	6.7	7.0	0.0	3.7	6.4
Namibia	..	..	..	..	..	..	..	..	..	..	1.8	..	..	1.8
Niger	..	14.0	13.3	13.1	10.1	11.5	9.8	10.2	12.3	15.3	12.8	11.1	13.6	11.7
Nigeria	5.7	49.6	41.7	47.6	45.4	40.8	42.4	34.3	39.7	31.4	21.4	7.7	38.0	36.5
Rwanda	1.7	4.6	5.4	5.7	5.0	8.2	7.9	9.0	27.7	11.3	6.5	2.5	4.7	10.8
São Tomé and Principe	..	10.0	14.0	8.8	12.3	16.2	15.5	16.8	14.9	15.6	4.9	..	10.9	13.7
Senegal	..	13.9	16.0	15.6	12.6	12.9	9.0	10.9	16.8	14.5	14.2	15.0	15.7	13.0
Seychelles	..	15.1	16.5	13.7	16.2	15.6	15.3	15.8	17.9	18.8	19.8	3.4	11.6	17.0
Sierra Leone	..	30.7	35.2	32.2	28.7	30.0	26.9	18.9	13.7	10.8	12.3	..	26.0	20.2
Somalia	..	..	..	..	..	..	..	..	..	..	..	..	..	..
South Africa	..	..	..	..	..	..	..	..	..	..	..	..	..	..
Sudan	..	..	..	..	..	..	..	..	..	..	..	..	..	..
Swaziland	..	..	..	..	..	..	..	..	..	..	..	..	..	..
Tanzania	..	13.7	14.2	15.6	13.2	13.2	12.2	13.1	13.9	15.3	20.8	8.1	12.4	14.5
Togo	14.3	12.5	14.6	14.7	11.3	12.6	12.9	15.9	21.9	15.4	13.0	18.1	14.8	14.7
Uganda	..	..	..	6.3	4.9	6.9	15.5	9.7	7.8	5.7	6.0	..	6.3	8.1
Zaire	..	..	..	..	..	..	..	..	..	..	..	..	..	..
Zambia	10.9	30.7	23.4	22.1	23.7	24.4	27.5	41.8	36.5	33.6	32.2	12.2	28.6	31.4
Zimbabwe	27.6	13.3	13.9	14.4	14.1	13.9	15.7	17.9	20.4	24.2	23.9	24.8	13.5	18.6
NORTH AFRICA	..	..	..	..	..	..	..	..	..	..	..	..	..	..
Algeria	..	4.0	5.3	5.6	6.4	6.0	7.0	6.4	8.2	9.9	..	2.5	4.2	7.3
Egypt, Arab Republic	..	8.7	8.6	10.0	10.0	15.5	18.7	25.5	29.3	25.4	..	..	9.1	20.7
Libya	..	..	..	..	..	..	..	..	..	..	..	..	..	..
Morocco	..	..	..	..	..	..	..	..	..	..	..	..	..	..
Tunisia	..	..	..	..	..	..	..	..	..	..	..	..	..	..
ALL AFRICA	..	13.9	13.5	12.3	12.4	12.8	14.3	14.2	16.3	15.4	..	10.4	12.3	14.3

Note: 1996 data are preliminary (see page 3). Nigeria's fiscal data are for federal level only.

7-17. Government expenditure: subsidies and current transfers

	Percentage of total expenditure and lending minus repayments											Annual average		
	1980	1987	1988	1989	1990	1991	1992	1993	1994	1995	1996	75-84	85-89	90-MR
SUB-SAHARAN AFRICA	..	1.1	0.8	0.9	0.9	0.8	0.8	0.7	0.6	1.1	..	2.4	1.1	0.8
excluding South Africa	..	1.7	1.3	1.3	1.3	1.3	1.2	1.1	1.0	1.6	1.3	1.9	1.8	1.3
excl. S. Africa & Nigeria	..	2.0	1.8	1.9	1.9	1.8	1.7	1.5	1.4	1.3	1.7	2.7	2.0	1.6
Angola	..	..	..	..	..	..	..	..	..	..	..	..	..	..
Benin	..	0.0	0.0	9.5	9.9	10.9	13.8	15.6	9.7	9.2	14.0	..	1.9	11.9
Botswana	..	..	..	..	..	..	..	..	..	..	..	..	..	..
Burkina Faso	..	0.0	0.0	0.0	0.0	0.0	0.0	0.0	0.0	0.0	0.0	0.0	0.0	0.0
Burundi	10.9	3.4	4.3	7.0	6.7	6.0	8.0	5.6	7.3	6.4	5.4	10.1	6.5	6.5
Cameroon	11.2	0.0	0.0	0.0	0.0	0.0	0.0	0.0	0.0	0.0	0.0	8.6	0.0	0.0
Cape Verde	..	0.6	1.0	0.7	0.6	0.4	0.2	0.1	0.0	0.1	0.0	1.2	0.7	0.2
Central African Republic	..	..	..	..	..	..	..	..	..	..	..	..	..	..
Chad	..	0.0	0.0	0.0	0.0	0.0	0.0	0.0	0.0	0.0	0.0	..	0.0	0.0
Comoros	..	0.0	0.0	0.0	0.0	0.0	0.0	0.0	0.0	0.0	0.0	0.0	0.0	0.0
Congo	..	2.8	3.5	2.3	1.9	0.0	0.0	0.0	0.0	0.0	0.0	..	2.2	0.3
Côte d'Ivoire	..	0.0	0.0	0.0	0.0	0.0	0.0	3.0	3.7	3.9	7.8	0.0	0.0	2.6
Djibouti	..	..	..	..	..	..	..	..	..	..	..	..	..	..
Equatorial Guinea	..	..	..	..	..	..	..	..	..	..	..	..	..	..
Eritrea	..	0.0	0.0	0.0	..	..	..	..	..	..	0.0	0.0	0.0	0.0
Ethiopia	..	1.4	1.4	1.8	1.7	1.1	1.5	0.1	0.8	1.7	1.5	3.5	1.4	1.2
Gabon	..	0.0	0.0	0.0	0.0	0.0	0.0	0.0	0.0	0.0	0.0	0.0	0.0	0.0
Gambia, The	..	0.0	0.0	0.0	0.0	0.0	..	..	..	..	..	11.8	0.0	0.0
Ghana	17.5	15.7	16.6	18.7	16.3	14.7	15.3	18.0	15.9	14.8	14.5	15.9	10.2	15.6
Guinea	..	6.8	7.8	7.0	3.8	5.4	5.7	5.4	6.4	8.1	8.6	..	6.8	6.2
Guinea-Bissau	..	0.0	..	..	0.0	0.0	0.0	0.0	0.0	0.0	0.0	..	0.0	0.0
Kenya	0.1	1.5	1.3	1.7	1.9	2.2	1.7	0.0	0.0	0.0	0.3	0.3	1.5	0.9
Lesotho	..	..	..	..	..	..	..	..	..	..	..	..	..	..
Liberia	..	..	..	..	..	..	..	..	..	..	..	..	..	..
Madagascar	..	..	..	..	..	..	..	..	..	..	..	0.0	..	..
Malawi	..	0.0	0.0	0.0	0.0	0.0	0.0	0.0	0.0	0.0	0.0	0.0	0.0	0.0
Mali	..	0.0	0.0	0.0	0.0	0.0	0.0	0.0	0.0	0.0	0.0	0.0	0.0	0.0
Mauritania	..	0.0	0.0	0.0	0.0	0.0	0.0	0.0	0.0	0.0	0.0	..	0.0	0.0
Mauritius	..	4.6	3.6	3.2	3.2	2.7	2.6	1.7	0.9	1.4	2.8	19.9	3.6	2.2
Mozambique	17.9	9.3	6.1	4.3	3.9	3.4	3.1	2.3	0.9	0.6	0.5	17.6	14.4	2.1
Namibia	..	5.5	4.3	2.8	2.1	2.7	2.3	3.8	2.4	2.4	2.3	5.4	4.3	2.6
Niger	..	6.9	5.6	5.2	7.4	6.7	6.9	12.9	6.6	4.1	6.0	9.4	6.6	7.3
Nigeria	0.0	0.8	0.0	0.0	0.0	..	..	..	..	2.4	0.2	0.0	1.1	0.9
Rwanda	0.0	8.0	4.3	5.8	9.4	1.6	3.7	0.7	0.0	0.0	0.0	0.6	3.9	2.2
São Tomé and Principe	..	..	0.0	0.0	3.6	2.6	1.9	0.9	1.0	0.0	0.0	..	0.0	1.4
Senegal	..	0.0	0.0	0.0	0.0	0.0	0.0	0.0	3.4	3.1	1.3	0.0	0.0	1.1
Seychelles	..	4.4	6.2	9.4	4.1	4.4	5.3	4.4	4.5	4.7	4.6	3.8	7.2	4.6
Sierra Leone	..	0.9	0.9	0.2	1.9	2.6	2.4	2.3	2.4	2.2	2.4	..	0.7	2.3
Somalia	..	..	..	..	..	..	..	..	..	..	..	..	..	..
South Africa	..	..	..	..	..	..	..	..	..	..	..	..	..	..
Sudan	..	..	..	..	..	..	..	..	..	..	..	..	..	..
Swaziland	..	..	..	..	..	..	..	..	..	..	..	..	..	..
Tanzania	..	0.0	0.0	0.0	0.0	0.0	0.0	0.0	0.0	0.0	0.0	0.0	0.0	0.0
Togo	..	-2.2	-2.3	4.2	4.4	5.1	5.9	4.6	9.0	6.7	5.1	2.3	-0.4	5.8
Uganda	..	0.0	0.0	0.0	0.0	0.0	0.0	0.0	0.0	0.0	0.0	0.0	0.0	0.0
Zaire	..	..	..	..	..	..	..	..	..	..	..	..	..	..
Zambia	13.7	12.2	16.5	13.5	10.9	11.6	2.5	0.6	0.0	0.0	0.0	9.9	11.9	3.6
Zimbabwe	29.3	9.0	6.7	5.6	5.9	7.7	8.3	5.0	1.4	0.5	0.3	23.2	8.5	4.1
NORTH AFRICA	..	..	..	..	..	..	..	..	..	..	..	..	..	..
Algeria	..	0.0	0.0	0.0	0.4	1.0	10.4	9.1	7.8	5.3	..	..	0.0	5.7
Egypt, Arab Republic	..	10.7	10.2	9.7	11.4	12.2	14.2	7.7	5.8	6.6	..	..	10.2	9.7
Libya	..	..	..	..	..	..	..	..	..	..	..	..	..	..
Morocco	..	..	..	..	..	..	..	..	..	..	..	..	..	..
Tunisia	..	..	..	..	..	..	..	..	..	..	..	..	..	..
ALL AFRICA	..	2.0	1.8	1.7	2.0	2.3	4.5	3.4	2.8	2.7	..	0.9	1.6	3.0

Note: 1996 data are preliminary (see page 3). Nigeria's fiscal data are for federal level only.

7-18. Government expenditure: capital and net lending

	Percentage of total expenditure and lending minus repayments											Annual average		
	1980	1987	1988	1989	1990	1991	1992	1993	1994	1995	1996	75-84	85-89	90-MR
SUB-SAHARAN AFRICA	36.9	27.4	26.0	20.7	22.0	21.6	20.9	21.9	22.0	22.4	..	35.7	26.8	21.8
excluding South Africa	..	33.7	32.8	26.9	26.8	27.1	26.0	26.8	28.3	29.3	26.7	38.3	33.5	27.3
excl. S. Africa & Nigeria	..	35.8	31.9	26.6	26.3	25.5	24.5	25.4	27.5	26.7	26.3	38.4	32.4	26.0
Angola	..	..	..	..	..	..	..	..	..	..	..	..	..	..
Benin	..	0.0	0.0	27.6	27.6	28.4	24.3	28.0	34.5	37.5	31.7	40.5	5.5	30.3
Botswana	..	..	..	..	..	..	..	..	..	..	..	..	..	..
Burkina Faso	..	52.8	45.7	36.0	27.8	44.5	43.3	34.4	40.8	46.3	48.3	52.5	45.3	40.8
Burundi	113.6	56.3	44.2	45.9	41.9	43.7	47.9	43.6	29.6	34.5	26.1	119.7	69.8	38.2
Cameroon	32.5	56.6	34.8	23.8	26.2	23.2	15.3	13.8	17.3	6.4	5.5	40.3	43.0	15.4
Cape Verde	..	57.3	51.7	45.9	38.7	47.8	59.4	55.9	60.2	51.5	50.7	67.8	57.5	52.0
Central African Republic	..	42.7	37.1	41.9	41.4	42.4	40.2	41.0	46.0	49.4	21.6	100.0	54.0	40.3
Chad	..	66.4	63.2	59.8	54.9	32.3	45.0	38.0	47.5	50.4	49.1	37.1	61.0	45.3
Comoros	..	54.3	56.9	20.0	18.7	20.4	34.4	15.7	32.6	21.3	21.9	54.8	60.0	23.6
Congo	..	15.3	20.8	18.3	13.3	8.0	4.9	4.6	7.5	9.1	16.5	45.8	24.6	9.1
Côte d'Ivoire	38.3	63.6	43.7	7.8	7.6	8.9	9.5	10.3	16.9	21.2	20.5	57.4	43.3	13.6
Djibouti	..	..	..	..	..	22.5	18.3	16.4	12.9	9.4	11.3	..	..	15.1
Equatorial Guinea	..	..	..	..	..	..	..	..	..	..	..	..	..	..
Eritrea	..	28.7	29.9	30.3	31.8	33.3	34.9	36.5	38.2	..	12.4	28.8	29.8	31.2
Ethiopia	..	34.6	29.9	33.5	25.1	24.6	22.6	36.0	42.2	38.1	35.7	27.2	33.0	32.0
Gabon	..	26.9	21.9	16.7	16.5	19.6	18.9	17.7	22.2	20.9	24.3	100.0	35.4	20.0
Gambia, The	32.0	28.6	28.2	28.4	25.7	21.2	..	..	..	..	..	32.7	30.6	23.4
Ghana	17.5	50.2	53.4	50.2	45.4	46.3	44.6	40.6	44.1	50.3	57.5	14.5	43.8	47.0
Guinea	..	41.7	44.7	46.0	49.8	45.6	47.0	49.4	46.3	48.5	44.9	..	42.5	47.4
Guinea-Bissau	..	62.0	71.3	64.0	63.4	61.5	67.7	64.5	59.1	49.6	56.0	64.3	63.1	60.3
Kenya	29.5	22.9	23.6	24.3	23.7	18.9	17.9	18.7	22.8	20.4	21.9	24.2	21.8	20.6
Lesotho	..	..	..	..	..	..	..	..	..	..	..	..	..	..
Liberia	..	..	..	..	..	..	..	..	..	..	..	..	..	..
Madagascar	40.4	37.3	40.3	49.3	46.6	40.4	41.2	41.1	35.2	35.8	38.0	37.1	39.0	39.8
Malawi	41.8	26.5	29.3	24.4	22.4	20.5	42.0	29.8	31.5	26.3	19.7	37.7	27.7	27.5
Mali	..	39.5	37.5	35.0	35.6	36.1	35.7	38.1	45.9	49.7	49.8	35.7	40.4	41.6
Mauritania	..	31.2	32.9	39.3	33.6	22.4	24.5	41.3	33.0	27.6	27.7	..	30.4	30.0
Mauritius	..	20.7	20.6	19.4	18.3	18.7	19.6	19.1	17.0	17.8	24.0	13.9	19.4	19.2
Mozambique	38.0	42.9	50.5	47.9	50.3	52.3	48.9	49.3	51.7	57.6	54.6	39.0	35.3	52.1
Namibia	..	16.5	20.9	16.5	14.5	15.1	13.7	15.6	13.2	10.3	14.8	23.5	18.4	13.9
Niger	..	41.1	39.8	38.5	39.0	30.4	21.9	21.5	28.6	27.0	29.6	46.9	40.8	28.3
Nigeria	57.4	28.6	34.9	27.6	28.0	31.3	29.7	30.2	30.5	35.7	27.7	60.8	36.1	30.5
Rwanda	0.0	35.4	30.7	34.1	29.4	32.0	30.6	32.2	16.6	39.4	41.7	32.6	34.1	31.7
São Tomé and Principe	..	35.5	36.6	61.1	60.4	58.9	57.4	52.3	57.9	68.9	48.0	..	44.4	57.7
Senegal	8.7	13.3	14.5	13.4	12.2	15.0	23.3	20.3	23.6	26.5	28.2	15.3	13.5	21.3
Seychelles	..	20.8	20.3	29.4	23.4	22.5	19.7	23.1	17.1	16.0	15.5	23.5	24.1	19.6
Sierra Leone	..	16.0	14.3	16.7	17.8	21.2	21.8	25.1	23.4	13.4	19.3	..	15.9	20.3
Somalia	..	..	..	..	..	..	..	..	..	..	..	..	..	..
South Africa	29.9	15.7	13.3	9.2	13.3	11.3	11.4	12.9	10.2	9.6	..	27.2	14.5	11.5
Sudan	..	..	..	..	..	..	..	..	..	..	..	..	..	..
Swaziland	..	..	..	..	..	..	..	..	..	..	..	..	..	..
Tanzania	..	25.9	29.3	16.9	17.7	10.9	16.7	21.5	20.1	14.6	17.3	24.3	22.0	17.0
Togo	49.9	29.6	25.6	26.0	25.7	17.7	16.0	8.8	9.1	15.6	13.2	34.5	30.8	15.1
Uganda	..	37.5	44.2	33.5	43.8	51.5	44.5	55.0	52.2	46.9	44.2	39.7	35.1	48.3
Zaire	..	..	..	..	..	..	..	..	..	..	..	..	..	..
Zambia	10.5	-5.8	6.0	8.7	18.9	15.5	12.1	10.7	12.5	16.4	20.2	11.6	2.2	15.2
Zimbabwe	43.1	15.5	18.3	18.7	18.2	20.3	18.0	16.8	17.6	14.5	12.9	42.7	15.7	16.9
NORTH AFRICA	..	..	..	..	..	..	..	..	..	..	..	..	..	..
Algeria	..	44.1	44.9	35.3	30.8	27.3	28.2	31.3	31.0	29.4	..	56.9	46.5	29.7
Egypt, Arab Republic	..	37.6	41.0	38.4	38.3	34.8	29.0	20.9	18.1	18.2	..	..	39.0	26.6
Libya	..	..	..	..	..	..	..	..	..	..	..	..	..	..
Morocco	..	..	..	..	..	..	..	..	..	..	..	..	..	..
Tunisia	..	..	..	..	..	..	..	..	..	..	..	..	..	..
ALL AFRICA	..	32.3	31.9	26.0	25.9	24.5	23.5	23.9	23.5	23.4	..	38.5	32.5	24.1

Note: 1996 data are preliminary (see page 3). Nigeria's fiscal data are for federal level only.

7-19. Government expenditure: trends in real defense spending

	Index 1980=100											Annual average		
	1980	1987	1988	1989	1990	1991	1992	1993	1994	1995	1996	75-84	85-89	90-MR
SUB-SAHARAN AFRICA	100.0	..	..	..	94.2	..	..	..	90.9	..	..	..	95.9	92.6
excluding South Africa	100.0	..	..	..	91.8	..	..	..	87.8	..	..	..	94.7	89.8
excl. S. Africa & Nigeria	100.0	..	..	..	94.2	..	..	..	95.0	..	..	..	95.9	94.6
Angola	..	..	..	..	..	..	..	..	..	..	..	..	..	..
Benin	..	..	..	..	..	..	..	..	..	..	..	..	..	..
Botswana	100.0	..	..	..	300.2	..	..	..	341.8	..	..	..	100.0	321.0
Burkina Faso	100.0	..	..	..	162.8	..	..	..	292.5	..	..	..	121.5	227.6
Burundi	100.0	..	..	..	..	..	..	..	66.7	..	..	..	95.9	66.7
Cameroon	100.0	..	..	..	..	..	..	..	102.9	..	..	..	190.5	102.9
Cape Verde	..	..	..	..	..	..	..	..	..	..	..	..	..	..
Central African Republic	100.0	..	..	..	133.9	..	..	..	249.4	..	..	..	109.2	191.6
Chad	..	..	..	..	..	..	..	..	..	..	..	..	..	..
Comoros	..	..	..	..	..	..	..	..	..	..	..	..	..	..
Congo	100.0	..	..	..	89.4	..	..	..	38.3	..	..	..	125.2	63.9
Côte d'Ivoire	100.0	..	..	..	89.1	..	..	..	87.8	..	..	..	81.0	88.5
Djibouti	..	..	..	..	..	..	..	..	..	..	..	..	..	..
Equatorial Guinea	..	..	..	..	..	..	..	..	..	..	..	..	..	..
Eritrea	..	..	..	..	..	..	..	..	..	..	..	..	..	..
Ethiopia	..	..	..	..	..	..	..	..	..	..	..	..	..	..
Gabon	100.0	..	..	..	116.8	..	..	..	151.2	..	..	..	162.1	134.0
Gambia, The	..	..	..	..	..	..	..	..	..	..	..	..	..	..
Ghana	100.0	..	..	..	56.3	..	..	..	76.8	..	..	..	99.8	66.5
Guinea	..	..	..	..	..	..	..	..	..	..	..	..	..	..
Guinea-Bissau	..	..	..	..	..	..	..	..	..	..	..	..	..	..
Kenya	100.0	..	..	..	81.2	..	..	..	36.6	..	..	..	60.6	58.9
Lesotho	..	..	..	..	..	..	..	..	..	..	..	..	..	..
Liberia	100.0	..	..	..	..	..	..	..	..	..	..	..	69.3	..
Madagascar	100.0	..	..	..	51.9	..	..	..	41.9	..	..	..	76.3	46.9
Malawi	100.0	..	..	..	23.0	..	..	..	21.1	..	..	..	59.0	22.1
Mali	..	..	..	..	..	..	..	..	..	..	..	..	..	..
Mauritania	..	..	..	..	..	..	..	..	..	..	..	..	..	..
Mauritius	100.0	..	..	..	110.7	..	..	..	149.5	..	..	..	56.8	130.1
Mozambique	..	..	..	..	..	..	..	..	..	..	..	..	..	..
Namibia	..	..	..	..	..	..	..	..	..	..	..	..	..	..
Niger	100.0	..	..	..	235.6	..	..	..	187.4	..	..	..	83.2	211.5
Nigeria	100.0	..	..	..	21.0	..	..	..	16.8	..	..	..	40.1	18.9
Rwanda	100.0	..	..	..	94.2	..	..	..	..	..	..	..	98.3	94.2
São Tomé and Principe	..	..	..	..	..	..	..	..	..	..	..	..	..	..
Senegal	100.0	..	..	..	109.8	..	..	..	102.2	..	..	..	93.6	106.0
Seychelles	..	..	..	..	..	..	..	..	..	..	..	..	..	..
Sierra Leone	100.0	..	..	..	23.4	..	..	..	158.2	..	..	..	122.1	90.8
Somalia	100.0	..	..	..	..	..	..	..	..	..	..	..	34.1	..
South Africa	100.0	..	..	..	128.4	..	..	..	94.1	..	..	..	143.0	111.2
Sudan	100.0	..	..	..	239.2	..	..	..	..	..	..	..	140.8	239.2
Swaziland	100.0	..	..	..	110.9	..	..	..	131.2	..	..	..	61.0	121.0
Tanzania	..	..	..	..	..	..	..	..	..	..	..	..	..	..
Togo	100.0	..	..	..	156.1	..	..	..	..	..	..	..	124.1	156.1
Uganda	100.0	..	..	..	11.8	..	..	..	40.5	..	..	..	73.0	26.2
Zaire	100.0	..	..	..	47.6	..	..	..	0.0	..	..	..	184.3	23.8
Zambia	..	..	..	..	..	..	..	..	..	..	..	..	..	..
Zimbabwe	100.0	..	..	..	85.1	..	..	..	52.2	..	..	..	68.5	68.6
NORTH AFRICA	100.0	..	..	..	86.1	..	..	..	181.3	..	..	..	108.4	133.7
Algeria	100.0	..	..	..	148.2	..	..	..	267.1	..	..	..	111.2	207.6
Egypt, Arab Republic	100.0	..	..	..	61.9	..	..	..	..	..	..	..	108.4	61.9
Libya	..	..	..	..	..	..	..	..	..	..	..	..	..	..
Morocco	100.0	..	..	..	86.1	..	..	..	95.5	..	..	..	82.3	90.8
Tunisia	..	..	..	..	..	..	..	..	..	..	..	..	..	..
ALL AFRICA	100.0	..	..	..	91.8	..	..	..	94.8	..	..	..	97.1	93.3

Note: Nigeria's fiscal data are for federal level only.

7-20. Government expenditure: real per capita education spending

	Constant 1987 U.S. dollars											Annual average		
	1980	1987	1988	1989	1990	1991	1992	1993	1994	1995	1996	75-84	85-89	90-MR
SUB-SAHARAN AFRICA	..	..	..	..	..	..	..	..	..	..	..	..	..	..
excluding South Africa	..	..	..	..	..	..	..	..	..	..	..	..	..	..
excl. S. Africa & Nigeria	..	..	..	..	..	..	..	..	..	..	..	..	..	..
Angola	..	..	..	..	..	..	..	..	..	..	..	..	..	..
Benin	..	..	..	..	..	..	..	..	..	..	..	11.6	..	..
Botswana	67.9	100.9	115.7	111.8	132.7	142.8	153.5	170.1	164.4	..	..	60.7	98.5	152.7
Burkina Faso	4.4	4.8	7.2	6.8	6.9	7.6	7.9	7.7	..	..	..	4.3	5.8	7.5
Burundi	..	..	..	..	..	..	..	..	..	..	..	7.6	..	..
Cameroon	16.9	34.3	36.1	24.1	..	..	..	21.5	..	..	..	21.1	32.3	21.5
Cape Verde	..	..	..	..	..	..	..	..	..	..	..	..	..	..
Central African Republic	..	..	..	..	..	..	..	..	..	..	..	17.2	..	..
Chad	..	..	..	..	..	..	..	..	..	..	..	..	..	..
Comoros	..	44.1	..	..	..	..	..	..	..	..	..	51.1	44.1	..
Congo	..	..	..	..	..	..	..	..	..	..	..	56.5	..	..
Côte d'Ivoire	..	..	..	..	..	..	..	..	..	..	..	..	..	..
Djibouti	..	..	..	..	..	..	..	..	..	..	..	..	..	..
Equatorial Guinea	..	..	..	..	..	..	..	..	..	..	..	..	..	..
Eritrea	..	..	..	..	..	..	..	..	..	..	..	..	..	..
Ethiopia	..	4.3	4.3	4.3	4.1	3.3	3.4	..	..	..	..	4.3	4.1	3.6
Gabon	..	..	..	..	..	..	..	..	..	..	..	..	..	..
Gambia, The	10.4	..	..	..	7.6	..	..	..	..	..	..	9.1	..	7.6
Ghana	10.4	12.3	13.5	13.1	13.1	12.9	16.9	19.9	..	..	..	12.2	12.0	15.7
Guinea	..	..	..	..	..	..	..	..	..	..	..	..	..	..
Guinea-Bissau	..	5.0	..	2.7	..	..	..	..	..	..	..	10.7	6.0	..
Kenya	18.4	22.2	22.5	23.3	21.5	22.4	19.9	18.0	..	..	..	17.7	21.1	20.5
Lesotho	..	21.8	25.6	23.2	24.6	36.2	31.3	..	..	..	..	16.1	20.5	30.7
Liberia	20.2	18.6	..	..	..	..	..	..	..	..	..	24.7	20.1	..
Madagascar	..	..	5.5	5.6	5.9	5.7	5.6	6.0	4.2	4.0	..	..	5.6	5.2
Malawi	5.3	5.0	5.5	..	..	..	..	..	..	..	..	5.2	5.4	..
Mali	8.6	6.6	6.6	..	..	..	..	..	..	..	..	7.8	6.5	..
Mauritania	..	..	..	..	..	..	..	..	..	..	..	..	..	..
Mauritius	62.3	47.6	57.3	68.8	68.7	71.6	78.2	77.0	90.1	99.9	..	57.3	56.7	80.9
Mozambique	..	..	..	..	..	..	..	..	..	..	..	..	..	..
Namibia	..	..	..	..	..	..	..	..	..	..	..	..	..	..
Niger	15.3	..	..	..	..	..	..	..	..	..	..	11.2	..	..
Nigeria	..	1.8	..	..	..	..	..	..	..	..	..	8.1	2.6	..
Rwanda	..	..	..	..	..	..	..	..	..	..	..	..	..	..
São Tomé and Principe	..	..	..	..	..	..	..	..	..	..	..	..	..	..
Senegal	35.2	..	..	..	..	..	..	..	..	..	..	31.8	..	..
Seychelles	..	..	..	..	..	..	..	373.6	381.1	296.6	..	..	..	350.4
Sierra Leone	..	..	..	..	1.8	..	..	..	..	..	..	7.1	..	1.8
Somalia	..	..	..	..	..	..	..	..	..	..	..	2.7	..	..
South Africa	..	..	..	..	..	..	..	..	..	..	..	..	..	..
Sudan	15.1	..	..	..	..	..	..	..	..	..	..	10.9	..	..
Swaziland	46.1	51.4	44.5	45.4	..	..	..	..	..	..	..	42.6	48.3	..
Tanzania	..	..	..	..	..	..	..	..	..	..	..	5.2	2.8	..
Togo	..	24.1	..	..	..	..	..	..	..	..	..	21.7	20.5	..
Uganda	..	..	..	..	..	..	..	..	..	..	..	6.1	6.9	..
Zaire	5.6	..	..	..	..	..	1.1	0.0	0.0	0.1	..	5.7	..	0.3
Zambia	15.8	8.6	7.7	7.9	7.2	8.8	6.8	5.5	7.6	6.5	..	19.9	9.5	7.1
Zimbabwe	34.0	53.9	52.4	55.4	..	..	..	..	..	..	..	35.4	52.5	..
NORTH AFRICA	..	39.2	41.4	42.8	42.8	44.5	44.2	..	..	..	..	37.2	42.4	43.8
Algeria	..	..	..	..	..	..	..	..	..	..	..	..	..	..
Egypt, Arab Republic	..	35.0	36.4	36.3	35.0	38.1	36.9	40.3	..	..	..	30.2	38.3	37.6
Libya	..	..	..	..	..	..	..	..	..	..	..	..	..	..
Morocco	44.8	39.8	43.8	46.9	48.0	47.2	48.4	..	..	..	..	42.6	42.9	47.9
Tunisia	63.3	64.3	65.9	72.5	77.1	77.7	78.9	..	..	..	..	66.5	67.7	77.9
ALL AFRICA	..	..	..	..	..	..	..	..	..	..	..	..	..	..

Note: Nigeria's fiscal data are for federal level only.

Figure 7-1. Government deficit/surplus as percentage of GDP, 1990-96*

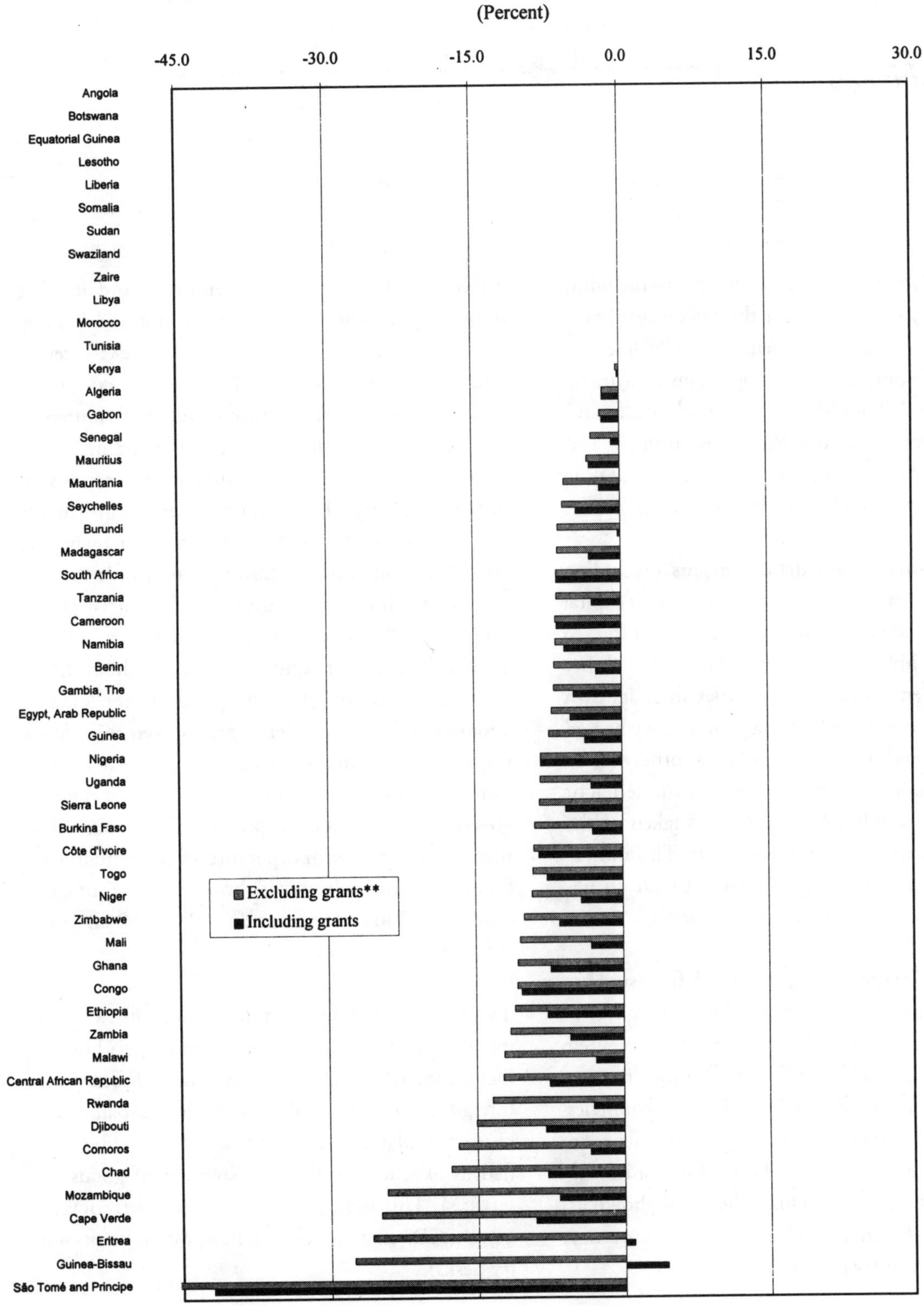

* Or most recent year available.

** Sorted by deficit excluding grants.

Note: Nigeria's ratios are distorted because of official exchange rate over-valuation affecting oil exports and oil value added.

Technical Notes

Tables

Table 7-1. Government deficit/surplus (including grants). Overall surplus/deficit is the difference between total revenue plus grants (as defined in *GFS* line A-I) and total expenditures and lending minus repayments (as defined in *GFS* line C-I). It represents the net financing requirement of the consolidated government. This indicator is shown as a percentage of current GDP in national currency (World Bank country desks).

Table 7-2. Government deficit/surplus (excluding grants). This is calculated as above, except that capital grants are excluded from receipts (as defined in *GFS* line A-II, less line C-I). It is a measure of the ability of a government to fund its activities from its own resources. Because some budgetary grants may be tied to certain expenditures that would not otherwise be incurred, excluding grants may overstate the deficit or understate the surplus if no account is taken of the expenditures dependent on these grants. This indicator is shown as a percentage of current GDP in national currency (World Bank country desks).

Table 7-3. Government primary deficit/surplus (–/+). The primary deficit or surplus is the government deficit or surplus including grants (as presented in Table 7-1) minus interest expenditures on both domestic and foreign debt (Table 7-5). In countries with large government interest payments, this ratio may provide a more reliable indicator for monitoring fiscal stabilization efforts. This indicator is shown as a percentage of current GDP in national currency (World Bank country desks).

Table 7-4. Government expenditure and lending minus repayments. Total expenditure and lending minus repayments (as defined in *GFS* line C-I) represents the government's total outlays for current or capital purposes. Expenditure includes all nonrepayable payments by the government. Lending minus repayments comprises government transactions in debt and equity claims upon others, acquired for purposes of public policy rather than for managing government liquidity or earning a return. It consists of gross lending and acquisition of financial equity minus repayments of past government lending and government sales of equities. (This definition differs from the concept of lending minus repayments adopted in the SNA, which is gross government lending minus repayments of past government lending minus net government borrowing.) In determining a government's deficit or surplus, lending minus repayments is grouped with expenditures rather than with financing. This indicator is shown as a percentage of current GDP in national currency (World Bank country desks).

Table 7-5. Government interest payments. Government interest payments (as defined in *GFS* line C2) include interest on all borrowings, both domestic and foreign, but exclude commission charges paid for assistance in placement of debt (which would be classified as expenditure for the payment of goods and services). This indicator is shown as a percentage of current GDP in national currency (World Bank country desks).

Table 7-6. Government revenue (excluding grants). Government revenue less grants (as defined in *GFS* line A-II) refers to current revenues (tax and nontax) and capital revenues, such as proceeds from the sale of real assets, including land. They do not include grant receipts from other governments or international organizations. This indicator is shown as a percentage of current GDP in national currency (World Bank country desks).

Table 7-7. Grants to government. These are unrequited, nonrepayable, noncompulsory government receipts from other governments or international institutions (as defined in *GFS* line A-II). Grants of goods and services in kind are excluded. This indicator is shown as a percentage of current GDP in national currency (World Bank country desks).

Table 7-8. Foreign financing. Includes all government financing transactions except grants (as defined in *GFS* line D-III) with nonresident individuals, enterprises, governments, international organizations, and other entities. It may be affected by trading in outstanding government securities between residents and nonresidents. The data also reflect changes, resulting from transactions but not revaluations, in government holdings of foreign exchange, deposits in nonresident financial institutions, and securities issued by nonresident entities held by government for liquidity purposes (reserves). This indicator is shown as a percentage of current GDP in national currency (World Bank country desks).

Table 7-9. Taxes on income and profits. These taxes (as defined in *GFS* line A1) are levied on the actual or presumptive net income of individuals and profits of enterprises. Also included are taxes levied on capital gains that are realized on land sales, securities, and other assets. This indicator is shown as a percentage of total revenue (as defined in *GFS* line A-II) (World Bank country desks).

Table 7-10. Taxes on international trade and transactions. Include import duties, export duties, profits of export or import monopolies remitted to government, and monopoly profits of monetary authorities made in foreign exchange transactions as well as taxes levied on the sale of foreign exchange (as defined in *GFS* line A6). This indicator is shown as a percentage of total revenue (as defined in *GFS* line A-II) (World Bank country desks).

Table 7-11. Indirect taxes. These are sales and excise taxes and duties (as defined in *GFS* line A-IV less A1). This indicator is shown as a percentage of total revenue (as defined in *GFS* line A-II) (World Bank country desks).

Table 7-12. Nontax revenue, excluding grants. This is all nonrepayable government receipts, other than compulsory unrequited receipts (taxes) and revenue from capital sales or government grants, plus all fines and penalties other than for noncompliance with taxes (as defined in *GFS* line A-V). For some mineral-exporting countries in Africa, this category is quite large, since royalties on the extraction of minerals, such as petroleum in Egypt and Nigeria and bauxite in Guinea, make up significant portions of total government revenues. This indicator is shown as a percentage of total revenue (as defined in *GFS* line A-II) (World Bank country desks).

Table 7-13. Government expenditure: wages and salaries. Are payments in cash, but not in kind, to employees in return for services, before withholding taxes and employee contributions to social security and pension funds are deducted (as defined in *GFS* line C1.1). Included are basic wages and salaries; pay for overtime, weekends, and nights; cost of living allowances; local allowances and expatriation allowances; and similar compensation. Reimbursement to employees for expenses incurred as part of their employment are excluded. This indicator is shown as a percentage of total expenditure and lending minus repayments (as defined in *GFS* line C-I) (World Bank country desks).

Table 7-14. Government expenditure: trends in real wages and salaries. Includes expenditure on wages and salaries as discussed above (as defined in *GFS* line C1.1), deflated by the CPI. For most countries the trend is shown in index numbers beginning with 100 in 1987 (World Bank country desks).

Table 7-15. Government expenditure: other goods and services. Includes expenditures for all goods and services (except fixed capital assets and wages and salaries) bought on the market, goods and services to be used to produce fixed capital assets, strategic or emergency stocks, stocks held by market regulatory organizations, and land and intangible assets. This category encompasses purchases of materials, office supplies, fuel and lighting, travel services, and payment of rent, as well as payments in kind to certain civil servants (as defined in *GFS* line C1.3). This indicator is presented as a percentage of total expenditure and lending minus repayments (as defined in *GFS* lines C-I) (World Bank country desks).

Table 7-16. Government expenditure: interest payments. Are payments for the use of all borrowed money, excluding commission charges paid for assistance in placing debt, which would be classified as expenditures for payment of other goods and services (as defined in *GFS* line C2). This indicator is presented as a percentage of total expenditure and lending minus repayments (as defined in *GFS* lines C-I) (World Bank country desks).

Table 7-17. Government expenditure: subsidies and current transfers. Are all unrequited, nonrepayable government payments for current purposes (as defined in *GFS* line C3). Transfers for capital purposes (that is, to permit the recipient to acquire capital assets) and transfers in kind are excluded. This indicator is presented as a percentage of total expenditure and lending minus repayments (as defined in *GFS* line C-I) (World Bank country desks).

Table 7-18. Government expenditure: capital and net lending. Represents payments for acquiring land, buildings, and other nonfinancial assets to be used for more than one year in the process of production, including transfers for capital assets as well as net lending (as defined in *GFS* lines C-IV plus C-V). This indicator is presented as a percentage of total expenditure and lending minus repayments (as defined in *GFS* line C-I) (World Bank country desks).

Table 7-19. Government expenditure: trends in real defense spending. Real defense spending has been calculated by deflating defense spending in current prices national currency (IMF, as defined in *GFS* line B2) by the national GDP deflator (Table 3-1). The results are presented in the form of 1980 base indexes.

Table 7-20. Government expenditure: real per capita education spending. Presents education spending (IMF, as defined in *GFS* line B4) deflated by the national GDP deflator (Table 3-1) and divided by total population (Table 2-1). The result is converted into 1987 US dollars by using the 1987 local currency/US dollar conversion factor (Table 3-6).

Figure

The following indicators have been used to derive the figure in this chapter.

Figure 7-1. Government deficit/surplus (Tables 7-1 and 7-2).

Methodology used for regional aggregations and period averages in chapter 7

	Aggregations[a]		*Period averages*[b]
Table	*(6)*	*(7)*	*(1)*
7-1	x		x
7-2	x		x
7-3	x		x
7-4	x		x
7-5	x		x
7-6	x		x
7-7	x		x
7-8	x		x
7-9	x		x
7-10	x		x
7-11	x		x
7-12	x		x
7-13	x		x
7-14		x	x
7-15	x		x
7-16	x		x
7-17	x		x
7-18	x		x
7-19		x	x
7-20	x		x

Note: Regional aggregations are shown in the rows for Sub-Saharan Africa, North Africa, and All Africa. Period averages are shown in the last three columns. This table shows only the methodologies used in this chapter. **For aggregation purposes, all data used in this chapter were converted to US dollars, using the conversion factors shown in Table 3-6.**

a. Regional aggregations: (1) simple total; (2) simple total of the first indicator divided by the simple total of the second indicator (same country coverage); (3) simple total of the gap-filled indicator; (4) simple total of the gap-filled main indicator divided by the simple total of the gap-filled secondary indicator; (5) simple total of the first gap-filled main indicator less the simple total of the second gap-filled main indicator, all divided by the simple total of the secondary indicator; (6) weighted total; (7) median; (8) no aggregation; (9) simple arithmetic mean.

b. Period averages: (1) arithmetic mean (using the same series as shown in the table, i.e., ratio if the rest of the table is shown as ratio, level if the rest of the table is shown as level, growth rate if the rest of the table is shown as growth rate); (2) least-squares growth rate (using main indicator); (3) least-squares growth rate (using main indicator in constant terms, with the rest of the table in current terms).

8

Agriculture

Agriculture is one of Africa's important sectors. African agriculture has two major components: food production and export commodities. Food production, including meat, is the livelihood for most Africans. Export crops provide many African countries with their main source of foreign exchange and thus the capacity to import, invest, and develop. The information in this chapter provides a basis for assessing recent trends in producer prices, aggregate agricultural production and trade, cereal imports, and food aid in Africa.

The data in this chapter are estimates based on a variety of sources whose quality and reliability vary from country to country and year to year. Furthermore, production and export data are probably underestimated for two reasons. It is difficult to estimate production levels of staple food crops, especially roots and tubers, when much of the output is consumed directly by farmers, rather than marketed. Moreover, parallel market activity, including trade, may not be fully accounted for.

8-1. Nominal producer prices

	ategory	1980	1983	1984	1985	1986	1987	1988	1989	1990	1991	1992	1993
		Local currency per kilogram											
ALGERIA													
Wheat (hard)	F1	1.2	1.4	1.6	2.0	2.2	2.2	2.7	3.7	4.6	4.9	9.9	..
Citrus (oranges)	F2	..	..	..	..	..	..	..	..	..	..	..	..
Dates	F3	4.5	6.5	7.0	10.0	11.3	11.5	..	..	..	..	..	..
Barley	NT1	0.8	0.8	1.0	1.4	1.4	1.7	1.7	2.3	2.3	2.3	4.7	..
Potatoes	NT2	1.3	1.9	1.9	2.5	2.6	2.8	2.7	3.0	3.3	3.3	6.5	..
ANGOLA													
Coffee	X1	..	..	67.0	67.0	67.0	67.0	67.0	67.0	135.0	158.0	..	..
Maize	F1	..	..	10.0	10.0	10.0	10.0	11.5	11.5	11.5	100.0	..	..
Millet	F2	4.0	10.0	10.0	10.0	10.0	10.0	10.0	10.0	10.0	100.0	..	..
Wheat	F3	4.5	17.5	17.5	17.5	17.5	17.5	17.5	17.5	17.5	200.0	..	..
Cassava	NT1	..	5.0	5.0	5.0	5.0	5.0	7.7	7.7	7.7	150.0	..	..
Sweet potatoes	NT2	2.5	..	7.5	7.5	7.5	7.5	14.0	14.0	14.0	200.0	..	..
BENIN													
Cotton (seed cotton)	X1	65.0	100.0	100.0	110.0	110.0	100.0	105.0	95.0	100.0	100.0	100.0	94.8
Palm kernels	X2	35.0	45.0	60.0	60.0	20.0	20.0	30.0	30.0	30.0	35.0	35.0	..
Maize	F1	40.0	..	94.0	83.0	65.0	68.0	64.0	55.0	85.0	58.0	62.0	53.0
Sorghum	F2	46.0	..	112.0	81.0	65.0	72.0	67.0	60.0	60.0	63.0	65.0	55.0
Cassava	NT1	30.0	..	66.0	56.0	15.0	20.0	16.0	16.0	16.0	17.0	17.5	18.2
Yams	NT2	32.0	..	78.0	87.0	50.0	58.0	49.0	49.0	49.0	49.0	50.0	52.0
BOTSWANA													
Groundnuts (in shell)	X1	0.2	269	273	..	0.7	0.7	0.7	0.7	0.7	1.1	1.0	1.4
Sorghum	F1	0.1	201	264	0.3	0.3	0.3	0.3	0.3	0.3	0.3	0.4	0.4
Maize	F2	0.1	185	230	0.2	0.3	0.3	0.3	0.3	0.3	0.3	0.3	0.4
BURKINA FASO													
Cotton (seed cotton)	X1	55.0	70.0	90.0	96.9	97.2	89.7	94.4	94.6	95.0	..	..	..
Groundnuts (in shell)	X2	54.0	92.0	92.0	80.0	50.0	60.0	55.0	60.0	60.0	..	..	..
Sesame seed	X3	70.0	96.0	96.0	95.0	80.0	55.0	65.0	85.0	80.0	..	..	..
Sorghum	F1	45.0	64.0	80.0	75.0	40.0	45.0	40.0	45.0	60.0	..	..	..
Millet	F2	45.0	66.0	80.0	75.0	40.0	45.0	40.0	45.0	60.0	..	..	..
Maize	F3	45.0	60.0	85.0	80.0	45.0	55.0	45.0	50.0	65.0	..	..	..
BURUNDI													
Coffee (green)	X1	..	..	..	..	..	..	..	..	..	..	..	..
Tea	X2	..	..	..	..	..	..	..	..	..	..	..	..
Cotton (seed)	X3	36.1	45.3	46.6	50.9	51.9	52.6	55.3	57.8	60.2	62.4	64.4	
Maize	F1	25.0	28.9	..	..	..	..	..	..	..	..	..	..
Sorghum	F2	20.0	19.8	..	..	..	..	..	..	..	..	..	..
Rice	F3	25.0	25.0	..	..	..	..	..	..	..	..	..	..
Millet	F4	20.0	19.8	..	..	..	..	..	..	..	..	..	..
Bananas	NT1	..	..	..	..	..	..	..	..	..	..	..	..
Cassava	NT1	10.9	7.9	..	..	..	..	..	..	..	..	..	..
CAMEROON													
Coffee (Arabica)	X1	320.0	370.0	430.0	450.0	475.0	475.0	475.0	458.0	186.0	165.0	..	..
Cocoa (grade 1, superior)	X2	300.0	370.0	410.0	420.0	420.0	420.0	42.0	250.0	220.0	200.0	200.0	200.0
Cotton (seed cotton, nonselected)	X3	70.0	105.0	117.0	130.0	130.0	130.0	140.0	95.0	95.0	95.0	85.0	..
Maize	F1	60.0	..	..	..	83.2	76.8	82.4	57.0	51.7	..	..	..
Sorghum	F2	40.0	..	..	..	38.9	60.6	47.2	43.0	77.9	..	..	..
Millet	F3	40.0	..	..	..	38.9	60.6	47.2	43.0	77.9	..	..	..
Rice (paddy)	F4	105.0	..	..	..	91.0	64.7	77.5	82.7	53.5	..	..	..
Cassava	NT1	19.0	..	..	..	48.0	46.6	41.7	..	..	..	..	..
Plantains	NT2	25.0	50.0	..	..	45.3	46.7	47.3	..	54.0	..	..	..
CENTRAL AFRICAN REPUBLIC													
Coffee (Robusta, cherries)	X1	120.0	135.0	135.0	135.0	135.0	135.0	190.0	..	..	..	..	..
Cotton (seed cotton)	X2	60.0	80.0	90.0	100.0	100.0	100.0	100.0	100.0	..	..	..	..
Sorghum	F1	..	40.0	60.0	115.9	103.5	128.3	107.7	..	..	..	..	..
Maize	F2	40.0	50.0	60.0	83.3	65.3	67.7	104.3	..	..	..	..	..
Groundnuts (unshelled)	F3	35.0	45.0	55.0	..	..	..	..	..	..	..	..	..
Cassava	NT1	30.0	35.0	40.0	82.0	76.2	89.5	57.5	..	..	..	..	..
Yams	NT2	25.0	25.0	25.0	97.4	107.1	91.0	124.5	..	..	..	..	..
CHAD													
Cotton (seed cotton, avg. white/yellow)	X1	..	80.0	100.0	98.6	99.0	99.0	97.0	88.0	88.0	88.0	77.0	89.0
Millet	F2	..	..	..	..	31.0	31.0	48.0	47.0	52.0	62.0	41.0	41.0
Groundnuts	F3	..	68.0	..	95.2	57.0	46.0	44.0	46.0	48.0	70.0	67.0	77.0

8-1. Nominal producer prices (continued)

		Local currency per kilogram											
	ategory	*1980*	*1983*	*1984*	*1985*	*1986*	*1987*	*1988*	*1989*	*1990*	*1991*	*1992*	*1993*
COMOROS													
Vanilla	X1	1,150.0	..	..	..	..	..	..	..	..	..	..	..
Cloves	X2	1,250.0	..	..	..	..	..	..	..	..	..	..	..
Ylang Ylang (flower)	X3	45.0	55.0	55.0	80.0	90.0	65.0	65.0	..	..	..	..	
Copra	X4	40.0	..	..	..	..	..	..	..	..	..	..	..
Bananas	F1	50.0	..	..	..	..	..	..	..	..	..	..	..
Cassava	NT1	40.0	..	..	..	..	..	..	..	..	..	..	..
CONGO													
Coffee	X1	146.0	135.0	135.0	148.0	215.0	215.0	115.0	115.0	115.0	115.0	115.0	115.0
Cocoa	X2	134.8	170.0	170.0	190.0	190.0	240.0	108.0	108.0	88.0	88.0	88.0	88.0
Maize	F1	43.0	65.0	68.0	73.0	73.0	85.0	60.0	60.0	60.0	60.0	100.0	100.0
Cassava	NT1	..	..	..	..	..	..	..	..	..	..	..	..
Plantains	NT2	..	..	..	..	..	..	..	..	..	..	..	..
COTE D'IVOIRE													
Coffee (Robusta, green)	X1	310.6	306.1	358.3	354.3	399.5	400.0	400.0	..	..	..	..	..
Cocoa (beans)	X2	300.0	350.0	375.0	400.0	400.0	400.0	400.0	..	..	..	..	..
Palm oil	X3	..	135.0	230.0	180.0	..	..	..	..	..	..	..	..
Rice (paddy)	F1	50.0	68.0	80.0	80.0	84.0	..	..	..	..	..	..	..
Maize	F2	68.0	65.0	72.0	60.0	76.0	..	..	..	..	..	..	..
Cassava	NT1	49.0	40.0	43.0	36.0	46.0	..	..	..	..	..	..	..
Yams	NT2	59.0	87.0	93.0	75.0	99.9	..	..	..	..	..	..	..
EGYPT													
Cotton	X1	0.3	0.4	0.5	0.6	0.6	0.7	0.9	1.3	1.7	2.0	..	..
Rice (96% humidity)	X2	0.1	0.1	0.1	0.2	0.2	0.2	0.3	0.4	0.4	0.4	..	..
Wheat (94% humidity)	F1	0.1	0.1	0.1	0.2	0.2	0.2	0.2	0.4	0.5	0.5	..	..
Sugarcane	F2	0.0	0.0	0.0	0.0	0.0	0.0	0.0	0.1	0.1	0.1	..	..
Broadbeans	NT1	0.1	..	..	..	..	..	..	..	..	..	..	..
EQUATORIAL GUINEA													
Cocoa (first grade dried beans)	X1	..	..	..	..	..	..	..	..	..	..	..	..
Coffee (Robusta, cherry)	X2	..	..	..	..	..	..	..	..	..	..	..	..
Cassava	NT1	..	..	..	..	..	..	..	..	..	..	..	..
Plantains	NT2	..	..	..	..	..	..	..	..	..	..	..	..
ETHIOPIA													
Coffee (Arabica, beans)	X1	2.6	2.6	3.0	2.9	3.7	4.1	4.2	4.2	4.2	3.1	3.1	..
Sesame seed	X2	..	1.4	1.4	1.3	1.1	1.1	1.3	1.3	1.4	1.7	..	..
Sorghum (mixed)	F1	..	0.4	0.8	0.8	0.5	0.4	0.5	0.5	0.5	0.8	0.8	..
Maize	F2	..	0.3	0.6	0.7	0.5	0.4	0.4	0.5	0.4	0.6	0.7	..
Barley (non-white mixed)	NT1	..	0.4	0.7	0.8	0.5	0.4	0.5	0.5	0.5	0.7	0.9	..
GABON													
Cocoa (first quality)	X1	320.0	375.0	..	..	..	..	..	..	..	..	..	..
Coffee (merchant, processed)	X2	180.0	180.0	..	..	..	..	..	..	..	..	..	..
Maize	F1	..	..	..	..	..	..	..	..	..	..	..	..
Cassava	NT1	139.5	150.0	..	..	..	..	..	..	..	..	..	..
Yams	NT3	124.5	127.5	..	..	..	..	..	..	..	..	..	..
GAMBIA, THE													
Groundnuts (unshelled)	X1	0.5	0.5	0.6	1.1	1.8	1.5	1.1	1.5	1.8	..	..	..
Cotton (seed cotton)	X2	0.5	0.6	0.7	1.1	1.3	..	..	..	..	..	..	..
Palm kernels	X3	0.3	0.3	0.3	0.3	0.3	..	..	..	..	..	..	..
Millet	F1	0.5	1.0	0.8	1.0	1.1	1.2	1.2	1.5	1.9	1.9	..	..
Rice (paddy)	F2	..	1.5	..	..	..	2.1	2.1	3.4	2.8	2.7	..	..
Maize	F3	..	..	1.1	1.1	..	1.2	1.2	1.4	2.1	1.9	..	..
Sorghum	F4	0.3	0.4	0.4	0.8	0.9	..	..	1.2	..	1.9	..	..
GHANA													
Cocoa	X1	4.0	14.0	26.7	52.2	80.3	101.3	153.8	..	..	..	..	..
Maize	F1	4.1	38.6	18.0	20.0	25.0	42.0	48.0	35.8	86.9	69.5	83.5	93.7
Millet	F2	5.3	..	..	..	24.2	36.0	83.3	89.7	77.9	113.5	141.4	149.9
Groundnuts	F3	8.4	72.3	..	..	..	..	..	..	..	..	..	..
Cassava	NT1	1.5	..	..	..	8.8	10.8	12.9	10.0	10.0	15.8	22.5	25.3
Plantains	NT2	1.9	22.0	..	..	15.0	18.6	43.0	45.9	27.8	26.8	35.5	91.4

8-1. Nominal producer prices (continued)

	ategory	Local currency per kilogram											
		1980	*1983*	*1984*	*1985*	*1986*	*1987*	*1988*	*1989*	*1990*	*1991*	*1992*	*1993*
GUINEA													
Coffee (Robusta)	X1	49.0	45.0	55.0	70.0	400.0	400.0	..	..	..	..	..	..
Palm kernels	X2	6.0	7.0	10.0	13.0	60.0	60.0	..	..	..	..	..	..
Rice (paddy)	F1	9.0	12.0	12.0	15.0	..	..	..	..	..	..	..	..
Maize	F2	7.0	10.0	10.0	13.0	..	..	..	..	..	..	..	..
Groundnuts (unshelled)	F3	11.0	15.0	15.0	20.0	..	..	..	..	..	..	..	..
Cassava	NT1	5.0	7.0	7.0	7.0	..	..	..	..	..	..	..	..
Plantains	NT2	4.5	14.0	14.0	14.0	..	..	..	..	..	..	..	..
GUINEA-BISSAU													
Cashew nuts	X1	..	9.5	17.5	28.5	38.5	125.0	230.0	350.0	450.0	550.0	1,000.0	3,500.0
Groundnuts (unshelled, grade 1)	X2	..	9.2	15.5	25.0	32.5	40.0	80.0	140.0	225.0	275.0	500.0	7,778.7
Palm kernels	X3	..	6.0	11.5	19.0	..	..	..	..	..	..	..	..
Rice (paddy, grade 1)	F1	8.5	9.5	14.5	24.0	37.5	50.0	85.0	180.0	225.0	400.0	650.0	1,100.0
Sorghum	F2	..	8.5	13.5	21.0	..	..	..	..	..	..	..	..
Maize (grade 1)	F3	..	8.5	13.5	21.0	..	..	..	..	..	..	..	740.0
KENYA													
Coffee (Arabica, washed bean, grade 1-6)	X1	26.4	34.9	38.4	46.6	54.8	34.1	43.0	43.1	36.4	46.5	49.4	98.9
Tea	X2	15.9	21.8	51.8	33.7	33.8	25.0	26.8	27.2	35.2	38.5	47.5	92.4
Sugar (cane)	X3	0.1	0.2	0.2	0.3	0.3	0.3	0.4	0.4	0.5	0.5	0.6	0.8
Sisal	X4	4.2	6.3	6.7	7.1	7.4	7.1	7.4	8.9	9.2	9.4	9.8	9.9
Maize	F1	1.0	1.5	1.8	1.9	2.1	2.1	2.2	2.7	2.6	3.1	4.7	8.1
Wheat	F2	1.6	2.2	2.7	2.7	2.9	3.0	3.2	3.4	4.5	5.0	5.6	5.7
LESOTHO													
Wheat	X1	0.2	0.3	0.3	0.4	0.4	0.5	0.5	0.6	..	..	..	..
Beans	X2	0.5	0.9	1.0	1.1	1.1	1.3	1.3	1.4	..	..	..	..
Peas	X3	0.4	0.6	0.5	0.5	0.9	0.9	1.1	1.2	..	..	..	..
Maize	X4	0.1	0.2	0.2	0.3	0.3	0.3	0.4	0.4	..	..	..	..
Sorghum	F1	0.2	0.2	0.2	0.2	0.2	0.3	0.3	0.3	..	..	..	..
LIBERIA													
Rubber (nonspec. coagul.)	X1	0.8	1.0	1.0	0.9	1.0	1.0	..	..	..	..	..	..
Coffee (Robusta)	X2	2.1	2.5	2.8	1.5	1.6	1.6	..	..	..	..	..	..
Cocoa (fair average quality)	X3	2.1	2.0	2.5	2.2	2.3	2.3	..	..	..	..	..	..
Rice	F1	0.3	0.3	0.3	0.3	0.3	0.3	0.3	..	..	..	..	..
Cassava	NT1	0.0	0.1	0.1	0.1	0.1	0.1	0.1	..	..	..	..	..
LIBYA													
Wheat	F1	..	0.2	0.2	0.2	..	..	..	..	..	..	..	..
Olives	F2	..	..	..	..	..	..	..	..	..	..	..	..
Oranges	F3	..	..	..	..	..	..	..	..	..	..	..	..
Barley	NT1	..	0.2	0.2	0.2	..	..	..	..	..	..	..	..
MADAGASCAR													
Coffee (Robusta)	X1	215.0	280.0	330.0	395.0	600.0	800.0	950.0	950.0	950.0	..	..	..
Vanilla (green)	X2	600.0	1,000.0	1,000.0	1,000.0	1,100.0	1,200.0	1,700.0	2,000.0	2,000.0	2,000.0	..	..
Cloves	X3	395.0	435.0	435.0	435.0	525.0	600.0	600.0	600.0	600.0	..	..	..
Rice (paddy)	F1	42.5	65.0	72.5	83.0	100.0	127.5	180.0	250.0	250.0	274.0	..	..
Cassava	NT1	7.0	..	50.0	50.0	55.0	55.0	..	..	..	124.0	..	..
Sweet potatoes	NT2	..	..	50.0	60.0	60.0	60.0	..	..	..	..	..	..
MALAWI													
Tobacco (flue-cured)	X1	0.0	0.0	0.0	0.0	0.0	0.0	0.0	0.0	0.0	..	..	..
Tobacco (Northen division dark-fired, G2)	X1	0.4	0.7	0.8	1.0	1.0	1.0	1.1	1.7	2.5	2.8	2.8	2.8
Tea (dry leaves)	X2	0.0	0.0	0.0	0.0	0.0	0.0	0.0	0.0	0.0	0.0	0.0	..
Groundnuts (shelled)	X3	0.3	0.5	0.6	0.7	0.7	0.7	0.7	0.7	0.9	..	1.7	2.2
Cotton (seed cotton)	X4	0.2	0.4	0.4	0.4	0.5	0.5	0.6	0.7	0.8	..	..	..
Maize	F1	0.1	0.1	0.1	0.1	0.1	0.2	0.2	0.3	0.3	0.3	0.4	0.5
Sorghum	F2	0.1	0.1	0.1	0.1	0.2	0.1	..	..	..	..	0.7	0.8
Rice (paddy, grade 1)	F3	0.1	0.1	0.2	0.2	0.2	0.2	0.3	0.3	..	0.4	0.5	0.9
Cassava	NT1	0.0	0.0	0.0	..	..	..	..	..	..	..	..	..
MALI													
Cotton (seed cotton)	X1	55.0	65.0	65.0	75.0	85.0	85.0	85.0	85.0	85.0	85.0	85.0	..
Groundnuts (unshelled)	X2	40.0	45.0	..	..	70.0	60.0	..	..	..	..	..	..
Millet	F1	35.0	50.0	50.0	55.0	55.0	55.0	..	..	77.0	41.5	42.0	..
Rice (paddy)	F2	37.5	60.0	65.0	70.0	70.0	70.0	70.0	70.0	70.0	70.0	68.0	..
Sorghum	F3	35.0	50.0	50.0	55.0	55.0	55.0	58.0	60.0	61.0	..	..	..
Maize	F4	35.0	50.0	50.0	55.0	55.0	55.0	..	..	54.0	35.0	35.0	..

8-1. Nominal producer prices (continued)

	Category	Local currency per kilogram											
		1980	1983	1984	1985	1986	1987	1988	1989	1990	1991	1992	1993
MAURITANIA													
Sorghum	F1	11.0	14.0	14.0	15.4	15.4	15.4	16.0	16.0	16.0	16.5	16.5	
Millet	F2	11.0	14.0	14.0	..	..	..	..	..	..	..	..	..
Rice (paddy)	F3	10.0	12.5	14.0	14.0	..	..	..	..	..	..	..	..
Maize	F4	15.0	15.0	15.0	..	..	..	..	..	..	..	..	..
MAURITIUS													
Sugarcane	X1	..	..	..	..	..	..	..	..	..	..	..	..
Tea	X2	..	11.9	19.5	12.9	9.2	7.4	10.3	10.4	13.5	13.4	16.8	16.4
Maize (12% moisture)	F1	2.0	2.9	3.2	3.9	4.3	4.3	4.8	4.8	4.8	4.8	5.0	5.0
Rice (paddy, 14% moisture)	F2	1.4	4.9	4.9	4.9	4.9	4.9	5.0	7.0	..	..	..	..
Potatoes	NT1	2.2	2.4	2.2	1.8	1.9	2.5	2.5	2.8	3.1	3.7	4.1	4.7
Onions	NT2	4.2	5.3	5.0	4.7	4.2	4.8	5.8	5.7	7.1	7.8	7.7	7.6
MOROCCO													
Citrus	X1	1.3	1.5	1.5	1.6	1.6	1.6	1.7	1.8	1.9	2.0	2.1	
Cotton	X3	3.2	4.0	5.0	5.5	6.0	6.0	6.0	6.7	..	6.7	5.7	5.7
Wheat (hard)	F1	1.5	1.8	2.2	2.5	2.2	2.4	2.3	2.5	2.7	2.7	3.2	..
Sugarbeet (16.5% sugar)	F2	0.1	0.2	0.2	0.2	0.2	0.2	0.2	0.2	0.2	0.3	0.3	0.3
Barley	NT1	1.3	1.4	1.5	1.5	1.3	1.3	1.2	1.3	1.5	1.5	2.0	..
MOZAMBIQUE													
Cashew nuts	X1	7.5	7.5	13.2	13.2	13.2	86.0	..	..	..	..	..	..
Cotton (seed, prime grade)	X2	11.0	12.5	12.5	16.0	16.0	65.0	..	..	..	..	..	..
Tea	X3	25.6	..	..	..	..	..	..	..	..	..	..	..
Maize	F1	..	..	..	..	..	..	..	..	..	..	..	..
Rice	F2	6.2	10.0	10.0	16.0	16.0	48.0	..	..	..	..	..	..
Cassava	NT1	2.0	4.5	4.5	..	..	..	..	..	..	..	..	..
NAMIBIA													
Wheat	F1	..	..	..	..	0.4	0.4	0.4	0.4	0.5	0.6	0.7	0.7
Maize (white)	F2	..	..	..	0.3	0.3	0.3	0.4	0.4	0.4	0.5	0.5	0.6
NIGER													
Cowpeas	X1	45.0	90.0	100.0	120.0	80.0	80.0	..	..	..	..	..	..
Cotton (unginned, top grade)	X2	62.0	62.0	80.0	120.0	120.0	120.0	120.0	130.0	110.0	70.0	70.0	77.0
Groundnuts (shelled)	X3	50.0	90.0	90.0	100.0	130.0	130.0	130.0	132.0	133.0	134.0	135.0	
Millet	F1	50.0	80.0	100.0	80.0	..	..	..	..	..	..	..	..
Sorghum (red)	F2	50.0	70.0	100.0	80.0	..	..	..	..	..	..	..	..
NIGERIA													
Cocoa (bean)	X1	1.3	1.4	1.5	1.6	3.5	7.5	11.0	10.1	8.5	10.2	12.7	..
Palm kernels	X2	0.2	0.2	0.4	0.4	0.4	0.9	1.0	1.3	1.2	..	..	..
Cotton (seed cotton)	X3	0.4	0.6	0.7	0.9	1.0	4.0	4.5	2.4	2.6	4.2	3.8	..
Groundnuts (in shell)	X4	0.4	0.5	0.7	0.8	1.0	2.3	2.3	4.8	4.3	6.3	6.8	19.7
Sorghum	F1	0.2	0.2	0.4	0.5	0.6	0.8	1.6	2.0	1.7	3.6	4.7	7.0
Millet	F2	0.2	0.2	0.4	0.5	0.6	0.6	1.3	2.1	1.7	3.4	5.7	6.6
Maize	F3	0.2	0.2	0.4	0.5	0.5	0.6	1.6	2.7	2.1	3.3	5.5	7.5
Rice (paddy)	F4	0.3	0.4	0.5	0.7	1.0	2.3	3.8	6.3	6.3	7.5	12.6	18.8
Yams	NT1	..	0.6	0.7	..	1.0	0.9	2.0	2.4	2.3	2.6	5.9	11.7
Cassava (gari)	NT2	..	0.4	0.6	0.2	0.3	0.4	0.8	1.2	2.2	2.1	2.3	4.6
RWANDA													
Coffee	X1	120.0	120.0	120.0	120.0	122.5	125.0	125.0	125.0	..	..	..	..
Tea	X2	75.0	75.0	75.0	75.0	75.0	75.0	..	..	..	..	..	..
Beans (dry)	F1	20.3	23.3	33.7	35.8	22.3	28.6	28.0	..	..	..	..	..
Sorghum	F2	12.7	16.0	23.5	23.6	20.2	20.2	20.6	..	..	..	..	..
Maize	F3	11.9	10.5	17.0	21.8	15.6	15.4	13.3	..	..	..	..	..
Bananas	NT1	7.6	6.4	9.5	12.0	9.7	9.8	10.3	10.5	10.7	..	..	
Sweet potatoes	NT2	5.7	6.5	7.6	9.9	6.1	6.2	5.3	..	..	..	..	..
SAO TOME & PRINCIPE													
Cocoa	X1	16.5	21.0	22.0	23.0	24.0	25.0	26.0	27.0	28.0	29.0	30.0	
Maize	F1	1.9	2.4	2.4	2.5	2.5	2.6	2.6	2.7	2.7	2.8	2.8	
Cassava	NT1	2.1	2.5	2.6	2.6	2.7	2.7	2.8	2.8	2.9	2.9	3.0	
SENEGAL													
Groundnuts (in shell)	X1	50.0	70.0	70.0	90.0	90.0	90.0	70.0	70.0	..	..	..	..
Cotton (seed cotton, first quality)	X2	60.0	70.0	70.0	100.0	100.0	100.0	100.0	100.0	..	..	..	..
Millet	F1	40.0	55.0	60.0	70.0	70.0	70.0	..	..	..	..	..	..
Rice (paddy)	F2	41.5	60.0	66.0	85.0	85.0	85.0	85.0	85.0	..	..	..	..
Maize	F3	37.0	50.0	60.0	70.0	70.0	70.0	..	..	..	..	..	..
Sorghum	F4	40.0	55.0	60.0	70.0	70.0	70.0	74.4	78.8	83.1	86.8	90.3	

8-1. Nominal producer prices (continued)

	ategory	1980	1983	1984	1985	1986	1987	1988	1989	1990	1991	1992	1993
		Local currency per kilogram											
SIERRA LEONE													
Cocoa	X1	2.1	2.3	4.0	4.0	17.8	30.2	..	..	..	..	..	..
Coffee (Robusta)	X2	2.0	2.7	4.7	8.4	25.0	40.3	..	..	..	..	..	..
Palm kernels	X3	0.2	0.3	0.6	0.7	1.1	1.3	..	..	..	..	..	..
Rice (paddy)	F1	0.4	0.9	1.1	1.3	2.8	7.4	22.2	29.0	37.0	44.4	..	..
Cassava	NT1	0.3	0.6	1.5	2.9	4.9	..	..	..	..	..	..	..
SOMALIA													
Bananas	X1	..	..	..	..	..	..	..	..	..	..	..	..
Maize	F1	2.9	25.1	22.8	21.4	34.5	..	..	..	..	..	..	..
Sorghum	F2	4.1	18.3	18.8	18.9	22.7	..	..	..	..	..	..	..
Sesame (seed)	NT1	25.3	58.6	62.6	61.6	76.4	..	..	..	..	..	..	..
SOUTH AFRICA													
Maize	X1	0.1	0.2	0.2	0.2	0.2	0.3	0.3	0.3	0.3	0.4	0.5	0.4
Wheat	X2	0.2	0.3	0.3	0.3	0.4	0.4	0.4	0.4	0.5	0.6	0.7	0.7
Sugar cane	X3	0.0	0.0	0.0	0.0	0.0	0.0	0.0	0.1	0.1	0.1	0.1	0.1
Sorghum	F1	0.1	0.2	0.2	0.2	0.2	0.2	0.2	0.2	0.2	0.3	0.5	0.4
Barley	F2	0.2	0.2	0.3	0.2	0.3	0.3	0.3	0.4	0.4	0.5	0.6	0.7
SUDAN													
Cotton (seed cotton, long-staple, grade 1)	X1	..	..	..	..	..	..	..	..	..	..	..	25.2
Groundnuts (El-Obeid, in shell)	X2	0.2	0.2	0.3	1.0	1.1	1.2	1.8	4.4	23.5	21.1	22.6	..
Sesame (El-Obeid, mixed)	X3	0.3	0.5	0.7	1.4	1.3	1.6	5.0	6.5	12.7	30.9	41.6	..
Gum arabic (El-Obeid)	X4	0.4	0.8	1.3	2.2	6.9	6.9	9.4	9.1	10.1	..	..	..
Sorghum	F1	0.1	0.2	0.3	0.5	0.2	0.8	0.9	1.9	11.4	6.6	11.8	..
Wheat	F2	0.2	0.3	0.4	0.7	0.7	1.0	2.3	2.9	5.7	8.3	11.4	33.3
SWAZILAND													
Sugarcane (sucrose)	X1	0.0	0.0	0.0	0.0	0.0	0.0	0.0	0.0	..	..	..	..
Citrus	X2	0.2	0.2	0.3	0.4	0.4	0.2	0.4	0.4	0.5	0.6	0.7	
Pineapple	X3	0.0	0.1	0.1	0.2	0.3	0.2	0.2	0.3	0.4	0.5	0.5	
Cotton (seed cotton)	X4	0.3	..	0.6	0.8	0.8	0.8	1.0	1.0	..	..	..	..
Maize	F1	0.1	0.2	0.2	0.3	0.3	0.3	0.3	0.4	..	..	..	..
TANZANIA													
Coffee (Arabica) (parchment)	X1	9.0	16.8	23.5	28.2	50.8	66.0	90.0	..	..	..	..	..
Cotton (seed cotton, AR)	X2	3.2	6.0	8.4	13.0	16.9	19.5	22.4	28.0	41.0	..	..	..
Tea (green leaves)	X3	1.5	2.8	4.1	5.0	7.6	9.9	13.4	..	..	..	..	..
Maize	F1	1.0	2.2	4.0	5.3	6.3	8.2	9.0	11.0	13.0	..	..	..
Sorghum	F2	1.0	2.0	3.0	4.0	4.8	6.0	..	..	..	..	..	..
Rice (paddy)	F3	1.8	4.0	6.0	8.0	9.6	14.4	17.3	19.0	26.0	..	..	..
Millet	F4	1.5	2.0	3.0	4.0	4.8	6.0	6.6	7.3	..	..	..	..
Cassava (grade 1, Makopa)	NT1	0.7	1.2	2.0	3.0	3.6	4.5	5.0	5.5	..	..	..	..
TOGO													
Coffee (Robusta)	X1	200.0	235.0	290.0	315.0	365.0	400.0	400.0	400.0	..	..	..	..
Cocoa	X2	220.0	235.0	275.0	300.0	330.0	360.0	360.0	360.0	..	..	..	..
Cotton (seed cotton)	X3	52.0	57.0	75.0	90.0	105.0	105.0	95.0	95.0	..	..	..	..
Maize	F1	68.4	104.2	75.0	47.0	73.0	72.0	79.0	60.0	..	..	..	..
Sorghum	F2	68.0	110.8	89.0	58.0	76.0	66.0	98.0	69.0	..	..	..	..
Millet	F3	66.7	76.9	89.0	67.9	59.0	61.0	..	..	..	..	..	..
Cassava	NT1	20.3	34.9	38.0	28.7	30.0	32.0	26.0	30.0	..	..	..	..
Yams	NT2	48.5	88.7	81.0	63.9	61.0	63.0	63.0	68.0	..	..	..	..
TUNISIA													
Olives	X1	0.1	0.1	0.1	0.1	0.1	0.2	0.2	0.2	0.2	0.3	..	..
Citrus (oranges)	X2	0.1	0.2	0.1	0.2	0.1	0.2	0.2	0.2	0.3	0.3	..	..
Wheat	F1	0.1	0.1	0.1	0.2	0.2	0.2	0.2	0.2	0.2	0.2	..	..
Barley	NT1	0.1	0.1	0.1	0.1	0.1	0.1	0.1	0.1	0.2	0.2	..	..
UGANDA													
Coffee	X1	0.1	1.0	1.7	3.8	8.5	24.0	44.5	60.0	97.5	210.0	190.0	..
Cotton (seed cotton)	X2	0.2	0.7	1.3	2.7	4.0	19.0	56.0	105.0	175.0	286.7	340.0	..
Tea (greenleaf)	X3	0.0	0.2	0.7	1.3	5.0	10.0	20.0	35.0	38.3	45.0	70.0	..
Millet	F1	0.2	0.3	1.4	1.7	7.4	17.6	30.7	109.6	134.8	142.6	294.3	..
Maize	F2	0.1	0.2	1.0	1.6	4.6	11.3	26.0	82.9	72.0	80.0	225.0	..
Sorghum	F3	0.1	0.3	1.4	1.6	5.4	18.3	30.5	84.6	104.0	115.3	237.3	..
Cassava	NT1	0.1	0.1	0.6	0.8	2.3	9.3	22.5	35.5	39.5	76.0	163.0	..
Plantains	NT2	0.1	0.2	0.7	0.8	3.9	7.5	13.6	46.9	51.2	64.5	156.7	..

8-1. Nominal producer prices (continued)

	ategory	*Local currency per kilogram* 1980	1983	1984	1985	1986	1987	1988	1989	1990	1991	1992	1993
ZAIRE													
Coffee (Arabica, green beans)	X1	4.0	14.9	21.3	24.5	42.6	69.3	107.5	166.9	440.5	13,837.3	..	..
Palm oil	X2	2.1	6.5	20.5	23.2	23.0	37.6	59.4	93.8	247.7	7,778.7	..	..
Rubber (natural)	X3	..	33.0	..	..	..	..	..	..	..	..	..	..
Cocoa (beans)	X4	..	11.5	19.0	25.0	30.0	50.0	..	..	..	..	..	..
Maize	F1	1.2	3.3	5.1	5.9	7.5	10.1	25.8	40.3	106.4	..	..	..
Rice (paddy)	F2	2.0	5.0	10.0	10.0	11.5	17.0	28.7	45.2	119.4	..	..	..
Cassava	NT1	1.3	3.2	2.2	2.4	3.0	3.9	8.4	13.2	34.7	1,090.8	..	..
Plantains	NT2	2.9	3.6	..	..	..	..	..	..	..	..	..	..
ZAMBIA													
Cotton (seed cotton)	X1	0.5	0.5	0.6	0.7	1.0	1.6	3.0	3.6	9.7	15.5	..	..
Tobacco (Virginia)	X2	1.6	2.7	2.8	3.5	5.1	6.3	14.0	14.4	60.0	94.5	..	..
Sunflower (seeds)	X3	0.3	0.4	0.4	0.6	0.8	1.4	1.8	3.2	6.4	11.4	..	..
Maize	F1	0.1	0.2	0.3	0.3	0.6	0.9	0.9	1.2	3.2	5.6	..	..
Wheat	F2	0.2	0.4	0.5	0.5	1.0	1.2	2.1	2.5	5.4	8.6	..	..
Cassava	NT1	..	0.2	0.2	0.3	0.6	0.7	1.0	1.4	3.2	5.4	..	..
ZIMBABWE													
Tobacco	X1	0.8	1.9	2.1	2.7	3.1	2.2	3.9	4.0	6.5	11.6	8.1	6.5
Cotton (seed cotton)	X2	0.4	0.5	0.6	0.7	0.8	0.8	0.9	1.1	1.4	1.6	1.4	2.6
Sugarcane	X3	0.0	..	..	..	..	..	..	..	..	..	..	..
Maize	X4	0.1	0.1	0.1	0.2	0.2	0.2	0.2	0.2	0.2	0.3	0.6	0.9
Wheat	F1	0.2	0.2	0.3	0.3	0.3	0.3	0.4	0.4	0.5	0.5	1.0	1.5

Notes: The categories of crops are defined in the technical notes.

Categories are mutually exclusive, and ordering is intended to reflect relative importance of these crops as of 1986-88. In many cases official markets operate simultaneously with parallel or open market activites. Where a large majority of marketed production is believed to pass through the official channels, the official price is also reported as the farmgate price. In most cases, only very rough estimates of the share of marketed production passing through each channel is available.

The CPI is based in 1987 rescaled from price index based in 1980.
For each country one to four export crops (X1,...,X4) are presented in order of importance, in terms of value of total production.
Similarly, up to three traded food crops (F1,...,F3) and two nontraded staples (NT1,NT2) are included.

8-2. Agricultural production index

	Index (average 1989-91 = 100)											Average annual percentage growth		
	1980	*1986*	*1987*	*1988*	*1989*	*1990*	*1991*	*1992*	*1993*	*1994*	*1995*	*75-84*	*85-89*	*90-MR*
SUB-SAHARAN AFRICA	105	103	102	103	102	99	99	95	95	93	92	-1.5	0.5	-1.7
excluding South Africa	104	103	102	103	102	99	99	95	95	93	93	-1.5	0.4	-1.6
excl. S. Africa & Nigeria	105	104	102	103	102	99	99	95	95	93	92	-1.4	0.4	-1.7
Angola	129	113	111	108	102	98	99	100	94	87	86	-6.1	-1.9	-2.8
Benin	73	94	78	94	94	99	106	104	111	109	103	0.7	0.8	1.8
Botswana	103	108	93	97	96	100	103	101	98	102	94	-3.5	-3.2	-0.3
Burkina Faso	72	106	95	106	99	94	105	108	109	104	101	0.5	4.4	1.1
Burundi	103	106	107	106	96	101	101	101	95	79	82	-1.8	0.5	-3.6
Cameroon	111	113	97	104	100	99	100	96	94	93	94	-1.8	-1.3	-1.3
Cape Verde	76	75	118	127	109	100	89	86	118	91	184	0.9	17.1	6.1
Central African Republic	102	103	99	105	103	99	96	98	95	98	95	-0.6	1.7	-1.0
Chad	101	92	92	101	99	96	103	101	93	104	101	-1.9	4.5	0.4
Comoros	121	103	105	103	102	98	98	94	95	94	91	-3.1	0.4	-1.6
Congo	108	107	108	108	103	100	95	94	94	92	91	-0.6	-1.0	-1.9
Côte d'Ivoire	105	101	102	103	103	101	94	89	93	91	90	-0.5	1.2	-2.2
Djibouti	98	107	104	102	118	106	74	77	69	71	70	3.9	2.8	-8.3
Equatorial Guinea	141	105	109	107	101	100	97	95	93	86	84	-1.6	-1.6	-3.2
Eritrea	..	..	..	..	..	..	..	..	..	..	..	..	..	..
Ethiopia	..	..	..	..	..	..	..	..	..	..	..	..	..	..
Gabon	115	102	102	103	101	100	98	96	94	94	91	-1.3	-0.1	-1.7
Gambia, The	101	122	123	109	123	85	90	70	78	78	82	-4.6	0.0	-5.3
Ghana	103	103	103	105	109	87	102	102	107	117	130	-4.0	1.2	4.3
Guinea	117	101	95	91	97	99	103	106	104	106	105	-0.5	-3.3	1.4
Guinea-Bissau	82	100	99	95	100	103	96	99	99	102	101	-0.3	0.3	0.1
Kenya	93	102	99	104	103	100	96	90	84	86	87	-1.1	3.3	-3.3
Lesotho	117	101	101	108	106	111	81	86	93	105	78	-1.6	-0.7	-3.1
Liberia	..	..	..	..	..	..	..	..	..	..	..	..	..	..
Madagascar	116	108	103	101	102	100	97	94	94	88	89	-1.6	-2.1	-2.5
Malawi	123	114	107	107	100	97	101	79	101	80	93	-0.5	-3.7	-2.1
Mali	97	97	92	103	102	95	102	95	93	98	94	1.1	2.8	-1.0
Mauritania	110	95	95	96	99	99	100	90	84	86	86	0.3	1.0	-3.1
Mauritius	85	108	109	100	97	101	101	104	102	96	100	-1.1	0.3	0.0
Mozambique	124	100	98	97	100	103	96	79	88	86	97	-4.4	-0.1	-1.9
Namibia	147	97	104	100	104	97	98	98	100	105	93	-5.4	2.3	-0.6
Niger	142	99	85	112	99	88	112	109	103	102	99	-0.7	3.6	0.8
Nigeria	82	87	84	91	95	98	106	111	114	112	113	-2.1	3.3	3.1
Rwanda	112	109	106	98	102	97	100	94	86	67	71	0.8	-2.2	-6.8
São Tomé and Principe	146	127	120	122	108	98	93	114	113	114	108	-5.2	-1.9	1.8
Senegal	78	109	117	97	107	95	97	88	96	96	100	-6.2	5.1	-0.7
Seychelles	118	144	110	93	99	97	103	89	90	108	107	-0.4	-6.2	1.1
Sierra Leone	100	106	102	101	102	99	97	89	85	90	77	-0.8	0.1	-4.1
Somalia	..	..	..	..	..	..	..	..	..	..	..	..	..	..
South Africa	117	98	100	101	104	98	97	81	89	90	76	-1.9	1.2	-4.2
Sudan	134	118	107	120	100	93	106	114	100	114	108	-1.8	-2.2	2.1
Swaziland	108	112	104	100	102	96	101	87	83	86	80	-0.1	-0.8	-4.0
Tanzania	104	106	103	99	103	99	97	90	90	85	85	-0.2	-0.9	-3.4
Togo	92	94	95	96	99	100	99	99	108	90	87	-1.3	2.5	-1.8
Uganda	93	93	94	95	100	100	99	95	98	97	99	-5.1	-0.1	-0.4
Zaire	101	100	99	99	99	100	100	99	97	89	85	-0.9	-0.3	-2.5
Zambia	104	98	93	116	112	92	94	76	106	89	82	-4.4	4.3	-3.1
Zimbabwe	106	109	94	113	103	99	97	66	88	88	67	-3.7	0.1	-5.6
NORTH AFRICA	94	97	96	93	96	97	104	100	105	94	81	-1.5	1.0	-2.0
Algeria	94	99	100	92	96	96	107	114	105	94	101	-2.3	0.5	0.3
Egypt, Arab Republic	95	97	99	96	96	101	101	106	106	104	107	-0.4	0.9	1.6
Libya	129	106	96	93	99	100	99	92	83	77	74	0.0	-3.7	-5.5
Morocco	73	90	83	96	100	95	104	80	78	101	70	-0.3	7.0	-4.3
Tunisia	94	85	96	65	81	97	120	100	108	79	81	-1.9	-3.2	-1.8
ALL AFRICA	104	103	100	101	101	99	99	95	95	93	91	-1.4	0.3	-1.7

8-3. Food production index

	Index (average 1989-91 = 100)											Average annual percentage growth		
	1980	*1986*	*1987*	*1988*	*1989*	*1990*	*1991*	*1992*	*1993*	*1994*	*1995*	*75-84*	*85-89*	*90-MR*
SUB-SAHARAN AFRICA	78	91	91	98	100	100	107	107	112	114	115	0.9	4.0	2.6
excluding South Africa	77	92	91	98	100	101	107	109	114	115	118	1.0	3.9	2.9
excl. S. Africa & Nigeria	81	94	93	99	100	99	104	103	107	108	110	1.0	3.3	1.7
Angola	92	100	101	100	98	98	103	108	105	102	104	-0.6	0.8	1.0
Benin	61	84	75	90	94	99	106	109	110	116	112	3.1	3.8	3.2
Botswana	73	95	84	90	93	100	106	107	107	115	110	0.0	0.1	2.9
Burkina Faso	58	96	88	102	97	92	109	116	122	119	119	2.4	6.6	4.5
Burundi	78	94	97	99	93	102	104	107	105	88	96	0.3	3.6	-0.7
Cameroon	82	99	90	94	96	99	103	103	107	108	111	0.7	1.5	2.3
Cape Verde	64	70	111	121	106	100	92	91	128	102	213	1.9	19.3	9.2
Central African Republic	80	92	92	98	100	99	100	106	107	110	110	2.0	4.9	2.0
Chad	86	89	88	98	98	96	105	111	106	122	122	1.0	6.1	4.2
Comoros	85	89	94	96	98	98	102	101	106	109	110	0.7	3.8	2.2
Congo	79	95	99	101	100	100	98	100	103	104	105	2.5	2.3	1.0
Côte d'Ivoire	70	86	90	98	99	100	100	103	109	110	114	4.1	4.0	2.5
Djibouti	53	87	90	94	114	107	77	81	75	78	78	11.1	9.3	-6.2
Equatorial Guinea	87	95	105	105	99	100	100	99	100	93	93	0.0	2.2	-1.2
Eritrea	87	95	105	105	99	100	100	99	100	93	93	0.0	2.2	-1.2
Ethiopia	..	..	..	..	..	..	..	..	..	..	..	..	..	..
Gabon	80	90	92	96	97	100	101	102	103	106	105	3.2	2.9	1.3
Gambia, The	71	104	109	101	118	86	95	75	88	91	95	-1.8	4.3	-2.2
Ghana	74	91	94	99	106	87	105	108	116	131	148	-1.6	4.5	7.1
Guinea	94	94	91	87	94	98	106	113	113	119	123	1.2	-1.1	4.6
Guinea-Bissau	67	91	92	90	98	103	98	103	106	112	114	3.3	2.3	2.5
Kenya	66	90	90	98	100	99	100	98	93	101	102	2.1	7.5	0.1
Lesotho	88	88	92	106	105	111	82	83	94	111	80	0.9	3.2	-2.4
Liberia	..	..	..	..	..	..	..	..	..	..	..	..	..	..
Madagascar	83	93	93	95	98	100	101	101	104	101	105	1.7	1.4	0.9
Malawi	90	99	99	103	97	97	105	78	112	92	107	1.8	1.1	0.9
Mali	75	88	85	100	99	95	105	98	104	112	112	3.3	5.2	2.5
Mauritania	85	86	88	91	96	99	103	95	91	95	98	2.9	3.5	-0.5
Mauritius	77	103	105	97	96	101	102	107	105	101	107	0.0	1.6	1.3
Mozambique	101	97	95	96	99	103	97	81	93	93	109	-1.4	1.0	0.2
Namibia	109	86	96	94	101	96	101	105	108	117	106	-2.7	5.4	2.2
Niger	103	87	77	105	95	88	115	117	114	117	118	2.7	6.8	4.4
Nigeria	61	77	77	86	92	97	109	118	125	127	132	0.8	6.1	6.5
Rwanda	84	96	96	91	99	97	103	98	93	78	82	4.0	0.4	-3.9
São Tomé and Principe	115	116	112	117	106	98	95	120	120	124	121	-2.5	0.5	4.0
Senegal	59	98	108	91	105	95	99	92	103	106	113	-3.6	8.4	1.7
Seychelles	111	140	107	93	99	96	103	90	92	113	113	0.6	-5.3	2.2
Sierra Leone	85	98	95	97	100	99	100	92	91	98	86	0.7	2.1	-2.0
Somalia	..	..	..	..	..	..	..	..	..	..	..	..	..	..
South Africa	91	89	93	96	102	98	99	85	97	101	87	0.6	4.0	-1.5
Sudan	103	106	97	114	96	92	110	123	112	130	124	1.4	1.4	5.4
Swaziland	81	103	99	95	98	96	105	98	94	102	97	3.3	1.5	-0.1
Tanzania	74	93	93	93	100	99	99	94	96	96	99	3.6	2.2	-0.4
Togo	76	86	86	91	98	103	98	100	118	98	101	1.3	3.6	0.6
Uganda	67	79	83	88	96	101	102	103	109	109	114	-1.7	3.7	2.7
Zaire	72	87	89	92	96	100	103	106	109	102	101	2.3	3.3	0.9
Zambia	75	86	86	108	108	94	97	83	115	102	95	-1.3	8.0	-0.2
Zimbabwe	76	97	83	108	100	102	96	58	88	96	66	-1.7	4.3	-5.1
NORTH AFRICA	73	91	95	94	100	106	116	115	114	117	116	1.6	4.7	2.3
Algeria	72	89	93	88	93	96	110	120	112	102	114	0.3	3.5	2.7
Egypt, Arab Republic	68	85	91	90	93	101	104	111	112	115	121	2.2	4.2	4.1
Libya	..	..	..	..	..	..	..	..	..	..	..	..	..	..
Morocco	59	82	77	92	98	94	106	84	83	110	77	1.9	9.8	-2.3
Tunisia	74	78	90	61	79	96	123	104	114	85	88	0.4	-1.1	0.0
ALL AFRICA	77	91	92	97	100	101	108	108	112	114	115	1.1	4.1	2.5

8-4. Nonfood production index

	Index (average 1989-91 = 100)											Average annual percentage growth		
	1980	1986	1987	1988	1989	1990	1991	1992	1993	1994	1995	75-84	85-89	90-MR
SUB-SAHARAN AFRICA	85	95	92	97	100	99	100	98	97	..	..	1.9	1.0	-0.7
excluding South Africa	85	95	93	98	100	98	100	98	97	..	..	2.1	1.1	-0.6
excl. S. Africa & Nigeria	85	95	94	98	100	98	100	98	97	..	..	1.9	1.1	-0.6
Angola	324	150	118	122	120	87	93	86	91	..	..	-21.8	-4.5	-5.6
Benin	12	83	49	80	74	100	126	116	152	..	..	8.3	3.7	17.3
Botswana	100	100	100	100	100	100	100	100	100	..	..	0.0	0.0	0.0
Burkina Faso	35	94	84	84	90	111	100	100	92	..	..	8.8	10.5	-0.5
Burundi	59	95	111	105	96	98	106	110	82	..	..	5.0	3.5	-2.1
Cameroon	89	111	81	117	101	94	105	86	71	..	..	3.0	0.6	-7.7
Cape Verde	94	131	61	94	177	94	28	12	12	..	..	-19.2	41.2	-52.9
Central African Republic	92	106	102	125	110	97	93	64	63	..	..	0.3	0.9	-14.2
Chad	51	55	77	85	93	97	109	76	61	..	..	-4.3	11.1	-10.3
Comoros	90	95	95	97	97	101	102	103	103	..	..	0.6	0.7	1.3
Congo	178	109	90	100	107	94	99	98	98	..	..	0.9	-9.7	-1.3
Côte d'Ivoire	82	95	99	83	102	109	89	64	76	..	..	-0.8	12.5	-10.5
Djibouti	..	..	..	..	..	..	..	..	..	..	..	..	..	..
Equatorial Guinea	..	..	..	..	..	..	..	..	..	..	..	..	..	..
Eritrea	..	..	..	..	..	..	..	..	..	..	..	..	..	..
Ethiopia	96	94	94	96	99	100	101	103	..	..	..	0.4	4.8	1.2
Gabon	76	150	194	199	216	34	51	22	29	..	..	19.5	10.7	-36.1
Gambia, The	55	47	37	79	132	73	95	135	135	..	..	22.5	3.9	6.7
Ghana	90	56	59	54	70	91	139	170	231	..	..	-6.6	4.0	35.2
Guinea	48	27	27	66	92	103	106	105	114	..	..	0.9	11.5	4.7
Guinea-Bissau	116	167	167	167	85	111	104	56	78	..	..	60.4	-9.3	-8.2
Kenya	67	86	87	97	100	101	99	94	97	..	..	5.7	2.7	-1.3
Lesotho	88	103	55	79	103	98	99	95	95	..	..	2.6	-4.8	-1.8
Liberia	181	199	191	192	192	72	36	64	28	..	..	1.6	-0.5	-33.0
Madagascar	91	105	95	97	106	99	94	88	90	..	..	-0.7	1.0	-4.4
Malawi	58	73	73	80	90	99	111	111	118	..	..	6.5	2.3	6.6
Mali	55	66	76	73	94	95	111	127	97	..	..	7.7	11.7	3.5
Mauritania	..	..	..	..	..	..	..	..	..	..	..	..	..	..
Mauritius	85	132	121	118	99	99	102	102	105	..	..	5.2	-5.3	1.4
Mozambique	245	75	89	72	87	99	114	99	99	..	..	-6.8	-4.2	2.6
Namibia	279	144	122	123	117	110	74	62	93	..	..	-6.7	-1.0	-9.7
Niger	84	169	165	126	125	85	90	129	90	..	..	-4.8	4.3	-2.4
Nigeria	46	48	57	62	83	108	109	114	114	..	..	-7.8	21.1	7.1
Rwanda	63	116	119	123	100	109	92	118	93	..	..	6.0	2.1	-0.6
São Tomé and Principe	321	118	48	166	43	198	59	70	107	..	..	1.1	-20.6	8.2
Senegal	50	71	99	100	79	90	131	124	129	..	..	2.0	-2.5	14.0
Seychelles	..	..	..	..	..	..	..	..	..	..	..	..	..	..
Sierra Leone	41	90	94	98	99	100	101	101	96	..	..	12.7	5.1	-0.6
Somalia	129	130	195	187	100	100	100	59	182	..	..	7.4	0.5	7.1
South Africa	105	93	91	97	102	99	99	89	72	..	..	0.7	0.0	-7.7
Sudan	92	113	125	108	110	105	84	82	60	..	..	-1.6	-7.2	-13.6
Swaziland	86	71	54	95	115	92	93	65	177	..	..	-3.5	12.0	5.3
Tanzania	101	102	107	96	97	95	108	106	106	..	..	-2.7	3.3	2.9
Togo	37	67	87	87	86	88	126	130	129	..	..	3.2	21.1	12.8
Uganda	85	104	107	98	110	87	102	81	102	..	..	-4.9	1.3	-2.3
Zaire	84	92	92	93	99	107	94	92	86	..	..	0.7	0.6	-4.3
Zambia	49	76	53	116	108	79	113	61	134	..	..	4.1	7.7	1.9
Zimbabwe	77	91	91	99	99	90	111	103	117	..	..	2.2	1.8	4.8
NORTH AFRICA	72	91	93	93	98	100	102	100	105	..	..	3.9	1.0	1.4
Algeria	46	91	94	93	98	98	104	107	108	..	..	10.0	1.0	2.7
Egypt, Arab Republic	178	140	122	110	101	99	100	118	137	..	..	0.5	-6.7	8.1
Libya	103	95	87	87	96	100	105	92	77	..	..	0.1	-1.7	-4.8
Morocco	46	87	93	98	99	102	99	93	88	..	..	1.1	5.9	-3.1
Tunisia	72	87	93	92	95	103	102	100	105	..	..	4.3	4.1	1.6
ALL AFRICA	85	95	93	97	99	99	100	98	97	..	..	2.1	1.1	-0.6

8-5. Food production per capita index

	Index (average 1989-91 = 100)											Average annual percentage growth		
	1980	1986	1987	1988	1989	1990	1991	1992	1993	1994	1995	75-84	85-89	90-MR
SUB-SAHARAN AFRICA	..	..	..	..	..	..	..	..	..	..	..	..	..	..
excluding South Africa	..	..	..	..	..	..	..	..	..	..	..	..	..	..
excl. S. Africa & Nigeria	..	..	..	..	..	..	..	..	..	..	..	..	..	..
Angola	92	100	101	100	98	98	103	108	105	102	104	-0.6	0.8	1.0
Benin	61	84	75	90	94	99	106	109	110	116	112	3.1	3.8	3.2
Botswana	73	95	84	90	93	100	106	107	107	115	110	0.0	0.1	2.9
Burkina Faso	58	96	88	102	97	92	109	116	122	119	119	2.4	6.6	4.5
Burundi	78	94	97	99	93	102	104	107	105	88	96	0.3	3.6	-0.7
Cameroon	82	99	90	94	96	99	103	103	107	108	111	0.7	1.5	2.3
Cape Verde	64	70	111	121	106	100	92	91	128	102	213	1.9	19.3	9.2
Central African Republic	80	92	92	98	100	99	100	106	107	110	110	2.0	4.9	2.0
Chad	86	89	88	98	98	96	105	111	106	122	122	1.0	6.1	4.2
Comoros	85	89	94	96	98	98	102	101	106	109	110	0.7	3.8	2.2
Congo	79	95	99	101	100	100	98	100	103	104	105	2.5	2.3	1.0
Côte d'Ivoire	70	86	90	98	99	100	100	103	109	110	114	4.1	4.0	2.5
Djibouti	53	87	90	94	114	107	77	81	75	78	78	11.1	9.3	-6.2
Equatorial Guinea	87	95	105	105	99	100	100	99	100	93	93	0.0	2.2	-1.2
Eritrea	..	..	..	..	..	..	..	..	..	..	..	..	..	..
Ethiopia	..	..	..	..	..	..	..	..	..	..	..	..	..	..
Gabon	80	90	92	96	97	100	101	102	103	106	105	3.2	2.9	1.3
Gambia, The	71	104	109	101	118	86	95	75	88	91	95	-1.8	4.3	-2.2
Ghana	74	91	94	99	106	87	105	108	116	131	148	-1.6	4.5	7.1
Guinea	94	94	91	87	94	98	106	113	113	119	123	1.2	-1.1	4.6
Guinea-Bissau	67	91	92	90	98	103	98	103	106	112	114	3.3	2.3	2.5
Kenya	66	90	90	98	100	99	100	98	93	101	102	2.1	7.5	0.1
Lesotho	88	88	92	106	105	111	82	83	94	111	80	0.9	3.2	-2.4
Liberia	..	..	..	..	..	..	..	..	..	..	..	..	..	..
Madagascar	83	93	93	95	98	100	101	101	104	101	105	1.7	1.4	0.9
Malawi	90	99	99	103	97	97	105	78	112	92	107	1.8	1.1	0.9
Mali	75	88	85	100	99	95	105	98	104	112	112	3.3	5.2	2.5
Mauritania	85	86	88	91	96	99	103	95	91	95	98	2.9	3.5	-0.5
Mauritius	77	103	105	97	96	101	102	107	105	101	107	0.0	1.6	1.3
Mozambique	101	97	95	96	99	103	97	81	93	93	109	-1.4	1.0	0.2
Namibia	109	86	96	94	101	96	101	105	108	117	106	-2.7	5.4	2.2
Niger	103	87	77	105	95	88	115	117	114	117	118	2.7	6.8	4.4
Nigeria	61	77	77	86	92	97	109	118	125	127	132	0.8	6.1	6.5
Rwanda	84	96	96	91	99	97	103	98	93	78	82	4.0	0.4	-3.9
São Tomé and Principe	115	116	112	117	106	98	95	120	120	124	121	-2.5	0.5	4.0
Senegal	59	98	108	91	105	95	99	92	103	106	113	-3.6	8.4	1.7
Seychelles	111	140	107	93	99	96	103	90	92	113	113	0.6	-5.3	2.2
Sierra Leone	85	98	95	97	100	99	100	92	91	98	86	0.7	2.1	-2.0
Somalia	..	..	..	..	..	..	..	..	..	..	..	..	..	..
South Africa	91	89	93	96	102	98	99	85	97	101	87	0.6	4.0	-1.5
Sudan	103	106	97	114	96	92	110	123	112	130	124	1.4	1.4	5.4
Swaziland	81	103	99	95	98	96	105	98	94	102	97	3.3	1.5	-0.1
Tanzania	74	93	93	93	100	99	99	94	96	96	99	3.6	2.2	-0.4
Togo	76	86	86	91	98	103	98	100	118	98	101	1.3	3.6	0.6
Uganda	67	79	83	88	96	101	102	103	109	109	114	-1.7	3.7	2.7
Zaire	72	87	89	92	96	100	103	106	109	102	101	2.3	3.3	0.9
Zambia	75	86	86	108	108	94	97	83	115	102	95	-1.3	8.0	-0.2
Zimbabwe	76	97	83	108	100	102	96	58	88	96	66	-1.7	4.3	-5.1
NORTH AFRICA	..	..	..	..	..	..	..	..	..	..	..	..	..	..
Algeria	72	89	93	88	93	96	110	120	112	102	114	0.3	3.5	2.7
Egypt, Arab Republic	68	85	91	90	93	101	104	111	112	115	121	2.2	4.2	4.1
Libya	85	92	86	87	95	100	103	99	92	88	88	4.8	0.0	-2.1
Morocco	59	82	77	92	98	94	106	84	83	110	77	1.9	9.8	-2.3
Tunisia	74	78	90	61	79	96	123	104	114	85	88	0.4	-1.1	0.0
ALL AFRICA	..	..	..	..	..	..	..	..	..	..	..	..	..	..

8-6. Volume of food output, by major food crop

	Category	1980	1986	1987	1988	1989	1990	1991	1992	1993	1994	1995	75-84	85-89	90-MR
		Thousands of metric tons											Average annual percentage growth		
ALGERIA															
Wheat	F1	1,511	1,229	1,175	614	1,152	750	1,869	1,837	1,017	714	1,600	-4.3	-3.8	1.0
Citrus	F2	294	175	193	219	189	199	237	270	271	276	277	-7.5	1.8	7.2
Dates	F3	201	189	224	196	210	206	209	261	262	317	318	2.5	2.3	8.7
Barley	NT1	794	1,083	820	390	790	833	1,810	1,398	408	234	540	1.4	-4.7	-16.9
Potatoes	NT2	591	812	905	899	1,001	809	1,077	1,158	1,065	716	720	0.6	11.0	-4.3
ANGOLA															
Maize	F1	360	280	300	270	204	180	299	369	274	201	235	-5.9	-2.6	2.0
Millet	F2	57	54	60	60	63	63	67	75	40	53	62	-4.7	5.3	-3.2
Cassava	NT1	1,150	1,430	1,470	1,500	1,530	1,650	1,670	1,863	1,861	1,600	1,700	-1.7	3.6	1.3
Sweet potatoes	NT2	165	170	170	170	165	165	170	180	185	200	200	0.5	-0.4	3.8
BENIN															
Palm oil	X2	34	25	25	25	20	20	14	14	14	9	9	0.0	-9.9	-12.6
Maize	F1	271	378	277	423	424	410	431	460	483	492	492	4.5	0.5	3.4
Sorghum	F2	56	89	91	97	106	99	115	110	106	113	113	-0.6	5.1	1.3
Cassava	NT1	583	724	572	880	977	937	1,046	1,041	1,040	1,146	1,146	0.5	6.6	3.2
Yam	NT2	694	884	835	922	1,010	1,046	1,178	1,125	1,150	1,250	1,250	5.0	4.7	3.5
BOTSWANA															
Livestock (1,000 heads)	X1	3,853	4,075	4,157	4,205	4,267	..	..	..	..	..		1.0	1.8	..
Rabbits/chickens (1,000s)		913	1,279	1,383	1,400	1,400	..	..	..	..	..		5.9	10.4	..
Sorghum	F1	29	16	18	94	53	38	33	11	38	37	38	-22.3	60.3	-3.2
Maize	F2	12	4	3	8	20	12	15	3	6	11	5	..	..	-17.1
Millet	F3	2	1	0	3	2	2	1	1	2	2	2	..	..	2.5
BURKINA FASO															
Groundnuts	F4	54	152	115	164	131	134	99	170	206	203	203	-0.3	8.5	10.8
Sorghum	F1	547	1,011	848	1,009	991	751	1,238	1,292	1,310	1,232	1,232	-0.7	9.2	6.3
Millet	F2	351	680	632	817	649	449	849	784	899	831	831	1.5	11.2	7.5
Maize	F3	105	155	131	227	257	258	315	341	271	350	350	2.2	23.1	5.1
Rice		40	38	22	39	42	48	39	47	54	61	61	..	-3.3	7.1
BURUNDI															
Maize	F1	140	164	173	178	135	168	172	176	172	123	153	1.5	0.8	-0.9
Sorghum	F2	52	61	63	63	69	64	65	67	66	45	66	13.8	5.7	-2.9
Rice	F3	10	21	28	27	28	40	40	40	39	38	27	7.7	10.2	-0.8
Millet	F4	9	12	13	13	14	13	13	14	13	11	14	2.4	5.9	-1.2
Bananas	NT1	1,100	1,436	1,485	1,575	1,634	1,547	1,586	1,626	1,585	1,487	1,421	-0.7	5.8	-1.8
Cassava	NT2	400	554	574	614	642	569	584	598	584	527	501	2.1	5.2	-3.2
CAMEROON															
Maize	F1	331	541	236	418	343	329	400	380	400	350	426	-1.1	7.2	2.8
Sorghum	F2	24	24	22	27	31	25	30	35	40	40	40	9.1	-4.5	7.4
Millets	F3	1,634	2,109	1,959	1,794	1,806	2,213	2,190	2,205	2,300	2,380	2,080	-1.2	-2.6	2.2
Rice	F4	414	389	387	367	387	369	450	380	430	450	654	-2.3	1.9	7.1
Cassava	NT1	105	69	44	66	60	71	73	76	76	78	78	0.0	-0.7	3.7
Plantains	NT2	104	107	107	124	97	102	108	109	114	117	117	-3.9	1.7	3.2
CENTRAL AFRICAN REP															
Sorghum	F1	36	62	39	49	37	20	18	21	20	21	23	1.9	2.5	-4.3
Maize	F2	41	94	66	70	62	57	58	59	58	63	71	0.5	8.5	2.2
Groundnuts	F3	123	112	88	97	103	80	63	71	72	84	86	-1.1	7.1	-1.1
Cassava	NT1	920	601	529	533	516	547	586	580	575	518	402	-1.7	-4.8	-3.1
Yam	NT2	150	180	180	190	200	230	230	260	250	250	250	1.6	1.1	3.3
CHAD															
Sorghum	F1	250	299	238	258	237	280	286	387	306	379	379	-6.1	-0.1	7.7
Millet	F2	200	276	214	316	179	168	226	293	234	307	307	-8.0	8.4	10.7
Groundnuts	F3	99	96	94	93	152	108	97	147	190	207	207	-1.2	11.9	10.9
COMOROS															
Bananas	F1	32	39	48	49	50	50	54	54	55	57	58	..	7.3	2.6
Cassava	NT1	33	29	43	44	45	45	45	47	48	52	52	-3.8	14.1	2.9
CONGO															
Maize	F1	9	21	19	20	25	25	25	26	26	26	26	-4.8	12.2	0.8
Cassava	NT1	628	693	736	761	699	700	585	600	632	630	630	3.1	0.9	-1.6
Plantains	NT2	56	59	64	63	70	75	80	85	90	95	95	6.8	4.9	5.5
COTE D'IVOIRE															
Palm oil	X3	189	211	221	195	193	214	228	261	256	259	249	1.8	3.9	4.6
Rice	F1	420	560	580	610	635	660	687	714	890	988	1,045	-0.7	4.3	9.6
Maize	F2	380	420	435	460	480	497	515	538	529	517	517	8.1	-1.4	1.2
Cassava	NT1	1,010	1,250	1,300	1,400	1,460	1,393	1,465	1,585	1,535	1,564	1,564	4.1	3.4	1.7
Yams	NT2	2,040	2,300	2,400	2,500	2,600	2,528	2,556	2,910	2,850	2,824	2,824	2.3	0.9	2.1

8-6. Volume of food output, by major food crop (continued)

	Category	1980	1986	1987	1988	1989	1990	1991	1992	1993	1994	1995	75-84	85-89	90-MR
		Thousands of metric tons											Average annual percentage growth		
EGYPT															
Rice	X2	2,382	2,445	2,406	2,132	2,679	3,167	3,448	3,910	4,161	4,583	4,822	0.2	1.9	10.1
Wheat	F1	1,736	1,928	2,721	2,838	3,182	4,268	4,483	4,618	4,833	4,437	5,722	0.0	13.4	7.1
Sugarcane	F3	8,618	10,832	8,424	10,795	11,213	11,095	11,624	11,708	12,412	13,822	14,000	1.7	3.2	4.3
Dry Broadbeans	NT1	213	282	323	362	360	375	283	215	252	317	288	1.0	6.2	-3.9
EQUATORIAL GUINEA															
Cassava	NT1	32	44	44	44	44	45	46	47	47	47	47	1.8	1.4	1.1
Plantains	NT2	..	..	..	..	..	..	..	..	..	..	..	..	..	..
ETHIOPIA															
Sorghum	F1	0	0	0	0	0	0	0	0	1,079	1,125	1,232	..	..	..
Maize	F2	0	0	0	0	0	0	0	0	1,644	2,011	2,189	..	..	..
Barley	NT1	0	0	0	0	0	0	0	0	996	1,284	1,417	..	..	..
Teff (mixed)	NT2	..	..	..	..	..	..	..	..	..	..	..	..	..	..
GABON															
Oil palm	X2	..	..	..	..	..	..	..	..	..	..	..	..	..	..
Maize	F1	10	20	25	25	20	22	23	24	25	26	27	5.7	13.2	4.8
Cassava	NT1	250	171	179	198	212	210	200	200	210	230	210	1.2	4.7	0.7
Yam	NT3	79	90	95	100	100	110	110	110	110	120	120	5.7	3.6	2.6
Plantains	NT4	175	229	220	230	233	235	240	242	245	250	250	6.1	0.9	1.3
GAMBIA, THE															
Groundnuts	X1	60	110	120	98	130	75	84	55	77	81	84	-3.5	5.6	-4.3
Palm oil	X3	3	3	3	3	3	3	3	3	3	3	3	-0.6	0.0	0.0
Millet	F1	25	51	50	48	51	47	58	46	52	53	53	2.0	2.6	0.9
Rice	F2	43	24	20	29	21	21	21	19	12	20	20	0.4	-2.1	-2.8
Maize	F3	6	17	15	16	14	14	20	18	24	13	22	15.0	-3.4	5.1
Sorghum	F4	5	9	7	7	11	8	12	12	9	9	13	4.9	-0.8	1.6
GHANA															
Maize	F1	382	559	598	751	715	553	932	731	961	940	1,042	0.7	2.8	8.3
Millet	F2	82	110	173	139	180	75	112	133	198	168	201	..	7.8	9.4
Groundnuts	F3	142	190	191	206	200	113	67	100	100	176	176	0.8	6.1	3.3
Cassava	NT1	1,858	2,876	2,726	3,300	3,327	2,717	3,600	4,000	4,500	6,025	6,899	2.2	9.3	15.4
Plantains	NT2	734	1,087	1,078	1,200	1,040	799	1,178	1,082	1,322	1,475	1,642	-2.1	-6.7	10.2
GUINEA															
Palm oil	X2	40	40	40	40	40	40	40	40	40	50	50	0.8	0.0	4.1
Rice	F1	480	350	320	303	358	424	501	512	531	532	532	0.5	-3.8	6.3
Maize	F2	90	100	80	62	68	74	80	88	88	88	89	4.3	-9.7	4.6
Groundnuts	F3	84	70	60	44	59	78	104	139	122	128	170	0.4	-9.2	16.7
Cassava	NT1	480	420	320	270	317	372	437	512	485	512	512	-2.9	-11.6	8.1
Plantains	NT2	350	350	350	350	380	400	410	420	429	429	429	3.1	1.2	2.0
GUINEA-BISSAU															
Groundnuts	X1	30	29	20	14	16	18	15	16	18	18	18	-3.4	-14.5	1.9
Palm kernels	X2	9	14	10	10	10	7	10	8	7	8	8	0.3	3.7	-2.7
Rice	F1	42	110	105	98	110	123	123	124	126	131	133	8.7	-0.1	2.6
Sorghum	F2/F3	18	20	15	16	9	11	13	11	14	14	16	..	-13.8	8.5
Maize	F4	12	10	10	8	10	14	13	10	13	14	15	11.5	-1.9	4.4
KENYA															
Sugarcane	X3	4,532	4,112	4,248	4,395	4,825	4,750	4,600	4,170	4,470	3,780	4,300	8.8	3.0	-2.9
Maize	F1	1,620	2,898	2,416	2,761	2,631	2,290	2,340	2,430	2,089	3,085	2,750	-1.5	9.8	2.2
Wheat	F2	216	252	207	234	244	190	195	126	150	277	330	2.1	7.5	5.1
LESOTHO															
Wheat	F3	28	11	19	19	30	33	7	12	8	21	2	-14.5	10.7	-27.2
Dry Beans	NT1	4	4	3	7	10	8	2	1	2	3	2	-19.6	53.4	-21.5
Dry Peas	NT2	5	2	1	3	1	3	1	2	1	1	2	-6.7	-19.6	-0.4
Maize	F1	106	86	95	160	137	172	49	61	92	175	27	-0.9	13.8	-14.0
Sorghum	F2	59	33	31	53	31	36	10	19	52	60	10	-5.3	-1.8	-2.6
LIBERIA															
Rice	F1	243	288	298	298	294	250	130	110	65	50	50	2.2	0.2	-28.1
Cassava	NT1	300	306	372	447	446	350	350	390	425	450	450	-0.1	15.9	2.6
LIBYA															
Wheat	F1	141	190	172	161	185	129	150	160	175	155	167	14.8	0.5	0.8
Olives	F2	161	120	58	62	65	68	70	68	55	60	62	..	-15.9	-2.2
MADAGASCAR															
Rice Paddy	F1	2,109	2,230	2,178	2,149	2,380	2,420	2,342	2,450	2,550	2,360	2,596	0.5	1.4	1.1
Cassava	NT1	1,683	2,421	2,178	2,186	2,277	2,292	2,307	2,280	2,350	2,413	2,420	5.0	1.4	1.1
Sweet potatoes	NT2	373	467	467	467	483	486	481	450	500	560	560	3.8	0.9	2.8

8-6. Volume of food output, by major food crop (continued)

		Thousands of metric tons											Average annual percentage growth		
	Category	*1980*	*1986*	*1987*	*1988*	*1989*	*1990*	*1991*	*1992*	*1993*	*1994*	*1995*	*75-84*	*85-89*	*90-MR*
MALAWI															
Groundnuts	F2	177	166	163	141	62	37	58	26	55	31	32	-3.6	-5.7	-8.2
Maize	F1	1,186	1,295	1,202	1,424	1,510	1,343	1,589	612	2,034	1,040	1,661	2.0	1.3	0.1
Sorghum	F3	20	21	15	22	20	15	19	4	22	17	45	-23.2	4.2	10.6
Cassava	NT1	292	218	169	135	155	145	168	129	216	200	200	-1.6	-11.1	6.1
MALI															
Groundnuts	X2	135	107	101	172	157	180	151	127	131	215	215	-11.5	23.5	4.2
Millet	F1	407	806	694	1,000	842	737	890	582	708	858	858	1.7	8.3	0.5
Rice	F2	132	225	237	288	338	282	454	410	428	469	469	-5.6	20.8	7.2
Sorghum	F3	301	465	513	672	731	531	770	602	694	746	746	2.2	13.9	2.3
Maize	F4	45	213	179	215	225	197	257	193	283	322	322	2.5	15.6	8.0
MAURITANIA															
Sorghum	F1	56	89	91	97	106	99	115	110	106	113	113	-0.6	5.1	1.3
Millet	F2	3	6	7	7	14	3	2	2	4	7	7	-4.3	23.1	1.0
Rice	F3	11	33	53	51	55	52	42	51	65	59	59	25.9	24.5	3.3
Maize	F4	5	3	1	7	3	2	2	3	7	6	6	2.2	13.2	22.9
MAURITIUS															
Sugarcane	X1	4,564	6,025	6,231	5,517	5,436	5,548	5,621	5,781	5,402	5,000	5,200	-0.5	1.2	-1.4
Potatoes	NT1	12	17	17	14	20	18	17	19	14	19	19	..	-4.8	-0.9
Dry Onions	NT2	2	3	2	3	3	3	3	3	4	4	4	..	-5.1	6.4
MOROCCO															
Citrus	X1	1,079	1,201	993	1,227	1,438	1,033	1,456	1,094	1,221	1,310	990	..	6.3	-2.9
Wheat	F1	1,811	3,809	2,427	4,019	3,927	3,614	4,939	1,562	1,573	5,523	1,091	0.4	13.9	-13.7
Sugarbeet	NT1	2,241	2,625	2,750	2,990	2,877	2,984	3,036	2,754	3,162	3,144	2,717	3.1	4.6	-0.1
Barley	F2	2,210	3,563	1,543	3,454	2,999	2,138	3,253	1,081	1,027	3,720	608	-4.3	11.7	-15.9
MOZAMBIQUE															
Cashew nuts	X1	71	30	35	45	50	23	31	54	24	23	30	-17.3	20.2	-6.1
Maize	F1	380	459	271	322	330	453	327	133	533	526	734	-1.2	-4.1	12.0
Rice	F2	75	93	90	93	95	96	56	33	65	98	113	-0.2	2.4	2.6
Cassava	NT1	3,600	3,600	3,700	3,600	3,700	4,056	3,690	3,239	3,511	3,294	4,178	1.6	0.1	-0.4
NAMIBIA															
Wheat	F1	2	6	5	5	4	4	6	3	6	6	3	16.4	1.4	-0.2
Maize	F2	32	23	7	16	24	29	50	13	26	44	15	2.9	-3.8	-4.3
NIGER															
Cowpeas	NT1	..	..	..	..	..	..	..	..	..	..	..	..	..	..
Groundnuts	X1	126	60	41	50	26	18	46	57	60	65	65	-3.6	-3.9	22.1
Sorghum	F2	368	360	366	560	422	281	463	387	421	420	420	2.1	13.8	2.5
Millet	F1	1,364	1,383	997	1,766	1,333	1,111	1,833	1,788	1,658	1,725	1,725	3.5	9.0	5.7
NIGERIA															
Groundnuts	X2	471	896	687	815	1,017	992	1,361	1,297	1,323	1,453	1,502	-6.1	12.5	7.0
Palm oil	X3	675	760	800	834	857	730	760	792	825	837	871	1.4	4.3	1.5
Sorghum	F1	3,690	5,425	5,455	5,182	4,831	4,185	5,367	5,909	6,051	6,197	6,184	1.8	1.2	6.1
Millet	F2	2,450	4,111	3,905	3,949	4,770	5,136	4,109	4,501	4,602	4,757	4,900	-2.3	5.7	0.1
Maize	F3	653	3,550	4,612	5,268	5,008	5,768	5,810	5,840	6,291	6,902	7,240	1.2	35.4	5.7
Rice	F4	1,090	1,416	1,780	2,082	3,303	2,500	3,226	3,260	2,305	2,427	2,548	14.3	18.8	-4.1
Yam	NT1	5,281	5,209	4,886	9,132	9,609	13,624	16,956	19,781	24,121	23,153	23,264	-5.0	17.3	15.6
Cassava	NT2	11,500	14,000	15,500	15,439	15,425	19,043	26,004	29,185	29,900	31,005	31,404	0.9	5.4	12.3
RWANDA															
Sorghum	F1	179	193	188	141	147	183	205	154	109	85	72	4.1	-7.1	-14.3
Maize	F2	85	90	91	135	95	101	104	109	74	60	71	5.0	1.7	-7.7
Plantains	NT1	2,063	2,266	2,290	2,400	3,020	2,747	2,800	2,900	2,900	2,600	2,600	3.3	5.6	-1.9
Sweet potatoes	NT2	871	893	895	849	772	857	1,000	1,063	1,150	800	1,100	4.3	-1.9	3.9
SENEGAL															
Groundnuts	X1	523	843	963	723	844	703	724	578	628	718	791	-6.6	9.8	-1.0
Millet	F1	451	502	690	485	639	505	593	446	654	548	667	-3.1	4.5	1.4
Rice	F2	65	143	136	146	168	181	170	177	193	162	155	1.1	2.9	-1.2
Maize	F3	57	108	114	123	131	133	103	115	138	108	107	6.8	2.8	-2.6
Sorghum	F4	102	132	111	110	127	157	78	117	99	132	127	-2.8	0.1	-0.4
SIERRA LEONE															
Palm oil	X2	47	49	50	51	49	50	51	52	47	50	45	1.7	0.2	-1.1
Palm kernels	X4	30	37	37	33	29	27	30	35	33	32	29	-2.5	-5.4	1.6
Rice	F1	513	525	466	493	518	504	504	479	486	405	284	-1.7	1.2	-7.8
Cassava	NT1	95	113	115	116	118	123	123	117	106	244	219	2.5	2.9	11.6
SOMALIA															
Bananas	X1	60	94	108	115	105	110	90	70	55	43	45	-5.8	14.5	-16.1
Maize	F1	110	336	286	353	299	315	100	101	79	150	146	9.8	3.0	-12.9
Sorghum	F2	140	237	244	235	334	250	145	92	80	252	136	5.7	6.7	-11.0
Sesame	NT1	38	45	45	46	50	45	35	20	22	22	25	3.2	1.4	-13.2

8-6. Volume of food output, by major food crop (continued)

	Category	1980	1986	1987	1988	1989	1990	1991	1992	1993	1994	1995	75-84	85-89	90-MR
		Thousands of metric tons											*Average annual percentage growth*		
SOUTH AFRICA															
Maize	X1	10,896	8,321	7,353	7,014	12,035	8,709	8,179	3,061	9,991	13,275	4,670	-5.3	12.3	-6.2
Wheat	X2	1,470	2,322	3,146	3,540	2,026	1,730	2,147	1,318	1,984	1,840	2,125	2.2	5.3	0.7
Sugarcane	X3	14,062	18,252	21,021	19,811	18,636	18,083	20,078	12,955	11,244	15,683	16,782	0.3	-1.7	-4.1
Sorghum	F1	701	446	616	604	470	293	260	101	515	520	291	-4.0	0.9	1.4
Barley	F2	60	199	280	126	291	241	173	100	230	275	300	11.6	2.4	2.3
SUDAN															
Groundnuts	X2	707	364	432	587	218	123	179	380	428	714	630	-8.2	-1.1	31.1
Sesame	X3	221	216	233	194	140	80	97	266	175	170	195	-5.1	4.8	11.7
Sorghum	F1	2,084	3,277	1,363	4,425	1,536	1,180	3,540	4,042	2,386	3,648	2,600	-1.8	4.4	13.1
Wheat	F2	231	199	157	181	247	408	680	895	453	475	520	-5.7	13.8	7.9
SWAZILAND															
Sugarcane	X1	2,782	4,084	3,870	3,690	3,797	3,842	3,900	3,700	3,500	3,786	3,798	8.6	1.4	-0.5
Citrus (oranges)	X2	45	50	42	40	30	35	37	40	30	48	35	-0.1	-7.6	3.2
Maize	F1	97	156	95	113	133	94	139	54	73	99	76	-4.1	-6.3	-7.6
TANZANIA															
Maize	F1	1,726	2,210	2,359	2,339	3,125	2,445	2,332	2,226	2,282	2,159	2,567	5.8	8.3	-3.0
Sorghum	F3	510	650	663	410	537	368	550	587	719	478	839	8.8	-1.0	7.9
Rice	F2	291	548	645	615	718	740	625	392	600	614	723	1.8	14.6	-1.4
Millet	F4	340	380	291	219	300	200	200	263	210	218	411	8.4	-6.2	4.3
Cassava	NT1	4,828	8,124	6,838	6,944	6,896	7,792	7,460	7,112	6,833	7,209	5,969	5.2	-3.2	-2.4
TOGO															
Maize	F1	138	127	172	296	287	285	231	278	393	270	296	4.6	9.1	1.9
Sorghum	F2	95	131	98	119	153	115	141	112	126	85	85	..	4.8	-8.5
Millet	F3	43	82	71	56	97	58	50	75	75	45	45	-7.8	0.7	-8.2
Cassava	NT1	408	411	355	413	409	593	511	452	389	412	469	-0.1	-2.7	-2.1
Yam	NT2	484	409	360	379	405	392	376	368	530	375	375	-0.1	2.4	0.1
TUNISIA															
Olive oil	X1	130	131	105	63	143	179	281	133	226	87	103	-3.6	-1.4	-9.0
Citrus	X2	160	252	250	230	261	236	225	185	298	206	199	3.9	4.2	-2.8
Wheat	F1	869	474	1,360	220	420	1,122	1,786	1,584	1,413	503	530	-0.9	-18.3	-4.0
Barley	F2	296	132	537	63	200	478	721	570	478	145	80	..	-20.4	-18.0
UGANDA															
Millet	F1	459	427	518	578	610	560	576	634	610	610	643	-4.8	11.4	1.4
Maize	F2	286	322	357	440	624	602	567	657	804	900	950	-5.2	11.5	9.0
Sorghum	F3	299	280	315	344	347	360	363	375	383	390	398	-3.2	6.3	2.3
Cassava	NT1	2,072	2,900	3,101	3,271	3,568	3,420	3,229	2,896	3,139	2,080	2,625	1.7	4.6	-6.7
Plantains	NT2	5,699	6,565	7,039	7,293	7,469	7,842	8,080	7,806	8,222	9,000	9,519	-4.4	3.8	3.7
ZAIRE															
Palm oil	X2	168	155	165	178	178	179	180	180	181	181	181	-2.1	3.3	0.3
Maize	F1	594	800	850	900	960	1,008	1,030	1,052	1,201	1,198	1,170	4.3	6.2	4.0
Rice	F2	234	315	330	350	370	392	418	440	458	414	425	3.4	4.9	2.2
Cassava	NT1	13,087	16,300	16,820	17,400	18,000	18,715	19,500	20,210	20,835	18,051	17,500	2.8	3.6	-0.3
Plantains	NT2	1,563	1,870	1,880	1,900	1,950	2,097	2,160	2,224	2,291	2,424	2,262	2.7	1.7	2.9
ZAMBIA															
Sunflower seeds	X3	28	31	17	18	15	20	11	1	21	10	16	15.8	-21.4	-1.9
Maize	F1	937	1,231	1,063	1,943	1,845	1,093	1,096	483	1,598	1,021	738	-6.1	16.2	-8.6
Wheat	F2	10	18	28	37	47	55	65	58	71	43	50	24.6	30.1	-0.8
Cassava	NT1	290	320	335	355	480	520	530	560	570	600	600	6.7	7.1	3.7
ZIMBABWE															
Sugarcane	X3	2,528	4,135	3,339	3,199	3,671	3,093	3,236	125	538	3,420	3,943	4.6	-0.5	-4.8
Maize	F1	1,511	2,546	1,131	2,341	2,019	1,972	1,586	362	2,012	2,326	840	-4.2	4.4	-7.1
Wheat	F2	191	248	215	257	284	326	259	58	276	239	83	1.2	17.9	-14.1

Notes: Crops shown represent same major food crops as in Table 8-1, Nominal producer prices, excluding beverages (coffee, tea, cocoa), cotton, and tobacco.

The following commodities are in their least-processed form unless otherwise indicated:

Groundnuts, unshelled
Rice, paddy
Sunflower, seeds
Citrus, total for country
Sesame, seeds
Livestock = combined total head of cattle, sheep, goats, pigs, horses, asses, and mules
Chickens/rabbits = combined total

For South Africa, barley production is for white areas only.

Countries excluded from listing: Cape Verde, Djibouti, Eritrea, São Tomé and Principe, and Seychelles.

8-7. Value of agricultural exports

	Millions of U.S. dollars (current prices)											Average annual percentage growth		
	1980	1986	1987	1988	1989	1990	1991	1992	1993	1994	1995	75-84	85-89	90-MR
SUB-SAHARAN AFRICA	12,608	11,142	10,525	10,321	10,963	10,575	9,469	9,125	8,832	3,641	3,862	1.9	1.7	-17.3
excluding South Africa	10,091	9,917	9,119	8,948	9,137	8,796	7,844	7,345	7,140	3,641	3,862	2.1	0.7	-14.7
excl. S. Africa & Nigeria	9,645	9,541	8,861	8,512	8,860	8,510	7,564	7,107	6,872	3,641	3,862	2.5	0.7	-14.2
Angola	172	55	36	22	16	6	5	5	3	3	1	-12.8	-30.5	-28.3
Benin	55	72	73	44	79	84	86	93	84	83	115	3.0	-4.2	3.9
Botswana	52	86	77	74	79	79	90	91	96	96	97	5.5	2.7	3.9
Burkina Faso	80	54	91	87	66	116	112	75	89	..	..	5.3	5.1	1.5
Burundi	64	160	79	128	74	71	90	69	64	61	101	8.8	-3.7	0.9
Cameroon	699	626	527	510	661	563	342	356	361	245	393	2.6	5.1	-10.7
Cape Verde	1	1	1	1	2	2	2	2	1	1	0	18.6	36.1	-22.9
Central African Republic	61	58	47	54	68	45	46	33	36	36	37	6.8	3.1	-8.6
Chad	115	80	88	112	114	135	123	132	84	84	118	13.2	-7.4	-4.3
Comoros	7	18	9	18	13	11	20	17	18	18	8	8.6	13.5	-2.3
Congo	13	12	10	10	8	15	14	17	9	9	7	-1.8	-14.8	-5.6
Côte d'Ivoire	2,009	2,418	2,071	1,721	1,809	1,620	1,507	1,401	1,358	1,615	1,599	7.0	-2.7	-1.7
Djibouti	3	4	6	7	11	9	4	5	4	3	4	7.9	18.8	-16.7
Equatorial Guinea	12	14	13	12	8	8	6	5	5	3	4	-4.0	-10.3	-15.3
Eritrea	..	..	..	..	..	..	..	..	1	..	..	..	..	..
Ethiopia	392	457	341	398	416	261	160	168	..	..	..	5.5	2.8	-27.5
Gabon	14	10	6	8	7	3	6	7	2	4	5	13.2	-1.2	-7.9
Gambia, The	28	13	8	13	10	14	12	11	9	15	15	-5.0	-21.9	3.4
Ghana	744	509	539	481	426	413	366	320	336	302	358	-5.1	3.2	-4.3
Guinea	33	26	26	32	31	28	23	31	43	43	45	5.3	10.7	9.8
Guinea-Bissau	6	7	12	13	10	13	16	4	14	..	..	8.9	2.9	-5.2
Kenya	693	909	678	735	669	688	639	612	719	975	916	6.5	-1.8	6.5
Lesotho	16	10	15	25	21	13	13	15	14	12	13	7.0	7.7	-5.1
Liberia	151	108	107	119	135	71	23	25	22	32	24	5.7	0.6	-21.6
Madagascar	334	250	273	180	206	176	157	151	147	..	..	2.6	-4.9	-8.0
Malawi	251	232	258	274	249	382	447	372	282	..	..	9.2	-0.6	2.2
Mali	192	172	222	208	240	254	268	259	266	..	..	12.3	3.8	2.3
Mauritania	39	32	31	32	33	43	39	40	40	..	..	7.3	-1.0	3.2
Mauritius	303	283	356	356	346	383	367	402	383	..	..	-1.1	13.2	2.6
Mozambique	157	36	53	47	44	41	45	51	32	..	..	-8.0	1.4	-4.5
Namibia	189	86	137	135	142	123	123	138	132	..	..	-8.0	15.1	-0.3
Niger	86	57	47	51	54	62	59	54	55	..	..	7.8	-5.9	-1.1
Nigeria	446	376	258	437	276	286	281	238	268	..	..	-4.4	-1.4	-2.4
Rwanda	66	169	131	99	113	95	85	60	47	..	..	5.5	8.6	-19.8
São Tomé and Principe	19	6	6	6	5	4	5	3	3	..	..	0.1	-10.1	-11.9
Senegal	115	105	118	153	204	219	135	131	98	..	..	-5.6	7.7	-17.9
Seychelles	3	1	1	1	1	1	1	1	2	..	..	-1.7	-16.3	31.9
Sierra Leone	59	49	42	31	21	18	24	11	9	..	..	-0.3	-11.6	-19.6
Somalia	125	95	99	76	75	74	41	62	70	..	..	4.9	3.6	-3.1
South Africa	2,517	1,225	1,406	1,373	1,827	1,779	1,625	1,780	1,691	..	..	0.6	8.2	-1.5
Sudan	553	325	514	507	662	522	384	371	448	..	..	1.9	5.8	-10.6
Swaziland	211	138	255	275	258	357	333	299	261	..	..	6.7	21.6	-1.5
Tanzania	406	346	251	289	306	280	243	272	265	..	..	-0.2	-0.2	-3.1
Togo	77	96	99	100	92	120	101	103	81	..	..	5.4	4.8	-3.8
Uganda	344	410	320	284	280	175	168	136	173	..	..	1.1	-7.4	-11.4
Zaire	235	378	212	165	182	140	77	83	51	..	..	-1.7	-8.5	-26.6
Zambia	14	25	17	13	20	24	30	34	27	..	..	-8.1	10.3	10.3
Zimbabwe	453	543	565	609	592	750	731	584	629	..	..	4.4	5.0	-1.3
NORTH AFRICA	1,544	1,308	1,356	1,312	1,297	1,469	1,641	1,428	1,319	495	615	-2.1	1.0	-15.3
Algeria	120	27	30	30	35	50	54	76	73	97	35	-12.7	-9.4	5.9
Egypt, Arab Republic	677	669	673	514	533	427	391	401	360	360	553	-1.9	-6.9	-1.1
Libya	..	1	2	2	1	63	49	31	30	38	27	-43.0	4.9	33.5
Morocco	606	450	457	572	520	647	670	581	509	..	..	0.4	11.9	-1.5
Tunisia	140	161	194	193	208	283	477	338	347	..	..	-2.7	8.0	12.7
ALL AFRICA	14,152	12,450	11,881	11,633	12,260	12,044	11,110	10,553	10,151	4,136	4,476	1.3	1.6	-17.1

8-8. Volume of cereal imports

	Thousands of metric tons											Average annual percentage growth		
	1980	1986	1987	1988	1989	1990	1991	1992	1993	1994	1995	75-84	85-89	90-MR
SUB-SAHARAN AFRICA	8,132	8,387	8,179	8,072	7,537	8,800	10,683	17,124	14,006	11,710	..	10.3	-9.3	12.3
excluding South Africa	7,973	7,575	7,617	7,682	7,148	7,885	9,309	12,275	11,573	10,798	..	5.7	-5.7	10.5
excl. S. Africa & Nigeria	6,145	6,206	7,022	7,203	6,647	7,408	8,505	11,054	9,780	9,720	..	8.7	-2.6	8.9
Angola	341	159	280	249	266	368	309	307	346	475	..	-1.1	-4.3	8.0
Benin	61	77	73	137	95	151	151	183	128	107	..	26.7	3.7	0.9
Botswana	68	113	94	140	111	106	91	139	133	175	..	21.0	-7.5	10.1
Burkina Faso	77	123	123	132	127	144	187	132	121	110	..	9.1	-7.1	-4.4
Burundi	18	13	13	15	6	18	31	19	22	105	..	1.5	-13.2	50.9
Cameroon	140	191	289	350	370	384	285	424	281	226	..	1.3	27.1	-8.2
Cape Verde	65	81	61	49	67	67	75	133	69	87	..	-0.1	-3.2	5.7
Central African Republic	12	40	35	33	28	40	27	30	34	52	..	18.5	15.7	8.0
Chad	16	36	59	62	40	30	72	61	59	50	..	26.7	-12.7	9.0
Comoros	14	35	19	34	33	35	32	38	36	34	..	9.3	3.0	1.1
Congo	88	94	78	113	83	79	110	143	136	86	..	8.9	-2.3	6.0
Côte d'Ivoire	469	580	739	535	542	535	588	469	576	466	..	10.6	0.6	-2.2
Djibouti	32	48	37	50	28	50	43	43	52	52	..	4.0	-3.5	9.6
Equatorial Guinea	2	8	9	15	14	13	9	8	11	9	..	24.0	20.6	-7.6
Eritrea	..	..	..	..	..	..	..	..	116	281	..	..	..	..
Ethiopia	..	..	..	..	..	..	..	..	428	928	..	..	..	..
Gabon	27	53	55	59	51	46	70	79	77	64	..	14.3	-1.8	8.5
Gambia, The	47	59	73	114	55	96	100	93	87	97	..	-2.1	2.8	7.2
Ghana	247	145	223	257	244	320	402	396	361	311	..	-4.4	10.5	4.6
Guinea	171	151	173	179	203	210	296	338	335	384	..	4.4	5.9	14.4
Guinea-Bissau	21	22	60	55	53	47	64	82	70	68	..	-7.4	15.3	7.8
Kenya	387	179	257	86	154	351	322	654	555	622	..	36.7	-24.0	29.6
Lesotho	107	115	73	144	100	130	148	130	131	99	..	6.2	0.2	-0.4
Liberia	99	118	100	102	157	70	172	141	137	121	..	5.1	4.2	1.5
Madagascar	110	212	178	86	123	134	77	135	110	140	..	3.9	-10.8	1.9
Malawi	36	16	61	132	190	151	213	439	576	506	..	5.8	62.0	31.6
Mali	87	228	132	158	124	74	229	97	83	70	..	15.0	-12.8	-9.2
Mauritania	166	188	201	250	211	198	341	235	279	206	..	11.1	-4.6	1.5
Mauritius	181	162	189	176	209	203	198	207	270	255	..	2.6	1.8	5.6
Mozambique	368	244	425	619	467	451	553	1,027	527	496	..	4.8	3.1	4.0
Namibia	54	75	102	92	91	88	94	168	121	112	..	6.0	5.3	7.8
Niger	90	68	144	135	75	113	143	135	136	155	..	10.1	-8.0	12.6
Nigeria	1,828	1,369	595	479	501	477	804	1,222	1,793	1,078	..	-3.1	-26.2	26.5
Rwanda	16	27	11	10	10	19	17	14	111	97	..	15.7	-23.2	60.0
São Tomé and Principe	9	7	9	5	18	9	12	9	9	11	..	4.0	2.4	-7.4
Senegal	452	520	450	511	561	704	612	588	574	579	..	5.1	-3.5	-1.4
Seychelles	9	9	10	13	14	13	15	9	13	11	..	-1.4	13.2	-5.1
Sierra Leone	83	124	149	119	145	160	183	133	136	141	..	-3.0	16.1	-2.7
Somalia	221	258	302	212	188	195	214	338	207	129	..	23.7	-2.9	-3.5
South Africa	159	813	563	390	390	915	1,375	4,849	2,433	913	..	70.7	-31.1	27.3
Sudan	236	658	745	723	609	650	1,273	654	725	1,022	..	21.0	-3.9	6.7
Swaziland	20	44	57	79	88	77	81	81	55	75	..	30.2	10.4	-5.1
Tanzania	399	230	185	148	64	92	152	212	215	195	..	19.1	-25.9	27.5
Togo	41	61	71	136	114	117	91	150	63	69	..	21.1	12.6	-10.6
Uganda	52	13	21	22	21	19	28	33	80	56	..	10.9	-1.0	30.5
Zaire	350	408	476	415	323	391	301	219	240	253	..	1.5	4.2	-8.2
Zambia	498	165	135	169	123	142	55	718	353	35	..	5.9	-10.9	-2.8
Zimbabwe	156	54	47	84	52	118	41	1,408	596	100	..	73.1	-28.5	39.6
NORTH AFRICA	12,987	17,575	18,039	19,236	21,264	18,806	17,426	18,140	20,741	22,021	..	7.0	3.3	1.5
Algeria	3,414	4,611	3,865	5,368	8,179	5,040	4,555	5,180	5,948	7,760	..	5.4	9.9	1.0
Egypt, Arab Republic	6,028	8,407	9,348	8,561	8,361	8,342	7,618	7,127	7,206	9,200	..	7.8	-0.5	-0.1
Libya	908	1,635	1,422	1,547	1,707	2,378	2,373	1,722	2,892	1,790	..	8.8	10.4	1.5
Morocco	1,821	1,610	2,236	1,643	1,363	1,605	1,957	3,095	3,652	1,678	..	7.2	-11.0	12.0
Tunisia	817	1,312	1,168	2,116	1,655	1,440	923	1,015	1,044	1,592	..	5.9	16.1	-3.0
ALL AFRICA	21,119	25,963	26,219	27,308	28,801	27,606	28,110	35,264	34,747	33,731	..	8.3	-1.1	5.0

8-9. Food aid

	Thousands of metric tons											Average annual percentage growth		
	1980	*1986*	*1987*	*1988*	*1989*	*1990*	*1991*	*1992*	*1993*	*1994*	*1995*	*75-84*	*85-89*	*90-MR*
SUB-SAHARAN AFRICA	2,171	2,761	2,944	2,169	2,139	2,414	3,417	5,912	3,254	2,954	..	18.0	-11.4	9.1
excluding South Africa	2,171	2,761	2,944	2,169	2,139	2,414	3,417	5,912	3,254	2,954	..	18.0	-11.4	9.1
excl. S. Africa & Nigeria	2,171	2,761	2,944	2,169	2,139	2,414	3,416	5,912	3,254	2,954	..	18.0	-11.4	9.1
Angola	25	69	109	80	113	97	116	111	217	..	..	36.0	9.6	15.6
Benin	11	8	11	15	13	8	7	19	26	15	..	5.0	-3.5	17.3
Botswana	11	44	53	33	5	..	0	10	8	7	..	22.5	-27.4	39.0
Burkina Faso	51	22	42	49	44	56	85	30	27	19	..	15.6	-18.7	-19.0
Burundi	12	2	4	6	2	3	1	4	63	48	..	11.6	-24.5	111.7
Cameroon	10	7	2	6	..	9	8	1	2	2	..	2.9	-27.9	-35.3
Cape Verde	31	59	54	54	55	57	58	45	57	65	..	16.8	1.6	1.8
Central African Republic	3	6	6	..	4	3	3	5	6	1	..	29.5	-20.4	-13.4
Chad	14	29	22	15	27	30	61	3	12	14	..	21.1	-33.5	-22.4
Comoros	2	10	11	2	2	5	6	6	6	10	..	12.3	-20.7	25.0
Congo	2	1	1	2	7	15	10	7	1	12	..	-12.1	45.7	-15.4
Côte d'Ivoire	..	..	1	19	26	59	36	41	45	56	..	-2.3	159.8	9.4
Djibouti	14	16	10	12	6	7	16	21	8	23	..	21.7	-16.7	22.4
Equatorial Guinea	2	1	2	3	1	4	4	3	5	3	..	78.1	-23.3	15.3
Eritrea	..	..	..	..	..	..	..	39	235	140	..	..	..	..
Ethiopia	..	..	..	..	..	..	..	833	652	720	..	..	..	..
Gabon	..	..	..	..	..	..	..	..	..	..	..	..	..	..
Gambia, The	16	15	17	10	11	11	10	6	11	2	..	15.2	-13.3	-21.1
Ghana	94	66	110	46	73	72	191	75	126	101	..	7.4	-8.3	7.0
Guinea	34	92	26	42	25	12	30	30	46	29	..	3.5	-15.1	14.8
Guinea-Bissau	26	10	13	8	14	7	12	9	9	2	..	10.9	-15.7	-25.0
Kenya	173	107	119	112	62	63	166	287	251	102	..	61.3	-22.8	22.9
Lesotho	44	34	55	34	30	31	29	45	29	15	..	15.6	-11.5	-8.6
Liberia	26	2	56	28	28	153	129	156	144	177	..	51.4	6.2	30.3
Madagascar	27	151	81	76	31	38	49	58	26	26	..	48.2	-15.7	-4.8
Malawi	17	10	105	223	175	181	259	635	67	204	..	35.0	142.7	-3.7
Mali	50	77	26	62	38	37	41	34	29	17	..	31.3	-28.3	-13.3
Mauritania	106	38	54	70	72	101	36	42	59	22	..	15.9	-12.9	-19.0
Mauritius	21	15	31	21	9	7	9	5	2	..	..	1.0	15.7	-30.5
Mozambique	155	364	480	434	493	454	556	958	371	320	..	20.8	9.8	-6.1
Namibia	..	..	..	1	4	10	6	26	..	..	..	..	..	64.0
Niger	11	17	23	83	35	79	40	26	31	32	..	-3.8	-24.2	-9.9
Nigeria	..	..	..	..	..	..	1	..	..	..	..	..	..	..
Rwanda	15	16	8	2	7	9	10	82	87	269	..	6.7	-36.7	118.2
São Tomé and Principe	2	8	9	7	4	13	7	6	7	6	..	18.7	-9.5	-2.6
Senegal	153	80	109	53	61	39	61	71	38	16	..	19.6	-15.4	-17.5
Seychelles	1	1	0	0	0	0	0	..	..	..	..	4.1	-28.2	..
Sierra Leone	12	43	58	38	37	17	64	29	30	30	..	16.9	7.3	-0.2
Somalia	330	161	154	74	90	74	113	318	78	30	..	14.0	-18.3	-11.8
South Africa	..	..	..	..	..	..	..	..	..	..	..	..	..	..
Sudan	195	890	615	200	335	453	586	238	274	132	..	35.3	-23.7	-18.2
Swaziland	1	3	8	15	7	4	5	40	10	1	..	19.5	99.4	-20.1
Tanzania	236	55	76	76	22	24	15	35	48	118	..	4.2	-20.2	38.1
Togo	4	6	16	11	11	16	14	3	11	8	..	1.6	-5.9	-11.3
Uganda	57	15	29	17	35	61	28	59	44	62	..	-8.7	11.9	7.9
Zaire	77	56	177	55	107	84	121	27	26	83	..	40.1	-5.4	-16.3
Zambia	84	116	145	66	3	4	335	535	11	11	..	35.8	-40.3	31.7
Zimbabwe	18	38	14	10	13	8	86	900	16	4	..	..	-40.1	-3.7
NORTH AFRICA	2,113	2,988	2,405	1,987	1,919	2,439	1,330	831	413	237	..	8.3	-5.3	-37.2
Algeria	29	4	5	38	11	26	19	15	13	23	..	-20.3	61.5	4.4
Egypt, Arab Republic	1,865	1,977	1,646	1,427	1,210	1,864	1,026	482	230	179	..	7.1	-8.9	-37.8
Libya	..	..	..	..	..	..	..	..	..	..	..	..	..	..
Morocco	120	611	340	237	219	200	197	234	124	13	..	22.2	-9.1	-35.8
Tunisia	99	396	415	284	479	348	88	100	46	22	..	8.0	27.2	-45.7
ALL AFRICA	4,284	5,749	5,349	4,156	4,057	4,853	4,747	6,743	3,667	3,191	..	12.4	-8.9	-4.7

8-10. Fertilizer use

	Thousands of metric tons											Average annual percentage growth		
	1980	1986	1987	1988	1989	1990	1991	1992	1993	1994	1995	75-84	85-89	90-MR
SUB-SAHARAN AFRICA	1,973	1,852	1,770	1,926	1,913	1,972	1,931	1,995	2,294	2,094	..	4.4	-0.6	2.7
excluding South Africa	909	1,014	1,057	1,090	1,137	1,180	1,192	1,262	1,450	1,262	..	5.3	2.2	3.5
excl. S. Africa & Nigeria	735	752	764	778	759	780	762	764	944	868	..	2.4	0.8	3.6
Angola	17	12	10	16	24	10	7	9	8	10	..	-0.5	16.0	-12.1
Benin	1	11	9	7	3	11	12	15	17	17	..	7.5	-15.0	32.4
Botswana	1	1	1	1	1	1	1	1	1	1	..	-5.7	2.7	2.4
Burkina Faso	4	16	18	15	21	21	20	21	21	23	..	23.4	11.1	1.9
Burundi	1	3	3	3	5	2	1	5	4	3	..	11.4	15.1	6.1
Cameroon	32	52	50	34	29	17	18	19	22	30	..	12.9	-9.8	3.4
Cape Verde	0	0	0	..	..	..	..	..	..	..	..	-0.6	22.3	..
Central African Republic	1	1	1	1	1	1	1	1	1	1	..	-11.1	-17.6	9.8
Chad	1	4	5	5	5	6	9	10	5	7	..	-4.9	-7.3	4.8
Comoros	..	..	..	..	..	..	0	0	0	0	..	..	..	0.0
Congo	1	3	2	1	1	2	1	2	2	2	..	4.0	-33.9	23.4
Côte d'Ivoire	53	29	33	41	39	36	44	56	54	63	..	1.4	-0.6	11.7
Djibouti	1	0	0	..	..	..	..	..	..	..	..	-44.2	..	..
Equatorial Guinea	0	..	..	..	..	..	..	..	..	..	..	0.0	..	..
Eritrea	0	..	..	..	..	..	..	..	..	..	..	0.0	..	..
Ethiopia	..	..	..	..	..	..	..	..	140	46	..	..	..	..
Gabon	0	2	2	1	1	1	1	1	0	0	..	28.9	-18.8	-22.2
Gambia, The	2	4	3	1	2	1	1	1	1	1	..	7.9	-13.3	-10.2
Ghana	12	8	11	13	8	13	8	10	8	10	..	-0.9	1.3	-1.6
Guinea	0	1	1	1	1	1	2	1	2	1	..	-15.8	29.7	3.1
Guinea-Bissau	0	..	1	0	1	1	1	0	0	1	..	9.8	..	-12.1
Kenya	62	123	102	125	117	116	95	100	103	138	..	6.1	6.4	1.5
Lesotho	5	4	4	5	5	5	6	6	6	6	..	18.1	2.3	6.2
Liberia	3	2	4	3	3	0	..	..	..	..	..	-11.1	24.9	..
Madagascar	9	11	6	11	6	11	9	8	11	11	..	3.1	-1.5	8.4
Malawi	33	37	48	51	55	48	70	74	74	36	..	12.4	7.4	-2.0
Mali	14	15	16	13	18	15	15	23	25	21	..	14.3	-16.4	8.1
Mauritania	1	1	1	3	2	4	5	7	5	4	..	-9.6	28.4	10.9
Mauritius	27	25	33	28	32	28	28	27	26	29	..	0.7	3.3	-2.0
Mozambique	28	6	7	2	2	3	5	5	3	7	..	6.5	-13.1	18.5
Namibia	..	..	..	..	..	..	..	..	..	..	..	..	..	..
Niger	3	2	3	2	3	2	1	1	2	1	..	23.0	-2.8	-12.0
Nigeria	174	262	293	312	378	400	429	498	506	394	..	23.8	5.5	3.1
Rwanda	0	1	2	1	1	3	2	1	3	1	..	11.8	-18.3	5.4
São Tomé and Principe	0	..	..	..	..	..	..	..	..	..	..	94.4	..	..
Senegal	19	21	21	26	13	12	15	17	25	20	..	-8.9	-3.3	14.1
Seychelles	..	..	..	..	..	..	..	..	..	..	..	..	..	..
Sierra Leone	2	4	1	1	2	1	1	1	3	3	..	-3.5	-17.8	20.8
Somalia	1	2	4	2	3	3	..	..	..	..	..	7.3	-7.4	..
South Africa	1,064	838	713	836	776	792	740	733	844	832	..	3.6	-3.9	1.5
Sudan	81	46	50	47	49	89	93	74	52	72	..	-1.5	-3.8	0.2
Swaziland	20	12	13	14	12	13	12	12	12	13	..	4.0	9.6	0.9
Tanzania	36	45	48	41	49	51	50	48	50	40	..	-1.0	5.7	-3.2
Togo	3	11	11	12	12	12	12	12	10	11	..	8.6	10.2	-2.2
Uganda	1	0	1	0	0	0	1	1	2	2	..	-16.2	-5.2	60.1
Zaire	8	2	6	3	8	6	8	2	4	4	..	0.1	-9.8	-15.3
Zambia	79	77	95	85	79	60	63	85	86	59	..	2.2	6.1	-0.3
Zimbabwe	173	158	140	166	149	177	148	108	157	171	..	2.0	-0.3	0.1
NORTH AFRICA	1,221	1,632	1,653	1,708	1,585	1,589	1,555	1,457	1,642	1,420	..	6.5	1.3	-1.5
Algeria	236	272	241	170	117	139	96	97	131	123	..	1.6	-11.9	0.3
Egypt, Arab Republic	664	867	897	1,034	965	965	963	875	973	852	..	7.5	3.5	-2.0
Libya	53	72	89	88	79	78	85	89	106	67	..	14.2	0.3	0.4
Morocco	207	315	321	315	321	326	312	290	336	290	..	5.4	3.0	-1.4
Tunisia	62	106	104	101	104	83	99	106	96	89	..	6.3	3.2	-0.8
ALL AFRICA	3,194	3,484	3,423	3,634	3,498	3,561	3,486	3,453	3,936	3,514	..	5.3	0.2	0.9

8-11. Fertilizer imports

	Thousands of metric tons											Average annual percentage growth		
	1980	1986	1987	1988	1989	1990	1991	1992	1993	1994	1995	75-84	85-89	90-MR
SUB-SAHARAN AFRICA	1,021	1,036	1,142	1,104	1,215	1,090	1,138	1,294	1,339	..	..	5.9	0.4	3.7
excluding South Africa	791	875	956	974	1,034	957	976	1,095	1,182	..	..	6.8	1.0	4.1
excl. S. Africa & Nigeria	615	654	694	809	814	760	769	845	893	..	..	3.8	4.7	3.0
Angola	17	12	10	22	24	7	7	9	8	..	..	-0.2	19.3	-17.9
Benin	1	13	8	7	3	11	12	16	16	..	..	6.7	-16.1	43.0
Botswana	1	1	1	1	1	1	1	1	1	..	..	-5.7	2.7	2.1
Burkina Faso	5	16	18	19	23	19	20	21	21	..	..	23.7	14.8	-0.5
Burundi	1	3	3	3	5	2	1	6	5	..	..	11.9	13.6	13.1
Cameroon	32	45	50	40	29	17	18	20	22	..	..	13.2	-9.4	-3.4
Cape Verde	0	0	0	..	..	..	..	..	..	..	..	-0.6	22.3	..
Central African Republic	1	1	1	1	1	1	1	1	1	..	..	-11.1	-17.6	13.3
Chad	1	4	5	5	5	6	9	10	5	..	..	-4.9	-7.3	7.1
Comoros	..	..	..	..	..	..	0	0	0	..	..	..	..	..
Congo	1	4	0	1	1	2	1	2	2	..	..	34.9	-38.7	33.1
Côte d'Ivoire	45	31	44	43	41	35	42	60	55	..	..	6.4	-6.9	11.6
Djibouti	1	0	0	..	..	..	..	..	..	..	..	-44.2	..	..
Equatorial Guinea	0	..	..	..	..	..	..	..	..	..	..	0.0	..	..
Eritrea	..	..	..	..	..	..	..	..	..	..	..	..	..	..
Ethiopia	50	62	54	79	97	112	99	133	141	..	..	4.0	14.6	9.5
Gabon	0	2	2	1	1	1	1	1	0	..	..	28.0	-18.8	-26.0
Gambia, The	2	3	3	1	2	1	1	1	1	..	..	7.9	-15.0	-14.1
Ghana	12	8	11	13	23	7	8	11	7	..	..	-2.3	15.5	-17.6
Guinea	0	1	1	1	1	1	2	1	2	..	..	-16.0	29.7	5.0
Guinea-Bissau	0	..	1	0	1	1	1	0	0	..	..	9.8	..	-20.9
Kenya	62	123	99	139	120	116	95	100	120	..	..	5.2	7.7	-1.4
Lesotho	5	4	4	5	5	5	6	6	6	..	..	18.1	2.3	8.5
Liberia	3	2	4	3	3	0	..	..	..	..	..	-11.1	24.9	..
Madagascar	9	11	6	11	6	11	9	8	8	..	..	3.1	-1.5	2.4
Malawi	33	37	48	51	55	48	76	68	86	..	..	13.9	4.8	13.3
Mali	14	15	16	13	18	19	13	30	25	..	..	14.3	-16.4	12.0
Mauritania	1	1	1	3	2	5	7	9	7	..	..	-9.6	28.4	34.6
Mauritius	17	31	23	25	30	26	25	28	24	..	..	0.0	5.5	-3.7
Mozambique	20	6	7	2	2	3	5	5	3	..	..	24.2	-23.1	9.1
Namibia	..	..	..	..	..	..	..	..	..	..	..	..	..	..
Niger	3	2	3	2	3	2	1	1	2	..	..	23.0	-2.8	-15.7
Nigeria	177	221	263	165	220	197	208	251	288	..	..	23.0	-9.1	8.1
Rwanda	0	2	2	1	2	1	2	1	2	..	..	11.8	1.3	1.5
São Tomé and Principe	..	..	..	..	..	..	..	..	..	..	..	..	..	..
Senegal	16	7	9	23	24	29	31	27	37	..	..	-7.7	6.8	8.2
Seychelles	..	..	..	..	..	..	..	..	..	..	..	..	..	..
Sierra Leone	2	4	1	1	2	1	1	2	3	..	..	-4.1	-17.7	17.4
Somalia	2	2	4	2	3	3	..	..	..	..	..	0.9	20.5	..
South Africa	229	161	186	130	181	132	162	199	157	..	..	2.9	-3.2	1.2
Sudan	81	46	50	47	49	89	93	74	67	..	..	0.0	-6.8	4.4
Swaziland	18	12	13	14	15	13	12	12	12	..	..	1.2	13.1	-5.2
Tanzania	20	24	40	52	56	38	53	40	50	..	..	4.0	14.1	-1.6
Togo	3	9	9	14	13	12	6	12	9	..	..	7.6	9.6	-6.1
Uganda	1	0	1	0	0	0	1	1	2	..	..	-13.1	-5.2	64.6
Zaire	8	2	6	3	11	6	8	2	4	..	..	0.1	-5.6	-25.4
Zambia	69	66	94	85	101	67	63	86	83	..	..	-1.1	42.7	-1.4
Zimbabwe	56	43	42	78	40	44	41	41	55	..	..	5.9	5.3	6.1
NORTH AFRICA	588	521	499	449	474	491	426	370	404	..	..	-2.2	-0.1	-5.8
Algeria	189	164	121	30	51	40	31	28	28	..	..	-1.8	-18.3	-14.5
Egypt, Arab Republic	182	91	115	150	182	184	102	96	89	..	..	-10.2	3.6	-18.8
Libya	53	72	95	80	74	68	83	87	108	..	..	11.5	4.2	10.6
Morocco	133	183	159	166	159	172	196	147	172	..	..	3.3	3.0	0.0
Tunisia	30	10	8	23	8	28	15	12	7	..	..	-0.7	5.2	-10.3
ALL AFRICA	1,608	1,557	1,641	1,553	1,689	1,581	1,564	1,664	1,743	..	..	3.1	0.2	1.1

8-12. Area under major crops

	Thousands of hectares											Average annual percentage growth		
	1980	1986	1987	1988	1989	1990	1991	1992	1993	1994	1995	75-84	85-89	90-MR
SUB-SAHARAN AFRICA	136,496	142,065	142,624	143,835	144,092	144,409	145,200	145,805	158,442	157,907	..	0.6	0.6	2.1
excluding South Africa	123,242	128,896	129,455	130,661	130,918	131,235	132,026	132,626	145,263	144,728	..	0.7	0.7	2.3
excl. S. Africa & Nigeria	92,857	97,536	97,975	98,949	99,030	99,161	99,691	100,169	112,684	112,028	..	0.8	0.7	2.9
Angola	3,400	3,400	3,400	3,400	3,400	3,400	3,450	3,500	3,500	3,500	..	0.0	0.0	0.7
Benin	1,795	1,838	1,840	1,860	1,860	1,860	1,870	1,880	1,880	1,880	..	0.3	0.4	0.3
Botswana	400	400	400	400	400	421	420	420	420	420	..	0.0	0.0	0.7
Burkina Faso	2,785	3,085	3,140	3,564	3,564	3,563	3,563	3,563	3,565	3,565	..	1.9	4.0	0.0
Burundi	1,180	1,180	1,180	1,180	1,180	1,180	1,180	1,180	1,180	1,180	..	0.0	0.0	0.0
Cameroon	6,930	6,990	6,995	7,008	7,008	7,008	7,020	7,040	7,040	7,040	..	1.1	0.1	0.1
Cape Verde	40	40	40	42	42	43	43	45	45	45	..	0.0	1.1	1.5
Central African Republic	1,945	2,004	2,005	2,006	2,006	2,006	2,006	2,020	2,020	2,020	..	0.5	0.3	0.2
Chad	3,150	3,205	3,205	3,205	3,205	3,205	3,205	3,256	3,256	3,256	..	0.6	0.4	0.4
Comoros	91	98	98	99	100	100	100	100	100	100	..	0.4	1.1	0.0
Congo	148	168	165	168	168	168	169	170	170	170	..	-0.6	1.1	0.3
Côte d'Ivoire	3,095	3,620	3,640	3,660	3,660	3,690	3,690	3,710	3,710	3,710	..	1.5	0.9	0.3
Djibouti	..	..	..	..	..	..	..	..	..	..	..	..	..	..
Equatorial Guinea	230	230	230	230	230	230	230	230	230	230	..	0.0	0.0	0.0
Eritrea	..	..	..	..	..	..	..	..	580	519	..	..	..	..
Ethiopia	..	..	..	..	..	..	..	..	11,650	11,012	..	..	..	..
Gabon	452	452	452	452	452	457	457	460	460	460	..	2.3	0.0	0.3
Gambia, The	159	177	184	199	181	187	196	162	161	172	..	1.0	2.5	-2.5
Ghana	3,500	4,000	4,000	4,000	4,000	4,000	4,320	4,320	4,320	4,320	..	1.3	0.0	1.8
Guinea	702	726	726	726	728	728	730	730	730	730	..	0.4	0.3	0.1
Guinea-Bissau	285	335	335	335	335	340	340	340	340	340	..	0.9	1.3	0.2
Kenya	4,280	4,490	4,490	4,495	4,498	4,500	4,510	4,520	4,520	4,520	..	0.4	0.7	0.1
Lesotho	292	287	326	339	301	317	319	320	320	320	..	-2.3	1.5	1.0
Liberia	371	371	371	373	373	373	373	375	375	375	..	0.1	0.1	0.1
Madagascar	3,000	3,065	3,067	3,078	3,092	3,102	3,102	3,105	3,105	3,105	..	1.5	0.4	0.1
Malawi	1,332	1,590	1,610	1,630	1,650	1,670	1,690	1,700	1,700	1,700	..	1.4	2.9	0.6
Mali	2,050	2,076	2,076	2,093	2,093	2,093	2,103	2,203	2,503	2,503	..	1.0	0.4	4.3
Mauritania	195	201	201	201	205	205	205	208	208	208	..	0.5	0.7	0.4
Mauritius	107	107	107	106	106	106	106	106	106	106	..	0.1	-0.2	0.0
Mozambique	3,080	3,090	3,090	3,100	3,100	3,130	3,130	3,180	3,180	3,180	..	0.0	0.1	0.5
Namibia	657	662	662	662	662	662	662	662	662	662	..	0.1	0.0	0.0
Niger	3,552	3,540	3,592	3,600	3,605	3,605	3,605	3,605	3,605	3,605	..	4.3	0.5	0.0
Nigeria	30,385	31,360	31,480	31,712	31,888	32,074	32,335	32,457	32,579	32,700	..	0.3	0.7	0.5
Rwanda	1,015	1,130	1,142	1,153	1,153	1,155	1,160	1,170	1,170	1,170	..	2.3	0.9	0.3
São Tomé and Principe	36	37	37	37	41	42	39	40	41	41	..	0.0	1.9	-0.1
Senegal	2,350	2,350	2,350	2,350	2,350	2,350	2,350	2,351	2,350	2,350	..	0.0	0.0	0.0
Seychelles	5	6	6	6	6	6	7	7	7	7	..	2.0	0.0	3.6
Sierra Leone	499	534	539	540	540	540	540	540	540	540	..	1.1	0.7	0.0
Somalia	1,000	1,030	1,035	1,039	1,039	1,039	1,039	1,038	1,020	1,020	..	0.5	0.4	-0.4
South Africa	13,254	13,169	13,169	13,174	13,174	13,174	13,174	13,179	13,179	13,179	..	-0.2	0.0	0.0
Sudan	12,417	12,708	12,758	12,800	12,900	12,900	12,900	12,975	12,975	12,975	..	0.4	0.4	0.1
Swaziland	189	164	177	190	204	192	192	191	191	191	..	-0.7	3.4	-1.0
Tanzania	2,830	3,235	3,367	3,634	3,522	3,500	3,500	3,500	3,500	3,500	..	0.7	4.9	-0.1
Togo	2,360	2,360	2,360	2,360	2,410	2,410	2,430	2,430	2,430	2,430	..	0.0	0.3	0.2
Uganda	5,680	6,705	6,705	6,705	6,705	6,710	6,750	6,770	6,770	6,800	..	1.8	0.6	0.3
Zaire	7,600	7,850	7,850	7,850	7,850	7,860	7,880	7,900	7,900	7,900	..	0.4	0.2	0.1
Zambia	5,108	5,188	5,208	5,238	5,268	5,268	5,268	5,273	5,273	5,273	..	0.4	0.4	0.0
Zimbabwe	2,565	2,812	2,814	2,836	2,838	2,840	2,842	2,874	2,876	2,878	..	1.1	0.2	0.3
NORTH AFRICA	24,738	25,628	25,907	25,948	26,544	26,832	27,072	27,925	28,384	27,956	..	0.2	0.8	1.3
Algeria	7,509	7,533	7,624	7,642	7,673	7,675	7,837	8,126	8,096	8,043	..	0.0	0.5	1.2
Egypt, Arab Republic	2,445	2,567	2,547	2,581	2,571	2,648	2,643	2,900	3,246	3,500	..	-1.5	0.7	6.6
Libya	2,080	2,137	2,145	2,145	2,150	2,155	2,160	2,170	2,170	2,170	..	0.3	0.3	0.2
Morocco	8,004	8,491	8,731	8,754	9,273	9,503	9,575	9,848	9,920	9,291	..	1.2	1.9	0.5
Tunisia	4,700	4,900	4,860	4,826	4,877	4,851	4,857	4,881	4,952	4,952	..	0.0	-0.5	0.4
ALL AFRICA	161,234	167,693	168,531	169,783	170,636	171,241	172,272	173,730	186,826	185,863	..	0.5	0.6	2.0

8-13. Agricultural yields by major crop

	Category	1980	1986	1987	1988	1989	1990	1991	1992	1993	1994	1995	75-84	85-89	90-MR
		Thousands of hectograms per hectare											*Average annual percentage growth*		
ALGERIA															
Wheat	F1	7.3	8.1	7.8	6.0	7.8	4.8	10.8	9.9	8.1	8.0	11.4	-0.8	1.0	6.8
Citrus	F2	..	..	..	..	..	..	..	..	..	..	..	..	..	..
Dates	F3	..	..	..	..	..	..	..	..	..	..	..	..	..	..
Barley	NT1	8.4	8.9	7.5	5.8	7.5	6.9	12.1	9.0	6.2	6.5	5.4	-1.0	0.9	-6.2
Potatoes	NT2	77.8	83.7	84.6	91.7	96.3	79.3	99.7	108.2	110.9	95.5	94.7	-1.4	5.0	1.5
ANGOLA															
Coffee(green)	X1	2.2	0.8	0.5	0.4	0.5	0.2	0.3	0.3	0.3	0.1	0.2	-13.9	-11.5	-15.4
Maize	F1	6.0	3.5	3.5	3.0	2.4	2.7	4.0	4.4	4.0	2.9	3.4	-4.4	-10.8	4.2
Millet	F2	7.1	6.0	6.0	6.0	5.7	5.7	4.8	4.8	4.0	1.3	1.6	-2.1	-3.0	-22.2
Wheat	F3	5.8	6.7	6.7	6.7	6.7	10.0	10.0	7.5	7.5	10.0	16.7	-5.2	2.4	9.2
Cassava	NT1	33.8	34.9	35.0	34.9	35.6	37.5	38.0	42.3	42.3	40.0	41.5	-0.6	0.7	2.5
Sweet potatoes	NT2	91.7	89.5	89.5	89.5	86.8	86.8	89.5	90.0	88.1	90.9	90.9	0.3	-0.4	0.8
BENIN															
Cotton lint	X1	..	..	..	..	..	..	..	..	..	..	..	..	..	..
Maize	F1	7.4	8.5	7.1	8.7	8.9	9.0	9.3	9.8	9.8	10.2	10.2	-1.2	0.6	2.7
Sorghum	F2	6.3	8.0	7.7	7.3	7.7	7.3	7.8	7.7	7.7	7.8	7.8	-2.3	0.2	0.6
Cassava	NT1	66.3	70.3	65.7	74.6	80.1	79.4	83.0	84.0	83.2	81.3	81.3	-0.1	2.7	0.3
Yams	NT2	97.7	110.5	103.1	106.0	113.5	111.3	114.4	106.1	106.5	108.7	108.7	-1.7	2.0	-0.9
BOTSWANA															
Sorghum	F1	2.2	1.6	1.6	3.9	2.6	2.5	3.7	2.2	3.8	2.5	3.8	-13.3	18.9	4.1
Maize	F2	2.6	4.4	6.0	2.4	3.8	2.9	4.1	3.0	2.0	3.1	3.3	..	..	-3.5
Millet	F3	1.4	1.0	0.0	3.3	1.7	2.2	2.0	3.3	3.3	2.5	2.5	..	..	7.3
BURKINA FASO															
Cotton lint	X1	..	..	..	..	..	..	..	..	..	..	..	..	..	..
Groundnuts	X2	8.4	5.7	3.8	4.9	5.3	7.4	3.5	4.9	5.1	5.1	6.1	..	..	0.2
Sorghum	F1	8.0	4.9	4.6	5.3	6.5	7.4	6.0	5.8	5.9	5.7	6.1	..	..	-2.6
Millet	F2	6.3	3.7	3.5	3.9	4.2	6.0	3.9	4.9	4.9	4.9	4.8	..	..	0.6
Maize	F3	16.1	7.3	6.5	5.6	5.8	9.9	8.2	9.3	9.0	9.1	8.3	..	..	3.5
BURUNDI															
Coffee	X1	9.3	6.1	7.0	9.3	5.7	10.0	5.2	7.0	8.0	6.3	8.0	..	..	2.0
Tea	X2	8.8	0.0	10.0	10.0	5.0	8.0	3.3	3.3	6.7	2.5	5.0	..	..	-5.7
Maize	F1	12.3	10.7	11.5	9.9	11.4	12.1	11.5	13.3	11.3	10.8	11.2	..	..	-1.1
Sorghum	F2	10.0	9.0	10.0	10.0	9.5	10.0	9.6	9.6	10.0	10.0	10.0	..	..	0.7
Rice, paddy	F3	29.2	25.0	16.7	20.0	23.3	40.0	20.0	15.0	30.0	25.0	20.0	11.3	7.1	-3.5
Millet	F4	11.0	8.9	9.0	7.8	9.0	10.0	9.1	9.2	9.0	10.0	10.0	..	..	1.1
Bananas	NT1	..	..	..	..	..	..	..	..	..	..	..	..	..	..
Cassava	NT2	87.8	89.7	90.0	90.5	90.9	90.0	90.9	91.8	91.7	90.9	92.0	64.9	66.7	0.2
CAMEROON															
Coffee	X1	3.1	3.5	4.2	4.2	4.2	3.8	3.6	3.3	3.6	3.7	3.7	-0.4	4.4	-1.6
Cocoa	X2	0.0	0.1	0.1	0.1	0.0	0.1	0.1	0.1	0.1	0.1	0.1	1.6	3.5	7.2
Cotton lint	X3	..	..	..	..	..	..	..	..	..	..	..	..	..	..
Maize	F1	8.3	19.3	19.2	19.6	18.6	18.5	18.0	18.1	18.7	20.2	21.8	1.6	1.8	2.5
Sorghum	F2	8.7	10.6	7.0	8.2	7.0	8.5	7.7	7.6	7.8	7.3	8.0	-3.5	2.4	0.4
Millet	F3	7.6	12.4	8.7	10.0	10.8	10.5	10.5	10.0	10.3	10.0	11.1	-3.5	7.0	-0.1
Rice	F4	23.0	45.0	43.3	45.0	56.4	50.0	60.0	60.0	60.0	43.8	50.0	..	7.1	-2.2
Cassava	NT1	59.0	148.1	142.1	125.1	157.1	163.7	187.5	187.5	193.8	200.0	162.5	4.2	-1.0	1.9
Plantains	NT2	..	..	..	..	..	..	..	..	..	..	..	..	..	..
CENTRAL AFRICAN REPUBLIC															
Coffee	X1	3.6	8.0	7.2	8.3	6.0	5.8	7.2	6.1	4.1	8.3	4.7	3.1	2.6	-2.0
Cotton lint	X2	..	..	..	..	..	..	..	..	..	..	..	..	..	..
Sorghum	F1	6.5	12.4	8.3	9.8	9.5	5.6	6.4	8.1	7.4	5.8	5.8	3.2	-2.1	-4.4
Maize	F2	3.8	12.1	10.2	10.1	9.4	8.1	8.2	9.1	9.1	8.5	8.6	-0.9	8.5	-0.3
Groundnuts	F3	10.1	10.7	9.9	10.3	11.7	9.2	8.5	9.7	9.7	10.0	9.5	-0.4	5.1	-1.2
Cassava	NT1	30.7	36.9	32.1	31.9	30.9	28.5	33.7	34.5	31.9	28.8	22.3	1.7	-4.6	-3.5
Yams	NT2	60.0	60.0	60.0	63.3	66.7	65.7	65.7	74.3	71.4	71.4	71.4	1.6	0.1	1.6
CHAD															
Cotton lint	X1	..	..	..	..	..	..	..	..	..	..	..	..	..	..
Sorghum	F1	5.1	6.4	6.3	7.4	5.5	6.4	5.3	7.4	5.9	6.6	6.6	-0.5	3.1	2.6
Millet	F2	4.7	5.4	4.6	5.4	3.4	3.4	4.8	5.2	4.1	4.9	4.9	-0.8	-2.7	6.2
Groundnuts	F3	5.8	7.3	6.3	7.2	14.8	5.8	6.3	9.8	6.9	7.0	7.0	1.4	12.7	-6.2
COMOROS															
Bananas	F1	..	..	..	..	..	..	..	..	..	..	..	..	..	..
Cassava	NT1	47.1	41.4	47.8	48.9	50.0	50.0	46.3	52.2	53.3	57.8	57.8	-0.8	4.6	3.1

8-13. Agricultural yields by major crop (continued)

	Category	Thousands of hectograms per hectare											Average annual percentage growth		
		1980	1986	1987	1988	1989	1990	1991	1992	1993	1994	1995	75-84	85-89	90-MR
CONGO															
Coffee	X1	..	..	..	..	..	..	..	..	..	..	..	..	..	..
Cocoa beans	X2	5.0	4.0	4.0	3.3	4.0	2.0	7.5	1.7	1.7	1.7	1.7	-2.2	-6.4	-14.8
Maize	F1	8.2	8.4	7.6	8.0	8.9	8.9	6.1	9.3	9.3	9.3	9.3	2.1	4.9	2.2
Cassava	NT1	69.0	72.2	71.5	71.8	63.5	64.8	54.9	74.1	65.8	65.6	65.6	3.6	-1.7	1.1
Plantains	NT2	..	..	..	..	..	..	..	..	..	..	..	..	..	..
COTE D'IVOIRE															
Coffee	X1	2.4	2.4	2.4	1.6	2.3	2.2	3.2	1.0	1.1	1.1	1.4	-6.6	12.2	-13.1
Cocoa	X2	5.0	5.2	5.4	5.3	5.7	5.1	4.4	5.2	5.5	5.4	5.7	0.1	1.0	1.3
Oil Palm, fruit	X3	..	..	..	..	..	..	..	..	..	..	..	..	..	..
Rice	F1	11.7	11.0	11.3	11.8	11.7	11.5	11.7	11.0	17.6	15.8	16.1	-0.9	-1.1	7.4
Maize	F2	8.1	7.0	6.8	7.0	7.1	7.2	4.8	7.8	7.7	7.5	7.5	5.8	-5.1	2.7
Cassava	NT1	52.3	55.1	56.5	58.8	59.6	55.1	50.6	52.8	50.0	50.5	50.5	1.8	1.8	-2.4
Yams	NT2	90.7	95.0	96.4	98.0	100.0	95.0	74.5	116.4	109.6	108.6	108.6	1.8	0.3	3.3
EGYPT															
Cotton lint	X1	..	..	..	..	..	..	..	..	..	..	..	..	..	..
Rice, paddy	X2	58.4	57.8	58.3	60.6	64.9	72.6	52.0	76.5	77.2	79.2	81.7	1.0	2.8	4.6
Wheat	F1	31.2	38.0	47.2	47.5	49.4	52.0	33.3	52.5	53.0	50.0	54.2	0.7	7.1	2.4
Sugarcane	F3	..	..	..	..	..	..	..	..	..	..	..	..	..	..
Dry Broadbeans	NT1	..	..	..	..	..	..	..	..	..	..	..	..	..	..
EQUATORIAL GUINEA															
Cocoa	X1	1.1	0.8	1.1	1.1	0.9	1.0	0.9	0.8	0.9	0.8	0.8	-2.8	2.6	-3.1
Coffee(green)	X2	3.3	3.7	3.7	3.7	3.7	3.7	3.3	3.7	3.7	3.7	3.7	1.2	-0.8	0.4
Cassava	NT1	24.6	29.3	29.3	29.3	29.3	25.0	23.8	26.1	26.1	26.1	26.1	0.9	0.4	-0.6
ETHIOPIA															
Coffee(green)	X1	..	..	..	..	..	..	..	..	..	..	..	..	..	..
Sorghum	F1	..	..	..	..	..	..	..	..	..	..	..	..	..	..
Maize	F2	..	..	..	..	..	..	..	..	..	..	..	..	..	..
Barley	NT1	..	..	..	..	..	..	..	..	..	..	..	..	..	..
GABON															
Coffee(green)	X2	3.3	2.5	5.0	5.0	5.0	0.0	0.0	0.0	0.0	0.0	0.0	..	14.7	..
Oil palm, fruit	X3	..	..	..	..	..	..	..	..	..	..	..	..	..	..
Maize	F1	16.7	14.3	16.7	16.7	14.3	15.7	15.0	17.1	17.9	17.3	18.0	1.9	-2.1	3.9
Cassava	NT1	50.0	50.3	49.7	49.5	50.5	50.0	50.2	50.0	50.0	51.1	50.0	0.0	0.0	0.0
Taro (cocoyam)	NT2	..	..	..	..	..	..	..	..	..	..	..	..	..	..
Yams	NT3	56.4	60.0	63.3	62.5	62.5	64.7	55.8	64.7	64.7	66.7	66.7	1.3	1.5	1.4
GAMBIA,THE															
Groundnuts	X1	8.7	13.8	12.6	10.3	15.1	8.4	10.5	8.5	12.2	10.8	10.6	-1.4	1.7	-1.4
Cotton lint	X2	..	..	..	..	..	..	..	..	..	..	..	..	..	..
Oil Palm, fruit	X3	..	..	..	..	..	..	..	..	..	..	..	..	..	..
Millet	F1	9.6	11.3	11.4	10.9	9.6	9.2	6.4	11.2	10.2	10.6	10.8	3.6	-3.0	4.0
Rice,paddy	F2	19.5	16.0	12.5	15.3	15.0	14.0	11.0	17.3	15.0	15.4	16.7	4.5	-9.2	3.0
Maize	F3	10.0	15.5	11.5	12.3	12.7	12.7	6.7	15.0	16.0	11.8	12.9	4.6	-4.4	2.8
Sorghum	F4	8.3	10.0	7.8	8.8	11.0	6.2	6.0	9.2	11.3	11.3	10.8	5.1	-1.7	6.6
GHANA															
Cocoa	X1	2.3	2.5	2.3	2.8	3.0	2.8	2.3	3.1	2.4	2.7	3.3	-2.8	7.1	0.8
Maize	F1	8.7	11.8	10.9	13.9	12.6	11.9	10.7	12.0	15.1	14.9	15.6	-4.6	6.6	5.2
Millet	F2	5.9	7.1	7.4	6.1	7.4	6.0	6.0	6.3	9.7	8.8	8.9	..	3.8	6.6
Groundnuts	F3	16.9	11.7	12.6	15.7	12.6	8.9	9.5	7.7	7.7	20.0	20.0	-1.6	4.5	10.5
Cassava	NT1	80.8	74.3	69.9	93.2	80.2	84.1	78.1	72.5	77.9	115.9	132.7	2.9	-0.1	8.0
Plantains	NT2	..	..	..	..	..	..	..	..	..	..	..	..	..	..
GUINEA															
Coffee(green)	X1	3.1	2.3	2.3	2.5	5.1	5.0	3.3	5.4	5.3	5.5	5.5	-1.2	7.9	3.1
Oil Palm, fruit	X2	..	..	..	..	..	..	..	..	..	..	..	..	..	..
Rice, paddy	F1	9.0	8.0	8.4	9.7	10.9	9.7	8.9	13.3	13.8	13.8	13.8	-1.8	8.6	6.9
Maize	F2	10.0	11.1	10.0	9.5	9.9	10.1	10.8	10.7	10.4	10.0	9.8	..	..	-0.3
Groundnuts	F3	6.6	5.6	5.5	5.5	6.6	7.6	6.5	10.1	8.8	8.8	11.6	-0.5	0.8	8.5
Cassava	NT1	69.6	70.0	72.7	73.0	81.3	77.5	69.9	72.1	68.3	72.1	72.1	0.0	2.9	-1.9
GUINEA-BISSAU															
Groundnuts	X1	3.5	5.5	6.7	10.0	8.9	10.0	3.8	10.0	10.0	11.3	11.3	-3.4	20.8	7.1
Rice, paddy	F1	7.0	20.0	21.0	20.0	20.0	20.5	6.0	19.1	19.7	20.2	19.0	1.2	11.1	3.6
Sorghum	F2	6.4	8.0	10.0	16.0	7.5	8.5	7.1	9.2	9.3	9.3	9.4	0.0	9.3	4.2
Millet	F3	7.2	9.0	10.0	15.3	9.4	8.5	6.2	8.5	8.4	7.8	9.2	4.0	7.5	0.3
Maize	F4	10.0	7.7	9.1	13.3	10.0	10.8	6.7	9.1	10.0	9.3	10.0	..	..	0.4

8-13. Agricultural yields by major crop (continued)

	Category	1980	1986	1987	1988	1989	1990	1991	1992	1993	1994	1995	75-84	85-89	90-MR
		Thousands of hectograms per hectare											Average annual percentage growth		
KENYA															
Coffee(green)	X1	8.9	7.3	6.8	8.3	7.6	6.8	7.8	5.5	4.7	5.0	6.0	0.9	1.8	-6.3
Tea	X2	11.7	16.6	18.4	18.9	20.8	20.3	12.6	18.1	20.1	19.7	23.1	4.0	6.8	2.6
Sugarcane	X3	1,224.9	790.8	849.6	1,022.1	1,176.8	1,187.5	727.2	851.0	894.0	840.0	860.0	5.4	4.0	-5.0
Sisal	X4	9.8	11.4	10.6	10.6	10.6	12.1	8.0	11.3	11.7	11.3	11.3	1.7	-4.5	1.6
Maize	F1	12.0	20.3	17.2	19.0	18.5	15.8	16.3	17.3	16.0	21.3	19.6	1.9	4.0	2.7
Wheat	F2	21.6	18.1	13.1	15.5	15.9	18.6	14.8	12.6	9.7	17.9	21.3	2.1	-0.6	1.3
LESOTHO															
Wheat	X1	9.7	5.8	6.8	6.3	6.8	8.0	14.5	8.6	6.2	16.2	5.0	-4.9	5.3	-1.4
Dry Peas	X2	8.3	5.0	2.5	6.0	5.0	2.5	10.0	5.0	5.0	2.5	4.0	-4.8	0.9	-4.7
Dry Beans	X3	5.7	2.4	2.3	3.0	5.6	20.0	14.0	2.5	4.0	3.8	3.3	-7.2	24.4	-19.7
Maize	X4	9.6	7.0	6.7	9.2	10.5	11.0	15.8	5.8	8.9	20.6	6.8	-1.9	7.9	-2.2
Sorghum	F1	9.7	6.3	4.4	7.0	7.8	10.0	14.8	5.9	13.0	12.0	6.7	-3.9	1.9	-0.8
LIBERIA															
Rubber	X1	..	..	..	..	..	..	..	..	..	..	..	..	..	..
Coffee(green)	X2	4.6	4.7	2.0	2.0	2.5	1.0	5.0	1.5	1.5	1.5	1.5	7.4	-19.7	-6.6
Cocoa	X3	2.5	1.5	1.0	1.2	3.0	2.0	2.2	0.0	0.0	0.0	0.0	-1.3	-2.3	..
Rice, paddy	F1	12.3	12.4	12.6	12.8	11.7	10.0	12.4	9.2	10.8	11.1	11.1	0.6	-1.1	-0.3
Cassava	NT1	66.7	63.8	79.1	86.0	74.3	70.0	63.3	70.9	70.8	71.4	71.4	0.1	9.4	0.1
LIBYA															
Wheat	F1	..	..	..	..	..	..	..	..	..	..	..	..	..	..
MADAGASCAR															
Coffee	X1	3.7	3.7	3.6	3.7	3.8	3.5	4.6	4.3	3.7	3.6	3.7	-1.0	1.1	-0.9
Vanilla	X2	..	..	..	..	..	..	..	..	..	..	..	..	..	..
Cloves	X3	..	..	..	..	..	..	..	..	..	..	..	..	..	..
Rice	F1	17.6	18.8	19.8	19.3	20.8	20.8	17.6	21.2	21.1	20.0	21.3	-0.7	2.5	0.7
Cassava	NT1	60.8	67.4	70.0	65.6	66.6	66.4	66.3	83.2	70.1	71.8	72.0	-1.0	2.0	1.6
Sweet potatoes	NT2	48.4	49.7	50.8	51.9	53.1	53.4	53.2	48.4	54.9	58.9	58.9	-0.8	2.0	2.0
MALAWI															
Tobacco leaves	X1	8.6	6.8	7.4	8.1	9.6	10.1	7.8	9.7	10.0	8.8	10.2	3.5	3.4	0.5
Tea	X2	16.7	21.7	17.8	21.1	21.7	20.5	18.8	15.6	20.5	18.4	17.9	3.1	-0.7	-2.5
Groundnuts	X3	7.1	9.4	7.8	8.0	4.4	7.7	7.0	4.1	9.0	5.6	4.6	0.3	-7.7	-0.8
Cotton lint	X4	..	..	..	..	..	..	..	..	..	..	..	..	..	..
Maize	F1	12.2	10.9	10.2	11.7	11.9	10.0	13.2	4.5	15.2	9.2	13.5	0.6	-0.3	1.3
Sorghum	F2	6.7	6.6	4.8	7.3	6.7	4.8	9.2	1.4	5.0	3.1	6.1	-5.8.	-0.1	-6.1
Cassava	NT1	58.4	29.9	26.0	21.8	21.2	23.4	62.0	20.2	28.8	26.7	26.7	-7.0	-7.5	0.6
MALI															
Cotton lint	X1	..	..	..	..	..	..	..	..	..	..	..	..	..	..
Groundnuts	X2	8.3	11.5	8.0	10.4	10.7	7.3	11.5	7.3	8.2	8.4	8.4	-4.5	7.0	-2.6
Millet	F1	6.2	9.8	8.9	8.4	7.8	6.1	5.1	5.4	5.5	6.1	6.1	-0.2	2.7	-2.2
Rice, paddy	F2	9.8	11.8	14.5	13.5	15.4	14.3	11.2	16.0	16.6	16.5	16.5	-3.8	15.1	3.2
Sorghum	F3	6.7	11.1	10.4	9.9	9.4	6.6	5.6	7.1	6.9	7.6	7.6	2.1	-1.3	-0.4
Maize	F4	11.0	16.5	15.2	15.0	12.9	11.6	8.8	10.1	11.0	11.3	11.3	3.2	2.8	-0.7
MAURITANIA															
Sorghum	F1	3.2	5.3	7.8	6.6	7.6	5.2	3.7	5.0	5.9	5.8	6.4	-4.9	19.1	0.7
Rice	F2	36.7	47.1	48.2	42.5	39.3	32.5	20.0	39.2	29.5	27.9	34.3	5.7	-1.6	-1.1
Millet	F3	2.3	6.0	3.5	5.4	5.0	2.5	2.5	3.3	2.5	2.8	3.6	12.6	-7.3	-2.6
Maize	F4	1.3	5.0	10.0	1.8	5.0	5.0	3.8	5.0	3.3	1.5	20.0	0.9	-3.3	6.2
MAURITIUS															
Sugarcane	X1	577.7	772.4	798.8	716.5	706.0	730.0	743.5	770.8	730.0	675.7	702.7	-0.2	1.5	-0.7
Potatoes	NT1	120.0	170.0	170.0	140.0	200.0	180.0	110.0	190.0	140.0	190.0	190.0	6.4	-4.8	0.7
Onions	NT2	..	..	..	..	..	..	..	..	..	..	..	..	..	..
MOROCCO															
Wheat	F1	10.6	17.1	10.6	17.4	14.9	13.3	6.3	7.0	6.8	18.1	5.5	0.8	6.4	-7.8
Sugarbeet	F2	355.7	477.3	450.8	490.2	456.7	466.3	307.1	529.6	510.0	499.0	468.4	3.4	0.8	2.6
Barley	NT1	10.3	14.4	6.7	13.8	12.5	8.9	5.8	4.8	4.8	14.4	3.9	-4.7	9.6	-9.3
MOZAMBIQUE															
Cotton lint	X2	..	..	..	..	..	..	..	..	..	..	..	..	..	..
Tea	X3	10.5	7.1	6.0	4.0	6.0	6.7	9.4	5.0	6.7	6.7	7.5	-0.6	-10.5	1.2
Maize	F1	5.4	4.6	2.7	3.2	3.3	4.5	7.2	1.6	6.3	5.6	6.8	-4.1	-8.0	9.3
Rice, paddy	F2	8.3	9.3	8.6	8.9	8.6	8.7	8.5	3.0	6.2	8.1	8.7	-3.5	0.4	-1.6
Cassava	NT1	41.4	40.0	41.1	40.0	41.1	43.0	41.9	33.3	41.6	36.3	42.4	0.1	0.1	-0.9
NAMIBIA															
Wheat	F1	20.0	30.0	25.0	25.0	40.0	13.3	20.0	15.0	20.0	20.0	15.0	12.8	12.0	-7.3
Maize	F2	12.3	12.8	7.0	12.3	12.0	12.6	12.5	3.3	9.0	13.3	8.3	0.0	2.0	-4.6

8-13. Agricultural yields by major crop (continued)

	Category	Thousands of hectograms per hectare											Average annual percentage growth		
		1980	1986	1987	1988	1989	1990	1991	1992	1993	1994	1995	75-84	85-89	90-MR
NIGER															
Cowpeas	X1	..	..	..	..	..	..	..	..	..	..	..	..	..	..
Groundnuts	X3	6.6	5.1	2.6	3.8	4.3	2.9	4.7	3.3	3.3	3.6	3.6	0.9	7.0	-1.7
Millet	F1	4.4	4.3	3.3	5.0	3.7	2.4	4.1	3.6	3.5	3.5	3.5	-1.0	5.7	1.5
Sorghum	F2	4.8	3.3	2.7	3.8	2.6	1.3	4.7	1.5	1.9	1.8	1.8	-4.4	4.7	-4.3
NIGERIA															
Cocoa	X1	3.9	2.5	3.8	4.1	4.0	4.0	5.1	3.6	3.4	3.3	3.3	-3.0	3.7	-5.0
Oil Palm, fruit	X2	..	..	..	..	..	..	..	..	..	..	..	..	..	..
Cotton lint	X3	..	..	..	..	..	..	..	..	..	..	..	..	..	..
Groundnuts	X4	8.4	10.6	7.9	8.9	11.0	14.0	7.9	12.4	11.8	9.2	8.5	2.8	3.7	-4.2
Sorghum	F1	11.2	10.8	16.0	12.2	9.8	10.0	9.6	9.9	11.0	10.8	10.1	8.0	-4.3	1.5
Millet	F2	8.7	10.5	10.2	11.1	11.7	10.7	8.3	7.9	9.2	9.7	9.6	8.3	-7.0	-2.5
Maize	F3	14.0	11.8	11.5	11.0	11.1	11.3	12.7	11.2	11.9	12.7	13.2	0.2	-1.0	2.4
Rice, paddy	F4	19.8	20.2	23.9	23.9	18.7	20.7	16.6	19.6	13.8	14.2	13.6	0.5	0.5	-6.6
Yams	NT1	106.0	56.4	65.1	84.0	87.4	106.8	115.4	113.5	131.0	114.0	109.8	-8.0	10.6	3.4
Cassava	NT2	95.8	107.7	124.0	124.7	94.1	116.5	100.0	105.9	106.8	105.9	106.8	-1.1	1.2	0.9
RWANDA															
Coffee(green)	X1	6.7	8.5	8.4	8.0	5.7	6.4	6.6	6.8	5.5	0.7	5.5	5.3	-9.8	-15.8
Tea	X2	7.8	9.1	10.0	10.0	10.8	10.8	10.0	10.8	10.0	7.1	7.1	-4.8	6.8	-7.2
Sorghum	F1	12.3	12.9	12.1	9.3	11.1	12.2	11.3	10.3	10.9	10.6	10.7	0.6	-1.0	-1.5
Maize	F2	11.8	11.4	14.9	15.0	14.6	13.5	11.0	13.6	14.8	15.0	39.4	1.9	5.6	13.3
Plantains	NT1	..	..	..	..	..	..	..	..	..	..	..	..	..	..
Sweet potatoes	NT2	76.4	70.9	71.0	65.3	47.7	53.6	76.3	66.4	69.7	59.3	73.3	-0.4	-5.2	5.1
SENEGAL															
Groundnuts	X1	4.9	10.4	11.4	8.0	10.8	7.7	4.7	6.0	8.5	8.0	9.4	-4.4	7.6	1.0
Cotton lint	X2	..	..	..	..	..	..	..	..	..	..	..	..	..	..
Millet	F1	4.7	5.9	7.3	5.4	6.7	5.8	4.1	5.8	6.7	5.9	7.5	-3.8	4.7	3.0
Rice, paddy	F2	9.7	20.1	18.4	18.5	21.3	24.8	10.0	23.9	24.7	20.8	22.5	3.8	0.0	2.6
Maize	F3	7.3	11.4	11.5	11.2	14.1	11.4	10.4	11.0	12.7	10.1	10.9	0.2	0.3	-2.8
Sorghum	F4	7.7	9.6	8.7	8.5	9.7	9.1	6.8	8.9	7.9	9.3	8.6	-0.4	-0.3	-0.6
SIERRA LEONE															
Cocoa	X1	13.3	35.0	40.0	48.0	40.0	40.0	8.3	25.0	25.0	30.0	33.3	8.4	9.3	-0.1
Coffee(green)	X2	12.5	20.9	21.8	22.7	26.0	23.6	12.5	23.6	22.7	18.7	16.7	8.9	5.2	-4.2
Palm oil	X3	..	..	..	..	..	..	..	..	..	..	..	..	..	..
Rice, paddy	F1	12.5	15.4	13.1	12.7	12.9	12.8	14.6	13.5	12.7	12.3	12.3	-3.8	4.7	-1.2
Cassava	NT1	38.0	51.4	41.1	41.4	59.0	58.6	49.4	53.2	46.1	58.1	57.6	-3.8	4.7	-0.6
SOMALIA															
Bananas	X1	..	..	..	..	..	..	..	..	..	..	..	..	..	..
Maize	F1	10.1	13.7	11.0	12.6	11.3	11.5	7.4	10.1	9.9	4.1	4.2	0.2	-1.4	-15.5
Sorghum	F2	3.1	6.2	4.7	4.1	6.1	5.6	3.2	3.1	2.9	4.1	3.4	1.5	3.5	-8.4
Sesame	NT1	4.6	5.6	4.3	4.2	4.5	4.5	5.5	3.3	3.1	3.1	3.4	-3.5	-2.0	-7.6
SOUTH AFRICA															
Maize	X1	25.2	20.5	18.3	19.2	31.9	25.1	21.9	8.9	22.8	28.5	13.2	..	..	-8.0
Wheat	X2	9.1	12.1	16.3	17.8	11.1	11.2	10.9	17.4	18.5	17.6	15.4	..	..	9.1
Sugarcane	X3	660.2	676.0	793.2	747.6	665.6	664.8	876.0	471.1	416.4	408.4	576.7	..	..	-7.4
Sorghum	F1	28.8	14.5	19.6	19.3	16.7	11.9	18.3	7.5	21.5	22.5	16.0	..	..	4.8
Barley	F2	8.8	21.9	28.0	15.8	22.2	18.5	8.2	12.5	19.8	22.9	24.0	..	..	5.6
SUDAN															
Cotton lint	X1	..	..	..	..	..	..	..	..	..	..	..	..	..	..
Groundnuts	X2	7.9	6.7	6.3	8.6	4.0	5.5	9.2	7.0	5.5	8.0	8.0	..	..	8.6
Sesame	X3	2.6	2.3	2.4	1.7	1.3	1.7	2.5	2.0	1.4	1.3	1.3	..	..	-4.3
Sorghum	F1	7.1	6.6	4.0	7.9	4.0	4.3	7.1	6.5	5.1	5.7	5.4	..	..	4.0
Wheat	F2	12.1	13.2	13.3	12.6	15.0	15.8	10.9	24.1	13.8	13.3	17.9	0.0	2.0	1.5
SWAZILAND															
Sugarcane	X1	1,070.0	1,166.9	1,075.0	1,025.0	1,054.7	1,038.4	996.0	925.0	875.0	946.5	999.5	-0.2	0.3	-1.7
Cotton lint	X3	10.2	11.1	11.5	9.8	9.0	9.5	9.8	9.5	11.1	11.1	..	-3.5	-3.7	..
Maize	F1	13.6	19.5	14.6	14.3	13.6	10.3	17.3	9.4	12.2	10.6	12.7	-3.1	-7.4	-1.8
TANZANIA															
Coffee	X1	4.2	5.0	5.3	4.2	3.9	4.2	5.0	4.1	4.2	3.1	3.6	0.5	-3.8	-3.6
Cotton lint	X2	..	..	..	..	..	..	..	..	..	..	..	..	..	..
Tea	X3	10.7	10.8	13.1	12.3	15.4	13.8	10.6	9.5	11.1	11.6	11.6	5.0	-5.4	-4.1
Maize	F1	12.3	11.6	13.7	12.6	15.8	15.0	12.8	11.7	12.5	13.3	15.5	3.7	2.1	-1.1
Rice	F2	11.9	20.0	18.4	17.8	18.6	19.2	16.9	12.8	16.9	17.4	15.1	-2.2	4.8	-2.9
Sorghum	F3	6.9	8.1	8.7	8.6	11.0	9.7	9.2	8.6	11.2	7.2	12.2	5.5	-2.3	-0.4
Millet	F4	7.6	11.4	10.0	8.0	10.0	11.2	7.8	8.5	6.5	6.4	10.9	5.5	-5.1	-3.7
Cassava	NT1	107.3	113.5	102.4	102.6	92.3	132.1	123.5	104.0	104.0	103.9	102.0	5.6	-3.3	-1.2

8-13. Agricultural yields by major crop (continued)

	Category	Thousands of hectograms per hectare											Average annual percentage growth		
		1980	1986	1987	1988	1989	1990	1991	1992	1993	1994	1995	75-84	85-89	90-MR
TOGO															
Coffee(green)	X1	4.8	3.8	6.7	7.1	5.7	6.2	6.8	6.8	7.0	6.8	4.2	-6.5	28.2	-2.4
Cocoa	X2	4.4	3.6	3.1	2.2	2.2	2.1	1.4	1.1	1.9	1.4	1.4	-3.6	-8.1	-6.5
Cotton lint	X3	..	..	..	..	..	..	..	..	..	..	..	..	..	..
Maize	F1	9.2	6.4	7.6	11.1	10.7	9.6	9.1	10.1	11.6	8.3	8.5	-3.6	4.3	-2.6
Sorghum	F2	7.5	10.3	7.2	6.6	7.8	6.3	7.3	7.7	6.4	5.5	5.5	..	0.4	-5.1
Millet	F3	2.6	7.1	5.5	4.7	7.7	4.1	3.8	5.6	5.0	3.8	3.8	1.7	-14.3	-7.0
Cassava	NT1	102.0	73.4	78.9	67.7	73.0	77.0	77.4	68.5	68.2	53.5	58.6	-14.6	3.1	-5.3
Yams	NT2	86.4	99.8	85.7	102.4	106.6	91.2	89.5	83.6	103.9	58.6	62.5	-2.4	-0.8	-8.0
TUNISIA															
Wheat	F1	10.2	8.8	14.0	7.6	7.5	12.7	17.0	17.0	13.7	10.7	7.1	-0.6	-4.1	-2.7
Barley	F2	7.7	3.0	8.4	4.2	4.9	9.4	13.1	11.9	9.3	5.9	3.3	-1.2	-6.7	-8.4
UGANDA															
Coffee(green)	X1	6.0	7.1	7.4	6.7	7.1	4.8	5.4	4.2	5.5	7.5	8.4	-2.9	1.8	5.1
Cotton lint	X2	..	..	..	..	..	..	..	..	..	..	..	..	..	..
Millet	F1	16.5	12.5	16.0	15.6	16.0	15.0	15.0	16.0	15.1	14.8	15.3	0.1	7.5	-0.6
Maize	F2	11.1	10.0	11.6	12.8	14.5	15.0	13.5	15.0	16.0	16.0	16.0	0.1	6.7	2.1
Sorghum	F3	17.9	13.5	15.5	14.8	15.0	15.0	14.8	15.0	15.0	15.0	15.0	2.7	2.8	0.0
Cassava	NT1	68.6	80.1	89.9	90.6	91.0	83.0	83.0	80.0	85.1	65.0	75.0	5.9	3.4	-3.7
Plantains	NT2	..	..	..	..	..	..	..	..	..	..	..	..	..	..
ZAIRE															
Coffee(green)	X1	3.7	3.3	3.7	3.7	3.7	3.3	3.2	3.7	2.2	3.1	3.0	-0.6	2.2	-3.8
Palm oil	X2	..	..	..	..	..	..	..	..	..	..	..	..	..	..
Maize	F1	8.0	8.0	8.5	8.1	8.1	8.2	8.1	8.1	9.2	8.2	8.4	1.7	-0.3	0.8
Rice	F2	8.0	8.0	8.0	8.0	8.0	8.0	8.1	8.5	8.6	8.2	7.2	1.1	-1.2	-0.8
Cassava	NT1	70.0	80.5	80.6	80.6	80.7	80.7	80.7	82.5	83.3	87.0	83.3	-0.1	1.7	1.0
Plantains	NT2	..	..	..	..	..	..	..	..	..	..	..	..	..	..
ZAMBIA															
Cotton	X1	3.0	4.0	3.4	4.7	3.7	3.0	4.2	2.7	4.7	4.8	4.7	2.0	-4.5	6.6
Tobacco leaves	X2	10.0	10.0	20.0	8.0	8.0	8.0	20.0	4.0	5.4	5.4	5.4	2.3	-6.4	-11.1
Sunflower	X3	9.0	5.4	5.3	4.0	3.3	4.5	3.1	0.3	5.4	6.3	5.0	1.3	-14.7	9.0
Maize	F1	16.9	20.9	17.4	26.9	18.1	14.3	17.2	7.3	25.2	15.0	14.2	3.6	3.1	-0.9
Wheat	F2	50.0	45.0	40.0	41.1	47.0	42.3	43.3	44.6	39.4	23.9	27.8	..	2.5	-9.6
Cassava	NT1	50.0	50.0	50.0	50.7	49.5	50.5	50.5	50.9	49.6	52.2	52.2	0.7	0.0	0.7
ZIMBABWE															
Tobacco leaves	X1	19.5	18.7	20.9	20.5	22.8	21.7	24.9	24.3	22.0	24.6	24.1	5.9	-0.5	1.1
Cotton	X2	18.6	19.2	14.1	16.2	14.5	12.5	10.8	8.7	11.0	10.0	6.7	-1.7	-5.6	-9.3
Sugarcane	X3	1,011.2	1,253.0	1,077.1	999.7	1,079.7	966.6	1,011.3	89.3	597.8	1,068.8	1,159.7	-0.1	-0.7	-0.4
Maize	F1	13.4	19.4	9.2	18.1	17.1	17.2	14.4	4.1	16.3	16.6	6.0	-8.1	6.8	-10.5
Wheat	F2	50.3	59.0	58.1	57.1	56.8	58.2	56.3	48.3	70.8	55.6	20.8	4.7	0.0	-9.8

Notes: The following commodities are in their least-processed form unless otherwise indicated:

Cotton, seed cotton
Groundnuts, unshelled
Coffee, green or roasted
Rice, paddy
Cloves, whole
Cocoa, beans
Tobacco, leaves
Sunflower, seeds
1 hectogram = 100 grams = 3.527 oz.

Countries excluded from listing: Cape Verde, Djibouti, Sao Tome and Principe, and Seychelles.

For livestock "yield", see Table 8.6. Food Output by Major Crops.

8-14. Incidence of drought

	D=Significant shortage of rain												
	1983	*1984*	*1985*	*1986*	*1987*	*1988*	*1989*	*1990*	*1991*	*1992*	*1993*	*1994*	*1995*
SUB-SAHARAN AFRICA	..	..	..	..	..	..	..	..	..	..	..	..	..
excluding South Africa	..	..	..	..	..	..	..	..	..	..	..	..	..
excluding South Africa & Nigeria	..	..	..	..	..	..	..	..	..	..	..	..	..
Angola	..	..	..	..	..	..	..	..	..	..	..	..	..
Benin	..	..	..	..	..	..	..	..	..	..	..	..	..
Botswana	D	D	D	D	D	..	..	..	..	D	..	..	D
Burkina Faso	D	D	..	..	..	..	..	..	..	..	..	..	..
Burundi	D	D	..	..	..	..	..	..	..	..	..	..	..
Cameroon	D	..	..	..	..	..	..	..	..	..	..	..	..
Cape Verde	D	D	D	..	..	..	..	..	..	..	D	D	..
Central African Republic	D	D	..	..	..	..	..	..	..	..	..	..	..
Chad	D	D	..	..	..	..	..	..	..	..	D	..	D
Comoros	..	..	..	..	..	..	..	..	..	..	..	..	..
Congo	..	..	..	..	..	..	..	..	..	..	..	..	..
Côte d'Ivoire	D	..	..	..	..	..	..	..	..	..	..	..	..
Djibouti	..	..	..	..	..	..	..	..	..	..	..	..	..
Equatorial Guinea	..	..	..	..	..	..	..	..	..	..	..	..	..
Ethiopia	..	D	D	..	D	D	..	..	D	D	..	D	..
Gabon	..	..	..	..	..	..	..	..	..	..	..	..	..
Gambia, The	..	..	..	..	..	..	..	..	..	..	..	..	..
Ghana	D	D	..	..	..	..	..	..	..	..	..	..	..
Guinea	..	..	..	..	..	..	..	..	..	..	..	..	..
Guinea-Bissau	..	..	..	..	..	..	..	..	..	..	..	..	..
Kenya	..	D	..	..	..	..	..	..	..	D	D	..	..
Lesotho	D	..	..	..	..	..	..	..	..	D	..	..	D
Liberia	..	..	..	..	..	..	..	..	..	..	..	..	..
Madagascar	..	..	..	..	..	..	..	..	..	..	..	..	..
Malawi	..	..	..	..	..	..	..	..	..	D	..	D	D
Mali	D	D	..	..	..	..	..	..	..	..	..	..	..
Mauritania	D	D	..	..	..	..	..	..	..	..	..	..	..
Mauritius	D	..	..	..	..	..	..	..	..	..	..	..	..
Mozambique	..	..	..	..	..	..	..	..	..	D	..	..	D
Namibia	..	..	..	..	..	..	..	..	..	D	..	..	D
Niger	D	D	..	..	D	..	..	D	..	..	..	..	D
Nigeria	..	..	..	..	..	..	..	..	..	..	..	..	..
Rwanda	..	D	..	..	..	..	..	..	..	..	..	..	D
São Tomé and Principe	D	..	..	..	..	..	..	..	..	..	..	..	..
Senegal	D	D	..	..	..	..	..	..	..	..	..	..	..
Seychelles	..	..	..	..	..	..	..	..	..	..	..	..	..
Sierra Leone	..	..	..	..	..	..	..	..	..	..	..	..	..
Somalia	D	..	..	..	..	..	..	..	..	..	..	..	..
South Africa	..	..	..	..	..	..	..	..	..	D	..	..	D
Sudan	..	D	..	..	D	..	D	D	..	..	..	..	D
Swaziland	..	..	..	..	D	..	..	..	..	D	..	..	D
Tanzania	..	D	D	..	..	..	..	..	..	D	..	..	..
Togo	D	..	..	..	..	..	..	..	..	..	..	..	..
Uganda	..	..	..	..	..	..	..	..	..	..	..	..	..
Zaire	..	..	..	..	..	..	..	..	..	..	..	..	..
Zambia	D	D	..	..	..	..	..	..	..	D	..	D	D
Zimbabwe	D	D	..	..	..	..	..	..	..	D	..	D	D
NORTH AFRICA	..	..	..	..	..	..	..	..	..	..	..	..	..
Algeria	..	..	..	..	..	D	D	..	..	..	D	D	D
Egypt, Arab Republic	..	..	..	..	..	..	..	..	..	..	..	..	..
Libya	..	..	..	..	..	..	..	..	..	..	..	..	..
Morocco	..	..	..	..	..	..	..	..	..	..	..	..	D
Tunisia	..	..	..	D	..	D	D	..	..	..	..	..	D
ALL AFRICA	..	..	..	..	..	..	..	..	..	..	..	..	..

Figure 8-1. Agricultural production index, 1995*

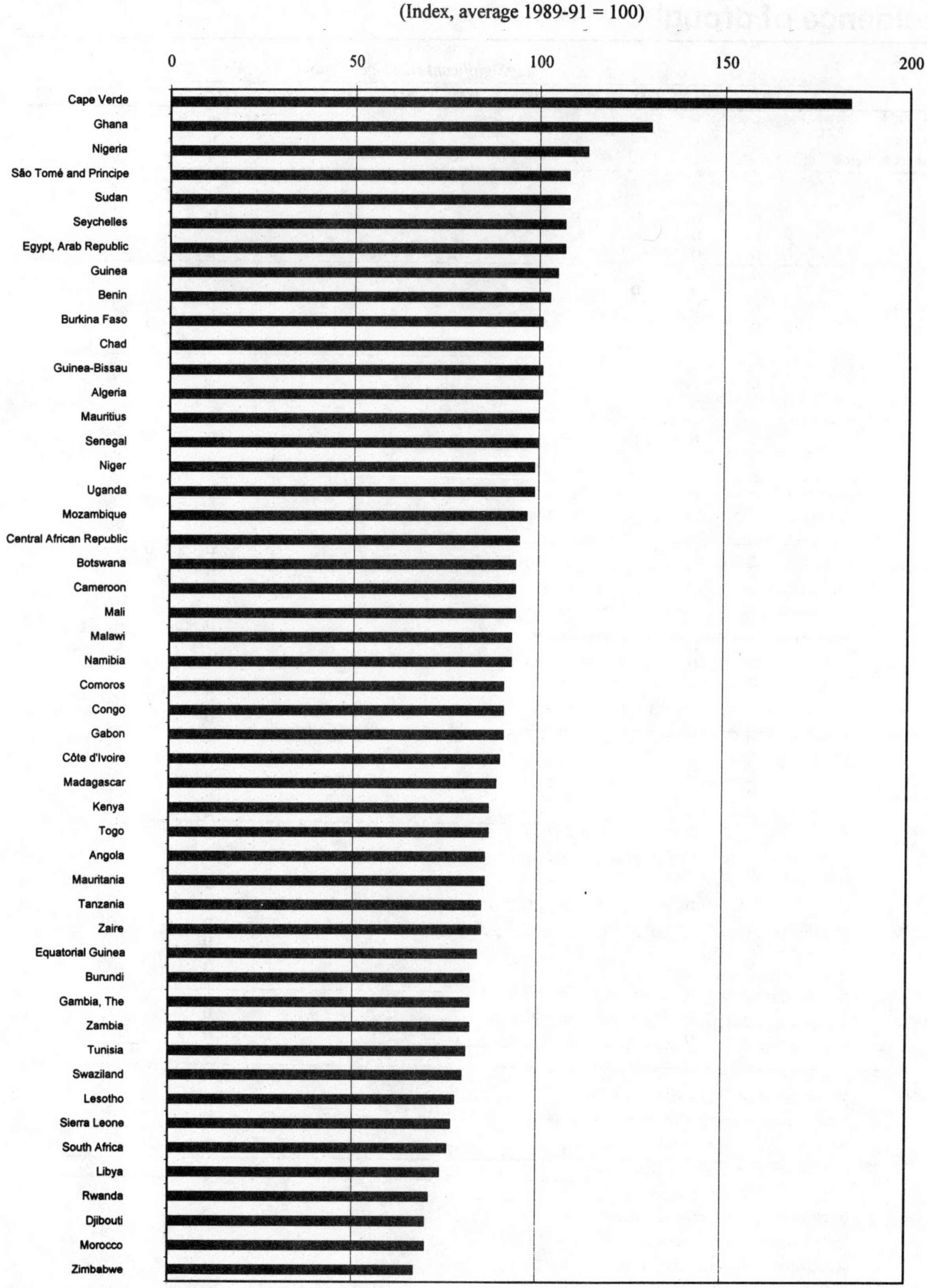

* Or most recent year available.

Figure 8-2. Food production per capita index, 1995*

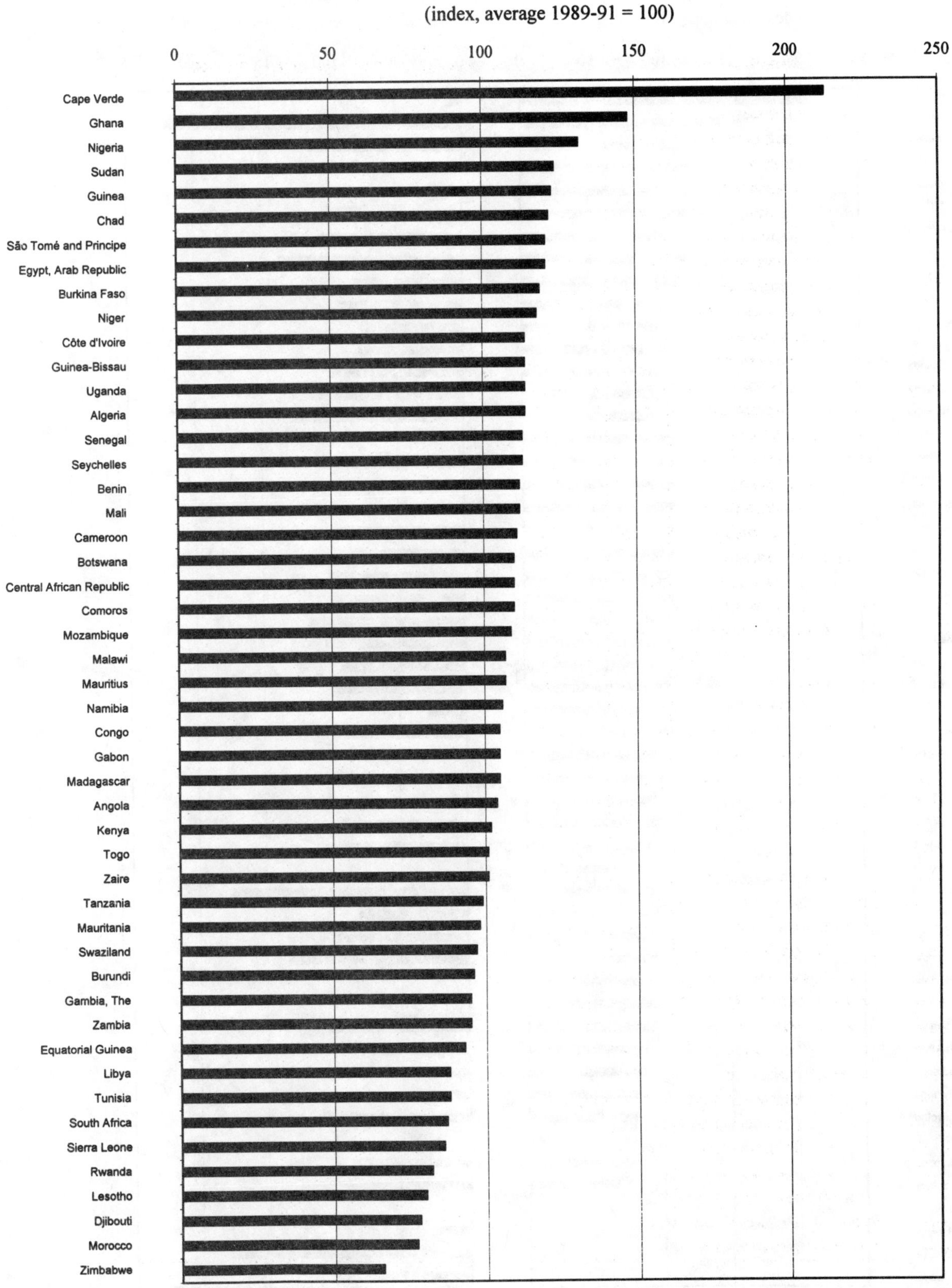

* Or most recent year available.

Figure 8-3. Food and nonfood production index, 1995*

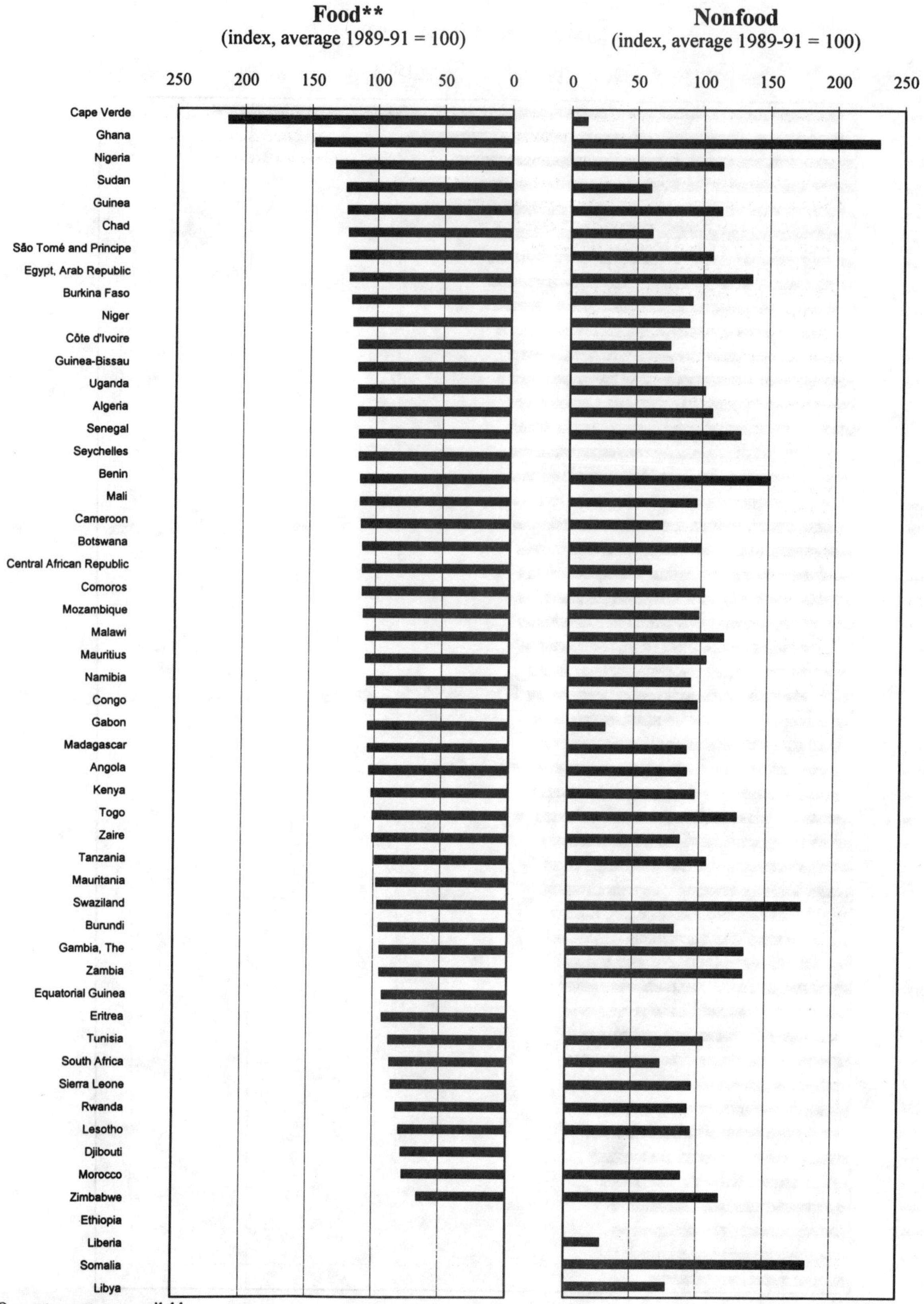

* Or most recent year available.

** Sorted by food production.

Figure 8-4. Agricultural exports, 1995*

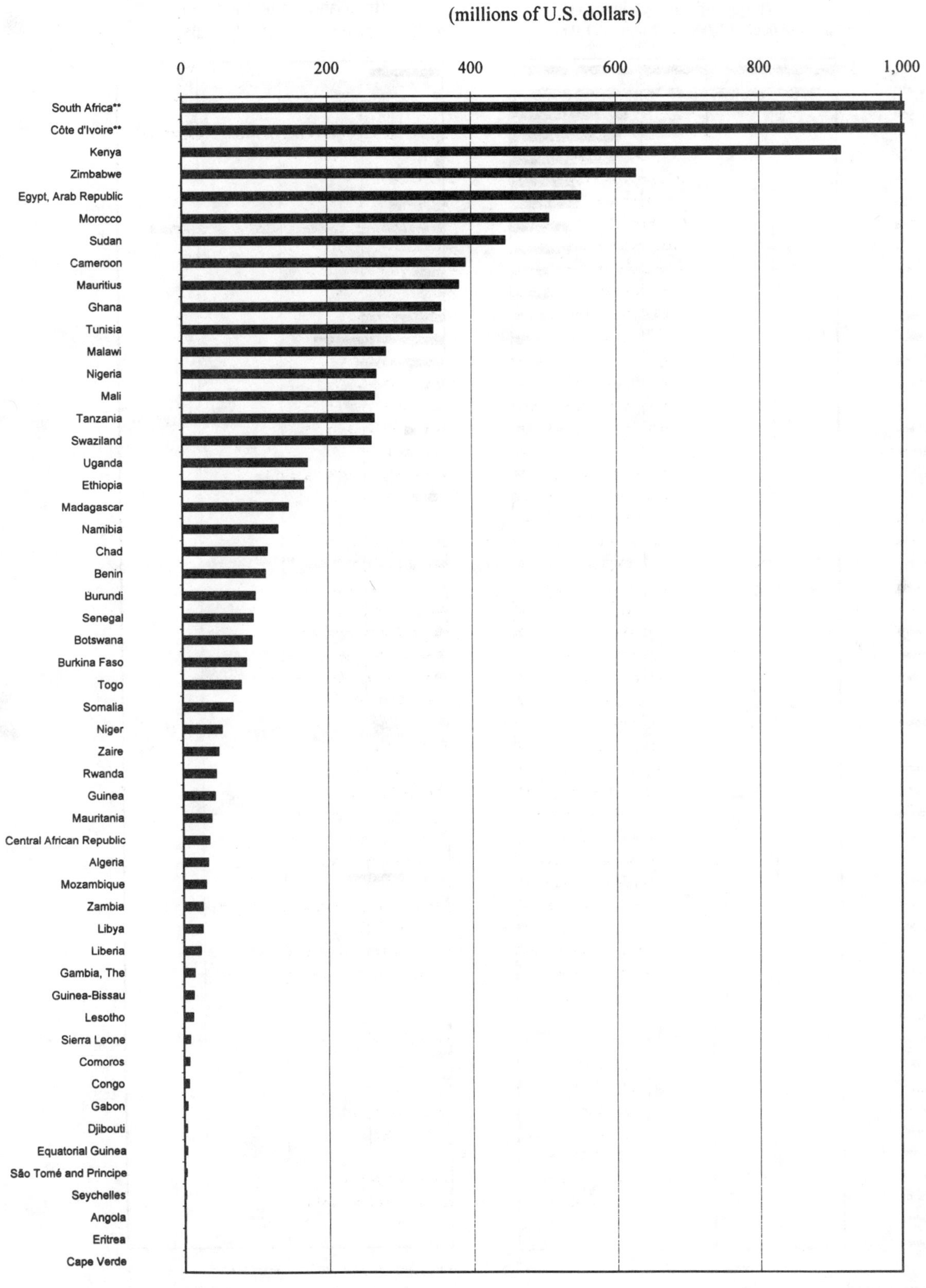

* Or most recent year available.

** Agricultural exports are greater than 1000.

Figure 8-5. Food imports, 1994*

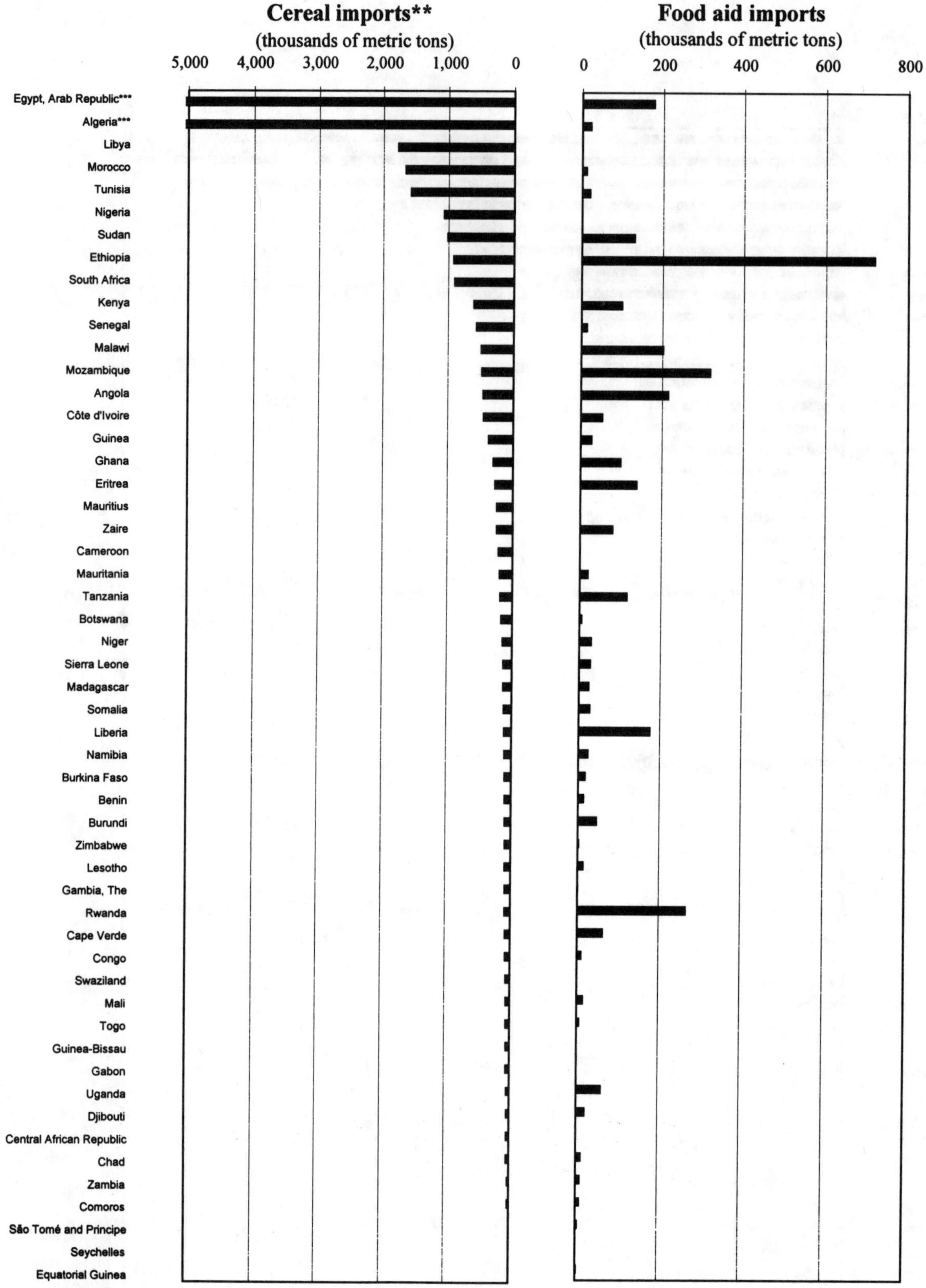

* Or most recent year available.
** Sorted by cereal imports.
*** Cereal imports are greater than 5000.

Technical Notes

Tables

Table 8-1. Nominal producer prices. Data on nominal producer prices are compiled from the FAO. In general, the figures reflect the average annual price received by farmers in the most important producing regions. But given the wide regional and seasonal variation and the lack of precision in recording specifics about prices quoted, the data should be interpreted only as a rough indication of price levels for an entire country during an entire year.

Unlike *ADI 1992*, because of lack of recent information, this volume does not differentiate between official producer prices and farmgate prices. In most cases they happen to be the same.

Crop years for most countries span parts of two calendar years; planting takes place in the first calendar year, while harvest and marketing take place at the end of the first and beginning of the second year. For consistency, producer prices are listed corresponding to the calendar year during which planting decisions are made. For example, producer prices for the crop year 1987/88 are listed as 1987.

For each country, up to four export crops and five food crops are included, which represent the most important commodities for that country in terms of value of total production during the early 1980s. The food crops include up to three cereals of "traded" grains (those commonly imported or exported) and up to two "nontraded" staples, generally roots and tubers, which are not normally imported or exported by African countries. In the table, these categories of crops are designated by the following symbols: X1 through X4 for export crops; Fl through F3 for traded food crops; and NT1 and NT2 for nontraded staple food crops. The categorization is consistent across countries, but the numbering of crops within categories in each country depends on which crops are most important.

Where commodities may be marketed in several different forms, the form is generally specified (for instance, shelled or unshelled groundnuts). When not specified, the form of the commodity is the most common (for instance, shelled and dried maize). Where commodities are graded, an average grade has been used unless otherwise specified.

Table 8-2. Agricultural production index. These are derived from production figures for 197 primary commodities (FAO data).

Table 8-3. Food production index. These indexes are based on 169 commodities that provide calories when consumed (FAO data). Some of these (such as cottonseed, cocoa, and vanilla) are not, however, a significant part of African diets, but are produced primarily for export.

Table 8-4. Nonfood production index. Data in this table are derived from 29 products that are not considered nutritious, including coffee, rubber, cotton lint, and tobacco leaves (FAO data).

Table 8-5. Food production per capita index. These are derived as the ratio of the food production index (Table 8-3) and estimated total midyear population figures (Table 1-2).

Table 8-6. Volume of food output, by major food crop. The table covers, with only a few differences, the same major food crops as presented in Table 8-1, excluding beverages (coffee, tea, cocoa), cotton, and tobacco. Included also are figures for livestock, which represent the combined total head of cattle, sheep, goats, pigs, horses, asses, and mules, and figures for the total head of rabbits (FAO data).

Table 8-7. Value of agricultural exports. Value of agricultural exports is expressed in current US dollars at f.o.b. prices (FAO data).

Table 8-8. Volume of cereal imports. The volume of cereal imports is the weighted sum of different cereals (including SITC groups 041 and 046) expressed in metric tons, with weights based on export unit values (FAO data).

Table 8-9. Food aid. Data are deliveries of all cereals, converted to grain equivalent, as defined and reported by the FAO database for *Food Aid in Figures*. Noncereal food aid is not included. Data are compiled for marketing years July through June and are shown in the tables under the calendar year corresponding to the second half of the split year (for instance, totals for 1988 refer to the 1987/88 marketing year).

Tables 8-10 and 8-11. Fertilizer use and imports. Figures are in metric tons and represent the aggregate of nitrogenous, phosphate, and potash fertilizers (FAO database for *Fertilizer Yearbook*).

Table 8-12. Area under major crops. Reflects arable land and land under permanent crops as defined and reported by the FAO.

Table 8-13. Agricultural yields by major crop. This table follows closely the selection of commodities of Table 8-1. Units are in thousands of hectograms (which are equivalent to hundreds of kilograms) per hectare. Most of the data come from the database for the FAO *Production Yearbook*, with additional information taken from World Bank agricultural sector reports.

Table 8-14. Incidence of drought. This is the only indicator in this chapter based on subjective considerations. Data on rainfall levels from other sources are usually presented to suit different purposes, without considering seasonal and regional characteristics of the producing regions. A low rainfall level might not harm agricultural production, if it did not adversely affect the regions where the main crops are produced, whereas an average rainfall level might be associated with difficulties in the producing regions, due to delay, for example. Therefore, simply presenting the annual rainfall levels would not necessarily enrich the agricultural data.

For each country, a binary classification was thus created. A "D" was assigned to a country if a significant shortage of rain unfavorably affected its agricultural production. For normal or average rainfall, the standard sign was given, as in the cases of insufficient information or "not applicable." (Specialists who work on the relevant countries were surveyed, as well as World Bank agricultural and environmental experts. In addition, the Federal Early Warning System project of the U.S. Agency for International Development provided information for 1993–94 for about half of the countries listed.)

Figures

The following indicators have been used to derive the figures in this chapter.

Figure 8-1. Agricultural production index (Table 8-2).

Figure 8-2. Food production per capita index (Table 8-5).

Figure 8-3. Food production index (Table 8-3); nonfood production index (Table 8-4).

Figure 8-4. Agricultural exports (Table 8-7).

Figure 8-5. Volume of cereal imports (Table 8-8); food aid imports (Table 8-9).

Methodology used for regional aggregations and period averages in chapter 8

Table	*Aggregations*[a]				*Period averages*[b]
	(1)	*(6)*	*(7)*	*(8)*	*(2)*
8-1				x	
8-2			x		x
8-3		x			x
8-4			x		
8-5			x		x
8-6				x	x
8-7	x				x
8-8	x				x
8-9	x				x
8-10	x				x
8-11	x				x
8-12	x				x
8-13				x	x
8-14				x	

Note: Regional aggregations are shown in the rows for Sub-Saharan Africa, North Africa, and All Africa. Period averages are shown in the last three columns. This table shows only the methodologies used in this chapter.

a. Regional aggregations: (1) simple total; (2) simple total of the first indicator divided by the simple total of the second indicator (same country coverage); (3) simple total of the gap-filled indicator; (4) simple total of the gap-filled main indicator divided by the simple total of the gap-filled secondary indicator; (5) simple total of the first gap-filled main indicator less the simple total of the second gap-filled main indicator, all divided by the simple total of the secondary indicator; (6) weighted total; (7) median; (8) no aggregation; (9) simple arithmetic mean.

b. Period averages: (1) arithmetic mean (using the same series as shown in the table, i.e., ratio if the rest of the table is shown as ratio, level if the rest of the table is shown as level, growth rate if the rest of the table is shown as growth rate); (2) least-squares growth rate (using main indicator); (3) least-squares growth rate (using main indicator in constant terms, with the rest of the table in current terms).

9

Power, Communications, and Transportation

This chapter provides data on the power, communications, and transportation sectors of the economy.

An adequate and reliable supply of power is a vital ingredient for the economic development of African countries. This chapter presents information on electric power production and distribution losses. Data are from the International Energy Agency's (IEA's) *Energy Statistics and Balances of Non-OECD Countries, 1993–94* (1996).

Telecommunications are also an essential ingredient of a modern economy. In this chapter telephone main lines represent the supply side of the system, which in Africa is well short of demand. In fact, waiting time for telephone lines is the highest of any other geographical region. Data on telecommunications are from the International Telecommunications Union's (ITU) *World Telecommunications Development Report* (1995).

In addition to power and communication, countries must have a solid transportation sector to underpin expansion of their economies and ensure support to the activities of households, producers, and government. This chapter presents data on vehicle use, roads, and railway traffic. Data are from the World Bank databases and from the International World Road Federation's *World Road Statistics* (1995).

9-1. Electric production per capita

	KWH											Annual average		
	1980	1986	1987	1988	1989	1990	1991	1992	1993	1994	1995	75-84	85-89	90-MR
SUB-SAHARAN AFRICA	419.5	567.6	569.5	570.4	574.9	452.4	451.6	438.4	440.3	570.8	..	447.0	568.8	470.7
excluding South Africa	169.7	161.2	163.7	159.4	161.2	133.3	135.7	132.3	128.6	151.1	..	148.9	160.6	136.2
excl. S. Africa & Nigeria	187.6	174.7	177.3	171.1	170.3	131.5	134.4	131.0	127.3	153.8	..	160.2	172.6	135.6
Angola	96.2	98.1	96.0	93.9	91.6	86.4	98.1	96.4	93.8	91.4	..	98.7	96.0	93.2
Benin	2.9	2.4	2.3	2.2	2.2	2.1	2.0	2.0	1.9	1.1	..	2.7	2.3	1.8
Botswana	..	..	..	..	..	..	..	..	..	..	..	..	..	..
Burkina Faso	16.2	..	..	..	..	21.3	20.8	20.5	20.0	..	..	15.9	..	20.6
Burundi	0.2	..	..	..	..	20.0	24.1	18.5	19.6	..	..	0.4	..	20.6
Cameroon	166.9	238.7	244.4	238.4	242.0	235.5	229.3	223.4	217.4	212.3	..	212.1	241.1	223.6
Cape Verde	34.6	..	..	..	..	105.4	103.3	104.0	101.8	..	..	38.2	..	103.6
Central African Republic	29.0	..	..	..	..	32.4	31.3	31.3	30.9	..	..	28.2	..	31.5
Chad	14.3	..	..	..	..	14.8	14.6	14.2	14.2	..	..	14.0	..	14.4
Comoros	..	..	..	..	..	..	..	..	..	..	..	..	..	..
Congo	93.5	135.0	136.0	136.8	180.1	223.2	205.3	176.9	173.0	169.8	..	110.3	150.0	189.6
Côte d'Ivoire	212.8	176.1	211.7	207.7	204.6	191.7	154.1	144.4	144.6	169.5	..	201.1	197.1	160.8
Djibouti	416.4	..	..	..	..	360.4	345.5	329.2	317.0	..	..	396.5	..	338.0
Equatorial Guinea	82.9	..	..	..	..	51.1	50.4	52.1	50.8	..	..	64.7	..	51.1
Eritrea	..	..	..	..	..	..	..	..	..	..	..	..	..	..
Ethiopia	18.3	20.5	19.4	18.4	17.8	17.7	18.4	22.9	24.3	23.6	..	19.9	19.3	21.4
Gabon	806.1	1,087.4	1,036.1	1,011.0	984.1	978.6	937.1	909.6	887.1	878.8	..	911.8	1,038.4	918.3
Gambia, The	62.4	..	..	..	..	75.8	72.6	70.7	70.0	..	..	59.8	..	72.3
Ghana	495.1	342.3	350.1	351.7	366.0	393.2	401.7	421.6	388.9	367.5	..	361.0	330.8	394.6
Guinea	112.1	..	..	..	..	90.0	88.3	87.2	85.7	..	..	108.5	..	87.8
Guinea-Bissau	17.3	..	..	..	..	41.5	41.7	40.9	41.1	..	..	15.9	..	41.3
Kenya	90.0	111.5	124.2	125.8	127.8	129.9	134.4	130.3	134.0	136.0	..	99.2	119.4	132.9
Lesotho	..	..	..	..	..	..	..	..	..	..	..	..	..	..
Liberia	479.0	..	..	..	..	232.0	181.2	181.3	184.9	..	..	530.7	..	194.9
Madagascar	48.9	..	..	..	..	50.7	48.6	48.0	46.6	..	..	47.8	..	48.5
Malawi	70.2	..	..	..	..	84.4	87.6	88.1	86.1	..	..	69.5	..	86.6
Mali	16.7	..	..	..	..	36.1	35.7	36.1	35.8	..	..	16.2	..	35.9
Mauritania	65.8	..	..	..	..	69.9	69.6	69.3	67.6	..	..	63.6	..	69.1
Mauritius	453.4	..	..	..	..	719.0	780.5	855.7	900.6	..	..	440.0	..	814.0
Mozambique	1,157.5	29.6	32.0	34.1	34.5	29.8	29.4	24.8	32.5	31.5	..	446.2	34.4	29.6
Namibia	..	..	..	..	..	..	..	..	..	..	..	..	..	..
Niger	24.7	..	..	..	..	21.5	21.2	20.9	20.5	..	..	30.7	..	21.1
Nigeria	100.4	125.6	127.6	128.3	137.0	139.9	140.8	137.4	133.5	143.8	..	108.7	128.8	139.1
Rwanda	31.6	..	..	..	..	34.7	33.7	34.0	38.6	..	..	29.9	..	35.2
São Tomé and Principe	117.3	..	..	..	..	132.2	128.4	125.7	123.0	..	..	113.7	..	127.3
Senegal	115.0	115.6	121.5	121.7	122.3	121.8	121.3	128.3	123.8	121.3	..	116.6	120.1	123.3
Seychelles	792.9	..	..	..	..	1,485.3	1,539.8	1,561.6	1,551.5	..	..	811.3	..	1,534.5
Sierra Leone	75.7	..	..	..	..	56.0	56.6	55.9	56.1	..	..	82.2	..	56.1
Somalia	11.2	..	..	..	..	29.9	32.1	31.1	29.9	..	..	10.6	..	30.7
South Africa	3,392.2	4,328.5	4,348.6	4,423.3	4,478.4	4,461.9	4,440.4	4,329.2	4,404.0	4,632.5	..	3,793.2	4,371.5	4,453.6
Sudan	58.9	57.8	60.2	59.1	57.9	55.2	54.1	52.8	51.8	50.9	..	61.6	60.0	53.0
Swaziland	..	..	..	..	..	..	..	..	..	..	..	..	..	..
Tanzania	53.7	48.0	50.6	52.0	58.5	61.4	66.6	66.4	68.1	66.5	..	52.9	52.2	65.8
Togo	36.3	..	..	..	..	16.7	24.5	24.3	23.6	..	..	51.7	..	22.3
Uganda	50.8	..	..	..	..	47.4	46.3	45.0	43.7	..	..	49.7	..	45.6
Zaire	164.6	165.0	159.2	154.0	165.7	141.7	159.6	154.9	150.3	130.5	..	156.5	161.4	147.4
Zambia	1,649.2	1,427.7	1,198.6	1,143.4	892.3	813.2	978.1	944.0	918.1	892.2	..	1,638.7	1,231.3	909.1
Zimbabwe	609.9	785.0	962.9	873.3	967.9	971.8	890.7	801.1	708.9	680.4	..	598.6	855.7	810.6
NORTH AFRICA	442.2	691.7	739.7	770.8	787.5	800.8	815.0	822.0	838.5	864.2	..	520.8	730.4	828.1
Algeria	381.5	576.8	549.5	587.4	628.3	639.5	676.8	696.5	723.0	725.1	..	460.4	580.6	692.2
Egypt, Arab Republic	463.3	701.6	774.3	790.6	812.7	829.3	860.2	859.0	886.4	914.5	..	544.6	751.1	869.9
Libya	1,588.2	3,369.3	3,809.5	3,898.9	3,799.8	3,696.4	3,573.0	3,483.2	3,374.2	3,411.0	..	1,948.5	3,601.2	3,507.6
Morocco	270.7	351.0	354.1	389.3	383.1	400.4	375.2	388.3	388.1	426.2	..	302.5	363.4	395.6
Tunisia	458.0	570.4	591.4	629.8	647.2	678.0	687.9	724.9	739.7	759.1	..	495.0	598.4	717.9
ALL AFRICA	423.8	596.2	608.6	616.3	623.3	516.9	518.7	508.8	513.3	636.4	..	461.5	605.8	538.8

9-2. Energy production and use

	Energy production (KT oil equivalent)		*Commercial energy use (KT oil equivalent)*		*Traditional energy use as % of energy consumption*	
	1980	*1994*	*1980*	*1994*	*1980*	*1993*
SUB-SAHARAN AFRICA	203,255	286,982	93,040	133,679	..	..
excluding South Africa	136,515	169,292	33,990	46,684	64	62
excl. S. Africa & Nigeria	31,005	65,982	24,111	28,637	64	64
Angola	7,700	24,914	937	931	65	59
Benin	0	315	149	107	85	93
Botswana	260	248	384	549	..	..
Burkina Faso	0	0	144	160	91	93
Burundi	1	5	58	143	93	14
Cameroon	2,855	5,782	774	1,335	71	73
Cape Verde	0	0	105	114	..	..
Central African Republic	17	22	59	93	91	89
Chad	0	0	93	100	95	90
Comoros	0	0	15	18	..	..
Congo	3,387	9,428	262	847	56	58
Côte d'Ivoire	192	425	1,435	1,406	..	53
Djibouti	0	0	517	548	..	..
Equatorial Guinea	1	1	19	31	83	..
Eritrea	..	..	..	..	..	..
Ethiopia	55	156	624	1,193	91	90
Gabon	9,151	15,998	759	692	27	51
Gambia, The	0	0	53	60	78	78
Ghana	554	523	1,303	1,542	56	71
Guinea	38	57	356	418	67	69
Guinea-Bissau	0	0	31	39	76	72
Kenya	91	488	1,991	2,872	75	77
Lesotho	0	0	0	0	..	..
Liberia	85	105	793	108	55	92
Madagascar	38	83	391	479	86	80
Malawi	99	152	334	370	83	86
Mali	21	42	164	205	85	87
Mauritania	0	0	214	229	0	0
Mauritius	21	34	339	431	48	47
Mozambique	1,293	161	1,123	619	73	85
Namibia	0	0	0	0	..	..
Niger	14	55	..	..	78	79
Nigeria	105,510	103,310	9,879	18,047	63	60
Rwanda	29	46	190	209	85	86
São Tomé and Principe	2	3	13	23	..	..
Senegal	0	0	875	803	48	57
Seychelles	0	0	70	122	..	..
Sierra Leone	0	0	310	323	85	70
Somalia	0	0	389	61	73	97
South Africa	66,740	117,690	59,050	86,995	..	..
Sudan	58	81	1,140	1,732	87	76
Swaziland	155	180	191	232	..	..
Tanzania	86	165	1,023	975	89	89
Togo	1	0	195	183	38	59
Uganda	153	179	320	425	94	88
Zaire	1,478	1,877	1,487	1,902	81	83
Zambia	1,146	890	1,685	1,286	55	71
Zimbabwe	2,024	3,567	2,797	4,722	34	25
NORTH AFRICA	203,407	244,658	41,903	85,717	5	4
Algeria	66,730	103,830	12,078	24,834	3	2
Egypt, Arab Republic	33,374	60,931	15,176	34,071	5	3
Libya	96,537	74,658	7,048	13,039	..	..
Morocco	617	463	4,518	8,509	5	4
Tunisia	6,149	4,776	3,083	5,264	15	13
ALL AFRICA	406,662	531,640	134,943	219,396	..	..

9-3. Telephone services availability

	Mainlines (per 1,000 persons)		Faults (per 100 lines)	
	1985-90	1991-95	1985-90	1991-95
SUB-SAHARAN AFRICA	10	11	..	63
excluding South Africa	4	5	..	75
excl. S. Africa & Nigeria	4	5	..	75
Angola	8	6	..	150
Benin	3	5	..	76
Botswana	21	41	..	55
Burkina Faso	2	3	..	83
Burundi	1	3	72	64
Cameroon	4	4	..	74
Cape Verde	24	57	..	36
Central African Republic	2	2	..	..
Chad	1	1	149	87
Comoros	8	9	..	68
Congo	7	8	94	61
Côte d'Ivoire	6	8	107	80
Djibouti	11	12	..	11
Equatorial Guinea	4	6	..	50
Eritrea	..	5	..	138
Ethiopia	2	3	116	74
Gabon	22	29	..	74
Gambia, The	7	18	..	45
Ghana	3	4	..	112
Guinea	2	2	..	172
Guinea-Bissau	6	9	..	..
Kenya	7	9	..	191
Lesotho	7	9	..	..
Liberia	4	2	..	283
Madagascar	3	2	..	78
Malawi	3	3	..	..
Mali	1	2	..	..
Mauritania	3	4	..	327
Mauritius	53	131	..	98
Mozambique	3	4	..	60
Namibia	39	51	..	78
Niger	1	1	88	79
Nigeria	3	4	350	327
Rwanda	1	2	..	38
São Tomé and Principe	19	19	..	76
Senegal	6	10	..	40
Seychelles	128	180	32	43
Sierra Leone	3	4	..	10
Somalia	2	2	..	..
South Africa	89	95	..	8
Sudan	3	3	..	20
Swaziland	17	22	250	206
Tanzania	3	3	..	201
Togo	3	5	25	83
Uganda	2	2	..	80
Zaire	1	1	..	7
Zambia	8	9	69	123
Zimbabwe	13	14	225	190
NORTH AFRICA	29	46	..	137
Algeria	32	42	..	73
Egypt, Arab Republic	31	47	23	..
Libya	48	59	..	230
Morocco	17	44	95	49
Tunisia	37	58	130	79
ALL AFRICA	13	18	..	66

9-4. Intensity of vehicle use

	Units per 1000 persons											Annual average		
	1980	1986	1987	1988	1989	1990	1991	1992	1993	1994	1995	75-84	85-89	90-MR
SUB-SAHARAN AFRICA	..	..	..	..	..	..	..	..	..	..	..	..	..	..
excluding South Africa	..	..	..	..	..	..	..	..	..	..	..	..	..	..
excl. S. Africa & Nigeria	..	..	..	..	..	..	..	..	..	..	..	..	..	..
Angola	..	..	..	..	..	..	..	..	..	..	..	..	..	..
Benin	..	..	..	..	..	..	..	..	..	..	..	..	..	..
Botswana	27.3	..	..	..	..	..	..	..	..	..	..	27.3	..	..
Burkina Faso	..	..	..	..	..	..	..	..	..	..	..	..	..	..
Burundi	..	..	..	..	..	..	..	..	..	..	..	..	..	..
Cameroon	7.7	..	..	..	..	8.2	..	..	..	..	..	7.7	..	8.2
Cape Verde	..	..	..	..	..	..	..	..	25.8	..	..	..	..	25.8
Central African Republic	7.5	..	..	..	..	..	..	..	..	0.4	..	7.5	..	0.4
Chad	..	..	..	..	..	..	..	..	..	3.3	..	..	..	3.3
Comoros	..	..	..	..	..	..	..	..	..	..	..	..	..	..
Congo	..	..	..	..	..	..	19.0	19.0	18.2	..	..	..	..	18.7
Côte d'Ivoire	24.3	..	..	..	..	..	..	..	..	..	..	24.3	..	..
Djibouti	..	..	..	..	..	..	..	..	..	..	..	..	..	..
Equatorial Guinea	..	..	..	..	..	..	..	..	..	..	..	..	..	..
Eritrea	..	..	..	..	..	..	..	..	..	..	..	..	..	..
Ethiopia	1.7	..	..	..	1.2	1.1	1.1	..	..	..	..	1.7	1.2	1.1
Gabon	..	..	..	..	..	..	..	..	..	..	..	..	..	..
Gambia, The	..	..	..	..	..	..	..	..	..	..	..	..	..	..
Ghana	..	..	..	..	..	..	..	..	..	..	..	..	..	..
Guinea	..	..	..	..	..	..	..	6.0	..	..	..	..	..	6.0
Guinea-Bissau	..	..	..	..	..	..	..	..	..	..	..	..	..	..
Kenya	8.4	..	..	..	11.9	13.4	14.0	14.0	14.0	..	..	8.4	11.9	13.9
Lesotho	9.6	..	..	..	..	..	..	..	12.6	..	..	9.6	..	12.6
Liberia	1.2	..	..	..	..	..	..	..	..	..	..	1.2	..	..
Madagascar	..	..	..	..	..	..	..	..	..	..	..	..	..	..
Malawi	4.8	..	..	..	..	..	..	..	..	..	..	4.8	..	..
Mali	..	..	..	..	..	..	..	..	..	..	..	..	..	..
Mauritania	..	..	..	..	..	..	..	..	..	..	..	..	..	..
Mauritius	43.5	..	..	..	54.0	59.0	62.0	..	..	..	..	43.5	54.0	60.5
Mozambique	..	..	..	..	..	..	..	..	2.2	2.5	..	..	..	2.3
Namibia	..	..	..	..	..	78.0	..	..	..	87.0	..	..	..	82.5
Niger	5.8	..	..	..	5.4	5.3	..	..	..	..	..	5.8	5.4	5.3
Nigeria	4.0	..	..	..	..	..	..	..	..	..	..	4.0	..	..
Rwanda	2.4	..	..	..	1.5	1.4	..	..	..	..	..	2.4	1.5	1.4
São Tomé and Principe	..	..	..	..	..	..	..	..	..	..	..	..	..	..
Senegal	18.9	..	..	..	..	..	..	..	13.0	..	..	18.9	..	13.0
Seychelles	..	..	..	..	..	..	..	..	..	..	..	..	..	..
Sierra Leone	..	..	..	..	10.0	10.0	10.0	11.0	11.0	..	..	..	10.0	10.5
Somalia	..	..	..	..	..	..	..	..	..	..	..	..	..	..
South Africa	132.7	..	..	..	159.8	160.3	161.0	160.1	156.7	156.7	..	132.7	159.8	159.0
Sudan	..	..	..	..	..	..	..	..	..	..	..	..	..	..
Swaziland	52.0	..	..	..	63.2	64.8	..	..	..	..	..	52.0	63.2	64.8
Tanzania	2.9	..	..	..	..	..	..	..	..	..	..	2.9	..	..
Togo	..	..	..	..	1.2	1.5	1.5	1.4	0.9	..	..	..	1.2	1.3
Uganda	1.5	..	..	..	..	..	..	..	..	..	..	1.5	..	..
Zaire	..	..	..	..	..	..	25.0	28.0	28.0	29.0	..	..	..	27.5
Zambia	..	..	..	..	..	..	..	..	..	..	..	..	..	..
Zimbabwe	..	..	..	..	..	..	..	32.7	..	..	..	..	..	32.7
NORTH AFRICA	..	..	..	..	37.8	29.7	30.2	30.9	32.2	..	..	..	37.8	30.8
Algeria	..	..	..	..	54.0	..	..	..	33.0	..	..	..	54.0	33.0
Egypt, Arab Republic	..	..	..	..	26.3	26.4	26.7	26.8	27.4	28.1	..	..	26.3	27.1
Libya	..	..	..	..	..	..	..	..	..	..	..	..	..	..
Morocco	..	..	..	..	..	37.0	38.0	40.0	42.0	..	..	..	..	39.3
Tunisia	37.8	..	..	..	62.0	..	..	..	..	..	..	37.8	62.0	..
ALL AFRICA	..	..	..	..	..	..	..	..	..	..	..	..	..	..

9-5. Road/population ratio

	Road 1000 km/1 million persons											Annual average		
	1980	*1986*	*1987*	*1988*	*1989*	*1990*	*1991*	*1992*	*1993*	*1994*	*1995*	*75-84*	*85-89*	*90-MR*
SUB-SAHARAN AFRICA	3.3	..	..	..	..	2.4	..	..	..	..	..	3.3	3.0	2.4
excluding South Africa	3.1	..	..	..	..	2.2	..	..	..	..	..	3.1	2.8	2.2
excl. S. Africa & Nigeria	3.5	..	..	..	..	2.6	..	..	..	..	..	3.5	3.2	2.6
Angola	10.3	..	..	..	..	7.9	..	7.4	7.6	..	..	11.1	9.0	7.6
Benin	2.1	..	..	..	1.3	1.8	1.2	1.2	..	..	..	2.1	1.6	1.4
Botswana	9.1	12.1	..	..	..	7.0	..	..	..	..	..	11.7	9.9	7.0
Burkina Faso	1.1	1.4	..	..	..	..	..	1.4	..	..	..	1.7	1.2	1.4
Burundi	1.2	..	..	..	..	1.1	..	2.5	..	..	..	1.8	0.6	1.8
Cameroon	7.2	5.1	5.0	..	..	6.1	..	..	..	0.0	..	6.6	5.5	3.1
Cape Verde	..	..	..	..	..	..	..	..	3.0	..	..	..	..	3.0
Central African Republic	9.8	7.6	..	..	8.3	8.0	7.9	7.7	7.6	..	..	9.8	7.9	7.8
Chad	6.0	..	..	..	..	4.8	..	..	..	..	..	6.7	5.4	4.8
Comoros	..	..	..	..	..	..	..	..	..	..	..	2.3	..	..
Congo	5.0	..	..	..	..	..	5.4	5.3	5.1	..	..	5.5	4.5	5.3
Côte d'Ivoire	5.0	..	..	..	..	4.1	..	..	..	..	..	5.6	4.7	4.1
Djibouti	..	7.1	..	..	6.1	5.8	5.5	..	..	..	..	7.6	6.8	5.7
Equatorial Guinea	..	..	..	..	..	..	..	..	..	..	..	5.2	..	..
Eritrea	..	..	..	..	..	..	..	..	..	..	..	..	..	..
Ethiopia	1.0	0.8	0.8	..	0.4	0.5	0.5	..	..	..	..	0.9	0.7	0.5
Gabon	10.2	..	..	..	..	..	7.6	7.4	7.2	..	..	10.9	9.5	7.4
Gambia, The	3.4	..	..	..	..	2.6	..	..	..	..	..	3.0	4.2	2.6
Ghana	3.0	..	..	..	2.6	2.6	..	..	..	..	..	2.8	2.7	2.6
Guinea	5.4	..	..	..	..	..	..	2.6	..	..	..	4.2	5.8	2.6
Guinea-Bissau	..	..	..	..	..	..	..	..	..	..	..	4.6	..	..
Kenya	3.1	..	..	..	2.7	2.6	2.6	..	..	..	..	3.2	3.0	2.6
Lesotho	2.9	..	..	..	..	..	..	2.8	2.8	..	..	2.6	2.6	2.8
Liberia	2.9	3.6	3.5	..	..	2.4	..	..	..	..	..	3.9	3.2	2.4
Madagascar	5.8	4.8	4.7	4.5	1.3	..	2.9	2.8	2.7	..	..	4.9	4.1	2.8
Malawi	1.8	..	..	..	1.4	3.2	..	..	..	..	..	1.9	1.5	3.2
Mali	2.0	1.8	1.8	1.8	1.7	1.7	1.7	..	..	..	..	2.1	1.8	1.7
Mauritania	4.7	..	..	..	..	3.6	..	..	..	..	..	4.7	4.1	3.6
Mauritius	1.8	1.7	1.8	1.7	1.7	1.7	1.7	..	..	..	..	2.2	1.7	1.7
Mozambique	2.9	1.9	1.9	1.9	1.9	2.5	..	..	..	..	..	3.3	2.0	2.5
Namibia	..	..	..	..	..	28.7	..	..	..	..	..	..	..	28.7
Niger	2.9	2.8	2.7	..	..	1.5	..	..	..	..	..	2.4	2.8	1.5
Nigeria	1.5	..	..	..	..	1.2	..	..	..	..	..	1.5	1.3	1.2
Rwanda	2.1	1.9	1.9	..	1.8	1.9	..	..	..	..	..	1.7	1.9	1.9
São Tomé and Principe	..	..	..	..	..	..	..	..	..	2.4	..	..	..	2.4
Senegal	2.5	2.3	..	..	..	2.0	..	..	..	..	..	2.4	2.2	2.0
Seychelles	..	..	..	..	..	..	..	..	..	..	..	..	..	..
Sierra Leone	2.4	..	..	..	..	..	..	2.8	..	..	..	2.6	2.3	2.8
Somalia	2.5	..	..	..	..	2.5	..	..	..	..	..	2.8	2.7	2.5
South Africa	6.3	5.4	5.3	5.1	5.0	5.0	4.8	..	..	..	..	6.8	5.3	4.9
Sudan	0.5	..	..	..	..	0.4	..	..	..	..	..	0.7	0.4	0.4
Swaziland	5.8	..	..	..	3.7	3.5	3.5	3.5	..	..	..	5.1	4.4	3.5
Tanzania	2.5	..	..	..	..	..	2.1	2.1	3.2	..	..	2.5	3.8	2.4
Togo	2.7	2.4	2.3	2.3	..	2.1	2.1	2.0	2.0	..	..	2.8	2.3	2.0
Uganda	2.1	..	..	..	..	1.8	..	1.7	..	..	..	2.1	2.0	1.7
Zaire	5.4	..	..	..	..	..	3.8	3.6	3.5	..	..	5.4	4.6	3.6
Zambia	6.3	5.3	5.2	..	4.9	4.8	4.7	4.5	..	..	..	6.4	5.2	4.7
Zimbabwe	12.0	..	..	..	..	..	..	8.9	..	..	..	12.0	9.4	8.9
NORTH AFRICA	2.1	1.5	..	1.5	1.6	..	1.9	1.6	..	..	..	2.1	1.6	1.7
Algeria	3.9	..	..	..	..	..	3.5	3.6	..	..	..	4.1	3.6	3.6
Egypt, Arab Republic	0.7	0.7	0.7	0.7	0.9	0.9	0.9	0.9	0.8	..	..	0.7	0.7	0.9
Libya	..	..	..	..	..	..	..	..	..	..	..	..	..	..
Morocco	3.0	2.7	..	2.6	2.5	..	2.4	1.1	..	..	..	2.9	2.6	1.8
Tunisia	3.7	3.6	3.6	3.5	3.7	..	..	..	..	..	..	3.4	3.6	..
ALL AFRICA	3.1	..	..	..	..	2.3	..	..	..	..	..	3.1	2.9	2.3

9-6. Paved primary roads

	KM / 1 Million persons								Percent in good condition
	1985	*1986*	*1987*	*1988*	*1989*	*1990*	*1991*	*1992*	*1989*
SUB-SAHARAN AFRICA	..	..	..	..	..	..	..	432.3	39.4
excluding South Africa	..	..	..	..	..	..	..	341.2	39.4
excl. S. Africa & Nigeria	..	..	..	..	..	..	..	329.8	40.9
Angola	..	..	..	..	..	..	..	..	..
Benin	..	..	..	..	..	..	..	241.0	13.0
Botswana	..	..	..	..	..	..	..	1,976.9	94.0
Burkina Faso	..	..	..	..	..	..	..	158.0	70.0
Burundi	..	..	..	..	..	..	..	177.0	75.0
Cameroon	..	..	..	..	..	..	..	299.5	25.0
Cape Verde	..	..	..	..	..	..	..	..	14.0
Central African Republic	..	..	..	..	..	..	..	135.0	30.0
Chad	..	..	..	..	..	..	..	56.0	..
Comoros	..	..	..	..	..	..	..	..	43.0
Congo	..	..	..	..	..	..	..	509.0	50.0
Côte d'Ivoire	..	..	..	..	..	..	..	357.4	75.0
Djibouti	..	..	..	..	..	..	..	..	51.0
Equatorial Guinea	..	..	..	..	..	..	..	..	27.0
Eritrea	..	..	..	..	..	..	..	..	..
Ethiopia	..	..	..	..	..	..	..	77.0	47.0
Gabon	..	..	..	..	..	..	..	511.0	30.0
Gambia, The	..	..	..	..	..	..	..	772.0	22.0
Ghana	..	..	..	..	..	..	..	474.0	28.0
Guinea	..	..	..	..	..	..	..	229.0	50.0
Guinea-Bissau	..	..	..	..	..	..	..	..	39.0
Kenya	..	..	..	..	..	..	..	324.0	32.0
Lesotho	..	..	..	..	..	..	..	452.0	53.0
Liberia	..	..	..	..	..	..	..	..	85.0
Madagascar	..	..	..	..	..	..	..	433.0	56.0
Malawi	..	..	..	..	..	..	..	277.8	56.0
Mali	..	..	..	..	..	..	..	308.3	70.0
Mauritania	..	..	..	..	..	..	..	803.8	58.0
Mauritius	..	..	..	..	..	..	..	1,549.0	95.0
Mozambique	..	..	..	..	..	..	..	342.6	19.0
Namibia	..	..	..	..	..	..	..	2,722.0	..
Niger	..	..	..	..	..	..	..	400.0	67.0
Nigeria	..	..	..	..	..	..	..	375.6	34.0
Rwanda	..	..	..	..	..	..	..	162.0	41.0
São Tomé and Principe	..	..	..	..	..	..	..	..	..
Senegal	..	..	..	..	..	..	..	542.5	28.0
Seychelles	..	..	..	..	..	..	..	..	..
Sierra Leone	..	..	..	..	..	..	..	295.0	62.0
Somalia	..	..	..	..	..	..	..	..	52.0
South Africa	..	..	..	..	..	..	..	1,394.0	..
Sudan	..	..	..	..	..	..	..	..	27.0
Swaziland	..	..	..	..	..	..	..	..	35.0
Tanzania	..	..	..	..	..	..	..	142.0	39.0
Togo	..	..	..	..	..	..	..	470.0	75.0
Uganda	..	..	..	..	..	..	..	117.7	10.0
Zaire	..	..	..	..	..	..	..	..	20.0
Zambia	..	..	..	..	..	..	..	795.0	40.0
Zimbabwe	..	..	..	..	..	..	..	1,406.0	70.0
NORTH AFRICA	..	..	..	..	..	..	..	1,047.0	..
Algeria	..	..	..	..	..	..	..	2,403.0	..
Egypt, Arab Republic	..	..	..	..	..	..	..	633.0	..
Libya	..	..	..	..	..	..	..	..	..
Morocco	..	..	..	..	..	..	..	179.0	..
Tunisia	..	..	..	..	..	..	..	2,080.0	..
ALL AFRICA	..	..	..	..	..	..	..	557.5	39.4

9-7. Rail traffic to GDP ratio

	Rail traffic units per million U.S. dollars of GDP											Annual average		
	1980	*1986*	*1987*	*1988*	*1989*	*1990*	*1991*	*1992*	*1993*	*1994*	*1995*	*75-84*	*85-89*	*90-MR*
SUB-SAHARAN AFRICA	62.3	78.9	64.3	58.8	..	56.0	..	..	..	..	..	66.3	73.3	56.0
excluding South Africa	22.1	21.5	..	..	..	..	..	..	..	..	..	22.0	23.3	..
excl. S. Africa & Nigeria	..	..	..	..	..	..	..	..	..	..	..	29.1	..	..
Angola	..	..	..	..	..	..	..	..	..	..	..	..	..	..
Benin	..	..	..	..	..	..	..	..	..	..	..	..	..	..
Botswana	..	..	..	..	..	..	..	..	..	..	..	..	..	..
Burkina Faso	..	..	..	..	..	..	..	..	..	..	..	..	..	..
Burundi	..	..	..	..	..	..	..	..	..	..	..	..	..	..
Cameroon	12.2	12.1	9.1	8.5	10.7	10.9	9.0	10.6	8.3	13.9	..	14.5	11.7	10.5
Cape Verde	..	..	..	..	..	..	..	..	..	..	..	..	..	..
Central African Republic	..	..	..	..	..	..	..	..	..	..	..	..	..	..
Chad	..	..	..	..	..	..	..	..	..	..	..	..	..	..
Comoros	..	..	..	..	..	..	..	..	..	..	..	..	..	..
Congo	19.8	53.6	36.9	..	..	..	34.7	25.9	21.3	25.8	..	22.8	44.9	26.9
Côte d'Ivoire	18.2	12.8	9.8	..	..	4.6	4.5	4.1	3.3	4.8	..	20.5	13.8	4.3
Djibouti	..	..	..	..	..	..	..	..	..	..	..	..	..	..
Equatorial Guinea	..	..	..	..	..	..	..	..	..	..	..	..	..	..
Eritrea	..	..	..	..	..	..	..	..	..	..	..	..	..	..
Ethiopia	..	..	..	..	5.2	..	2.2	..	..	..	..	5.7	5.2	2.2
Gabon	0.8	4.5	6.4	7.8	5.8	..	..	..	7.1	10.5	..	2.2	5.8	8.8
Gambia, The	..	..	..	..	..	..	..	..	..	..	..	..	..	..
Ghana	14.9	6.4	8.1	9.2	..	5.9	..	..	..	..	..	13.1	7.9	5.9
Guinea	..	..	..	..	..	..	..	..	..	..	..	..	..	..
Guinea-Bissau	..	..	..	..	..	..	..	..	..	..	..	..	..	..
Kenya	41.1	33.6	31.3	31.1	32.4	30.7	29.1	22.3	29.4	22.8	..	43.6	34.0	26.9
Lesotho	..	..	..	..	..	..	..	..	..	..	..	..	..	..
Liberia	..	..	..	..	..	..	..	..	..	..	..	..	..	..
Madagascar	..	..	..	..	..	..	..	..	..	..	..	..	..	..
Malawi	25.3	18.4	18.0	13.7	12.2	10.0	8.1	7.8	5.3	6.9	8.4	22.7	16.3	7.7
Mali	16.1	26.4	20.1	20.3	22.6	19.0	18.6	9.7	..	..	..	23.7	25.7	15.8
Mauritania	..	..	..	..	..	..	..	..	..	..	..	..	..	..
Mauritius	..	..	..	..	..	..	..	..	..	..	..	..	..	..
Mozambique	..	..	..	..	..	..	..	..	..	..	..	..	..	..
Namibia	..	..	..	..	..	73.9	52.3	46.0	44.6	38.1	36.6	..	..	48.6
Niger	..	..	..	..	..	..	..	..	..	..	..	..	..	..
Nigeria	2.5	6.0	6.6	3.3	4.8	4.6	..	..	..	..	..	4.2	5.0	4.6
Rwanda	..	..	..	..	..	..	..	..	..	..	..	..	..	..
São Tomé and Principe	..	..	..	..	..	..	..	..	..	..	..	..	..	..
Senegal	13.5	15.3	13.5	13.6	13.5	13.1	11.7	10.5	9.5	14.6	..	16.1	15.1	11.9
Seychelles	..	..	..	..	..	..	..	..	..	..	..	..	..	..
Sierra Leone	..	..	..	..	..	..	..	..	..	..	..	..	..	..
Somalia	..	..	..	..	..	..	..	..	..	..	..	..	..	..
South Africa	126.4	175.1	129.1	114.5	117.2	107.3	84.6	75.5	78.7	77.5	71.0	142.9	147.3	82.4
Sudan	45.4	10.7	..	..	..	..	15.7	..	..	..	..	33.5	13.0	15.7
Swaziland	..	..	..	..	..	..	..	..	..	..	..	..	..	..
Tanzania	..	..	..	..	..	..	64.8	63.1	89.9	10.7	..	37.2	49.6	57.1
Togo	..	..	..	..	..	..	..	..	..	..	..	..	..	..
Uganda	..	6.7	4.6	3.1	6.7	11.9	6.0	6.8	6.0	6.1	..	11.4	5.9	7.3
Zaire	15.0	25.6	26.7	25.4	..	..	..	..	..	..	..	19.3	27.0	..
Zambia	..	152.6	118.6	47.7	..	56.7	65.7	70.1	67.9	36.4	16.2	75.7	108.1	52.2
Zimbabwe	134.3	149.8	123.4	99.1	94.0	94.0	95.0	126.6	108.1	86.0	81.3	120.2	124.6	98.5
NORTH AFRICA	27.4	32.4	..	..	..	40.1	50.7	48.1	46.2	43.0	..	29.8	31.4	45.6
Algeria	10.7	7.9	7.6	8.9	9.8	9.2	12.7	11.0	10.7	10.7	..	9.8	8.6	10.9
Egypt, Arab Republic	58.3	75.1	..	..	..	106.5	139.7	133.6	128.2	117.6	..	63.1	68.4	125.1
Libya	..	..	..	..	..	..	..	..	..	..	..	..	..	..
Morocco	25.1	37.6	35.3	34.2	28.2	27.6	23.9	24.9	23.1	21.2	..	35.7	36.5	24.2
Tunisia	29.3	30.1	30.3	30.3	30.6	23.1	21.7	19.8	20.9	20.7	..	30.2	30.5	21.2
ALL AFRICA	47.7	59.8	47.0	..	..	48.9	52.1	..	..	..	..	51.5	57.6	50.5

9-8. Rail load to locomotive ratio

	Million rail ton-km/locomotive											Annual average		
	1980	*1986*	*1987*	*1988*	*1989*	*1990*	*1991*	*1992*	*1993*	*1994*	*1995*	*75-84*	*85-89*	*90-MR*
SUB-SAHARAN AFRICA	..	12.0	12.5	..	..	..	..	..	..	..	..	12.8	12.4	..
excluding South Africa	..	7.3	..	..	..	..	..	..	..	..	..	..	7.3	..
excl. S. Africa & Nigeria	..	..	..	..	..	..	..	..	..	..	..	..	..	..
Angola	..	..	..	..	..	..	..	..	..	..	..	..	..	..
Benin	..	..	..	..	..	..	..	..	..	..	..	..	..	..
Botswana	..	..	..	..	..	..	..	..	..	..	..	..	..	..
Burkina Faso	..	..	..	..	..	..	..	..	..	..	..	..	..	..
Burundi	..	..	..	..	..	..	..	..	..	..	..	..	..	..
Cameroon	10.9	9.1	7.3	6.5	9.0	10.1	8.9	9.6	8.6	12.4	..	9.8	8.4	9.9
Cape Verde	..	..	..	..	..	..	..	..	..	..	..	..	..	..
Central African Republic	..	..	..	..	..	..	..	..	..	..	..	..	..	..
Chad	..	..	..	..	..	..	..	..	..	..	..	..	..	..
Comoros	..	..	..	..	..	..	..	..	..	..	..	..	..	..
Congo	..	9.9	8.3	..	..	..	14.8	9.4	..	5.8	..	11.3	9.4	10.0
Côte d'Ivoire	12.8	13.0	13.1	..	..	8.0	6.7	6.8	4.5	4.5	..	12.3	12.3	6.1
Djibouti	..	..	..	..	..	..	..	..	..	..	..	..	..	..
Equatorial Guinea	..	..	..	..	..	..	..	..	..	..	..	..	..	..
Eritrea	..	..	..	..	..	..	..	..	..	..	..	..	..	..
Ethiopia	..	..	..	..	6.1	..	2.3	..	..	..	..	..	6.1	2.3
Gabon	2.1	5.7	5.4	4.6	3.3	..	..	4.8	5.2	5.1	..	4.2	5.4	5.0
Gambia, The	..	..	..	..	..	..	..	..	..	..	..	..	..	..
Ghana	..	1.6	..	..	..	3.3	..	..	..	..	..	..	1.6	3.3
Guinea	..	..	..	..	..	..	..	..	..	..	..	..	..	..
Guinea-Bissau	..	..	..	..	..	..	..	..	..	..	..	..	..	..
Kenya	6.9	8.3	8.1	..	9.2	8.8	9.0	..	..	..	..	9.2	8.7	8.9
Lesotho	..	..	..	..	..	..	..	..	..	..	..	..	..	..
Liberia	..	..	..	..	..	..	..	..	..	..	..	..	..	..
Madagascar	..	..	..	..	..	..	..	..	..	..	..	..	..	..
Malawi	..	2.2	1.9	1.4	1.4	1.4	1.5	1.1	1.1	0.9	3.4	3.5	1.9	1.6
Mali	..	12.5	7.7	6.7	7.8	7.8	7.8	7.9	..	..	..	18.4	9.0	7.8
Mauritania	..	..	..	..	..	..	..	..	..	..	..	..	..	..
Mauritius	..	..	..	..	..	..	..	..	..	..	..	..	..	..
Mozambique	..	..	..	..	..	..	..	..	..	..	..	..	..	..
Namibia	..	..	..	..	..	..	14.6	14.1	13.0	14.3	..	..	..	14.0
Niger	..	..	..	..	..	..	..	..	..	..	..	..	..	..
Nigeria	3.8	2.5	1.5	..	..	..	..	0.3	..	..	..	5.0	2.5	0.3
Rwanda	..	..	..	..	..	..	..	..	..	..	..	..	..	..
São Tomé and Principe	..	..	..	..	..	..	..	..	..	..	..	..	..	..
Senegal	13.3	19.6	18.3	18.4	16.7	20.9	18.0	16.4	14.6	9.7	..	14.3	18.0	15.9
Seychelles	..	..	..	..	..	..	..	..	..	..	..	..	..	..
Sierra Leone	..	..	..	..	..	..	..	..	..	..	..	..	..	..
Somalia	..	..	..	..	..	..	..	..	..	..	..	..	..	..
South Africa	..	19.9	20.1	19.9	23.2	25.4	23.6	22.6	25.8	26.4	27.0	18.2	20.5	25.1
Sudan	8.0	4.8	..	..	..	..	4.5	..	..	..	..	7.1	4.8	4.5
Swaziland	..	..	..	..	..	..	..	..	..	..	..	..	..	..
Tanzania	..	..	..	..	8.4	..	11.7	11.4	13.9	..	..	7.8	8.2	12.3
Togo	..	..	..	..	..	..	..	..	..	..	..	..	..	..
Uganda	..	1.1	1.3	2.1	2.0	3.1	2.7	2.0	2.3	3.5	..	1.4	1.5	2.7
Zaire	11.7	11.5	10.7	10.9	..	11.2	..	..	..	1.0	..	12.0	11.5	6.1
Zambia	16.1	20.1	19.7	23.0	22.7	20.3	15.4	14.6	15.1	9.9	5.6	17.2	21.1	13.5
Zimbabwe	21.7	22.4	20.0	13.0	..	13.6	13.8	16.0	17.5	27.9	27.5	20.7	18.4	19.4
NORTH AFRICA	..	..	..	..	..	..	..	..	..	..	..	..	..	..
Algeria	..	..	..	..	..	..	..	..	..	..	..	..	..	..
Egypt, Arab Republic	..	..	..	..	..	..	..	..	..	..	..	..	..	..
Libya	..	..	..	..	..	..	..	..	..	..	..	..	..	..
Morocco	..	..	..	..	..	..	..	..	..	..	..	..	..	..
Tunisia	..	..	..	..	..	..	..	..	..	..	..	..	..	..
ALL AFRICA	..	..	..	..	..	..	..	..	..	..	..	..	..	..

Technical Notes

Tables

Table 9-1. Electricity production per capita. This table refers to gross production per capita in kilowatt-hours. It covers electricity generated from all primary sources of energy—coal, oil, gas, nuclear, hydro, geothermal, wind, tide and wave, and combustible renewables—where data are available (IEA).

Table 9-2. Energy production and use. This table presents three indicators. *Energy production* refers to commercial forms of primary energy—petroleum (crude oil, natural gas liquids, and oil from nonconventional sources), natural gas, solid fuels, and primary electricity—all converted into oil equivalent (IEA and UN *Energy Statistics Yearbook*). *Commercial energy use* is indigenous production plus imports and stock changes, minus exports and international marine bunkers (IEA and UN *Energy Statistics Yearbook*). *Traditional energy use* includes estimates of the consumption of fuelwood, charcoal, bagasse, and animal and vegetable wastes (WRI). This is expressed as a percentage of energy consumption, which comprises commercial energy plus traditional fuel use.

Table 9-3. Telephone services availability. This table presents data for mainlines and faults per line. Telephone mainlines (ITU) refer to telephone lines connecting a customer's equipment to the public switched telephone network, where mainline is normally identified by a unique number. Mainlines are presented for every 1,000 people (Table 1.2). Faults per 100 mainlines per year (ITU) are defined as the number of reported faults for the year indicated. Some operators include malfunctioning customer premises equipment as faults while others include only technical faults.

Table 9-4. Intensity of vehicle use. Vehicles (International Road Federation) include all forms of road transportation, except buses. They are expressed as a ratio of 1,000 people (Table 1.2).

Table 9-5. Road-to-population ratio. This table presents the ratio of 1,000 kilometers of paved or unpaved road (International Road Federation) per 1 million people (Table 1.2).

Table 9-6. Paved primary roads. This table presents paved primary roads (International Road Federation) as a ratio to the country's population (Table 1.2) and then shows the percentage that is in good condition (World Bank data).

Table 9-7. Rail traffic-to-GDP ratio. This the number of rail traffic units (the sum of passenger-kilometers and ton-kilometers) per million US dollars of GDP (World Bank data).

Table 9-8. Rail load-to-locomotive ratio. This is the volume of rail transported goods (measured in millions of metric tons times kilometers traveled) per single locomotive (World Bank data).

Methodology used for regional aggregations and period averages in chapter 9

Table	*Aggregations*[a] (1)	(6)	*Period averages*[b] (1)
9-1		x	x
9-2			
Columns 1-4	x		
Columns 5-6		x	
9-3		x	
9-4		x	x
9-5		x	x
9-6		x	
9-7		x	x
9-8		x	x

Note: Regional aggregations are shown in the rows for Sub-Saharan Africa, North Africa, and All Africa. Period averages are shown in the last three columns. This table shows only the methodologies used in this chapter.

a. Regional aggregations: (1) simple total; (2) simple total of the first indicator divided by the simple total of the second indicator (same country coverage); (3) simple total of the gap-filled indicator; (4) simple total of the gap-filled main indicator divided by the simple total of the gap-filled secondary indicator; (5) simple total of the first gap-filled main indicator less the simple total of the second gap-filled main indicator, all divided by the simple total of the secondary indicator; (6) weighted total; (7) median; (8) no aggregation; (9) simple arithmetic mean.

b. Period averages: (1) arithmetic mean (using the same series as shown in the table, i.e., ratio if the rest of the table is shown as ratio, level if the rest of the table is shown as level, growth rate if the rest of the table is shown as growth rate); (2) least-squares growth rate (using main indicator); (3) least-squares growth rate (using main indicator in constant terms, with the rest of the table in current terms).

10

Public Enterprises

Public enterprises (PEs) account for a significant share of output, investment, and employment in Sub-Saharan Africa. They usually dominate public utilities and mining, account on average for nearly half of the output in transportation and communications, and are important in other productive sectors. Data presented here are for nonfinancial PEs only and exclude financial PEs and public agencies. Most PEs listed are government majority-owned. In common usage, the term "public enterprise" is synonymous with the term "state-owned enterprise." They are generally majority-owned by government, and their borrowing is implicitly or explicitly guaranteed by the government. PEs are singled out from other government activities because they are expected to earn most of their income from the sale of goods and services and to be financially self-sufficient. PEs have a separate legal identity, and their accounts are conventionally separated from government finance accounts, in part because their productive activities use different accounting conventions.

This chapter provides data on the size and importance of the PE sector, PE financial results and financial flows between PEs and governments, and the extent of PE reform efforts. A measure of the importance of PEs in the economy is the amount of resources they use, that is, their share of total investment, credit, and employment compared with their share of total goods and services produced (GDP). Another important measure is the fiscal impact of PEs, of which PE net financial results, or aggregate sector profits less aggregate sector losses, is an important determinant. PE financial results influence the level and composition of government expenditure, domestic credit, and external debt.

This chapter contains data on more than 31 Sub-Saharan African countries, although for most indicators, data are available for considerably fewer. Major mineral or commodity-exporting enterprises that weigh heavily on the size and performance of the sector are included in PE sectoral data for most countries. Financial enterprises and regulatory, educational, health, and promotional agencies are excluded, except where otherwise indicated in the table notes. Data on Algeria refer to the entire PE sector, not just industrial PEs, a major difference between numbers published here and in other reports. Data for Benin, Botswana, Congo, The Gambia, Ghana, Malawi, Mali, Morocco, Namibia, Niger, Nigeria, Rwanda, São Tome, Togo, and Zimbabwe refer to selected or major PEs only. Data for Cape Verde, Seychelles, and Sierra Leone refer to all PEs.

Most of the data in this chapter have been derived from two sources: the World Bank study *Bureaucrats in Business*, and an ongoing study on privatization in Sub-Saharan Africa being carried out by the Private Sector Finance Department of the Africa Region of the Bank.

The data in this section have serious limitations. First, time-series data are incomplete; for many indicators, the data are available for only one or two years, and data for some years are scarce (in particular for 1991 and 1992, because no comprehensive studies are available). Second, the quality of the data is sometimes inadequate; insufficient information on government lending to PEs, on cross debts among public entities, and on PE arrears impairs the assessment of government and PE financial flows. Subsidies, or loans provided by the government at below market value, are often not reflected in the government accounts. As governments undergo more stringent supervision by multilateral organizations regarding subsidies and transfers, some PEs have resorted to not paying taxes as a way to circumvent the detection of these transfers. Also, technical assistance provided by donor agencies and the World Bank might not be reflected as a form of transfer to PEs. Third, data consistency over time and comparability across countries for data series are compromised by varying definitions and accounting conventions. Trends shown for country groups may be distorted by changes in country coverage. National aggregates may be unduly biased by the inclusion or exclusion of some large enterprises that dominate the sector but may not be representative of PE operations. The table notes provide details on data coverage for most indicators. Technical notes and sources offer more information on each indicator and on the nature of the data. Despite these limitations, the data in this section are a step toward better monitoring of PE activities at the national and regional level.

10-1. Contribution of public enterprises to gross domestic product

	Percent											
	1980	*1983*	*1984*	*1985*	*1986*	*1987*	*1988*	*1989*	*1990*	*1991*	*1992*	*1993*
SUB-SAHARAN AFRICA	..	..	..	..	..	..	..	..	..	..	..	..
excluding South Africa	..	..	..	..	..	..	..	..	..	..	..	..
excl. S. Africa & Nigeria	..	..	..	..	..	..	..	..	..	..	..	..
Angola	..	..	..	..	..	..	..	..	..	..	..	..
Benin	..	..	..	..	..	..	..	..	..	..	..	..
Botswana	3.2	5.7	4.7	6.2	5.6	7.0	6.8	4.5	5.4	6.0	..	..
Burkina Faso	..	..	..	..	..	..	..	..	..	..	..	..
Burundi	..	..	5.4	..	5.0	7.9	..	..	9.0	..	..	..
Cameroon	..	..	..	18.4	..	17.7	..	..	17.8	..	..	..
Cape Verde	..	..	..	..	..	..	..	..	..	..	..	..
Central African Republic	..	4.4	4.3	4.1	3.3	3.5	3.5	..	..	..	..	..
Chad	..	..	..	..	..	..	..	..	..	..	..	..
Comoros	..	..	5.6	..	..	..	11.1	..	..	12.8	..	..
Congo	11.0	9.8	9.8	10.7	17.7	15.0	16.0	16.2	..	..	..	..
Côte d'Ivoire	..	..	..	..	..	..	..	..	..	..	..	..
Djibouti	..	..	..	..	..	..	..	..	..	..	..	..
Equatorial Guinea	..	..	..	..	..	..	..	..	..	..	..	..
Eritrea	..	..	..	..	..	..	..	..	..	..	..	..
Ethiopia	..	..	..	..	..	..	..	..	..	..	..	..
Gabon	..	..	..	..	..	..	..	..	..	..	..	..
Gambia, The	..	..	..	4.9	4.2	4.3	4.9	5.1	..	..	..	..
Ghana	..	..	4.6	5.5	10.6	11.9	8.3	8.0	7.3	4.9	..	..
Guinea	..	..	..	..	8.6	..	..	..	8.7	..	..	..
Guinea-Bissau	..	..	..	..	..	..	..	..	..	..	..	..
Kenya	..	..	8.0	12.0	11.7	11.7	10.9	11.4	11.6	..	..	..
Lesotho	..	..	..	..	..	..	..	..	..	..	..	..
Liberia	..	..	..	..	..	..	..	..	..	..	..	..
Madagascar	..	..	..	..	..	..	..	..	..	..	..	..
Malawi	9.5	6.8	6.0	4.9	3.9	4.1	..	..	..	..	..	..
Mali	11.7	..	..	..	..	..	..	..	..	..	..	..
Mauritania	..	25.0	..	..	..	..	..	..	..	..	..	..
Mauritius	2.0	2.2	2.0	2.0	1.8	1.8	..	..	..	..	..	..
Mozambique	..	..	..	..	..	..	..	..	..	..	..	..
Namibia	..	..	..	..	..	..	..	..	..	..	..	..
Niger	..	4.4	4.8	5.3	5.8	4.6	4.7	..	..	5.5	..	..
Nigeria	..	13.6	13.9	12.9	14.8	..	..	..	..	..	..	..
Rwanda	..	..	..	..	..	..	..	10.0	..	..	..	..
São Tomé and Principe	..	..	..	..	..	..	..	..	..	..	..	..
Senegal	8.4	8.9	10.3	9.6	6.1	5.8	6.3	6.7	..	..	..	..
Seychelles	..	..	..	..	..	..	..	..	..	..	..	..
Sierra Leone	24.1	..	..	..	..	..	..	..	..	..	..	..
Somalia	..	..	..	..	..	..	..	..	..	..	..	..
South Africa	12.9	14.4	15.2	15.2	16.0	15.3	14.7	13.3	..	..	..	..
Sudan	..	..	..	..	..	..	..	..	..	..	..	..
Swaziland	..	..	..	..	..	..	..	..	..	..	..	..
Tanzania	..	11.5	10.4	10.3	8.5	12.1	13.1	13.4	20.0	..	..	..
Togo	11.8	..	..	..	..	..	..	14.4	10.5	10.6	..	..
Uganda	..	..	..	..	..	..	..	..	..	..	..	..
Zaire	..	..	..	..	..	..	..	..	..	..	..	..
Zambia	..	30.9	31.5	35.0	..	23.9	29.4	40.0	32.8	21.8	..	..
Zimbabwe	..	..	..	..	..	..	..	..	..	..	..	..
NORTH AFRICA	..	..	..	..	..	..	..	..	..	..	..	..
Algeria	66.7	72.2	70.6	68.3	63.4	65.2	59.9	45.9	..	..	..	..
Egypt, Arab Republic	..	..	..	..	..	27.2	..	..	..	32.8	..	..
Libya	..	..	..	..	..	..	..	..	..	..	..	..
Morocco	20.0	9.1	11.8	15.4	..	20.0	..	..	15.0	..	..	..
Tunisia	32.1	31.2	31.4	30.2	..	..	..	..	..	29.8	..	..
ALL AFRICA	..	..	..	..	..	..	..	..	..	..	..	..

10-2. Share of public enterprises in non agricultural activity

	Percentage of nonagricultural GDP											
	1980	*1983*	*1984*	*1985*	*1986*	*1987*	*1988*	*1989*	*1990*	*1991*	*1992*	*1993*
SUB-SAHARAN AFRICA	..	..	..	..	..	..	..	..	..	..	..	..
excluding South Africa	..	..	..	..	..	..	..	..	..	..	..	..
excl. S. Africa & Nigeria	..	..	..	..	..	..	..	..	..	..	..	..
Angola	..	..	..	..	..	..	..	..	..	..	..	..
Benin	..	..	..	..	..	..	..	..	..	..	..	..
Botswana	3.6	6.3	5.1	6.5	5.9	7.3	7.0	4.7	5.6	6.3	..	..
Burkina Faso	..	..	..	..	..	..	..	..	..	..	..	..
Burundi	..	..	11.9	..	10.5	15.9	..	..	16.8	..	..	..
Cameroon	..	..	..	23.0	..	23.8	..	..	23.5	..	..	..
Cape Verde	..	..	..	..	..	..	..	..	..	..	..	..
Central African Republic	..	7.1	7.1	7.4	6.4	6.3	6.6	..	..	..	..	..
Chad	..	..	..	..	..	..	..	..	..	..	..	..
Comoros	..	..	8.2	..	..	..	17.5	..	..	21.6	..	..
Congo	12.3	10.5	10.5	11.5	19.9	16.9	18.3	18.4	..	..	..	..
Côte d'Ivoire	..	..	..	..	..	..	..	..	..	..	..	..
Djibouti	..	..	..	..	..	..	..	..	..	..	..	..
Equatorial Guinea	..	..	..	..	..	..	..	..	..	..	..	..
Eritrea	..	..	..	..	..	..	..	..	..	..	..	..
Ethiopia	..	..	..	..	..	..	..	..	..	..	..	..
Gabon	..	..	..	..	..	..	..	..	..	..	..	..
Gambia, The	..	..	..	6.9	5.7	6.3	7.0	6.8	..	..	..	..
Ghana	..	..	7.7	9.0	15.2	17.7	13.0	12.6	9.9	6.8	..	..
Guinea	..	..	..	..	12.3	..	..	..	11.5	..	..	..
Guinea-Bissau	..	..	..	..	..	..	..	..	..	..	..	..
Kenya	..	..	8.1	12.2	11.9	11.9	11.0	11.6	12.0	..	..	..
Lesotho	..	..	..	..	..	..	..	..	..	..	..	..
Liberia	..	..	..	..	..	..	..	..	..	..	..	..
Madagascar	..	..	..	..	..	..	..	..	..	..	..	..
Malawi	11.7	7.8	5.8	6.1	..	..	..	..	9.9	6.0	..	..
Mali	19.8	..	..	..	..	..	..	..	..	..	..	..
Mauritania	..	33.9	..	..	..	..	..	..	..	..	..	..
Mauritius	2.2	2.5	2.3	2.2	2.0	2.0	..	..	..	..	..	..
Mozambique	..	..	..	..	..	..	..	..	..	..	..	..
Namibia	..	..	..	..	..	..	..	..	..	..	..	..
Niger	..	7.8	9.4	8.2	8.9	6.8	7.5	..	..	8.5	..	..
Nigeria	..	17.0	17.4	16.1	18.5	..	..	..	..	..	..	..
Rwanda	..	..	..	..	..	..	..	14.7	..	..	..	..
São Tomé and Principe	..	..	..	..	..	..	..	..	..	..	..	..
Senegal	..	10.7	12.6	11.0	7.1	5.8	6.2	6.9	..	..	..	..
Seychelles	..	..	..	..	..	..	..	..	..	..	..	..
Sierra Leone	36.4	..	..	..	..	..	..	..	..	..	..	..
Somalia	..	..	..	..	..	..	..	..	..	..	..	..
South Africa	13.5	15.1	16.0	16.0	16.8	16.2	15.6	14.1	..	..	..	..
Sudan	..	..	..	..	..	..	..	..	..	..	..	..
Swaziland	..	..	..	..	..	..	..	..	..	..	..	..
Tanzania	..	19.6	17.4	18.2	15.7	21.5	24.0	24.7	33.2	..	..	..
Togo	14.8	..	..	..	..	..	..	21.2	15.4	15.6	..	..
Uganda	..	..	..	..	..	..	..	..	..	..	..	..
Zaire	..	..	..	..	..	..	..	..	..	..	..	..
Zambia	..	35.0	35.8	39.0	..	26.0	31.7	43.7	35.8	24.0	..	..
Zimbabwe	..	..	..	..	..	..	..	..	..	..	..	..
NORTH AFRICA	..	..	..	..	..	..	..	..	..	..	..	..
Algeria	71.0	76.8	74.2	71.8	66.3	66.5	63.7	48.8	..	..	..	..
Egypt, Arab Republic	..	..	..	..	..	35.3	..	..	..	42.6	..	..
Libya	..	..	..	..	..	..	..	..	..	..	..	..
Morocco	23.5	19.1	19.9	17.7	24.6	..	..	17.8	..	21.1	..	..
Tunisia	37.2	36.2	37.0	34.8	..	..	..	..	..	34.3	..	..
ALL AFRICA	..	..	..	..	..	..	..	..	..	..	..	..

10-3. Share of public enterprises in gross domestic investment

	Percent											
	1980	*1983*	*1984*	*1985*	*1986*	*1987*	*1988*	*1989*	*1990*	*1991*	*1992*	*1993*
SUB-SAHARAN AFRICA	..	..	..	..	..	..	..	..	..	..	..	..
excluding South Africa	..	..	..	..	..	..	..	..	..	..	..	..
excl. S. Africa & Nigeria	..	..	..	..	..	..	..	..	..	..	..	..
Angola	..	..	..	..	..	..	..	..	..	..	..	..
Benin	..	..	..	51.9	11.7	14.8	15.9	23.3	13.4	..	..	..
Botswana	6.4	23.0	26.9	43.6	9.5	18.4	28.6	20.8	..	..	..	..
Burkina Faso	..	..	..	..	..	..	..	..	..	..	..	..
Burundi	42.7	31.2	36.1	42.6	44.9	46.3	39.6	39.6	33.7	..	..	..
Cameroon	..	..	..	..	..	..	..	..	..	..	..	..
Cape Verde	..	..	..	..	..	..	..	..	..	..	..	..
Central African Republic	..	..	..	..	13.4	..	..	..	..	..	..	..
Chad	..	..	..	..	..	..	..	..	..	..	..	..
Comoros	..	22.1	11.7	15.2	15.8	..	..	..	..	..	..	..
Congo	..	39.8	..	..	..	..	..	..	..	..	..	..
Côte d'Ivoire	7.7	23.9	28.3	21.5	21.1	15.8	15.4	17.6	20.7	22.0	..	..
Djibouti	..	..	..	..	..	..	..	..	..	..	..	..
Equatorial Guinea	..	..	..	..	..	..	..	..	..	..	..	..
Eritrea	..	..	..	..	..	..	..	..	..	..	..	..
Ethiopia	..	..	..	..	..	..	..	..	..	..	..	..
Gabon	..	..	..	..	..	..	..	..	..	..	..	..
Gambia, The	17.4	..	..	..	..	..	..	..	..	..	..	..
Ghana	27.6	17.4	8.2	20.4	24.4	16.8	16.9	26.4	0.6	62.8	..	..
Guinea	..	..	..	..	..	..	..	..	..	..	..	..
Guinea-Bissau	..	..	..	..	..	..	..	..	..	..	..	..
Kenya	24.6	24.0	22.7	18.8	22.2	18.5	17.3	20.8	25.0	..	..	..
Lesotho	..	..	..	..	..	..	..	..	..	..	..	..
Liberia	..	..	..	..	..	..	..	..	..	..	..	..
Madagascar	..	..	..	..	..	..	..	..	..	..	..	..
Malawi	49.6	6.1	7.3	4.9	10.5	8.0	12.3	10.2	..	..	..	..
Mali	8.1	..	..	..	..	..	..	..	..	..	..	..
Mauritania	49.2	..	28.1	19.1	24.7	30.0	25.8	5.6	10.8	18.8	..	..
Mauritius	..	..	7.2	..	..	..	..	..	..	..	..	..
Mozambique	..	..	..	..	..	..	..	..	..	..	..	..
Namibia	13.2	21.2	15.2	15.8	14.3	13.2	11.7	8.8	7.8	8.2	..	..
Niger	..	10.6	..	33.5	14.5	..	..	..	..	..	..	..
Nigeria	..	20.0	10.6	14.0	15.1	..	..	..	..	..	..	..
Rwanda	..	..	..	..	..	..	..	..	..	..	..	..
São Tomé and Principe	..	..	..	..	..	..	..	..	..	..	..	..
Senegal	..	80.1	33.7	46.1	28.7	20.9	18.6	19.9	..	..	..	..
Seychelles	..	..	..	..	..	..	..	..	..	..	..	..
Sierra Leone	..	1.2	1.1	..	..	..	..	..	..	..	..	..
Somalia	..	..	..	..	..	..	..	..	..	..	..	..
South Africa	25.8	17.9	18.4	20.9	18.4	16.1	13.4	15.6	16.1	..	..	..
Sudan	..	..	..	..	..	..	..	..	..	..	..	..
Swaziland	..	..	..	..	..	..	..	..	..	..	..	..
Tanzania	..	21.0	19.4	23.4	26.8	27.2	33.8	44.0	24.9	23.2	..	..
Togo	..	..	..	10.2	9.1	21.6	13.0	10.4	13.7	..	..	..
Uganda	..	..	..	..	..	..	..	..	..	..	..	..
Zaire	..	..	..	..	..	..	..	..	..	..	..	..
Zambia	54.8	58.8	57.2	..	..	..	..	..	..	..	..	..
Zimbabwe	..	..	..	..	..	..	..	..	..	..	..	..
NORTH AFRICA	..	..	..	..	..	..	..	..	..	..	..	..
Algeria	69.5	42.0	36.8	32.2	28.1	..	..	..	..	..	..	..
Egypt, Arab Republic	..	53.0	56.1	68.5	79.3	79.6	54.5	59.4	51.9	..	..	..
Libya	..	..	..	..	..	..	..	..	..	..	..	..
Morocco	22.0	24.0	27.0	23.0	17.0	18.0	18.0	22.0	18.0	..	..	..
Tunisia	33.8	37.7	38.6	33.7	35.8	34.0	28.2	26.8	27.2	30.5	..	..
ALL AFRICA	..	..	..	..	..	..	..	..	..	..	..	..

10-4. Share of investment of public enterprises

	Percentage of GDP											
	1980	*1983*	*1984*	*1985*	*1986*	*1987*	*1988*	*1989*	*1990*	*1991*	*1992*	*1993*
SUB-SAHARAN AFRICA	..	..	..	..	..	..	..	..	..	..	..	..
excluding South Africa	..	..	..	..	..	..	..	..	..	..	..	..
excl. S. Africa & Nigeria	..	..	..	..	..	..	..	..	..	..	..	..
Angola	..	..	..	..	..	..	..	..	..	..	..	..
Benin	..	..	..	4.6	1.6	1.9	2.0	2.7	1.9	..	..	..
Botswana	2.4	6.9	7.1	13.2	1.5	4.5	2.1	8.5	..	..	..	..
Burkina Faso	..	..	..	..	..	..	..	..	..	..	..	..
Burundi	5.9	7.1	6.6	5.9	5.2	10.5	6.0	6.5	4.9	..	..	..
Cameroon	..	..	..	..	..	..	..	..	..	..	..	..
Cape Verde	..	..	..	..	..	..	..	..	..	..	..	..
Central African Republic	..	..	..	..	1.9	..	..	..	..	..	..	..
Chad	..	..	..	..	..	..	..	..	..	..	..	..
Comoros	..	6.7	5.3	5.0	3.7	..	..	..	..	..	..	..
Congo	..	15.3	..	..	..	..	..	..	..	..	..	..
Côte d'Ivoire	2.0	4.4	3.3	2.8	3.2	2.3	2.3	1.9	1.7	1.8	..	..
Djibouti	..	..	..	..	..	..	..	..	..	..	..	..
Equatorial Guinea	..	..	..	..	..	..	..	..	..	..	..	..
Eritrea	..	..	..	..	..	..	..	..	..	..	..	..
Ethiopia	..	..	..	..	..	..	..	..	..	..	..	..
Gabon	..	..	..	..	..	..	..	..	..	..	..	..
Gambia, The	4.6	..	..	..	..	..	..	..	..	..	..	..
Ghana	1.6	0.7	0.6	2.0	2.4	2.3	1.9	3.5	0.1	10.0	..	..
Guinea	..	..	..	..	..	..	..	..	..	..	..	..
Guinea-Bissau	..	..	..	..	..	..	..	..	..	..	..	..
Kenya	7.2	5.0	4.7	4.9	4.8	4.5	4.3	5.1	6.0	..	..	..
Lesotho	..	..	..	..	..	..	..	..	..	..	..	..
Liberia	..	..	..	..	..	..	..	..	..	..	..	..
Madagascar	..	..	..	..	..	..	..	..	..	..	..	..
Malawi	12.3	1.4	0.9	0.9	1.3	1.3	2.3	2.2	..	..	..	..
Mali	1.3	..	..	..	..	..	..	..	..	..	..	..
Mauritania	17.8	..	7.0	5.5	7.5	8.7	7.2	1.0	2.2	3.4	..	..
Mauritius	..	..	1.6	..	..	..	..	..	..	..	..	..
Mozambique	..	..	..	..	..	..	..	..	..	..	..	..
Namibia	3.9	4.2	2.6	1.7	1.3	2.0	2.1	1.5	2.1	1.6	..	..
Niger	..	1.4	..	5.1	1.9	..	..	..	..	..	..	..
Nigeria	..	2.9	1.0	1.3	2.3	..	..	..	..	..	..	..
Rwanda	..	..	..	..	..	..	..	..	..	..	..	..
São Tomé and Principe	..	..	..	..	..	..	..	..	..	..	..	..
Senegal	..	9.5	3.9	4.9	3.4	2.6	2.4	2.5	..	..	..	..
Seychelles	..	..	..	..	..	..	..	..	..	..	..	..
Sierra Leone	..	0.2	0.1	..	..	..	..	..	..	..	..	..
Somalia	..	..	..	..	..	..	..	..	..	..	..	..
South Africa	7.3	4.4	4.7	4.2	3.4	2.9	2.7	3.2	2.7	..	..	..
Sudan	..	..	..	..	..	..	..	..	..	..	..	..
Swaziland	..	..	..	..	..	..	..	..	..	..	..	..
Tanzania	..	4.1	3.2	4.1	5.2	6.6	9.6	13.2	9.1	8.0	..	..
Togo	..	..	..	1.7	1.7	3.8	2.1	2.6	3.6	..	..	..
Uganda	..	..	..	..	..	..	..	..	..	..	..	..
Zaire	..	..	..	..	..	..	..	..	..	..	..	..
Zambia	12.8	8.1	8.4	..	..	..	..	..	..	..	..	..
Zimbabwe	..	..	..	..	..	..	..	..	..	..	..	..
NORTH AFRICA	..	..	..	..	..	..	..	..	..	..	..	..
Algeria	27.2	15.8	12.9	10.7	9.4	..	..	..	..	..	..	..
Egypt, Arab Republic	..	15.2	15.4	18.3	18.8	20.8	19.0	18.9	15.0	..	..	..
Libya	..	..	..	..	..	..	..	..	..	..	..	..
Morocco	5.3	5.8	6.8	6.2	3.9	3.8	3.8	5.2	4.5	..	..	..
Tunisia	9.9	12.6	13.9	10.2	9.5	8.0	5.8	6.4	7.4	7.9	..	..
ALL AFRICA	..	..	..	..	..	..	..	..	..	..	..	..

10-5. Share of public enterprises in formal sector employment

	Percent											
	1980	*1983*	*1984*	*1985*	*1986*	*1987*	*1988*	*1989*	*1990*	*1991*	*1992*	*1993*
SUB-SAHARAN AFRICA	..	..	..	..	..	..	..	..	..	..	..	..
excluding South Africa	..	..	..	..	..	..	..	..	..	..	..	..
excl. S. Africa & Nigeria	..	..	..	..	..	..	..	..	..	..	..	..
Angola	..	..	..	..	..	..	..	..	..	..	..	..
Benin	25.6	25.2	26.0	..	..	..	..	..	..	..	..	..
Botswana	..	..	..	7.6	6.2	5.8	6.6	6.0	5.7	5.3	..	..
Burkina Faso	..	..	..	..	..	..	..	..	..	..	..	..
Burundi	35.0	27.9	..	..	28.1	33.0	35.7	31.4	..	..	..	..
Cameroon	..	..	..	10.4	..	10.0	..	..	..	..	..	..
Cape Verde	..	..	..	..	..	..	..	..	..	..	..	..
Central African Republic	..	..	..	..	..	..	..	..	..	..	..	..
Chad	..	..	..	..	..	..	..	..	..	..	..	..
Comoros	..	..	..	..	..	..	..	..	..	..	..	..
Congo	..	..	..	21.8	18.9	..	..	..	..	..	..	..
Côte d'Ivoire	7.7	22.9	26.1	18.8	20.4	..	..	..	..	..	..	..
Djibouti	..	..	..	..	..	..	..	..	..	..	..	..
Equatorial Guinea	..	..	..	..	..	..	..	..	..	..	..	..
Eritrea	..	..	..	..	..	..	..	..	..	..	..	..
Ethiopia	..	..	..	..	..	..	..	..	..	..	..	..
Gabon	..	..	..	..	..	..	26.2	25.5	26.0	25.1	..	..
Gambia, The	..	..	..	..	..	..	25.0	..	..	..	..	..
Ghana	..	..	27.6	..	27.8	27.4	33.3	44.9	38.0	45.1	..	..
Guinea	68.8	..	75.0	..	..	..	..	..	..	..	..	..
Guinea-Bissau	..	..	..	..	..	..	..	..	..	..	..	..
Kenya	..	9.0	8.5	7.7	8.2	7.6	8.1	8.1	8.1	..	..	..
Lesotho	..	..	..	..	..	..	..	..	..	..	..	..
Liberia	..	..	..	..	..	..	..	..	..	..	..	..
Madagascar	..	..	..	..	..	..	..	..	..	..	..	..
Malawi	11.2	11.9	11.9	12.0	12.0	..	..	..	..	..	..	..
Mali	17.4	..	..	..	..	..	..	..	..	..	..	..
Mauritania	..	..	..	..	..	..	..	..	..	..	20.0	20.0
Mauritius	..	..	7.2	6.0	..	..	..	..	..	..	..	..
Mozambique	..	..	..	..	..	..	..	..	..	..	..	..
Namibia	..	..	..	..	..	..	2.7	..	..	..	..	..
Niger	..	..	..	..	..	..	..	..	..	..	..	20.0
Nigeria	..	..	..	..	..	..	..	..	..	..	..	..
Rwanda	..	..	..	..	..	..	..	..	..	..	..	..
São Tomé and Principe	..	..	..	..	..	..	..	..	..	..	..	..
Senegal	..	23.4	22.1	21.2	19.4	20.9	21.7	19.0	..	..	..	..
Seychelles	..	..	..	..	..	..	..	..	..	..	..	..
Sierra Leone	..	..	..	..	..	..	..	..	..	..	..	..
Somalia	..	..	..	..	..	..	..	..	..	..	..	..
South Africa	..	..	..	..	..	..	..	..	..	..	..	..
Sudan	..	..	..	..	..	..	..	..	..	..	..	..
Swaziland	..	..	..	..	..	..	..	..	..	..	..	..
Tanzania	23.2	22.1	25.4	17.2	21.1	21.9	21.7	23.2	23.8	..	..	..
Togo	..	24.0	..	..	..	..	..	..	..	..	..	..
Uganda	..	..	..	..	..	..	..	..	..	..	..	..
Zaire	..	..	..	10.0	..	..	..	..	..	..	..	..
Zambia	43.4	34.9	..	..	..	..	..	..	..	..	..	..
Zimbabwe	..	..	..	..	..	..	..	..	..	..	..	..
NORTH AFRICA	..	..	..	..	..	..	..	..	..	..	..	..
Algeria	8.1	8.3	7.9	7.9	7.3	7.4	7.2	7.3	7.0	7.0	..	..
Egypt, Arab Republic	..	13.6	13.6	14.7	14.2	13.7	13.7	13.5	13.2	13.5	..	..
Libya	..	..	..	..	..	..	..	..	..	..	..	..
Morocco	..	..	..	..	..	..	..	..	..	..	..	..
Tunisia	..	18.5	..	..	..	..	..	..	..	..	..	..
ALL AFRICA	..	..	..	..	..	..	..	..	..	..	..	..

10-6. Gross domestic credit to public enterprises

	Percentage of GDP											
	1980	*1983*	*1984*	*1985*	*1986*	*1987*	*1988*	*1989*	*1990*	*1991*	*1992*	*1993*
SUB-SAHARAN AFRICA	..	..	..	..	..	..	..	..	..	..	..	..
excluding South Africa	..	..	..	..	..	..	..	..	..	..	..	..
excl. S. Africa & Nigeria	..	..	..	..	..	..	..	..	..	..	..	..
Angola	..	..	..	..	..	..	..	..	..	..	..	..
Benin	23.5	31.7	28.6	32.1	30.4	29.1	29.7	21.1	22.4	14.6	13.2	9.2
Botswana	0.8	-0.7	-9.3	-22.9	-41.2	-54.5	-52.2	-46.3	-53.0	-46.6	-47.5	-48.3
Burkina Faso	16.0	13.6	12.8	12.1	12.1	11.2	11.5	13.5	13.7	11.8	9.9	9.3
Burundi	15.8	23.8	21.6	20.6	20.3	21.0	23.0	19.5	19.6	19.2	16.9	17.5
Cameroon	26.8	27.5	23.6	22.2	24.5	20.5	26.7	30.2	31.2	37.9	26.0	25.5
Cape Verde	26.2	36.4	36.6	39.6	40.5	31.4	30.6	34.0	38.4	45.5	49.7	54.0
Central African Republic	23.8	21.8	18.9	14.9	15.0	14.2	13.1	13.1	13.1	15.8	13.8	14.1
Chad	32.8	20.4	19.8	20.8	31.7	31.8	22.1	19.0	14.4	17.4	20.5	21.0
Comoros	..	14.4	17.9	11.3	10.6	11.0	13.2	15.9	17.5	19.1	20.6	14.5
Congo	22.3	22.0	21.0	22.7	34.0	28.8	30.9	30.4	29.1	29.9	30.6	21.1
Côte d'Ivoire	39.3	51.3	45.2	42.1	42.9	45.7	47.7	44.2	44.5	44.0	45.2	43.8
Djibouti	..	..	..	49.5	52.4	47.2	45.8	47.0	43.2	41.5	43.3	42.5
Equatorial Guinea	..	..	..	37.3	42.2	34.3	31.0	33.9	31.2	63.3	50.1	31.5
Eritrea	..	..	..	..	..	..	..	..	..	..	..	..
Ethiopia	..	32.8	38.1	35.3	37.1	38.6	41.4	44.5	50.3	49.7	55.2	44.5
Gabon	19.6	16.4	15.2	17.3	27.9	34.8	32.0	28.3	20.0	21.9	21.0	20.5
Gambia, The	47.8	61.7	63.7	61.4	33.5	13.8	14.8	11.1	3.6	0.0	9.4	7.1
Ghana	22.2	17.6	18.0	22.7	23.3	27.5	18.6	17.1	13.2	19.0	23.8	27.6
Guinea	..	..	..	..	..	..	..	..	..	5.5	6.2	5.9
Guinea-Bissau	..	..	..	..	45.6	36.5	33.4	37.2	43.5	27.8	18.9	16.1
Kenya	30.1	32.6	32.1	31.9	34.9	37.5	34.7	32.5	35.8	37.4	37.3	29.1
Lesotho	20.3	35.0	31.4	33.9	38.1	39.7	41.0	37.4	27.4	25.0	10.6	2.3
Liberia	25.4	42.4	42.9	49.3	53.9	59.4	70.7	81.0	..	..	..	..
Madagascar	39.9	40.2	42.9	42.9	42.1	41.7	34.2	28.6	26.2	27.5	30.9	31.0
Malawi	33.2	41.2	35.5	35.2	38.0	33.0	20.8	20.3	17.3	17.3	26.1	22.3
Mali	38.7	41.5	20.6	22.9	24.4	23.1	17.1	16.7	13.4	12.8	11.9	13.2
Mauritania	36.0	41.9	42.5	38.4	35.9	35.1	34.7	49.6	54.7	53.3	47.9	46.5
Mauritius	51.0	63.1	64.6	60.7	55.6	48.0	47.5	45.9	45.1	50.2	53.5	58.8
Mozambique	..	..	..	..	..	..	..	..	..	..	..	..
Namibia	..	..	..	..	..	..	..	..	21.0	20.6	32.9	39.9
Niger	15.7	20.2	20.5	19.8	20.3	17.8	17.8	16.3	16.2	14.9	15.1	12.4
Nigeria	21.1	48.5	47.9	44.1	49.9	37.0	34.9	20.5	23.7	21.5	29.2	38.3
Rwanda	3.2	8.4	8.5	9.5	10.3	12.5	14.5	16.4	17.0	13.5	16.2	19.1
São Tomé and Principe	..	..	57.4	73.7	153.8	146.4	103.7	..	..	..	..	..
Senegal	47.3	51.8	49.9	47.9	42.4	40.3	40.1	38.9	33.7	32.9	31.3	31.1
Seychelles	20.1	29.0	29.4	31.1	32.8	31.9	36.5	39.4	38.3	42.5	41.2	46.0
Sierra Leone	32.8	39.9	33.0	42.2	26.2	19.8	18.4	16.6	26.3	18.5	11.8	9.4
Somalia	22.3	15.0	15.4	13.2	11.5	20.5	18.0	17.7	..	..	..	..
South Africa	52.7	57.0	59.2	61.5	57.4	56.5	59.2	58.0	58.4	..	64.3	64.1
Sudan	44.6	37.3	36.2	38.0	37.1	39.4	34.2	34.6	29.9	25.9	31.1	25.8
Swaziland	8.1	22.0	20.7	20.9	19.1	15.4	11.3	6.5	7.6	2.3	3.4	6.4
Tanzania	..	47.4	49.7	52.0	43.5	49.7	42.0	35.1	42.8	38.5	38.9	44.3
Togo	29.8	27.5	23.6	19.8	27.5	27.1	26.0	19.2	21.3	23.0	21.5	28.4
Uganda	16.6	11.9	13.7	16.1	12.4	..	..	..	..	..	17.8	11.6
Zaire	9.2	13.4	6.3	5.4	7.3	6.7	9.9	11.2	25.3	18.1	14.3	16.4
Zambia	60.8	76.1	72.1	59.7	45.0	32.7	66.9	74.6	68.4	83.8	..	31.7
Zimbabwe	18.7	23.5	29.1	29.1	28.5	31.7	27.6	29.2	29.1	27.1	31.8	39.3
NORTH AFRICA	..	..	..	..	..	..	..	..	..	..	..	..
Algeria	62.5	79.4	84.8	86.2	93.7	97.2	97.6	87.7	74.7	56.6	59.6	64.4
Egypt, Arab Republic	85.3	108.0	110.7	113.7	116.7	101.8	102.2	102.6	103.6	96.6	80.0	75.8
Libya	11.5	33.4	44.2	42.3	47.4	48.7	61.1	103.1	..	..	..	..
Morocco	42.1	52.8	50.5	50.1	46.6	49.3	46.1	47.8	42.9	44.9	49.5	52.4
Tunisia	44.4	54.7	56.0	59.5	63.1	61.2	59.2	66.4	62.5	60.8	59.4	58.5
ALL AFRICA	..	..	..	..	..	..	..	..	..	..	..	..

10-7. Share of public enterprises in domestic credit outstanding

	Percent											Annual average		
	1980	1986	1987	1988	1989	1990	1991	1992	1993	1994	1995	75-84	85-89	90-MR
SUB-SAHARAN AFRICA	..	..	..	..	..	..	..	..	..	..	..	..	..	..
excluding South Africa	..	..	..	..	..	..	..	..	..	..	..	..	..	..
excl. S. Africa & Nigeria	..	..	..	..	..	..	..	..	..	..	..	..	..	..
Angola	..	..	..	..	..	..	..	..	..	..	..	..	..	..
Benin	..	..	..	..	..	..	..	..	..	..	..	..	..	..
Botswana	27.3	-3.4	-1.5	-1.3	-2.2	-1.7	-1.8	-2.0	-2.3	-3.0	..	-14.7	-2.9	-2.2
Burkina Faso	..	..	..	..	..	..	..	..	..	..	..	..	..	..
Burundi	12.9	19.8	19.9	22.2	25.0	25.1	20.3	18.8	7.3	8.3	..	12.1	21.1	15.9
Cameroon	..	..	..	13.6	18.0	17.5	13.6	9.3	6.5	4.9	..	..	15.8	10.4
Cape Verde	52.2	32.1	26.4	46.5	42.0	38.5	34.7	30.5	17.9	3.1	..	37.0	37.1	24.9
Central African Republic	..	..	..	9.1	12.2	21.1	15.2	8.4	9.0	8.8	..	..	10.6	12.5
Chad	..	..	..	49.6	39.3	33.5	36.0	18.0	11.0	9.0	..	..	44.4	21.5
Comoros	..	..	..	..	..	..	..	..	..	..	..	..	..	..
Congo	..	..	..	19.1	13.9	12.3	12.0	11.3	7.0	6.1	..	..	16.5	9.7
Côte d'Ivoire	..	..	..	..	..	..	..	..	..	..	..	..	..	..
Djibouti	..	1.5	1.5	1.9	0.7	1.8	1.5	1.2	1.4	1.1	..	2.1	1.5	1.4
Equatorial Guinea	..	..	..	2.1	3.9	5.7	0.2	1.4	3.2	3.5	..	..	3.0	2.8
Eritrea	..	..	..	..	..	..	..	..	..	..	..	..	..	..
Ethiopia	..	..	..	..	..	..	..	..	..	..	..	..	..	..
Gabon	..	..	..	6.2	6.0	5.9	6.0	2.8	3.1	2.6	..	..	6.1	4.1
Gambia, The	..	..	..	..	..	..	..	..	..	..	..	..	..	..
Ghana	20.7	17.0	9.8	4.1	16.9	11.8	12.0	10.8	8.6	14.7	..	17.3	13.8	11.6
Guinea	..	..	..	..	..	..	2.0	1.5	1.4	1.4	..	..	..	1.6
Guinea-Bissau	..	9.2	15.5	23.4	16.6	12.8	12.4	13.9	9.2	11.7	..	..	16.2	12.0
Kenya	2.1	4.3	7.2	6.4	4.9	4.5	4.7	4.1	4.0	3.6	..	2.6	5.6	4.2
Lesotho	..	..	..	..	..	..	..	..	..	..	..	..	..	..
Liberia	15.2	9.1	5.7	5.9	4.7	..	4.7	4.8	6.2	4.6	..	12.3	6.8	5.1
Madagascar	..	..	..	..	..	..	..	..	..	..	..	..	..	..
Malawi	17.1	13.6	15.5	15.0	13.8	14.5	20.4	8.1	13.6	6.0	..	17.4	14.8	12.5
Mali	..	..	..	..	0.1	0.1	0.1	0.1	0.1	0.1	..	..	0.1	0.1
Mauritania	..	..	..	..	..	..	..	..	..	..	..	..	..	..
Mauritius	..	..	..	..	..	..	..	..	..	..	..	..	..	..
Mozambique	..	..	..	..	..	..	..	..	..	..	..	..	..	..
Namibia	..	..	..	..	..	0.3	3.7	1.6	1.3	1.0	..	..	..	1.6
Niger	..	..	..	..	..	..	..	..	..	..	..	..	..	..
Nigeria	..	..	..	..	..	..	..	1.2	1.1	0.1	..	..	..	0.8
Rwanda	..	..	..	..	..	..	..	..	..	..	..	..	..	..
São Tomé and Principe	..	71.6	69.5	70.6	..	..	..	..	..	..	..	32.9	59.7	..
Senegal	..	..	..	..	..	..	..	..	..	..	..	..	..	..
Seychelles	..	..	..	..	..	..	..	..	..	..	..	..	..	..
Sierra Leone	0.9	0.6	0.0	0.7	0.4	0.2	0.1	0.1	0.1	0.0	..	1.2	0.5	0.1
Somalia	..	..	..	..	..	..	..	..	..	..	..	..	..	..
South Africa	..	..	..	..	..	..	..	..	..	..	..	..	..	..
Sudan	21.3	20.4	20.3	18.1	15.1	11.8	5.3	6.3	4.3	4.6	..	19.6	18.7	6.4
Swaziland	..	..	..	..	..	..	..	..	..	..	..	..	..	..
Tanzania	..	..	..	..	..	..	..	..	..	..	..	..	..	..
Togo	..	..	..	..	..	..	..	..	..	..	..	..	..	..
Uganda	..	..	..	..	..	..	..	..	..	..	..	..	..	..
Zaire	0.1	0.9	0.5	1.3	1.1	1.6	5.3	0.3	0.2	3.4	7.3	0.6	0.9	3.0
Zambia	..	..	..	..	..	..	..	..	..	..	..	..	..	..
Zimbabwe	26.5	41.6	28.9	26.7	25.8	19.5	12.5	6.6	8.6	5.1	..	36.3	33.0	10.4
NORTH AFRICA	..	..	..	..	..	..	..	..	..	..	..	..	..	..
Algeria	..	..	..	..	..	..	..	44.1	16.0	24.5	..	..	..	28.2
Egypt, Arab Republic	23.5	22.7	22.3	21.7	22.0	23.8	26.9	22.2	25.2	22.8	..	22.9	22.5	24.2
Libya	..	..	..	..	..	..	..	..	..	..	..	..	..	..
Morocco	..	..	..	..	..	..	..	..	..	..	..	..	..	..
Tunisia	..	..	..	..	..	..	..	..	..	..	..	..	..	..
ALL AFRICA	..	..	..	..	..	..	..	..	..	..	..	..	..	..

10-8. Share of public enterprises in external debt outstanding

	Percent											Annual average		
	1980	1986	1987	1988	1989	1990	1991	1992	1993	1994	1995	75-84	85-89	90-MR
SUB-SAHARAN AFRICA	14.4	10.6	9.5	8.6	7.4	6.3	6.1	5.7	5.4	4.9	4.6	15.3	9.5	5.5
excluding South Africa	14.4	10.6	9.5	8.6	7.4	6.3	6.1	5.7	5.4	4.9	4.6	15.3	9.5	5.5
excl. S. Africa & Nigeria	16.0	11.3	10.4	9.3	8.0	6.8	6.4	5.7	5.3	4.8	4.4	16.4	10.2	5.6
Angola	..	13.9	11.5	9.5	7.1	6.8	6.7	6.8	7.1	6.2	6.1	..	10.8	6.6
Benin	32.8	28.4	28.9	27.9	10.1	4.7	4.5	3.7	3.2	3.0	1.2	25.7	24.7	3.4
Botswana	17.7	34.0	31.5	29.5	26.9	26.5	23.6	19.3	15.6	14.6	13.0	11.2	30.8	18.8
Burkina Faso	7.6	7.7	6.6	5.3	5.2	4.1	2.1	1.4	1.1	0.6	0.5	7.6	6.7	1.6
Burundi	1.2	1.9	0.9	0.7	0.5	0.2	0.1	0.3	0.3	0.4	0.3	2.8	1.2	0.3
Cameroon	38.5	20.0	19.3	16.4	11.0	9.1	8.5	6.2	5.6	3.3	2.7	33.6	17.8	5.9
Cape Verde	0.0	32.0	24.3	22.9	20.4	19.2	17.0	16.2	13.4	10.6	7.9	18.8	26.9	14.0
Central African Republic	24.1	13.2	13.6	12.6	11.8	6.4	6.2	5.7	5.2	4.5	4.6	26.7	12.7	5.4
Chad	25.9	18.6	21.9	21.2	8.8	9.4	8.0	7.3	6.5	6.4	5.9	17.2	16.8	7.3
Comoros	0.0	8.4	11.3	12.6	2.3	3.2	0.6	0.5	0.5	0.0	0.0	0.9	8.4	0.8
Congo	24.4	20.7	15.7	16.4	13.9	8.4	4.5	3.5	2.8	1.4	1.2	20.6	18.1	3.6
Côte d'Ivoire	18.9	9.6	7.9	6.0	5.1	3.2	2.4	1.7	1.4	1.2	1.1	20.3	8.0	1.8
Djibouti	66.0	63.0	49.6	45.0	32.5	37.8	46.3	44.2	39.5	37.7	36.1	64.4	47.3	40.3
Equatorial Guinea	7.9	3.2	3.6	2.8	0.9	0.8	0.8	0.8	0.4	0.3	0.7	3.8	2.8	0.6
Eritrea	..	..	..	..	..	..	..	..	..	..	..	..	..	..
Ethiopia	12.5	15.4	15.9	15.6	12.8	10.9	14.6	13.6	11.4	9.8	8.4	12.2	15.3	11.5
Gabon	14.3	7.2	6.8	5.6	4.6	3.9	3.5	3.7	3.4	1.8	1.0	11.8	6.3	2.9
Gambia, The	8.0	5.9	4.3	1.5	1.5	0.3	0.3	0.0	0.0	0.0	0.0	6.4	4.4	0.1
Ghana	13.6	8.5	7.9	7.7	6.2	5.4	4.8	4.2	3.5	2.9	2.5	11.6	8.0	3.9
Guinea	1.0	1.1	0.9	0.5	0.3	0.2	0.2	0.2	0.2	0.2	0.2	1.5	1.0	0.2
Guinea-Bissau	2.1	1.2	0.6	0.0	0.0	0.0	0.0	0.0	0.0	0.0	0.0	1.5	0.6	0.0
Kenya	19.2	15.4	15.9	15.3	16.2	14.5	13.8	14.3	13.1	10.8	10.8	18.3	15.3	12.9
Lesotho	0.0	3.5	3.5	2.8	2.4	2.0	3.1	5.9	10.0	11.0	13.8	0.1	3.2	7.6
Liberia	10.8	6.9	6.7	7.1	7.0	6.9	6.5	6.4	6.1	5.6	5.7	11.6	6.9	6.2
Madagascar	24.6	16.5	16.8	15.8	12.5	9.5	9.1	9.0	8.8	8.6	8.2	27.2	15.8	8.9
Malawi	16.4	4.7	4.7	4.1	4.3	3.7	2.5	1.9	1.5	1.6	1.3	12.1	4.7	2.1
Mali	3.7	1.1	0.9	0.5	0.5	0.4	0.4	0.4	0.4	0.3	0.2	3.8	0.9	0.4
Mauritania	7.8	21.2	20.5	20.0	18.6	16.1	14.7	15.2	14.3	13.9	12.0	14.5	20.3	14.4
Mauritius	3.9	3.9	6.0	18.2	19.4	21.4	28.2	28.5	28.9	29.7	24.5	3.4	10.2	26.9
Mozambique	..	14.4	11.0	9.6	10.5	7.3	5.7	4.5	3.9	3.6	2.3	..	11.7	4.5
Namibia	..	..	..	..	..	..	..	..	..	..	..	..	..	..
Niger	12.5	6.3	5.5	4.0	2.8	2.7	3.1	2.8	3.0	1.5	1.4	9.1	5.3	2.4
Nigeria	5.1	7.9	6.1	5.8	4.8	4.4	4.8	5.5	5.5	5.6	5.3	9.3	6.8	5.2
Rwanda	0.0	0.0	0.0	0.0	0.0	0.0	0.0	0.0	0.0	0.0	0.0	0.0	0.0	0.0
São Tomé and Principe	0.0	0.0	0.0	0.0	0.0	0.0	0.0	0.0	0.0	0.0	0.0	0.0	0.0	0.0
Senegal	12.3	6.8	7.1	6.4	5.4	4.8	4.7	4.0	3.6	1.8	1.5	11.2	6.5	3.4
Seychelles	3.6	6.8	8.6	7.8	8.4	10.8	11.1	11.6	11.0	10.0	9.7	3.3	7.7	10.7
Sierra Leone	8.7	5.2	4.4	4.0	3.4	3.0	2.6	1.7	1.4	1.0	1.1	9.6	4.8	1.8
Somalia	3.0	0.8	0.8	0.8	0.8	0.7	0.7	0.7	0.7	0.6	0.6	2.6	0.8	0.7
South Africa	..	..	..	..	..	..	..	..	..	..	..	..	..	..
Sudan	3.3	1.2	1.1	0.9	0.8	0.7	0.7	0.7	0.7	0.6	0.6	3.5	1.1	0.7
Swaziland	22.9	17.6	16.9	15.5	12.3	5.7	5.0	3.8	3.6	2.5	1.6	14.4	15.8	3.7
Tanzania	19.1	10.4	9.2	7.4	7.3	6.1	5.5	3.8	3.5	3.1	2.9	15.2	9.3	4.2
Togo	6.3	4.6	4.6	4.4	3.8	4.0	3.5	3.3	3.3	3.1	1.5	3.9	4.5	3.1
Uganda	4.1	4.2	4.0	3.8	3.4	3.3	3.1	2.5	1.9	1.5	1.3	2.8	3.8	2.3
Zaire	25.3	15.7	14.9	13.4	13.4	13.5	14.3	13.4	12.7	12.3	12.0	28.8	14.7	13.1
Zambia	16.9	16.3	16.0	14.0	14.0	12.7	10.9	9.5	8.7	7.9	6.8	22.8	15.5	9.4
Zimbabwe	2.5	20.4	18.1	14.8	11.9	9.7	7.9	6.1	8.1	9.6	9.2	14.8	17.7	8.4
NORTH AFRICA	42.0	31.7	31.8	30.3	29.6	34.3	30.0	29.9	30.0	26.8	22.7	37.5	30.9	29.0
Algeria	79.9	71.4	76.6	72.9	69.5	70.5	66.5	68.2	68.7	53.9	40.8	78.0	73.2	61.4
Egypt, Arab Republic	13.0	15.9	15.3	15.1	15.6	24.1	13.2	13.1	13.0	13.1	12.3	11.7	15.3	14.8
Libya	..	..	..	..	..	..	..	..	..	..	..	..	..	..
Morocco	27.2	18.2	16.2	13.7	12.7	11.6	13.2	12.6	13.9	15.8	16.9	22.6	15.9	14.0
Tunisia	30.9	25.9	24.9	21.2	19.1	17.2	15.7	13.9	13.4	13.3	12.2	27.1	23.6	14.3
ALL AFRICA	27.4	19.5	18.4	17.4	16.3	16.1	14.1	13.7	13.3	12.1	10.5	25.6	18.3	13.3

10-9. External debt of public enterprises

	Percentage of GDP										
	1980	*1986*	*1987*	*1988*	*1989*	*1990*	*1991*	*1992*	*1993*	*1994*	*1995*
SUB-SAHARAN AFRICA	3.1	5.9	5.7	5.0	4.4	3.9	3.9	3.5	3.6	3.6	3.2
excluding South Africa	4.4	8.4	8.6	7.8	6.9	6.2	6.4	6.1	6.4	6.7	5.9
excl. S. Africa & Nigeria	6.5	8.4	8.8	7.8	7.0	6.4	6.5	6.2	6.3	6.6	5.6
Angola	..	8.0	8.5	7.5	5.5	6.3	13.2	12.5	17.4	10.2	11.2
Benin	9.9	20.1	21.2	18.3	8.1	3.2	3.2	3.2	2.3	3.2	0.9
Botswana	2.7	11.1	11.2	7.1	5.4	4.7	4.0	3.2	2.7	2.5	2.1
Burkina Faso	1.5	2.6	2.6	1.9	1.6	1.2	0.7	0.5	0.4	0.4	0.3
Burundi	0.2	0.9	0.6	0.6	0.4	0.2	0.1	0.3	0.3	0.4	0.4
Cameroon	14.8	7.8	7.3	6.3	5.4	5.4	4.7	4.0	3.5	3.4	3.2
Cape Verde	0.0	25.4	13.6	10.9	9.7	8.5	7.2	6.4	6.0	5.5	4.0
Central African Republic	5.9	5.6	7.1	6.7	6.6	3.1	3.6	3.3	3.6	4.5	3.8
Chad	10.2	6.5	9.3	8.0	3.5	4.1	3.9	4.0	4.9	6.4	5.1
Comoros	0.0	8.6	11.7	12.0	2.0	2.4	0.4	0.4	0.4	0.0	0.0
Congo	21.8	39.4	29.5	30.3	25.0	14.8	8.0	5.7	7.5	4.3	3.3
Côte d'Ivoire	13.8	12.0	10.7	7.9	7.7	5.1	4.2	2.8	2.6	2.8	2.0
Djibouti	..	21.6	24.2	20.8	14.5	18.4	19.5	18.1	18.9	19.1	19.1
Equatorial Guinea	..	5.1	5.8	4.7	1.8	1.5	1.5	1.3	0.6	0.8	1.2
Eritrea	..	..	..	..	..	..	..	..	..	..	..
Ethiopia	..	5.3	6.2	6.6	5.5	4.8	6.4	8.0	7.3	8.4	7.4
Gabon	5.0	3.5	4.6	4.1	3.7	2.6	2.8	2.5	3.0	1.7	0.9
Gambia, The	4.7	10.8	6.4	2.2	2.1	0.3	0.3	0.0	0.0	0.0	0.0
Ghana	4.3	4.1	5.2	4.6	4.0	3.6	3.2	2.9	3.0	3.0	2.3
Guinea	..	1.0	0.9	0.5	0.3	0.2	0.2	0.2	0.2	0.2	0.2
Guinea-Bissau	2.8	3.8	1.8	0.0	0.0	0.0	0.0	0.0	0.0	0.0	0.0
Kenya	8.9	9.8	11.5	10.4	11.4	11.9	12.7	12.0	16.3	10.4	8.7
Lesotho	0.0	2.5	2.4	1.8	1.6	1.3	2.4	4.3	7.5	8.6	10.8
Liberia	6.6	9.1	10.0	9.8	9.8	..	..	..	..	..	..
Madagascar	7.6	15.1	24.0	23.7	17.2	11.5	13.3	11.7	10.0	11.9	11.1
Malawi	10.9	4.7	5.5	4.2	4.0	3.2	1.9	1.7	1.3	2.5	1.9
Mali	1.6	1.2	0.9	0.5	0.5	0.4	0.5	0.4	0.4	0.4	0.3
Mauritania	9.3	46.3	46.4	43.5	37.9	33.8	29.1	27.3	32.9	31.5	27.7
Mauritius	1.6	1.8	2.6	7.5	7.6	8.1	10.5	9.8	9.3	11.9	11.2
Mozambique	0.0	16.6	33.4	33.1	34.5	23.6	18.7	18.6	14.3	14.0	9.1
Namibia	0.0	0.0	0.0	0.0	0.0	0.0	0.0	0.0	0.0	0.0	0.0
Niger	4.3	4.8	4.2	3.1	2.0	1.9	2.1	1.9	2.2	1.5	1.2
Nigeria	0.7	8.7	7.6	7.6	6.1	5.2	5.8	5.5	7.3	7.4	7.7
Rwanda	0.0	0.0	0.0	0.0	0.0	0.0	0.0	0.0	0.0	0.0	0.0
São Tomé and Principe	0.0	0.0	0.0	0.0	0.0	0.0	0.0	0.0	0.0	0.0	0.0
Senegal	6.0	5.8	6.2	5.0	3.8	3.1	3.1	3.6	3.3	1.7	1.2
Seychelles	2.0	4.8	6.0	4.6	4.5	5.6	5.9	4.7	3.7	3.5	3.1
Sierra Leone	3.2	5.1	5.5	3.3	3.1	4.0	4.2	3.2	2.7	1.7	1.5
Somalia	3.3	1.5	1.6	1.5	1.6	1.9	..	..	..	..	..
South Africa	0.0	0.0	0.0	0.0	0.0	0.0	0.0	0.0	0.0	0.0	0.0
Sudan	2.6	0.9	0.7	1.0	1.0	1.2	1.4	1.7	..	..	..
Swaziland	8.2	10.9	8.9	5.9	4.6	1.7	1.5	0.9	0.9	0.6	0.4
Tanzania	..	6.8	14.7	12.6	10.4	10.0	8.3	6.0	6.3	6.5	5.1
Togo	5.8	4.6	4.6	3.9	3.3	3.2	3.0	2.7	3.5	4.8	1.8
Uganda	2.2	1.5	1.2	1.1	1.4	2.0	2.6	2.6	1.8	1.3	0.8
Zaire	8.1	13.9	17.0	13.0	13.7	14.9	17.0	18.0	16.0	26.1	25.7
Zambia	14.2	56.3	46.8	25.8	23.6	28.0	23.8	20.8	16.7	14.1	11.3
Zimbabwe	0.4	10.8	9.6	6.2	5.1	4.6	4.1	4.4	6.2	7.3	6.8
NORTH AFRICA	16.8	18.7	19.5	20.6	20.2	18.9	18.7	16.2	16.0	15.4	12.6
Algeria	36.5	25.7	29.0	32.3	34.3	31.8	40.5	37.6	35.9	38.7	32.1
Egypt, Arab Republic	10.8	17.7	16.7	20.0	18.1	18.7	11.8	8.9	8.6	8.3	7.0
Libya	0.0	0.0	0.0	0.0	0.0	..	..	..	..	..	..
Morocco	13.4	18.8	17.8	12.8	12.1	10.6	10.0	9.4	10.7	11.2	11.5
Tunisia	12.5	17.1	17.5	14.3	13.2	10.8	9.9	7.6	8.0	7.9	6.7
ALL AFRICA	7.6	11.1	11.1	10.8	10.2	9.5	8.9	8.1	8.3	8.1	6.8

Note: Nigeria's ratios are distorted for 1994-95 because of official exchange rate over-valuation affecting oil exports and oil value added (see chapter 3).

10-10. Net Financial flows between government and public enterprises

	Percentage of GDP											
	1980	*1983*	*1984*	*1985*	*1986*	*1987*	*1988*	*1989*	*1990*	*1991*	*1992*	*1993*
SUB-SAHARAN AFRICA	..	..	..	..	..	..	..	..	..	..	..	..
excluding South Africa	..	..	..	..	..	..	..	..	..	..	..	..
excl. S. Africa & Nigeria	..	..	..	..	..	..	..	..	..	..	..	..
Angola	..	..	..	..	..	..	..	..	..	..	..	..
Benin	0.7	0.4	..	..	..	..	..	..	..	..	..	..
Botswana	-5.6	-10.6	-7.1	-12.5	-8.1	-7.6	-13.0	-18.5	-15.4	-13.8	..	..
Burkina Faso	..	..	..	..	..	-0.5	-0.4	..	..	..	..	..
Burundi	1.3	0.3	..	..	..	1.6	2.0	3.8	3.4	-1.0	..	..
Cameroon	..	1.2	2.0	1.4	2.1	0.2	..	..	..	..	..	..
Cape Verde	..	..	..	..	..	..	..	..	..	..	..	..
Central African Republic	..	1.1	1.2	..	..	..	..	..	..	..	..	..
Chad	..	..	..	..	..	..	..	..	..	..	..	..
Comoros	..	..	..	..	..	..	..	..	..	..	..	..
Congo	..	0.9	..	..	..	..	..	..	..	..	..	..
Côte d'Ivoire	2.5	..	0.6	5.2	..	..	..	..	..	..	..	..
Djibouti	..	..	..	..	..	..	..	..	..	..	..	..
Equatorial Guinea	..	..	..	..	..	..	..	..	..	..	..	..
Eritrea	..	..	..	..	..	..	..	..	..	..	..	..
Ethiopia	..	..	..	..	..	..	..	..	..	..	..	..
Gabon	..	..	..	..	..	..	..	..	..	..	..	..
Gambia, The	..	..	..	0.4	6.6	8.1	0.4	1.7	3.2	..	..	..
Ghana	0.5	0.1	0.2	0.2	0.5	0.6	0.3	0.4	..	..	..	..
Guinea	..	..	..	..	..	..	..	..	..	..	..	..
Guinea-Bissau	..	0.8	-0.9	-0.3	..	..	..	..	..	..	..	..
Kenya	2.3	0.5	1.1	1.5	-0.2	-0.2	0.0	0.0	0.4	..	..	..
Lesotho	..	..	..	..	..	..	..	..	..	..	..	..
Liberia	..	..	..	..	..	..	..	..	..	..	..	..
Madagascar	..	..	..	..	..	..	..	..	..	..	..	..
Malawi	6.1	1.0	0.4	0.7	0.7	0.6	1.1	1.0	..	..	..	..
Mali	..	..	..	..	-0.9	-0.6	..	..	..	..	..	..
Mauritania	..	..	..	..	..	..	..	..	..	..	..	..
Mauritius	..	2.4	1.1	1.0	-0.8	-0.9	-0.6	0.6	-1.0	..	..	..
Mozambique	..	..	..	..	..	..	..	..	..	..	..	..
Namibia	..	..	..	..	3.5	5.3	1.7	1.0	1.0	..	..	..
Niger	0.3	-0.3	..	..	..	..	..	..	..	..	..	..
Nigeria	..	-4.9	-6.2	-5.3	..	..	..	..	..	..	..	..
Rwanda	-0.3	..	0.2	0.3	0.6	0.5	0.2	0.4	0.4	-0.1	..	..
São Tomé and Principe	-19.0	-3.8	-7.4	..	..	..	-4.0	-4.9	-0.9	-1.2	..	..
Senegal	..	6.9	2.3	2.4	8.3	2.9	..	..	..	..	..	..
Seychelles	2.4	0.5	3.5	8.3	7.3	-0.7	0.4	1.6	-0.3	2.3	..	..
Sierra Leone	-0.2	1.7	..	0.2	0.3	-0.1	0.1	-0.2	..	..	..	..
Somalia	..	..	..	..	..	..	..	..	..	..	..	..
South Africa	..	..	..	..	..	..	..	..	..	..	..	..
Sudan	..	..	..	..	..	..	..	..	..	..	..	..
Swaziland	..	..	..	..	..	..	..	..	..	..	..	..
Tanzania	..	0.8	-1.3	-2.3	..	..	..	..	..	..	..	..
Togo	..	..	..	..	..	3.6	2.1	-0.8	..	..	..	..
Uganda	..	..	..	..	..	..	..	..	..	..	..	..
Zaire	..	..	..	..	..	..	..	..	..	..	..	..
Zambia	0.8	-2.9	-3.6	..	-3.1	..	..	..	..	..	..	..
Zimbabwe	..	..	..	..	..	..	..	..	..	..	..	..
NORTH AFRICA	..	..	..	..	..	..	..	..	..	..	..	..
Algeria	..	..	..	..	..	..	..	..	..	..	..	..
Egypt, Arab Republic	..	..	..	..	..	..	..	..	..	..	..	..
Libya	..	..	..	..	..	..	..	..	..	..	..	..
Morocco	..	..	..	..	..	..	..	..	..	..	..	..
Tunisia	..	..	..	..	..	..	..	..	..	..	..	..
ALL AFRICA	..	..	..	..	..	..	..	..	..	..	..	..

Note: Nigeria's ratios are distorted for 1994-95 because of official exchange rate over-valuation affecting oil exports and oil value added (see chapter 3).

10-11. Overall balance of public enterprises before transfers

	Percentage of GDP											
	1980	*1983*	*1984*	*1985*	*1986*	*1987*	*1988*	*1989*	*1990*	*1991*	*1992*	*1993*
SUB-SAHARAN AFRICA	..	..	..	..	..	..	..	..	..	..	..	..
excluding South Africa	..	..	..	..	..	..	..	..	..	..	..	..
excl. S. Africa & Nigeria	..	..	..	..	..	..	..	..	..	..	..	..
Angola	..	..	..	..	..	..	..	..	..	..	..	..
Benin	..	-1.5	..	..	..	..	..	..	..	..	..	..
Botswana	-4.5	-6.0	-14.0	-0.3	-2.3	-2.6	-4.1	-3.3	-4.5	-10.0	..	..
Burkina Faso	..	..	..	..	..	..	..	..	..	..	..	..
Burundi	..	..	0.4	..	..	..	..	..	..	..	..	..
Cameroon	..	-2.3	-1.2	..	..	..	..	..	..	..	..	..
Cape Verde	..	..	..	..	..	..	..	..	..	..	..	..
Central African Republic	..	-1.0	-0.7	-1.7	-3.0	-4.2	-2.2	..	..	..	..	..
Chad	..	..	..	..	..	..	..	..	..	..	..	..
Comoros	..	..	..	..	..	..	..	..	..	..	..	..
Congo	..	-3.4	-2.9	-2.6	..	..	..	..	..	..	..	..
Côte d'Ivoire	..	-4.1	-4.6	-5.0	..	..	..	..	..	..	..	..
Djibouti	..	..	..	..	..	..	..	..	..	..	..	..
Equatorial Guinea	..	..	..	..	..	..	..	..	..	..	..	..
Eritrea	..	..	..	..	..	..	..	..	..	..	..	..
Ethiopia	..	..	..	..	..	..	..	..	..	..	..	..
Gabon	..	..	..	..	..	..	..	..	..	..	..	..
Gambia, The	..	-9.0	2.3	-3.3	-4.4	..	..	..	..	..	..	..
Ghana	-0.2	-0.3	-0.4	0.1	0.9	-0.6	-0.1	-2.0	2.5	..	..	..
Guinea	..	..	..	..	..	..	..	..	..	..	..	..
Guinea-Bissau	..	..	..	..	..	..	..	..	..	..	..	..
Kenya	..	..	-4.0	..	..	..	..	..	..	..	..	..
Lesotho	..	..	..	..	..	..	..	..	..	..	..	..
Liberia	..	..	..	..	..	..	..	..	..	..	..	..
Madagascar	..	..	..	..	..	..	..	..	..	..	..	..
Malawi	-12.0	0.0	0.5	-0.2	-2.5	-1.0	..	..	..	..	..	..
Mali	..	-0.8	-1.6	-1.4	-0.6	..	..	..	..	..	..	..
Mauritania	-0.3	-0.6	..	..	..	..	..	..	..	..	..	..
Mauritius	-2.9	-3.5	-1.8	..	..	..	..	..	..	..	..	..
Mozambique	..	..	..	..	..	..	..	..	..	..	..	..
Namibia	..	-3.8	-2.1	-1.8	-1.4	-1.2	-0.8	-0.5	-0.3	0.1	..	..
Niger	..	-1.3	-0.9	0.3	0.0	-0.5	-0.2	..	..	..	..	..
Nigeria	..	0.7	2.3	..	1.0	..	..	..	..	..	..	..
Rwanda	..	0.3	1.0	1.0	1.0	1.0	..	..	..	..	..	..
São Tomé and Principe	..	..	..	..	..	..	..	..	..	..	..	..
Senegal	..	-9.0	-2.9	-2.9	1.3	-1.5	..	..	..	..	..	..
Seychelles	-9.3	-9.8	-13.9	-20.3	-24.3	-9.0	-14.6	..	..	..	..	..
Sierra Leone	..	-1.7	-0.3	1.4	..	..	..	..	..	..	..	..
Somalia	..	..	..	..	..	..	..	..	..	..	..	..
South Africa	..	..	..	..	..	..	..	..	..	..	..	..
Sudan	..	..	..	..	..	..	..	..	..	..	..	..
Swaziland	..	..	..	..	..	..	..	..	..	..	..	..
Tanzania	..	1.1	1.1	3.2	-4.0	-8.2	-11.6	-16.2	-7.6	..	..	..
Togo	..	0.1	0.1	..	..	..	..	0.0	..	..	..	..
Uganda	..	..	..	..	..	..	..	..	..	..	..	..
Zaire	..	..	..	..	..	..	..	..	..	..	..	..
Zambia	1.0	4.6	7.1	..	..	..	..	..	..	..	..	..
Zimbabwe	..	..	..	..	..	..	..	..	..	..	..	..
NORTH AFRICA	..	..	..	..	..	..	..	..	..	..	..	..
Algeria	..	..	..	..	..	..	..	..	..	..	..	..
Egypt, Arab Republic	..	..	..	..	..	..	..	..	..	..	..	..
Libya	..	..	..	..	..	..	..	..	..	..	..	..
Morocco	..	..	..	..	..	..	..	..	..	..	..	..
Tunisia	..	..	..	..	..	..	..	..	..	..	..	..
ALL AFRICA	..	..	..	..	..	..	..	..	..	..	..	..

Note: Nigeria's ratios are distorted for 1994-95 because of official exchange rate over-valuation affecting oil exports and oil value added (see chapter 3).

10-12. Summary of privatizations of public enterprises

	No. of PEs		Total no. of trans- actions	Total sales value (US$m)	Transactions completed				Transactions by sector					
	Before 1990	1995			Before 1990	1993	1994	1995	Agric. prod. & process	Financial	Manu- facturing	Services	Trade	Other
SUB-SAHARAN AFRICA	6,069	4,058	2,040	2,325	316	196	292	370	378	121	695	339	290	114
excluding South Africa	6,043	4,035	2,037	1,688	314	196	292	370	378	118	695	339	290	114
excl. S. Africa & Nigeria	5,413	3,517	1,926	2,034	301	184	283	352	347	96	668	313	290	109
Angola	545	276	269	25	..	..	..	..	77	0	102	11	73	6
Benin	60	25	46	63	17	5	3	5	6	1	13	13	5	8
Botswana	48	47	1	..	..	0	0	0	0	0	0	0	0	1
Burkina Faso	71	57	16	10	0	5	5	3	1	4	7	1	1	2
Burundi	86	51	26	11	4	7	1	..	3	0	2	1	3	6
Cameroon	209	172	37	..	10	1	5	5	10	0	22	2	1	2
Cape Verde	35	14	21	24	0	1	10	10	5	0	9	7	0	0
Central African Republic	52	28	24	..	22	0	0	0	..	..	..	..	..	..
Chad	43	19	25	..	0	0	12	12	7	5	2	6	2	3
Comoros	15	11	4	0	0	4	..	..	0	0	0	3	1	0
Congo	82	73	9	..	9	0	0	0	..	..	..	..	..	..
Côte d'Ivoire	140	108	32	174	0	3	8	14	8	0	6	8	0	10
Djibouti	19	19	1	0	0	0	0	0	0	0	0	0	0	1
Equatorial Guinea	20	17	3	0	0	2	..	..	0	0	1	1	0	1
Eritrea	0	0	0	0	0	0	0	0	0	0	0	0	0	0
Ethiopia	58	58	0	0	0	0	0	0	0	0	0	0	0	0
Gabon	32	13	19	0	19	0	0	0	..	..	..	..	..	..
Gambia, The	39	9	30	8	8	4	3	0	7	2	5	13	3	0
Ghana	329	227	102	406	3	8	30	11	16	2	58	17	4	5
Guinea	166	54	115	76	77	16	3	4	10	7	49	11	30	8
Guinea-Bissau	39	8	31	18	2	1	3	11	4	0	5	17	3	2
Kenya	255	146	109	59	0	20	15	64	47	2	40	18	2	0
Lesotho	33	25	8	..	0	0	0	8	0	1	1	3	0	0
Liberia	16	16	0	0	0	0	0	0	0	0	0	0	0	0
Madagascar	173	114	58	16	11	1	3	3	1	25	8	0	6	6
Malawi	135	100	35	5	0	2	1	0	27	1	7	0	0	0
Mali	77	31	48	38	2	..	..	..	1	27	10	4	3	0
Mauritania	58	28	31	..	6	..	..	3	4	0	14	4	5	6
Mauritius	33	33	0	0	0	0	0	0	0	0	0	0	0	0
Mozambique	1200	690	510	133	65	43	135	112	47	0	211	128	123	1
Namibia	41	41	1	0	0	0	0	0	0	0	0	0	0	1
Niger	64	34	31	3	20	1	1	2	1	2	4	2	3	19
Nigeria	485	404	81	207	15	8	0	0	22	24	19	12	0	4
Rwanda	29	29	..	..	..	..	..	..	..	..	..	..	..	..
São Tomé and Principe	44	35	10	2	0	3	0	1	2	0	1	1	1	5
Senegal	108	69	39	57	12	..	..	..	9	6	17	0	2	0
Seychelles	35	35	1	0	0	0	0	0	0	0	0	0	0	1
Sierra Leone	26	20	9	..	0	6	1	1	0	2	4	0	3	0
Somalia	52	52	0	0	0	0	0	0	0	0	0	0	0	0
South Africa	26	23	3	637	2	0	0	0	0	3	0	0	0	0
Sudan	111	86	26	..	0	12	3	..	5	1	9	9	1	1
Swaziland	14	14	0	0	0	0	0	0	0	0	0	0	0	0
Tanzania	420	327	93	127	0	33	17	31	30	1	20	11	5	6
Togo	50	28	24	37	12	0	2	1	4	0	12	4	1	3
Uganda	171	137	33	84	0	4	9	18	9	1	8	14	0	1
Zaire	138	138	2	..	..	..	0	2	0	0	0	0	0	2
Zambia	160	92	75	91	0	6	20	49	15	2	29	18	8	3
Zimbabwe	27	25	2	13	0	0	2	0	0	2	0	0	1	0
NORTH AFRICA	..	..	..	..	..	..	..	..	..		..	..	..	..
Algeria	..	..	..	..	..	..	..	..	..	..	..	..	..	..
Egypt	441	..	..	..	..	..	..	..	..	..	..	..	..	..
Libya	..	..	..	..	..	..	..	..	..	..	..	..	..	..
Morocco	73	..	..	..	..	..	..	..	..	..	..	..	..	..
Tunisia	105	..	..	..	..	..	..	..	..	..	..	..	..	..
ALL AFRICA	..	..	..	..	..	..	..	..	..		..	..	..	..

10-13. Progress in privatization: divestiture methods employed, 1988-95

	Sales of shares				*Sale of Assets*			*Other methods*							
	Competitive trade	*Direct sale*	*Pre-emption rights*	*Public flotation*	*Liquidation*	*Competitive sale*	*Direct sale*	*Debt/ Equity swaps*	*Leases*	*Joint ventures*	*Mgmt./ employee buyouts*	*Mgmt. contracts*	*Trustees*	*Restitution*	*Other*
SUB-SAHARAN AFRICA	765	279	78	64	339	165	25	4	160	23	23	41	11	29	34
excluding South Africa	763	279	78	64	339	165	25	4	160	23	23	41	11	29	33
excl. S. Africa & Nigeria	754	275	78	28	339	137	25	3	160	23	22	41	11	29	31
Angola	0	192	0	0	0	0	0	0	77	0	0	0	0	0	0
Benin	0	2	0	0	23	13	4	0	1	0	0	2	1	0	0
Botswana	0	0	0	0	0	0	0	0	0	0	0	1	0	0	0
Burkina Faso	7	5	0	0	1	1	..	0	0	0	0	1	..	1	0
Burundi	6	3	0	0	11	4	0	0	0	0	1	1	0	0	0
Cameroon	3	1	0	0	23	..	0	0	0	0	0	1	0	0	9
Cape Verde	5	3	..	0	5	1	..	0	0	0	6	0	..	..	1
Central African Republic	0	0	0	0	15	0	0	0	0	0	0	2	0	0	7
Chad	11	0	0	0	13	0	0	0	0	0	0	1	0	0	0
Comoros	2	0	0	0	1	0	0	0	1	0	0	0	0	0	0
Congo	0	0	0	0	9	0	0	0	0	0	0	0	0	0	0
Côte d'Ivoire	2	10	0	10	0	6	1	0	2	0	0	0	0	0	1
Djibouti	0	0	0	0	0	0	0	0	0	0	0	0	0	0	1
Equatorial Guinea	0	0	0	0	1	0	0	0	1	0	0	1	0	0	0
Eritrea	0	0	0	0	0	0	0	0	0	0	0	0	0	0	0
Ethiopia	0	0	0	0	0	0	0	0	0	0	0	0	0	0	0
Gabon	14	0	0	0	5	0	0	0	0	..	0	0	0	0	0
Gambia, The	13	7	0	0	3	1	0	0	5	0	1	0	0	0	0
Ghana	20	14	0	10	22	15	9	0	2	7	0	1	0	0	2
Guinea	41	0	0	0	63	0	0	0	2	0	0	5	0	0	4
Guinea-Bissau	8	2	..	..	8	2	0	..	2	1	0	8	0	0	0
Kenya	1	5	69	7	0	21	5	0	0	0	0	0	0	0	1
Lesotho	3	1	0	0	4	0	0	0	0	0	0	0	0	0	0
Liberia	0	0	0	0	0	0	0	0	0	0	0	0	0	0	0
Madagascar	5	11	0	0	7	14	5	0	0	1	3	3	0	8	1
Malawi	18	0	0	0	0	14	0	0	0	0	0	0	3	0	0
Mali	8	9	0	0	25	0	0	0	2	0	0	2	0	0	2
Mauritania	10	0	0	0	20	0	0	0	0	0	0	1	0	0	0
Mauritius	0	0	0	0	0	0	0	0	0	0	0	0	0	0	0
Mozambique	466	0	0	0	0	0	0	0	34	10	0	0	0	0	0
Namibia	0	0	0	0	0	0	0	0	0	0	0	0	0	0	1
Niger	13	0	0	0	17	0	0	0	1	0	0	0	0	0	0
Nigeria	9	4	0	36	0	28	0	1	0	0	1	0	0	0	2
Rwanda	0	0	0	0	0	0	0	0	0	0	0	0	0	0	0
São Tomé and Principe	4	1	0	0	2	0	0	0	1	0	1	1	0	0	0
Senegal	16	0	0	0	20	1	0	1	1	0	0	0	0	0	0
Seychelles	0	0	0	0	0	0	..	0	0	0	0	1	0	0	0
Sierra Leone	0	0	0	0	1	0	0	0	5	0	0	3	0	0	0
Somalia	0	0	0	0	0	0	0	0	0	0	0	0	0	0	0
South Africa	2	0	0	0	0	0	0	0	0	0	0	0	0	0	1
Sudan	25	0	0	0	0	0	0	0	0	0	0	1	0	0	0
Swaziland	0	0	0	0	0	0	0	0	0	0	0	0	0	0	0
Tanzania	34	4	0	0	20	5	0	0	19	3	2	1	2	2	1
Togo	0	4	0	0	4	10	1	0	3	0	0	2	0	0	0
Uganda	3	0	1	0	0	16	0	1	0	1	2	0	4	5	0
Zaire	0	0	0	0	0	0	0	0	0	0	0	2	0	0	0
Zambia	15	0	8	1	16	13	0	1	1	0	6	0	1	13	0
Zimbabwe	1	1	0	0	0	0	0	0	0	0	0	0	0	0	0
NORTH AFRICA	..	..	..		..	..	..	..	..	..	..	..	..		
Algeria	..	..	..	..	..	..	..	..	..	..	..	..	..	..	..
Egypt	..	..	..	..	..	..	..	..	..	..	..	..	..	..	..
Libya	..	..	..	..	..	..	..	..	..	..	..	..	..	..	..
Morocco	..	..	..	..	..	..	..	..	..	..	..	..	..	..	..
Tunisia	..	..	..	..	..	..	..	..	..	..	..	..	..	..	..
ALL AFRICA	765	279	78	64	339	165	25	4	160	23	23	41	11	29	34

10-14. Progress in privatization: ownership and control changes

	Transfer of majority ownership to private shareholders	Government retention of majority ownership	Sales of minority government interest	Government retention of minority interest	Total share transaction	Total sales of assets	Transactions not known	Total transactions
SUB-SAHARAN AFRICA	1,027	216	85	159	1,487	469		2,040
excluding South Africa	..	..	..		..	..		..
excl. S. Africa & Nigeria	..	..	..		..	..		..
Angola	192	77	0	0	269	0	..	269
Benin	3	4	2	1	10	36	..	46
Botswana	..	..	..	..	..	..	1	1
Burkina Faso	2	1	2	10	15	..	1	16
Burundi	7	0	2	1	10	16	..	26
Cameroon	..	..	..	..	..	..	37	37
Cape Verde	5	..	..	3	8	12	1	21
Central African Republic	..	2	..	..	2	15	7	24
Chad	11	1	..	..	12	13	..	25
Comoros	2	1	..	..	3	1	..	4
Congo	..	..	..	..	0	9	..	9
Côte d'Ivoire	15	1	5	10	31	1	..	32
Djibouti	..	..	..	..	0	..	1	1
Equatorial Guinea	..	2	..	..	2	1	..	3
Eritrea	..	..	..	..	0	..	..	0
Ethiopia	..	..	..	..	0	..	..	0
Gabon	14	..	..	..	14	5	..	19
Gambia, The	22	4	..	..	26	4	..	30
Ghana	30	10	9	8	57	45	..	102
Guinea	24	8	1	15	48	63	4	115
Guinea-Bissau	11	10	..	..	21	10	..	31
Kenya	23	..	42	44	109	0	..	109
Lesotho	4	..	..	..	4	..	4	8
Liberia	..	..	..	..	0	..	..	0
Madagascar	11	3	..	15	29	29	..	58
Malawi	18	..	2	..	20	12	3	35
Mali	14	..	3	4	21	25	2	48
Mauritania	7	1	..	3	11	20	..	31
Mauritius	..	..	..	..	0	..	..	0
Mozambique	466	44	..	..	510	..	..	510
Namibia	..	..	..	..	0	..	1	1
Niger	10	1	3	..	14	17	..	31
Nigeria	42	1	..	7	50	29	2	81
Rwanda	..	..	..	..	0	..	..	0
São Tomé and Principe	5	2	..	..	7	3	..	10
Senegal	8	3	..	7	18	21	..	39
Seychelles	..	1	..	..	1	..	..	1
Sierra Leone	..	8	..	..	8	1	..	9
Somalia	..	..	..	..	0	..	..	0
South Africa	2	..	..	..	2	..	1	3
Sudan	25	1	..	..	26	..	..	26
Swaziland	..	..	..	..	0	..	..	0
Tanzania	20	23	..	20	63	27	3	93
Togo	..	3	5	1	9	15	..	24
Uganda	8	..	1	4	13	4	16	33
Zaire	..	2	..	..	2	..	..	2
Zambia	24	2	8	6	40	35	..	75
Zimbabwe	2	..	..	..	2	..	..	2
NORTH AFRICA	..	..	..	..	..	..	..	..
Algeria	..	..	..	..	..	..	..	..
Egypt	..	..	..	..	..	..	..	..
Libya	..	..	..	..	..	..	..	..
Morocco	..	..	..	..	..	..	..	..
Tunisia	..	..	..	..	..	..	..	..
ALL AFRICA	..	..	..	..	..	..	..	..

Technical Notes

Tables

Table 10-1. Contribution of public enterprises to gross domestic product. This is the sum of PE value added (World Bank data) as a share of total GDP (at market prices) (Table 2-5). PE value added is estimated as the sales revenue minus the cost of intermediate inputs, or the sum of the operating surplus (balance) and wage payments.

For Egypt, the value added series are estimated from three data points based on published studies pointing to little change in the contribution of PEs to economic activity. For Ghana, value added numbers for 1988–91 are estimated from the average value added share of 13 core nonfinancial PEs in total nonfinancial PEs value added for 1984–87. For Mauritius, value added figures are from the national accounts and refer to government enterprises in the manufacturing, construction, transport, and communications sectors. For Zambia, value added figures for 1987–91 are estimated based on share of the Zambia Industrial and Mining Corporation (ZIMCO) in PE value added for 1981–84. ZIMCO alone averaged a 14.3 percent share of GDP for 1987–92.

Table 10-2. Share of public enterprises in nonagricultural activity. This table is calculated as the sum of PE value added (World Bank data) as a share of nonagricultural GDP (at market prices) (World Bank country desks).

Table 10-3. Share of public enterprises in gross domestic investment. This table is calculated as the ratio of fixed capital formation (World Bank data) to gross domestic investment (World Bank country desks).

For Congo, investment figures are based on the government's investment budget and thus exclude any PE investment carried outside of that budget. For Côte d'Ivoire, investment figures are for all PEs. For Egypt, investment figures include financial and insurance PEs, but these represent a very small share of total PE sector investment. For Togo, investment figures refer to eight major PEs.

Table 10-4. Share of investment of public enterprises in gross domestic product. This table represents the ratio of fixed capital formation of public enterprises (World Bank data) to the country's GDP (at market prices) (Table 2-5).

Table 10-5. Share of public enterprises in formal sector employment. This table is calculated as the ratio of the number of people employed in PEs (World Bank data) to total formal sector employment. Formal sector employment is defined as full-time employees, although seasonal and temporary workers also constitute part of the PE workforce. All employment data, including total formal sector employment, must be viewed as approximations, since survey techniques and accuracy may vary widely across countries, and these differences among countries will be reflected in the ratios. Formal sector implies wage employment, although definitions may vary. In some countries, PE employment includes those employed in financial PEs.

For Algeria, employment numbers are for industrial enterprises only. For Benin, PE employment was estimated using the share of civil service employment in PEs and the share of total civil service employment for

1981–83. Employment figures for Burundi, Cameroon, Congo, Guinea, Kenya, Madagascar, Mali, Mauritius, Senegal, Togo, and Zambia refer to the share in formal or modern sector employment. For Malawi, PE employment in 1982–86 is estimated based on a 15 percent share of PE employment in aggregate PE and private sector employment.

Table 10-6. Gross domestic credit to public enterprises. This table shows the ratio of gross domestic credit to nonfinancial PEs (IMF, IFS, line 32C) to GDP (at market prices) (Table 2-5). Gross domestic credit is defined as the sum of outstanding gross credit from the financial system to the private sector, the PE sector, and the government. The use of gross instead of net credit provides a more consistent cross-country comparison and eliminates distortions and negative ratios that may otherwise arise if government deposits with the central bank exceed central bank credit to the government.

Table 10-7. Share of public enterprises in domestic credit outstanding. This table shows the ratio of gross domestic credit to nonfinancial PEs to the country's total gross domestic credit outstanding (IMF, IFS, line 32).

Table 10-8. Share of public enterprises in external debt outstanding. This table is calculated by dividing the PEs' external debt (World Bank, DRS) by the country's external debt (World Bank, DRS). The share of external debt attributable to PEs is defined as debt outstanding and disbursed that has been borrowed directly by PEs; it generally does not include debt that has been assumed or incurred by the government on behalf of PEs. The figures may thus understate the actual share of PEs in external debt. Totals are for long-term debt (see Tables 6-22, 6-23, and 6-26).

Table 10-9. External debt of public enterprises. This table shows the share of external debt attributed to PEs (Table 10-8) as a percentage of GDP (at market prices) (Table 2-5).

Table 10-10. Net financial flows between government and public enterprises. This is calculated as the difference between total PE payments to the government (World Bank data) and total government payments to PEs (World Bank data). Figures for PE payments to government (taxes, dividends, and net profits) may be underestimated because data on trading profits transferred to government are sometimes not available for major exporting PEs (for instance, the petroleum company in Cameroon). Taxes paid by PEs are treated as a transfer of financial resources from the PE to the government. Net financial flows exclude government loans to PEs as well as interest payments and principle repayments to government. Implicit flows, such as the accumulation or retirement of arrears between PEs and government and government assumption of PEs debt, are also excluded. Government payments to PEs consists of capital transfers (unrequited receipts to acquire capital or equity), debt servicing, and subsidies. Debt servicing takes two forms: government forgiveness of its own outstanding loans to PEs (through write-offs and equity conversions) and debt service payments on behalf of PEs to third parties, mainly domestic and external banks. Data on government assumptions of PE debt are not available.

For Cape Verde, net transfers are based only on transfer from government to PEs. For Morocco, net transfers data for 1985–90 are for 10 major nonfinancial PEs that account for more than 80 percent of PEs investment.

Table 10-11. Overall balance of public enterprises before transfers. This table shows the savings-investment gap of PEs (World Bank data) before transfers as a percentage of GDP at market prices (Table 2-5). PEs' savings are the sum of net operating and net non-operating revenues. Unless otherwise noted, net operating revenue (or operating surplus or balances) refers to gross operating profits, or operating revenue minus the costs of intermediate inputs, wages, factors rentals, and depreciation. The sum of operating surplus and net non-operating revenue is PE savings. In turn, PEs' savings-investment balance is obtained as PEs' savings minus PE net capital expenditure.

For Côte d'Ivoire, overall balance figures for 1978–79 are from Floyd, Gray, and Short (1984). For Kenya, Malawi, and Namibia, overall balance figures are estimated as operating balance minus capital expenditure.

Table 10-12. Summary of privatizations of public enterprises. For most countries, the number of enterprises measures the changes brought about by the creation, dissolution, or privatization of PEs. In a few cases, improved monitoring or reclassification have resulted in revised figures, especially in recent years. In this table, "privatization" refers to the transfer of government assets or enterprises from the government to private control and ownership. Experience has shown that, depending on the privatization method used, the end result of the process does not necessarily translate into transfer of ownership and/or control. The process, however, accomplishes divestiture. Therefore, the term "privatization" can be substituted by the word "transaction," and the term "proceeds" by "sale value" of the transaction. Proceeds here is defined narrowly as meaning the amount of cash paid to the government or its privatization agency, while sale value captures the different types of payments involved in the transaction (for example, installments and other deferred terms). The data classifying privatizations by sectors have not been reconciled with the total number of privatizations, but are indicative. The data are from national privatization agencies and the World Bank.

Table 10-13. Progress in privatization: divestiture methods employed. This table shows the various methods employed in each country's privatization approach. The data cover only countries for which information is available. They also indicate the lack of divestiture in some countries. Eleven broad categories have been used to classify the different approaches employed in the different countries.

Sale of shares in general is divided into two categories: sale of shares privately and sale of shares to the public. Sale of shares privately is further divided into three categories to reflect the level of negotiations. Competitive sales of shares are mostly those processed through tender, while direct sale of shares includes negotiations with prequalified bidders, transfer of shares to identified investors or other government entities (municipals), and restitution. Preemptive right equally reflects lack of competition, but the negations can be complex. Public flotation is when government shares are offered for subscription to the public at large through the stock market.

Sale of assets of an enterprise is divided into three categories: liquidation, competitive, and direct. Liquidation involves full divestiture, as is usually applied to insolvent companies that have ceased productive activity. Competitive sale of assets includes sale of the liquidated enterprises' assets in whole or piecemeal. This is achieved through tender or other competitive means (auction) to identify the buyers and the sale of assets through receivership. Direct sale of assets is accomplished through management buyouts.

Debt conversion is defined in two different ways. In some countries, the other shareholder requires the government to exchange its equity for its debt to the enterprise, and it is referred to as a debt-equity conversion. In other countries, international practice was applied where investors bought stock of debt in foreign currency at the secondary market at a discount of more than 60 percent. Through auctioning of the stock to the central bank, the investors get a lower discount rate (50 percent) and then receive corresponding funds in local currency for investment in privatized enterprises.

Leases transfer management and operations of the enterprise to the private sector without transferring ownership. Lease arrangements provide private sector management, technology, and skills to the enterprise for an agreed period. Most leases are seen as an intermediate step toward full privatization and are used to improve operations and profitability of an enterprise.

Joint ventures is not defined in its legal terms. Instead, it is defined as occurring when a portion of government shares are sold, or assets are offered as equity contribution, to a private enterprise to form a new private enterprise. The private enterprise normally contributes cash to the newly created entity to restore and increase its working capital. Joint ventures allow for rehabilitation of the assets and expansion of enterprises' operations.

Management employee buyouts (MBO) is the acquisition by management or by employees generally of the shares or principal assets of an enterprise, usually leading to full privatization. Buyouts can be accomplished through either a competitive process (with or without the management-employee team being given preferred terms) or a noncompetitive process. There can be confusion as to how to categorize an MBO and distinguish it from employee participation.

Management contract is also termed as an intermediate step toward full privatization where private management is injected into the enterprise for a specific period of time. Maintenance and renewal obligations and other costs are defined between the private investor (management team) and government.

Trustees is the transfer of shares to a trust (whether public or private) or to a privately managed investment fund. It is considered to represent a change of ownership (that is, privatization) if government ceases to exercise any ownership rights. A transfer of shares happens when a government cedes ownership to another institution without financial consideration. The reason for the transfer may be for warehousing the shares for later direct or indirect sale to the public or for government to provide an additional revenue source to a government-sponsored institution that takes full responsibility for portfolio management.

Restitution is a return of assets or shares to former owners from whom they have been acquired by the government through nationalization or confiscation without adequate compensation. It is sometimes called deconfiscation.

Table 10-14. Progress in privatization: ownership and control changes. Since the main goal of privatization is to transfer ownership and control of public enterprises to the private sector, this table shows the progress achieved to date. Majority ownership is defined as an entity that owns more than 50 percent of the shares.

Transfer of majority ownership to private shareholders means that the government has sold all its shares to the private sector, and a complete privatization is achieved from the transaction.

Government retains majority ownership is when the transaction dilutes government ownership and (maybe) control, but still holds more than 50 percent of the shares. Methods that bring about this situation include share dilution, joint ventures, leases, and management contracts.

Sale of minority government interest is when the government sells off all its minority shares, and thus full privatization is achieved.

Government retains minority interest is when the government maintains minority interest (for example, for political reasons). This type of transaction produces partial privatization of ownership, but not necessarily of control. Joint ventures are such an example.

Total share transactions are transactions that involve selling enterprise shares, while *total sale of assets* are transactions that eliminate the enterprise completely (dissolution).

Methodology used for regional aggregations and period averages in chapter 10

	Aggregations[a]			Period averages[b]
Table	*(1)*	*(2)*	*(8)*	*(1)*
10-1			x	
10-2			x	
10-3			x	
10-4			x	
10-5			x	
10-6			x	
10-7			x	x
10-8		x		x
10-9		x		
10-10			x	
10-11			x	
10-12	x			
10-13	x			
10-14	x			

Note: Regional aggregations are shown in the rows for Sub-Saharan Africa, North Africa, and All Africa. Period averages are shown in the last three columns. This table shows only the methodologies used in this chapter.

a. Regional aggregations: (1) simple total; (2) simple total of the first indicator divided by the simple total of the second indicator (same country coverage); (3) simple total of the gap-filled indicator; (4) simple total of the gap-filled main indicator divided by the simple total of the gap-filled secondary indicator; (5) simple total of the first gap-filled main indicator less the simple total of the second gap-filled main indicator, all divided by the simple total of the secondary indicator; (6) weighted total; (7) median; (8) no aggregation; (9) simple arithmetic mean.

b. Period averages: (1) arithmetic mean (using the same series as shown in the table, i.e., ratio if the rest of the table is shown as ratio, level if the rest of the table is shown as level, growth rate if the rest of the table is shown as growth rate); (2) least-squares growth rate (using main indicator); (3) least-squares growth rate (using main indicator in constant terms, with the rest of the table in current terms).

11

Labor Force and Employment

This chapter presents data on the level and structure of the labor force. The distribution of the labor force into various industrial activities is also given, as well as the participation rates of the population in economic activities. Information is also presented on average wages in different sectors.

The treatment of statistics on public sector employment is not consistent among countries. The scope covered often varies. While some countries include education and health sectors, others leave them out. Staff of local, regional, and state or provincial governments are likewise treated differently.

The stipulations on wages take different forms among the countries where such practice exists. While some countries have a minimum wage per hour worked, others stipulate a minimum monthly wage for a worker. To permit some measure of comparability, we have computed and reported the monthly average earnings per wage earner. These earnings are further converted to US dollars at the *Atlas* exchange rate. These data should be used with caution since some countries have more than one minimum wage rate based on the industry and the occupation within the industry as well as on the region of the country concerned.

The definition of labor force or economically active population is that used by the International Labour Organization (ILO), which follows the UN system of national accounts (SNA). The labor force is measured by dividing economically active persons into two categories: employed and unemployed. Caution in the use of the data is necessary because, as pointed out in the ILO's *World Labor Report 1* (1987), there are many persons who do not clearly come within one of these categories or the other. Many are visibly underemployed in that they work less than full time. Others work full time but earn less than a subsistence income. Some of the unemployed may even be voluntarily idle.

The comparability of the data is further hampered by the fact that practices vary among countries as regards the treatment of such groups as armed forces, inmates of institutions, persons living on reservations, persons seeking their first job, seasonal workers, and persons engaged in part-time economic activities. In some countries, all or part of these groups are included among the economically active, while in others they are treated as inactive. In addition, the extent to which family workers who assist in family enterprises are included among the enumerated economically active population, particularly females, varies considerably from country to country. Further, in some countries the statistics of the economically active relate only to employed and unemployed persons above a specified age, while in others there is no such age provision.

The reference period is also an important factor of difference, especially when it comes to the classification of the labor force according to industry. In some countries, such classification refers to the actual position of each individual on the day of the census or survey date, while in others the data recorded refer to the usual position of each person, generally without reference to any given period of time.

The sources for the tables in this chapter are various issues of the ILO's *Yearbook of Labor Statistics*, and electronic ILO files kept in World Bank BESD.

11-1. Number and gender structure of the labor force

	Total labor force (thousands)			Percentage of total labor force that are females		
	1970	1980	1995	1970	1980	1995
SUB-SAHARAN AFRICA	135,265	172,592	257,147	42.3	42.3	42.2
excluding South Africa	126,877	161,647	240,960	42.9	42.8	42.5
excl. S. Africa & Nigeria	103,695	132,128	196,818	44.3	44.3	44.0
Angola	2,894	3,474	4,959	47.4	47.1	46.4
Benin	1,425	1,659	2,476	48.6	47.1	47.6
Botswana	290	396	633	53.1	50.1	45.7
Burkina Faso	3,308	3,995	5,428	48.9	47.5	46.8
Burundi	1,958	2,270	3,366	50.5	50.2	48.8
Cameroon	3,012	3,639	5,410	37.3	36.8	37.5
Cape Verde	88	94	146	28.4	33.7	38.4
Central African Republic	1,051	1,216	1,579	49.3	48.2	46.8
Chad	1,831	2,231	3,130	42.5	43.4	44.4
Comoros	131	152	219	42.7	42.9	42.2
Congo	549	702	1,088	41.2	42.6	43.3
Côte d'Ivoire	2,319	3,282	5,009	32.9	32.2	33.1
Djibouti	..	..	..	..	..	..
Equatorial Guinea	136	95	169	36.8	35.1	34.8
Eritrea	950	1,220	1,806	47.5	47.5	47.4
Ethiopia	13,373	16,927	25,425	42.4	42.3	40.9
Gabon	277	372	503	45.8	44.9	44.4
Gambia, The	248	330	546	44.8	44.7	44.9
Ghana	4,010	5,090	7,957	50.6	51.0	50.7
Guinea	2,067	2,293	3,184	47.8	47.1	47.3
Guinea-Bissau	274	406	509	39.4	39.7	40.2
Kenya	5,595	7,795	12,789	45.2	46.0	46.0
Lesotho	465	572	806	39.4	38.4	36.8
Liberia	600	790	1,103	38.2	38.5	39.2
Madagascar	3,502	4,314	6,468	45.5	45.2	45.0
Malawi	2,359	3,090	4,736	50.6	50.6	49.1
Mali	2,898	3,393	4,862	46.5	46.7	46.4
Mauritania	619	744	1,039	46.7	45.1	44.0
Mauritius	251	344	471	20.3	25.6	31.5
Mozambique	5,260	6,684	8,471	49.2	49.0	48.4
Namibia	365	447	641	39.5	40.0	40.6
Niger	2,135	2,752	4,316	45.2	44.6	44.2
Nigeria	23,182	29,519	44,143	36.8	36.2	35.9
Rwanda	1,973	2,637	4,011	49.4	49.1	48.8
São Tomé and Principe	..	..	..	..	..	..
Senegal	1,978	2,541	3,783	41.6	42.3	42.5
Seychelles	..	..	..	..	..	..
Sierra Leone	1,064	1,249	1,651	35.6	35.5	36.1
Somalia	2,299	3,073	4,278	43.9	43.4	43.4
South Africa	8,388	10,945	16,187	32.7	35.1	37.4
Sudan	4,744	6,837	9,923	20.0	26.9	28.3
Swaziland	160	202	318	33.1	33.8	37.4
Tanzania	7,327	9,508	15,189	50.6	49.9	49.4
Togo	910	1,143	1,699	38.9	39.2	40.0
Uganda	5,209	6,619	9,477	48.2	48.0	47.7
Zaire	9,512	12,006	18,472	45.2	44.5	43.6
Zambia	1,898	2,398	3,741	44.6	45.4	44.8
Zimbabwe	2,381	3,148	5,031	44.4	44.4	44.4
NORTH AFRICA	19,040	29,267	44,744	9.2	27.3	29.0
Algeria	2,993	4,850	8,628	5.9	21.4	24.2
Egypt, Arab Republic	9,983	14,319	20,951	8.0	26.5	28.6
Libya	668	945	1,543	6.0	18.6	20.5
Morocco	4,049	6,966	10,281	13.9	33.5	34.6
Tunisia	1,347	2,188	3,341	12.8	28.9	30.4
ALL AFRICA	154,305	201,859	301,891	38.2	40.1	40.2

11-2. Children under 14 working in the labor force

	As percentage of population aged 10 to 14			
	1970	*1980*	*1990*	*1995*
SUB-SAHARAN AFRICA	36.2	34.8	32.1	30.4
excluding South Africa	39.0	37.3	34.4	32.4
excl. S.Africa & Nigeria	41.1	39.3	36.1	34.2
Angola	31.4	29.7	28.1	27.1
Benin	34.5	30.4	28.6	27.5
Botswana	32.3	25.9	19.4	16.9
Burkina Faso	75.1	70.9	58.7	51.0
Burundi	50.8	50.0	49.4	49.0
Cameroon	38.9	33.9	27.5	25.3
Cape Verde	17.4	16.0	14.7	14.1
Central African Republic	45.1	39.4	33.8	31.2
Chad	41.9	41.6	40.0	38.3
Comoros	45.8	44.8	41.0	39.3
Congo	28.3	27.5	26.6	26.0
Côte d'Ivoire	34.6	28.4	22.3	20.5
Djibouti	..	..	..	..
Equatorial Guinea	42.9	40.5	35.8	33.9
Eritrea	46.1	43.8	40.8	39.6
Ethiopia	48.5	46.3	43.5	42.3
Gabon	35.6	29.1	22.7	18.4
Gambia, The	45.9	44.4	40.2	37.0
Ghana	16.3	16.2	14.6	13.3
Guinea	43.3	41.2	37.0	34.0
Guinea-Bissau	45.2	43.3	40.4	38.6
Kenya	45.0	45.1	43.4	41.3
Lesotho	30.9	27.6	23.5	22.1
Liberia	31.1	25.7	21.9	18.6
Madagascar	41.7	40.2	37.6	35.8
Malawi	50.7	45.2	38.9	35.2
Mali	62.5	61.2	57.9	54.5
Mauritania	33.3	29.6	25.8	24.0
Mauritius	5.7	4.8	4.0	3.0
Mozambique	40.7	39.5	35.2	33.8
Namibia	40.1	33.6	26.0	21.7
Niger	48.8	47.8	46.8	45.2
Nigeria	30.8	29.2	27.6	25.8
Rwanda	43.3	42.5	42.1	41.7
São Tomé and Principe	..	..	..	..
Senegal	46.9	42.9	35.4	31.4
Seychelles	..	..	..	..
Sierra Leone	21.7	19.4	17.1	15.5
Somalia	39.9	37.7	34.5	32.9
South Africa	2.7	0.9	0.0	0.0
Sudan	27.0	33.3	31.4	29.4
Swaziland	19.1	17.2	15.3	13.8
Tanzania	45.6	42.8	42.1	39.5
Togo	40.4	36.1	30.4	28.6
Uganda	50.4	48.9	46.8	45.3
Zaire	36.5	33.2	30.5	29.6
Zambia	21.1	19.0	16.9	16.3
Zimbabwe	41.1	36.7	31.8	29.4
NORTH AFRICA	12.7	15.1	8.8	6.7
Algeria	7.4	7.1	3.3	1.6
Egypt, Arab Republic	15.0	18.3	13.2	11.2
Libya	10.8	8.7	0.5	0.2
Morocco	13.3	20.9	10.6	5.6
Tunisia	11.7	5.8	0.0	0.0
ALL AFRICA	31.4	31.0	27.9	26.3

11-3. Unpaid family workers in the total labor force

	Percentage of unpaid family workers in total labor force (most recent year available between 1980-93)		
	Female	*Male*	*Total*
SUB-SAHARAN AFRICA	..	..	..
excluding South Africa	..	..	..
excl. S.Africa & Nigeria	..	..	..
Angola	..	..	..
Benin	12.2	18.3	30.5
Botswana	6.0	11.1	17.1
Burkina Faso	..	..	..
Burundi	42.5	15.9	58.4
Cameroon	12.3	5.7	18.0
Cape Verde	1.1	0.9	2.0
Central African Republic	4.5	3.7	8.1
Chad	..	..	..
Comoros	..	..	..
Congo	..	..	..
Côte d'Ivoire	..	..	..
Djibouti	..	..	..
Equatorial Guinea	22.3	7.7	29.9
Eritrea	..	..	..
Ethiopia	22.7	11.3	34.0
Gabon	..	..	..
Gambia, The	9.1	5.2	14.3
Ghana	7.7	4.4	12.2
Guinea	..	..	..
Guinea-Bissau	..	..	..
Kenya	..	..	..
Lesotho	19.2	17.6	36.8
Liberia	9.4	5.0	14.4
Madagascar	..	..	..
Malawi	47.5	30.1	77.6
Mali	12.6	29.9	42.5
Mauritania	..	..	..
Mauritius	0.9	1.0	1.9
Mozambique	..	..	..
Namibia	..	..	..
Niger	..	..	..
Nigeria	..	..	..
Rwanda	..	..	..
São Tomé and Principe	..	..	..
Senegal	..	..	..
Seychelles	..	..	..
Sierra Leone	..	..	..
Somalia	..	..	..
South Africa	..	..	..
Sudan	..	..	..
Swaziland	..	..	..
Tanzania	..	..	..
Togo	..	..	..
Uganda	..	..	..
Zaire	..	..	..
Zambia	..	..	..
Zimbabwe	..	..	..
NORTH AFRICA	6.0	5.7	11.7
Algeria	0.0	2.0	2.1
Egypt, Arab Republic	8.6	7.8	16.4
Libya	..	..	..
Morocco	6.0	14.8	20.9
Tunisia	..	..	..
ALL AFRICA	..	..	..

11-4. Industrial structure of the labor force

	Percentage of labor force working in								
	Agriculture			Industry			Services		
	1970	1980	1990	1970	1980	1990	1970	1980	1990
SUB-SAHARAN AFRICA	78	72	67	8	9	9	14	20	24
excluding South Africa	82	76	71	6	7	7	12	18	22
excl. S.Africa & Nigeria	84	80	77	6	6	7	10	13	16
Angola	78	76	75	7	8	8	15	16	17
Benin	81	67	64	5	7	8	14	26	28
Botswana	82	64	46	5	10	20	13	26	33
Burkina Faso	92	92	92	3	3	2	5	5	6
Burundi	94	93	92	2	2	3	4	5	6
Cameroon	85	73	70	5	8	9	10	19	21
Cape Verde	47	37	31	27	31	30	27	33	40
Central African Republic	89	85	80	2	3	3	8	12	16
Chad	92	88	83	2	3	4	5	9	13
Comoros	83	81	77	7	8	9	10	11	13
Congo	66	58	49	11	13	15	23	29	37
Côte d'Ivoire	76	65	60	6	8	10	19	27	30
Djibouti	..	..	..	..	..	..	..	..	..
Equatorial Guinea	82	78	75	5	5	5	14	17	20
Eritrea	86	83	80	4	5	5	10	12	15
Ethiopia	91	89	86	2	2	2	7	9	12
Gabon	79	65	52	9	12	16	12	22	33
Gambia, The	87	84	82	5	7	8	8	9	11
Ghana	60	61	59	15	13	13	25	25	28
Guinea	92	91	87	1	1	2	7	8	11
Guinea-Bissau	89	87	85	1	2	2	9	11	13
Kenya	86	82	80	5	6	7	9	11	13
Lesotho	43	40	40	36	34	28	21	26	32
Liberia	81	76	72	7	6	6	12	17	22
Madagascar	84	82	78	5	6	7	11	13	15
Malawi	91	87	87	4	5	5	5	7	8
Mali	93	89	86	1	2	2	6	9	12
Mauritania	84	72	55	3	7	10	12	22	34
Mauritius	34	27	17	25	28	43	41	45	40
Mozambique	86	84	83	6	7	8	8	8	9
Namibia	64	56	49	15	15	15	21	29	36
Niger	93	91	90	2	3	4	5	5	6
Nigeria	71	54	43	11	8	7	19	38	50
Rwanda	94	93	92	3	3	3	4	4	5
São Tomé and Principe	..	..	..	..	..	..	..	..	..
Senegal	83	81	77	6	6	8	12	13	16
Seychelles	..	..	..	..	..	..	..	..	..
Sierra Leone	76	70	67	12	14	15	12	16	17
Somalia	81	78	75	6	7	8	13	14	16
South Africa	31	17	14	30	35	32	39	48	54
Sudan	77	72	69	6	8	8	17	20	22
Swaziland	65	50	39	13	19	22	22	31	38
Tanzania	90	86	84	3	4	5	7	10	11
Togo	74	69	66	9	10	10	17	22	24
Uganda	90	87	85	3	4	5	7	9	11
Zaire	75	72	68	11	12	13	14	16	19
Zambia	79	76	75	7	8	8	14	16	17
Zimbabwe	77	72	68	11	12	8	12	15	24
NORTH AFRICA	51	51	37	18	20	25	31	29	38
Algeria	47	36	26	21	27	31	31	37	43
Egypt, Arab Republic	52	57	40	16	16	22	32	27	38
Libya	29	25	11	25	24	23	46	51	66
Morocco	58	56	45	17	20	25	25	24	31
Tunisia	42	39	28	26	30	33	33	31	39
ALL AFRICA	75	69	63	9	10	11	16	21	26

Note: Figures may not add up to 100 because of rounding.

11-5. Labor force participation rate

	Percentage of population of all ages in the labor force								
	Total			Female			Male		
	1970	1980	1990	1970	1980	1990	1970	1980	1990
SUB-SAHARAN AFRICA	47.5	45.9	44.9	20.4	19.7	19.2	27.1	26.2	25.8
excluding South Africa	48.1	46.5	45.4	21.0	20.2	19.5	27.2	26.4	25.9
excl. S.Africa & Nigeria	49.2	47.5	46.6	22.1	21.3	20.7	27.1	26.3	25.9
Angola	51.8	49.5	46.6	24.6	23.3	21.7	27.2	26.2	24.9
Benin	53.6	47.8	45.0	26.0	22.5	21.5	27.6	25.3	23.6
Botswana	46.5	44.2	43.8	24.7	22.2	20.3	21.8	22.1	23.5
Burkina Faso	58.7	57.4	53.9	28.7	27.3	25.2	30.0	30.1	28.7
Burundi	55.7	55.0	53.9	28.1	27.6	26.5	27.6	27.4	27.4
Cameroon	46.3	41.6	40.3	17.3	15.3	14.9	29.0	26.3	25.4
Cape Verde	33.0	32.9	37.2	9.4	11.1	14.4	23.6	21.8	22.9
Central African Republic	56.8	52.6	49.2	28.0	25.3	23.1	28.8	27.2	26.0
Chad	50.1	49.8	47.5	21.3	21.6	20.9	28.8	28.2	26.6
Comoros	..	52.2	55.4	..	22.4	23.6	..	29.9	31.9
Congo	43.5	42.1	41.1	17.9	17.9	17.8	25.6	24.1	23.3
Côte d'Ivoire	42.1	40.1	37.3	13.8	12.9	12.1	28.2	27.2	25.2
Djibouti	..	..	..	..	..	..	..	..	..
Equatorial Guinea	46.7	44.7	43.5	17.2	15.7	14.8	29.6	29.0	28.7
Ethiopia	..	..	..	..	..	..	..	..	..
Eritrea	46.2	43.3	41.1	19.6	18.3	16.8	26.6	25.0	24.3
Gabon	55.0	53.8	49.0	25.2	24.2	21.6	29.8	29.7	27.4
Gambia, The	53.4	51.6	50.3	23.9	23.1	22.5	29.5	28.5	27.7
Ghana	46.6	47.4	47.1	23.5	24.1	24.0	23.0	23.2	23.1
Guinea	53.7	51.4	49.0	25.7	24.2	23.3	28.0	27.2	25.8
Guinea-Bissau	52.2	49.6	48.3	20.6	19.7	19.4	31.6	29.9	28.9
Kenya	48.7	47.3	48.3	22.0	21.8	22.2	26.7	25.5	26.1
Lesotho	43.7	41.8	40.7	17.2	16.1	14.9	26.5	25.8	25.8
Liberia	43.3	41.9	42.9	16.5	16.1	16.8	26.8	25.8	26.2
Madagascar	51.9	51.5	51.2	23.6	23.3	23.1	28.3	28.2	28.1
Malawi	52.2	50.7	54.2	26.4	25.6	26.8	25.8	25.1	27.4
Mali	54.3	53.7	54.7	25.3	25.1	25.5	29.1	28.6	29.2
Mauritania	50.7	47.9	45.5	23.7	21.6	20.1	27.0	26.3	25.4
Mauritius	30.3	35.6	40.8	6.2	9.1	12.4	24.1	26.5	28.4
Mozambique	56.0	55.2	53.0	27.5	27.1	25.7	28.5	28.2	27.4
Namibia	46.1	43.4	41.8	18.2	17.4	16.9	27.9	26.0	24.9
Niger	51.5	50.5	49.0	23.3	22.5	21.6	28.2	28.0	27.4
Nigeria	43.6	42.0	40.0	16.1	15.2	14.1	27.5	26.8	25.8
Rwanda	52.9	51.1	52.2	26.1	25.1	25.5	26.8	26.0	26.7
São Tomé and Principe	..	..	..	..	..	..	..	..	..
Senegal	47.6	45.9	44.2	19.8	19.4	18.7	27.8	26.5	25.4
Seychelles	..	..	..	..	..	..	..	..	..
Sierra Leone	40.1	38.6	37.4	14.3	13.7	13.3	25.8	24.9	24.1
Somalia	53.3	53.5	49.2	23.4	23.2	21.3	29.9	30.3	27.9
South Africa	37.3	37.5	38.6	12.2	13.2	14.3	25.1	24.4	24.4
Sudan	34.2	36.6	36.3	6.8	9.8	9.8	27.4	26.7	26.5
Swaziland	38.2	35.6	31.9	12.6	12.0	11.8	25.5	23.5	20.0
Tanzania	53.5	51.2	51.6	27.1	25.5	25.6	26.4	25.7	26.0
Togo	45.0	43.7	42.0	17.5	17.2	16.7	27.5	26.6	25.2
Uganda	53.1	52.9	55.6	25.6	25.4	26.6	27.5	27.5	29.0
Zaire	46.9	44.4	42.5	21.2	19.8	18.6	25.7	24.6	23.8
Zambia	45.3	41.8	41.8	20.2	19.0	18.9	25.1	22.8	23.0
Zimbabwe	45.4	45.7	47.0	20.2	20.3	20.8	25.2	25.4	26.2
NORTH AFRICA	27.9	34.6	34.9	2.7	9.6	9.8	25.2	25.0	25.1
Algeria	21.8	26.1	28.1	1.3	5.6	5.9	20.5	20.5	22.1
Egypt, Arab Republic	30.2	37.5	37.5	2.4	9.9	10.1	27.8	27.6	27.4
Libya	33.6	24.9	17.6	6.3	5.6	4.7	27.3	19.3	12.9
Morocco	26.4	36.0	37.6	3.7	12.1	13.0	22.8	23.9	24.6
Tunisia	26.3	34.3	34.7	3.4	9.9	10.1	22.9	24.3	24.6
ALL AFRICA	45.0	44.3	43.5	18.2	18.2	17.8	26.8	26.1	25.7

11-6. Wages in non-agricultural activities

	Monthly earnings in current US dollars											
	1980	*1984*	*1985*	*1986*	*1987*	*1988*	*1989*	*1990*	*1991*	*1992*	*1993*	*1994*
SUB-SAHARAN AFRICA	..	..	..	..	..	..	..	..	..	..	..	..
excluding South Africa	..	..	..	..	..	..	..	..	..	..	..	..
excl. S. Africa & Nigeria	..	..	..	..	..	..	..	..	..	..	..	..
Angola	..	..	..	..	..	..	..	..	..	..	..	..
Benin	..	..	..	..	..	..	..	..	..	..	..	..
Botswana	..	200	164	158	170	206	200	237	250	293	..	..
Burkina Faso	..	..	..	..	..	..	..	..	..	..	..	..
Burundi	109	140	140	149	139	..	..	..	..	..	..	..
Cameroon	..	..	..	..	..	..	..	..	..	..	..	..
Cape Verde	..	..	..	..	..	..	..	..	..	..	..	..
Central African Republic	..	..	..	..	..	..	..	..	..	..	..	..
Chad	..	..	..	..	..	..	..	..	..	..	..	..
Comoros	..	..	..	..	..	..	..	..	..	..	..	..
Congo	..	..	..	..	..	..	..	..	..	..	..	..
Côte d'Ivoire	..	..	..	..	..	..	..	..	..	..	..	..
Djibouti	..	..	..	..	..	..	..	..	..	..	..	..
Equatorial Guinea	..	..	..	..	..	..	..	..	..	..	..	..
Eritrea	..	..	..	..	..	..	..	..	..	..	..	..
Ethiopia	..	..	..	..	..	..	..	..	..	..	..	..
Gabon	..	..	..	..	..	..	..	..	..	..	..	..
Gambia, The	..	64	77	55	51	..	..	..	..	..	..	..
Ghana	48	37	48	83	72	68	90	92	96	..	..	..
Guinea	..	..	..	..	..	..	..	..	..	..	..	..
Guinea-Bissau	..	..	..	..	..	..	..	..	..	..	..	..
Kenya	175	130	123	136	143	151	139	136	123	..	..	..
Lesotho	..	..	..	..	..	..	..	..	..	..	..	..
Liberia	..	..	..	..	..	..	..	..	..	..	..	..
Madagascar	..	..	..	..	..	..	..	..	..	..	..	..
Malawi	87	64	58	58	55	54	60	64	64	..	..	..
Mali	..	..	..	..	..	..	..	..	..	..	..	..
Mauritania	..	..	..	..	..	..	..	..	..	..	..	..
Mauritius	..	153	141	172	188	230	239	258	278	314	294	349
Mozambique	..	..	..	..	..	..	..	..	..	..	..	..
Namibia	..	..	..	..	..	..	..	..	..	..	..	..
Niger	..	..	..	..	..	..	..	..	..	..	..	..
Nigeria	..	..	..	..	..	..	..	..	..	..	..	..
Rwanda	..	..	..	..	..	..	..	..	..	..	..	..
São Tomé and Principe	..	..	..	..	..	..	..	..	..	..	..	..
Senegal	..	..	..	..	..	..	..	..	..	..	..	..
Seychelles	239	280	289	340	401	380	374	424	442	516	525	..
Sierra Leone	74	48	30	17	13	..	..	..	..	..	..	..
Somalia	..	..	..	..	..	..	..	..	..	..	..	..
South Africa	..	..	..	..	..	..	..	..	..	..	..	..
Sudan	..	..	..	..	..	53	..	18	..	15	..	..
Swaziland	460	433	328	339	532	440	285	381	351	448	..	..
Tanzania	..	..	..	..	..	..	..	..	..	..	..	..
Togo	..	..	..	..	..	..	..	..	..	..	..	..
Uganda	..	..	..	..	..	..	..	..	..	..	..	..
Zaire	..	..	..	..	..	..	..	..	..	..	..	..
Zambia	..	..	..	..	..	..	..	..	..	..	..	..
Zimbabwe	325	274	210	255	284	251	278	293	226	189	171	152
NORTH AFRICA	..	..	..	..	..	..	..	..	..	..	..	..
Algeria	..	..	..	..	..	..	..	..	..	..	..	..
Egypt, Arab Republic	..	..	144	137	128	105	109	106	84	83	..	..
Libya	..	..	..	..	..	..	..	..	..	..	..	..
Morocco	..	..	..	..	..	..	..	..	..	..	..	..
Tunisia	..	..	..	..	..	..	..	..	..	..	..	..
ALL AFRICA	..	..	..	..	..	..	..	..	..	..	..	..

11-7. Wages in manufacturing

	Monthly earnings in current US dollars											
	1980	*1984*	*1985*	*1986*	*1987*	*1988*	*1989*	*1990*	*1991*	*1992*	*1993*	*1994*
SUB-SAHARAN AFRICA	..	..	..	..	..	..	..	..	..	..	..	..
excluding South Africa	..	..	..	..	..	..	..	..	..	..	..	..
excl. S. Africa & Nigeria	..	..	..	..	..	..	..	..	..	..	..	..
Angola	..	..	..	..	..	..	..	..	..	..	..	..
Benin	..	..	..	..	..	..	..	..	..	..	..	..
Botswana	..	185	155	148	157	196	173	198	213	242	272	214
Burkina Faso	..	..	..	..	..	..	..	..	..	..	..	..
Burundi	102	144	144	154	142	..	..	..	..	..	..	..
Cameroon	..	..	..	..	..	..	..	..	..	..	..	..
Cape Verde	..	..	..	..	..	..	..	..	..	..	..	..
Central African Republic	..	..	..	..	..	..	..	..	..	..	..	..
Chad	..	..	..	..	..	..	..	..	..	..	..	..
Comoros	..	..	..	..	..	..	..	..	..	..	..	..
Congo	..	..	..	..	..	..	..	..	..	..	..	..
Côte d'Ivoire	..	..	..	..	..	..	..	..	..	..	..	..
Djibouti	..	..	..	..	..	..	..	..	..	..	..	..
Equatorial Guinea	..	..	..	..	..	..	..	..	..	..	..	..
Eritrea	..	..	..	..	..	..	..	..	..	..	..	..
Ethiopia	..	..	..	..	..	..	..	..	..	..	..	..
Gabon	..	..	..	..	..	..	..	..	..	..	..	..
Gambia, The	..	38	53	33	36	..	..	..	..	..	..	..
Ghana	57	56	66	98	104	106	136	138	93	..	..	..
Guinea	..	..	..	..	..	..	..	..	..	..	..	..
Guinea-Bissau	..	..	..	..	..	..	..	..	..	..	..	..
Kenya	169	127	117	128	139	139	136	134	121	..	..	..
Lesotho	..	..	..	..	..	..	..	..	..	..	..	..
Liberia	..	..	..	..	..	..	..	..	..	..	..	..
Madagascar	..	..	..	..	..	..	..	..	..	..	..	..
Malawi	75	51	52	54	57	55	53	65	49	..	..	..
Mali	..	..	..	..	..	..	..	..	..	..	..	..
Mauritania	..	..	..	..	..	..	..	..	..	..	..	..
Mauritius	..	124	115	144	160	181	184	209	228	255	251	290
Mozambique	..	..	..	..	..	..	..	..	..	..	..	..
Namibia	..	..	..	..	..	..	..	..	..	..	..	..
Niger	..	..	..	..	..	..	..	..	..	..	..	..
Nigeria	..	..	..	..	..	..	..	..	..	..	..	..
Rwanda	..	..	..	..	..	..	..	..	..	..	..	..
São Tomé and Principe	..	..	..	..	..	..	..	..	..	..	..	..
Senegal	..	..	..	..	..	..	..	..	..	..	..	..
Seychelles	212	263	274	324	371	346	350	410	428	459	474	..
Sierra Leone	78	55	39	21	11	..	..	..	..	..	..	..
Somalia	..	..	..	..	..	..	..	..	..	..	..	..
South Africa	475	483	361	399	513	534	548	642	685	770	749	..
Sudan	..	..	..	..	..	60	..	31	..	17	..	..
Swaziland	571	546	396	414	507	416	398	534	513	522	..	..
Tanzania	..	..	..	..	..	..	..	..	..	..	..	..
Togo	..	..	..	..	..	..	..	..	..	..	..	..
Uganda	..	..	..	..	..	..	..	..	..	..	..	..
Zaire	..	..	..	..	..	..	..	..	..	..	..	..
Zambia	..	..	..	..	..	..	..	..	..	..	..	..
Zimbabwe	327	304	270	283	318	327	315	325	271	218	190	179
NORTH AFRICA	..	..	..	..	..	..	..	..	..	..	..	..
Algeria	..	..	..	..	..	..	..	..	..	..	..	..
Egypt, Arab Republic	..	..	131	133	128	100	102	104	79	80	..	..
Libya	..	..	..	..	..	..	..	..	..	..	..	..
Morocco	..	..	..	..	..	..	..	..	..	..	..	..
Tunisia	..	..	..	..	..	..	..	..	..	..	..	..
ALL AFRICA	..	..	..	..	..	..	..	..	..	..	..	..

11-8. Wages in minning and quarrying

	Monthly earnings in current US dollars											
	1980	1984	1985	1986	1987	1988	1989	1990	1991	1992	1993	1994
SUB-SAHARAN AFRICA	..	..	..	..	..	..	..	..	..	..	..	..
excluding South Africa	..	..	..	..	..	..	..	..	..	..	..	..
excl. S. Africa & Nigeria	..	..	..	..	..	..	..	..	..	..	..	..
Angola	..	..	..	..	..	..	..	..	..	..	..	..
Benin	..	..	..	..	..	..	..	..	..	..	..	..
Botswana	..	271	218	243	268	311	323	433	452	435	539	435
Burkina Faso	..	..	..	..	..	..	..	..	..	..	..	..
Burundi	..	77	78	85	79	..	..	..	..	..	..	..
Cameroon	..	..	..	..	..	..	..	..	..	..	..	..
Cape Verde	..	..	..	..	..	..	..	..	..	..	..	..
Central African Republic	..	..	..	..	..	..	..	..	..	..	..	..
Chad	..	..	..	..	..	..	..	..	..	..	..	..
Comoros	..	..	..	..	..	..	..	..	..	..	..	..
Congo	..	..	..	..	..	..	..	..	..	..	..	..
Côte d'Ivoire	..	..	..	..	..	..	..	..	..	..	..	..
Djibouti	..	..	..	..	..	..	..	..	..	..	..	..
Equatorial Guinea	..	..	..	..	..	..	..	..	..	..	..	..
Eritrea	..	..	..	..	..	..	..	..	..	..	..	..
Ethiopia	..	..	..	..	..	..	..	..	..	..	..	..
Gabon	..	..	..	..	..	..	..	..	..	..	..	..
Gambia, The	..	..	..	..	..	..	..	..	..	..	..	..
Ghana	64	55	138	134	116	57	64	117	75	..	..	..
Guinea	..	..	..	..	..	..	..	..	..	..	..	..
Guinea-Bissau	..	..	..	..	..	..	..	..	..	..	..	..
Kenya	157	121	105	106	110	104	106	101	93	..	..	..
Lesotho	..	..	..	..	..	..	..	..	..	..	..	..
Liberia	..	..	..	..	..	..	..	..	..	..	..	..
Madagascar	..	..	..	..	..	..	..	..	..	..	..	..
Malawi	36	50	27	29	20	17	17	20	39	..	..	..
Mali	..	..	..	..	..	..	..	..	..	..	..	..
Mauritania	..	..	..	..	..	..	..	..	..	..	..	..
Mauritius	..	163	136	185	202	245	231	256	272	302	280	374
Mozambique	..	..	..	..	..	..	..	..	..	..	..	..
Namibia	..	..	..	..	..	..	..	..	..	..	..	..
Niger	..	..	..	..	..	..	..	..	..	..	..	..
Nigeria	..	..	..	..	..	..	..	..	..	..	..	..
Rwanda	..	..	..	..	..	..	..	..	..	..	..	..
São Tomé and Principe	..	..	..	..	..	..	..	..	..	..	..	..
Senegal	..	..	..	..	..	..	..	..	..	..	..	..
Seychelles	212	220	240	283	327	334	317	348	379	444	455	..
Sierra Leone	..	..	30	16	20	..	..	..	..	..	..	..
Somalia	..	..	..	..	..	..	..	..	..	..	..	..
South Africa	330	328	247	278	371	397	403	477	514	561	542	..
Sudan	..	..	..	..	..	58	..	37	..	..	..	..
Swaziland	822	480	425	422	560	485	310	395	368	395	..	..
Tanzania	..	..	..	..	..	..	..	..	..	..	..	..
Togo	..	..	..	..	..	..	..	..	..	..	..	..
Uganda	..	..	..	..	..	..	..	..	..	..	..	..
Zaire	..	..	..	..	..	..	..	..	..	..	..	..
Zambia	358	169	..	..	..	..	..	..	..	..	..	..
Zimbabwe	229	236	211	222	240	254	243	254	215	178	152	157
NORTH AFRICA	..	..	..	..	..	..	..	..	..	..	..	..
Algeria	..	..	..	..	..	..	..	..	..	..	..	..
Egypt, Arab Republic	..	..	225	282	199	149	191	220	182	167	..	..
Libya	..	..	..	..	..	..	..	..	..	..	..	..
Morocco	..	..	..	..	..	..	..	..	..	..	..	..
Tunisia	..	..	..	..	..	..	..	..	..	..	..	..
ALL AFRICA	..	..	..	..	..	..	..	..	..	..	..	..

11-9. Wages in construction

	Monthly earnings in current US dollars											
	1980	*1984*	*1985*	*1986*	*1987*	*1988*	*1989*	*1990*	*1991*	*1992*	*1993*	*1994*
SUB-SAHARAN AFRICA	..	..	..	..	..	..	..	..	..	..	..	..
excluding South Africa	..	..	..	..	..	..	..	..	..	..	..	..
excl. S. Africa & Nigeria	..	..	..	..	..	..	..	..	..	..	..	..
Angola	..	..	..	..	..	..	..	..	..	..	..	..
Benin	..	..	..	..	..	..	..	..	..	..	..	..
Botswana	..	161	125	112	137	160	161	176	209	211	240	222
Burkina Faso	..	..	..	..	..	..	..	..	..	..	..	..
Burundi	70	66	67	72	68	..	..	..	..	..	..	..
Cameroon	..	..	..	..	..	..	..	..	..	..	..	..
Cape Verde	..	..	..	..	..	..	..	..	..	..	..	..
Central African Republic	..	..	..	..	..	..	..	..	..	..	..	..
Chad	..	..	..	..	..	..	..	..	..	..	..	..
Comoros	..	..	..	..	..	..	..	..	..	..	..	..
Congo	..	..	..	..	..	..	..	..	..	..	..	..
Côte d'Ivoire	..	..	..	..	..	..	..	..	..	..	..	..
Djibouti	..	..	..	..	..	..	..	..	..	..	..	..
Equatorial Guinea	..	..	..	..	..	..	..	..	..	..	..	..
Eritrea	..	..	..	..	..	..	..	..	..	..	..	..
Ethiopia	..	..	..	..	..	..	..	..	..	..	..	..
Gabon	..	..	..	..	..	..	..	..	..	..	..	..
Gambia, The	..	54	62	60	49	..	..	..	..	..	..	..
Ghana	37	26	34	57	47	43	51	59	71	..	..	..
Guinea	..	..	..	..	..	..	..	..	..	..	..	..
Guinea-Bissau	..	..	..	..	..	..	..	..	..	..	..	..
Kenya	133	102	96	91	97	98	96	99	95	..	..	..
Lesotho	..	..	..	..	..	..	..	..	..	..	..	..
Liberia	..	..	..	..	..	..	..	..	..	..	..	..
Madagascar	..	..	..	..	..	..	..	..	..	..	..	..
Malawi	60	37	33	31	29	29	29	30	31	..	..	..
Mali	..	..	..	..	..	..	..	..	..	..	..	..
Mauritania	..	..	..	..	..	..	..	..	..	..	..	..
Mauritius	..	147	125	153	170	220	245	255	297	364	324	368
Mozambique	..	..	..	..	..	..	..	..	..	..	..	..
Namibia	..	..	..	..	..	..	..	..	..	..	..	..
Niger	..	..	..	..	..	..	..	..	..	..	..	..
Nigeria	..	..	..	..	..	..	..	..	..	..	..	..
Rwanda	..	..	..	..	..	..	..	..	..	..	..	..
São Tomé and Principe	..	..	..	..	..	..	..	..	..	..	..	..
Senegal	..	..	..	..	..	..	..	..	..	..	..	..
Seychelles	..	..	..	..	..	..	..	..	..	..	..	..
Sierra Leone	57	38	26	18	14	..	..	..	..	..	..	..
Somalia	..	..	..	..	..	..	..	..	..	..	..	..
South Africa	371	363	271	289	347	368	348	394	372	475	424	..
Sudan	..	..	..	..	..	60	..	66	..	18	..	..
Swaziland	525	344	248	292	335	268	193	247	253	470	..	..
Tanzania	..	..	..	..	..	..	..	..	..	..	..	..
Togo	..	..	..	..	..	..	..	..	..	..	..	..
Uganda	..	..	..	..	..	..	..	..	..	..	..	..
Zaire	..	..	..	..	..	..	..	..	..	..	..	..
Zambia	172	90	..	..	..	..	..	..	..	..	..	..
Zimbabwe	238	206	191	197	209	200	182	179	153	109	101	81
NORTH AFRICA	..	..	..	..	..	..	..	..	..	..	..	..
Algeria	..	..	..	..	..	..	..	..	..	..	..	..
Egypt, Arab Republic	..	..	149	149	135	110	113	106	87	80	..	..
Libya	..	..	..	..	..	..	..	..	..	..	..	..
Morocco	..	..	..	..	..	..	..	..	..	..	..	..
Tunisia	..	..	..	..	..	..	..	..	..	..	..	..
ALL AFRICA	..	..	..	..	..	..	..	..	..	..	..	..

11-10. Wages in transport, storage and communication

	Monthly earnings in current US dollars											
	1980	*1984*	*1985*	*1986*	*1987*	*1988*	*1989*	*1990*	*1991*	*1992*	*1993*	*1994*
SUB-SAHARAN AFRICA	..	..	..	..	..	..	..	..	..	..	..	..
excluding South Africa	..	..	..	..	..	..	..	..	..	..	..	..
excl. S. Africa & Nigeria	..	..	..	..	..	..	..	..	..	..	..	..
Angola	..	..	..	..	..	..	..	..	..	..	..	..
Benin	..	..	..	..	..	..	..	..	..	..	..	..
Botswana	..	210	172	165	177	260	300	333	445	457	46	520
Burkina Faso	..	..	..	..	..	..	..	..	..	..	..	..
Burundi	183	146	147	156	145	..	..	..	..	..	..	..
Cameroon	..	..	..	..	..	..	..	..	..	..	..	..
Cape Verde	..	..	..	..	..	..	..	..	..	..	..	..
Central African Republic	..	..	..	..	..	..	..	..	..	..	..	..
Chad	..	..	..	..	..	..	..	..	..	..	..	..
Comoros	..	..	..	..	..	..	..	..	..	..	..	..
Congo	..	..	..	..	..	..	..	..	..	..	..	..
Côte d'Ivoire	..	..	..	..	..	..	..	..	..	..	..	..
Djibouti	..	..	..	..	..	..	..	..	..	..	..	..
Equatorial Guinea	..	..	..	..	..	..	..	..	..	..	..	..
Eritrea	..	..	..	..	..	..	..	..	..	..	..	..
Ethiopia	..	..	..	..	..	..	..	..	..	..	..	..
Gabon	..	..	..	..	..	..	..	..	..	..	..	..
Gambia, The	..	59	62	39	49	..	..	..	..	..	..	..
Ghana	55	38	48	117	38	89	96	100	106	..	..	..
Guinea	..	..	..	..	..	..	..	..	..	..	..	..
Guinea-Bissau	..	..	..	..	..	..	..	..	..	..	..	..
Kenya	237	177	165	183	195	207	193	187	171	..	..	..
Lesotho	..	..	..	..	..	..	..	..	..	..	..	..
Liberia	..	..	..	..	..	..	..	..	..	..	..	..
Madagascar	..	..	..	..	..	..	..	..	..	..	..	..
Malawi	99	59	52	50	47	49	62	63	70	..	..	..
Mali	..	..	..	..	..	..	..	..	..	..	..	..
Mauritania	..	..	..	..	..	..	..	..	..	..	..	..
Mauritius	..	188	179	235	231	290	289	307	339	380	353	376
Mozambique	..	..	..	..	..	..	..	..	..	..	..	..
Namibia	..	..	..	..	..	..	..	..	..	..	..	..
Niger	..	..	..	..	..	..	..	..	..	..	..	..
Nigeria	..	..	..	..	..	..	..	..	..	..	..	..
Rwanda	..	..	..	..	..	..	..	..	..	..	..	..
São Tomé and Principe	..	..	..	..	..	..	..	..	..	..	..	..
Senegal	..	..	..	..	..	..	..	..	..	..	..	..
Seychelles	299	339	352	..	..	..	..	..	..	..	..	..
Sierra Leone	74	36	49	22	17	..	..	..	..	..	..	..
Somalia	..	..	..	..	..	..	..	..	..	..	..	..
South Africa	..	557	399	434	571	583	577	700	794	1,110	1,076	..
Sudan	..	..	..	..	..	52	..	29	..	19	..	..
Swaziland	520	292	248	207	243	243	192	364	442	357	..	..
Tanzania	..	..	..	..	..	..	..	..	..	..	..	..
Togo	..	..	..	..	..	..	..	..	..	..	..	..
Uganda	..	..	..	..	..	..	..	..	..	..	..	..
Zaire	..	..	..	..	..	..	..	..	..	..	..	..
Zambia	153	144	..	..	..	..	..	..	..	..	..	..
Zimbabwe	537	391	335	368	400	425	430	466	353	285	281	235
NORTH AFRICA	..	..	..	..	..	..	..	..	..	..	..	..
Algeria	..	..	..	..	..	..	..	..	..	..	..	..
Egypt, Arab Republic	..	..	..	..	..	..	..	..	..	..	..	..
Libya	..	..	..	..	..	..	..	..	..	..	..	..
Morocco	..	..	..	..	..	..	..	..	..	..	..	..
Tunisia	..	..	..	..	..	..	..	..	..	..	..	..
ALL AFRICA	..	..	..	..	..	..	..	..	..	..	..	..

11-11. Wages in agriculture

	Monthly earnings in current US dollars											
	1980	*1984*	*1985*	*1986*	*1987*	*1988*	*1989*	*1990*	*1991*	*1992*	*1993*	*1994*
SUB-SAHARAN AFRICA	..	..	..	..	..	..	..	..	..	..	..	..
excluding South Africa	..	..	..	..	..	..	..	..	..	..	..	..
excl. S. Africa & Nigeria	..	..	..	..	..	..	..	..	..	..	..	..
Angola	..	..	..	..	..	..	..	..	..	..	..	..
Benin	..	..	..	..	..	..	..	..	..	..	..	..
Botswana	..	58	40	46	51	59	72	77	103	97	..	..
Burkina Faso	..	..	..	..	..	..	..	..	..	..	..	..
Burundi	..	79	80	85	79	..	..	..	..	..	..	..
Cameroon	..	..	..	..	..	..	..	..	..	..	..	..
Cape Verde	..	..	..	..	..	..	..	..	..	..	..	..
Central African Republic	..	..	..	..	..	..	..	..	..	..	..	..
Chad	..	..	..	..	..	..	..	..	..	..	..	..
Comoros	..	..	..	..	..	..	..	..	..	..	..	..
Congo	..	..	..	..	..	..	..	..	..	..	..	..
Côte d'Ivoire	..	..	..	..	..	..	..	..	..	..	..	..
Djibouti	..	..	..	..	..	..	..	..	..	..	..	..
Equatorial Guinea	..	..	..	..	..	..	..	..	..	..	..	..
Eritrea	..	..	..	..	..	..	..	..	..	..	..	..
Ethiopia	..	..	..	..	..	..	..	..	..	..	..	..
Gabon	..	..	..	..	..	..	..	..	..	..	..	..
Gambia, The	..	..	..	..	..	..	..	..	..	..	..	..
Ghana	34	38	36	64	54	52	73	64	107	..	..	..
Guinea	..	..	..	..	..	..	..	..	..	..	..	..
Guinea-Bissau	..	..	..	..	..	..	..	..	..	..	..	..
Kenya	59	41	39	44	48	53	48	47	45	..	..	..
Lesotho	..	..	..	..	..	..	..	..	..	..	..	..
Liberia	..	..	..	..	..	..	..	..	..	..	..	..
Madagascar	..	..	..	..	..	..	..	..	..	..	..	..
Malawi	20	17	15	14	13	12	13	15	16	..	..	..
Mali	..	..	..	..	..	..	..	..	..	..	..	..
Mauritania	..	..	..	..	..	..	..	..	..	..	..	..
Mauritius	80	62	57	70	74	87	89	95	114	134	138	140
Mozambique	..	..	..	..	..	..	..	..	..	..	..	..
Namibia	..	..	..	..	..	..	..	..	..	..	..	..
Niger	..	..	..	..	..	..	..	..	..	..	..	..
Nigeria	..	..	..	..	..	..	..	..	..	..	..	..
Rwanda	..	..	..	..	..	..	..	..	..	..	..	..
São Tomé and Principe	..	..	..	..	..	..	..	..	..	..	..	..
Senegal	..	..	..	..	..	..	..	..	..	..	..	..
Seychelles	139	181	199	245	305	304	305	348	367	434	442	..
Sierra Leone	..	..	..	..	..	..	..	..	..	..	..	..
Somalia	..	..	..	..	..	..	..	..	..	..	..	..
South Africa	..	..	..	..	..	..	..	..	..	..	..	..
Sudan	..	..	..	..	..	..	..	..	..	..	..	..
Swaziland	..	503	400	390	310	507	..	..	..	..	..	..
Tanzania	..	..	..	..	..	..	..	..	..	..	..	..
Togo	..	..	..	..	..	..	..	..	..	..	..	..
Uganda	..	..	..	..	..	..	..	..	..	..	..	..
Zaire	..	..	..	..	..	..	..	..	..	..	..	..
Zambia	112	..	..	..	..	..	..	..	..	..	..	..
Zimbabwe	59	78	64	69	73	76	72	75	59	33	37	..
NORTH AFRICA	..	..	..	..	..	..	..	..	..	..	..	..
Algeria	..	..	..	..	..	..	..	..	..	..	..	..
Egypt, Arab Republic	..	..	113	89	84	61	64	66	56	53	..	..
Libya	..	..	..	..	..	..	..	..	..	..	..	..
Morocco	..	..	..	..	..	..	..	..	..	..	..	..
Tunisia	..	85	79	83	80	77	70	100	96	100	..	..
ALL AFRICA	..	..	..	..	..	..	..	..	..	..	..	..

Technical Notes

Tables

Table 11-1. Number and gender structure of the labor force. This table (ILO data) provides the total number of persons in the labor force and the percentage that is female. Labor force refers to "economically active" persons, including the armed forces and the unemployed but excluding housewives and students. The "economically active" population comprises all persons of either gender who furnish the labor to produce economic goods and services, as defined by the SNA, during a specified period. The production of economic goods and services should include all production and processing of primary products, whether for the market, for barter, or for own consumption; the production of all other goods and services for the market; and, for households that produce such goods and services for the markets, the corresponding production for own consumption.

Table 11-2. Children under 14 working in the labor force. This table (ILO data) shows the percentage of children between the ages of 10 to 14 that participate in the labor force.

Table 11-3. Unpaid family workers in the total labor force. This table (ILO data) shows the percentage of family members—male and female—that participate in the labor force without receiving compensation for their services.

Table 11-4. Industrial structure of the labor force. The industrial structure of the labor force can often indicate the relative level of development of the economy. This table (ILO data) shows the distribution of the labor force among the various sectors of economic activities. The agriculture sector includes farming, animal husbandry, hunting, forestry, and fishing. The industry sector includes mining and quarrying, manufacturing, construction and public works, electricity, water, and gas. All other branches of activity are included in services.

Table 11-5. Labor force participation rate. This is the percentage of the male and female population of all ages that participates in economic activities (either employed or unemployed) (ILO data). Figures given are crude activity rates, that is, the ratios of the total economically active population to the total population of all ages. It should be recalled that the sex-age structure of the population, that is, the proportion of population in each sex-age group (particularly those under 15 years of age) will affect the participation rates shown. Further, the activity (participation) rate for females may be difficult to compare among countries, since in many countries relatively large numbers of women work on farms or in other family enterprises without pay, and there are differences from one country to another in the criteria adopted for determining the extent to which such workers are to be counted among the "economically active."

Table 11-6. Wages in nonagricultural activities. Data are from ILO, *Yearbook of Labor Statistics* (1988, 1993, 1994, and 1995) and show the monthly earnings at the average wage converted to US dollars at the *Atlas* exchange rates in the countries concerned. Earnings here are limited to wages and salaries of employees only unless otherwise specified. They include remuneration for time not worked, such as for annual vacation, other paid leave or holidays, bonuses and gratuities, and housing and family allowances paid by the employer to the employee. They exclude employers' contributions to social security and pension schemes and the benefits received by employees under these schemes, as well as severance and termination pay.

It should be remembered that these earnings do not reflect worker's disposable or net earnings since they include gross wages before deductions, such as taxes or social security contributions.

The series shown in this table comprise wages paid in the following sectors: mining and quarrying; electricity, gas and water; construction; wholesale and retail trade; restaurants and hotels; transport, storage, and communication; financing, insurance, real estate, and business services; and community, social, and personal services.

Data for Botswana include agriculture, hunting, forestry, and fishing, and exclude government sector. Data for Burundi include family allowances. Data for the Gambia exclude mining and quarrying. Data for Ghana include agriculture, hunting, forestry, and fishing. Data for Mauritius exclude sugar and tea factories. Data for Seychelles include agriculture, forestry, and fishing, and beginning in 1988 earnings are exempted from income tax. Data for Swaziland include agriculture and forestry and refer to skilled male workers only. Data for Tanzania include agriculture, forestry, and fishing. Data for Zambia exclude domestic services. Data for Zimbabwe refer to all workers engaged (skilled and unskilled).

Figures for Egypt and Sierra Leone were converted from weekly to monthly earnings using a rate of 4.3 weeks per month. Figures for the Gambia were converted from daily to monthly earnings using a rate of 22 days per month.

Table 11-7. Wages in manufacturing. Data are from ILO, *Yearbook of Labor Statistics* (1988, 1993, 1994, and 1995). Refer to the definitions in Table 11-6.

Data for Burundi include family allowances. Data for Egypt are for establishments with 10 or more persons employed. Data for the Gambia are for establishments with five or more persons employed. Data for Mauritius exclude sugar and tea factories. Data for Seychelles include electricity and water before 1992, and beginning in 1988 earnings are exempted from income tax. Data for Swaziland refer to skilled male workers only. Data for Zimbabwe include the value of payments in kind and refer to all persons engaged.

Figures for Egypt and Sierra Leone were converted from weekly to monthly earnings using a rate of 4.3 weeks per month. Figures for The Gambia were converted from daily to monthly earnings using a rate of 22 days per month.

Table 11-8. Wages in mining and quarrying. Data are from ILO, *Yearbook of Labor Statistics* (1988, 1993, 1994, and 1995). Refer to the definitions in Table 11-6.

Data for Burundi include family allowances. Data for Egypt are for establishments with 10 or more persons employed. Data for Kenya include the value of payments in kind. Data for Swaziland refer to skilled male workers only. Data for Seychelles include construction, and beginning in 1988 earnings are exempted from income tax. Data for South Africa exclude salt and iron works. Data for Swaziland refer to skilled male workers only. Data for Zimbabwe include the value of payments in kind and refer to all persons engaged.

Figures for Egypt and Sierra Leone were converted from weekly to monthly earnings using a rate of 4.3 weeks per month.

Table 11-9. Wages in construction. Data are from ILO, *Yearbook of Labor Statistics* (1988, 1993, 1994, and 1995). Refer to the definitions in Table 11-6.

Data for Burundi include family allowances. Data for Egypt are for establishments with 10 or more persons employed. Data for the Gambia are for establishments with five or more persons employed. Data for Kenya include the value of payments in kind. Data for Swaziland refer to skilled male workers only. Data for South Africa include private construction. Data for Swaziland refer to skilled male workers only. Data for

Zimbabwe include the value of payments in kind and refer to all persons engaged.

Figures for Egypt and Sierra Leone were converted from weekly to monthly earnings using a rate of 4.3 weeks per month. Figures for the Gambia were converted from daily to monthly earnings using a rate of 22 days per month.

Table 11-10. Wages in transport, storage, and communications. Data are from ILO, *Yearbook of Labor Statistics* (1988, 1993, 1994, and 1995). Refer to the definitions in Table 11-6.

Data for Burundi include family allowances. Data for Egypt are for establishments with 10 or more persons employed. Data for the Gambia are for establishments with five or more persons employed. Data for Kenya include the value of payments in kind. Data for Swaziland refer to skilled male workers only. Data for Zimbabwe include the value of payments in kind and refer to all persons engaged.

Figures for Egypt and Sierra Leone were converted from weekly to monthly earnings using a rate of 4.3 weeks per month. Figures for the Gambia were converted from daily to monthly earnings using a rate of 22 days per month.

Table 11-11. Wages in agriculture. Data are from ILO, *Yearbook of Labor Statistics* (1988, 1993, 1994, and 1995) and refer in most cases to general farm laborers.

International comparisons of wages in agriculture should be interpreted with caution because they entail wide coverage variations mainly as a result of the form of remuneration, the nature of the work, and the length of the working day.

For the following countries wages are paid entirely in cash: Botswana, Burundi, Egypt, Malawi, Mauritius, Seychelles, Swaziland, Tanzania, Tunisia, and Zambia.

For the following countries, wages shown are cash portion only, although the workers receive other payments in kind in addition: Ghana, Kenya, and Zimbabwe. Wages for these three countries include the value of food and lodging allowances.

Data for Burundi include family allowances. Data for Egypt are for establishments with 10 or more persons employed. Data for Ghana include forestry and fishing. Data for Kenya include the value of payments in kind. Data for Malawi include forestry and fishing. Data for Mauritius include sugar and tea factories. Data for Seychelles exclude hunting. Data for Swaziland include forestry and refer to skilled male workers only. Data for Zimbabwe include forestry and refer to all persons engaged.

Figures for Egypt were converted from weekly to monthly earnings using a rate of 4.3 weeks per month. Figures for Mauritius and Tunisia were converted from daily to monthly earnings using a rate of 22 days per month.

Methodology used for regional aggregations and period averages in chapter 11

Table	*Aggregations*[a]		
	(1)	*(6)*	*(8)*
11-1			
Col. 1-3	x		
Col. 4-6		x	
11-2		x	
11-3			x
11-4		x	
11-5		x	
11-6			x
11-7			x
11-8			x
11-9			x
11-10			x
11-11			x

Note: Regional aggregations are shown in the rows for Sub-Saharan Africa, North Africa, and All Africa. Period averages are shown in the last three columns. This table shows only the methodologies used in this chapter.

a. Regional aggregations: (1) simple total; (2) simple total of the first indicator divided by the simple total of the second indicator (same country coverage); (3) simple total of the gap-filled indicator; (4) simple total of the gap-filled main indicator divided by the simple total of the gap-filled secondary indicator; (5) simple total of the first gap-filled main indicator less the simple total of the second gap-filled main indicator, all divided by the simple total of the secondary indicator; (6) weighted total; (7) median; (8) no aggregation; (9) simple arithmetic mean.

12

Aid Flows

Official development assistance (ODA) consists of concessional financial flows that aim to promote economic development and welfare. ODA disbursements from bilateral and multilateral sources became increasingly important to Africa in the second half of the 1980s. For many countries, the foreign savings made available to them through ODA flows are equivalent to a sizable share of GDP and to the bulk of their domestic investment. Thus, monitoring aid flows is of special importance because of their significance for the economic performance of the region.

The tables in this chapter show data on net ODA flows and their relative importance to key economic and demographic indicators in recipient countries, real growth in net ODA flows to Sub-Saharan Africa in the 1980s and early 1990s from major donors or donor groups, and the share of each donor's worldwide aid portfolio allocated to Sub-Saharan Africa.

These flows are concessional in character and contain a grant element of at least 25 percent (based on a standard 10 percent discount rate). Net ODA disbursements equal gross ODA disbursements less principal repayments (amortization) of previous ODA loans.

ODA includes both grants (inflows of unrequited transfers from official sources) for current and capital expenditures and disbursements of concessional loans. However, because of different sources and definitions of data, the ODA flows shown in this chapter will not necessarily equal those that could be calculated by adding net disbursements of official concessional long-term loans (Table 6-1 less Table 6-4) and net official transfers (Tables 5-6 and 5-9). For example, one of the reasons for differences is that the flows shown here include "off-shore" disbursements of grants, primarily for technical cooperation, which are generally excluded from transfers as recorded in the balance of payments (Tables 5-6 and 5-9). Other reasons include possible differences in the timing of the recording of disbursements and in the recording of multilateral ODA.

The data on net ODA disbursements are taken from the most recent electronic version of OECD, *Geographical Distribution of Financial Flows to Developing Countries.* The tables include only those flows for which the recipient is specified in creditor reports.

Growth rates (based on constant price series) presented in this chapter may differ from those presented in *ADI 1992* because import price deflators (from World Bank) have been used to deflate the current price series, regardless of the type of donor, to indicate the volume of imports that aid can finance over time. In *ADI 1992*, donor country GNP deflators were used to deflate each DAC donor's aid flows (with the GNP deflators for DAC countries taken from the 1988 DAC chairman's report) thereby indicating the real resource transfer from individual donors, and the ODA flows from multilateral agencies and non-DAC donors were deflated by the average import price deflator for Sub-Saharan countries.

12-1. Net ODA from all donors, nominal

	Millions of U.S. dollars (current prices)											Annual average		
	1980	*1986*	*1987*	*1988*	*1989*	*1990*	*1991*	*1992*	*1993*	*1994*	*1995*	*75-84*	*85-89*	*90-MR*
SUB-SAHARAN AFRICA	7,394	10,475	12,094	13,725	14,521	17,283	16,996	18,279	16,830	18,152	17,914	5,837	11,868	17,576
excluding South Africa	7,394	10,475	12,094	13,725	14,521	17,283	16,996	18,279	16,555	17,857	17,528	5,837	11,868	17,416
excl. S.Africa & Nigeria	7,358	10,416	12,024	13,605	14,176	17,032	16,733	18,021	16,276	17,667	17,316	5,793	11,743	17,174
Angola	53	131	136	159	171	270	280	351	298	453	424	51	138	346
Benin	90	135	135	159	269	269	268	270	290	257	282	72	158	273
Botswana	106	102	156	151	160	149	136	114	134	87	91	83	133	118
Burkina Faso	212	281	277	295	270	335	424	439	470	436	487	165	264	432
Burundi	117	193	198	202	207	266	259	312	218	313	288	96	188	276
Cameroon	265	217	204	276	453	447	519	716	545	731	444	187	261	567
Cape Verde	64	109	89	88	89	111	107	124	120	122	112	42	89	116
Central African Republic	111	136	180	205	190	251	175	178	173	166	168	80	163	185
Chad	35	164	205	263	256	317	266	241	228	215	239	80	214	251
Comoros	43	46	54	52	45	46	65	49	50	40	43	30	49	49
Congo	92	107	149	87	91	218	134	114	123	362	125	82	101	179
Côte d'Ivoire	210	175	241	425	396	689	633	758	765	1,594	1,212	136	271	942
Djibouti	73	115	106	93	75	195	108	113	134	129	106	60	94	131
Equatorial Guinea	9	21	53	48	57	62	63	62	53	30	34	7	39	51
Eritrea	0	0	0	0	0	0	0	0	68	158	150	0	0	63
Ethiopia	212	629	627	963	749	1,020	1,097	1,182	1,094	1,075	888	208	736	1,059
Gabon	56	79	83	106	133	132	143	69	102	182	145	50	92	129
Gambia, The	55	103	105	85	100	100	103	113	87	71	48	38	88	87
Ghana	192	360	413	577	718	563	882	613	618	546	653	137	453	646
Guinea	90	169	222	257	365	296	382	450	410	360	416	68	226	386
Guinea-Bissau	59	71	113	103	118	132	118	108	97	177	119	49	92	125
Kenya	397	445	560	836	1,064	1,187	921	886	911	677	732	319	667	886
Lesotho	94	87	106	111	137	143	126	145	143	117	115	71	107	131
Liberia	98	97	78	65	59	112	158	120	123	64	123	78	78	117
Madagascar	230	310	332	298	349	399	456	363	363	289	303	148	295	362
Malawi	143	195	277	375	433	505	525	573	498	469	434	115	279	501
Mali	267	367	360	436	451	488	458	435	366	443	545	194	398	456
Mauritania	176	230	195	185	253	240	220	202	328	269	231	177	214	248
Mauritius	33	54	63	57	60	89	68	46	26	14	22	36	52	44
Mozambique	169	421	667	918	821	1,008	1,073	1,471	1,188	1,231	1,103	141	626	1,179
Namibia	0	16	17	23	59	123	184	143	155	138	187	0	24	155
Niger	170	312	363	379	305	398	377	370	347	377	270	165	333	357
Nigeria	36	59	69	120	345	250	263	259	279	190	212	44	125	242
Rwanda	155	208	242	249	230	293	364	354	358	715	711	131	222	466
São Tomé and Principe	4	12	17	25	46	56	53	58	47	51	79	7	23	57
Senegal	263	579	666	601	710	823	639	676	504	644	668	254	569	659
Seychelles	22	29	24	21	20	36	23	19	19	13	13	15	23	21
Sierra Leone	91	91	67	102	100	63	105	135	209	277	207	51	85	166
Somalia	433	509	589	433	427	494	186	654	890	538	191	283	462	492
South Africa	0	0	0	0	0	0	0	0	275	295	386	0	0	159
Sudan	625	945	898	938	773	827	881	550	458	413	236	541	936	561
Swaziland	50	34	44	37	28	55	54	54	53	56	56	33	34	55
Tanzania	679	666	900	1,016	918	1,175	1,081	1,343	953	969	882	513	797	1,067
Togo	91	171	122	206	200	261	202	224	98	126	190	81	162	183
Uganda	114	192	300	397	452	671	667	728	612	750	828	85	304	709
Zaire	428	422	675	553	731	898	476	269	178	246	195	318	537	377
Zambia	318	455	426	478	374	481	883	1,036	872	719	2,035	204	411	1,004
Zimbabwe	164	225	294	273	265	341	393	792	500	560	489	114	259	513
NORTH AFRICA	2,710	2,448	2,645	2,450	2,453	7,166	6,981	5,354	3,696	3,859	2,910	2,680	2,573	4,994
Algeria	176	165	214	172	159	263	340	406	349	420	312	137	177	348
Egypt, Arab Republic	1,387	1,673	1,726	1,498	1,545	5,439	5,025	3,604	2,401	2,695	2,022	1,775	1,640	3,531
Libya	17	11	7	6	17	20	26	6	6	7	8	9	9	12
Morocco	898	377	421	457	450	1,051	1,232	947	713	631	496	536	494	845
Tunisia	232	222	277	318	283	393	357	390	228	107	71	223	252	258
ALL AFRICA	10,104	12,923	14,738	16,175	16,974	24,448	23,976	23,633	20,526	22,011	20,824	8,517	14,441	22,570

Note: In 1995, Zambia completed a 3 year Rights Arrangement Program permitting disbursment of 833.4 M SDR under a new SAF/ESAF arrangement.

12-2. Net ODA from DAC donors, nominal

	Millions of U.S. dollars (current prices)											Annual average		
	1980	1986	1987	1988	1989	1990	1991	1992	1993	1994	1995	75-84	85-89	90-MR
SUB-SAHARAN AFRICA	4,350	6,621	7,639	8,972	9,061	10,820	10,272	10,778	10,171	10,332	9,886	3,429	7,517	10,376
excluding South Africa	4,350	6,621	7,639	8,972	9,061	10,820	10,272	10,778	9,987	10,117	9,567	3,429	7,517	10,257
excl. S.Africa & Nigeria	4,333	6,582	7,588	8,875	8,751	10,648	10,100	10,641	9,916	10,070	9,495	3,402	7,414	10,145
Angola	36	94	98	106	110	165	159	195	156	226	248	30	94	191
Benin	36	73	77	93	149	126	160	171	148	142	177	37	88	154
Botswana	83	82	124	125	120	121	104	93	80	57	54	63	102	85
Burkina Faso	151	175	196	219	199	239	270	268	255	265	251	112	182	258
Burundi	60	90	88	83	90	158	123	149	126	109	107	50	85	128
Cameroon	171	177	180	240	301	339	377	579	528	397	345	130	205	428
Cape Verde	39	76	64	61	61	77	81	82	83	82	72	28	61	79
Central African Republic	75	85	109	107	99	100	98	107	117	94	122	52	92	106
Chad	20	102	120	146	131	183	138	148	146	104	127	44	119	141
Comoros	13	21	33	35	32	31	31	23	29	18	22	11	28	25
Congo	55	101	131	78	81	202	118	102	116	253	105	49	88	149
Côte d'Ivoire	152	138	221	226	260	531	435	527	709	820	727	105	191	625
Djibouti	32	65	60	71	64	88	83	92	94	94	80	35	61	88
Equatorial Guinea	1	11	33	25	36	44	35	36	28	17	22	2	22	30
Eritrea	0	0	0	0	0	0	0	0	48	96	95	0	0	40
Ethiopia	91	397	313	560	379	510	464	457	417	567	525	86	413	490
Gabon	49	59	71	99	121	127	141	65	98	161	136	42	80	121
Gambia, The	17	59	51	55	56	57	55	50	50	38	25	16	50	46
Ghana	107	121	131	236	352	265	449	333	312	332	359	75	187	341
Guinea	33	98	120	160	192	139	173	234	185	186	220	20	126	189
Guinea-Bissau	34	41	48	52	67	78	65	59	58	125	79	29	46	77
Kenya	277	383	444	610	621	735	608	520	427	401	459	244	477	525
Lesotho	64	56	63	70	74	85	74	69	74	46	62	44	63	68
Liberia	60	69	52	48	39	42	57	26	25	36	31	53	54	36
Madagascar	91	176	181	214	175	268	274	216	228	190	195	77	169	228
Malawi	76	85	170	181	182	216	209	208	159	251	221	63	134	211
Mali	131	204	222	260	301	313	280	239	221	243	285	104	248	263
Mauritania	54	105	98	114	162	106	110	116	196	128	126	45	116	131
Mauritius	25	48	50	45	52	76	62	35	27	8	10	24	43	36
Mozambique	115	319	535	732	579	752	772	1,010	817	733	702	104	477	798
Namibia	0	7	16	17	36	39	95	98	123	113	144	0	16	102
Niger	105	184	215	242	200	255	264	262	254	262	190	97	209	248
Nigeria	17	39	51	97	310	173	172	138	71	47	72	27	103	112
Rwanda	97	124	138	137	132	183	233	188	201	487	338	83	127	272
São Tomé and Principe	1	7	4	9	23	32	25	27	29	27	56	2	9	33
Senegal	182	316	359	369	537	589	421	454	364	475	397	157	355	450
Seychelles	18	21	19	18	15	33	17	15	7	7	11	14	17	15
Sierra Leone	57	51	44	53	72	40	68	74	106	54	60	28	50	67
Somalia	139	354	399	311	267	270	116	497	688	438	119	93	299	355
South Africa	0	0	0	0	0	0	0	0	183	214	318	0	0	119
Sudan	272	469	443	502	436	420	369	188	164	175	130	211	499	241
Swaziland	33	25	30	23	12	36	31	27	33	28	38	22	21	32
Tanzania	524	514	719	786	692	844	764	816	650	570	587	383	617	705
Togo	52	92	86	128	108	155	125	135	77	64	115	46	93	112
Uganda	42	77	87	188	164	244	285	255	348	345	422	31	112	316
Zaire	317	296	339	403	434	633	343	163	99	97	117	221	336	242
Zambia	234	349	346	407	314	409	583	699	511	434	439	156	326	512
Zimbabwe	112	191	265	233	228	296	359	536	310	280	348	86	226	355
NORTH AFRICA	1,661	2,133	2,269	2,199	2,095	4,221	5,342	4,405	2,640	3,077	2,381	1,427	2,192	3,678
Algeria	118	119	137	121	96	232	307	376	265	374	290	116	123	307
Egypt, Arab Republic	1,187	1,566	1,575	1,435	1,409	3,172	4,157	2,996	1,824	2,311	1,689	959	1,533	2,691
Libya	10	8	3	2	7	8	3	2	2	2	3	4	5	3
Morocco	188	292	351	404	403	595	611	734	422	318	347	189	354	505
Tunisia	158	147	203	237	180	214	264	298	127	73	51	160	178	171
ALL AFRICA	6,011	8,754	9,908	11,171	11,156	15,042	15,613	15,184	12,810	13,408	12,267	4,857	9,709	14,054

12-3. Net ODA from non-DAC bilateral donors, nominal

	Millions of U.S. dollars (current prices)											Annual average		
	1980	*1986*	*1987*	*1988*	*1989*	*1990*	*1991*	*1992*	*1993*	*1994*	*1995*	*75-84*	*85-89*	*90-MR*
SUB-SAHARAN AFRICA	685	445	368	196	99	457	131	42	36	14	11	561	317	115
excluding South Africa	685	445	368	196	99	457	131	42	36	14	11	561	317	115
excl. S.Africa & Nigeria	684	445	368	196	99	457	131	42	36	14	11	561	317	115
Angola	1	1	2	3	3	2	2	1	3	0	0	0	1	1
Benin	1	3	1	1	5	0	-2	0	0	3	7	1	2	1
Botswana	0	-1	0	1	-2	-2	2	-2	7	1	0	3	0	1
Burkina Faso	0	11	7	2	0	11	10	2	0	1	6	2	5	5
Burundi	3	8	12	4	4	0	-3	-2	-2	-3	-3	4	7	-2
Cameroon	23	3	0	-4	0	-3	-2	-1	0	0	1	7	0	-1
Cape Verde	2	2	1	1	1	0	0	0	1	0	0	1	1	0
Central African Republic	2	3	8	2	-1	2	3	0	0	-1	0	1	3	1
Chad	0	0	0	0	0	2	2	0	3	1	1	3	0	1
Comoros	17	2	0	0	0	0	0	0	0	0	0	7	1	0
Congo	15	-1	0	0	0	0	0	0	0	0	0	10	0	0
Côte d'Ivoire	0	0	0	0	0	0	0	0	0	0	0	0	0	0
Djibouti	32	29	24	3	1	88	3	-1	10	12	3	16	14	19
Equatorial Guinea	0	0	0	0	0	0	6	0	0	0	0	0	0	1
Eritrea	0	0	0	0	0	0	0	0	1	12	5	0	0	3
Ethiopia	1	-1	-2	-1	-2	68	1	0	1	0	0	11	1	12
Gabon	0	14	5	-2	-1	0	0	0	0	0	-1	3	3	0
Gambia, The	7	-1	0	-2	-1	0	2	-2	-2	-2	-2	5	-1	-1
Ghana	26	3	-5	13	2	1	9	-4	-4	-6	-6	7	2	-2
Guinea	0	4	12	14	18	4	-1	-2	-4	-2	6	12	10	0
Guinea-Bissau	1	4	9	6	2	0	1	3	1	0	0	3	5	1
Kenya	0	5	4	3	0	5	3	-4	-4	-5	2	4	7	-1
Lesotho	-1	0	-1	-1	0	0	-1	1	1	0	0	0	0	0
Liberia	9	0	0	0	0	0	0	0	0	0	0	3	0	0
Madagascar	48	-2	-2	-1	-2	-1	0	0	0	0	0	12	-2	0
Malawi	-1	0	0	0	0	0	0	0	0	0	0	0	0	0
Mali	33	40	8	6	3	15	5	4	-4	-11	-14	17	16	-1
Mauritania	86	63	14	-4	-5	25	1	-7	-6	-10	-16	83	26	-2
Mauritius	0	2	3	3	-1	1	-2	-1	0	-1	-2	1	2	-1
Mozambique	20	7	3	3	3	0	0	2	3	2	2	3	4	2
Namibia	0	0	0	0	0	0	0	0	0	0	0	0	0	0
Niger	1	5	9	6	2	4	4	0	2	5	0	17	5	2
Nigeria	1	0	0	0	0	0	0	0	0	0	0	0	0	0
Rwanda	1	6	6	3	6	10	3	0	2	1	0	2	5	3
São Tomé and Principe	0	0	0	0	0	0	0	0	0	0	0	0	0	0
Senegal	2	33	30	24	12	2	22	16	14	1	12	19	27	11
Seychelles	1	1	1	0	0	0	0	0	1	0	-1	0	1	0
Sierra Leone	4	6	4	10	0	0	0	0	0	0	0	2	4	0
Somalia	128	-9	1	4	1	82	0	10	9	0	0	81	7	17
South Africa	0	0	0	0	0	0	0	0	0	0	0	0	0	0
Sudan	161	191	208	104	25	8	16	20	2	0	1	183	148	8
Swaziland	0	0	0	0	0	0	0	0	0	0	0	0	0	0
Tanzania	27	5	0	0	1	3	-3	-3	-1	6	4	12	3	1
Togo	0	8	3	-1	-1	-1	-1	-2	0	0	0	1	4	0
Uganda	2	3	5	0	28	43	51	15	1	11	7	6	7	21
Zaire	5	0	0	0	0	77	0	1	0	0	0	3	0	13
Zambia	22	0	0	0	0	0	0	0	0	0	0	11	0	0
Zimbabwe	5	-2	0	-3	-2	9	-1	-3	-1	-3	-4	6	-2	0
NORTH AFRICA	738	190	214	35	47	2,655	985	455	389	110	101	794	176	782
Algeria	41	28	52	27	22	8	2	4	1	2	-12	7	28	1
Egypt, Arab Republic	4	54	74	-16	-14	2,186	510	409	380	94	117	453	14	616
Libya	0	0	0	0	0	0	0	0	0	0	0	0	0	0
Morocco	644	70	62	20	-2	361	470	53	18	29	19	299	111	158
Tunisia	49	39	27	3	42	100	3	-10	-9	-15	-23	36	23	8
ALL AFRICA	1,423	634	582	231	147	3,112	1,116	497	425	124	112	1,355	493	898

12-4. Net ODA from multilateral donors, nominal

	Millions of U.S. dollars (current prices)											Annual average		
	1980	1986	1987	1988	1989	1990	1991	1992	1993	1994	1995	75-84	85-89	90-MR
SUB-SAHARAN AFRICA	2,359	3,410	4,087	4,557	5,361	6,005	6,593	7,459	6,624	7,806	8,018	1,847	4,035	7,084
excluding South Africa	2,359	3,410	4,087	4,557	5,361	6,005	6,593	7,459	6,532	7,726	7,950	1,847	4,035	7,044
excl. S.Africa & Nigeria	2,341	3,390	4,068	4,534	5,325	5,927	6,502	7,338	6,324	7,583	7,810	1,830	4,012	6,914
Angola	16	37	36	50	58	103	119	156	139	227	177	20	42	154
Benin	53	60	57	64	115	144	111	100	142	112	98	34	68	118
Botswana	23	22	32	25	42	29	30	23	47	29	37	17	31	32
Burkina Faso	61	95	75	73	71	85	143	169	215	171	230	52	77	169
Burundi	54	95	98	115	113	108	139	165	95	208	183	42	95	149
Cameroon	71	37	24	40	153	111	143	138	17	334	98	51	56	140
Cape Verde	23	31	24	26	27	34	27	43	36	40	40	13	27	37
Central African Republic	34	47	63	96	91	149	74	71	57	73	45	27	68	78
Chad	15	62	85	117	125	131	126	92	79	110	112	33	95	108
Comoros	13	23	21	17	13	16	34	26	21	22	22	12	20	23
Congo	22	7	17	9	10	16	16	12	7	109	20	23	13	30
Côte d'Ivoire	58	37	20	199	135	159	198	231	57	774	486	31	80	317
Djibouti	9	22	22	18	10	18	23	22	30	23	24	9	19	23
Equatorial Guinea	8	10	20	23	21	18	22	26	25	14	12	4	17	20
Eritrea	0	0	0	0	0	0	0	0	19	50	50	0	0	20
Ethiopia	120	234	316	404	372	442	632	725	675	507	362	111	322	557
Gabon	7	6	7	9	13	6	3	5	5	20	10	5	9	8
Gambia, The	31	44	54	32	45	43	46	65	39	35	24	17	39	42
Ghana	59	236	287	328	363	297	425	285	310	221	301	55	264	306
Guinea	57	68	91	83	156	153	210	219	229	175	190	36	90	196
Guinea-Bissau	24	27	56	45	49	54	52	46	38	52	40	18	41	47
Kenya	120	57	112	223	444	448	310	371	488	281	271	71	183	361
Lesotho	31	31	44	42	64	58	53	74	68	71	53	27	44	63
Liberia	29	28	27	17	20	70	101	93	98	28	92	21	24	80
Madagascar	91	136	153	86	176	132	182	147	135	99	108	59	128	134
Malawi	68	110	106	194	252	289	316	365	339	218	213	52	144	290
Mali	103	123	131	170	147	160	174	192	149	210	274	73	134	193
Mauritania	36	62	83	74	96	109	109	93	138	151	121	49	72	120
Mauritius	8	5	10	9	10	13	8	11	-1	7	14	12	7	9
Mozambique	34	95	129	183	238	256	301	459	367	496	400	34	145	380
Namibia	0	9	1	5	23	84	89	46	32	25	43	0	8	53
Niger	64	123	140	132	103	140	108	108	91	111	80	51	118	107
Nigeria	18	20	18	23	36	78	91	121	208	143	140	17	23	130
Rwanda	57	78	99	109	92	100	127	166	155	226	373	46	90	191
São Tomé and Principe	3	5	13	16	23	24	28	31	19	24	23	5	13	25
Senegal	79	230	277	209	162	231	196	205	126	168	259	78	187	197
Seychelles	3	7	5	3	5	3	6	4	12	6	3	2	5	6
Sierra Leone	30	34	19	40	28	23	37	61	103	223	147	21	31	99
Somalia	166	164	189	118	159	143	70	146	193	100	72	109	157	121
South Africa	0	0	0	0	0	0	0	0	92	80	68	0	0	40
Sudan	192	286	248	333	312	399	496	342	292	238	105	147	289	312
Swaziland	17	9	15	14	17	19	23	27	20	29	18	12	12	22
Tanzania	128	147	180	230	225	327	319	530	304	392	291	118	177	361
Togo	39	71	33	79	93	107	78	91	20	62	75	34	65	72
Uganda	70	112	209	210	261	384	331	459	264	395	399	49	186	372
Zaire	106	126	336	150	297	188	134	105	79	148	78	93	201	122
Zambia	62	105	80	71	60	72	301	337	361	285	1,596	37	85	492
Zimbabwe	47	36	28	43	39	36	35	259	191	282	145	22	34	158
NORTH AFRICA	311	125	162	216	311	290	654	493	667	673	427	459	204	534
Algeria	17	18	25	24	41	23	31	27	83	44	35	14	26	40
Egypt, Arab Republic	196	53	78	79	150	81	358	199	198	290	216	363	93	223
Libya	7	3	4	4	10	13	23	5	4	5	5	6	5	9
Morocco	66	15	8	32	49	94	151	161	273	285	129	48	30	182
Tunisia	25	37	46	77	61	79	91	102	110	49	43	28	51	79
ALL AFRICA	2,670	3,535	4,248	4,773	5,672	6,295	7,248	7,952	7,291	8,479	8,445	2,306	4,239	7,618

Note: In 1995, Zambia completed a 3 year Rights Arrangement Program permitting disbursment of 833.4 M SDR under a new SAF/ESAF arrangement.

12-5. Net ODA from all donors, real

	Millions of U.S. dollars (constant 1987 prices)											Average annual percentage growth		
	1980	1986	1987	1988	1989	1990	1991	1992	1993	1994	1995	75-84	85-89	90-MR
SUB-SAHARAN AFRICA	7,622	11,329	12,094	12,979	13,510	15,110	15,293	16,499	15,936	16,784	15,505	6.7	9.9	2.4
excluding South Africa	7,622	11,329	12,094	12,979	13,510	15,110	15,293	16,499	15,675	16,512	15,171	6.7	9.9	2.0
excl. S. Africa & Nigeria	7,585	11,265	12,024	12,865	13,189	14,891	15,057	16,266	15,411	16,336	14,988	6.9	9.6	2.1
Angola	55	142	136	150	159	236	252	317	282	419	367	19.7	9.3	14.5
Benin	93	146	135	150	250	235	242	244	274	238	244	2.4	19.8	0.2
Botswana	109	111	156	143	149	130	122	103	126	80	79	5.4	7.3	-9.6
Burkina Faso	219	304	277	278	251	293	381	396	445	403	421	4.0	4.5	8.7
Burundi	121	209	198	191	193	232	233	281	207	289	249	9.4	4.7	4.0
Cameroon	273	234	204	261	422	391	467	646	516	676	384	1.5	14.5	3.3
Cape Verde	66	118	89	83	82	97	97	112	113	112	97	13.3	1.8	3.4
Central African Republic	114	147	180	194	176	220	157	160	164	154	145	6.4	7.8	-4.4
Chad	36	177	205	249	238	277	239	217	215	199	207	-4.4	11.7	-4.2
Comoros	44	50	54	49	42	41	58	44	48	37	37	3.0	-1.8	-2.5
Congo	95	116	149	82	85	191	120	103	117	335	109	2.7	-2.2	6.8
Côte d'Ivoire	216	189	241	402	368	603	569	684	724	1,474	1,049	-0.6	27.5	20.3
Djibouti	75	124	106	88	70	170	97	102	127	119	92	4.9	-7.5	1.4
Equatorial Guinea	9	22	53	45	53	54	57	56	50	28	29	11.3	29.9	-10.8
Eritrea	0	0	0	0	0	0	0	0	64	146	130	..	..	..
Ethiopia	219	681	627	910	697	892	987	1,067	1,036	994	768	5.5	9.1	2.0
Gabon	58	85	83	100	124	116	129	63	97	168	125	2.2	9.0	1.8
Gambia, The	57	111	105	80	93	87	92	102	82	66	41	15.4	9.9	-10.6
Ghana	198	389	413	546	668	493	794	553	585	505	565	5.4	25.3	-2.7
Guinea	93	183	222	243	340	258	344	406	388	333	360	16.7	21.0	2.9
Guinea-Bissau	61	77	113	97	109	115	106	97	92	164	103	16.9	13.6	1.3
Kenya	409	481	560	791	990	1,038	829	800	862	626	633	9.7	17.1	-7.9
Lesotho	97	94	106	105	127	125	114	131	135	108	99	12.2	2.2	-3.0
Liberia	101	105	78	61	55	98	142	108	116	59	107	18.1	-17.5	2.8
Madagascar	237	336	332	282	325	349	410	327	344	268	262	8.3	12.7	-4.7
Malawi	147	211	277	355	403	442	472	517	471	434	375	6.5	21.4	-0.9
Mali	275	397	360	412	419	426	412	393	347	409	472	4.5	1.9	0.4
Mauritania	181	248	195	175	235	210	198	182	311	249	200	0.4	-0.4	1.1
Mauritius	34	59	63	54	56	78	61	41	25	13	19	1.2	11.6	-24.1
Mozambique	174	456	667	868	763	881	965	1,328	1,124	1,139	955	38.3	26.0	4.9
Namibia	0	17	17	21	55	108	166	129	146	128	162	..	54.9	13.2
Niger	175	337	363	358	284	348	339	334	329	349	234	-1.0	7.6	-2.2
Nigeria	37	64	69	114	321	219	236	234	264	176	184	-11.8	50.6	-6.9
Rwanda	160	225	242	236	214	256	327	319	339	661	615	4.7	3.8	20.0
São Tomé and Principe	4	13	17	23	43	49	47	52	45	47	68	13.0	25.1	4.6
Senegal	271	626	666	569	661	719	575	610	478	596	578	6.6	12.6	-3.4
Seychelles	23	31	24	20	18	31	21	17	18	12	11	3.3	-1.6	-11.9
Sierra Leone	94	99	67	97	93	55	94	122	198	256	179	14.9	6.5	22.9
Somalia	446	550	589	410	397	432	168	590	843	497	166	10.5	0.7	-2.6
South Africa	0	0	0	0	0	0	0	0	261	272	334	..	..	..
Sudan	644	1,022	898	887	719	723	793	496	434	382	204	10.4	-2.8	-18.3
Swaziland	52	36	44	35	26	48	49	49	50	52	48	2.1	-0.7	7.3
Tanzania	700	721	900	961	854	1,027	972	1,213	903	896	763	7.0	10.7	-2.4
Togo	94	185	122	195	186	228	182	202	92	116	164	4.0	9.1	-8.2
Uganda	118	208	300	376	421	586	600	657	580	694	717	19.6	20.2	7.0
Zaire	441	457	675	523	680	785	428	243	169	227	169	0.8	15.9	-23.8
Zambia	328	492	426	452	348	420	795	935	826	664	1,761	10.9	5.5	23.1
Zimbabwe	169	243	294	258	246	298	354	715	474	518	423	64.9	-3.9	11.4
NORTH AFRICA	2,794	2,648	2,645	2,317	2,282	6,265	6,281	4,832	3,499	3,568	2,518	-5.3	-5.1	-4.9
Algeria	181	179	214	163	147	230	306	367	330	388	270	-6.9	0.2	11.1
Egypt, Arab Republic	1,430	1,809	1,726	1,417	1,437	4,755	4,521	3,253	2,273	2,492	1,750	-7.8	-7.3	-4.8
Libya	18	12	7	5	16	18	24	6	6	6	7	-8.7	12.7	-18.7
Morocco	926	408	421	432	418	918	1,109	855	675	584	429	6.6	-4.4	-4.6
Tunisia	239	241	277	300	263	344	321	352	215	99	62	-5.2	9.0	-22.8
ALL AFRICA	10,416	13,977	14,738	15,296	15,792	21,376	21,575	21,332	19,435	20,353	18,024	2.4	6.9	0.7

Note: In 1995, Zambia completed a 3 year Rights Arrangement Program permitting disbursment of 833.4 M SDR under a new SAF/ESAF arrangement.

12-6. Net ODA from DAC donors, real

	Millions of U.S. dollars (constant 1987 prices)											Average annual percentage growth		
	1980	*1986*	*1987*	*1988*	*1989*	*1990*	*1991*	*1992*	*1993*	*1994*	*1995*	*75-84*	*85-89*	*90-MR*
SUB-SAHARAN AFRICA	4,484	7,161	7,639	8,484	8,430	9,460	9,243	9,729	9,630	9,553	8,556	7.2	10.6	0.4
excluding South Africa	4,484	7,161	7,639	8,484	8,430	9,460	9,243	9,729	9,456	9,355	8,281	7.2	10.6	-0.2
excl. S. Africa & Nigeria	4,467	7,119	7,588	8,392	8,142	9,309	9,088	9,605	9,389	9,311	8,218	7.6	10.0	0.2
Angola	37	101	98	100	103	144	143	176	147	209	214	23.4	10.1	11.3
Benin	37	78	77	88	139	110	144	155	140	131	153	1.2	22.8	2.2
Botswana	86	89	124	119	112	106	94	84	76	52	47	3.9	12.9	-14.0
Burkina Faso	156	190	196	207	185	209	243	242	241	245	217	6.0	8.3	2.9
Burundi	62	97	88	79	83	138	111	134	119	100	93	8.9	-0.3	-0.8
Cameroon	176	191	180	227	280	296	339	523	500	367	299	3.6	11.4	3.7
Cape Verde	40	83	64	57	57	67	72	74	79	76	62	25.4	5.1	2.0
Central African Republic	77	92	109	102	92	87	88	96	111	87	106	8.0	6.7	2.3
Chad	21	111	120	138	122	160	124	134	138	96	110	-4.0	11.8	-4.3
Comoros	13	22	33	33	30	27	27	21	27	16	19	-0.7	11.2	-8.1
Congo	57	109	131	73	75	177	106	92	110	234	91	2.3	3.5	4.2
Côte d'Ivoire	157	149	221	214	242	464	391	476	671	758	629	2.0	16.1	17.0
Djibouti	33	70	60	67	59	77	75	83	89	87	69	-0.9	3.1	3.1
Equatorial Guinea	1	11	33	23	33	38	32	32	26	15	19	..	36.8	-12.5
Eritrea	0	0	0	0	0	0	0	0	46	88	82	..	..	..
Ethiopia	94	429	313	529	352	446	418	413	395	524	455	0.1	7.9	3.8
Gabon	51	63	71	93	113	111	126	58	92	149	117	3.5	10.6	1.4
Gambia, The	18	64	51	52	52	50	49	45	47	35	22	16.1	8.3	-11.3
Ghana	110	130	131	223	327	232	404	300	296	307	310	1.5	25.0	0.3
Guinea	34	106	120	151	178	122	156	211	175	172	190	19.9	30.1	3.7
Guinea-Bissau	35	44	48	49	62	68	58	53	55	116	68	7.3	14.8	4.8
Kenya	286	414	444	577	577	643	547	469	404	370	397	8.7	12.8	-8.6
Lesotho	66	61	63	66	68	74	67	62	70	42	53	13.6	0.2	-6.4
Liberia	62	75	52	46	36	37	51	24	23	33	27	24.0	-19.9	-6.5
Madagascar	94	191	181	202	163	234	247	195	216	176	169	11.9	11.3	-2.2
Malawi	78	92	170	172	169	189	188	188	150	232	191	-0.7	30.0	2.0
Mali	135	220	222	246	280	273	252	216	209	225	246	5.8	0.5	-3.4
Mauritania	56	114	98	108	151	93	99	105	186	118	109	11.1	9.3	0.5
Mauritius	26	52	50	42	48	66	55	31	25	7	8	3.6	13.5	-31.3
Mozambique	119	345	535	692	539	657	694	912	774	678	607	39.7	26.5	1.9
Namibia	0	7	16	16	34	34	86	88	116	104	125	..	74.2	25.9
Niger	108	199	215	229	186	223	238	236	240	242	164	-0.9	7.4	-0.7
Nigeria	18	42	51	92	288	151	154	124	67	44	63	-17.1	74.2	-24.5
Rwanda	100	134	138	130	123	160	210	169	191	451	293	4.1	3.0	17.8
São Tomé and Principe	1	8	4	8	21	28	23	24	27	25	48	10.7	32.8	9.0
Senegal	188	341	359	349	499	515	379	410	344	439	344	8.5	13.5	-5.3
Seychelles	19	22	19	17	14	29	15	14	6	7	10	2.0	0.2	-16.1
Sierra Leone	59	55	44	50	67	35	61	67	100	50	52	17.0	18.0	1.5
Somalia	143	383	399	294	248	236	104	449	651	405	103	29.3	6.4	1.0
South Africa	0	0	0	0	0	0	0	0	174	198	276	..	..	..
Sudan	280	507	443	474	405	367	332	169	155	161	113	23.0	-1.7	-20.0
Swaziland	34	27	30	21	11	32	28	24	32	25	33	1.7	-7.6	11.3
Tanzania	540	556	719	743	644	738	687	737	616	527	508	5.3	11.1	-5.2
Togo	54	99	86	121	100	135	112	122	73	59	99	2.8	14.1	-7.3
Uganda	43	84	87	178	152	214	257	230	329	319	365	25.0	30.4	14.0
Zaire	327	320	339	381	404	553	308	147	94	90	101	-0.7	12.9	-27.4
Zambia	241	378	346	385	292	358	524	631	483	401	380	8.7	9.4	3.4
Zimbabwe	115	207	265	220	212	259	323	484	294	259	301	59.2	-3.5	3.5
NORTH AFRICA	1,712	2,307	2,269	2,079	1,949	3,691	4,806	3,976	2,499	2,845	2,061	8.4	-4.7	-3.5
Algeria	122	129	137	114	89	203	276	339	251	345	251	-5.4	-7.3	15.7
Egypt, Arab Republic	1,224	1,694	1,575	1,357	1,311	2,773	3,741	2,704	1,727	2,137	1,462	18.3	-7.6	-3.4
Libya	10	9	3	2	6	7	3	1	2	2	3	-12.4	4.2	-18.3
Morocco	194	316	351	382	375	521	550	662	400	294	301	1.5	5.4	-7.3
Tunisia	163	159	203	224	168	187	237	269	120	67	44	-4.3	6.1	-21.3
ALL AFRICA	6,196	9,468	9,908	10,563	10,379	13,151	14,049	13,705	12,129	12,398	10,617	7.4	6.6	-0.7

12-7. Net ODA from non DAC donors, real

	Millions of U.S. dollars (constant 1987 prices)											Average annual percentage growth		
	1980	1986	1987	1988	1989	1990	1991	1992	1993	1994	1995	75-84	85-89	90-MR
SUB-SAHARAN AFRICA	706	481	368	186	92	400	118	38	34	13	9	1.9	-28.4	-41.4
excluding South Africa	706	481	368	186	92	400	118	38	34	13	10	1.9	-28.4	-41.3
excl. S. Africa & Nigeria	705	481	368	186	92	400	118	38	34	13	10	1.9	-28.4	-41.4
Angola	1	1	2	2	2	2	2	0	3	0	0	..	18.6	-35.6
Benin	1	3	1	1	5	0	-2	0	0	3	6	-0.4	-3.5	-3.6
Botswana	0	-1	0	1	-2	-1	1	-2	7	1	0	..	..	-31.3
Burkina Faso	0	11	7	2	0	10	9	2	0	0	5	..	-54.0	9.5
Burundi	3	9	12	3	4	0	-2	-1	-2	-3	-3	10.3	-21.3	..
Cameroon	24	3	0	-4	0	-2	-2	-1	0	0	1	5.6	-73.4	..
Cape Verde	2	2	1	1	0	0	0	0	0	0	0	..	-20.1	-17.4
Central African Republic	2	4	8	2	-1	2	2	0	0	-1	0	-20.4	94.9	-32.3
Chad	0	0	0	0	0	2	2	0	2	1	1	-29.3	..	-21.8
Comoros	18	3	0	0	0	0	0	0	0	0	0	15.2	-54.6	..
Congo	15	-1	0	0	0	0	0	0	0	0	0	11.4	..	..
Côte d'Ivoire	0	0	0	0	0	0	0	0	0	0	0	..	..	..
Djibouti	33	31	24	3	1	77	3	-1	9	11	3	-13.7	-47.6	1.4
Equatorial Guinea	0	0	0	0	0	0	6	0	0	0	0	..	..	-1.1
Eritrea	0	0	0	0	0	0	0	0	1	11	5	..	..	..
Ethiopia	1	-2	-2	-1	-2	59	1	0	1	0	0	14.5	..	-67.4
Gabon	0	15	5	-1	-1	0	0	0	0	0	-1	..	..	..
Gambia, The	7	-1	0	-2	-1	0	2	-2	-2	-2	-1	-3.8	..	..
Ghana	27	4	-5	13	2	1	8	-4	-4	-5	-5	16.1	..	..
Guinea	0	5	12	13	17	4	-1	-2	-4	-2	5	13.7	7.8	..
Guinea-Bissau	1	4	9	6	2	0	1	2	1	0	0	-3.5	5.4	-27.5
Kenya	0	5	4	3	0	4	3	-3	-4	-5	2	22.7	-48.0	..
Lesotho	-1	0	-1	-1	0	0	-1	1	1	0	0	..	..	..
Liberia	9	0	0	0	0	0	0	0	0	0	0	-26.8	..	..
Madagascar	49	-2	-2	-1	-2	-1	0	0	0	0	0	43.0	..	..
Malawi	-1	0	0	0	0	0	0	0	0	0	0	..	..	..
Mali	34	43	8	5	3	13	4	3	-4	-10	-12	3.2	-33.2	-3.4
Mauritania	89	68	14	-3	-4	22	1	-7	-5	-10	-14	-5.9	-33.1	..
Mauritius	0	2	3	3	-1	1	-1	-1	0	-1	-1	..	1.0	
Mozambique	21	7	3	3	3	0	0	2	3	2	2	5.0	-10.5	25.6
Namibia	0	0	0	0	0	0	0	0	0	0	0	..	..	..
Niger	1	6	9	5	2	3	4	0	2	4	0	13.9	-8.6	-18.5
Nigeria	1	0	0	0	0	0	0	0	0	0	0	..	..	..
Rwanda	1	7	6	3	6	9	3	0	2	1	0	-11.2	-9.4	-31.6
São Tomé and Principe	0	0	0	0	0	0	0	0	0	0	0	..	..	..
Senegal	2	36	30	23	11	2	20	15	14	1	11	13.6	-27.1	-4.7
Seychelles	1	2	1	0	0	0	0	0	1	0	0	..	17.7	..
Sierra Leone	4	6	4	10	0	0	0	0	0	0	0	..	-23.2	..
Somalia	132	-10	1	4	1	72	0	9	9	0	0	-12.3	-44.2	-26.2
South Africa	0	0	0	0	0	0	0	0	0	0	0	..	..	..
Sudan	166	206	208	98	23	7	14	18	2	0	1	0.7	-27.6	-54.6
Swaziland	0	0	0	0	0	0	0	0	0	0	0	..	..	..
Tanzania	28	6	0	0	1	3	-2	-2	0	5	4	27.6	-48.5	22.7
Togo	0	9	3	-1	-1	0	-1	-2	0	0	0	-3.0	1.7	..
Uganda	2	3	5	0	26	37	46	13	1	10	6	-12.5	191.4	-31.8
Zaire	5	0	0	0	0	67	0	1	0	0	0	-0.1	..	..
Zambia	23	0	0	0	0	0	0	0	0	0	0	12.4	..	..
Zimbabwe	5	-2	0	-3	-1	8	-1	-2	-1	-2	-3	..	..	..
NORTH AFRICA	761	205	214	33	44	2,321	886	411	368	102	88	-28.4	-24.0	-16.6
Algeria	42	30	52	26	21	7	2	4	1	2	-10	..	13.5	-38.9
Egypt, Arab Republic	4	58	74	-15	-13	1,911	459	369	359	87	101	-58.8	..	-43.1
Libya	0	0	0	0	0	0	0	0	0	0	0	..	..	..
Morocco	664	75	62	19	-2	316	423	47	17	26	17	17.0	-38.8	-49.7
Tunisia	51	42	27	3	39	87	2	-9	-9	-14	-20	-9.4	14.6	..
ALL AFRICA	1,467	686	582	219	136	2,721	1,004	449	402	114	97	-14.1	-28.2	-25.6

12-8. Net ODA from multilateral donors, real

	Millions of U.S. dollars (constant 1987 prices)											Average annual percentage growth		
	1980	1986	1987	1988	1989	1990	1991	1992	1993	1994	1995	75-84	85-89	90-MR
SUB-SAHARAN AFRICA	2,432	3,688	4,087	4,309	4,988	5,250	5,933	6,732	6,272	7,218	6,940	7.1	12.3	6.2
excluding South Africa	2,432	3,688	4,087	4,309	4,988	5,250	5,933	6,732	6,184	7,144	6,881	7.1	12.3	6.0
excl. S. Africa & Nigeria	2,413	3,666	4,068	4,288	4,955	5,182	5,851	6,623	5,988	7,012	6,760	7.2	12.3	5.7
Angola	16	39	36	48	54	90	107	141	132	210	153	19.6	7.3	19.7
Benin	55	65	57	61	107	126	100	90	134	103	84	3.2	16.1	-2.8
Botswana	24	23	32	23	39	25	27	20	44	27	32	5.8	0.1	-0.1
Burkina Faso	63	103	75	69	66	74	129	152	204	158	199	0.6	-0.5	20.8
Burundi	56	103	98	109	106	94	125	148	90	192	159	8.9	12.8	8.6
Cameroon	73	40	24	38	142	97	129	124	16	309	84	-3.9	31.1	-4.6
Cape Verde	24	34	24	25	25	30	24	38	34	37	35	2.6	-3.3	6.5
Central African Republic	35	51	63	90	84	130	66	64	53	68	39	4.1	9.0	-12.9
Chad	15	67	85	111	116	114	113	83	75	102	97	-2.6	11.8	-4.2
Comoros	13	25	21	16	12	14	31	23	20	21	19	7.4	-12.3	6.7
Congo	23	8	17	9	9	14	14	11	7	101	18	-2.3	-17.1	19.6
Côte d'Ivoire	60	40	20	188	126	139	178	208	53	716	420	-11.4	83.8	22.5
Djibouti	9	23	22	17	9	16	20	20	29	22	20	25.0	-14.6	12.3
Equatorial Guinea	8	11	20	22	20	16	19	24	24	13	11	23.4	22.3	-7.1
Eritrea	0	0	0	0	0	0	0	0	18	47	43	..	..	..
Ethiopia	124	253	316	382	346	387	569	654	639	469	314	9.0	11.1	0.8
Gabon	7	7	7	8	12	5	3	4	4	19	9	3.5	7.1	8.4
Gambia, The	32	48	54	31	42	37	41	58	37	32	21	14.1	14.3	-8.6
Ghana	61	255	287	310	338	260	382	257	294	204	260	12.5	23.7	-5.3
Guinea	59	73	91	79	145	133	189	197	217	162	165	29.5	18.3	3.3
Guinea-Bissau	25	29	56	43	45	48	47	41	36	48	34	20.9	13.0	-3.8
Kenya	124	62	112	211	413	391	279	334	462	260	235	11.6	36.1	-6.9
Lesotho	32	34	44	39	59	50	47	67	64	65	46	9.4	7.9	0.3
Liberia	30	30	27	16	19	61	91	84	93	26	80	7.9	-10.0	9.9
Madagascar	94	147	153	81	164	116	164	133	128	92	94	3.6	11.1	-8.1
Malawi	70	119	106	183	234	253	284	330	321	202	185	16.5	16.3	-3.7
Mali	106	133	131	161	137	140	156	174	141	195	237	2.1	8.6	8.2
Mauritania	37	67	83	70	89	95	98	84	130	140	105	1.9	8.7	5.7
Mauritius	8	5	10	9	9	11	7	10	-1	7	12	-6.9	16.4	1.1
Mozambique	35	103	129	173	221	224	271	414	347	458	346	10.8	25.0	11.4
Namibia	0	10	1	5	21	73	80	41	30	23	37	..	33.4	-5.5
Niger	66	133	140	124	96	123	98	98	86	103	69	-4.9	9.3	-5.0
Nigeria	19	22	18	22	33	68	82	109	197	132	121	-0.8	8.2	24.3
Rwanda	59	85	99	103	86	87	115	150	146	209	323	6.7	5.7	23.8
São Tomé and Principe	3	6	13	15	21	21	25	28	18	22	20	9.5	20.7	-1.7
Senegal	81	249	277	197	151	202	176	185	119	155	224	1.8	24.3	0.9
Seychelles	3	7	5	2	4	3	6	4	11	5	2	4.0	0.8	-1.2
Sierra Leone	31	37	19	38	26	20	33	55	98	206	127	10.4	-1.9	45.8
Somalia	171	178	189	111	148	125	63	132	183	92	62	12.2	-5.2	-7.3
South Africa	0	0	0	0	0	0	0	0	87	74	58	..	..	..
Sudan	198	309	248	315	290	349	447	309	276	220	91	8.3	4.2	-16.0
Swaziland	18	10	15	14	16	17	20	24	19	26	15	3.5	8.9	3.0
Tanzania	132	159	180	217	209	286	287	478	287	363	252	11.6	10.9	3.7
Togo	40	77	33	75	87	93	70	82	19	58	65	6.2	5.6	-10.6
Uganda	72	121	209	198	243	336	297	414	249	365	345	24.7	13.2	3.8
Zaire	109	136	336	142	277	164	120	95	75	137	68	5.2	20.8	-16.5
Zambia	64	114	80	67	56	63	270	304	342	263	1,381	18.9	-7.5	57.5
Zimbabwe	48	39	28	40	36	31	32	234	180	261	125	59.6	-4.9	41.5
NORTH AFRICA	321	136	162	204	289	253	589	445	632	622	370	-4.3	2.3	9.7
Algeria	18	19	25	23	38	20	28	24	78	41	30	-11.2	19.7	6.3
Egypt, Arab Republic	202	58	78	75	140	71	322	179	187	268	187	-3.2	-5.3	11.3
Libya	7	3	4	3	9	11	21	4	4	5	5	-3.5	21.8	-18.1
Morocco	68	16	8	30	46	82	136	145	259	263	112	6.5	3.9	22.3
Tunisia	26	39	46	73	57	69	82	92	104	45	37	-4.6	14.5	-6.5
ALL AFRICA	2,752	3,823	4,248	4,514	5,277	5,504	6,521	7,178	6,903	7,840	7,309	4.6	11.6	6.4

Note: In 1995, Zambia completed a 3 year Rights Arrangement Program permitting disbursment of 833.4 M SDR under a new SAF/ESAF arrangement.

12-9. Net ODA from all donors as share of recipient GDP

	Percentage of GDP											*Annual average*		
	1980	*1986*	*1987*	*1988*	*1989*	*1990*	*1991*	*1992*	*1993*	*1994*	*1995*	*75-84*	*85-89*	*90-MR*
SUB-SAHARAN AFRICA	2.6	5.0	5.0	5.5	5.7	6.1	6.0	6.2	5.8	6.6	6.1	2.7	5.1	6.1
excluding South Africa	3.8	7.1	7.6	8.5	8.8	9.8	10.0	10.7	10.3	12.3	11.2	4.1	7.6	10.7
excl. S. Africa & Nigeria	6.3	8.2	8.9	9.8	10.1	11.5	11.7	12.9	12.1	15.0	13.2	6.0	8.9	12.7
Angola	..	2.1	1.8	2.0	1.8	3.0	6.2	6.5	7.0	6.6	6.9	..	1.8	6.0
Benin	6.4	10.1	8.6	9.7	17.9	14.6	14.1	16.6	13.6	16.8	13.6	7.0	11.1	14.9
Botswana	10.9	8.1	10.1	6.7	5.8	4.7	3.7	3.1	3.5	2.2	2.1	11.7	7.8	3.2
Burkina Faso	12.4	15.1	12.9	12.4	11.4	12.1	15.2	14.7	16.7	23.5	20.9	12.4	13.1	17.2
Burundi	12.7	16.1	17.5	18.6	18.6	23.5	22.2	28.7	23.2	32.2	27.1	12.0	16.6	26.2
Cameroon	3.9	2.0	1.7	2.2	4.1	4.0	4.2	6.3	4.6	9.3	5.6	3.6	2.4	5.7
Cape Verde	60.0	75.1	37.7	33.1	33.0	36.5	33.6	34.7	36.1	35.0	26.6	47.0	48.8	33.7
Central African Republic	13.9	12.4	15.3	16.4	15.3	17.2	12.7	12.8	13.8	18.5	14.7	12.9	14.3	15.0
Chad	4.8	21.8	25.0	25.2	25.3	25.9	20.1	18.2	22.1	25.9	22.7	12.2	24.4	22.5
Comoros	34.8	28.5	27.6	25.0	22.5	18.6	26.3	18.5	17.9	19.9	18.6	37.0	29.0	20.0
Congo	5.4	5.8	6.5	3.9	3.8	7.8	4.9	3.9	6.4	20.5	6.0	6.4	4.6	8.2
Côte d'Ivoire	2.1	1.9	2.4	4.1	4.1	6.4	6.0	6.8	7.4	20.8	12.1	1.9	2.8	9.9
Djibouti	..	31.5	28.0	23.3	18.8	45.8	23.8	24.1	28.4	26.5	21.7	..	25.1	28.4
Equatorial Guinea	..	20.8	44.5	37.8	50.8	46.8	48.3	39.2	34.0	23.5	20.1	1.0	35.1	35.3
Eritrea	..	..	..	..	..	..	..	..	..	..	..	..	..	..
Ethiopia	..	9.0	8.4	12.5	9.2	11.8	11.5	16.1	15.1	18.4	15.0	5.1	9.9	14.6
Gabon	1.3	2.0	2.1	2.8	3.2	2.2	2.7	1.2	2.3	4.3	2.8	1.6	2.3	2.6
Gambia, The	23.6	69.1	47.6	36.6	41.5	34.4	31.0	35.0	23.7	19.7	13.1	19.6	44.7	26.2
Ghana	4.3	6.3	8.1	11.1	13.7	9.6	13.4	9.6	10.9	10.6	10.6	3.6	8.7	10.8
Guinea	..	8.5	10.9	10.8	15.0	10.5	12.8	15.1	12.9	10.6	11.3	..	11.3	12.2
Guinea-Bissau	56.0	54.5	67.2	64.9	58.4	55.8	49.8	48.4	41.1	75.2	46.7	37.5	56.3	52.8
Kenya	5.5	6.1	7.0	9.8	12.8	13.9	11.3	10.8	15.8	9.1	8.0	5.5	8.6	11.5
Lesotho	25.6	31.3	28.7	24.8	26.8	22.9	21.4	21.5	20.2	15.2	13.6	24.6	29.9	19.2
Liberia	8.8	9.0	6.9	5.4	4.9	..	..	..	..	..	..	7.4	6.9	..
Madagascar	5.7	9.5	12.9	12.2	14.0	13.0	17.0	12.1	10.8	9.7	9.5	4.6	11.0	12.0
Malawi	11.6	16.5	23.8	28.1	28.5	27.2	24.1	30.9	24.5	36.6	29.6	11.1	21.4	28.8
Mali	15.8	21.4	18.3	22.0	22.0	19.7	18.9	15.3	13.7	23.9	22.1	15.9	22.8	18.9
Mauritania	24.8	28.6	21.4	19.3	25.8	23.5	19.5	17.0	34.8	26.2	21.6	27.8	25.1	23.8
Mauritius	2.9	3.7	3.3	2.7	2.8	3.4	2.4	1.5	0.8	0.4	0.6	3.6	3.0	1.5
Mozambique	8.3	14.0	49.3	76.3	61.7	69.9	74.8	118.5	84.2	85.9	75.4	10.0	42.6	84.8
Namibia	0.0	1.0	0.9	1.1	2.8	5.4	7.7	5.2	6.1	4.7	5.9	0.0	1.2	5.8
Niger	6.7	16.4	16.3	16.8	13.9	16.1	16.2	15.8	15.6	24.1	14.4	10.0	16.9	17.0
Nigeria	0.1	0.3	0.3	0.5	1.4	0.9	1.0	0.9	1.2	0.8	0.9	0.1	0.5	0.9
Rwanda	13.3	10.7	11.3	10.4	9.5	11.3	19.8	18.4	19.4	98.0	57.8	12.5	10.5	37.5
São Tomé and Principe	9.3	19.3	31.2	50.5	99.3	112.3	92.6	127.3	99.6	102.8	172.8	20.8	47.3	117.9
Senegal	8.7	15.4	14.5	12.1	15.3	14.4	11.6	16.8	12.4	16.6	13.7	10.5	13.7	14.3
Seychelles	14.9	13.8	9.7	7.3	6.4	9.6	6.1	4.3	4.0	2.6	2.5	14.3	10.1	4.9
Sierra Leone	7.6	10.1	8.0	8.0	8.5	7.0	13.0	19.5	27.1	29.8	23.9	4.6	8.0	20.0
Somalia	71.7	54.7	58.3	41.7	39.1	53.9	..	..	..	..	..	42.1	46.8	53.9
South Africa	0.0	0.0	0.0	0.0	0.0	0.0	0.0	0.0	0.2	0.2	0.3	0.0	0.0	0.1
Sudan	9.2	6.8	5.5	8.9	7.1	9.2	12.1	9.2	..	..	..	7.5	7.9	10.1
Swaziland	8.6	7.5	7.5	5.3	3.9	6.2	6.0	5.6	5.7	5.7	5.2	7.7	6.2	5.7
Tanzania	..	9.5	26.1	29.3	23.1	30.4	25.8	32.6	25.6	28.7	21.0	10.1	19.4	27.3
Togo	8.0	16.1	9.7	14.9	14.8	16.0	12.6	13.3	8.0	13.5	14.7	10.0	14.0	13.0
Uganda	9.0	4.9	4.8	6.1	8.6	15.6	20.1	25.5	19.0	18.8	14.6	7.0	5.9	18.9
Zaire	2.9	5.2	8.8	6.2	8.1	9.6	5.2	3.3	2.0	4.2	3.2	2.7	6.5	4.6
Zambia	8.2	27.3	18.8	12.8	9.4	14.6	26.2	32.5	24.5	19.3	49.5	6.3	16.5	27.8
Zimbabwe	3.1	4.5	5.5	4.3	4.0	5.0	6.0	14.5	9.0	9.6	7.4	2.0	4.7	8.6
NORTH AFRICA	2.1	1.7	1.7	1.7	1.6	5.0	5.6	3.8	2.7	2.8	1.9	3.0	1.7	3.6
Algeria	0.4	0.3	0.3	0.3	0.3	0.4	0.7	0.8	0.7	1.0	0.8	0.5	0.3	0.7
Egypt, Arab Republic	6.1	4.7	4.3	4.3	3.9	12.6	13.6	7.8	5.1	5.2	3.3	10.3	4.4	7.9
Libya	0.0	0.1	0.0	0.0	0.1	..	..	..	..	..	..	0.0	0.0	..
Morocco	4.8	2.2	2.2	2.1	2.0	4.1	4.4	3.3	2.7	2.1	1.5	3.8	2.9	3.0
Tunisia	2.7	2.5	2.9	3.1	2.8	3.2	2.7	2.5	1.6	0.7	0.4	3.5	2.6	1.8
ALL AFRICA	2.4	3.6	3.7	4.1	4.2	5.7	5.8	5.4	4.7	5.2	4.6	2.8	3.8	5.3

Note: Nigeria's ratios are distorted for 1994-95 because of official exchange rate over-valuation affecting oil exports and oil value added (see chapter 3).

12-10. Net ODA from DAC donors as share of recipient GDP

	Percentage of GDP											Annual average		
	1980	*1986*	*1987*	*1988*	*1989*	*1990*	*1991*	*1992*	*1993*	*1994*	*1995*	*75-84*	*85-89*	*90-MR*
SUB-SAHARAN AFRICA	1.5	3.1	3.2	3.6	3.5	3.8	3.6	3.6	3.5	3.7	3.3	1.6	3.2	3.6
excluding South Africa	2.2	4.5	4.8	5.5	5.5	6.2	6.0	6.3	6.2	6.9	6.1	2.4	4.8	6.3
excl. S. Africa & Nigeria	3.7	5.2	5.6	6.4	6.2	7.2	7.1	7.6	7.4	8.5	7.2	3.5	5.6	7.5
Angola	..	1.5	1.3	1.3	1.2	1.8	3.5	3.6	3.7	3.3	4.0	..	1.2	3.3
Benin	2.6	5.4	4.9	5.7	9.9	6.8	8.4	10.5	7.0	9.3	8.5	3.6	6.1	8.4
Botswana	8.6	6.5	8.1	5.6	4.4	3.8	2.8	2.5	2.1	1.4	1.3	9.0	5.9	2.3
Burkina Faso	8.8	9.4	9.1	9.2	8.4	8.6	9.7	9.0	9.1	14.3	10.8	8.3	8.9	10.2
Burundi	6.5	7.5	7.7	7.7	8.0	13.9	10.5	13.7	13.4	11.2	10.1	6.3	7.5	12.1
Cameroon	2.5	1.7	1.5	1.9	2.7	3.0	3.0	5.1	4.4	5.1	4.3	2.5	1.9	4.2
Cape Verde	36.6	52.4	27.0	22.9	22.8	25.2	25.2	22.9	25.1	23.5	17.0	30.6	32.7	23.1
Central African Republic	9.4	7.8	9.2	8.6	8.0	6.8	7.1	7.7	9.3	10.5	10.7	8.2	8.2	8.7
Chad	2.8	13.6	14.6	14.0	12.9	15.0	10.4	11.2	14.1	12.5	12.0	6.7	13.7	12.5
Comoros	10.5	12.8	16.9	16.6	16.0	12.2	12.4	8.8	10.3	8.9	9.2	14.0	15.6	10.3
Congo	3.2	5.4	5.7	3.5	3.4	7.2	4.3	3.5	6.1	14.3	5.0	3.9	4.0	6.7
Côte d'Ivoire	1.5	1.5	2.2	2.2	2.7	4.9	4.1	4.7	6.8	10.7	7.3	1.5	2.0	6.4
Djibouti	..	17.7	15.8	17.9	16.0	20.8	18.2	19.6	19.9	19.3	16.2	..	16.2	19.0
Equatorial Guinea	..	10.6	27.9	19.5	31.9	33.0	27.0	22.6	17.7	12.8	12.8	0.0	19.7	21.0
Eritrea	..	..	..	..	..	..	..	..	..	..	..	..	..	..
Ethiopia	..	5.7	4.2	7.2	4.6	5.9	4.9	6.2	5.8	9.7	8.9	1.9	5.6	6.9
Gabon	1.1	1.5	1.8	2.6	2.9	2.1	2.6	1.2	2.2	3.8	2.6	1.3	2.0	2.4
Gambia, The	7.3	39.8	23.1	23.5	23.3	19.5	16.6	15.6	13.7	10.6	6.9	8.7	25.5	13.8
Ghana	2.4	2.1	2.6	4.5	6.7	4.5	6.8	5.2	5.5	6.4	5.8	2.0	3.6	5.7
Guinea	..	4.9	5.9	6.7	7.9	4.9	5.8	7.9	5.8	5.5	6.0	..	6.3	6.0
Guinea-Bissau	32.2	31.2	28.5	32.6	33.1	32.9	27.3	26.6	24.6	53.2	31.2	22.0	28.2	32.6
Kenya	3.8	5.3	5.6	7.2	7.4	8.6	7.5	6.3	7.4	5.4	5.0	4.3	6.2	6.7
Lesotho	17.4	20.3	16.9	15.7	14.4	13.7	12.6	10.3	10.4	5.9	7.3	15.1	17.6	10.0
Liberia	5.4	6.4	4.5	4.0	3.2	..	..	..	..	..	..	5.1	4.8	..
Madagascar	2.3	5.4	7.1	8.7	7.0	8.7	10.2	7.2	6.8	6.4	6.1	2.4	6.3	7.6
Malawi	6.1	7.2	14.7	13.6	11.9	11.6	9.6	11.2	7.8	19.6	15.1	6.3	10.4	12.5
Mali	7.8	11.9	11.3	13.1	14.7	12.6	11.6	8.4	8.3	13.1	11.5	8.5	14.3	10.9
Mauritania	7.6	13.1	10.7	11.9	16.5	10.4	9.8	9.8	20.8	12.5	11.8	6.7	13.4	12.5
Mauritius	2.2	3.3	2.6	2.1	2.4	2.9	2.2	1.1	0.8	0.2	0.2	2.3	2.5	1.2
Mozambique	5.7	10.6	39.6	60.8	43.6	52.1	53.8	81.3	58.0	51.2	48.0	7.5	32.6	57.4
Namibia	0.0	0.4	0.8	0.8	1.7	1.7	4.0	3.5	4.8	3.8	4.6	0.0	0.8	3.7
Niger	4.1	9.7	9.6	10.7	9.1	10.3	11.4	11.2	11.4	16.7	10.1	5.9	10.7	11.8
Nigeria	0.0	0.2	0.2	0.4	1.3	0.6	0.6	0.5	0.3	0.2	0.3	0.1	0.4	0.4
Rwanda	8.3	6.4	6.4	5.7	5.5	7.1	12.7	9.8	10.9	66.8	27.5	7.9	6.0	22.5
São Tomé and Principe	2.3	10.9	7.8	17.8	49.7	64.4	44.1	59.3	60.5	54.7	122.9	6.4	19.0	67.7
Senegal	6.0	8.4	7.8	7.4	11.6	10.3	7.7	11.3	8.9	12.2	8.2	6.5	8.6	9.8
Seychelles	12.2	10.0	7.5	6.3	4.9	8.8	4.5	3.5	1.4	1.5	2.1	13.0	7.2	3.6
Sierra Leone	4.8	5.7	5.3	4.1	6.1	4.4	8.4	10.7	13.7	5.8	6.9	2.4	4.7	8.3
Somalia	23.0	38.0	39.5	30.0	24.4	29.4	..	..	..	..	..	13.4	30.1	29.4
South Africa	0.0	0.0	0.0	0.0	0.0	0.0	0.0	0.0	0.2	0.2	0.2	0.0	0.0	0.1
Sudan	4.0	3.4	2.7	4.8	4.0	4.7	5.0	3.1	..	..	..	2.8	4.2	4.3
Swaziland	5.7	5.5	5.1	3.2	1.6	4.1	3.5	2.8	3.6	2.8	3.5	5.0	4.1	3.4
Tanzania	..	7.4	20.9	22.7	17.4	21.8	18.2	19.8	17.4	16.9	14.0	7.2	15.0	18.0
Togo	4.6	8.6	6.9	9.3	8.0	9.5	7.8	8.0	6.4	6.8	8.9	5.7	8.0	7.9
Uganda	3.3	2.0	1.4	2.9	3.1	5.7	8.6	8.9	10.8	8.7	7.5	2.9	2.1	8.4
Zaire	2.1	3.7	4.4	4.5	4.8	6.8	3.8	2.0	1.1	1.7	1.9	1.9	4.1	2.9
Zambia	6.0	21.0	15.3	10.9	7.9	12.4	17.3	22.0	14.3	11.7	10.7	4.8	12.9	14.7
Zimbabwe	2.1	3.8	4.9	3.7	3.5	4.3	5.4	9.8	5.6	4.8	5.3	1.5	4.1	5.9
NORTH AFRICA	1.3	1.5	1.4	1.5	1.4	2.9	4.3	3.2	1.9	2.2	1.6	1.4	1.5	2.7
Algeria	0.3	0.2	0.2	0.2	0.2	0.4	0.7	0.8	0.5	0.9	0.7	0.4	0.2	0.7
Egypt, Arab Republic	5.2	4.4	3.9	4.1	3.6	7.4	11.2	6.5	3.9	4.5	2.8	4.6	4.1	6.0
Libya	0.0	0.0	0.0	0.0	0.0	..	..	..	..	..	..	0.0	0.0	..
Morocco	1.0	1.7	1.9	1.8	1.8	2.3	2.2	2.6	1.6	1.0	1.1	1.5	1.9	1.8
Tunisia	1.8	1.6	2.1	2.3	1.8	1.7	2.0	1.9	0.9	0.5	0.3	2.5	1.9	1.2
ALL AFRICA	1.4	2.5	2.5	2.8	2.8	3.5	3.8	3.5	3.0	3.2	2.7	1.5	2.6	3.3

Note: Nigeria's ratios are distorted for 1994-95 because of official exchange rate over-valuation affecting oil exports and oil value added (see chapter 3).

12-11. Net ODA from multilateral donors as share of recipient GDP

	Percentage of GDP											Annual average		
	1980	1986	1987	1988	1989	1990	1991	1992	1993	1994	1995	75-84	85-89	90-MR
SUB-SAHARAN AFRICA	0.8	1.6	1.7	1.8	2.1	2.1	2.3	2.6	2.3	2.9	2.7	0.9	1.7	2.5
excluding South Africa	1.2	2.3	2.6	2.8	3.3	3.4	3.8	4.4	4.1	5.4	5.1	1.3	2.6	4.4
excl. S. Africa & Nigeria	2.0	2.7	3.0	3.3	3.8	4.0	4.5	5.3	4.7	6.5	5.9	1.9	3.0	5.2
Angola	..	0.6	0.5	0.6	0.6	1.1	2.6	2.9	3.3	3.3	2.9	..	0.6	2.7
Benin	3.8	4.5	3.6	4.0	7.6	7.8	5.8	6.1	6.7	7.3	4.7	3.3	4.8	6.4
Botswana	2.4	1.7	2.1	1.1	1.5	0.9	0.8	0.6	1.2	0.7	0.8	2.4	1.9	0.9
Burkina Faso	3.6	5.1	3.5	3.1	3.0	3.1	5.1	5.6	7.6	9.2	9.9	3.9	3.9	6.8
Burundi	5.9	7.9	8.7	10.6	10.2	9.5	11.9	15.1	10.1	21.4	17.3	5.2	8.4	14.2
Cameroon	1.1	0.4	0.2	0.3	1.4	1.0	1.2	1.2	0.1	4.3	1.2	1.0	0.5	1.5
Cape Verde	21.6	21.5	10.2	9.8	10.0	11.2	8.3	11.9	10.9	11.5	9.5	15.6	15.4	10.5
Central African Republic	4.3	4.3	5.4	7.6	7.3	10.2	5.4	5.1	4.5	8.1	3.9	4.4	5.9	6.2
Chad	2.1	8.2	10.4	11.2	12.4	10.7	9.5	7.0	7.7	13.3	10.6	5.1	10.8	9.8
Comoros	10.5	14.2	10.8	8.3	6.3	6.2	13.9	9.7	7.6	11.1	9.3	13.9	12.3	9.6
Congo	1.3	0.4	0.7	0.4	0.4	0.6	0.6	0.4	0.4	6.2	1.0	1.9	0.6	1.5
Côte d'Ivoire	0.6	0.4	0.2	1.9	1.4	1.5	1.9	2.1	0.5	10.1	4.9	0.5	0.8	3.5
Djibouti	..	5.9	5.9	4.6	2.5	4.3	5.0	4.7	6.4	4.8	4.8	..	5.1	5.0
Equatorial Guinea	..	10.1	16.5	18.3	18.7	13.8	16.5	16.5	16.2	10.7	7.2	0.6	15.3	13.5
Eritrea	..	..	..	..	..	..	..	..	..	..	..	..	..	..
Ethiopia	..	3.3	4.2	5.2	4.6	5.1	6.6	9.8	9.3	8.7	6.1	2.8	4.3	7.6
Gabon	0.2	0.2	0.2	0.2	0.3	0.1	0.1	0.1	0.1	0.5	0.2	0.2	0.2	0.2
Gambia, The	13.3	29.9	24.6	13.9	18.8	14.7	13.8	20.1	10.6	9.7	6.6	8.5	19.5	12.6
Ghana	1.3	4.1	5.7	6.3	6.9	5.1	6.4	4.4	5.5	4.3	4.9	1.4	5.1	5.1
Guinea	..	3.4	4.4	3.5	6.4	5.4	7.0	7.4	7.2	5.2	5.2	..	4.4	6.2
Guinea-Bissau	22.8	20.6	33.4	28.5	24.1	23.0	22.0	20.5	16.0	21.9	15.6	13.2	25.2	19.8
Kenya	1.7	0.8	1.4	2.6	5.3	5.2	3.8	4.5	8.5	3.8	3.0	1.2	2.3	4.8
Lesotho	8.4	11.2	11.9	9.3	12.5	9.3	8.9	11.1	9.6	9.2	6.3	9.4	12.1	9.1
Liberia	2.6	2.6	2.3	1.4	1.7	..	..	..	..	..	..	2.1	2.1	..
Madagascar	2.3	4.2	6.0	3.5	7.0	4.3	6.8	4.9	4.0	3.3	3.4	1.9	4.8	4.5
Malawi	5.5	9.3	9.2	14.5	16.5	15.6	14.5	19.7	16.7	17.0	14.6	4.8	11.0	16.3
Mali	6.1	7.2	6.6	8.6	7.2	6.4	7.2	6.8	5.6	11.4	11.1	6.0	7.5	8.1
Mauritania	5.1	7.7	9.1	7.7	9.7	10.7	9.6	7.8	14.6	14.7	11.3	7.6	8.2	11.5
Mauritius	0.7	0.3	0.5	0.4	0.4	0.5	0.3	0.4	0.0	0.2	0.4	1.2	0.4	0.3
Mozambique	1.7	3.2	9.5	15.2	17.9	17.8	21.0	37.0	26.0	34.6	27.3	2.3	9.8	27.3
Namibia	0.0	0.6	0.0	0.3	1.1	3.7	3.7	1.6	1.2	0.9	1.4	0.0	0.4	2.1
Niger	2.5	6.5	6.2	5.8	4.7	5.7	4.7	4.6	4.1	7.1	4.3	3.1	6.0	5.1
Nigeria	0.0	0.1	0.1	0.1	0.1	0.3	0.3	0.4	0.9	0.6	0.6	0.0	0.1	0.5
Rwanda	4.9	4.0	4.6	4.6	3.8	3.9	6.9	8.7	8.4	31.0	30.3	4.3	4.2	14.9
São Tomé and Principe	7.0	8.4	23.5	32.7	49.7	48.0	48.5	67.9	39.1	47.8	50.1	14.8	28.3	50.2
Senegal	2.6	6.1	6.0	4.2	3.5	4.1	3.6	5.1	3.1	4.3	5.3	3.2	4.4	4.2
Seychelles	2.0	3.1	1.9	0.9	1.6	0.9	1.7	0.9	2.4	1.2	0.5	1.2	2.5	1.3
Sierra Leone	2.5	3.8	2.3	3.1	2.3	2.5	4.6	8.8	13.4	24.0	16.9	2.0	2.9	11.7
Somalia	27.5	17.7	18.7	11.4	14.6	15.6	..	..	..	..	..	15.9	16.0	15.6
South Africa	0.0	0.0	0.0	0.0	0.0	0.0	0.0	0.0	0.1	0.1	0.1	0.0	0.0	0.0
Sudan	2.8	2.1	1.5	3.2	2.9	4.4	6.8	5.7	..	..	..	2.0	2.4	5.6
Swaziland	2.9	2.0	2.5	2.1	2.3	2.1	2.5	2.8	2.1	2.9	1.7	2.7	2.1	2.4
Tanzania	..	2.1	5.2	6.6	5.7	8.5	7.6	12.8	8.1	11.6	6.9	2.6	4.3	9.3
Togo	3.4	6.7	2.7	5.8	6.9	6.6	4.9	5.4	1.7	6.7	5.8	4.2	5.7	5.2
Uganda	5.5	2.8	3.3	3.2	5.0	8.9	10.0	16.1	8.2	9.9	7.1	4.0	3.7	10.0
Zaire	0.7	1.6	4.4	1.7	3.3	2.0	1.5	1.3	0.9	2.5	1.3	0.8	2.5	1.6
Zambia	1.6	6.3	3.5	1.9	1.5	2.2	8.9	10.6	10.1	7.7	38.8	1.1	3.6	13.1
Zimbabwe	0.9	0.7	0.5	0.7	0.6	0.5	0.5	4.7	3.4	4.9	2.2	0.4	0.6	2.7
NORTH AFRICA	0.2	0.1	0.1	0.1	0.2	0.2	0.5	0.3	0.5	0.5	0.3	0.5	0.1	0.4
Algeria	0.0	0.0	0.0	0.0	0.1	0.0	0.1	0.1	0.2	0.1	0.1	0.1	0.0	0.1
Egypt, Arab Republic	0.9	0.1	0.2	0.2	0.4	0.2	1.0	0.4	0.4	0.6	0.4	2.2	0.2	0.5
Libya	0.0	0.0	0.0	0.0	0.0	..	..	..	..	..	..	0.0	0.0	..
Morocco	0.4	0.1	0.0	0.1	0.2	0.4	0.5	0.6	1.0	0.9	0.4	0.3	0.2	0.6
Tunisia	0.3	0.4	0.5	0.8	0.6	0.6	0.7	0.7	0.8	0.3	0.2	0.4	0.5	0.5
ALL AFRICA	0.6	1.0	1.1	1.2	1.4	1.5	1.7	1.8	1.7	2.0	1.9	0.7	1.1	1.8

Note: Nigeria's ratios are distorted for 1994-95 because of official exchange rate over-valuation affecting oil exports and oil value added (see chapter 3).

12-12. Net ODA from all donors as share of recipient GDI

	Percentage of GDI											Annual average		
	1980	*1986*	*1987*	*1988*	*1989*	*1990*	*1991*	*1992*	*1993*	*1994*	*1995*	*75-84*	*85-89*	*90-MR*
SUB-SAHARAN AFRICA	11.1	28.4	28.1	29.2	30.8	35.5	34.6	36.4	36.3	37.4	32.6	12.2	28.6	35.5
excluding South Africa	18.3	41.4	42.9	47.3	51.5	57.2	55.3	56.7	60.6	67.1	60.6	20.4	44.9	59.6
excl. S. Africa & Nigeria	31.7	46.9	49.3	54.7	59.2	65.7	69.1	77.7	72.6	81.3	71.1	30.5	51.4	72.9
Angola	..	11.2	9.9	13.7	15.1	25.3	41.2	45.2	48.4	46.6	48.9	..	11.5	42.6
Benin	42.3	75.2	66.6	75.9	151.6	102.5	98.6	120.9	89.5	109.0	71.5	40.9	94.1	98.7
Botswana	29.0	49.7	41.2	91.7	14.3	11.5	9.0	7.5	13.2	8.8	8.5	33.1	45.0	9.8
Burkina Faso	72.8	69.6	61.5	62.6	52.8	58.9	73.7	69.0	84.5	122.1	93.9	64.1	60.5	83.7
Burundi	91.6	138.1	77.2	124.0	113.0	161.3	154.0	161.4	131.6	346.8	246.8	89.4	108.0	200.3
Cameroon	18.7	8.0	6.7	10.6	23.8	22.5	25.0	46.7	27.7	60.7	38.4	15.0	11.3	36.8
Cape Verde	116.2	155.5	125.8	82.1	85.3	91.0	84.2	64.9	65.6	57.9	46.3	94.8	113.8	68.3
Central African Republic	198.8	88.6	111.3	139.4	129.3	120.0	99.8	102.7	117.7	140.2	102.5	129.3	112.7	113.8
Chad	..	238.7	243.9	319.3	281.3	144.6	274.0	217.0	201.6	138.5	126.9	202.5	277.3	183.8
Comoros	105.0	120.8	109.5	114.6	129.3	94.4	129.6	82.3	107.5	117.7	108.3	114.3	120.2	106.6
Congo	15.1	19.7	32.8	21.1	27.0	45.3	24.9	18.8	22.2	38.7	16.6	19.6	22.2	27.7
Côte d'Ivoire	7.8	12.7	16.3	27.7	37.4	75.6	75.3	123.1	88.3	165.7	81.1	8.9	21.4	101.5
Djibouti	..	..	..	..	..	..	165.5	126.3	164.6	226.2	253.1	..	..	187.2
Equatorial Guinea	..	156.7	215.7	202.1	248.7	176.4	111.6	162.1	135.1	101.9	..	6.6	234.0	137.4
Eritrea	..	..	..	..	..	..	..	..	..	..	..	..	..	..
Ethiopia	..	75.8	58.6	75.8	94.4	133.1	161.0	170.6	101.8	121.3	91.5	51.0	84.6	129.9
Gabon	4.8	4.9	7.0	7.8	12.1	10.3	10.0	5.5	10.4	19.8	13.3	4.1	7.1	11.6
Gambia, The	89.8	341.8	243.6	210.6	236.0	187.7	157.2	177.6	112.9	94.0	62.6	96.9	242.7	132.0
Ghana	76.8	65.0	60.7	98.4	103.5	66.3	84.2	74.7	73.8	66.4	56.8	60.8	74.6	70.3
Guinea	..	56.9	67.0	63.0	87.4	59.9	77.8	91.8	79.6	77.8	77.8	..	68.6	77.5
Guinea-Bissau	189.2	229.3	184.3	139.5	141.5	180.8	148.2	98.2	133.2	467.7	204.5	158.5	156.8	205.4
Kenya	18.7	28.2	28.9	39.3	51.7	57.3	53.9	63.9	89.9	49.1	41.9	24.2	35.0	59.3
Lesotho	60.3	68.0	63.2	51.7	44.2	32.4	27.6	26.2	26.0	17.9	13.6	73.2	60.7	23.9
Liberia	32.1	92.7	..	..	..	..	..	..	..	..	..	44.5	94.0	..
Madagascar	38.0	105.4	128.1	91.8	104.4	87.5	161.3	107.0	94.1	89.1	87.7	47.1	101.1	104.4
Malawi	46.7	134.7	152.0	150.0	134.6	142.2	119.6	164.3	201.0	276.4	194.8	49.5	125.0	183.0
Mali	96.6	105.1	90.0	104.9	103.4	87.7	83.0	69.8	62.7	91.9	85.0	103.7	117.1	80.0
Mauritania	68.6	93.6	73.3	68.8	139.2	117.9	108.4	83.0	148.1	180.7	119.4	86.4	95.9	126.2
Mauritius	14.1	16.9	13.0	8.7	8.9	10.9	8.3	5.0	2.6	1.2	2.2	15.0	11.6	5.0
Mozambique	..	85.6	136.8	176.4	152.1	156.5	163.8	242.8	154.8	164.6	148.7	48.0	124.0	171.8
Namibia	0.0	11.8	5.7	6.0	15.8	20.3	40.4	23.0	34.7	19.5	28.8	0.0	8.7	27.8
Niger	18.3	123.5	154.1	87.2	102.4	198.3	176.4	291.6	273.0	232.3	190.8	84.3	121.0	227.1
Nigeria	0.2	1.9	1.8	2.9	8.2	6.0	4.1	3.1	6.2	4.1	4.8	0.6	3.2	4.7
Rwanda	82.6	67.5	71.8	71.8	71.1	95.5	166.8	124.5	121.9	..	437.8	85.9	68.5	189.3
São Tomé and Principe	27.2	89.8	204.2	256.9	377.3	382.1	295.2	329.2	245.4	250.2	300.3	66.5	205.1	300.4
Senegal	57.1	131.8	116.9	95.0	120.1	106.5	94.8	120.7	93.9	121.6	87.7	78.2	114.0	104.2
Seychelles	39.0	60.4	49.1	28.6	23.7	39.6	27.7	21.0	14.4	11.4	10.7	43.2	43.9	20.8
Sierra Leone	44.0	96.1	99.2	99.9	86.5	74.3	123.3	237.0	350.3	350.0	425.7	31.7	86.9	260.1
Somalia	169.2	217.1	175.1	174.6	128.9	347.8	..	..	..	..	..	156.0	166.2	347.8
South Africa	0.0	0.0	0.0	0.0	0.0	0.0	0.0	0.0	1.6	1.4	1.5	0.0	0.0	0.8
Sudan	61.4	52.6	35.8	59.8	50.3	67.3	94.9	..	..	..	..	47.0	88.3	81.1
Swaziland	28.3	37.5	50.9	22.6	16.8	29.4	32.1	25.6	25.0	31.8	30.3	24.5	30.8	29.0
Tanzania	..	49.4	107.2	103.3	77.1	83.4	74.5	104.2	78.9	91.5	67.9	45.8	77.3	83.4
Togo	28.2	85.5	55.2	93.2	60.5	60.4	73.7	91.1	152.1	101.7	102.7	39.6	76.5	96.9
Uganda	148.8	58.0	49.2	56.6	77.3	122.7	132.3	159.9	124.7	127.9	89.3	107.1	59.9	126.1
Zaire	28.7	39.6	62.2	43.3	56.7	106.1	94.0	47.5	112.6	53.6	42.0	23.8	47.2	76.0
Zambia	35.2	114.7	147.9	115.8	86.7	84.6	237.4	273.7	234.6	140.2	381.0	34.1	112.2	225.3
Zimbabwe	13.5	19.9	31.7	19.8	21.4	21.6	23.9	56.9	42.3	48.1	42.3	8.9	23.2	39.2
NORTH AFRICA	7.2	6.8	7.3	7.0	6.7	17.7	21.8	15.7	11.5	11.9	8.5	9.4	7.2	14.5
Algeria	1.1	0.8	1.1	1.1	1.0	1.5	2.4	2.8	2.4	3.1	2.4	1.1	1.0	2.4
Egypt, Arab Republic	22.0	19.7	16.3	12.2	12.3	43.8	64.2	42.7	31.4	31.3	20.5	33.9	15.9	39.0
Libya	0.2	..	..	..	..	..	..	..	..	..	..	0.2	..	..
Morocco	19.7	9.7	10.6	9.8	8.3	16.2	19.5	14.8	12.6	9.8	7.3	14.4	12.1	13.3
Tunisia	9.0	9.3	12.1	15.2	11.7	11.8	10.5	8.6	5.5	2.7	1.7	11.3	10.9	6.8
ALL AFRICA	9.5	17.7	18.5	19.6	20.2	27.3	29.5	27.6	25.6	26.8	23.1	10.8	18.6	26.7

Note: Nigeria's ratios are distorted for 1994-95 because of official exchange rate over-valuation affecting oil exports and oil value added (see chapter 3).

12-13. Net ODA from DAC donors as share of recipient GDI

	Percentage of GDI											Annual average		
	1980	*1986*	*1987*	*1988*	*1989*	*1990*	*1991*	*1992*	*1993*	*1994*	*1995*	*75-84*	*85-89*	*90-MR*
SUB-SAHARAN AFRICA	6.4	18.0	17.7	19.0	19.2	22.3	21.0	21.6	21.9	21.1	18.0	7.1	18.1	21.0
excluding South Africa	10.6	26.2	27.1	30.8	32.1	36.0	33.5	33.7	36.6	37.7	33.1	11.9	28.4	35.1
excl. S. Africa & Nigeria	18.3	29.7	31.1	35.6	36.5	41.3	41.8	46.2	44.3	46.0	39.0	17.8	32.4	43.1
Angola	..	8.0	7.2	9.1	9.7	15.4	23.4	25.1	25.2	23.2	28.5	..	7.8	23.5
Benin	16.9	40.3	38.1	44.6	84.2	47.9	58.8	76.6	45.7	60.2	45.0	21.0	51.7	55.7
Botswana	22.7	39.9	32.9	76.3	10.7	9.4	6.9	6.2	7.9	5.8	5.1	25.4	35.4	6.9
Burkina Faso	51.8	43.4	43.4	46.5	39.0	41.9	47.0	42.1	45.8	74.1	48.5	43.3	41.5	49.9
Burundi	47.0	64.2	34.2	51.2	48.8	95.8	73.1	77.0	75.8	120.2	92.1	48.0	49.4	89.0
Cameroon	12.1	6.5	5.9	9.2	15.8	17.1	18.2	37.8	26.8	33.0	29.9	10.1	8.7	27.1
Cape Verde	70.8	108.4	90.0	56.7	59.0	62.8	63.2	42.8	45.5	38.9	29.7	58.6	76.9	47.2
Central African Republic	134.3	55.5	67.2	72.9	67.8	47.7	56.0	61.6	79.3	79.4	74.8	84.5	63.8	66.5
Chad	..	149.0	142.6	177.2	143.6	83.8	141.9	133.7	129.1	66.8	67.3	109.3	154.6	103.7
Comoros	31.7	54.3	66.7	76.2	92.0	62.2	60.9	39.0	61.7	52.4	53.8	42.8	67.4	55.0
Congo	9.0	18.5	29.0	18.8	24.0	42.0	21.9	16.8	20.9	27.0	13.9	11.8	19.5	23.8
Côte d'Ivoire	5.6	10.0	15.0	14.7	24.6	58.2	51.7	85.7	81.8	85.3	48.6	7.0	15.3	68.5
Djibouti	..	..	..	..	..	..	126.7	102.8	115.6	164.6	189.6	..	..	139.8
Equatorial Guinea	..	79.9	135.1	104.2	156.0	124.3	62.3	93.7	70.4	55.5	..	0.0	122.9	81.2
Eritrea	..	..	..	..	..	..	..	..	..	..	..	..	..	..
Ethiopia	..	47.8	29.2	44.1	47.7	66.5	68.2	66.0	38.8	64.0	54.1	17.9	47.7	59.6
Gabon	4.2	3.7	5.9	7.3	11.0	9.8	9.8	5.2	9.9	17.6	12.5	3.5	6.2	10.8
Gambia, The	27.8	196.7	117.9	135.5	132.4	106.8	84.2	79.2	65.1	50.6	32.9	45.0	139.4	69.8
Ghana	42.8	21.8	19.2	40.2	50.8	31.2	42.8	40.5	37.3	40.3	31.2	32.7	30.8	37.2
Guinea	..	32.8	36.1	39.1	45.9	28.1	35.3	47.6	35.9	40.3	41.1	..	38.5	38.1
Guinea-Bissau	109.0	131.1	78.1	70.0	80.3	106.4	81.4	54.0	79.8	330.8	136.3	92.8	79.4	131.5
Kenya	13.0	24.3	22.9	28.7	30.1	35.5	35.6	37.5	42.1	29.0	26.3	18.7	25.3	34.3
Lesotho	41.1	44.0	37.2	32.7	23.7	19.4	16.2	12.5	13.4	7.0	7.3	43.9	35.9	12.6
Liberia	19.7	65.8	..	..	..	..	..	..	..	..	..	32.5	66.7	..
Madagascar	15.0	59.8	69.9	65.8	52.4	58.7	97.0	63.6	59.0	58.5	56.4	25.0	57.7	65.5
Malawi	24.8	58.7	93.5	72.5	56.4	60.8	47.6	59.6	64.1	147.9	99.0	26.2	61.3	79.8
Mali	47.4	58.3	55.5	62.6	69.0	56.2	50.7	38.4	37.8	50.4	44.4	55.7	73.4	46.3
Mauritania	21.0	42.8	36.8	42.5	89.1	52.3	54.4	47.8	88.5	86.0	65.3	22.2	52.4	65.7
Mauritius	10.7	14.9	10.3	6.8	7.7	9.3	7.6	3.8	2.7	0.7	1.0	9.8	9.7	4.2
Mozambique	..	64.8	109.8	140.6	107.4	116.7	117.8	166.7	106.5	98.0	94.5	36.3	94.5	116.7
Namibia	0.0	5.0	5.4	4.6	9.7	6.5	20.8	15.7	27.6	15.9	22.2	0.0	5.3	18.1
Niger	11.3	72.7	91.2	55.7	67.0	126.7	123.7	206.4	199.8	161.0	133.9	51.0	76.1	158.6
Nigeria	0.1	1.3	1.4	2.4	7.3	4.1	2.7	1.6	1.6	1.0	1.6	0.4	2.6	2.1
Rwanda	51.7	40.1	40.9	39.5	40.7	59.7	106.9	66.0	68.5	..	208.2	54.3	39.2	101.9
São Tomé and Principe	6.8	50.7	50.8	90.5	189.1	218.9	140.6	153.5	149.1	133.2	213.5	18.4	80.8	168.1
Senegal	39.5	71.9	63.0	58.2	90.7	76.3	62.5	81.1	67.7	89.7	52.1	48.6	71.2	71.6
Seychelles	31.9	43.7	38.2	24.6	18.0	36.1	20.3	16.8	5.1	6.5	9.1	38.6	31.3	15.6
Sierra Leone	27.6	54.0	65.1	51.2	62.5	47.2	79.8	130.2	177.4	68.1	122.8	16.6	51.5	104.3
Somalia	54.3	151.0	118.5	125.4	80.6	189.7	..	..	..	..	..	49.5	107.6	189.7
South Africa	0.0	0.0	0.0	0.0	0.0	0.0	0.0	0.0	1.1	1.0	1.3	0.0	0.0	0.6
Sudan	26.7	26.1	17.7	32.0	28.4	34.2	39.7	..	..	..	..	17.7	48.7	36.9
Swaziland	18.7	27.7	34.2	13.8	6.9	19.3	18.5	12.7	15.8	15.6	20.6	15.8	20.4	17.1
Tanzania	..	38.1	85.7	79.9	58.1	59.9	52.6	63.3	53.8	53.9	45.1	32.9	60.0	54.8
Togo	16.1	45.9	39.0	58.0	32.6	35.8	45.4	54.9	120.3	51.3	62.1	21.5	43.5	61.6
Uganda	54.8	23.3	14.2	26.8	28.0	44.7	56.6	55.9	70.8	58.7	45.5	45.9	21.2	55.4
Zaire	21.3	27.8	31.2	31.5	33.7	74.8	67.6	28.7	62.6	21.2	25.2	16.6	29.5	46.7
Zambia	25.9	88.1	120.2	98.7	72.8	72.0	156.7	184.7	137.4	84.7	82.3	26.2	88.8	119.6
Zimbabwe	9.2	16.9	28.6	16.9	18.4	18.7	21.8	38.5	26.2	24.1	30.1	6.9	20.3	26.6
NORTH AFRICA	4.4	5.9	6.3	6.3	5.7	10.4	16.7	12.9	8.2	9.5	6.9	4.5	6.2	10.8
Algeria	0.7	0.6	0.7	0.8	0.6	1.3	2.1	2.5	1.8	2.8	2.2	0.9	0.7	2.1
Egypt, Arab Republic	18.8	18.4	14.9	11.7	11.2	25.5	53.1	35.5	23.8	26.9	17.1	15.3	14.9	30.3
Libya	0.1	..	..	..	..	..	..	..	..	..	..	0.1	..	..
Morocco	4.1	7.5	8.9	8.7	7.4	9.2	9.6	11.4	7.5	4.9	5.1	5.5	8.3	8.0
Tunisia	6.2	6.1	8.9	11.3	7.5	6.4	7.8	6.6	3.0	1.9	1.2	8.0	7.7	4.5
ALL AFRICA	5.6	12.0	12.5	13.6	13.3	16.9	19.3	17.9	16.0	16.3	13.7	5.9	12.5	16.7

Note: Nigeria's ratios are distorted for 1994-95 because of official exchange rate over-valuation affecting oil exports and oil value added (see chapter 3).

12-14. Net ODA from multilateral donors as share of recipient GDI

	Percentage of GDI											Annual average		
	1980	1986	1987	1988	1989	1990	1991	1992	1993	1994	1995	75-84	85-89	90-MR
SUB-SAHARAN AFRICA	3.6	9.3	9.5	9.7	11.4	12.4	13.3	14.8	14.3	16.3	14.6	3.8	9.7	14.3
excluding South Africa	5.9	13.6	14.5	15.8	19.1	20.0	21.3	23.0	23.9	29.4	27.5	6.4	15.2	24.2
excl. S. Africa & Nigeria	10.1	15.3	16.7	18.3	22.3	22.9	26.7	31.4	28.2	35.3	32.1	9.6	17.6	29.4
Angola	..	3.1	2.6	4.3	5.1	9.7	17.5	20.1	22.6	23.3	20.3	..	3.6	18.9
Benin	24.9	33.4	28.1	30.8	64.6	54.8	40.7	44.5	43.8	47.4	24.8	19.5	40.8	42.6
Botswana	6.3	10.5	8.4	15.0	3.8	2.2	2.0	1.5	4.6	3.0	3.4	6.9	9.5	2.8
Burkina Faso	20.9	23.6	16.6	15.6	13.8	15.0	24.9	26.5	38.7	47.8	44.4	20.1	17.9	32.9
Burundi	42.3	67.9	38.3	70.7	61.8	65.4	82.6	85.2	57.3	229.9	157.2	39.1	54.8	112.9
Cameroon	5.0	1.4	0.8	1.5	8.0	5.6	6.9	9.0	0.9	27.7	8.4	4.3	2.6	9.7
Cape Verde	41.8	44.6	34.1	24.3	25.8	27.9	20.8	22.2	19.8	19.0	16.6	34.4	35.1	21.0
Central African Republic	60.9	31.0	39.0	65.0	62.0	71.1	42.2	41.0	38.4	61.6	27.4	43.0	47.1	47.0
Chad	..	89.7	101.3	142.3	137.7	59.8	129.9	83.3	70.2	71.1	59.3	88.5	122.7	78.9
Comoros	31.7	60.3	42.7	38.2	36.4	31.7	68.7	43.3	45.4	65.3	54.5	42.6	49.0	51.5
Congo	3.6	1.4	3.8	2.2	3.0	3.3	3.0	2.0	1.2	11.7	2.7	5.8	2.8	4.0
Côte d'Ivoire	2.1	2.7	1.3	13.0	12.8	17.4	23.6	37.5	6.5	80.5	32.5	1.9	6.1	33.0
Djibouti	..	..	..	..	..	..	34.5	24.7	37.1	40.8	56.0	..	..	38.6
Equatorial Guinea	..	76.1	80.1	97.9	91.8	51.9	38.2	68.4	64.5	46.4	..	4.5	110.7	53.9
Eritrea	..	..	..	..	..	..	..	..	..	..	..	..	..	..
Ethiopia	..	28.2	29.5	31.8	46.9	57.7	92.8	104.6	62.9	57.3	37.4	28.0	36.7	68.8
Gabon	0.6	0.4	0.6	0.7	1.1	0.4	0.2	0.4	0.5	2.2	0.9	0.5	0.7	0.8
Gambia, The	50.6	147.8	125.6	80.3	106.9	80.1	69.8	101.7	50.5	46.0	31.6	41.7	105.0	63.3
Ghana	23.6	42.6	42.2	55.9	52.4	35.0	40.5	34.7	37.0	26.8	26.1	24.9	43.6	33.4
Guinea	..	22.7	27.3	20.5	37.2	30.9	42.8	44.5	44.6	37.9	35.6	..	26.9	39.4
Guinea-Bissau	77.0	86.5	91.7	61.2	58.4	74.5	65.5	41.7	52.0	136.1	68.2	54.3	69.0	73.0
Kenya	5.7	3.6	5.8	10.5	21.6	21.6	18.1	26.7	48.2	20.4	15.5	5.1	9.3	25.1
Lesotho	19.9	24.4	26.3	19.3	20.6	13.1	11.5	13.5	12.4	10.9	6.3	28.9	24.5	11.3
Liberia	9.5	26.8	..	..	..	..	..	..	..	..	..	10.9	27.2	..
Madagascar	15.0	46.1	59.0	26.5	52.7	29.0	64.3	43.5	35.1	30.6	31.3	19.9	44.3	39.0
Malawi	22.2	75.9	58.4	77.5	78.1	81.3	72.0	104.7	137.0	128.5	95.8	23.2	63.7	103.2
Mali	37.3	35.3	32.6	41.0	33.8	28.7	31.5	30.9	25.5	43.7	42.7	38.7	38.0	33.8
Mauritania	14.0	25.2	31.1	27.6	52.6	53.5	53.6	38.2	62.2	101.7	62.5	24.9	32.0	61.9
Mauritius	3.4	1.4	2.0	1.4	1.4	1.5	0.9	1.3	-0.1	0.6	1.4	4.9	1.4	0.9
Mozambique	..	19.4	26.4	35.2	44.1	39.8	45.9	75.7	47.8	66.3	53.8	11.1	28.6	54.9
Namibia	0.0	6.9	0.3	1.5	6.1	13.8	19.5	7.3	7.2	3.6	6.6	0.0	3.4	9.7
Niger	6.9	48.6	59.2	30.3	34.6	69.8	50.7	85.4	71.7	68.4	56.6	26.3	43.2	67.1
Nigeria	0.1	0.7	0.5	0.6	0.8	1.9	1.4	1.4	4.6	3.1	3.2	0.2	0.6	2.6
Rwanda	30.4	25.4	29.2	31.5	28.5	32.5	58.4	58.5	52.6	..	229.8	29.6	27.7	86.4
São Tomé and Principe	20.4	39.1	153.4	166.4	189.1	163.2	154.6	175.7	96.3	116.5	87.1	49.2	124.3	132.2
Senegal	17.2	52.5	48.6	33.0	27.4	29.9	29.1	36.7	23.5	31.6	33.9	23.1	36.3	30.8
Seychelles	5.3	13.7	9.5	3.4	5.7	3.7	7.5	4.5	8.8	5.1	2.1	4.2	11.0	5.3
Sierra Leone	14.5	36.0	28.7	38.8	23.8	27.0	43.5	106.8	172.9	281.9	302.1	13.7	31.1	155.7
Somalia	64.9	70.1	56.3	47.5	48.1	100.5	..	..	..	..	..	58.5	56.2	100.5
South Africa	0.0	0.0	0.0	0.0	0.0	0.0	0.0	0.0	0.5	0.4	0.3	0.0	0.0	0.2
Sudan	18.9	15.9	9.9	21.2	20.3	32.5	53.5	..	..	..	..	12.7	25.0	43.0
Swaziland	9.6	9.8	16.7	8.8	9.9	10.1	13.5	12.9	9.2	16.2	9.7	8.8	10.4	11.9
Tanzania	..	10.9	21.5	23.3	18.9	23.2	22.0	41.1	25.1	37.1	22.4	11.6	17.0	28.5
Togo	12.1	35.7	15.1	35.9	28.1	24.7	28.6	36.9	31.5	50.4	40.5	17.3	30.7	35.4
Uganda	91.4	33.7	34.1	29.8	44.6	70.2	65.6	100.7	53.7	67.4	43.0	60.3	37.4	66.8
Zaire	7.1	11.8	31.0	11.8	23.0	22.2	26.4	18.5	50.1	32.3	16.8	7.0	17.7	27.7
Zambia	6.9	26.6	27.7	17.1	13.9	12.7	80.8	89.0	97.2	55.5	298.7	6.2	23.4	105.7
Zimbabwe	3.9	3.1	3.0	3.1	3.1	2.2	2.1	18.6	16.1	24.3	12.5	1.7	3.0	12.7
NORTH AFRICA	0.8	0.3	0.4	0.6	0.8	0.7	2.0	1.4	2.1	2.1	1.2	1.6	0.6	1.6
Algeria	0.1	0.1	0.1	0.2	0.3	0.1	0.2	0.2	0.6	0.3	0.3	0.1	0.1	0.3
Egypt, Arab Republic	3.1	0.6	0.7	0.6	1.2	0.7	4.6	2.4	2.6	3.4	2.2	7.2	0.9	2.6
Libya	0.1	..	..	..	..	..	..	..	..	..	..	0.1	..	..
Morocco	1.4	0.4	0.2	0.7	0.9	1.4	2.4	2.5	4.8	4.4	1.9	1.3	0.7	2.9
Tunisia	1.0	1.5	2.0	3.7	2.5	2.4	2.7	2.2	2.6	1.3	1.0	1.4	2.2	2.0
ALL AFRICA	2.5	4.9	5.3	5.8	6.8	7.0	8.8	9.1	9.0	10.4	9.3	2.9	5.4	8.9

Note: Nigeria's ratios are distorted for 1994-95 because of official exchange rate over-valuation affecting oil exports and oil value added (see chapter 3).

12-15. Net ODA per capita from all donors

	U.S. dollars (current prices)											Annual average		
	1980	*1986*	*1987*	*1988*	*1989*	*1990*	*1991*	*1992*	*1993*	*1994*	*1995*	*75-84*	*85-89*	*90-MR*
SUB-SAHARAN AFRICA	19	23	26	29	29	34	32	34	30	32	31	15	25	32
excluding South Africa	21	25	28	31	32	36	35	36	32	34	32	16	27	34
excl. S.Africa & Nigeria	26	31	35	38	39	45	43	45	40	42	40	20	34	43
Angola	8	16	16	18	19	29	29	36	29	43	39	7	16	34
Benin	26	32	31	36	59	57	55	54	56	48	51	21	36	54
Botswana	118	92	135	126	129	116	103	84	96	61	63	91	114	87
Burkina Faso	30	35	33	35	31	37	46	46	48	43	47	24	32	44
Burundi	28	40	39	39	39	48	46	54	37	51	46	23	37	47
Cameroon	30	21	19	25	41	39	44	59	44	57	33	22	24	46
Cape Verde	221	347	277	268	265	325	308	349	329	327	293	144	276	322
Central African Republic	48	51	66	74	66	86	58	58	55	52	51	35	59	60
Chad	8	32	39	49	46	56	46	40	37	34	37	18	40	42
Comoros	128	119	136	127	106	107	147	107	107	83	88	119	123	107
Congo	55	54	72	41	41	96	57	47	49	141	48	49	49	73
Côte d'Ivoire	26	17	22	38	34	58	51	59	58	117	87	17	25	72
Djibouti	260	281	245	206	159	392	208	207	233	214	168	212	220	237
Equatorial Guinea	41	63	159	140	163	176	177	170	142	79	85	27	116	138
Eritrea	..	..	..	..	..	0	0	0	20	45	42	0	..	18
Ethiopia	6	14	14	20	15	20	21	22	21	20	16	5	16	20
Gabon	81	96	98	122	149	142	145	68	98	170	132	73	108	126
Gambia, The	86	133	130	101	114	108	106	112	83	66	43	58	109	86
Ghana	18	28	31	41	50	38	58	39	38	33	38	13	33	41
Guinea	20	33	42	47	65	51	64	74	65	56	63	15	42	62
Guinea-Bissau	73	79	123	110	124	137	120	107	95	170	111	63	100	123
Kenya	24	22	26	38	47	51	38	36	36	26	27	19	31	36
Lesotho	69	54	65	66	79	80	69	78	75	60	58	52	65	70
Liberia	52	43	34	28	25	46	64	47	47	24	45	40	34	45
Madagascar	26	30	31	27	31	34	38	29	28	22	22	17	28	29
Malawi	23	26	36	47	53	59	60	64	54	49	44	19	36	55
Mali	41	48	46	55	55	58	53	49	40	47	56	29	51	50
Mauritania	113	127	105	97	130	120	107	96	152	121	102	115	115	116
Mauritius	34	53	61	55	58	84	63	42	24	13	20	37	51	41
Mozambique	14	31	48	66	58	71	75	100	79	79	68	11	45	79
Namibia	0	13	13	18	45	91	133	100	106	92	121	0	19	107
Niger	31	46	52	53	41	52	48	45	41	43	30	30	48	43
Nigeria	1	1	1	1	4	3	3	3	3	2	2	1	1	2
Rwanda	30	33	38	38	34	42	51	48	48	115	111	26	34	69
São Tomé and Principe	43	118	162	227	411	495	451	485	389	406	609	70	208	473
Senegal	47	88	98	86	99	111	84	86	63	78	79	45	83	83
Seychelles	349	436	366	311	294	528	334	275	274	177	177	245	349	294
Sierra Leone	28	25	18	27	26	16	26	32	49	63	46	16	23	38
Somalia	65	63	72	52	50	57	23	79	103	60	20	42	56	57
South Africa	0	0	0	0	0	0	0	0	7	7	9	0	0	4
Sudan	33	43	40	41	33	34	36	22	18	16	9	29	42	22
Swaziland	88	49	62	50	37	69	66	64	62	64	62	60	47	65
Tanzania	37	30	39	42	37	46	41	50	34	34	30	28	34	39
Togo	35	55	38	62	59	74	56	60	25	32	46	31	50	49
Uganda	9	13	20	26	29	41	39	42	34	40	43	7	20	40
Zaire	16	13	20	16	20	24	12	7	4	6	4	12	16	10
Zambia	55	64	59	64	49	62	110	126	103	82	227	35	57	118
Zimbabwe	23	26	33	30	28	35	39	77	47	52	44	15	29	49
NORTH AFRICA	31	24	25	22	22	63	60	45	30	31	23	31	24	42
Algeria	9	7	9	7	6	11	13	15	13	15	11	8	8	13
Egypt, Arab Republic	34	35	35	30	30	104	94	66	43	47	35	44	34	65
Libya	6	3	2	1	4	4	6	1	1	1	2	3	2	3
Morocco	46	17	19	20	19	44	50	38	28	24	19	28	22	34
Tunisia	36	30	36	40	36	48	43	46	26	12	8	36	33	30
ALL AFRICA	22	23	26	27	28	39	37	36	30	32	29	18	25	34

12-16. Net ODA per capita from DAC donors

	U.S. dollars (current prices)											Annual average		
	1980	1986	1987	1988	1989	1990	1991	1992	1993	1994	1995	75-84	85-89	90-MR
SUB-SAHARAN AFRICA	11	15	16	19	18	21	20	20	18	18	17	9	16	19
excluding South Africa	12	16	18	20	20	23	21	21	19	19	18	10	17	20
excl. S.Africa & Nigeria	15	20	22	25	24	28	26	27	24	24	22	12	21	25
Angola	5	11	12	12	12	18	17	20	15	22	23	4	11	19
Benin	10	17	18	21	33	27	33	34	29	27	32	11	20	30
Botswana	92	74	108	105	97	95	79	69	58	40	37	70	88	63
Burkina Faso	22	22	24	26	23	26	29	28	26	26	24	16	22	27
Burundi	15	18	17	16	17	29	22	26	21	18	17	12	17	22
Cameroon	20	17	17	22	27	30	32	48	42	31	26	15	19	35
Cape Verde	135	242	198	185	183	225	231	230	228	220	188	95	188	220
Central African Republic	32	32	40	39	35	34	33	35	37	29	37	22	34	34
Chad	4	20	23	27	24	32	24	25	24	16	20	10	22	23
Comoros	39	53	83	84	75	71	69	51	62	37	44	44	69	55
Congo	33	50	64	36	37	89	50	42	47	99	40	30	42	61
Côte d'Ivoire	19	13	21	20	23	44	35	41	54	60	52	13	18	48
Djibouti	114	157	138	158	135	178	159	168	164	156	126	125	141	158
Equatorial Guinea	5	32	99	72	102	124	99	98	74	43	54	8	66	82
Eritrea	..	..	..	..	..	0	0	0	14	27	26	0	..	11
Ethiopia	2	9	7	12	8	10	9	8	8	10	9	2	9	9
Gabon	71	71	83	114	136	136	142	64	93	151	123	61	94	118
Gambia, The	27	76	63	65	64	62	57	50	48	35	23	25	62	46
Ghana	10	9	10	17	24	18	29	21	19	20	21	7	14	21
Guinea	7	19	23	29	34	24	29	38	29	29	33	4	23	31
Guinea-Bissau	42	45	52	55	70	81	66	59	57	120	74	37	50	76
Kenya	17	19	21	28	27	31	25	21	17	15	17	15	22	21
Lesotho	47	35	38	41	42	48	41	37	39	23	31	32	38	37
Liberia	32	31	22	21	16	17	23	10	9	13	11	27	24	14
Madagascar	10	17	17	20	16	23	23	17	18	14	14	9	16	18
Malawi	12	11	22	23	22	25	24	23	17	26	23	10	17	23
Mali	20	27	29	33	37	37	32	27	24	26	29	16	32	29
Mauritania	35	58	52	60	83	53	54	55	91	58	56	29	62	61
Mauritius	26	47	48	43	50	72	58	32	24	7	9	24	42	34
Mozambique	10	23	39	52	41	53	54	69	54	47	43	8	34	53
Namibia	0	5	13	13	27	29	68	69	84	75	93	0	12	70
Niger	19	27	31	34	27	33	33	32	30	30	21	18	30	30
Nigeria	0	0	1	1	3	2	2	1	1	0	1	0	1	1
Rwanda	19	20	21	21	19	26	33	26	27	78	53	16	20	40
São Tomé and Principe	11	67	40	80	206	284	215	226	236	216	433	21	84	268
Senegal	33	48	53	53	75	80	55	58	45	57	47	28	52	57
Seychelles	285	315	284	267	224	481	244	221	96	101	150	217	256	215
Sierra Leone	18	14	12	14	18	10	17	18	25	12	13	8	13	16
Somalia	21	44	48	37	31	31	14	60	80	49	13	13	36	41
South Africa	0	0	0	0	0	0	0	0	5	5	8	0	0	3
Sudan	15	21	20	22	18	17	15	7	6	7	5	11	22	10
Swaziland	58	36	42	31	15	45	38	32	39	31	42	39	30	38
Tanzania	28	23	31	33	28	33	29	30	23	20	20	21	26	26
Togo	20	29	27	39	32	44	34	36	20	16	28	18	29	30
Uganda	3	5	6	12	10	15	17	15	19	19	22	2	7	18
Zaire	12	9	10	12	12	17	9	4	2	2	3	8	10	6
Zambia	41	49	48	55	41	53	73	85	60	50	49	27	45	62
Zimbabwe	16	22	30	25	24	30	36	52	29	26	32	11	25	34
NORTH AFRICA	19	21	21	20	19	37	46	37	22	25	19	16	21	31
Algeria	6	5	6	5	4	9	12	14	10	14	10	6	5	12
Egypt, Arab Republic	29	33	32	29	27	60	78	55	33	40	29	23	31	49
Libya	3	2	1	0	2	2	1	0	0	0	1	1	1	1
Morocco	10	13	16	18	17	25	25	29	17	12	13	10	16	20
Tunisia	25	20	26	30	23	26	32	35	15	8	6	25	23	20
ALL AFRICA	13	16	17	19	18	24	24	23	19	19	17	10	17	21

12-17. Net ODA per capita from multilateral donors

	U.S. dollars (current prices)											Annual average		
	1980	*1986*	*1987*	*1988*	*1989*	*1990*	*1991*	*1992*	*1993*	*1994*	*1995*	*75-84*	*85-89*	*90-MR*
SUB-SAHARAN AFRICA	6	8	9	9	11	12	13	14	12	14	14	5	9	13
excluding South Africa	7	8	9	10	12	13	14	15	13	15	15	5	9	14
excl. S.Africa & Nigeria	8	10	12	13	15	16	17	18	15	18	18	6	12	17
Angola	2	4	4	6	6	11	13	16	14	22	16	3	5	15
Benin	15	14	13	14	25	30	23	20	27	21	18	10	16	23
Botswana	26	19	28	21	34	23	23	17	34	21	25	19	27	24
Burkina Faso	9	12	9	9	8	9	15	18	22	17	22	7	9	17
Burundi	13	19	19	22	21	20	25	28	16	34	29	10	19	25
Cameroon	8	4	2	4	14	10	12	11	1	26	7	6	5	11
Cape Verde	80	99	75	79	80	100	76	120	99	107	105	46	84	101
Central African Republic	15	18	23	34	32	51	25	23	18	23	14	12	25	26
Chad	3	12	16	22	23	23	22	15	13	18	17	7	18	18
Comoros	39	59	53	42	30	36	78	56	45	46	44	44	50	51
Congo	13	4	8	4	5	7	7	5	3	43	8	14	7	12
Côte d'Ivoire	7	4	2	18	12	13	16	18	4	57	35	4	7	24
Djibouti	32	52	52	41	22	36	43	40	53	39	37	28	45	41
Equatorial Guinea	37	31	59	68	60	52	60	72	68	36	31	18	50	53
Eritrea	..	..	..	..	..	0	0	0	6	14	14	0	..	6
Ethiopia	3	5	7	8	8	9	12	13	13	9	6	3	7	10
Gabon	10	8	8	10	14	6	3	5	4	19	9	8	10	8
Gambia, The	48	57	67	39	51	46	47	64	37	32	22	26	48	41
Ghana	5	18	21	23	25	20	28	18	19	13	18	5	19	19
Guinea	13	13	17	15	28	26	35	36	37	27	29	8	17	32
Guinea-Bissau	30	30	61	48	51	56	53	46	37	49	37	22	45	46
Kenya	7	3	5	10	20	19	13	15	19	11	10	4	8	15
Lesotho	23	19	27	25	37	32	29	40	36	36	27	19	26	33
Liberia	15	12	12	7	8	29	41	37	38	11	34	11	10	31
Madagascar	10	13	14	8	16	11	15	12	11	8	8	7	12	11
Malawi	11	15	14	24	31	34	36	41	37	23	22	8	18	32
Mali	16	16	17	21	18	19	20	21	16	22	28	11	17	21
Mauritania	23	34	44	39	49	54	53	44	64	68	53	31	39	56
Mauritius	8	4	9	9	9	12	7	11	-1	7	12	12	7	8
Mozambique	3	7	9	13	17	18	21	31	24	32	25	3	10	25
Namibia	0	8	1	4	17	62	64	32	22	17	28	0	7	37
Niger	12	18	20	18	14	18	14	13	11	13	9	9	17	13
Nigeria	0	0	0	0	0	1	1	1	2	1	1	0	0	1
Rwanda	11	13	15	16	14	14	18	23	20	36	58	9	14	28
São Tomé and Principe	32	51	122	147	206	211	236	259	152	189	177	50	124	204
Senegal	14	35	41	30	23	31	26	26	16	20	31	14	27	25
Seychelles	48	99	71	38	71	50	90	59	168	79	34	24	82	80
Sierra Leone	9	9	5	10	7	6	9	15	24	51	33	6	8	23
Somalia	25	20	23	14	19	17	9	18	22	11	8	16	19	14
South Africa	0	0	0	0	0	0	0	0	2	2	2	0	0	1
Sudan	10	13	11	14	13	17	20	14	11	9	4	8	13	12
Swaziland	30	13	20	20	22	24	28	32	23	33	20	21	17	27
Tanzania	7	7	8	10	9	13	12	20	11	14	10	6	8	13
Togo	15	23	10	24	27	30	22	24	5	16	18	13	20	19
Uganda	5	8	14	14	17	24	20	26	15	21	21	4	12	21
Zaire	4	4	10	4	8	5	3	3	2	3	2	3	6	3
Zambia	11	15	11	10	8	9	38	41	43	33	178	6	12	57
Zimbabwe	7	4	3	5	4	4	4	25	18	26	13	3	4	15
NORTH AFRICA	4	1	2	2	3	3	6	4	5	5	3	5	2	4
Algeria	1	1	1	1	2	1	1	1	3	2	1	1	1	2
Egypt, Arab Republic	5	1	2	2	3	2	7	4	4	5	4	9	2	4
Libya	2	1	1	1	2	3	5	1	1	1	1	2	1	2
Morocco	3	1	0	1	2	4	6	6	11	11	5	2	1	7
Tunisia	4	5	6	10	8	10	11	12	13	6	5	4	7	9
ALL AFRICA	6	6	7	8	9	10	11	12	11	12	12	5	7	11

Figure 12-1. Total net ODA as a share of recipient's GDP, 1995*

(percent)

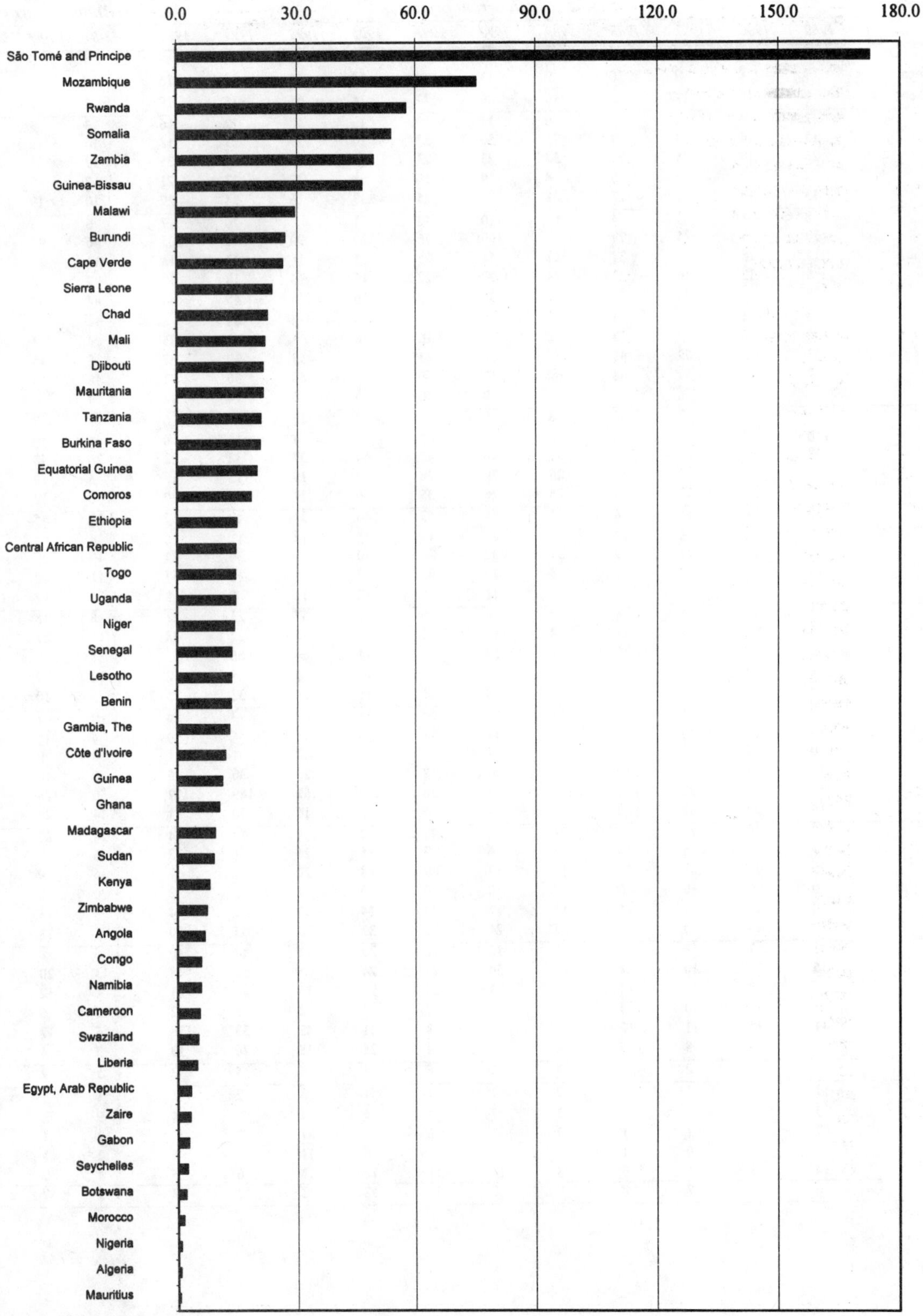

* Or most recent year available.

Note: Nigeria's ratio is distorted because of official exchange rate over-valuation affecting oil exports and oil value added .

Figure 12-2. Total net ODA per capita, 1995

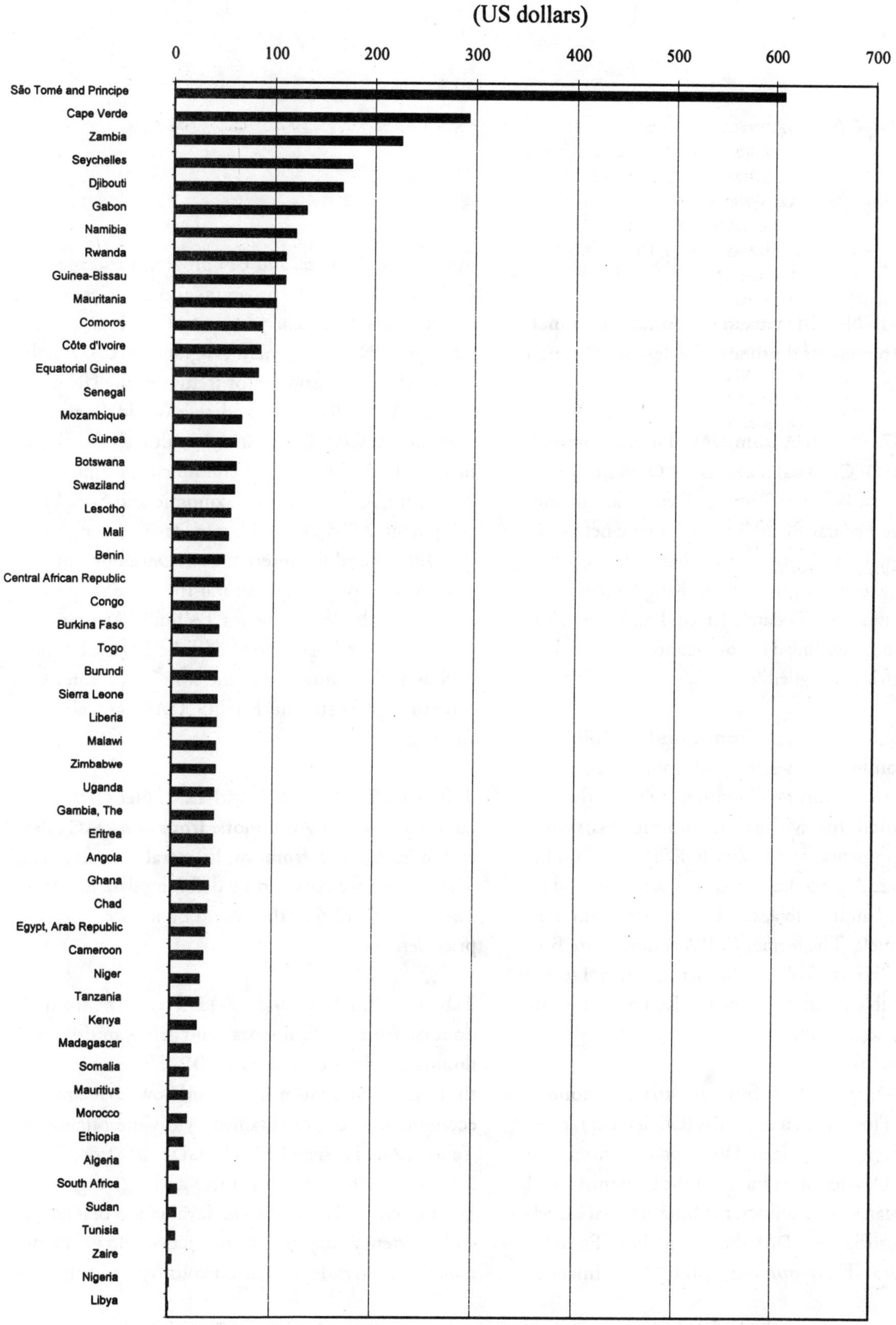

Technical Notes

Tables

Table 12-1. Net ODA from all donors, nominal. This table represents the total of Tables 12-2 through 12-4.

Table 12-2. Net ODA from DAC donors, nominal. This table (OECD data) includes net ODA from Australia, Austria, Belgium, Canada, Denmark, Finland, France, the Federal Republic of Germany before reunification, Italy, Japan, the Netherlands, Norway, Sweden, Switzerland, the United Kingdom, and the United States (OECD data). (Ireland and New Zealand have been excluded in compilation because their ODA to Africa is negligible.)

Table 12-3. Net ODA from non-DAC bilateral donors, nominal. This is net ODA from Organization of Petroleum Exporting Countries (OPEC), the former Council for Mutual Economic Assistance (CMEA) countries, and China (OECD data). OPEC countries are Algeria, Iran, Iraq, Kuwait, Libya, Nigeria, Qatar, Saudi Arabia, the United Arab Emirates, and Venezuela. The former CMEA countries are Bulgaria, Czechoslovakia, the former German Democratic Republic, Hungary, Poland, Romania, and the former Soviet Union.

Table 12-4. Net ODA from multilateral donors, nominal. This includes net ODA (OECD data), most notably from the African Development Fund, the European Development Fund for the Commission of the European Communities, the International Development Association (IDA), the International Fund for Agricultural Development, Arab/OPEC-financed multilateral agencies, and UN programs and agencies (OECD data). The UN programs and agencies include mainly the UN regular program of Technical Assistance, the UN Development Programme (UNDP), the UN High Commissioner for Refugees, the UN Children's Fund (UNICEF), and the World Food Programme. Arab/OPEC-financed multilateral agencies include the Arab Bank for Economic Development in Africa, the Arab Fund for Economic and Social Development (AFESD), the Islamic Development Bank, the OPEC Fund for International Development, the Arab Authority for Agricultural Investment and Development, the Arab Fund for Technical Assistance to African and Arab Countries, and the Islamic Solidarity Fund. ODA flows from the IMF Trust Fund and Structural Adjustment Facility (SAF) are also included.

Tables 12-5, 12-6, 12-7, and 12-8. Net ODA from all donors, from DAC donors, from non-DAC bilateral donors, and from multilateral donors, real. These tables are obtained by deflating data in Tables 12-1 through 12-4 by the World Bank LIMIC import price deflator.

Tables 12-9, 12-10, and 12-11. Net ODA from all donors, from DAC donors, and from multilateral donors as a share of recipient GDP. These tables show the relative importance of these aid flows to recipients' economies. They are obtained by dividing figures in Tables 12-1, 12-2, and 12-4 by GDP data from Table 2-5, which reflect current prices and exchange rates. For a given level of aid flows, devaluation of a recipient's currency may inflate the ratios shown in the table. Thus, trends for a given country and comparisons across countries that have implemented different exchange rate policies should be interpreted carefully.

Tables 12-12, 12-13, and 12-14. Net ODA from all donors, from DAC donors, and from multilateral donors as a share of recipient GDI. These tables are obtained by dividing figures in Tables 12-1, 12-2, and 12-4 by GDI (World Bank country desks). These tables highlight the relative importance of the indicated aid flows in maintaining and increasing investment in these economies. The same caveats mentioned above apply to their interpretation. Furthermore, aid flows do not exclusively finance investment (for example, food aid finances consumption), and the share of ODA going to investment varies across countries.

Tables 12-15, 12-16, and 12-17. Net ODA per capita from all donors, from DAC donors, and from multilateral donors. These tables are calculated by dividing figures in Tables 12-1, 12-2, and 12-4 by midyear population (Table 1-2). These ratios offer some indication of the importance of aid flows in sustaining per capita income and consumption levels (shown in Tables 2-19 and 2-20, respectively), although comparisons must be done carefully because exchange rate fluctuations, the actual rise of ODA flows, and other factors vary across countries and over time.

Figures

The following indicators have been used to derive the figures in this chapter.

Figure 12-1. Total net ODA as a share of recipient's GDP (Table 12-9).

Figure 12-2. Total net ODA per capita (Table 12-15).

Methodology used for regional aggregations and period averages in chapter 12

	Aggregations[a]		*Period averages*[b]	
Table	*(1)*	*(2)*	*(1)*	*(2)*
12-1	x		x	
12-2	x		x	
12-3	x		x	
12-4	x		x	
12-5	x			x
12-6	x			x
12-7	x			x
12-8	x			x
12-9		x	x	
12-10		x	x	
12-11		x	x	
12-12		x	x	
12-13		x	x	
12-14		x	x	
12-15		x	x	
12-16		x	x	
12-17		x	x	

Note: Regional aggregations are shown in the rows for Sub-Saharan Africa, North Africa, and All Africa. Period averages are shown in the last three columns. This table shows only the methodologies used in this chapter.

a. Regional aggregations: (1) simple total; (2) simple total of the first indicator divided by the simple total of the second indicator (same country coverage); (3) simple total of the gap-filled indicator; (4) simple total of the gap-filled main indicator divided by the simple total of the gap-filled secondary indicator; (5) simple total of the first gap-filled main indicator less the simple total of the second gap-filled main indicator, all divided by the simple total of the secondary indicator; (6) weighted total; (7) median; (8) no aggregation; (9) simple arithmetic mean.

b. Period averages: (1) arithmetic mean (using the same series as shown in the table, i.e., ratio if the rest of the table is shown as ratio, level if the rest of the table is shown as level, growth rate if the rest of the table is shown as growth rate); (2) least-squares growth rate (using main indicator); (3) least-squares growth rate (using main indicator in constant terms, with the rest of the table in current terms).

13

Social Indicators

This chapter provides indicators in the areas of demography, health, education, and gender issues in development. These indicators can be useful in evaluating and monitoring the social impact of development progress, aid flows, and structural adjustment policies.

The chapter presents such indicators as dependency ratio, urbanization, crude death rate, life expectancy at birth, infant mortality rate, child mortality rate, immunization rates for children, maternal death rate, and number of population per physician. These indicators are an indirect measure of the physical well-being of the population. In the same vein, such indicators as literacy rate among adults, school enrollment ratios by gender, and pupil-teacher ratio give some picture of the progress being made in education and training. Social indicators refer to phenomena that are inherently more qualitative than macroeconomic variables and thus need to be interpreted cautiously. Further caution is called for because of the particular limitations of the data. One of these limitations is the paucity—or even nonexistence—of data on certain indicators in many of the countries covered. This is especially true of indicators dealing with gender issues. Many countries have no data showing the gender breakdown of several social indicators.

Even when data are available, comparison among countries is limited due to varied practices in data gathering and reporting. Often the countries report survey data that cover different portions of the nation. Sometimes surveys are limited to just the urban areas to cover only the largest cities or the capital city alone. This is especially true of the health indicators. Such indicators as immunization rates for children under one year of age, percentage of births attended by health personnel, infant mortality rate, child mortality rate, and maternal death rate are often based on surveys of a handful of hospitals in the urban areas.

Another source of limitation is the definition of terms, which may differ from country to country. Some countries, for example, consider an institution as a "private school" only if it receives no form of financial support from the government, while others classify as "private" all schools not run by the government, whether or not they receive financial support from the government. In like manner, some countries include personnel other than doctors and trained nurses in the term "medical personnel."

Cultural norms may also affect the reported data. This is especially true for gender issues. In some countries, it is assumed that no woman can be the head of any household that also contains an adult male. In population censuses, therefore, enumerators and respondents simply take such assumptions for granted, reporting a male rather than a female as head of the household or family (see United Nations, *The World's Women, 1970–90*). This distorts the true picture of the percentage of households headed by women.

The main source for this chapter is the World Bank Socioeconomic Database (BESD), which contains electronic information as reported by a number of institutions and agencies in the socioeconomic field, such as the United Nations, UNICEF, UNESCO, World Health Organization (WHO), the UNDP, and the ECA. Other sources of data also include reports and publications on children, health, human development, education, and population from various agencies including the World Bank.

In this chapter, columns headed by a period (for example, 1990–93) show data for the latest available year within the period.

13-1. Age and gender structure of the population

	Females as percentage of total population		*Age groups as percentage of total population*						*Age dependency ratio*	
			1980			*1995*				
	1980	*1995*	*0-14*	*15-64*	*65+*	*0-14*	*15-64*	*65+*	*1980*	*1995*
SUB-SAHARAN AFRICA	50.6	50.4	45.2	51.9	2.9	45.4	51.7	2.9	0.9	0.9
excluding South Africa	50.6	50.4	45.6	51.6	2.8	46.0	51.2	2.7	0.9	1.0
excl. S.Africa & Nigeria	50.6	50.3	45.9	51.2	2.8	46.2	50.9	2.8	1.0	1.0
Angola	50.9	50.6	44.6	52.5	3.0	47.8	49.2	2.9	0.9	1.0
Benin	50.7	51.3	45.5	51.4	3.1	46.8	50.4	2.8	0.9	1.0
Botswana	52.2	51.6	48.4	49.5	2.1	43.6	54.2	2.2	1.0	0.8
Burkina Faso	50.5	50.7	43.9	53.3	2.8	46.7	50.3	3.0	0.9	1.0
Burundi	51.9	50.8	44.7	51.8	3.5	46.8	50.6	2.6	0.9	1.0
Cameroon	50.6	50.4	44.4	52.0	3.6	44.7	51.8	3.5	0.9	0.9
Cape Verde	54.0	53.6	46.0	47.8	6.3	42.4	52.6	4.7	1.1	0.9
Central African Republic	..	51.6	41.6	54.4	4.0	42.5	53.6	3.8	0.8	0.9
Chad	50.8	50.6	41.9	54.5	3.6	42.9	53.4	3.7	0.8	0.9
Comoros	49.9	50.4	47.9	49.5	2.6	47.8	51.0	2.6	1.0	1.0
Congo	51.2	51.0	45.1	51.5	3.4	46.0	50.2	3.8	0.9	1.0
Côte d'Ivoire	48.9	49.4	46.5	51.0	2.5	45.9	51.4	2.8	1.0	0.9
Djibouti	50.5	51.1	43.8	53.7	2.5	42.1	55.2	2.7	0.9	0.8
Equatorial Guinea	51.2	50.9	41.6	54.7	3.7	43.5	53.0	4.0	0.8	0.9
Eritrea	50.4	50.1	..	..	..	45.0	52.7	2.3	..	0.9
Ethiopia	50.6	49.8	46.1	51.2	2.7	47.3	50.0	2.8	1.0	1.0
Gabon	50.9	50.7	32.6	61.7	5.7	37.4	55.0	5.6	0.6	0.8
Gambia, The	50.7	50.6	42.6	54.4	3.0	42.0	55.3	2.8	0.8	0.8
Ghana	50.4	50.4	44.9	52.3	2.8	45.0	52.0	3.0	0.9	0.9
Guinea	50.1	49.7	45.8	51.6	2.6	46.4	51.0	2.6	0.9	1.0
Guinea-Bissau	50.9	51.2	38.9	57.1	4.0	43.9	53.0	3.1	0.8	0.9
Kenya	50.0	50.3	50.1	46.5	3.4	46.5	50.8	2.8	1.2	1.0
Lesotho	51.8	51.0	42.0	54.5	3.5	41.3	54.8	3.8	0.8	0.8
Liberia	49.5	49.4	44.3	52.0	3.6	45.2	52.2	2.6	0.9	0.9
Madagascar	50.7	49.8	44.9	52.2	2.9	45.6	51.4	3.0	0.9	0.9
Malawi	51.6	50.8	47.5	50.3	2.3	46.7	50.8	2.6	1.0	1.0
Mali	51.2	51.5	46.8	50.7	2.6	48.0	49.4	2.7	1.0	1.0
Mauritania	50.7	50.5	43.8	53.2	3.0	43.0	53.7	3.2	0.9	0.9
Mauritius	50.7	50.2	35.6	60.7	3.7	27.6	66.7	5.8	0.6	0.5
Mozambique	50.8	50.9	43.4	53.4	3.1	44.5	52.5	3.1	0.9	0.9
Namibia	50.6	50.3	43.1	53.3	3.6	42.7	53.7	3.6	0.9	0.9
Niger	50.8	50.6	46.8	50.8	2.5	48.1	49.3	2.6	1.0	1.0
Nigeria	50.6	50.8	44.3	53.1	2.6	45.2	52.3	2.5	0.9	0.9
Rwanda	50.6	50.6	48.8	48.8	2.4	49.3	48.6	2.1	1.0	1.1
São Tomé and Principe	..	50.4	..	..	..	39.5	54.3	5.4	..	0.8
Senegal	50.0	50.1	45.3	51.8	2.8	46.6	51.0	2.5	0.9	1.0
Seychelles	..	48.7	..	..	..	32.7	63.9	6.8	..	0.6
Sierra Leone	51.0	50.9	43.0	53.9	3.1	43.3	47.3	2.4	0.9	1.0
Somalia	50.6	50.4	46.0	51.0	3.0	47.0	49.8	3.2	1.0	1.0
South Africa	50.2	50.3	40.3	55.8	3.9	37.5	58.3	4.2	0.8	0.7
Sudan	49.9	49.8	44.9	52.4	2.7	43.3	53.9	2.8	0.9	0.9
Swaziland	50.9	50.6	45.8	51.2	3.0	46.0	51.3	2.7	1.0	0.9
Tanzania	50.8	50.5	47.6	50.1	2.3	45.9	51.6	2.5	1.0	0.9
Togo	50.7	50.5	44.5	52.3	3.2	46.0	50.5	2.9	0.9	1.0
Uganda	50.5	50.8	47.8	49.7	2.5	49.3	48.2	2.4	1.0	1.1
Zaire	51.1	50.6	46.0	51.1	2.8	47.9	49.3	2.8	1.0	1.0
Zambia	51.1	50.6	49.4	48.2	2.4	47.0	50.7	2.3	1.1	1.0
Zimbabwe	50.4	50.1	47.9	49.5	2.6	42.8	54.4	2.8	1.0	0.8
NORTH AFRICA	49.5	49.2	42.2	53.9	3.9	37.5	58.2	4.0	0.9	0.7
Algeria	50.4	49.4	46.5	49.6	3.9	38.3	57.9	3.7	1.0	0.7
Egypt, Arab Republic	49.2	49.1	39.5	56.5	4.0	37.3	57.9	4.1	0.8	0.7
Libya	47.1	47.8	46.6	51.1	2.2	45.6	51.9	2.6	1.0	0.9
Morocco	49.9	50.0	43.2	52.7	4.1	36.0	59.9	4.1	0.9	0.7
Tunisia	49.3	49.6	41.6	54.6	3.8	35.0	60.5	4.5	0.8	0.7
ALL AFRICA	50.4	50.2	44.6	52.3	3.1	44.0	52.9	3.1	0.9	0.9

Note: Some age groups may not add up to 100 due to rounding up error.

13-2. Poverty

	GDP per capita, based on PPP, 1995	National poverty headcount as % of population 1984-1995	% of the population below 2/3 of national mean per capita income, 1991-95		Gini coefficients 1991-95		Percentage of household income spent on food, 1991-95
			Urban	Rural	Urban	Rural	
SUB-SAHARAN AFRICA	1577	..	22	57	..	..	55
excluding South Africa	1233	..	22	57	..	..	55
excl. S. Africa & Nigeria	1207	..	22	57	..	..	55
Angola	1170	..	..	..	..	..	..
Benin	..	33	..	..	..	..	..
Botswana	5630	..	..	..	..	..	..
Burkina Faso	790	..	13	65	38	46	57
Burundi	640	36	..	..	..	..	..
Cameroon	2300	40	..	..	..	..	55
Cape Verde	..	..	..	..	..	..	..
Central African Republic	1080	..	77	33	51	63	60
Chad	710	..	..	..	..	..	..
Comoros	1320	..	..	..	..	..	..
Congo	2480	..	..	..	..	..	..
Côte d'Ivoire	1770	..	31	49	39	33	30
Djibouti	..	..	..	..	..	..	..
Equatorial Guinea	..	..	..	..	..	..	..
Ethiopia	..	..	..	..	..	..	..
Eritrea	460	..	..	..	..	..	..
Gabon	..	..	..	..	..	..	..
Gambia, The	950	64	21	73	43	35	59
Ghana	2030	31	26	45	34	36	39
Guinea	..	..	18	57	..	..	56
Guinea-Bissau	800	49	29	65	55	56	..
Kenya	1430	42	12	69	51	52	54
Lesotho	1240	49	..	..	..	..	..
Liberia	..	..	..	..	..	..	..
Madagascar	680	..	21	59	..	..	70
Malawi	770	..	..	..	..	57	..
Mali	560	..	..	..	53	55	..
Mauritania	1620	57	..	..	34	33	..
Mauritius	13270	11	..	..	..	..	..
Mozambique	910	..	..	..	..	..	..
Namibia	4100	..	..	..	..	..	..
Niger	750	..	14	43	39	31	32
Nigeria	1310	34	32	52	44	46	67
Rwanda	540	51	..	..	..	..	..
São Tomé and Principe	..	..	..	..	..	..	..
Senegal	1830	..	21	78	..	..	61
Seychelles	..	..	..	..	..	..	..
Sierra Leone	620	..	..	..	..	..	..
Somalia	..	..	..	..	..	..	..
South Africa	5240	..	41	82	..	..	48
Sudan	..	..	..	..	..	..	..
Swaziland	2950	..	..	..	..	..	..
Tanzania	1160	51	20	52	..	..	70
Togo	670	32	..	..	..	..	..
Uganda	1490	55	16	46	35	44	63
Zaire	..	..	..	..	..	..	..
Zambia	990	86	16	75	40	46	75
Zimbabwe	2140	26	..	..	..	..	..
NORTH AFRICA	4292	..	..	..	..	..	..
Algeria	5600	..	..	..	..	..	..
Egypt, Arab Republic	3890	..	..	..	..	..	..
Libya	..	..	..	..	..	..	..
Morocco	3470	13	..	..	..	..	..
Tunisia	5260	14	..	..	..	..	..
ALL AFRICA	2124	..	22	57	..	..	55

13-3. Income distribution

	Share of income held by population groups			
	Richest 10%	Richest 20%	Poorest 10%	Poorest 20%
	1986-95	1986-95	1986-95	1986-95
SUB-SAHARAN AFRICA	..	..	..	..
excluding South Africa	..	..	..	..
excl. S. Africa & Nigeria	..	..	..	..
Angola	..	..	..	..
Benin	..	..	..	..
Botswana	42.9	58.9	..	3.6
Burkina Faso	..	..	..	..
Burundi	..	..	..	..
Cameroon	..	..	..	..
Cape Verde	..	..	..	..
Central African Republic	..	..	..	..
Chad	..	..	..	..
Comoros	..	..	..	..
Congo	..	..	..	..
Côte d'Ivoire	28.5	44.1	2.8	6.8
Djibouti	..	..	..	..
Equatorial Guinea	..	..	..	..
Eritrea	..	..	..	..
Ethiopia	..	..	..	..
Gabon	..	..	..	..
Gambia, The	..	..	..	..
Ghana	27.3	42.2	3.4	7.9
Guinea	31.7	50.2	0.9	3.0
Guinea-Bissau	42.4	58.9	0.5	2.1
Kenya	47.7	62.1	1.2	3.4
Lesotho	43.4	60.1	0.9	2.8
Liberia	..	..	..	..
Madagascar	34.9	50.0	2.3	5.8
Malawi	..	..	..	..
Mali	..	..	..	..
Mauritania	30.4	46.5	0.7	3.6
Mauritius	..	..	..	..
Mozambique	..	..	..	..
Namibia	..	..	..	..
Niger	29.3	44.1	3.0	7.5
Nigeria	31.3	49.3	1.3	4.0
Rwanda	..	..	..	..
São Tomé and Principe	..	..	..	..
Senegal	42.8	58.6	1.4	3.5
Seychelles	..	..	..	..
Sierra Leone	..	..	..	..
Somalia	..	..	..	..
South Africa	47.3	63.3	1.4	3.3
Sudan	..	..	..	..
Swaziland	..	..	..	..
Tanzania	30.2	45.4	2.9	6.9
Togo	..	..	..	..
Uganda	33.4	48.1	3.0	6.8
Zaire	..	..	..	..
Zambia	31.3	50.4	1.5	3.9
Zimbabwe	46.9	62.3	1.8	4.0
NORTH AFRICA	..	..	..	..
Algeria	31.5	46.1	2.8	6.9
Egypt, Arab Republic	26.7	41.1	3.9	8.7
Libya	..	..	..	..
Morocco	30.5	46.3	2.8	6.6
Tunisia	30.7	46.3	2.3	5.9
ALL AFRICA	..	..	..	..

13-4. Urbanization

	Total population (millions)			Average annual percentage growth of total population			Urban population as percentage of total population			Average annual percentage growth of urban population		
	1980	1987	1995	75-79	80-87	88-95	1980	1987	1995	75-79	80-87	88-95
SUB-SAHARAN AFRICA	380.5	466.6	583.7	2.8	2.9	2.8	23.3	26.6	31.1	4.9	4.9	4.8
excluding South Africa	351.4	432.0	542.2	2.9	3.0	2.8	21.2	24.8	29.6	5.4	5.3	5.1
excl. S. Africa & Nigeria	280.2	343.7	431.0	2.8	2.9	2.8	19.7	22.8	27.1	5.2	5.1	5.1
Angola	7.0	8.4	10.8	2.6	2.6	3.1	21.0	26.0	32.2	6.0	5.7	5.7
Benin	3.5	4.3	5.5	2.6	3.1	3.0	31.6	36.2	41.8	7.6	5.2	4.8
Botswana	0.9	1.2	1.5	3.6	3.5	2.9	15.1	21.7	30.8	8.5	8.6	7.2
Burkina Faso	7.0	8.3	10.4	2.3	2.5	2.8	8.5	14.0	27.2	7.9	9.1	11.2
Burundi	4.1	5.0	6.3	2.1	2.8	2.7	4.3	5.6	7.5	8.1	6.7	6.3
Cameroon	8.7	10.5	13.3	3.1	2.7	2.9	31.4	37.5	44.9	6.6	5.3	5.1
Cape Verde	0.3	0.3	0.4	0.7	1.5	2.1	23.5	37.5	54.3	2.6	7.8	6.7
Central African Republic	2.3	2.7	3.3	2.3	2.3	2.3	35.1	36.8	39.3	3.3	3.0	3.2
Chad	4.5	5.3	6.4	2.1	2.3	2.5	18.7	20.0	21.4	6.0	3.4	3.4
Comoros	0.3	0.4	0.5	..	2.5	2.6	21.2	24.0	27.8	..	4.3	4.4
Congo	1.7	2.1	2.6	2.8	3.0	3.0	41.0	49.9	58.8	5.9	5.9	5.1
Côte d'Ivoire	8.2	10.7	14.0	3.9	3.8	3.3	34.8	38.7	43.6	5.7	5.4	4.8
Djibouti	0.3	0.4	0.6	6.2	6.3	4.8	73.7	78.9	82.8	7.8	7.3	5.4
Equatorial Guinea	0.2	0.3	0.4	-2.8	6.5	2.0	27.4	32.2	42.2	-2.5	8.5	5.4
Eritrea	..	..	3.6	..	..	2.6	12.2	14.0	17.2	..	..	5.6
Ethiopia	37.7	46.1	56.4	2.7	2.8	2.4	10.5	11.8	13.4	4.7	4.6	4.0
Gabon	0.7	0.8	1.1	3.1	2.9	3.5	35.8	42.8	50.0	6.3	5.5	5.4
Gambia, The	0.6	0.8	1.1	3.2	3.2	4.1	18.2	21.2	25.5	5.1	5.3	6.5
Ghana	10.7	13.5	17.1	1.7	3.2	2.9	31.2	33.0	36.3	2.4	4.0	4.1
Guinea	4.5	5.3	6.6	1.4	2.3	2.8	19.1	23.7	29.6	4.6	5.4	5.6
Guinea-Bissau	0.8	0.9	1.1	5.4	1.9	1.9	16.8	18.8	22.2	6.5	3.5	4.0
Kenya	16.6	21.4	26.7	3.7	3.7	2.8	16.1	21.2	27.7	8.2	7.7	6.1
Lesotho	1.4	1.6	2.0	2.8	2.7	2.3	13.3	17.4	23.1	6.6	6.7	6.0
Liberia	1.9	2.3	2.7	3.1	3.0	2.1	35.0	40.4	45.0	6.0	5.2	3.9
Madagascar	8.7	10.6	13.7	2.7	2.8	3.2	18.3	22.1	27.1	5.3	5.4	5.6
Malawi	6.1	7.7	9.8	3.1	3.2	3.0	9.1	11.0	13.5	6.7	5.9	5.6
Mali	6.6	7.8	9.8	2.2	2.3	2.9	18.5	22.1	27.0	4.8	4.9	5.4
Mauritania	1.6	1.9	2.3	2.4	2.6	2.5	29.0	41.6	53.8	9.8	7.9	5.7
Mauritius	1.0	1.0	1.1	1.7	1.0	1.1	42.4	41.0	40.6	1.4	0.6	1.0
Mozambique	12.1	13.8	16.2	2.8	2.1	1.9	13.1	22.4	34.2	11.4	9.7	7.8
Namibia	1.0	1.2	1.5	2.7	2.7	2.7	22.8	28.8	37.4	4.7	5.9	6.0
Niger	5.5	7.0	9.0	3.1	3.4	3.2	13.2	17.5	23.1	7.5	7.5	6.6
Nigeria	71.1	88.3	111.3	3.0	3.1	2.9	27.1	32.7	39.3	5.9	5.8	5.2
Rwanda	5.2	6.4	6.4	3.3	3.2	0.1	4.7	5.4	6.1	6.7	5.1	1.7
São Tomé and Principe	0.1	0.1	0.1	3.0	1.9	2.4	32.2	39.5	46.7	5.9	5.1	4.5
Senegal	5.5	6.8	8.5	2.9	2.8	2.8	35.9	38.7	42.3	3.8	3.9	4.0
Seychelles	0.1	0.1	0.1	1.5	0.7	1.3	42.8	54.8	65.1	6.6	4.4	3.7
Sierra Leone	3.2	3.8	4.5	2.0	2.1	2.3	24.5	29.9	36.2	5.0	4.9	4.8
Somalia	6.7	8.2	9.5	4.0	3.1	1.3	22.2	23.6	25.7	3.7	3.9	4.0
South Africa	29.2	34.6	41.5	2.6	2.5	2.2	48.1	48.7	50.8	2.6	2.6	2.8
Sudan	18.7	22.5	26.7	3.1	2.7	2.1	20.0	21.6	24.6	4.5	3.8	4.4
Swaziland	0.6	0.7	0.9	3.2	3.2	2.9	17.8	23.6	31.2	8.3	7.2	7.0
Tanzania	18.6	23.2	29.6	3.1	3.2	3.1	14.8	18.9	24.4	11.0	6.9	6.3
Togo	2.6	3.2	4.1	2.6	2.9	3.1	22.9	27.3	30.8	9.3	5.8	4.7
Uganda	12.8	14.8	19.2	2.7	2.1	3.2	8.8	10.4	12.5	3.8	4.4	5.5
Zaire	27.0	33.9	43.8	2.9	3.2	3.2	28.7	28.0	29.1	2.4	2.8	3.7
Zambia	5.7	7.2	9.0	3.2	3.5	2.7	39.8	41.3	43.1	6.0	4.2	3.6
Zimbabwe	7.0	8.9	11.0	2.8	3.4	2.7	22.3	26.5	32.1	5.5	5.9	5.1
NORTH AFRICA	88.4	106.4	127.1	2.5	2.7	2.2	44.6	47.3	50.6	3.5	3.6	3.0
Algeria	18.7	23.2	28.0	3.1	3.1	2.4	43.4	49.2	55.8	4.4	4.9	3.9
Egypt, Arab Republic	40.9	48.9	58.2	2.3	2.6	2.2	43.8	43.9	44.8	2.5	2.6	2.4
Libya	3.0	4.1	5.4	4.3	4.3	3.5	69.6	79.2	86.0	7.4	6.2	4.5
Morocco	19.4	22.6	26.6	2.3	2.2	2.0	41.0	44.8	48.4	4.0	3.7	3.0
Tunisia	6.4	7.7	9.0	2.5	2.6	2.0	51.4	53.7	57.3	3.3	3.3	2.7
ALL AFRICA	468.9	573.0	710.8	2.8	2.9	2.7	27.3	30.5	34.6	4.5	4.5	4.3

Note: Minus sign indicates population outflow.

13-5. Components of population change

	Total fertility rate			Crude birth rate			Crude death rate		
	1982	1987	1995	1982	1987	1995	1982	1987	1995
SUB-SAHARAN AFRICA	..	6.3	5.7	47.1	45.2	38.2	17.0	15.5	13.2
excluding South Africa	..	6.4	5.8	48.1	46.2	38.8	17.5	15.9	13.6
excl. S. Africa & Nigeria	..	6.5	5.9	47.7	46.6	38.1	17.6	16.1	13.6
Angola	7.0	7.2	6.9	50.8	51.3	48.8	22.8	21.3	18.8
Benin	6.5	6.5	6.0	49.3	47.8	43.4	18.1	15.7	15.1
Botswana	6.8	5.3	4.4	46.8	38.5	34.3	12.8	6.8	11.5
Burkina Faso	7.5	7.2	6.7	46.9	47.5	46.0	19.9	18.6	18.1
Burundi	6.8	6.8	6.5	46.1	46.6	43.8	17.6	17.2	17.5
Cameroon	6.5	5.9	5.7	46.3	41.3	41.0	14.7	12.5	11.1
Cape Verde	6.3	4.7	4.0	38.3	36.0	33.9	11.3	9.9	8.2
Central African Republic	5.7	5.7	5.1	41.5	41.4	38.4	18.6	17.4	16.6
Chad	5.9	5.9	5.9	44.2	44.4	43.0	21.4	19.6	17.6
Comoros	6.6	6.4	5.9	45.5	45.2	42.6	16.8	15.7	11.8
Congo	6.3	6.3	6.0	45.9	47.8	47.0	14.5	15.6	15.7
Côte d'Ivoire	7.4	6.8	5.3	50.2	49.9	37.1	15.7	14.7	12.2
Djibouti	6.6	6.2	5.8	47.9	46.3	46.0	19.1	17.9	15.9
Equatorial Guinea	5.8	5.9	5.9	43.3	43.8	43.5	21.1	19.6	17.3
Eritrea	..	5.8	5.8	..	..	42.9	..	..	16.1
Ethiopia	7.0	7.0	7.0	49.3	52.8	46.6	20.7	18.8	16.7
Gabon	4.5	5.0	5.2	33.8	36.5	38.7	18.1	16.6	14.9
Gambia, The	6.5	6.2	5.3	48.2	46.5	41.0	23.1	20.7	18.2
Ghana	6.5	6.2	5.1	45.2	46.2	37.0	14.2	13.4	10.1
Guinea	6.2	6.5	6.5	46.8	48.5	47.6	23.5	21.6	19.8
Guinea-Bissau	6.0	6.0	6.0	43.3	42.9	45.2	24.7	23.0	24.9
Kenya	7.7	6.3	4.7	49.7	42.1	34.7	12.1	11.1	9.3
Lesotho	5.5	5.3	4.6	40.4	36.3	32.6	13.9	12.3	10.7
Liberia	6.8	6.8	6.5	47.2	47.3	46.7	16.7	15.8	19.3
Madagascar	6.5	6.5	5.8	45.8	45.8	41.4	15.4	14.0	11.0
Malawi	7.6	7.6	6.6	56.6	55.6	46.8	22.3	21.4	20.3
Mali	7.1	7.1	6.8	49.0	50.1	49.4	21.6	19.4	16.5
Mauritania	6.1	5.7	5.2	42.3	41.0	38.5	18.5	15.9	13.8
Mauritius	2.5	2.1	2.2	22.2	18.7	19.1	6.0	6.5	6.5
Mozambique	6.5	6.5	6.2	45.7	45.6	43.6	20.1	19.0	17.9
Namibia	5.8	5.6	5.0	40.3	39.0	36.9	13.5	12.0	11.7
Niger	7.5	7.4	7.4	51.7	51.6	51.6	22.2	20.5	18.8
Nigeria	6.9	6.1	5.5	49.6	44.6	41.7	17.1	15.2	13.5
Rwanda	8.1	7.0	6.2	50.4	45.1	40.7	18.6	16.6	22.0
São Tomé and Principe	5.3	5.3	4.8	38.7	36.6	34.7	10.2	9.3	7.4
Senegal	6.7	6.5	5.7	46.0	45.0	40.1	19.4	17.2	13.7
Seychelles	3.5	3.0	2.4	24.1	24.9	21.6	7.4	7.4	6.5
Sierra Leone	6.5	6.5	6.5	48.9	49.1	48.2	28.6	27.1	29.5
Somalia	7.0	7.0	7.0	49.6	48.9	48.5	21.8	20.1	17.6
South Africa	4.8	4.4	3.9	35.5	32.9	29.8	11.1	9.7	8.2
Sudan	6.4	5.4	4.8	43.5	36.9	34.6	15.8	14.0	12.2
Swaziland	6.0	5.3	4.6	43.1	39.8	34.3	13.7	12.5	9.0
Tanzania	6.7	6.4	5.8	46.5	45.2	42.4	14.8	13.8	14.0
Togo	6.6	6.6	6.4	44.9	44.7	43.5	15.7	14.1	14.6
Uganda	7.3	7.1	6.7	49.1	50.5	48.9	17.6	17.6	19.1
Zaire	6.7	6.7	..	48.3	47.8	..	16.2	15.0	..
Zambia	6.9	6.5	5.7	49.0	47.4	44.8	14.8	14.1	17.6
Zimbabwe	6.6	5.4	3.8	49.1	38.8	30.6	12.7	8.0	9.6
NORTH AFRICA	..	4.6	3.5	38.9	35.2	26.8	11.6	9.7	7.1
Algeria	6.4	5.3	3.5	40.6	35.5	26.2	10.7	8.3	5.4
Egypt, Arab Republic	5.1	4.3	3.4	39.1	35.1	26.3	12.7	10.8	8.1
Libya	7.2	6.9	6.1	45.6	44.0	40.7	10.9	9.4	7.4
Morocco	5.1	4.4	3.4	37.3	35.6	26.7	11.4	9.8	7.1
Tunisia	4.9	3.9	2.9	33.7	29.2	24.0	8.4	7.2	6.1
ALL AFRICA	..	5.9	5.2	45.6	43.3	36.2	16.0	14.4	12.1

13-6. Survival prospects

	Life expectancy at birth (years)		*Infant mortality (per thousand)*		*Mortality of children under 5 years (per thousand)*	*Maternal mortality (per 100,000 live births)*	*Adult HIV-1 seroprevalence (per 100 adults)*
	1982	*1995*	*1982*	*1995*	*1995*	*1995 or MR available*	*1994*
SUB-SAHARAN AFRICA	48	52	111	92	157	..	4.3
excluding South Africa	47	51	114	94	163	..	4.4
excl. S. Africa & Nigeria	48	51	119	99	159	..	4.9
Angola	42	47	149	124	209	..	1.0
Benin	48	50	118	95	156	..	1.2
Botswana	60	68	64	56	74	220	18.0
Burkina Faso	45	49	117	99	164	939	6.7
Burundi	48	49	117	98	162	1,327	2.7
Cameroon	51	57	88	56	86	..	3.0
Cape Verde	60	65	66	46	68	..	..
Central African Republic	47	48	114	98	160	649	5.8
Chad	43	48	143	117	197	1,594	2.7
Comoros	50	56	120	87	143	460	0.1
Congo	51	51	87	90	144	822	7.2
Côte d'Ivoire	53	55	105	86	138	887	6.8
Djibouti	45	50	132	108	181	..	3.0
Equatorial Guinea	44	49	137	111	185	430	1.1
Eritrea	44	48	..	131	196	929	3.2
Ethiopia	40	49	159	112	188	1,528	2.5
Gabon	49	55	112	89	145	483	2.3
Gambia, The	41	46	154	126	213	..	2.1
Ghana	53	59	98	73	116	742	2.3
Guinea	40	44	157	128	220	880	0.6
Guinea-Bissau	39	38	163	136	233	..	3.1
Kenya	56	58	66	58	90	..	8.3
Lesotho	54	61	100	76	121	598	3.1
Liberia	51	54	153	172	239	544	1.3
Madagascar	51	52	130	89	127	..	0.1
Malawi	45	43	163	133	225	620	13.6
Mali	43	50	180	123	192	1,249	1.3
Mauritania	47	51	117	96	158	..	0.7
Mauritius	67	71	28	16	20	112	0.1
Mozambique	44	47	135	113	190	1,512	5.8
Namibia	54	59	84	62	78	518	6.5
Niger	42	47	146	119	200	593	1.0
Nigeria	46	53	96	80	176	..	2.2
Rwanda	46	39	124	133	200	1,512	7.2
São Tomé and Principe	63	69	80	60	78	..	..
Senegal	45	50	87	62	97	..	1.4
Seychelles	69	72	19	15	19	..	..
Sierra Leone	35	40	189	179	236	..	3.0
Somalia	43	49	143	128	218	1,725	0.3
South Africa	58	64	63	50	67	404	3.2
Sudan	49	54	92	77	109	607	1.0
Swaziland	52	58	110	69	96	..	3.8
Tanzania	51	51	98	82	133	748	6.4
Togo	50	56	105	88	128	626	8.5
Uganda	48	42	116	98	160	506	14.5
Zaire	50	..	107	..	144	..	3.7
Zambia	51	46	88	109	180	..	17.1
Zimbabwe	56	57	80	55	83	..	17.4
NORTH AFRICA	59	65	99	50	67	..	0.0
Algeria	60	70	88	34	42	140	0.1
Egypt, Arab Republic	57	63	112	56	76	..	0.0
Libya	58	65	97	61	75	..	0.1
Morocco	60	65	92	55	75	372	..
Tunisia	63	69	62	39	50	138	0.0
ALL AFRICA	50	55	109	86	145	..	3.6

13-7. Immunization and ORT use

	Percentage of children (0-1 years) immunized against						*ORT use among the under fives (percent)*
	DPT			*Measles*			
	1986	*1992*	*1995*	*1986*	*1992*	*1995*	*1992-93*
SUB-SAHARAN AFRICA	..	..	58	..	..	59	49
excluding South Africa	..	..	57	..	..	58	49
excl. S. Africa & Nigeria	..	..	60	..	..	61	49
Angola	9	26	21	..	39	32	48
Benin	21	67	79	..	70	72	28
Botswana	66	..	78	64	..	68	64
Burkina Faso	34	37	47	64	42	55	15
Burundi	65	83	57	55	75	44	49
Cameroon	..	56	48	..	52	31	84
Cape Verde	54	..	73	59	..	66	5
Central African Republic	19	82	40	24	82	70	24
Chad	10	10	18	..	25	24	15
Comoros	29	..	59	26	..	59	70
Congo	71	..	50	..	..	39	67
Côte d'Ivoire	22	48	40	..	42	57	16
Djibouti	26	..	49	19	..	42	56
Equatorial Guinea	..	..	64	..	..	61	40
Eritrea	..	..	45	..	..	45	..
Ethiopia	7	44	57	10	37	54	68
Gabon	48	..	48	58	64	50	25
Gambia, The	72	..	93	..	..	88	51
Ghana	35	43	71	63	39	68	44
Guinea	2	41	73	9	39	69	82
Guinea-Bissau	29	..	74	..	..	68	26
Kenya	72	36	84	65	36	73	69
Lesotho	..	..	56	..	..	82	78
Liberia	15	..	43	..	..	44	15
Madagascar	22	46	67	18	33	59	26
Malawi	70	81	98	65	78	99	50
Mali	3	35	46	5	40	49	41
Mauritania	..	..	50	..	..	53	54
Mauritius	86	..	89	75	..	85	..
Mozambique	32	19	57	39	23	71	60
Namibia	..	..	61	..	..	57	75
Niger	5	18	19	..	24	38	17
Nigeria	16	..	44	17	..	50	80
Rwanda	77	89	90	63	89	88	36
São Tomé and Principe	65	70	79	58	..	74	50
Senegal	..	46	80	69	43	80	27
Seychelles	94	..	97	95	..	99	..
Sierra Leone	..	..	41	..	..	44	60
Somalia	17	18	18	25	30	30	78
South Africa	..	67	73	..	63	76	..
Sudan	14	63	76	11	58	74	47
Swaziland	73	..	96	66	..	94	85
Tanzania	74	79	79	97	75	75	83
Togo	23	73	73	..	61	65	33
Uganda	21	77	79	32	74	79	45
Zaire	32	..	35	39	..	41	46
Zambia	66	79	76	..	76	78	90
Zimbabwe	75	89	80	74	87	78	..
NORTH AFRICA	..	..	84	..	..	82	38
Algeria	..	89	75	..	83	69	27
Egypt, Arab Republic	80	86	82	78	89	82	34
Libya	53	62	91	52	59	89	80
Morocco	53	79	93	48	76	92	14
Tunisia	72	90	90	67	80	89	22
ALL AFRICA	..	..	62	..	..	63	48

Notes: ORT = Oral re-hydration therapy; DPT = diphtheria, pertussis (whopping cough), and tetanus.

13-8. Child malnutrition

	Percentage of children (1986-94): exclusively breastfed (0-3 months)	breastfed, plus other food (6-9 months)	still breastfeading (20-23 months)	Percentage of infants with low birth weight 1988	1991-94	Percentage of under-five (1984-95) suffering from moderate to severe Underweight	Wasting	Stunting
SUB-SAHARAN AFRICA	..	..	..	..	..	..	..	..
excluding South Africa	..	..	..	..	..	..	..	..
excl. S. Africa & Nigeria	..	..	..	..	..	..	..	..
Angola	3	83	53	21	..	20	..	..
Benin	..	..	..	..	..	36	7	34
Botswana	41	82	23	..	..	15	..	..
Burkina Faso	3	44	..	11	12	46	13	33
Burundi	89	66	73	..	..	31	6	47
Cameroon	7	77	35	10	13	14	3	26
Cape Verde	..	..	..	..	..	15	6	24
Central African Republic	..	..	..	15	18	30	..	28
Chad	..	..	..	..	..	35	..	13
Comoros	..	..	..	7	..	..	..	..
Congo	43	..	27	..	15	24	6	28
Côte d'Ivoire	..	..	..	15	14	12	..	24
Djibouti	..	..	..	11	..	40	11	22
Equatorial Guinea	..	..	..	..	..	..	2	40
Eritrea	..	..	..	..	..	..	18	49
Ethiopia	74	..	35	..	..	47	8	64
Gabon	..	..	..	10	10	25	..	18
Gambia, The	..	..	61	..	35	20	7	24
Ghana	8	36	53	5	5	27	11	26
Guinea	..	..	..	..	18	18	11	27
Guinea-Bissau	..	..	..	13	13	..	5	22
Kenya	17	90	54	15	18	23	8	34
Lesotho	..	..	..	10	10	21	2	33
Liberia	15	56	26	..	..	..	3	37
Madagascar	47	80	45	10	10	32	7	50
Malawi	3	88	56	10	10	27	5	49
Mali	8	45	44	13	10	25	11	24
Mauritania	12	39	..	..	..	30	16	57
Mauritius	16	29	..	8	..	24	14	10
Mozambique	..	..	..	11	16	..	..	48
Namibia	22	65	23	..	..	..	9	28
Niger	..	..	..	..	..	49	16	32
Nigeria	2	52	43	..	18	43	9	43
Rwanda	90	68	..	..	..	28	4	48
São Tomé and Principe	..	..	..	7	3	17	5	26
Senegal	7	41	48	..	..	20	9	22
Seychelles	..	..	..	10	9	6	2	5
Sierra Leone	..	94	41	13	..	23	9	35
Somalia	..	..	..	..	..	..	..	30
South Africa	..	..	..	..	..	43	3	23
Sudan	14	45	44	..	17	..	13	34
Swaziland	..	..	..	..	..	10	1	30
Tanzania	32	59	57	16	..	28	6	43
Togo	10	86	68	32	..	24	4	34
Uganda	63	71	24	..	..	23	2	38
Zaire	..	..	..	10	13	35	10	45
Zambia	13	88	34	..	..	27	5	46
Zimbabwe	11	94	26	5	15	16	6	23
NORTH AFRICA	..	..	..	..	..	10	..	..
Algeria	..	..	..	..	..	9	6	18
Egypt, Arab Republic	38	52	..	12	..	9	3	24
Libya	..	..	..	5	5	..	3	15
Morocco	65	35	..	..	9	9	2	23
Tunisia	12	53	16	..	7	8	4	23
ALL AFRICA	..	..	..	..	..	..	..	..

13-9. Access to sanitation facilities

	Percentage of population with access to sanitation facilities					
	1985			1993-95		
	Total	*Urban*	*Rural*	*Total*	*Urban*	*Rural*
SUB-SAHARAN AFRICA	..	..	..	..	..	..
excluding South Africa	..	45	..	..	..	..
excl. S. Africa & Nigeria	..	..	20	..	..	..
Angola	18	27	16	16	..	..
Benin	10	45	4	22	49	7
Botswana	36	79	13	55	91	41
Burkina Faso	9	38	5	14	..	..
Burundi	52	90	25	48	71	47
Cameroon	36	..	..	40	73	21
Cape Verde	10	36	9	..	..	..
Central African Republic	19	36	9	..	..	..
Chad	14	..	..	32	..	..
Comoros	..	..	..	..	..	..
Congo	40	..	..	9	11	7
Côte d'Ivoire	..	..	..	54	..	..
Djibouti	37	43	19	..	..	..
Equatorial Guinea	..	28	..	50	33	52
Eritrea	..	..	..	..	..	..
Ethiopia	..	..	5	10	..	..
Gabon	50	..	..	76	79	67
Gambia, The	..	..	..	34	..	..
Ghana	26	47	17	29	61	11
Guinea	..	..	..	6	24	10
Guinea-Bissau	25	..	..	20	32	19
Kenya	44	75	39	43	69	35
Lesotho	..	..	..	35	..	..
Liberia	21	24	20	24	..	..
Madagascar	..	8	..	17	..	..
Malawi	60	88	56	63	82	68
Mali	21	90	5	44	..	..
Mauritania	..	7	..	..	..	..
Mauritius	97	100	95	100	..	..
Mozambique	..	..	..	23	53	12
Namibia	..	..	..	36	89	15
Niger	9	36	3	15	..	..
Nigeria	..	30	..	63	89	45
Rwanda	..	60	60	..	..	..
São Tomé and Principe	15	..	..	21	..	..
Senegal	..	87	..	..	..	..
Seychelles	99	..	..	..	..	99
Sierra Leone	21	43	10	..	..	..
Somalia	15	44	5	..	..	..
South Africa	..	..	..	46	..	..
Sudan	5	20	1	..	85	45
Swaziland	..	100	25	..	..	..
Tanzania	..	90	78	86	97	83
Togo	14	34	8	20	..	..
Uganda	13	40	10	60	..	..
Zaire	..	..	10	9	..	..
Zambia	47	56	41	42	76	34
Zimbabwe	26	100	5	58	98	50
NORTH AFRICA	..	..	..	..	..	..
Algeria	..	..	..	..	..	..
Egypt, Arab Republic	..	..	..	..	..	..
Libya	91	100	53	..	..	..
Morocco	46	..	..	63	96	32
Tunisia	52	84	16	72	100	36
ALL AFRICA	..	..	..	..	..	..

13-10. Access to safe water

	Percentage of population with access to safe water					
	1988			*1993-95*		
	Total	*Urban*	*Rural*	*Total*	*Urban*	*Rural*
SUB-SAHARAN AFRICA	..	..	..	..	..	..
excluding South Africa	..	..	..	44	73	33
excl. S. Africa & Nigeria	..	..	..	..	..	..
Angola	..	75	18	32	..	..
Benin	..	79	35	70	82	63
Botswana	56	100	33	70	100	53
Burkina Faso	35	50	26	..	..	..
Burundi	..	..	27	58	..	55
Cameroon	..	47	27	41	71	24
Cape Verde	..	..	49	..	..	..
Central African Republic	19	29	14	..	..	..
Chad	..	..	..	29	..	..
Comoros	..	..	..	48	..	..
Congo	..	..	..	60	..	8
Côte d'Ivoire	..	60	77	82	97	73
Djibouti	..	..	..	..	..	..
Equatorial Guinea	..	..	..	..	..	48
Eritrea	..	..	..	..	..	..
Ethiopia	10	..	..	27	90	20
Gabon	52	..	50	67	80	30
Gambia, The	..	..	..	61	87	86
Ghana	..	..	40	56	76	46
Guinea	27	62	15	49	78	51
Guinea-Bissau	21	19	22	27	18	47
Kenya	..	..	..	49	74	43
Lesotho	40	..	40	57	..	..
Liberia	..	50	25	40	..	..
Madagascar	..	..	..	32	..	..
Malawi	51	66	49	54	..	41
Mali	..	48	17	44	..	25
Mauritania	..	..	..	..	49	86
Mauritius	95	100	92	100	..	..
Mozambique	19	50	12	28	44	17
Namibia	..	..	..	57	97	37
Niger	..	..	..	57	58	..
Nigeria	..	..	..	43	69	11
Rwanda	77	..	..	..	..	..
São Tomé and Principe	..	..	..	70	..	..
Senegal	..	..	..	..	..	..
Seychelles	90	..	..	97	99	80
Sierra Leone	..	86	20	..	..	..
Somalia	..	..	..	..	..	..
South Africa	..	..	..	..	..	..
Sudan	35	..	20	..	..	73
Swaziland	..	..	..	60	80	42
Tanzania	..	80	..	49	65	45
Togo	..	..	..	67	64	..
Uganda	..	45	12	42	..	..
Zaire	36	62	16	25	..	..
Zambia	..	..	..	47	76	43
Zimbabwe	65	100	14	74	99	65
NORTH AFRICA	..	91	..	..	..	..
Algeria	77	86	55	..	..	..
Egypt, Arab Republic	..	100	..	..	..	..
Libya	90	..	..	..	..	..
Morocco	47	74	17	59	100	18
Tunisia	78	100	52	86	100	67
ALL AFRICA	..	..	..	..	..	..

13-11. Access to health services

	Percentage of population with access to health services								
	1985			*1988*			*1991-93*		
	Total	*Urban*	*Rural*	*Total*	*Urban*	*Rural*	*Total*	*Urban*	*Rural*
SUB-SAHARAN AFRICA	..	..	..	..	..	..	..	..	..
excluding South Africa	..	..	..	..	..	..	..	..	..
excl. S.Africa & Nigeria	51	..	..	..	..	..	..	..	..
Angola	..	..	..	..	..	..	24	..	..
Benin	..	..	..	18	..	..	42	..	..
Botswana	..	..	..	86	..	..	..	..	..
Burkina Faso	70	..	..	..	..	..	..	..	..
Burundi	45	..	..	..	..	..	80	..	..
Cameroon	..	..	..	15	..	..	..	..	..
Cape Verde	..	..	..	82	..	..	..	..	..
Central African Republic	..	..	..	13	..	..	..	..	..
Chad	30	..	..	..	..	..	26	..	..
Comoros	82	..	..	..	..	..	..	..	..
Congo	..	..	..	..	..	..	..	..	..
Côte d'Ivoire	..	..	..	60	..	..	..	..	..
Djibouti	..	..	..	..	100	95	..	..	..
Equatorial Guinea	..	..	..	..	..	..	..	..	..
Eritrea	..	..	..	..	..	..	..	..	..
Ethiopia	44	..	..	45	..	..	55	..	..
Gabon	80	..	..	87	..	..	..	..	..
Gambia, The	..	..	..	..	..	..	..	..	..
Ghana	64	..	..	65	..	..	25	..	..
Guinea	13	..	..	32	..	..	45	..	..
Guinea-Bissau	64	..	..	..	..	..	..	..	..
Kenya	..	..	..	..	..	..	..	..	..
Lesotho	50	..	..	80	..	..	..	..	..
Liberia	35	..	..	34	..	..	..	..	..
Madagascar	65	..	..	65	..	..	..	..	..
Malawi	54	..	..	80	..	..	..	..	..
Mali	..	..	..	..	..	..	..	..	..
Mauritania	30	..	..	..	..	..	..	..	..
Mauritius	100	100	100	100	100	100	99	..	..
Mozambique	40	..	..	30	..	..	..	..	..
Namibia	..	..	..	..	..	..	..	..	..
Niger	48	..	..	..	..	..	30	..	17
Nigeria	..	..	..	..	..	..	67	87	62
Rwanda	..	..	..	..	..	..	..	..	..
São Tomé and Principe	..	..	..	88	..	..	..	..	..
Senegal	..	..	..	40	..	..	..	..	..
Seychelles	99	..	..	99	..	..	99	..	..
Sierra Leone	36	..	..	..	..	..	..	88	..
Somalia	20	50	15	..	..	..	..	..	..
South Africa	..	..	..	..	..	..	..	..	..
Sudan	70	..	..	70	..	..	70	..	..
Swaziland	..	..	..	..	..	..	55	..	..
Tanzania	73	..	..	..	..	..	93	94	73
Togo	..	..	..	..	..	..	..	..	..
Uganda	42	..	..	71	..	..	..	..	..
Zaire	33	..	..	..	..	..	59	..	..
Zambia	70	..	..	75	100	50	..	..	..
Zimbabwe	71	..	..	..	90	80	..	..	..
NORTH AFRICA	..	..	..	..	100	93	88	..	78
Algeria	..	..	..	..	100	80	..	..	..
Egypt, Arab Republic	99	100	99	99	100	99	99	100	99
Libya	100	100	100	100	100	100	100	..	..
Morocco	..	..	..	..	..	..	62	100	30
Tunisia	..	..	..	..	..	..	90	..	..
ALL AFRICA	..	..	..	..	..	..	..	..	..

13-12. Health care

	Population per physician		*Population per nursing personnel*		*Percentage of births attended by trained health personnel*	*Health expenditure as % of GDP*
	1981	*1990-93*	*1981*	*1990-93*	*1990-93*	*1991-95*
SUB-SAHARAN AFRICA	..	..	..	..	..	..
excluding South Africa	..	..	..	..	..	..
excl. S.Africa & Nigeria	..	..	..	..	..	..
Angola	..	23,725	..	..	16	4.0
Benin	16,989	..	1,658	4,182	34	1.7
Botswana	7,411	..	700	..	..	1.9
Burkina Faso	55,721	..	3,073	..	33	2.3
Burundi	..	17,153	..	4,778	26	0.9
Cameroon	..	11,996	..	1,999	25	1.0
Cape Verde	..	4,288	..	1,640	49	..
Central African Republic	22,766	25,920	2,143	11,309	..	1.7
Chad	..	30,030	..	..	21	1.8
Comoros	..	7,579	..	2,787	..	..
Congo	..	3,713	..	1,401	..	3.6
Côte d'Ivoire	..	11,739	..	3,244	..	1.4
Djibouti	4,291	5,913	957	724	..	..
Equatorial Guinea	..	3,556	..	2,286	..	..
Eritrea	..	..	..	..	..	1.1
Ethiopia	88,119	..	4,998	..	..	1.1
Gabon	2,184	..	..	..	..	0.5
Gambia, The	..	..	..	..	65	1.8
Ghana	..	..	621	..	42	1.0
Guinea	45,457	7,445	5,056	5,166	76	0.9
Guinea-Bissau	..	..	..	..	..	1.1
Kenya	10,071	21,970	983	8,675	..	1.9
Lesotho	..	24,095	..	2,040	..	3.5
Liberia	9,473	..	2,965	..	..	..
Madagascar	9,891	8,385	1,721	3,736	71	1.0
Malawi	53,605	..	3,024	..	41	2.3
Mali	25,997	..	2,279	..	..	1.3
Mauritania	..	15,772	..	2,261	..	1.5
Mauritius	1,817	..	575	..	91	2.2
Mozambique	36,969	..	5,610	..	29	4.6
Namibia	..	4,328	..	317	71	3.9
Niger	..	53,986	..	3,765	21	2.2
Nigeria	..	..	..	..	45	..
Rwanda	32,318	..	10,314	..	28	..
São Tomé and Principe	2,525	..	564	..	63	..
Senegal	12,683	18,192	1,931	13,174	..	..
Seychelles	..	764	..	244	99	..
Sierra Leone	18,973	..	2,078	..	..	1.6
Somalia	25,334	..	..	..	2	..
South Africa	..	..	..	..	..	3.6
Sudan	9,582	..	1,408	..	..	..
Swaziland	..	9,566	743	628	67	..
Tanzania	..	..	..	..	..	2.8
Togo	21,357	11,385	1,657	3,060	..	1.7
Uganda	21,405	..	2,009	..	..	1.8
Zaire	..	15,150	..	1,355	..	..
Zambia	7,956	10,917	1,693	..	43	..
Zimbabwe	7,074	7,384	997	1,594	49	2.1
NORTH AFRICA	5,936	1,280	799	..	..	..
Algeria	..	1,062	..	..	..	3.3
Egypt, Arab Republic	733	1,317	762	489	24	..
Libya	612	957	355	340	68	..
Morocco	18,558	..	898	..	..	1.6
Tunisia	3,642	1,549	956	411	50	3.0
ALL AFRICA	..	..	..	..	..	..

13-13. Illiteracy rate

	Percentage of population 15 years of age and above that is illiterate								
	1985			*1990*			*1995*		
	Total	*Male*	*Female*	*Total*	*Male*	*Female*	*Total*	*Male*	*Female*
SUB-SAHARAN AFRICA	57	45	68	..	..	64	43	33	52
excluding South Africa	57	45	68	53	41	64	46	35	56
excl. S. Africa & Nigeria	56	45	68	..	..	..	47	35	56
Angola	64	50	77	58	44	72	..	..	..
Benin	81	74	88	77	68	84	63	51	74
Botswana	30	19	40	26	16	35	30	20	40
Burkina Faso	86	77	94	82	72	91	81	71	91
Burundi	58	47	68	50	39	60	65	51	78
Cameroon	52	39	64	46	34	57	37	25	48
Cape Verde	..	..	..	..	..	..	28	19	36
Central African Republic	69	55	81	62	48	75	40	32	48
Chad	77	66	88	70	58	82	52	38	65
Comoros	..	..	..	..	..	..	43	36	50
Congo	48	34	62	43	30	56	25	17	33
Côte d'Ivoire	51	38	66	46	33	60	60	50	70
Djibouti	..	..	..	..	..	..	54	40	67
Equatorial Guinea	55	41	69	50	36	63	..	10	32
Eritrea	..	..	..	..	..	..	..	..	..
Ethiopia	..	..	..	..	..	..	65	55	75
Gabon	44	30	57	39	27	52	37	26	47
Gambia, The	80	70	90	73	61	84	61	47	75
Ghana	47	36	58	40	30	49	..	24	47
Guinea	83	75	92	76	65	87	..	50	78
Guinea-Bissau	70	57	82	64	50	76	45	32	58
Kenya	35	23	47	31	20	42	22	14	30
Lesotho	26	38	16	..	..	..	29	19	38
Liberia	68	57	79	61	50	71	..	46	78
Madagascar	23	14	32	20	12	27	..	..	..
Malawi	59	48	69	..	..	..	44	28	58
Mali	77	69	85	68	59	76	69	61	77
Mauritania	73	60	84	66	53	79	..	50	74
Mauritius	17	11	23	..	..	..	17	13	21
Mozambique	72	61	84	67	55	79	60	42	77
Namibia	..	..	..	..	..	..	..	..	..
Niger	79	68	89	72	60	83	86	79	93
Nigeria	57	45	69	49	38	61	43	33	53
Rwanda	55	41	68	50	36	63	40	30	48
São Tomé and Principe	..	..	..	..	..	..	..	..	..
Senegal	68	55	81	62	48	75	67	57	77
Seychelles	..	..	..	..	..	..	21	..	..
Sierra Leone	87	79	94	79	69	89	..	55	82
Somalia	83	73	91	76	64	86	..	..	..
South Africa	..	..	..	..	..	..	18	18	18
Sudan	76	61	90	73	57	88	54	42	65
Swaziland	32	30	34	..	..	..	23	22	24
Tanzania	..	..	..	..	..	..	32	21	43
Togo	62	49	75	57	44	69	48	33	63
Uganda	57	43	71	52	38	65	38	26	50
Zaire	34	21	47	..	..	..	33	13	32
Zambia	33	23	41	27	19	35	22	14	29
Zimbabwe	38	30	45	33	26	40	15	10	20
NORTH AFRICA	54	40	68	47	35	61	47	34	59
Algeria	51	37	65	43	30	55	38	26	51
Egypt, Arab Republic	55	40	71	52	37	66	49	36	61
Libya	44	30	60	36	25	50	..	12	37
Morocco	58	46	71	51	39	62	56	43	69
Tunisia	42	32	53	32	26	44	33	21	45
ALL AFRICA	56	44	68	51	39	63	44	33	54

13-14. Primary school gross enrollment ratio

	Total			Males			Females		
	1980	1989	1992-93	1980	1989	1992-93	1980	1989	1992-93
SUB-SAHARAN AFRICA	79	71	73	85	79	80	64	62	66
excluding South Africa	78	71	69	85	79	76	64	62	61
excl. S. Africa & Nigeria	71	64	62	76	..	69	57	..	56
Angola	175	99	..	0	103	..	0	95	..
Benin	64	55	72	87	73	..	41	37	..
Botswana	91	114	115	83	110	113	100	118	118
Burkina Faso	18	35	39	23	44	48	14	27	31
Burundi	26	71	69	32	79	76	21	63	62
Cameroon	98	103	91	107	111	95	89	95	86
Cape Verde	114	122	131	119	125	132	110	119	130
Central African Republic	71	71	..	92	88	..	51	55	..
Chad	..	57	56	..	79	76	..	35	36
Comoros	88	73	75	100	85	81	75	61	69
Congo	..	..	..	..	..	..	..	..	..
Côte d'Ivoire	79	73	69	95	85	80	63	61	58
Djibouti	37	..	36	..	..	41	..	..	31
Equatorial Guinea	135	..	..	..	..	..	..	..	..
Eritrea	..	25	47	..	26	52	..	24	41
Ethiopia	34	34	27	44	40	33	23	28	21
Gabon	..	..	..	..	..	..	..	..	..
Gambia, The	51	64	67	67	74	79	35	53	56
Ghana	80	74	..	89	82	..	71	67	..
Guinea	36	34	46	48	47	61	25	21	30
Guinea-Bissau	68	..	..	94	..	..	43	..	..
Kenya	115	..	91	120	..	92	110	..	91
Lesotho	102	..	98	85	..	90	120	..	105
Liberia	48	..	..	61	..	..	34	..	..
Madagascar	136	101	73	139	103	75	133	99	72
Malawi	60	68	82	72	74	84	48	61	80
Mali	26	23	30	33	29	37	18	17	23
Mauritania	37	49	69	47	57	76	26	40	62
Mauritius	93	..	106	94	..	107	91	..	106
Mozambique	99	65	60	114	74	69	84	56	51
Namibia	..	129	134	..	123	133	..	136	136
Niger	25	28	28	33	36	35	18	20	21
Nigeria	105	88	90	118	100	101	92	76	79
Rwanda	63	69	..	66	70	..	60	68	..
São Tomé and Principe	..	..	..	..	..	..	..	..	..
Senegal	46	58	60	55	68	67	37	49	53
Seychelles	..	..	..	..	..	..	..	..	..
Sierra Leone	52	56	..	61	66	..	43	45	..
Somalia	19	..	..	24	..	..	14	..	..
South Africa	85	..	115	..	..	116	..	..	115
Sudan	50	..	55	59	..	61	41	..	48
Swaziland	103	0	120	104	0	123	102	0	116
Tanzania	93	69	70	99	69	71	86	68	69
Togo	118	105	102	146	127	122	91	82	81
Uganda	50	..	67	56	..	74	43	..	59
Zaire	92	..	68	108	..	78	77	..	58
Zambia	90	94	..	97	..	..	83	..	..
Zimbabwe	85	126	115	..	128	119	..	124	111
NORTH AFRICA	84	46	96	97	51	104	70	40	88
Algeria	94	98	104	108	106	111	81	89	97
Egypt, Arab Republic	73	0	97	84	0	105	61	0	89
Libya	125	..	110	129	..	110	120	..	110
Morocco	83	69	77	102	82	89	63	55	64
Tunisia	103	115	118	118	122	123	88	107	113
ALL AFRICA	80	65	78	87	72	85	65	57	70

13-15. Pupil progression and efficiency indicator

	Pecentage of cohort reaching grade 4 (1989-93)			*Age efficiency ratio*	
				Primary	*Secondary*
	Total	*Male*	*Female*	*1989-93*	*1989-93*
SUB-SAHARAN AFRICA	..	..	..	..	..
excluding South Africa	..	..	..	..	..
excl. S. Africa & Nigeria	..	..	..	..	..
Angola	44	49	37	..	..
Benin	58	58	58	80	..
Botswana	95	94	95	83	80
Burkina Faso	88	88	89	81	79
Burundi	78	77	78	74	72
Cameroon	..	..	..	74	..
Cape Verde	..	..	..	82	..
Central African Republic	84	..	..	82	..
Chad	71	74	66	..	..
Comoros	..	..	..	61	..
Congo	87	..	..	..	..
Côte d'Ivoire	84	85	83	71	..
Djibouti	83	..	..	83	..
Equatorial Guinea	..	..	..	66	..
Eritrea	..	..	..	55	74
Ethiopia	..	..	..	75	..
Gabon	..	..	..	..	..
Gambia, The	..	..	..	82	96
Ghana	..	..	..	..	..
Guinea	81	84	77	42	73
Guinea-Bissau	..	..	..	..	..
Kenya	..	..	..	..	..
Lesotho	81	76	86	67	63
Liberia	..	..	..	..	..
Madagascar	63	64	61	69	..
Malawi	71	73	68	77	38
Mali	92	87	84	70	75
Mauritania	86	85	87	..	..
Mauritius	99	99	99	..	..
Mozambique	58	60	54	68 ..	
Namibia	64	65	64	66	55
Niger	..	..	..	87	88
Nigeria	81	88	73	..	..
Rwanda	74	73	75	93	78
São Tomé and Principe	..	..	..	72	..
Senegal	..	..	..	83	78
Seychelles	..	..	..	100	..
Sierra Leone	..	..	..	..	..
Somalia	..	..	..	..	..
South Africa	..	..	..	82	65
Sudan	..	..	..	..	..
Swaziland	85	85	86	78	..
Tanzania	89	89	90	72	..
Togo	82	84	79	68	..
Uganda	..	..	..	..	..
Zaire	73	77	68	79	67
Zambia	..	..	..	..	..
Zimbabwe	..	..	..	..	..
NORTH AFRICA	..	..	..	81	73
Algeria	97	97	96	91	54
Egypt, Arab Republic	98	..	..	76	81
Libya	..	..	..	96	..
Morocco	85	85	84	76	84
Tunisia	94	93	93	83	59
ALL AFRICA	..	..	..	..	..

Notes: In Seychelles and Sudan, a policy of automatic promotion is practiced at the primary level of education. Tanzanian figures refer to mainland only.

13-16. Net primary enrollment ratio

	Total			*Males*			*Females*		
	1980	*1989*	*1992-93*	*1980*	*1989*	*1992-93*	*1980*	*1989*	*1992-93*
SUB-SAHARAN AFRICA	15	..	..	14	..	..	13	..	..
excluding South Africa	16	..	..	14	..	..	13	..	..
excl. S. Africa & Nigeria	20	..	..	18	..	..	16	..	..
Angola	0	..	..	0	..	..	0	..	..
Benin	0	43	..	0	56	..	0	29	..
Botswana	75	94	96	69	91	93	82	98	99
Burkina Faso	15	..	32	19	..	39	11	..	25
Burundi	20	..	51	23	..	56	16	..	47
Cameroon	0	76	..	0	81	..	0	71	..
Cape Verde	90	100	100	93	100	100	88	99	100
Central African Republic	56	58	..	73	71	..	41	46	..
Chad	..	..	..	..	..	..	..	..	..
Comoros	0	..	51	0	..	55	0	..	46
Congo	..	..	..	..	..	..	..	..	..
Côte d'Ivoire	0	..	..	0	..	..	0	..	..
Djibouti	0	..	30	..	..	34	..	..	26
Equatorial Guinea	..	..	..	..	..	..	..	..	..
Eritrea	..	..	26	..	..	27	..	..	24
Ethiopia	0	..	21	0	..	24	0	..	17
Gabon	..	..	..	..	..	..	..	..	..
Gambia, The	48	53	55	63	62	64	33	45	46
Ghana	0	..	..	0	..	..	0	..	..
Guinea	0	..	40	0	..	..	0	..	..
Guinea-Bissau	47	..	..	63	..	..	31	..	..
Kenya	91	..	..	92	..	..	89	..	..
Lesotho	66	..	65	54	..	59	78	..	71
Liberia	..	..	..	..	..	..	..	..	..
Madagascar	0	64	..	0	64	..	0	63	..
Malawi	43	51	63	48	53	61	38	50	65
Mali	20	..	23	0	..	28	0	..	18
Mauritania	0	..	..	0	..	..	0	..	..
Mauritius	79	..	94	80	..	94	79	..	94
Mozambique	36	..	41	39	..	46	33	..	35
Namibia	..	87	89	..	..	86	..	..	93
Niger	21	..	..	0	..	..	0	..	..
Nigeria	0	..	..	0	..	..	0	..	..
Rwanda	59	66	..	62	66	..	57	65	..
São Tomé and Principe	..	..	..	..	..	..	..	..	..
Senegal	37	48	50	44	55	..	30	41	..
Seychelles	..	..	..	..	..	..	..	..	..
Sierra Leone	0	..	..	0	..	..	0	..	..
Somalia	14	..	..	18	..	..	10	..	..
South Africa	0	..	..	..	..	..	..	..	..
Sudan	0	..	..	0	..	..	0	..	..
Swaziland	80	82	93	0	80	93	0	84	93
Tanzania	68	..	50	0	..	50	0	..	51
Togo	0	73	69	0	86	80	0	60	58
Uganda	0	..	..	0	..	..	0	..	..
Zaire	0	..	54	0	..	60	0	..	47
Zambia	77	..	..	81	81	..	73	73	..
Zimbabwe	0	..	..	100	..	..	100	..	..
NORTH AFRICA	40	..	86	46	..	92	34	..	79
Algeria	81	91	95	91	97	99	71	84	90
Egypt, Arab Republic	0	..	89	0	..	95	0	..	82
Libya	100	..	97	100	..	98	100	..	96
Morocco	62	..	66	75	..	76	47	..	56
Tunisia	83	..	98	93	..	100	72	..	95
ALL AFRICA	20	..	..	21	..	..	17	..	..

13-17. Number of school teachers

	Primary						Secondary					
	Total teaching staff			Percentage females			Total teaching staff			Percentage females		
	1980	1989	1992-94	1980	1989	1992-94	1980	1989	1992-94	1980	1989	1992-94
SUB-SAHARAN AFRICA	..	..	..	29	34	39	..	..	..	..	..	..
excluding South Africa	..	..	..	29	34	35	..	..	..	..	..	..
excl. S. Africa & Nigeria	..	..	..	28	..	32	..	..	..	..	..	..
Angola	..	..	..	..	..	..	..	..	..	..	..	..
Benin	7,994	13,693	12,890	23	25	..	..	..	..	..	..	..
Botswana	5,316	8,529	11,726	72	80	77	..	..	5,678	..	..	..
Burkina Faso	3,700	8,572	10,300	20	27	23	..	..	..	..	..	..
Burundi	4,805	9,049	10,400	47	46	47	..	..	2	..	..	25,950
Cameroon	26,763	37,804	40,970	20	30	32	..	..	..	..	..	..
Cape Verde	1,436	2,028	2,657	..	60	59	..	..	..	..	..	..
Central African Republic	4,130	3,581	..	25	26	..	..	..	..	..	..	..
Chad	..	7,327	8,905	..	6	7	..	..	..	..	..	..
Comoros	1,292	1,900	1,737	7	..	..	..	..	..	..	..	..
Congo	7,186	7,639	6,891	25	33	34	..	..	7,861	..	..	..
Côte d'Ivoire	26,460	38,722	39,691	15	19	20	..	..	..	..	..	..
Djibouti	419	711	932	..	..	33	..	..	..	..	..	..
Equatorial Guinea	647	..	1,381	..	..	27	..	..	566	..	..	11
Eritrea	..	3,035	5,583	..	46	35	..	..	..	..	..	..
Ethiopia	33,322	65,450	75,736	22	24	27	..	..	22,600	..	..	10
Gabon	3,441	4,289	4,782	27	36	..	..	2,091	..	..	..	..
Gambia, The	1,808	2,451	3,193	34	32	31	..	..	1,054	..	..	100
Ghana	47,921	62,859	72,925	42	37	35	..	..	..	..	..	..
Guinea	7,165	8,113	9,718	14	22	22	..	..	4,719	..	..	13
Guinea-Bissau	3,257	..	..	24	..	..	..	..	..	..	..	..
Kenya	102,489	163,609	179,200	..	36	44	..	..	..	..	..	..
Lesotho	5,097	6,275	7,433	75	80	79	..	..	..	..	..	..
Liberia	9,099	..	..	23	..	..	..	..	..	..	..	..
Madagascar	39,474	37,932	37,676	..	..	56	..	..	..	..	..	..
Malawi	12,540	20,580	45,775	..	34	38	..	..	..	..	..	..
Mali	6,862	8,405	8,363	20	24	23	..	..	..	..	..	..
Mauritania	2,183	3,497	4,970	9	16	17	..	..	1,938	..	..	11
Mauritius	6,379	6,324	5,931	43	44	47	..	..	..	..	..	..
Mozambique	17,030	21,031	22,396	22	22	23	..	..	4,809	..	..	20
Namibia	..	..	10,912	..	..	65	..	..	3,999	..	..	46
Niger	5,518	8,462	12,216	30	32	28	..	..	2,394	..	..	18
Nigeria	369,636	331,915	435,210	33	43	46	..	..	152,596	..	..	36
Rwanda	11,912	18,524	18,937	38	46	47	..	..	3,413	..	..	21
São Tomé and Principe	588	559	..	..	52	..	..	..	..	..	..	..
Senegal	9,175	11,859	14,436	24	26	25	..	..	..	..	..	..
Seychelles	658	781	588	80	82	87	..	..	757	..	..	50
Sierra Leone	9,528	11,280	..	..	..	..	..	..	..	..	..	..
Somalia	8,122	..	..	29	..	..	..	..	..	..	..	..
South Africa	160,286	..	213,890	..	..	58	..	..	128,784	..	..	64
Sudan	43,451	..	66,268	31	..	58	..	..	30,642	..	..	33
Swaziland	3,278	4,890	5,887	79	78	77	..	..	..	..	..	..
Tanzania	81,153	98,392	101,816	37	41	42	..	..	10,735	..	..	20
Togo	9,193	10,739	12,487	21	19	16	..	..	..	..	..	..
Uganda	38,422	81,418	79,024	30	..	31	..	..	16,163	..	..	..
Zaire	..	..	112,041	..	..	24	..	..	59,325	..	..	10
Zambia	21,455	..	36,697	40	..	44	..	..	..	..	..	..
Zimbabwe	28,118	58,362	52,415	..	40	42	..	..	21,403	..	..	32
NORTH AFRICA	..	..	..	..	45	47	..	..	..	..	..	..
Algeria	88,481	144,945	166,771	37	40	43	..	..	..	..	..	..
Egypt, Arab Republic	..	261,613	288,939	..	51	54	..	..	..	..	..	..
Libya	36,591	..	103,791	47	..	64	..	..	..	..	..	..
Morocco	56,908	86,588	106,393	30	36	38	..	..	..	..	..	..
Tunisia	27,375	46,366	58,738	29	43	48	..	..	..	..	..	..
ALL AFRICA	..	..	..	30	37	41	..	..	..	..	..	..

Note: Figures include both part-time and full-time teachers.

13-18. Pupil / teacher ratio

	Number of pupils per teacher					
	Primary			Secondary		
	1980	1989	1992-94	1980	1989	1992-94
SUB-SAHARAN AFRICA	..	..	..	..	..	..
excluding South Africa	..	..	..	..	..	..
excl. S. Africa & Nigeria	..	..	..	..	..	..
Angola	..	..	..	..	..	..
Benin	48	31	49	..	..	..
Botswana	32	32	26	..	..	16
Burkina Faso	54	55	58	..	..	..
Burundi	37	66	63	..	..	27,857
Cameroon	52	51	46	..	..	..
Cape Verde	40	33	29	..	..	..
Central African Republic	60	90	..	..	..	..
Chad	..	67	61	..	..	..
Comoros	46	36	45	..	..	..
Congo	54	64	73	..	..	27
Côte d'Ivoire	39	36	41	..	..	..
Djibouti	40	44	38	..	..	..
Equatorial Guinea	69	..	55	..	..	29
Eritrea	..	38	40	..	..	..
Ethiopia	64	41	30	..	..	32
Gabon	45	48	44	..	..	..
Gambia, The	24	31	30	..	..	25
Ghana	29	27	28	..	..	..
Guinea	36	38	49	..	..	..
Guinea-Bissau	23	..	..	..	..	..
Kenya	38	33	31	..	..	..
Lesotho	48	56	49	..	..	..
Liberia	16	..	..	..	..	..
Madagascar	44	40	40	..	..	..
Malawi	65	64	62	..	..	..
Mali	42	39	60	..	..	..
Mauritania	41	44	53	..	..	24
Mauritius	20	22	21	..	..	..
Mozambique	81	58	55	..	..	..
Namibia	..	..	32	..	..	..
Niger	41	41	32	..	..	33
Nigeria	37	41	37	..	..	29
Rwanda	59	57	58	..	..	28
São Tomé and Principe	28	35	..	..	..	..
Senegal	46	58	54	..	..	..
Seychelles	22	19	17	..	..	12
Sierra Leone	33	35	..	..	..	..
Somalia	33	..	..	..	..	..
South Africa	27	..	37	..	..	28
Sudan	34	..	36	..	..	23
Swaziland	34	32	33	..	..	..
Tanzania	41	33	37	..	..	18
Togo	55	56	53	..	..	..
Uganda	34	31	31	..	..	16
Zaire	..	..	44	..	..	23
Zambia	49	..	41	..	..	..
Zimbabwe	44	38	45	..	..	30
NORTH AFRICA	33	26	27	..	..	..
Algeria	35	28	27	..	..	..
Egypt, Arab Republic	..	25	27	..	..	..
Libya	18	..	13	..	..	..
Morocco	38	25	28	..	..	..
Tunisia	39	30	25	..	..	..
ALL AFRICA	..	..	..	..	..	..

Note: Figures include both part-time and full-time teachers.

13-19. Secondary school gross enrollment ratio

	Total			Males			Females		
	1980	*1989*	*1992-93*	*1980*	*1989*	*1992-93*	*1980*	*1989*	*1992-93*
SUB-SAHARAN AFRICA	13	..	25	18	..	28	9	..	24
excluding South Africa	14	17	20	18	..	23	9	..	17
excl. S. Africa & Nigeria	13	..	16	17	..	..	9	..	..
Angola	20	12	..	0	..	..	0	..	..
Benin	16	10	..	24	..	..	9	..	..
Botswana	19	38	57	17	36	53	20	40	60
Burkina Faso	3	7	9	4	9	12	2	5	6
Burundi	3	5	7	4	6	8	2	4	5
Cameroon	18	26	27	24	31	33	13	21	22
Cape Verde	8	20	27	9	21	28	7	20	26
Central African Republic	14	12	..	21	17	..	7	6	..
Chad	..	7	8	..	12	13	..	3	3
Comoros	23	17	19	30	20	21	15	15	17
Congo	..	..	..	..	..	..	..	..	..
Côte d'Ivoire	19	22	25	27	30	33	12	14	17
Djibouti	12	..	12	..	..	14	..	..	10
Equatorial Guinea	..	..	..	..	..	..	..	..	..
Eritrea	..	15	15	..	16	17	..	15	13
Ethiopia	8	14	11	11	16	11	6	12	10
Gabon	..	..	..	..	..	..	..	..	..
Gambia, The	11	15	19	16	21	25	7	10	13
Ghana	41	39	..	51	47	..	31	31	..
Guinea	17	7	12	24	11	18	10	3	6
Guinea-Bissau	6	..	..	10	..	..	2	..	..
Kenya	20	..	25	23	..	28	16	..	23
Lesotho	18	..	26	14	..	22	21	..	31
Liberia	22	..	..	31	..	..	12	..	..
Madagascar	0	23	14	0	23	14	0	22	14
Malawi	3	4	5	5	5	6	2	3	4
Mali	8	6	8	12	8	11	5	4	6
Mauritania	11	..	15	17	..	19	4	..	11
Mauritius	50	53	59	51	54	58	49	53	60
Mozambique	5	..	7	8	..	9	3	..	6
Namibia	..	42	59	..	37	53	..	48	65
Niger	5	6	7	7	9	9	3	4	4
Nigeria	16	24	29	22	27	31	11	20	26
Rwanda	3	8	..	4	9	..	3	6	..
São Tomé and Principe	..	..	..	..	..	..	..	..	..
Senegal	11	16	16	15	21	21	7	11	11
Seychelles	..	..	..	..	..	..	..	..	..
Sierra Leone	14	17	..	20	23	..	8	12	..
Somalia	8	..	..	11	..	..	4	..	..
South Africa	0	..	77	..	..	71	..	..	84
Sudan	16	..	..	20	..	..	12	..	..
Swaziland	38	..	51	39	..	51	37	..	50
Tanzania	3	4	5	4	5	6	2	4	5
Togo	33	24	23	51	36	34	16	12	12
Uganda	5	..	11	7	..	14	3	..	8
Zaire	24	..	24	35	..	33	13	..	15
Zambia	16	..	..	22	..	..	11	..	..
Zimbabwe	8	..	44	..	..	49	..	..	39
NORTH AFRICA	40	..	62	49	..	67	32	..	56
Algeria	33	62	62	40	70	66	26	54	57
Egypt, Arab Republic	50	..	76	61	..	81	39	..	69
Libya	76	..	97	88	..	..	63	..	..
Morocco	26	36	37	32	42	43	20	29	31
Tunisia	27	45	52	34	50	55	20	39	49
ALL AFRICA	18	..	33	25	..	37	14	..	31

Note: "Secondary" refers to secondary general education.

13-20. Public expenditure on education

	As percentage of Total public expenditure			As percentage of GDP		
	1980	1989	1991-93	1980	1989	1991-93
SUB-SAHARAN AFRICA	..	..	..	..	..	..
excluding South Africa	..	..	..	..	..	..
excl. S. Africa & Nigeria	..	..	..	..	..	..
Angola	..	..	..	..	..	..
Benin	..	..	..	..	..	..
Botswana	22.2	20.3	20.6	..	3.9	5.0
Burkina Faso	15.5	18.3	17.3	1.7	..	..
Burundi	..	..	..	..	..	3.3
Cameroon	12.4	12.0	18.0	..	..	..
Cape Verde	..	..	..	..	..	2.8
Central African Republic	..	..	..	3.5	..	..
Chad	..	..	..	..	..	2.2
Comoros	..	..	..	..	..	3.0
Congo	..	..	..	4.9	..	..
Côte d'Ivoire	..	..	..	..	..	..
Djibouti	..	..	..	..	3.2	..
Equatorial Guinea	..	..	..	..	..	..
Eritrea	..	..	..	..	..	..
Ethiopia	10.2	9.9	14.2	..	2.6	2.7
Gabon	..	..	..	..	..	..
Gambia, The	12.3	..	..	..	2.6	..
Ghana	22.0	24.3	22.0	1.1	2.4	..
Guinea	..	..	..	..	..	1.6
Guinea-Bissau	..	2.7	..	..	..	..
Kenya	19.6	19.8	18.8	5.2	..	5.3
Lesotho	..	14.7	20.8	6.0	..	7.4
Liberia	11.9	..	..	..	..	..
Madagascar	..	12.9	14.3	3.1	..	..
Malawi	9.0	..	..	2.0	2.1	2.9
Mali	15.7	..	..	2.8	..	..
Mauritania	..	..	..	..	..	3.5
Mauritius	17.6	15.3	15.0	4.0	2.8	..
Mozambique	..	..	..	..	2.3	..
Namibia	..	..	..	..	..	..
Niger	18.0	..	..	..	..	..
Nigeria	..	..	..	..	..	..
Rwanda	..	..	..	..	..	..
São Tomé and Principe	..	..	..	..	..	..
Senegal	23.0	..	..	3.8	..	..
Seychelles	..	..	13.0	..	..	..
Sierra Leone	..	..	..	..	0.7	..
Somalia	..	..	..	..	..	..
South Africa	..	..	..	..	..	..
Sudan	9.8	..	..	3.4	..	..
Swaziland	24.6	24.5	..	3.9	3.6	5.4
Tanzania	13.3	..	..	..	2.2	..
Togo	..	..	..	4.5	..	4.1
Uganda	14.9	..	..	..	..	..
Zaire	18.9	..	0.2	..	..	..
Zambia	11.4	11.5	15.5	3.2	1.7	..
Zimbabwe	15.5	23.4	..	6.0	..	7.8
NORTH AFRICA	..	..	..	..	..	..
Algeria	..	..	..	..	..	..
Egypt, Arab Republic	..	13.4	12.3	..	..	..
Libya	..	..	..	..	..	..
Morocco	17.3	17.1	17.9	..	4.7	4.2
Tunisia	17.0	16.3	17.5	..	..	5.0
ALL AFRICA	..	..	..	..	..	..

13-21. Economic opportunities of women

	Female / male ratio of participation in economic activity 1994	*Female as percentage of male in occupational group, 1990*			
		Administrative and managerial	*Professional and technical*	*Clerical and sales*	*Services*
SUB-SAHARAN AFRICA	57	11	42	..	..
excluding South Africa	57	10	37	..	..
excl. S.Africa & Nigeria	59	..	..	..	..
Angola	58	..	..	..	..
Benin	85	..	..	..	..
Botswana	49	57	159	151	238
Burkina Faso	81	16	35	168	28
Burundi	82	16	44	..	..
Cameroon	46	11	32	59	46
Cape Verde	36	30	94	170	134
Central African Republic	74	10	23	146	13
Chad	25	..	..	..	..
Comoros	63	..	29	..	..
Congo	61	7	40	..	..
Côte d'Ivoire	54	..	..	..	..
Djibouti	64	2	25	..	..
Equatorial Guinea	63	2	37	..	..
Eritrea	..	..	..	..	..
Ethiopia	56	13	31	..	..
Gabon	55	..	..	..	..
Gambia, The	62	18	31	..	..
Ghana	63	10	56	..	..
Guinea	61	..	..	..	..
Guinea-Bissau	61	..	..	..	..
Kenya	62	..	..	..	..
Lesotho	69	50	130	144	209
Liberia	41	..	..	..	..
Madagascar	60	..	..	..	..
Malawi	62	5	53	58	39
Mali	17	25	23	130	71
Mauritania	29	8	26	33	81
Mauritius	35	17	71	44	70
Mozambique	85	13	26	..	..
Namibia	30	26	69	..	..
Niger	83	9	..	..	..
Nigeria	51	6	35	140	13
Rwanda	83	9	47	48	35
São Tomé and Principe	..	..	..	..	..
Senegal	60	..	..	..	..
Seychelles	72	40	139	143	141
Sierra Leone	45	9	47	191	18
Somalia	59	..	..	..	..
South Africa	54	21	88	..	196
Sudan	30	3	40	..	..
Swaziland	60	17	119	116	82
Tanzania	85	..	..	..	..
Togo	52	9	27	..	..
Uganda	65	..	..	..	..
Zaire	52	10	20	..	..
Zambia	41	6	47	136	29
Zimbabwe	49	18	67	52	42
NORTH AFRICA	16	19	39	31	14
Algeria	11	6	38	13	23
Egypt, Arab Republic	12	19	40	40	9
Libya	12	..	..	..	..
Morocco	26	34	46	..	..
Tunisia	33	8	21	..	..
ALL AFRICA	50	13	41	..	..

13-22. Household and economic participation of women

	Percentage of households headed by women (latest available between 1991-95)	Percentage of women in occupational group 1991-93: Agriculture	Mining	Utilities & manufacturing	Construction, transport, storage & communications	Service industries	Community, social & personal services
SUB-SAHARAN AFRICA	..	..	..	..	..	..	..
excluding South Africa	..	..	..	..	..	..	..
excl. S.Africa & Nigeria	..	..	..	..	..	..	..
Angola	..	..	..	..	..	..	..
Benin	..	..	..	..	..	..	..
Botswana	..	2	0	12	9	35	41
Burkina Faso	6	..	..	..	..	..	..
Burundi	..	..	..	..	..	..	..
Cameroon	18	..	..	..	..	..	..
Cape Verde	..	..	..	..	..	..	..
Central African Republic	16	..	..	..	..	..	..
Chad	..	14	0	14	14	14	43
Comoros	..	..	..	..	..	..	..
Congo	..	..	..	..	..	..	..
Côte d'Ivoire	13	..	..	..	..	..	..
Djibouti	..	..	..	..	..	..	..
Equatorial Guinea	..	..	..	..	..	..	..
Eritrea	..	..	..	..	..	..	..
Ethiopia	..	..	..	..	..	..	..
Gabon	..	..	..	..	..	..	..
Gambia, The	1	..	..	..	..	..	..
Ghana	32	..	..	..	..	..	..
Guinea	8	..	..	..	..	..	..
Guinea-Bissau	10	..	..	..	..	..	..
Kenya	17	20	0	8	5	11	57
Lesotho	..	..	..	..	..	..	..
Liberia	..	..	..	..	..	..	..
Madagascar	18	..	..	..	..	..	..
Malawi	..	73	0	7	2	4	14
Mali	..	..	..	..	..	..	..
Mauritania	23	..	..	..	..	..	..
Mauritius	..	12	0	64	2	7	15
Mozambique	..	..	..	..	..	..	..
Namibia	..	..	..	..	..	..	..
Niger	6	5	5	20	25	25	25
Nigeria	13	..	..	..	..	..	..
Rwanda	..	..	..	..	..	..	..
São Tomé and Principe	..	..	..	..	..	..	..
Senegal	8	..	..	..	..	..	..
Seychelles	..	..	..	..	..	..	..
Sierra Leone	..	..	..	..	..	..	..
Somalia	..	..	..	..	..	..	..
South Africa	26	..	..	..	..	..	..
Sudan	..	..	..	..	..	..	..
Swaziland	..	23	0	16	4	20	36
Tanzania	12	..	..	..	..	..	..
Togo	..	..	..	..	..	..	..
Uganda	3	..	..	..	..	..	..
Zaire	..	..	..	..	..	..	..
Zambia	19	..	..	..	..	..	..
Zimbabwe	..	38	1	6	3	10	42
NORTH AFRICA	..	..	..	..	..	..	..
Algeria	..	..	..	..	..	..	..
Egypt, Arab Republic	..	39	0	13	7	11	30
Libya	..	..	..	..	..	..	..
Morocco	..	..	..	..	..	..	..
Tunisia	..	..	..	..	..	..	..
ALL AFRICA	..	..	..	..	..	..	..

Figure 13-1. Life expectancy, 1995

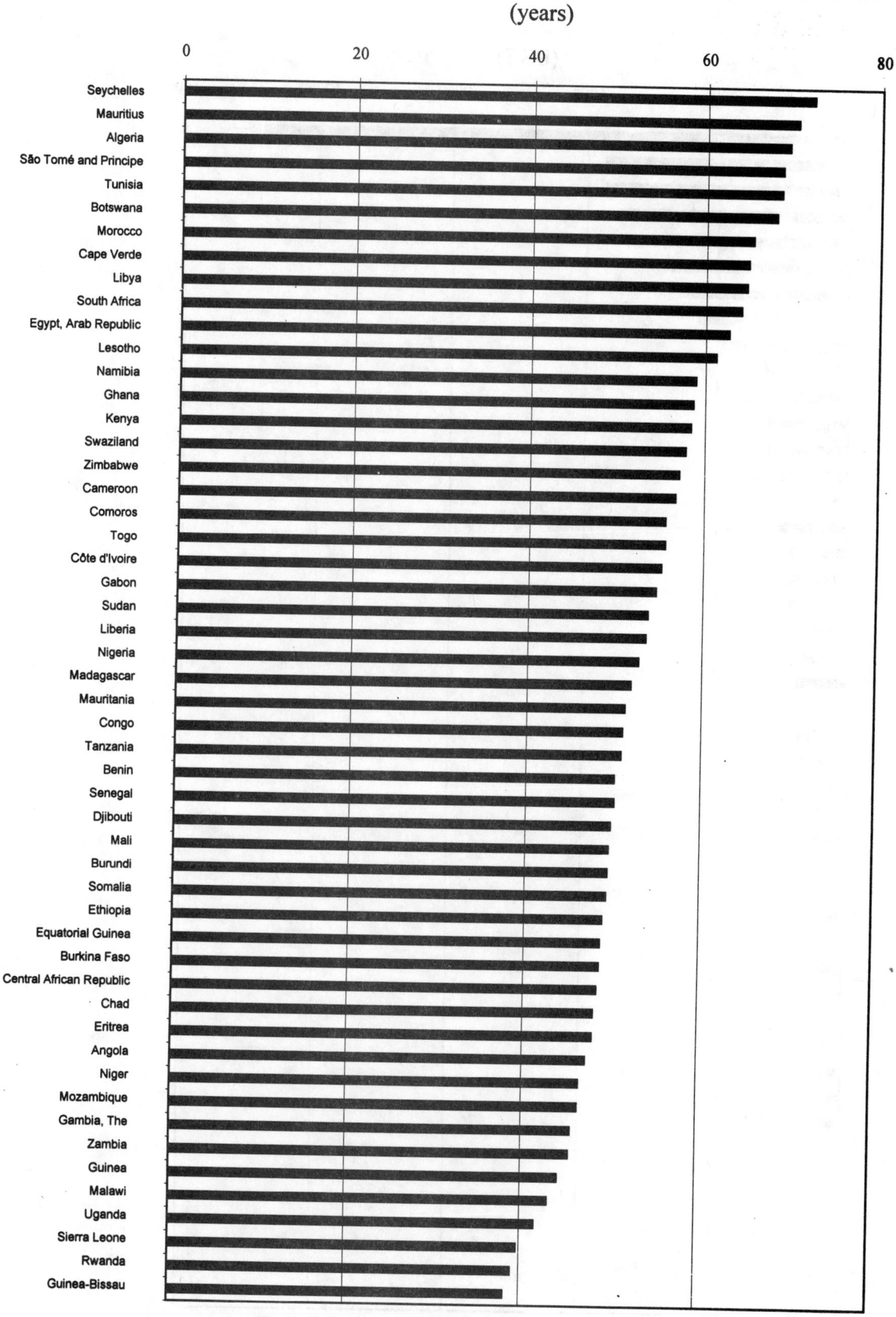

Figure 13-2. GDP per capita based on PPP, 1995

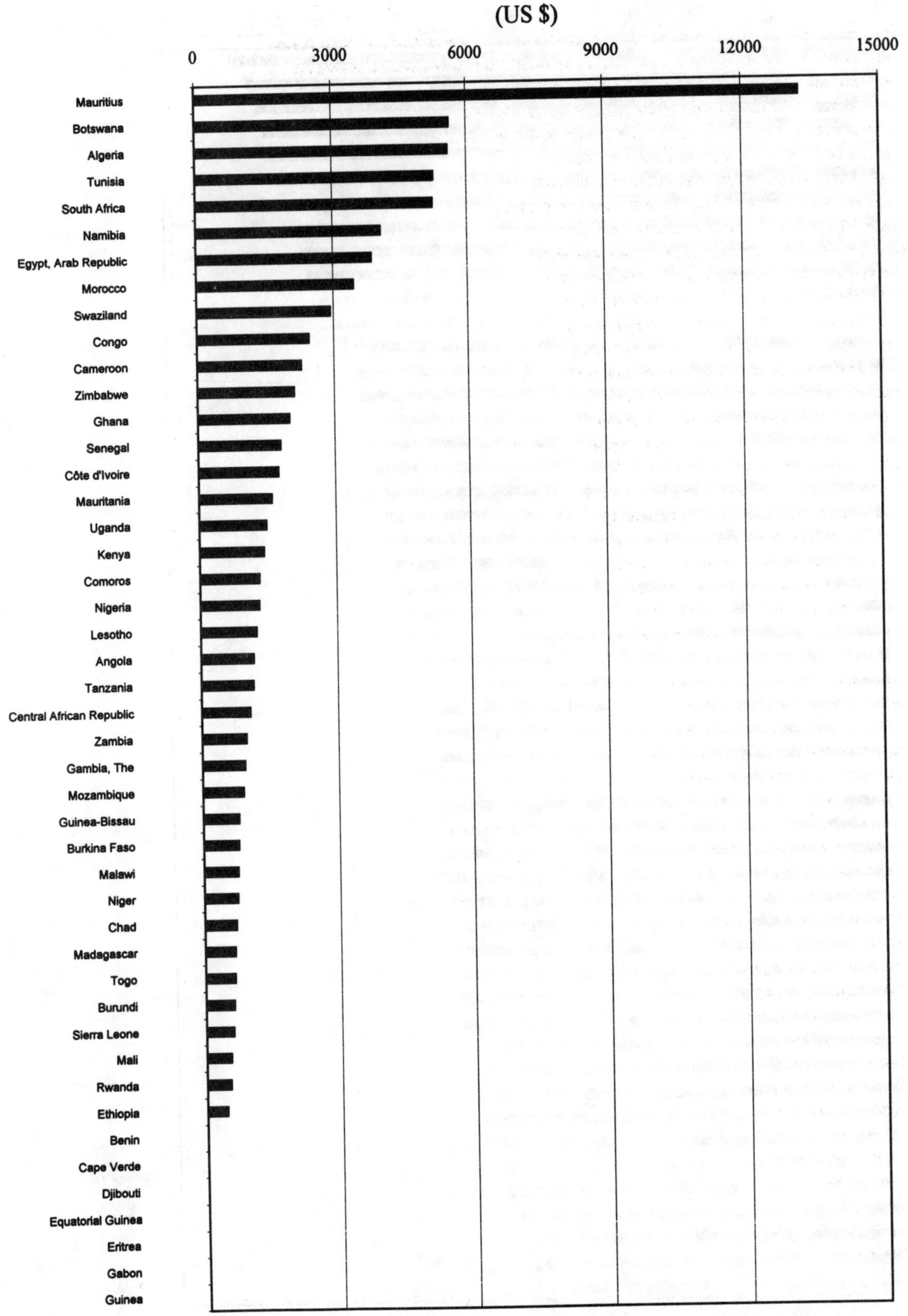

Figure 13-3. Urban population as percentage of total population, 1995*

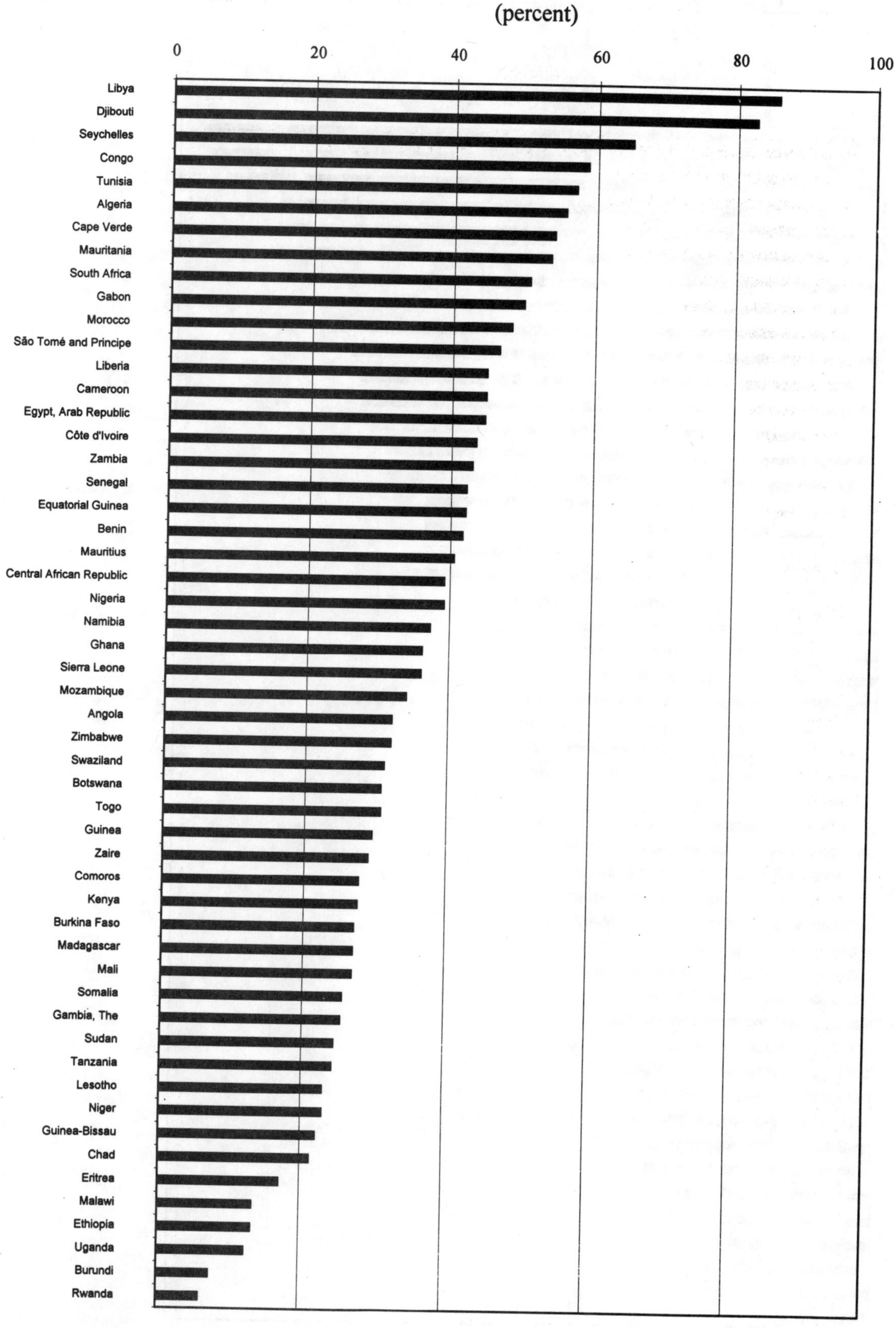

* Or most recent year available.

Figure 13-4. Primary school gross enrollment ratio, 1993*

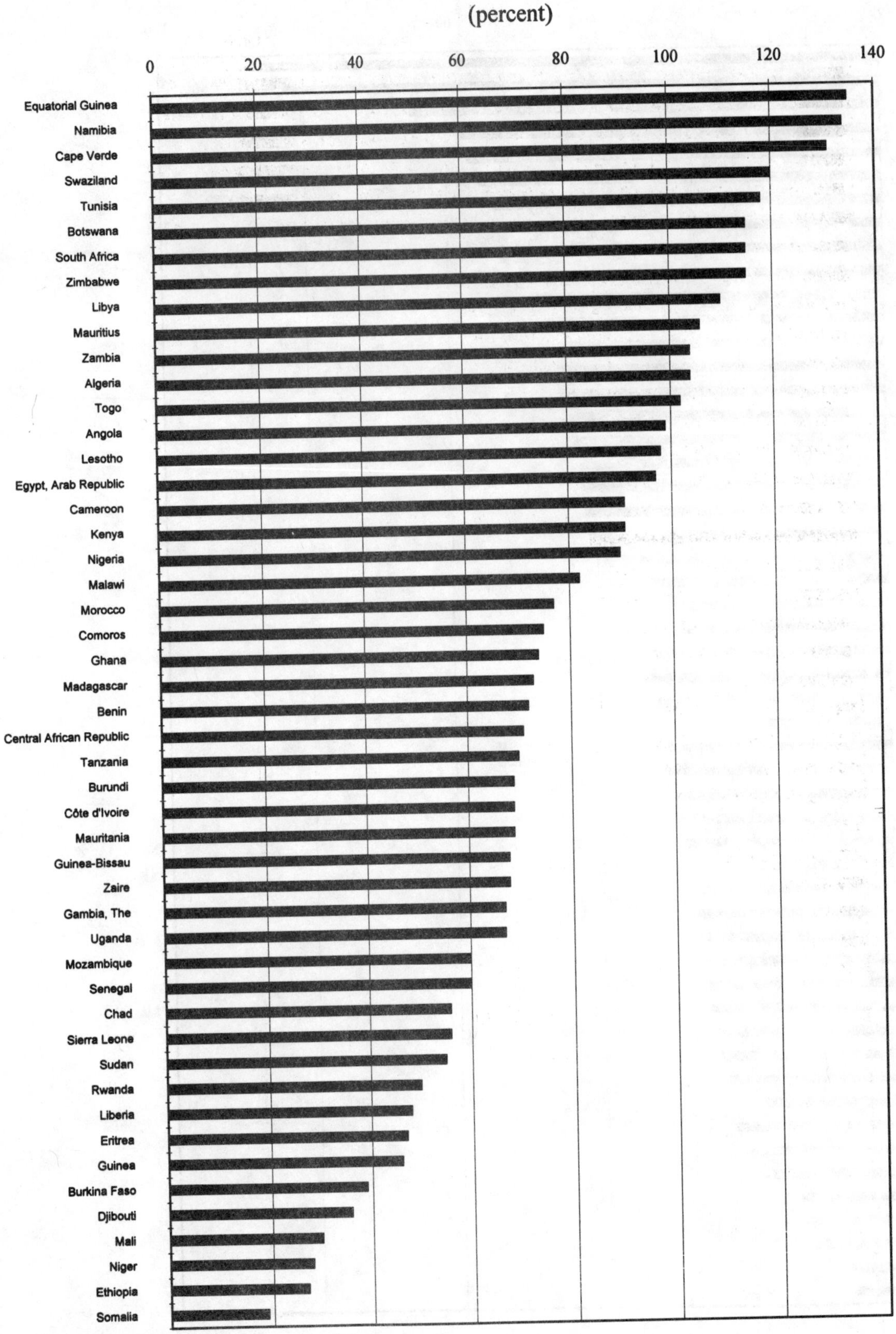

*Or most recent year available

Figure 13-5. Maternal mortality, 1995*

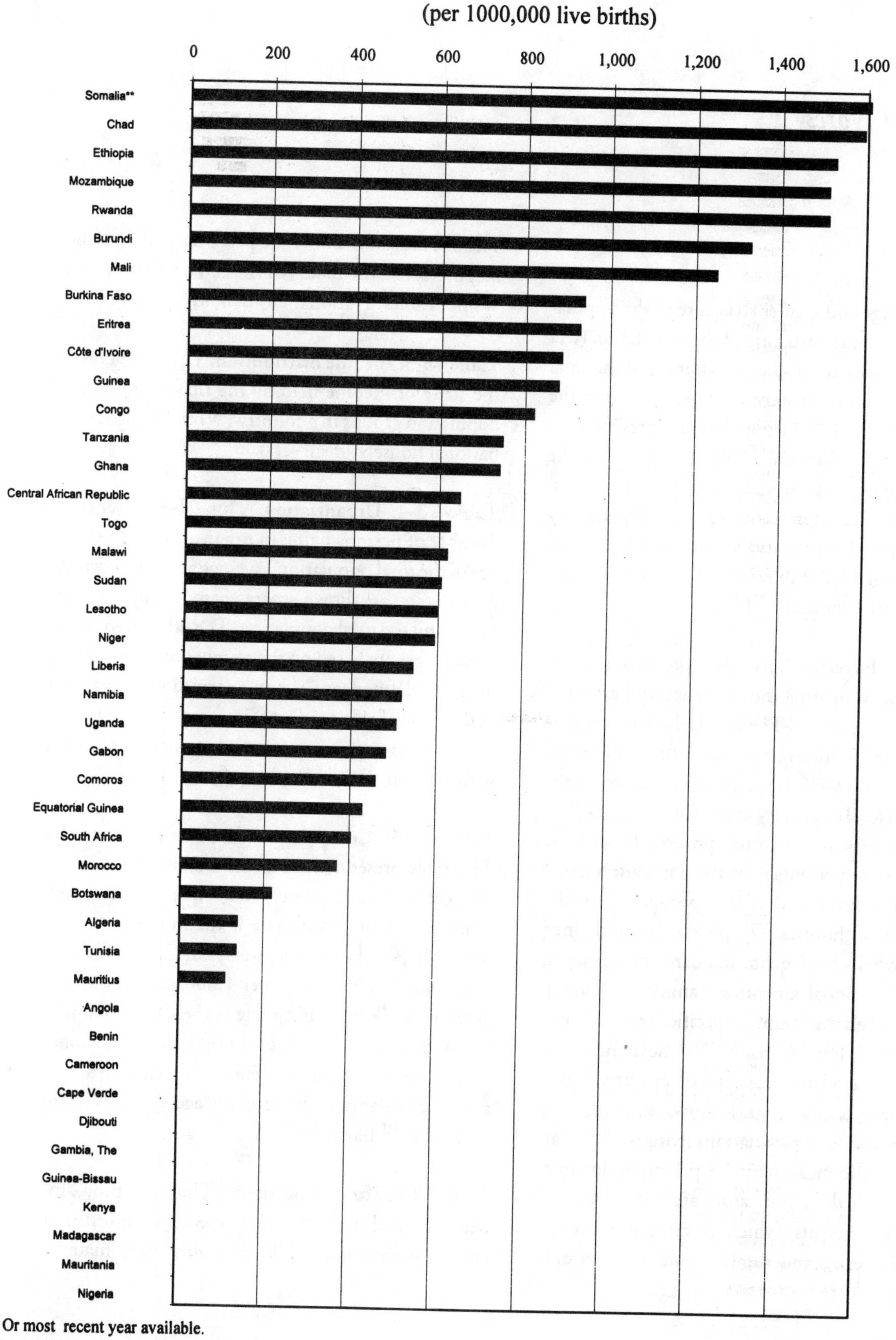

* Or most recent year available.

** Maternal mortality is greater than 1600.

Technical Notes

Tables

Table 13-1. Age and gender structure of the population. Age and gender structure of the population (UN and World Bank data) is the distribution of the total population according to age and gender. Only the female composition of the population is presented, as the male composition can easily be figured as the residual. Figures relate to midyear populations as estimated from the latest censuses. Age dependency ratio is calculated as the ratio of dependents—population under age 15 and above age 65—to the working age population—those aged 15 to 64.

Table 13-2. Poverty. This table presents selected indicators for comparing the incidence and extent of urban and rural poverty. The first indicator uses purchasing power parities rather than official exchange rates to calculate GDP per capita: a measure of the overall mean level of poverty at the national level. The next indicator is the national poverty headcount, which shows the percentage of the population living below the poverty line deemed appropriate for the country by its authorities. The poverty line is defined as the below which adequate standards of nutrition, shelter, and personal amenities cannot be assured. Since these levels are country specific, cross-country comparisons cannot be made. The next indicator, however, uses a relative concept of poverty, which does allow such comparisons. It shows the percentage of the urban and rural populations living on less than two-thirds of the mean national per capita income. Associated with these indicators are the urban and rural Gini coefficients, which describe the level of inequality in urban and rural income distributions. The last indicator shows the percentage of household income spent on food (UNDP, World Bank, Penn World Tables, National Household Surveys).

Table 13-3. Income distribution. This table presents the share of income held by the richest and poorest population groups in a country (World Bank data and national household surveys).

Table 13-4. Urbanization. This table presents the number of persons living in urban areas as a percentage of the total population. Average annual percentage growth rates are shown separately for the urban population and the total population. The urban population percentages are based on the number of persons living in areas defined as "urban" according to national definitions of this concept. Since national definitions differ, cross-country comparisons should be made with caution (World Bank data).

Table 13-5. Components of population change. This table presents three determinants of population change: total fertility rate, crude birth rate, and crude death rate. Crude birth rate is the number of births per 1,000 population in a given year. Crude death rate is the number of deaths per 1,000 population in a given year. Total fertility rate is the average number of children that would be born alive to a woman during her lifetime, if she were to bear children at each age in accordance with prevailing age-specific fertility rates (World Bank data).

Table 13-6. Survival prospects. This table shows five health-related indicators: life expectancy at birth, infant mortality rate, child mortality rate, maternal mortality rate, and adult HIVs sero prevalence.

Life expectancy at birth is the number of years a newborn infant would live if prevailing patterns of mortality at the time of its birth were to stay the same throughout its life. Infant mortality rate is the number of deaths of infants under one year of age per 1,000 live births in a given year. Child mortality rate is the number of deaths of children under five years of age per 1,000 live births in a given year. Maternal mortality rate is the annual number of deaths of women from pregnancy-related causes per 100,000 live births. Adult HIV-1 sero prevalence reflects the estimated rate of infection in each country's adult population (aged 15 and older) (WHO and World Bank data).

Table 13-7. Immunization and ORT use. This is the percentage of children under one year of age immunized against tuberculosis, DPT, polio, and measles. It also gives the use rate of oral rehydration therapy (ORT) among children under five years of age. DPT refers to diphtheria, pertussis (whooping cough), and tetanus. ORT use is the percentage of all cases of diarrhea in children under five years of age treated with oral rehydration salts or an appropriate household solution (WHO data).

Table 13-8. Child malnutrition. Data reported on this table give the percentage of children and babies suffering from nutrition-related problems of low birthweight, underweight, wasting, and stunting. Figures are also given on the extent of breastfeeding among nursing mothers.

Low birthweight refers to babies born weighing less than 2,500 grams. Underweight refers to children under the age of five weighing two standard deviations below the median weight for age of the reference population. Wasting refers to children of ages 12 through 23 months weighing two standard deviations below the median weight for height of the reference population. Stunting refers to children of ages 24 through 59 months standing two standard deviations below the median height-for-age of the reference population (UNDP 1995, WHO and World Bank data).

Table 13-9. Access to sanitation facilities. Table 13-9 shows the percentage of the population with access to sanitation facilities (WHO data). Urban areas with access to sanitation facilities are defined as urban populations served by connections to public sewers or household systems, such as pit privies, pour-flush latrines, septic tanks, communal toilets, and other such facilities. Rural populations with access were defined as those with adequate disposal, such as pit privies and pour-flush latrines. Application of these definitions may vary, and comparisons can therefore be misleading.

Table 13-10. Access to safe water. This table refers to the percentage of the population with reasonable access to safe water supply, which includes treated surface waters or untreated, but uncontaminated water, such as that from springs, sanitary wells, and protected boreholes. In an urban area, this may be a public fountain or standpost located not more than 200 meters away. In rural areas, it implies that members of the household do not have to spend a disproportionate part of the day fetching water. Data are presented separately for total, urban and rural population (WHO data).

Table 13-11. Access to health services. Access to health services refers to the percentage of the population that can reach appropriate local health services by the local means of transport in no more than one hour. Data are presented separately for total, urban, and rural population (WHO data).

Table 13-12. Health care. Indicators presented here are population per physician, population per nursing personnel, and the percentage of births attended by trained health personnel. The figure for physicians includes, in addition to the total number of registered practitioners in the country, medical assistants whose medical training is less than that of qualified physicians, but who nevertheless dispense similar medical services, including simple surgical operations. The definition of recognized medical practitioners differs among countries. Nursing persons include graduate, practical, assistant, and auxiliary nurses, as well as paraprofessional personnel such as health workers, first-aid workers, and traditional birth attendants. Inclusion of auxiliary and paraprofessional personnel provides a more realistic estimate of available nursing and health care overall. Births attended refers to births attended by physicians, nurses, midwives, trained primary healthcare workers, or trained traditional birth attendants (WHO and World Bank data).

Table 13-13. Illiteracy rate. This table shows the share of illiterate adults in total adult population aged 15 years and over. Literacy is defined as the ability to read and write. A person who can, with understanding, both read and write a short, simple statement about his everyday life is literate. Persons who can read, but cannot write, are included with illiterates. Figures are shown separately for males, females, and both genders combined (UNESCO data).

Tables 13-14. Primary school gross enrollment ratio. This is the total number of pupils enrolled at the primary level of education, regardless of age, expressed as a percentage of the population corresponding to the official school age of primary education in a given country. Data are given separately for males, females, and both genders combined. Figures shown may be more than 100 percent since total enrollment includes pupils above and pupils below the primary school age, as well as repeaters (UNESCO data).

Tables 13-15. Pupil progression and efficiency indicator. This table provides two education indicators. *Percentage of cohort reaching grade 4 of primary school* shows the percentage of children starting primary school, who eventually attain grade 4. The estimate is based on the Reconstructed Cohort Method, which uses data on enrollment and repeaters for two consecutive years. *Age efficiency ratio* is the ratio of net enrollment to gross enrollment at the primary and secondary levels (UNESCO and World Bank data).

Table 13-16. Net primary enrollment ratio. This is the ratio of the number of children of official school age enrolled in school to the number of children of official school age in the population (UNESCO data).

Table 13-17. Number of school teachers. Teachers in both public and private schools are covered in this table. Data refer to both full-time and part-time teachers, excluding other instructional personnel without teaching functions. Figures are shown here separately for primary and secondary schools. Percentage females means the number of female teachers expressed as a percentage of total teaching staff (UNESCO data).

Table 13-18. Pupil/teacher ratio. This ratio gives the average number of pupils per teacher. Figures are given separately for primary and secondary schools. As teaching staff includes both full-time and part-time teachers, comparability of this ratio between countries may be affected as the proportion of part-time teachers varies greatly from one country to another (UNESCO data).

Table 13-19. Secondary school gross enrollment ratio. This is the secondary school equivalent of the data presented in Table 13-14. It gives the total number of students enrolled at the secondary level of education, regardless of age, expressed as a percentage of the population corresponding to the official school age of secondary education. Data are presented separately for males, females, and both genders combined. Second level, general refers to education in secondary schools that provides general or specialized instruction based upon at least four years of previous instruction at the first or primary level, which do not specifically aim at preparing the pupils directly for a given trade or occupation. Such schools may be called high schools, middle schools, or lyceums and offer courses of study whose completion is a minimum condition for admission into universities. In some countries, some of these schools provide both academic and vocational training. These composite secondary schools are considered as equivalent to the academic type of secondary school and are thus classified as second level, general (UNESCO data).

Table 13-20. Public expenditure on education. This table presents the public expenditure on education (UNESCO) first as a percentage of total public expenditure (IMF/GFS) and then as a percentage of current GDP (Table 2-5).

Table 13-21. Economic opportunities of women. This table shows two indicators. Female/male ratio of participation in economic activity shows the number of female workers in relation to the number of male workers. Females as percentage of males in occupational group shows the breakdown of the first indicator for occupational categories (UNDP data).

Table 13-22. Household and economic participation of women. This table presents indicators on gender issues in development. Households headed by women (World Bank data) refers to families in which a woman is acknowledged as the head by the other members. The occupational statistics are based on UN, *Statistical Yearbook 1992–93.*

Figures

The following indicators have been used to derive the figures in this chapter.

Figure 13-1. Life expectancy (Table 13-6).

Figure 13-2. GDP per capita, based on PPP, 1995 (Table 13-2).

Figure 13-3. Percentage of urban population in total population (Table 13-4).

Figure 13-4. Primary school enrollment ratio (Table 13-14).

Figure 13-5. Maternal mortality (Table 13-6).

Methodology used for regional aggregations and period averages in chapter 13

Table	*Aggregations*[a]					*Period averages*[b]	
	(1)	*(2)*	*(6)*	*(7)*	*(8)*	*(1)*	*(2)*
13-1							
Col. 1–8		x					
Col. 9–10			x				
13-2							
Col. 1			x				
Col. 2			x				
Col. 3–4, 7				x			
Col. 5–6					x		
13-3					x		
13-4							
Col. 1–3	x						
Col. 4–6							x
Col. 7–9			x				
Col. 10–12							x
13-5							
Col. 1–3			x				
Col. 4–6		x					
Col. 7–9		x					
13-6			x				
13-7			x				
13-8			x				
13-9			x				
13-10			x				
13-11			x				
13-12			x				
13-13			x				
13-14			x				
13-15			x				
13-16			x				
13-17							
Col. 1–3, 7–9					x		
Col. 4–6, 10–12			x				
13-18			x				
13-19			x				
13-20			x				
13-21			x				
13-22					x		

Note: Regional aggregations are shown in the rows for Sub-Saharan Africa, North Africa, and All Africa. Period averages are shown in the last three columns. This table shows only the methodologies used in this chapter.

a. Regional aggregations: (1) simple total; (2) simple total of the first indicator divided by the simple total of the second indicator (same country coverage); (3) simple total of the gap-filled indicator; (4) simple total of the gap-filled main indicator divided by the simple total of the gap-filled secondary indicator; (5) simple total of the first gap-filled main indicator less the simple total of the second gap-filled main indicator, all divided by the simple total of the secondary indicator; (6) weighted total; (7) median; (8) no aggregation; (9) simple arithmetic mean.

b. Period averages: (1) arithmetic mean (using the same series as shown in the table, i.e., ratio if the rest of the table is shown as ratio, level if the rest of the table is shown as level, growth rate if the rest of the table is shown as growth rate); (2) least-squares growth rate (using main indicator); (3) least-squares growth rate (using main indicator in constant terms, with the rest of the table in current terms).

14

Environmental Indicators

This chapter was drawn entirely from the World Resources Institute and reflects tables published in their *World Resources 1994–95* and *World Resources 1996–97* volumes. It includes data on natural resources—their use by sector and the trends in their use—protected resources and those in danger of extinction, commercial energy consumption and its components, the extent and the scope of greenhouse gas discharges, and participation in major global conventions.

Until the early 1970s, environmental issues were mainly focused on problems of industrial countries and on such issues as water and air pollution, acid rain, and greenhouse gas emissions. Since the publication of the Club of Rome's *The Limit to Growth* in 1972, however, issues of natural resource depletion and degradation have received considerable attention in assessing environmental factors and their impacts on the development prospects of developing nations. At the national level, environmental concerns revolve around population expansion, desertification, deforestation, and the by-products of energy consumption.

Environmental destruction is not, however, confined by geographic borders. For instance, global warming, said to be caused by greenhouse gas emissions, has become a major global environmental concern. The issue of the greenhouse effect may be subject to controversy at the theoretical level and difficult to prove at the practical level. The fact that industrial wastes generated in one country cross frontiers and cause environmental damage to other nations is, however, widely acknowledged. Common interests, therefore, compel the international community to jointly work toward a common goal of preserving the environment.

Increasing emphasis on the links between the environment and development, both at the national and international levels, is reflected in the growing number of scientific and analytical studies. Challenging the hegemony of the SNA national income accounting convention, numerous scholarly endeavors are under way to internalize environmental consequences in national income calculations. The argument is made that the SNA methodology overstates national income levels for two reasons. First, it does not account for both the direct and indirect costs of drawing down natural resources. Second, it counts expenditure on resources for environmental protection activities as income. The changes both in methodology and emphasis have created an urgent demand for physical data. The information in this chapter aims to meet this growing demand, notwithstanding the limitations in data coverage and reliability.

The rate of deforestation is of particular concern because the cost of deforestation goes far beyond the loses of forest products, such as timber and fuelwood. There are equally significant indirect costs, including soil erosion; the substitution of animal and agricultural residues for cooking, which would otherwise be used for fertilizer; and climate changes. Deforestation is caused by many factors, including increased demand for settlement area, cultivation, woodfuel, or a combination thereof. The information in this chapter provides an empirical framework for assessing policy alternatives in reversing the continuing depletion of natural resources.

Data on roundwood production and consumption are important in monitoring the causes of deforestation. In addition, since roundwood is a primary source of energy in developing nations, data on roundwood consumption is essential in analyzing air pollution. For instance, for 1985–87, Africa used close to 88 percent of its roundwood production for fuel and charcoal production, while approximately 12 percent of the roundwood production went to industrial uses. To put these figures in perspective, the corresponding figures for Europe are 16 and 84 percent.

Information on fresh water resources available and on the extent and the methods of their uses can provide a partial basis for analyzing Africa's agricultural performance, its potential hydroelectric power, and its populations' health conditions. Almost all Sub-Saharan African countries use a very small fraction of their internal renewable water resources. For instance, Ethiopia, a nation that has suffered from repeated droughts, uses only 2 percent of its water resources. The major problem rests in the uneven geographic distribution of water resources with respect to population density and the state of freshwater drawing technology. The quality of water is as important as the quantity of water available. Water-related disease accounts for 80 percent of all sicknesses and for 90 percent of the 15 million deaths in developing countries each year.

Data on energy use consist of information on energy consumption and on related environmental consequences. Biomass fuel, comprising woodfuel and animal and agricultural residues, accounts for 40 to 90 percent of total energy used in Sub-Saharan Africa.

The data on greenhouse heating effects provide information on the global climate warming that is caused by a change in chemical composition of the atmosphere due to the emission of industrial and agricultural greenhouse gases. The tables highlight data that provide a continental perspective of potential environmental damage associated with fossil fuel consumption, deforestation, and other industrial activities as well as each country's contribution to the problem.

Data on global conventions indicate the intentions of countries to safeguard the environment and protect the use of natural resources for future generations.

14-1. Land area and use, 1981-93

	Land area (000 hectares)	Population density (per 1,000 hectares) 1993	Domesticated land as a percentage of land area (a)	Land use (000 hectares): Cropland 1991-93	Cropland: Percentage change since 1981-83	Permanent pasture 1991-93	Permanent pasture: Percentage change since 1981-83	Forest and woodland 1991-93	Forest and woodland: Percentage change since 1981-83	Other land 1991-93	Other land: Percentage change since 1981-83
SUB-SAHARAN AFRICA	..	..	..	..	..	..	..	..	..	..	..
excluding South Africa	..	..	..	..	..	..	..	..	..	..	..
excl. S. Africa & Nigeria	..	..	..	..	..	..	..	..	..	..	..
Angola	124,670	82	26	3,483	2.5	29,000	0.0	51,917	-3.1	40,270	-3.9
Benin	11,062	460	21	1,877	4.1	442	0.0	3,407	-12.0	5,337	-7.3
Botswana	56,673	25	46	420	5.0	25,600	0.0	26,500	0.0	4,153	0.5
Burkina Faso	27,360	357	35	3,564	23.5	6,000	0.0	13,800	0.0	3,996	17.0
Burundi	2,568	2,347	89	1,357	3.9	915	0.5	85	0.0	211	26.3
Cameroon	46,540	269	19	7,033	1.2	2,000	0.0	35,900	0.0	1,607	5.2
Cape Verde	..	..	..	..	..	..	..	..	..	..	..
Central African Republic	62,298	51	8	2,015	2.9	3,000	0.0	46,700	0.0	10,583	0.5
Chad	125,920	48	38	3,239	2.8	45,000	0.0	32,400	0.0	45,281	0.2
Comoros											
Congo	34,150	72	30	170	11.6	10,000	0.0	21,120	-0.9	2,860	-6.4
Côte d'Ivoire	31,800	419	53	3,703	16.7	13,000	0.0	7,080	-24.4	8,017	-21.9
Djibouti	..	..	..	..	..	..	..	..	..	..	..
Equatorial Guinea	2,805	135	12	230	0.0	104	0.0	1,297	0.1	1,174	0.1
Eritrea	10,100	331	60	1,280	..	1,600	..	2,000	..	5,220	93.5
Ethiopia	110,100	471	53	13,930	0.0	44,825	-1.0	26,950	-3.4	24,395	-5.8
Gabon	25,767	48	20	459	1.5	4,700	0.0	19,900	-0.5	708	-12.7
Gambia, The	1,000	1,042	27	180	13.0	90	0.0	280	0.0	450	4.6
Ghana	22,754	723	41	4,320	23.4	5,000	0.0	7,943	-8.0	5,491	2.4
Guinea	24,572	257	25	730	2.4	5,500	0.0	14,480	-3.9	3,862	-14.6
Guinea-Bissau	2,812	366	50	340	13.7	1,080	0.0	1,070	0.0	322	12.7
Kenya	56,914	464	45	4,517	5.5	21,300	0.0	16,800	0.0	14,297	1.7
Lesotho	3,035	640	76	320	10.4	2,000	0.0	80	-4.8	635	4.1
Liberia	9,675	294	63	374	0.9	5,700	0.0	1,707	-13.2	1,894	-13.6
Madagascar	58,154	238	47	3,104	3.3	24,000	0.0	23,200	0.0	7,850	1.3
Malawi	9,408	1,118	38	1,697	22.1	1,840	0.0	3,700	-1.1	2,171	12.3
Mali	122,019	83	27	2,270	10.6	30,000	0.0	6,907	-3.9	82,843	-0.1
Mauritania	102,522	21	38	207	6.2	39,250	0.0	4,413	-2.1	58,652	-0.1
Mauritius	203	5,374	56	106	-0.9	7	0.0	44	-24.1	46	-32.6
Mozambique	78,409	193	60	3,163	2.7	44,000	0.0	14,053	-7.7	17,192	-6.3
Namibia	82,329	18	47	662	0.5	38,000	0.0	18,030	-1.8	25,637	-1.3
Niger	126,670	67	10	3,605	1.5	8,913	-3.4	2,500	0.8	111,652	-0.2
Nigeria	91,077	1,156	79	32,368	6.1	40,000	0.0	11,400	-20.3	7,309	-14.1
Rwanda	2,467	3,062	66	1,167	8.5	453	-15.2	550	-4.8	297	-5.8
São Tomé and Principe	..	..	..	..	..	..	..	..	..	..	..
Senegal	19,253	410	28	2,350	0.0	3,100	0.0	10,467	-4.4	3,336	-14.5
Seychelles	..	..	..	..	..	..	..	..	..	..	..
Sierra Leone	7,162	600	38	540	5.6	2,203	-0.1	2,043	-2.9	2,376	-1.4
Somalia	62,734	143	70	1,032	2.2	43,000	0.0	16,000	6.7	2,702	37.8
South Africa	122,104	325	77	13,177	-0.1	81,378	0.0	8,200	0.0	19,349	-0.1
Sudan	237,600	112	52	12,950	3.6	110,000	12.2	44,340	-6.1	70,310	13.6
Swaziland	1,720	470	73	191	35.4	1,070	-6.5	118	15.7	341	-2.5
Tanzania	88,359	317	44	3,500	19.2	35,000	0.0	33,500	-14.4	16,359	-31.0
Togo	5,439	714	48	2,430	3.0	200	0.0	933	-8.5	1,876	-0.9
Uganda	19,965	999	43	6,763	13.4	1,800	0.0	5,503	-7.7	5,898	5.8
Zaire	226,705	182	10	7,893	2.9	15,000	0.0	173,860	-1.7	29,952	-9.6
Zambia	74,339	120	47	5,271	2.2	30,000	0.0	28,727	-2.3	10,341	-5.5
Zimbabwe	38,685	278	20	2,864	3.4	4,856	0.0	8,800	-7.4	22,165	-2.7
NORTH AFRICA	..	..	..	..	..	..	..	..	..	..	..
Algeria	238,174	112	16	7,938	7.0	30,752	-3.2	3,969	-9.5	195,516	-0.5
Egypt	99,545	606	8	2,760	11.7	4,934	12.7	31	0.0	91,820	0.9
Libya	175,954	29	9	2,167	3.5	13,300	0.8	840	35.1	159,647	0.2
Morocco	44,630	581	69	9,781	15.9	20,900	0.0	8,290	6.0	5,659	32.0
Tunisia	15,536	552	52	4,897	2.2	3,525	5.1	664	18.8	6,451	5.9
ALL AFRICA	2,943,737	232	38	188,395	6	854,336	0	762,497	-2	1,138,509	1

Source: Food and Agriculture Organization of the United Nations, The United Nations Statistical Commission and Economic Commission for Europe, and other sources.

Notes: a. Domesticated land is the sum of cropland and permanent pasture.

0 = zero or less than half the unit of measure; .. = not available

For additional information, see Sources and Technical notes.

14-2. Forest resources, 1981-90

	Forest and other wooded land	Forest area						Other wooded land		Annual logging (000 ha)		
		Total forest		Natural forest		Plantation						
	Extent (000 ha) 1990	Extent (000 ha) 1990	Annual % change 1981-90	Extent (000 ha) 1990	Annual % change 1981-90	Extent (000 ha) 1990	Annual % change 1981-90	Extent (000 ha) 1990	Annual % change 1981-90	Extent 1990	% of closed forest	% that is primary forest
SUB-SAHARAN AFRICA	..	..	..	..	..	..	..	..	..	..	..	..
excluding South Africa	..	..	..	..	..	..	..	..	..	..	..	..
excl. S. Africa & Nigeria	..	..	..	..	..	..	..	..	..	..	..	..
Angola	77,198	23,194	-0.7	23,074	-0.7	120	0.9	54,004	..	1	0.0	5
Benin	11,497	4,961	-1.2	4,947	-1.2	14	6.7	6,536	..	0	0.3	57
Botswana	26,561	14,262	-0.5	14,261	-0.5	1	0.0	12,299	..	..	..	..
Burkina Faso	13,813	4,436	-0.6	4,416	-0.7	20	12.7	9,377	..	0	0.0	0
Burundi	1,314	325	2.5	233	-0.6	92	59.4	989	..	0	0.0	0
Cameroon	35,905	20,366	-0.6	20,350	-0.6	16	29.0	15,539	..	333	4.5	89
Cape Verde	78	16	7.8	6	0.0	10	23.3	62	..	..	..	..
Central African Republic	46,753	30,568	-0.4	30,562	-0.4	6	1,190.0	16,185	..	3	0.0	93
Chad	32,450	11,438	-0.7	11,434	-0.7	4	7.8	21,012	..	0	0.0	81
Comoros	41	11	-3.1	11	-3.1	0	..	30	..	..	..	..
Congo	25,285	19,902	-0.1	19,865	-0.2	37	21.7	5,383	..	78	0.4	89
Côte d'Ivoire	18,952	10,967	-1.0	10,904	-1.0	63	10.0	7,985	..	85	7.6	34
Djibouti	1,320	22	0.0	22	0.0	0	..	1,298	..	..	..	..
Equatorial Guinea	2,719	1,829	-0.4	1,826	-0.4	3	0.0	890	..	5	0.3	88
Ethiopia (a)	41,991	14,354	-0.2	14,165	-0.3	189	17.5	27,637	..	0	0.0	92
Gabon	19,966	18,256	-0.6	18,235	-0.6	21	5.8	1,710	..	126	0.7	93
Gambia, The	286	98	-0.8	97	-0.8	1	0.0	188	..	0	1.1	0
Ghana	18,013	9,608	-1.2	9,555	-1.3	53	2.5	8,405	..	11	0.7	19
Guinea	17,484	6,696	-1.1	6,692	-1.1	4	5.8	10,788	..	9	0.5	87
Guinea-Bissau	2,162	2,022	-0.7	2,021	-0.7	1	0.0	140	..	5	0.6	90
Kenya	16,816	1,305	-0.4	1,187	-0.5	118	1.6	15,511	..	2	0.6	86
Lesotho	..	..	..	..	..	..	..	..	..	..	..	..
Liberia	6,632	4,639	-0.5	4,633	-0.5	6	1.0	1,993	..	79	1.7	87
Madagascar	23,225	15,999	-0.8	15,782	-0.8	217	1.7	7,226	..	20	0.3	31
Malawi	3,724	3,612	-1.1	3,486	-1.3	126	12.4	112	..	0	0.0	0
Mali	28,791	12,158	-0.8	12,144	-0.8	14	143.8	16,633	..	0	0.0	0
Mauritania	4,536	556	0.0	554	0.0	2	101.1	3,980	..	0	0.1	0
Mauritius	44	12	1.3	3	0.0	9	1.8	32	..	..	..	..
Mozambique	55,881	17,357	-0.7	17,329	-0.7	28	5.4	38,524	..	1	0.0	..
Namibia	26,296	12,569	-0.3	12,569	-0.3	0	..	13,727	..	..	..	..
Niger	10,442	2,562	0.0	2,550	0.0	12	17.9	7,880	..	0	0.0	0
Nigeria	65,654	15,785	-0.7	15,634	-0.7	151	3.2	49,869	..	127	2.3	31
Rwanda	946	252	1.8	164	-0.2	88	9.4	694	..	1	0.4	5
São Tomé and Principe	..	..	..	..	..	..	..	..	..	..	..	..
Senegal	13,400	7,656	-0.5	7,544	-0.6	112	118.0	5,744	..	0	0.0	5
Seychelles	..	..	..	..	..	..	..	..	..	..	..	..
Sierra Leone	6,969	1,895	-0.6	1,889	-0.6	6	3.5	5,074	..	1	0.2	0
Somalia	15,945	758	-0.4	754	-0.4	4	0.0	15,187	..	1	0.6	0
South Africa	41,543	8,208	-0.5	7,243	-0.8	965	1.9	33,335	..	..	..	..
Sudan	68,955	43,179	-1.0	42,976	-1.0	203	7.6	25,776	..	0	0.0	0
Swaziland	146	146	0.0	74	0.0	72	0.1	0	..	..	..	..
Tanzania	68,497	33,709	-1.1	33,555	-1.2	154	12.5	34,788	..	2	0.2	77
Togo	4,566	1,370	-1.3	1,353	-1.4	17	23.3	3,196	..	1	0.3	47
Uganda	16,023	6,366	-0.9	6,346	-0.9	20	0.0	9,657	..	1	0.1	61
Zaire	166,076	113,317	-0.6	113,275	-0.6	42	16.7	52,759	..	26	0.0	95
Zambia	60,337	32,349	-1.0	32,301	-1.0	48	7.8	27,988	..	5	0.2	34
Zimbabwe	26,144	8,981	-0.6	8,897	-0.6	84	2.0	17,163	..	0	0.2	14
NORTH AFRICA	..	..	..	..	..	..	..	..	..	..	..	..
Algeria	3,945	2,039	-0.9	1,554	-2.0	485	6.1	1,906	..	..	..	..
Egypt	34	34	2.0	0	..	34	2.0	0	..	..	..	..
Libya	846	400	3.8	190	..	210	11.0	446	..	..	..	..
Morocco	5,744	3,864	-0.4	3,543	-0.7	321	4.3	1,880	..	..	..	..
Tunisia	569	569	0.9	368	-1.5	201	12.6	0	..	..	..	..
ALL AFRICA	1,136,510	544,968	-0.2	540,539	-0.6	6,326	36.3	591,533	..	..	..	..

Sources: Food and Agriculture Organization of the United Nations and the United Nations Economic Commission for Europe.

Notes: a. Ethiopia includes Eritrea

0 = zero or less than half the unit of measure; negative numbers indicate reduction in forest area; .. = not available.

For additional information, see Sources and Technical Notes.

14-3. Wood production and trade, 1981-93

	Roundwood production						Processed wood production				Paper production		Average annual net trade in roundwood (a) (000 cubic meters)	
	Total		Fuel and charcoal		Industrial roundwood		Sawnwood		Panels					
	(000 cubic meters) 1991-93	Percent change since 1981-83	(000 cubic meters) 1991-93	Percent change since 1981-83	(000 cubic meters) 1991-93	Percent change since 1981-83	(000 cubic meters) 1991-93	Percent change since 1981-83	(000 cubic meters) 1991-93	Percent change since 1981-83	(000 metric tons) 1991-93	Percent change since 1981-83	981-83	1991-93
SUB-SAHARAN AFRICA	..	..	..	..	..	..	..	..	..	..	..	..	..	..
excluding South Africa	..	..	..	..	..	..	..	..	..	..	..	..	..	..
excl. S. Africa & Nigeria	..	..	..	..	..	..	..	..	..	..	..	..	..	..
Angola	6,382	30.7	5,483	31.5	899	25.8	5	-37.5	11	-68.3	0	-100.0	..	..
Benin	5,374	35.1	5,075	34.6	299	44.6	25	177.8	..	..	..	..	..	..
Botswana	1,399	35.8	1,312	35.8	86	35.6	..	..	..	..	..	..	..	..
Burkina Faso	9,254	30.2	8,836	30.2	418	28.6	2	0.0	..	..	..	..	..	..
Burundi	4,484	33.6	4,431	33.5	53	44.1	3	200.0	..	..	..	..	..	..
Cameroon	14,483	35.1	11,490	37.1	2,993	27.7	481	-0.1	78	7.3	5	0.0	-428	-732
Cape Verde	..	..	..	..	..	..	..	..	..	..	..	..	..	..
Central African Rep	3,628	16.3	3,185	21.9	443	-12.3	63	-3.1	2	-83.9	..	..	..	..
Chad	4,164	24.9	3,569	24.7	595	26.2	2	100.0	..	..	..	..	..	..
Comoros	..	..	..	..	..	..	..	..	..	..	..	..	..	..
Congo	3,438	45.5	2,155	33.8	1,283	70.4	53	-22.9	36	-50.2	..	..	..	..
Côte d'Ivoire	13,370	12.9	10,498	45.8	2,872	-38.1	606	-12.5	229	39.8	..	..	-2,254	-323
Djibouti	..	..	..	..	..	..	..	..	..	..	..	..	..	..
Equatorial Guinea	613	16.5	447	2.1	166	87.6	10	-42.6	7	400.0	..	..	..	..
Ethiopia (b)	44,937	27.9	43,227	29.2	1,711	1.1	12	-76.8	9	-35.7	5	-46.0	0	0
Gabon	4,345	39.4	2,712	41.0	1,633	36.8	32	-70.4	140	-26.2	..	..	..	..
Gambia, The	948	16.6	927	16.4	21	26.0	1	0.0	..	..	..	..	..	..
Ghana	16,965	15.9	15,512	12.9	1,453	62.8	407	70.6	60	-6.8	..	..	..	..
Guinea	4,359	34.9	3,792	36.1	567	27.7	66	-26.7	0	-100.0	..	..	-13	-15
Guinea-Bissau	572	3.4	422	0.0	150	14.5	16	0.0	..	..	..	..	..	..
Kenya	37,324	40.9	35,513	41.1	1,811	37.8	185	26.1	52	132.8	148	124.2	-8	0
Lesotho	635	29.8	635	29.8	..	..	..	..	..	..	..	..	..	..
Liberia	6,000	40.6	5,040	34.4	960	86.0	411	131.8	8	84.6	..	..	-236	-234
Madagascar	8,600	32.7	7,793	37.4	807	0.0	235	0.6	5	275.0	5	6.7	..	..
Malawi	9,730	56.9	9,235	57.5	496	46.1	44	26.0	17	108.3	..	..	..	..
Mali	5,955	35.4	5,575	35.3	380	36.5	13	116.7	..	..	..	..	..	..
Mauritania	13	30.0	8	33.3	5	25.0	..	..	..	..	..	..	..	..
Mauritius	15	-54.0	2	-90.0	13	30.0	5	40.0	0	..	..	..	1	16
Mozambique	15,980	11.7	15,022	12.5	958	-0.3	21	-55.9	4	22.2	2	-16.7	-5	-7
Namibia	..	..	..	..	..	..	..	..	..	..	..	..	..	..
Niger	5,292	38.1	4,965	38.1	326	38.3	2	..	..	..	..	..	..	..
Nigeria	114,704	35.2	106,441	38.3	8,263	4.5	2,723	1.7	109	-48.0	63	372.5	-59	-49
Rwanda	5,647	10.0	5,392	10.8	255	-4.1	27	247.8	2	0.0	..	..	..	..
São Tomé and Principe	..	..	..	..	..	..	..	..	..	..	..	..	..	..
Senegal	4,953	34.4	4,281	33.5	672	40.5	23	109.1	..	..	..	..	..	..
Seychelles									..	..	..	..	..	..
Sierra Leone	3,227	25.6	3,106	28.3	121	-17.9	9	-55.7	..	..	..	..	..	..
Somalia	8,761	27.6	8,655	27.7	106	18.7	14	0.0	0	-100.0	..	..	0	0
South Africa	19,747	-0.6	7,146	1.1	12,601	-1.5	1,792	8.5	350	-10.9	1,735	25.1	-72	-1,066
Sudan	24,108	33.8	21,877	34.0	2,231	32.2	3	-68.0	2	0.0	3	-66.7	..	..
Swaziland	2,297	3.3	560	0.0	1,737	4.4	103	-1.0	8	14.3	..	..	-199	0
Tanzania	34,911	41.9	32,849	40.3	2,062	74.0	156	72.1	15	150.0	25	..	0	-9
Togo	1,265	80.1	1,072	90.4	192	38.4	3	100.0	..	..	..	..	0	-1
Uganda	15,099	34.9	13,103	34.8	1,996	35.9	64	179.7	4	160.0	3	..	0	0
Zaire	43,252	48.0	40,101	49.2	3,151	33.6	105	1.0	28	-7.7	2	0.0	-62	-111
Zambia	13,778	43.9	12,952	42.5	826	69.8	106	137.3	81	1,513.3	3	-23.1	9	-4
Zimbabwe	8,033	16.7	6,269	12.5	1,764	34.9	250	41.8	79	102.6	86	33.0	-9	-6
NORTH AFRICA	..	..	..	..	..	..	..	..	..	..	..	..	..	..
Algeria	2,305	33.1	2,006	32.0	298	40.7	13	0.0	50	0.0	91	-12.8	..	..
Egypt	2,352	27.4	2,243	27.4	109	27.6	..	..	76	110.2	203	66.7	232	74
Libya	646	2.4	536	0.0	110	15.7	31	0.0	..	..	6	20.0	45	-1
Morocco	2,296	38.1	1,426	28.3	869	58.0	83	-36.6	34	-66.9	106	10.0	213	376
Tunisia	3,324	25.6	3,169	24.9	155	42.2	10	222.2	102	60.5	67	150.0	33	40
ALL AFRICA	538,961	24.6	480,046	24.1	58,916	26.1	8,213	28.9	1,595	48.6	2,558	10.2	-2,811	-2,051

Source: Food and Agriculture Organization of the United Nations.

Notes: a. Imports of roundwood are shown as positive numbers; exports are represented by negative numbers.

b. Ethiopia includes Eritrea

0 = zero or less than half of the unit of measure; .. = not available.

For additional information, see Sources and Technical Notes.

14-4. National protection of natural areas, 1994

	All protected areas (IUCN categories I-V)			Totally protected areas (IUCN categories I-III)		Partially protected areas (IUCN categories IV-V)		Percentage of protected areas (IUCN categories I -V) at least	
	Number	Area (000 ha)	Percent of land area	Number	Area (000 ha)	Number	Area (000 ha)	100,000 ha in size	1 million ha in size
SUB-SAHARAN AFRICA	..	..	..	..	..	..	..	..	..
excluding South Africa	..	..	..	..	..	..	..	..	..
excl. S. Africa & Nigeria	..	..	..	..	..	..	..	..	..
Angola	5	2,641	2	1	790	4	1,851	60	0
Benin	2	778	7	2	778	0	0	100	0
Botswana	9	10,663	18	5	9,731	4	932	89	33
Burkina Faso	12	2,662	10	3	489	9	2,173	42	8
Burundi	3	89	3	0	0	3	89	0	0
Cameroon	14	2,050	4	7	1,032	7	1,019	57	0
Cape Verde	..	..	..	..	..	..	..	..	..
Central African Republic	13	6,106	10	5	3,188	8	2,918	92	23
Chad	9	11,494	9	2	414	7	11,080	100	22
Comoros	..	..	..	..	..	..	..	..	..
Congo	10	1,177	3	1	127	9	1,051	30	0
Côte d'Ivoire	12	1,993	6	10	1,891	2	102	33	8
Djibouti	..	..	..	..	..	..	..	..	..
Equatorial Guinea	0	0	0	0	0	0	0	0	0
Ethiopia	23	6,023	5	12	3,040	11	2,982	70	0
Gabon	6	1,045	4	1	15	5	1,030	33	0
Gambia, The	5	23	2	3	18	2	5	0	0
Ghana	9	1,104	5	7	1,097	2	7	33	0
Guinea	3	164	1	3	164	0	0	33	0
Guinea-Bissau	0	0	0	0	0	0	0	0	0
Kenya	36	3,504	6	32	3,451	4	52	19	3
Lesotho	1	7	0	0	0	1	7	0	0
Liberia	1	129	1	1	129	0	0	100	0
Madagascar	36	1,115	2	16	740	20	375	3	0
Malawi	9	1,059	9	5	696	4	362	33	0
Mali	11	4,012	3	1	350	10	3,662	55	18
Mauritania	4	1,746	2	3	1,496	1	250	75	25
Mauritius	1	4	2	0	0	1	4	0	0
Mozambique	1	2	0	0	0	1	2	0	0
Namibia	12	10,218	12	6	9,000	6	1,218	50	25
Niger	5	8,416	7	1	220	4	8,196	60	20
Nigeria	19	2,971	3	6	2,226	13	745	47	0
Rwanda	2	327	12	2	327	0	0	50	0
São Tomé and Principe	..	..	..	..	..	..	..	..	..
Senegal	9	2,180	11	5	1,012	4	1,168	33	0
Seychelles	..	..	..	..	..	..	..	..	..
Sierra Leone	2	82	1	0	0	2	82	0	0
Somalia	1	180	0	0	0	1	180	100	0
South Africa	238	6,970	6	55	4,280	183	2,689	3	0
Sudan	16	9,383	4	9	8,514	7	869	44	25
Swaziland	3	40	2	0	0	3	40	0	0
Tanzania	31	13,936	15	12	4,100	19	9,836	61	10
Togo	11	647	11	3	357	8	290	27	0
Uganda	31	1,909	8	7	876	24	1,033	19	0
Zaire	8	9,917	4	8	9,917	0	0	100	50
Zambia	21	6,364	8	21	6,364	0	0	52	5
Zimbabwe	25	3,068	8	11	2,704	14	364	24	4
NORTH AFRICA	..	..	..	..	..	..	..	..	..
Algeria	19	11,919	5	12	11,801	7	118	11	11
Egypt	12	793	1	4	99	8	695	8	0
Libya	6	173	0	3	51	3	122	0	0
Morocco	11	369	1	6	62	5	307	9	0
Tunisia	6	44	0	6	44	0	0	0	0
ALL AFRICA	723	149,493	4	297	91,591	426	57,902	33	5

Source: World Conservation Monitoring Centre.

Notes: 0 = zero or less than half the unit of measure. .. = not available or indeterminate.

For additional information, see Sources and Technical Notes.

14-5. International and marine protected areas, 1994

	International protection systems (a)						*Marine protected areas*		
	Biosphere reserves		*World heritage sites*		*Wetlands of international importance*				*Regional priority sites (b)*
	Number	*Area (000 ha)*	*Number*	*Area (000 ha)*	*Number*	*Area (000 ha)*	*Number*	*Area (000 ha)*	*Number*
SUB-SAHARAN AFRICA	..	..	..	..	..	..	..	..	..
excluding South Africa	..	..	..	..	..	..	..	..	..
excl. S. Africa & Nigeria	..	..	..	..	..	..	..	..	..
Angola	0	0	0	0	0	0	3	2,465,200	0
Benin	1	880	0	0	0	0	..	..	..
Botswana	0	0	0	0	0	0	..	..	..
Burkina Faso	1	19	0	0	3	299	..	..	..
Burundi	0	0	0	0	0	0	..	..	..
Cameroon	3	850	1	526	0	0	1	160,000	0
Cape Verde	..	..	..	..	..	..	..	..	..
Central African Republic	2	1,640	1	1,740	0	0	..	..	..
Chad	0	0	0	0	1	195	..	..	..
Comoros	..	..	..	..	..	..	..	..	..
Congo	2	172	0	0	0	0	..	..	..
Côte d'Ivoire	2	1,480	3	1,485	0	0	..	..	..
Djibouti	..	..	..	..	..	..	2	..	..
Equatorial Guinea	0	0	0	0	0	0	..	..	..
Ethiopia	0	0	1	22	0	0	..	..	..
Gabon	1	15	0	0	3	1,080	1	200,000	0
Gambia, The	0	0	0	0	0	0	3	18,440	1
Ghana	1	8	0	0	6	178	..	..	..
Guinea	2	133	1	13	6	225	..	..	..
Guinea-Bissau	0	0	0	0	1	39	1	0	0
Kenya	5	1,335	0	0	1	19	10	79,559	1
Lesotho	0	0	0	0	0	0	..	..	..
Liberia	0	0	0	0	0	0	..	..	..
Madagascar	1	140	1	152	0	0	1	1,000	0
Malawi	0	0	1	9	0	0	..	..	..
Mali	1	771	1	400	3	162			
Mauritania	0	0	1	1,200	1	1,173	2	1,186,000	1
Mauritius	1	4	0	0	0	0	6	8,400	0
Mozambique	0	0	0	0	0	0	4	1,027,000	2
Namibia	0	0	0	0	0	0	..	..	..
Niger	0	0	1	7,736	1	220	..	..	..
Nigeria	1	0	0	0	0	0	..	..	..
Rwanda	1	15	0	0	0	0	..	..	..
São Tomé and Principe	..	..	..	..	..	..	..	..	..
Senegal	3	1,094	2	929	4	100	6	84,186	1
Seychelles	..	..	..	..	..	..	15	..	0
Sierra Leone	0	0	0	0	0	0	..	..	..
Somalia	0	0	0	0	0	0	..	..	..
South Africa	0	0	0	0	12	228	22	..	0
Sudan	2	1,901	0	0	0	0	2	..	0
Swaziland	0	0	0	0	0	0	..	..	..
Tanzania	2	2,338	4	7,381	0	0	7		3
Togo	0	0	0	0	0	0	..	..	..
Uganda	1	220	2	132	1	15	..	..	..
Zaire	3	298	4	5,482	0	0	1	..	0
Zambia	0	0	1	4	2	333	..	..	..
Zimbabwe	0	0	2	1,095	0	0	..	..	..
NORTH AFRICA	..	..	..	..	..	..	..	..	..
Algeria	2	7,276	1	300	2	5	2	76,568	0
Egypt	2	2,577	0	0	2	106	6	708,300	0
Libya	0	0	0	0	0	0	..	..	..
Morocco	0	0	0	0	4	11	3	56,900	0
Tunisia	4	32	1	13	1	13	2	4,480	0
ALL AFRICA	44	23,198	29	28,619	54	4,400	100	6,076,033	9

Source: World Conservation Monitoring Centre, Great Barrier Reef Marine Park Authority, The World Bank, The World Conservation Union (IUCN), United Nations Office for Ocean Affairs and the Law of the Sea.

Notes:
a. Areas listed often include nationally protected systems .
b. Regional priorities as defined by The Great Barrier Reef Marine Park Authority.
0 = zero or less than half the unit of measure. .. = not available or indeterminate.
For additional information, see Sources and Technical Notes.

14-6. Habitat extent and loss, 1980s

	Habitat types													
	Forests						Savannah/ grassland		Desert/ scrub		Wetlands/ marsh		Mangroves	
	All forests		Dry forests		Moist forests									
	Current extent (000 ha)	% lost	Current extent (000 ha)	% lost	Current extent (000 ha)	% lost	Current extent (000 ha)	% lost	Current extent (000 ha)	% lost	Current extent (000 ha)	% lost	Current extent (000 ha)	% lost
SUB-SAHARAN AFRICA	..	..	..	..	..	..	..	..	..	..	..	..	..	..
excluding South Africa	..	..	..	..	..	..	..	..	..	..	..	..	..	..
excl. S. Africa & Nigeria	..	..	..	..	..	..	..	..	..	..	..	..	..	..
Angola	51,428	45	40,261	45	11,167	48	24,590	17	456	20	..	..	..	..
Benin	4,448 b	62 b	4,406	55	42	97	0	0	0	0	..	..	110	50
Botswana	11,293	62	11,293	62	0	0	12,247	53	0	0	0	0	7	..
Burkina Faso	4,964	80	4,964	80	0	0	768	70	0	0	2,331	10	0	0
Burundi	117	91	114	91	3	95	246	80	0	0	0	0	0	0
Cameroon	18,468	59	2,949	69	15,519	56	376	72	0	0	14	..	0	0
Cape Verde	..	..	..	..	..	..	..	..	0	0	16	80	486	40
Central African Republic	27,933	55	14,667	51	13,266	59	0	0	..	..	..	..	..	..
Chad {a}	5,848	80	5,848	80	0	0	11,958	72	0	0	0	0	0	0
Comoros	..	..	..	..	..	..	..	..	0	0	66	90	0	0
Congo	17,442	49	0	0	17,442	49	0	0	..	..	..	..	..	..
Côte d'Ivoire	6,308 b	80 b	3,562	60	2,746	88	0	0	0	0	290	..	2	0
Djibouti	0	0	0	0	0	0	1,000	50	0	0	32	..	3	..
Equatorial Guinea	1,285	50	0	0	1,285	50	0	0	120	20	0	0	9	70
Ethiopia	5,570	86	5,570	86	0	0	27,469	61	0	0	0	0	12	60
Gabon	17,245	35	0	0	17,245	35	0	0	525	30	0	0	0	0
Gambia, The	122 b	89 b	72	90	50	88	0	0	0	0	0	0	115	50
Ghana	4,254 b	82 b	2,670	71	1,584	89	0	0	0	0	0	0	50	..
Guinea	7,440	69	1,799	71	5,641	69	0	0	0	0	853	..	2	..
Guinea-Bissau	512	80	0	0	512	80	0	0	0	0	525	..	120	60
Kenya	2,274	71	2,130	67	144	90	27,682	43	0	0	0	0	315	70
Lesotho	851	67	851	67	0	0	141	70	0	0	0	0	93	70
Liberia	1,424	87	8	20	1,416	87	0	0	0	0	0	0	0	0
Madagascar	13,049	75	11,401	62	1,648	84	1,509	78	0	0	40	..	36	70
Malawi	3,977	56	3,977	56	0	0	0	0	0	0	197	..	130	40
Mali {a}	7,670	78	7,670	78	0	0	8,368	80	0	0	112	60	0	0
Mauritania {a}	6	90	6	90	0	0	4,610	88	0	0	2,000	..	0	0
Mauritius	11 c	..	..	..	..	..	..	..	0	0	0	0	0	0
Mozambique	33,137	57	33,137	57	0	0	696	20	..	..	..	..	0	..
Namibia	15,020	52	15,020	52	0	0	14,741	59	0	0	171	10	276	60
Niger {a}	2,278	80	2,278	80	0	0	10,985	75	14,570	0	225	10	0	0
Nigeria	18,201 b	80 b	14,339	70	3,862	91	498	80	0	0	38	80	0	0
Rwanda	184	80	184	80	0	0	157	90	0	0	42	80	1,052	..
São Tomé and Principe	..	..	..	..	..	..	..	..	0	0	80	..	0	0
Senegal	2,455 b	82	2,250	80	205	93	1,120	80	..	..	..	..	..	..
Seychelles	..	..	..	..	..	..	..	..	0	0	2	..	185	..
Sierra Leone	554 b	92 b	48	40	506	93	0	0	..	..	..	..	..	..
Somalia	642	67	642	67	0	0	36,374	40	0	0	0	0	102	..
South Africa	20,444	46	20,444	46	0	0	32,257	62	712	4	0	0	54	70
Sudan {a}	15,367	74	15,162	73	205	91	36,007	68	880	0	0	0	45	50
Swaziland	772	56	772	56	0	0	0	0	0	0	11,170	..	0	0
Tanzania	36,137	40	35,867	39	270	80	14,352	49	0	0	0	0	0	0
Togo	1,758 b	69 b	1,622	57	136	92	0	0	0	0	1,545	..	212	60
Uganda	3,371	79	2,062	67	1,309	86	1,042	71	0	0	0	0	0	..
Zaire	83,255	57	9,135	54	74,120	57	5,405	30	0	0	1,420	..	0	0
Zambia	44,606	30	44,606	30	0	0	8,175	18	0	0	215	50	125	50
Zimbabwe	17,169	56	17,169	56	0	0	0	0	0	0	1,106	10	0	0
NORTH AFRICA	..	..	..	..	..	..	..	..	0	0	0	0	0	0
Algeria	..	..	..	..	..	..	..	..	..	..	..	..	..	..
Egypt	..	..	..	..	..	..	..	..	..	..	730	..	0	0
Libya	..	..	..	..	..	..	..	..	..	..	809	..	..	..
Morocco	..	..	..	..	..	..	..	..	..	..	..	..	0	0
Tunisia	..	..	..	..	..	..	..	..	..	..	33	..	0	0
ALL AFRICA {a}	..	..	..	..	..	..	..	..	..	..	868	..	0	0
	..	..	..	..	..	..	..	..	..	..	..	..	..	..

Sources: World Conservation Union, The Woods Hole Research Center, World Conservation Monitoring Centre, and other sources.

Notes: a. Data are for sub-Saharan region only. b. Includes mangroves. c. Protected private and crown forest lands.

.. = not available; 0 = zero or less than half the unit of measure.

For additional information, see Sources and Technical Notes.

14-7. Globally threatened species: mammals, birds, and higher plants, 1990s

	Mammals				Birds				Higher plants			
	Total number of known species			Number of species per 10,000 square km (a)	Total number of known species			Number of species per 10,000 square km (a)	Total number of known species			Number of species per 10,000 square km (a)
	All species	Endemic species	Threatened species		All species	Endemic species	Threatened species		All species (b)	Endemic species	Threatened species	
SUB-SAHARAN AFRICA	..	..	..	..	..	..	..	..	..	..	..	..
excluding South Africa	..	..	..	..	..	..	..	..	..	..	..	..
excl. S. Africa & Nigeria	..	..	..	..	..	..	..	..	..	..	..	..
Angola	276	7	16	56	909	13	13	185	5,000	1,260	25	1,017
Benin	188	0	7	85	423	0	1	190	2,000	..	3	899
Botswana	164	0	8	43	550	0	5	144	..	17	4	..
Burkina Faso	147	0	6	49	453	0	1	152	1,100	..	0	369
Burundi	107	0	6	76	596	0	5	425	2,500	..	1	1,783
Cameroon	297	13	21	83	874	8	14	244	8,000	156	74	2,237
Cape Verde	..	..	..	..	..	..	..	..	..	..	..	..
Central African Republic	209	2	9	53	662	0	2	169	3,600	100	0	921
Chad	134	1	13	27	532	0	3	107	1,600	..	12	322
Comoros	..	..	..	..	..	..	..	..	..	..	..	..
Congo	200	2	13	62	569	0	3	177	4,350	1,200	3	1,356
Côte d'Ivoire	230	1	16	73	694	0	11	221	3,517	62	66	1,118
Djibouti	..	..	..	..	..	..	..	..	..	..	..	..
Equatorial Guinea	184	3	12	131	322	3	4	229	3,000	66	9	2,135
Ethiopia	255	31	21	54	813	28	17	172	6,500	1,000	153	1,378
Gabon	190	2	12	64	629	0	4	213	6,500	..	78	2,197
Gambia, The	108	0	3	104	504	0	1	484	966	..	0	928
Ghana	222	1	12	78	725	1	7	255	3,600	43	32	1,264
Guinea	190	1	13	66	552	0	11	192	3,000	88	35	1,043
Guinea-Bissau	108	0	5	71	319	0	1	209	1,000	12	0	655
Kenya	359	21	16	94	1,068	6	22	280	6,000	265	158	1,571
Lesotho	33	0	2	23	281	0	3	195	1,576	2	7	1,093
Liberia	193	0	13	91	581	1	13	274	2,200	103	1	1,037
Madagascar	105	77	33	27	253	103	28	66	9,000	6,500	189	2,347
Malawi	195	0	6	86	645	0	9	285	3,600	49	61	1,592
Mali	137	0	12	28	622	0	5	127	1,741	11	14	355
Mauritania	61	1	10	13	541	0	3	117	1,100	..	3	239
Mauritius	4	2	3	7	81	9	9	137	700	325	222	1,183
Mozambique	179	1	9	42	678	0	13	160	5,500	219	92	1,294
Namibia	154	3	12	36	609	1	6	142	3,128	..	23	729
Niger	131	0	10	27	482	0	2	98	1,170	..	0	237
Nigeria	274	6	22	62	862	2	8	194	4,614	205	9	1,036
Rwanda	151	0	14	110	666	0	6	484	2,288	26	0	1,662
São Tomé and Principe	..	..	..	..	..	..	..	..	..	..	..	..
Senegal	155	0	9	58	610	0	5	228	2,062	26	32	771
Seychelles	..	..	..	..	..	..	..	..	..	..	..	..
Sierra Leone	147	0	12	77	622	0	12	325	2,090	74	12	1,091
Somalia	171	11	12	43	649	10	8	165	3,000	500	57	761
South Africa	247	27	25	51	790	7	16	162	23,000	..	953	4,711
Sudan	267	11	16	43	937	0	9	151	3,132	50	8	506
Swaziland	47	0	4	39	485	0	4	404	2,636	4	41	2,197
Tanzania	322	14	16	72	1,005	19	30	224	10,000	1,122	406	2,229
Togo	196	1	8	110	558	0	1	315	2,000	..	0	1,128
Uganda	338	6	15	119	992	3	10	350	5,000	..	6	1,762
Zaire	415	28	23	69	1,096	22	26	181	11,000	1,100	7	1,817
Zambia	229	3	7	55	736	1	10	177	4,600	211	9	1,105
Zimbabwe	270	1	9	81	648	0	7	193	4,200	95	94	1,253
NORTH AFRICA	..	..	..	..	..	..	..	..	..	..	..	..
Algeria	92	2	11	15	375	1	7	62	3,100	250	145	509
Egypt	98	7	7	21	439	0	10	96	2,066	70	84	452
Libya	76	5	8	14	323	0	2	59	1,800	134	57	327
Morocco	105	4	7	30	416	0	11	119	3,600	625	195	1,028
Tunisia	78	1	5	31	356	0	6	142	2,150	..	24	855
ALL AFRICA	..	..	..	..	..	..	..	..	..	..	..	..

Source: World Conservation Monitoring Centre.

Notes: a. Values are standardized using a species-area curve. b. Flowering plants only.
Threatened species data are as of June 1993. .. = not available.
For additional information, see Sources and Technical Notes.

14-8. Globally threatened species: reptiles, amphibians, and fish, 1990s

	Reptiles: Total number of known species: All species	Reptiles: Total number of known species: Endemic species	Reptiles: Total number of known species: Threatened species	Reptiles: Number of species per 10,000 square km {a}	Amphibians: Total number of known species: All species	Amphibians: Total number of known species: Endemic species	Amphibians: Total number of known species: Threatened species	Amphibians: Number of species per 10,000 square km {a}	Total number of known freshwater fish species: All species	Total number of known freshwater fish species: Threatened species
SUB-SAHARAN AFRICA	..	..	..	..	..	..	..	..	..	..
excluding South Africa	..	..	..	..	..	..	..	..	..	..
excl. S. Africa & Nigeria	..	..	..	..	..	..	..	..	..	..
Angola	..	18	5	..	..	22	0	..	..	0
Benin	..	1	2	..	..	0	0	..	..	0
Botswana	157	2	0	41	38	0	0	10	92	0
Burkina Faso	..	3	1	..	..	0	0	..	..	0
Burundi	..	0	0	..	..	2	0	..	..	0
Cameroon	..	19	3	..	..	66	1	..	..	20
Cape Verde	..	..	..	..	..	..	..	..	..	..
Central African Republic	..	0	1	..	..	0	0	..	..	0
Chad	..	1	1	..	..	0	0	..	..	0
Comoros	..	..	..	..	..	..	..	..	..	..
Congo	..	1	2	..	..	1	0	..	..	0
Côte d'Ivoire	..	2	4	..	..	3	1	..	..	0
Djibouti	..	..	..	..	..	..	..	..	..	..
Equatorial Guinea	..	3	3	..	..	2	1	..	..	0
Ethiopia	..	6	2	..	..	32	0	..	..	0
Gabon	..	3	3	..	..	4	0	..	..	0
Gambia, The	..	1	1	..	..	0	0	..	79	0
Ghana	..	1	4	..	..	4	0	..	..	0
Guinea	..	3	3	..	..	3	1	..	..	0
Guinea-Bissau	..	2	3	..	..	1	0	..	..	0
Kenya	187	15	3	49	88	11	0	23	..	..
Lesotho	..	2	1	..	..	1	2	..	8	1
Liberia	62	2	3	29	38	4	1	18	..	0
Madagascar	252	197	10	66	144	143	0	38	40	10
Malawi	124	6	0	55	69	3	0	31	..	0
Mali	16	2	1	3	..	1	0	..	..	0
Mauritania	..	1	3	..	..	0	0	..	..	0
Mauritius	11	8	6	19	0	0	0	0	..	0
Mozambique	..	5	6	..	62	1	1	15	..	1
Namibia	..	26	2	..	32	1	1	7	102	5
Niger	..	0	0	..	..	0	0	..	..	0
Nigeria	> 135	7	3	0	>109	1	0	0	260	0
Rwanda	..	1	0	..	..	0	0	..	..	0
São Tomé and Principe	..	..	..	..	..	..	..	..	..	..
Senegal	..	1	6	..	..	1	0	..	83	0
Seychelles	..	..	..	..	..	..	..	..	..	..
Sierra Leone	..	1	3	..	..	2	0	..	..	0
Somalia	193	48	2	49	27	3	0	7	..	1
South Africa	299	81	36	61	95	45	16	19	94	34
Sudan	..	6	2	..	..	1	0	..	..	0
Swaziland	102	1	2	85	40	0	1	33	40	0
Tanzania	245	56	4	55	121	43	0	27	..	..
Togo	..	1	3	..	..	3	0	..	..	0
Uganda	149	2	0	53	50	1	0	18	291	..
Zaire	..	33	3	..	..	53	0	..	..	1
Zambia	..	2	1	..	83	1	0	20	..	0
Zimbabwe	153	2	0	46	120	3	0	36	112	0
NORTH AFRICA	..	..	..	..	..	..	..	..	..	..
Algeria	..	3	0	..	..	0	0	..	..	1
Egypt	83	0	4	18	6	0	0	1	70	1
Libya	..	1	2	..	..	0	0	..	..	0
Morocco	..	8	1	..	..	1	0	..	..	1
Tunisia	..	1	1	..	..	0	0	..	..	0
ALL AFRICA	..	..	..	..	..	..	..	..	..	..

Source: World Conservation Monitoring Centre.

Notes: a. Values are standardized using a species-area curve.
Threatened species data are as of 1994. ..= not available.
For additional information, see Sources and Technical Notes.

14-9. Net trade in wildlife and wildlife products reported by CITES, 1990

	CITES reporting equirement met {a} (percent)	Mammals: Live primates (number)		Mammals: Cat skins (number)		Birds: Live birds (number)		Reptiles: Reptile skins {b} (number)		Plants: Live cacti (number)		Plants: Live orchids (number)	
		Imports	Exports	Imports	Exports	Imports	Exports	Imports	Exports	Imports	Exports	Imports	Exports
SUB-SAHARAN AFRICA	..	..	..	..	..	..	..	..	..	..	..	..	..
excluding South Africa	..	..	..	..	..	..	..	..	..	..	..	..	..
excl. S. Africa & Nigeria	..	..	..	..	..	..	..	..	..	..	..	..	..
Angola {c}	NA	0	4	2	0	0	2	..	..	..	..	..	..
Benin	0	..	..	..	..	0	510	..	..	..	..	..	..
Botswana	86	..	..	122	0	0	1,974	0	380	..	..	..	..
Burkina Faso	0	..	..	..	..	0	0	..	..	..	..	..	..
Burundi	0	..	..	..	..	0	5	..	..	..	..	..	..
Cameroon	92	..	..	9	0	0	18,194	0	72,351	..	..	..	..
Cape Verde	..	..	..	..	..	..	..	..	..	..	..	..	..
Central African Republic	50	..	..	..	..	0	1	0	1	..	..	..	..
Chad	0	..	..	..	..	0	2	0	13,180	..	..	..	..
Comoros	..	..	..	..	..	..	..	..	..	..	..	..	..
Congo	100	0	3	0	2	0	45	0	546	..	..	0	20
Côte d'Ivoire	NA	..	..	..	..	0	5,850	..	..	..	..	..	..
Djibouti	..	..	..	0	2	..	..	..	..	..	..	..	..
Equatorial Guinea	..	..	..	..	..	..	..	..	..	..	..	..	..
Ethiopia													
Eritrea	75	0	287	0	3	..	..	0	2,075	..	..	..	..
Gabon	67	14	0	13	0	0	29	..	..	..	..	0	123
Gambia, The	20	..	..	..	..	..	..	..	..	..	..	..	..
Ghana	81	0	457	..	..	0	6,015	0	21	..	..	0	723
Guinea	45	0	2	0	2	0	121,887	0	7,648	..	..	..	..
Guinea-Bissau	0	..	..	..	..	0	1	0	165	..	..	..	..
Kenya	54	0	1,929	0	100	0	11	0	2,201	..	..	0	3
Lesotho {c}	NA	..	..	..	..	..	..	..	..	..	..	..	..
Liberia	73	..	..	0	1	0	2,939	..	..	..	..	..	..
Madagascar	82	0	7	..	..	0	1,923	0	853	0	101	0	18,558
Malawi	70	..	..	0	2	..	..	0	1,070	..	..	0	22
Mali {c}	NA	..	..	0	1	0	89,033	0	240,695	..	..	..	..
Mauritania {c}	NA	..	..	..	..	..	..	1	0	..	..	..	..
Mauritius	88	0	1,929	..	..	76	0	12	0	..	..	0	26
Mozambique	73	0	20	0	5	0	21,322	0	590	..	..	..	..
Namibia	0	..	..	0	16	53	0	1	0	..	..	..	..
Niger	41	2	0	..	..	46	0	0	1	..	..	..	..
Nigeria	18	..	..	0	1	0	15	0	52	..	..	0	12
Rwanda	27	..	..	..	..	..	..	..	..	..	..	..	..
São Tomé and Principe	..	..	..	..	..	..	..	..	..	..	..	..	..
Senegal	80	0	62	1	0	0	270,671	0	11,568	..	..	..	..
Seychelles	..	..	..	..	..	..	..	..	..	..	..	..	..
Sierra Leone {c}	NA	..	..	..	..	0	4,019	..	..	..	..	..	..
Somalia	17	..	..	..	..	0	1	..	..	..	..	..	..
South Africa	94	0	178	0	52	7,751	0	3,302	0	..	..	0	73
Sudan	44	..	..	2	0	37	0	0	95,288	..	..	..	..
Swaziland {c}	NA	..	..	1	0	..	..	..	..	..	..	..	..
Tanzania	75	0	1,455	0	27	0	122,761	0	1,556	..	..	..	..
Togo	69	0	484	..	..	0	4,643	0	10,393	..	..	..	..
Uganda	0	..	..	..	..	..	..	..	..	..	..	0	568
Zaire	69	0	3	..	..	0	711	0	1	..	..	..	..
Zambia	45	3	0	0	10	0	1	0	2,290	..	..	..	..
Zimbabwe	83	..	..	0	134	0	1,156	0	13,683	..	..	..	..
NORTH AFRICA	..	..	..	..	..	..	..	..	..	..	..	..	..
Algeria	50	..	..	..	..	1	0	..	..	..	..	..	..
Egypt	0	31	0	..	..	1,000	0	0	16,949	..	..	..	..
Libya {c}	NA	..	..	..	..	20	0	4	0	..	..	..	..
Morocco	44	..	..	..	..	0	37	60	0	..	..	..	..
Tunisia	100	..	..	..	..	1	0	..	..	..	..	..	..
ALL AFRICA	..	50	6,820	150	358	8,985	673,758	3,380	493,557	0	101	0	20,128

Source: World Conservation Monitoring Centre.

Notes: a. Includes all trade reported by members of the Convention on International Trade in Endangered Species of Wild Flora and Fauna (CITES) as of May 1993

b. Reptile skins include skins of snakes, lizards, and crocodilians. c. Not a member of CITES as of May 1993

0 = zero or less than half the unit of measurement; .. = not available; NA = not applicable.

For additional information, see Sources and Technical Notes.

14-10. Commercial energy production, 1973-93

	Total		Solid		Liquid		Gas		Primary electricity (a): Geothermal & wind		Primary electricity (a): Hydro		Primary electricity (a): Nuclear	
	Peta-joules 1993	Percent change since 1973	Peta-joules 1993	Percent change since 1973	Peta-joules 1993	Percent change since 1973	Peta-joules 1993	Percent change since 1973	Peta-joules 1993	Percent change since 1973	Peta-joules 1993	Percent change since 1973	Peta-joules 1993	Percent change since 1973
SUB-SAHARAN AFRICA	..	..	..	..	..	..	..	..	..	..	..	..	..	..
excluding South Africa	..	..	..	..	..	..	..	..	..	..	..	..	..	..
excl. S. Africa & Nigeria	..	..	..	..	..	..	..	..	..	..	..	..	..	..
Angola	1,066	207	0	..	1,055	209	7	175	0	..	5	102	0	..
Benin	13	..	0	..	13	..	0	..	0	..	0	..	0	..
Botswana	..	..	0	..	..	..	0	..	0	..	0	..	0	..
Burkina Faso	..	..	0	..	..	..	0	..	0	..	0	..	0	..
Burundi	1	3,312	0	..	..	..	0	..	0	..	0	..	0	..
Cameroon	270	6,879	0	..	260	..	0	..	0	..	10	145	0	..
Cape Verde	..	..	..	..	..	..	..	..	..	..	..	..	..	..
Central African Republic	0	..	0	..	..	..	0	..	0	..	0	74	0	..
Chad	..	..	0	..	..	..	0	..	0	..	0	..	0	..
Comoros	..	..	..	..	..	..	..	..	..	..	..	..	..	..
Congo	365	313	0	..	363	315	0	..	0	..	2	550	0	..
Côte d'Ivoire	18	2,880	0	..	14	..	0	..	0	..	4	385	0	..
Djibouti	..	..	..	..	..	..	..	..	..	..	..	..	..	..
Equatorial Guinea	0	..	0	..	..	..	0	..	0	..	0	20	0	..
Ethiopia	7	494	0	..	..	..	0	..	3	..	4	269	0	..
Gabon	637	89	0	..	631	98	4	-78	0	..	3	14,100	0	..
Gambia, The	..	..	0	..	..	..	0	..	0	..	0	..	0	..
Ghana	22	58	0	..	0	..	0	..	0	..	22	84	0	..
Guinea	1	256	0	..	..	..	0	..	0	..	1	151	0	..
Guinea-Bissau	..	..	0	..	..	..	0	..	0	..	0	..	0	..
Kenya	21	1,328	0	..	..	..	0	..	10	..	11	646	0	..
Lesotho	..	..	0	..	..	..	0	..	0	..	0	..	0	..
Liberia	1	-7	0	..	..	..	0	..	0	..	1	-34	0	..
Madagascar	1	71	0	..	..	..	0	..	0	..	1	145	0	..
Malawi	3	341	0	..	..	..	0	..	0	..	3	364	0	..
Mali	1	694	0	..	..	..	0	..	0	..	1	506	0	..
Mauritania	0	..	0	..	..	..	0	..	0	..	0	..	0	..
Mauritius	0	..	0	..	..	..	0	..	0	..	0	52	0	..
Mozambique	1	-90	1	-90	..	..	0	..	0	..	0	-82	0	..
Namibia	..	..	0	..	..	..	0	..	0	..	0	..	0	..
Niger	5	..	5	..	..	..	0	..	0	..	0	..	0	..
Nigeria	4,140	-3	3	-63	3,935	-8	191	1,513	0	..	12	121	0	..
Rwanda	1	112	0	..	..	..	0	..	0	..	1	89	0	..
São Tomé and Principe	..	..	..	..	..	..	..	..	..	..	..	..	..	..
Senegal	..	..	0	..	..	..	0	..	0	..	0	..	0	..
Seychelles	..	..	..	..	..	..	..	..	..	..	..	..	..	..
Sierra Leone	..	..	0	..	..	..	0	..	0	..	0	..	0	..
Somalia	..	..	0	..	..	..	0	..	0	..	0	..	0	..
South Africa (b)	4,146	169	4,064	164	..	..	0	..	0	..	3	-1	79	..
Sudan	3	316	0	..	..	..	0	..	0	..	3	836	0	..
Swaziland	..	..	0	..	..	..	0	..	0	..	0	..	0	..
Tanzania	2	78	0	..	..	..	0	..	0	..	2	95	0	..
Togo	0	..	0	..	..	..	0	..	0	..	0	50	0	..
Uganda	3	1	0	..	..	..	0	..	0	..	3	-6	0	..
Zaire	78	365	3	-7	54	..	0	..	0	..	22	75	0	..
Zambia	38	11	10	-57	..	..	0	..	0	..	28	154	0	..
Zimbabwe	160	79	154	122	..	..	0	..	0	..	6	-68	0	..
NORTH AFRICA	..	..	..	..	..	..	..	..	..	..	..	..	..	..
Algeria	4,584	99	1	162	2,481	16	2,102	1,190	0	..	1	-27	0	..
Egypt	2,435	546	0	..	2,028	471	376	10,960	0	..	31	66	0	..
Libya	3,054	-33	0	..	2,806	-37	248	107	0	..	0	..	0	..
Morocco	21	-8	18	29	0	..	1	-63	0	..	2	-73	0	..
Tunisia	209	24	0	..	196	21	13	144	0	..	0	21	0	..
ALL AFRICA	21,307	..	4,259	..	13,836	..	2,942	..	17	..	180	..	79	..

Source: United Nations Statistical Division.

Notes: a. The production of primary electricity was assessed at the equivalent of 100 percent efficiency for wind and hydroelectric generation (at the heat value of electricity: 1 kilowatt hour = 3.6 million joules), at 33 percent efficiency for nuclear power generation, and at 10 percent efficiency for geothermal generation.

b. Data are for the South Africa Customs Union (Botswana, Lesotho, Namibia, South Africa, and Swaziland).

1 petajoule = 1,000,000,000,000,000 joules = 947,800,000,000 Btus = 163,400 "U.N. standard" barrels of oil = 34,140 "U.N. standard" metric tons of coal.

0 = zero or less than half of the unit of measure; .. = not available or indeterminate.

For additional information, see Sources and Technical Notes.

14-11. Energy consumption, 1973-93

	Commercial energy consumption: Total peta-joules 1993	Per capita giga-joules 1993	Per constant 1987 US $ of GNP: Mega-joules 1993	Per constant 1987 US $ of GNP: Percent change since 1973	Imports as percentage of consumption 1973	Imports as percentage of consumption 1993	Traditional fuels: Total Peta-joules 1993	Total Percent change since 1973	Per capita Mega-joules 1993	Per capita Percent change since 1973	Percentage of total consumption 1993	Percentage of total consumption 1973
SUB-SAHARAN AFRICA	..	..	..	..	..	..	..	..	..	..	..	..
excluding South Africa	..	..	..	..	..	..	..	..	..	..	..	..
excl. S. Africa & Nigeria	..	..	..	..	..	..	..	..	..	..	..	..
Angola	26	3	..	..	-1,136	-3,835	56	-12	5,455	-50	68	63
Benin	7	1	4	-28	81	-71	48	67	9,482	-5	87	84
Botswana	..	..	0	..	..	..	13	102	9,420	2	100	100
Burkina Faso	8	1	3	57	30	100	85	62	8,652	-2	91	96
Burundi	3	0	2	77	30	100	44	60	7,222	-4	94	97
Cameroon	36	3	4	17	38	-639	114	72	9,130	-2	76	81
Cape Verde	..	..	..	..	..	..	..	..	..	..	..	..
Central African Republic	3	1	3	-2	82	133	34	67	10,694	4	92	89
Chad	1	0	1	-71	337	200	35	55	5,900	0	97	91
Comoros	..	..	..	..	..	..	..	..	..	..	..	..
Congo	24	10	10	67	-234	-1,379	22	77	8,945	-1	48	69
Côte d'Ivoire	109	8	11	115	40	119	103	111	7,723	-1	49	57
Djibouti	..	..	..	..	..	..	..	..	..	..	..	..
Equatorial Guinea	2	5	13	..	19	100	4	20	11,522	-20	69	84
Ethiopia	45	1	..	..	53	93	414	84	7,984	9	90	91
Gabon	32	26	7	-52	-926	-1,859	26	138	21,166	10	45	24
Gambia, The	3	3	10	59	28	100	9	27	8,579	-38	75	89
Ghana	67	4	10	10	53	75	152	101	9,213	15	69	64
Guinea	15	2	6	..	72	100	35	43	5,594	-8	70	69
Guinea-Bissau	3	3	13	6	49	100	4	11	4,012	-38	58	72
Kenya	90	3	10	-14	86	97	344	84	13,049	-11	79	80
Lesotho	..	..	0	..	..	..	6	168	3,338	56	100	100
Liberia	5	2	..	..	373	100	48	56	17,045	-17	91	62
Madagascar	15	1	5	-10	127	93	76	56	5,483	-17	84	77
Malawi	11	1	8	-20	59	82	133	198	12,596	39	92	86
Mali	7	1	3	12	52	100	54	68	5,279	-2	88	90
Mauritania	39	18	37	297	17	118	0	58	37	-4	0	1
Mauritius	21	19	8	-20	56	143	17	-13	15,392	-31	44	67
Mozambique	14	1	7	..	274	114	147	57	9,758	4	91	71
Namibia	..	..	0	..	..	..	0	..	0	..	..	..
Niger	15	2	6	175	28	67	47	83	5,484	-3	76	86
Nigeria	705	7	19	220	-590	-481	1,010	82	9,590	3	59	80
Rwanda	7	1	3	154	15	100	53	16	6,986	-37	88	97
São Tomé and Principe	..	..	..	..	..	..	..	..	..	..	..	..
Senegal	38	5	8	28	168	126	49	75	6,257	1	57	61
Seychelles	..	..	..	..	..	..	..	..	..	..	..	..
Sierra Leone	6	1	10	-59	154	233	30	49	6,903	-2	83	64
Somalia	..	..	..	..	..	..	71	143	7,975	39	100	89
South Africa (a)	3,578	79	42	..	0	-15	131	13	3,314	-31	4	100
Sudan	48	2	..	..	170	110	220	78	8,261	1	82	61
Swaziland	..	..	0	..	..	..	18	111	22,852	19	100	66
Tanzania	30	1	6	-56	142	100	330	135	11,769	25	92	79
Togo	9	2	8	61	53	100	10	139	2,665	34	53	48
Uganda	16	1	2	..	94	81	137	85	6,870	-2	90	81
Zaire	73	2	..	..	58	4	365	70	8,854	-9	83	81
Zambia	51	6	22	-32	78	33	130	91	14,536	-2	72	52
Zimbabwe	208	19	32	1	11	25	70	57	6,513	-16	25	26
NORTH AFRICA	..	..	..	..	..	..	..	..	..	..	..	..
Algeria	1,183	44	18	144	-176	-274	19	64	714	-8	2	5
Egypt	1,226	20	30	36	-6	-84	45	59	752	-2	4	9
Libya	457	91	..	..	-982	-562	5	18	1,037	-47	1	7
Morocco	297	11	13	19	33	108	14	147	529	57	4	5
Tunisia	218	25	18	42	-40	7	31	55	3,593	-2	12	25
ALL AFRICA	8,751	8	416	23	-21	-114	4,810	64	368,122	-2	57	58

Sources: United Nations Statistical Division and The World Bank.

Notes: Commercial energy consumption does not include bunkers (fuel for aircraft and ships in international transport) or additions to stocks.
Imports are net imports (gross imports minus exports) and may exceed consumption due to additions to stocks and use for bunkers.
a. Data are for the South African Customs Union (Botswana, Lesotho, Namibia, South Africa, and Swaziland). 1 petajoule = 1,000,000,000,000,000 joules = 947,800,000,000 Btus = 163,400 "U.N. standard" barrels of oil = 34,140 "U.N. standard" metric tons of coal. 1 gigajoule = 1,000,000,000 joules = 947,800 Btus; 1 megajoule = 1,000,000 joules = 947.8 Btus. 0 = zero or less than half of the unit of measure, .. = not available or indeterminate, GNP = gross national product. For additional info., see Sources & Technical Notes.

14-12. Reserves and resources of commercial energy, 1993

	Anthracite and bituminous coals (million metric tons) 1993		*Subbituminous and lignite coals (million metric tons) 1993*		*Crude oil (million metric tons) 1993*	*Natural gas (billion cubic meters) 1993*	*Uranium (metric tons)*		*Hydroelectric (megawatts)*	
	Proved reserves in place	**Proved recoverable reserves**	**Proved reserves in place**	**Proved recoverable reserves**	**proved recoverable reserves**	**proved recoverable reserves**	**Recoverable at less than $80 per kg 1993**	**Recoverable at less than $130 per kg 1993**	**Known exploitable potential**	**Installed capacity 1993**
SUB-SAHARAN AFRICA	..	..	..	..	..	..	..	..	..	..
excluding South Africa	..	..	..	..	..	..	..	..	..	..
excl. S. Africa & Nigeria	..	..	..	..	..	..	..	..	..	..
Angola	..	..	..	..	736	51	..	..	100,000	322
Benin	..	..	..	..	4	..	..	..	500 a	0
Botswana	7,000	3,500	..	..	..	..	..	..	1 a	0
Burkina Faso	..	..	..	..	..	..	..	..	200 a	30
Burundi	..	..	..	..	..	..	..	..	1,366	36
Cameroon	..	..	..	..	54	110	..	..	115,000	725
Cape Verde	..	..	..	..	..	..	..	..	..	..
Central African Republic	..	..	4	4	..	..	8,000	8,000	2,000 a	22
Chad	..	..	..	..	..	..	..	..	30 a	0
Comoros	..	..	..	..	..	..	..	..	..	..
Congo	..	..	..	..	113	77	..	..	50,000	89
Côte d'Ivoire	..	..	..	..	7	14	..	..	14,000	900
Djibouti	..	..	..	..	..	..	..	..	..	..
Equatorial Guinea	..	..	..	..	2	37	..	..	2,000 a	..
Ethiopia	..	..	14	..	..	23	..	..	162,000	378
Gabon	..	..	..	..	182	14	9,780	4,650	32,500	326
Gambia, The	..	..	..	..	..	..	..	..	..	0
Ghana	..	..	..	..	0	23	..	..	11,550	1,072
Guinea	..	..	..	..	..	..	..	..	26,000	61
Guinea-Bissau	..	..	..	..	..	..	..	..	300	0
Kenya	..	..	..	..	..	..	..	..	30,000	611
Lesotho	..	..	..	..	..	..	..	..	2,000	0
Liberia	..	..	..	..	..	..	..	..	11,000	81
Madagascar	1,000	..	75	..	..	2	..	..	23,061	130
Malawi	15	2	..	..	..	..	..	..	6,000	146
Mali	..	..	..	..	..	..	..	..	10,000	45
Mauritania	..	..	..	..	..	..	..	..	..	61
Mauritius	..	..	..	..	..	..	..	..	65 a	59
Mozambique	..	240	..	..	..	77	..	..	72,000	2,081
Namibia	..	..	..	..	..	147	80,620	16,000	1,060	249
Niger	..	70	..	..	..	..	159,170	6,650	235 a	0
Nigeria	..	21	338	169	1,693	3,451	..	..	40,000	1,970
Rwanda	..	..	..	..	..	57	..	..	3,000	59
São Tomé and Principe	..	..	..	..	..	..	..	..	..	..
Senegal	..	..	..	..	..	..	..	..	500 a	0
Seychelles	..	..	..	..	..	..	..	..	..	..
Sierra Leone	..	..	..	..	..	..	..	..	6,800	..
Somalia	..	..	..	..	..	6	0	6,600	50 a	0
South Africa	121,218	55,333	..	..	6	27	144,400	96,440	..	593
Sudan	..	..	..	..	41	86	..	..	1,900	225
Swaziland	1,000	116	..	999	..	..	..	..	400	51
Tanzania	304	200	..	..	..	116	..	..	20,000	339
Togo	..	..	..	..	..	..	..	..	270 a	73
Uganda	..	..	..	..	..	..	..	..	10,200	155
Zaire	720	88	..	..	25	1	1,800	..	530,000	2,829
Zambia	..	..	69	55	..	..	1,800	..	309,009	2,259
Zimbabwe	1,535	734	965	..	..	..	..	..	19,281	666
NORTH AFRICA	..	..	..	..	..	..	..	..	..	..
Algeria	..	43	..	..	1,183	3,700	26,000	..	287 a	274
Egypt	25	13	..	40	472	706	..	..	3,210 a	2,825
Libya	..	..	..	..	5,931	1,296	..	..	..	0
Morocco	134	45	44	..	0	3	..	..	4,000	713
Tunisia	..	..	..	..	45	92	..	..	65 a	79
AFRICA	132,951	60,405	1,509	1,267	10,493	10,116	431,570	138,340	1,621,840	20,534

Sources: World Energy Council, United Nations Statistical Division.

Notes: a. Technical potential.

0 = zero or less than half of the unit of measures. .. = not available.

For additional information, see Sources and Technical Notes.

14-13. Freshwater resources and withdrawals

	Annual internal renewable water resources (a)		*Annual river flows*			*Annual withdrawals*			*Sectoral withdrawals (b) (percent)*		
	Total (cubic km)	*1995 per capita (cubic meters)*	*From other countries (cubic km)*	*To other countries (cubic km)*	*Year of data*	*Total (cubic km)*	*Percentage of water esources (a)*	*Per capita (cubic meters)*	*Domestic*	*ndustry*	*Agriculture*
SUB-SAHARAN AFRICA	..	..	..	..	..	..	..	..	..	..	..
excluding South Africa	..	..	..	..	..	..	..	..	..	..	..
excl. S. Africa & Nigeria	..	..	..	..	..	..	..	..	..	..	..
Angola	184	16,618	..	..	1987	0.5	0	57	14	10	76
Benin	26	4,770	16	..	1994	0.1	1	28	23	10	67
Botswana	15	9,886	12	..	1992	0.1	1	83	32	20	48
Burkina Faso	28	2,713	..	..	1992	0.4	1	40	19	0	81
Burundi	4	563	..	..	1987	0.1	3	20	36	0	64
Cameroon	268	20,252	0	0	1987	0.4	0	38	46	19	35
Cape Verde	..	..	..	..	..	..	..	..	..	..	..
Central African Republic	141	42,534	..	..	1987	0.1	0	26	21	5	74
Chad	43	6,760	28	..	1987	0.2	0	34	16	2	82
Comoros	..	..	..	..	..	..	..	..	..	..	..
Congo	832	321,236	610	..	1987	0.0	0	20	62	27	11
Côte d'Ivoire	78	5,451	1	..	1987	0.7	1	66	22	11	67
Djibouti	..	..	..	..	..	..	..	..	..	..	..
Equatorial Guinea	30	75,000	0	..	1987	0.0	0	15	81	13	6
Eritrea	9	2,492	6	..	..	..	..	..	..	..	..
Ethiopia	110	1,998	0	..	1987	2.2	2	51	11	3	86
Gabon	164	124,242	0	..	1987	0.1	0	57	72	22	6
Gambia, The	8	7,156	5	..	1982	0.0	0	30	7	2	91
Ghana	53	3,048	23	..	1970	0.3	1	35	35	13	52
Guinea	226	33,731	0	..	1987	0.7	0	140	10	3	87
Guinea-Bissau	27	25,163	11	..	1991	0.0	0	17	60	4	36
Kenya	30	1,069	10	..	1990	2.0	7	87	20	4	76
Lesotho	5	2,551	0	..	1987	0.1	1	30	22	22	56
Liberia	232	76,341	32	..	1987	0.1	0	56	27	13	60
Madagascar	337	22,827	0	0	1984	16.3	5	1,584	1	0	99
Malawi	19	1,678	1	..	1994	0.9	5	86	10	3	86
Mali	67	6,207	40	..	1987	1.4	2	162	2	1	97
Mauritania	11	5,013	11	..	1985	1.6	14	923	6	2	92
Mauritius	2	1,979	0	0	1974	0.4	16	410	16	7	77
Mozambique	208	12,997	111	0	1992	0.6	0	41	9	2	89
Namibia	46	29,545	39	..	1991	0.2	1	180	29	3	68
Niger	33	3,552	29	..	1988	0.5	2	69	16	2	82
Nigeria	280	2,506	59	..	1987	3.6	1	41	31	15	54
Rwanda	6	792	..	..	1993	0.8	12	102	5	2	94
São Tomé and Principe	..	..	..	..	..	..	..	..	..	..	..
Senegal	39	4,740	13	..	1987	1.4	3	202	5	3	92
Seychelles	..	..	..	..	..	..	..	..	..	..	..
Sierra Leone	160	35,485	0	..	1987	0.4	0	99	7	4	89
Somalia	14	1,459	8	..	1987	0.8	6	98	3	0	97
South Africa	50	1,206	5	..	1990	13.3	27	359	17	11	72
Sudan	154	5,481	119	57	1995	17.8	12	633	4	1	94
Swaziland	5	5,275	2	..	1980	0.7	15	1,171	2	2	96
Tanzania	89	2,998	9	..	1994	1.2	1	40	9	2	89
Togo	12	2,900	1	..	1987	0.1	1	28	62	13	25
Uganda	66	3,099	27	..	1970	0.2	0	20	32	8	60
Zaire	1,019	23,211	84	..	1990	0.4	0	10	61	16	23
Zambia	116	12,267	36	..	1994	1.7	1	186	16	7	77
Zimbabwe	20	1,776	6	..	1987	1.2	6	136	14	7	79
NORTH AFRICA	..	..	..	..	..	..	..	..	..	..	..
Algeria	15	528	0	1	1990	4.5	30	180	25	15	60
Egypt	58	923	56	0	1992	56.4	97	956	6	9	85
Libya	1	111	0	0	1994	4.6	767	880	11	2	87
Morocco	30	1,110	0	0	1992	10.9	36	427	5	3	92
Tunisia	4	443	0	0	1990	3.1	78	381	9	3	89
ALL AFRICA	3,996	5,488	..	..	..	145	4	199	7	5	88

Source: Compiled by World Resources Institute

Notes: a. Annual Internal Renewable Water Resources usually include river flows from other countries.

b. Sectoral percentages date are the same as for annual withdrawal data.

Total withdrawals may exceed 100 percent due to ground water drawdowns or river inflows.

0 = zero or less than half the unit of measure; .. = not available. For additional information, see Sources and Technical Notes.

14-14. CO_2 emissions from industrial processes, 1993

	Carbon dioxide emissions (000 metric tons)						Per capita carbon dioxide emissions	
	Solid	Liquid	Gas	Gas flaring	Cement manufacture	Total	(metric tons)	Bunker fuels (000 metric tons)
SUB-SAHARAN AFRICA	..	..	..	..	..	..	..	..
excluding South Africa	..	..	..	..	..	..	..	..
excl. S. Africa & Nigeria	..	..	..	..	..	..	..	..
Angola	0	1,249	319	2,459	498	4,525	0.4	0
Benin	0	425	0	0	183	612	0.1	0
Botswana	2,173	0	0	0	0	2,173	1.6	0
Burkina Faso	0	557	0	0	0	557	0.1	0
Burundi	15	180	0	0	0	191	0.0	0
Cameroon	4	1,920	0	0	308	2,231	0.2	0
Cape Verde	..	..	..	..	..	..	..	..
Central African Republic	0	216	0	0	0	216	0.1	0
Chad	0	253	0	0	0	253	0.0	0
Comoros	..	..	..	..	..	..	..	..
Congo	0	3,748	7	169	51	3,972	1.7	0
Côte d'Ivoire	0	6,060	0	0	249	6,309	0.5	0
Djibouti	..	..	..	..	..	..	..	..
Equatorial Guinea	0	117	0	0	0	117	0.3	0
Ethiopia	0	2,744	0	0	161	2,906	0.0	0
Gabon	0	2,154	99	3,261	59	5,569	4.5	0
Gambia, The	0	198	0	0	0	198	0.2	0
Ghana	7	3,265	0	0	509	3,781	0.2	0
Guinea	0	1,026	0	0	0	1,026	0.2	0
Guinea-Bissau	0	209	0	0	0	209	0.2	0
Kenya	297	4,287	0	0	758	5,342	0.2	0
Lesotho	..	..	..	..	..	..	..	..
Liberia	0	275	0	0	4	278	0.1	0
Madagascar	4	912	0	0	29	945	0.1	0
Malawi	33	561	0	0	59	652	0.1	0
Mali	0	432	0	0	11	443	0.0	0
Mauritania	15	2,807	0	0	44	2,869	1.4	0
Mauritius	165	1,191	0	0	0	1,356	1.2	0
Mozambique	161	821	0	0	15	997	0.1	0
Namibia	..	..	..	..	..	..	..	..
Niger	458	616	0	0	11	1,085	0.1	0
Nigeria	180	37,285	9,405	47,896	1,744	96,513	0.8	0
Rwanda	0	421	0	4	29	451	0.1	0
São Tomé and Principe	..	..	..	..	..	..	..	..
Senegal	0	2,510	0	0	300	2,810	0.4	0
Seychelles	..	..	..	..	..	..	..	..
Sierra Leone	0	432	0	0	0	432	0.1	0
Somalia	0	0	0	0	15	15	0.0	0
South Africa	239,138	47,544	0	0	3,613	290,291	7.3	0
Sudan	0	3,338	0	0	125	3,462	0.1	0
Swaziland	267	0	0	0	0	267	0.3	0
Tanzania	0	1,832	0	0	271	2,103	0.1	0
Togo	0	539	0	0	194	733	0.2	0
Uganda	0	931	0	0	26	953	0.0	0
Zaire	931	3,151	0	0	99	4,181	0.1	0
Zambia	883	1,411	0	0	187	2,481	0.3	0
Zimbabwe	15,664	2,565	0	0	447	18,675	1.8	0
NORTH AFRICA	..	..	..	..	..	..	..	..
Algeria	3,558	26,165	38,772	7,694	2,982	79,172	3.0	0
Egypt	2,524	57,353	16,118	0	8,002	83,997	1.5	0
Libya	15	23,721	10,501	4,155	1,129	39,520	8.1	0
Morocco	4,869	19,265	48	0	3,166	27,344	1.0	0
Tunisia	385	9,746	1,784	22	1,627	13,560	1.6	0
ALL AFRICA	271,744	274,430	77,054	65,659	26,905	715,773	..	0

Sources: Carbon Dioxide Information Analysis Center.

Notes: Estimates are of the carbon dioxide emitted, 3.664 times the carbon it contains.
Emissions from Bunker Fuels are included in other categories as well.
0 = zero or less than half the unit of measure, .. = not available.
For additional information, see Sources and Technical Notes.

14-15. Other greenhouse gas emissions, 1993

	Carbon dioxide emissions from land-use change (000 metric tons)	Methane from anthropogenic sources (000 metric tons)					
		Solid waste	Coal mining	Oil and gas production	Wet rice agriculture	Livestock	Total
SUB-SAHARAN AFRICA	..	..	..	..	..	..	..
excluding South Africa	..	..	..	..	..	..	..
excl. S. Africa & Nigeria	..	..	..	..	..	..	..
Angola	16,000	34	..	180	8	120	340
Benin	3,200	15	..	..	2	47	65
Botswana	3,200	4	..	..	..	100	110
Burkina Faso	3,400	29	..	..	23	210	260
Burundi	130	5	..	..	8	20	33
Cameroon	28,000	54	..	..	5	200	260
Cape Verde	..	..	..	..	..	..	..
Central African Republic	23,000	12	..	..	3	99	110
Chad	7,100	12	..	..	23	210	240
Comoros	..	..	..	..	..	..	..
Congo	14,000	14	..	12	1	4	31
Côte d'Ivoire	15,000	57	..	..	..	51	110
Djibouti	..	..	..	..	..	..	..
Equatorial Guinea	3,000	2	..	..	..	0	2
Ethiopia	8,000	68	..	..	..	1,100	1,200
Gabon	51,000	6	..	240	..	3	250
Gambia, The	130	3	..	..	2	15	20
Ghana	18,000	29	..	..	23	76	130
Guinea	10,000	19	..	..	440	59	520
Guinea-Bissau	1,800	2	..	..	38	19	59
Kenya	1,400	74	..	..	4	460	540
Lesotho	..	4	..	..	..	40	44
Liberia	9,600	12	..	..	15	3	31
Madagascar	21,000	38	..	..	480	350	860
Malawi	11,000	14	..	..	21	37	72
Mali	8,400	27	..	..	66	260	350
Mauritania	1	11	..	..	6	120	140
Mauritius	9	4	..	..	..	2	5
Mozambique	15,000	54	0	..	..	44	98
Namibia	1,800	5	..	..	..	91	96
Niger	..	15	2	..	6	140	160
Nigeria	24,000	3	1	3,600	220	760	4,500
Rwanda	170	4	..	0	2	28	34
São Tomé and Principe	..	..	..	..	..	..	..
Senegal	4,700	32	..	..	16	140	190
Seychelles	..	..	..	..	..	..	..
Sierra Leone	1,800	15	..	..	120	14	150
Somalia	430	22	..	..	1	510	540
South Africa	14,000	180	1,600	..	1	590	2,400
Sudan	38,000	63	..	..	1	1,000	1,100
Swaziland	370	3	0	..	..	22	25
Tanzania	22,000	68	..	..	190	500	760
Togo	2,100	12	..	..	9	25	45
Uganda	5,000	25	..	..	28	200	250
Zaire	280,000	120	1	..	190	81	380
Zambia	34,000	36	0	..	6	110	150
Zimbabwe	5,300	33	47	..	..	150	230
NORTH AFRICA	..	..	..	..	..	..	..
Algeria	6,900	140	0	1,400	..	160	1,700
Egypt	..	160	..	150	360	370	1,000
Libya	76	42	..	400	..	33	480
Morocco	4,700	110	9	0	3	230	360
Tunisia	640	44	..	7	..	81	130
ALL AFRICA	730,000	1,700	1,700	6,000	2,400	9,000	21,000

Source: World Resources Institute

Notes: Estimates are of the carbon dioxide emitted, 3.664 times the carbon it contains.

0 = zero or less than half the unit of measure; .. = not available.

For additional information, see Sources and Technical Notes

14-16. Participation in major global conventions--wildlife, habitat, and oceans, 1993

	Antarctic treaty and convention 1959 & 1980	Wildlife and habitat: Wetlands (Ramsar) 1971	World heritage 1972	Endangered species (CITES) 1973	Migratory species 1979	Biodiversity 1992	Oceans: Ocean dumping 1972	Ship pollution (MARPOL) 1978	Law of the sea {a} 1982
SUB-SAHARAN AFRICA									
excluding South Africa									
excl. S. Africa & Nigeria									
Angola			CP			S			CP
Benin			CP	CP	CP	S			S
Botswana				CP		S			CP
Burkina Faso		CP	CP	CP	CP	CP			S
Burundi			CP	CP		S			S
Cameroon			CP	CP	CP	S			CP
Cape Verde	..	..	..	..	..	..	..	..	..
Central African Republic			CP	CP	S	S			S
Chad		CP		CP	S	S	S		S
Comoros	..	..	..	..	..	..	..	..	..
Congo			CP	CP		S			S
Côte d'Ivoire			CP		S	S	CP	CP	CP
Djibouti				CP		S		CP	CP
Equatorial Guinea									S
Ethiopia									S
Gabon		CP	CP	CP		S	CP	CP	S
Gambia, The			CP	CP		S		CP	CP
Ghana		CP	CP	CP	CP	S		CP	CP
Guinea		CP	CP	CP		CP			CP
Guinea-Bissau		CP		CP		S			CP
Kenya		CP	CP	CP		S	CP	CP	CP
Lesotho		CP		S		S	S		S
Liberia				CP		S	S	CP	S
Madagascar			CP	CP	S	S			S
Malawi			CP	CP		S			S
Mali		CP	CP		CP	S			CP
Mauritania		CP	CP			S			S
Mauritius				CP		S			S
Mozambique			CP	CP		S			S
Namibia				CP		S			CP
Niger		CP	CP	CP	CP	S			S
Nigeria			CP	CP	CP	S	CP		CP
Rwanda				CP		S			S
São Tomé and Principe	..	..	..	..	..	..	..	..	..
Senegal		CP	CP	CP	CP	S	S		CP
Seychelles	..	..	..	..	..	..	..	..	..
Sierra Leone									S
Somalia				CP	CP		S		CP
South Africa	CP, MLR	CP		CP	CP	S	CP	CP	S
Sudan			CP	CP		S			CP
Swaziland						S			S
Tanzania			CP	CP		S			CP
Togo				CP	S	S	S	CP	CP
Uganda		CP	CP	CP	S	CP			CP
Zaire			CP	CP	CP	S	CP		CP
Zambia		CP	CP	CP		CP			CP
Zimbabwe			CP	CP		S			S
NORTH AFRICA									
Algeria		CP	CP	CP		S		CP	S
Egypt		CP	CP	CP	CP	S		CP	CP
Libya			CP			S	CP		S
Morocco		CP	CP	CP	S	S	CP		S
Tunisia		CP	CP	CP	CP	CP	CP	CP	CP
ALL AFRICA									

Sources: Environmental Law Information System of the World Conservation Union Environmental Law Centre and the United Nations Environment Programme.

Notes: a. Convention will enter into force November 16, 1994.

CP = contracting party (has ratified or taken equivalent action); S = signatory (has signed but not ratified); MLR = contracting party to the Convention on the Conservation of Antarctic Marine Living Resources.

For formal titles of the conventions and protocols listed, and for additional information, see Sources and Technical Notes.

14-17. Participation in major global conventions--atmosphere and hazardous substances, 1993

	Global conventions							*Regional agreements {b}*	
	Atmosphere				*Hazardous substances*				
	Ozone layer 1985	*CFC control 1987*	*Climate change {a} 1992*	*Biological and toxin weapons 1972*	*Nuclear accident notification 1986*	*Nuclear accident assistance 1986*	*Hazardous waste movement {a} 1989*	*UNEP regional seas*	*Other regional agreements*
SUB-SAHARAN AFRICA									
excluding South Africa									
excl. S. Africa & Nigeria									
Angola			S						
Benin	CP	CP	S	CP				WCA*	AFC*, HW*
Botswana	CP	CP	S	CP					AFC*
Burkina Faso	CP	CP	CP	CP					HW*
Burundi			S	S					AFC*, HW*
Cameroon	CP	CP	S		S	S		WCA	AFC, HW*
Cape Verde	..	..	..	..	..	..	..	..	..
Central African Republic	CP		S	S					AFC, HW*
Chad	CP		S						AFC*, HW*
Comoros	..	..	..	..	..	..	..	..	..
Congo		S	S	CP				WCA	AFC
Côte d'Ivoire	CP	CP	S	S	S	S		WCA	AFC, HW*
Djibouti			S						AFC, HW*
Equatorial Guinea	CP			CP					
Ethiopia									
Gabon			S	S				WCA	AFC*
Gambia, The	CP	CP	S	S				WCA	AFC*
Ghana	CP	CP	S	CP				WCA	AFC
Guinea	CP	CP	CP					WCA	AFC*, HW*
Guinea-Bissau			S	CP					HW*
Kenya	CP	CP	S	CP				EA+	AFC
Lesotho			S	CP					AFC*, HW*
Liberia			S					WCA*	AFC
Madagascar			S	S				EA*	AFC
Malawi	CP	CP	S	S					AFC
Mali			S	S	S	S			AFC, HW*
Mauritania			S					WCA*	AFC*
Mauritius			S	CP					AFC*
Mozambique			S						AFC
Namibia			S						
Niger	CP		S	CP	S	S			AFC, HW*
Nigeria	CP	CP	S	CP	CP	CP	CP	WCA	AFC
Rwanda			S	CP					AFC, HW*
São Tomé and Principe	..	..	..	..	..	..	..	..	..
Senegal		CP	S	CP	S	S	CP	WCA	AFC, EC, HW*
Seychelles	..	..	..	..	..	..	..	..	..
Sierra Leone			S	CP	S	S			AFC*
Somalia				S				EA*, RS	AFC*, HW*
South Africa	CP	CP	S	CP	CP	CP			
Sudan	CP	CP	S		S	S		RS	AFC
Swaziland	CP	CP	S						AFC, HW*
Tanzania	CP	CP	S	S			CP		AFC, HW*
Togo	CP	CP	S	CP				WCA	AFC, HW*
Uganda	CP	CP	CP						AFC
Zaire			S	CP	S	S			AFC
Zambia	CP	CP	CP						AFC
Zimbabwe	CP	CP	CP	CP	S	S			HW
NORTH AFRICA									
Algeria	CP	CP	CP		S	S		M+	AFC
Egypt	CP	CP	S	S	CP	CP		M+, RS	AFC, HW*
Libya	CP	CP	S	CP		CP		M+	AFC*, HW*
Morocco	S	S	S	S	S	S		M+	AFC
Tunisia	CP	CP	CP	CP	CP	CP		M+	AFC, HW
ALL AFRICA									

Sources: Environmental Law Information System of the World Conservation Union Environmental Law Centre and the United Nations Environment Program (UNEP).

Notes: a. Convention not yet in force. b. Regional agreement letter codes (M, ML, etc.) indicate ratification of specific regional agreements.
CP = contracting party (has ratified or taken equivalent action); S = signatory; + = has signed or ratified at least two protocols to this convention. * = signatory to regional agreement. UNEP Regional Seas agreements; M = Mediterranean convention;
WCA = West and Central African convention; EA = East African convention; RS = Red Sea and Gulf of Aden convention;
Other Regional Agreements: AFC = African conservation convention;HW = African hazardous waste convention; EC = European conservation convention;
For formal titles of the conventions and protocols listed, and for additional information, see Sources and Technical Notes.

Technical Notes

Tables

These notes are based on technical notes for each table as presented in WRI (1994 and 1996). They have been edited and shortened for this volume. Readers are urged to consult the original source for details.

Table 14-1. Land area and use, 1981–93. Land area and land use data are provided to the FAO by national governments in response to annual questionnaires. The FAO also compiles data from national agricultural censuses. The FAO often adjusts the definitions of land use categories and sometimes substantially revises earlier data.

Land use data are periodically revised and may change significantly from year to year. For the most recent land use statistics, see the latest *FAO Production Yearbook*.

Land area data are for 1993. They exclude major inland water bodies, national claims to the continental shelf, and Exclusive Economic Zones.

Population density was derived by using the population figures for 1994 published by the United Nations Population Division and 1993 land area data from the FAO. Although the population figures were published in 1994, actual censuses and estimates were made in prior years.

Cropland includes land under temporary and permanent crops, temporary meadows, market and kitchen gardens, and land that is temporarily fallow. Permanent crops are those that do not need to be replanted after each harvest, such as cocoa, coffee, rubber, fruit, and vines. This category excludes land used to grow trees for wood or timber.

Permanent pasture is land used for five or more years for forage, including natural crops and cultivated crops. This category is difficult for countries to assess because it includes wildland used for pasture. In addition, few countries regularly report data on permanent pasture. As a result, the absence of a change in permanent pasture area may indicate differences in land classification and data reporting rather than actual conditions. Grassland not used for forage is included under other land.

Forest and woodland includes land under natural or planted stands of trees, as well as logged-over areas that will be reforested in the near future.

Other land includes uncultivated land, grassland not used for pasture, built-up areas, wetlands, wastelands, and roads.

Table 14-2. Forest resources, 1981–90. Data from tropical and temperate countries are not strictly comparable, and FAO and UNECE (UN Economic Commission for Europe)/FAO have slightly different definitions depending on the respective forest ecosystem. The FAO defines a natural forest in tropical countries as either a closed forest or an open forest. A tropical forest encompasses all stands, except plantations and includes stands that have been degraded to some degree by agriculture, fire, logging, or acid precipitation.

UNECE/FAO defines a forest as land where tree crowns cover more than 20 percent of the area. Also included are open forest formations; forest roads and firebreaks; small, temporarily cleared areas; young stands expected to achieve at least 20 percent crown cover upon maturity; and windbreaks and shelterbelts exceeding 0.5 hectare in size. Plantation area is included under temperate country estimates of natural forest extent.

Other wooded land encompasses forest fallows (closed and open forests) and shrubs in tropical countries. In the temperate zone, other wooded land consists of open woodland and scrub, shrub, and brushland. The category also includes wooded areas used for rangeland, but excludes orchards, wood lots under 0.5 hectare, and tree hedgerows.

Annual deforestation refers to the "clearing of forest lands for all forms of agricultural uses (shifting cultivation, permanent agriculture and ranching) and for other land uses such as settlements, other infrastructure, and mining."

Logging of closed broadleaf forest provides averages of the total area of primary (undisturbed) and thus secondary (previously logged) forest logged each year. Many "primary" forests are essentially old secondary forests.

Plantations refer to forest stands established artificially by afforestation and reforestation for industrial and nonindustrial usage. Reforestation does not include regeneration of old tree crops. Many trees are also planted for nonindustrial uses, such as village wood lots. Reforestation data often exclude this component.

Protected forests in tropical countries are protected areas such as national parks and reserves occurring within mapped moist forest zones. Totals for African countries do not include areas protected as forest reserves. Protected forests for temperate countries consist primarily of national parks and nature reserves found within forests and other wooded lands, although other protected area categories apply.

Table 14-3. Wood production and trade, 1981–93. Total roundwood production refers to all wood in the rough, whether destined for industrial or fuelwood uses.

Fuel and charcoal production covers all rough wood used for cooking, heating, and power production. Wood intended for charcoal production, pit kilns, and portable ovens is included.

Industrial roundwood production comprises all roundwood products other than fuelwood and charcoal.

Processed wood production includes sawnwood and panels.

Paper production includes newsprint, printing and writing paper, and other paper and paperboard.

Average annual net trade in roundwood is the balance of imports minus exports.

Table 14-4. National protection of natural areas, 1994. All protected areas combine natural areas in five World Conservation Union, formerly the International Union for Conservation of Nature and Natural Resources (IUCN), management categories (areas at least 1,000 hectares).

Totally protected areas are maintained in a natural state and are closed to extractive uses. They encompass the following three management categories: *category I,* scientific reserves and strict nature reserves; *category II*, national parks and provincial parks; and *category III*, natural monuments and natural landmarks.

Partially protected areas are areas that may be managed for specific uses, such as recreation or tourism, or areas that provide optimum conditions for certain species or communities of wildlife. Some extractive use within these areas is allowed. They encompass two management categories: *category IV*, managed nature reserves wildlife sanctuaries; and *category V*, protected landscapes and seascapes.

Protected areas between at least 100,000 hectares and 1 million hectares in size refer to all IUCN category I–V protected areas that fall within these two classifications.

The values in this table do not include locally or provincially protected sites, or privately owned areas.

Table 14-5. International and marine protected areas, 1994. Internationally protected areas usually include sites that are listed under national protection systems.

Biosphere reserves are representative of terrestrial

and coastal environments that have been internationally recognized under the Man and the Biosphere Programme of UNESCO.

World heritage sites represent areas of "outstanding universal value" for their natural features, their cultural value, or for both natural and cultural values. The table includes only natural and mixed natural and cultural sites.

Any party to the Convention on Wetlands of International Importance, Especially as Waterfowl Habitat that agrees to respect the site's integrity and to establish wetland reserves can designate wetlands of international importance.

Marine and coastal protected areas refer to all protected areas greater than 1,000 hectares with littoral, coral, island, marine, or estuarine components. The area given is the whole protected area.

Table 14-6. Habitat extent and loss, 1980s. Except where otherwise defined below, habitat is variously defined as wildland, undisturbed vegetation, and natural vegetation, depending on the source. Most mangrove data are total estimates of current mangrove cover, regardless of degree of degradation. Except where otherwise indicated, percentage lost refers to habitat lost since pre-agricultural times. Original habitat extent is estimated based on potential vegetation maps, which generally predict vegetation cover from the physical characteristics of a region, such as temperature and rainfall patterns.

Forests comprise dry and moist forests. Dry forests include upland montane forest/nonforest, dry forest, and woodland; moist forests include lowland rainforest. Savannah/grassland includes salt-pan vegetation, brushland/thicket, shrubland, grassland, and halophytic. Mangroves includes mangrove forest and swamp.

Table 14-7. Globally threatened species: mammals, birds, and higher plants, 1990s. The total number of known species may include introductions in some instances. Data on mammals exclude cetaceans (whales and porpoises), except where otherwise indicated. Threatened bird species are listed for countries included within their breeding or wintering ranges. Higher plants refer to numbers of native vascular plant species. Total plant species numbers may differ from earlier estimates published in previous editions of WRI (1994), as totals are of full species only, rather than of species and subspecies. The number of endemic species refers to those species known to be found only within the countries listed. Figures are not necessarily comparable among countries because taxonomic concepts and the extent of knowledge vary (for the latter reason, country totals of species and endemics may be underestimates). In general, numbers of mammals and birds are fairly well known, while plants have not been as well inventoried.

The World Conservation Union classifies threatened and endangered species in six categories.

Endangered. "Taxa in danger of extinction and whose survival is unlikely if the causal factors continue operating."

Vulnerable. "Taxa believed likely to move into the endangered category in the near future if the causal factors continue operating."

Rare. "Taxa with world populations that are not at present endangered or vulnerable, but are at risk."

Indeterminate. "Taxa known to be endangered, vulnerable, or rare but where there is not enough information to say which of the three categories is appropriate."

Out of danger. "Taxa formerly included in one of the above categories, but which are now considered relatively secure because effective conservation measures have been taken or the previous threat to their survival has been removed."

Insufficiently known. "Taxa that are suspected but not definitely known to belong to any of the above categories."

The number of threatened species listed for all countries includes full species that are endangered, vulnerable, rare, indeterminate, and insufficiently known, but excludes introduced species or those known to be extinct.

Number of species per 10,000 square kilometers provides a relative estimate for comparing numbers of species among countries of differing size. Because the relationship between area and species number is nonlinear (that is, as the area sampled increases, the number of new species located decreases), a species-area curve has been used to standardize these species numbers.

Table 14-8. Globally threatened species: reptiles, amphibians, and fish, 1990s. Threatened marine turtles and marine fish are excluded from country totals. Endangered fish species numbers do not include approximately 250 haplochromine and 2 tilapiine species of Lake Victoria cichlids, since the ranges of these species are undetermined.

The number of species per 10,000 square kilometers provides a relative estimate for comparing numbers of species among countries of differing size.

Table 14-9. Net trade in wildlife and wildlife products reported by CITES, 1990. Convention on International Trade in Endangered Species of Wild Flora and Fauna (CITES) members agree to prohibit commercial international trade in endangered species and to closely monitor trade in species that may become depleted by trade. Parties to the Convention are required to submit annual reports, including trade records, to the CITES Secretariat in Switzerland. The World Conservation Monitoring Center compiles these data from those reports. Figures refer primarily to legal trade, though illegal trade is included when known.

"CITES reporting requirements met" refers to the percentage of years for which a country has submitted an annual report to the CITES Secretariat since it became a party to the Convention, through 1991 (1992 for a few countries that had submitted reports for this year as of May 1993). Countries that had ratified the CITES treaty by May 1993 are listed as members.

Live primates include all species of monkeys, apes, and prosimians.

Cat skins include skins of all species of felidae, excluding a small number of skins reported only by weight or length.

Live birds include parrots, macaws, cockatoos, and other species.

Reptile skins include whole skins, reported by number, of all crocodilians and many commonly traded lizard and snake species.

Live cacti include wild and artificially propagated Cactaceae plants.

Live orchids include wild and artificially propagated Orchidaceae plants.

This table shows trade in wild and captive-bred species. The impact of international trade on a particular species can be greater than the numbers reported because of mortality (during capture or collection, transit, and quarantine), illegal trade, trade to or from countries that are not CITES members, and omission of domestic trade data.

Table 14-10. Commercial energy production, 1973–93. Total production of commercially traded fuels includes solid, liquid, and gaseous fuels and primary electricity production. Solid fuels include bituminous coal, lignite, peat, and oil shale burned directly. Liquid fuels include crude petroleum and liquid natural gas. Gas includes natural gas and other petroleum gases.

Primary electricity is valued differently depending on its source. Wind, tide, wave, solar, and hydroelectric power generation is expressed at the energy value of electricity (1 kilowatt hour = 3.6 million joules). Nuclear and geothermal power generation is valued on a fossil-fuel-avoided basis rather than an energy-output basis. Electricity production data generally refer to gross production. Data for Zambia and Zimbabwe refer to net production. Gross production is the amount of electricity produced by a generating station before consumption by station auxiliaries and transformer losses within the station are deducted. Net production is the amount of electricity remaining after these deductions. Typically, net production is 5 to 10 percent less than gross production. Energy production from pumped storage is not included in gross or net electricity generation. Electricity production includes both public and self-producer power plants. Fuelwood, charcoal, bagasse, animal and vegetal wastes, and all forms of solar energy are excluded from production figures, even when traded commercially.

One petajoule (1,015 joules) is the same as 0.0009478 quads (1,015 British Thermal Units) and is the equivalent of 163,400 "UN standard" barrels of oil or 34,140 "UN standard" metric tons of coal. The heat content of various fuels has been converted to coal-equivalent and then to petajoule-equivalent values using country-specific and other conversion factors.

South Africa refers to the South Africa Customs Union: Botswana, Lesotho, Namibia, South Africa, and Swaziland.

For additional information, refer to the United Nations *Energy Statistics Yearbook 1993.*

Table 14-11. Energy consumption, 1973–93. Commercial energy consumption refers to "apparent consumption" and is defined as domestic production plus net imports, minus net stock increases, minus aircraft and marine bunkers. Total consumption includes energy from solid, liquid, and gaseous fuels, plus primary electricity. Energy consumption per constant 1987 US dollars of GNP is calculated using GNP data from the World Bank and is a measure of relative energy efficiency. Included under imports as percentage of consumption are imports minus exports. A negative value (in parentheses) indicates that exports are greater than imports.

Traditional fuels includes estimate of the consumption of fuelwood, charcoal, bagasse, and animal and vegetal wastes. Fuelwood and charcoal consumption data are estimated from population data and country-specific per capita consumption figures.

A petajoule is one quadrillion (1,015) joules. A gigajoule is one billion (109) joules. A megajoule is one million (106) joules.

Table 14-12. Reserves and resources of commercial energy, 1993. Energy resource estimates are based on geological, economic, and technical criteria. Resources are first graded according to the degree of confidence in the extent and location of the resource, based on available geological information, and are then judged on the technical and economic feasibility of their exploitation.

Proved reserves in place are the total resource that is known to exist in specific locations and in specific quantities and qualities. Proved recoverable reserves are the fraction of proved reserves in place that can be extracted under present and expected local economic conditions with existing technology. Additional energy resources, comprising those that are not currently economic, are not shown in this table.

The coal, oil, and gas sectors of the energy industry each have their own categories for estimating reserves.

Crude oil also includes liquids obtained by condensation or extraction from natural gas.

Uranium data refer to known uranium deposits of a size and quality that could be recovered within specified production cost ranges (under $80 per kilogram and $80 to $130 per kilogram) using currently proven mining and processing technologies.

Known exploitable potential of hydroelectric power refers to that part of a country's annual gross theoretical capacity (the amount of energy that would be obtained if all flows were exploited with 100 percent efficiency) that could be exploited using current technology and under current and expected local economic conditions. This includes both large- and small-scale schemes. Hydroelectric technical potential refers to the annual energy potential of all sites where it is physically possible to construct dams, with no consideration of economic return or adverse effects of site development.

Installed capacity refers to the combined generating capacity of hydroelectric plants installed in the country as of December 31, 1993.

Table 14-13. Freshwater resources and withdrawals. Annual internal renewable water resources refers to the average annual flow of rivers and groundwater generated from endogenous precipitation. Caution should be used when comparing different countries because these estimates are based on differing sources and dates. These annual averages also disguise large seasonal, inter-annual, and long-term variations.

When data for annual river flows from and to other countries are not shown, the internal renewable water resources figure may include these flows. Per capita annual internal renewable water resource data were calculated using 1995 population estimates.

Annual withdrawals as a percentage of water resources refer to total water withdrawals, not counting evaporative losses from storage basins, as a percentage of internal renewable water resources and river flows from other countries. Water withdrawals also include water from desalination plants in countries where that source is a significant part of all water withdrawals.

Per capita annual withdrawals were calculated using national population data for the year of data shown for withdrawals.

Sectoral withdrawals are classified as domestic (drinking water, homes, commercial establishments, public services [for example, hospitals], and municipal use or provision); industry (including water withdrawn to cool thermoelectric plants); and agriculture (irrigation and livestock).

Table 14-14. CO2 emissions from industrial processes, 1993. This table includes data on industrial additions to the carbon dioxide flux from solid fuels, liquid fuels, gas fuels, gas flaring, and cement manufacture. The Carbon Dioxide Information Analysis Center (CDIAC) annually calculates emissions of CO_2 from the burning of fossil fuels and the manufacture of cement for most of the countries of the world. Estimates of total and per capita national emissions do not include bunker fuels used in international transport because of the difficulty of apportioning these fuels among the countries benefiting from that transport. Emissions from bunker fuels are shown separately for the country where the fuel was delivered.

Emissions of CO2 are often calculated and reported in terms of their content of elemental carbon. CDIAC reports them that way. For this table, CDIAC's figures were converted to the actual mass by 3.664 (the ratio of the mass of carbon to that of CO2).

Solid, liquid, and gas fuels are primarily, but not exclusively, coals, petroleum products, and natural gas. Gas flaring is the practice of burning off gas released in the process of petroleum extraction, a practice that is declining. During cement manufacture, cement is calcined to produce calcium oxide. In the process, 0.498 metric ton of CO2 is released for each metric ton of cement produced. Total emissions consist of the sum of the CO2 produced during the consumption of solid, liquid, and gas fuels, and from gas flaring and the manufacture of cement.

Combustion of different fossil fuels releases CO2 at different rates for the same level of energy production. Burning oil releases about 1.5 times the amount of CO2 released from burning natural gas; burning coal releases about twice as much CO2 as natural gas.

Table 14-15. Other greenhouse gas emissions, 1993. CO2, CH4, CFC-11, and CFC-12 are the four most important greenhouse gases. This table provides estimates of annual emissions of CO2 from land use change (that is, deforestation), CH4 emissions by source, and current annual emissions of CFC-11 and CFC-12 combined. Nitrous oxide, tropospheric ozone, and other CFCs are also important to the greenhouse effect but have not been well studied and are more difficult to estimate, especially at the national level. Tropospheric ozone has an average lifetime measured in hours and is a product of chemical processes involving the precursors CH4, carbon monoxide, nitrogen oxides, and nonmethane hydrocarbons in the presence of sunlight. Nitrous oxide emissions by country have proven difficult to estimate, in part because significant emissions are poorly understood. Production estimates and emission parameters from CFCs other than CFC-11 and CFC-12 are not available.

Tables 14-16 and 14-17. Participation in major global conventions: wildlife, habitat, and oceans, 1993, and atmosphere and hazardous substances, 1993. A country becomes a signatory of a treaty when a person given authority by the national government signs the treaty. Unless otherwise provided in the treaty, a signatory is under no duty to perform the obligations stipulated before the treaty comes into force for the country. The authorized signature indicates a commitment to undertake domestic action to ratify, accept, approve, or accede to the treaty. A country is a contracting party when the treaty comes into force in that country. Typically, this occurs when the country has ratified the treaty or otherwise adopted the treaty's provisions as national law, and when a prescribed number of countries indicate consent to be bound by the treaty and register instruments of ratification, acceptance, approval, or accession with the treaty's depositary (which may be a national government, a UN organization, or another international organization; some treaties have multiple depositaries).

15

Household Welfare Indicators for Selected Countries

The absence of reliable information on poverty in Sub-Saharan Africa led to the implementation of poverty monitoring programs. Major components of these programs included data collection, capacity building of statistical Offices, Institutions, and policy analysis. This chapter presents a set of standardized household welfare indicators derived from household surveys carried out in 17 African countries: Burkina Faso, Central African Republic, Côte d'Ivoire, the Gambia, Ghana, Guinea, Guinea-Bissau, Kenya, Madagascar, Niger, Nigeria, Senegal, South Africa, Sierra Leone, Tanzania, Uganda, and Zambia. Most of these countries are among the 35 countries that were assisted in establishing a poverty monitoring program under the Social Dimensions of Adjustment (SDA) project. Five countries have been added to last year's country data sets. In the country data set for Guinea-Bissau, some corrections were made to the weighting coefficient, which resulted in changes to the figures published last year.

All statistics are based on nationally representative household surveys. Survey results have been disaggregated by urban and rural expenditure quintiles. Welfare indicators are grouped into five classes: demographic, education and literacy, household structure, household expenditure, and household amenities. The technical notes provide definitions of indicators, which sometimes differ from country to country. Differences in definitions and in the way in which variables have been computed may be a source of discrepancy between indicators published by the national statistical offices and the ones given here.

The robustness and completeness of expenditures and household variables vary according to the type of survey used to collect the data. The three household surveys types referred to are traditional household budget surveys, integrated surveys or living standards measurement surveys (LSMS), and priority surveys. Household budget surveys involve multiple visits to a household during a year, provide the most complete record of expenditures, and capture seasonal variations in expenditure patterns. They are limited, however, in terms of additional social indicators. The integrated and LSMS surveys involve two visits to the household within a fortnight and provide a more complete picture of household living standards. The expenditure data are generally complete, but seasonal and month-to-month variation in expenditure patterns are not well captured, which can lead to biases in the results. The priority surveys were designed to provide a rapid way to collect socioeconomic indicators, involve one visit to a household, and may have expenditure levels that are underestimated. While the *absolute* expenditure levels may be affected by type of survey used, the *relative* ranking of households within a country—the grouping of households into expenditure quintiles—is less affected.

Expenditure surveys were used in Niger, Nigeria, and Sierra Leone. Integrated or LSMS surveys were used in Ghana, Madagascar, South Africa, Tanzania, and Uganda. Priority surveys were used in Burkina Faso, Central African Republic, Côte d'Ivoire, the Gambia, Guinea, Guinea-Bissau, Kenya, Senegal, and Zambia.

Generic definitions

Household is defined as a group of related or unrelated people, who live in a dwelling unit or its equivalent, eat from the same pot, and share common housekeeping arrangements.

Expenditure quintiles are derived by ranking sample households according to per capita expenditure. Individuals rather than households are used as the basis for estimating expenditures quintiles. Quintiles are constructed such that the first quintile represents the poorest 20 percent, the second quintile the next poorest 20 percent (less poor), and so on; the fifth quintile represents the wealthiest group.

Price deflators, when available, are used to adjust expenditures for regional price differences. In many countries, deflators were not available. When price deflators are not used, urban-rural differences are overestimated.

Demographic indicators

Population below 15 years is estimated by taking the ratio of all individuals below age 15 to the total number of individuals in the population. The calculation is repeated for men and women.

Number of household in each quintile varies due to differences in household size, although the total number of individuals in each quintile is the same.

Average household size is estimated for each quintile as well as for regional and national levels by taking the weighted average household size in each quintile.

Education and literacy indicators

Net primary enrollment rate is defined as the total number of children of primary school age (6 to 13 years) enrolled as a proportion of the total number of children of primary school age.

Net secondary enrollment rate is the total number of children of secondary school age (14 to 18 years) enrolled as a proportion of the total number of children of secondary school age.

Literacy rate is the proportion of the population above 15 years old able to read and write. When the literacy level is not specified, however, the individual is considered illiterate.

Head of household indicators

Monogamous male-headed refers to a male-headed household having no more than one spouse.

Polygamous male-headed refers to a male-headed household with more than one spouse. Differences exist in the way in which countries define polygamous households, depending, in some cases, on whether or not the wives live under the same roof.

Single male-headed refers to a male-headed household where the head is either divorced or has never been married.

Defacto female-headed refers to a household where the husband is not present and the wife is head by default and the main decisionmaker in his absence.

Dejure female-headed is a single female-headed household where the head has never been married or is divorced or widowed.

Educational level of the head shows the percentage of household heads who have completed primary or secondary education or who have never attended any school.

Employment of head is classified into two broad categories: agro-pastoral and nonagricultural. Agro-pastoralist is used when the main source of income of the household is farming and/or livestock. Nonagricultural activities include services, industry, and other nonagricultural activities.

Household expenditure indicators

These indicators provide information on per capita expenditure in local currency (including the value of own-produced food consumed in the household) and the share of food in household expenditures. Price deflators, when available, are used to compensate for regional price differences.

Per capita expenditure, in local currency, is estimated as the weighted average per capita household expenditure. *It includes the value of own produce consumed.*

Poverty line is a relative poverty line defined as 2/3 the national mean per capita expenditure. This definition may differ from country-specific definitions used by national statistical offices.

Food share in total expenditure provides a weighted estimate of total per capita household expenditure allocated to food, including a valuation of own-produced food consumed by the household.

Household amenities indicators

These indicators provide estimates of the percentage of households using different household amenities.

Type of fuel for cooking includes firewood, gas and kerosene, charcoal, and electricity.

Access to safe sanitation refers to households equipped with a flush toilet or pit latrine.

Access to water indicates the percentage of households with access to different sources of drinking water.

Age pyramids

These indicators represent the population derived from each survey by age group. Unlike the tables, which describe literacy rates for adults over age 15, the shaded area shows the proportion in each age group who is attending or has attended school. Therefore, the shaded areas of the pyramids do not represent literacy rates. These pyramids have been adjusted for age misreporting using the methodology of the U.S. National Academy of Science.

15-1. Burkina Faso: household welfare indicators

			Expenditure quintile											
			Rural						Urban					
Indicator	*Unit of measure*	*National total*	*All*	*1*	*2*	*3*	*4*	*5*	*All*	*1*	*2*	*3*	*4*	*5*
Demographic indicators														
Sample size	Number	8,628	5,912	943	991	1,123	1,298	1,557	2,716	427	481	497	541	770
Total population	Thousands	9,385	7,865	1,573	1,573	1,574	1,573	1,572	1,521	304	305	304	304	304
Female	Percent	50	50	51	51	51	49	50	49	50	50	50	49	47
Population below 15 years	Percent	46	48	53	52	50	47	44	42	49	47	43	42	35
Female	Percent	49	48	48	48	47	45	49	51	49	50	50	52	52
Number of households	Thousands	1,204	975	140	164	184	219	267	234	35	40	44	47	68
Average household size	Number	7.8	8.1	11.2	9.6	8.6	7.2	5.9	6.5	8.7	7.7	6.9	6.4	4.4
Education and literacy														
Net primary enrollment (total)	Percent	33	27	17	20	23	32	43	70	53	66	72	80	85
Male	Percent	38	32	22	27	30	38	45	75	58	69	78	86	93
Female	Percent	28	21	13	12	15	25	41	65	48	63	66	74	77
Net secondary enrollment (total)	Percent	16	9	4	5	8	8	19	46	25	35	48	56	64
Male	Percent	20	12	5	8	12	13	24	52	31	39	55	62	76
Female	Percent	13	5	2	3	4	4	13	40	19	31	40	49	56
Literacy rate (total)	Percent	7	4	2	3	3	4	7	20	9	15	19	23	32
Male	Percent	2	2	2	1	2	2	2	1	1	0	1	0	0
Female	Percent	11	6	3	4	3	6	13	41	15	29	37	49	72
Head of household														
Marital status of head														
Monogamous male-headed	Percent	55	53	45	51	52	58	57	58	51	57	60	63	56
Polygamous male-headed	Percent	26	31	42	37	36	28	20	15	28	22	18	12	5
Single male-headed	Percent	10	8	8	6	6	7	12	15	8	8	10	14	26
Defacto female-headed	Percent	2	2	2	2	1	2	3	4	5	4	3	3	4
Dejure female-headed	Percent	6	6	4	4	4	5	9	9	8	9	9	7	9
Education level of head														
Completed primary	Percent	10	4	2	2	2	3	10	23	7	15	23	30	32
Completed secondary	Percent	4	1	0	0	0	0	4	11	0	1	3	9	32
Illiterate	Percent	85	95	98	98	98	97	86	66	92	83	75	62	36
Employment of head														
Agro-pastoral activities	Percent	65	86	88	92	92	90	75	19	51	30	18	9	4
Household expenditure														
Mean per capita expenditure (CFAF)	Thousands	67	49	18	27	36	50	112	161	39	73	112	171	412
Population below relative poverty line	Percent	56	65	100	100	100	24	0	13	67	0	0	0	0
Food share in total expenditure	Percent	57	59	62	65	62	59	50	43	50	46	45	41	32
Household amenities														
Type of fuel for cooking														
Firewood	Percent	89	94	93	93	93	94	93	78	94	92	86	80	53
Gas, kerosine	Percent	3	1	1	1	1	1	2	9	1	2	3	5	25
Charcoal	Percent	2	0	0	0	0	0	1	5	0	1	4	4	11
Electricity	Percent	0	0	0	0	0	0	0	0	0	0	0	1	0
Other	Percent	6	5	6	6	6	5	4	8	5	5	7	10	11
Access to sanitation	Percent	37	14	7	8	9	12	28	87	70	84	88	92	95
Access to water														
Pipe	Percent	26	3	2	1	2	2	7	74	51	69	77	79	86
Well/borne	Percent	66	86	87	88	87	87	82	24	47	30	21	19	12
Other	Percent	8	11	11	11	11	11	11	2	2	1	3	1	2

Source: 1995 Household Priority Survey.

Burkina Faso

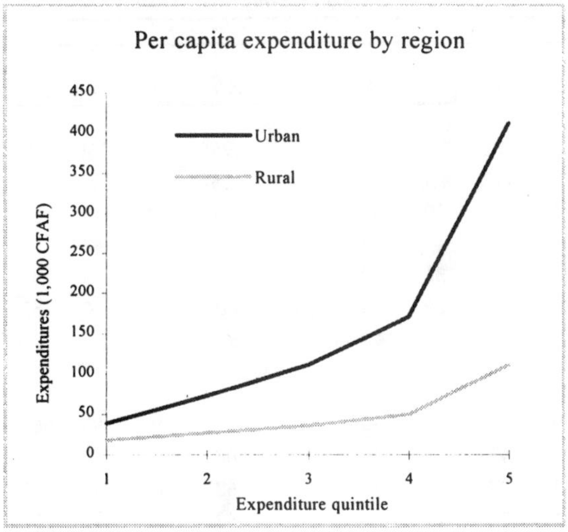

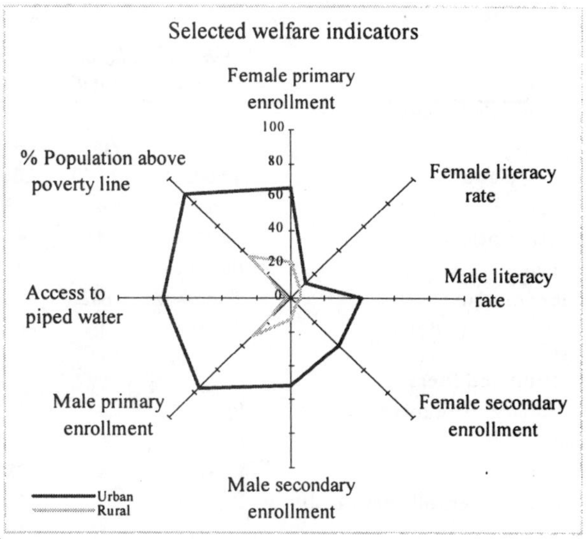

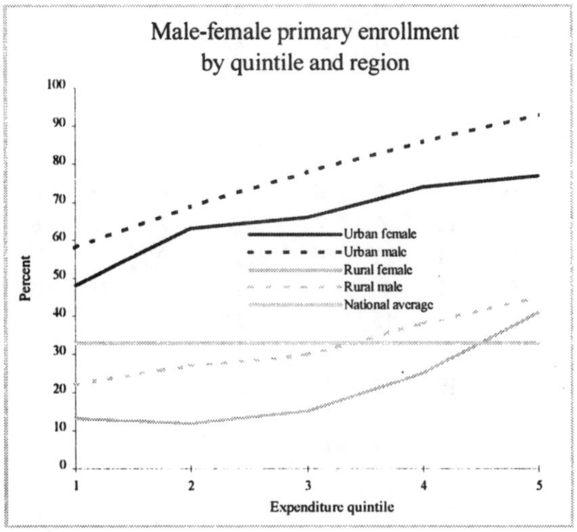

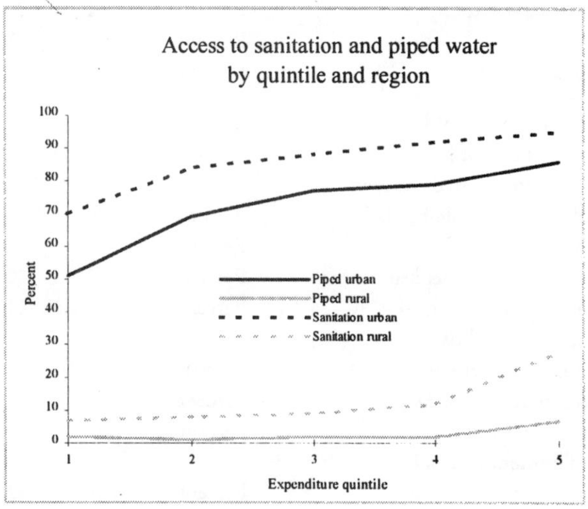

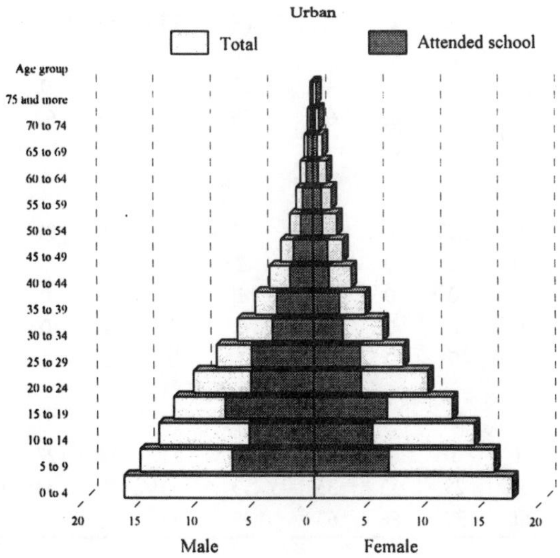

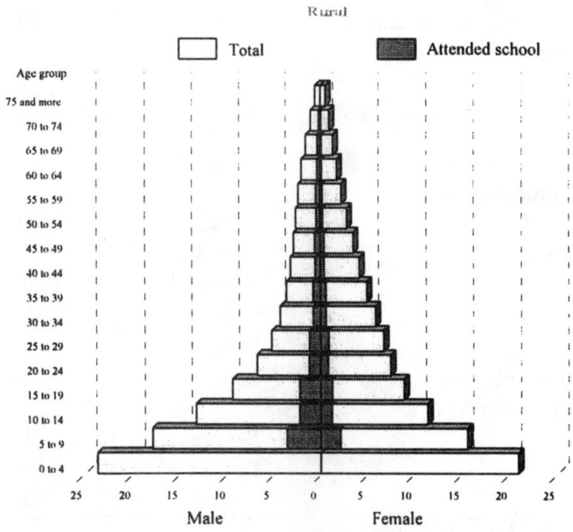

15-2. Central African Republic: household welfare indicators

			Expenditure quintile											
			Rural						Urban					
Indicator	*Unit of measure*	*National total*	*All*	*1*	*2*	*3*	*4*	*5*	*All*	*1*	*2*	*3*	*4*	*5*
Demographic indicators														
Sample size	Number	7,417	4,462	815	701	773	943	1,230	2,955	578	539	514	547	777
Total population	Thousands	3,340	2,085	417	417	416	417	417	1,257	251	251	251	251	251
Female	Percent	49	49	50	50	50	50	48	50	51	50	50	50	48
Population below 15 years	Percent	47	46	52	50	47	44	40	48	49	48	51	49	44
Female	Percent	49	49	48	47	51	50	49	49	50	48	50	49	49
Number of households	Thousands	682	466	76	81	89	98	121	215	44	40	37	40	54
Average household size	Number	4.9	4.5	5.5	5.2	4.7	4.2	3.4	5.8	5.7	6.3	6.6	6.4	4.6
Education and literacy														
Net primary enrollment (total)	Percent	48	37	29	35	37	40	48	65	46	65	69	73	76
Male	Percent	54	46	39	42	46	48	58	68	50	70	71	74	78
Female	Percent	41	28	19	27	27	33	38	62	42	59	66	71	74
Net secondary enrollment (total)	Percent	36	23	21	27	19	27	22	52	42	49	52	57	62
Male	Percent	50	39	35	48	36	42	32	64	53	62	63	71	72
Female	Percent	23	9	8	8	6	13	13	42	28	36	43	46	54
Literacy rate (total)	Percent	41	30	22	26	26	32	40	61	43	55	61	70	73
Male	Percent	57	47	39	43	41	51	55	75	59	74	76	83	80
Female	Percent	27	14	8	12	12	13	24	48	29	39	47	58	64
Head of household														
Marital status of head														
Monogamous male-headed	Percent	51	54	58	58	56	60	42	46	48	48	46	46	42
Polygamous male-headed	Percent	8	9	11	11	11	7	7	5	7	6	6	4	2
Single male-headed	Percent	13	13	5	8	11	11	25	12	9	9	10	9	20
Defacto female-headed	Percent	12	10	10	9	10	9	10	17	13	17	19	20	16
Dejure female-headed	Percent	16	14	16	15	12	13	16	21	23	20	19	21	20
Education level of head														
Completed primary	Percent	27	22	16	17	19	27	28	39	26	38	46	46	40
Completed secondary	Percent	4	1	0	0	1	1	4	10	2	4	6	14	20
Illiterate	Percent	69	77	84	83	80	73	68	52	73	58	48	40	40
Employment of head														
Agro-pastoral activities	Percent	68	82	94	92	89	85	62	38	80	54	31	18	10
Household expenditure														
Mean per capita expenditure (CFAF)	Thousands	54	35	4	10	16	28	118	84	13	33	56	87	230
Population below relative poverty line	Percent	61	77	100	100	100	87	0	33	100	65	0	0	0
Food share in total expenditure	Percent	60	61	52	60	64	65	62	59	58	62	62	60	53
Household amenities														
Type of fuel for cooking														
Firewood	Percent	99	99	100	99	100	100	98	97	99	98	99	98	90
Gas, kerosine	Percent	1	0	0	0	0	0	1	2	0	1	0	1	6
Charcoal	Percent	0	0	0	0	0	0	0	1	0	0	0	0	3
Electricity	Percent	0	0	0	0	0	0	0	0	0	0	0	0	0
Other	Percent	0	0	0	0	0	0	1	1	1	1	1	1	1
Access to sanitation	Percent													
Access to water														
Pipe	Percent	10	1	2	1	1	1	2	28	11	22	27	36	40
Well/borne	Percent	39	33	34	31	29	33	35	53	53	52	54	54	52
Other	Percent	51	66	64	68	70	66	63	19	36	26	19	11	8

Source: 1993 Household Priority Survey.

Central African Republic

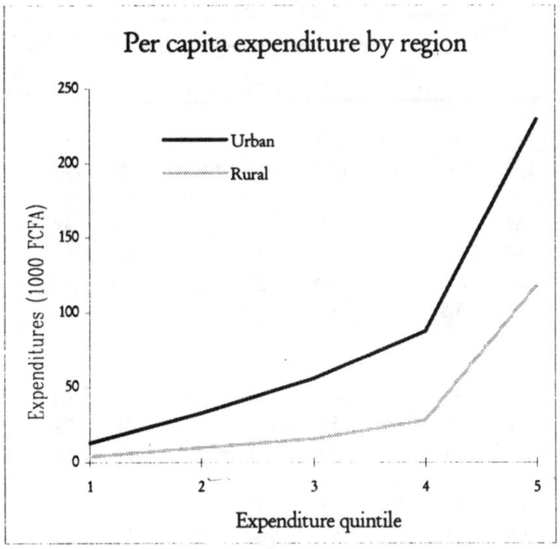

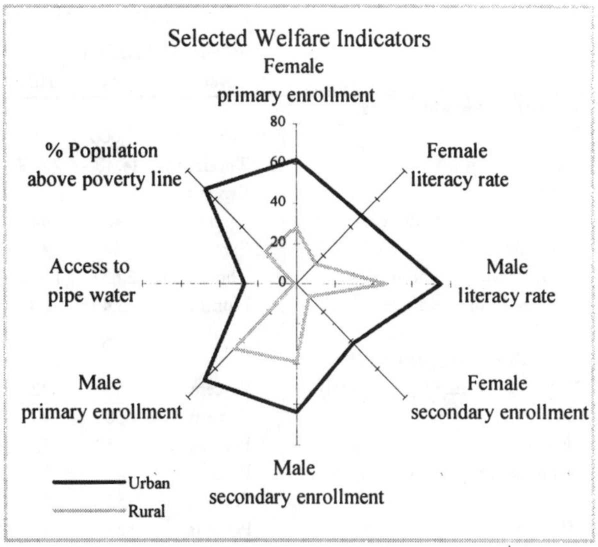

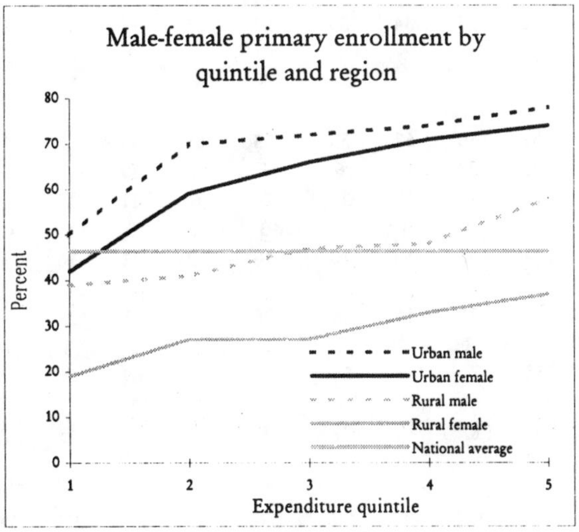

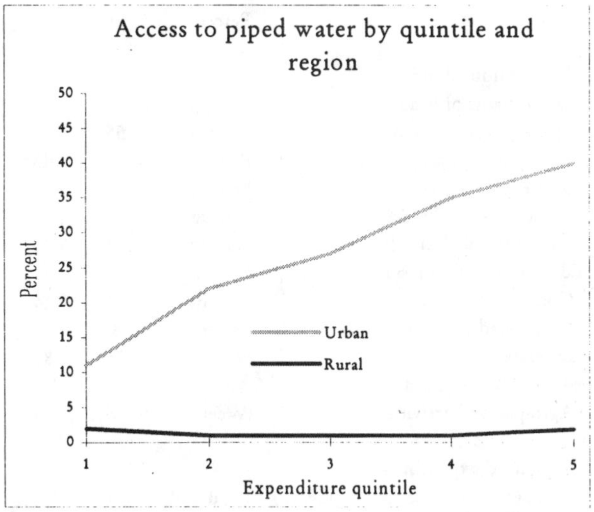

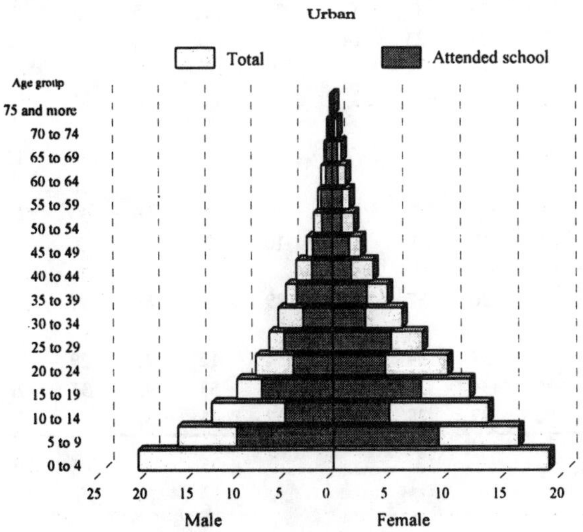

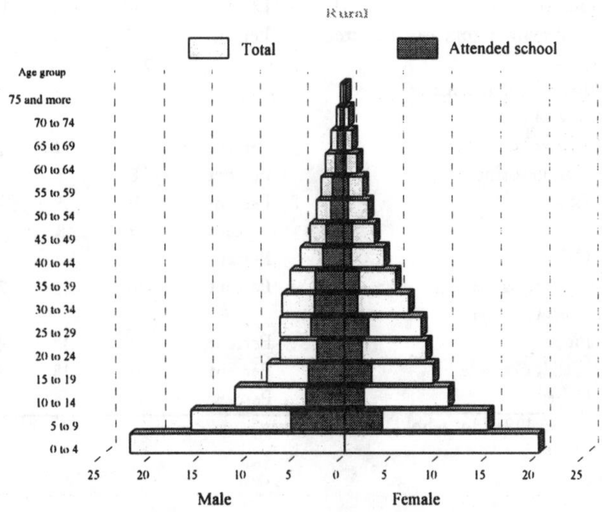

15-3. Côte d'Ivoire: household welfare indicators

Indicator	*Unit of measure*	*National total*	*Expenditure quintile* — *Rural* *All*	*1*	*2*	*3*	*4*	*5*	*Urban* *All*	*1*	*2*	*3*	*4*	*5*
Demographic indicators														
Sample size	Number	1,000	520	71	80	95	99	175	480	72	75	86	89	158
Total population	Thousands	14,400	7,418	1,480	1,491	1,467	1,488	1,491	6,982	1,387	1,406	1,403	1,382	1,403
Female	Percent	51	47	45	52	50	47	45	54	50	57	54	52	56
Population below 15 years	Percent	42	44	57	51	47	49	31	41	50	49	48	40	29
Female	Percent	49	43	40	47	44	43	43	54	49	54	54	52	59
Number of households	Thousands	2,653	1,380	188	212	252	263	464	1,273	191	199	228	236	419
Average household size	Number	5.4	5.4	7.9	7	5.8	5.7	3.2	5.5	7.3	7.1	6.2	5.9	3.3
Education and literacy														
Net primary enrollment (total)	Percent	53	42	34	36	42	52	47	66	53	58	66	79	83
Male	Percent	58	45	37	41	39	56	53	76	57	71	76	92	97
Female	Percent	48	37	30	31	46	44	40	58	49	47	57	67	73
Net secondary enrollment (total)	Percent	40	26	28	35	19	22	27	50	39	45	54	59	52
Male	Percent	52	34	36	45	24	31	31	70	55	78	66	78	72
Female	Percent	27	15	9	16	13	9	23	34	27	20	41	39	41
Literacy rate (total)	Percent	44	33	23	27	28	39	43	62	43	47	65	70	74
Male	Percent	51	39	28	33	34	44	51	70	55	60	71	77	81
Female	Percent	36	27	19	21	23	34	35	53	31	36	59	63	66
Head of household														
Marital status of head														
Monogamous male-headed	Percent	55	56	62	51	56	62	53	53	65	55	60	51	45
Polygamous male-headed	Percent	12	15	20	22	22	15	6	8	12	19	5	9	2
Single male-headed	Percent	18	17	7	12	12	12	29	20	6	11	16	18	34
Defacto female-headed	Percent	3	2	3		4	1	2	3	4	5	2	2	3
Dejure female-headed	Percent	13	10	8	14	6	10	10	16	12	11	16	20	17
Education level of head														
Completed primary	Percent	21	14	8	15	21	11	14	28	18	25	27	35	30
Completed secondary	Percent	8	1			2	2	2	16	4	5	8	16	31
Illiterate	Percent	71	85	92	85	77	87	85	56	78	69	65	49	39
Employment of head														
Agro-pastoral activities	Percent	47	83	90	91	87	76	79	8	17	7	13	7	3
Household expenditure														
Mean per capita expenditure (CFAF)	Thousands	246	203	87	130	170	240	385	291	107	164	227	314	644
Population below relative poverty line	Percent	40	49	100	100	46	0	0	31	100	55	0	0	0
Food share in total expenditure	Percent	30	21	20	20	21	23	24	40	43	46	39	38	34
Household amenities														
Type of fuel for cooking														
Firewood	Percent	57	86	91	94	95	91	76	25	43	37	30	15	12
Gas, kerosine	Percent	8	1				2	1	15		3	10	15	31
Charcoal	Percent	26	5	3	2	3	5	7	50	53	56	53	62	37
Electricity	Percent	9	8	6	4	2	2	16	10	4	4	7	8	20
Other	Percent													
Access to sanitation	Percent	61	35	25	39	26	37	41	89	79	88	91	89	94
Access to water														
Pipe	Percent	36	38	42	44	37	34	36	34	12	21	29	37	52
Well/bore hole	Percent	36	38	31	36	34	38	44	34	53	47	37	27	21
Other	Percent	28	24	27	20	29	28	20	32	35	32	34	36	27

Source: 1995 Household Priority Survey.

Côte d'Ivoire

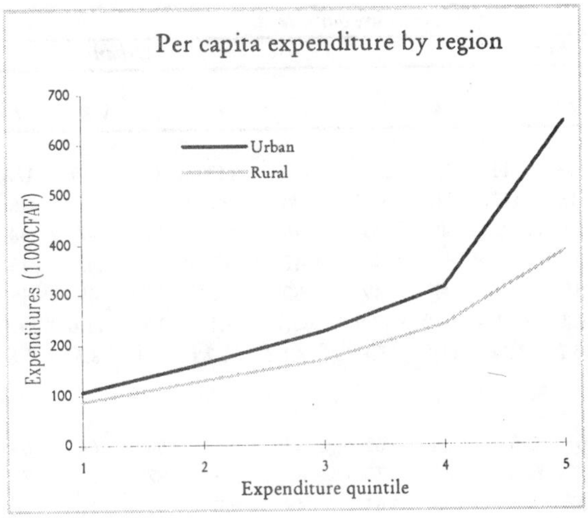

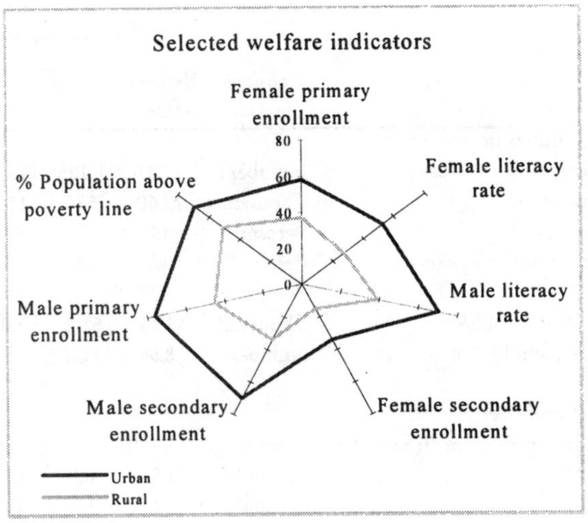

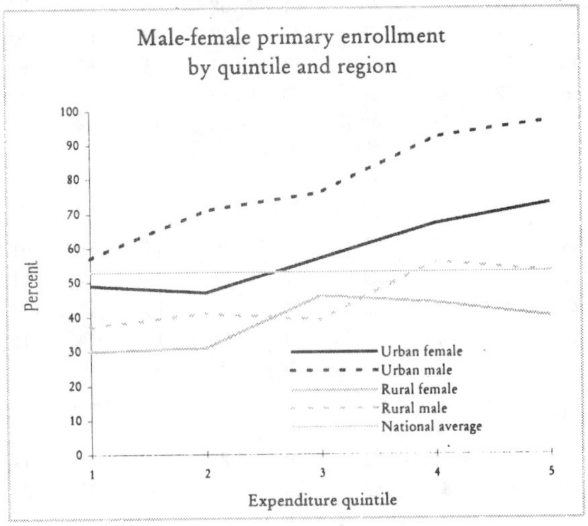

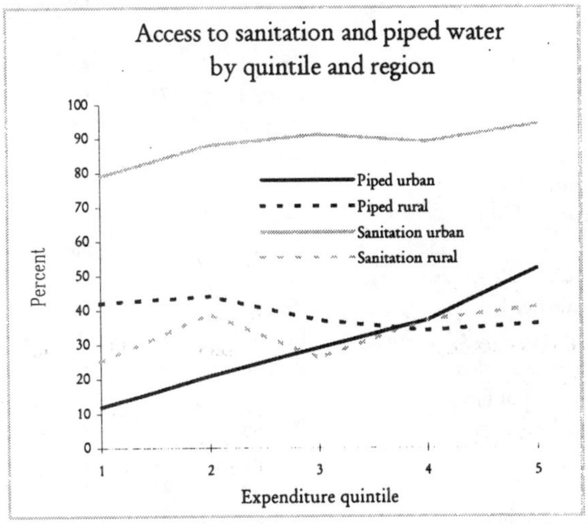

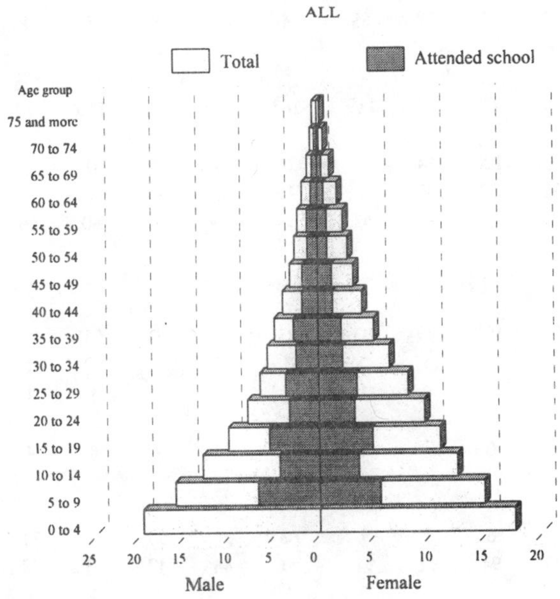

15-4. Gambia: household welfare indicators

			Expenditure quintile											
			Rural						*Urban*					
Indicator	*Unit of measure*	*National total*	*All*	*1*	*2*	*3*	*4*	*5*	*All*	*1*	*2*	*3*	*4*	*5*
Demographic indicators														
Sample size	Number	2,031	1,185	191	204	211	234	345	846	113	109	135	172	317
Total population	Thousands	1,060	580	116	116	117	115	116	480	96	96	96	96	96
Female	Percent	49	50	51	52	50	49	49	46	47	49	47	48	44
Population below 15 years	Percent	47	50	51	53	54	51	47	42	47	46	48	45	34
Female	Percent	49	49	51	51	47	47	49	50	52	51	49	49	50
Number of households	Thousands	119.1	51.0	8.2	8.8	9.1	10.0	14.9	68.1	9.4	9.3	11.6	14.1	23.6
Average household size	Number	8.9	11.4	14	13.2	12.8	11.5	7.8	7.1	10.2	10.3	8.3	6.8	4.1
Education and literacy														
Net primary enrollment (total)	Percent	63	61	53	65	58	65	65	58	65	58	64	69	65
Male	Percent	68	67	61	72	61	73	70	67	69	67	75	71	67
Female	Percent	57	55	45	57	55	55	61	49	60	49	51	66	63
Net secondary enrollment (total)	Percent	54	51	45	50	53	55	50	55	58	55	65	61	61
Male	Percent	69	69	65	65	68	71	75	68	68	68	68	72	73
Female	Percent	40	31	23	35	38	32	23	42	49	42	63	49	48
Literacy rate (total)	Percent	52	43	39	43	38	44	47	53	63	53	59	61	63
Male	Percent	71	63	58	66	57	65	67	73	79	73	75	80	77
Female	Percent	34	24	23	25	22	25	27	29	46	29	44	42	49
Head of household														
Marital status of head														
Monogamous male-headed	Percent	54	58	62	54	55	62	57	51	46	45	58	61	47
Polygamous male-headed	Percent	20	32	33	38	36	32	25	12	19	26	12	11	3
Single male-headed	Percent	15	7	4	6	5	3	12	21	20	12	13	12	34
Defacto female-headed	Percent	10	3	2	2	4	2	6	14	12	14	14	13	16
Dejure female-headed	Percent	1	0				1		2	3	3	3	2	1
Education level of head														
Completed primary	Percent	7	6	8	6	5	6	5	7	8	9	5	5	8
Completed secondary	Percent	10	10	8	10	8	11	12	10	8	5	12	11	11
Illiterate	Percent	83	84	84	84	87	83	82	83	85	86	83	84	81
Employment of head														
Agro-pastoral activities	Percent	37	80	94	90	85	78	65	4	9	9	2	4	2
Household expenditure														
Mean per capita expenditure (Dalasis)	Value	105	57	17	34	49	67	119	163	49	83	115	161	409
Population below relative poverty line	Percent	49	73	100	100	100	64	0	21	100	4	0	0	0
Female	Percent	49	50	51	52	50	49	.	45	47	43	.	.	.
Food share in total expenditure	Percent	59	60	59	61	63	61	57	58	64	64	60	56	47
Household amenities														
Type of fuel for cooking														
Firewood	Percent	89	97	98	99	100	99	93	83	88	93	91	94	68
Gas, kerosine	Percent	2	1				1	2	3	1			1	9
Charcoal	Percent	1	1	1	0		0	1	1			1	1	1
Electricity	Percent	0							1					1
Other	Percent	8	1	1	1	0		4	12	11	7	8	4	21
Access to sanitation	Percent													
Access to water														
Pipe	Percent	42	7	2	7	6	8	9	68	56	50	56	71	84
Well/bore hole	Percent	57	93	98	93	94	92	91	31	44	47	43	28	15
Other	Percent	1	0					0	1		3	1	1	1

Source: 1993/94 Household Integrated Survey

Gambia

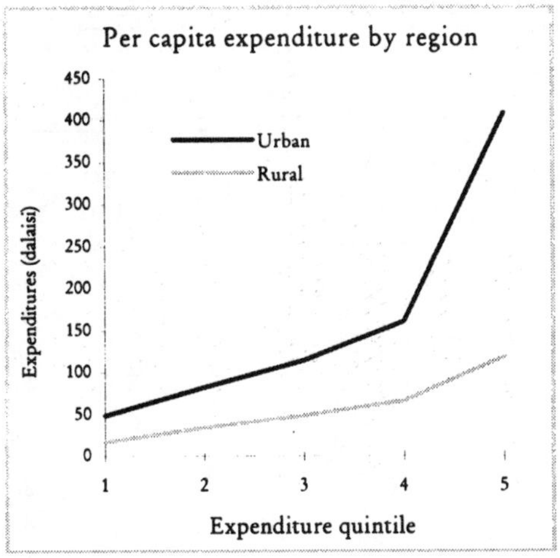
Per capita expenditure by region
Expenditures (dalaisi)
0 50 100 150 200 250 300 350 400 450
Urban
Rural
1 2 3 4 5
Expenditure quintile

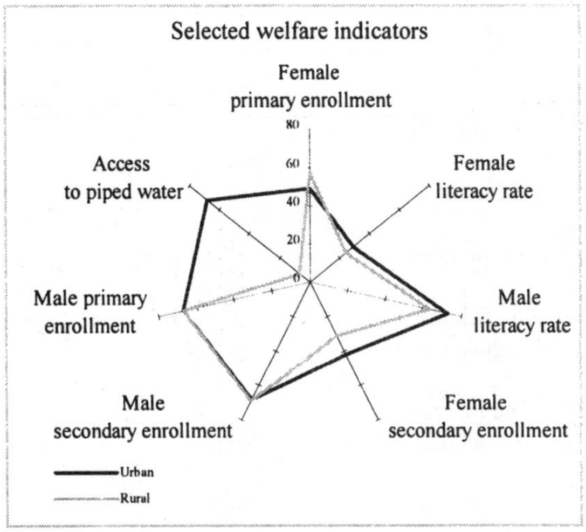
Selected welfare indicators
Female primary enrollment
80 60 40 20 0
Female literacy rate
Male literacy rate
Female secondary enrollment
Male secondary enrollment
Male primary enrollment
Access to piped water
Urban
Rural

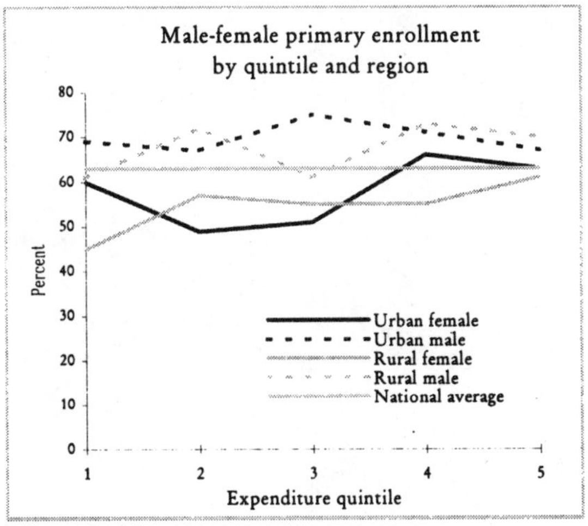
Male-female primary enrollment by quintile and region
Percent
0 10 20 30 40 50 60 70 80
Urban female
Urban male
Rural female
Rural male
National average
1 2 3 4 5
Expenditure quintile

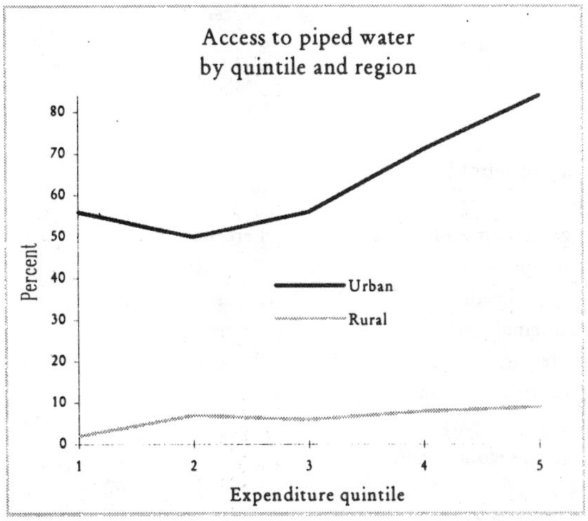
Access to piped water by quintile and region
Percent
0 10 20 30 40 50 60 70 80
Urban
Rural
1 2 3 4 5
Expenditure quintile

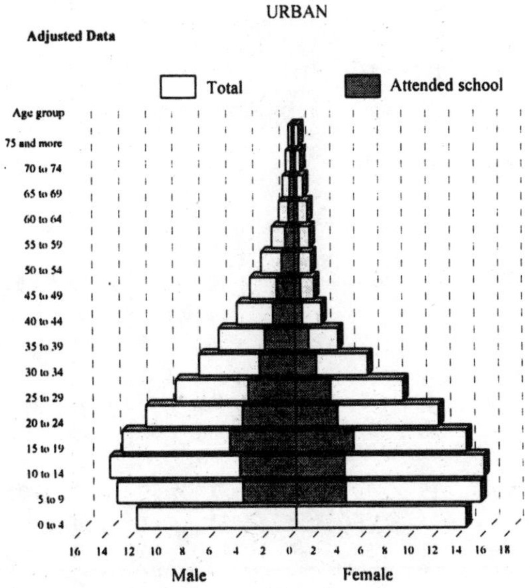
URBAN
Adjusted Data
Total
Attended school
Age group
75 and more
70 to 74
65 to 69
60 to 64
55 to 59
50 to 54
45 to 49
40 to 44
35 to 39
30 to 34
25 to 29
20 to 24
15 to 19
10 to 14
5 to 9
0 to 4
16 14 12 10 8 6 4 2 0 2 4 6 8 10 12 14 16 18
Male
Female

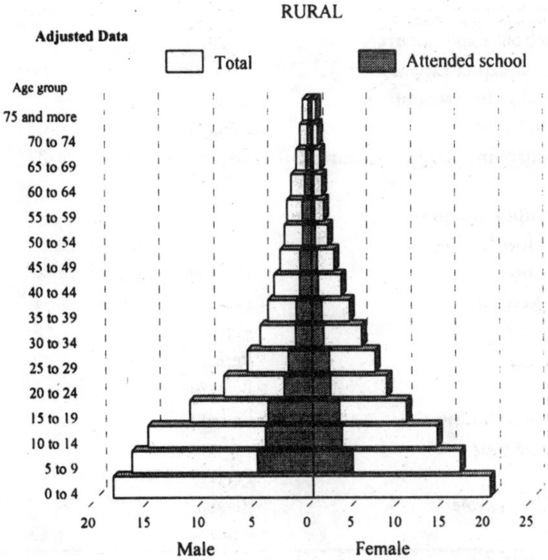
RURAL
Adjusted Data
Total
Attended school
Age group
75 and more
70 to 74
65 to 69
60 to 64
55 to 59
50 to 54
45 to 49
40 to 44
35 to 39
30 to 34
25 to 29
20 to 24
15 to 19
10 to 14
5 to 9
0 to 4
20 15 10 5 0 5 10 15 20 25
Male
Female

15-5. Ghana: household welfare indicators

Indicator	*Unit of measure*	*National total*	*Expenditure quintile* — *Rural* — *All*	*1*	*2*	*3*	*4*	*5*	*Urban* — *All*	*1*	*2*	*3*	*4*	*5*
Demographic indicators														
Sample size	Number	4,523	2,945	398	465	517	596	969	1578	205	241	286	317	529
Total population	Thousands	16,700	11,164	2,236	2,230	2,231	2,231	2,235	5,536	1,107	1,104	1,109	1,109	1,107
Female	Percent	51	51	49	50	54	52	49	53	51	54	53	53	52
Population below 15 years	Percent	44	46	57	52	51	47	36	41	54	50	44	41	31
Female	Percent	49	49	45	47	53	50	48	51	47	50	49	49	55
Number of households	Thousands	3,728	2,427	328	383	426	491	799	1,301	169	199	236	261	436
Average household size	Number	4.5	4.6	6.8	5.8	5.2	4.5	2.8	4.3	6.6	5.6	4.7	4.2	2.5
Education and literacy														
Net primary enrollment (total)	Percent	72	66	59	72	70	74	81	84	74	82	86	87	92
Male	Percent	77	73	63	71	73	78	84	86	80	84	87	89	98
Female	Percent	72	67	55	73	68	69	77	80	67	80	84	86	88
Net secondary enrollment (total)	Percent	60	57	50	61	56	60	57	65	61	69	68	64	66
Male	Percent	67	64	56	68	62	68	65	74	68	77	74	73	80
Female	Percent	52	48	39	52	50	51	47	58	51	62	59	58	56
Literacy rate (total)	Percent	52	43	32	42	42	47	50	69	53	62	71	71	81
Male	Percent	64	57	44	56	56	61	62	78	63	74	82	81	86
Female	Percent	42	31	22	31	31	35	37	61	45	52	62	63	76
Head of household														
Marital status of head														
Monogamous male-headed	Percent	45	48	58	57	54	51	33	40	49	52	41	45	27
Polygamous male-headed	Percent	5	7	13	9	7	5	3	2	8	2	1	2	0
Single male-headed	Percent	18	17	5	6	7	14	34	19	3	7	12	16	38
Defacto female-headed	Percent	0	0	1	0	0	1	0	0	1		1		0
Dejure female-headed	Percent	32	29	24	27	32	28	30	38	39	39	44	38	35
Education level of head														
Completed primary	Percent	28	24	16	22	21	26	28	37	24	35	36	41	40
Completed secondary	Percent	10	5	2	4	3	5	7	19	11	12	14	18	30
Illiterate	Percent	62	71	82	74	76	69	64	44	65	53	50	41	30
Employment of head														
Agro-pastoral activities	Percent	56	74	86	81	78	74	65	19	33	24	19	14	14
Household expenditure														
Mean per capita expenditure (CEDI)	Thousands	168	149	59	90	120	162	311	208	78	121	163	224	455
Population below relative poverty line	Percent	39	45	100	100	26	0	0	26	100	28	0	0	0
Food share in total expenditure	Percent	39	37	36	35	36	36	41	45	47	47	47	45	39
Household amenities														
Type of fuel for cooking														
Firewood	Percent	67	87	94	90	93	86	80	30	55	40	33	25	19
Gas, kerosine	Percent	4	1	0	1		0	2	11	2	5	6	9	19
Charcoal	Percent	25	8	2	4	4	9	15	56	43	54	60	63	55
Electricity	Percent	1	0					0	2		0	0	1	5
Other	Percent	3	4	4	5	3	5	3	1		1	1	2	2
Access to sanitation	Percent	64	66	59	65	66	70	68	60	52	58	55	60	66
Access to water														
Pipe	Percent	36	14	9	9	15	14	18	77	59	72	75	82	84
Well/bore hole	Percent	29	37	39	39	34	36	38	13	21	18	15	10	9
Other	Percent	35	49	52	52	51	50	44	10	20	10	10	8	7

Source: 1992 Ghana Living Standards Survey 3.

Ghana

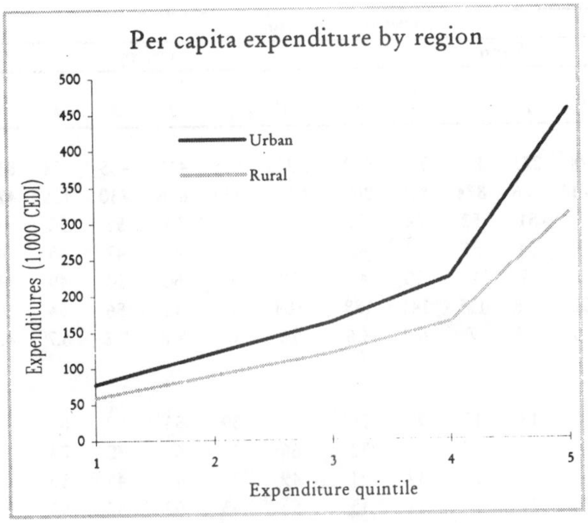
Per capita expenditure by region
Expenditures (1,000 CEDI)
500
450
400
350
300
250
200
150
100
50
0
Urban
Rural
1
2
3
4
5
Expenditure quintile

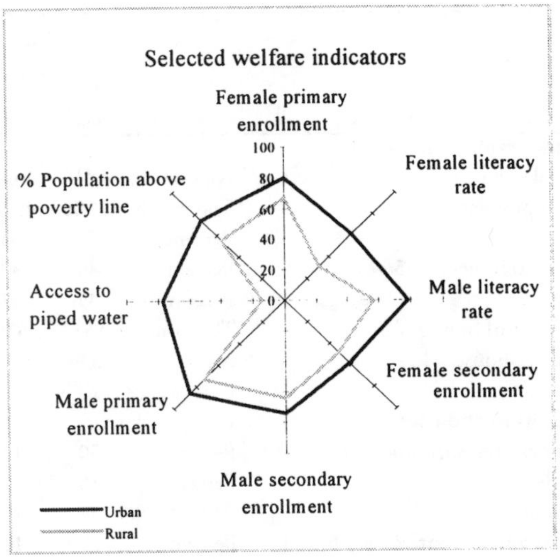
Selected welfare indicators
Female primary enrollment
100
80
60
40
20
0
Female literacy rate
Male literacy rate
Female secondary enrollment
Male secondary enrollment
Male primary enrollment
Access to piped water
% Population above poverty line
Urban
Rural

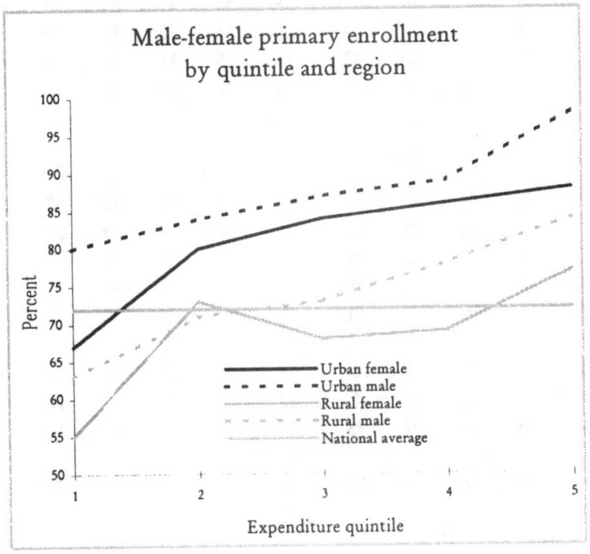
Male-female primary enrollment by quintile and region
Percent
100
95
90
85
80
75
70
65
60
55
50
Urban female
Urban male
Rural female
Rural male
National average
1
2
3
4
5
Expenditure quintile

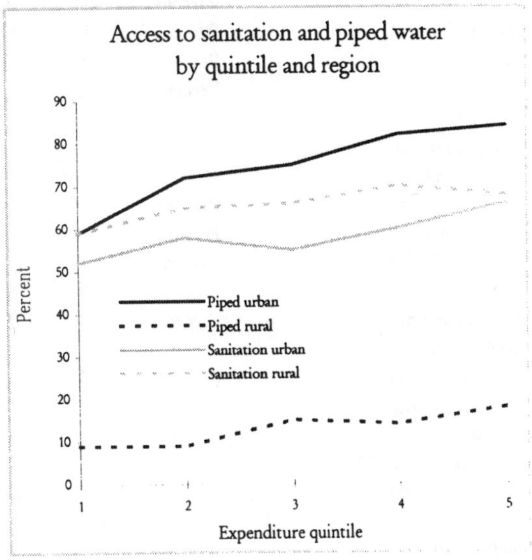
Access to sanitation and piped water by quintile and region
Percent
90
80
70
60
50
40
30
20
10
0
Piped urban
Piped rural
Sanitation urban
Sanitation rural
1
2
3
4
5
Expenditure quintile

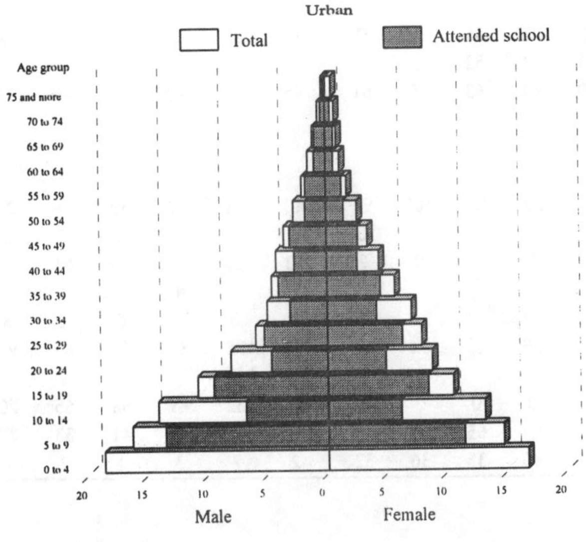
Urban
Total
Attended school
Age group
75 and more
70 to 74
65 to 69
60 to 64
55 to 59
50 to 54
45 to 49
40 to 44
35 to 39
30 to 34
25 to 29
20 to 24
15 to 19
10 to 14
5 to 9
0 to 4
20
15
10
5
0
5
10
15
20
Male
Female

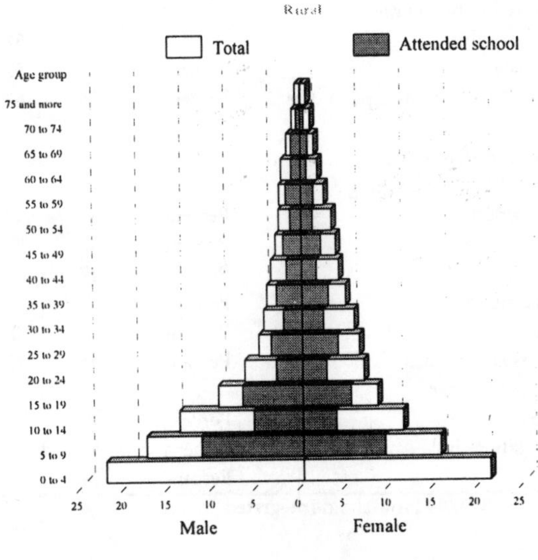
Rural
Total
Attended school
Age group
75 and more
70 to 74
65 to 69
60 to 64
55 to 59
50 to 54
45 to 49
40 to 44
35 to 39
30 to 34
25 to 29
20 to 24
15 to 19
10 to 14
5 to 9
0 to 4
25
20
15
10
5
0
5
10
15
20
25
Male
Female

15-6. Guinea: household welfare indicators

			Expenditure quintile											
			Rural						*Urban*					
Indicator	*Unit of measure*	*National total*	*All*	*1*	*2*	*3*	*4*	*5*	*All*	*1*	*2*	*3*	*4*	*5*
Demographic indicators														
Sample size	Number	4,416	1,680	228	273	318	359	502	2,736	425	413	485	574	839
Total population	Thousands	6,500	4,360	871	876	874	869	869	2,140	429	426	430	428	429
Female	Percent	51	53	53	51	52	54	52	50	51	51	51	50	49
Population below 15 years	Percent	46	49	55	54	51	47	43	45	51	47	47	45	40
Female	Percent	49	47	48	47	45	50	47	50	49	50	50	49	50
Number of households	Thousands	983	675	102	118	125	141	188	308	49	48	56	64	92
Average household size	Number	6.6	6.5	8.5	7.4	7	6.2	4.6	6.9	8.7	8.8	7.8	6.7	4.7
Education and literacy														
Net primary enrollment (total)	Percent	30	18	14	13	15	22	28	57	39	55	59	66	72
Male	Percent	35	23	21	16	17	33	32	66	47	65	70	74	80
Female	Percent	24	12	5	9	12	12	23	49	31	46	48	59	65
Net secondary enrollment (total)	Percent	29	12	8	12	13	11	15	53	43	52	57	55	59
Male	Percent	38	19	12	20	21	20	23	66	50	65	71	73	76
Female	Percent	17	3	3	0	3	3	6	38	31	35	40	35	45
Literacy rate (total)	Percent	15	10	6	8	11	11	14	25	16	22	21	25	37
Male	Percent	27	23	13	18	26	24	29	35	25	31	32	36	48
Female	Percent	6	1	1	0	1	2	2	15	8	14	11	15	25
Head of household														
Marital status of head														
Monogamous male-headed	Percent	47	44	42	41	41	43	51	52	44	49	52	58	53
Polygamous male-headed	Percent	32	36	46	42	42	38	22	23	37	33	29	20	10
Single male-headed	Percent	4	3	1	4	2	2	6	7	3	2	3	4	16
Defacto female-headed	Percent	9	9	5	7	9	10	10	10	7	8	8	9	13
Dejure female-headed	Percent	8	7	5	6	6	7	11	8	9	8	7	9	7
Education level of head														
Completed primary	Percent	8	3	1	2	3	2	6	19	8	15	16	19	27
Completed secondary	Percent	4	0			0	0	1	11	2	6	7	12	19
Illiterate	Percent	88	96	99	98	96	97	93	71	89	79	77	70	53
Employment of head														
Agro-pastoral activities	Percent	60	84	89	87	86	85	78	8	19	13	6	5	3
Household expenditure														
Mean per capita expenditure (FG)	Thousands	468	342	136	207	281	388	698	724	241	394	542	769	1,675
Population below relative poverty line	Percent	44	57	100	100	85	0	0	18	88	0	0	0	0
Female	Percent	52	52	53	51	52	.	.	51	51	.	.	.	.
Food share in total expenditure	Percent	56	62	60	62	63	65	61	45	55	48	46	40	34
Household amenities														
Type of fuel for cooking														
Firewood	Percent	81	99	99	100	99	100	97	42	71	52	39	36	27
Gas, kerosine	Percent	0	0			0		0	1			1	0	3
Charcoal	Percent	17	1		0	1	0	2	53	29	46	60	61	60
Electricity	Percent	1							1		1		1	2
Other	Percent	1	0	1				1	3	0	1	0	2	8
Access to sanitation	Percent	55	40	41	39	43	34	42	86	78	86	85	89	90
Access to water														
Pipe	Percent	19	1	0	0	0		3	58	32	49	58	65	70
Well/bore hole	Percent	57	65	75	60	65	64	65	40	61	48	41	33	29
Other	Percent	24	34	25	40	35	36	32	2	7	3	1	2	1

Source: 1993/94 Household Integrated Survey

Guinea

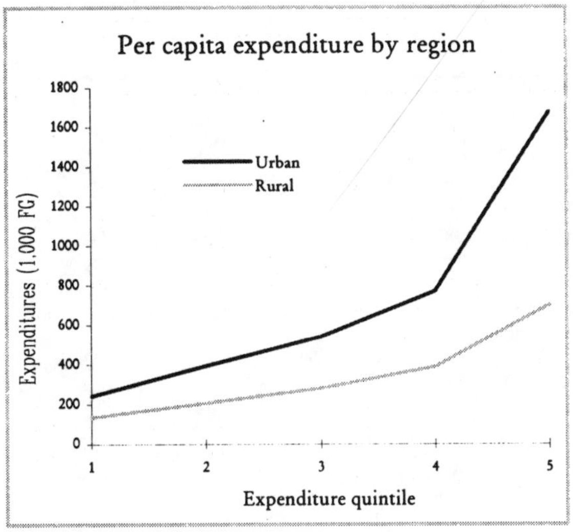
Per capita expenditure by region
Expenditures (1,000 FG)
Urban
Rural
Expenditure quintile

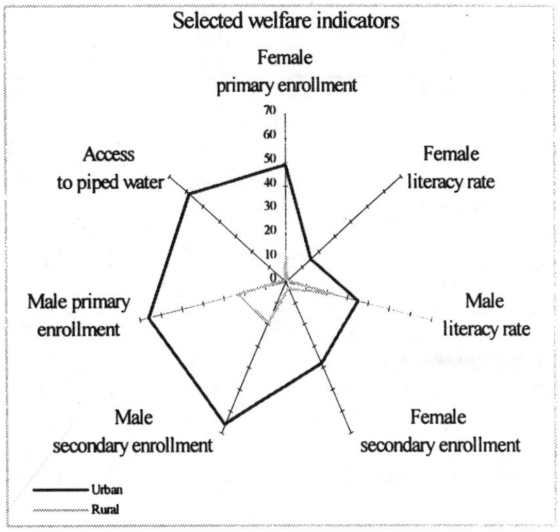
Selected welfare indicators
Female primary enrollment
Female literacy rate
Male literacy rate
Female secondary enrollment
Male secondary enrollment
Male primary enrollment
Access to piped water
Urban
Rural

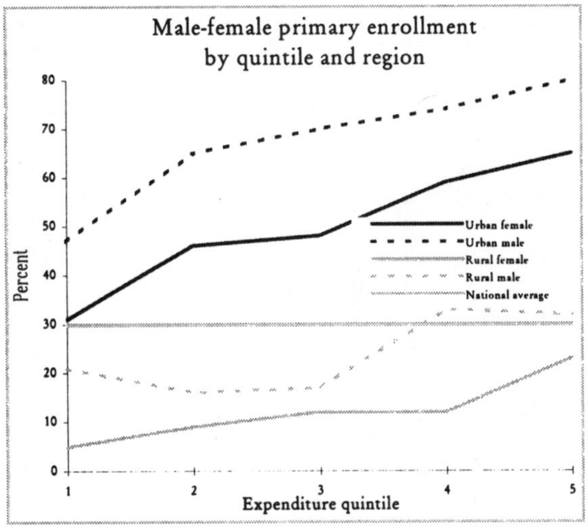
Male-female primary enrollment by quintile and region
Percent
Urban female
Urban male
Rural female
Rural male
National average
Expenditure quintile

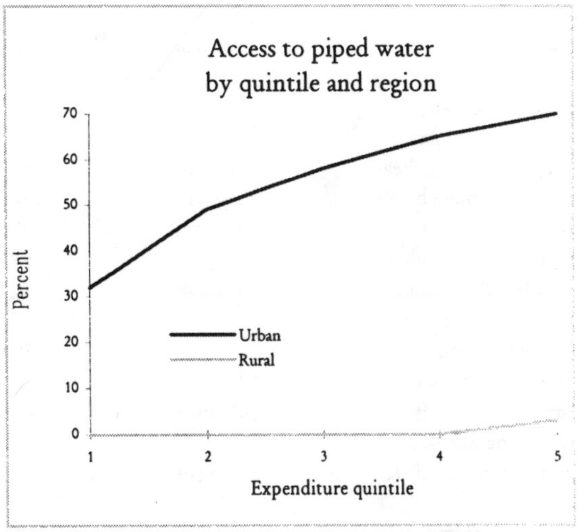
Access to piped water by quintile and region
Percent
Urban
Rural
Expenditure quintile

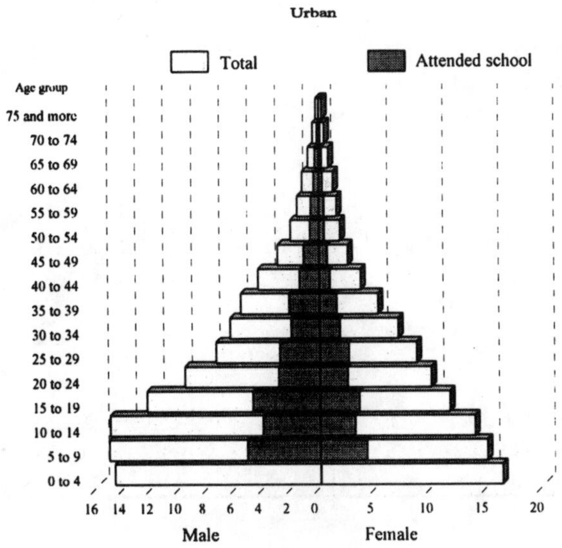
Urban
Total
Attended school
Age group
Male
Female

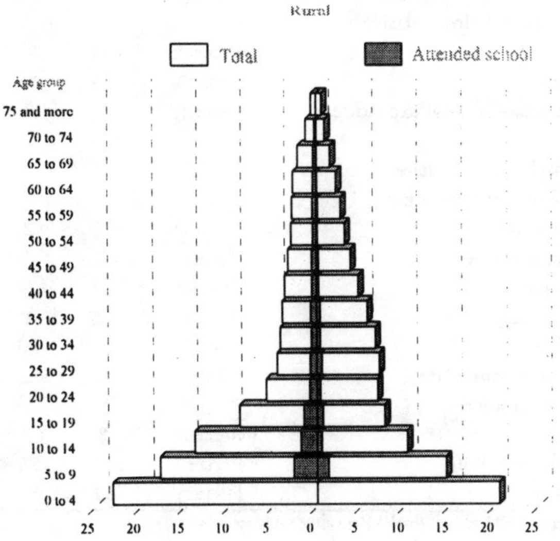
Rural
Total
Attended school
Age group

15-7. Guinea-Bissau: household welfare indicators

			Expenditure quintile											
			Rural						*Urban*					
Indicator	*Unit of measure*	*National total*	*All*	*1*	*2*	*3*	*4*	*5*	*All*	*1*	*2*	*3*	*4*	*5*
Demographic indicators														
Sample size	Number	1,617	1,178	232	230	227	243	246	439	106	92	84	86	71
Total population	Thousand	1,060	720	144	144	144	144	144	340	68	69	69	69	68
Female	Percent	45	46	46	47	45	44	47	44	46	47	47	38	41
Population below 15 years	Percent	52	52	50	54	54	50	53	51	48	47	55	52	57
Female	Percent	47	47	46	48	48	48	47	47	54	51	45	42	38
Number of households	Thousand	136	99	20	19	19	20	20	37	8	8	8	7	7
Average household size	Number	7.8	7.3	7.1	7.7	7.5	7	7.2	9.1	8.2	9	8.8	9.7	10.1
Education and literacy														
Net primary enrollment (total)	Percent	30	20	14	15	14	26	32	48	43	49	56	46	47
Male	Percent	34	26	20	23	20	32	36	48	49	55	56	39	44
Female	Percent	25	13	8	7	6	19	25	49	36	42	57	55	53
Net secondary enrollment (total)	Percent	19	8	5	2	3	6	27	37	38	18	30	28	61
Male	Percent	..	..	..	..	..	..	..	..	..	..	..	..	..
Female	Percent	..	..	..	..	..	..	..	..	..	..	..	..	..
Literacy rate (total)	Percent	24	12	8	8	12	14	18	50	45	41	59	53	56
Male	Percent	37	22	15	17	21	26	30	69	60	66	76	70	73
Female	Percent	12	4	3	1	4	4	6	32	27	19	41	35	41
Head of household														
Marital status of head														
Monogamous male-headed	Percent	52	50	45	46	52	57	49	58	38	61	68	57	69
Polygamous male-headed	Percent	8	6	8	8	7	5	5	14	25	10	13	15	5
Single male-headed	Percent	1	0	0		0	0	1	3	2	2	3	3	5
Defacto female-headed	Percent	28	33	34	34	31	29	36	17	24	20	8	17	13
Dejure female-headed	Percent	10	10	12	12	9	10	9	8	12	7	7	8	8
Education level of head														
Completed primary	Percent	24	19	12	17	15	23	25	37	30	40	42	33	38
Completed secondary	Percent	7	2	1	0	3	2	4	20	12	14	17	29	31
Illiterate	Percent	69	79	87	83	82	74	70	43	57	45	41	38	30
Employment of head														
Agro-pastoral activities	Percent	68	87	85	89	90	87	82	19	24	15	13	17	26
Household expenditure														
Mean per capita expenditure (GBpeso)	Thousand	251	192	19	61	110	197	574	377	71	172	261	399	986
Population below relative poverty line	Percent	54	65	100	100	100	27	0	29	100	47	0	0	0
Female	Percent	44	45	46	47	45	40	.	43	46	41	.	.	.
Food share in total expenditure	Percent		..	..	..	..	..	..	..	..	..	..	..	..
Household amenities														
Type of fuel for cooking														
Firewood	Percent	10	2	1	4	2	2	3	30	17	21	31	41	47
Gas, kerosine	Percent	3	1	1	0	1	1	2	7	2	3	4	11	16
Charcoal	Percent	69	76	74	78	71	78	77	52	67	70	56	37	28
Electricity	Percent	2	1		1	1	1	3	6	6	4	3	9	9
Other	Percent	16	20	24	17	25	18	15	4	8	2	6	2	
Access to sanitation	Percent	..	..	..	..	..	..	..	..	..	..	..	..	..
Access to water														
Pipe	Percent	8	2	1	1	1	3	3	25	20	20	28	27	33
Well/bore hole	Percent	81	86	85	85	87	86	86	70	78	77	70	59	60
Other	Percent	11	12	14	14	12	11	11	5	2	3	2	14	7

Source: 1991 Household Priority Survey

Guinea Bissau

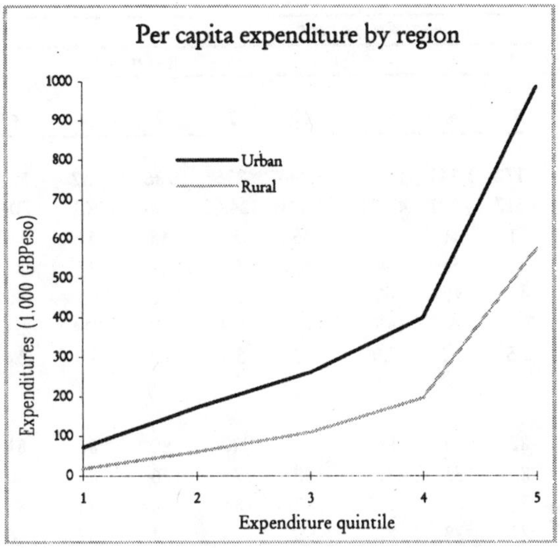

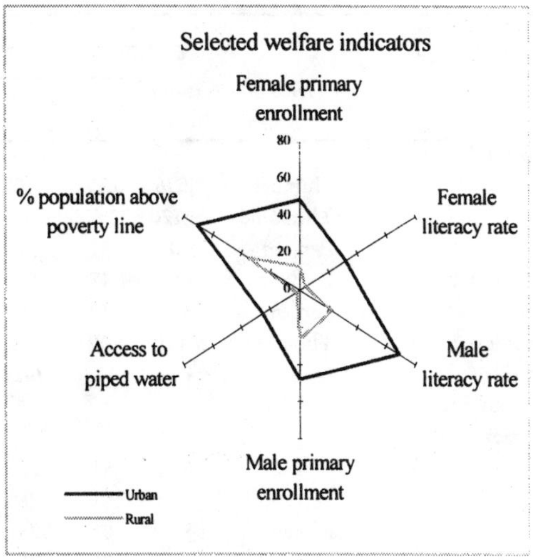

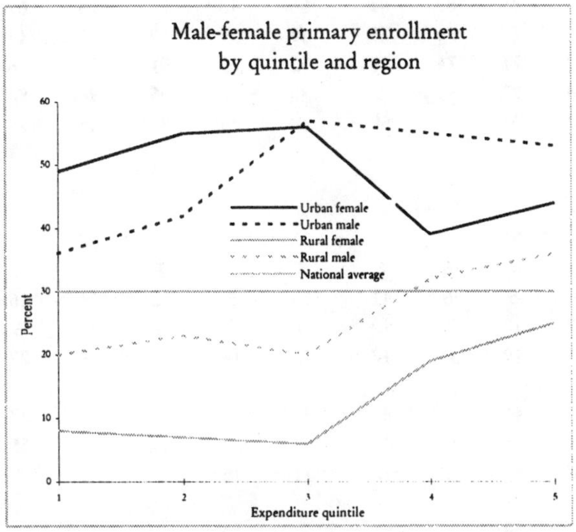

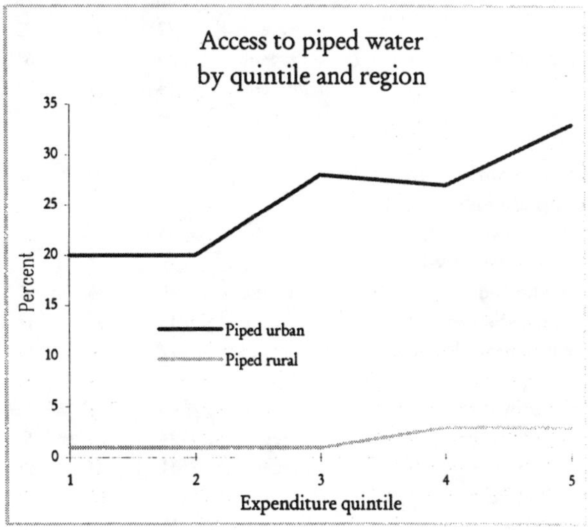

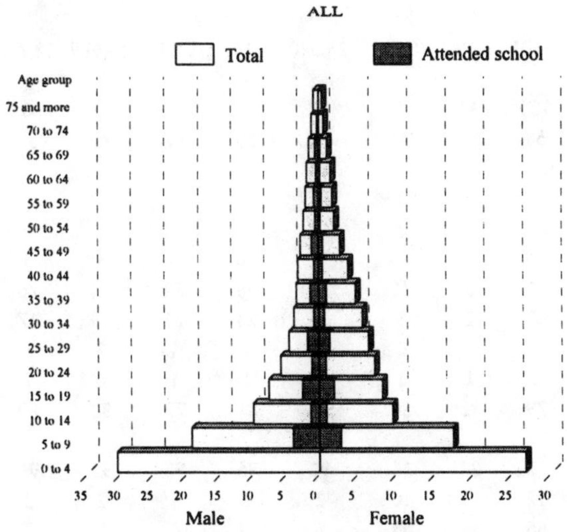

15-8. Kenya: household welfare indicators

			Expenditure quintile											
			Rural						Urban					
Indicator	*Unit of measure*	*National total*	*All*	*1*	*2*	*3*	*4*	*5*	*All*	*1*	*2*	*3*	*4*	*5*
Demographic indicators														
Sample size	Number	8,096	6,352	1,102	1,111	1,172	1,241	1,726	1,744	236	286	332	391	499
Total population	Thousands	26,120	22,600	4,520	4,521	4,517	4,521	4,520	3,521	704.05	706	701	706	703
Female	Percent	50	51	51	52	51	51	50	46	50	48	51	46	41
Population below 15 years	Percent	45	48	54	53	51	46	40	33	51	42	37	29	22
Female	Percent	49	49	50	50	48	49	50	49	50	50	55	49	44
Number of households	Thousands	5,453	4,327	734	753	825	863	1151	1126	134	171	214	270	336
Average household size	Number	4.8	5.2	6.2	6	5.5	5.2	3.9	3.1	5.2	4.1	3.3	2.6	2.1
Education and literacy														
Net primary enrollment (total)	Percent	81	81	76	81	82	85	89	86	80	80	87	81	97
Male	Percent	81	81	76	81	82	83	86	80	75	76	82	80	95
Female	Percent	83	83	75	81	83	86	91	87	84	84	92	82	98
Net secondary enrollment (total)	Percent	76	78	75	77	79	78	82	56	44	64	59	56	58
Male	Percent	80	81	78	79	81	82	84	66	48	73	74	69	70
Female	Percent	72	75	72	76	77	74	79	49	39	59	47	43	51
Literacy rate (total)	Percent	75	71	61	69	71	74	78	92	85	91	91	96	96
Male	Percent	84	81	74	78	80	83	87	96	92	95	94	97	98
Female	Percent	66	63	50	62	63	67	69	89	78	87	88	94	94
Head of household														
Marital status of head														
Monogamous male-headed	Percent	55	55	54	57	51	58	53	57	61	69	57	55	52
Polygamous male-headed	Percent	6	7	9	7	7	6	6	3	8	1	5	2	2
Single male-headed	Percent	8	6	4	5	5	6	11	16	5	12	14	16	25
Defacto female-headed	Percent	13	15	14	17	18	17	12	5	8	4	6	6	4
Dejure female-headed	Percent	17	17	19	15	19	14	17	18	18	15	19	22	17
Education level of head														
Completed primary	Percent	45	47	44	50	46	51	46	37	45	43	37	37	30
Completed secondary	Percent	24	17	9	13	14	17	27	53	38	49	55	55	57
Illiterate	Percent	31	36	47	37	41	32	27	11	16	8	9	8	13
Employment of head														
Agro-pastoral activities	Percent	60	74	82	80	79	72	61	7	10	6	9	6	4
Household expenditure														
Mean per capita expenditure (KSH)	Value	8,838	6,578	1,440	2,708	4,101	6,190	18,451	23,340	5,180	9,592	13,989	22,177	65,829
Population below relative poverty line	Percent	61	69	100	100	100	43	0	12	61	0	0	0	0
Food share in total expenditure	Percent	54	56	62	62	58	52	43	41	55	47	42	33	28
Household amenities														
Type of fuel for cooking														
Firewood	Percent	73	92	98	97	96	94	80	5	16	5	4	3	3
Gas, kerosine	Percent	19	4	1	1	2	3	11	75	58	72	74	76	80
Charcoal	Percent	6	3	0	1	2	2	8	16	24	21	19	17	8
Electricity	Percent	1	0			0		0	3	1	1	2	3	8
Other	Percent	1	1	1	1	0	1	1	1	1	1	0	1	1
Access to sanitation	Percent	80	80	70	75	79	82	89	78	81	77	80	80	75
Access to water														
Pipe	Percent	39	25	20	21	22	24	35	92	86	93	93	91	96
Well/bore hole	Percent	9	12	10	15	12	11	10	2	2	1	2	2	1
Other	Percent	52	63	70	64	66	65	55	6	12	6	5	7	3

Source: 1992/93 Welfare Monitoring Survey.

Kenya

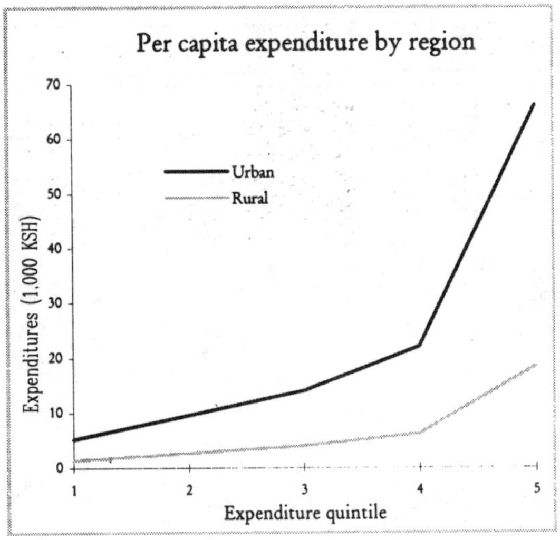
Per capita expenditure by region
Urban
Rural
Expenditures (1,000 KSH)
70
60
50
40
30
20
10
0
1
2
3
4
5
Expenditure quintile

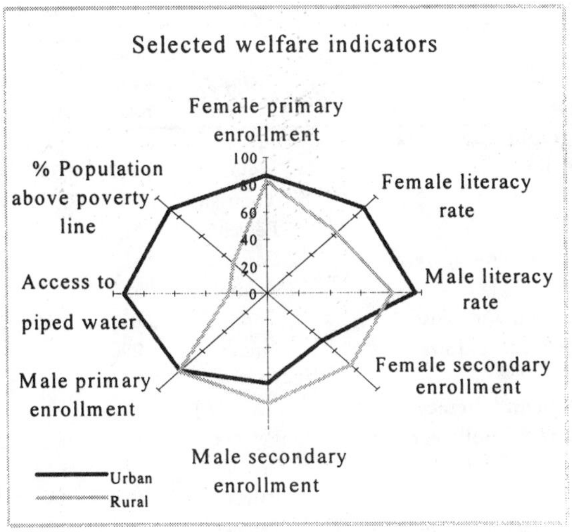
Selected welfare indicators
Female primary enrollment
Female literacy rate
Male literacy rate
Female secondary enrollment
Male secondary enrollment
Male primary enrollment
Access to piped water
% Population above poverty line
100
80
60
40
20
0
Urban
Rural

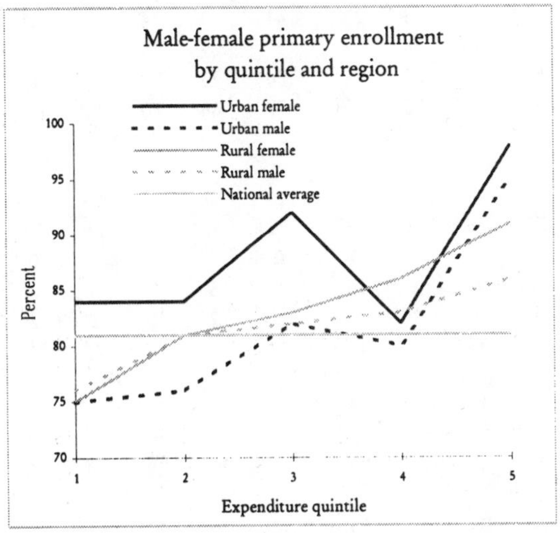
Male-female primary enrollment by quintile and region
Urban female
Urban male
Rural female
Rural male
National average
Percent
100
95
90
85
80
75
70
1
2
3
4
5
Expenditure quintile

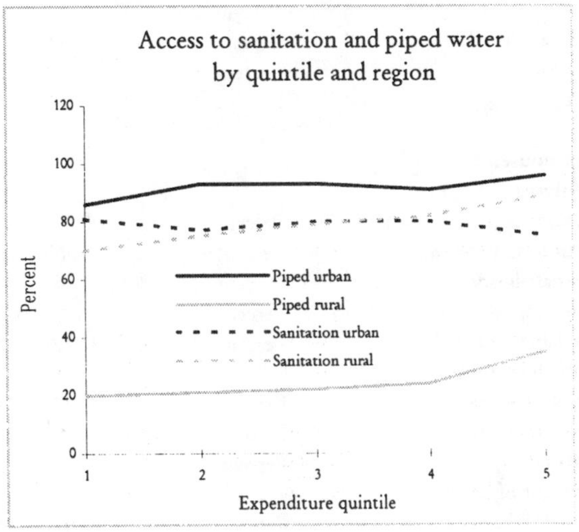
Access to sanitation and piped water by quintile and region
120
100
80
60
40
20
0
Percent
Piped urban
Piped rural
Sanitation urban
Sanitation rural
1
2
3
4
5
Expenditure quintile

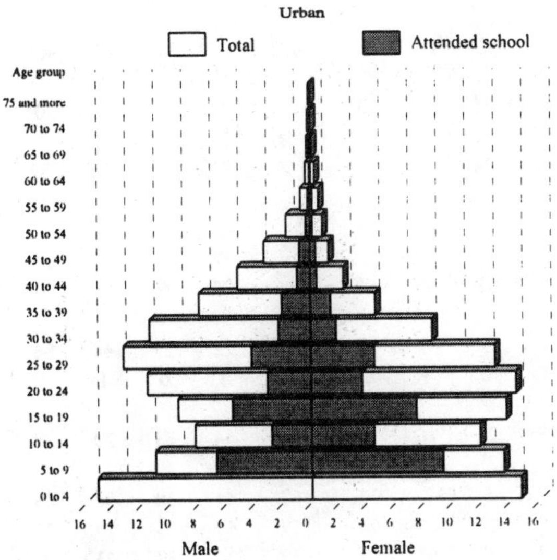
Urban
Total
Attended school
Age group
75 and more
70 to 74
65 to 69
60 to 64
55 to 59
50 to 54
45 to 49
40 to 44
35 to 39
30 to 34
25 to 29
20 to 24
15 to 19
10 to 14
5 to 9
0 to 4
16 14 12 10 8 6 4 2 0 2 4 6 8 10 12 14 16
Male
Female

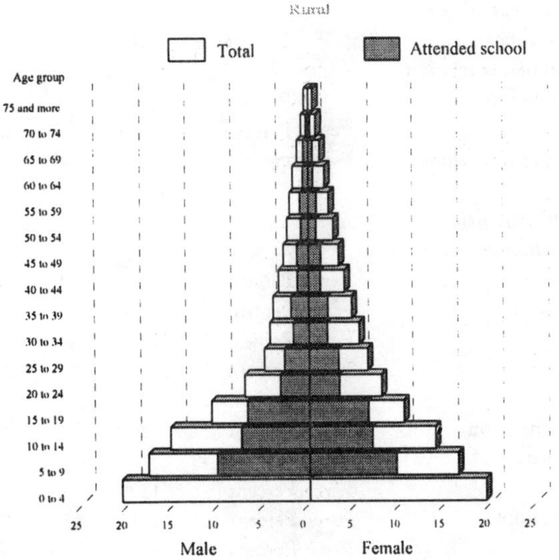
Rural
Total
Attended school
Age group
75 and more
70 to 74
65 to 69
60 to 64
55 to 59
50 to 54
45 to 49
40 to 44
35 to 39
30 to 34
25 to 29
20 to 24
15 to 19
10 to 14
5 to 9
0 to 4
25 20 15 10 5 0 5 10 15 20 25
Male
Female

15-9. Madagascar: household welfare indicators

			Expenditure quintile												
			Rural						Urban						
Indicator	*Unit of measure*	*National total*	*All*	*1*	*2*	*3*	*4*	*5*	*All*	*1*	*2*	*3*	*4*	*5*
Demographic indicators															
Sample size	Number	4,500	2,557	434	443	473	554	653	1,943	263	282	402	439	557
Total population	Thousands	13,100	10,297	2,059	2,059	2,059	2,062	2,060	2,803	560	559	562	560	560
Female	Percent	51	50	50	51	51	49	48	52	53	51	53	50	52
Population below 15 years	Percent	42	45	53	51	47	44	36	39	49	46	42	37	29
Female	Percent	50	50	49	52	50	48	50	51	53	50	51	50	50
Number of households	Thousands	2,654	2,100	342	369	387	448	554	554	84	96	111	118	144
Average household size	Number	4.9	4.9	6	5.6	5.3	4.6	3.7	5.1	6.7	5.8	5	4.8	3.9
Education and literacy															
Net primary enrollment (total)	Percent	39	32	21	26	33	39	51	66	54	62	66	76	77
Male	Percent	39	32	19	26	31	40	54	66	54	61	67	78	78
Female	Percent	40	33	22	27	36	38	49	65	53	63	66	74	76
Net secondary enrollment (total)	Percent	19	12	7	7	10	15	20	41	24	28	43	54	59
Male	Percent	18	11	9	7	6	13	19	42	25	22	45	57	64
Female	Percent	19	12	4	6	13	18	22	41	24	34	41	51	55
Literacy rate (total)	Percent	58	51	35	45	53	56	62	82	69	75	83	90	91
Male	Percent	64	57	40	52	59	62	68	86	73	79	87	92	94
Female	Percent	53	45	31	37	48	50	56	79	66	70	80	87	89
Head of household															
Marital status of head															
Monogamous male-headed	Percent	72	73	71	75	75	74	69	70	69	76	68	73	67
Polygamous male-headed	Percent	0	0		1		0	0	0				0	
Single male-headed	Percent	8	9	7	6	6	8	13	6	5	5	4	6	10
Defacto female-headed	Percent	2	2	2	1	1	1	3	2	2	1	1	2	2
Dejure female-headed	Percent	18	17	20	17	18	16	14	22	25	18	28	19	21
Education level of head															
Completed primary	Percent	19	15	4	8	12	16	26	36	17	30	32	46	46
Completed secondary	Percent	3	1		0	0	0	2	11	1	1	3	14	29
Illiterate	Percent	78	85	96	92	87	84	72	53	83	69	65	40	25
Employment of head															
Agro-pastoral activities	Percent	80	91	94	94	95	90	85	40	56	59	41	32	24
Household expenditure															
Mean per capita expenditure (FMG)	Thousands	237	185	55	101	139	199	433	427	112	191	284	439	1,108
Population below relative poverty line	Percent	51	59	100	100	95	0	0	21	100	7	0	0	0
Female	Percent	51	51	50	51	51	.	.	51	53	49	.	.	.
Food share in total expenditure	Percent	70	72	74	74	74	73	65	64	71	71	66	59	50
Household amenities															
Type of fuel for cooking															
Firewood	Percent	85	95	100	98	99	95	88	44	75	70	51	31	15
Gas, kerosine	Percent	0	0					0	2		1		0	7
Charcoal	Percent	14	4	0	1	1	4	12	51	22	29	48	66	72
Electricity	Percent	1	1	0	1	0	1	0	3	3	0	1	3	6
Other	Percent													
Access to sanitation	Percent	33	23	10	19	25	26	31	70	54	55	70	78	84
Access to water															
Pipe	Percent	18	6	4	4	5	7	11	62	44	38	58	76	76
Well/bore hole	Percent	21	22	21	19	13	26	28	19	19	25	19	20	16
Other	Percent	61	72	75	77	82	67	61	19	37	37	23	4	8

Source: 1993 Household Integrated Survey

Madagascar

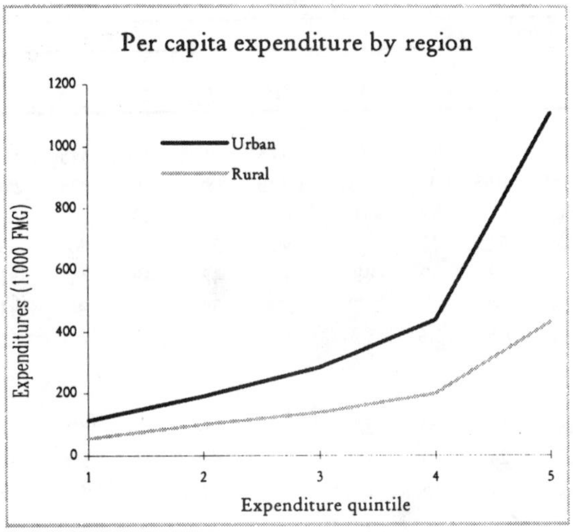
Per capita expenditure by region
Urban
Rural
Expenditures (1,000 FMG)
Expenditure quintile

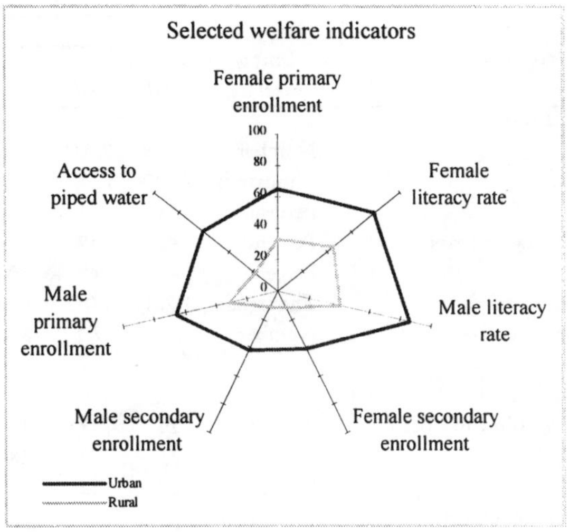
Selected welfare indicators
Female primary enrollment
Female literacy rate
Male literacy rate
Female secondary enrollment
Male secondary enrollment
Male primary enrollment
Access to piped water
Urban
Rural

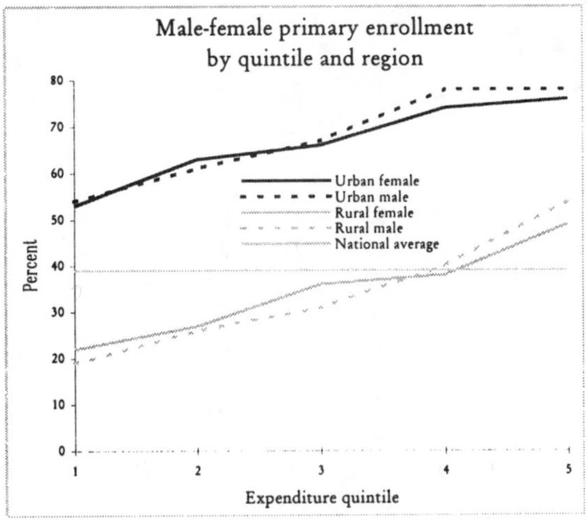
Male-female primary enrollment by quintile and region
Urban female
Urban male
Rural female
Rural male
National average
Percent
Expenditure quintile

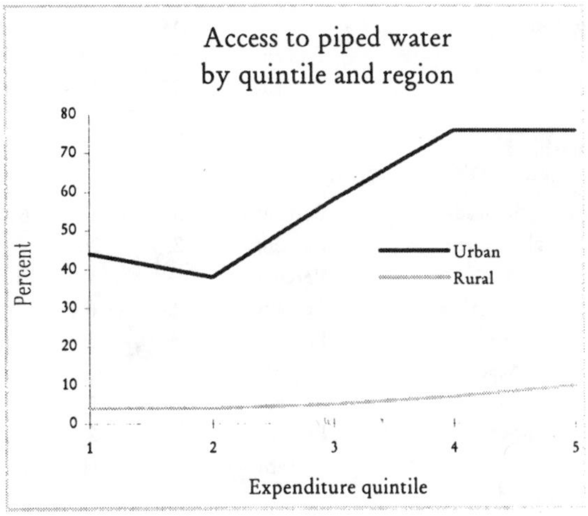
Access to piped water by quintile and region
Urban
Rural
Percent
Expenditure quintile

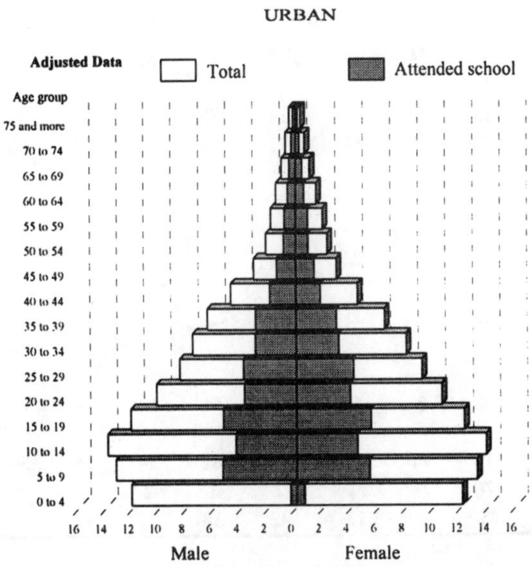
URBAN
Adjusted Data
Total
Attended school
Age group
Male
Female

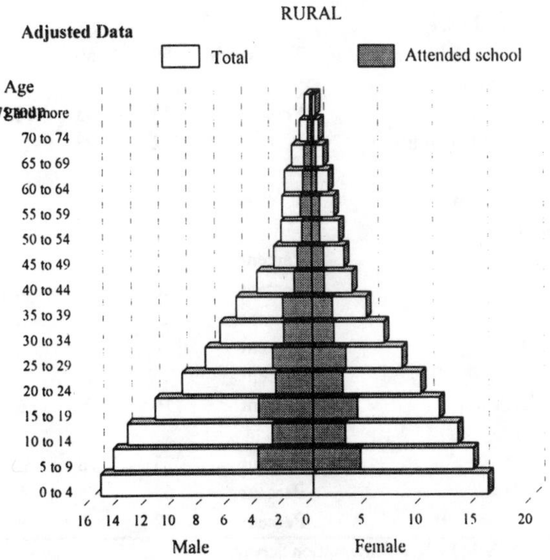
RURAL
Adjusted Data
Total
Attended school
Age group
Male
Female

15-10. Niger: household welfare indicators

Indicator	Unit of measure	National total	Expenditure quintile: Rural All	Rural 1	Rural 2	Rural 3	Rural 4	Rural 5	Urban All	Urban 1	Urban 2	Urban 3	Urban 4	Urban 5
Demographic indicators														
Sample size	Number	3,799	2,024	330	352	363	418	561	1,775	293	323	345	358	456
Total population	Thousands	8,710	7,265	1,454	1,455	1,453	1,451	1,453	1,445	289	290	289	290	290
Female	Percent	51	51	51	50	51	52	51	51	50	50	51	52	49
Population below 15 years	Percent	49	49	53	52	52	48	43	50	55	52	52	49	44
Female	Percent	49	49	50	48	49	50	49	49	47	49	50	51	47
Number of households	Thousands	1,221	1,017	166	174	185	220	272	204	35	36	40	41	54
Average household size	Number	7.1	7.1	8.8	8.3	7.9	6.6	5.3	7.1	8.4	8.2	7.3	7.1	5.4
Education and literacy														
Net primary enrollment (total)	Percent	26	17	13	19	17	20	22	65	58	66	67	74	78
Male	Percent	33	24	18	25	24	25	28	74	64	73	73	83	81
Female	Percent	20	12	7	12	11	15	15	61	50	60	60	65	74
Net secondary enrollment (total)	Percent	..	..	..	..	..	..	..	..	..	..	..	..	..
Male	Percent	..	..	..	..	..	..	..	..	..	..	..	..	..
Female	Percent	..	..	..	..	..	..	..	..	..	..	..	..	..
Literacy rate (total)	Percent	38	36	28	30	33	38	48	47	38	43	45	49	57
Male	Percent	54	53	42	47	52	56	64	62	54	61	61	65	69
Female	Percent	23	21	16	15	17	22	33	33	25	28	31	35	46
Head of household														
Marital status of head														
Monogamous male-headed	Percent	59	60	61	58	61	60	59	54	55	54	60	55	48
Polygamous male-headed	Percent	25	26	25	26	30	27	22	23	26	27	22	25	19
Single male-headed	Percent	4	4	3	4	1	3	7	6	3	4	4	5	13
Defacto female-headed	Percent	6	6	7	8	4	6	6	3	5	4	3	2	3
Dejure female-headed	Percent	6	5	4	4	3	4	7	13	11	12	11	13	17
Education level of head														
Completed primary	Percent	6	5	5	5	4	4	6	11	4	7	11	14	14
Completed secondary	Percent	3	2	1	1	0	1	4	11	2	2	6	8	27
Illiterate	Percent	91	94	94	94	96	95	90	79	94	92	83	78	59
Employment of head														
Agro-pastoral activities	Percent	76	88	92	92	89	91	82	13	19	17	16	12	6
Household expenditure														
Mean per capita expenditure (CFAF)	Thousands	58	50	21	32	42	54	99	98	33	53	73	104	226
Population below relative poverty line	Percent	38	43	100	100	15	0	0	14	73	0	0	0	0
Food share in total expenditure	Percent	32	29	27	27	26	29	35	51	57	56	54	50	40
Household amenities														
Type of fuel for cooking														
Firewood	Percent	..	..	..	..	..	..	..	..	..	..	..	..	..
Gas, kerosine	Percent	..	..	..	..	..	..	..	..	..	..	..	..	..
Charcoal	Percent	..	..	..	..	..	..	..	..	..	..	..	..	..
Electricity	Percent	..	..	..	..	..	..	..	..	..	..	..	..	..
Other	Percent	..	..	..	..	..	..	..	..	..	..	..	..	..
Access to sanitation	Percent	16	5	6	2	4	3	9	72	51	64	74	76	84
Access to water														
Pipe	Percent	25	18	17	17	19	21	17	56	61	54	56	54	57
Well/bore hole	Percent	63	75	75	79	76	74	71	2	1	2	2	3	1
Other	Percent	12	7	8	4	5	5	12	42	38	44	42	43	42

Source: 1993 Household Budget Consumption Survey.

Niger

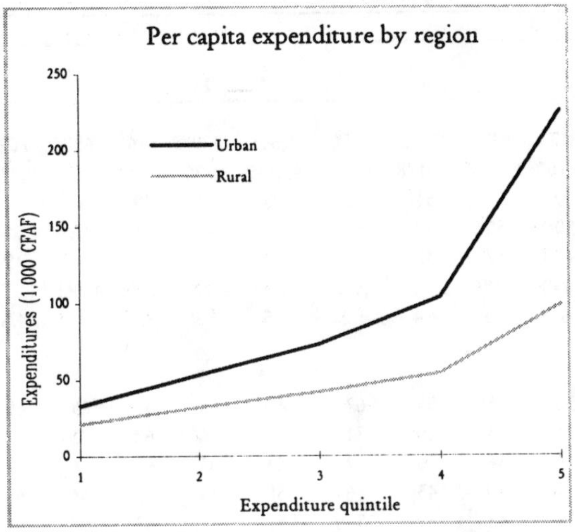

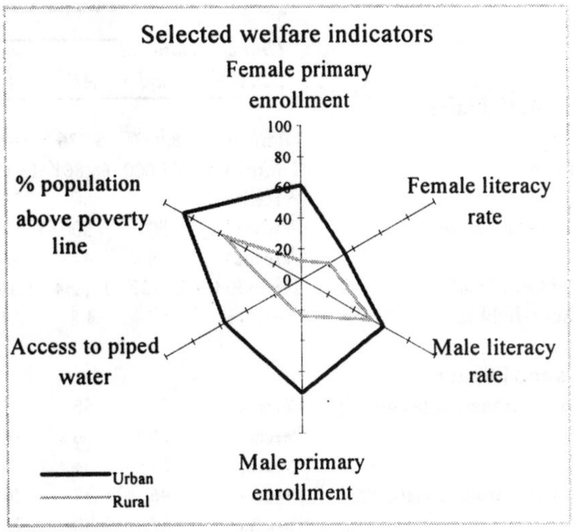

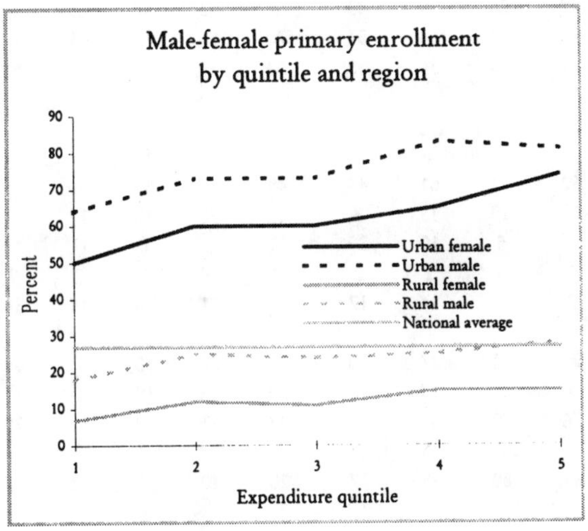

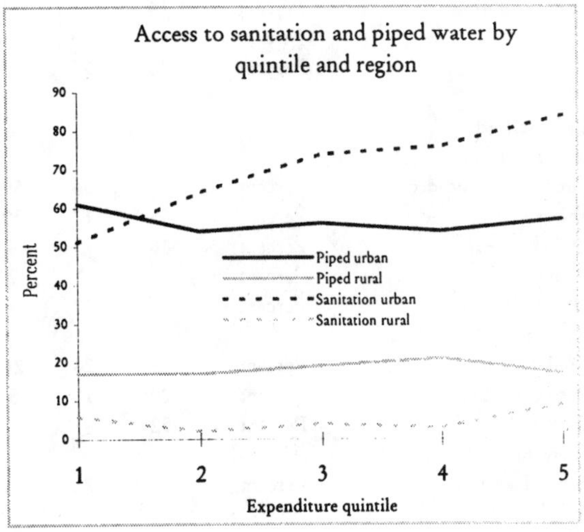

Urban

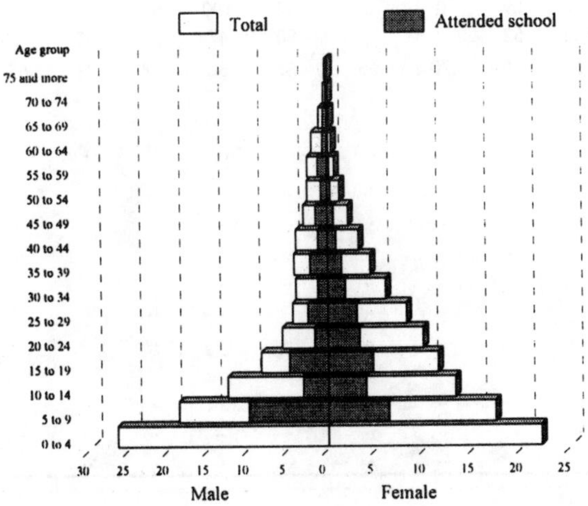

Rural

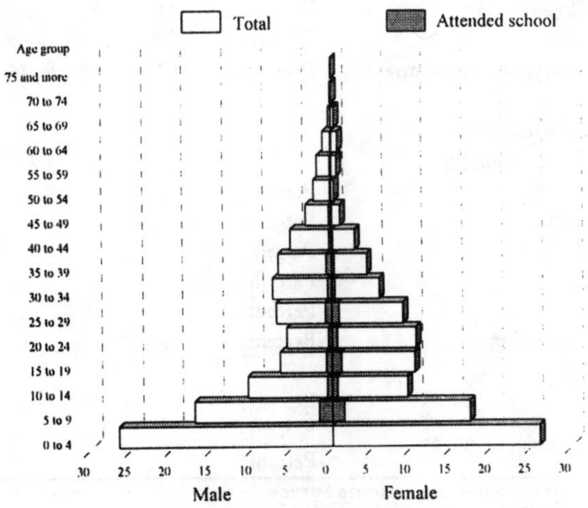

15-11. Nigeria: household welfare indicators

Indicator	Unit of measure	National total	Expenditure quintiles: Rural All	Rural 1	Rural 2	Rural 3	Rural 4	Rural 5	Urban All	Urban 1	Urban 2	Urban 3	Urban 4	Urban 5
Demographic Indicators														
Sample size	Number	8,937	5,276	686	817	917	1,100	1,756	3,661	479	616	658	702	1,206
Total population	Thousands	107,000	65,861	13,183	13,160	13,177	13,178	13,163	41,139	8,220	8,226	8,251	8,220	8,221
Female	Percent	50	50	50	50	50	51	50	50	47	49	52	51	49
Population below 15 years	Percent	50	50	50	50	50	51	50	50	47	49	52	51	49
Female	Percent	48	47	48	47	47	47	48	49	49	50	50	49	47
Number of households	Thousands	22,739	13,654	1,863	2,190	2,486	2,962	4,153	9,085	1,119	1,425	1,541	1,777	3,223
Average household size	Number	4.7	4.8	7.1	6	5.3	4.4	3.2	4.5	7.3	5.8	5.4	4.6	2.6
Education and literacy														
Net primary enrollment (total)	Percent	59	55	48	50	55	58	67	65	55	63	69	69	74
Male	Percent	60	56	48	51	54	59	71	66	56	62	71	72	74
Female	Percent	58	54	47	49	56	56	62	64	55	65	66	67	73
Net secondary enrollment (total)	Percent	46	38	26	34	40	45	46	58	41	59	64	63	61
Male	Percent	48	40	23	38	43	49	50	59	42	67	67	61	64
Female	Percent	45	36	29	30	37	42	42	56	39	50	61	66	58
Literacy rates (total)	Percent	44	33	23	27	28	39	43	62	43	47	65	70	74
Male	Percent	51	39	28	33	34	44	51	70	55	60	71	77	81
Female	Percent	36	27	19	21	23	34	35	53	31	36	59	63	66
Head of household														
Marital status of head														
Monogamous male-headed	Percent	53	56	59	62	64	61	44	49	52	58	60	59	33
Polygamous male-headed	Percent	15	17	30	26	19	13	8	12	31	18	12	9	4
Single male-headed	Percent	16	13	4	3	5	10	29	21	5	8	11	15	41
Defacto female-headed	Percent	2	2	2	1	3	2	2	2	2	1	2	2	2
Dejure female-headed	Percent	13	12	4	7	9	14	17	16	11	14	15	14	21
Education level of head														
Completed primary	Percent	28	26	24	20	23	27	30	32	28	30	36	39	29
Completed econdary	Percent	20	11	5	4	7	13	18	33	19	19	29	33	47
Illiterate	Percent	52	63	71	76	70	60	52	35	53	52	35	29	23
Employment of head														
Agro-pastoral activities	Percent	52	73	91	84	80	69	57	20	40	26	18	17	13
Household Expenditure														
Mean per capita expenditure (Naira)	Value	744	708	161	328	483	702	1866	802	264	471	657	891	1729
Population below relative poverty line	Percent	44	52	100	100	59	0	0	32	100	61	0	0	0
Female	Percent	50	51	48	52	52	.	.	50	47	51	50	.	.
Food share in total expenditure	Percent	67	68	76	76	76	70	65	66	80	78	71	67	61
Household Amenities														
Type of fuel for cooking														
Firewood	Percent	..	..	..	..	..	..	..	..	..	..	..	..	..
Gas, Kerosine	Percent	..	..	..	..	..	..	..	..	..	..	..	..	..
Charcoal	Percent	..	..	..	..	..	..	..	..	..	..	..	..	..
Electricity	Percent	..	..	..	..	..	..	..	..	..	..	..	..	..
Other	Percent	..	..	..	..	..	..	..	..	..	..	..	..	..
Access to Sanitation	Percent	..	..	..	..	..	..	..	..	..	..	..	..	..
Access to Water														
Pipe	Percent	..	..	..	..	..	..	..	..	..	..	..	..	..
Well	Percent	..	..	..	..	..	..	..	..	..	..	..	..	..
Other	Percent	..	..	..	..	..	..	..	..	..	..	..	..	..

Source: 1992 Consumer Expenditure Survey

Nigeria

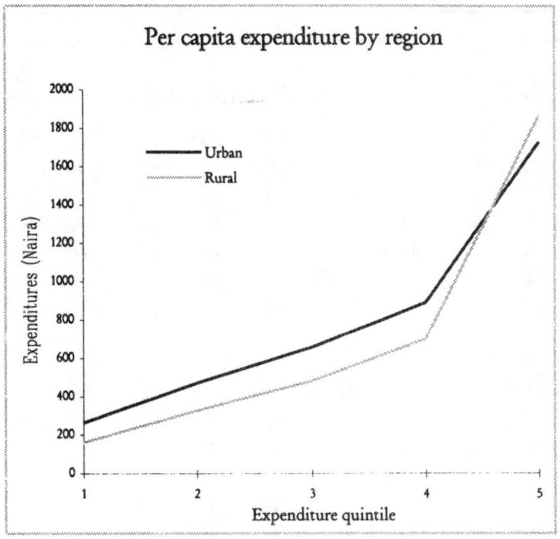
Per capita expenditure by region
Urban
Rural
Expenditures (Naira)
2000
1800
1600
1400
1200
1000
800
600
400
200
0
1
2
3
4
5
Expenditure quintile

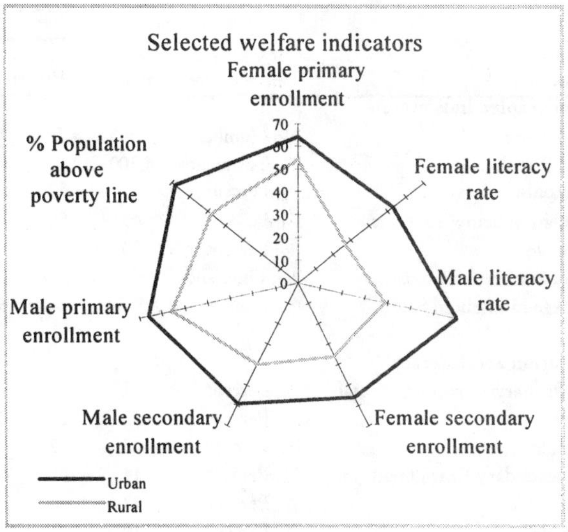
Selected welfare indicators
Female primary enrollment
Female literacy rate
Male literacy rate
Female secondary enrollment
Male secondary enrollment
Male primary enrollment
% Population above poverty line
70
60
50
40
30
20
10
0
Urban
Rural

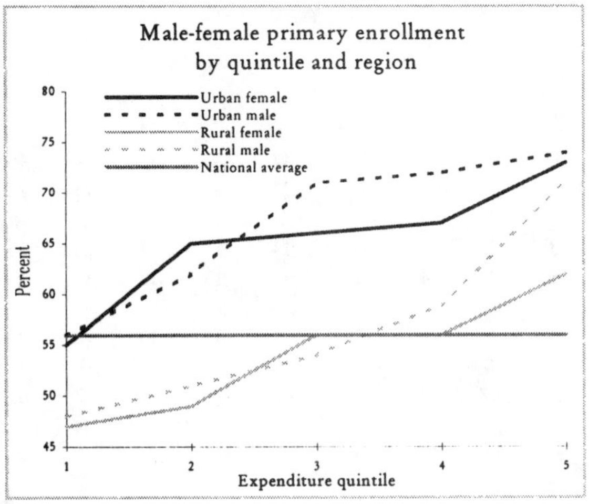
Male-female primary enrollment by quintile and region
Urban female
Urban male
Rural female
Rural male
National average
Percent
80
75
70
65
60
55
50
45
1
2
3
4
5
Expenditure quintile

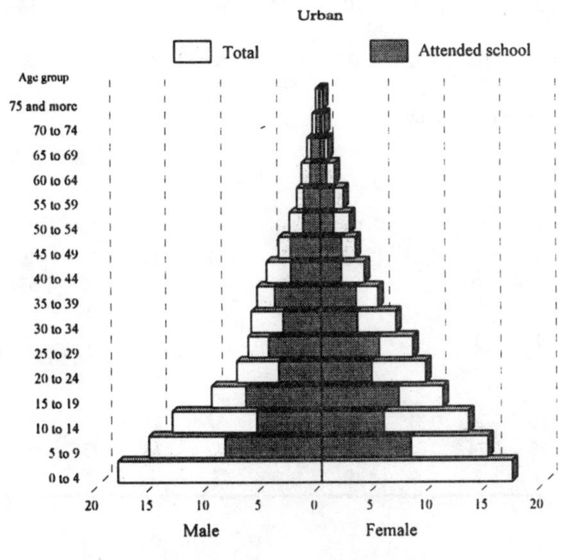
Urban
Total
Attended school
Age group
75 and more
70 to 74
65 to 69
60 to 64
55 to 59
50 to 54
45 to 49
40 to 44
35 to 39
30 to 34
25 to 29
20 to 24
15 to 19
10 to 14
5 to 9
0 to 4
20
15
10
5
0
5
10
15
20
Male
Female

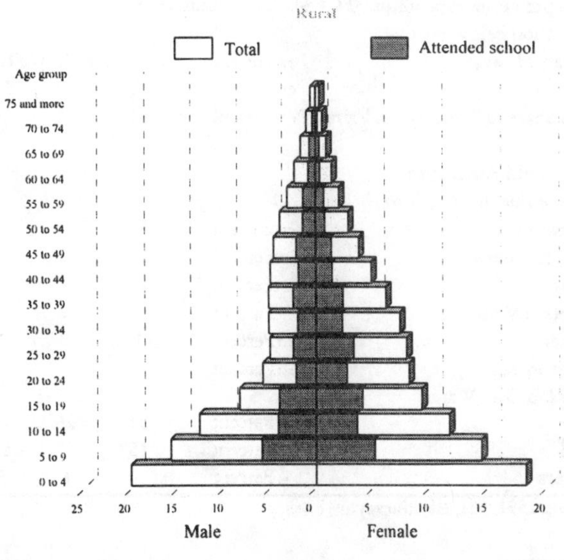
Rural
Total
Attended school
Age group
75 and more
70 to 74
65 to 69
60 to 64
55 to 59
50 to 54
45 to 49
40 to 44
35 to 39
30 to 34
25 to 29
20 to 24
15 to 19
10 to 14
5 to 9
0 to 4
25
20
15
10
5
0
5
10
15
20
Male
Female

15-12. Senegal: household welfare indicators

			Expenditure quintiles											
			Rural						*Urban*					
Indicator	*Unit of measure*	*National total*	*All*	*1*	*2*	*3*	*4*	*5*	*All*	*1*	*2*	*3*	*4*	*5*
Demographic indicators														
Sample Size	Number	9,955	4,158	760	744	788	816	1,050	5,797	709	859	981	1,203	2,045
Total Population	Thousands	8,300	4,948	991	989	990	990	990	3,352	670	674	668	670	670
Female	Percent	51	52	51	51	53	53	54	51	52	52	52	51	49
Population below 15 Years	Percent	45	50	52	51	50	49	47	42	51	48	46	43	36
Female	Percent	50	49	49	48	50	48	50	50	49	50	51	49	51
Number of Households	Thousands	951	548	102	98	105	108	136	403	59	64	69	83	128
Average Household Size	Number	8.7	9	9.7	10.1	9.5	9.2	7.3	8.3	11.4	10.5	9.6	8.1	5.2
Education and Literacy														
Net Primary Enrollment (total)	Percent	31	17	15	13	16	20	22	54	39	51	54	61	71
Male	Percent	35	22	21	18	19	24	27	58	45	54	58	65	73
Female	Percent	27	12	9	8	13	15	18	50	33	48	50	57	70
Net Secondary Enrollment (total)	Percent	14	3	2	2	1	3	5	27	16	17	25	28	53
Male	Percent	18	4	4	3	2	5	8	34	24	24	32	37	61
Female	Percent	10	1	1	1	1	2	2	20	8	11	18	21	45
Literacy Rates (total)	Percent	45	33	30	34	33	31	38	61	47	54	59	64	77
Male	Percent	67	56	47	55	58	57	63	80	72	76	77	82	87
Female	Percent	27	15	16	16	13	12	19	44	27	34	42	47	65
Household Head														
Marital Status of Head														
Monogamous Male-headed	Percent	47	47	48	48	48	51	43	47	43	42	44	46	52
Polygamous Male-headed	Percent	30	35	41	42	38	31	28	23	31	26	25	21	16
Single Male-headed	Percent	4	3	2	2	3	3	4	5	2	2	3	4	10
Defacto Female-headed	Percent	11	9	4	3	7	11	18	13	11	17	15	14	10
Dejure Female-headed	Percent	8	5	5	5	5	4	6	13	13	13	13	15	12
Education Level of Head														
Completed Primary	Percent	11	4	3	3	3	4	6	21	10	15	20	25	28
Completed Secondary	Percent	5	1			0	0	2	10	1	0	3	6	27
Illiterate	Percent	84	96	97	97	97	95	92	68	89	85	77	69	45
Employment of Head														
Agro-pastoral Activities	Percent	46	74	90	85	80	71	54	7	18	8	7	5	3
Household Expenditure														
Mean per capita expenditure (FCFA)	Thousands	8	4	1	2	3	5	10	14	4	7	9	14	38
Population below relative poverty Line	Percent	55	78	100	100	100	92	0	21	100	6	0	0	0
Female		52	52	51	51	53	53	.	52	52	52	.	.	.
Food Share in Total Expenditure	Percent	61	65	56	69	71	69	61	55	68	63	58	50	36
Household Amenities														
Type of Fuel for Cooking														
Firewood	Percent	61	94	98	98	98	96	84	16	47	25	16	9	2
Gas, Kerosene	Percent	16	2	1	1	1	2	6	35	10	20	25	36	60
Charcoal	Percent	21	4		0	0	2	10	46	42	53	58	53	33
Electricity	Percent	1	0					0	1	0	0	0	1	1
Other	Percent	1	0	1	1	1	0	0	2	1	2	1	1	4
Access to Sanitation	Percent													
Access to Safe Water														
Pipe	Percent	51	26	14	19	23	31	39	86	67	81	85	90	94
Well	Percent	45	68	81	78	74	63	51	13	32	18	13	8	4
Others	Percent	4	6	5	3	3	6	10	2	2	1	2	3	2

Source: 1991 Priority Survey.

Senegal

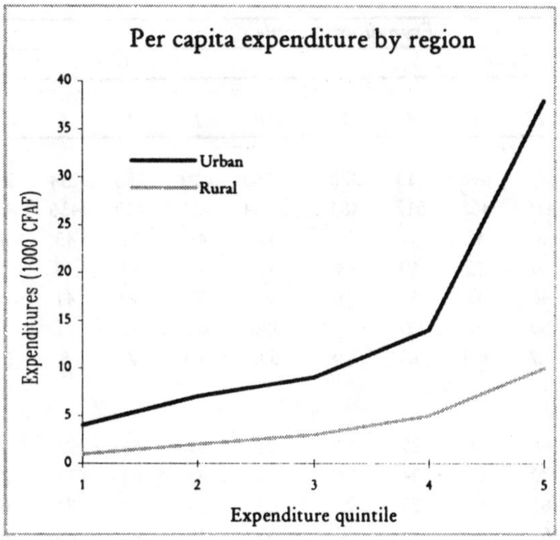
Per capita expenditure by region
Urban
Rural
Expenditures (1000 CFAF)
Expenditure quintile

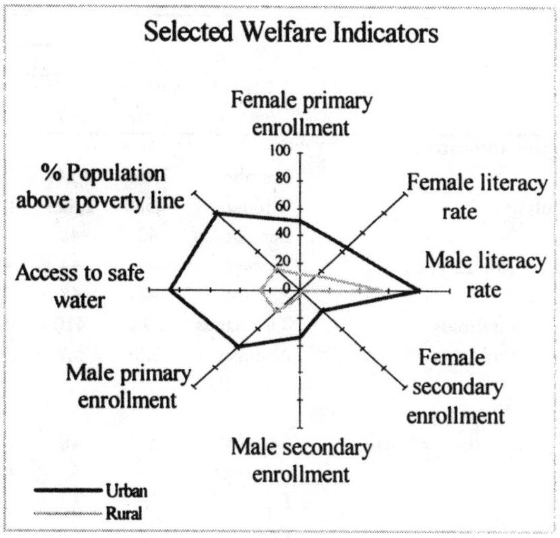
Selected Welfare Indicators
Female primary enrollment
Female literacy rate
Male literacy rate
Female secondary enrollment
Male secondary enrollment
Male primary enrollment
Access to safe water
% Population above poverty line
Urban
Rural

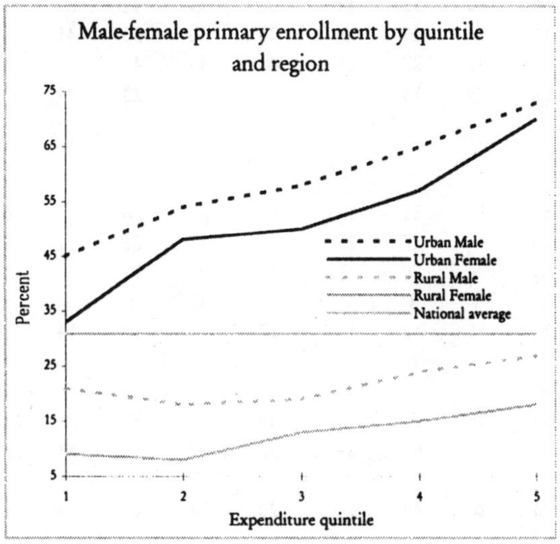
Male-female primary enrollment by quintile and region
Urban Male
Urban Female
Rural Male
Rural Female
National average
Percent
Expenditure quintile

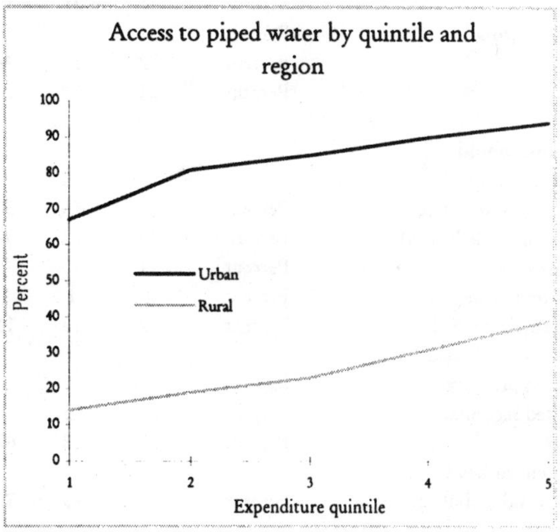
Access to piped water by quintile and region
Urban
Rural
Percent
Expenditure quintile

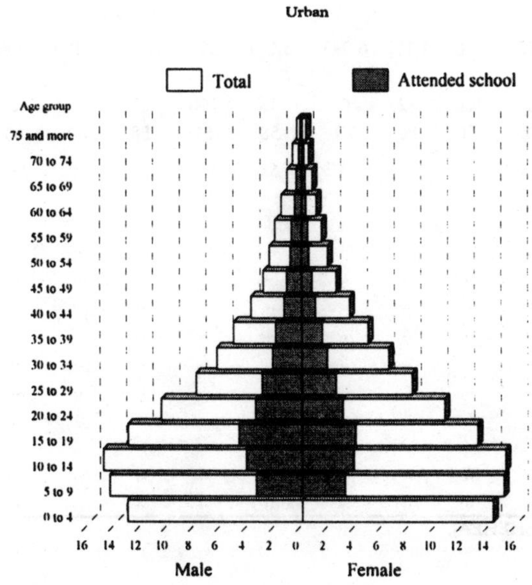
Urban
Total
Attended school
Age group
Male
Female

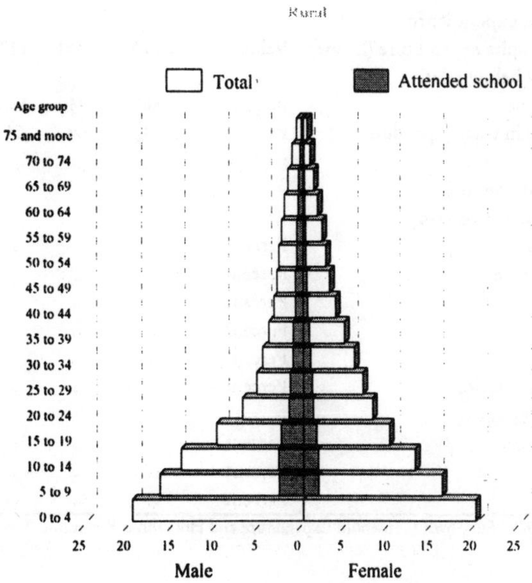
Rural
Total
Attended school
Age group
Male
Female

15-13. Sierra Leone: household welfare indicators

			Expenditure quintile											
			Rural						*Urban*					
Indicator	*Unit of measure*	*National total*	*All*	*1*	*2*	*3*	*4*	*5*	*All*	*1*	*2*	*3*	*4*	*5*
Demographic indicators														
Sample size	Number	3,407	2,244	202	363	596	713	370	1,163	200	186	234	244	299
Total population	Thousands	4,580	2,426	471	486	468	517	484	2,154	431	429	436	429	431
Female	Percent	48	48	49	46	47	50	50	47	49	51	45	47	44
Population below 15 years	Percent	45	44	48	50	42	40	44	47	43	49	49	48	46
Female	Percent	47	48	49	46	47	49	48	45	50	49	41	46	39
Number of households	Thousands	796	410	36	60	96	127	91	386	68	61	72	78	105
Average household size	Number	5.8	5.9	13.1	8.2	4.9	4.1	5.3	5.6	6.3	7	6	5.5	4.1
Education and literacy														
Net primary enrollment (total)	Percent	55	48	63	66	66	29	23	62	62	55	77	68	75
Male	Percent	63	53	66	70	67	34	24	72	65	61	78	71	81
Female	Percent	54	47	59	61	64	23	22	63	59	50	75	65	66
Net secondary enrollment (total)	Percent	47	42	50	62	50	17	17	53	42	46	63	62	58
Male	Percent	53	48	59	66	58	22	17	59	45	49	65	72	69
Female	Percent	40	35	40	56	40	12	17	46	39	42	60	52	40
Literacy rate (total)	Percent	32	27	36	41	37	19	9	38	36	33	41	39	40
Male	Percent	42	37	48	53	46	27	15	47	43	45	53	48	48
Female	Percent	23	19	26	28	29	11	4	28	29	23	29	29	29
Head of household														
Marital status of head														
Monogamous male-headed	Percent	57	55	30	57	71	51	53	59	63	56	57	60	60
Polygamous male-headed	Percent	19	22	57	29	9	17	25	16	17	22	22	12	10
Single male-headed	Percent	11	10	2	2	5	20	9	12	5	11	6	14	19
Defacto female-headed	Percent	1	1	1	0	1	1	0	1	0	1	1	2	0
Dejure female-headed	Percent	12	13	11	11	15	12	13	12	14	10	14	13	10
Education level of head														
Completed primary	Percent	8	7	5	8	7	7	8	9	8	8	9	10	8
Completed secondary	Percent	29	25	28	35	35	24	8	34	30	33	33	33	38
Illiterate	Percent	63	68	67	58	58	69	84	57	62	58	58	57	53
Employment of head														
Agro-pastoral activities	Percent	33	45	35	24	20	49	82	20	24	27	23	17	15
Household expenditure														
Mean per capita expenditure (Leone)	Value	2,275	1,551	117	157	226	1,117	6,083	3,091	303	1,231	2,280	3,585	8,057
Population below relative poverty line	Percent	56	74	100	100	100	72	0	36	100	83	0	0	0
Food share in total expenditure	Percent	64	69	51	62	71	80	79	58	51	58	60	60	61
Household amenities														
Type of fuel for cooking														
Firewood	Percent	..	..	..	..	..	..	..	..	..	..	..	..	..
Gas, kerosine	Percent	..	..	..	..	..	..	..	..	..	..	..	..	..
Charcoal	Percent	..	..	..	..	..	..	..	..	..	..	..	..	..
Electricity	Percent	..	..	..	..	..	..	..	..	..	..	..	..	..
Other	Percent	..	..	..	..	..	..	..	..	..	..	..	..	..
Access to sanitation	Percent	..	..	..	..	..	..	..	..	..	..	..	..	..
Access to water														
Pipe	Percent	..	..	..	..	..	..	..	..	..	..	..	..	..
Well/bore hole	Percent	..	..	..	..	..	..	..	..	..	..	..	..	..
Other	Percent	..	..	..	..	..	..	..	..	..	..	..	..	..

Source: 1989/90 Survey of Household Expenditure and Household Economic Activities (SHEHEA).

Sierra Leone

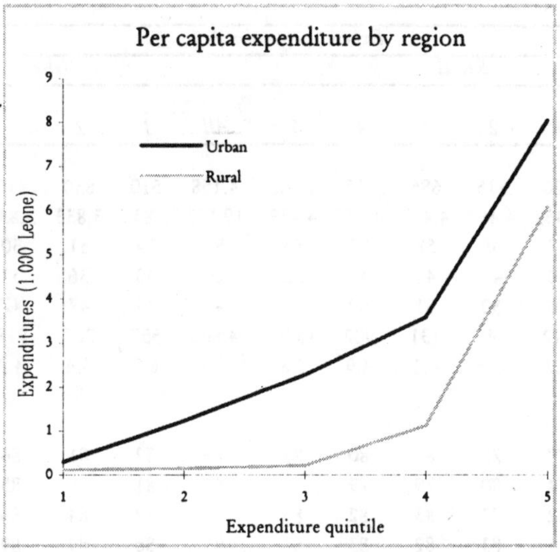

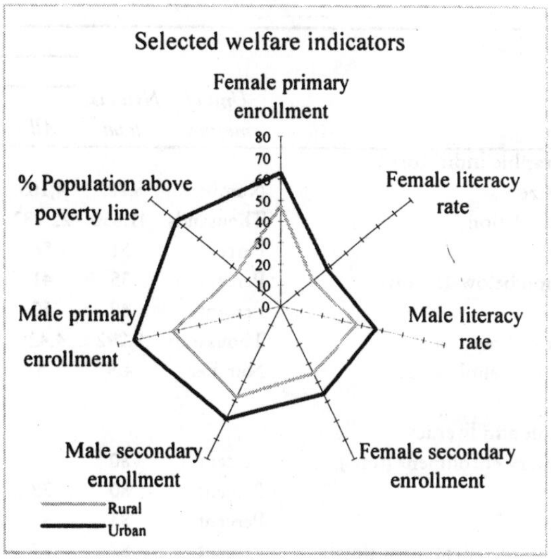

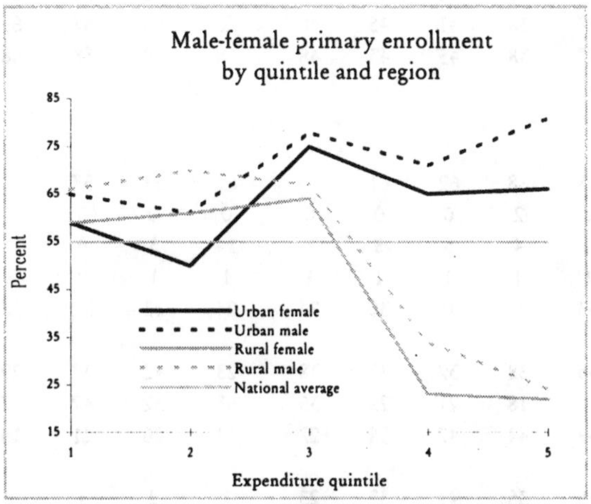

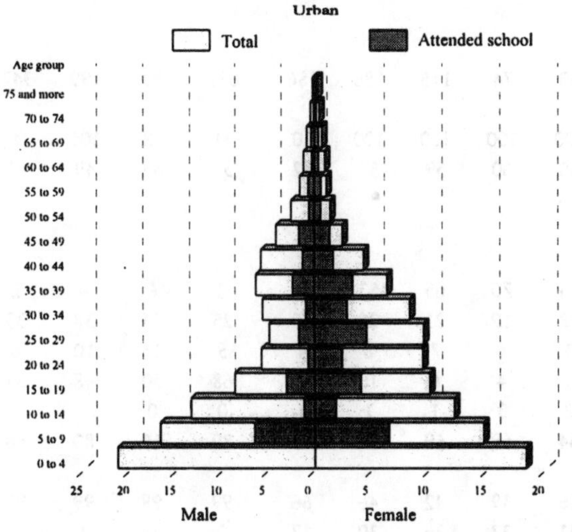

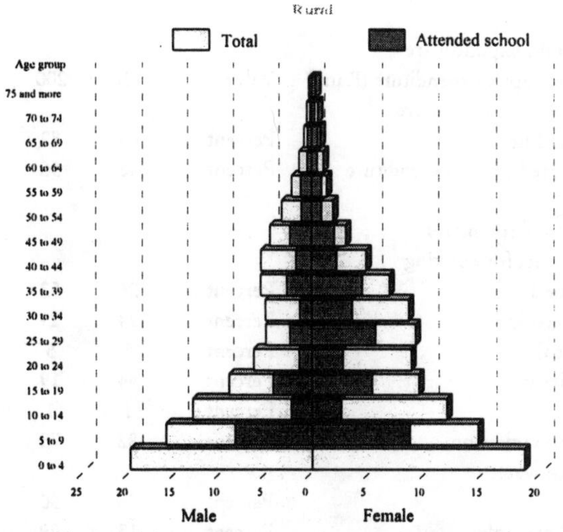

15-14. South Africa: household welfare indicators

			Expenditure quintile											
			Rural						*Urban*					
Indicator	*Unit of measure*	*National total*	*All*	*1*	*2*	*3*	*4*	*5*	*All*	*1*	*2*	*3*	*4*	*5*
Demographic indicators														
Sample size	Number	8,782	4,165	520	615	695	855	1,480	4,158	510	630	813	1,000	1,205
Total population	Thousands	41,650	22,287	4,455	4,460	4,457	4,457	4,459	19,173	3,834	3,833	3,838	3,834	3,833
Female	Percent	51	56	57	56	58	57	53	51	54	51	50	50	50
Population below 15 years	Percent	35	41	50	47	46	43	32	29	40	36	32	27	20
Female	Percent	49	50	50	50	51	50	49	49	49	47	47	50	49
Number of households	Thousands	9,292	4,426	542	645	731	902	1,607	4,866	557	707	918	1,172	1,511
Average household size	Number	4.5	5	8.2	6.9	6.1	4.9	2.8	3.9	6.9	5.4	4.2	3.3	2.5
Education and literacy														
Net primary enrollment (total)	Percent	80	80	78	78	81	80	83	79	82	81	86	85	82
Male	Percent	80	78	74	80	79	79	81	82	81	79	85	86	76
Female	Percent	83	81	82	77	83	82	85	85	82	84	86	85	88
Net secondary enrollment (total)	Percent	87	83	85	83	82	83	84	91	88	89	89	96	95
Male	Percent	87	84	85	84	83	84	86	91	90	90	88	96	94
Female	Percent	86	83	86	82	80	81	84	91	86	89	89	97	95
Literacy rate (total)	Percent	55	42	37	38	42	44	47	69	48	58	68	77	85
Male	Percent	55	42	37	38	41	45	46	70	48	57	69	77	87
Female	Percent	54	42	37	38	43	43	48	68	48	58	68	78	83
Head of household														
Marital status of head														
Monogamous male-headed	Percent	58	54	63	68	62	61	39	61	53	57	60	63	65
Polygamous male-headed	Percent	0	1	2	2	0	0	0	0	0	0		0	
Single male-headed	Percent	15	17	2	4	5	8	36	14	3	9	11	16	20
Defacto female-headed	Percent	1	1	1	1	1	1	1	1	1	2	2	1	1
Dejure female-headed	Percent	26	28	33	25	31	30	24	24	43	32	27	19	14
Education level of head														
Completed primary	Percent	30	37	35	38	37	37	38	23	42	37	29	19	7
Completed secondary	Percent	46	26	16	18	21	25	35	65	32	42	57	71	87
Illiterate	Percent	24	37	49	44	42	38	27	13	26	21	14	10	5
Employment of head														
Agro-pastoral activities	Percent	12	30	35	35	41	33	23	2	2	4	2	2	2
Household expenditure														
Mean per capita expenditure (Rand)	Value	402	200	40	74	115	186	586	632	90	199	347	670	1,853
Population below relative poverty line	Percent	63	82	100	100	100	100	10	41	100	100	4	0	0
Food share in total expenditure	Percent	48	56	60	60	59	57	42	39	55	49	42	31	18
Household amenities														
Type of fuel for cooking														
Firewood	Percent	26	52	74	70	65	53	30	2	6	4	2	1	0
Gas, kerosine	Percent	24	23	18	19	21	28	25	25	53	38	33	21	8
Charcoal	Percent	5	5	3	4	7	8	4	5	11	10	6	3	0
Electricity	Percent	44	19	3	4	6	10	40	68	30	48	59	75	92
Other	Percent	1	1	2	3	1	1	1	0	0			0	
Access to sanitation	Percent	82	75	64	68	69	74	85	89	66	80	86	94	99
Access to water														
Pipe	Percent	76	50	36	39	42	46	66	99	98	99	99	100	100
Well/bore hole	Percent	13	29	41	37	35	30	17	0	0	1	0	0	0
Other	Percent	11	21	23	24	23	24	17	1	2	0	1	0	0

Source: 1993 Living Standards and Development Survey.

South Africa

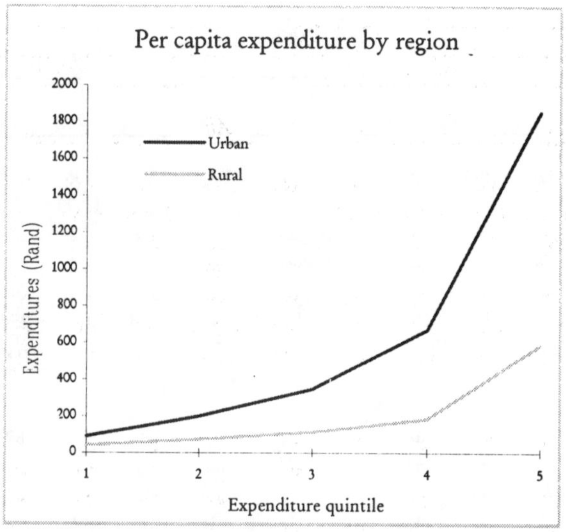

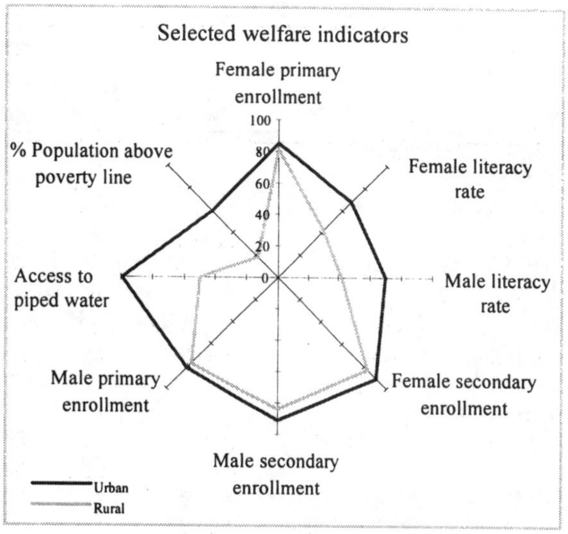

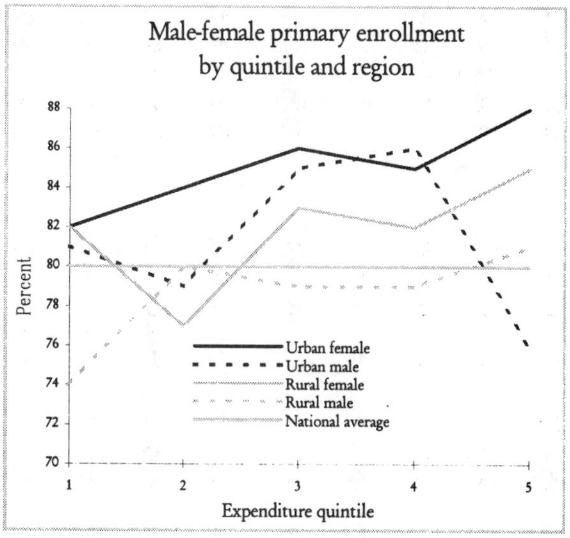

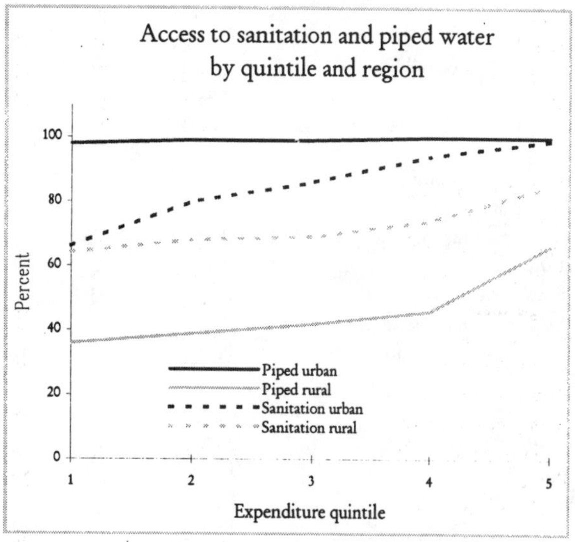

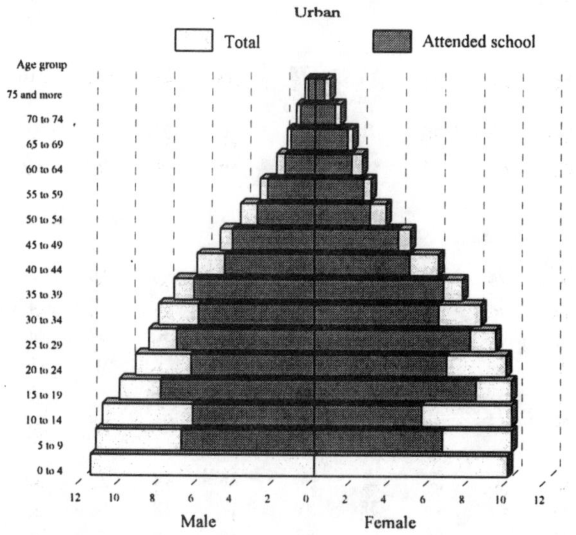

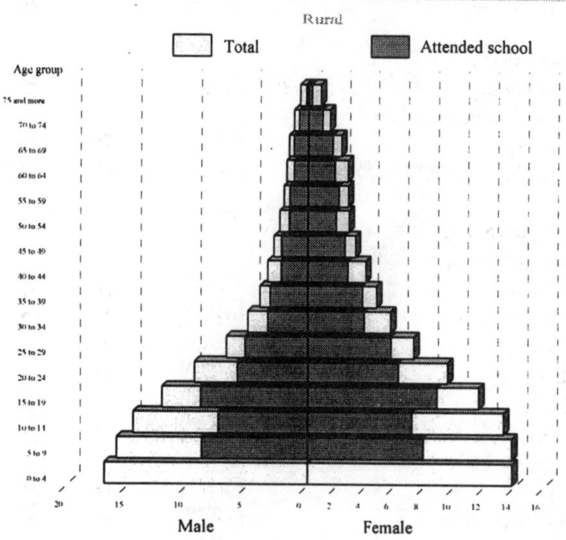

15-15. Tanzania: household welfare indicators

			Expenditure quintile											
			Rural						Urban					
Indicator	*Unit of measure*	*National total*	*All*	*1*	*2*	*3*	*4*	*5*	*All*	*1*	*2*	*3*	*4*	*5*
Demographic indicators														
Sample size	Number	5,184	2,262	321	383	420	503	635	2,922	278	405	426	728	1,085
Total population	Thousands	27,530	19,567	3,910	3,903	3,928	3,912	3,914	7,963	1,597	1,592	1,586	1,597	1,593
Female	Percent	51	51	52	52	50	49	51	51	52	52	52	51	49
Population below 15 years	Percent	46	49	54	54	50	49	42	43	52	49	48	42	37
Female	Percent	49	49	49	49	48	48	51	49	49	50	50	52	47
Number of households	Thousands	4,544	3,120	505	564	597	662	793	1,423	223	245	258	303	393
Average household size	Number	6.1	6.3	7.7	6.9	6.6	5.9	4.9	5.6	7.2	6.5	6.2	5.3	4.1
Education and literacy														
Net primary enrollment (total)	Percent	68	65	58	64	67	69	78	77	76	77	82	78	73
Male	Percent	69	66	61	61	64	67	81	76	71	73	83	77	75
Female	Percent	70	67	54	67	70	73	76	79	80	82	80	79	72
Net secondary enrollment (total)	Percent	12	8	2	4	9	10	13	21	5	14	24	26	38
Male	Percent	13	10	2	5	14	13	15	20	5	14	18	24	41
Female	Percent	10	5	2	3	4	6	11	22	5	15	32	29	34
Literacy rate (total)	Percent	74	70	62	66	73	73	76	81	70	81	80	85	88
Male	Percent	83	80	74	75	83	83	83	88	81	87	85	90	95
Female	Percent	66	62	52	59	63	63	69	75	61	75	75	79	81
Head of household														
Marital status of head														
Monogamous male-headed	Percent	76	77	71	77	81	79	76	74	78	78	73	72	69
Polygamous male-headed	Percent	7	9	15	10	7	9	7	3	5	3	6	2	1
Single male-headed	Percent	3	3	2	2	2	2	5	5	1	3	3	7	8
Defacto female-headed	Percent	1	1	1	0	1	1	2	1	2	0	2	0	2
Dejure female-headed	Percent	12	10	11	11	9	10	11	17	14	16	17	18	20
Education level of head														
Completed primary	Percent	66	66	61	61	70	69	68	64	66	66	63	65	63
Completed secondary	Percent	11	8	5	8	7	9	11	18	11	17	14	21	25
Illiterate	Percent	23	25	34	31	23	22	21	17	24	17	23	15	12
Employment of head														
Agro-pastoral activities	Percent	64	81	88	84	83	79	75	28	46	36	33	24	12
Household expenditure														
Mean per capita expenditure (TZS)	Thousands	106	86	33	52	70	96	178	154	53	84	116	164	356
Population below relative poverty line	Percent	42	52	100	100	58	0	0	20	97	0	0	0	0
Food share in total expenditure	Percent	70	72	73	73	74	73	70	63	69	66	60	64	55
Household amenities														
Type of fuel for cooking														
Firewood	Percent	79	96	100	98	98	97	93	42	69	59	45	37	18
Gas, kerosine	Percent	2	0		0		0	1	7	1	3	4	8	14
Charcoal	Percent	17	3	0	2	2	3	6	47	30	37	50	51	60
Electricity	Percent	1							3		1	1	4	7
Other	Percent	1	1			0		0	1	0		0	0	1
Access to sanitation	Percent	94	92	88	93	91	93	93	97	96	98	98	95	98
Access to water														
Pipe	Percent	12	2	1	1	1	2	4	35	14	20	27	40	57
Well/bore hole	Percent	31	38	34	43	33	38	39	17	38	16	23	11	5
Other	Percent	57	60	65	56	66	60	57	48	48	64	50	49	38

Source: 1993 Human Resource Development Survey.

Tanzania

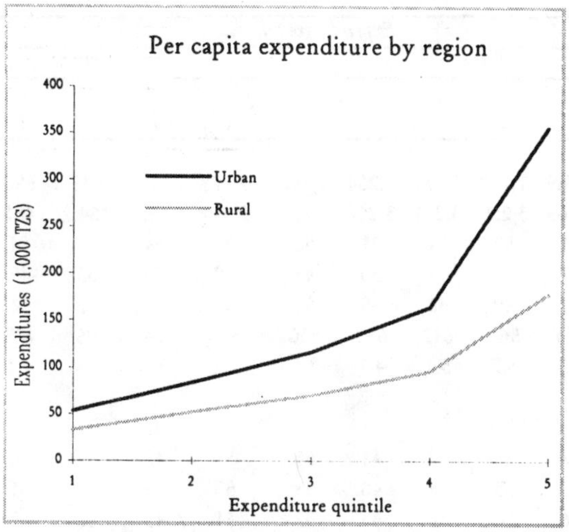
Per capita expenditure by region
Expenditures (1,000 TZS)
Urban
Rural
Expenditure quintile

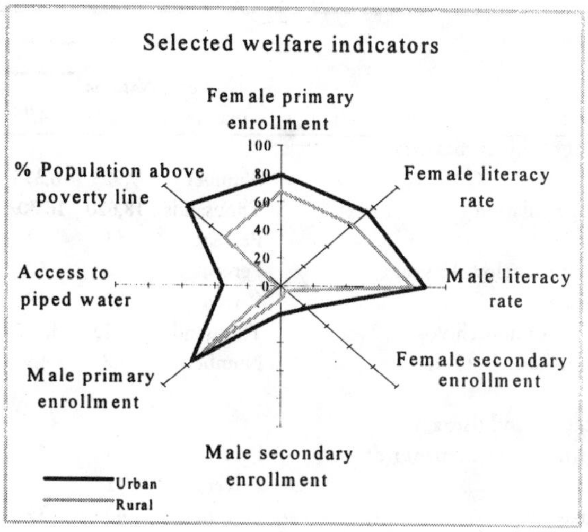
Selected welfare indicators
Female primary enrollment
Female literacy rate
Male literacy rate
Female secondary enrollment
Male secondary enrollment
Male primary enrollment
Access to piped water
% Population above poverty line
Urban
Rural

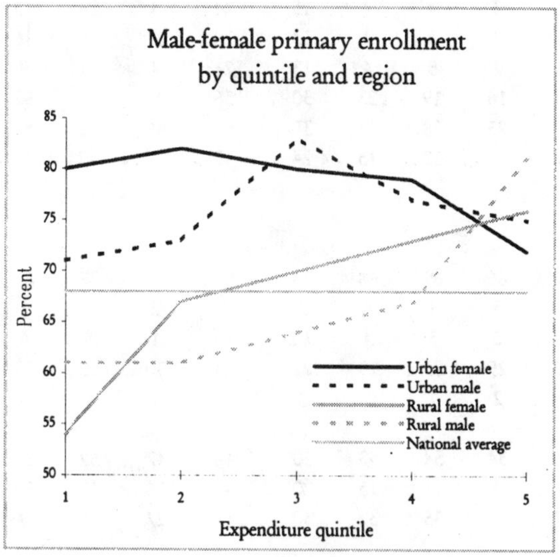
Male-female primary enrollment by quintile and region
Percent
Urban female
Urban male
Rural female
Rural male
National average
Expenditure quintile

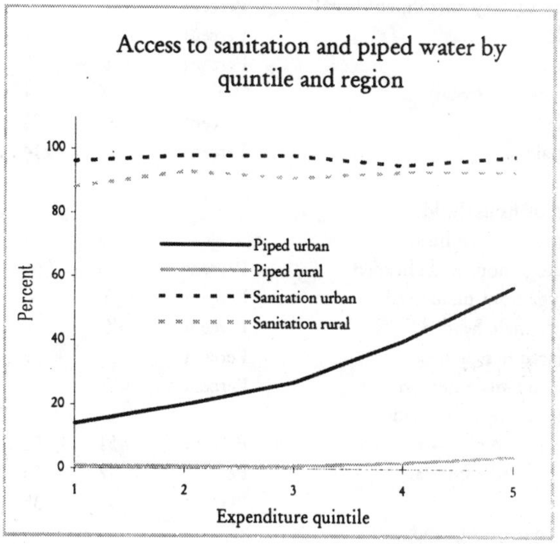
Access to sanitation and piped water by quintile and region
Percent
Piped urban
Piped rural
Sanitation urban
Sanitation rural
Expenditure quintile

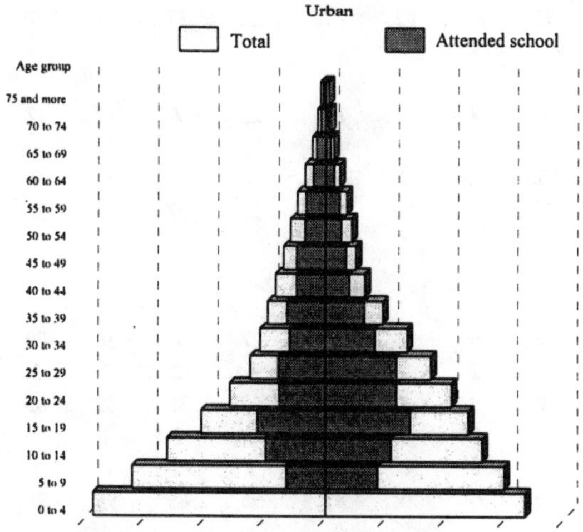
Urban
Total
Attended school
Age group
Male
Female

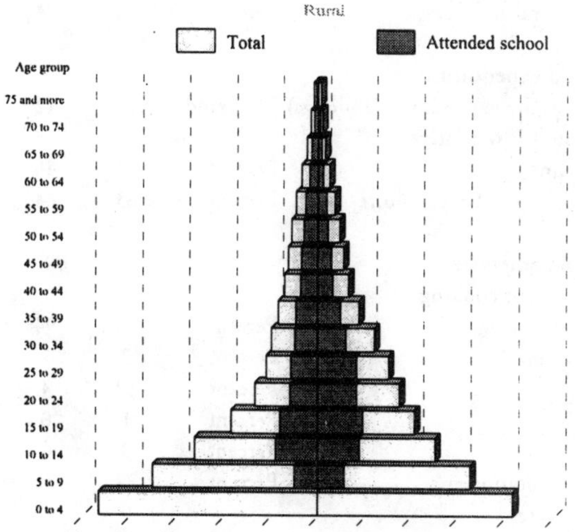
Rural
Total
Attended school
Age group
Male
Female

15-16. Uganda: household welfare indicators

			Expenditure quintile											
			Rural						*Urban*					
Indicator	*Unit of measure*	*National total*	*All*	*1*	*2*	*3*	*4*	*5*	*All*	*1*	*2*	*3*	*4*	*5*
Demographic indicators														
Sample size	Number	9,923	6,395	1,069	1,112	1,212	1,254	1,748	3,528	688	637	688	679	836
Total population	Thousands	18,620	16,307	3,265	3,259	3,261	3,262	3,261	2,312	462	464.2	461	466.3	459.9
Female	Percent	53	52	51	52	51	51	53	55	54	54	54	49	61
Population below 15 years	Percent	50	50	57	54	53	50	43	48	55	53	49	45	40
Female	Percent	50	49	49	49	48	48	50	51	52	52	54	44	53
Number of households	Thousands	3,913	3,347	514	569	642	690	930	566	84	96	108	121	157
Average household size	Number	4.8	4.9	6.3	5.7	5.1	4.7	3.5	4.1	5.5	4.9	4.3	3.9	2.9
Education and literacy														
Net primary enrollment (total)	Percent	39	37	27	36	37	44	55	57	42	52	56	57	62
Male	Percent	41	39	29	35	38	46	53	55	39	57	61	62	61
Female	Percent	40	39	26	36	37	43	57	51	45	48	53	51	62
Net secondary enrollment (total)	Percent	9	6	1	3	4	4	15	24	8	14	13	26	44
Male	Percent	9	6	1	4	3	4	17	28	11	18	16	33	47
Female	Percent	8	5	1	2	5	4	13	21	4	11	9	21	41
Literacy rate (total)	Percent	26	21	11	16	19	23	30	56	35	45	52	62	71
Male	Percent	33	28	17	23	28	31	37	63	48	51	58	68	75
Female	Percent	19	14	6	10	12	15	24	49	25	40	46	55	68
Head of household														
Marital status of head														
Monogamous male-headed	Percent	65	66	66	66	69	68	63	60	63	57	65	64	53
Polygamous male-headed	Percent	3	4	6	5	4	4	2	1	2	0	1	1	0
Single male-headed	Percent	5	5	1	2	3	4	10	10	1	5	6	10	20
Defacto female-headed	Percent	23	23	26	25	23	23	21	23	30	32	23	18	18
Dejure female-headed	Percent	3	2	1	2	1	2	3	6	4	4	5	7	9
Education level of head														
Completed primary	Percent	51	52	48	54	54	53	50	44	47	52	52	44	33
Completed secondary	Percent	17	13	5	9	11	15	20	44	26	33	39	46	62
Illiterate	Percent	32	35	47	37	35	32	30	11	27	15	9	10	4
Employment of head														
Agro-pastoral activities	Percent	75	84	92	90	88	82	75	22	37	34	17	17	14
Household expenditure														
Mean per capita expenditure (Shillings)	Thousands	13	12	4	7	9	13	24	25	7	12	17	25	62
Population below relative poverty line	Percent	42	46	100	100	29	0	0	16	78	0	0	0	0
Food share in total expenditure	Percent	63	64	63	65	65	66	63	51	57	55	53	51	42
Household amenities														
Type of fuel for cooking														
Firewood	Percent	85	94	98	98	96	94	90	27	61	36	29	19	8
Gas, kerosine	Percent	2	2	1	1	2	2	2	5	2	1	3	3	11
Charcoal	Percent	12	4	1	1	2	4	8	62	35	62	65	74	66
Electricity	Percent	1	0	0	0	0	0	0	5	2	1	2	3	13
Other	Percent	0	0	0	0	0	0	0	1	0	0	1	1	2
Access to sanitation	Percent	78	75	61	69	77	79	81	95	89	95	95	96	98
Access to water														
Pipe	Percent	7	2	1	1	2	2	3	35	19	26	28	40	49
Well/bore hole	Percent	54	55	53	54	55	54	57	51	56	57	59	46	44
Other	Percent	39	43	46	45	43	44	40	14	25	17	13	14	7

Source: 1993 Integrated Household Survey.

Uganda

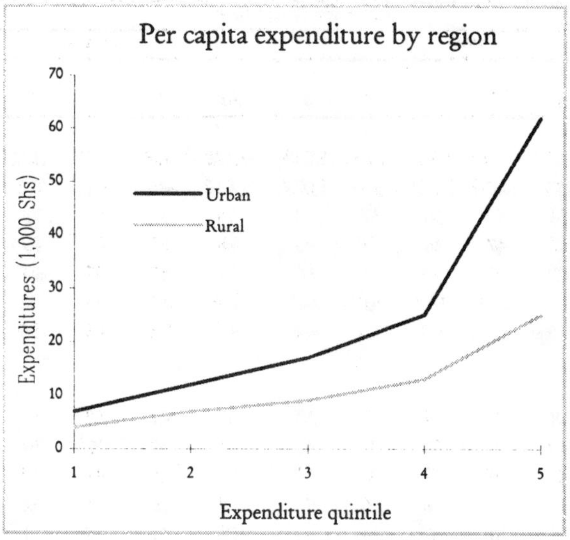
Per capita expenditure by region
Urban
Rural
Expenditures (1,000 Shs)
70
60
50
40
30
20
10
0
1
2
3
4
5
Expenditure quintile

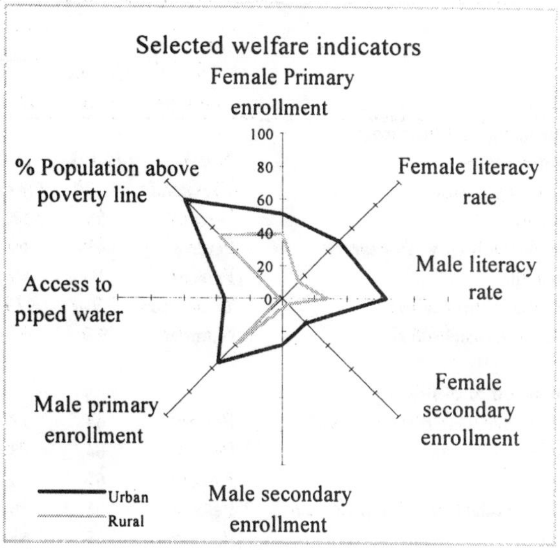
Selected welfare indicators
Female Primary enrollment
Female literacy rate
Male literacy rate
Female secondary enrollment
Male secondary enrollment
Male primary enrollment
Access to piped water
% Population above poverty line
100
80
60
40
20
0
Urban
Rural

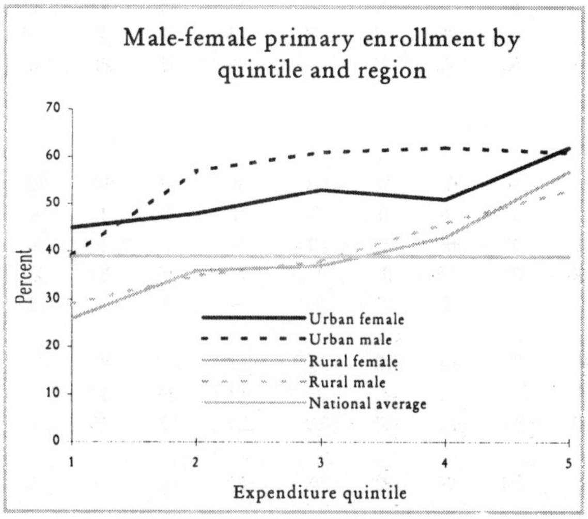
Male-female primary enrollment by quintile and region
Percent
70
60
50
40
30
20
10
0
Urban female
Urban male
Rural female
Rural male
National average
1
2
3
4
5
Expenditure quintile

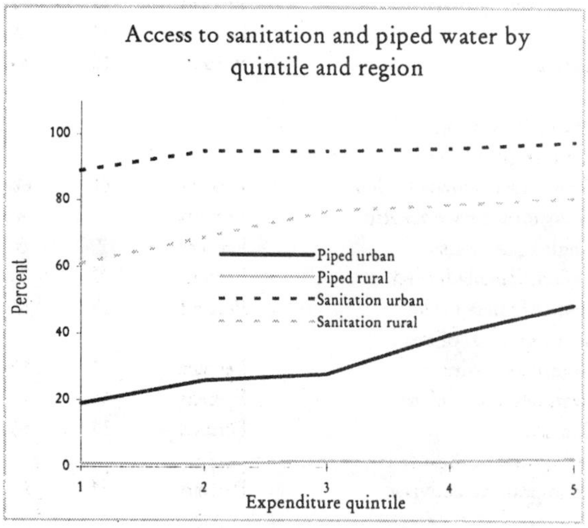
Access to sanitation and piped water by quintile and region
Percent
100
80
60
40
20
0
Piped urban
Piped rural
Sanitation urban
Sanitation rural
1
2
3
4
5
Expenditure quintile

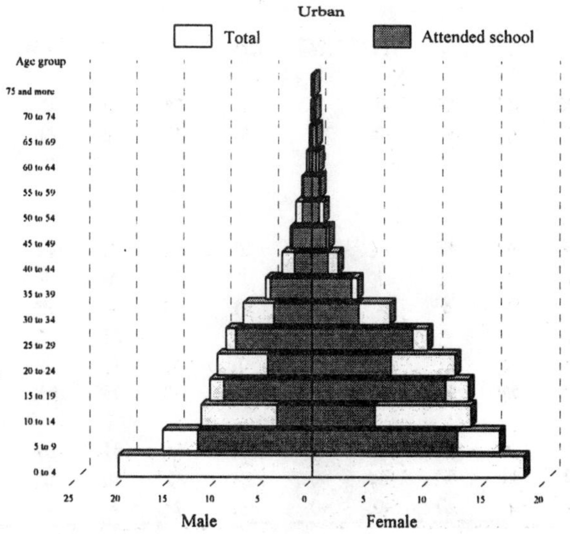
Urban
Total
Attended school
Age group
75 and more
70 to 74
65 to 69
60 to 64
55 to 59
50 to 54
45 to 49
40 to 44
35 to 39
30 to 34
25 to 29
20 to 24
15 to 19
10 to 14
5 to 9
0 to 4
25
20
15
10
5
0
5
10
15
20
Male
Female

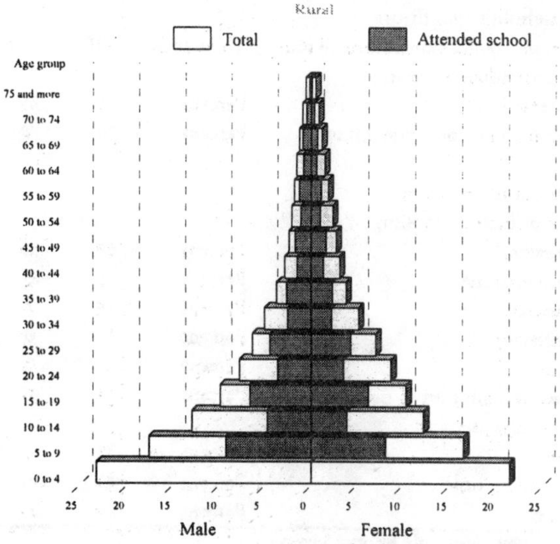
Rural
Total
Attended school
Age group
75 and more
70 to 74
65 to 69
60 to 64
55 to 59
50 to 54
45 to 49
40 to 44
35 to 39
30 to 34
25 to 29
20 to 24
15 to 19
10 to 14
5 to 9
0 to 4
25
20
15
10
5
0
5
10
15
20
25
Male
Female

15-17. Zambia: household welfare indicators

			Expenditure quintile											
			Rural						Urban					
Indicator	*Unit of measure*	*National total*	*All*	*1*	*2*	*3*	*4*	*5*	*All*	*1*	*2*	*3*	*4*	*5*
Demographic indicators														
Sample size	Number	10,128	3,900	631	670	740	810	1,049	6,228	986	1,022	1,171	1,293	1,756
Total population	Thousands	8,790	5,383	1,077	1,076	1,077	1,076	1,077	3,407	682	682	682	682	682
Female	Percent	55	57	56	57	56	57	56	54	55	55	55	55	53
Population below 15 years	Percent	43	44	47	47	46	43	40	43	48	47	46	43	36
Female	Percent	50	50	49	49	50	51	50	50	49	50	50	51	51
Number of households	Thousands	1,516	973	166	171	183	204	247	544	88	93	103	111	149
Average household size	Number	5.8	5.5	6.5	6.3	5.9	5.3	4.4	6.3	7.7	7.3	6.6	6.1	4.6
Education and literacy														
Net primary enrollment (total)	Percent	64	57	48	55	59	61	70	77	68	75	75	76	83
Male	Percent	64	58	47	53	60	61	71	74	68	75	74	75	84
Female	Percent	65	58	48	56	58	61	69	75	67	76	77	77	81
Net secondary enrollment (total)	Percent	62	56	50	52	56	59	65	71	62	73	72	71	77
Male	Percent	69	63	58	61	60	66	73	78	70	79	78	80	85
Female	Percent	55	49	41	42	53	52	57	64	55	67	66	62	71
Literacy rate (total)	Percent	22	12	6	8	10	11	22	38	22	30	37	42	57
Male	Percent	27	16	8	11	13	15	29	45	27	37	44	49	63
Female	Percent	17	8	4	5	7	8	15	31	17	23	30	34	50
Head of household														
Marital status of head														
Monogamous male-headed	Percent	71	68	66	67	70	72	66	75	76	80	80	79	66
Polygamous male-headed	Percent	2	3	3	3	3	2	2	1	2	1	1	1	0
Single male-headed	Percent	7	6	4	3	5	5	10	9	6	5	6	7	17
Defacto female-headed	Percent	1	1	2	2	1	1	1	1	1	1	1	1	0
Dejure female-headed	Percent	19	22	25	25	20	19	20	14	15	13	12	12	16
Education level of head														
Completed primary	Percent	65	43	18	29	40	42	65	85	68	82	88	91	88
Completed secondary	Percent	1	0			0		1	2	0	0	1	1	6
Illiterate	Percent	33	56	82	71	60	58	34	12	32	17	11	9	6
Employment of head														
Agro-pastoral activities	Percent	60	89	97	94	92	88	79	9	18	8	7	7	6
Household expenditure														
Mean per capita expenditure (Kwacha)	Thousands	3,710	2,051	434	968	1,475	2,212	5,168	6,331	1,931	3,377	4,724	6,815	14,810
Population below relative poverty line	Percent	52	75	100	100	100	77	0	16	79	0	0	0	0
Food share in total expenditure	Percent	75	78	75	81	82	80	72	70	73	72	71	69	63
Household amenities														
Type of fuel for cooking														
Firewood	Percent	64	93	97	95	92	94	87	14	38	18	12	7	4
Gas, kerosine	Percent	0	0					0	1	0	1	1	1	1
Charcoal	Percent	24	7	2	5	8	6	11	54	50	58	59	59	48
Electricity	Percent	11	0				0	2	31	11	23	27	33	47
Other	Percent	1	0	1			0		0	1	0	1	0	0
Access to sanitation	Percent	73	61	47	56	65	66	73	96	94	95	95	96	97
Access to water														
Pipe	Percent	33	4	2	2	3	4	8	85	73	81	86	88	91
Well/bore hole	Percent	41	57	62	62	57	56	52	12	20	15	10	10	7
Other	Percent	26	39	36	36	40	40	40	3	7	4	4	2	2

Source: 1993 Household Priority Survey II.

Zambia

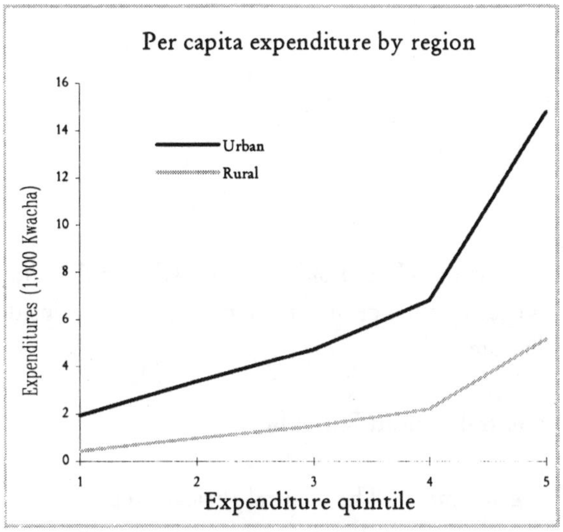
Per capita expenditure by region
Expenditures (1,000 Kwacha)
16
14
12
10
8
6
4
2
0
Urban
Rural
1
2
3
4
5
Expenditure quintile

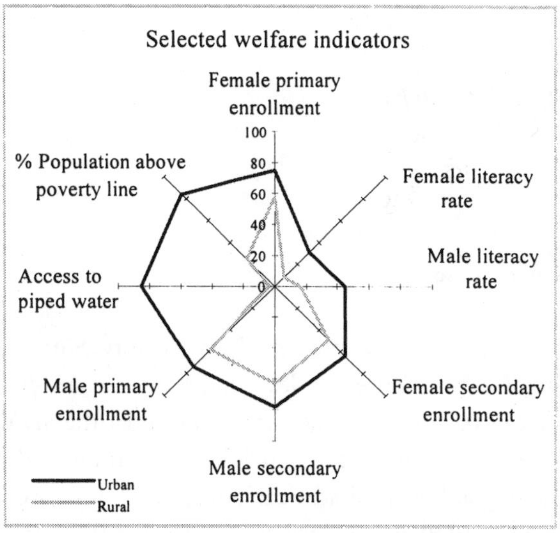
Selected welfare indicators
Female primary enrollment
100
80
60
40
20
0
Female literacy rate
Male literacy rate
Female secondary enrollment
Male secondary enrollment
Male primary enrollment
Access to piped water
% Population above poverty line
Urban
Rural

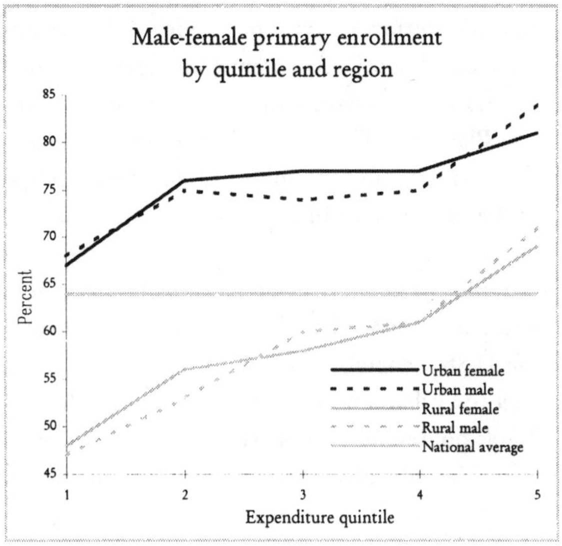
Male-female primary enrollment by quintile and region
Percent
85
80
75
70
65
60
55
50
45
Urban female
Urban male
Rural female
Rural male
National average
1
2
3
4
5
Expenditure quintile

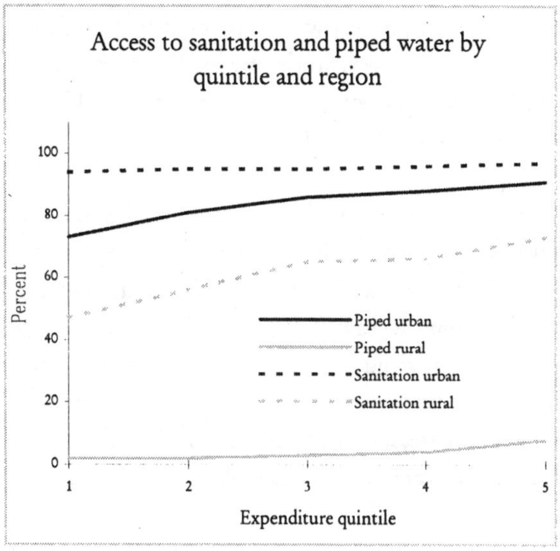
Access to sanitation and piped water by quintile and region
Percent
100
80
60
40
20
0
Piped urban
Piped rural
Sanitation urban
Sanitation rural
1
2
3
4
5
Expenditure quintile

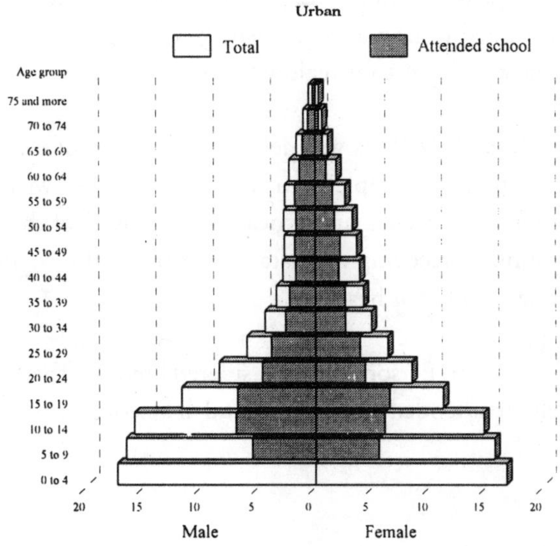
Urban
Total
Attended school
Age group
75 and more
70 to 74
65 to 69
60 to 64
55 to 59
50 to 54
45 to 49
40 to 44
35 to 39
30 to 34
25 to 29
20 to 24
15 to 19
10 to 14
5 to 9
0 to 4
20
15
10
5
0
5
10
15
20
Male
Female

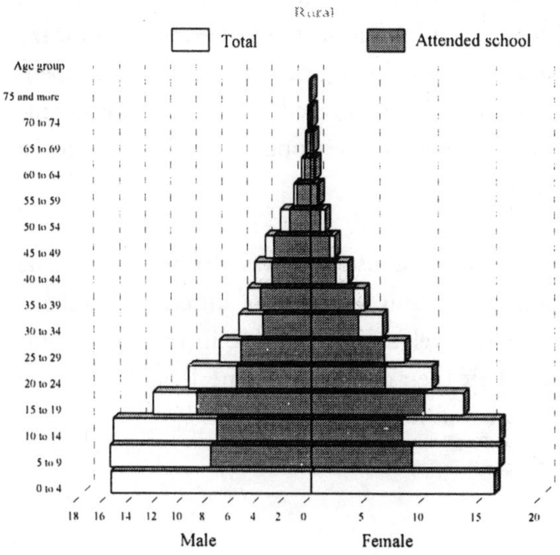
Rural
Total
Attended school
Age group
75 and more
70 to 74
65 to 69
60 to 64
55 to 59
50 to 54
45 to 49
40 to 44
35 to 39
30 to 34
25 to 29
20 to 24
15 to 19
10 to 14
5 to 9
0 to 4
18
16
14
12
10
8
6
4
2
0
5
10
15
20
Male
Female

Technical Notes

Burkina Faso

Data source. The Burkina Faso Priority Survey, (Enquête prioritaire sur les conditions de vie des ménages au Burkina) was carried out under the SDA project by the Institut national de la statistique et de la démographie, the Statistical Unit of the Ministry of Finance and Planning. Initiated in October 1994, the data collection process was completed in September 1995. The project was funded by the World Bank, the African Development Bank (ADB), and the United Nations through the UNDP.

Sample. The survey used a two-stage stratified random sample and was nationally representative. The country was divided into seven strata (two urban and five rural) and data were collected in all urban and rural regions. Approximately 20 households were sampled without repeat and with equal probability from 434 enumeration areas, producing a sample size of 8,442, of which 2,718 were urban households and 5,724 rural.

Expenditure data. Total household expenditures on health, food, and nonfood items were recorded for the 30 days preceding the enumerator's visit, while expenditure on education covered the 1993/94 academic year. Price deflators were applied to adjust for spatial differences.

Household. A household was defined as a basic socioeconomic unit made up of different members, not necessary related, who reside in the same compound, share their resources and meals, and recognize one member as head.

Literacy. Household members who could read and write a sentence in any language were considered literate.

Central African Republic

Data source. The Central African Republic Priority Survey (L'Enquête prioritaire sur les conditions de vie des ménages) was carried out under Le Projet dimensions sociales de l'ajustement et du développement by the Statistics Department of the Ministry of Finance and Planning. The data collection process started in the urban area in September 1992 and was completed in the rural area in June 1994.

Sample. The survey was a nationally representative household survey, based on the enumeration areas of the 1988 General Population Census (which delineated the urban and rural areas). The sample size was 7,500 households. Approximately 2,960 households were selected from urban and 4,540 from rural areas.

Expenditure data. Expenditure information was collected during a single visit. No adjustments were made to correct for regional price differences.

Household. This was defined as a group of related or unrelated people who live in the same dwelling unit, have been sharing meals for at least 6 of the 12 months preceding the data collection, and recognize one member as head.

Literacy. Persons were considered literate if they had either attended any school and had completed elementary education level or were older than 15 and could read and write a short note in French, even though they may never have attended any school.

Côte d'Ivoire

Data source. The Côte d'Ivoire 1995 Priority Survey (Enquête Niveau de Vie) was carried out under the SDA project by the Direction de la Statistique, unit of the Ministry of Economics, Finance, and Planning. The project was jointly funded by the government of Côte d'Ivoire, IDA, and the ADB.

Sample. This was a nationwide household survey based on the priority survey 1993 master sample. It was a two stage, self-weighted, stratified random sampling. In the first stage, 100 clusters were randomly selected from the 480 clusters of households. In the second sampling stage, 10 households were selected from each cluster, producing a total sample size of 1,000 households.

Expenditure data. Expenditure data collected detailed information on household expenditure on health during the past three months preceding the enumerator's visit. Detailed information on other household expenditure items was collected either over a 1-month or 12-month recall period. Regional price indices were used to account for spatial differences, with the Abidjan CPI as base.

Household. This was defined as a person or a group of people who have been living under the same roof for the past 12 months, share the same meal, and recognize one member as head.

Literacy. Household members who could read and write a sentence in any language were considered literate.

The Gambia

Data source. The Gambia Priority Survey was carried out under the SDA program by the Central Statistics Department of the Ministry of Finance and Economic Affairs. The data were collected from late February to early May 1992. The project was funded by the government of the Gambia, the World Bank, and the African Development Bank (ADB).

Sample. A multistage sample using probability proportional to size was used in the sample selection. The total sample size was 2,031 households, of which 1,185 were rural and 846 urban.

Expenditure data. The survey collected information on household expenditure incurred during the previous month on selected items, and/or over a year for education expenses. Total household expenditure on food was collected on five items, and home-produced and consumed food was not accounted for in estimating total household expenditure.

Household. This was defined as a group of people who normally live and eat together and accept the authority of one member as head. A household may also consist of one person, and its members may or may not be related.

Literacy. Literacy was defined as the ability to read and write a simple sentence in any language (English/Arabic).

Access to sanitation. This priority survey did not collect data on household access to sanitation and type of toilet facilities.

Ghana

Data source. The third round of a series of Ghana Living Standards Survey was financed by the World Bank and the Ghanaian government and was carried out by the Ghana Statistical Service from September 1991 to September 1992.

Sample. This was a nationwide household survey

based on the master sample of enumeration areas as defined by the 1984 population census. A multistage sampling design was used to select the sample. A total of 407 clusters were selected, of which 110 clusters were urban and 297 rural. This design provided a sample of 4,565 households, of which 3,080 were rural and 1,485 urban.

Expenditure data. Multiple visits were made to each household over a one-month period. Regional and spatial differences were adjusted by using price deflators.

Household. This was defined as a person living alone or any group of people staying together and sharing the same catering arrangements.

Literacy. Persons were considered literate if they had either completed primary education or had attended a literary course, and if they could read a sentence in English or perform written calculations.

Access to sanitation. Households with access to sanitation consist of those equipped with a flush toilet, KVIP, pit latrine, or pan/bucket.

Guinea

Data source. The Guinean Integrated Survey (Enquête Integrale sur les Conditions de Vie des Menages) was carried out under *Le Project dimensions sociales de l'ajustement structurel* by the Statistical Unit of the Ministry of Finance and Planning. The data collection was carried out between January 1994 and February 1995. The project was funded by the government of Guinea, IDA, CIDA, and the ADB.

Sample. A multistage stratified random sample was used, with the strata defined as the main agroeconomic regions. The Guinean Priority Survey was a nationwide household survey. Data were collected in urban and rural areas, and the total sample size was 4,416 households, of which 1,680 were rural and 2,736 urban.

Expenditure data. The survey collected expenditure data over two visits. Expenditure data were adjusted to correct for regional and seasonal price differences.

Household. This was defined as a group of related or unrelated people who have been living in the same dwelling unit and sharing meals for at least 6 of the 12 months preceding the data collection and who recognize one member as head.

Literacy. Persons were considered literate if they had completed at least primary education.

Guinea-Bissau

Data source. The Guinea-Bissau Priority Survey (Inquérito Ligeiro Junta as Familias) was part of the SDA project. The survey was implemented by the Direcção General de Estatistica under the Ministério de Economica e Financas in 1991. Funding for the survey was provided by the UNDP, ADB, the World Bank, and a number of donors and organizations.

Sample. The sample was based on administrative boundaries in regions and sectoral subdivisions. The sample size was 1,630 households.

Expenditure data. Total expenditure was estimated as the sum of cash expenditure on consumption goods and services; the value of own-produced food, transfers, and remittances received (in cash and in kind); and goods received in barter. Items excluded from the household expenditure data include the purchase of buildings, land, and the imputed value of owner occupied houses and vehicles.

Household. This was defined as a group of people who have been living in the same dwelling unit and sharing meals for at least 6 of the past 12 months preceding the data collection and who recognize one member as head.

Literacy. Persons were considered literate if they could read and write a simple sentence.

Access to sanitation. Information on household sanitation was not collected during the survey.

Kenya

Data source. The National Welfare Monitoring Survey I was a household priority survey carried out in November/December 1992 by the Central Bureau of Statistics in the Ministry of Planning and National Development. The data were collected in 44 districts, excluding Turkana, Marsabit, and Samburu. In the North Eastern province, the data were collected only from the urban clusters.

Sample. A total of 1,205 clusters were sampled, with 10 households sampled from each cluster, providing a sample of 12,050 households. Implementation difficulties led to the loss of a significant number of responses, approximately 4,000 households. The final sample size was 8,123 households.

Expenditure data. The survey collected information on household expenditure on essential commodities incurred during the month before the data collection. Price deflators were used to correct for regional price differences.

Household. This was defined as a person or a group of people living in the same compound (fenced or unfenced), answerable to the same head, and sharing a common source of food and/or income.

Literacy. Persons were considered literate if they could read and write a sentence in English.

Madagascar

Data source. The Madagascar Integrated Survey (Enquête permanente Aupres des Menages) was carried out under the Project dimensions sociales de l'ajustement structurel by the Statistical Service (Office Statistique et informatique pour la Programmation du Développement). Initiated in April 1993, the data collection was completed in October 1993. The project was funded by the government of Madagascar, the World Bank, and the UNDP.

Sample. The survey used a three-stage stratified random sample. The sample was stratified by urban and rural areas. The sample size was 4,500 households, of which 2,557 were rural and 1,943 urban.

Expenditure data. The survey collects data on all aspects of household expenditures (food and nonfood). In urban areas, a daily diary was used to record consumption expenditure, with a view of reducing nonsampling and recall errors.

Household. This was defined as a person or group of people living together and sharing the same food, as well as other household items and facilities.

Literacy. Household members were considered literate if they had completed primary education, attended any literacy course, or could read and write a sentence in French.

Niger

Data source. The Household Budget Consumption Survey (Enquête nationale du budget et de la consomation des ménages) was carried out in two phases by the Statistical Unit (Direction de la Statistique et des Comptes Nationaux) under the Ministry of Finance and Planning between 1989 and 1993. The survey was part of the Programme d'appui à la gestion économique et financière and was funded by the World Bank, PNUD, and the governments of France and the Netherlands.

Sample. This was a two-stage nationwide household survey based on a master sample drawn from the 1988 population census. The survey was based on a multistage stratified random sample. A total of 3,799 households were selected, of which 1,775 were from urban areas and 2,024 from rural areas.

Expenditure data. The survey used three reference periods: day, month, and year. Household diaries were used to reduce errors associated with the recall period. The urban and rural data initially collected in two different periods were consolidated after adjustment for regional and over-time price differences and are expressed in 1992 constant CFAF.

Household. This was defined as a group of people who live together in the same dwelling unit, share meals, and recognize one member as head.

Literacy. Persons were considered literate if they had attended any school. However, since primary school students below a certain class may not be able to read or write, these figures are likely to be high.

Access to sanitation. Households with access to safe sanitation refer to those equipped with a flush toilet.

Nigeria

Data source. The National Consumer Survey was part of the National Integrated Survey of Households, sponsored by the United Nations through the National Household Survey Capabilities Programme. The data collection started in April 1992 and was completed in March 1993, with national coverage. The survey and data collection process was conducted by the Federal Office of Statistics.

Sample. This was a nationwide household survey based on enumeration areas defined by the 1991 population census. The survey used a two-stage stratified random sample. Overall, a sample of about 10,000 households was drawn from 120 enumeration areas selected from each of the 21 states and the Federal Capital territory.

Expenditure data. The survey included information on most household expenditure items: food, nonfood, and own-produced and consumed food items. Price deflators were used to adjust for regional price differences.

Household. This was defined as a group of related or unrelated people, living in a dwelling unit or its equivalent, eating from the same pot, and sharing common housekeeping arrangements.

Literacy. Persons were considered literate if they had completed primary education.

Access to sanitation. Information on household sanitation was not collected during survey.

Access to water. Information on household access to water was not collected during survey.

Senegal

Data source. The Senegal Priority Survey (Enquête sur les Priorités) was carried out under the Projet dimensions sociales de l'ajustement structurel, by the statistical division, Direction de la Prevision et de la Statistique of the Ministry of Economic and Finance. Initiated in October 1991, the data collection was completed in January 1992. The project was funded by the government of Senegal and the World Bank.

Sample. A two-stage stratified random sample was used. In the first stage, the districts de recensement were sampled with probability proportional to size, and households were sampled in the second stage. The strata were divided along the main geographical regions. The total sample size was 9,955 households, of which 4,158 were rural and 5,797 urban.

Expenditure data. The survey collected information on household expenditure on essential commodities incurred during the previous month or the current school year for expenditure on education. Average household expenditure in urban areas was significantly larger than the rural estimate. The discrepancy was attributed to the fact that home-produced and -consumed goods were not accounted for in the estimation of rural household expenditure, and price deflators were not used to correct for regional price differences.

Household. This was defined as a person or group of people living in the same compound, answerable to the same head, and sharing a common source of food and/or income.

Literacy. People were considered literate if they could read and write a sentence in French.

Access to sanitation. The survey did not collect data on household access to sanitation and type of toilet facilities.

Sierra Leone

Data source. The Survey of Household Expenditure and Household Economic Activities was carried out between October 1989 and September 1990 by the Central Statistics Office. Funding and technical assistance were provided by the UNDP, ECA, UNICEF, ILO, UNFPA, and FAO.

Sample. The survey covered the entire country, including provinces in urban and rural areas, and was based on administrative subdivisions and enumeration areas of the 1985 population census. A two-stage stratified random sample was used. A total sample size of 2,800 households was drawn. A total of 1,940 households were selected from the urban area (1,560 from large towns and 380 from the small towns), and 860 households were from rural areas.

Expenditure data. These include consumption expenditures on food, imputed value of consumption of own-produced goods, and monetary value of gifts received, purchased, and other acquisition of nonfood items. The nonconsumption component of taxes, insurance premiums, income transfers, and remittances were left out. Nominal figures were not deflated with a regional price index.

Household. This was defined as a group of people living in the same dwelling unit or its equivalent, eating from the same pot, and sharing the common housekeeping arrangements.

Literacy. People were considered literate if they had completed primary education.

Access to sanitation. Information on household sanitation was not collected during the survey.

Access to water. Information on household access to water was not collected during the survey.

South Africa

Data source. The South African Living Standards and Development Survey was a nationwide household survey conducted between July 1993 and April 1994 by the Southern Africa Labor and Development Research Unit in the School of Economics at the University of Cape Town. Funding for the project was provided by the governments of Denmark, Netherlands, and Norway through the World Bank.

Sample. The sampling frame was based on the existing census enumeration areas. The sample was a two-stage, self-weighting design in which the first stage units were the Census Enumerators Sub-Districts, and the second stage units were households. Enumerators collected detailed information on 9,000 households, of which approximately 4,230 were rural and 4,770 urban.

Expenditure data. The survey collected data on household key expenditure items classified into two groups: food and nonfood. Nearly 748 households failed to report nonfood consumption, and only 1,462 households provided information on remittances expenditure. No price adjustment was made to account for seasonality and regional price variation.

Household. Two definitions of households were used to avoid double counting. One was used in the first part of the questionnaire (household roster), which referred to individuals who lived under one roof or within the same compound at least 15 days during the past year, shared food from a common source, and contributed to a common resource pool. Visitors were not included. The second was used in the second part of the questionnaire and included household members who had lived "under this roof for more than 15 of the past 30 days."

Literacy. People were considered literate if they had completed a standard form 7 or higher.

Tanzania

Data source. The Human Resource Development Survey was carried out by the World Bank with the University of Dar es Salaam and the Tanzanian Planning Commission. The data collection lasted from September 1993 to March 1994. The project was funded by the British Overseas Development Administration (ODA), the government of Japan, and the World Bank.

Sample. This was a nationwide household survey based on the national master sample revised in 1990. The sample was based on a two-stage stratified random sample. Approximately 25 households were randomly selected from each enumeration area, which produced a sample of 5,184 households, of which 2,262 were rural and 2,922 were urban.

Expenditure data. The survey collected information on household expenditure incurred over different referenced periods (day, week, and month). No adjustment was made for regional and seasonal price differences.

Household. This was defined as a person living alone or any group of people staying together and sharing the same catering arrangements.

Literacy. People were considered literate if they could read a newspaper, write a letter, or perform written calculations.

Uganda

Data source. The Uganda Integrated Household Survey was conducted by the Statistics Department of the Ministry of Planning and Economic Development. It consists of three surveys: the integrated survey, the small-scale enterprise survey, and the community survey. Except for few parishes, the integrated survey covered most districts in Uganda and was implemented over a 12-month period, between 1992 and 1993.

Sample. This was based on a two-stage stratified sample. The sample size was 9,921 households, of which 6,398 were rural and 3,523 urban.

Expenditure data. The survey collected data on all household expenditures (food and nonfood). Adjustments were made to correct for regional and seasonal price differences.

Household. This was defined as a group of people who normally eat and live together. These people may or may not be related by blood, but make common provision for food and other essentials for living and have one person whom they regard as the head of the household.

Literacy. Persons were considered literate if they had completed primary education.

Zambia

Data source. The Zambia Priority Survey was conducted under the SDA project between October and November 1991 by the Central Statistical Office in the Ministry of Planning.

Sample. This was a nationwide survey which collected data at the household and individual levels. The sample consisted of 4,144 households.

Expenditure data. The survey collected data on household consumption on various items. Household expenditures recorded during one month were aggregated to obtain a household monthly consumption expenditure. No adjustment for regional price differences was made.

Household. This was defined as a group of people who normally eat and live together and have one person whom they regard as the head of household.

Literacy. People were considered literate if they had completed the standard grade 5 or higher.

References

Association for the Development of African Education. 1995. *A Statistical Profile of Education in Sub-Saharan Africa, 1990–93*. Paris, France.

Candoy-Sekse, Rebecca. 1988. *Techniques of Privatization of State-Owned Enterprises. Volume III. Inventory of Country Experience and Reference Materials*. World Bank Technical Paper 90. Washington, D.C.

Central African Republic, Division of Statistics and Economic Studies. 1994. "Enquete prioritaire sur les conditions de vie des menages." Bangui.

Club of Rome. 1972. *The Limit to Growth*. Rome.

Côte d'Ivoire, Institut National de Statistique. 1994. "Enquete prioritaire." Abidjan.

Currency Data & Intelligence Inc. Monthly. *Global Currency Report*. New York.

Floyd, Robert, Clive Gray, and R. P. Short. 1984. *Public Enterprise in Mixed Economies: Some Macroeconomic Aspects*. Washington, D.C.: International Monetary Fund.

Food and Agriculture Organization (FAO). 1987. *Agrostat Code Book*. Rome.

___. annual. *Fertilizer Yearbook*. Rome.

___. annual. *Food and Agriculture Organization Production Yearbook*. Rome.

___. annual. *Food Aid in Figures*. Rome.

___. annual. *Trade Yearbook*. Rome.

___. annual. *Yearbook of Forest Products*. Rome.

Galal, Ahmed. 1990. "Public Enterprise Reform: A Challenge for the World Bank." PRE Working Paper 407. World Bank, Country Economics Department, Washington, D.C. Processed.

___. 1991. *Public Enterprise Reform: Lessons from the Past and Issues for the Future*. World Bank Discussion Paper 119. Washington, D.C., World Bank.

The Gambia, Ministry of Finance. 1993. "Report on the 1992 Priority Survey." Banjul.

Grootaert, Christian, and Timothy Marchant. 1991. *The Social Dimensions of Adjustment Priority Survey: An Instrument for the Rapid Identification and Monitoring of Policy Targeting Groups*. SDA Working Paper 12. Washington, D.C.: World Bank.

Guinea, Ministry of Planning and Finance. 1991. "Rapport Final: Enquete sur les informations prioritaire: Dimensions Sociales de l'Adjustment Structurel." Conakry.

Guinea-Bissau, National Institute of Statistics and Census. 1992. "Relatorio Final: Inquerito Ligeiro Junto as Familias." Bissau.

Hemming, Richard, and Ali M. Mansoor. 1988. *Privatization and Public Enterprises.* IMF Occasional Paper 56. Washington, D.C.

International Energy Agency (IEA). 1996. *Energy Statistics and Balances of Non-OECD Countries, 1993–94.* Paris.

International Labour Organization (ILO). annual. *Yearbook of Labor Statistics.* Geneva.

___. 1968. *International Standard Classification of Occupations.* Geneva.

___. 1987. *World Labor Report* 1. Oxford: Oxford University Press.

International Monetary Fund (IMF). 1986. *Manual on Government Finance Statistics.* Washington, D.C.

___. 1993. *Balance of Payments Manual,* Fifth ed. Washington, D.C.

___. annual. *Balance of Payments Yearbook.*Washington, D.C. various years.

___. annual. *Government Finance Statistics Yearbook.* Washington, D.C. various years.

___. monthly. *International Financial Statistics.* Washington, D.C.

___. various issues. *Recent Economic Development.* Washington, D.C.

International Telecommunication Union (ITU). 1995. *World Telecommunication Development Report.* Geneva.

International Road Federation. 1995. *World Road Statistics, 1990–94.* Geneva.

Jager, William, and Charles Humphreys. 1988. "The Effect of Policy Reforms on Africa." *American Journal of Agricultural Economics* 70 (50): 1036–43.

Kenya, Central Bureau of Statistics. 1993. "Welfare Monitoring Survey." Nairobi.

Metallgesellschaft AG. annual. *Metallstatistik.* Frankfurt am Main.

Mukui, John Thinguri. 1994. "Kenya: Poverty Profiles, 1982–92." Prepared for the Office of the Vice-President and Ministry of Planning and National Development, Nairobi, Kenya.

Nair, Govindan, and Anastosios Filppides. 1988. "How Much Do State-Owned Enterprises Contribute to Public Sector Deficits in Developing Countries?" PPR Working Paper 45. World Bank, Development Economics Vice Presidency, Washington, D.C. Processed.

Organisation for Economic Cooperation and Development (OECD). Various issues. *Geographical Distribution of Financial Flows to Developing Countries.* Paris.

Republic of South Africa. 1990. *South Africa Statistics.* Pretoria: Government Printer.

Swanson, Daniel, and Teferra Wolde-Semait. 1989. *Africa's Public Enterprise Sector and Evidence of Reforms.* World Bank Technical Paper 95. Washington, D.C.

Uganda, Ministry of Finance and Economic Planning. 1993. "Report on the Uganda National Integrated Household Survey 1992–93." Entebbe.

United Nations. 1950. *Index Numbers of Industrial Production.* New York.

___. 1989. *Compendium of Statistics and Indicators on the Situation of Women.* New York.

___. 1992. *The World's Women, 1970–90.* New York.

___. annual. *Population and Vital Statistics Report.* New York.

___. annual. *Yearbook. G., International Trade Statistics.* New York.

United Nations Children's Fund (UNICEF). annual. *The State of the World's Children.* New York.

United Nations Development Programme (UNDP). 1994. *Human Development Report 1994.* New York.

United Nations Development Programme and the World Bank. 1989. *African Economic and Financial Data.* Washington, D.C.

___. 1992. *African Development Indicators.* Washington, D.C.

United Nations Statistical Office (UNSO). 1975, 1986. "United National Standard International

Trade Classification," revisions 2 and 3 (SITC, rev. 2 and 3). Statistical Papers, series M. no. 34, rev. 2 and 3. New York.

———. *United Nations International Standard Classification of All Economic Activities*, revision 2 (ISIC, rev. 2). New York.

———. annual. *Energy Statistics Yearbook*. New York.

United Nations Educational, Scientific, and Cultural Organization (UNESCO). 1982. *Conferences of Ministers of Education and Those Responsible for Economic Planning in African Member States*. Paris.

———. 1986. *Regional Bulletin of Education Statistics BREDA – STAT*. Regional Office for Education in Africa. Paris.

———. 1989. *Trends and Projections of Enrollment by Level of Education and by Age, 1960–2025 (as assessed in 1989)*. Division of Statistics on Education. Paris.

———. 1990. *Basic Education and Literacy: World Statistical Indicators*. Paris.

———. annual. *Statistical Yearbook*. Paris.

Wadda, Rohey, and Russel Craig. 1993. "Report on the 1992 Priority Survey." Central Statistics, Ministry of Finance and Economic Affairs, Banjul, The Gambia.

World Bank. 1988. *Education in Sub-Saharan Africa: Policies for Adjustment, Revitalization, and Expansion*. Washington, D.C.

———. 1993a. "Africa Adjustment Study P.E. Sector Reform: Case Studies." Washington, D.C. Processed.

———. 1993b. "Public Enterprise Reform and Privatization in Africa." Washington, D.C. Processed.

———. 1994a. "Kenya Poverty Assessment." Eastern Africa Department, Africa Region. Washington, D.C.

———. 1994b. "A Statistical Profile of Education in Sub-Saharan Africa in the 1980s." Africa Technical Department. Washington, D.C. Processed.

———. 1994c. *World Population Projections, 1994-95*. Washington, D.C.

———. 1994d. "Zambia Poverty Assessment." Southern Africa Department. Washington D.C.

———. 1995. *Bureaucrats in Business*. New York: Oxford University Press.

———. annual. *Commodity Trade and Price Trends*. Washington, D.C.

———. annual. *Global Development Finance* (was *World Debt Tables* up to 1996).

———. annual. *Social Indicators of Development*. Washington, D.C.

———. annual. *Trends in Development Economies*. Washington, D.C.

———. annual. *World Bank Atlas*. Washington, D.C.

———. annual. *World Debt Tables* (until 1996; now *Global Development Finance*). Washington, D.C.

———. annual. *World Development Report*. New York: Oxford University Press.

———. annual. *World Tables*. Washington, D.C.

World Resources Institute. 1994. *World Resources, 1994–95*. Washington, D.C.

———. 1996. *World Resources 1996–97*. Washington, D.C.

World Bureau of Metal Statistics. monthly. *World Metal Statistics*. London.

World Health Organization (WHO). annual. *World Health Statistics Annual*. Geneva.

———. various issues. *World Health Statistics Quarterly*. Geneva.

Zambia, Central Statistical Office. 1993. "Social Dimensions of Adjustment: Priority Survey I, 1991." Lusaka.